Eastern Hemisphere

HOLT

PEOPLE, PLACES, AND CHANGE

An Introduction to World Studies

HOLT, RINEHART AND WINSTON

A Harcourt Education Company

Orlando • **Austin** • New York • San Diego • Toronto • London

THE AUTHORS

Prof. David M. Helgren is Director of the Center for Geographic Education at San Jose State University in California, where he is also Chair of the Department of Geography. Prof. Helgren received his Ph.D. in geography from the University of Chicago. He is the coauthor of several geography textbooks and has written many articles on the geography of Africa. Awards from the National Geographic Society, the National Science Foundation, and the L. S. B. Leakey Foundation have supported his many field research projects. Prof. Helgren is a former president of the California Geographical Society and a founder of the Northern California Geographic Alliance.

Prof. Robert J. Sager is Chair of Earth Sciences at Pierce College in Lakewood, Washington. Prof. Sager received his B.S. in geology and geography and M.S. in geography from the University of Wisconsin and holds a J.D. in international law from Western State University College of Law. He is the coauthor of several geography and earth science textbooks and has written many articles and educational media programs on the geography of the Pacific. Prof. Sager has received several National Science Foundation study grants and has twice been a recipient of the University of Texas NISOD National Teaching Excellence Award. He is a founding member of the Southern California Geographic Alliance and former president of the Association of Washington Geographers.

Prof. Alison S. Brooks is Professor of Anthropology at George Washington University and a Research Associate in Anthropology at the Smithsonian Institution. She received her A.B., M.A., and Ph.D. in Anthropology from Harvard University. Since 1964, she has carried out ethnological and archaeological research in Africa, Europe, and Asia and is the author of more than 300 scholarly and popular publications. She has served as a consultant to Smithsonian exhibits and to National Geographic, Public Broadcasting, the Discovery Channel, and other public media. In addition, she is a founder and editor of *Anthro Notes: The National Museum of Natural History Bulletin for Teachers* and has received numerous grants and awards to develop and lead in-service training institutes for teachers in grades 5–12. She served as the American Anthropological Association's representative to the NCSS task force on developing Scope and Sequence guidelines for Social Studies Education in grade K–12.

While the details of the young people's stories in the chapter openers are real, their identities have been changed to protect their privacy.

Cover and Title Page Photo Credits: (child image) Steve Vidler/Nawrocki Stock Photo; (bkgd) Image Copyright © 2003 PhotoDisc, Inc./HRW

Printed in the United States of America

ISBN 0-03-037577-0

1 2 3 4 5 6 7 8 9 032 07 06 05 04

CONTENT REVIEWERS

Robin Datel
Instructor in Geography
California State University,
Sacramento

David Dickason
Professor of Geography
Western Michigan University

Dennis Dingemans
Professor of Geography
University of California, Davis

Robert Gabler
Professor of Geography
Western Illinois University

Jeffrey Gritzner
Professor of Geography
University of Montana

W. A. Douglas Jackson
Professor of Geography, Emeritus
University of Washington

Robert B. Kent
Professor of Geography
and Planning
University of Akron

Kwadwo Konadu-Agyemang
Professor of Geography
and Planning
University of Akron

Nancy Lewis
Professor of Geography
University of Hawaii

Bill Takizawa
Professor of Geography
San Jose State University

EDUCATIONAL REVIEWERS

Patricia Britt
Durant Middle School
Durant, Oklahoma

Marcia Caldwell
Lamar Middle School
Austin, Texas

Marcia Clevenger
Roosevelt Junior High School
Charleston, West Virginia

James Corley
Durant Middle School
Durant, Oklahoma

Maureen Dempsey
Spring Creek Middle School
Spring Creek, Nevada

Jean Eldredge
Teague Middle School
Altamonte, Florida

Cindy Herring
Old Town Elementary School
Round Rock, Texas

Lois Jordan
Pearl/Cohn Comprehensive
High School
Nashville, Tennessee

Kay A. Knowles
Montross Middle School
Montross, Virginia

Wendy Mason
Corbett Junior High School
Schertz, Texas

Rebecca Minnear
Burkholder Middle School
Las Vegas, Nevada

Jane Palmer
District Supervisor for
Social Studies
Sanford, Florida

Sandra Rojas
Adams City Middle School
Commerce City, Colorado

JoAnn Sadler
Curriculum Supervisor
Buffalo City Schools
Buffalo, New York

Celeste Smith
Crockett High School
Austin, Texas

Frank Thomas
Crockett High School
Austin, Texas

Susan Walker
Beaufort County School District
Beaufort, South Carolina

Field Test Teachers
Ricky A. Blackman
Rawlinson Road Middle School
Rock Hill, South Carolina

Lisa Klien
Daniels Middle School
Raleigh, North Carolina

Deborah D. Larry
Garland V. Stewart Middle School
Tampa, Florida

Linda P. Moore
Cramerton Middle School
Cramerton, North Carolina

Earl F. Sease
Portage Area School District
Portage, Pennsylvania

Christi Sherrill
Grier Middle School
Gastonia, North Carolina

John W. Watkins, Jr.
Clark Middle School
East St. Louis, Illinois

It's All About

INTERVIEWS with young people from around the world begin each chapter, making real world peer connections for your students. Plus students can read the interviews in their entirety on our Web site.

The first step to success in the social studies classroom is capturing and sustaining the interest of your students. *HOLT PEOPLE, PLACES, AND CHANGE* is designed to be open and friendly to all students, so that they develop an enthusiasm for learning and an appreciation for their world.

HOLT PEOPLE, PLACES, AND CHANGE offers
- Built-in Reading Support
- Technology with Instructional Value
- Standardized Testing Strategies and Skill Building
- The Best Teacher's Management System in the Industry

RELEVANCE

CNNfyi.com™ is designed to give students in grades 6–12 access to the news about people, places, and environments around the globe while offering "real-world" articles, career and college resources, and online activities.

In-Text Features that Put Geography into Perspective

- Case Study
- Connecting to Art
- Connecting to History
- Connecting to Literature
- Connecting to Math
- Connecting to Science
- Connecting to Technology
- Daily Life
- Focus on Culture

- Focus on Economy
- Focus on Environment
- Focus on Government
- Focus on Regions
- Geo Skills
- Hands On Geography
- Our Amazing Planet
- Why It Matters

Reading for

At Holt, we don't assume that students know how or have any desire to make sense of what they're reading, and we develop our programs based on that assumption. We don't just ask students questions about content, we give them strategies to get to that content. Through design, research, and the help of experts like Dr. Judith Irvin, we make sure students' reading needs are covered with our programs.

Helping Students Make Sense of What They're Reading

An Essay by Dr. Judith Irvin, Ph.D.

Who in middle and high schools helps students become more successful at reading and writing informational text? When I ask this question of a school faculty, the Language Arts/English teachers point to the social studies and science teachers because they are the ones with this type of textbook. The social studies and science teachers point to the Language Arts/English teachers because they are the ones that "do" words.

I advocate teachers taking an active role in helping students learn how to use text structure and context to understand what they read. Through consistent and systematic instruction that includes modeling of effective reading behavior, teachers can assist students in becoming better readers while at the same time helping them learn more content material.

The strategies in this book are designed to assist students with getting started, maintaining focus with reading, and organizing information for later retrieval. They engage students in learning material, provide the vehicle for them to organize and reorganize concepts, and extend their understanding through writing.

When teachers combine the teaching of reading and the teaching of content together into meaningful, systematic, and corrected instruction, students can apply what they have learned to understanding increasingly more difficult and complex texts as they progress through the school years.

READING STRATEGIES FOR THE SOCIAL STUDIES CLASSROOM

by Dr. Judith Irvin,
Ph.D., Reading Education

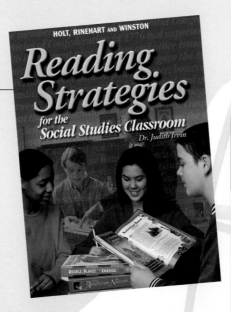

HOLT, RINEHART AND WINSTON
Reading Strategies *for the* Social Studies Classroom
Dr. Judith Irvin

Additional Reading Support

- Graphic Organizer Activities
- Guided Reading Strategies
- Main Idea Activities for English Language Learners and Special-Needs Students
- Audio CD Program

MEANING

Section 2   The Countries of Northeastern Europe

Read to Discover
1. What peoples contributed to the early history of northeastern Europe?
2. How was northeastern Europe's culture influenced by other cultures?
3. How has the political organization of this region changed since World War II?

Vocabulary
Indo-European

Places
Estonia
Poland
Czech Republic
Slovakia

Hungary
Lithuania
Latvia
Prague
Tallinn
Riga
Warsaw

Vistula River
Bratislava
Budapest

People
Vaclav Havel

Reading Strategy

READING ORGANIZER Before you read, draw a circle in the center of a sheet of paper. Draw seven surrounding circles connected by lines to the center circle. Label the center circle Northeastern Europe. As you read, write information about each of the seven countries in the outer circles.

The Teutonic knights, a German order of soldier monks, brought Christianity and feudalism to northeastern Europe. They built this castle at Malbork, Poland, in the 1200s.

430   Chapter 19

History

Migrants and warring armies have swept across Eastern Europe over the centuries. Each group of people brought its own language, religion, and customs. Together these groups contributed to the mosaic of cultures we see in Eastern Europe today.

Early History Among the region's early peoples were the Balts. The Balts lived on the eastern coast of the Baltic Sea. They spoke **Indo-European** languages. The Indo-European language family includes many languages spoken in Europe. These include Germanic, Baltic, and Slavic languages. More than 3,500 years ago, hunters from the Ural Mountains moved into what is now Estonia. They spoke a very different, non-Indo-European language. The language they spoke provided the early roots of today's Estonian and Finnish languages. Beginning around A.D. 400, a warrior people called the Huns invaded the region from Asia. Later, the Slavs came to the region from the plains north of the Black Sea.

In the 800s the Magyars moved into the Great Hungarian Plain. They spoke a language related to Turkish. In the 1200s the Mongols rode out of Central Asia into Hungary. At the same time German settlers pushed eastward, colonizing Poland and Bohemia—the western region of the present-day Czech Republic.

Emerging Nations Since the Middle Ages, Austria, Russia, Sweden, and the German state of Prussia have all ruled parts of Eastern Europe. After World War I ended in 1918, a new map of Eastern Europe was drawn. The peace treaty created two new countries: Yugoslavia and Czechoslovakia. Czechoslovakia included the old regions of Bohemia, Moravia, and Slovakia. At about the same time, Poland, Lithuania, Latvia, and Estonia also became independent countries.

✓ **READING CHECK:** *Places and Regions* What peoples contributed to the region's early history? Balts, hunters from Ural Mountains, Huns, Slavs, Magyars, Mongols, Germans

Hungarian dancers perform in traditional dress.

Interpreting the Visual Record
Region How does this Hungarian costume compare to those you have seen from other countries?

Culture

The culture and festivals of this region show the influence of the many peoples who contributed to its history. As in Scandinavia, Latvians celebrate a midsummer festival. The festival marks the summer solstice, the year's longest day. Poles celebrate major Roman Catholic festivals. Many of these have become symbols of the Polish nation. The annual pilgrimage, or journey, to the shrine of the Black Madonna of Częstochowa (chen-stuh-KOH-vuh) is an example.

Traditional Foods The food of the region reflects German, Russian, and Scandinavian influences. As in northern Europe, potatoes and sausages are important in the diets of Poland and the Baltic countries. Although the region has only limited access to the sea, the fish of lakes and rivers are often the center of a meal. These fish often include trout and carp. Many foods are preserved to last through the long winter. These include pickles, fruits in syrup, dried or smoked hams and sausages, and cured fish.

The Arts, Literature, and Science Northeastern Europe has made major contributions to the arts, literature, and sciences. For example, Frédéric Chopin (1810–1849) was a famous Polish pianist and composer. Marie Curie (1867–1934), one of the first female physicists, was also born in Poland. The writer Franz Kafka (1883–1924) was born to Jewish parents in Prague (PRAHG), the

Eastern Europe • 431

Successful Readers must have:

1 AN ENGAGING NARRATIVE

Great care is taken in selecting and presenting content in a way that students will find motivating and engaging. Features such as **Youth Interviews** help students connect their own lives to the lives and cultures of other students around the world.

2 A FORECAST OF WHAT THEY WILL LEARN

Read to Discover questions give students insight into the content they will cover in the chapter to come. In features such as **Why It Matters**, students gain insight into regional issues.

3 VOCABULARY DEFINED IN CONTEXT

Important new terms are identified at the beginning of every section and are defined in context so students will develop an understanding of the contextual meaning of all terms.

4 STRATEGIES FOR UNDERSTANDING WHAT THEY READ

Through the design of the text, students are led through the content using built-in reading strategies. For example, **Reading Checks** in the text are used as a comprehension tool. The checks remind students to stop and engage with what they have read, functioning as a "Tutor in the Text."

Get Your Students

Your students love activities that get them involved with the content. That's why Holt offers active-learning resources that link directly to program content and provide a multitude of different lessons for large-group, small-group, and individual projects.

CREATIVE TEACHING STRATEGIES

These innovative teaching strategies can be utilized at various points in your lesson. The wide range of cooperative-learning activities, including learning stations and simulations, motivate your students and help them develop critical-thinking skills.

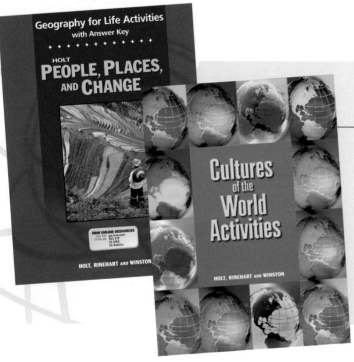

HANDS-ON GEOGRAPHY ACTIVITIES

From hands-on study of world cultures to hands-on practice with skill building, the following booklets cover it all. *Cultures of the World Activities* is a stand-alone booklet containing recipes, games, and craft activities. *Geography for Life Activities with Answer Key* contains a a problem-solving activity for each chapter, reflecting the skills and knowledge called for in the **National Geography Standards**.

GEOGRAPHY APPLICATIONS

For use in geography as well as earth science courses, here are two stand-alone booklets that organize applications with special relevance. *Environmental and Global Issues Activities* contains activities related to current environmental and global issues. *Lab Activities for Geography and Earth Science* contains laboratory activities related to physical geography and earth science.

Involved in Learning

Resources for Active Lessons

- **Block Scheduling Handbook**
- **Creative Strategies for Teaching World Geography**
- **Critical Thinking Activities**
- **Cultures of the World Activities**
- **Environmental and Global Issues Activities**
- **Geography and Cultures Visual Resources with Teaching Activities**
- **Geography for Life Activities**
- **Interdisciplinary Activities for the Middle Grades**
- **Lab Activities for Geography and Earth Science**
- **Map Activities**
- **Regions of the World Map Posters**
- **World and Regional Outline Maps**
- **World History and Geography Document-Based Questions Activities**

Joining Forces

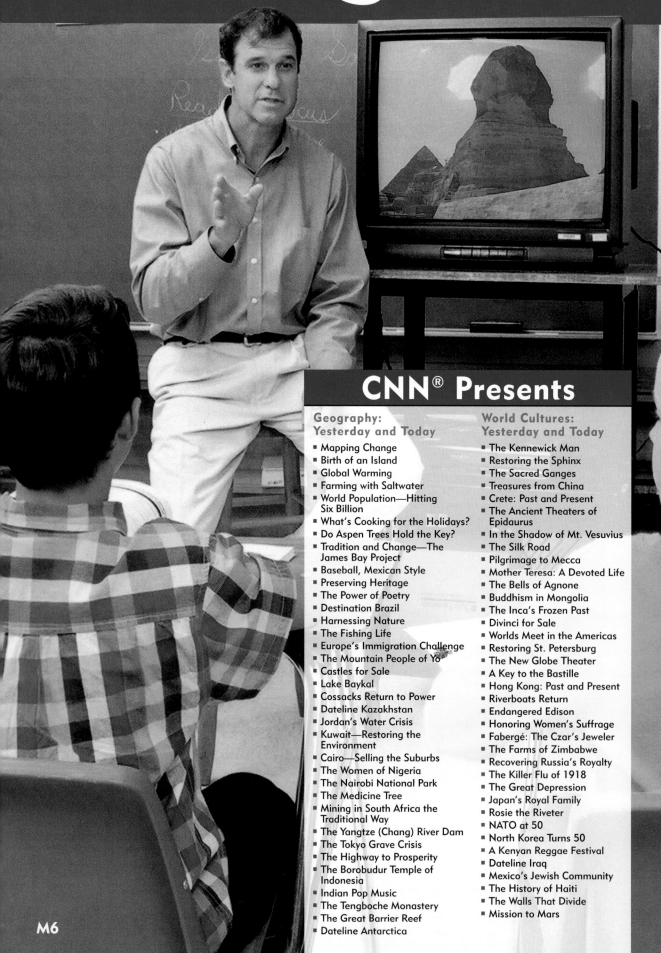

CNN® Presents

Geography: Yesterday and Today

- Mapping Change
- Birth of an Island
- Global Warming
- Farming with Saltwater
- World Population—Hitting Six Billion
- What's Cooking for the Holidays?
- Do Aspen Trees Hold the Key?
- Tradition and Change—The James Bay Project
- Baseball, Mexican Style
- Preserving Heritage
- The Power of Poetry
- Destination Brazil
- Harnessing Nature
- The Fishing Life
- Europe's Immigration Challenge
- The Mountain People of Yo
- Castles for Sale
- Lake Baykal
- Cossacks Return to Power
- Dateline Kazakhstan
- Jordan's Water Crisis
- Kuwait—Restoring the Environment
- Cairo—Selling the Suburbs
- The Women of Nigeria
- The Nairobi National Park
- The Medicine Tree
- Mining in South Africa the Traditional Way
- The Yangtze (Chang) River Dam
- The Tokyo Grave Crisis
- The Highway to Prosperity
- The Borobudur Temple of Indonesia
- Indian Pop Music
- The Tengboche Monastery
- The Great Barrier Reef
- Dateline Antarctica

World Cultures: Yesterday and Today

- The Kennewick Man
- Restoring the Sphinx
- The Sacred Ganges
- Treasures from China
- Crete: Past and Present
- The Ancient Theaters of Epidaurus
- In the Shadow of Mt. Vesuvius
- The Silk Road
- Pilgrimage to Mecca
- Mother Teresa: A Devoted Life
- The Bells of Agnone
- Buddhism in Mongolia
- The Inca's Frozen Past
- Divinci for Sale
- Worlds Meet in the Americas
- Restoring St. Petersburg
- The New Globe Theater
- A Key to the Bastille
- Hong Kong: Past and Present
- Riverboats Return
- Endangered Edison
- Honoring Women's Suffrage
- Fabergé: The Czar's Jeweler
- The Farms of Zimbabwe
- Recovering Russia's Royalty
- The Killer Flu of 1918
- The Great Depression
- Japan's Royal Family
- Rosie the Riveter
- NATO at 50
- North Korea Turns 50
- A Kenyan Reggae Festival
- Dateline Iraq
- Mexico's Jewish Community
- The History of Haiti
- The Walls That Divide
- Mission to Mars

to Enrich Your Classroom

CNNfyi.com

At **CNNfyi.com**, students will love exploring news stories written by experienced journalists as well as student bureau reporters. Stories link to homework help and lesson plans.

CNN PRESENTS VIDEO LIBRARY

The **CNN PRESENTS** video collection tackles the issue of making content relevant to students head on. Real-world news stories enable students to see the connections between classroom curriculum and today's issues and events around the nation and the world.

CNN PRESENTS...

- **America: Yesterday and Today, Beginnings to 1914**
- **America: Yesterday and Today, 1850 to Present**
- **America: Yesterday and Today, Modern Times**
- **Geography: Yesterday and Today**
- **World Cultures: Yesterday and Today**
- **American Government**
- **Economics**
- **September 11, 2001, Part One**
- **September 11, 2001, Part Two**

Holt is proud to team up with CNN/TURNER LEARNING® to provide you and your students with exceptional current and historical news videos and online resources that add depth and relevance to your daily instruction. This information collection takes your classroom to the far corners of the globe without students ever leaving their desks!

Your Multitalented Classroom

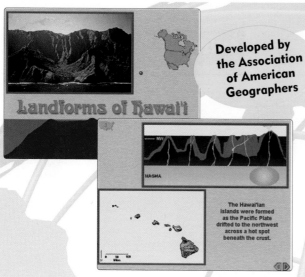

Developed by the Association of American Geographers

Landforms of Hawai'i

The Hawai'ian islands were formed as the Pacific Plate drifted to the northwest across a hot spot beneath the crust.

ACTIVITIES AND READINGS IN THE GEOGRAPHY OF THE WORLD

Integrate real geography into the topic you're studying with *Activities and Readings in the Geography of the World (ARGWorld).* This CD–ROM features world geography case studies with a multitude of activities that focus around geographical themes, population geography, economic geography, political geography, and environmental issues. Case studies will help teachers address the National Geography Standards.

HOLT RESEARCHER ONLINE: WORLD HISTORY AND CULTURES

New and online—students can access this outstanding research tool at **www.hrw.com**. A fully searchable database provides biographies, nation profiles and statistics, a glossary, and powerful graphic capabilities.

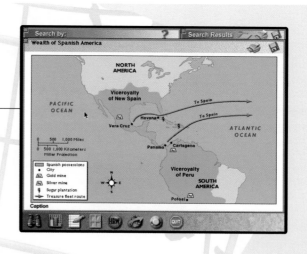

GLOBAL SKILL BUILDER CD-ROM

This CD-ROM is a comprehensive program containing interactive lessons that motivate your students to strengthen their map, graph, and computer skills. A handy *User's Guide and Teacher's Manual* provides student project sheets for each lesson along with optional suggestions for using the Internet to help complete the activity.

Guided Tour
1 Navigating the Internet
2 Mapping the Earth
3 Understanding Map Projections
4 Determining Absolute and Relative Location
5 Understanding Time Zones
6 Using Map Legends and Symbols
7 Identifying Different Types of Maps
8 Comparing Maps

Global Skill Builder
CD-ROM for Macintosh® and Windows®

needs Multimedia Tools

THE WORLD TODAY VIDEODISC PROGRAM

This unique resource offers a stimulating outlook on world geography by showing your students the different ways geographers organize the world, and challenging them to contemplate and discuss significant world issues. Compelling video segments with in-depth content cover contemporary culture in every major world region.

PEOPLE, PLACES, AND CHANGE AUDIO CD PROGRAM

The *Audio CD Program* provides in-depth audio section summaries and self-check activity sheets to help those students who respond to auditory learning. Available in English and Spanish.

Other Multimedia Products

- **CNN Presents Geography: Modern Times**
- **CNN Presents Geography: Yesterday and Today**
- **CNN Presents World Cultures: Yesterday and Today**
- **Holt Researcher Online: World History and Cultures**

Technology with

go.hrw.com FOR TEACHERS

Throughout the *Annotated Teacher's Edition*, you'll find **Internet Connect** boxes that take you to specific chapter activities, links, current events, and more that correlate directly to the section you are teaching. Through **go.hrw.com** you'll find a wealth of teaching resources at your fingertips for fun, interactive lessons.

DIRECT LAUNCH TO
CHAPTER ACTIVITIES

GUIDED ONLINE ACTIVITIES

LINKS FOR EVERY SECTION

MAPS AND CHARTS

INTERACTIVE PRACTICE AND REVIEW

RUBRICS FOR SUBJECTIVE GRADING

UP-TO-DATE INFORMATION

CLASSROOM PRESENTATION SUPPORT

PRACTICE FOR READING SUCCESS

WEB RESOURCES FOR CURRENT ISSUES

print out materials
Planner CD–ROM

forcement, and
Resources

Activity S1
view
.1
maries and Review
Summary 2.1
Summary 2.1

Activity S2
eview
4.2
maries and Review
Summary 4.2
Summary 4.2

Activity S3
eview
.3
maries and Review
Summary 4.3
Summary 4.3

Activity S4
view

maries and Review
Summary 4.4
Summary 4.4

internet connect

HRW ONLINE RESOURCES

GO TO: go.hrw.com
Then type in a keyword.

TEACHER HOMEPAGE
    KEYWORD: SK5 TEACHER

CHAPTER INTERNET ACTIVITIES
    KEYWORD: SK5 GT4

Choose an activity to:
• learn more about the development of writing.
• explore the Persian Empire.
• trace the spread of the Mongol Empire.

CHAPTER ENRICHMENT LINKS
KEYWORD: SK5 CH4

CHAPTER MAPS
KEYWORDS: SK5 MAPS4

ONLINE ASSESSMENT
Homework Practice
    KEYWORD: SK5 HP 4
    Standardized Test Prep Online
    KEYWORD: SK5 STP4
    Rubrics
    KEYWORD: SS Rubrics

COUNTRY INFORMATION
    KEYWORD: SK5 Almanac

CONTENT UPDATES
    KEYWORD: SS Contents Updates

HOLT PRESENTATION MAKER
    KEYWORD: SK5 PPT4

ONLINE READING SUPPORT
    KEYWORD: SS Strategies

CURRENT EVENTS
    KEYWORD: SS Current Events

Chapter Review and Assessment

E	Readings in World Geography, History, and Culture 50
SM	Critical Thinking Activity 4
REV	Chapter 4 Review and Practice
REV	Chapter Summaries and Review
ELL	Vocabulary Activity 4
A	Chapter 4 Test
A	Chapter 4 Test Generator (on the One-Stop Planner)
	Audio CD program, Chapter 4
A	Chapter 4 Test for English Language Learners and Special Needs Students
	HRW Go site

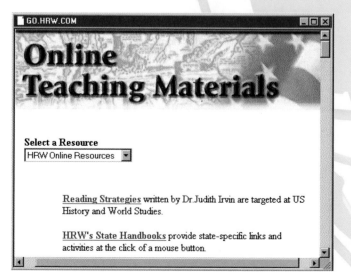

GO.HRW.COM

Online Teaching Materials

Select a Resource
HRW Online Resources

Reading Strategies written by Dr. Judith Irvin are targeted at US History and World Studies.

HRW's State Handbooks provide state-specific links and activities at the click of a mouse button.

Instructional Value

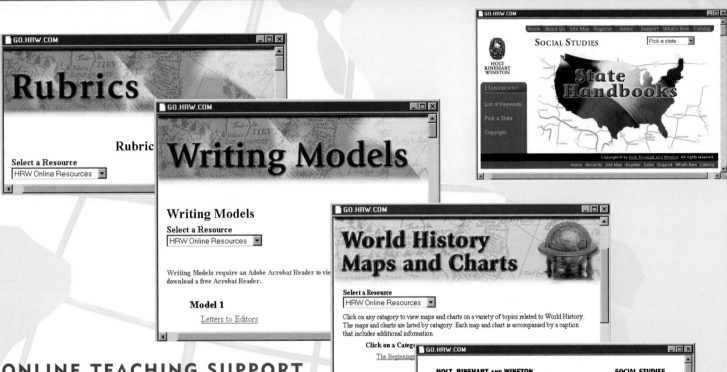

ONLINE TEACHING SUPPORT

Teacher materials on **go.hrw.com** offer you multiple resources for keeping content current. From **World History Maps and Charts** to **State Handbooks,** we've got it all.

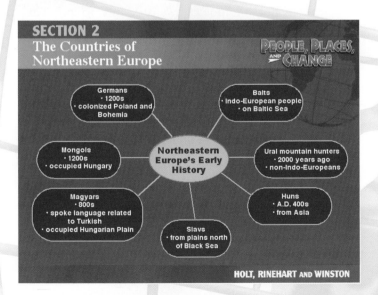

CLASSROOM PRESENTATION SUPPORT

Lecture notes and animated graphic organizers help add visual support to your classroom presentations.

Technology that

go.hrw.com FOR STUDENTS

Your students can access interactive activities, homework help, up-to-date maps, and more when they visit **go.hrw.com** and type in the keywords they find in their text.

ONLINE WORLD TRAVEL

When you log on to **go.hrw.com**, you and your students gain passage to **GeoTreks**—a site with guided Internet activities that integrate program content, spark imaginations, and promote online research skills. You'll find:

Interactive templates for creating newspapers, postcards, travel brochures, guided research reports, and more

GeoMaps—Interactive satellite maps of the world's regions for content review

Drag-and-drop exercises to review chapter content in short, fun activities

Chapter Web Links for prescreened, age-appropriate Web sites and current events

HOMEWORK PRACTICE

This helpful tool allows students to practice and review content by chapter anywhere there is a computer.

HRW ONLINE ATLAS AND HISTORICAL MAPS

The helpful online atlas contains over 300 well-rendered and clearly labeled country and state maps. Available in English and Spanish, these maps are continually updated so you can rest assured that you and your students have the latest and most accurate geographical content.

Online historical maps provide fascinating visual "snapshots" of the past. Students will relish the chance to explore medieval European trade routes, explorers' routes, ancient African kingdoms, and more.

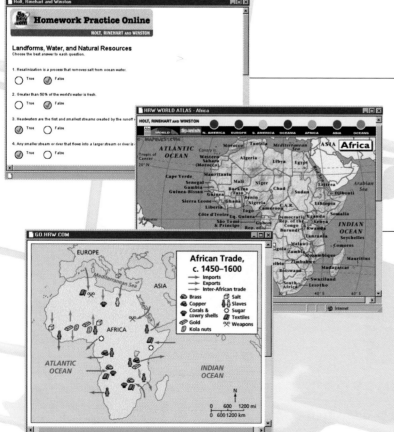

Delivers Content

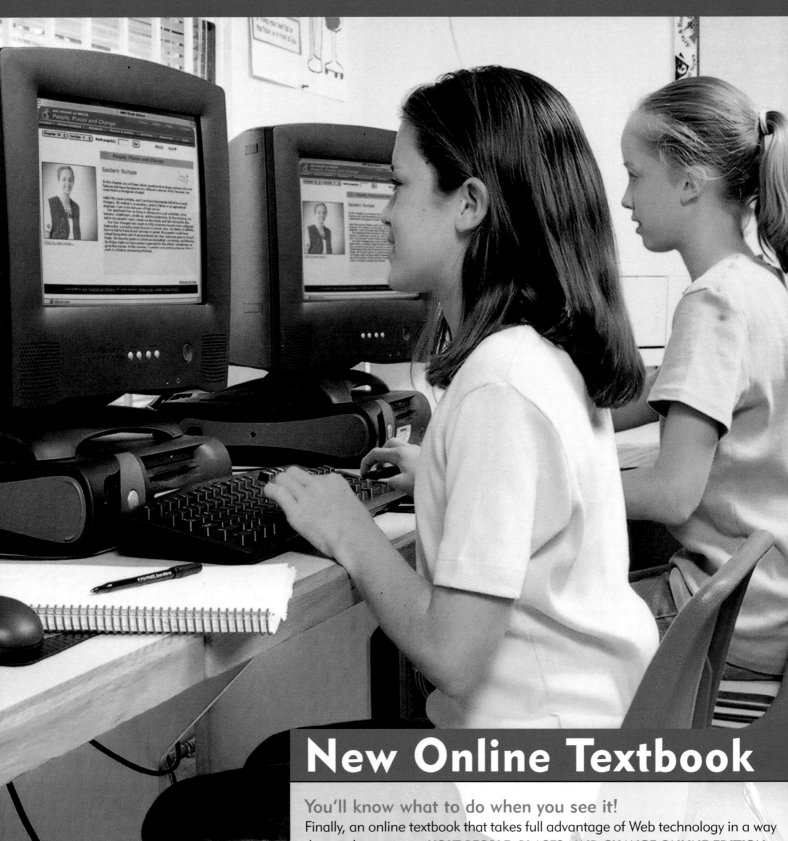

New Online Textbook

You'll know what to do when you see it!
Finally, an online textbook that takes full advantage of Web technology in a way that makes sense—*HOLT PEOPLE, PLACES, AND CHANGE ONLINE EDITION.*

- **Entire student edition online, formatted to match printed text**
- **User-friendly navigation**
- **Hot links to interactive activities, practice, and assessment**
- **Student Notebook for online responses**

Unique Teacher's

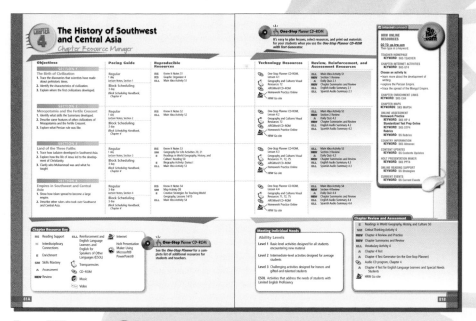

In-Text Chapter Planning

TEACHER TO TEACHER

These strategies are offered in the columns of your *Annotated Teacher's Edition* and provide you with valuable, classroom-tested ideas and activities that have been developed and successfully applied by your peers.

FOOD FESTIVAL

Kolaches are popular Czech or Polish pastries. For a shortcut version, use frozen bread dough. Or, make a sweetened yeast dough from scratch. After the dough has risen, roll it out, cut it into circles 2–3 inches across, and indent the center of each. Add a filling of fruit preserves, cottage cheese with egg and sugar, or a sweetened poppyseed paste. Let rise again. Sprinkle with a streusel topping of sugar, cinnamon, butter, and a little flour. Bake at 375° for 15–20 minutes. There are many *kolache* recipes on the Internet. *Kolacky* and *kolachke* are alternate spellings.

OBJECTIVE-BASED LESSON CYCLE

With lively activities and presentation strategies such as **Let's Get Started, Building Vocabulary,** and **Graphic Organizers,** your step-by-step lesson cycle makes planning your lessons easy and productive.

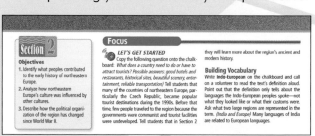

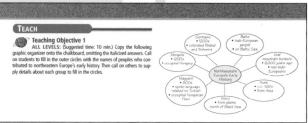

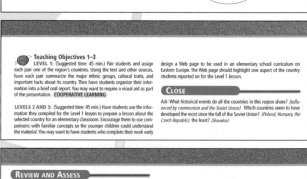

Side-Column Annotations that Spark Curiosity

- **Across the Curriculum: Art**
- **Across the Curriculum: History**
- **Across the Curriculum: Literature**
- **Across the Curriculum: Math**
- **Across the Curriculum: Science**
- **Across the Curriculum: Technology**
- **Cooperative Learning**
- **Cultural Kaleidoscope**
- **Daily Life**
- **Eye on Earth**
- **Geography sidelight**
- **Global Perspectives**
- **Historical Geography**
- **Linking Past to Present**
- **National Geography Standards**
- **People in the Profile**
- **Using Illustrations**

Management System

Everything you need is on one disc!

ONE-STOP PLANNER® CD–ROM WITH TEST GENERATOR

Holt brings you the most user-friendly management system in the industry with the **One-Stop Planner CD–ROM with Test Generator.** Plan and manage your lessons from this single disc containing all the teaching resources for **Holt People, Places, and Change,** valuable planning and assessment tools, and more.

- **Editable lesson plans**
- **Classroom Lecture Notes and Animated Graphic Organizers**
- **Easy-to-use test generator**
- **Previews of all teaching and video resources**
- **Easy printing feature**
- **Direct launch to go.hrw.com**

BLOCK SCHEDULING HANDBOOK

This is more than a pacing guide—it provides daily lesson plans that suggest practical ways to cover more than one textbook section in an extended class period and ways to make interdisciplinary connections.

PRESENTATIONS THAT BENEFIT LEARNING

Classroom presentations and lecture notes can be accessed with ease when you use Holt's **Presentation** tool found on the **One-Stop Planner CD–ROM**. This resource helps you spice up your presentations and gives you ideas to build on. You'll find Microsoft® PowerPoint® presentations that include lecture notes and animated graphic organizers for each chapter and section of your text.

M15

Assessment for

Section Review 1

Define and explain: exotic rivers, wadis, fossil water

Working with Sketch Maps On a map of the Arabian Peninsula, Iraq, Iran, and Afghanistan that you draw or that your teacher provides, label the following: Persian Gulf, Arabian Peninsula, Red Sea, Arabian Sea, Tigris River, Euphrates River, Elburz Mountains, Zagros Mountains, Hindu Kush, and Rub' al-Khali.

Reading for the Main Idea
1. *Places and Regions* Why do you think Mesopotamia was important in ancient times?
2. *Places and Regions* What is the region's climate?

Critical Thinking
3. **Drawing Inferences and Conclusions** Why do you think the Persian Gulf is important to international trade?
4. **Drawing Inferences and Conclusions** What settlement pattern might you find in this region?

Organizing What You Know
5. **Summarizing** Copy the following graphic organizer. Use it to list as many details of landforms, resources, and climate as you can. Place them in the correct part of the diagram.

Arabian Peninsula — Iraq — Iran and Afghanistan

go.hrw.com **Homework Practice Online**
Keyword: SK5 HP6

THE SUPERIOR TEST GENERATOR THAT REALLY WORKS!

M16

CHAPTER 4 Review and Practice

Define and Identify

Identify each of the following:

1. hominid
2. land bridges
3. irrigation
4. Sumerians
5. Fertile Crescent
6. Persians
7. cuneiform
8. Judaism
9. Abraham
10. Christianity
11. Jesus
12. Muhammad
13. mosques
14. Genghis Khan
15. Ottoman Turks

Review the Main Ideas

16. What are the four characteristics of civilization?
17. How did the development of agriculture lead to the growth of villages and towns?
18. What were some of the Sumerians' achievements?
19. How did the Assyrians rule?
20. What do Judaism, Christianity, and Islam have in common?

21. What event convinced Jesus' followers that he w the Messiah?
22. What were some achievements of the Islamic Empire?
23. How were the Mongols able to conquer so much territory?

Think Critically

24. **Drawing Conclusions** Why is the ability to make and use tools an important step in human development?
25. **Drawing Inferences** Why are the developme a calendar, a system of counting, and a system o writing so important to a civilization?
26. **Analyzing Information** According to traditio how did the Jews escape slavery in Egypt?
27. **Contrasting** On what issue do the Sunni and Shia disagree?
28. **Evaluating** How did the Muslim Empire becom powerful?

Map Activity

29. Identify the places marked on the map.
    Sumer
    Mesopotamia
    Palestine
    Arabia
    Baghdad

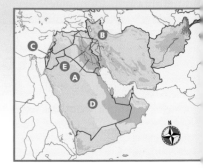

Every Student

ACCESS ONLINE RUBRICS
FOR GRADING PROJECTS AND
PORTFOLIO ASSIGNMENTS

Writing Activity

Imagine that you are a merchant who comes to Mesopotamia to do business. Write a diary entry about what you see both in the cities and in the countryside. First, choose a time period in which to set your "visit." Then review which culture controlled the area at the time and what life was like during that time. You may want to pay particular attention to the technologies that you see demonstrated and how those technologies affect your business deals. For example, how might the Persian road system have affected your ability to bring goods to market? Use the illustrations in the chapter to help you add detail to your diary entry.

internet connect

Internet Activity: go.hrw.com
KEYWORD: SK5 GT4

Choose a topic to explore about the history of Southwest and Central Asia:
• Learn more about the development of writing.
• Explore the Persian Empire.
• Trace the spread of the Mongol Empire.

Social Studies Skills Practice

Interpreting Maps

Study the following map about trade routes from Mesopotamia. Then answer the questions.

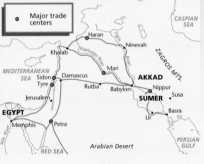

1. What role did the Tigris and Euphrates play in trade?
2. According to this map, how far west did the trade routes from Mesopotamia extend?
3. Why do you think there were no routes through the Arabian Desert?
4. What major trade center was located in Sumer?

Analyzing Primary Sources

Read the following passage from the Code of Hammurabi. Then answer the questions.

"If any one open his ditches to water his crop, but is careless, and the water flood the field of his neighbor, then he shall pay his neighbor corn for his loss. . . . If a man let in the water, and the water overflow the plantation of his neighbor, he shall pay ten gur of corn for every ten gan of land."

1. What is the main purpose of this portion of the Code of Hammurabi?
2. Based on your knowledge of ancient civilizations, why would this issue be important?
3. Based on your understanding of this quote, what do you think a *gur* and a *gan* are?
4. Does the punishment in the code seem just and fair? Why or why not?

SOCIAL STUDIES
SKILLS REVIEW

WORLD HISTORY AND GEOGRAPHY DOCUMENT-BASED QUESTIONS ACTIVITIES

This resource provides a wide variety of primary sources and thought-provoking questions to help students develop intelligent, well-formed opinions. Important historical and geographical themes are grouped together, allowing for scaffolded instruction.

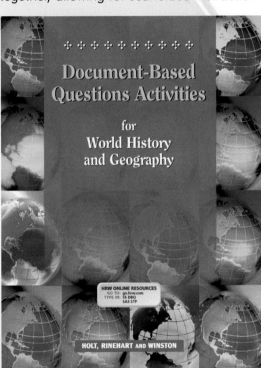

✦ ✦ ✦ ✦ ✦ ✦ ✦ ✦ ✦ ✦
Document-Based
Questions Activities
for
World History
and Geography

HRW ONLINE RESOURCES
GO TO: go.hrw.com
TYPE IN: SS DBQ
SA3 STP

HOLT, RINEHART AND WINSTON

Additional Print and Technology Assessment Resources

■ **Daily Quizzes**

■ **Chapter Tutorials for Students, Parents, Mentors, and Peers**

■ **Chapter and Unit Tests**

■ **Chapter and Unit Tests for English Language Learners and Special-Needs Students**

■ **Alternative Assessment Handbook**

■ **Test Generator (located on the One-Stop Planner)**

PEOPLE, PLACES, AND CHANGE

Eastern Hemisphere

CONTENTS

UNIT 1 An Introduction to World Geography and Cultures 1

Notes from the Field

UNIT 3 Africa 162

Notes from the Field

UNIT 5 East and Southeast Asia 342
Notes from the Field

FEATURES

FEATURES

Connecting to Science

Connecting to Technology

FOCUS ON

FEATURES

MAPS

FEATURES

FEATURES

DIAGRAMS, CHARTS, and TABLES

ATLAS CONTENTS

WORLD: PHYSICAL

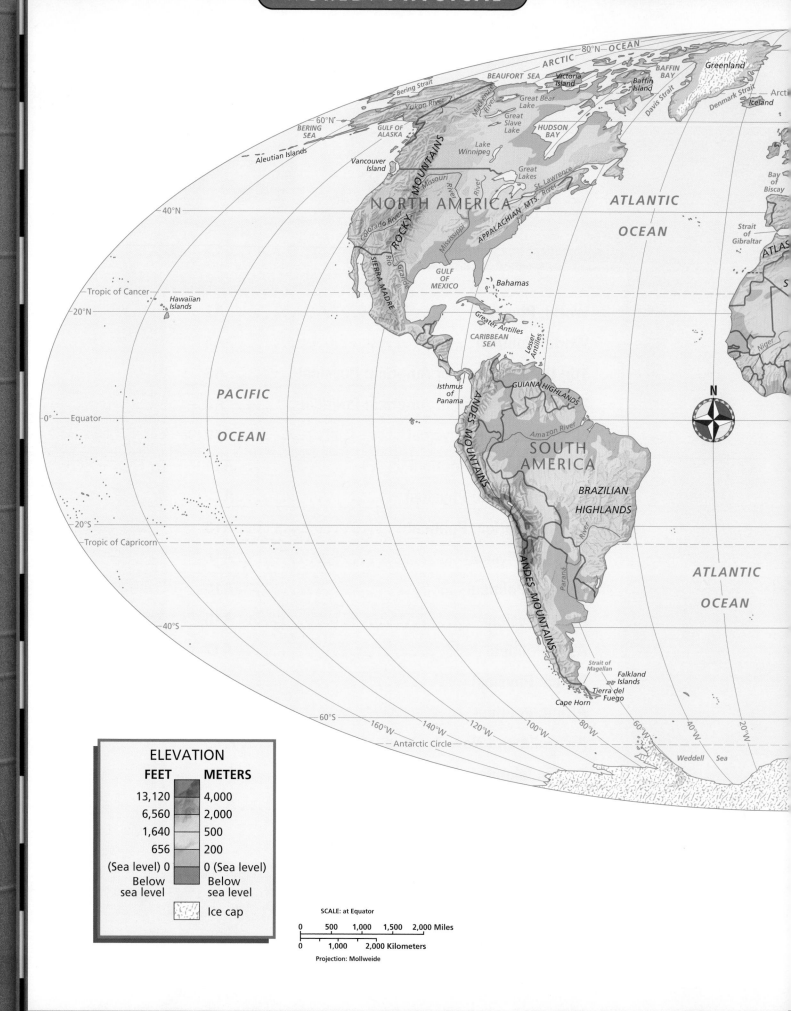

ARCTIC OCEAN

80°N

BEAUFORT SEA

Victoria Island

BAFFIN BAY

Baffin Island

Greenland

Bering Strait

Yukon River

Mackenzie River

Great Bear Lake

Great Slave Lake

HUDSON BAY

Davis Strait

Denmark Strait

Iceland

Arcti

60°N

BERING SEA

GULF OF ALASKA

Lake Winnipeg

Bay of Biscay

Aleutian Islands

Vancouver Island

ROCKY MOUNTAINS

Missouri River

Great Lakes

St. Lawrence River

APPALACHIAN MTS.

ATLANTIC OCEAN

Strait of Gibraltar

ATLAS

40°N

Colorado River

NORTH AMERICA

Mississippi

SIERRA MADRE

Rio Grande

GULF OF MEXICO

Bahamas

S

Tropic of Cancer

20°N

Hawaiian Islands

Greater Antilles

CARIBBEAN SEA

Lesser Antilles

Niger

PACIFIC

Isthmus of Panama

GUIANA HIGHLANDS

N

0° Equator

OCEAN

ANDES MOUNTAINS

Amazon River

SOUTH AMERICA

BRAZILIAN HIGHLANDS

20°S

Tropic of Capricorn

Parana River

ATLANTIC

40°S

ANDES MOUNTAINS

OCEAN

Strait of Magellan

Falkland Islands

Tierra del Fuego

Cape Horn

60°S

160°W 140°W 120°W 100°W 80°W 60°W 40°W 20°W

Antarctic Circle

Weddell Sea

ELEVATION

FEET	METERS
13,120	4,000
6,560	2,000
1,640	500
656	200
(Sea level) 0	0 (Sea level)
Below sea level	Below sea level

Ice cap

SCALE: at Equator

0   500   1,000   1,500   2,000 Miles

0   1,000   2,000 Kilometers

Projection: Mollweide

ARCTIC 80°N OCEAN

North Cape
BARENTS SEA
KARA SEA
LAPTEV SEA
EAST SIBERIAN SEA

BALTIC SEA
EUROPE

Yenisei River
Ob River
Lena River
Kolyma River

60°N

SEA OF OKHOTSK
KAMCHATKA PENINSULA

ALPS

BLACK SEA

Volga River

URAL MOUNTAINS

ARAL SEA

Baiqash Lake

Lake Baikal

Amur River

Sakhalin Island

MEDITERRANEAN SEA

CASPIAN SEA

Tigris River
Euphrates River

Persian Gulf

ALTAY MOUNTAINS

GOBI

ASIA

Huang He

40°N

Hokkaido

SEA OF JAPAN

Honshu

HIMALAYAS

Chang River

Shikoku
Kyushu

SAHARA

NILE RED SEA
ARABIAN PENINSULA

THAR DESERT
Ganges River

Tigris River

EAST CHINA SEA

Taiwan

Tropic of Cancer

AFRICA

Congo River

ARABIAN SEA

Bay of Bengal

Mekong River

SOUTH CHINA SEA

Philippine Islands

PACIFIC

20°N

OCEAN

Lake Tanganyika
Lake Victoria

Sri Lanka

Strait of Malacca

MALAY PENINSULA

Sumatra

Borneo

Celebes

New Guinea

Solomon Islands

Equator 0°

INDIAN OCEAN

Java

Madagascar

Mozambique Channel

CORAL SEA

New Hebrides

Fiji Islands

KALAHARI DESERT

GREAT SANDY DESERT

AUSTRALIA

GREAT VICTORIA DESERT

Darling River

GREAT DIVIDING RANGE

New Caledonia

20°S

Tropic of Capricorn

Cape of Good Hope

TASMAN SEA

North Island

NEW ZEALAND

Tasmania

South Island

20°E 40°E 60°E 80°E 100°E 120°E 140°E 160°E

60°S

ANTARCTICA

Denmark Strait
Iceland

North Cape

20°E 30°E 40°E

BARENTS SEA

KARA SEA

KJÖLEN MTS.

URAL MTS.

N

0 250 500 750 Miles
0 250 500 750 Kilometers

Projection: Mollweide

60°N

NORTH SEA

BALTIC SEA

Volga River

British Isles

Rhine River

ALPS

Danube River

BLACK SEA

50°N

ATLANTIC OCEAN

Bay of Biscay

40°N

MEDITERRANEAN SEA

Euphrates R.
Tigris R.

Strait of Gibraltar

Crete

WORLD: POLITICAL

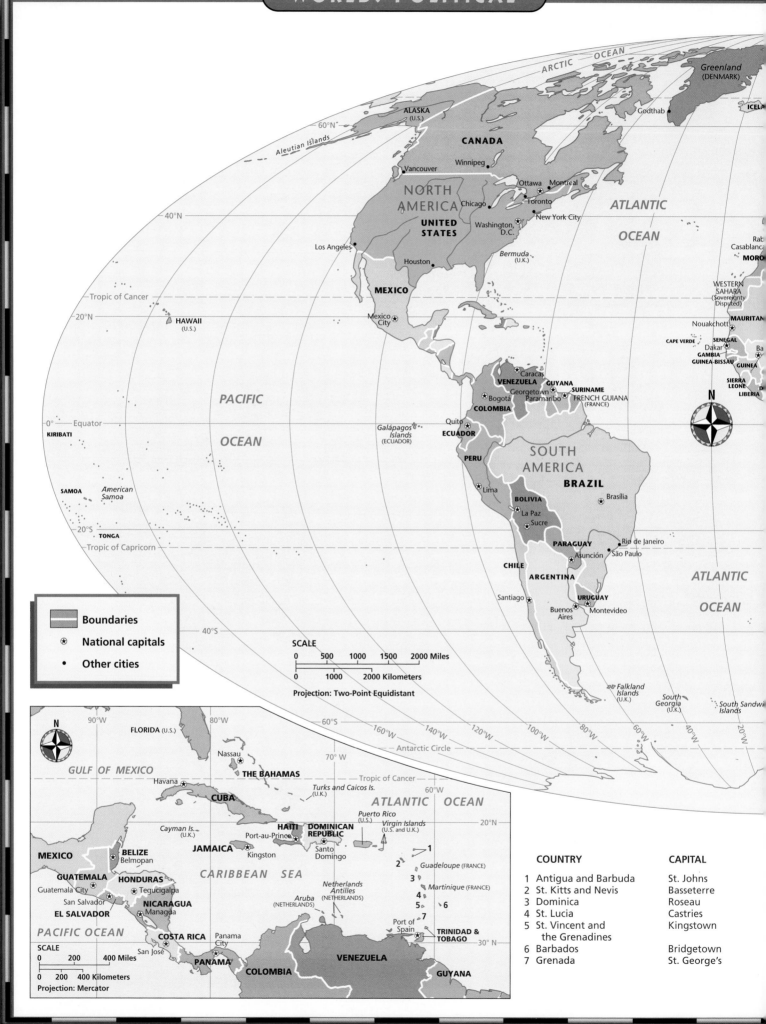

ARCTIC OCEAN

Greenland (DENMARK)

Godthab

ICELA

ALASKA (U.S.)

60°N

CANADA

Vancouver   Winnipeg
                        Ottawa   Montreal
NORTH AMERICA   Chicago   Toronto
                        New York City
40°N

UNITED STATES   Washington, D.C.

ATLANTIC OCEAN

Los Angeles

Houston

Bermuda (U.K.)

MEXICO

Rab
Casablanca
MORO

Tropic of Cancer

20°N

HAWAII (U.S.)

Mexico City

WESTERN SAHARA (Sovereignty Disputed)

Nouakchott   MAURITAN

MAURITAN

CAPE VERDE   SENEGAL
                        Dakar   Ba
                        GAMBIA
                        GUINEA-BISSAU   GUINEA

PACIFIC

Caracas
VENEZUELA   GUYANA
Georgetown   SURINAME
Bogotá   Paramaribo   FRENCH GUIANA (FRANCE)
COLOMBIA

SIERRA LEONE
LIBERIA

N

0°   Equator

KIRIBATI

OCEAN

Quito
ECUADOR

Galápagos Islands (ECUADOR)

PERU

SOUTH AMERICA

BRAZIL

Brasília

SAMOA

American Samoa

Lima

BOLIVIA
La Paz
Sucre

20°S

TONGA

Tropic of Capricorn

PARAGUAY   Rio de Janeiro
                        Asunción   São Paulo

CHILE   ARGENTINA

URUGUAY

ATLANTIC OCEAN

Santiago

Buenos Aires   Montevideo

Legend

	Boundaries
✪	National capitals
•	Other cities

40°S

SCALE

0   500   1000   1500   2000 Miles

0   1000   2000 Kilometers

Projection: Two-Point Equidistant

Falkland Islands (U.K.)

South Georgia (U.K.)

South Sandwich Islands

60°S

160°W   140°W   120°W   100°W   80°W   60°W   40°W   20°W

Antarctic Circle

Inset map (Caribbean)

N

90°W   80°W

FLORIDA (U.S.)

Nassau

GULF OF MEXICO   THE BAHAMAS

Havana

CUBA

Turks and Caicos Is. (U.K.)

70°W

Puerto Rico (U.S.)   Virgin Islands (U.S. and U.K.)

ATLANTIC OCEAN

20°N

Cayman Is. (U.K.)

HAITI   DOMINICAN REPUBLIC
Port-au-Prince

60°W

1

MEXICO

JAMAICA
Kingston

Santo Domingo

2   Guadeloupe (FRANCE)

BELIZE
Belmopan

CARIBBEAN SEA

3   Martinique (FRANCE)

Netherlands Antilles (NETHERLANDS)

4

GUATEMALA   HONDURAS
Guatemala City   Tegucigalpa
San Salvador
NICARAGUA
EL SALVADOR   Managua

Aruba (NETHERLANDS)

5   6

7

Port of Spain

PACIFIC OCEAN

COSTA RICA   Panama City

San José

TRINIDAD & TOBAGO

30°N

SCALE

0   200   400 Miles

0   200   400 Kilometers

Projection: Mercator

PANAMA

VENEZUELA

COLOMBIA

GUYANA

COUNTRY	CAPITAL
1 Antigua and Barbuda	St. Johns
2 St. Kitts and Nevis	Basseterre
3 Dominica	Roseau
4 St. Lucia	Castries
5 St. Vincent and the Grenadines	Kingstown
6 Barbados	Bridgetown
7 Grenada	St. George's

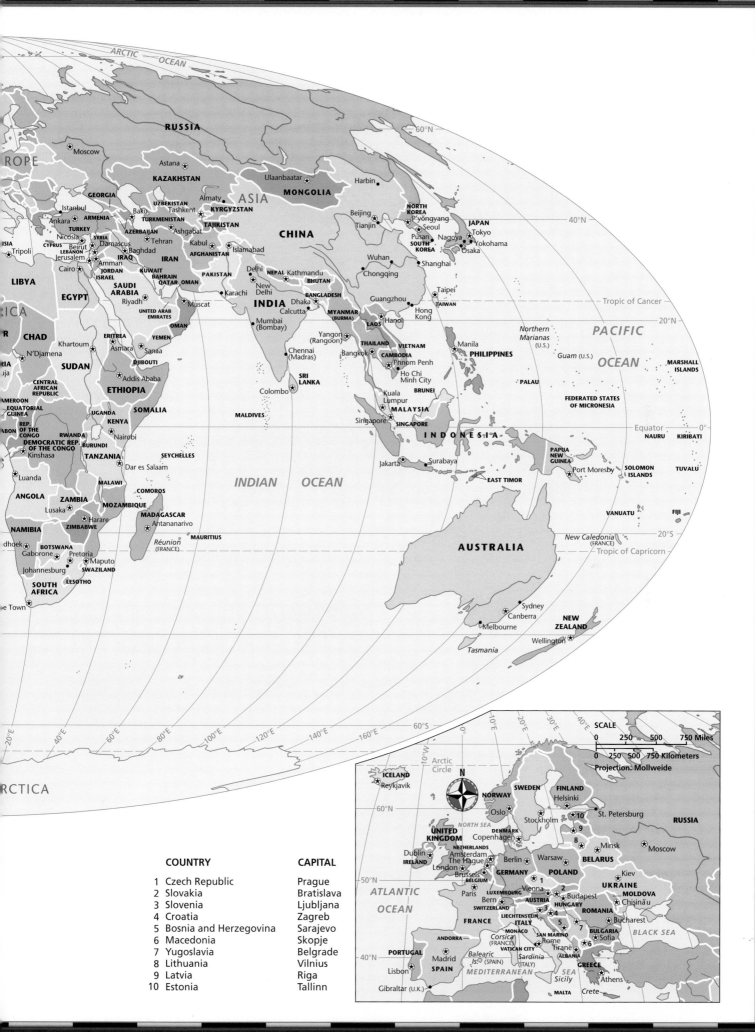

ARCTIC OCEAN

RUSSIA

Moscow

EUROPE

KAZAKHSTAN

Astana

GEORGIA

Istanbul

Ankara

ARMENIA

TURKEY

Baku

AZERBAIJAN

Almaty

UZBEKISTAN

Tashkent

KYRGYZSTAN

Ashgabat

TAJIKISTAN

TURKMENISTAN

ASIA

Ulaanbaatar

MONGOLIA

Harbin

Beijing

Tianjin

NORTH KOREA

P'yŏngyang

Seoul

SOUTH KOREA

Pusan

JAPAN

Nagoya

Tokyo

Yokohama

Osaka

Nicosia

CYPRUS

SYRIA

LEBANON

Beirut

Damascus

Tehran

Kabul

Islamabad

CHINA

Wuhan

Chongqing

Shanghai

60°N

40°N

Tripoli

Jerusalem

ISRAEL

Amman

JORDAN

IRAQ

Baghdad

IRAN

AFGHANISTAN

Cairo

KUWAIT

BAHRAIN

QATAR

PAKISTAN

Delhi

New Delhi

NEPAL

Kathmandu

BHUTAN

Guangzhou

Taipei

TAIWAN

Hong Kong

Tropic of Cancer

LIBYA

EGYPT

SAUDI ARABIA

Riyadh

UNITED ARAB EMIRATES

OMAN

Muscat

Karachi

INDIA

Mumbai (Bombay)

Calcutta

BANGLADESH

Dhaka

MYANMAR (BURMA)

Hanoi

LAOS

Yangon (Rangoon)

THAILAND

VIETNAM

Manila

PHILIPPINES

Northern Marianas (U.S.)

Guam (U.S.)

PACIFIC OCEAN

20°N

AFRICA

CHAD

N'Djamena

Khartoum

ERITREA

Asmara

YEMEN

Sanaa

SUDAN

DJIBOUTI

Addis Ababa

ETHIOPIA

Chennai (Madras)

SRI LANKA

Colombo

Bangkok

CAMBODIA

Phnom Penh

Ho Chi Minh City

BRUNEI

Kuala Lumpur

MALAYSIA

SINGAPORE

Singapore

PALAU

FEDERATED STATES OF MICRONESIA

MARSHALL ISLANDS

CENTRAL AFRICAN REPUBLIC

CAMEROON

EQUATORIAL GUINEA

GABON

REP. OF THE CONGO

DEMOCRATIC REP. OF THE CONGO

Kinshasa

RWANDA

BURUNDI

UGANDA

KENYA

Nairobi

SOMALIA

TANZANIA

Dar es Salaam

SEYCHELLES

MALDIVES

INDONESIA

Jakarta

Surabaya

EAST TIMOR

PAPUA NEW GUINEA

Port Moresby

SOLOMON ISLANDS

NAURU

KIRIBATI

Equator

TUVALU

0°

Luanda

ANGOLA

ZAMBIA

Lusaka

MALAWI

MOZAMBIQUE

COMOROS

MADAGASCAR

Antananarivo

INDIAN OCEAN

VANUATU

FIJI

NAMIBIA

ZIMBABWE

Harare

Réunion (FRANCE)

MAURITIUS

New Caledonia (FRANCE)

20°S

dhoek

BOTSWANA

Gaborone

Pretoria

Maputo

SWAZILAND

AUSTRALIA

Tropic of Capricorn

Johannesburg

LESOTHO

SOUTH AFRICA

e Town

Sydney

Canberra

Melbourne

NEW ZEALAND

Tasmania

Wellington

20°E

40°E

60°E

80°E

100°E

120°E

140°E

160°E

60°S

ARCTICA

COUNTRY — CAPITAL

	COUNTRY	CAPITAL
1	Czech Republic	Prague
2	Slovakia	Bratislava
3	Slovenia	Ljubljana
4	Croatia	Zagreb
5	Bosnia and Herzegovina	Sarajevo
6	Macedonia	Skopje
7	Yugoslavia	Belgrade
8	Lithuania	Vilnius
9	Latvia	Riga
10	Estonia	Tallinn

SCALE

0 250 500 750 Miles

0 250 500 750 Kilometers

Projection: Mollweide

Arctic Circle

ICELAND

Reykjavik

NORWAY

SWEDEN

FINLAND

Helsinki

St. Petersburg

RUSSIA

60°N

NORTH SEA

Oslo

Stockholm

10

9

8

UNITED KINGDOM

DENMARK

Copenhagen

Minsk

Moscow

Dublin

IRELAND

NETHERLANDS

Amsterdam

The Hague

London

Berlin

Warsaw

BELARUS

GERMANY

POLAND

Kiev

ATLANTIC OCEAN

Brussels

BELGIUM

LUXEMBOURG

Paris

Vienna

1

2

Budapest

HUNGARY

UKRAINE

MOLDOVA

Chişinău

50°N

Bern

SWITZERLAND

AUSTRIA

LIECHTENSTEIN

3

4

ROMANIA

Bucharest

FRANCE

ITALY

5

7

BULGARIA

Sofia

BLACK SEA

ANDORRA

Corsica (FRANCE)

MONACO

SAN MARINO

Rome

VATICAN CITY

Sardinia (ITALY)

Tiranë

ALBANIA

6

PORTUGAL

Madrid

Balearic Is. (SPAIN)

GREECE

40°N

Lisbon

SPAIN

MEDITERRANEAN SEA

Sicily

Athens

Gibraltar (U.K.)

MALTA

Crete

45°N

130°W

125°W

Strait of
Juan De Fuca

Puget
Sound

Mount Rainier
14,410 ft.
(4,392 m)

COAST RANGES

CASCADE RANGE

Columbia River

COLUMBIA PLATEAU

BITTERROOT RANGE

Salmon River Range

SALMON RIVER MTS.

SAWTOOTH MTS.

Franklin D.
Roosevelt
Lake

Pend
Oreille

Clark Fork

Flathead River

Flathead
Lake

LEWIS RANGE

R O C K Y

Milk River

Missouri River

Fort Peck
Lake

Yellowstone River

G R E A T

Red River

Lake
Sakakawea

40°N

PACIFIC
OCEAN

Cape
Mendocino

Klamath River

Goose
Lake

Snake River

Yellowstone Lake

GRAND TETONS

CONTINENTAL

WIND RIVER RANGE

Gannett Peak
13,804 ft.
(4,207 m)

M O U N T A I N S

BIGHORN MTS.

Bighorn River

Powder River

Cheyenne River

BLACK
HILLS

Niobrara River

White River

James River

Lake
Oahe

Lake

Minne

I N T E R I O R

35°N

125°W

San Francisco Bay

Monterey
Bay

COAST RANGES

SIERRA NEVADA

CENTRAL VALLEY

San Joaquin River

Sacramento River

Shasta
Lake

Pyramid
Lake

Lake Tahoe

GREAT
BASIN

Great
Salt
Lake

Utah
Lake

WASATCH RANGE

UINTA MTS.

Green River

Colorado River

DIVIDE

FRONT RANGE

RIVER

Mount Elbert
14,433 ft.
(4,400 m)

DIVIDE

South Platte River

North Platte River

Pikes Peak
14,110 ft.
(4,301 m)

Republican River

P L A I N S

Smoky Hill River

Kansas

Platte River

Mount Whitney
14,494 ft.
(4,419 m)

DEATH VALLEY

MOJAVE
DESERT

Lake
Mead

Colorado River

GRAND
CANYON

COLORADO

PLATEAU

PAINTED DESERT

San Juan River

Lake
Powell

SAN LUIS
VALLEY

SANGRE DE CRISTO MTS.

DIVIDE

Arkansas

Keystone Lake

Eufaula
Lake

30°N

Channel Islands

Salton
Sea

IMPERIAL
VALLEY

Gila River

SONORA
DESERT

CONTINENTAL

Canadian River

Lake
Texoma

120°W

115°W

Gulf of
California

Pecos River

Rio
Grande

Amistad
Reservoir

Colorado River

Brazos

Trini

G U L

To understand the relative locations of Alaska and Hawaii,
as well as the vast distances separating them from the rest
of the United States, see the world map.

Nueces River

MEXICO

Falcon
Lake

Padre
Island

25°N

Hawaii inset

Kauai

Niihau

Oahu

Molokai

Maui

Lanai

Kahoolawe

Mauna Kea
13,796 ft.
(4,206 m)

Hawaii

PACIFIC OCEAN

22°N

19°N

160°W

155°W

N

SCALE
0   75   150 Miles
0   75   150 Kilometers

Alaska inset

180°

ARCTIC OCEAN

Arctic Circle

RUSSIA

Bering Strait

St. Lawrence
Island

St. Matthew
Island

Nunivak
Island

BROOKS RANGE

Yukon River

Kuskokwim River

Tanana River

ALASKA RANGE

Mount McKinley
20,320 ft.
(6,194 m)

CANADA

65°N

60°N

Kodiak
Island

GULF OF
ALASKA

Alexander
Archipelago

140°W

130°W

55°N

Attu Island

BERING SEA

SCALE
0   250   500 Miles
0   250   500 Kilometers

Projection: Albers Equal Area

A l e u t i a n   I s l a n d s

PACIFIC
OCEAN

170°E

55°N

50°N

170°W

160°W

150°W

CANADA

MESABI RANGE
Isle Royale
Lake Superior
Lake Huron
Lake Michigan
Mississippi River
Wisconsin River
Des Moines River

PLAINS

Lake of the Ozarks
Illinois River
Wabash River
Ohio River
Scioto River
Allegheny River

OZARK PLATEAU
OUACHITA MTS.
White River
Mississippi River
Kentucky Lake
Lake Barkley
Cumberland River
Tennessee River
Red River

Lake Erie

Finger Lakes

Lake Ontario

St. Lawrence River
St. Lawrence Seaway

ADIRONDACK MTS.

Lake Champlain
GREEN MTS.
WHITE MTS.
LONGFELLOW MTS.
St. John River
Penobscot River
Connecticut River

CATSKILL MTS.

PLATEAU

ALLEGHENY

Susquehanna River
Monongahela R.
Kanawha River
Potomac River

APPALACHIAN MOUNTAINS

Delaware R.
Hudson R.
Cape Cod
Long Island Sound
Long Island

Delaware Bay
Chesapeake Bay

James River
Roanoke River

BLUE RIDGE MOUNTAINS

GREAT SMOKY MTS.

CUMBERLAND PLATEAU

PIEDMONT

ATLANTIC COASTAL PLAIN

Pamlico Sound
Cape Hatteras

COASTAL PLAIN

Tombigbee River
Coosa River
Oconee River
Savannah River
Alabama R.
Chattahoochee River
Altamaha River
Pearl River
Sea Islands

Okefenokee Swamp

Chandeleur Islands
Mississippi Delta

GULF OF MEXICO

FLORIDA PENINSULA

Cape Canaveral

Lake Okeechobee

The Everglades

Cape Sable
Florida Key

ATLANTIC OCEAN

THE BAHAMAS

Straits of Florida

CUBA

ELEVATION

FEET	METERS
13,120	4,000
6,560	2,000
1,640	500
656	200
(Sea level) 0	0 (Sea level)
Below sea level	Below sea level
Ice cap	

N

SCALE
0   250   500 Miles
0   250   500 Kilometers
Projection: Albers Equal Area

THE UNITED STATES OF AMERICA: POLITICAL

PACIFIC OCEAN

Strait of Juan de Fuca

Puget Sound
Seattle
Tacoma
Olympia
WASHINGTON
Spokane

Franklin D. Roosevelt Lake

Pend Oreille

Portland
Columbia River

Salem

Eugene

OREGON

Flathead Lake

Helena ★ **MONTANA**

Fort Peck Lake

Billings

Missouri River

Yellowstone River

NORTH DAKOTA
Bismarck ★
Fargo

Lake Sakakawea

Red River

IDAHO

Boise ★

Snake River

Yellowstone Lake

WYOMING

Pocatello

Casper

Cheyenne ★

Lake Oahe

SOUTH DAKOTA
Pierre ★

Sioux Falls

Minne...

Cape Mendocino

Goose Lake

Shasta Lake

Sacramento River

Pyramid Lake

Reno
Carson City ★
Lake Tahoe

NEVADA

Great Salt Lake

Utah Lake
Salt Lake City ★
Provo

UTAH

Green River

Denver ★

COLORADO

Colorado Springs

NEBRASKA

Platte River

Omaha
Lincoln ★

Berkeley
Oakland
San Francisco
San Francisco Bay
Sacramento
Stockton
Modesto
San Joaquin R.
San Jose
Monterey Bay

Fresno

CALIFORNIA

Bakersfield

Los Angeles
Long Beach
Channel Islands
Anaheim
Santa Ana

San Diego

Salton Sea

Las Vegas

Lake Mead

Colorado River

Lake Powell

ARIZONA

Phoenix ★

Gila River

Tucson

Santa Fe ★

Albuquerque

NEW MEXICO

Topeka ★

KANSAS

Wichita

Arkansas River

Keystone Lake

OKLAHOMA

Amarillo

Oklahoma City ★

Eufaula Lake

Canadian River

Lubbock

Lake Texo...

Abilene

Fort Worth

Dallas

TEXAS

Brazos River

Waco

Odessa

Pecos River

Colorado River

Austin ★

El Paso

Rio Grande

Amistad Reservoir

San Antonio

Corpus Christi

Laredo

MEXICO

Padre Island

Gulf of California

Inset Maps

To understand the relative locations of Alaska and Hawaii as well as the vast distances separating them from the rest of the United States, see the world map.

Hawaii
Kauai
Niihau
Oahu
Honolulu ★
Molokai
Lanai
Kahoolawe
Maui
Hawaii
HAWAII
PACIFIC OCEAN

SCALE
0   75   150 Miles
0   75   150 Kilometers

N

Alaska
ARCTIC OCEAN
Arctic Circle
RUSSIA
Bering Strait
Nome
St. Lawrence Island
St. Matthew Island
Nunivak Island
Yukon River
Fairbanks
ALASKA
CANADA
Anchorage
Kodiak Island
GULF OF ALASKA
Juneau ★
Alexander Archipelago

BERING SEA
Attu Island
Aleutian Islands
PACIFIC OCEAN

SCALE
0   250   500 Miles
0   250   500 Kilometers
Projection: Albers Equal Area

N

CANADA

MINNESOTA
Duluth

Lake Superior

Minneapolis
St. Paul
WISCONSIN
Madison
Milwaukee

IOWA
Cedar Rapids
Davenport
Des Moines

Rockford
Chicago

MICHIGAN
Grand Rapids
Lansing
Ann Arbor
Detroit
Flint

Lake Michigan
Lake Huron

Gary
South Bend
Fort Wayne

Peoria
Springfield
INDIANA
Indianapolis

ILLINOIS

Toledo
Cleveland

Lake Erie

OHIO
Columbus
Dayton
Cincinnati

Youngstown
Akron

Pittsburgh

PENNSYLVANIA
Allentown
Harrisburg
Philadelphia

Susquehanna River

Buffalo
Rochester
Syracuse
Albany

NEW YORK

Lake Ontario

St. Lawrence River

Lake Champlain

MAINE
Augusta

Montpelier

VT.
N.H.
Concord

MASS.
Boston
Springfield
Worcester
CONN.
Providence
R.I.
Hartford
New Haven
Bridgeport
Cape Cod

Newark
New York City
Jersey City
Trenton
N.J.

Long Island Sound
Long Island

Hudson River
Connecticut River

St. Louis
Jefferson City

Lake of the Ozarks

MISSOURI
Springfield

Evansville

Louisville

Frankfort
Lexington

KENTUCKY

Ohio River
Wabash River

Lake Barkley
Kentucky Lake

WEST VIRGINIA
Charleston

VIRGINIA
Richmond
Roanoke
Newport News
Portsmouth

Arlington
Alexandria

Baltimore
MD.
Annapolis
Washington, D.C.

DELAWARE
Dover

Delaware Bay

Chesapeake Bay

Norfolk

Cape Hatteras

Kansas City

Fayetteville

ARKANSAS
Little Rock

TENNESSEE
Nashville
Chattanooga
Memphis
Huntsville
Knoxville

Winston-Salem
Greensboro
Durham
Raleigh

NORTH CAROLINA
Charlotte

SOUTH CAROLINA
Columbia

MISSISSIPPI
Jackson

ALABAMA
Birmingham
Montgomery

GEORGIA
Atlanta
Macon
Columbus

Savannah River

Shreveport

LOUISIANA
Baton Rouge
Beaumont
New Orleans

Mobile

Chandeleur Islands

Tallahassee

Jacksonville

Savannah

Sea Islands

Chattahoochee River

Mississippi River
Red River

GULF OF MEXICO

FLORIDA
Orlando
Cape Canaveral
Tampa
St. Petersburg
Lake Okeechobee

Fort Lauderdale
Miami

Cape Sable

Florida Keys
Straits of Florida

THE BAHAMAS

CUBA

ATLANTIC OCEAN

Boundaries
⊛ National capitals
★ State capitals
• Other cities

N

SCALE
0   250   500 Miles
0   250   500 Kilometers

Projection: Albers Equal Area

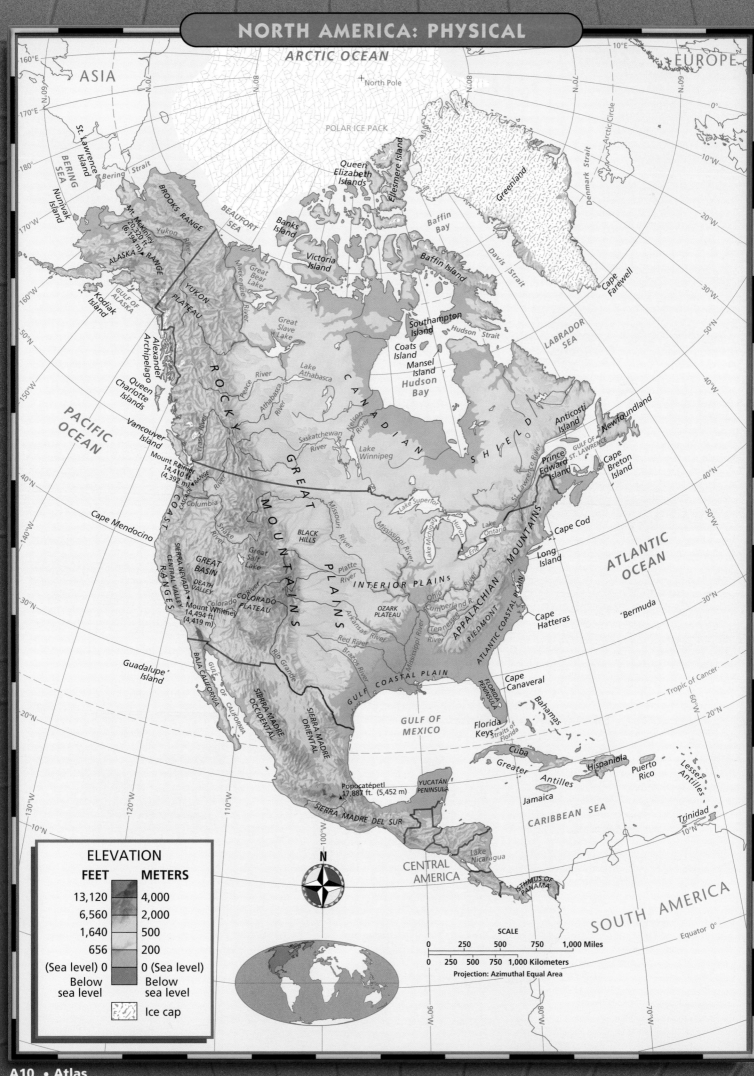

NORTH AMERICA: PHYSICAL

ARCTIC OCEAN

ASIA

EUROPE

North Pole

POLAR ICE PACK

St. Lawrence Island

BERING SEA

Nunivak Island

Bering Strait

BEAUFORT SEA

Queen Elizabeth Islands

Ellesmere Island

Greenland

Denmark Strait

BROOKS RANGE

Mt. McKinley 20,320 ft. (6,194 m)

Yukon River

Banks Island

Victoria Island

Baffin Bay

Baffin Island

Davis Strait

Cape Farewell

ALASKA RANGE

GULF OF ALASKA

Kodiak Island

YUKON PLATEAU

Mackenzie River

Great Bear Lake

Southampton Island

Hudson Strait

LABRADOR SEA

Alexander Archipelago

Queen Charlotte Islands

Great Slave Lake

Coats Island

Mansel Island

Vancouver Island

PACIFIC OCEAN

Peace River

Athabasca River

Lake Athabasca

C A N A D I A N

Hudson Bay

S H I E L D

Anticosti Island

Newfoundland

Mount Rainier 14,410 ft. (4,392 m)

R O C K Y

Saskatchewan River

Nelson River

Lake Winnipeg

Prince Edward Island

GULF OF ST. LAWRENCE

Cape Breton Island

Columbia River

CASCADE RANGE

G R E A T

Missouri River

Lake Superior

St. Lawrence River

Cape Mendocino

COAST RANGES

Snake River

M O U N T A I N S

BLACK HILLS

Lake Michigan

Lake Huron

Lake Ontario

APPALACHIAN MOUNTAINS

Cape Cod

Long Island

ATLANTIC OCEAN

SIERRA NEVADA

CENTRAL VALLEY

GREAT BASIN

Great Salt Lake

P L A I N S

Platte River

Mississippi River

Ohio River

Cumberland R.

PIEDMONT

Cape Hatteras

Bermuda

DEATH VALLEY

Mount Whitney 14,494 ft. (4,419 m)

COLORADO PLATEAU

Colorado River

INTERIOR PLAINS

Arkansas River

OZARK PLATEAU

Tennessee River

Red River

ATLANTIC COASTAL PLAIN

Guadalupe Island

BAJA CALIFORNIA

GULF OF CALIFORNIA

Rio Grande

Brazos River

GULF COASTAL PLAIN

FLORIDA PENINSULA

Cape Canaveral

Tropic of Cancer

SIERRA MADRE OCCIDENTAL

SIERRA MADRE ORIENTAL

GULF OF MEXICO

Florida Keys

Straits of Florida

Bahamas

Cuba

Greater Antilles

Hispaniola

Puerto Rico

Lesser Antilles

Popocatépetl 17,887 ft. (5,452 m)

YUCATÁN PENINSULA

Jamaica

CARIBBEAN SEA

Trinidad

SIERRA MADRE DEL SUR

Lake Nicaragua

CENTRAL AMERICA

ISTHMUS OF PANAMA

SOUTH AMERICA

Equator 0°

ELEVATION

FEET	METERS
13,120	4,000
6,560	2,000
1,640	500
656	200
(Sea level) 0	0 (Sea level)
Below sea level	Below sea level

Ice cap

N

SCALE

0 250 500 750 1,000 Miles

0 250 500 750 1,000 Kilometers

Projection: Azimuthal Equal Area

NORTH AMERICA: POLITICAL

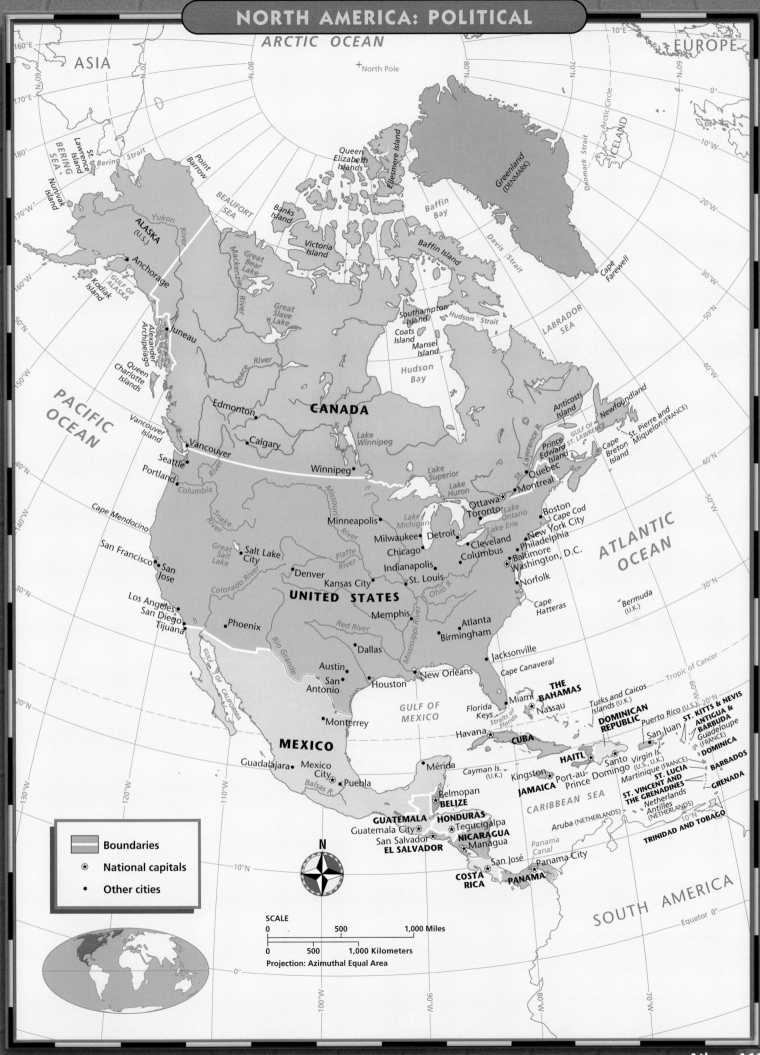

ARCTIC OCEAN

North Pole

EUROPE

ASIA

ICELAND

BERING SEA

St. Lawrence Island

Bering Strait

Nunivak Island

Point Barrow

BEAUFORT SEA

Banks Island

Queen Elizabeth Islands

Ellesmere Island

Greenland (DENMARK)

Denmark Strait

ALASKA (U.S.)

Yukon River

Victoria Island

Great Bear Lake

Baffin Island

Baffin Bay

Davis Strait

Cape Farewell

Anchorage

GULF OF ALASKA

Kodiak Island

Juneau

Alexander Archipelago

Mackenzie River

Great Slave Lake

Southampton Island

Coats Island

Mansel Island

Hudson Strait

LABRADOR SEA

PACIFIC OCEAN

Queen Charlotte Islands

Peace River

CANADA

Hudson Bay

Anticosti Island

Newfoundland

Vancouver Island

Edmonton

Lake Winnipeg

St. Lawrence R.

Prince Edward Island

GULF OF ST. LAWRENCE

Cape Breton Island

St. Pierre and Miquelon (FRANCE)

Vancouver

Calgary

Winnipeg

Lake Superior

Quebec

Seattle

Portland

Columbia R.

Snake River

Missouri River

Lake Michigan

Lake Huron

Ottawa

Toronto

Lake Ontario

Lake Erie

Montreal

Boston

Cape Cod

New York City

ATLANTIC OCEAN

Minneapolis

Milwaukee

Detroit

Cleveland

Philadelphia

Cape Mendocino

Great Salt Lake

Salt Lake City

Platte River

Chicago

Columbus

Baltimore

Washington, D.C.

San Francisco

San Jose

Denver

Colorado River

Kansas City

Indianapolis

St. Louis

Ohio R.

Norfolk

Los Angeles

San Diego

Tijuana

Phoenix

UNITED STATES

Red River

Memphis

Mississippi River

Atlanta

Birmingham

Cape Hatteras

Bermuda (U.K.)

Dallas

Jacksonville

Cape Canaveral

Tropic of Cancer

Austin

San Antonio

Houston

New Orleans

Rio Grande

GULF OF CALIFORNIA

Monterrey

GULF OF MEXICO

Florida Keys

Miami

Nassau

THE BAHAMAS

Turks and Caicos Islands (U.K.)

Straits of Florida

DOMINICAN REPUBLIC

Puerto Rico (U.S.)

ST. KITTS & NEVIS

ANTIGUA & BARBUDA

MEXICO

Havana

CUBA

Guadalajara

Mexico City

Mérida

San Juan

Guadeloupe (FRANCE)

DOMINICA

Puebla

Cayman Is. (U.K.)

HAITI

Santo Domingo

Virgin Is. (U.S., U.K.)

Martinique (FRANCE)

BARBADOS

Balsas R.

Kingston

Port-au-Prince

ST. LUCIA

JAMAICA

ST. VINCENT AND THE GRENADINES

GRENADA

Belmopan

Netherlands Antilles (NETHERLANDS)

BELIZE

CARIBBEAN SEA

GUATEMALA

HONDURAS

Aruba (NETHERLANDS)

TRINIDAD AND TOBAGO

Guatemala City

San Salvador

Tegucigalpa

NICARAGUA

EL SALVADOR

Managua

Panama Canal

San José

Panama City

COSTA RICA

PANAMA

SOUTH AMERICA

Equator 0°

Legend

Boundaries

⊛ National capitals

• Other cities

N

SCALE

0 — 500 — 1,000 Miles

0 — 500 — 1,000 Kilometers

Projection: Azimuthal Equal Area

SOUTH AMERICA: PHYSICAL

CENTRAL AMERICA

CARIBBEAN SEA

Panama Canal

GULF OF PANAMA

Malpelo Island

Margarita Island

Tobago
Trinidad

Orinoco River Delta

N

ATLANTIC OCEAN

Lake Maracaibo

LLANOS

Orinoco River

Angel Falls

GUIANA HIGHLANDS

Devil's Island
Cape Orange

Cauca River

Meta River

▲ Mount Tolima
18,425 ft. (5,616 m)

Magdalena River

Orinoco River

Rio Negro

Amazon River Delta

Caquetá River

Japurá River

AMAZON BASIN

Amazon River

Equator 0°

Galápagos Islands

Equator

▲ Mount Chimborazo
20,561 ft. (6,267 m)

GULF OF GUAYAQUIL

Marañón River

Amazon River

Juruá River

Purus River

Madeira River

Tapajós River

Xingu River

Tocantins River

Parnaíba River

ANDES

Ucayali River

Mamoré River

10°S

Mount Huascarán
22,205 ft. (6,768 m)

Beni River

MATO GROSSO PLATEAU

BRAZILIAN HIGHLANDS

PACIFIC OCEAN

Lake Titicaca

▲ Ancohuma Peak
20,958 ft. (6,388 m)

Araguaia River

São Francisco River

10°S

Lake Poopó

ATACAMA DESERT

CHACO

BRAZILIAN PLATEAU

San Ambrosio Island

Pilcomayo River

San Félix Island

Tropic of Capricorn

ANDES

Paraguay River

Salado River

20°S

Tropic of Capricorn

Juan Fernández Islands

Salado River

Paraná River

Paraguay River

Uruguay River

Río de la Plata

ATLANTIC OCEAN

30°S

Mount Aconcagua
22,834 ft. (6,960 m)

PAMPAS

Colorado River

GULF OF SAN MATÍAS

Chiloé Island

CHONOS ARCHIPELAGO

PATAGONIA

GULF OF SAN JORGE

Cape Tres Puntas

Falkland Islands

40°S

South Georgia Islands

Bahía Grande

Strait of Magellan

TIERRA DEL FUEGO

CAPE HORN

50°S

ELEVATION

FEET		METERS
13,120		4,000
6,560		2,000
1,640		500
656		200
(Sea level) 0		0 (Sea level)
Below sea level		Below sea level

SCALE

0   250   500   750   1,000 Miles

0   250   500   750   1,000 Kilometers

Projection: Azimuthal Equal Area

SOUTH AMERICA: POLITICAL

CENTRAL AMERICA

CARIBBEAN SEA

ATLANTIC OCEAN

N

Barranquilla
Cartagena
Caracas
Lake Maracaibo

VENEZUELA

Georgetown
Paramaribo
Cayenne

GUYANA

SURINAME
FRENCH GUIANA (FRANCE)

Medellín

⊛ Bogotá

COLOMBIA

Cali

Malpelo Island (COLOMBIA)

Orinoco River

Rio Negro

Amazon River

Equator 0°

Quito ⊛

ECUADOR

Guayaquil

Galápagos Islands (ECUADOR)

0° Equator

Belém

Amazon River

BRAZIL

Marañón River

Ucayali River

PERU

Trujillo

Callao

⊛ Lima

Recife

São Francisco River

PACIFIC OCEAN

Lake Titicaca

BOLIVIA

⊛ La Paz

Arequipa

Lake Poopó

⊛ Sucre

⊛ Brasília

Salvador

Belo Horizonte

PARAGUAY

Paraguay River

⊛ Asunción

Campinas

São Paulo

Curitiba

Rio de Janeiro

Tropic of Capricorn

Tropic of Capricorn

San Ambrosio Island (CHILE)

San Félix Island (CHILE)

CHILE

Paraná River

Uruguay River

Pôrto Alegre

Córdoba

Juan Fernández Islands (CHILE)

Valparaíso

Santiago ⊛

Rosario

URUGUAY

⊛ Montevideo

Buenos Aires ⊛

Río de la Plata

ATLANTIC OCEAN

ARGENTINA

Legend

▨	Boundaries
⊛	National capitals
•	Other cities

SCALE

0 250 500 750 1,000 Miles

0 250 500 750 1,000 Kilometers

Projection: Azimuthal Equal Area

Strait of Magellan

Falkland Islands (U.K.)

Tierra del Fuego

South Georgia Island (U.K.)

EUROPE: PHYSICAL

ASIA

URAL MOUNTAINS

NORTHERN EUROPEAN PLAIN

CASPIAN SEA

Mt. Elbrus (5,642 m)
18,510 ft.
CAUCASUS MTS.

SOUTHWEST ASIA

BARENTS SEA

Pechora River

Dvina River

North Dvina River

Kama River

Ural River

Volga River

Don River

SEA OF AZOV

CRIMEAN PENINSULA

BLACK SEA

KOLA PENINSULA

White Sea

Lake Onega

Lake Ladoga

Rybinsk Reservoir

Dnipro River

Dnestr River

Nistru River

BALKAN PENINSULA

SEA OF MARMARA

AEGEAN SEA

Rhodes

Crete

North Cape

PLAINS

GULF OF FINLAND

Daugava R.

Dzvina R.

BALTIC SEA

Vistula River

Oder River

CARPATHIAN MTS.

TRANSYLVANIAN ALPS

Danube River

DINARIC ALPS

ADRIATIC SEA

KJØLEN MOUNTAINS

GULF OF BOTHNIA

Lake Vättern

Lake Vänern

Kattegat

Skagerrak

Elbe River

Rhine River

Danube River

Po River

APENNINES

Tiber River

Corsica

Sardinia

TYRRHENIAN SEA

Sicily

Malta

MEDITERRANEAN SEA

AFRICA

ARCTIC OCEAN

Arctic Circle

NORWEGIAN SEA

Iceland

Faeroe Islands

Shetland Islands

Orkney Islands

Hebrides

British Isles

IRISH SEA

PENNINES

Thames River

English Channel

NORTH SEA

ALPS

Lake Geneva

15,781 ft. Mont Blanc (4,810 m)

Seine River

Loire River

Rhône River

Garonne River

PYRENEES

Bay of Biscay

Ebro River

Cape Finisterre

IBERIAN PENINSULA

Douro River

Tagus River

Guadiana River

Guadalquivir River

Strait of Gibraltar

ATLANTIC OCEAN

N

ELEVATION

FEET	METERS
13,120	4,000
6,560	2,000
1,640	500
656	200
(Sea level) 0	0 (Sea level)
Below sea level	Below sea level

Ice cap

SCALE

0   250   500 Miles

0   250   500 Kilometers

Projection: Azimuthal Equal Area

ASIA

URAL MOUNTAINS

RUSSIA

Nizhny Novgorod

Moscow

St. Petersburg

BARENTS SEA

WHITE SEA

ARCTIC OCEAN

North Cape

FINLAND

SWEDEN

NORWAY

Helsinki

GULF OF BOTHNIA

Stockholm

Göteborg

Oslo

Bergen

ESTONIA
Tallinn

LATVIA
Riga

LITHUANIA
Vilnius

RUSSIA

BELARUS
Minsk

BALTIC SEA

POLAND
Warsaw

Kraków

UKRAINE
Kiev

Dnipro River

MOLDOVA
Chişinău

CASPIAN SEA

BLACK SEA

SOUTHWEST ASIA

ROMANIA
Bucharest

Danube River

BULGARIA
Sofia

SERBIA AND MONTENEGRO
Belgrade

MACEDONIA
Skopje

ALBANIA
Tiranë

GREECE
Athens

AEGEAN SEA

Rhodes

Crete

SLOVAKIA
Bratislava

HUNGARY
Budapest

CZECH REPUBLIC
Prague

Dresden

Berlin

Hamburg

Elbe River

GERMANY
Cologne
Bonn

DENMARK
Copenhagen

NORTH SEA

NETHERLANDS
The Hague
Amsterdam

BELGIUM
Brussels

LUXEMBOURG
Luxembourg

Munich

Danube River

AUSTRIA
Vienna

SLOVENIA
Ljubljana

CROATIA
Zagreb

BOSNIA & HERZEGOVINA
Sarajevo

LIECHTENSTEIN
Vaduz

SWITZERLAND
Bern
Geneva
Lake Geneva

Rhine River

SAN MARINO
San Marino

MONACO
Monaco

ITALY
Rome
Naples

VATICAN CITY

Milan
Po River

ADRIATIC SEA

Sicily

MALTA
Valletta

MEDITERRANEAN SEA

Corsica (FRANCE)

Sardinia (ITALY)

Balearic Islands (SPAIN)

FRANCE
Paris

Seine River

Loire River

Rhône River

Lyons

Marseilles

Bay of Biscay

ANDORRA
Andorra la Vella

PYRENEES

Barcelona

Valencia

SPAIN
Madrid

Seville

Tagus River

PORTUGAL
Lisbon

Gibraltar (U.K.)

Strait of Gibraltar

AFRICA

ATLANTIC OCEAN

ALPS

ICELAND
Reykjavík

Faeroe Islands (DENMARK)

Shetland Islands

SCOTLAND
Edinburgh

UNITED KINGDOM

NORTHERN IRELAND
Belfast

IRELAND
Dublin

ENGLAND
Liverpool
London

WALES

Thames R.

English Channel

Channel Islands (U.K.)

British Isles

Arctic Circle

Danube River

Ural River

Don River

Volga River

N

Atlas • A15

Boundaries
National capitals
Other cities

SCALE

0   250   500 Miles

0   250   500 Kilometers

Projection: Azimuthal Equal Area

Boundaries
⊛ National capitals
• Other cities

PACIFIC OCEAN

AUSTRALIA

IRIAN JAYA

EAST TIMOR

ARAFURA SEA

CELEBES SEA

JAVA SEA

PHILIPPINES

SOUTH CHINA SEA

INDONESIA

BRUNEI

Bandar Seri Begawan

MALAYSIA

SINGAPORE

Kuala Lumpur

Sujung Pandang

Semarang

Surabaya

Jakarta

Bandung

Medan

BRUNEI

EAST CHINA SEA

Taipei

TAIWAN

Hong Kong

Macao

Hainan (CHINA)

Luzon Strait

Tropic of Cancer

Ryukyu Islands (JAPAN)

Manila

VIETNAM

Hanoi

Vientiane

LAOS

CAMBODIA

Phnom Penh

THAILAND

Bangkok

GULF OF THAILAND

Ho Chi Minh City

Mekong River

ANDAMAN SEA

MYANMAR (BURMA)

Yangon (Rangoon)

Mandalay

Andaman Islands (INDIA)

Nicobar Islands (INDIA)

BEJING SEA

SEA OF OKHOTSK

Sakhalin Island

Kuril Islands (RUSSIA)

Aleutian Islands

Sapporo

JAPAN

Tokyo

Yokohama

Nagoya

Osaka

Kyoto

Hiroshima

Nagasaki

SEA OF JAPAN

Vladivostok

NORTH KOREA

P'yongyang

Seoul

SOUTH KOREA

Pusan

YELLOW SEA

Harbin

Changchun

Fushun

Dalian

Beijing

Shanghai

Qingdao

Nanjing

Wuhan

Huang River

Great Wall of China

Chang River

Chengdu

Chongqing

Guangzhou

Xi'an

CHINA

MONGOLIA

Ulaanbaatar

Lake Baykal

Irkutsk

Yakutsk

Lena River

Angara River

Yenisey River

RUSSIA

Novosibirsk

Omsk

Ob River

Irtysh River

Yekaterinburg

Chelyabinsk

URAL MOUNTAINS

KARA SEA

LAPTEV SEA

BARENTS SEA

Arctic Circle

Moscow

RUSSIA

EUROPE

MEDITERRANEAN SEA

AFRICA

RED SEA

GULF OF ADEN

Socotra (YEMEN)

ARABIAN SEA

BLACK SEA

CASPIAN SEA

Istanbul

TURKEY

Ankara

Izmir

Aleppo

CYPRUS

Nicosia

LEBANON

Beirut

Tel Aviv

Jerusalem

ISRAEL

Damascus

SYRIA

Amman

JORDAN

Mecca

Jidda

SAUDI ARABIA

Riyadh

YEMEN

Sanaa

GEORGIA

T'bilisi

ARMENIA

Yerevan

AZERBAIJAN

Baku

Tabriz

Mosul

Baghdad

IRAQ

Basra

Kuwait City

KUWAIT

BAHRAIN

Manama

QATAR

Doha

UNITED ARAB EMIRATES

Abu Dhabi

OMAN

Masqat (Muscat)

PERSIAN GULF

Tigris River

Euphrates River

IRAN

Tehran

Isfahan

Shiraz

Mashhad

TURKMENISTAN

Ashgabat

KAZAKHSTAN

Astana

Almaty

Lake Balkhash

ARAL SEA

Ural River

UZBEKISTAN

Tashkent

KYRGYZSTAN

Bishkek

TAJIKISTAN

Dushanbe

AFGHANISTAN

Kabul

PAKISTAN

Islamabad

Lahore

Faisalabad

Karachi

Indus River

INDIA

New Delhi

Delhi

Jaipur

Ahmadabad

Mumbai (Bombay)

Bhopal

Nagpur

Hyderabad

Bangalore

Chennai (Madras)

Kolkata (Calcutta)

Ganges River

Brahmaputra River

NEPAL

Kathmandu

BHUTAN

Thimphu

BANGLADESH

Dhaka

Chittagong

Bay of Bengal

SRI LANKA

Colombo

MALDIVES

Male

Lakshadweep Islands (INDIA)

INDIAN OCEAN

N

SCALE

0   500   1000 Miles

0   500   1000 Kilometers

Projection: Two-Point Equidistant

AFRICA: PHYSICAL

EUROPE

CENTRAL ASIA

SOUTHWEST ASIA

Azores

MEDITERRANEAN SEA

Madeira Islands

Strait of Gibraltar

ATLAS MOUNTAINS

Canary Islands

GULF OF SIDRA

LIBYAN DESERT

QATTARA DEPRESSION

Cape Blanc

SAHARA

AHAGGAR MOUNTAINS

TIBESTI MOUNTAINS

AIR MTS.

Suez Canal

Nile River

Lake Nasser

NUBIAN DESERT

RED SEA

PERSIAN GULF

Tropic of Cancer

Cape Verde Islands

SAHEL

Cape Verde

Senegal R.

Niger River

SUDAN

Black Volta R.

White Volta R.

CHAD BASIN

Lake Chad

Blue Nile

White Nile

Lake Tana

GULF OF ADEN

HORN OF AFRICA

SOMALI PENINSULA

FOUTA DJALLON

Lake Volta

Benue River

SUDAN BASIN

ETHIOPIAN HIGHLANDS

Cape Palmas

GULF OF GUINEA

ADAMAWA MTS.

Lake Turkana

RIFT VALLEY

Cape Lopez

Ubangi River

Congo River

CONGO BASIN

Lake Albert

Lake Edward

Mount Kenya 17,058 ft. (5,199 m)

ATLANTIC OCEAN

Equator

Kasai River

Lake Kivu

Lake Victoria

Mount Kilimanjaro 19,340 ft. (5,895 m)

SERENGETI PLAIN

MASAI STEPPE

INDIAN OCEAN

N

MITUMBA MOUNTAINS

WESTERN RIFT VALLEY

EASTERN RIFT VALLEY

Lake Tanganyika

Zanzibar

Seychelles

Ascension

Cuanza River

Lake Mweru

Lake Rukwa

Cape Delgado

Lake Malawi (Nyasa)

Comoro Islands

Lake Kariba

Zambezi River

Madagascar

Mozambique Channel

Mauritius

NAMIB DESERT

Okavango Delta

Victoria Falls

KALAHARI BASIN

Réunion

ELEVATION

FEET		METERS
13,120		4,000
6,560		2,000
1,640		500
656		200
(Sea level) 0		0 (Sea level)
Below sea level		Below sea level

Limpopo River

KALAHARI DESERT

Tropic of Capricorn

Vaal River

Orange River

DRAKENSBERG MOUNTAINS

GREAT KARROO

Cape of Good Hope

SCALE

| 0 | 500 | 1,000 Miles |
| 0 | 500 | 1,000 Kilometers |

Projection: Azimuthal Equal Area

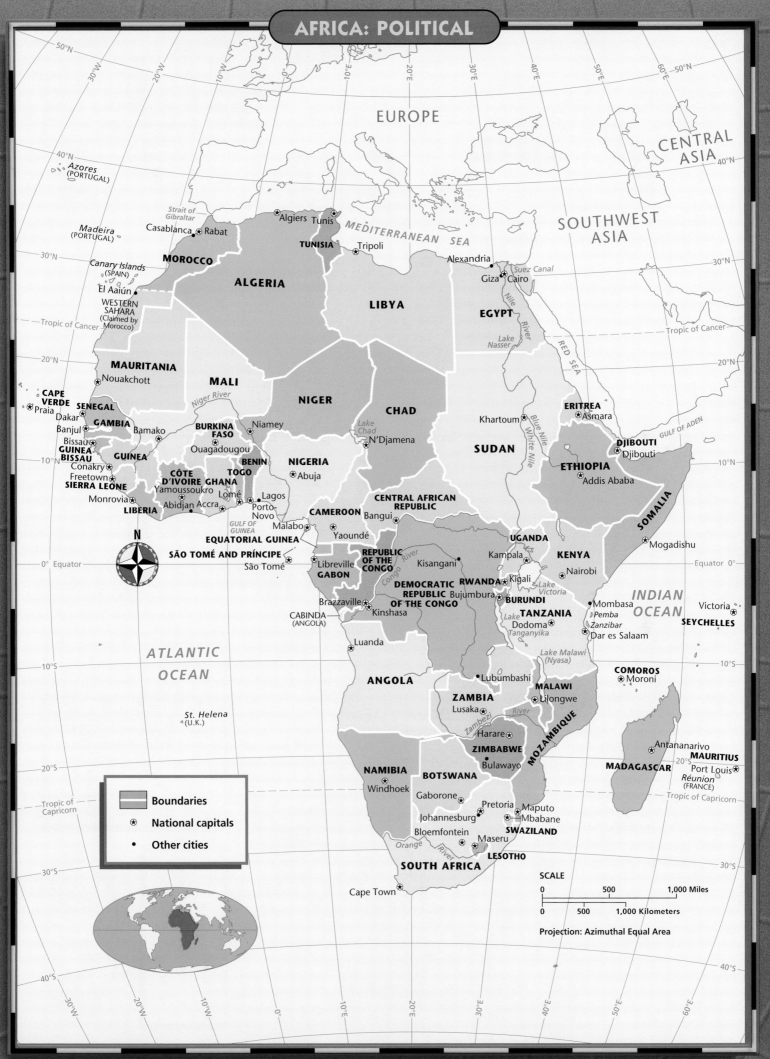

AFRICA: POLITICAL

EUROPE

CENTRAL ASIA

SOUTHWEST ASIA

MEDITERRANEAN SEA

Azores (PORTUGAL)

Madeira (PORTUGAL)

Strait of Gibraltar

Casablanca · Rabat

Algiers · Tunis

Tripoli ⊛

TUNISIA

MOROCCO

Canary Islands (SPAIN)

El Aaiún ·

WESTERN SAHARA (Claimed by Morocco)

ALGERIA

LIBYA

EGYPT

Alexandria ·

Giza · Cairo ⊛

Suez Canal

Tropic of Cancer

Lake Nasser

Nile River

RED SEA

Tropic of Cancer

MAURITANIA

Nouakchott ⊛

MALI

NIGER

CHAD

Khartoum ⊛

SUDAN

ERITREA

Asmara ⊛

GULF OF ADEN

DJIBOUTI

Djibouti ⊛

CAPE VERDE

Praia ⊛

SENEGAL

Dakar ⊛

GAMBIA

Banjul ⊛

Bamako ·

Niger River

Niamey ⊛

BURKINA FASO

Ouagadougou ⊛

Lake Chad

N'Djamena ⊛

ETHIOPIA

Addis Ababa ·

SOMALIA

Bissau ⊛

GUINEA-BISSAU

GUINEA

Conakry ⊛

Freetown ⊛

SIERRA LEONE

Monrovia ·

LIBERIA

CÔTE D'IVOIRE

Yamoussoukro ⊛

Abidjan ·

GHANA

Accra ⊛

TOGO

BENIN

Lomé ⊛

Porto-Novo ⊛

NIGERIA

Abuja ⊛

Lagos ·

CAMEROON

Yaoundé ⊛

Malabo ⊛

EQUATORIAL GUINEA

GULF OF GUINEA

SÃO TOMÉ AND PRÍNCIPE

São Tomé ⊛

CENTRAL AFRICAN REPUBLIC

Bangui ⊛

UGANDA

Kampala ⊛

Kisangani ·

Congo River

REPUBLIC OF THE CONGO

GABON

Libreville ⊛

Brazzaville ⊛

CABINDA (ANGOLA)

Kinshasa ⊛

DEMOCRATIC REPUBLIC OF THE CONGO

RWANDA

Kigali ⊛

Bujumbura ⊛

BURUNDI

Lake Victoria

KENYA

Nairobi ⊛

Mogadishu ·

TANZANIA

Dodoma ⊛

Lake Tanganyika

Mombasa ·

Pemba

Zanzibar

Dar es Salaam ·

INDIAN OCEAN

Victoria ·

SEYCHELLES

Luanda ⊛

ATLANTIC OCEAN

N

St. Helena (U.K.)

Equator 0°

Equator

ANGOLA

Lubumbashi ·

ZAMBIA

Lusaka ⊛

MALAWI

Lilongwe ⊛

Lake Malawi (Nyasa)

COMOROS

Moroni ⊛

MOZAMBIQUE

Zambezi River

Harare ⊛

ZIMBABWE

Bulawayo ·

Antananarivo ·

MAURITIUS

MADAGASCAR

Port Louis ⊛

Réunion (FRANCE)

Tropic of Capricorn

NAMIBIA

Windhoek ⊛

BOTSWANA

Gaborone ⊛

Pretoria ⊛

Johannesburg ·

Maputo ⊛

Mbabane ⊛

SWAZILAND

Maseru ⊛

LESOTHO

Bloemfontein ·

Orange River

SOUTH AFRICA

Cape Town ·

Tropic of Capricorn

Legend

▭	Boundaries
⊛	National capitals
·	Other cities

SCALE

0 ... 500 ... 1,000 Miles

0 ... 500 ... 1,000 Kilometers

Projection: Azimuthal Equal Area

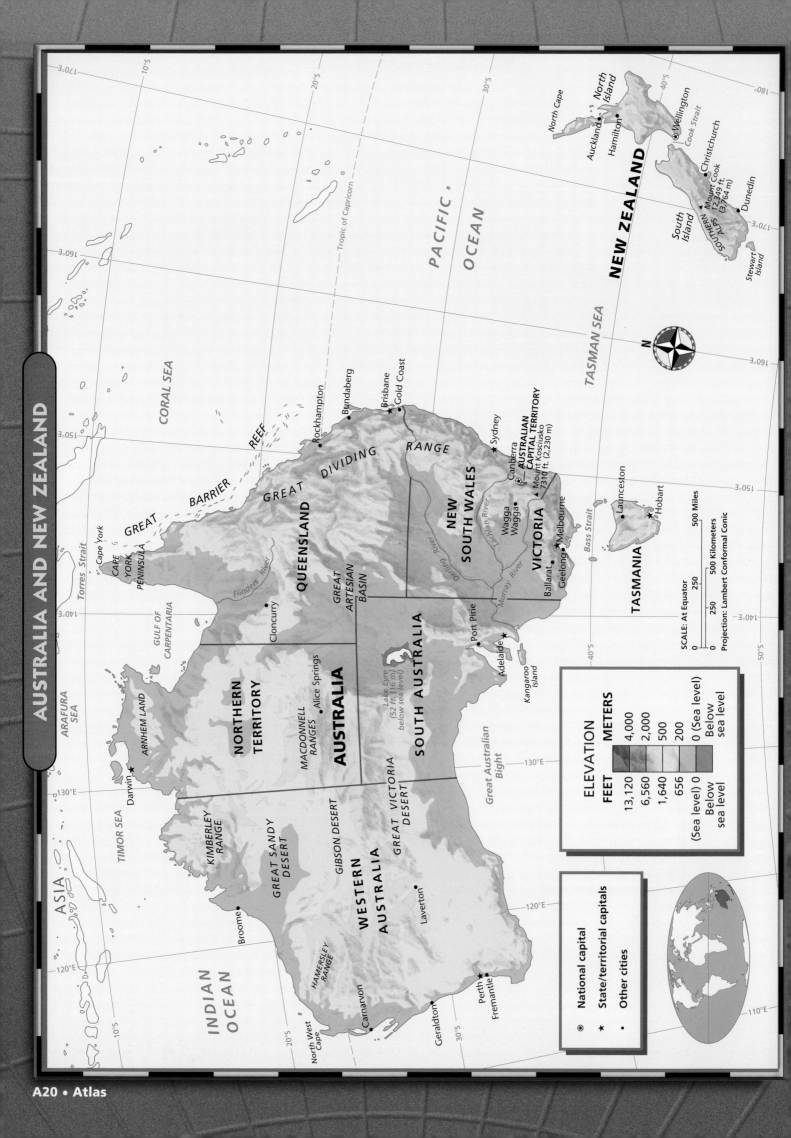

ASIA

INDIAN OCEAN

TIMOR SEA

ARAFURA SEA

ARNHEM LAND

Darwin

KIMBERLEY RANGE

GREAT SANDY DESERT

GIBSON DESERT

HAMERSLEY RANGE

North West Cape

Carnarvon

Broome

Laverton

Geraldton

Perth
Fremantle

WESTERN AUSTRALIA

GREAT VICTORIA DESERT

NORTHERN TERRITORY

MACDONNELL RANGES

Alice Springs

AUSTRALIA

SOUTH AUSTRALIA

Lake Eyre
(52 ft. [16 m]
below sea level)

Great Australian Bight

Kangaroo Island

Adelaide

Port Pirie

Cloncurry

GREAT ARTESIAN BASIN

Flinders River

GULF OF CARPENTARIA

Cape York

CAPE YORK PENINSULA

Torres Strait

GREAT

BARRIER

REEF

CORAL SEA

QUEENSLAND

GREAT DIVIDING RANGE

Rockhampton

Bundaberg

Brisbane
Gold Coast

Sydney

NEW SOUTH WALES

Canberra
AUSTRALIAN CAPITAL TERRITORY
Mount Kosciusko
7310 ft. (2,230 m)

Darling River

Lachlan River

Wagga Wagga

Murray River

VICTORIA

Ballarat

Geelong Melbourne

Bass Strait

Launceston

Hobart

TASMANIA

PACIFIC OCEAN

Tropic of Capricorn

TASMAN SEA

NEW ZEALAND

North Cape

North Island

Auckland
Hamilton

Wellington

Cook Strait

Christchurch

Mount Cook
12,349 ft.
(3,764 m)

SOUTHERN ALPS

South Island

Dunedin

Stewart Island

N

ELEVATION

FEET	METERS
13,120	4,000
6,560	2,000
1,640	500
656	200
(Sea level) 0	0 (Sea level)
Below sea level	Below sea level

SCALE: At Equator

0   250   500 Miles

0   250   500 Kilometers

Projection: Lambert Conformal Conic

⊛ National capital
★ State/territorial capitals
• Other cities

NORTH AMERICA

ASIA

JAPAN

AUSTRALIA

NEW ZEALAND

NORTH PACIFIC OCEAN

SOUTH PACIFIC OCEAN

INDIAN OCEAN

PHILIPPINE SEA

SOUTH CHINA SEA

TIMOR SEA

ARAFURA SEA

CORAL SEA

TASMAN SEA

Tropic of Cancer

Equator 0°

Tropic of Capricorn

International Date Line

30°N
15°N
15°S
30°S
45°S

120°W
135°W
150°W
165°W
180°
165°E
150°E
135°E
120°E

POLYNESIA

MICRONESIA

MELANESIA

Boundaries
National capitals ⊛
Other cities •

SCALE
1,000 Miles
500
0
1,000 Kilometers
500
0
Projection: Mercator

N

Hawaiian Islands
Hawaii (U.S.)

Midway Island (U.S.)
Johnston Island (U.S.)
Wake Island (U.S.)
Bonin Islands (JAPAN)
Volcano Islands (JAPAN)
Northern Marianas (U.S.)
Guam (U.S.) • Agana
Truk Is.

PALAU ⊛ Koror
FEDERATED STATES OF MICRONESIA Palikir ⊛
MARSHALL ISLANDS
Eniwetok I.
Kwajalein Island
⊛ Majuro
Gilbert Islands
⊛ Tarawa
NAURU Yaren ⊛
KIRIBATI
Kingman Reef (U.S.)
Washington Island
Palmyra Island (U.S.)
Fanning Island
Jarvis I. (U.S.)
Howland I. (U.S.)
Baker I. (U.S.)
McKean I.
Gardner
Phoenix Islands
Starbuck Island
Manihiki Island
Cook Islands (NEW ZEALAND)
Rarotonga Island
Tokelau (N.Z.)
SAMOA Apia ⊛
American Samoa
Pago Pago ⊛
Niue (N.Z.)
TONGA Nuku'alofa ⊛
Wallis & Futuna (FRANCE)
TUVALU Funafuti ⊛
FIJI Suva ⊛

Marquesas Islands (FRANCE)
Tuamotu Archipelago (FRANCE)
French Polynesia
Society Islands (FRANCE)
Tahiti (FRANCE)
Papeete •
Tubuai Islands (FRANCE)
Rapa Island (FRANCE)
Pitcairn (U.K.)
Pitcairn Island
Ducie Island
Easter Island (CHILE)

SOLOMON ISLANDS Honiara ⊛
Guadalcanal I.
Espiritu Santo I.
VANUATU Port-Vila ⊛
Malekula I.
New Caledonia (FRANCE) Noumea •
Loyalty Islands (FRANCE)
Norfolk Island (AUSTRALIA)
Kermadec Islands (NEW ZEALAND)
Chatham Islands (N.Z.)
Bounty Islands (N.Z.)
Auckland Islands (NEW ZEALAND)

PAPUA NEW GUINEA Port Moresby ⊛
Bismarck Archipelago
New Guinea

Christmas Island (AUSTRALIA)

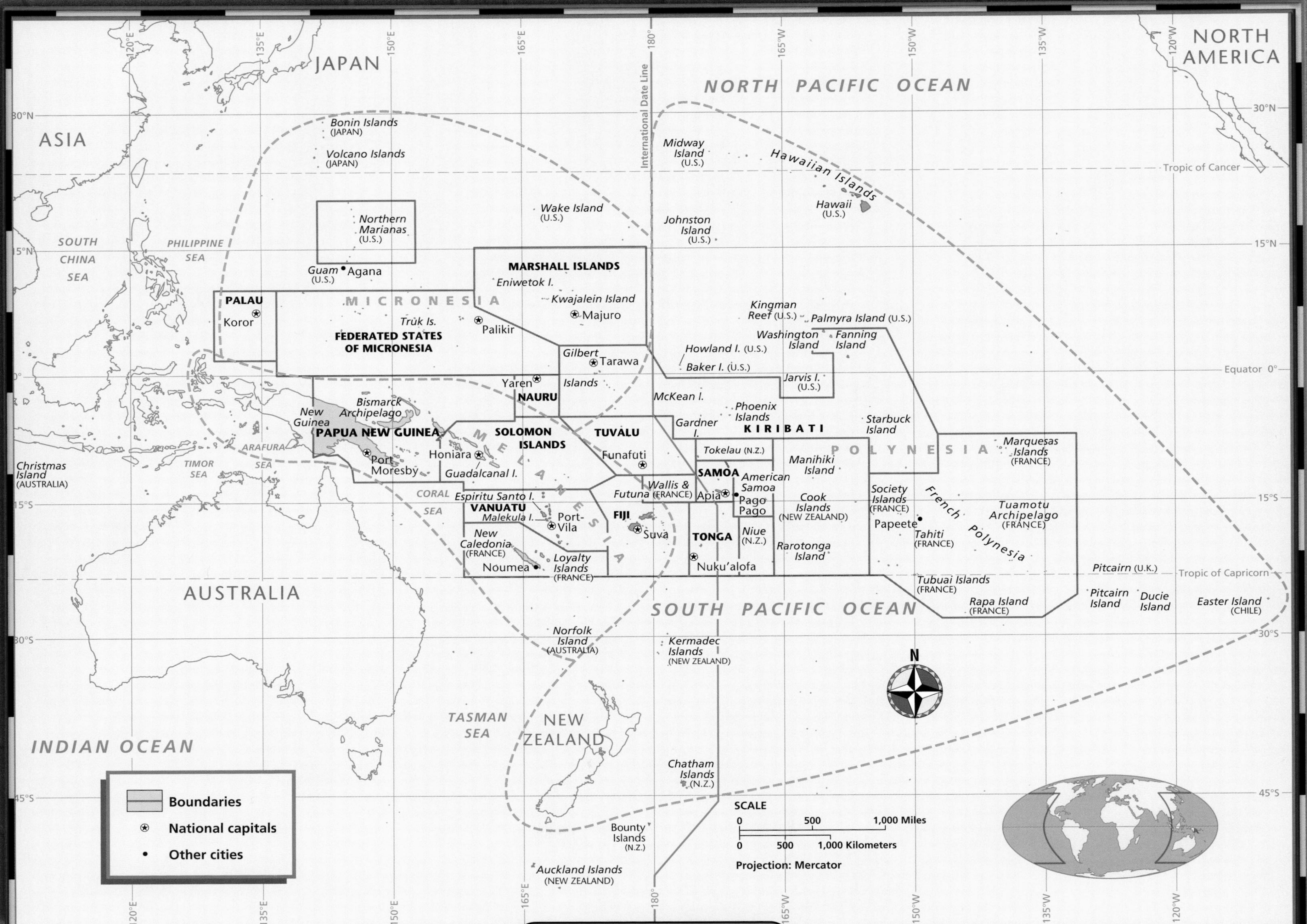

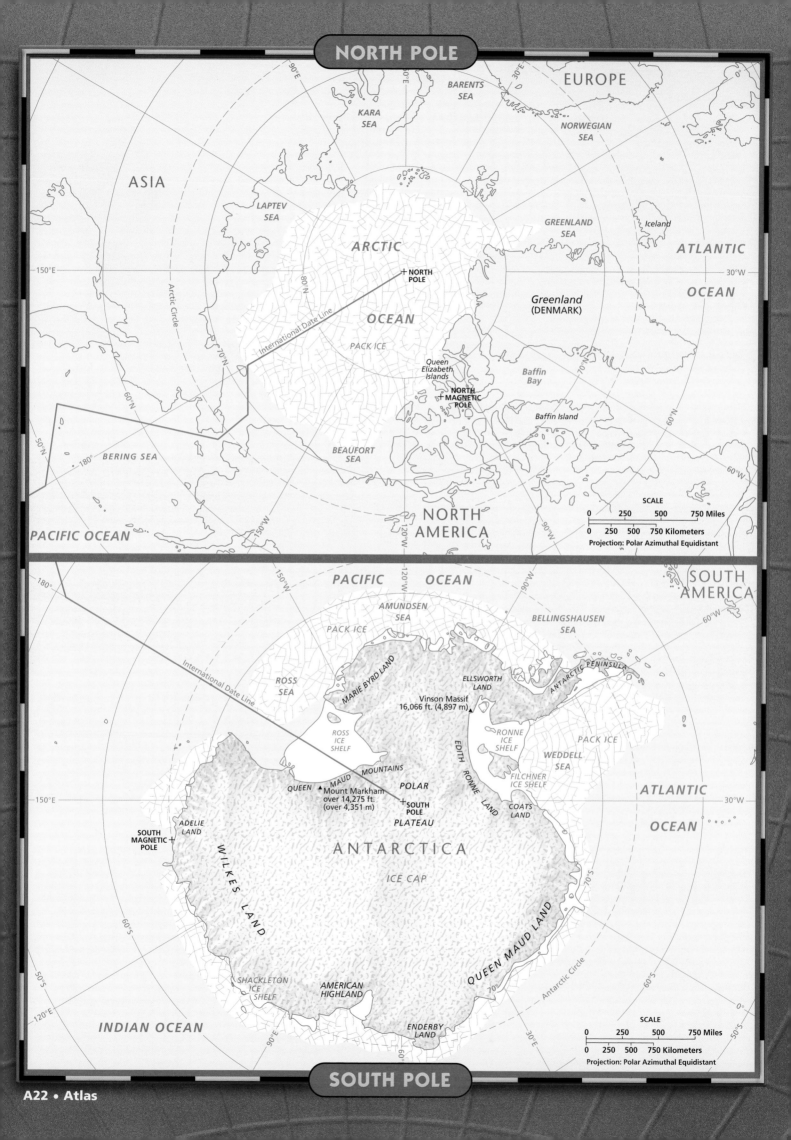

ASIA

KARA SEA

BARENTS SEA

EUROPE

LAPTEV SEA

NORWEGIAN SEA

GREENLAND SEA

Iceland

ARCTIC

150°E

80°N

North Pole

ATLANTIC

OCEAN

OCEAN

30°W

Greenland (DENMARK)

PACK ICE

70°N

Queen Elizabeth Islands

Baffin Bay

NORTH MAGNETIC POLE

Baffin Island

180°

BERING SEA

60°N

50°N

BEAUFORT SEA

60°N

NORTH AMERICA

PACIFIC OCEAN

120°W

90°W

SCALE

0 — 250 — 500 — 750 Miles

0 — 250 — 500 — 750 Kilometers

Projection: Polar Azimuthal Equidistant

180°

PACIFIC OCEAN

120°W

SOUTH AMERICA

AMUNDSEN SEA

90°W

BELLINGSHAUSEN SEA

PACK ICE

International Date Line

ROSS SEA

MARIE BYRD LAND

ELLSWORTH LAND

ANTARCTIC PENINSULA

60°W

Vinson Massif 16,066 ft. (4,897 m)

ROSS ICE SHELF

RONNE ICE SHELF

PACK ICE

EDITH RONNE LAND

WEDDELL SEA

MOUNTAINS

QUEEN MAUD

▲ Mount Markham over 14,275 ft. (over 4,351 m)

POLAR

SOUTH POLE

FILCHNER ICE SHELF

ATLANTIC

150°E

COATS LAND

30°W

SOUTH MAGNETIC POLE

ADELIE LAND

PLATEAU

OCEAN

0°

WILKES LAND

ANTARCTICA

ICE CAP

QUEEN MAUD LAND

70°S

60°S

Antarctic Circle

70°

50°S

120°E

SHACKLETON ICE SHELF

AMERICAN HIGHLAND

60°E

ENDERBY LAND

30°E

60°S

50°S

INDIAN OCEAN

90°E

SCALE

0 — 250 — 500 — 750 Miles

0 — 250 — 500 — 750 Kilometers

Projection: Polar Azimuthal Equidistant

GEOGRAPHY & MAP SKILLS HANDBOOK

CONTENTS

Studying geography requires the ability to understand and use various tools. This Skills Handbook explains how to use maps, charts, and other graphics to help you learn about geography and the various regions of the world. Throughout this textbook, you will have the opportunity to improve these skills and build upon them.

GEOGRAPHIC Vocabulary

- globe
- grid
- latitude
- equator
- parallels
- degrees
- minutes
- longitude
- prime meridian
- meridians
- hemispheres
- continents
- islands
- ocean
- map
- map projections
- compass rose
- scale
- legend

MAPPING THE EARTH

The Globe

A **globe** is a scale model of Earth. It is useful for looking at the entire Earth or at large areas of Earth's surface.

The pattern of lines that circle the globe in east-west and north-south directions is called a **grid**. The intersection of these imaginary lines helps us find places on Earth.

The east-west lines in the grid are lines of **latitude**. These imaginary lines measure distance north and south of the **equator**. The equator is an imaginary line that circles the globe halfway between the North and South Poles. Lines of latitude are called **parallels** because they are always parallel to the equator. Parallels measure distance from the equator in **degrees**. The symbol for degrees is °. Degrees are further divided into **minutes**. The symbol for minutes is ´. There are 60 minutes in a degree. Parallels north of the equator are labeled with an *N*. Those south of the equator are labeled with an *S*.

The north-south lines are lines of **longitude**. These imaginary lines pass through the Poles. They measure distance east and west of the **prime meridian**. The prime meridian is an imaginary line that runs through Greenwich, England. It represents 0° longitude. Lines of longitude are called **meridians**.

Lines of latitude range from 0°, for locations on the equator, to 90°N or 90°S, for locations at the Poles. See **Figure 1**. Lines of longitude range from 0° on the prime meridian to 180° on a meridian in the mid-Pacific Ocean. Meridians west of the prime meridian to 180° are labeled with a *W*. Those east of the prime meridian to 180° are labeled with an *E*. See **Figure 2**.

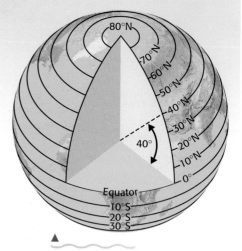

Figure 1: The east-west lines in the grid are lines of latitude.

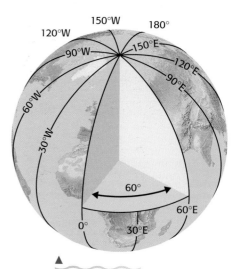

Figure 2: The north-south lines are lines of longitude.

NORTHERN HEMISPHERE

Figure 3: The hemispheres

SOUTHERN HEMISPHERE

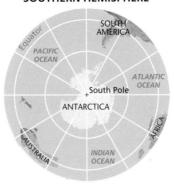

EASTERN HEMISPHERE

WESTERN HEMISPHERE

The equator divides the globe into two halves, called **hemispheres**. See Figure 3. The half north of the equator is the Northern Hemisphere. The southern half is the Southern Hemisphere. The prime meridian and the 180° meridian divide the world into the Eastern Hemisphere and the Western Hemisphere. The prime meridian separates parts of Europe and Africa into two different hemispheres. To prevent this, some mapmakers divide the Eastern and Western hemispheres at 20° W. This places all of Europe and Africa in the Eastern Hemisphere.

Our planet's land surface is organized into seven large landmasses, called **continents**. They are identified in Figure 3. Landmasses smaller than continents and completely surrounded by water are called **islands**. Geographers also organize Earth's water surface into parts. The largest is the world **ocean**. Geographers divide the world ocean into the Pacific Ocean, the Atlantic Ocean, the Indian Ocean, and the Arctic Ocean. Lakes and seas are smaller bodies of water.

YOUR TURN

1. Look at the Student Atlas map on page A4. What islands are located near the intersection of latitude 20° N and longitude 160° W?
2. Name the four hemispheres. In which hemispheres is the United States located?
3. Name the continents of the world.
4. Name the oceans of the world.

SKILL SIDELIGHT

Point out to students that phrases such as "Western influences," "Western world," and "Western society" do not refer to the Western Hemisphere. Rather, these phrases refer to ideas and ways of life associated with western Europe and North America.

Your Turn

Answers

1. The Hawaiian Islands
2. The United States is located in the Northern and Western Hemispheres. The other two hemispheres are the Southern and Eastern.
3. North America, South America, Africa, Europe, Asia, Australia, Antarctica
4. Pacific, Atlantic, Indian, Arctic

MAPMAKING

A **map** is a flat diagram of all or part of Earth's surface. Mapmakers have different ways of showing our round Earth on flat maps. These different ways are called **map projections**. Because our planet is round, all flat maps lose some accuracy. Mapmakers must choose the type of map projection that is best for their purposes. Many map projections are one of three kinds: cylindrical, conic, or flat-plane.

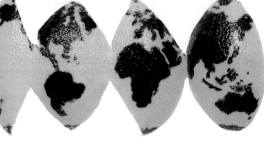

Figure 4: If you remove the peel from the orange and flatten the peel, it will stretch and tear. The larger the piece of peel, the more its shape is distorted as it is flattened. Also distorted are the distances between points on the peel.

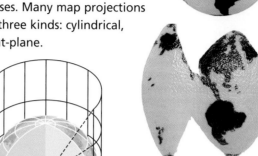

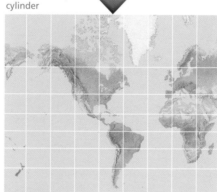

Figure 5A: Paper cylinder

Cylindrical projections are designed from a cylinder wrapped around the globe. See **Figure 5A**. The cylinder touches the globe only at the equator. The meridians are pulled apart and are parallel to each other instead of meeting at the Poles. This causes landmasses near the Poles to appear larger than they really are. **Figure 5B** is a Mercator projection, one type of cylindrical projection. The Mercator projection is useful for navigators because it shows true direction and shape. The Mercator projection for world maps, however, emphasizes the Northern Hemisphere. Africa and South America appear smaller than they really are.

Figure 5B: A Mercator projection, although accurate near the equator, distorts distances between regions of land. This projection also distorts the sizes of areas near the poles.

Conic projections are designed from a cone placed over the globe. See **Figure 6A**. A conic projection is most accurate along the lines of latitude where it touches the globe. It retains almost true shape and size. Conic projections are most useful for areas that have long east-west dimensions, such as the United States. See the map in **Figure 6B**.

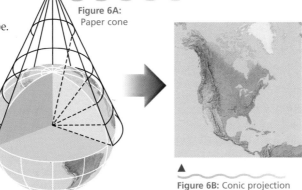

Figure 6A: Paper cone

Figure 6B: Conic projection

Flat-plane projections are designed from a plane touching the globe at one point, such as at the North Pole or South Pole. See **Figures 7A** and **7B**. A flat-plane projection is useful for showing true direction for airplane pilots and ship navigators. It also shows true area. However, it distorts true shape.

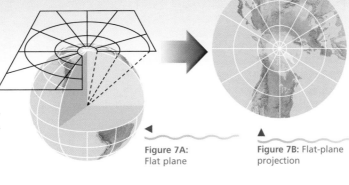

Figure 7A: Flat plane

Figure 7B: Flat-plane projection

The Robinson projection is a compromise between size and shape distortions. It often is used for world maps, such as the map on page 76. The minor distortions in size at high latitudes on Robinson projections are balanced by realistic shapes at the middle and low latitudes.

YOUR TURN

1. What are three major kinds of map projections?
2. Why is a Robinson projection often used for world maps?
3. What kind of projection is a Mercator map?
4. When would a mapmaker choose to use a conic projection?

Answers
1. cylindrical, conic, flat-plane
2. The minor distortions in size at high latitudes are balanced by realistic shapes at the middle and low latitudes.
3. cylindrical
4. when mapping areas that have long east-west dimensions, such as the United States

MAP ESSENTIALS

In some ways, maps are like messages sent out in code. Mapmakers provide certain elements that help us translate these codes. These elements help us understand the message they are presenting about a particular part of the world. Of these elements, almost all maps have directional indicators, scales, and legends, or keys. **Figure 8**, a map of East Asia, has all three elements.

A directional indicator shows which directions are north, south, east, and west. Some mapmakers use a "north arrow," which points toward the North Pole. Remember, "north" is not always at the top of a map. The way a map is drawn and the location of directions on that map depend on the perspective of the mapmaker. Maps in this textbook indicate direction by using a **compass rose** ①. A compass rose has arrows that point to all four principal directions, as shown in **Figure 8**.

▲
Figure 8: East and Southeast Asia—Physical

Mapmakers use scales to represent distances between points on a map. Scales may appear on maps in several different forms. The maps in this textbook provide a line **scale** ②. Scales give distances in miles and kilometers (km).

To find the distance between two points on the map in **Figure 8**, place a piece of paper so that the edge connects the two points. Mark the location of each point on the paper with a line or dot. Then, compare the distance between the two dots with the map's line scale. The number on the top of the scale gives the distance in miles. The number on the bottom gives the distance in kilometers. Because the distances are given in intervals, you will have to approximate the actual distance on the scale.

ELEVATION

FEET		METERS
13,120		4,000
6,560		2,000
1,640		500
656		200
(Sea level) 0		0 (Sea level)
Below sea level		Below sea level

Size comparison of Canada to the contiguous United States

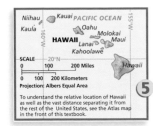

The **legend** ③, or key, explains what the symbols on the map represent. Point symbols are used to specify the location of things, such as cities, that do not take up much space on a large-scale map. Some legends, such as the one in **Figure 8**, show which colors represent certain elevations. Other maps might have legends with symbols or colors that represent things such as roads. Legends can also show economic resources, land use, population density, and climate.

Physical maps at the beginning of each unit have size comparison maps ④. An outline of the mainland United States (not including Alaska and Hawaii) is compared to the area under study in that chapter. These size comparison maps help you understand the size of the areas you are studying in relation to the size of the United States.

Inset maps are sometimes used to show a small part of a larger map. Mapmakers also use inset maps to show areas that are far away from the areas shown on the main map. Maps of the United States, for example, often include inset maps of Alaska and Hawaii ⑤. Those two states are too far from the other 48 states to accurately represent the true distance on the main map. Subject areas in inset maps can be drawn to a scale different from the scale used on the main map.

YOUR TURN

Look at the Student Atlas map on pages A4 and A5.

1. Locate the compass rose. What country is directly west of Madagascar in Africa?
2. What island country is located southeast of India?
3. Locate the distance scale. Using the inset map, find the approximate distance in miles and kilometers from Oslo, Norway, to Stockholm, Sweden.
4. What is the capital of Brazil? What other cities are shown in Brazil?

Your Turn

Answers
1. Mozambique
2. Sri Lanka
3. less than 500 miles (800 km)
4. Brasília is the capital. Rio de Janeiro and São Paulo are also shown.

Global Skill Builder CD–ROM

You might wish to use **Using Different Types of Maps** and **Comparing Maps** from the interactive Global Skill Builder CD–ROM to reinforce students' work with different kinds of maps.

WORKING
WITH MAPS

The Atlas at the front of this textbook includes two kinds of maps: physical and political. At the beginning of most units in this textbook, you will find five kinds of maps. These physical, political, climate, population, and land use and resources maps provide different kinds of information about the region you will study in that unit. These maps are accompanied by questions. Some questions ask you to show how the information on each of the maps might be related.

Mapmakers often combine physical and political features into one map. Physical maps, such as the one in **Figure 8** on page S6, show important physical features in a region, including major mountains and mountain ranges, rivers, oceans and other bodies of water, deserts, and plains. Physical-political maps also show important political features, such as national borders, state and provincial boundaries, and capitals and other important cities. You will find a physical-political map at the beginning of most chapters.

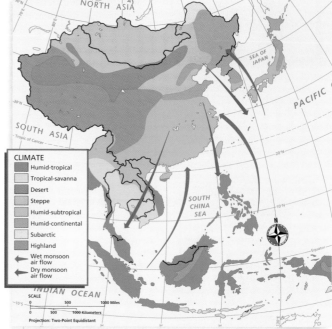

Figure 9: East and Southeast Asia—Climate

Mapmakers use climate maps to show the most important weather patterns in certain areas. Climate maps throughout this textbook use color to show the various climate regions of the world. See **Figure 9**. Colors that identify climate types are found in a legend with each map. Boundaries between climate regions do not indicate an immediate change in the main weather conditions between two climate regions. Instead, boundaries show the general areas of gradual change between climate regions.

Answers

1. to show the most important weather patterns in certain areas
2. more than 520 persons per square mile (200 per sq km)
3. oil

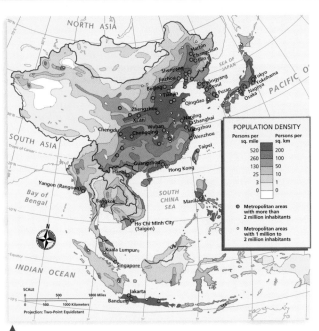

Figure 10: East and Southeast Asia—Population

Population maps show where people live in a particular region. They also show how crowded, or densely populated, regions are. Population maps throughout this textbook use color to show population density. See **Figure 10**. Each color represents a certain number of people living within a square mile or square kilometer. Population maps also use symbols to show metropolitan areas with populations of a particular size. These symbols and colors are shown in a legend.

Land Use and Resources maps show the important resources of a region. See **Figure 11**. Symbols and colors are used to show information about economic development, such as where industry is located or where farming is most common. The meanings of each symbol and color are shown in a legend.

Figure 11: East and Southeast Asia—Land Use and Resources

YOUR TURN

1. What is the purpose of a climate map?
2. Look at the population map. What is the population density of the area around Qingdao in northern China?
3. What energy resource is found near Ho Chi Minh City?

Skills Handbook • S9

USING

GRAPHS, DIAGRAMS, CHARTS, AND TABLES

Bar graphs are a visual way to present information. The bar graph in **Figure 12** shows the imports and exports of the countries of southern Europe. The amount of imports and exports in billions of dollars is listed on the left side of the graph. Along the bottom of the graph are the names of the countries of southern Europe. Above each country or group of countries is a vertical bar. The top of the bar corresponds to a number along the left side of the graph. For example, Italy imports $200 billion worth of goods.

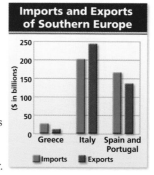

▲
Figure 12: Reading a bar graph

Often, line graphs are used to show such things as trends, comparisons, and size. The line graph in **Figure 13** shows the population growth of the world over time. The information on the left shows the number of people in billions. The years being studied are listed along the bottom. Lines connect points that show the population in billions at each year under study. This line graph projects population growth into the future.

◄
Figure 13: Reading a line graph

A pie graph shows how a whole is divided into parts. In this kind of graph, a circle represents the whole. The wedges represent the parts. Bigger wedges represent larger parts of the whole. The pie graph in **Figure 14** shows the percentages of the world's coffee beans produced by various groups of countries. Brazil is the largest grower. It grows 25 percent of the world's coffee beans.

Major Producers of Coffee

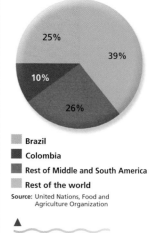

■ Brazil
■ Colombia
■ Rest of Middle and South America
■ Rest of the world

Source: United Nations, Food and Agriculture Organization

▲
Figure 14: Reading a pie graph

Age structure diagrams show the number of males and females by age group. These diagrams are split into two sides, one for male and one for female. Along the bottom are numbers that show the number of males or females in the age groups. The age groups are listed on the side of the diagram. The wider the base of a country's diagram, the younger the population of that country. The wider the top of a country's diagram, the older the population.

Some countries have so many younger people that their age structure diagrams are shaped like pyramids. For this reason, these diagrams are sometimes called population pyramids. However, in some countries the population is more evenly distributed by age group. For example, see the age structure diagram for Germany in **Figure 15**. Germany's population is older. It is not growing as fast as countries with younger populations.

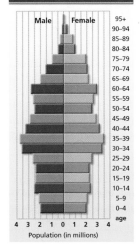

Germany's Population 2000

Source: U.S. Census Bureau

Figure 15: Reading an age structure diagram

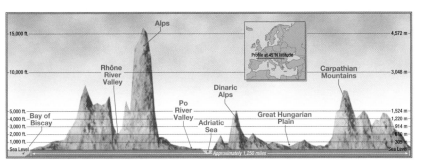

Figure 16: Reading an elevation profile

Each unit atlas includes an elevation profile. See **Figure 16**. It is a side view, or profile, of a region along a line drawn between two points.

Vertical and horizontal distances are figured differently on elevation profiles. The vertical distance (the height of a mountain, for example) is exaggerated when compared to the horizontal distance between the two points. This technique is called vertical exaggeration. If the vertical scale were not exaggerated, even tall mountains would appear as small bumps on an elevation profile.

SKILL SIDELIGHT

Direct students' attention to the statistical chart on this page. Point out that most chapters contain statistical charts that provide information about the populations of countries within a region. Each statistical chart also includes information for the United States. The U.S. statistical information is provided for comparison.

Global Skill Builder CD–ROM

You might wish to use **Using Time Lines, Reading Graphs, Presenting Data Graphically,** and **Creating Graphic Organizers** from the interactive Global Skill Builder CD–ROM to reinforce students' understanding of charts, tables, and diagrams.

In each unit and chapter on the various regions of the world, you will find tables that provide basic information about the countries under study.

The countries of Spain and Portugal are listed on the left in the table in **Figure 17**. You can match statistical information on the right with the name of each country listed on the left. The categories of information are listed across the top of the table.

Graphic organizers can help you understand certain ideas and concepts. For example, the diagram in **Figure 18** helps you think about the uses of water. In this diagram, one water use goes in each oval. Graphic organizers can help you focus on key facts in your study of geography.

Time lines provide highlights of important events over a period of time. The time line in **Figure 19** begins at the left with 5000 B.C., when rice was first cultivated in present-day China. The time line highlights important events that have shaped the human and political geography of China.

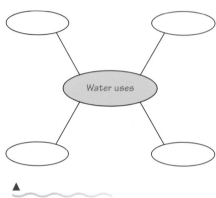

Spain and Portugal

Country	Population/ Growth Rate	Life Expectancy	Literacy Rate	Per Capita GDP
Portugal	10,102,022 0.1%	72, male 80, female	93%	$18,000
Spain	40,217,413 0.1%	75, male 82, female	97%	$20,700
United States	290,342,554 0.9%	74, male 80, female	97%	$37,600

Source: Central Intelligence Agency, *The World Factbook 2003*

▲
Figure 17: Reading a table

Water uses

▲
Figure 18: Graphic organizer

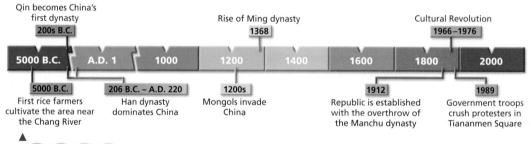

Historic China: A Time Line

Qin becomes China's first dynasty
200s B.C.

Rise of Ming dynasty
1368

Cultural Revolution
1966–1976

| 5000 B.C. | A.D. 1 | 1000 | 1200 | 1400 | 1600 | 1800 | 2000 |

5000 B.C.
First rice farmers cultivate the area near the Chang River

206 B.C. – A.D. 220
Han dynasty dominates China

1200s
Mongols invade China

1912
Republic is established with the overthrow of the Manchu dynasty

1989
Government troops crush protesters in Tiananmen Square

▲
Figure 19: Reading a time line

Corn: From Field to Consumer

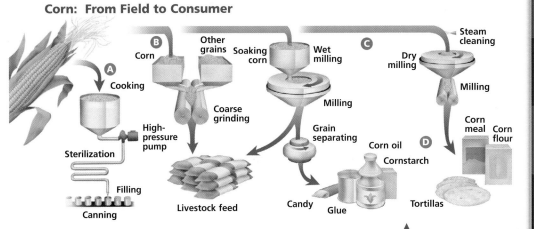

A Corn can be processed in a variety of ways. Some corn is cooked and then canned.

B Corn is ground and used for livestock feed.

C Corn also might be wet-milled or dry-milled. Then grain parts are used to make different products.

D Corn by-products, such as cornstarch and corn syrup, are used to make breads, breakfast cereals, puddings, and snack foods. Corn oil is used for cooking.

Figure 20: Reading a flowchart

Flowcharts are visual guides that explain different processes. They lead the reader from one step to the next, sometimes providing both illustrations and text. The flowchart in **Figure 20** shows the different steps involved in harvesting corn and preparing it for use by consumers. The flowchart takes you through the steps of harvesting and processing corn. Captions guide you through flowcharts.

YOUR TURN

1. Look at the statistical table for Spain and Portugal in Figure 17. Which countries have the highest literacy rate?

2. Look at the China time line in Figure 19. Name two important events in China's history between 1200 and 1400.

3. Look at Figure 20. What are three corn products?

Your Turn

Answers

1. Spain and the United States

2. Mongols invade China, rise of Ming dynasty

3. Students should name three of the following products: livestock feed, candy, glue, corn oil, cornstarch, tortillas, cornmeal, corn flour

READING
A TIME-ZONE MAP

The sun is not directly overhead everywhere on Earth at the same time. Clocks are set to reflect the difference in the sun's position. Our planet rotates on its axis once every 24 hours. In other words, in one hour, it makes one twenty-fourth of a complete rotation. Since there are 360 degrees in a circle, we know that the planet turns 15 degrees of longitude each hour. ($360° \div 24 = 15°$) We also know that the planet turns in a west-to-east direction. Therefore, if a place on Earth has the sun directly overhead at this moment (noon), then a place 15 degrees to the west will have the sun directly overhead one hour from now. During that hour the planet will have rotated 15 degrees. As a result, Earth is divided into 24 time zones. Thus, time is an hour earlier for each 15 degrees you move westward on Earth. Time is an hour later for each 15 degrees you move eastward on Earth.

By international agreement, longitude is measured from the prime meridian. This meridian passes through the Royal Observatory in Greenwich, England. Time also is measured from Greenwich and is called Greenwich mean time (GMT). For each time zone east of the prime meridian, clocks must be set one hour ahead of GMT. For each time zone west of Greenwich, clocks are set back one hour from GMT. When it is noon in London, it is 1:00 P.M. in Oslo, Norway, one time zone east. However, it is 7 A.M. in New York City, five time zones west.

WORLD TIME ZONES

As you can see by looking at the map below, time zones do not follow meridians exactly. Political boundaries are often used to draw time-zone lines. In Europe and Africa, for example, time zones follow national boundaries. The mainland United States, meanwhile, is divided into four major time zones: Eastern, Central, Mountain, and Pacific. Alaska and Hawaii are in separate time zones to the west of the mainland.

Some countries have made changes in their time zones. For example, most of the United States has daylight savings time in the summer in order to have more evening hours of daylight.

The international date line is a north-south line that runs through the Pacific Ocean. It is located at 180°, although it sometimes varies from that meridian to avoid dividing countries.

At 180°, the time is 12 hours from Greenwich time. There is a time difference of 24 hours between the two sides of the 180° meridian. The 180° meridian is called the international date line because when you cross it, the date and day change. As you cross the date line from the west to the east, you gain a day. If you travel from east to west, you lose a day.

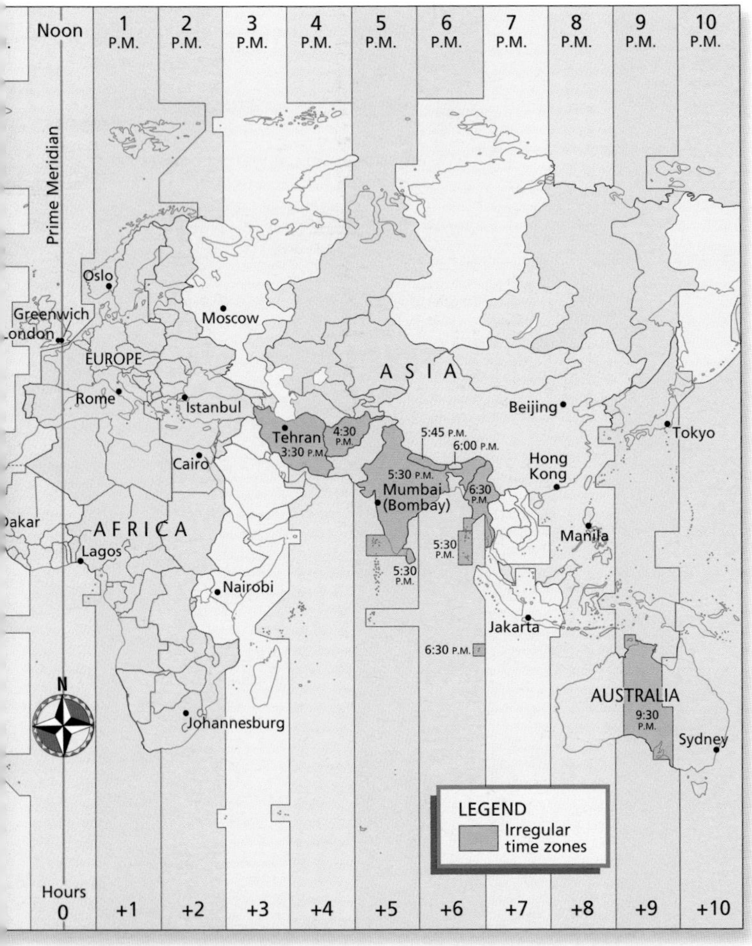

Noon	1 P.M.	2 P.M.	3 P.M.	4 P.M.	5 P.M.	6 P.M.	7 P.M.	8 P.M.	9 P.M.	10 P.M.

Tehran 4:30 P.M.
3:30 P.M.
5:45 P.M.
6:00 P.M.
Mumbai (Bombay) 5:30 P.M.
6:30 P.M.
5:30 P.M.
5:30 P.M.
6:30 P.M.
AUSTRALIA 9:30 P.M.

LEGEND
Irregular time zones

Hours 0	+1	+2	+3	+4	+5	+6	+7	+8	+9	+10

YOUR TURN

1. In which time zone do you live? Check your time now. What time is it in New York?
2. How many hours behind New York is Anchorage, Alaska?
3. How many time zones are there in Africa?
4. If it is 9 A.M. in the middle of Greenland, what time is it in São Paulo?

Skills Handbook • S15

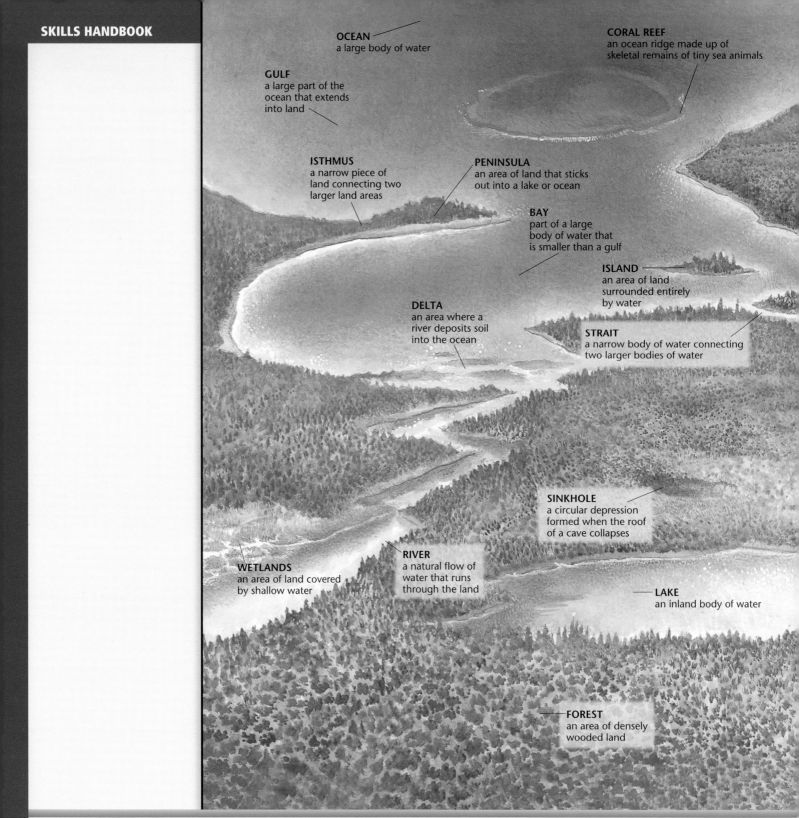

OCEAN
a large body of water

CORAL REEF
an ocean ridge made up of
skeletal remains of tiny sea animals

GULF
a large part of the
ocean that extends
into land

ISTHMUS
a narrow piece of
land connecting two
larger land areas

PENINSULA
an area of land that sticks
out into a lake or ocean

BAY
part of a large
body of water that
is smaller than a gulf

ISLAND
an area of land
surrounded entirely
by water

DELTA
an area where a
river deposits soil
into the ocean

STRAIT
a narrow body of water connecting
two larger bodies of water

SINKHOLE
a circular depression
formed when the roof
of a cave collapses

WETLANDS
an area of land covered
by shallow water

RIVER
a natural flow of
water that runs
through the land

LAKE
an inland body of water

FOREST
an area of densely
wooded land

COAST
an area of land
near the ocean

VALLEY
an area of low
land between hills
or mountains

MOUNTAIN
an area of rugged
land that generally
rises higher than
2,000 feet

VOLCANO
an opening in the Earth's crust
where lava, ash, and gases erupt

CANYON
a deep, narrow valley
with steep walls

GLACIER
a large area of
slow-moving ice

HILL
a rounded, elevated
area of land smaller
than a mountain

PLAIN
a nearly
flat area

DUNE
a hill of sand
shaped by wind

DESERT
an extremely dry area with
little water and few plants

OASIS
an area in the desert
with a water source

PLATEAU
a large, flat, elevated
area of land

UNIT OBJECTIVES

1. Introduce geography as a field of study.
2. Explain the formation of the shapes on Earth's surface.
3. Analyze the interrelationships of wind, climate, and natural environments.
4. Identify major resources and how people use them.
5. Describe the development of cultures and the results of population expansion.
6. Learn to draw sketch maps and use them as geographic tools.

Your Classroom Time Line

To help you create a time line to display in your classroom, the most important dates and time periods discussed in each unit's chapters are compiled for you. Some additional dates have been inserted for clarity and continuity. Note that many dates, particularly those in the distant past, are approximate. In each unit, the lists begin in the sidebar on the page with the political map. You may want to have students use colored markers to differentiate among political, scientific, religious, and artistic events or achievements. You might also want to create your own categories.

UNIT 1

An Introduction to World Geography and Cultures

CHAPTER 1
A Geographer's World

CHAPTER 2
Planet Earth

CHAPTER 3
The World's People

Iceberg in sea ice, Antarctica

Carnival parade in Valletta, Malta

USING THE ILLUSTRATIONS

Direct students' attention to the photographs on these pages. Point out that in this unit students will learn there are two major branches of geography. One is physical geography, which deals with land, water, climate, and similar topics; the other is human geography, which involves people. Ask students which photos may relate more closely to physical geography (rosettes, tropical landscape, iceberg) and which relate more to human geography (Carnival scene).

Ask which photo shows a cold climate (iceberg), and which shows a warm climate (La Digue Island). On what familiar images or clues do we depend for the answers? (Possible answers: ice, lush vegetation, palm trees) Ask why the photo of the rosette plants does not give us much information about how warm or cold the climate may be. (Because the plant is not familiar to most of us, we do not know where it grows.)

You may want to invite students to speculate about the construction or meaning of the costumes in the Carnival photo. Lead a discussion about what kinds of parades are held in your community and what costumes the participants wear.

A Physical Geographer in Mountain Environments

Professor Francisco Pérez studies tropical mountain environments. He is interested in the natural processes, plants, and environments of mountains. **WHAT DO YOU THINK?** *What faraway places would you like to study?*

I became attracted to mountains when I was a child. While crossing the Atlantic Ocean in a ship, I saw snow-capped Teide Peak in the Canary Islands rising from the water. It was an amazing sight.

As a physical geographer, I am interested in the unique environments of high mountain areas. This includes geological history, climate, and soils. The unusual conditions of high mountain environments have influenced plant evolution. Plants and animals that live on separate mountains sometimes end up looking similar. This happens because they react to their environments in similar ways. For example, several types of tall, weird-looking plants called giant rosettes grow in the Andes, Hawaii, East Africa, and the Canary Islands. Giant rosettes look like the top of a pineapple at the end of a tall stem.

I have found other strange plants, such as rolling mosses. Mosses normally grow on rocks. However, if a moss plant falls to the ground, ice crystals on the soil surface lift the moss. This allows it to "roll" downhill while it continues to grow in a ball shape!

I like doing research in mountains. They are some of the least explored regions of our planet. Like most geographers, I cannot resist the attraction of strange landscapes in remote places.

Rosette plants, Ecuador

La Digue Island, Seychelles

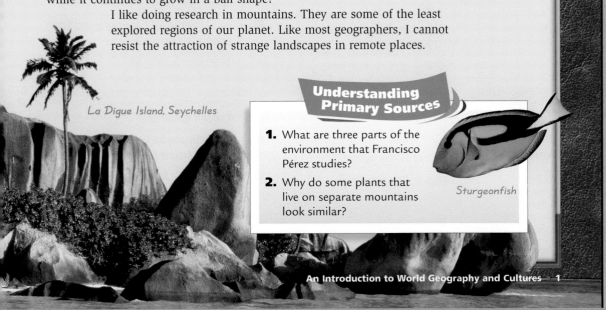

Understanding Primary Sources

1. What are three parts of the environment that Francisco Pérez studies?

2. Why do some plants that live on separate mountains look similar?

Sturgeonfish

MORE FROM THE FIELD

Living things that are not related sometimes develop similar physical traits because they live in similar environments. This process is called convergent evolution. For example, tuna (fish) and dolphins (mammals) both have streamlined bodies and fins for living in the water.

For a land-based example, compare the serval of Africa, a cat, and the maned wolf of South America, a dog. Both have long necks, long legs, and large ears. They hunt small animals in grassy plains areas. Their long legs and necks elevate their ears above the grass. As a result, they can hear the slightest sound made by their prey.

Understanding Primary Sources
Answers
1. geological history, climate, soils
2. because they react to their environments in similar ways

CHAPTERS

CHAPTER 1

A Geographer's World
Chapter Resource Manager

Objectives	Pacing Guide	Reproducible Resources
SECTION 1 **Developing a Geographic Eye** 1. Explain the role perspective plays in the study of geography. 2. Describe some issues and topics that geographers study. 3. Identify the three levels geographers use to view the world.	**Regular** 1 day Lecture Notes, Section 1 **Block Scheduling** .5 day *Block Scheduling Handbook, Chapter 1*	**RS** Know It Notes **RS** Graphic Organizer **E** Geography for Life Activity 1 **ELL** Main Idea Activity S1
SECTION 2 **Themes and Essential Elements of Geography** 1. Identify the tools geographers use to study the world. 2. Identify what shapes Earth's features. 3. Examine how humans shape the world. 4. Explain how studying geography helps us understand the world.	**Regular** 1 day Lecture Notes, Section 2 **Block Scheduling** .5 day *Block Scheduling Handbook, Chapter 1*	**RS** Know It Notes S2 **RS** Graphic Organizer 1 **SM** Map Activity 1 **E** Creative Strategies for Teaching World Geography, Lessons 1–3 **E** Lab Activities for Geography and Earth Science, Hands-On 2 **ELL** Main Idea Activity S2
SECTION 3 **Being a Geographer** 1. Explain the study of human geography. 2. Describe the study of physical geography. 3. Investigate the types of work that geographers do.	**Regular** 1 day Lecture Notes, Section 3 **Block Scheduling** .5 day *Block Scheduling Handbook, Chapter 1*	**RS** Know It Notes S3 **E** Lab Activities for Geography and Earth Science, Hands-On 1 **E** Biography Activity: John Snow **ELL** Main Idea Activity S3

Chapter Resource Key

RS Reading Support

IC Interdisciplinary Connections

E Enrichment

SM Skills Mastery

A Assessment

REV Review

ELL Reinforcement and English Language Learners and English for Speakers of Other Languages (ESOL)

 Transparencies

 CD–ROM

 Music

 Video

 Internet

 Holt Presentation Maker Using Microsoft® PowerPoint®

 One-Stop Planner CD–ROM

See the ***One-Stop Planner*** for a complete list of additional resources for students and teachers.

One-Stop Planner CD–ROM

It's easy to plan lessons, select resources, and print out materials for your students when you use the *One-Stop Planner CD–ROM with Test Generator.*

Technology Resources

- One-Stop Planner CD-ROM, Lesson 1.1
- Global Skill Builder CD-ROM, Project 1
- *ARGWorld* CD–ROM
- Homework Practice Online
- HRW Go site

- One-Stop Planner CD-ROM, Lesson
- *ARGWorld* CD–ROM
- Homework Practice Online
- HRW Go site

- One-Stop Planner CD-ROM, Lesson
- *ARGWorld* CD–ROM
- Homework Practice Online
- HRW Go site

Review, Reinforcement, and Assessment Resources

ELL	Main Idea Activity S1
REV	Section 1 Review
A	Daily Quiz 1.1
REV	Chapter Summaries and Review
ELL	English Audio Summary 1.1
ELL	Spanish Audio Summary 1.1

ELL	Main Idea Activity S2
REV	Section 2 Review
A	Daily Quiz 1.2
REV	Chapter Summaries and Review
ELL	English Audio Summary 1.2
ELL	Spanish Audio Summary 1.2

ELL	Main Idea Activity S3
REV	Section 3 Review
A	Daily Quiz 1.3
REV	Chapter Summaries and Review
ELL	English Audio Summary 1.3
ELL	Spanish Audio Summary 1.3

internet connect

HRW ONLINE RESOURCES

GO TO: go.hrw.com
Then type in a keyword.

TEACHER HOME PAGE
KEYWORD: SJ5 TEACHER

CHAPTER INTERNET ACTIVITIES
KEYWORD: SJ5 GT1

Choose an activity to:
- learn to use online maps.
- be a virtual geographer for a day.
- compare regions around the world.

CHAPTER ENRICHMENT LINKS
KEYWORD: SJ5 CH1

CHAPTER MAPS
KEYWORDS: SJ5 MAPS1

ONLINE ASSESSMENT
Homework Practice
KEYWORD: SJ5 HP1
Standardized Test Prep Online
KEYWORD: SJ5 STP1
Rubrics
KEYWORD: SS Rubrics

COUNTRY INFORMATION
KEYWORD: SJ5 Almanac

CONTENT UPDATES
KEYWORD: SS Content Updates

HOLT PRESENTATION MAKER
KEYWORD: SJ5 PPT1

ONLINE READING SUPPORT
KEYWORD: SS Strategies

CURRENT EVENTS
KEYWORD: S5 Current Events

Meeting Individual Needs

Ability Levels

Level 1 Basic-level activities designed for all students encountering new material

Level 2 Intermediate-level activities designed for average students

Level 3 Challenging activities designed for honors and gifted-and-talented students

ESOL Activities that address the needs of students with Limited English Proficiency

Chapter Review and Assessment

SM	Critical Thinking Activity 1
REV	Chapter 1 Review and Practice
REV	Chapter Summaries and Review
ELL	Vocabulary Activity 1
A	Chapter 1 Test
A	Chapter 1 Test Generator (on the One-Stop Planner)
	Audio CD program, Chapter 1
A	Chapter 1 Test for English Language learners and Special Needs Students
	HRW Go site

1B

A Geographer's World
Previewing Chapter Resources

Holt Online Learning

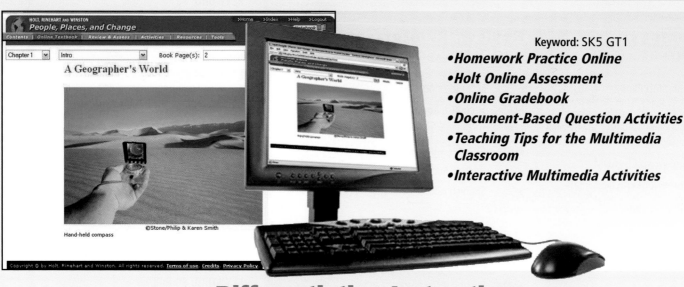

Keyword: SK5 GT1

- *Homework Practice Online*
- *Holt Online Assessment*
- *Online Gradebook*
- *Document-Based Question Activities*
- *Teaching Tips for the Multimedia Classroom*
- *Interactive Multimedia Activities*

Differentiating Instruction

Reading and Writing Support

◀ *Graphic Organizer Activity*
- *Vocabulary Activity*
- *Chapter Summary and Review*
- *Know It Notes S1–3*
- *Audio CD*

Active Learning

◀ *Block Scheduling Handbook*
- *Cultures of the World Activity*
- *Interdisciplinary Activity*
- *Map Activity*
- *Critical Thinking Activity 1*

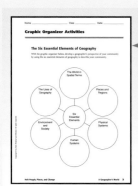

Primary Sources and Advanced Learners

- *Geography for Life Activity: Spatial Perspective*
◀ *Map Activity: Absolute and Relative Location*
- *Readings in World Geography, History and Culture:*
  - *1 Ancient Geographers*
  - *2 Mapping Earth from Space*

Assessment Program

◀ *Daily Quizzes S1–3*
- *Chapter Test*
- *Chapter Test for English Language Learners and Special-Needs Students*

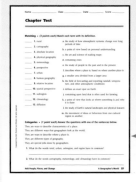

Spanish and ESOL

- *Vocabulary Activity*
- *Main Idea Activities for English Language Learners and Special-Needs Students*
- *Chapter Summary and Review*
- *Spanish Audio Summary*
- *Know It Notes S1–3*
◀ *Chapter Test for English Language Learners and Special-Needs Students*

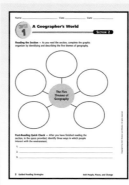

Special Education Modifications

Your **I.D.E.A. Works! CD-ROM** will provide modified versions of the following teaching materials:

◀ *Guided Reading Strategies S1–3*
- *Vocabulary Activity*
- *Main Idea Activities S1–3*
- *Daily Quizzes S1–3*
- *Chapter 1 Test*
- *Flash cards of chapter vocabulary terms*

Teacher Resources

Books for Teachers

Gould, Peter. *Becoming a Geographer.* Syracuse University Press, 1999.

Lippard, Lucy R. *The Lure of the Local: Senses of Place in a Multicentered Society.* New Press, 1997.

Sack, Robert David. *Homo Geographicus: A Framework for Action, Awareness, and Moral Concern.* Johns Hopkins University Press, 1997.

Schama, Simon. *Landscape and Memory.* Knopf, 1995.

Books for Students

Baicker-McKee, Carol. *Mapped Out!: The Search for Snookums.* Gibbs Smith, 1997. Interactive mystery teaches map-reading and problem-solving skills.
SHELTERED ENGLISH

Dunn, Margery G., ed. *Exploring Your World: The Adventure of Geography.* National Geographic Society, 1993. Presents more than 300 topics in physical and human geography.

Geography on File. Facts On File, 1999. Overview of physical and human geography from global and regional perspectives.

Multimedia Materials

Compton's Interactive World Atlas (Classic). CD–ROM. The Learning Company.

Eartha Global Explorer. CD–ROM. DeLorme.

My City. CD–ROM. Glencoe.

Videos and CDs

Videos

- **CNN** *Presents Geography: Yesterday and Today, Segment 1 Mapping Change*
- *ARG World*

Holt Researcher

http://researcher.hrw.com

- *Rural and Urban Populations in the United States, 1900-1990*
- *World*
- *Vital Statistics of Selected Countries, 2000*
- *Communications Technologies in Selected Countries*
- *Total GDP for Selected Countries*

Transparency Packages

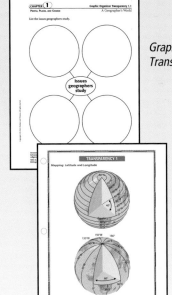

Graphic Organizer Transparencies 1.1–3

Geography and Cultures Visual Resources Transparencies
1 *Latitude and Longitude*
2 *Earth's Hemispheres*
3 *Mercator Projection*
4 *Comic Projection*
5 *Flat-Plane Projections*
6 *Reading a Time Zone Map*

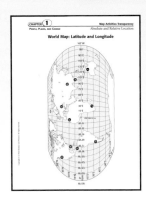

Map Activities Transparency 01 Absolute and Relative Location

WHY IT MATTERS

You may want to share with your students the following reasons for gaining a basic understanding of geography as a field of study:

▶ Knowing the fundamentals of geography will help students learn more about all aspects of their world.

▶ Getting an overview from Chapter 1 will make it easier to grasp details in later chapters.

▶ Throughout the book, connections are made to the five themes and six essential elements of geography. These ideas are explained fully in Chapter 1.

▶ Geography is an expanding field that includes a wide range of specializations. Students may want to consider geography as a career.

CHAPTER 1

A Geographer's World

Hand-held compass

Chart of the Mediterranean and Europe, 1559

GPS (global positioning satellite) receiver

2 • Chapter 1

CHAPTER PROJECT

Different cultures use different methods for showing directions and locations. For example, long ago Polynesians developed shell maps to help them navigate in the vast Pacific Ocean. Have students work in groups to devise new ways to record information about a region familiar to them. Ask them to include a standard map of the area along with the new map. They should also write a legend or key for the new map.

STARTING THE CHAPTER

Ask students to name a country they would like to visit and to give a reason why they want to travel to that particular country. (Examples: France, for the food; China, to see the Great Wall) Point out that their interests could probably be the subject of serious study by a geographer. (Examples: A geographer may study patterns in food preferences among French people or the regional use of ingredients and cooking techniques. Another may use satellite technology to find forgotten sections of the Great Wall.) Use several of the students' suggestions to show geography's wide range. Then ask students to create "geographic studies" based on their classmates' chosen destinations.

Section 1 — Developing a Geographic Eye

Read to Discover

1. What role does perspective play in the study of geography?
2. What are some issues or topics that geographers study?
3. At what three levels can geographers view the world?

Vocabulary

perspective
spatial perspective
geography
urban
rural

Reading Strategy

VISUALIZING INFORMATION Look at the photographs in this section. What do you see in the photographs that would tell you about some of the topics geographers study? Write your answers on a sheet of paper.

SECTION 1 RESOURCES

Reproducible
- Lecture Notes, Section 1
- Block Scheduling Handbook, Chapter 1
- Know It Notes S1
- Geography for Life Activity 1

Technology
- One-Stop Planner CD–ROM, Lesson 1.1
- Homework Practice Online
- Global Skill Builder CD–ROM, Project 1
- HRW Go site

Reinforcement, Review, and Assessment
- Section 1 Review
- Daily Quiz 1.1
- Main Idea Activity S1
- Chapter Summaries and Review
- English Audio Summary 1.1
- Spanish Audio Summary 1.1

Perspectives

People look at the world in different ways. Their experiences shape the way they understand the world. This personal understanding is called **perspective**. Your perspective is your point of view. A geographer's point of view looks at where something is and why it is there. This point of view is known as **spatial perspective**. Geographers apply this perspective when they study the arrangement of towns in a state. They might also use this perspective to examine the movement of cars and trucks on busy roads.

Geographers also work to understand how things are connected. Some connections are easy to see, like highways that link cities. Other connections are harder to see. For example, a dry winter in Colorado could mean that farms as far away as northern Mexico will not have enough water.

Geography is a science. It describes the physical and cultural features of Earth. Studying geography is important. Geographically informed people can see meaning in the arrangement of things on Earth. They know how people and places are related. Above all, they can apply a spatial perspective to real life. In other words, people familiar with geography can understand the world around them.

This fish-eye view of a large city shows highway patterns.

✓ READING CHECK: *The World in Spatial Terms* What role does perspective play in the study of geography? Geographers use perspective when they study where something is and why it is there.

Section 1

Objectives

1. Explain the role perspective plays in the study of geography.
2. Describe some issues or topics that geographers study.
3. Identify the three levels geographers use to view the world.

FOCUS

Bellringer

Select several photographs of scenes from around the world and display them in the classroom. Copy the following instructions on the chalkboard: *Choose one of the photographs and write down three questions you would like to ask about the place in the picture.* Call on students to read their questions aloud, and use their questions as the basis for a discussion about the issues that professional geographers study. Tell students that in Section 1 they will learn more about developing a geographic eye.

Building Vocabulary

Write the vocabulary terms on the chalkboard. Tell students that **perspective** is based on a word meaning "to look" and that **spatial** is based on a word meaning "space." Then, as a class, decide on a definition for **spatial perspective**. Compare this definition to the one in Section 1. Then, point out that **geography** is based on two Greek roots: *geō-,* which means "Earth," and *graphein,* which means "to write." Ask students to compare the meaning of the root words to the textbook's definition and explain the relationship. Finally, have students read the definitions for **urban** and **rural** and then provide examples of urban and rural areas in their region.

PHYSICAL SYSTEMS

Islanders and Their Tiny Island Geographers study how people all around the world react to Earth's processes. Tristan da Cunha is one of a group of small islands in the South Atlantic Ocean about midway between Africa and South America. It is a British territory.

A volcano 6,760 feet (2,060 m) high dominates the island. Its peak is often shrouded in clouds. Lava flows have continually shaped the island's landscape. A volcanic eruption in 1961 forced the evacuation of the island's residents. After the danger passed, most of the Tristanians returned to their isolated island.

Critical Thinking: How have Earth's physical processes affected Tristanians?

Answer: They were forced to evacuate their homeland because of a volcano.

Visual Record Answer ▲

Answers will vary, but students may mention possible political instability, a negative or fearful atmosphere, or fewer people to fill jobs.

▶

The movement of people is one issue that geographers study. For example, political and economic troubles led many Albanians to leave their country in 1991. Many packed onto freighters like this one for the trip. Geographers want to know how this movement affects the environment and other people.

Interpreting the Visual Record

(*Movement*) **How do you think Albania has been affected by so many people leaving the country?**

Geographic Issues

Issues geographers study include Earth's processes and their impact on people. Geographers study the relationship between people and environment in different places. For example, geographers study tornadoes to find ways to reduce loss of life and property damage. They ask how people prepare for tornadoes. Do they prepare differently in different places? When a tornado strikes, how do people react?

Geographers also study how governments change and how those changes affect people. Czechoslovakia, for example, split into Slovakia and the Czech Republic in 1993. These types of political events affect geographic boundaries. People react differently to these changes. Some people are forced to move. Others welcome the change.

Other issues geographers study include religions, diet (or food), **urban** areas, and **rural** areas. Urban areas contain cities. Rural areas contain open land that is often used for farming.

✓ READING CHECK: (*The Uses of Geography*) What issues or topics do geographers study? Earth's processes, the relationship between people and environment, changes of government, religions, diet, urban areas, and rural areas

Local, Regional, and Global Geographic Studies

With any topic, geographers must decide how large an area to study. They can focus their study at a local, regional, or global level.

Local Studying your community at the local, or close-up, level will help you learn geography. You know where homes and stores are located. You know how to find parks, ball fields, and other fun places. Over time, you see your community change. New buildings are constructed. People move in and out of your neighborhood. New stores open their doors, and others go out of business.

internet connect

GO TO: go.hrw.com
KEYWORD: SK5 CH1
FOR: Web sites about the geographer's world

4 • Chapter 1

TEACH

Teaching Objective 1

ALL LEVELS: (Suggested time: 10 min.) Discuss geographers' use of spatial perspective. Then have students examine the aerial photograph on the previous page and suggest why the highways are located where they are. **ESOL,** [LS] **VISUAL-SPATIAL**

Teaching Objectives 2–3

ALL LEVELS: (Suggested time: 20 min.) Copy the following graphic organizer onto the chalkboard, omitting the blue answers. Use it to help students understand the issues geographers study and the level at which they view the world. **ESOL,** [LS] **VISUAL-SPATIAL**

STUDY OF GEOGRAPHY	
Issues/Topics	Levels
Earth's processes	local
relationships between people and environment	regional
governments	global
religion and food	local, regional
urban and rural areas	local, regional

 The southwest is a region within the United States. One well-known place that characterizes the landscape of the southwest is the Grand Canyon. The Grand Canyon is shown in the photo at left and in the satellite image at right.

Regional Regional geographers organize the world into convenient parts for study. For example, this book separates the world into big areas like Africa and Europe. Regional studies cover larger areas than local studies. Some regional studies might look at connections like highways and rivers. Others might examine the regional customs.

Global Geographers also work to understand global issues and the connections between events. For example, many countries depend on oil from Southwest Asia. If those oil supplies are threatened, some countries might rush to secure oil from other areas. Oil all over the world could then become much more expensive.

✓ **READING CHECK:** *The World in Spatial Terms* What levels do geographers use to focus their study of an issue or topic? *local, regional, or global*

Homework Practice Online
go.hrw.com
Keyword: SK5 HP1

Define and explain: perspective, spatial perspective, geography, urban, rural

Reading for the Main Idea

1. How can a spatial perspective be used to study the world?

2. Why is it important to study geography?

Critical Thinking

3. **Drawing Inferences and Conclusions** How do threatening weather patterns affect people, and why do geographers study these patterns?

4. **Drawing Inferences and Conclusions** Why is it important to view geography on a global level?

Organizing What You Know

5. **Finding the Main Idea** Copy the following graphic organizer. Use it to examine the issues geographers study. Write a paragraph on one of these issues.

Issues geographers study

A Geographer's World • 5

Define For definitions, see the glossary.

Reading for the Main Idea

1. to understand how things are connected **(NGS 3)**

2. to see meaning in the arrangement of things on Earth and to understand the world **(NGS 17, 18)**

Critical Thinking

3. They can cause loss of life or property damage; to help people protect themselves from dangerous weather situations **(NGS 15)**

4. Answers will vary but might include to gain an understanding of how events in one region can affect other regions.

Organizing What You Know

5. Answers will vary but should be issues geographers study.

CLOSE

Ask students to imagine that they are geographers from the planet Geog who have landed on Earth. Have students list what human activities they would study first and what sources they would use in their research.

Have students complete Main Idea Activity S1. Then have them illustrate one of the section's topics. Ask students to explain their illustrations. **ESOL,** LS **VISUAL-SPATIAL**

REVIEW, ASSESS, RETEACH

Have students complete the Section Review. Then have students work in groups to create short quizzes based on the section's material. Have groups exchange quizzes and complete another group's quiz. Then have students complete Daily Quiz 1.1. **COOPERATIVE LEARNING**

EXTEND

Have interested students conduct research on the history of the field of geography and its influence on society. They may want to concentrate on ancient Greek or Arabic achievements. Ask them to create illustrated charts showing their research. **BLOCK SCHEDULING**

Visual Record Answer ▶

in northern Egypt, near the pyramids

Section 2 — Themes and Essential Elements of Geography

Read to Discover

1. What tools do geographers use to study the world?
2. What shapes Earth's features?
3. How do humans shape the world?
4. How does studying geography help us understand the world?

Vocabulary

absolute location
relative location
place
region

movement
diffusion
human-environment interaction

Reading Strategy

TAKING NOTES Taking notes while you read will help you understand and remember the information in this section. Write down the headings in the section. As you read, fill in notes under each heading. Underline the most important details you find.

▲
The location of a place can be described in many ways.

Interpreting the Visual Record

(Location) Looking at the photo of this hotel in Giza, Egypt, and at the map, how would you describe Giza's location?

Learning Geography

The study of geography has long been organized according to five important themes, or topics of study. One theme, location, deals with the exact or relative spot of something on Earth. Place includes the physical and human features of a location. Human-environment interaction covers the ways people and environments affect each other. Movement involves how people change locations and how goods are traded as well as the effects of these movements. For example, when people move they may bring animals, diseases, and their own culture to a new place. Region organizes Earth into geographic areas with one or more shared characteristics.

Another way to look at geography, however, is to study its essential elements, or most important parts. In 1994, several geographers and teachers created national geography standards called *Geography For Life*. The six essential elements they created to organize the study of geography are The World in Spatial Terms, Places and Regions, Physical Systems, Human Systems, Environment and Society, and The Uses of Geography. Because the six essential elements and the five themes share many of the same properties, both will be used throughout this textbook. Look for labels on questions, photographs, maps, graphs, and charts that show which geography theme or essential element is the main focus. In this section we discuss several topics related to the geography themes and essential elements. Here you will discover the relationship between these two ways of learning about our world.

✓ **READING CHECK:** (The Uses of Geography) What are the five themes of geography? What are the six essential elements? location, place, human-environment interaction, movement, region; the world in spatial terms, places and regions, physical systems, human systems, environment and society, the uses of geography

Section 2

Objectives

1. Identify tools geographers use to study the world.
2. Identify what shapes Earth's features.
3. Examine how humans shape the world.
4. Explain how studying geography helps us understand the world.

FOCUS

 Bellringer

Write the following question on the chalkboard: *Where is your favorite shopping mall or movie theater located?* Have students respond to the question. If a student names the actual address for the building, explain that he or she has provided its absolute location. Tell students that in Section 1 they will learn about the difference between absolute and relative location and other topics of geography.

Building Vocabulary

Write the vocabulary terms on the chalkboard. Ask what we mean when we say "It's all relative" and "Absolutely!" Ask students for suggestions on how those phrases could relate to **absolute location** and **relative location**. Have students look up the remaining vocabulary terms in the text or glossary and write sentences using them.

The World in Spatial Terms

This element focuses on geography's spatial perspective. As you learned in Section 1, geographers apply spatial perspective when they look at the location of something and why it is there.

Location The term location can be used in two ways. **Absolute location** defines an exact spot on Earth. For example, the address of the Smithsonian American Art Museum is an absolute location. The address is at 8th and G Streets, N.W., in Washington, D.C. City streets often form a grid. This system tells anyone looking for an address where to go. The grid formed by latitude and longitude lines also pinpoints absolute location. Suppose you asked a pilot to take you to 52° north latitude by 175° west longitude. You would land at a location on Alaska's Aleutian Islands.

Relative location describes the position of a place in relation to another place. Measurements of direction, distance, or time can define relative location. For example, the following sentences give relative location. "The hospital is one mile north of our school." "Canada's border is about an hour's drive from Great Falls, Montana."

A geographer must be able to use maps and other geographic tools and technologies to determine spatial perspective. A geographer must also know how to organize and analyze information about people, places, and environments using geographic tools.

✓ **READING CHECK:** (*The World in Spatial Terms*) What two ways describe location? absolute location and relative location

Places and Regions

To help explain why many areas of the world are similar to or different from one another, geographers organize Earth's surface into different places and regions. The Places and Regions essential element deals with how people have created regions based on Earth's features and how culture and other factors affect how we see places and regions.

Place Our world has a vast number of unique places and regions. A **place** can be described both by its physical location and by its physical and human features. Physical features include coastlines and landforms. They can also include lakes, rivers, or soil types. For example, Colorado is flat in the east but mountainous in the west. This is an example of a place being described in terms of its landforms. A place can also be described by its climate. For example, Greenland has long, cold winters. Florida has mild winters and hot, humid summers.

Channeled Scablands Geographers study not just the unique features of places and regions, but also how those features came to be. For example, geographers think that large Ice Age floods originating in western Montana created the Channeled Scablands in eastern Washington state. A glacier blocked a river and created a glacial lake near Missoula in present-day Montana. When this ice dam broke, a wall of water perhaps 2,000 feet (610 m) high crashed through the region, carving out unusual landforms such as the Channeled Scablands—an area marked by channels, cliffs, and steep-sided canyons. Scientists suspect that water poured from the lake at 60 or more miles per hour and that the glacial lake near Missoula may have filled and emptied dozens of times.

▲
(**Place**) Places can be described by what they do not have. This photo shows the result of a long period without rain.

TEACH

Teaching Objectives 1–2
ALL LEVELS: (Suggested time: 20 min.) Pair students and have each pair create a geography fact sheet for the school. Fact sheets should include the school's absolute and relative location as well as several of its physical or human characteristics. Ask volunteers to read their fact sheets to the class. Then discuss why pairs may have chosen different identifying features. **ESOL, COOPERATIVE LEARNING**

Teaching Objectives 3–4
ALL LEVELS: (Suggested time: 30 min.) Have students draw maps of their neighborhoods, including homes, stores, streets, and other landmarks. Then have them locate their neighborhoods on a map of their town, city, or county. Tell students to label items on their maps that represent the relationship between environment and society. (such as dams, recycling plants, airports, train stations, and highways) Ask volunteers to share their maps with the class. **ESOL,** **LS** **VISUAL-SPATIAL**

PHYSICAL SYSTEMS

Permafrost Some of the factors in a physical system aren't immediately apparent. Some, for example, lie far underground. Permafrost lies under some 20 to 25 percent of the world's land surface. It occurs in more than 50 percent of Russia and Canada and more than 80 percent of Alaska.

Permafrost gives scientists a window into the plant and animal life of the past. The various layers of permafrost contain plant and animal remains from different periods of Earth's history. Some of these layers are more than 30,000 years old.

Scientists also use permafrost to assess the rate of global warming. By studying ground temperatures and preserved plant and animal life, scientists can understand past climatic conditions and current temperature change.

Critical Thinking: What may the presence of oak tree remains in a layer of permafrost indicate about past temperatures in a region near the North Pole?

Answer: that long ago the region was warmer

Visual Record Answer ▶

It represents a human adaptation to Egypt's environment.

Movement People travel from place to place on miles of new roadway.

▼

Men in rural Egypt wear a long shirt called a *galabia*. This loose-fitting garment is ideal for people living in Egypt's hot desert climate. In addition, the galabia is made from cotton, an important agricultural product of Egypt.

Interpreting the Visual Record

Human-Environment Interaction How does the *galabia* show how people have adapted to their environment?

▶

8 • Chapter 1

Region A **region** is an area of Earth's surface with one or more shared characteristics. Many of the characteristics that describe places can also be used to describe regions. Regions vary in size. Some are very large, like North America. Others are much smaller, like the Florida Keys. Regions are also different from the surrounding areas. For example, Silicon Valley is a region in California that is known for its many computer companies and engineers.

What defines a region? Some regions have boundaries that are easy to define. For example, natural vegetation regions have similar plants. Deserts, forests, and grasslands are examples of natural regions with fairly clear boundaries. A region can also be described as cultural, economic, or political.

✓ **READING CHECK:** *Places and Regions* What features can you use to describe a place? physical and human features

Physical Systems

Physical systems shape Earth's features. Geographers study earthquakes, mountains, rivers, volcanoes, weather patterns, and similar topics and how these physical systems have affected Earth's characteristics. For example, geographers might study how volcanic eruptions in the Hawaiian Islands spread lava, causing landforms to change. They might note that southern California's shoreline changes yearly, as winter and summer waves move beach sand.

Geographers also study how plants and animals relate to these nonliving physical systems. For example, deserts are places with cactus and other plants, as well as rattlesnakes and other reptiles, that can live in very dry conditions. Geographers also study how different types of plants, animals, and physical systems are distributed on Earth.

✓ **READING CHECK:** *Physical Systems* What types of physical systems do geographers study? earthquakes, mountains, rivers, volcanoes, weather patterns, plants and animals, and similar topics

Teaching Objective 4

ALL LEVELS: (Suggested time: 30 min.) Copy the following graphic organizer onto the chalkboard, omitting the blue answers. Use it to help students illustrate how regions and subregions help geographers understand our world. Using the United States as an example, tell students to identify regions (such as the East or the Midwest) and subregions (such as their state). Remind students that regions and subregions may vary in size and can be categorized as cultural, economic, or political. Then have students identify subregions of one subregion and classify each into one of these three categories. **ESOL**

REGIONS AND SUBREGIONS

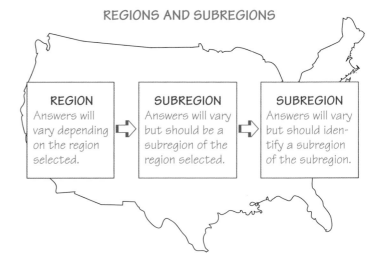

REGION	SUBREGION	SUBREGION
Answers will vary depending on the region selected.	Answers will vary but should be a subregion of the region selected.	Answers will vary but should identify a subregion of the subregion.

Human Systems

People are central to geography. Geographers study human systems, or the human activities, movements, and settlements that shape Earth's surface. Human systems also include peoples' customs, history, languages, and religions.

Movement Geographers study the **movement** of people and ideas. When people move, they may go to live in other countries or move within a country. Geographers want to know how and why people move from place to place.

People move for many reasons. Some move to start a new job. Some move to attend special schools. Others might move to be closer to family. People move either when they are pushed out of a place or when they are pulled toward another place. In the Dust Bowl, for example, crop failures pushed people out of Oklahoma in the 1930s. Many were pulled to California by their belief that they would find work there.

Geographers also want to know how ideas or behaviors move from one region to another. The movement of ideas occurs through communication. There are many ways to communicate. People visit with each other in person or on the phone. New technology allows people to communicate by e-mail. Ideas are also spread through films, magazines, newspapers, radio, and television. The movement of ideas or behaviors from one region to another is known as **diffusion**.

The things we produce and trade are also part of the study of human systems. Geographers study trading patterns and how countries depend on each other for certain goods. In addition, geographers look at the causes and results of conflicts between peoples. The study of governments we set up and the features of cities and other settlements we live in are also part of this study.

READING CHECK: (*Human Systems*) What are some reasons why people move? start a new job, attend schools, be closer to family, to find work

Environment and Society

Human actions, such as using oil or water, affect the environment. At the same time, Earth's physical systems, such as climate or natural hazards, affect human activities. Our survival depends on what Earth provides. Many geographers consider the relationship between people and the environment a central focus of geography.

Human-Environment Interaction Geographers study how people and their surroundings affect each other. This relationship between people and the environment, or **human-environment interaction**, can be examined in three ways. First, geographers study

▲
A satellite dish brings different images and ideas to people in a remote area of Brazil.
Interpreting the Visual Record How might resources have affected the use of technology here?

▲
This woman at a railway station in Russian Siberia sells some goods that were once unavailable in her country.

Megamalls At more than 5 million square feet (465,000 sq m), West Edmonton Mall in Alberta, Canada, is the largest indoor shopping and entertainment complex in the world. The Mall of America, near Minneapolis, Minnesota, is the largest mall in the United States. These malls combine hundreds of stores, full-scale amusement parks, and other attractions. They have become the top tourist destination in their regions and attract people from as far away as Asia and Europe.

Activity: Have students conduct research on sales at West Edmonton Mall and the Mall of America. Ask students to compare the sales at these malls, explain their differences, and identify what role these malls play in the movement of goods.

▲ **Visual Record Answer**

People in the region value the ability to obtain information from other parts of the world and have invested their apparently scant resources in costly technology.

TEACHER TO TEACHER

Rebecca Minnear of Las Vegas, Nevada, suggests the following activity to help students understand the six essential elements of geography. Prior to class, draw an outline map of your community on six transparencies. Organize the class into six groups and assign one element to each group. Give each group a transparency sheet and a marker. Each group should draw on the transparency ways its element relates to the community. For example, the "places and regions" group might draw features of the local landscape. The "environment and society" group might draw waterways, streets, airports, and so on. Groups should draw the parts of the community in their proper place so that when the transparencies are placed on top of each other there will be an overlap.

►**ASSIGNMENT:** Have students recall the most beautiful, interesting, or exciting place they have ever visited. Then have them write words or phrases that describe that place in terms of landforms, climate, animal life, plant life, language spoken, common religion, history, customs, or other physical or human characteristics. Ask students to consult primary or secondary sources for additional information. Then have students write a description of their chosen locale's relative location and find its absolute location by calculating latitude and longitude. You may also want to have students interpret the place in terms of the five themes of geography.

Section 2 Review

Answers to Section 2 Review

Define For definitions, see the glossary.

Reading for the Main Idea

1. with maps and other geographic tools (NGS 1)
2. physical systems such as earthquakes, mountains, rivers, volcanoes, weather patterns (NGS 7)

Critical Thinking

3. through their activities, movements, settlements, modifications
4. provides clues to the past and helps geographers plan for the future
5. The World in Spatial Terms—using maps and other geographic tools to look at the world with a spatial perspective; Places and Regions—studying the physical and human features of a place; Physical Systems—systems that have shaped Earth's features; Human Systems—how people have shaped Earth's surface; Environment and Society—how people and their surroundings affect each other; The Uses of Geography—how geography helps us understand relationships among people, places, and the environment over time

▲
Open-air markets like this one in Mali provide opportunities for farmers to sell their goods.

how humans depend on their physical environment to survive. Human life requires certain living and nonliving resources, such as freshwater and fertile soil for farming.

Geographers also study how humans change their behavior to be better suited to an environment. These changes or adaptations include the kinds of clothing, food, and shelter that people create. These changes help people live in harsh climates.

Finally, humans change the environment. For example, farmers who irrigate their fields can grow fruit in Arizona's dry climate. People in Louisiana have built levees, or large walls, to protect themselves when the Mississippi River floods.

✓ **READING CHECK:** *Environment and Society* How might people change to live in certain environments? by changing the kinds of clothing, food, and shelter they create

The Uses of Geography

Geography helps us understand the relationships among people, places, and the environment over time. Understanding how a relationship has developed can help in making plans for the future. For example, geographers can study how human use of the soil in a farming region has affected that region over time. Such knowledge can help them determine what changes have been made to the soil and whether any corrective measures need to be taken.

✓ **READING CHECK:** *The Uses of Geography* How can studying geography help plan for the future? by helping us understand the relationships among people, places, and environments over time

Homework Practice Online
Keyword: SK5 HP1

Define and explain: absolute location, relative location, place, region, movement, diffusion, human-environment interaction

Reading for the Main Idea

1. (The World in Spatial Terms) How do geographers study the world?
2. (Physical Systems) What shapes Earth's features? Give examples.

Critical Thinking

3. **Finding the Main Idea** How do humans shape the world in which they live?

4. **Analyzing Information** What benefits can studying geography provide?

Organizing What You Know

5. **Summarizing** Copy the following graphic organizer. Use it to identify and describe all aspects of each of the six essential elements.

Element	Description

CLOSE

Display a picture of a well-known local landmark. Call on students to suggest how the themes and essential elements of geography relate to it.

REVIEW, ASSESS, RETEACH

Have students complete the Section Review. Then organize students into groups of four or five. Assign each group a city that appears on one of the Atlas maps in the textbook. Have students create a travel guide that describes the region in which the city is located. Then have students complete Daily Quiz 1.2. **COOPERATIVE LEARNING**

Have students complete Main Idea Activity S2. Then organize students into groups and assign each group one of the six essential elements. Ask members of each group to write a paragraph describing their element in relation to your school. **ESOL,** [LS] **VISUAL-LINGUISTIC**

EXTEND

Ask interested students to imagine that they have been hired to submit a building plan for a recreation center in their community. Tell them to use the themes and essential elements of geography to determine the center's location and construction features. Ask students to include a drawing of the building and a map showing its location. **BLOCK SCHEDULING**

Section 3 Being a Geographer

Read to Discover
1. What is included in the study of human geography?
2. What is included in the study of physical geography?
3. What types of work do geographers do?

Vocabulary
human geography
physical geography
cartography
meteorology
climatology

Reading Strategy

READING ORGANIZER Before you read this section, create a three column chart. Title the columns Human Geography, Physical Geography, and Working as a Geographer. As you read, write information that you learn about each topic on your chart.

Human Geography

The study of people, past or present, is the focus of **human geography**. People's location and distribution over Earth, their activities, and their differences are studied. For example, people living in different countries create different kinds of governments. Political geographers study those differences. Economic geographers study the exchange of goods and services across Earth. Cultural geography, population geography, and urban geography are some other examples of human geography. A professional geographer might specialize in any of these branches.

✓ **READING CHECK:** *Human Systems* How is human geography defined? as the study of people, past or present

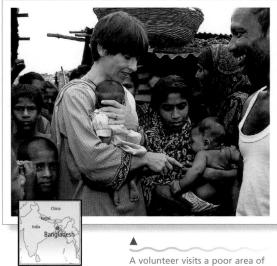

A volunteer visits a poor area of Bangladesh. Geographers study economic conditions in regions to help them understand human geography.

Physical Geography

The study of Earth's natural landscapes and physical systems, including the atmosphere, is the focus of **physical geography**. The world is full of different landforms such as deserts, mountains, and plains. Climates affect these landscapes. Knowledge of physical systems helps geographers understand how a landscape developed and how it might change.

A Geographer's World • 11

Section 3

Objectives
1. Explain the study of human geography.
2. Describe the study of physical geography.
3. Investigate the types of work that geographers do.

FOCUS

Bellringer
Ask students what they would do if they were lost in an unfamiliar part of town. Then have them work in pairs to list ways to find their way home. (asking for directions or consulting a map) Ask them to describe the advantages or disadvantages of these options. Have them choose one of these solutions and create a map or written directions for a place with which they are both familiar. Tell them to evaluate the effectiveness of the solution by presenting their work to another pair.

Building Vocabulary
Tell students that the word **cartography** contains the common suffix -*graphy*, which means "writing or representation." Ask students what other words they know that contain the suffix. Point out that the prefix *cart*- indicates maps, so the complete word means writing or representing maps. Divide **meteorology** also: *meteor*-, from a Greek word meaning "high in the air"; and -*logy*, meaning "a branch of learning." Then ask students to use what they just learned to define **climatology**.

FOOD FESTIVAL

The Geography of Food
Have students bring food items to class and use them to discuss human and physical geography. For example, a student may bring a can of green beans and note that certain soil, sunlight, and climate conditions must be present to grow the beans. Or a student may use the can to discuss how people in different parts of the country prepare green beans, or how farms and canneries affect local economies.

Connecting to Technology
Answers
1. It can help planners build roads, dams, or other structures.
2. greater knowledge about population, profitable economic activities, or change to the environment

CONNECTING TO Technology

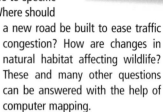

A mapmaker creates a digital map.

Maps are tools that can display a wide range of information. Traditionally, maps were drawn on paper and could not be changed to suit the user. However, computers have revolutionized the art of mapmaking.

Today, mapmakers use computers to create and modify maps for different uses. They do this by using a geographic information system, or GIS. A GIS is a computer system that combines maps and satellite photographs with other kinds of spatial data—information about places on the planet. This information might include soil types, population figures, or voting patterns.

Using a GIS, mapmakers can create maps that show geographic features and relationships. For example, a map showing rainfall patterns in a particular region might be combined with data on soil types or human settlement to show areas of possible soil erosion.

The flexibility of a GIS allows people to seek answers to specific questions. Where should a new road be built to ease traffic congestion? How are changes in natural habitat affecting wildlife? These and many other questions can be answered with the help of computer mapping.

Computer Mapping

Understanding What You Read
1. How could a GIS help people change their environment?
2. What social, environmental, or economic consequences might future advances in GIS technology have?

Knowledge of physical and human geography will help you understand the world's different regions and peoples. In your study of the major world regions, you will see how physical and human geography connect to each other.

✓ **READING CHECK:** (*Physical Systems*) What is included in the study of physical geography? Earth's natural landscapes and physical systems, including the atmosphere

---

Working as a Geographer

Geography plays a role in almost every occupation. Wherever you live and work, you should know local geography. School board members know where children live. Taxi drivers are familiar with city streets. Grocery store managers know which foods sell well in certain areas.

TEACH

Teaching Objectives 1–3
ALL LEVELS: (Suggested time: 20 min.) Copy the following graphic organizer onto the chalkboard, omitting the blue answers. Use it to help students distinguish between the study of human geography and the study of physical geography and to identify the types of work geographers do.
ESOL, LS **VISUAL-SPATIAL**

Geography helps us understand the world.

Physical Geography	Types of work	Human Geography
the study of • Earth's natural landscapes and physical systems • different landforms	include • cartography • meteorology • climatology	the study of • people, past or present • politics, economy, and culture

They also know where they can obtain these products throughout the year. Local newspaper reporters are familiar with town meetings and local politicians. Reporters also know how faraway places can affect their communities. Doctors must know if their towns have poisonous snakes or plants. City managers know whether nearby rivers might flood. Emergency workers in mountain towns check snow depth so they can give avalanche warnings. Local weather forecasters watch for powerful storms and track their routes on special maps.

Some specially trained geographers practice in the field of **cartography**. Cartography is the art and science of mapmaking. Today, most mapmakers do their work on computers. Geographers also work as weather forecasters. The field of forecasting and reporting rainfall, temperature, and other atmospheric conditions is called **meteorology**. A related field is **climatology**. These geographers, known as climatologists, track Earth's larger atmospheric systems. Climatologists want to know how these systems change over long periods of time. They also study how people might be affected by changes in climate.

Governments and a variety of organizations hire geographers to study the environment. These geographers might explore such topics as pollution, endangered plants and animals, or rain forests. Some geographers who are interested in education become teachers and writers. They help people of all ages learn more about the world. Modern technology allows people all over the world to communicate instantly. Therefore, it is more important than ever to be familiar with the geographer's world.

▲
Experts examine snow to help forecast avalanches. They study the type of snow, weather conditions, and landforms.

✓ **READING CHECK:** (*The Uses of Geography*) What types of work do geographers perform? They make maps, work as weather forecasters, track atmospheric systems, or work as teachers or writers.

Section Review 3

Define and explain: human geography, physical geography, cartography, meteorology, climatology

Reading for the Main Idea

1. (Human Systems) What topics are included in the study of human geography?

2. (The Uses of Geography) How do people who study the weather use geography?

Critical Thinking

3. Finding the Main Idea Why is it important to study physical geography?

go.hrw.com **Homework Practice Online**
Keyword: SK5 HP1

4. Making Generalizations and Predictions How might future discoveries in the field of geography affect societies, world economies, or the environment?

Organizing What You Know

5. Categorizing Copy the following graphic organizer. Use it to list geographers' professions and their job responsibilities.

Cartographer
—makes maps
—studies maps

A Geographer's World • 13

Section 3 Review

Answers to Section 3 Review

Define For definitions, see the glossary.

Reading for the Main Idea

1. Topics are the study of people, their location and distribution, their activities, and their differences. **(NGS 9)**

2. by tracking Earth's larger atmospheric systems **(NGS 18)**

Critical Thinking

3. to learn how a landscape developed and how it might change

4. by helping resolve problems regarding population, pollution, endangered plants and animals, or through increased economic activities **(NGS 18)**

Organizing What You Know

5. meteorologist—tracks weather and atmospheric conditions; climatologist—tracks atmospheric systems

CLOSE

Write the following statement on the chalkboard: *A cartographer's work is never done.* Ask students why might this be true. (Possible answers: changes required by physical processes, new roads and suburbs, and political boundary changes)

Have students complete Main Idea Activity S3. Then have them complete the following sentence: "I used my knowledge of geography today when I . . . " Ask volunteers to read their sentences to the class. **ESOL,** **LS** **INTERPERSONAL**

REVIEW, ASSESS, RETEACH

Have students complete the Section Review. Then pair students and have each pair locate newspaper or magazine articles that relate to some aspect of human or physical geography. Have pairs write a few sentences explaining the connection between the articles and human or physical geography. Then have students complete Daily Quiz 1.3. **COOPERATIVE LEARNING**

EXTEND

Have interested students conduct research on the history of cartography in an area that has been mapped since antiquity. Have them use copies of ancient maps to investigate how maps of that region have evolved over time and then present their findings to the class. **BLOCK SCHEDULING**

HISTORICAL GEOGRAPHY

Hurricanes and typhoons—as these large storms are called when they occur in the Pacific Ocean—have changed history. Here are just three examples.

In 1281 the Mongol ruler Kublai Khan was ready to invade Japan, but a typhoon scattered his huge fleet of ships. A second storm, dubbed the Great Hurricane, ravaged the Caribbean in October 1780. It killed approximately 22,000 people and may be the deadliest hurricane on record. British and French fleets involved in the American Revolutionary War were both ravaged. Finally, in December 1944, during World War II, a sudden typhoon east of the Philippines caught the U.S. Third Fleet by surprise. Three destroyers, 146 aircraft, and several hundred men were lost.

Critical Thinking: How could early storm warning technology have changed world history?

Answer: Answers will vary but students might mention a successful invasion by Kublai Khan, fewer deaths in the Caribbean, and fewer ships and lives lost during the Revolutionary War and World War II.

➤ This Case Study feature addresses National Geography Standards 4, 15, and 17.

CASE STUDY

HOW GEOGRAPHERS TRACK HURRICANES

As you learned in Chapter 1, geographers called climatologists study Earth's atmosphere. Sometimes large circulating storms called hurricanes develop in the atmosphere above tropical oceans. Hurricanes often move over land and into populated areas. When a hurricane approaches land, it brings strong winds, heavy rains, and large ocean waves.

Climatologists try to predict where these storms will travel. They want to be able to warn people in the hurricane's path. Early warnings can help people be better prepared for the deadly winds and rain. It is a difficult job because hurricanes can change course suddenly. Hurricanes are one of the most dangerous natural hazards.

The map below shows the path of Hurricane Fran in 1996. Notice how Fran moved to the west and became stronger until it reached land. It began as a tropical depression and became a powerful hurricane as it passed over warm ocean waters.

One way of determining a hurricane's strength is by measuring the atmospheric pressure inside it. The lower the pressure, the stronger the storm. Hurricanes are rated on a scale of one to five. Study Table 1 to see how wind speed and air pressure are used to help determine the strength of a hurricane.

Hurricane Mitch formed in October 1998. The National Weather Service (NWS) recorded Mitch's position and strength. They learned that Mitch's pressure was one of the lowest ever recorded. The

Table 1: Saffir-Simpson Scale

HURRICANE TYPE	WIND SPEED MPH	AIR PRESSURE MB (INCHES)
Category 1	74–95	more than 980 (28.94)
Category 2	96–110	965–979 (28.50–28.91)
Category 3	111–130	945–964 (27.91–28.47)
Category 4	131–155	920–944 (27.17–27.88)
Category 5	more than 155	less than 920 (27.17)

Source: Florida State University, <http://www.met.fsu.edu/explores/tropical.html>

Path of Hurricane Fran, 1996

Setting the Scene

Every year, hurricanes torment residents of the Caribbean islands, the coastlands bordering the Gulf of Mexico, and the East Coast of the United States. Because hurricanes get their strength from warm water, hurricane season lasts through summer and into fall. These storms carry tremendous energy. In one day an average hurricane releases at least 8,000 times the daily electrical power output of the United States. Severe hurricanes can cause billions of dollars of damage. Fewer lives are lost now than in years past, however, because early warning systems help predict the storms' paths and power. Coastal towns and cities evacuate people before the storms arrive. Satellites provide much of the information used to make storm predictions.

Building a Case

Have students read "Hurricane: Tracking a Natural Hazard" and follow the instructions in You Be the Geographer. Ask on what date the atmospheric pressure was lowest. (10/27) How did Mitch register on the Saffir-Simpson Scale that day? (category 5) Compare Hurricane Mitch with the hurricane that struck Galveston on September 8, 1900.

The storm headed for Galveston was first observed on August 30. The Weather Bureau placed Galveston under a storm warning on September 7. September 8 dawned rainy and gusty. Though the storm worsened, few residents left the city. At 6:30 P.M. a storm surge flooded the city. The lowest barometer reading was 27.91. Windspeed was estimated at more than 120 mph. By 10:00 P.M. much of the city was wrecked. As many as 8,000 city residents died.

Table 2: Hurricane Mitch, 1998 Position and Strength

DATE	LATITUDE (DEGREES)	LONGITUDE (DEGREES)	WIND SPEED (MPH)	PRESSURE (MILLIBARS)	STORM TYPE
10/22	12 N	78 W	30	1002	Tropical depression
10/24	15 N	78 W	90	980	Category 2
10/26	16 N	81 W	130	923	Category 4
10/27	17 N	84 W	150	910	Category 5
10/31	15 N	88 W	40	1000	Tropical storm
11/01	15 N	90 W	30	1002	Tropical depression
11/03	20 N	91 W	40	997	Tropical storm
11/05	26 N	83 W	50	990	Tropical storm

Source: <http://www.met.fsu.edu/explores/tropical.html>

NWS estimated that Mitch's maximum sustained surface winds reached 180 miles per hour.

Hurricanes like Mitch cause very heavy rains in short periods of time. These heavy rains are particularly dangerous. The ground becomes saturated, and mud can flow almost like water. The flooding and mudslides caused by Mitch killed an estimated 10,000 people in four countries. Many people predicted that the region would not recover without help from other countries.

In the southeastern United States, many places have emergency preparedness units. The people assigned to these groups organize their communities. They provide food, shelter, and clothing for those who must evacuate their homes.

You Be the Geographer

1. Trace a map of the Caribbean. Be sure to include latitude and longitude lines.

2. Use the data about Hurricane Mitch in Table 2 to plot its path. Make a key with symbols to show Mitch's strength at each location.

3. What happened to Mitch when it reached land?

▲ This satellite image shows the intensity of Hurricane Mitch. With advanced technology, hurricane tracking is helping to save lives.

You Be the Geographer

1. Students may trace the map on the previous page. Or, provide an outline map to students.

2. On student maps, from its first position Hurricane Mitch should progress north-northwest toward Cuba, swing southwest toward Nicaragua, then back northeast across the Yucatán Peninsula on its way to the open Atlantic Ocean.

3. When it reached land, Mitch's strength weakened.

internet connect

GO TO: go.hrw.com
KEYWORD: SG5 CH1
FOR: Web sites about hurricanes

Drawing Conclusions

Lead a discussion comparing the two storms. According to wind speed and air pressure, what level storm was the Galveston hurricane? (3) Which was the stronger storm? (Mitch) Which hurricane lasted longer? (Mitch) Why did the 1900 storm kill so many people in such a short time? (They had not evacuated the city.) If there had been no warning system, how might Hurricane Mitch have affected the Caribbean region? (It might have killed even more people.)

What might have happened if Galveston had been warned earlier? Have students prepare and present an alternate newscast for the morning of September 9, 1900, based on this possibility.

Going Further: Thinking Critically

Locate detailed maps of the Gulf of Mexico or Atlantic coasts of the United States. Use maps of different areas or concentrate on one region. Have students work in groups to answer some or all of these questions:

- What cities and towns might be threatened by a hurricane? Can students estimate how many people live in the area?
- What routes could residents use to evacuate? What factors might slow evacuation? If they could travel about 30 mph (48 km/h), how far could people travel in one day? two days?
- What would happen if residents were warned just a few hours before a hurricane? What effect might an early warning system have on this region?

Define and Identify

For definitions and identifications, see the glossary and index.

Review the Main Ideas

18. a science that describes the physical and cultural features of Earth

19. cities; open land that is often used for farming **(NGS 12)**

20. local, regional, or global

21. in terms of its absolute location or its relative location **(NGS 1)**

22. in terms of vegetation; also cultural, economic, or political **(NGS 5)**

23. to start a new job, attend schools, be closer to family, find work **(NGS 9)**

24. by changing kinds of clothing, food, and shelter **(NGS 15)**

25. possible answers: because accurate maps can help businesses, can help people enjoy travel, and even save lives **(NGS 3)**

26. possible answers: study pollution, endangered plants and animals, or rain forests; teach or write

Think Critically

27. Answers will vary, but students might mention that a geographer identifies where things are so that connections can be made.

28. when—daily; how— answers will vary; examples might include building dams and irrigating fields

29. Students might mention the movement of people, trade networks, or the diffusion of ideas between groups.

30. both human and physical characteristics

31. by helping us see meaning in the arrangement of things on Earth

Review and Practice

Define and Identify

Identify each of the following:

1. perspective
2. spatial perspective
3. geography
4. urban
5. rural
6. absolute location
7. relative location
8. place
9. region
10. movement
11. diffusion
12. human-environment interaction
13. human geography
14. physical geography
15. cartography
16. meteorology
17. climatology

Review the Main Ideas

18. What is geography?

19. What do urban areas contain? What do rural areas contain?

20. What are three ways to study geography? Give an example of when each type could be used.

21. What kind of directions would you give to indicate a place's absolute location? Its relative location?

22. How can a place be described?

23. What are some ways to define a region?

24. What are some reasons why people move?

25. How do some people adapt to better suit their environment?

26. Why is cartography important?

27. What types of jobs do geographers do?

Think Critically

28. Analyzing Information How can a geographer use spatial perspective to explain how things in our world are connected?

29. Drawing Inferences and Conclusions When and how do humans relate to the environment? Provide some examples of this relationship.

30. Summarizing How are patterns created by the movement of goods, ideas, and people?

31. Finding the Main Idea How are places and regions defined?

32. Finding the Main Idea How does studying geography help us understand the world?

Map Activity

33. On a separate sheet of paper, match the letters on the map with their correct labels.

Africa	Europe
Antarctica	North America
Asia	South America
Australia	

Map Activity

32. A. Europe
B. North America
C. Antarctica
D. South America
E. Asia
F. Australia
G. Africa

Writing Activity

Write a letter persuading another student to enroll in a geography class. Include examples of professions that use geography and relate that information to the everyday life of a student. Be sure to use standard grammar, spelling, sentence structure, and punctuation.

☑ internet connect ▬▬▬▬

Internet Activity: **go.hrw.com**
KEYWORD: SK5 GT1

Choose a topic to explore online:
- Learn to use online maps.
- Be a virtual geographer for a day.
- Compare regions around the world.

Social Studies Skills Practice

Interpreting Maps

Study the following map of the state of California. Use what you know about location to answer the questions.

1. How would you describe the relative location of Los Angeles?
2. If you were in San Francisco, how would you describe the relative location of Yosemite National Park?
3. What would you use on this map to find the absolute location of places?
4. What is the absolute location of Los Angeles?

Analyzing Primary Sources

Read the following quote from geographer Dr. Reginald G. Golledge. Then answer the questions.

"As I was growing up in Australia, my family moved frequently, largely from one small town to another . . . The small-town environment and the surrounding countryside favored the development of a state of mind that constantly asked, 'What's over the next hill? How far is it to the river? Where are the wild berries and fruits located?'"

Source: *Geographical Voices: Fourteen Autobiographical Essays*

1. Did Dr. Golledge grow up in a rural area or an urban area?
2. How do you think Dr. Golledge's childhood experiences led him to become a geographer?
3. As a child, was Golledge interested more in human geography or physical geography?
4. Which two of the five geography themes best describes the questions Dr. Golledge asks?

Writing Activity

Letters will vary, but should include various professions that use geography. Letters should also relate the use of geography to the everyday life of a student. Use Rubric 25, Personal Letters, to evaluate student work.

Interpreting Maps

1. on the southern coast of California
2. east of San Francisco, in the Sierra Nevada
3. lines of latitude and longitude
4. 118°W, 34°N

Analyzing Primary Sources

1. rural
2. by stimulating his curiosity about his surroundings
3. physical geography
4. possible answer: location and place

CHAPTER 1

REVIEW AND ASSESSMENT RESOURCES

Reproducible
- Readings in World Geography, History, and Culture 1, 2
- Critical Thinking Activity 1
- Vocabulary Activity 1

Technology
- Chapter 1 Test Generator (on the One-Stop Planner)

- Audio CD Program, Chapter 1
- HRW Go site

Reinforcement, Review, and Assessment
- Chapter 1 Review and Practice
- Chapter Summaries and Review

- Chapter 1 Test
- Chapter 1 Test for English Language Learners and Special-Needs Students

☑ internet connect

GO TO: **go.hrw.com**
KEYWORD: SG5 Teacher
FOR: a guide to using the Internet in your classroom

CHAPTER 2

Planet Earth
Chapter Resource Manager

Objectives	Pacing Guide	Reproducible Resources
SECTION 1 **The Land** 1. Describe the processes that build up the land. 2. Describe the processes that shape Earth's surface. 3. Show how topography has affected human history and culture.	**Regular** 1.5 day Lecture Notes, Section 1 **Block Scheduling** 1 day *Block Scheduling Handbook, Chapter 2*	**RS** Know It Notes **RS** Graphic Organizer **SM** Critical Thinking Activity 2 **E** Environmental and Global Issues Activity 3 Lab Activities for Geography and Earth Science, Hands-On 5, Demonstrations 3–10 Geography for Life Activity 4 **E** Readings in World Geography, History, and Culture, Reading 3 **E** Biography Activity: Louis Agassiz **ELL** Main Idea Activity S1
SECTION 2 **Water and Air** 1. Identify where water is found on Earth. 2. Analyze the water cycle. 3. Explore how people and water affect each other. 4. Explain the short-term and long-term results of air pollution.	**Regular** 1.5 day Lecture Notes, Section 2 **Block Scheduling** 1 day *Block Scheduling Handbook, Chapter 2*	**RS** Know It Notes S2 **IC** Lab Activities for Geography and Earth Sces, Demonstration 1 **ELL** Main Idea Activity S2
SECTION 3 **Climate, Weather and Vegetation** 1. Identify the factors that create climate and weather. 2. Describe how climate, plants, and animal life are related.	**Regular** 1.5 day Lecture Notes, Section 3 **Block Scheduling** 1 day *Block Scheduling Handbook, Chapter 2*	**RS** Know It Notes S3 **IC** Environmental and Global Issues Activities 1, 2 **E** Lab Activities for Geography and Earth Science, Hands-On 1, Demonstrations 11, 12 **E** Geography for Life Activities 2–4 Creative Strategies for Teaching World Geography, Lesson 13 **SM** Map Activity **ELL** Main Idea Activity S3
SECTION 4 **Natural Resources** 1. Identify the most important renewable resources. 2. Explain how the main energy resources differ. 3. Explore how we use mineral resources. 4. Discover how resources affect people.	**Regular** 1.5 day Lecture Notes, Section 4 **Block Scheduling** 1 day *Block Scheduling Handbook, Chapter 2*	**RS** Know It Notes **IC** Environmental and Global Issues Activities 1, 2, 4–8 **IC** Lab Activities for Geography and Earth Science, Hands-On 3, Demonstration 8 **E** Geography for Life Activity 4 **E** Readings in World Geography, History, and Culture, Readings 5, 7, 8 **SM** Map Activity 4 **E** Creative Strategies for Teaching World Geography, Lesson 8 **ELL** Main Idea Activity S4

Chapter Resource Key

RS Reading Support	**ELL** Reinforcement and English Language Learners and English for Speakers of Other Languages (ESOL)	Internet	
IC Interdisciplinary Connections		Holt Presentation Maker Using Microsoft® PowerPoint®	
E Enrichment			
SM Skills Mastery	Transparencies		
A Assessment	CD–ROM		
REV Review	Music		
	Video		

 One-Stop Planner CD–ROM

See the *One-Stop Planner* for a complete list of additional resources for students and teachers.

One-Stop Planner CD–ROM

It's easy to plan lessons, select resources, and print out materials for your students when you use the *One-Stop Planner CD–ROM with Test Generator.*

internet connect

HRW ONLINE RESOURCES

<u>GO TO: go.hrw.com</u>
Then type in a keyword.

TEACHER HOME PAGE
  KEYWORD: SJ5 TEACHER

CHAPTER INTERNET ACTIVITIES
  KEYWORD: SJ5 GT2

Choose an activity to:
• learn more about using weather maps.
• discover facts about Earth's water.
• investigate earthquakes.

CHAPTER ENRICHMENT LINKS
  KEYWORD: SJ5 CH2

CHAPTER MAPS
  KEYWORD: SJ5 MAPS2

ONLINE ASSESSMENT
Homework Practice
  KEYWORD: SJ5 HP2
  Standardized Test Prep Online
  KEYWORD: SJ5 STP2
  Rubrics
  KEYWORD: SS Rubrics

COUNTRY INFORMATION
  KEYWORD: SJ5 Almanac

CONTENT UPDATES
  KEYWORD: SS Content Updates

HOLT PRESENTATION MAKER
  KEYWORD: SJ5 PPT2

ONLINE READING SUPPORT
  KEYWORD: SS Strategies

CURRENT EVENTS
  KEYWORD: S5 Current Events

Technology Resources	Review, Reinforcement, and Assessment Resources	
One-Stop Planner CD-ROM, Lesson 2.1	ELL	Main Idea Activity S1
ARGWorld CD–ROM	REV	Section 1 Review
Homework Practice Online	A	Daily Quiz 2.1
HRW Go site	REV	Chapter Summaries and Review
	ELL	English Audio Summary 2.1
	ELL	Spanish Audio Summary 2.1
One-Stop Planner CD-ROM, Lesson 2.2	ELL	Main Idea Activity S2
Geography and Cultures Visual Resources 13	REV	Section 2 Review
ARGWorld CD–ROM	A	Daily Quiz 2.2
Homework Practice Online	REV	Chapter Summaries and Review
HRW Go site	ELL	English Audio Summary 2.2
	ELL	Spanish Audio Summary 2.2
One-Stop Planner CD-ROM, Lesson 2.3	ELL	Main Idea Activity S3
ARGWorld CD–ROM	REV	Section 3 Review
Homework Practice Online	A	Daily Quiz 2.3
HRW Go site	REV	Chapter Summaries and Review
	ELL	English Audio Summary 2.3
	ELL	Spanish Audio Summary 2.3
One-Stop Planner CD-ROM, Lesson 2.4	ELL	Main Idea Activity S4
ARGWorld CD–ROM	REV	Section 4 Review
Homework Practice Online	A	Daily Quiz 2.4
HRW Go site	REV	Chapter Summaries and Review
	ELL	English Audio Summary 2.4
	ELL	Spanish Audio Summary 2.4

Meeting Individual Needs

Ability Levels

Level 1 Basic-level activities designed for all students encountering new material

Level 2 Intermediate-level activities designed for average students

Level 3 Challenging activities designed for honors and gifted-and-talented students

ESOL Activities that address the needs of students with Limited English Proficiency

Chapter Review and Assessment

E	Readings in World Geography, History, and Culture 5–8
SM	Critical Thinking Activity 2
REV	Chapter 2 Review and Practice
REV	Chapter Summaries and Review
ELL	Vocabulary Activity 2
A	Chapter 2 Test
A	Chapter 2 Test Generator (on the One-Stop Planner)
	Audio CD program, Chapter 2
A	Chapter 2 Test for English Language learners and Special Needs Students
	HRW Go site

CHAPTER 2

Planet Earth

Previewing Chapter Resources

Holt Online Learning

Earth as seen from space

Digital Stock Corp./HRW

Keyword: SK5 GT2

- *Homework Practice Online*
- *Holt Online Assessment*
- *Online Gradebook*
- *Document-Based Question Activities*
- *Teaching Tips for the Multimedia Classroom*
- *Interactive Multimedia Activities*

Differentiating Instruction

Reading and Writing Support

- *Graphic Organizer Activity*
- ◀ *Vocabulary Activity*
- *Chapter Summary and Review*
- *Know It Notes*
- *Audio CD*

Active Learning

- *Block Scheduling Handbook*
- *Cultures of the World Activity*
- *Interdisciplinary Activity*
- *Map Activity*
- ◀ *Critical Thinking Activity: Volcanoes*

Primary Sources and Advanced Learners

- *Geography for Life Activity: Hurricane Season*
- ◀ *Map Activity: Earthquakes and Volcanoes*
- *Readings in World Geography, History and Culture:*
  - *3 Preparing for the Big One*
  - *4 Earth's Rotation in Our Daily Lives*

Assessment Program

- ◀ *Daily Quizzes S1–4*
- *Chapter Test*
- *Chapter Test for English Language Learners and Special-Needs Students*

Spanish and ESOL

- *Vocabulary Activity*
- *Main Idea Activities for English Language Learners and Special-Needs Students*
- *Chapter Summary and Review*
- *Spanish Audio Summary*
- *Know It Notes S1–4*
- ◀ *Chapter Test for English Language Learners and Special-Needs Students*

Special Education Modifications

Your **I.D.E.A. Works! CD-ROM** will provide modified versions of the following teaching materials:

- ◀ *Guided Reading Strategies S1–4*
- *Vocabulary Activity*
- *Main Idea Activities S1–4*
- *Daily Quizzes S1–4*
- *Chapter 2 Test*
- *Flash cards of chapter vocabulary terms*

17C

Teacher Resources

Books for Teachers

Jones, William Barrie. *Discovering the Solar System.* John Wiley & Sons, 1999.

Munsart, Craig A. *American History through Earth Science.* Teacher Ideas Press, 1997.

Windley, Brian F. *The Evolving Continents.* John Wiley & Sons, 1995.

Books for Students

Farndon, John. *How the Earth Works.* Reader's Digest, 1992. Descriptions, illustrations, and experiments about Earth. **SHELTERED ENGLISH**

Lauber, Patricia. *Volcano: The Eruption and Healing of Mount St. Helens.* Aladdin Paperbacks, 1993. Why it erupted, the destruction it caused, and the return of life to the mountain.

Redfern, Martin. *The Kingfisher Young People's Book of Space.* Kingfisher, 1998. Definitions of black holes, galaxies, the solar system, the Milky Way, and more.

Singh, Madanjeet, and UNESCO. *The Timeless Energy of the Sun.* Sierra Club Books, 1999. Explores the potential for integrating the latest solar technologies into traditional cultures.

Multimedia Materials

Earth Quest. CD–ROM. DK Family Learning.

Interactive Earth. CD–ROM. Worldlink.

On the Edge of the World. Video, 60 min. Films for the Humanities and Sciences.

Videos and CDs

Videos

- *CNN Presents Geography: Yesterday and Today, Segment 2 Birth of an Island; Segment 3 Global Warming*
- *ARG World*

Holt Researcher

http://researcher.hrw.com

- *Global Problem of Acid Rain*
- *Clean Air Act of 1970*
- *Clean Water Act (Federal Water Pollution Control Act Amendments)*
- *Water Quality Improvement Act*
- *World*

Transparency Packages

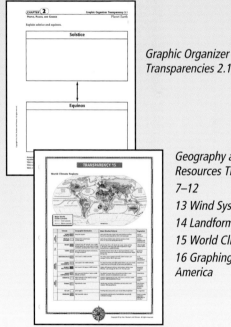

Graphic Organizer Transparencies 2.1–4

Geography and Cultures Visual Resources Transparencies 7–12
13 Wind Systems
14 Landforms and Precipitation
15 World Climate Regions
16 Graphing Climate in South America

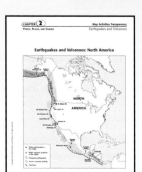

Map Activities Transparency 02 Earthquakes and Volcanoes

These are among the reasons why students should take an interest in this chapter's topics:

▶ By learning more about how land is formed and changed, we can save lives threatened by earthquakes, volcanoes, and other hazards.

▶ To protect our supplies of clean water and clean air, we should know more about these precious resources.

▶ We can plan daily activities better if we understand the weather and how it changes.

▶ We make decisions about using resources every day. We need to be informed to make good decisions.

CHAPTER 2

Planet Earth

Diver, coral, and fish, Fiji Islands

Quartz crystals

Erupting volcano

Tornado in Saskatoon, Canada

CHAPTER PROJECT

Have students research the origin of local or nearby landforms. (Possible origins include glacial action, volcanic action, and sedimentation.) To present their findings, have students label landforms on a topographic map according to how they were formed. You may want to have students design models that show the formation processes. Photograph the models and place the pictures in student portfolios.

STARTING THE CHAPTER

Write *air, earth, fire,* and *water* on the chalkboard. Tell students that long ago, people thought that these four were elements and that everything was made from them. Ask students to identify different forms of these "elements." Write their responses under the appropriate categories on the chalkboard. (Examples: air—wind, tornadoes, ozone; earth—dirt, landslides, mountains; fire—volcanoes, forest fires; water—rain, oceans, rivers, water from pipes and faucets) Tell students that although we now know that air, earth, fire, and water are not elements, understanding their characteristics and relationships helps us understand geography and life on Earth.

Section 1 The Land

Read to Discover

1. What processes build up the land?
2. What processes shape Earth's surfaces?
3. How has topography affected human history and culture?

Vocabulary

landforms
topography
plate tectonics
subduction
earthquakes
lava
fault
weathering

erosion
plain
alluvial fan
floodplain
delta
glaciers
terraces

Reading Strategy

TAKING NOTES | Taking notes while you read will help you understand and remember the information in this section. Write down the headings in the section. As you read, fill in notes under each heading. Underline the most important details you find.

Building Up the Land

Landforms are shapes on Earth's surface. The shape, height, and arrangement of landforms in a certain place is called **topography**. The theory of **plate tectonics** helps explain how Earth's topography formed and how it changes. According to this theory, Earth's surface is divided into several large plates, or pieces. There are also a number of smaller plates. These plates move very slowly — just inches per year.

Plate Tectonics

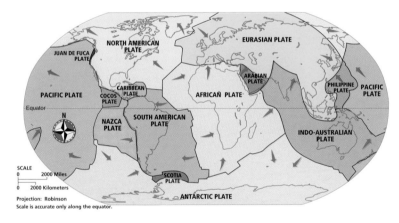

The plates that make up Earth's crust are moving, usually a few inches per year. This map shows the plates and the direction of their movement.

Section 1 RESOURCES

Reproducible
- Lecture Notes, Section 1
- Know It Notes S1
- Environmental and Global Issues Activity 3
- Lab Activities for Geography and Earth Science, Hands-On 5, Demonstrations 3–10
- Geography for Life Activity 4
- Readings in World Geography, History, and Culture, Reading 3
- Map Activity 2
- Critical Thinking Activity 2
- Main Idea Activity S1
- Biography Activity: Louis Agassiz

Technology
- One-Stop Planner CD-ROM, Lesson 2.1
- Homework Practice Online
- Geography and Cultures Visual Resources 11–13
- HRW Go Site

Reinforcement, Review, and Assessment
- Section 1 Review
- Daily Quiz 2.1
- Main Idea Activity S1
- Chapter Summaries and Review
- English Audio Summary 2.1
- Spanish Audio Summary 2.1

Section 1

Objectives

1. Describe the processes that build up the land.
2. Describe the processes that shape Earth's surface.
3. Show how topography has affected human history and culture.

FOCUS

 Bellringer

Write the following question on the chalkboard: *What do we mean when we say "solid as a rock," "mountain of strength," or "older than dirt"?* Use student responses to conduct a class discussion. Then ask students what the phrases suggest about Earth (that it is unchangeable and permanent). Tell students that in Section 1 they will learn that Earth is actually in motion and changes both slowly and quickly.

Building Vocabulary

Write the vocabulary words on slips of paper and have each student draw one from a hat. You will probably need to have duplicates of some terms. Ask students to find the definitions in the text and read them to the class. Then write *shapes on Earth's surface, slow movement,* and *fast change* on the chalkboard. Have the students determine the appropriate category for each term.

Linking Past to Present
Lava and Ice

According to some historical accounts, Iceland has experienced about 60 gigantic floods since the Vikings arrived in the A.D. 800s. Scientists had doubted the accuracy of these accounts. However, events in November 1996 showed how these floods could have occurred.

Water that had been melted by a volcanic eruption broke out from under the Vatnajökull ice cap. Ash and steam gushed up through the ice, melting a huge hole in it. The runoff carved a canyon in the ice—a canyon 500 feet deep and more than two miles long. Magma melted more of the ice cap's bottom layers. Billions of gallons of water drained into an ice-covered crater. The water raised the crater's thick lid of ice and then flowed downhill underneath the ice cap. Finally, the water burst out from under the ice. Blocks of ice as large as buildings ripped loose. When the flood crashed into a bridge it was flowing at 1.6 million cubic feet per second.

Visual Record Answer ▶

The mountains have been thrust up by the force of colliding plates.

Colliding Plates Some of the plates collide as they move, and one plate may move underneath the other. This process is called **subduction**. In subduction zones, volcanoes and **earthquakes** are common. An earthquake is a sudden, violent movement along a break within the outer layers of Earth's crust.

Look at the Plate Tectonics map on the previous page and find the Pacific plate. Where the Pacific plate moves against neighboring plates, volcanoes and earthquakes are common. In fact, the edge of the Pacific plate is called the Ring of Fire because it is rimmed by active volcanoes. The region's earthquakes and volcanoes have killed thousands of people and caused terrible destruction. Several major earthquakes have hit California in recent years. Local authorities along the West Coast are constantly preparing for future earthquakes. Scientists predict that one of the strongest earthquakes in U.S. history may occur in the San Francisco Bay area within the next 30 years.

In some places, colliding plates have other results. Instead of sinking, one of the plates may crumple up and form a mountain range. The Andes in South America and the Himalayas in Asia formed in this way.

Other Plate Movements In other parts of the world, plates move away from each other. From the gap, hot **lava**, or melted rock from deep in the Earth, may emerge. The lava may build up, forming a mountain range. This process is happening in the Atlantic Ocean where the Eurasian plate and the North American plate are moving away from each other.

Tectonic plates can also slide past each other. Earthquakes occur from these sudden changes in Earth's crust. In California the Pacific plate is sliding northwestward along the edge of the North American plate. This movement has created the San Andreas Fault zone. A **fault** is a fractured surface in Earth's crust where a mass of rock is in motion.

✓ **READING CHECK:** (*Physical Systems*) What are three ways that tectonic plates move? collide, move away from each other, slide past each other

These steep peaks in Chile are part of the Andes. **Interpreting the Visual Record** (Place) How do these mountains show the effects of colliding plates?

▼

TEACH

Teaching Objective 1

LEVEL 1: (Suggested time: 45 min.) Provide students with nature and tourism magazines. Have them find and cut out photographs of different types of topography and use the Geographic Dictionary at the front of this book to label them. Call on volunteers to display their labeled photos.

Then lead a class discussion about which photos may show landforms built up by tectonic action. **ESOL, LS KINESTHETIC**

LEVELS 2 AND 3: Provide extra time and additional resources for this activity. Have each student create a three-panel brochure titled "When Plates Collide." Each panel should contain a description of a landform created by colliding tectonic plates, a diagram of the process involved in creating the landform, and an example of a place where that process is occurring. Display brochures in the classroom. **LS VISUAL-SPATIAL**

Shaping Earth's Surface

The forces of plate tectonics build up the land. At the same time, water, wind, and ice constantly break down rock and move rocky material. This process of breaking down landforms and creating new ones is called **weathering**.

Heat, Water, and Chemical Action Weathering breaks rocks into smaller pieces in several ways. Heat can cause rocks to crack. Water may then get into the cracks. If the water freezes, the ice expands with a force great enough to break the rock. Water can also work its way underground and slowly dissolve minerals such as limestone. This process sometimes carves out caves. In some areas small plants called lichens attach to bare rock. Chemicals in the lichens gradually break down the stone. All these processes eventually break rock down into sediment, in the form of gravel, sand, silt, or clay. Then water, ice, or wind can move the sediment and create new topography with it. This process of moving rocky material or sediment to another place is called **erosion**.

Moving water is the most common force that erodes the land. Flowing water carries sediment. This sediment eventually forms different kinds of landforms depending on where it is deposited. For example, a river flowing from a mountain range onto a flat area, or **plain**, may deposit sediment there. The sediment sometimes builds up into a fan-shaped form called an **alluvial fan**. A **floodplain** is created when rivers flood their banks and deposit sediment. A **delta** forms where a river carries sediment all the way to the ocean. The sediment settles to the bottom where the river meets the ocean. The Nile and Mississippi Rivers have two of the world's largest deltas.

Waves in the ocean or lakes also shape the land they touch. Waves can shape beaches into great dunes, such as on the shore of Long Island. Oregon's jagged coastline also shows how waves can erode land.

▲

Erosion wears away Earth's surface at an island beach off the Florida coast. **Interpreting the Visual Record**
(Place) **What physical process is causing erosion on this beach?**

Ocean water turns muddy as the Mississippi River pushes sediment out of its delta.

▼

EYE ON EARTH

A Rapid Change Weathering and erosion are slow processes. Sometimes, however, landforms can break down very quickly.

For example, many years ago miners in Switzerland carved slate from the base of a mountain cliff, creating a huge overhang. Big cracks appeared in the cliff. Finally, on September 11, 1881, millions of cubic yards of rock fell. The avalanche of rocks didn't stop when it hit the valley floor. Instead, the broken rock continued up the valley's other side. More than 100 people were killed. This type of event is called a debris avalanche.

Critical Thinking: In what other ways do humans change their environment that may create conditions for debris avalanches?

Answer: cutting through mountains to build highways, constructing buildings on hillsides, cutting down trees, and other disturbances of steep slopes

▲ **Visual Record Answer**

wave action

TEACH

Teaching Objective 2

ALL LEVELS: (Suggested time: 45 min.) Organize students into teams and have them explore the school grounds or a nearby park to find examples of weathering and erosion. Ask them to collect rocks and try to figure out how they have been weathered. Also have students try to determine if and why any of the forces of weathering or erosion are not present in their region. Discuss results as a class. (Examples: Students in warm regions may state that ice is not a factor there. Inland areas are not subject to wave action.)
ESOL, LS KINESTHETIC

National Geography Standard 7

Creating Soil We can put aside concerns about soil erosion briefly to learn more about how soil is formed in the first place.

The next time you see a fallen tree in the forest, don't think of it as just a dead log. It's a soil factory! As the tree decays and crumbles, it adds nutrients to the forest soil. The fallen tree doesn't do its work alone, however.

When a tree falls, weevils, bark beetles, carpenter ants, termites, and other insects bore into the wood and start to break it down. Bacteria and other microorganisms invade the wood contribute to the process. In this way, fallen trees provide as much as one third of the organic matter in forest soil.

Ice and Wind Action In high mountain settings and in the coldest places on Earth one finds **glaciers**. These large, slow-moving rivers of ice can move tons of rock.

Glaciers covered most of Canada and the United States during the last ice age—or period of extreme cold. As they advanced, the glaciers carved out gashes in Earth's surface. Glaciers dug the Great Lakes. As the ice melted and retreated, tons of rock and sediment were left behind.

Wind also shapes the land. Strong winds can lift soil into the air and carry it far away. On beaches and in deserts, wind drops sand, which piles up into dunes. In addition, blowing sand can wear away rock. The sand acts like sandpaper to polish jagged edges and rough surfaces.

Erosion and Soil These processes of breaking down Earth's surface create deposits of soil. People need soil to grow food. Erosion, however, can also remove soil from farmers' fields. Heavy rainfall can wash away soil. Strong winds can blow it away.

Over the centuries, however, people have developed ways to conserve our precious soil. Some farmers plant rows of trees to block the wind. Others who farm on steep hillsides build **terraces** into the slope. Terraces are horizontal ridges like stair steps. By slowing the downhill rush of water the terraces keep the soil in place. They also provide more space for growing crops.

✓ **READING CHECK:** (*Physical Systems*) What forces cause erosion?
water, ice, and wind

Rice paddies like these in Indonesia are common throughout island Southeast Asia.

Interpreting the Visual Record
(*Human-Environment Interaction*)
How have farmers limited erosion in the rice paddies pictured below?
▼

22   Chapter 2

Visual Record Answer ▶

by building terraces

Teaching Objectives 1–2

LEVEL 2: (Suggested time: 20 min.) Copy the following graphic organizer onto the chalkboard, omitting the blue answers. Use it to help students describe the differences between landforms created by tectonic plate movement and those shaped by weathering and erosion. **ESOL**

Landforms created by tectonic plate movement	Landforms shaped by weathering and erosion
• created by subduction, colliding plates, or plates moving apart • masses of rock raised by volcanic eruptions • include mountains on land and under the oceans	• shaped by the actions of water, wind, and ice • include alluvial fans, floodplains, and deltas

People and Topography

Topography has quite a bit to do with human history and culture. Those effects are so big, however, that we may not see them easily.

Landforms and Life Why do you live where you live? Perhaps your parents moved to your city to take jobs in the tourist industry. Do tourists visit your area partly because of its landforms, such as mountains? Or maybe your town grew up on a river delta. People could farm the delta's fertile soil. They could also use either the river or the sea for trade and travel. What are some more ways that your area's topography may have influenced its growth?

Reading a Topographic Map

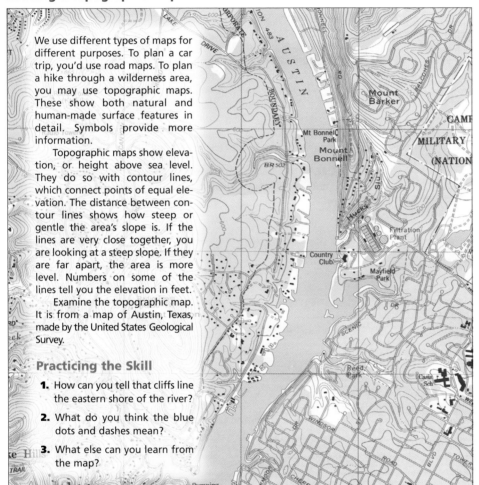

We use different types of maps for different purposes. To plan a car trip, you'd use road maps. To plan a hike through a wilderness area, you may use topographic maps. These show both natural and human-made surface features in detail. Symbols provide more information.

Topographic maps show elevation, or height above sea level. They do so with contour lines, which connect points of equal elevation. The distance between contour lines shows how steep or gentle the area's slope is. If the lines are very close together, you are looking at a steep slope. If they are far apart, the area is more level. Numbers on some of the lines tell you the elevation in feet.

Examine the topographic map. It is from a map of Austin, Texas, made by the United States Geological Survey.

Practicing the Skill

1. How can you tell that cliffs line the eastern shore of the river?

2. What do you think the blue dots and dashes mean?

3. What else can you learn from the map?

Cultural Kaleidoscope

Topography and Legends According to Irish legend, a giant named Finn Mac Cool built the Giant's Causeway, a formation of about 40,000 stone columns on the coast of Northern Ireland. By one account, Mac Cool drove the columns into place so he could walk to Scotland to fight a fellow giant. Later, his enemy broke the causeway so that Mac Cool couldn't reach him.

The basalt columns were actually formed 50 to 60 million years ago when lava cooled as it reached the sea. Pressure shaped the rock into columns with three to seven sides. The columns average 330 feet high.

Activity: Have students identify an unusual landform in your state and find out how it was formed. Then have them write and act out legends that describe the feature's origin.

Practicing the Skill
Answers

1. The contour lines are very close together.

2. creekbeds that may or may not have water in them

3. locations of roads, river, individual houses, radio towers, pumping station, vegetation, built-up areas, corporate boundaries, names of major streets, and other features

---

TEACHER TO TEACHER

Kay A. Knowles, of Montross, Virginia, suggests the following activity to help students identify landforms and predict where certain landforms may be found. Display a wall map and have students point out examples of these landforms: continent, isthmus, peninsula, plain, and plateau. Also, ask students to identify places where they would expect to find these landforms: alluvial fan, floodplain, and delta.

Teaching Objective 3

LEVEL 2: (Suggested time: 45 min.) Begin by asking students to name historical events with which they are familiar. From the suggestions, choose one that occurred where topography seems to have played a role in the event's outcome. (Examples may include a battle, invasion, or natural disaster.) Then lead a class discussion about how topography affected the event. Challenge students to confirm their suggestions by checking historical resources. Call on volunteers to find the place where the event happened in an atlas and relate its topography to its history.

LS INTERPERSONAL

Section 1 Review

Answers to Section 1 Review

Define For definitions, see the glossary.

Reading for the Main Idea

1. volcanoes and earthquakes **(NGS 7)**
2. by depositing sediment **(NGS 7)**

Critical Thinking

3. weathering—breaks down rock; erosion—moves rocky material or sediment
4. Ways of making a living, leisure activities, threats from natural hazards, ease of travel and communication, and other factors may all be different.

Organizing What You Know

5. heat—cracks rock; cold—ice cracks rock; water moving through limestone—dissolves minerals; chemicals in lichens—break down stone; waves—build up dunes or erode beaches; glaciers—carve and dig, leave rock and sediment as they melt; wind—carries soil away, deposits soil and sand, wears away rock if blown

Visual Record Answer

mountains

▲

In 1914 an enormous canal was completed across the Isthmus of Panama, linking the Pacific and Atlantic Oceans. Workers used millions of pounds of explosives and steam-powered shovels to cut through much of the landscape.

Interpreting the Visual Record

(**Human-Environment Interaction**)

Through what landforms did the Panama Canal workers have to dig?

Landforms affect the history of entire countries. For one example, start by looking at a map of India. You will see that the Ganges River crosses a broad plain before emptying into the Bay of Bengal. This river has brought sediment down from the Himalayas for countless centuries. It dropped the sediment on the plain, forming a vast area of excellent farmland. Many invaders have attacked India, trying to win this rich plain for themselves.

Here is an example of how landforms affected language. Find the island of New Guinea on a map of Southeast Asia. Notice how mountainous it is. These mountains have isolated New Guinea's peoples so much that many languages developed. In fact, more than 700 different languages are spoken on the island today.

Changing Landforms For thousands of years, people have changed Earth's surface to suit their needs. They have dug canals for irrigation ditches and carved terraces for farms. They have created artificial hills on which to build temples. People have even held back the sea to claim more dry land. Today, engineers build dams to control river flooding. They drill tunnels through mountains instead of laying roads over the mountains. Thus, while earthquakes, volcanoes, weathering, and erosion change Earth's surface, people do so also.

✓ **READING CHECK:** (**Environment and Society**) What are some landforms that could affect human history and culture? mountains, hills, plains, deltas, others

Homework Practice Online
Keyword: SK5 HP2

Section Review 1

Define and explain: landforms, topography, plate tectonics, subduction, earthquakes, lava, fault, weathering, erosion, plain, alluvial fan, floodplain, delta, glaciers, terraces

Reading for the Main Idea

1. (*Physical Systems*) What events are common where tectonic plates collide?
2. (*Physical Systems*) How do rivers create new landforms?

Critical Thinking

3. **Comparing and Contrasting** How are weathering and erosion different?

4. **Making Predictions** How may the lives of people who live in the mountains or on plains be different?

Organizing What You Know

5. **Categorizing** Copy the following graphic organizer. Use it to describe the results of each force of erosion or weathering.

heat ⇨
cold ⇨
water moving through limestone ⇨
chemicals in lichens ⇨
waves ⇨
glaciers ⇨
wind ⇨

CLOSE

Focus students' attention on the map on this section's first page. Point out that the shapes of South America and Africa provided an early clue in the development of the plate tectonics theory. Ask students what other kinds of evidence might indicate that now-distant continents were once joined. (Possible answers: corresponding fossils and mineral deposits)

REVIEW, ASSESS, RETEACH

Have students complete the Section Review. Then pair students and instruct pairs to write sentences that illustrate the connection between two of the vocabulary terms. (Example: Erosion can form an alluvial fan.) Call on vol-

unteers to read their sentences to the class. Continue until all major points have been covered. Then have students complete this section's Daily Quiz.

Have students complete Main Idea Activity S1. Then pair students and have them create brief descriptions of each main idea in the section. Have students consult atlases, globes, or encyclopedias to locate two examples of each feature or main idea. **ESOL**

EXTEND

Have interested students conduct research in newspapers, magazines, and online sources on how recent changes in Earth's surface have affected cities. Examples include volcanic eruptions, earthquakes, and landslides. **BLOCK SCHEDULING**

Section 2 Water and Air

Read to Discover
1. Where is water found on Earth?
2. What is the water cycle?
3. How do people and water affect each other?
4. What are short-term and long-term results of air pollution?

Vocabulary
tributary
groundwater
aquifers
water cycle
evaporation
water vapor

condensation
precipitation
acid rain
ozone layer
global warming
greenhouse effect

Reading Strategy

READING ORGANIZER Before you read this section, create a spider map. Label the circle Water and Air. Create a leg for each of these topics: Geographic Distribution of Water, The Water Cycle, Water and People, and The Air We Breathe. As you read the section, fill in the map with details about each topic.

Geographic Distribution of Water

Water is essential for life. The presence or absence of water in a place affects whether people can live there. Water, therefore, is part of both physical and human geography. Throughout this book, you will see how water or its lack determines what life is like around the world.

The oceans contain about 97 percent of Earth's water. Another 2 percent is locked in the ice of Earth's polar regions and glaciers. Only about 1 percent is freshwater in lakes, streams, rivers, and below Earth's surface.

Earth's freshwater resources are not evenly distributed. Some places are extremely dry. Dry states such as Nevada have few natural lakes. Others have many lakes and rivers. For example, in the United States, Minnesota has more than 11,000 lakes. Some areas have too much water. Floods can make survival difficult in places where rainfall is very heavy or where rivers burst their banks.

Mountain glaciers like this one can move slowly downhill. This photo shows the face of a glacier. Here chunks may break off, or calve, and form icebergs.

Interpreting the Visual Record What dangers may these kayakers face?

Planet Earth • 25

SECTION 2 RESOURCES

Reproducible
- Know It Notes S2
- Lab Activities for Geography and Earth Science, Demonstration 1
- Main Idea Activity S2

Technology
- One-Stop Planner CD-ROM, Lesson 2.2
- Homework Practice Online
- Geography and Cultures Visual Resources 13, 16
- HRW Go Site

Reinforcement, Review, and Assessment
- Section 2 Review
- Daily Quiz 2.2
- Main Idea Activity S2
- Chapter Summaries and Review
- English Audio Summary 2.2
- Spanish Audio Summary 2.2

▲ **Visual Record Answer**

being overturned by waves caused by calving glacier

Section 2

Objectives
1. Identify where water is found on Earth.
2. Analyze the water cycle.
3. Explore how people and water affect each other.
4. Explain the short-term and long-term results of air pollution.

FOCUS

Bellringer

Write the following instructions on the chalkboard: *Draw as many quick sketches as you can, in two minutes, of the ways you use water throughout the day.* Discuss completed drawings. Then ask students to write a summary sentence beneath their drawings. (Possible answers: We can't live without water. We use water every day in many ways.) Display sketches around the classroom. Tell students that in this section they will learn more about the role of water and air on Earth.

Building Vocabulary

Explain that adding *-tion* to a root verb usually turns the verb into a noun. Point out that verbs from which the words *evaporation, condensation,* and *precipitation* are formed (evaporate, condense, precipitate). Have students use these vocabulary words in sentences relating the words to bodies of water in their region. Students should use the U.S. map in the textbook's Atlas for help. (Example: Precipitation that falls in Illinois may end up in the Mississippi River.)

PHYSICAL SYSTEMS

Water from Earth's Refrigerator? Each year as many as 40,000 icebergs break off from the glaciers of Greenland. One of Greenland's biggest reported icebergs towered 550 feet (168 m) above the Atlantic Ocean's surface. If they stay in cold climates, gigantic icebergs like this one can last for years before melting.

Could we use the freshwater locked in icebergs? Experts have tried to design ways to tow icebergs to arid regions, but expense and other problems have hindered the task.

Activity: Have students determine why towing icebergs hasn't been successful by gathering information and then brainstorming possible solutions to the obstacles. Ask students to analyze the advantages and disadvantages of their proposals.

Visual Record Answer

by digging wells

not enough rainfall

In some areas where rainfall is scarce, there is enough groundwater to support agriculture.
Interpreting the Visual Record How do people gain access to groundwater?

Pivoting sprinklers irrigate these circular cornfields in Kansas.
Interpreting the Visual Record
(*Human-Environment Interaction*)
Why may irrigation be necessary in these fields?

26 • Chapter 2

Groundwater

Precipitation

Runoff

Well

Groundwater

Surface Water Water may collect at high elevations, where rivers begin. The first and smallest streams that form are called headwaters. When these headwaters meet and join, they form larger streams. In turn, these streams join with others to form rivers. Any smaller stream or river that flows into a larger river is a **tributary**. For example, the Missouri River is a major tributary of the Mississippi River.

A lake may form where a river flows into a low-lying area. Most lakes are freshwater, but some are salty. For example, the Dead Sea in Southwest Asia is actually a lake that is much saltier than the ocean. When the lake water evaporates, it leaves behind salts and minerals, making the lake salty.

Most of Earth's water is in the oceans. The Pacific, Atlantic, Indian, and Arctic Oceans are connected. This vast body of water covers about 70 percent of Earth's surface. These oceans also include smaller areas called seas and gulfs. The Gulf of Mexico and the Mediterranean Sea are two examples of smaller ocean areas.

Groundwater Not all surface water immediately returns to the atmosphere through evaporation. Some water from rain, snow, rivers, and lakes seeps into the ground. This **groundwater** trickles down until all the tiny spaces in the soil and rock are filled. In some places, the groundwater collects in water-bearing layers of rock, sand, or gravel called **aquifers**. Some aquifers are quite large. For example, the

Teaching Objective 1

LEVEL 1: (Suggested time: 15 min.) Pair students and tell each pair to create flash cards for the key terms that relate to how water is distributed on Earth. Student should write an appropriate vocabulary term on one side of a flash card and its definition on the reverse. Ask volunteers to share their flash cards with the class.
ESOL, COOPERATIVE LEARNING , **LS KINESTHETIC**

LEVELS 2 AND 3: (Suggested time: 20 min.) In advance, locate and duplicate a map of a river that flows through your community or region. Be sure that the map shows the river's full course. Give each student a copy of the map. Have students label the river's headwaters, tributaries, and other relevant features along the river's course. To conclude, lead a discussion about how water is distributed on Earth. **LS VISUAL-SPATIAL**

The Water Cycle

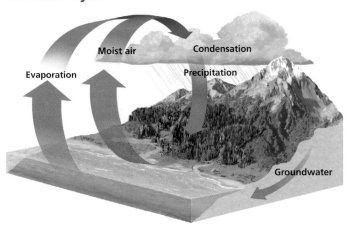

◄

The circulation of water from one part of the hydrosphere to another depends on energy from the Sun. Water evaporates, condenses, and falls to Earth as precipitation.

Interpreting the Visual Record (Place)

How would a seasonal increase in the amount of the Sun's energy received by an area change the water cycle in that area?

National Geography Standard 15

Wetlands, Animals, and People Wetlands are areas where the soil absorbs a great deal of water. Tidal flats, swamps, and bogs are different types of wetlands.

Wetlands play several important roles. By absorbing moisture, they help prevent floods. The plants that grow in wetlands can remove pollution from sewage. Wetlands also serve as nurseries for fish and shellfish. About one third of the rare and endangered animals in the United States live in wetlands. Migrating birds depend on wetlands for rest and food. Coastal wetlands can help prevent erosion.

By the mid-1970s the continental United States had lost more than 50 percent of its original wetlands. They are threatened worldwide.

Ogallala Aquifer stretches across the Great Plains from Texas to South Dakota. Many Americans get their water from wells—deep holes dug down to reach an aquifer's groundwater. Elsewhere, groundwater may bubble up from an aquifer as springs.

✓ **READING CHECK:** (*Physical Systems*) Where is most of Earth's surface water found? **in the oceans**

Flooded streets are a way of life during the wet monsoon season in Tamil Nadu, India.

▼

The Water Cycle

The circulation of water from Earth's surface to the atmosphere and back is called the **water cycle**. The total amount of water on the planet doesn't change. Water, however, does change its form and its location.

The Sun's energy drives the water cycle. **Evaporation** occurs when the Sun heats water on Earth's surface. The heated water evaporates, becoming a gas called **water vapor**. As the water vapor cools, **condensation** happens. This is the process by which water changes from a gas into tiny liquid droplets. These droplets join together to form clouds. If the droplets become heavy enough, **precipitation** occurs— that is, the water falls back to Earth. This water can be in the form of rain, hail, sleet, or snow. The entire cycle of evaporation, condensation, and precipitation repeats over and over.

✓ **READING CHECK:** (*Physical Systems*) What are the three main steps in the water cycle? **evaporation, condensation, precipitation**

▲ **Visual Record Answer**

It would increase evaporation, which may in turn increase condensation and precipitation.

Planet Earth • 27

Teaching Objective 2

LEVEL 1: (Suggested time: 20 min.) Pair students. Then, using the diagram of the water cycle as a guide, have each pair create a graphic organizer to show the role of evaporation, condensation, and precipitation in the cycle. **ESOL, COOPERATIVE LEARNING, LS VISUAL-SPATIAL**

LEVEL 2: (Suggested time: 20 min.) In advance, locate a map of your city, community, or region and make a transparency of the map. Call on students to suggest from where on the map the most evaporation occurs. (More evaporation will be occur in areas with heavy vegetation or areas of open water.) Lead a discussion on how evaporation in those areas may affect the rest of the region.

GLOBAL PERSPECTIVES

Dams: Pro and Con One way that people have conserved water is by building dams. They have been doing so for at least 5,000 years. More than 800,000 dams have been constructed around the world.

Dams and the reservoirs that form behind them can provide a steady water supply, hydroelectricity, protection from floods, and increased fish yields. However, they can also displace people, submerge farmland and cultural sites, disrupt animal migration patterns, and even increase the risk of certain diseases. Malaria, for example, is spread by mosquitoes that can breed in the standing water of reservoirs. For these and other reasons, dam construction has slowed in recent years.

Activity: Have students search news media for information on dams in your state. Students should concentrate on these questions: What controversies have arisen? What possible solutions have been suggested to address these controversies?

Visual Record Answer ▶

uses no electricity, wastes less water than some modern methods that spray water into the air over a large area

Davenport, Iowa, located on the Mississippi River, suffered severe flooding when heavy rains caused the river to rise above its banks.

An Omani man collects water from a local *falaj*, or aqueduct. These channels are dug to carry water from desert springs to farms and villages. **Interpreting the Visual Record** *Human-Environment Interaction* **How does this method of irrigation differ from modern methods?** ▶

28 • Chapter 2

Water and People

Water plays a vital role in our survival. As a result, you will often see events and problems related to water in the news. Some of those events are natural disasters. Some of them are issues that people create.

Water Hazards Water can be extremely destructive. Thunderstorms, especially when accompanied by hail or tornadoes, can damage buildings and ruin crops. Heavy rains can cause floods, the world's deadliest natural hazard. Of every ten people who die from natural disasters, four die in floods. Some floods occur in usually dry places when a large amount of rain falls in a short amount of time. Then the water collects on the surface instead of soaking into the hard, dry ground. Normally dry creekbeds can suddenly gush with rushing water. People and livestock are sometimes caught in these flash floods.

Floods also happen in low-lying places next to rivers and on coastlines. Too much rain or snowmelt entering a river can push the water over the river's banks. Powerful storms, especially hurricanes, can cause ocean waters to surge into coastal areas. Is your region ever threatened by floods? What causes floods where you live?

Water Conservation In those places where there isn't enough water, however, many people try to use as little as possible. Scientists have developed new water management methods for saving the precious liquid. Many modern factories now recycle water. Farmers can irrigate their crops more efficiently. Cities build water treatment plants to purify water that might otherwise be wasted. Some people in dry regions use desert plants instead of grass for landscaping. As a result, they use less water in their yards.

Teaching Objective 3

ALL LEVELS: (Suggested time: 20 min.) Copy the following graphic organizer onto the chalkboard, omitting the blue answers. Use it to help students explore how water affects people and how people affect water. Have students copy the organizer into their notebooks and complete it. Challenge students to add other topics, especially topics that have local significance. **ESOL, LS VISUAL-SPATIAL**

WATER AND PEOPLE
- damage from thunderstorms
- floods
- recycling
- efficient irrigation
- changes in gardening
- use of aquifers
- pollution of water by agriculture and industry
- pollution of water from other sources
- costs of pollution control
- spread of pollution

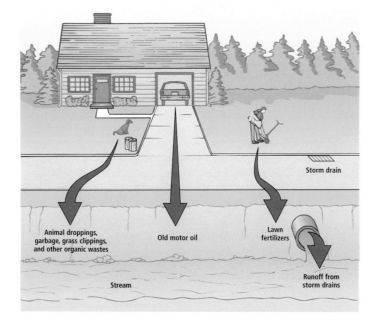

Most of the water that goes down drains, or wastewater, flows through pipes to a wastewater treatment plant. There the polluted water is treated before being returned to a river or a lake. Most of the wastewater from homes is easy to purify. However, industrial wastewater and storm runoff from streets and fields contain toxic substances that are difficult to purify.

Interpreting the Diagram What are some sources of pollution created by this single home?

ENVIRONMENT AND SOCIETY

Dangerous Water In some places, dangerous substances found in water didn't come from factories or other common sources of pollution. Bangladesh, a small country in South Asia, faces such a problem. Because Bangladesh experiences heavy flooding, which can ruin surface water supplies, the government has dug deep wells. Much of the groundwater, however, contains naturally occurring arsenic. Arsenic is a poison that causes serious health problems and, in large amounts, death.

The arsenic was first detected in 1993. Recent surveys report that about 75 million people are at risk for arsenic poisoning. The World Bank has committed $30 million to solve the problem, but Bangladesh will need much more money and time to provide totally clean drinking water.

Water management is often a local environmental issue. Growing cities may want to pump more groundwater from an aquifer, while farmers say they need that water for their crops. In dry areas, businesses that use large amounts of water, such as golf courses or fish farms, may draw criticism. What are the water management issues in your community?

Water Pollution Even where water is plentiful, it may not be clean enough to use. Polluted water can carry disease-causing bacteria or substances that harm people and animals.

Water pollution has many causes. Agriculture and industry are two main ones. When farmers use too many chemical fertilizers and pesticides, these chemicals ooze into local streams. Industrial waste may drain poisons or metals into the water supply. Heavy rain can wash motor oil from parking lots into groundwater. In addition, some poor communities don't have quality sewer systems for household wastes. Although most countries try to keep their water clean, sometimes the cost of doing so is higher than they can afford.

Pollution may spread far from its source. Rivers carry chemicals from distant factories to the oceans. There, pollution can sicken or kill fish and shellfish. People who eat these foods from polluted waters can get sick.

✓ **READING CHECK:** (*Environment and Society*) What are some causes of water pollution? agriculture, industry, motor oil, household wastes

▲ **Visual Record Answer**

animal droppings, garbage, grass clippings, other organic wastes, motor oil, lawn fertilizers

➤**ASSIGNMENT:** Supply copies of national, regional, or local newspapers. Have students search through the newspapers for stories about the interactions of water and people. Some students may want to use Internet resources to search English-language newspapers from other countries. (Stories may be about floods, dam construction, water rights, disputes over water use, water pollution, or other topics.) Ask each student to write a paragraph that summarizes the chosen news story. Call on volunteers to read their paragraphs to the class. Discuss the stories and the issues they raise.

Air and Borders Natural phenomena regularly cross international boundaries. For examples, wind, rain, and migrating animals pay no attention to borders. Similarly, pollution created in one country can contaminate the air of another country. Organize students into groups to study this process. Have each group select a major international border and report on pollution issues regarding that border. Instruct groups to identify the economic reasons why the controversy exists.

Visual Record Answer ▶

eye irritation, lung diseases, accumulation on buildings and other surfaces, acid rain

The Air We Breathe

Like water, air is necessary for survival. Just as human activities can pollute our water, they can also pollute our air.

Air Pollution Air pollution comes from several sources. Burning fuels for heating and running factories releases chemicals into the air. A major cause of air pollution is exhaust from the hundreds of millions of motor vehicles on the planet. Particularly in big cities, all these chemicals build up in the air. They create a mixture called smog.

Some cities have special problems with smog. Denver, Los Angeles, and Mexico City, for example, lie in bowl-shaped valleys that trap air pollution. On some days, the air in these cities gets so thick with smog that officials urge residents to stay indoors to protect their health.

When air pollution combines with moisture in the air, it can form an acid similar in strength to vinegar. When it falls to the ground, this liquid is called **acid rain**. It can damage or kill trees. Acid rain can even kill fish.

Many countries have laws to limit pollution. However, pollution is an international problem. Winds can blow polluted air away, but just to another place. Pollution can easily blow from one country to another. It can even pass across continents. As a result, countries that keep their own air clean can still suffer from other countries' pollution.

Pollution and Climate Change Smog and acid rain are short-term effects of air pollution. Air pollution may also have long-term effects by changing Earth's atmosphere. Certain kinds of pollution damage the **ozone layer** in the upper atmosphere. This ozone layer protects living things by absorbing harmful ultraviolet light from the Sun. Damage to Earth's ozone layer may cause human health problems such as skin cancer.

Another issue of growing concern is **global warming** — a slow increase in Earth's average temperature. The Sun constantly warms Earth's surface. The gases and water vapor in the atmosphere trap some of the heat. This process helps keep Earth warm. Without the atmosphere, heat would escape into space, and we would freeze. The process is called the **greenhouse effect**. In a greenhouse the Sun's heat passes through the glass roof but is then trapped inside. Evidence suggests that pollution causes the atmosphere to trap more heat. As a result, Earth would get warmer.

Heavy smog clouds the Los Angeles skyline. **Interpreting the Visual Record** *Human-Environment Interaction* **What problems do you think smog would create in everyday life?**

▼

Teaching Objective 4

ALL LEVELS: (Suggested time: 20 min.) First, lead a class discussion about the causes of air pollution. (Causes include burning fuels, running factories, and operating motor vehicles.) Then copy the following graphic organizer onto the chalkboard, omitting the blue answers. Have students complete it to learn the short- and long-term effects of air pollution.

Results of Air Pollution	
Short-term results	Long-term results
• smog	• damage to the ozone layer
• acid rain	• global warming

The Greenhouse Effect

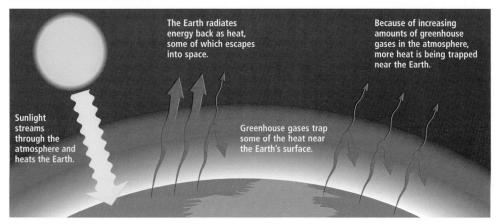

The Earth radiates energy back as heat, some of which escapes into space.

Because of increasing amounts of greenhouse gases in the atmosphere, more heat is being trapped near the Earth.

Sunlight streams through the atmosphere and heats the Earth.

Greenhouse gases trap some of the heat near the Earth's surface.

Scientists agree that Earth's climate has warmed during the last century. Not all agree, however, on the explanation. Most scientists say that air pollution caused by people has made temperatures rise. Burning fuels such as oil and coal is listed as the main culprit. Other scientists think warmer temperatures have resulted from natural causes. There is also disagreement about what has caused the thinning of the ozone layer.

 **READING CHECK:** (*Environment and Society*) How may air pollution affect Earth's climate? *may lead to global warming*

▲ The Earth's atmosphere acts like the glass in a greenhouse. Sunlight passes through the atmosphere and heats the Earth. As heat radiates up from the Earth, some heat escapes into space. The rest of the heat is trapped by gases in the atmosphere.

Interpreting the Diagram **What is one result of an increase in greenhouse gases in the atmosphere?**

Section Review 2

Define and explain: tributary, groundwater, aquifers, water cycle, evaporation, water vapor, condensation, precipitation, acid rain, ozone layer, global warming, greenhouse effect

Reading for the Main Idea

1. (*Environment and Society*) What are some hazards that water can create?

2. (*Environment and Society*) What are the main causes of air pollution?

 **Homework Practice Online**
Keyword: SK5 HP2

Critical Thinking

3. **Analyzing Information** Why would protecting groundwater from pollution be important?

4. **Making Generalizations and Predictions** What may happen if air pollution continues to increase?

Organizing What You Know

5. **Sequencing** Copy the following graphic organizer. Use it to describe the steps in the water cycle.

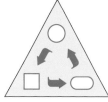

Answers to Section 2 Review

Define For definitions, see the glossary.

Reading for the Main Idea

1. damage from thunderstorms, floods **(NGS 7)**

2. burning fuels, running factories, operating motor vehicles **(NGS 14)**

Critical Thinking

3. Unless pollutants can be removed, polluted groundwater is no longer safe for human or animal consumption.

4. Health problems may increase due to loss of the ozone layer and increased irritants in the air, and global warming may increase.

Organizing What You Know

5. Graphic organizers should reflect the diagram of the water cycle in this section.

▲ **Diagram Answer**

global warming

CLOSE

Lead a class discussion about how students would cope if suddenly your community's water supply became too polluted for human use.

REVIEW, ASSESS, RETEACH

Have students complete the Section Review. Then have each student write a paragraph about how individuals can reduce water and air pollution. Then have students complete Daily Quiz 2.2. **LS** **INTRAPERSONAL**

Have students complete Main Idea Activity S2. Then have students describe the content of the section's photos and diagrams and relate the content to the section's text. **LS** **VISUAL-SPATIAL**

EXTEND

Have interested students conduct research on a significant flood that occurred in the past 10 years. Tell students to provide a map of the areas hurt by the flood as well as information on how the flood affected the area's people, plants, animals, and economy. Students should also note the long-term effects of the flood. **BLOCK SCHEDULING**

Visual Record Answer ▶

High elevations keep temperatures low.

Section 3 Climate, Weather, and Vegetation

Read to Discover
1. What factors create climate and weather?
2. How are climate, plants, and animal life related?

Vocabulary
weather
climate
prevailing winds
currents
rain shadow

Reading Strategy

FOLDNOTES: TRI-FOLD Create a **Tri-Fold** FoldNote as described in the Appendix. Label the columns "Know," "Want," and "Learn." Use the main ideas to write down what you know about weather and climate. Then write down what you want to know. After you study the section, write down what you learned.

Wildlife eat the summer vegetation in the Alaskan tundra.
Interpreting the Visual Record Why is there snow on the mountain peaks during summer?

32 • Chapter 2

Factors Affecting Climate and Weather

Weather is the condition of the atmosphere at a certain time and place. **Climate** refers to the weather conditions in an area over a long period of time. Weather and climate then help determine what kind of plants grow in a certain place.

Several factors determine a region's climate. Some of the forces that affect whether it will be sunny or rainy today are related to what is happening on the other side of the planet. Other forces are local.

The Sun Solar heat, or heat from the Sun, makes life possible on Earth. It also affects our weather and climate. The Sun doesn't heat Earth evenly, however. Because Earth is a sphere, areas closest to the North Pole and the South Pole don't receive direct rays from the Sun. Also, because Earth is tilted on its axis, areas away from the Sun receive less heat. Regions closer to the equator receive more heat. Therefore, the higher a place's latitude, the less solar heat it gets and the colder its climate.

Section 3

Objectives
1. Identify the factors that create climate and weather.
2. Describe how climate, plants, and animal life are related.

FOCUS

Bellringer
Copy the following instructions onto the chalkboard: *Write down three words or phrases you use to describe the climate or weather events in our area* (Possible answers include muggy, bone-chilling, gully-washer, nor'easter, raining cats and dogs.) Point out that having so many terms for our weather indicates that weather is very important to us. Tell students that in Section 3 they will also learn that climate and weather affect what plants and animals live in an area.

Building Vocabulary
Write the vocabulary terms on the chalkboard. Call on volunteers to find and read aloud the definitions from the text or glossary. Discuss the word *prevail* ("to be or become effective") as the root word for **prevailing winds**. You may want to introduce *orographic effect* as the term for what causes a **rain shadow**.

Each year is divided into periods of time called seasons. Each season is known for a certain type of weather, based on temperature and amount of precipitation. Winter, spring, summer, and fall are examples of seasons that are described by their average temperature. "Wet" and "dry" seasons are described by their precipitation. The seasons change as Earth orbits the Sun. As this happens, the amount of solar energy received in any given location changes.

Winds Solar heat doesn't stay in one place. It moves around the planet. Otherwise, some places would be much hotter and others much colder than they are now. Winds, created by changes in air pressure, move the heat.

You may think of air as weightless, but it isn't. Cold air weighs more than warm air. When air warms, it gets lighter and rises. Colder air then moves in to replace the rising air. Wind is the result of this process.

Winds blow in great streams of air around the planet. Winds that blow in the same direction over large areas of Earth are called **prevailing winds**. These winds then make a region warmer or colder, drier or wetter, depending on from where they blow.

Some regions on Earth, particularly in the tropics, have seasons tied to precipitation rather than temperature. Shifting wind patterns are one cause of seasonal change. For example, in January winds from the north bring dry air to India. By June the winds have shifted, coming from the southwest and bringing moisture from the Indian Ocean.

As Earth revolves around the Sun, the tilt of the poles toward and away from the Sun causes the seasons to change. The day when the Sun's vertical rays are farthest from the equator is called a solstice. Solstices occur twice a year—about June 21 and about December 22. The days when the Sun's rays strike the equator directly are called equinoxes. These days mark the beginning of spring and fall.

Interpreting the Diagram At what point is the North Pole tilted toward the Sun?

▼

The Seasons

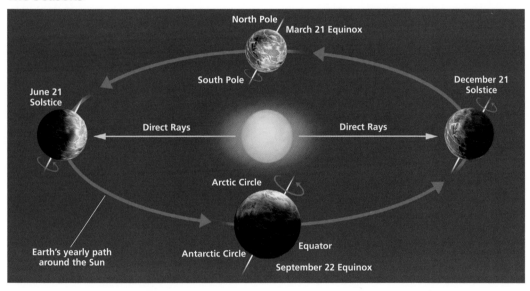

North Pole
March 21 Equinox
South Pole
June 21 Solstice
Direct Rays
Direct Rays
December 21 Solstice
Arctic Circle
Earth's yearly path around the Sun
Antarctic Circle
Equator
September 22 Equinox

Teaching Objective 1

LEVEL 1: (Suggested time: 30 min.) Pair students and have each pair create an informational brochure titled "The Study of Weather." In their brochures, students should identify and create a symbol for each of the factors that influence climate and weather. (Brochures should identify the Sun, winds, oceans and currents, and elevation and mountain effects.) Call on volunteers to display and discuss their brochures.
COOPERATIVE LEARNING, [LS] **VISUAL-SPATIAL**

➤**ASSIGNMENT:** Ask students to watch a weather forecast on television or listen to one on the radio. Have then write down any unfamiliar terms (examples: dew point, dry line, lake effect) in the forecast. In class, provide resource materials for students to research these terms and relate them to the text material.

EYE ON EARTH

Weird Waves We think of ocean waves as racing across miles of open water within hours. However, an odd type of waves called Rossby waves can take years to travel across the ocean. These waves may be only a few inches high, but they can be many miles long. Because they move slowly, Rossby waves can carry a "memory" of storms or other oceanic events that happened years earlier. For example, oceanographers mapped a Rossby wave in 1994 that seemed to show evidence of a 1982–83 El Niño. Understanding Rossby waves helps meteorologists predict the weather because the waves may push powerful ocean currents away from their usual paths.

Visual Record Answer ▶

the Southwest, from Arizona through West Texas

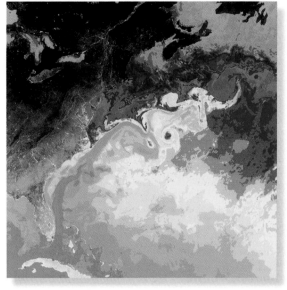

▲ This infrared satellite image shows the Gulf Stream moving warm water from lower latitudes to higher latitudes. The dark red shape alongside Florida's east coast is the Gulf Stream.

Weather maps show atmospheric conditions as they currently exist or as they are forecast for a particular time period. Most weather maps have legends that explain what the symbols on the map mean. This map shows a cold front sweeping through the central United States. A low-pressure system is at the center of a storm bringing rain and snow to the Midwest. Notice that temperatures behind the cold front are considerably cooler than those ahead of the front.

You Be the Geographer According to this map, what region is experiencing the highest temperatures?

Oceans and Currents Winds move ocean water in the same general directions as the air above it moves. Warm ocean water from near the equator moves in giant streams, or **currents**, to colder areas. Cold water flows from the polar regions to the tropics. So, just as wind moves heat between places, so do ocean currents.

The Gulf Stream is an important ocean current. It moves warm water north from the Gulf of Mexico to the east coast of the United States. It then moves across the Atlantic Ocean toward Europe. The warm air that moves with it keeps winters mild. As a result, much of western Europe has warmer winters than areas in Canada that are just as far north.

Distance from the ocean also affects a region's climate. Water heats and cools more slowly than land. Therefore, coastal areas don't have the wide differences in temperature that areas in the middle of continents have. For example, Kansas City has colder winters and hotter summers than San Francisco. The cities are at about the same latitude, but Kansas City is in the continent's interior. In contrast, San Francisco lies on the Pacific Ocean.

Reading a Weather Map

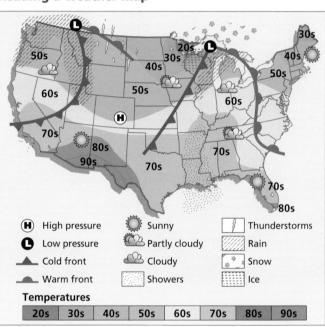

(H)	High pressure		☀	Sunny		⚡	Thunderstorms
(L)	Low pressure		⛅	Partly cloudy		▨	Rain
▲	Cold front		☁	Cloudy		❄	Snow
●	Warm front		▦	Showers		▦	Ice

Temperatures

| 20s | 30s | 40s | 50s | 60s | 70s | 80s | 90s |

LEVEL 2: (Suggested time: 30 min.) In advance, prepare photocopies of the local weather map from your daily newspaper or the U.S. weather map in a national paper. Review the "Reading a Weather Map" feature on this page. Have students circle and label the information on their maps that illustrates the conditions that affect weather. **LS KINESTHETIC**

LEVEL 3: (Suggested time: 30 min.) Have students look through this textbook for photographs that show or imply specific weather conditions. Challenge students to find the approximate location of the place in the photo in the appropriate unit's physical and climate maps and to speculate about what causes climate and weather conditions in that place. **ESOL**

Landforms and Precipitation

Windward (wet)　　　　　Leeward (dry)

Snow

Warming dry air

Rain

Cooling moist air

Rain Shadow

Ocean　　　　　　　　Inland

Moist air from the ocean cools as it moves up the windward side of a mountain. The water vapor in the air condenses and falls in the form of rain or snow. The drier air then moves down the leeward side of a mountain. This drier air brings very little precipitation to areas in the rain shadow.

◄

Pictured in the bottom photo are mountains in the western part of the Sierra Nevada in Sequoia National Park. The top photo shows part of the eastern slope of the same range near Bishop, California.
Place How does the vegetation of these places differ? What causes the difference?

▼

Planet Earth • 35

Cultural Kaleidoscope
Religion and Weather Cultural and religious explanations of climate and weather have influenced people's understanding of the physical world. In the American Southwest, the Hopi rain dance reveals that culture's attitude toward nature. By dancing and making offerings, the Hopi show respect to the kachinas, or spirits of ancestors, that they believe control the natural world. The Hopi believe the kachinas will return the favor by sending rain. Many other cultures have ceremonies designed to affect the weather.

Activity: Have students conduct research on ways that weather has been incorporated into other cultures' religious beliefs or folklore and analyze the similarities and differences. Have students present their findings to the class.

◄**Visual Record Answer**

The area in the top photo is drier because it is in a rain shadow caused by the Sierra Nevada.

Elevation and Mountain Effects

Have you seen photos of Kilimanjaro, a mountain in East Africa? The mountain has snow on it all year although it is only about 250 miles from the equator. How can this be?

An increase in elevation—height on Earth's surface above sea level—causes a drop in temperature. This happens because the air is less dense at higher elevations. Thus the base of a mountain may be hot while the top is covered with ice.

Elevation has another effect on weather and climate. Warm, moist air blowing against a mountainside will rise. As it rises, it cools and forms clouds. Precipitation falls from the clouds. The side of the mountain facing the wind often gets heavy rain. By the time the air reaches the other side of the mountain it has lost most of its moisture. This can create a dry area called a **rain shadow**. Compare some of the physical maps and climate maps in the unit atlases to find examples of this effect.

✓ **READING CHECK:** *Physical Systems*
What are the main factors affecting climate and weather? the Sun, winds, oceans and currents, elevation and mountain effects

Teaching Objective 2

ALL LEVELS: (Suggested time: 10 min.) Tell students to use the World Climate, Plant, and Animal Regions map on the following pages to locate the region where they live. Have them refer to the chart to identify the state's climate region. Then tell them to read the description of the weather patterns for their climate region. Ask whether the description corresponds to their observations of weather patterns in the area. **ESOL**

LEVEL 2: (Suggested time: 30 min.) Have students write trivia questions about each of the climate types. (At this point, they don't have to know the answers.) Tell students to refer to the world climate regions map on this page and the text atlas to help them write questions. (Examples of questions: What is the coldest temperature ever recorded at the South Pole? What is the hottest desert? What is the approximate temperature of the oval-shaped current in the North Atlantic Ocean?) Then have students consult reference materials to find the answers to their questions.
LS VERBAL-LINGUISTIC

Linking Past to Present
Changing

Climates Just because today an area has a certain climate— and the plants and animals that are typical of that climate— doesn't mean that it's always been that way. For example, the Sahara was once a vast grassland. Researchers recently concluded that the Sahara's transformation into a desert was triggered by changes in Earth's orbit and the tilt of its axis. These changes occurred in two phases, with the first happening some 6,700 to 5,500 years ago and the second 4,000 to 3,600 years ago.

The orbital changes caused fairly sudden changes in North Africa's climate. Rains stopped coming to the Sahara and regional temperatures rose. Within a few hundred years the moist Sahara became a desert scrubland. Researchers think that ancient civilizations in the Sahara may have moved to the Nile River valley in response to the climate changes.

Discussion: What ancient civilization with which the students may already be familiar developed as a result of the changing climate of North Africa?
(Egyptian civilization)

Climate Regions, Plants, and Animals

The chart below describes the 12 main climate types in terms of weather. Climate affects what kind of plants, or vegetation, can grow in a certain area. For example, if your region has a tundra climate, you won't be able to grow palm trees in your yard. Palm trees need a much warmer climate.

In turn, vegetation helps determine what animals are present. If you live in a desert, you won't see tree-dwelling monkeys, except in a zoo! What plants and animals live in your area?

World Climate, Plant, and Animal Regions

Climate	Major Weather Patterns	Vegetation	Animals You May See in the Climate Region (Animals Vary by Region.)
HUMID TROPICAL	warm and rainy all year	rain forest	bats, tree frogs, monkeys, jaguars, tigers, snakes, parrots
TROPICAL SAVANNA	warm all year, with rainy and dry seasons	grassland with scattered trees	anacondas, lions, elephants, gazelles, ostriches, hyenas, rhinoceroses, zebras
DESERT	dry and sunny	a few hardy plants such as cacti	lizards, scorpions, snakes, bats, bobcats, coyotes
STEPPE	semiarid, hot summers with cooler winters	grassland and a few trees	antelope, wild horses, kangaroos, coyotes, camels
MEDITERRANEAN	dry, sunny, warm winters and mild, wetter winters	scrub woodland and grassland	deer, elk, mountain lions, wolves
HUMID SUBTROPICAL	hot, humid summers and mild, humid winters; rain all year	mixed forest	alligators, deer, bears, squirrels, foxes, snakes, many species of birds
MARINE WEST COAST	cloudy, mild summers and cool, rainy winters	evergreen forest	wild boars, deer, bears, seals
HUMID CONTINENTAL	four distinct seasons; long, cold winters and short, warm summers	mixed forest	wolverines, wild boars, deer, badgers, beavers, ducks
SUBARCTIC	long, cold winters and short, warm summers; low	evergreen forest	rabbits, moose, elk, wolves, lynxes, bears
TUNDRA	cold all year, little precipitation	moss, lichens, low shrubs, marshes during the summer	rabbits, reindeer, wolves, foxes
ICE CAP	freezing cold all year	no vegetation	animals that depend on the sea, such as polar bears, seals, and penguins
HIGHLAND	wide range of temperatures and precipitation amounts, depending on elevation	forest to tundra vegetation, depending on location and elevation	wide range of animals, depending on location, elevation, and vegetation

➤**ASSIGNMENT:** Prepare a list of 10 to 20 major world cities. Include cities in all climate zones except for the ice cap zone. Give students copies of the list and have them locate the cities in the text's atlas. Then have them write down each city's climate type and temperatures, moisture, vegetation, sunlight levels, and storms that would be common there.

TEACHER TO TEACHER

Maureen Dempsey of Spring Creek, Nevada, suggests the following activity to help students summarize climate types: Organize students into small groups. Then have each group fold and staple 12 sheets of white paper together to create booklets entitled Climates of the World. Students should describe the climate on one page and illustrate it on the opposite page. They may draw pictures, cut them from magazines, or download images from the Internet. Each student's book should include a table of contents and a cover illustration.

World Climate Regions

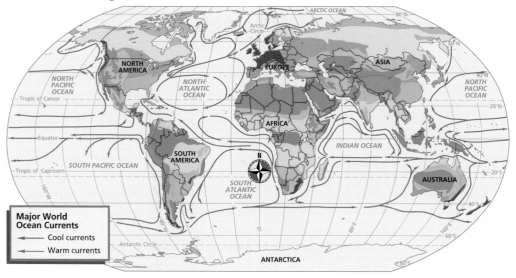

Low Latitudes		Middle Latitudes		High Latitudes	
HUMID TROPICAL		MEDITERRANEAN		SUBARCTIC	
TROPICAL SAVANNA		HUMID SUBTROPICAL		TUNDRA	
DESERT		MARINE WEST COAST		ICE CAP	
STEPPE		HUMID CONTINENTAL		HIGHLAND	

Dry

go.hrw.com

Homework Practice Online

Keyword: SK5 HP2

Section Review 3

Define and explain: weather, climate, prevailing winds, currents, rain shadow

Reading for the Main Idea

1. (*Physical Systems*) How does the Sun's heat affect temperature and winds?

2. (*Physical Systems*) What effect does the Gulf Stream have on Europe's climates?

Critical Thinking

3. **Drawing Inferences** From looking at the map, why do you think central Asia is very cold in winter and often hot in the summer?

4. **Finding the Main Idea** Why may a mountaintop and a nearby valley have wide differences in temperature?

Organizing What You Know

5. **Summarizing** Copy the following graphic organizer. Use it to summarize the 12 climate types.

Climate	Weather	Vegetation	Animals

Answers to Section 3 Review

Define For definitions, see the glossary.

Reading for the Main Idea

1. The higher a place's latitude, the less heat it receives from the Sun. The Sun's heat makes air get lighter and rise, causing wind. (NGS 7)

2. keeps Europe relatively warm (NGS 7)

Critical Thinking

3. The region is far from the ocean, which would otherwise moderate its climate.

4. because elevation keeps temperatures lower

Organizing What You Know

5. For climate types, latitudes, and characteristics, see the table in this section.

CLOSE

People live in almost every climate on Earth, including extreme climates. Have students suggest ways that people have adapted to them.

REVIEW, ASSESS, RETEACH

Have each student choose a climate type and write five adjectives to describe it. Have students read their adjectives to the class, and other students guess which climate type is being described. Then have students complete Daily Quiz 2.3. **LS INTERPERSONAL**

Have students complete Main Idea Activity S3. Then have them choose specific locations and write postcards from that place describing the weather there. **ESOL**

EXTEND

Have interested students perform a simple experiment to illustrate dew point—the temperature at which water vapor begins to condense. Put water into a coffee can, and gradually add ice cubes while stirring with a thermometer. Record the temperature at the moment when condensation forms on the outside of the coffee can. This temperature is the dew point. Have students conduct research on the relationship between relative humidity and dew point to explain the results of their experiment. Students may also want to investigate places in the world where very little rain falls and where dew sustains plants and animals. **BLOCK SCHEDULING**

Visual Record Answer ▶

They may reduce wind erosion.

Section 4 Natural Resources

Read to Discover

1. What are the most important renewable resources?
2. How do the main energy resources differ?
3. How do we use mineral resources?
4. How do resources affect people?

Vocabulary

renewable resources
nonrenewable resources
deforestation
reforestation
fossil fuels

petroleum
hydroelectric power
geothermal energy
solar power

Reading Strategy

TAKING NOTES As you read this section, list the natural resources mentioned in the text. Beside each resource, write R if the resource is renewable and N if the resource is nonrenewable.

A row of poplar trees divides farmland near Aix-en-Provence, France.
Human-Environment Interaction What effect will these trees have on erosion?

Using Renewable Resources

The landforms, water, climate, and weather of a place all affect the people who live there. Another factor that affects daily life is the resources available to them. A resource is any material that is part of Earth and that people need and value.

Some of Earth's resources are renewable, while others are nonrenewable. **Renewable resources**, such as soil and forests, are those that natural processes continuously replace. **Nonrenewable resources** are those that can't be replaced naturally after they have been used. Once they've been used, they're gone forever!

You read in Section 1 about the need to preserve soil, since it is essential to survival. Soil qualifies as a renewable resource because natural processes create more of it. For example, when a tree dies and falls to the forest floor, the tree decays and adds valuable nutrients to the soil. Bacteria and other organisms break down the wood and turn it into humus. However, these processes are very slow. Soil that required hundreds of years to build up can be washed away in a few seconds.

Section 4

Objectives

1. Identify the most important renewable resources.
2. Explain how the main energy resources differ.
3. Explore how we use mineral resources.
4. Discover how resources affect people.

FOCUS

 Bellringer

Copy the following riddle onto the chalkboard and ask students to solve it.

It lies all around us.
We don't give it a thought,
It puts food on the table.
What it gives can't be bought.

(The riddle refers to soil.) Tell students that in Section 4 they will learn more about the importance of soil and the other resources on which we depend.

Building Vocabulary

Write the vocabulary terms on the chalkboard. Point out that the prefix *re-* often means "again." So, renewable resources are those that can be new again. **Reforestation** indicates that a forest can grow again in the same place. Ask students what they already know about fossils and relate their knowledge to the term **fossil fuels**.

Forests Forests are renewable resources because we can plant new trees. People use trees for many products. Wood products include lumber for buildings and furniture. Plastics and some fabrics use wood in the manufacturing process. Cooking oils, medicines, nuts, and rubber are among the many products that trees supply. In addition, trees and other plants release oxygen into the atmosphere. We enjoy forests for hiking and camping. Wildlife depends on forests for food and shelter.

Like soil, forests can be destroyed much faster than they can grow. In some places, forests are not being replaced as quickly as they are cut down. This loss of forest areas is called **deforestation**. People can reverse the trend by planting new trees. This practice, called **reforestation**, is important for both people and wildlife.

Resources and Land Management The preservation of renewable resources is often part of larger land management issues. For example, suburbs spring up on what was valuable farmland. Fertile soil there can no longer grow food. Or, a developer may want to build a shopping mall in a forested area. Residents may prefer to preserve the trees within a park. These and similar local environmental issues are debated across the United States as towns and cities grow.

✓ **READING CHECK:** (*Environment and Society*) How can people help preserve forest resources? by planting new trees and by using wise resource and land management procedures

▲
Human-Environment Interaction
Villagers work on a reforestation project in Cameroon.

Human-Environment Interaction
Development at the edge of Danville, California, is replacing farmland and rangeland.
▼

Planet Earth 39

Linking Past to Present
Ancient Deforestation Although they didn't have access to modern technology, ancient peoples often dramatically affected natural landscapes. Some archaeologists think that during the Neolithic era—beginning about 8,000 years ago—people may have deforested large areas of central and western Europe. They chopped down trees to clear land for farming. They also used timber for fuel and building. For example, a single fort in the British Isles could use up several thousand trees.

Activity: Have students conduct research on ancient and recent deforestation. Challenge students to compare the deforestation of the two time periods in terms of causes, methods, and results.

🔲 **internet** connect
GO TO: **go.hrw.com**
KEYWORD: **SG5 CH2**
FOR: **Web sites about deforestation**

Teaching Objective 1
ALL LEVELS: (Suggested time: 15 min.) Copy the following graphic organizer onto the chalkboard, omitting the blue answers. Use it to help students understand the importance of preserving soil and forests. Call on students to supply the main ideas from this subsection on these resources. Then lead a class discussion about the question in the bottom oval. You may want to provide local newspapers to help students explore the issues. **ESOL,** 🔲 **INTERPERSONAL**

Soil and Forests: Important Renewable Resources

Soil	Forests
• essential for our survival	• wood used in many products
• created by natural processes	• produce oxygen
• from decayed plant materials	• important for recreation, wildlife
• can easily be washed away	• importance of reforestation

Resources and Land Management

What are the resources and land management issues in your community?

Across the Curriculum
SCIENCE

Energy from the Ocean Floor? There is a strange form of ice on the ocean floor called methane hydrate. A methane hydrate crystal consists of a natural gas molecule surrounded by water molecules. Methane hydrates resemble regular ice, but unlike ice they can burn! The compounds are abundant on the ocean floor and may provide new sources of energy. In fact, the amount of carbon locked in methane hydrates may be twice as big as the total amount of carbon in all other fossil fuels.

However, because they are formed under pressure, hydrates can disintegrate when removed from the ocean. Furthermore, in terms of its potential effect on global warming, methane as a greenhouse gas is 10 times worse than carbon dioxide, which is released in the burning of traditional fossil fuels.

Visual Record Answer ▶

People have taken advantage of a windy location by using turbines to generate power.

Human-Environment Interaction Deep underground, a miner digs coal in a narrow tunnel.

Wind turbines are just one source of electricity. **Interpreting the Visual Record** *Human-Environment Interaction* **How does this photo show human adaptation to the environment?** ▼

Energy Resources

Most of the energy we use comes from the three **fossil fuels**: coal, petroleum, and natural gas. Fossil fuels were formed from the remains of ancient plants and animals. These remains gradually decayed and were covered with sediment. Over long periods of time, pressure and heat changed these materials. They became completely different solids, liquids, or gases. All fossil fuels are nonrenewable resources.

For thousands of years, people have burned coal for heat. Burning coal pollutes the air, however. Modern ways of burning coal produce less pollution, but cost more money. **Petroleum** may be the fossil fuel with which you are most familiar. When it is first pumped out of the ground, petroleum is a dark oily liquid called crude oil. It is then processed into gasoline, diesel and jet fuels, and heating oil. Burning these fuels also creates air pollution. The cleanest-burning fossil fuel is natural gas, which is usually found near petroleum deposits.

Renewable Energy Resources Energy sources besides fossil fuels exist. Their big advantage is they are cleaner, in general. Renewable energy sources aren't available everywhere, however. They may also cost more money. Some of these energy sources have other drawbacks too.

Teaching Objective 2

LEVEL 1: (Suggested time: 45 min.) Organize the class into three groups and assign each group one of these topics: fossil fuels, clean energy sources, and nuclear power. Within each group, have students discuss the advantages and disadvantages of each type and then summarize their discussions for the class. **COOPERATIVE LEARNING**

LEVELS 2 AND 3: In advance, gather resource materials about various energy resources. Using the same groups as in the Level 1 activity, challenge students to locate statistical information on the assigned energy source. For example, the fossil fuel group may locate figures on how many tons of coal are mined and burned in the United States each year and how many tons of carbon dioxide are released into the atmosphere as a result. Or, students may calculate how these figures average out to consumption per person. **LS LOGICAL-MATHEMATICAL**

Water pours through Owen Falls Dam in Uganda. More than 99 percent of Uganda's electricity comes from hydroelectric power.
Interpreting the Visual Record What body of water is used to produce hydroelectric power?

France has 59 nuclear reactors like this one and depends on nuclear power for about 77 percent of its energy.

▼

Clean Energy Sources The most commonly used renewable energy source is **hydroelectric power** —the production of electricity by waterpower. Dams harness the energy of falling water from rivers to run generators that produce electricity. Although hydroelectric power doesn't pollute the air, it does affect the environment. The lakes that form when dams block rivers may drown farmland and forests. Fish and wildlife habitats are also affected.

Wind has powered sailing ships and windmills for centuries. Now wind has a new use. It can create electricity by turning a system of fan blades called a turbine. "Wind farms" with hundreds of wind turbines have been built in windy places. The heat of Earth's interior— **geothermal energy** —is another clean source of power. People can use the energy directly to heat water, or they can generate electricity with it. **Solar power** —heat and light from the Sun—can heat water or homes. Special solar panels also absorb solar energy to make electricity.

Nuclear Power The last major renewable energy resource is nuclear power. Although operating a nuclear power plant doesn't release pollution into the air, it does produce waste materials that will be deadly for many centuries. Management of these wastes is a serious problem. In addition, some nuclear power plants have had serious accidents. A nuclear accident in Chernobyl in Ukraine killed people, caused cancer in survivors, and poisoned farmland.

✓ **READING CHECK:** (*Environment and Society*) What are the main advantages of using renewable energy sources? They don't pollute and they are based on resources that won't run out.

Hot Times in Idaho
Geothermal energy is becoming a useful alternative energy source in some places in the United States. Idaho began harnessing geothermal power in 1892. The state has already developed 70 direct-use geothermal sites. Idaho uses geothermal energy for fish farms, greenhouses, heated swimming pools, and for other applications. In addition, the Idaho State Capitol is the only U.S. capitol building heated with hot water from deep in the Earth.

Other states also are developing geothermal potential. California generates the most geothermal energy in the country, followed by Nevada, Utah, and Hawaii. As our energy needs increase, we may find a renewable resource right under our feet.

▲ **Visual Record Answer**
a lake

Teaching Objective 3

ALL LEVELS: (Suggested time: 10 min.) First, discuss with students the guessing game of "animal, vegetable, or mineral," in which players describe unnamed common objects as belonging to one of these categories. Ask what the word *mineral* means in this context. (Possible answers: rocks, something that is not alive and never has been alive, or materials dug from the ground.) Using students' definitions, ask the class to list minerals and products made from minerals that they see or use in daily life. **LS** INTERPERSONAL

LEVEL 2: (Suggested time: 10 min.) Quiz the class on what they may already know about recycling in your community. Then have students write letters to the editor of your local newspaper urging the community to begin or expand a recycling program. **LS** VERBAL-LINGUISTIC

FOOD FESTIVAL

The Mineral on Your French Fries One of the most widely used minerals is salt. It is plentiful, cheap, and essential to good health. We are most familiar with salt as an ingredient in foods, but it is also used in many other products and processes.

Salt removes unwanted minerals from the water supply. Farm animals and poultry consume salt. Food processors such as pickle makers use tons of the mineral. Salt makes dyes colorfast in fabric. Film companies use salt in chemical solutions. Health spas offer salt baths and rubs. Salt producers have claimed that salt has 14,000 uses.

Have students examine labels of common packaged foods to find salt as an ingredient. You may also want to have them bring samples of different types of salt to class, such as rock salt, kosher salt, sea salt, or gourmet flavored salts.

Visual Record Answer ▶

for easier access for repairs

Human-Environment Interaction A mine employee shows the reddish ore of an iron mine located deep in the forest of northern Brazil.

Stretching from north to south across Alaska, a pipeline carries oil to the port of Sitka. **Interpreting the Visual Record** **Human-Environment Interaction** **Why do you think the pipeline is above ground?**

▼

42 Chapter 2

Mineral Resources

Energy resources are not the only nonrenewable resources that come out of the ground. We also use solid substances called minerals. Examples include metals, rocks, and salt.

Minerals fulfill many needs. Look around you to see just a few of the ways we use minerals. Your school is probably built on steel girders made from iron. The outside walls may be granite, limestone, or other types of rock. Window glass is made from quartz, a mineral found in sand. The "lead" in your pencil is actually graphite, another mineral. Metals are everywhere—from the staples through your homework papers to the coins in your wallet and the watch on your wrist.

Because they are nonrenewable, we need to conserve mineral resources. Recycling common items, such as aluminum cans, will make the supply of these resources last longer. It also reduces the amount of energy that factories use to convert metal into useful objects.

✓ **READING CHECK:** (*Environment and Society*) How can people conserve mineral resources? by recycling

Resources and People

Why does it matter what resources an area has, or how much it has of a resource? Actually, resources affect culture, history, and current events.

Resources and Wealth As you read this book, you will find that some places are rich in resources of many kinds. For example, the United States has fertile soil, forests, oil, metals, and many other resources. These riches have allowed our country to develop its economy. Our resources provide raw materials for various industries, from building houses to making cars. We also grow huge amounts of food. Partly because the United States has such a powerful economy, we also have great power in world affairs.

In contrast, some other countries are poor in resources. There, few industries grow, and people don't have many choices about how to earn a living. Some countries

Teaching Objective 4

ALL LEVELS: (Suggested time: 20 min.) Have students flip through this textbook looking for photographs that show or imply the relationship of people to the resources available to them. Then ask students to skim the text about that place for more information on how the resources in that place affect the people who live there. They may need to use the index to find information in other chapters. (Example: The lower photo on this page shows the Alaska pipeline. In the material on the United States, students will learn that oil provides significant income to that state.) After a discussion of their findings, ask students to write down a conclusion that they have drawn about people and resources. (Example: People with many available resources have many options about how to make a living.)

have large amounts of some resources but not of others. For example, Saudi Arabia is rich in oil but lacks water for growing food. Saudi Arabia pays other countries for food with the profit it earns on oil.

Resources and Daily Life The resources available to people affect how they live. In this country we have many resources. We can choose among many different ways to dress, build our homes, eat, travel, and entertain ourselves. People of other cultures may have fewer choices because they have fewer resources. Or, their environments may offer resources that we don't use.

Consider people who live in a rain forest, far from any city or factory. These people depend on the resources in their environment for all their needs. They may craft containers by weaving plant fibers together or canoes by hollowing out tree trunks. Their musical instruments are not electric guitars, but perhaps flutes made from bamboo. What kinds of songs would they sing? These forest people would be more likely to sing about finding food than about new cars.

This Brazilian rain forest is being cleared by burning.
Human-Environment Interaction
How do you think the loss of land affects people who live in the rain forest?

▼

✓ **READING CHECK:**
(*Environment and Society*) How does the lack of resources affect people? *affects the choices they have for many aspects of daily life*

Homework Practice Online
Keyword: SK5 HP2

Define and explain: renewable resources, nonrenewable resources, deforestation, reforestation, fossil fuels, petroleum, hydroelectric power, geothermal energy, solar power

Reading for the Main Idea

1. (*Environment and Society*) What are fossil fuels, and how are they used?

2. (*Environment and Society*) What are the main renewable energy sources?

Critical Thinking

3. Analyzing Information How are preserving soil and forest resources related to resource and land management?

4. Making Generalizations and Predictions How may a country that has only one or two valuable resources develop its economy?

Organizing What You Know

5. Categorizing Copy the following graphic organizer. Use it to describe the mineral resources that may be used in a typical home.

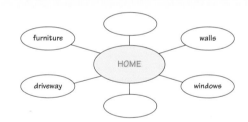

furniture — HOME — walls
driveway — windows

Answers to Section 4 Review

Define For definitions, see the glossary.

Reading for the Main Idea

1. fuels formed from the remains of ancient plants and animals; used in the form of coal, oil, or natural gas **(NGS 16)**

2. hydroelectric power, wind, geothermal energy, solar power **(NGS 16)**

Critical Thinking

3. Careful resource and land management can help preserve soil and forests. **(NGS 16)**

4. Possible answer: using profits from the sale or development of a resource to diversify the country's economy

Organizing What You Know

5. Answers will vary, but students should note a wide range of resources.

▲ **Visual Record Answer**

destroys plant life and the habitat of animals on which they depend

Planet Earth • 43

CLOSE

Ask students to suggest advertising slogans or logos for companies that harness and sell hydroelectric power, wind energy, geothermal energy, or solar energy.

REVIEW, ASSESS, RETEACH

Have students complete the Section Review. You may also have them prepare an outline of the section. Then have students complete Daily Quiz 2.4.

Have students complete Main Idea Activity S4. Then have them create crossword puzzles using the section's vocabulary terms. Ask students to exchange and solve another classmate's puzzle.
ESOL, LS **VERBAL-LINGUISTIC**

EXTEND

Have interested students conduct research on the Arctic National Wildlife Refuge (often abbreviated as ANWAR) and the controversy surrounding oil development there. **BLOCK SCHEDULING**

Define and Identify
For definitions, see the glossary.

Review the Main Ideas
11. It explains how Earth's topography formed and changes; Earth's surface is divided into plates which move very slowly. (NGS 7)

12. Hot lava may emerge and build up to form a mountain range. (NGS 7)

13. Ice cracks rocks; water dissolves underground minerals; water and ice move sediment; water waves shape beaches and coastlines. (NGS 7)

14. Rows of trees are planted to block wind; terraces are built into slopes of hillsides.

15. 1%; the Pacific, Atlantic, Indian, and Arctic Oceans, which are connected (NGS 7)

16. evaporation, condensation, and precipitation; the Sun's energy (NGS 7)

17. agriculture and industry

18. Wind blows polluted air from one place to another.

19. regions closer to the equator; because they receive the most direct rays from the Sun (NGS 7)

20. changes in air pressure as light, warm air rises and heavy, cold air moves in (NGS 7)

21. Distance from the ocean affects a region's climate, because water heats and cools more slowly than land. Because Kansas City is far from the ocean, its weather is not moderated by the ocean. (NGS 7)

22. An increase in elevation causes a drop in temperature because the air is less dense. (NGS 7)

23. The processes of renewal can take many years, while these resources can be used or destroyed within seconds.

24. They are nonrenewable resources, and they create air pollution.

CHAPTER 2 Review and Practice

Define and Identify
Idenfity each of the following:

1. topography
2. plate tectonics
3. erosion
4. tributary
5. water cycle
6. global warming
7. climate
8. rain shadow
9. nonrenewable resources
10. geothermal energy

Review the Main Idea
11. What is the theory of plate tectonics and how does it work?

12. What may occur when tectonic plates move away from each other?

13. How is water involved in erosion?

14. What methods are used to protect soil from erosion?

15. What percentage of Earth's water is freshwater? What covers 70% of Earth's surface?

16. What are the three phases of the water cycle? What drives the water cycle?

17. What are the two main causes of water pollution?

18. Why may one country suffer from another country's air pollution?

19. What parts of the Earth receive the most solar heat? Why?

20. What makes wind?

21. Explain why Kansas City has more extreme seasons than San Francisco.

22. Why may the base of a mountain be hot while the top is covered in ice?

23. Why is it important to preserve renewable resources such as soil and forests?

24. What problems are associated with fossil fuels?

25. What are some examples of renewable energy resources?

26. What are minerals used for?

Think Critically
27. **Drawing Inferences and Conclusions** Why are we developing alternative energy sources?

28. **Finding the Main Idea** How are the Earth's land, water, and atmosphere related?

29. **Understanding Cause and Effect** How may a dam affect a river and its surrounding areas?

30. **Drawing Inferences and Conclusions** How do the laws that govern and restrict pollution both help and hurt people?

31. **Making Generalizations and Predictions** Why is pollution a global concern?

Map Activity
32. Match the letters on the map with their correct labels.
> Humid subtropical
> Steppe climate
> Marine west coast climate
> Mediterranean climate
> Desert
> Humid tropical
> Tropical savanna

25. hydroelectric power, wind, geothermal energy, solar power, nuclear power (NGS 16)

26. Answers may vary but may include: salt; metals and rocks are used for building; glass is made from the mineral quartz; pencils; staples; coins; jewelry; aluminum and tin cans; cars (NGS 16)

Think Critically
27. Because fossil fuels are nonrenewable, they will eventually run out. Also, alternative energy resources may help to reduce air pollution.

28. Answers will vary but should include: water, wind, and ice break down land forms; weathering and erosion occur; winds lift and carry soil and wear down rocks; the water cycle moves water from Earth to the atmosphere and back to Earth.

29. A dam changes the flow of a river, which alters the river's ecosystem and that of its coastal areas. Land upstream from the dam will have more water, land downstream from the dam will have less water.

30. Limiting pollution keeps the air and ground cleaner and healthier for people. These limitations sometimes inhibit business and industry, which can hurt the economy.

31. Air and water pollution have no boundaries. All countries must address these issues in order to make a difference.

Writing Activity

Imagine you are writing a report about your region of the United States for students around the world. Use your text-book, the library, and the Internet to research the land-forms, climate, resources, and history of your region. Then write a few paragraphs highlighting what you discover.

internet connect

Internet Activity: **go.hrw.com**
KEYWORD: **SK5 GT2**

Choose a topic to explore online:
• Learn more about using weather maps.
• Discover facts about Earth's water.
• Investigate earthquakes.

Social Studies Skills Practice

Interpreting Graphs

The United States uses different resources to meet its energy needs. Study the following graph and answer the questions.

Energy Consumption in the United States, 2002

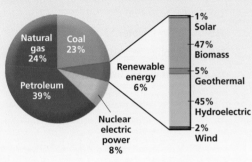

Natural gas 24%
Coal 23%
Petroleum 39%
Renewable energy 6%
Nuclear electric power 8%

1% Solar
47% Biomass
5% Geothermal
45% Hydroelectric
2% Wind

Source: Energy Information Administration

1. What percentage of the nation's energy consumption is renewable?
2. Which fossil fuel is used the most?
3. Based on what you have learned in this chapter, which renewable resources provide the cleanest energy?
4. Why do you think solar, wind, and geothermal energy are not a commonly used resource?

Analyzing Primary Sources

In 1906, San Francisco experienced the most powerful earthquake recorded in the United States. Read the follow-ing account of the disaster from Peter Bacigalupi, one of San Francisco's shop owners. Then answer the questions.

"I was awakened from a sound slumber by a terrific trem-bling, which acted in the same manner as would a buck-ing broncho . . . My bed was going up and down in all four directions at once, while all about me I heard screams, wails, and crashing of breaking china-ware and nick-nacks. A great portion of plaster right over the head of my bed fell all around me, and caused a cloud of dust, which was very hard to breathe through . . . I started to walk downtown, and arriving within eight blocks of the business section, noted that there were hardly any panes of glass left in any of the show windows . . . Buildings were tumbled over on their sides, others looked as though they had been cut off short with a cleaver."

1. Was there any warning that the earthquake was about to occur?
2. What effect did the earthquake have on Mr. Bacigalupi's house?
3. What did he witness when he walked around the city?
4. How do you think communities can prepare for earthquakes such as this one?

Planet Earth • 45

Map Activity

32. A. Desert climate
   B. Mediterranean climate
   C. Marine west coast climate
   D. Humid subtropical
   E. Tropical savanna
   F. Steppe climate
   G. Humid tropical

Writing Activity

Reports will vary but should include accurate information on the region's landforms, climate, resources, and history. Use Rubric 40, Writing to Describe, to evalu-ate student work.

Interpreting Graphs

1. 6%
2. petroleum
3. hydroelectric, solar, and wind power
4. Possible answer: The high cost of harnessing these resources limit their use.

Analyzing Primary Sources

1. No, the earthquake occurred without warning.
2. Chunks of plaster fell from the ceilings, and many items were broken.
3. Windows were broken, and buildings were demolished.
4. Builders can avoid fault lines and build earthquake-resistant structures. Communities prone to earthquakes can develop emergency response systems.

CHAPTER 2 REVIEW AND ASSESSMENT RESOURCES

Reproducible
♦ Readings in World Geography, History, and Culture 5–8
♦ Critical Thinking Activity 2
♦ Vocabulary Activity 2

Technology
♦ Chapter 2 Test Generator (on the One-Stop Planner)
♦ HRW Go site

♦ Audio CD Program, Chapter 2

Reinforcement, Review, and Assessment
♦ Chapter 2 Review and Practice
♦ Chapter Summaries and Review
♦ Chapter 2 Test

♦ Chapter 2 Test for English Language Learners and Special-Needs Students
♦ Unit Test
♦ Unit 1 Test for English Language Learners and Special-Needs Students

internet connect

GO TO: **go.hrw.com**
KEYWORD: **SG2 Teacher**
FOR: **a guide to using the Internet in your classoom**

CHAPTER 3

The World's People
Chapter Resource Manager

Objectives	Pacing Guide	Reproducible Resources
SECTION 1 **What is Culture** 1. Define Culture. 2. Identify the importance of cultural symbols. 3. Trace how cultures develop	**Regular** .5 day Lecture Notes, Section 1 **Block Scheduling** .5 day *Block Scheduling Handbook, Chapter 3*	**RS** Know It Notes S3 **E** Biography Activity: Ruth Benedict **E** Creative Strategies for Teaching World Geography, Lessons 4, 5 **E** Lab Activity for Geography and Earth Science, Hands-On 4 **SM** Geography for Life Activity 3 **SM** Map Activity 3 **ELL** Main Idea Activity S1
SECTION 2 **Economics and Population** 1. Define economics. 2. Compare how industrialized countries are different from developing countries. 3. Identify the different types of economic systems. 4. Explain where most people on Earth live.	**Regular** .5 day Lecture Notes, Section 2 **Block Scheduling** .5 day *Block Scheduling Handbook, Chapter 3*	**RS** Know It Notes S2 **RS** Graphic Organizer 3 **ELL** Main Idea Activity S2
SECTION 3 **Global Connections** 1. Define globalization and describe how people around the world are connected. 2. Explore refugees as a global problem, famine, and how people in need get help.	**Regular** 1 day Lecture Notes, Section 3 **Block Scheduling** .5 day *Block Scheduling Handbook, Chapter 3*	**RS** Know It Notes S3 **E** Environmental and Global Issues Activity 8 **ELL** Main Idea Activity S3

Chapter Resource Key

RS Reading Support

IC Interdisciplinary Connections

E Enrichment

SM Skills Mastery

A Assessment

REV Review

ELL Reinforcement and English Language Learners and English for Speakers of Other Languages (ESOL)

 go. hrw .com Internet

 Holt Presentation Maker Using Microsoft® PowerPoint®

 Transparencies

 CD–ROM

 Music

 Video

  One-Stop Planner CD–ROM

See the *One-Stop Planner* for a complete list of additional resources for students and teachers.

45A

One-Stop Planner CD–ROM

It's easy to plan lessons, select resources, and print out materials for your students when you use the *One-Stop Planner CD–ROM with Test Generator.*

☑ **internet** connect

HRW ONLINE RESOURCES

GO TO: go.hrw.com
Then type in a keyword.

TEACHER HOME PAGE
    KEYWORD: SJ5 TEACHER

CHAPTER INTERNET ACTIVITIES
    KEYWORD: SJ5 GT3

Choose an activity to:
• visit famous buildings and monuments around the world.
• compare facts about life in different countries.
• examine world population growth.

CHAPTER ENRICHMENT LINKS
    KEYWORD: SJ5 CH3

CHAPTER MAPS
    KEYWORDS: SJ5 MAPS3

ONLINE ASSESSMENT
Homework Practice
    KEYWORD: SJ5 HP3
    Standardized Test Prep Online
    KEYWORD: SJ5 STP3
    Rubrics
    KEYWORD: SS Rubrics

COUNTRY INFORMATION
    KEYWORD: SJ5 Almanac

CONTENT UPDATES
    KEYWORD: SS Content Updates

HOLT PRESENTATION MAKER
    KEYWORD: SJ5 PPT3

ONLINE READING SUPPORT
    KEYWORD: SS Strategies

CURRENT EVENTS
    KEYWORD: S5 Current Events

Technology Resources

 One-Stop Planner CD-ROM, Lesson 3.1

 ARGWorld CD–ROM

 Homework Practice Online

HRW Go site

 One-Stop Planner CD-ROM, Lesson 3.2

ARGWorld CD–ROM

Homework Practice Online

HRW Go site

 One-Stop Planner CD-ROM, Lesson 3.3

 Yourtown CD-ROM

 ARGWorld CD–ROM

Homework Practice Online

HRW Go site

Review, Reinforcement, and Assessment Resources

ELL	Main Idea Activity S1
REV	Section 1 Review
A	Daily Quiz 3.1
REV	Chapter Summaries and Review
ELL	English Audio Summary 3.1
ELL	Spanish Audio Summary 3.1

ELL	Main Idea Activity S2
REV	Section 2 Review
A	Daily Quiz 3.2
REV	Chapter Summaries and Review
ELL	English Audio Summary 3.2
ELL	Spanish Audio Summary 3.2

ELL	Main Idea Activity S3
REV	Section 3 Review
A	Daily Quiz 3.3
REV	Chapter Summaries and Review
ELL	English Audio Summary 3.3
ELL	Spanish Audio Summary 3.3

Chapter Review and Assessment

SM	Critical Thinking Activity 3
REV	Chapter 3 Review and Practice
REV	Chapter Summaries and Review
ELL	Vocabulary Activity 3
A	Chapter 3 Test
A	Chapter 3 Test Generator (on the One-Stop Planner)
	Audio CD program, Chapter 3
A	Chapter 3 Test for English Language Learners and Special-Needs Students
	HRW Go site

Meeting Individual Needs

Ability Levels

Level 1 Basic-level activities designed for all students encountering new material

Level 2 Intermediate-level activities designed for average students

Level 3 Challenging activities designed for honors and gifted-and-talented students

ESOL Activities that address the needs of students with Limited English Proficiency

CHAPTER 3

The World's People

Previewing Chapter Resources

Holt Online Learning

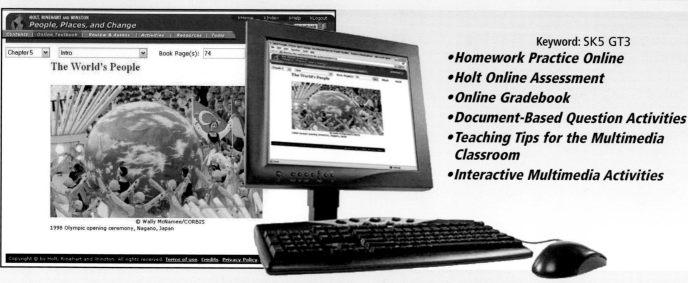

© Wally McNamee/CORBIS
1998 Olympic opening ceremony, Nagano, Japan

Keyword: SK5 GT3

- •**Homework Practice Online**
- •**Holt Online Assessment**
- •**Online Gradebook**
- •**Document-Based Question Activities**
- •**Teaching Tips for the Multimedia Classroom**
- •**Interactive Multimedia Activities**

Differentiating Instruction

Reading and Writing Support

◄ Graphic Organizer Activity
- •Vocabulary Activity
- •Chapter Summary and Review
- •Know It Notes
- •Audio CD

Active Learning

◄ Block Scheduling Handbook
- •Cultures of the World Activity
- •Interdisciplinary Activity
- •Map Activity
- •Critical Thinking Activity: Wheat and the World

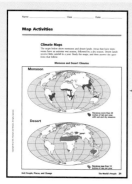

Primary Sources and Advanced Learners

- •Geography for Life Activity: What Region Do You Live In?
◄ Map Activity: Languages of Europe
- •Readings in World Geography, History and Culture:
  - • 9 How Many Is Too Many?
  - • 10 People and Migration

Assessment Program

◄ Daily Quizzes S1–3
- •Chapter Test
- •Chapter Test for English Language Learners and Special-Needs Students

Spanish and ESOL

- •Vocabulary Activity
◄ Main Idea Activities for English Language Learners and Special-Needs Students
- •Chapter Summary and Review
- •Spanish Audio Summary
- •Know It Notes S1–3
- •Chapter Test for English Language Learners and Special-Needs Students

Special Education Modifications

Your **I.D.E.A. Works! CD-ROM** will provide modified versions of the following teaching materials:

◄ Guided Reading Strategies S1–3
- •Vocabulary Activity
- •Main Idea Activities S1–3
- •Daily Quizzes S1–3
- •Chapter 3 Test
- •Flash cards of chapter vocabulary terms

Teacher Resources

Books for Teachers

Gallant, Roy A. *The Peopling of Planet Earth: Human Population Growth Through the Ages.* Macmillan Publishing Company, 1990.

Hirschman, Charles, Josh Dewind, and Philip Kasintz, eds. *The Handbook of International Migration.* Russell Sage Foundation, 1999.

Johnston, R.J., and David M. Smith, ed. *Dictionary of Human Geography.* Blackwell Publishing, 1994.

Books for Students

Ajerma, Maya, and Anna Rhesa Versola (contributor). *Children from Australia to Zimbabwe.* Charlebridge Publishing, 1997. Photographs of children at work, play, and worship showing the differences and similarities among civilizations. **SHELTERED ENGLISH**

Ellwood, Robert, ed. *The Encyclopedia of World Religions.* Facts on File, 1998. Maps, charts, and chronologies of major religions and related world events.

Pollack, Steve. *The Atlas of Endangered Peoples.* Facts on File, 1995. Human-made and natural problems threatening human life around the world and proposed solutions.

Roundtree, Lester. *Diversity amid Globalization.* Prentice Hall, 2000. Interconnections among the regions of the world.

Multimedia Materials

Folktales of Peace, Vol. I. Video, 22 min. The Video Project.

6.4 Billion: Will the Earth Drown in People? Video and Teacher's Guide, 60 min. Agency for Instructional Technology.

The World and Its People. Videodisc, 60 min. Glencoe.

Videos and CDs

Videos

- CNN *Presents Geography: Yesterday and Today, Segment 5 World Population—Hitting Six Billion*
- *ARG World*

Holt Researcher

http://researcher.hrw.com

- *Natural Increase in Population*
- *Population and Population Projections—Asia*
- *Total GDP for Selected Countries*
- *Immigrants to The United States by Region*
- *U.S. Trade with Selected Countries, 2000*
- *Major Religions of the World*

Transparency Packages

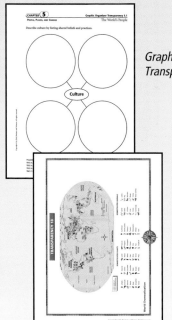

Graphic Organizer Transparencies 3.1–3

Geography and Cultures Visual Resources Transparencies
18 World Domestication
19 Age Structure Diagrams
20 Population Growth in the Americas

Map Activities Transparency 03 Languages of Europe

CHAPTER 3

The World's People

The Colosseum, Rome, Italy

1998 Olympic opening ceremony, Nagano, Japan

Easter Island, Chile

46 Chapter 3

Section 1 What Is Culture?

Read to Discover
1. What is culture?
2. Why are cultural symbols important?
3. What influences how cultures develop?
4. How did agriculture affect the development of culture?

Vocabulary
culture
culture region
culture traits
ethnic groups
multicultural
race
acculturation

symbol
ethnocentrism
domestication
subsistence agriculture
commercial agriculture
civilization

Reading Strategy
READING ORGANIZER Before you read, create a chart with columns titled Term, Definition, Example. Write each of the terms above in the left column. As you read write the definition and give an example in the other two columns.

Aspects of Culture

The people of the world's approximately 200 countries speak hundreds of different languages. They may dress in different ways and eat different foods. However, all societies share certain basic institutions, including a government, an educational system, an economic system, and religious institutions. These vary from society to society and are often based on that society's **culture**. Culture is a learned system of shared beliefs and ways of doing things that guides a person's daily behavior. Most people around the world have a national culture shared with people of their own country. They may also have religious practices, beliefs, and language in common with people from other countries. Sometimes a culture dominates a particular region. This is known as a **culture region**. In a culture region, people may share certain **culture traits**, or elements of culture, such as dress, food, or religious beliefs. West Africa is an example of a culture region. Culture can also be based on a person's job or age. People can belong to more than one culture and can choose which to emphasize.

Race and Ethnic Groups Cultural groups share beliefs and practices learned from parents, grandparents, and ancestors. These groups are sometimes called **ethnic groups**. An ethnic group's shared culture may include its religion, history, language, holiday traditions, and special foods.

When people from different cultures live in the same country, the country is described as **multicultural** or multiethnic. Many countries

Dance is an example of a culture trait. Dancers from central Texas perform a traditional Czech dance.

The World's People • 47

SECTION 1 RESOURCES
Reproducible
- Lecture Notes, Section 1
- Block Scheduling Handbook, Chapter 3
- Know It Notes S1
- Creative Strategies for Teaching World Geography, Lessons 4, 5
- Map Activity 3
- Geography for Life Activity 3
- Lab Activity for Geography and Earth Science, Hands-On 4
- Biography Activity: Ruth Benedict

Technology
- One-Stop Planner CD–ROM, Lesson 3.1
- Homework Practice Online
- HRW Go site

Reinforcement, Review, and Assessment
- Section 1 Review
- Daily Quiz 3.1
- Main Idea Activity S1
- Chapter Summaries and Review
- English Audio Summary 3.1
- Spanish Audio Summary 3.1

Section 1

Objectives
1. Define culture.
2. Identify the importance of cultural symbols.
3. Trace how cultures develop.
4. Explain how agriculture affected culture.

FOCUS

Bellringer

Copy the following instructions onto the chalkboard: *What are some organized events that occur regularly in our community?* Discuss responses. (Possible answers: parades, festivals, garage sales, sports tournaments, concerts) Point out that the events they listed are part of the community's culture. Ask if students know of similar events elsewhere. If so, compare those events with the students' lists to note ways in which other communities have different cultures. Tell students that in Section 1 they will learn more about culture.

Building Vocabulary

Write the vocabulary terms on the chalkboard. Underline the prefixes *multi-* and *sub-*. Explain that they mean, respectively, "many" and "below" or "almost." Ask students to find the terms' definitions in the text or glossary and to relate the prefix meanings to **multicultural** and **subsistence agriculture**. Call on students to read the remaining definitions. Ask each student to choose a vocabulary term and write a sentence to define it. Call on students to read their sentences. Continue until all of the terms have been covered.

The World's People 47

World Religions

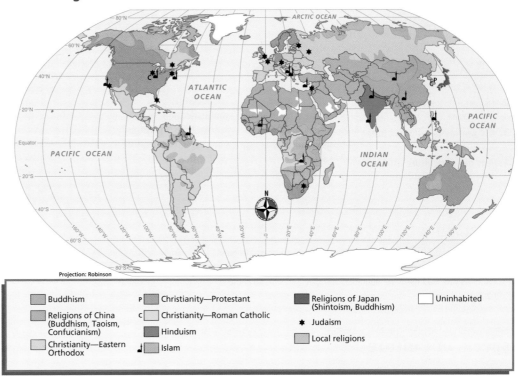

Legend:
- Buddhism
- Religions of China (Buddhism, Taoism, Confucianism)
- Christianity—Eastern Orthodox
- **P** Christianity—Protestant
- **C** Christianity—Roman Catholic
- Hinduism
- Islam
- Religions of Japan (Shintoism, Buddhism)
- ★ Judaism
- Local religions
- Uninhabited

Projection: Robinson

▲
Religion is one aspect of culture.

A disc jockey plays Cuban music for the large Cuban ethnic group of Miami, Florida.

▼

48 • Chapter 3

DAILY LIFE

Mancala! Peoples of many races and ethnic groups often enjoy the same entertainments. For example, a board game called *mancala* is popular in many parts of the world. *Mancala* is possibly the oldest board game in the world. Egyptians played this counting and strategy game before 1400 B.C. It is popular across Africa, among all ages and social classes.

Mancala is played on boards of different sizes and shapes or simply with shallow holes in the ground. Counters can be anything from seashells to seeds. Versions of *mancala* can be found thousands of miles from Africa, in Southeast Asia. The game's actual origin is not known, however.

Activity: Have students conduct research on the rules for playing *mancala*. Ask them to determine similarities and differences in rules from different countries. Then have them construct *mancala* boards from egg cartons. Hold a *mancala* tournament in your classroom.

internet connect

GO TO: go.hrw.com
KEYWORD: SG5 CH3
FOR: Web sites about mancala

are multicultural. In some countries, such as Belgium, different ethnic groups have cooperated to form a united country. In other cases, such as in French-speaking Quebec, Canada, ethnic groups have frequently been in conflict. Sometimes, people from one ethnic group are spread over two or more countries. For example, Germans live in different European countries: Germany, Austria, and the Czech Republic. The Kurds, who are a people with no country of their own, live mostly in Syria, Iran, Iraq, and Turkey.

Race is based on inherited physical or biological traits. It is sometimes confused with ethnic group. For example, the Hispanic ethnic group in the United States includes people who look quite different from each other. However, they share a common Spanish or Latin American heritage. As you know, people vary in physical appearance. Some of these differences have developed in response to climate factors like cold and sunlight. Because people have moved from region to region throughout history, these differences are not clear-cut. Each culture defines race in its own way, emphasizing particular biological and ethnic characteristics. An example can be seen in Rwanda, a country in East Africa. In this country, the Hutu and the Tutsi have carried on a bitter civil war. Although both are East African, each one

TEACH

Teaching Objectives 1 and 3

ALL LEVELS: (Suggested time: 30 min.) Ask students to write on a slip of paper three of the cultures or culture regions to which they belong. Collect the suggestions. (Responses may include ethnic groups, sports teams, state or regional affiliations, or many other possibilities.) On the chalkboard, draw three columns. Label them *Culture, History,* and *Environment.* Choose a range of the student suggestions. As you record each group on the chart, lead a discussion on how it fulfills the definition of culture and how history and environment helped shape that culture. **ESOL**

Teaching Objective 2

ALL LEVELS: Point out that gestures are symbols and that they vary among cultures. Call on volunteers to demonstrate how they would show appreciation after a school play or choir concert (polite applause) and after the home team's winning goal at a sports event (cheers, high fives). Then have students conduct research on how people in other countries display approval in similar situations. Ask them to speculate how history and the environment have shaped the customs. Tell them to consider the effect of having a culture region divided by political boundaries. How might gestures or symbols in general change? You may need to extend this activity to another class period so that students can use other sources. **ESOL**

considers itself different from the other. Their definition of race involves height and facial features. Around the world, people tend to identify races based on obvious physical traits. However, these definitions of race are based primarily on attitudes, not actual biological differences.

Cultural Change Cultures change over time. Humans invent new ways of doing things and spread these new ways to others. The spread of one culture's ways or beliefs to another culture is called diffusion. Diffusion may occur when people move from one place to another. The English language was once confined to England and parts of Scotland. It is now one of the world's most widely spoken languages. English originally spread because people from England founded colonies in other regions. More recently, as communication among cultures has increased, English has spread through English-language films and television programs. English has also become an international language of science and technology.

People sometimes may borrow aspects of another culture as the result of long-term contact with another society. This process is called **acculturation**. For example, people in one culture may adopt the religion of another. As a result, they might change other cultural practices to conform to the new religion. For example, farmers who become Muslim may quit raising pigs because Islam forbids eating pork.

✓ **READING CHECK:** (*Human Systems*) What is the definition of culture?
a learned system of shared beliefs and ways of doing things that guides a person's daily behavior

Cultural Differences

A **symbol** is a sign that stands for something else. A symbol can be many things such as a word, a shape, a color, or a flag. People learn symbols from their culture. The sets of sounds of a language are symbols. These symbols have meaning for the people who speak that language. The same sound may mean something different to people who speak another language. The word bad means "evil" in English, "cool" to teenagers, and "bath" in German.

If you traveled to another country, you might notice immediately that people behave differently. Some people, however, may see the differences in other cultures as inferior to their own. This view is called **ethnocentrism**. Many people may even have an ethnocentric view toward the foods some cultures eat. For example, they may think it is disgusting that the Inuit of Canada eat whale blubber. To the Inuit, however, eating blubber is perfectly normal.

✓ **READING CHECK:** (*Human Systems*) How do symbols reflect differences among societies and cultures? They show the societies' particular cultural expressions or belief systems.

▲ **Movement** Some immigrants from China settle in New York City's Chinatown.

📧 **internet** connect

GO TO: go.hrw.com
KEYWORD: SK5 CH3
FOR: Web sites about the world's people

Fans cheer for the U.S. Olympic soccer team.

Interpreting the Visual Record Why do you think symbols such as flags create strong emotions?

▼

The World's People • 49

CHAPTER 3, Section 1

National Geography Standard 10

Lost and Found Diffusion has carried elements of modern cultures into the far corners of the world, from vast deserts to rain forests.

In 1972, newspapers reported that a "lost" culture had been found in the Philippines. The Tasaday supposedly led an isolated existence and had never before encountered other cultures. However, in 1986 the story was revealed as a hoax. The Tasaday were well aware of modern cultures.

Discussion: Lead a discussion on these questions: Do isolated peoples have the right to be left alone? What may be the consequences of improved communication between these cultures and modern cultures?

◄**Visual Record Answer**

because they can evoke strong feelings of national pride

Teaching Objective 4

LEVEL 1: (Suggested time: 30 min.) Copy the following graphic organizer onto the chalkboard, omitting the blue answers. Use it to help students describe how agriculture affected culture. Call on students to fill in the boxes. Then have them choose a step and illustrate it. Display the illustrated diagrams. **ESOL,** 🅛🅢 **VISUAL-SPATIAL**

LEVELS 2 AND 3: (Suggested time: 45 min.) Organize students into groups. Have each group create a scenario that describes what human life would be like today if the progression from hunting and gathering to civilization had been interrupted. Instruct students to create feasible scenarios. You may want to have students act out their ideas. Have group members summarize in a paragraph the reasoning they used. **COOPERATIVE LEARNING,** 🅛🅢 **KINESTHETIC**

AGRICULTURE AND CIVILIZATION

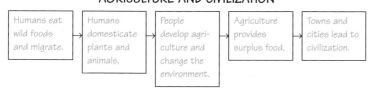

Humans eat wild foods and migrate. → Humans domesticate plants and animals. → People develop agriculture and change the environment. → Agriculture provides surplus food. → Towns and cities lead to civilization.

Linking Past to Present
Nile River

Cultures Without the Nile River, the civilization whose people built the pyramids and the Sphinx could never have existed. The thousands of workers who labored on these and other monumental projects could be fed only because the river made intensive agriculture possible. The Nile Valley and Delta have been densely populated for thousands of years. Hunter-gatherers may have started to move into the Nile Valley by 12,000 B.C. By about 3,000 B.C. a great civilization flourished.

Alexandria, Egypt, was built next to the Nile Delta. During the 200s B.C. Alexandria may have been the largest metropolis in the world. Cleopatra's palace was there. During the 1980s, archaeologists began excavating the ruins of the city, which is now under water. They mapped the Royal Quarter, where Cleopatra had lived. Today, Alexandria is Egypt's second-largest city, with more than 4 million inhabitants.

Visual Record Answer ▶

possible answers: streets narrower and appear to be laid out in a random pattern, houses closer together and with flat roofs

▲ A couple prepares for a wedding ceremony in Kazakhstan.

The layout of Marrakech, Morocco, is typical of many North African cities.

Interpreting the Visual Record (Place)
How are the streets and houses of Marrakech different from those in your community?

Development of a Culture

All people have the same basic needs for food, water, clothing, and shelter. People everywhere live in families and mark important family changes together. They usually have rituals or traditions that go with the birth of a baby, the wedding of a couple, or the death of a grandparent. All human societies need to deal with natural disasters. They must also deal with people who break the rules of behavior. However, people in different places meet these needs in unique ways. They eat different foods, build different kinds of houses, and form families in different ways. They have different rules of behavior. Two important factors that influence the way people meet basic needs are their history and environment.

History Culture is shaped by history. A region's people may have been conquered by the same outsiders. They may have adopted the same religion. They may have come from the same area and may share a common language. However, historical events may have affected some parts of a region but not others. For example, in North America French colonists brought their culture to Louisiana and Canada. However, they did not have a major influence on the Middle Atlantic region of the United States.

Cultures also shape history by influencing the way people respond to the same historical forces. Nigeria, India, and Australia were all colonized by the British. Today each nation still uses elements of the British legal system, but with important differences.

Environment The environment of a region can influence the development of culture. For example, in Egypt the Nile River is central to people's lives. The ancient Egyptians saw the fertile soils brought by the flooding of the Nile as the work of the gods. Beliefs in mountain spirits were important in many mountainous regions of the world. These areas include Tibet, Japan, and the Andes of South America.

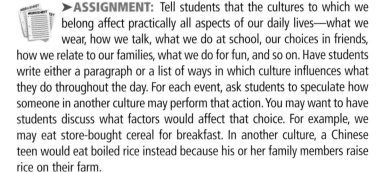

▶**ASSIGNMENT:** Tell students that the cultures to which we belong affect practically all aspects of our daily lives—what we wear, how we talk, what we do at school, our choices in friends, how we relate to our families, what we do for fun, and so on. Have students write either a paragraph or a list of ways in which culture influences what they do throughout the day. For each event, ask students to speculate how someone in another culture may perform that action. You may want to have students discuss what factors would affect that choice. For example, we may eat store-bought cereal for breakfast. In another culture, a Chinese teen would eat boiled rice instead because his or her family members raise rice on their farm.

TEACHER TO TEACHER

Lois Jordan of Nashville, Tennessee, suggests this research project to help students explore how minority groups can affect a country's development and culture. Organize the class into teams. Assign one country per team. Have each team use primary and secondary sources to research the country's minority groups and the geographical or historical reasons why the groups are there. Students should try to answer questions such as these: Are members of the minority groups spread throughout the country or concentrated in one area? In what ways are the minority cultures different from the majority culture? How do the majority and minority cultures relate to each other politically and socially? Have the students share their findings in a panel discussion.

Culture also determines how people use and shape their landscape. For example, city plans are cultural. Cities in Spain and its former colonies are organized around a central plaza, or square, with a church and a courthouse. On the other hand, Chinese cities are oriented to the four compass points. American cities often follow a rectangular grid plan. Many French city streets radiate out from a central core.

✓ **READING CHECK:** (*Human Systems*) What are some ways in which culture traits spread? *through historical events such as conquest by outsiders or colonization*

Development of Agriculture

For most of human history people ate only wild plants and animals. When the food ran out in one place, they migrated, or moved to another place. Very few people still live this way today. Thousands of years ago, humans began to help their favorite wild plant foods to grow. They probably cleared the land around their campsites and dumped seeds or fruits in piles of refuse. Plants took root and grew. People may also have dug water holes to encourage wild cattle to come and drink. People began cultivating the largest plants and breeding the tamest animals. Gradually, the wild plants and animals changed. They became dependent on people. This process is called **domestication**. A domesticated species has changed its form and behavior so much that it depends on people to survive. Domestic sheep can no longer leap from rock to rock like their wild ancestors. However, the wool of domestic sheep is more useful to humans. It can be combed and twisted into yarn.

Domestication happened in many parts of the world. In Peru llamas and potatoes were domesticated. People in ancient Mexico and Central America domesticated corn, beans, squash, tomatoes, and hot peppers. None of these foods was grown in Europe, Asia, or Africa before the time of Christopher Columbus's voyages to the Americas. Meanwhile, Africans had domesticated sorghum and a kind of rice. Cattle, sheep, and goats were probably first raised in Southwest Asia. Wheat and rye were first domesticated in Central Asia. The horse was also domesticated there. These domesticated plants and animals were unknown in the Americas before the time of Columbus.

▲

This ancient Egyptian wall painting shows domesticated cattle.

Interpreting the Visual Record Can you name other kinds of domesticated animals?

ENVIRONMENT AND SOCIETY

The Animals around Us
We know cats, dogs, cattle, horses, sheep, and other familiar animals have served or been dependent on humans for many centuries. Creatures we think of as living only in the wild have also been tamed.

Cheetahs were tamed perhaps 5,000 years ago. Ancient Egyptians and early rulers of India kept them as pets and trained them to hunt. Hunting with falcons and hawks has been known since before 700 B.C. Elephants have served as beasts of burden and have been used to drag heavy equipment over difficult terrain. As early as the 200s B.C. and as late as the 1940s elephants have been used in warfare.

Activity: What other examples of tamed animals can students find in books and nature television programs? To depict their findings, have them paint a mural in the style of a cave painting.

◀ **Visual Record Answer**

possible answers: cats, chickens, dogs, ducks, geese, goats, horses, pigs, sheep, turkeys

The World's People • 51

CLOSE

Call on students to suggest foods that are typical of a local culture. (Possible answers: pierogi, quesadillas, dim sum, gumbo, grits) Ask them to speculate how the popularity of that dish spread to the region. (Possible answers: television ads, families moving to new regions, national restaurant franchises) Point out how food is related to the main topics of the section.

REVIEW, ASSESS, RETEACH

Have students complete the Section Review. Then have them work in pairs to draw flow charts or other graphic organizers of the section material. Then have students complete Daily Quiz 3.1 **COOPERATIVE LEARNING**

Have students complete Main Idea Activity S1. Then have them work in groups to invent a previously unknown culture. Have them write sentences describing the features and development of their culture by using the vocabulary terms. Discuss the invented cultures to check on students' understanding of key concepts. **ESOL, COOPERATIVE LEARNING**

Answers to Section 1 Review

Define For definitions, see the glossary.

Reading for the Main Idea

1. People may belong to cultures based on where they live, their job, religious practices, beliefs, or age. **(NGS 10)**

2. Government, education, an economic system, religious institutions are basic to all. **(NGS 10)**

Critical Thinking

3. history—conquered by the same outsiders, have same religion or language; environment—affects religion, land use and planning; French colonists brought their culture to Louisiana; Nile River's influence on Egyptians

4. People built permanent settlements; surplus of food developed; population grew; civilizations formed.

Organizing What You Know

5. possible answers: religion, age, job, race, where we live, language and other cultural symbols

Our Amazing Planet

Thousands of years ago, domesticated dogs came with humans across the Bering Strait into North America. A breed called the Carolina dog may be descended almost unchanged from those dogs. The reddish yellow, short-haired breed also appears to be closely related to Australian dingoes.

Agriculture and Environment Agriculture changed the landscape. To make room for growing food, people cut down forests. They also built fences, dug irrigation canals, and terraced hillsides. Governments were created to direct the labor needed for these large projects. Governments also defended against outsiders and helped people resolve problems. People could now grow enough food for a whole year. Therefore, they stopped migrating and built permanent settlements.

Types of Agriculture Some farmers grow just enough food to provide for themselves and their own families. This type of farming is called **subsistence agriculture**. In the wealthier countries of the world, a small number of farmers can produce food for everyone. Each farm is large and may grow only one product. This type of farming is called **commercial agriculture**. In this system companies rather than individuals or families may own the farms.

Agriculture and Civilization Agriculture enabled farmers to produce a surplus of food—more than they could eat themselves. A few people could make things like pottery jars instead of farming. They traded or sold their products for food. With more food a family could feed more children. As a result, populations began to grow. More people became involved in trading and manufacturing. Traders and craftspeople began to live in central market towns. Some towns grew into cities, where many people lived and carried out even more specialized tasks. For example, cities often supported priests and religious officials. They were responsible for organizing and carrying out religious ceremonies. When a culture becomes highly complex, we sometimes call it a **civilization**.

✓ **READING CHECK:** (*Environment and Society*) In what ways did agriculture affect culture? Permanent settlements developed; a surplus of food developed; the population grew; civilizations developed.

go.hrw.com
Homework Practice Online
Keyword: SK5 HP3

Section Review 1

Define and explain: culture, culture region, culture trait, ethnic groups, multicultural, race, acculturation, symbol, ethnocentrism, domestication, subsistence agriculture, commercial agriculture, civilization

Reading for the Main Idea

1. (*Human Systems*) How can an individual belong to more than one cultural group?

2. (*Human Systems*) What institutions are basic to all societies?

Critical Thinking

3. **Drawing Inferences and Conclusions** In what ways do history and environment influence or shape a culture? What examples can you find in the text that explain this relationship?

4. **Analyzing Information** What is the relationship between the development of agriculture and culture?

Organizing What You Know

5. **Summarizing** Copy the following graphic organizer. Use it to describe culture by listing shared beliefs and practices.

Culture

EXTEND

Have interested students use primary and secondary sources to research how archaeology has shed light on when and where various plants and animals were domesticated for use as food. Then challenge them to choose a certain time period and region and write recipes appropriate to the available foods. Students may want to prepare an "ancient" meal for the class. Substitutions will be necessary. **BLOCK SCHEDULING**

Section 2 Economics and Population

Read to Discover

1. What is economics?
2. How are industrialized countries different from developing countries?
3. What are the different types of economic systems?
4. Where do most people on Earth live?

Vocabulary

gross national product
gross domestic product
industrialized countries
literacy rate
developing countries
third-world countries
free enterprise
market economy
command economy
tradition-based economy
mixed economy
one-crop economy
exports
imports
interdependence
birthrate
death rate
population density
overpopulation
migration
emigrant
immigrant

Reading Strategy

FOLDNOTES: FOUR-CORNER FOLD Create a **Four-Corner Fold** described in the Appendix. Title the flaps The Economy, Developed and Undeveloped Countries, Types of Economies, and Population. As you read, write what you learn about each topic beneath its flap.

SECTION 2 RESOURCES

Reproducible
◆ Lecture Notes, Section 2
◆ Know It Notes S2
◆ Graphic Organizer 3

Technology
◆ One-Stop Planner CD–ROM, Lesson 3.2
◆ Homework Practice Online
◆ HRW Go site

Reinforcement, Review, and Assessment
◆ Section 2 Review
◆ Daily Quiz 3.2
◆ Main Idea Activity S2
◆ Chapter Summaries and Review
◆ English Audio Summary 3.2
◆ Spanish Audio Summary 3.2

The Economy

All of the activities that people do to earn a living are part of a system called the economy. This includes people going to work, making things, selling things, buying things, and trading services. Economics is the study of the production, distribution, and use of goods and services.

Economic Indicators A common means of measuring a country's economy is the **gross national product** (GNP). The GNP is the value of all goods and services that a country produces in one year. It includes goods and services made by factories owned by that country's citizens but located in foreign countries. Most economists use **gross domestic product** (GDP) instead of GNP. GDP includes only those goods and services produced within a country. GDP divided by the country's population is called per capita GDP. This figure shows individual purchasing power and is useful for comparing levels of economic development.

Economic Activities Economists divide economic activities into four industries—primary, secondary, tertiary, and quaternary (see chart on the next page). A country's economy is usually based on one or more of these activities.

Shoppers crowd a street in Tokyo, Japan.
▼

The World's People ● 53

Section 2

Objectives

1. Define economics.
2. Compare how industrialized countries are different from developing countries.
3. Identify the different types of economic systems.
4. Explain where most people on Earth live.

Focus

Bellringer

Write these instructions on the chalkboard: *Everyone except those on the first row should move to the back third of the room. I will explain soon.* Then tell students the crowded area represents a densely populated country, such as India, and the front of the room a thinly populated one, such as Mongolia. Discuss with students the advantages and disadvantages they would experience as citizens of these countries, based on their population density. Tell students that in Section 2 they will learn more about population issues and economics.

Building Vocabulary

Write the vocabulary terms on the chalkboard. Call on volunteers to read the definitions aloud. Then label some of them according to these categories: Ways to Measure Economic Development (**gross national product, gross domestic product, industrialized countries,** and **developing countries**); Economic Systems (**free enterprise, market command, tradition-based economy**); and Concepts Related to Population (**population density, overpopulation, migration, emigrant,** and **immigrant**).

HUMAN SYSTEMS

Development in India India provides a good example of a country that has industries but is still usually considered a developing country. One factor that keeps India from reaching its development goals is its huge and growing population. The population surpassed 1 billion in the year 2000 and may surpass the population of China by 2050. For most of these people, the standard of living is still low. Many villages lack any telephone service. Industrial growth is hampered by lack of sufficient energy, transportation, and communication resources.

Economic Activities

ECONOMIC INDUSTRIES	DESCRIPTION	TYPES OF ACTIVITIES	EXAMPLE
Primary industry	Involves natural resources or raw materials	Farming, fishing, mining, forestry	Dairy farmer feeds his cows.
Secondary industry	Makes finished products using natural resources or raw materials	Manufacturing and construction	Factories make cheese.
Tertiary industry	Handles goods that are ready for sale	Trucking, restaurants, grocery stores	Grocery stores sell cheese.
Quaternary industry	Collects information	Research and management	A technician inspects dairy products in a lab.

▲

Interpreting the Chart **Which economic industry involves selling goods?**

A monorail in Sydney, Australia takes passengers throughout the city's central business district. **Interpreting the Visual Record** (Place) **What in this photo suggests that this is a city in an industrialized country?**

▼

Chart Answer ▲

tertiary

Visual Record Answer ▶

tall buildings, advanced transportation system, recreational facilities

Australia
Sydney

54 • Chapter 3

The World's Rich and Poor

Economists divide the countries of the world into two groups. They use various measures including GNP, GDP, per capita GDP, life expectancy, and literacy to determine a country's stage of development. Developed countries like the United States, Canada, Japan, and most European countries are the world's wealthiest. They are called **industrialized countries**.

Industrialization occurs when a country relies more on manufacturing and less on agriculture. In industrialized countries, many people work in manufacturing, service, and information industries. These countries have strong secondary, tertiary, and quaternary industries. They have good health care systems. Industrialized countries also have good systems of education. The **literacy rate**, or the percentage of people, who can read and write is high.

Most people in industrialized countries live in cities and have access to telecommunications systems — systems that allow long-distance communication. The level of technology in most countries is usually measured by how many telephones, televisions, or computers are in use.

TEACH

Teaching Objective 1

LEVEL 1: (Suggested time: 20 min.) Organize the class into groups. Have each group examine a common object (examples—dish, book, sock, eyeglasses) and discuss among themselves what role primary, secondary, tertiary, and quaternary industries have played in the object's "history." Then have students in each group create a flow chart to display their ideas. **ESOL, COOPERATIVE LEARNING**

LEVELS 2 AND 3: (Suggested time: 20 min.) Point out that students may play different roles in economies at different times—sometimes a consumer and sometimes a producer. Discuss these concepts. Then have each student write a brief essay titled "How I Participate in the Economy." Encourage students to consider not just the local economy, but the state, regional, national, and global economies. **LS INTRAPERSONAL**

Developing countries make up the second group. They are in different stages of moving toward development. About two thirds of the world's people live in developing countries. These countries are poor. People often work in farming or other primary industries earning low wages. Cities in developing countries are often very crowded. Many people move to cities to find work. Most people are not educated. They usually have little access to health care or telecommunications.

Some developing countries have made economic progress in recent decades. South Korea and Mexico are good examples. These countries are experiencing strong growth in manufacturing and trade. However, some of the world's poorest countries are developing slowly or not at all.

One Planet, Four Worlds Some people also refer to developing countries as **third-world countries**. These countries lack the economic opportunities of most industrialized countries. Some industrialized countries are called first-world and second-world countries. First-world countries include the United States, Canada, Western Europe, Japan and Australia. Second-world countries include Russia, the former Soviet republics, China, and Eastern Europe.

Third-world countries in Latin America, however, experience some economic growth. Countries like Haiti, however, show no economic growth. They are known as fourth-world countries.

✔ **READING CHECK:** What are some of the differences between industrialized and developing countries? differences in income; reliance on industry or agriculture; access to health care, education, and telecommunications

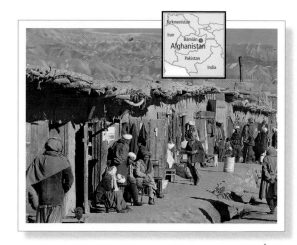

This photo shows daily life in a village in eastern Afghanistan.
Interpreting the Visual Record (Place)
What in this photo suggests that this village is in a developing country?

Interpreting the Chart Which countries have the highest literacy rates?

▼

Comparing Developed and Developing Countries

COUNTRY	POPULATION	POPULATION GROWTH RATE	PER CAPITA GDP	LIFE EXPECTANCY	LITERACY RATE	TELEPHONE LINES
United States	290.3 million	0.9%	$ 37,600	77	97%	194 million
France	60.1 million	0.4%	$ 26,000	79	99%	35 million
South Korea	48.2 million	0.7%	$ 19,600	75	98%	24 million
Mexico	104.9 million	1.4%	$ 8,900	72	92%	9.6 million
Poland	38.6 million	0.0%	$ 9,700	73	99%	8 million
Brazil	182.1 million	1.1%	$ 7,600	71	86%	17 million
Egypt	74.7 million	1.8%	$ 4,000	70	57%	3.9 million
Myanmar	42 million	0.5%	$ 1,700	55	83%	250,000
Mali	11.6 million	2.8%	$ 900	45	46%	23,000

Source: Central Intelligence Agency, *The World Factbook 2003*

The World's People • 55

Teaching Objective 2

LEVEL 1: (Suggested time: 20 min.) Copy the following graphic organizer onto the chalkboard, omitting the blue answers. Use it to help students learn the characteristics of industrialized and developing countries. **ESOL,** 🔲 **VISUAL-SPATIAL**

COMPARING COUNTRIES

Industrialized Countries		Developing Countries
• relies more on manufacturing		• relies more on agriculture
• strong secondary, tertiary, quaternary industries		• most people in primary industries
• good health care and education systems	↔	• people looking for work in crowded cities
• high literacy rates		• low levels of education
• most people in cities, have access to telecommunications		• little access to health care or telecommunications

LEVELS 2 AND 3: (Suggested time: 20 min.) Organize the class into two groups. Using the characteristics noted in the section, have one half write a what-I-did-today journal entry for a youngster in an imaginary developed country and the other half do the same for an imaginary developing country. Call on volunteers to read their entries. Lead a discussion on how the journal entries compare to the characteristics mentioned in the section. **COOPERATIVE LEARNING,** 🔲 **VERBAL-LINGUISTIC**

Across the Curriculum
MATH

Per Capita GDP A country's gross domestic product (GDP) indicates the total size of its economy. However, it may not be a clear indication of an average citizen's wealth. For that purpose per capita GDP is more useful.

For example, China's GDP for 1998 was estimated at $4.4 trillion, making China a major economic power. However, China's per capita GDP was only $3,600, because the GDP figure was divided among China's immense population of more than 1 billion. In contrast, Chile's GDP the same year was about $184.6 billion. With a population of about 15 million, Chile's per capita GDP was $12,500. This comparison indicates that an average citizen in Chile is probably better off financially than an average citizen in China.

Activity: Use an almanac to provide students with GDP and population figures for several countries. Have each student choose a country and divide its gross GDP by its population to calculate its per capita GDP. Ask them to write a brief paragraph describing the information they found.

Making a Living

Countries organize their economies in different ways. Most developed countries have an economic system called **free enterprise**. This system is organized around the production and distribution of goods and services. The United States operates under a free enterprise system. There are many benefits of this system. Companies are free to make whatever goods they wish. Employees can seek the highest wages for their work. People, rather than the government, control the factors of production. Factors of production are the things that determine what goods are produced in an economy. They include the natural resources that are available for making goods for sale. They also include the capital, or money, needed to pay for production and the labor needed to manufacture goods. The work of entrepreneurs is another factor of production. Entrepreneurs are people who start businesses in a free enterprise system.

Business owners in a free enterprise system sell their goods in a **market economy**. In such an economy, business owners and customers make decisions about what to make, sell, and buy. In contrast, the governments of some countries control the factors of production. The government decides what, and how much, will be produced. It also sets the prices of goods to be sold. This is called a **command economy**.

Some countries with a command economy are communist. Communism is a political system where the government owns almost all the factors of production. Only five countries in the world are communist today—China, Cuba, Laos, North Korea, and Vietnam.

The third type of economy is called a **tradition-based economy**. This type of economy is based on customs and tradition. Economic activities are based on laws, rituals, religious beliefs, or habits developed by the society long ago. The Mbuti people of the Democratic Republic of the Congo practice a tradition-based economy.

Large shopping malls, such as this one in New York City's Trump Tower, are common in countries that have market economies and a free enterprise system. Shoppers here can find a wide range of stores and goods concentrated in one area. ▼

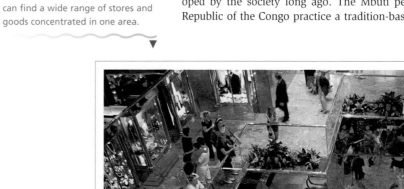

Teaching Objectives 3 and 4

ALL LEVELS: (Suggested time: 15 min.) Copy the following graphic organizer onto the chalkboard, omitting the blue answers. Use it to help students understand the connection between economics and politics. Point out that many countries do not follow the chart's model exactly but are a mixture of economic and political systems. **ESOL**

LEVELS 2 AND 3: (Suggested time: 20 min.) Have students formulate and write hypotheses to explain why developed countries are usually based on free enterprise and democracy and why the economies of developing countries are often controlled by the government. **LS VERBAL-LINGUISTIC**

ECONOMICS AND POLITICS

	Developed Countries	Developing Countries
Economy	free enterprise	government control, communism
Political System	democracy	communism

Another economic system is called a **mixed economy**. Most countries have this type of economy. Their economy is based on at least two of the economic systems you've learned about. For example, the United States has a market economy but certain things are regulated by the government.

Finally, some countries in tropical and subtropical regions have a **one-crop economy**. Their economy is based on a single crop, such as bananas, sugarcane, or cacao.

Buying and Selling International trade plays a large role in a country's economy. A country's **exports** include products sold to other countries. On the other hand, a country's **imports** include products a country buys from other countries. Imported products are usually things that aren't produced or available in the country that is buying the item. For example, Japan must import many agricultural products from other countries. Because Japan is a relatively small island, it does not have enough land suitable for crop growing.

Getting the Goods In international trade a condition known as **interdependence** occurs between countries when they depend on each other for resources or goods and services. An industrialized country may depend on the raw materials of a developing country. However, the developing country depends on the finished goods and technology of the industrialized country. For example, Mexico exports crude oil to the United States. In return, the United States exports computer equipment to Mexico.

✓ **READING CHECK:** (**Human Systems**) What are the four types of economies?
market, command, tradition-based, mixed, one-crop

▲
At a plantation in Costa Rica, workers wash bananas before shipping them around the world.

Interpreting the Visual Record
(Movement) **Why may having a one-crop economy cause problems for a country?**

The World's People • 57

Teaching Objective 4

LEVEL 1: (Suggested time: 15 min.) Lead a class discussion on why people live where they do in your state. Encourage students to consider issues such as climate, availability of jobs, cultural and educational opportunities, and proximity to transportation facilities. Then call on volunteers to suggest how state population patterns can be compared to entire countries. (People have the same basic needs and wants everywhere. More people live where their wants can be fulfilled most easily.) **ESOL**

LEVELS 2 AND 3: (Suggested time: 30 min.) In advance, prepare names of countries on slips of paper. Include densely populated nations (United Kingdom, Bangladesh, Japan) and sparsely populated ones (Mongolia, Australia, Canada). Have students pick a country and find population data on that country in the text or in other secondary sources. They should also look for information on the country's resources and climate. Then have students write a paragraph describing the influences on that country's population density. Ask students to use the Fast Facts features or a world almanac to calculate the population density for their chosen country.

Linking Past to Present

Population

Density and Disease In order to sustain themselves, many organisms that cause infectious diseases require large, dense populations like those found in cities.

In Rome, for example, about one-third of the population died of smallpox in A.D. 165, and measles caused 5000 deaths a day there in A.D. 251. In the 1300s the Black Death swept through densely populated cities from China to Europe. This disease–borne by flea-infested rodents–killed up to one-quarter of Europe's population between 1346 and 1352. The influenza epidemic of 1918–19 killed 21 million people worldwide–more than twice the number killed in World War I.

Today's jet travel provides rapid transit for contagious diseases. Some scientists warn that overuse of antibiotics and the immunity that can result have made our crowded cities vulnerable to another serious epidemic.

The regions on this map that are shaded dark purple have a high population density.

Interpreting the Map How do you think the patterns on this map will change over the next 100 years? Why?

World Population Density

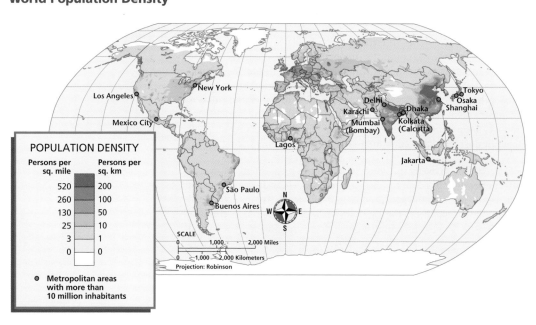

POPULATION DENSITY

Persons per sq. mile	Persons per sq. km
520	200
260	100
130	50
25	10
3	1
0	0

● Metropolitan areas with more than 10 million inhabitants

SCALE
0   1,000   2,000 Miles
0   1,000   2,000 Kilometers
Projection: Robinson

Six Billion and Counting

In 1960, the world's population hit three billion. Since then the world's population has grown to over six billion. More than 90 percent of this population growth was in the developing countries of Africa, Latin America, and Asia. More than a quarter of the world's six billion people are between the ages of 10 and 24. About 86 percent of these young people live in developing countries.

World of People Some countries are very crowded. Others are only thinly populated. People who study these differences in the world's population are called demographers. They collect information, or demographics, which include population size, and the ages and gender of the population. They also determine **population density**, or how many people live closely together. Population density is calculated by dividing a country's population by its area—stated in either square miles or square kilometers. When a country has an extremely high population density, it may be suffering from **overpopulation**. An overpopulated country usually cannot support its people without outside help.

People are spread unevenly across Earth. Some places are crowded with people, while others are empty. Where do most of the world's people live? Asia is the world's most populated region. China and India both have more than a billion people! In addition, Indonesia, Pakistan, Japan, and Bangladesh each have over 100 million people.

CLOSE

To illustrate the meaning of 6 billion, the approximate total world population, challenge students to calculate how long it would take for 6 billion seconds to go by (approximately 190 years).

REVIEW, ASSESS, RETEACH

Have students complete the Section Review. Then refer them to the list of vocabulary terms. Call on students to create a sentence that relates the first term to the second, then the second to the third, and so on. Then have students complete Daily Quiz 3.2.

Have students complete Main Idea Activity S2. Then have students work in pairs to create web diagrams to illustrate the section's main points.
ESOL, COOPERATIVE LEARNING

Growing Pains Births add to a country's population. Deaths subtract from it. The number of births per 1,000 people in a year is called the **birthrate**. Similarly, the **death rate** is the annual number of deaths per 1,000 people. The birthrate minus the death rate equals the rate of natural population increase. This number is expressed as a percentage. The birthrate in developing countries is more than double that of industrialized countries. For example, the birthrates of Niger and Bulgaria are very different. Niger has the world's highest birthrate. Most women in Niger have about seven children. On the other hand, Bulgaria has the world's lowest birthrate. Most Bulgarian women only have one child.

On the Move Throughout history, people have moved from place to place looking for better opportunities. People are constantly moving within their own country or across international borders. This movement of people is called **migration**. One person or a group migrate either for a short period of time or permanently. There are several different types of migration. Someone who leaves one place for another is called an **emigrant**.

On the other hand, an **immigrant** is someone arriving from another country. A migrant worker is someone looking for work by regularly moving from place to place. Some people move to other countries for opportunities they don't have in their homeland. Most people emigrate for economic reasons.

✓ **READING CHECK:** (*Human Systems*) What region of the world has the most people? Asia

Section Review 2

Define and explain: gross national product, gross domestic product, industrialized countries, literacy rate, developing countries, third-world countries, free enterprise, market economy, command economy, tradition-based economy, mixed economy, one-crop economy, exports, imports, interdependence, birthrate, death rate, population density, overpopulation, migration, emigrant, immigrant

Reading for the Main Idea

1. (*Environment and Society*) What geographic features influence population density?
2. (*Human Systems*) What characteristics do developed nations share?

Critical Thinking

3. **Finding the Main Idea** What are the different economic systems? Describe each.
4. **Drawing Inferences and Conclusions** What causes overpopulation and how can it be prevented?

Organizing What You Know

5. **Summarizing** Copy the following graphic organizer. Use it to study your local community and classify the businesses in your area.

Primary Industries	Secondary Industries	Tertiary Industries	Quaternary Industries
●	●	●	●
●	●	●	●

go.hrw.com **Homework Practice Online** Keyword: SK5 HP3

The World's People • 59

EXTEND

No longer does one have to live in a large city to be employed by a large company. Have interested students conduct research on the effects of telecommuting—using an electronic linkup with a central office to work out of one's home—on population densities in the United States. Students may want to concentrate on one of your state's major cities and the towns nearby. Have students report their findings in a bar graph.

BLOCK SCHEDULING

Section 3 Global Connections

Read to Discover

1. What is globalization? How are people around the world connected?
2. Why are refugees a global problem? What causes famine? How do people in need get help?

Vocabulary

globalization
popular culture
refugees
famine
humanitarian aid
drought

Reading Strategy

READING ORGANIZER Before you read, create a spider map. Label the center oval Global Connections. Draw seven legs and label them Technology, Cities, Travel, Trade, Sports, Refugees, and Assistance. As you read, write what you learn about these topics beneath each of the legs.

A Buddhist monk in Cambodia may use this laptop computer to log on to the Internet.

Living in a Small World

In just seconds an e-mail message sent by a teenager in India beams all the way to a friend in the United States. A businesswoman in Singapore takes a call from her cell phone from an investor in New York. With just a few taps on a computer's keyboard, anyone in the world can also immediately access the Internet. These are all examples of how small our world has become with the use of cell phones, e-mail, the Internet, and satellite television.

Global Tech Thanks to these technologies, people around the world communicate and do business with each other faster than anyone ever thought possible. **Globalization** is the term most often used to describe how time and distance in the world seem to be shrinking. Globalization is also used to describe how countries are increasingly linked through **popular culture** and a global economy. Popular culture includes things people across the world share such as movies, literature, music, clothing, and food. For example, you can find the American restaurant, McDonald's, in almost every major world city today. Kids throughout the world exchange Pokemon trading cards from Japan. Millions read Harry Potter.

Section 3

Objectives

1. Define globalization and describe how people around the world are connected.
2. Explore refugees as a global problem, famine, and how people in need get help.

FOCUS

Bellringer

Write the following questions on the chalkboard: *How many different brands can you write down that are for products made outside the United States? What kinds of products are they?* (Students will probably list many brands of electronic equipment, cars, and athletic shoes.) Discuss responses. Point out that these products illustrate one way in which countries are connected today—through trade. Tell students that in Section 3 they will learn more about these and other connections.

Building Vocabulary

Write the vocabulary terms on the chalkboard and have students find the definitions in the text. Point out that **globalization** and **popular culture** may be connected in some cases. For example, a singer or sports star from another country represents globalization and is a leading figure in the world of popular culture.

Speaking Globally Almost 6,000 languages are spoken today. English, however, is the language of globalization. As a result, a quarter of the world's population speaks English for global business, communications, higher education, diplomacy, aviation, the Internet, science, popular music, entertainment and international travel. American news channels and movies are seen everywhere. For example, CNN uses satellites to broadcast in English to millions of TV sets around the world.

Cultural Centers Even with fast communication, globalization wouldn't be possible without major cities. As transportation and cultural centers, cities provide the perfect place for different people to exchange goods and ideas. For example, Miami is sometimes called the "Gateway to Latin America." As an international port and multicultural city, many companies that operate in Latin America are headquartered in Miami. Many other global cities also depend on their geographical location for international business. Seattle and San Francisco have economic ties to major Asian cities located across the Pacific Ocean, such as Tokyo and Hong Kong.

This restaurant in Ecuador provides visitors with Internet access.

Ships dock in Miami, Florida.
Interpreting the Visual Record
Movement What in this photo suggests that Miami is a major international city?

USING ILLUSTRATIONS

E-Travel Focus students' attention on the photo of the Internet café on this page. Point out that modern telecommunications have made international travel much easier than it was a few decades ago. Ask students why this may be so. Remind them of advertisements or commercials related to the travel industry that they have seen. (Possible answers: Tourists can buy tickets, make hotel reservations, and get information about destinations online. Upon arrival, they can use ATM machines for cash instead of traveler's checks. Internet cafés or the tourist's own laptop can provide instant connections to friends, family, and coworkers back home.) Lead a discussion about how "e-travel" may affect students' interest in international travel.

◄**Visual Record Answer**
commercial and cruise ships, extensive dock facilities

TEACH

Teaching Objective 1
LEVEL 1: (Suggested time: 30 min.) Provide several copies of national newspapers or the main section of your local newspaper. Have students work in pairs to find examples of globalization in the newspapers. **ESOL, COOPERATIVE LEARNING**

LEVEL 2: You will need extra time for this activity. Point out that increased globalization has some critics. Provide research materials so students can conduct research on the criticism. (Critics charge that globalization is responsible for the eradication of native cultures, child labor abuses, and environmental damage, among other problems.) When students have com-

pleted their research, stage a debate about the benefits and costs of globalization. Ask each student to write a paragraph summarizing the arguments presented in the debate. **LS LOGICAL-MATHEMATICAL**

LEVEL 3: (Suggested time: 30 min.) Have students use what they have learned from the Level 2 activity to draw editorial cartoons about globalization. **LS VISUAL-SPATIAL**

FOOD FESTIVAL

Gobbling Up Globalization
The shrinkage of our world is evident in the expansion of our supermarkets. All kinds of foods from around the world—fresh, frozen, dried, canned, and packaged—flow into U.S. grocery stores. Shoppers in communities lacking big supermarkets can order many exotic foodstuffs from online suppliers.

Without telling students the purpose of their choice, have each student select a different country. Then challenge students to find a food product from that country in the local supermarket or from an online supplier. If circumstances permit, encourage students to bring their foods to class. Or, students may simply bring to class printed information about the products from the Internet.

Visual Record Answer ▶

because it combines both English and Japanese and celebrates a Japanese athlete playing for a U.S. team

Fans of Hideki Matsui—a professional baseball player from Japan—show their support as they watch him play for the New York Yankees.
Interpreting the Visual Record
(Movement) **How is this sign an example of globalization?**

▼

Travel Ills There's a downside, however, to life in a well-connected world. You can board a plane at any major airport today and travel to just about anywhere in the world. Some people, however, carry more than just their luggage on to these flights. They can also carry diseases. For example, in 2003, one woman who didn't realize she was infected with the contagious disease called SARS, traveled from China to Toronto, Canada. As she made contact with several people in Toronto, they too came down with the disease. However, steps are now taken to prevent people with contagious diseases from boarding international flights.

Quick Trades Globalization not only links the world's people, it also connects businesses and countries. For centuries, people have traded. But, never as fast as today. Through the use of the Internet it is quick and simple to order goods from anywhere in the world. For example, a shoe retailer in Chicago can find a Web site that links them to someone in China who makes the sneakers they need. The order is then flown to Chicago the following day. That afternoon the sneakers are sold to customers.

Made in the USA? Check the label on your shoes, other clothing, or book bag to see where it's made. It probably doesn't say the United States. Why? Most clothing and a lot of electronic equipment are imported to the United States from other countries. Many international companies build their factories in places where workers will work for less money than American workers. By hiring cheap labor, these companies lower their manufacturing costs. As a result, these products usually have a lower price tag than products made in the United States.

World Sports You've already learned that money, ideas, and goods are traded in the global economy. But, did you also know that people could be exchanged as well? For example, more and more baseball players from Latin America and Asia are now playing professionally in the United States. In addition, many American and European soccer teams frequently trade players across the Atlantic.

✓ **READING CHECK:**
(Human Systems) What are some examples of globalization?

spread of English language, use of telecommunications, spread of popular culture, growth of international cities, global trade, global trade in athletes

Teaching Objective 2

ALL LEVELS: (Suggested time: 45 min.) Pair students and have students re-read the "Helping People in Need" subsection aloud to each other. Then have them design book covers for an imaginary book of the same title. Pairs should include both text and pictures in their designs. **ESOL, LS VISUAL-SPATIAL**

ALL LEVELS: (Suggested time: 15 min.) Lead a class discussion about whether individuals in the United States can help refugees and victims of other problems in foreign countries and, if so, how to do so. Continue with a discussion of how nonprofit organizations can pool the efforts and funds of individuals, making the aid more effective. **LS INTERPERSONAL**

Helping People in Need

In a smaller world, global problems also connect the world's people. What happens in one part of the world affects the entire planet. Millions of people today suffer without life's necessities. In response to these problems, the global community tries to help as many people as possible.

Searching for Home One of the major global problems today are the 14 million people who seek refuge in other countries. These **refugees** require food, shelter, and help with finding jobs. Many international agencies help refugees start new lives. Unlike immigrants, however, refugees flee their countries because of persecution, war, or economic reasons. Some refugees even eventually become citizens in the country they settle in. For example, many Cuban refugees and their families are now United States citizens.

Hungry Planet A great shortage of food, or **famine**, affects millions of people throughout the world. International relief agencies provide **humanitarian aid** to famine areas. This aid includes medicine and millions of pounds of grain and other foods. These efforts, however, sometimes are not enough to relieve the problem. Today in Ethiopia more than 12 million people are at risk for starvation. The lack of rain, or **drought**, has prevented farmers from growing enough food to feed their country's population.

✓ **READING CHECK:** (*Human Systems*) What are some reasons why refugees flee their homeland? persecution, war, or economic reasons

Movement In the late 1990s unrest in Kosovo, Yugoslavia, disrupted the lives of hundreds of thousands of ethnic Albanians. Many people were forced from their homes. Here, refugees in neighboring Macedonia wait to be transported to nearby transition camps.

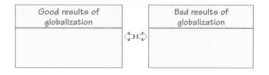

Section Review 3

Define and explain: globalization, popular culture, refugees, famine, humanitarian aid, drought

Reading for the Main Idea
1. (*Human Systems*) What are some effects of globalization?
2. (*Human Systems*) How does humanitarian aid help people?

Critical Thinking
3. **Drawing Conclusions** How has globalization made the world smaller?

go.hrw.com | **Homework Practice Online**
Keyword: SK5 HP3

4. **Making Predictions** What will happen if the number of refugees continues to grow?

Organizing What You Know
5. **Contrasting** Copy the following graphic organizer. Use it to discuss two arguments about globalization.

Good results of globalization		Bad results of globalization
	⟺	

The World's People • 63

CLOSE

Ask students how decisions they make now and in the future may reflect or affect globalization.

REVIEW, ASSESS, RETEACH

Have students complete the Section Review. Then have students work in groups to use the spider maps referenced in the Reading Strategy at the beginning of this section to review its main concepts. Then have students complete Daily Quiz 3.3. **COOPERATIVE LEARNING**

Have students complete Main Idea Activity S3. Then have students write one sentence per paragraph to summarize that paragraph.
LS VERBAL-LINGUISTIC

EXTEND

Some of the cheap foreign-made products we buy are made by children. Have interested students conduct research on Iqbal Masih, a Pakistani youngster who, from his own experiences as an exploited child worker, spoke out against child labor practices. Iqbal was killed to silence him. This tragic story inspired a Canadian boy named Craig Kielburger to found Free the Children, an organization that tries to help the millions of children who work long hours under miserable conditions. Ask students to report on the current state of child labor to the class. **BLOCK SCHEDULING**

Define and Identify
For definitions, see the glossary.

Review the Main Ideas

20. People study culture, which is a learned system of shared beliefs, to understand the different ways in which people live all over the world. (NGS 10)

21. People move from one place to another and bring their ways or beliefs to another culture.

22. history and environment

23. subsistence agriculture—produces only enough food to feed the farmer's family; commercial agriculture—large farms, often run by companies, produce food for many people

24. GNP—measures all goods and services a nation produces, even those manufactured in foreign countries; GDP—measures goods and services produced in a country

25. third-world countries—developing nations with some economic growth; fourth-world countries—those with no economic growth

26. to acquire things that aren't produced or available in the country importing the items

27. More and more people speak English, the language of globalization. They also use electronic technologies such as the Internet to communicate around the world.

28. Refugees flee their countries because of persecution, war, economic problems or other troubles; immigrants move of their own choice in search of economic opportunity.

Think Critically

29. People may use someone's appearance, which is more closely connected to his or her race, to define the person's ethnic group.

CHAPTER 3 Review and Practice

Define and Identify
Idenfity each of the following:

1. culture
2. ethnic groups
3. ethnocentrism
4. domestication
5. subsistence agriculture
6. civilization
7. gross national product
8. literacy rate
9. third-world countries
10. mixed economy
11. imports
12. birthrate
13. population density
14. migration
15. immigrant
16. globalization
17. popular culture
18. refugees
19. humanitarian aid

Review the Main Ideas

20. What is culture, and why should people study it?
21. How does diffusion occur?
22. What are two important factors that influence the way people meet basic needs?
23. What is the difference between subsistence and commercial agriculture?

24. How does gross national product differ from gross domestic product?
25. How do third-world countries differ from fourth-world nations?
26. Why do countries import products?
27. How has globalization affected how people communicate?
28. How do refugees differ from immigrants?

Think Critically

29. **Drawing Inferences and Conclusions** Why are ethnic groups sometimes confused with races?
30. **Identifying Cause and Effect** How did the development of agriculture affect the global population?
31. **Comparing and Contrasting** How do industrialized countries differ from developing countries?
32. **Summarizing** How have new technologies helped to create a global culture?
33. **Finding the Main Idea** How has globalization changed how countries trade with each other?

Map Activity

34. On a separate sheet of paper, match the letters on the map with their correct labels.
    Buddhism
    Christianity—Eastern Orthodox
    Christianity—Protestant
    Christianity—Roman Catholic
    Hinduism
    Islam

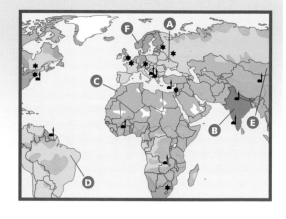

30. After the development of agriculture, the global population increased as the food supply increased.

31. industrialized countries—rely on industry, have educated populace, access to health care and communications; developing countries—agriculture or primary industries, poorly educated populace, little access to health and telecommunications

32. Technologies such as e-mail, the Internet, and satellite television have made it easier for people to share popular culture all over the globe.

33. Trade is faster, and some goods are available at lower prices.

Map Activity
34. **A.** Christianity—Eastern Orthodox
    B. Hinduism
    C. Islam
    D. Christianity—Roman Catholic
    E. Buddhism
    F. Christianity—Protestant

Writing Activity

Research the economy of your community. Has the economy grown or declined in the last 10 years? Why? What goods are exported from your community? What goods are imported to your community? Write about what you learn from your research. Then write about how you think your community might change in the future.

internet connect

Internet Activity: go.hrw.com
KEYWORD: SK5 GT3

Choose a topic to explore online:
- Visit famous buildings and monuments around the world.
- Compare facts about life in different countries.
- Examine world population growth.

go.hrw.com

Social Studies Skills Practice

Interpreting Cartoons

Study the following cartoon. Then answer the questions.

MARTIN GUHL

1. What is the main idea of this cartoon?
2. Why is the Earth in the middle of a maze?
3. Does the cartoonist believe it is difficult or easy to connect with people around the world by using the Internet? Why?
4. How is this cartoon an example of globalization?

Analyzing Primary Sources

Read the following quote from French-American film director Jean-Marc Barr. Then answer the questions.

"We believe Europe is going to exist because the English language allows it to culturally. Never on this continent has there been a language that all the classes can speak, from a Polish man to a Spaniard to an Icelandic. My biggest and most rewarding events in my life have been because I have been able to speak English with people all over the world."

1. What advantage does Barr see for Europe as English is used more?
2. Why would a film director such as Barr be especially interested in language?
3. Based on your knowledge of culture, why might some Europeans resist the use of English?
4. How do you think Barr feels about globalization?

The World's People • 65

Writing Activity

Answers will vary, but the information included should be consistent with text material. Students' predictions should be supported by logical arguments. Use Rubric 37, Writing Assignments, to evaluate student work.

Interpreting Cartoons

1. Once you find your way in the Internet you can find anything in the world.
2. Reaching the information may be difficult, but gaining the whole world makes it worthwhile.
3. By drawing a maze, the cartoonist shows that it may be hard to find what you are looking for on the Internet.
4. It shows how anyone can make global connections by using the Internet.

Analyzing Primary Sources

1. English provides a common language for all Europeans, no matter what their first language may be.
2. If more people can understand the language used in a movie, the potential audience will be much greater.
3. They may see English as replacing their native language and, in the process, destroying their native cultures.
4. He seems to feel that globalization is a good thing because it increases communication.

internet connect

GO TO: go.hrw.com
KEYWORD: SG5 CH3
FOR: a guide to using the Internet in your classroom

CHAPTER 3 REVIEW AND ASSESSMENT RESOURCES

Reproducible
- Readings in World Geography, History, and Culture 9 and 10
- Critical Thinking Activity 3
- Vocabulary Activity 3

Technology
- Chapter 3 Test Generator (on the One-Stop Planner)
- HRW Go site

- Audio CD Program, Chapter 3

Reinforcement, Review, and Assessment
- Chapter 3 Review and Practice
- Chapter Summaries and Review

- Chapter 3 Test
- Chapter 3 Test for English Language Learners and Special-Needs Students
- Unit 1 Test
- Unit 1 Test for English Language Learners and Special-Needs Students

GEOGRAPHY SIDELIGHT

Physical, political, economic, and cultural changes can affect the way we define regions and draw their boundaries.

Physical changes are often slow to occur, but they are important. Beaches erode. Rivers run dry. Forests grow up on abandoned farmland. Political changes also bring regional redefinitions. For example, one large country may break up into several smaller ones, or small countries may unite to form a larger country.

Economic changes occur as different resources or economic activities decline or increase in importance. For example, a community once known for its manufacturing industries may now be part of an area that focuses on services. Finally, changing cultural characteristics can reshape regions as people of various language, religious, or ethnic groups move across regional boundaries.

Critical Thinking: What factors affect how we define regions?

Answer: physical, political, economic, and cultural changes

➤ **This Focus On Regions feature addresses National Geography Standards 5 and 6.**

What is a Region?

Think about where you live, where you go to school, and where you shop. These places are all part of your neighborhood. In geographic terms, your neighborhood is a region. A region is an area that has common features that make it different from surrounding areas.

What regions do you live in? You live on a continent, in a country, and in a state. These are all regions that can be mapped.

Regions can be divided into smaller regions called subregions. For example, Africa is a major world region. Africa's subregions include North Africa, West Africa, East Africa, central Africa, and southern Africa. Each subregion can be divided into even smaller subregions.

Regional Characteristics Regions can be based on physical, political, economic, or cultural characteristics. Physical regions are based on Earth's natural features, such as continents, landforms, and climates. Political regions are based on countries and their subregions, such as states, provinces, and cities. Economic regions are based on money-making activities such as agriculture or industries. Cultural regions are based on features such as language, religion, or ethnicity.

▲
East Africa is a subregion of Africa. It is an area of plateaus, rolling hills, and savanna grasslands.

FOCUS ON REGIONS

Identifying Local Regions

Ask students to write down regions in which they live, go to school, shop, and pursue other daily activities. Call on volunteers for their responses. Record them on the chalkboard, placing the largest regions (continent, country) at the top and placing smaller regions (neighborhoods, boroughs, blocks) at the bottom. Note at what point descriptions of regions where students live differ from each other (probably at the town or neighborhood level). Draw a line separating these smaller divisions from the larger ones. Have students work in small groups to draw large maps showing these local regions and their relationships.

Major World Regions

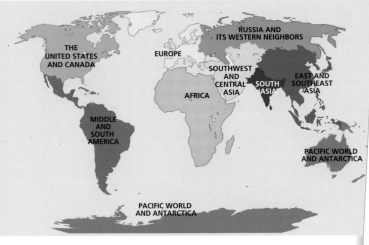

Understanding What You Read

Answers
1. Regions can be based on physical, political, economic, or cultural characteristics.

2. The three basic types of regions are: formal, functional, and perceived.

▲
The international border between Kenya and Tanzania is a clearly defined regional boundary.

Regional Boundaries All regions have boundaries, or borders. Boundaries are where the features of one region meet the features of a different region. Some boundaries, such as coastlines or country borders, can be shown as lines on a map. Other regional boundaries are less clear.

Transition zones are areas where the features of one region change gradually to the features of a different region. For example, when a city's suburbs expand into rural areas, a transition zone forms. In the transition zone, it may be hard to find the boundary between rural and urban areas.

Types of Regions There are three basic types of regions. The first is a formal region. Formal regions are based on one or more common features. For example, Japan is a formal region. Its people share a common government, language, and culture.

The second type of region is a functional region. Functional regions are based on movement and activities that connect different places. For example, Paris, France, is a functional region. It is based on the goods, services, and people that move throughout the city. A shopping center or an airport might also be a functional region.

The third type of region is a perceived region. Perceived regions are based on people's shared feelings and beliefs. For example, the neighborhood where you live may be a perceived region.

The three basic types of regions overlap to form complex world regions. The world can be divided into nine major world regions (see map above). Each has general features that make it different from the other major world regions. These differences include physical, cultural, economic, historical, and political features.

Understanding What You Read

1. Regions can be based on what types of characteristics?
2. What are the three basic types of regions?

Going Further: Thinking Critically

Have students compare their maps. Note areas where regions overlap and ask students how they might describe these areas (transition zones). Also have them look at how maps of the same regions have different boundaries. Point out that these are perceived regions. The word *perceived* has to do with getting information from one's senses. Therefore, perceived regions differ according to how one "sees" the region. Ask students how they decided on the boundaries that they drew. Use their responses to illustrate the differences in perceived regions. Finally, review formal and functional regions and ask whether any regions shown on the maps fulfill the definitions.

PRACTICING THE SKILL

1. The prime meridian extends through western Europe (England, western France, northeastern Spain) and western Africa (Algeria, Mali, Burkina Faso, Togo, Ghana).

2. Students' sketch maps should show the equator, Tropic of Cancer, Tropic of Capricorn, prime meridian, and continents in their approximate locations.

3. Answers will vary. Students might notice that the international date line does not cross any major landmasses, the Southern Hemisphere has much more water than land, South America extends farther south than Africa, or other similar facts.

➤ This GeoSkills feature addresses National Geography Standards 1, 2, and 3.

Geo SKILLS

Building Skills for Life: Drawing Mental Maps

We create maps in our heads of all kinds of places—our homes, schools, communities, country, and the world. Some of these places we know well. Others we have only heard about. These images we carry in our heads are shaped by what we see and experience. They are also influenced by what we learn from news reports or other sources. Geographers call the maps that we carry around in our heads mental maps.

We use mental maps to organize spatial information about people and places. For example, our mental maps help us move from classroom to classroom at school or get to a friend's home. A mental map of the United States helps us list the states we would pass through driving from New York City to Miami.

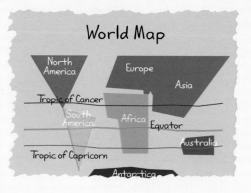

World Map

North America · Europe · Asia · Tropic of Cancer · South America · Africa · Equator · Australia · Tropic of Capricorn · Antarctica

We use our mental maps of places when we draw sketch maps. A sketch map showing the relationship between places and the relative size of places can be drawn using very simple shapes. For example, triangles and rectangles could be used to sketch a map of the world. This quickly drawn map would show the relative size and position of the continents.

Think about some simple ways we could make our map of the world more detailed. Adding the equator, Tropic of Cancer, and Tropic of Capricorn would be one way. Look at a map of the world in your textbook's Atlas. Note that the bulge in the continent of Africa is north of the equator. Also note that all of Asia is north of the equator. Next note that the Indian subcontinent extends south from the Tropic of Cancer. About half of Australia is located north of the Tropic of Capricorn. As your knowledge of the world increases, your mental map will become even more detailed.

PRACTICING THE SKILL

1. Look at the maps in your textbook's Atlas. Where does the prime meridian fall in relation to the continents?

2. On a separate sheet of paper, sketch a simple map of the world from memory. First draw the equator, Tropic of Cancer, Tropic of Capricorn, and prime meridian. Then sketch in the continents. You can use circles, rectangles, and triangles.

3. Draw a second map of the world from memory. This time, draw the international date line in the center of your map. Add the equator, Tropic of Cancer, and Tropic of Capricorn. Now sketch in the continents. What do you notice?

GEOSKILLS

Going Further: Thinking Critically

Prepare two sets of words on slips of paper. One set should consist of action words, such as *go, fly, run, skip, dig, walk, swim, climb,* and *drive.* The other set should consist of nouns having to do with places, such as *tree, house, cliff, beach, road, river, mountain, church, rock, cave, highway,* and *ocean.* Students will draw at least one word of each type from a hat. Using their chosen words at least once, students should write travel or adventure stories set in familiar places. You may want to require that the stories be a certain length or that the students mention a certain number of places in their stories. Tell students that when they finish they should be able to draw maps of the settings through which the characters travel. When all the students have completed their stories, have them exchange papers to draw maps of each other's story settings.

HANDS *on* GEOGRAPHY

Mental maps are personal. They change as we learn more about the world and the places in it. For example, they can include details about places that are of interest only to you.

What is your mental map of your neighborhood like? Sketch your mental map of your neighborhood. Include the features that you think are important and that help you find your way around. These guidelines will help you get started.

1. Decide what your map will show. Choose boundaries so that you do not sketch more than you need to.

2. Determine how much space you will need for your map. Things that are the same size in reality should be about the same size on your map.

3. Decide on and note the orientation of your map. Most maps use a directional indicator. On most maps, north is at the top.

4. Label reference points so that others who look at your map can quickly and easily figure out what they are looking at. For example, a major street or your school might be a reference point.

5. Decide how much detail your map will show. The larger the area you want to represent, the less detail you will need.

6. Use circles, rectangles, and triangles if you do not know the exact shape of an area.

7. As you think of them, fill in more details, such as names of places or major land features.

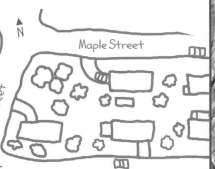

Lab Report

1. What are the most important features on your map? Why did you include them?

2. Compare your sketch map to a published map of the area. How does it differ?

3. At the bottom, list three ways that you could make your sketch map more complete.

UNIT OBJECTIVES

1. Describe how the physical geography and economic geography of Southwest Asia affect ways of life there.

2. Explore the development of ancient and modern cultures in the region.

3. Trace the history and development of religion in the region, and analyze the role that religion has played in events in Southwest Asia.

4. Identify the political, social, and environmental challenges facing the countries of Southwest Asia.

5. Understand the significance of the region's strategic location and natural resources.

6. Use special-purpose maps to interpret the relationships among climate, population patterns, and economic resources in Southwest Asia.

UNIT 2

Southwest and Central Asia

Bottle trees, Yemen

USING THE ILLUSTRATIONS

Direct students' attention to the photographs on these pages. Point out the young Israeli girls in the center. If students in your school wear uniforms, you may want to ask students to compare theirs with the uniforms the Israeli girls are wearing.

Ask students how they think the bottle trees have adapted to Yemen's rocky terrain and dry climate. (The trunks store water. Students may also suggest that because the trees have relatively few leaves they lose less water through evaporation.)

Ask which photo relates to religion. (Students should identify the family preparing a feast.) Tell students that Southwest Asia is the birthplace of three of the world's major religions—Judaism, Christianity, and Islam. Focus students' attention on the photo showing a family preparing a feast. Tell students similar photos could have been taken in any one of several countries, including the United States, because Islamic families around the world fast during the month of Ramadan. Feasts that mark the end of the fast are also common. You may want to read the More from the Field feature about Ramadan on the opposite page aloud to the students.

An Exchange Student in Turkey

Sara Lewis was an American exchange student in Turkey. Here she describes how teenagers live in Istanbul, Turkey's largest city, and the month-long fast of Ramadan. **WHAT DO YOU THINK?** *What would it be like to live in a place where you can see the remains of thousands of years of history?*

The people of Istanbul are very traditional and family-oriented, but today's Turk also has European-style tastes. Turkish teens go dancing and hang out in coffeehouses. All around them, though, are reminders of the past. There are many monuments left over from Greek, Roman, Byzantine, and Ottoman times.

Islam plays a big part in daily life. Five times every day I can hear the people being called to prayer. For more than a month, my host parents fasted during Ramadan. They didn't eat or drink anything while the sun was up. My host sister and I fasted for one day. By the time the sun went down we were starving! I'm glad we weren't expected to continue the fast. Then we shopped for new clothes. It is the custom to wear new clothes to the feast at the end of Ramadan. The fresh clothes seem to stand for the cleanliness one achieves during the month of fasting.

Family preparing food for the end of Ramadan

Jewish girls, Zefat, Israel

Understanding Primary Sources

1. What do modern Turkish teenagers do for fun?

2. How is Ramadan observed in Turkey?

Sooty falcon

MORE FROM THE FIELD

Islam teaches that Muslims should fast during Ramadan, the ninth month of the Islamic calendar. Muslims fast during Ramadan for several reasons. Fasting is said to help people focus on their spiritual lives, to teach self-control, and to promote compassion for the poor.

When Ramadan ends, Muslims celebrate 'Eid-ul-Fitr, or the Festival of Fast-Breaking. People wear their best clothes and attend morning prayers. People wish each other *Eid mubarak*—"a blessed 'Eid". It is customary to give to charity. Often children receive gifts.

Activity: Ask students to find information about how Muslims in your community or state observe Ramadan. Have them write newspaper articles to describe local observances.

Understanding Primary Sources
Answers
1. go dancing and hang out in coffeehouses
2. through fasting, wearing new clothes to the feast

CHAPTERS

PEOPLE IN THE PROFILE

The elevation profile crosses northern Saudi Arabia and southern Iraq, homeland of the nomadic Bedouins. A traditional Bedouin home is a long, low black tent made of woven goat hair. There are few household items besides carpets, utensils, and a portable stove. Long robes of thick material, a head covering, and sandals form the basic wardrobe. Milk products, dried fruit, and grains from villagers are staple foods.

In the 1900s life began to change for the Bedouin. The countries where they wandered exercised more control over their movement. The Bedouin had to reduce their raids and pursue peaceful commercial relationships. Many settled in urban areas. Airplanes, telephones, trucks, and other by-products of oil wealth continue to change Bedouin ways.

Critical Thinking: How did the Bedouin belief system affect their use of technology, and how has this changed as a result of their relationship with surrounding cultures?

Answer: Bedouins were nomads who did not use technology until countries where they lived began to control their movements and influence their use of technology.

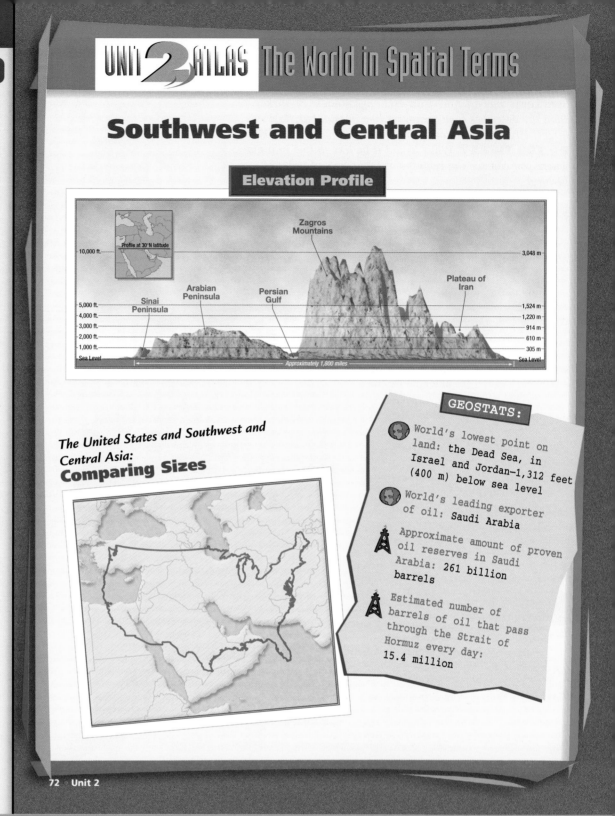

UNIT 2 ATLAS The World in Spatial Terms

Southwest and Central Asia

Elevation Profile

Profile at 30°N latitude

Zagros Mountains

Arabian Peninsula

Sinai Peninsula

Persian Gulf

Plateau of Iran

10,000 ft. — 3,048 m
5,000 ft. — 1,524 m
4,000 ft. — 1,220 m
3,000 ft. — 914 m
2,000 ft. — 610 m
1,000 ft. — 305 m
Sea Level — Sea Level

Approximately 1,800 miles

The United States and Southwest and Central Asia:
Comparing Sizes

GEOSTATS:

World's lowest point on land: the Dead Sea, in Israel and Jordan—1,312 feet (400 m) below sea level

World's leading exporter of oil: Saudi Arabia

Approximate amount of proven oil reserves in Saudi Arabia: 261 billion barrels

Estimated number of barrels of oil that pass through the Strait of Hormuz every day: 15.4 million

OVERVIEW

In this unit, students will learn about the geography, ancient history, and rapid modernization of the region often referred to as the Middle East.

Some of the world's earliest civilizations developed in the Fertile Crescent, in what is now Iraq. Wave after wave of conquerors have invaded the region. In the A.D. 600s Islam spread from the Arabian Peninsula across much of the area. Tensions between major Islamic groups date back to the religion's early years and continue today.

Two other major faiths—Judaism and Christianity—also originated in Southwest Asia. Over the centuries there have been many conflicts among followers of the three religions.

Arid and semiarid climates dominate Southwest Asia. Farming is possible only in limited areas, so nomadic herding is common. Overall population density is low.

The discovery of immense oil reserves in the early 1900s changed the region's economy dramatically. Some countries, particularly those along the Persian Gulf, have become very wealthy. Oil wealth has brought political power to several Southwest Asian countries. However, many people still live in poverty.

Southwest and Central Asia:
Physical

internet connect

ONLINE ATLAS
GO TO: go.hrw.com
KEYWORD: SK5 MapsU2
FOR: Web links to online maps of the region

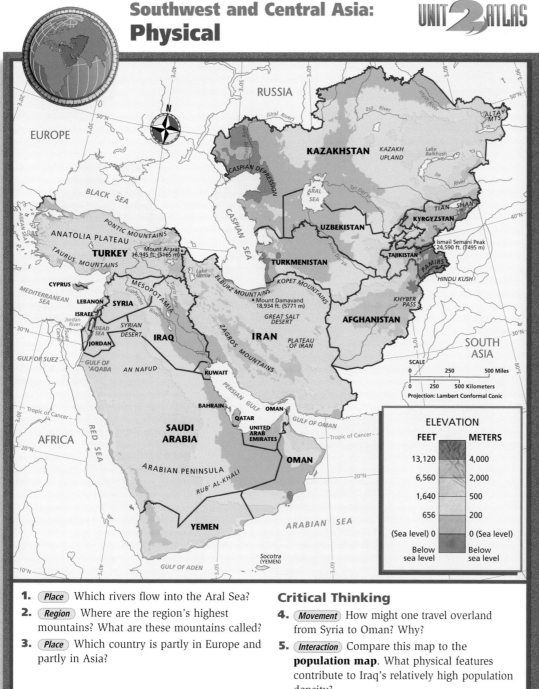

1. (Place) Which rivers flow into the Aral Sea?

2. (Region) Where are the region's highest mountains? What are these mountains called?

3. (Place) Which country is partly in Europe and partly in Asia?

Critical Thinking

4. (Movement) How might one travel overland from Syria to Oman? Why?

5. (Interaction) Compare this map to the **population map**. What physical features contribute to Iraq's relatively high population density?

Physical Map
Answers
1. Syr Dar'ya, Amu Dar'ya
2. far eastern part of the region; Pamirs, Hindu Kush, Tian Shan
3. Turkey

Critical Thinking
4. down the Euphrates River and through the Persian Gulf and Gulf of Oman; avoids deserts
5. the Tigris and Euphrates rivers, a large area of open plains

Southwest and Central Asia • 73

USING THE PHYSICAL MAP

Focus students' attention on the **physical map** on this page. Most of Southwest Asia lacks certain physical features that are important to other places the class has studied. What are these features? (major rivers and lakes) Call on a volunteer to point out where in Southwest Asia the lack of water appears to be most severe. (Arabian Peninsula) Ask students to suggest what residents of the region might do to increase their access to water. You may want to remind students about desalinization plants at this point.

Your Classroom Time Line

These are the major dates and time periods for this unit. Have students enter them on the time line you created earlier. You may want to watch for these dates as students progress through the unit.

500s B.C. The Persian Empire is established; Persians conquer Mesopotamia.

330s B.C. Alexander the Great conquers Asia Minor.

60s B.C. The Roman Empire conquers Palestine.

c.* 610 Muhammad begins to preach the religion of Islam.

*c. stands for circa *and means "about."*

Political Map

Answers
1. Kazakhstan; Bahrain
2. Kuwait City

Critical Thinking
3. because in the desert there are few natural features that would help define boundaries

Southwest and Central Asia: Political

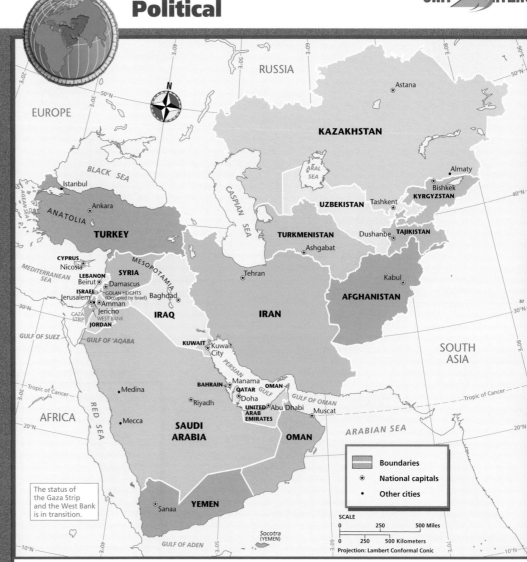

The status of the Gaza Strip and the West Bank is in transition.

1. (Place) What is the region's largest country? the region's smallest?

2. (Location) Which capital lies near latitude 30°N and longitude 50°E?

Critical Thinking

3. (Region) Examine the **climate map**. Why do you think so many of the boundaries in this region are straight lines?

3. (Movement) Which countries lie along the Persian Gulf and the Gulf of Oman? Why might conflicts occur among these countries?

USING THE POLITICAL MAP

While students focus on the **political map** on this page, ask which three continents meet at Southwest Asia. (Europe, Asia, Africa) How might this location have affected the region's history and culture? (invasions, trade, and ideas from many directions) Which small countries border the Persian Gulf? (Kuwait, Bahrain, Qatar, United Arab Emirates, Oman) Which small countries border the Mediterranean Sea? (Syria, Lebanon, Israel) What nearby small country is landlocked? (Jordan) What is the largest country that doesn't have access to the oceans? (Kazakhstan) Why may all these countries want to get or keep access to the sea? (for trade, travel, communication with other countries)

Southwest and Central Asia:
Climate

UNIT 2 ATLAS

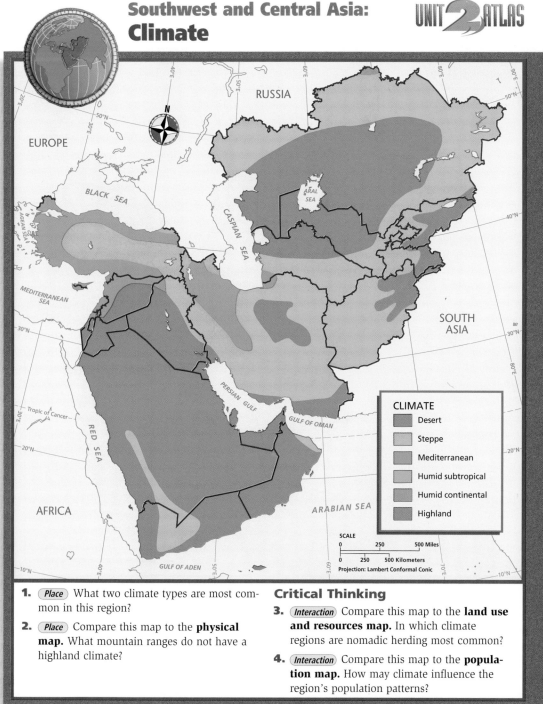

CLIMATE
- Desert
- Steppe
- Mediterranean
- Humid subtropical
- Humid continental
- Highland

SCALE
0   250   500 Miles
0   250   500 Kilometers
Projection: Lambert Conformal Conic

1. **Place** What two climate types are most common in this region?

2. **Place** Compare this map to the **physical map.** What mountain ranges do not have a highland climate?

Critical Thinking

3. **Interaction** Compare this map to the **land use and resources map.** In which climate regions are nomadic herding most common?

4. **Interaction** Compare this map to the **population map.** How may climate influence the region's population patterns?

Southwest and Central Asia • 75

Your Classroom Time Line, (continued)

A.D. **600s** Arabs conquer Mesopotamia and Palestine.

1000s The Seljuk Turks invade Asia Minor.

1000s–1200s The Crusades occur.

1099 Crusaders capture Jerusalem.

1258 Mongols destroy Baghdad.

1500s Mesopotamia becomes part of the Ottoman Empire.

1700s Kuwait is established.

late 1800s The Zionist movement begins.

1925–1979 Shahs rule Iran.

1930 Constantinople is renamed Istanbul.

1930s Oil is discovered on the Arabian Peninsula.

1932 The kingdom of Saudi Arabia is founded.

Climate Map
Answers
1. steppe, desert
2. Zagros, Kopet, Elburz, Pontic, and Taurus ranges

Critical Thinking
3. steppe and desert
4. In general, desert areas have low population densities.

USING THE CLIMATE MAP

Have students look at the **climate map** of Southwest and Central Asia on this page. Ask them to list the region's climate types in the order of the amount of area each one appears to cover (desert, steppe, Mediterranean, highland, humid continental, humid subtropical). Refer students to the **political map** on the preceding page and ask which countries they would choose to live in or visit based solely on climate.

*Your Classroom Time Line,
(continued)*

1932 The kingdom of Iraq is founded.

1940s Syria, Lebanon, and Jordan gain independence.

1948 The State of Israel is created.

1948–74 Israel and its Arab neighbors fight several wars.

1950s Iraqi army officers overthrow the government.

1952–99 King Hussein rules Jordan.

1968 The Ba'ath Party gains power in Iraq.

1970s A civil war begins in Lebanon.

1979 The Iranian Revolution overthrows Iran's shah.

late 1970s Saddam Hussein becomes president of Iraq.

1979 The Soviet Union invades Afghanistan.

Population Map

Answers

1. Yemen

2. Tashkent, Uzbekistan

Critical Thinking

3. Trade from the Black Sea and areas to the north must pass through Istanbul on its way to the Mediterranean.

4. large number of people involved in livestock raising, commercial farming, and subsistence farming

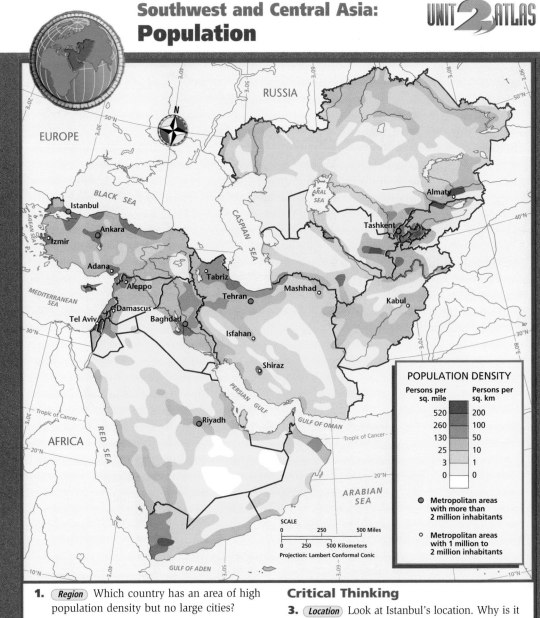

POPULATION DENSITY

Persons per sq. mile	Persons per sq. km
520	200
260	100
130	50
25	10
3	1
0	0

● Metropolitan areas with more than 2 million inhabitants

○ Metropolitan areas with 1 million to 2 million inhabitants

SCALE
0   250   500 Miles
0   250   500 Kilometers
Projection: Lambert Conformal Conic

1. **Region** Which country has an area of high population density but no large cities?

2. **Region** What is the largest city in the easternmost part of the region?

Critical Thinking

3. **Location** Look at Istanbul's location. Why is it good for a large city?

4. **Region** Compare this map to the **land use and resources map**. Why do you think the southwestern tip of the Arabian Pennisula has a high population density?

USING THE POPULATION MAP

Have students examine the **population map** of Southwest and Central Asia on this page. Ask a volunteer to compare the map to the **physical map** of the region and to name the most densely populated country in the region. (Israel) Ask students to point out the country in the region with the largest area that is sparsely populated or uninhabited. (Saudi Arabia)

internet connect

ONLINE ATLAS
GO TO: go.hrw.com
KEYWORD: SK5 MapsU2

Southwest and Central Asia:
Land Use and Resources

UNIT **2** ATLAS

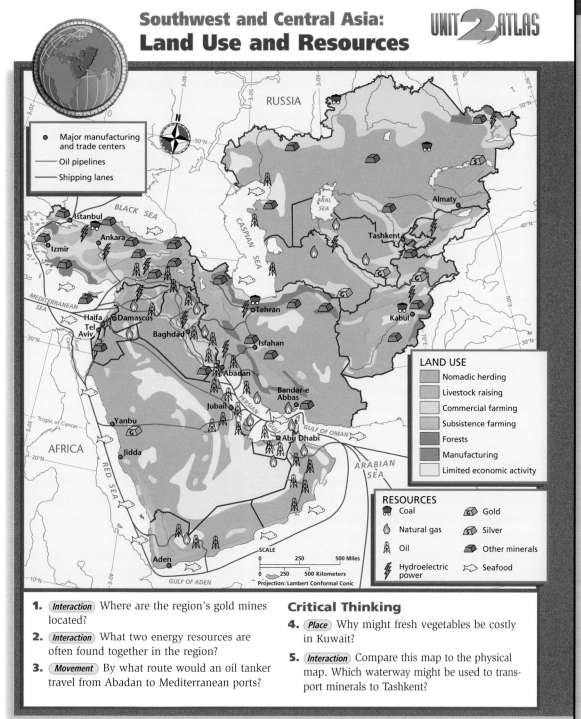

Major manufacturing and trade centers
— Oil pipelines
— Shipping lanes

RUSSIA

BLACK SEA

İstanbul
Ankara
İzmir

CASPIAN SEA

ARAL SEA

Almaty

Tashkent

MEDITERRANEAN SEA

Haifa Damascus
Tel Aviv
Baghdad
Isfahan
Abadan
Bandar-e Abbas
Jubail
Yanbu
Jidda
Aden

Tehran
Kabul

PERSIAN GULF
GULF OF OMAN

Tropic of Cancer

AFRICA

RED SEA

ARABIAN SEA

GULF OF ADEN

Abu Dhabi

LAND USE
- Nomadic herding
- Livestock raising
- Commercial farming
- Subsistence farming
- Forests
- Manufacturing
- Limited economic activity

RESOURCES
- 🪣 Coal
- 💧 Natural gas
- 🛢 Oil
- ⚡ Hydroelectric power
- ⑱ Gold
- Ⓢ Silver
- Other minerals
- 🐟 Seafood

SCALE
0   250   500 Miles
0   250   500 Kilometers
Projection: Lambert Conformal Conic

1. (*Interaction*) Where are the region's gold mines located?

2. (*Interaction*) What two energy resources are often found together in the region?

3. (*Movement*) By what route would an oil tanker travel from Abadan to Mediterranean ports?

Critical Thinking

4. (*Place*) Why might fresh vegetables be costly in Kuwait?

5. (*Interaction*) Compare this map to the physical map. Which waterway might be used to transport minerals to Tashkent?

Southwest and Central Asia • 77

UNIT 2 ATLAS

Your Classroom Time Line, (continued)

1980 Iraq invades Iran.

1989 Soviet troops withdraw from Afghanistan.

1990 Iraq invades Kuwait.

1991 Persian Gulf War ends.

1990s Israel agrees to turn over parts of the Occupied Territories.

mid-1990s The Taliban rise to power in Afghanistan.

2001 United States attacks Taliban and terrorist targets in Afghanistan.

2003 U.S. forces topple the regime of Saddam Hussein in Iraq and later capture him.

Land Use and Resources Map

Answers

1. southern Turkmenistan and Uzbekistan, northern Afghanistan, western Saudi Arabia

2. natural gas and oil

3. southeast through Persian Gulf and Gulf of Oman to the Arabian Sea, southwest to Gulf of Aden, northwest through Red Sea, and through Suez Canal to Mediterranean Sea

Critical Thinking

4. No farmland is indicated on the map; fruits, grains, and vegetables would have to be imported, driving up prices.

5. Syr Dar'ya

USING THE LAND USE AND RESOURCES MAP

Ask students to look at the **land use and resources map** on this page. Have them identify the economic activities and resources that seem to dominate Southwest Asia. (nomadic herding, oil) Refer students to the **climate map** and ask how the region's harsh climate affects these two economic activities. (limits nomadic herd-

ing to some extent, has no effect on oil industry) Also, have students compare this map to the **population map** of the region and identify the type of farming that takes place in the areas with the greatest population density. (commercial farming)

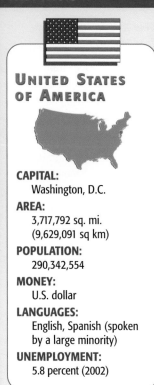

UNITED STATES OF AMERICA

CAPITAL:
Washington, D.C.

AREA:
3,717,792 sq. mi.
(9,629,091 sq km)

POPULATION:
290,342,554

MONEY:
U.S. dollar

LANGUAGES:
English, Spanish (spoken by a large minority)

UNEMPLOYMENT:
5.8 percent (2002)

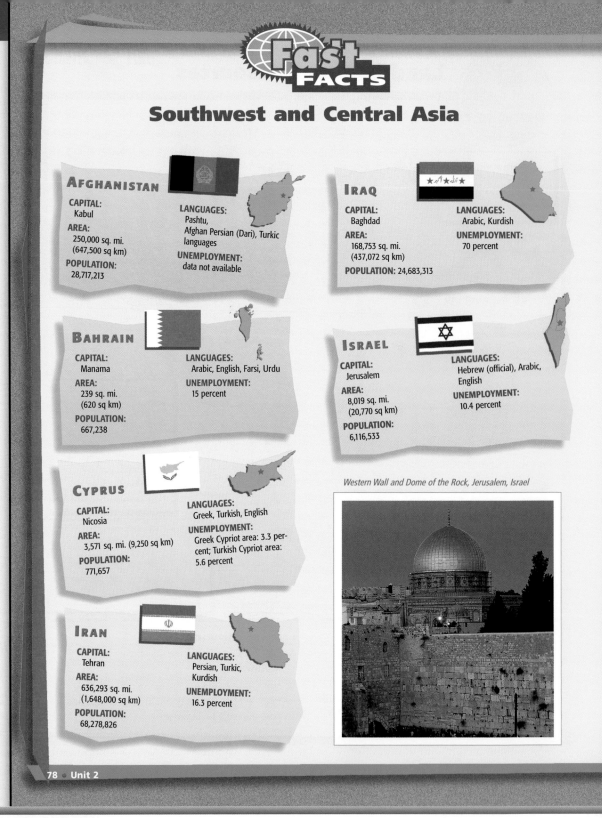

Fast FACTS

Southwest and Central Asia

AFGHANISTAN

CAPITAL:
Kabul

AREA:
250,000 sq. mi.
(647,500 sq km)

POPULATION:
28,717,213

LANGUAGES:
Pashtu,
Afghan Persian (Dari), Turkic languages

UNEMPLOYMENT:
data not available

IRAQ

CAPITAL:
Baghdad

AREA:
168,753 sq. mi.
(437,072 sq km)

POPULATION: 24,683,313

LANGUAGES:
Arabic, Kurdish

UNEMPLOYMENT:
70 percent

BAHRAIN

CAPITAL:
Manama

AREA:
239 sq. mi.
(620 sq km)

POPULATION:
667,238

LANGUAGES:
Arabic, English, Farsi, Urdu

UNEMPLOYMENT:
15 percent

ISRAEL

CAPITAL:
Jerusalem

AREA:
8,019 sq. mi.
(20,770 sq km)

POPULATION:
6,116,533

LANGUAGES:
Hebrew (official), Arabic, English

UNEMPLOYMENT:
10.4 percent

CYPRUS

CAPITAL:
Nicosia

AREA:
3,571 sq. mi. (9,250 sq km)

POPULATION:
771,657

LANGUAGES:
Greek, Turkish, English

UNEMPLOYMENT:
Greek Cypriot area: 3.3 percent; Turkish Cypriot area:
5.6 percent

Western Wall and Dome of the Rock, Jerusalem, Israel

IRAN

CAPITAL:
Tehran

AREA:
636,293 sq. mi.
(1,648,000 sq km)

POPULATION:
68,278,826

LANGUAGES:
Persian, Turkic, Kurdish

UNEMPLOYMENT:
16.3 percent

78 • Unit 2

FAST FACTS ACTIVITIES

LEVEL 1: (Suggested time: 15 min.) Call on students to name the countries that have unemployment rates of 15 percent or more (Bahrain, Iran, Iraq, Jordan, Lebanon, Saudi Arabia, Syria, Tajikistan, and Yemen). Ask students for possible reasons for the high rates of unemployment. (Students may suggest warfare, large numbers of refugees, or the change from a communist to a free-market economy.) Challenge students to look in news sources to determine if recent events have improved the percentages.

LEVEL 2: (Suggested time: 35 min.) Have the students refer to the **political map** and **land use and resources map** in this unit's atlas to identify two countries whose economies depend on oil production and two that depend more on other resources. Have students use the *CIA World Factbook* to create a bar graph showing the per capita GDP of citizens in their selected countries. What can they conclude?

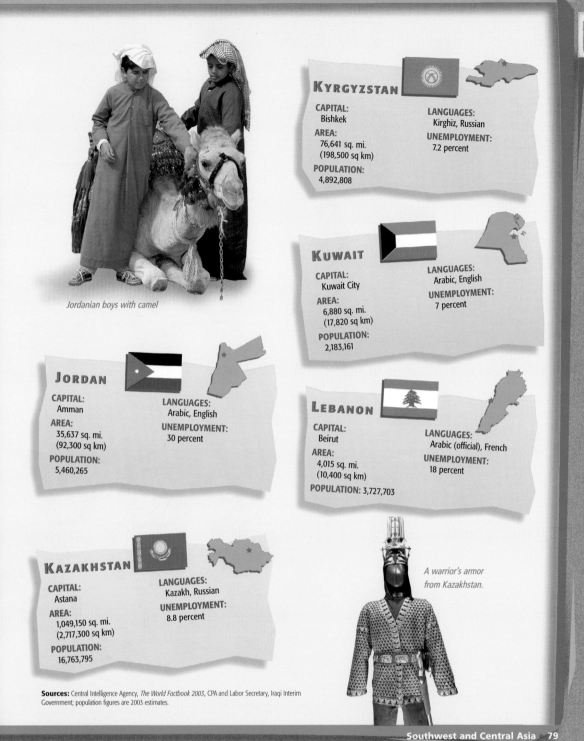

Reproducible
◆ Unit 2 Test
◆ Unit 2 Test for English Language Learners and Special-Needs Students

Jordanian boys with camel

KYRGYZSTAN

CAPITAL:
Bishkek
AREA:
76,641 sq. mi.
(198,500 sq km)
POPULATION:
4,892,808

LANGUAGES:
Kirghiz, Russian
UNEMPLOYMENT:
7.2 percent

KUWAIT

CAPITAL:
Kuwait City
AREA:
6,880 sq. mi.
(17,820 sq km)
POPULATION:
2,183,161

LANGUAGES:
Arabic, English
UNEMPLOYMENT:
7 percent

JORDAN

CAPITAL:
Amman
AREA:
35,637 sq. mi.
(92,300 sq km)
POPULATION:
5,460,265

LANGUAGES:
Arabic, English
UNEMPLOYMENT:
30 percent

LEBANON

CAPITAL:
Beirut
AREA:
4,015 sq. mi.
(10,400 sq km)
POPULATION: 3,727,703

LANGUAGES:
Arabic (official), French
UNEMPLOYMENT:
18 percent

KAZAKHSTAN

CAPITAL:
Astana
AREA:
1,049,150 sq. mi.
(2,717,300 sq km)
POPULATION:
16,763,795

LANGUAGES:
Kazakh, Russian
UNEMPLOYMENT:
8.8 percent

A warrior's armor from Kazakhstan.

Sources: Central Intelligence Agency, *The World Factbook 2003*, CPA and Labor Secretary, Iraqi Interim Government; population figures are 2003 estimates.

 internet connect

COUNTRY STATISTICS
GO TO: go.hrw.com
KEYWORD: SK5 FactsU2

Highlights of Country Statistics
Links to online country statistics for Southwest Asia include:
• *CIA World Factbook*
• Library of Congress country studies
• Flags of the world

FAST FACTS ACTIVITIES

LEVEL 3: (Suggested time: 40 min.) Ask students to imagine that they live in Southwest Asia and have a pen pal in the United States. Have them write letters describing how modernization and Western culture have influenced their way of life. Students should indicate if they feel the effects on their region have been positive or negative. They should back up their opinions with examples from the unit.

OMAN

CAPITAL:
Muscat

AREA:
82,031 sq. mi.
(212,460 sq km)

POPULATION: 2,807,125

LANGUAGES:
Arabic (official), English

UNEMPLOYMENT:
data not available

SYRIA

CAPITAL:
Damascus

AREA:
71,498 sq. mi.
(185,180 sq km)

POPULATION: 17,585,540

LANGUAGES:
Arabic (official), Kurdish

UNEMPLOYMENT:
20 percent

QATAR

CAPITAL:
Doha

AREA:
4,416 sq. mi.
(11,437 sq km)

POPULATION:
817,052

LANGUAGES:
Arabic (official),
English

UNEMPLOYMENT:
2.7 percent

TAJIKISTAN

CAPITAL:
Dushanbe

AREA:
55,251 sq. mi.
(143,100 sq km)

POPULATION:
6,863,752

LANGUAGES:
Tajik (official), Russian

UNEMPLOYMENT:
40 percent (and many underemployed)

SAUDI ARABIA

CAPITAL:
Riyadh

AREA:
756,981 sq. mi.
(1,960,582 sq km)

POPULATION:
24,293,844

LANGUAGES:
Arabic

UNEMPLOYMENT:
25 percent

Children learning Islam in Tajikistan

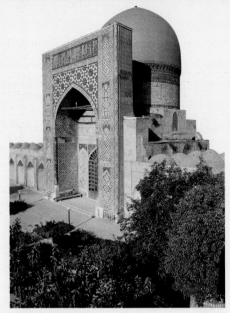

Mosque in Uzbekistan

UNITED ARAB EMIRATES

CAPITAL: Abu Dhabi

AREA:
32,000 sq. mi.
(82,880 sq km)

POPULATION: 2,484,818

LANGUAGES:
Arabic (official), Persian

UNEMPLOYMENT:
data not available

UZBEKISTAN

CAPITAL:
Tashkent

AREA:
172,741 sq. mi.
(447,400 sq km)

POPULATION:
25,981,647

LANGUAGES:
Uzbek, Russian, Tajik

UNEMPLOYMENT:
10 percent (and many underemployed)

TURKEY

CAPITAL: Ankara

AREA:
301,382 sq. mi.
(780,580 sq km)

POPULATION:
68,109,469

LANGUAGES:
Turkish (official), Kurdish

UNEMPLOYMENT:
10.8 percent (6.1 percent underemployed)

YEMEN

CAPITAL:
Sanaa

AREA:
203,849 sq. mi.
(527,970 sq km)

POPULATION:
19,349,881

LANGUAGES:
Arabic

UNEMPLOYMENT:
30 percent

TURKMENISTAN

CAPITAL:
Ashgabat

AREA:
188,455 sq. mi.
(488,100 sq km)

POPULATION: 4,775,544

LANGUAGES:
Turkmen, Uzbek, Russian

UNEMPLOYMENT:
data not available

---

internet connect

COUNTRY STATISTICS
GO TO: go.hrw.com
KEYWORD: SK5 FactsU2
FOR: more facts about
Southwest and Central Asia

Sources: Central Intelligence Agency, *The World Factbook 2003*, CPA and Labor Secretary, Iraqi Interim Government; population figures are 2003 estimates.

CHAPTER 4
The History of Southwest and Central Asia

Chapter Resource Manager

Objectives	Pacing Guide	Reproducible Resources
SECTION 1		
The Birth of Civilization 1. Trace the discoveries that scientists have made about prehistoric times. 2. Identify the characteristics of civilization. 3. Explain where the first civilizations developed.	**Regular** 1 day Lecture Notes, Section 1 **Block Scheduling** .5 day *Block Scheduling Handbook, Chapter 4*	**RS** Know It Notes S1 **RS** Graphic Organizer 4 **ELL** Main Idea Activity S1
SECTION 2		
Mesopotamia and the Fertile Crescent 1. Identify what skills the Sumerians developed. 2. Describe some features of other civilizations of Mesopotamia and the Fertile Crescent. 3. Explore what Persian rule was like.	**Regular** 1 day Lecture Notes, Section 2 **Block Scheduling** .5 day *Block Scheduling Handbook, Chapter 4*	**RS** Know It Notes S2 **ELL** Main Idea Activity S2
SECTION 3		
Land of the Three Faiths 1. Trace how Judaism developed in Southwest Asia. 2. Explore how the life of Jesus led to the development of Christianity. 3. Clarify who Muhammad was and what he taught.	**Regular** 1 day Lecture Notes, Section 3 **Block Scheduling** .5 day *Block Scheduling Handbook, Chapter 4*	**RS** Know It Notes S3 **SM** Geography for Life Activities 20, 21 **E** Readings in World Geography, History, and Culture: Reading 50 **E** Biography Activity: Darius I **ELL** Main Idea Activity S3
SECTION 4		
Empires in Southwest and Central Asia 1. Show how Islam spread to become a large empire. 2. Describe other rulers who took over Southwest and Central Asia.	**Regular** .5 day Lecture Notes, Section 4 **Block Scheduling** .5 day *Block Scheduling Handbook, Chapter 4*	**RS** Know It Notes S4 **SM** Map Activity 20 **E** Creative Strategies for Teaching World Geography, Lessons 14/15 **ELL** Main Idea Activity S4

Chapter Resource Key

RS Reading Support

IC Interdisciplinary Connections

E Enrichment

SM Skills Mastery

A Assessment

REV Review

ELL Reinforcement and English Language Learners and English for Speakers of Other Languages (ESOL)

 Transparencies

 CD–ROM

 Music

 Video

 Internet

 Holt Presentation Maker Using Microsoft® PowerPoint®

  One-Stop Planner CD–ROM

See the *One-Stop Planner* for a complete list of additional resources for students and teachers.

One-Stop Planner CD–ROM

It's easy to plan lessons, select resources, and print out materials for your students when you use the *One-Stop Planner CD–ROM with Test Generator.*

Technology Resources	Review, Reinforcement, and Assessment Resources	
One-Stop Planner CD-ROM, Lesson 4.1	ELL	Main Idea Activity S1
Geography and Cultures Visual Resources 72	REV	Section 1 Review
ARGWorld CD–ROM	A	Daily Quiz 4.1
Homework Practice Online	REV	Chapter Summaries and Review
HRW Go site	ELL	English Audio Summary 4.1
	ELL	Spanish Audio Summary 4.1
One-Stop Planner CD-ROM, Lesson 4.2	ELL	Main Idea Activity S2
Geography and Cultures Visual Resources 72	REV	Section 2 Review
ARGWorld CD–ROM	A	Daily Quiz 4.2
Homework Practice Online	REV	Chapter Summaries and Review
HRW Go site	ELL	English Audio Summary 4.2
	ELL	Spanish Audio Summary 4.2
One-Stop Planner CD-ROM, Lesson 4.3	ELL	Main Idea Activity S3
Geography and Cultures Visual Resources 71, 72, 75	REV	Section 3 Review
ARGWorld CD–ROM	A	Daily Quiz 4.3
Homework Practice Online	REV	Chapter Summaries and Review
HRW Go site	ELL	English Audio Summary 4.3
	ELL	Spanish Audio Summary 4.3
One-Stop Planner CD-ROM, Lesson 4.4	ELL	Main Idea Activity S4
Geography and Cultures Visual Resources 71, 72, 75	REV	Section 4 Review
ARGWorld CD–ROM	A	Daily Quiz 4.4
Homework Practice Online	REV	Chapter Summaries and Review
HRW Go site	ELL	English Audio Summary 4.4
	ELL	Spanish Audio Summary 4.4

internet connect

HRW ONLINE RESOURCES

GO TO: go.hrw.com
Then type in a keyword.

TEACHER HOMEPAGE
KEYWORD: SK5 TEACHER

CHAPTER INTERNET ACTIVITIES
KEYWORD: SK5 GT4

Choose an activity to:
• learn more about the development of writing.
• explore the Persian Empire.
• trace the spread of the Mongol Empire.

CHAPTER ENRICHMENT LINKS
KEYWORD: SK5 CH4

CHAPTER MAPS
KEYWORDS: SK5 MAPS4

ONLINE ASSESSMENT
Homework Practice
KEYWORD: SK5 HP 4
Standardized Test Prep Online
KEYWORD: SK5 STP4
Rubrics
KEYWORD: SS Rubrics

COUNTRY INFORMATION
KEYWORD: SK5 Almanac

CONTENT UPDATES
KEYWORD: SS Contents Updates

HOLT PRESENTATION MAKER
KEYWORD: SK5 PPT4

ONLINE READING SUPPORT
KEYWORD: SS Strategies

CURRENT EVENTS
KEYWORD: SS Current Events

Meeting Individual Needs

Ability Levels

Level 1 Basic-level activities designed for all students encountering new material

Level 2 Intermediate-level activities designed for average students

Level 3 Challenging activities designed for honors and gifted-and-talented students

ESOL Activities that address the needs of students with Limited English Proficiency

Chapter Review and Assessment

E	Readings in World Geography, History, and Culture 50
SM	Critical Thinking Activity 4
REV	Chapter 4 Review and Practice
REV	Chapter Summaries and Review
ELL	Vocabulary Activity 4
A	Chapter 4 Test
A	Chapter 4 Test Generator (on the One-Stop Planner)
	Audio CD program, Chapter 4
A	Chapter 4 Test for English Language Learners and Special Needs Students
	HRW Go site

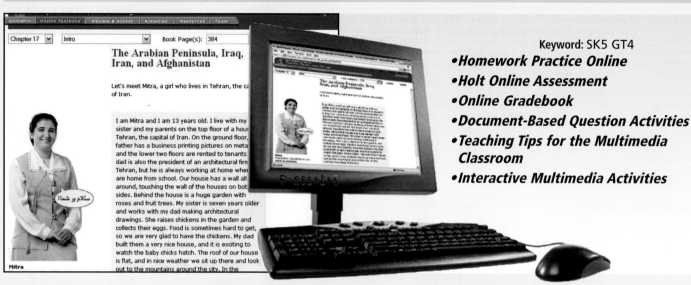

| Contents | Online Textbook | Review & Assess | Activities | Resources | Tests |

Chapter 17 ▾ Intro ▾ Book Page(s): 384

The Arabian Peninsula, Iraq, Iran, and Afghanistan

Let's meet Mitra, a girl who lives in Tehran, the capital of Iran.

I am Mitra and I am 13 years old. I live with my sister and my parents on the top floor of a house in Tehran, the capital of Iran. On the ground floor, my father has a business printing pictures on metal, and the lower two floors are rented to tenants. My dad is also the president of an architectural firm in Tehran, but he is always home when we are home from school. Our house has a wall all around, touching the wall of the houses on both sides. Behind the house is a huge garden with roses and fruit trees. My sister is seven years older and works with my dad making architectural drawings. She raises chickens in the garden and collects their eggs. Food is sometimes hard to get, so we are very glad to have the chickens. My dad built them a very nice house, and it is exciting to watch the baby chicks hatch. The roof of our house is flat, and in nice weather we sit up there and look out to the mountains around the city. In the

Mitra

سلام بر شما

Keyword: SK5 GT4

- *Homework Practice Online*
- *Holt Online Assessment*
- *Online Gradebook*
- *Document-Based Question Activities*
- *Teaching Tips for the Multimedia Classroom*
- *Interactive Multimedia Activities*

Differentiating Instruction

Reading and Writing Support

◀ Graphic Organizer Activity
- *Vocabulary Activity*
- *Chapter Summary and Review*
- *Know-It Notes S1–4*
- *Audio CD*

Active Learning

◀ Block Scheduling Handbook
- *Cultures of the World Activity*
- *Interdisciplinary Activity: Religious Architecture*
- *Map Activity*

Primary Sources and Advanced Learners

◀ Map Activity: Islam
- *Readings in World Geography, History and Culture:*
  - *46 Exploring Central Asia*
  - *50 The Islamic City*

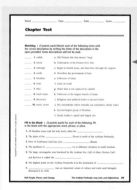

Assessment Program

- *Daily Quizzes S1–4*
◀ Chapter Test
- *Chapter Test for English Language Learners and Special-Needs Students*

Spanish and ESOL

- *Vocabulary Activity*
◀ Main Idea Activities for English Language Learners and Special-Needs Students
- *Chapter Summary and Review*
- *Spanish Audio Summary*
- *Know-It Notes S1–4*
- *Chapter Test for English Language Learners and Special-Needs Students*

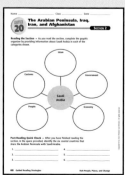

Special Education Modifications

Your **I.D.E.A. Works! CD-ROM** will provide modified versions of the following teaching materials:

◀ Guided Reading Strategies S1–4
- *Vocabulary Activity*
- *Main Idea Activities S1–4*
- *Daily Quizzes S1–4*
- *Chapter 4 Test*
- *Flash cards of chapter vocabulary terms*

Teacher Resources

Books for Teachers

Hawkes, Jaquetta. *The Atlas of Early Man: The Rise of Man Across the Globe from 35, 000 B.C. to A.D. 500.* St. Martin's Press, 1993.

Dalley, Stephanie, ed., *Myths from Mesopotamia.* Oxford University Press, 1998.

Leick, Gwendolyn. *The Babylonians: An Introduction.* Routledge, 2002.

Halevi, Yossi K. *At the Entrance to the Garden of Eden: A Jew's Search for Hope with Christians and Muslims in the Holy Land.* Perennial, 2002

Books for Students

Brooks, Philip. *Prehistoric Peoples: Discover the Long-Ago World of the First Humans.* Lorenz Books, 2000.

Pilbeam, Mavis and John Malam. *Mesopotamia and the Fertile Cresent.* Raintree/Steck-Vaughn, 1999. Traces Mesopotamia's history, technological innovations, people, and culture from 10,000 to 539 B. C.

Connolly, Peter. *The Holy Land.* Oxford University Press, 1999. Features the geography of the eastern Mediterranean, Jewish history, and the beginnings of Christianity.

Morris, Neil. *The Atlas of Islam: People, Daily Life and Traditions.* Barrons Educational Series, 2003.

Multimedia Materials

Mesopotamia. Video, Time-Life.

Islam-Empire of Faith. Video, PBS Home Video.

Christianity-The First Thousand Years. Video, A&E Entertainment.

The Kingdom of David-The Saga of the Israelites. Video, PBS Home Video.

Videos and CDs

Videos

• CNN. *Presents World Cultures: Yesterday and Today, Segment 9 Pilgrimage to Mecca*
• *ARG World*

Holt Researcher

http://researcher.hrw.com

• *Hammurabi*
• *Cyrus the Great*
• *Sargon*
• *Sassanid Empire*
• *David*
• *Muhammad*
• *Development of Cuneiform*
• *The First Civilizations*

Transparency Packages

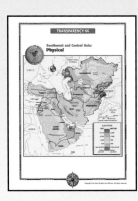

Geography and Cultures Visual Resources Transparencies
66 Southwest and Central Asia: Physical
73 Qanat Irrigation System
74 Nomadic Encampment

Map Activities Transparency
20 Islam

WHY IT MATTERS

Use these points to emphasize the importance of knowing more about the history of Southwest and Central Asia:

▶ The study of ancient remains and artifacts from the region affects our understanding of our place on Earth.

▶ The development of agriculture was key to the development of civilizations in Southwest and Central Asia. Agriculture is still a key issue, since the world still needs to be fed.

▶ Some areas where ancient civilizations thrived in the past are in conflict today.

▶ The region is the birthplace of three faiths, which together claim billions of followers.

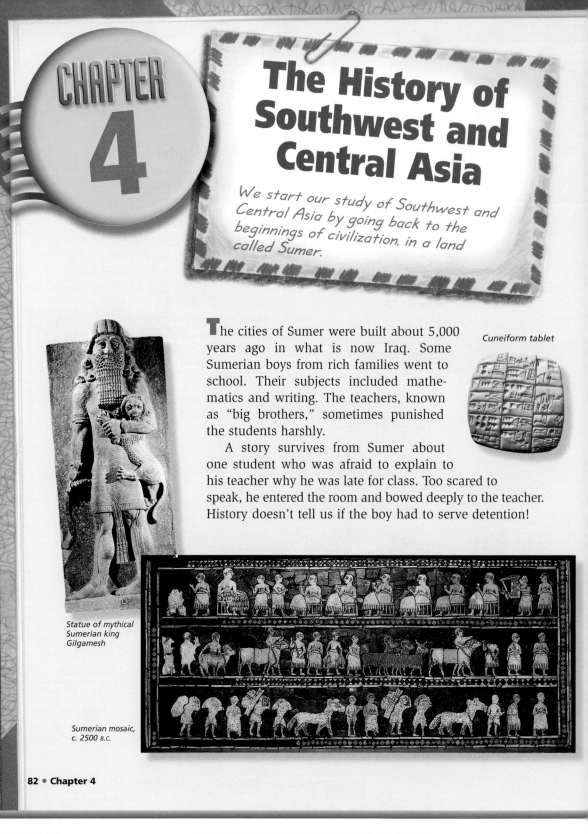

CHAPTER 4

The History of Southwest and Central Asia

We start our study of Southwest and Central Asia by going back to the beginnings of civilization, in a land called Sumer.

The cities of Sumer were built about 5,000 years ago in what is now Iraq. Some Sumerian boys from rich families went to school. Their subjects included mathematics and writing. The teachers, known as "big brothers," sometimes punished the students harshly.

A story survives from Sumer about one student who was afraid to explain to his teacher why he was late for class. Too scared to speak, he entered the room and bowed deeply to the teacher. History doesn't tell us if the boy had to serve detention!

Cuneiform tablet

Statue of mythical Sumerian king Gilgamesh

Sumerian mosaic, c. 2500 B.C.

CHAPTER PROJECT

Ask students to imagine that they are archaeologists excavating a site once inhabited by one of the civilizations discussed in this chapter. Have them create a list of objects they think they may find that would indicate what life was like in that civilization. Then have students write explanations or pictures of each item. Place explanations or pictures in student portfolios.

STARTING THE CHAPTER

Point out to students that the word *history* specifically refers to events since people developed writing, about 5,000 years ago. Times before that go under the word *prehistory.* Then tell students that one of the cultures they will study in this chapter developed in an area called Sumer, and some historians say "History starts at Sumer." Invite students to analyze this quote, based on the meaning of *history.* (The people of Sumer are usually credited with being the first people to develop a writing system.) Emphasize, though, that people had been going about their business for thousands of years already when writing was developed. Students will learn more about Sumer and other cultures of Southwest and Central Asia in this chapter.

Section 1 The Birth of Civilization

Get Ready to Read

1. What discoveries have scientists made about prehistoric times?
2. What are the characteristics of civilization?
3. Where did the first civilizations develop?

Vocabulary

hominids
prehistory
nomads
land bridges

irrigation
division of labor
history

Reading Strategy

VISUALIZING INFORMATION Look at the photographs in this section. What information do they show about past civilizations? Write your answers on a sheet of paper. As you read, write what you learn about these civilizations.

Looking into the Past

Peoples of Southwest and Central Asia created some of the greatest civilizations the world has ever seen. However, for our study of the region's history, we need to start by looking further back into the past. In fact, we must start with the dawn of humanity. The story begins in Africa.

In the late 1970s in Tanzania, a country in East Africa, scientist Mary Leakey discovered fossilized footprints millions of years old. She concluded the footprints were those of **hominids**, early humanlike creatures. This find was one of many discoveries in the same region. Ancient skulls and skeletons, along with objects found near them, provide clues about hominid life. For example, scientists can tell that hominids walked upright and used primitive tools made of stone.

Archaeologists dig carefully through layers of soil and rubble to find clues about how people lived long ago.
Interpreting the Visual Record What kinds of objects may these archaeologists be hoping to find?

SECTION 1 RESOURCES

Reproducibles
- Lecture Notes, Section 1
- Block Scheduling Handbook, Chapter 4
- Know It Notes S1

Technology
- One-Stop Planner CD-ROM, Lesson 4.1
- Geography and Cultures Visual Resources 72
- Homework Practice Online
- HRW Go Site

Review, Reinforcement, and Assessment Resources
- Section 1 Review
- Daily Quiz 4.1
- Main Idea Activity S1
- Chapter Summaries and Review
- English Audio Summary 4.1
- Spanish Audio Summary 4.1

◄Visual Record Answer

skeletal remains and stone tools

Section 1

Objectives

1. Trace the discoveries that scientists have made about prehistoric times.
2. Identify the characteristics of civilization.
3. Explain where the first civilizations developed.

FOCUS

Bellringer

Copy the following questions onto the chalkboard. *How would you survive if you were stranded on a remote island? How would you get food? What would you use for tools and shelter?* Discuss responses. (Possible answers: food—hunt fish and small animals, gather seeds, nuts, berries; tools—sticks, rocks; shelter—branches, caves) Point out to students that early people had to survive in much the same way. Tell students that in Section 1 they will learn about early people and how they lived.

Building Vocabulary

Write the vocabulary terms on the chalkboard. Remind students that the prefix *pre-* means "before." Ask students to infer the meaning of **prehistory** ("before history"). Ask students to identify other words that begin with the prefix *pre-*. Point out that the suffix *-tion* at the end of a word indicates a process or an action. Have students infer the meaning of the word **irrigation** using what they know about the base word and the suffix. Call on volunteers to read the definitions for all the terms.

USING ILLUSTRATIONS

An Ancient Art Gallery
Focus students' attention on the lower photo on this page. Four teenagers discovered the Lascaux cave in 1940. While exploring a hole left by a large fallen pine tree, the boys suddenly found themselves in a cavern filled with magnificent prehistoric paintings. The paintings had been naturally preserved when soil built up and sealed the entrance to the cave. Lack of exposure to outside air kept the paintings in perfect condition. The chambers of the Lascaux cave contain some 600 painted and drawn animals and symbols, as well as nearly 1,500 engravings.

Shortly after its discovery, the cave was opened to visitors. However, exposure and use of artificial lighting caused the colors to fade and algae to grow over the paintings. As a result, the cave was closed to tourists in 1963. A replica opened nearby in 1983 so that people could enjoy the pictures without destroying them.

internet connect

GO TO: go.hrw.com
KEYWORD: SK5 CH4
FOR: Web sites about archaeology

Visual Record Answer ▶

horses, cattle

▲
These stone ax heads date from the Stone Age. They were found in Italy. The ivory tool in the shape of a dagger was found in China.

Shown in beautiful detail, this cave painting in Lascaux, France, is an example of Stone Age art. People may have drawn on cave walls to express ideas.
Interpreting the Visual Record What kinds of animals did the Lascaux artists paint on this wall?

▶

The period during which hominids and early humans lived is called **prehistory**. This means that no written records exist for those times. The period of prehistory in which stone tools were used is called the Stone Age. It began about 2.5 million years ago and lasted until about 3500 B.C.

The First Humans Early humans that looked like modern people may have first appeared during the Stone Age between 200,000 and 100,000 years ago. These first humans, called *Homo sapiens*, lived in Africa. They were **nomads** who moved from place to place in search of food. They gathered seeds, fruits, and nuts from wild plants. In time they also began to hunt small animals. Dangerous times lay ahead, though.

Migration Within the last 1.8 million years, Earth has gone through several periods of very cold weather. Together these periods are known as the Ice Age. During each period, large parts of Earth's surface were covered with ice. Sea levels dropped, leaving strips of dry land called **land bridges** between continents. Humans walked over these land bridges to new regions. They may have been following the animals they hunted. Slowly, humans spread out to all parts of the world.

An important discovery helped people survive during the Ice Age. They learned how to control fire and use it for warmth and cooking.

Later Developments In time humans began to make more advanced tools, including spears. As a result, they could hunt larger animals. They made clothes from animal skins. Perhaps as early as 40,000 years ago, people began to create art. Carved ivory figures show that some groups had time for activities besides hunting, gathering, and tool making. Beautiful paintings on the walls of caves in France and Spain show animals such as lions, bulls, and horses in great detail.

Later, between 10,000 and 5,500 years ago, people learned to make sharper tools by grinding and polishing stone. People developed better hunting methods. They made bows and arrows, which meant that hunters could attack prey from a safer distance. The hunters shaped

TEACH

Teaching Objective 1

ALL LEVELS: (Suggested time: 15 min.) Ask students to look in the text for examples of the types of information scientists have gathered about prehistoric times. Then ask students to provide specific examples for each one. (Example: type of information—how early humans got food; specific examples—gathered plants, hunted, developed agriculture)

LEVEL 1: (Suggested time: 30 min.) Have students complete the All Levels activity. Then copy the graphic organizer onto the chalkboard, omitting the blue answers. Use it to help students examine the kinds of resources early people used to survive. Have students work in pairs to complete it.
ESOL, COOPERATIVE LEARNING, LS **VISUAL-SPATIAL**

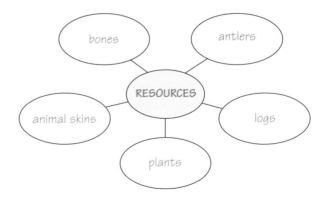

Emergence of Agriculture

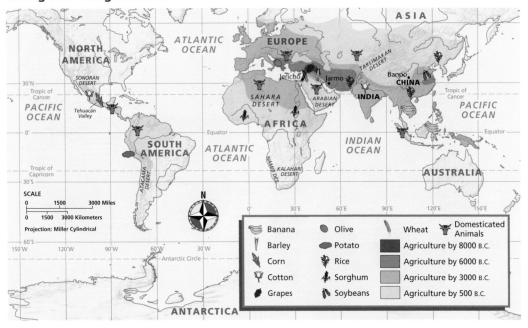

The spread of agriculture meant that people no longer had to travel in search of food. As a result, civilization began to develop.

Interpreting the Map What crops were grown in Southwest and Central Asia?

fishhooks and harpoons from bones and antlers. People hollowed out logs to make canoes for fishing in deep water and crossing rivers. Also at about this time, people tamed dogs. Dogs helped locate prey and warned of wild animals or strangers approaching.

In the late Stone Age, people began to practice agriculture. We don't know exactly how people made the change from gathering plants to growing them. We do know that life changed drastically when they did. Instead of moving from place to place to hunt animals and gather wild plants, people began to stay in one place. They became farmers. People also domesticated animals such as cattle and sheep. That means people tamed animals that had been living wild.

The Importance of Agriculture Agriculture changed how people interacted with their surroundings. To grow food, people learned to control and change their environment. They created fields by clearing forested areas. People became farmers by gathering the seeds or pieces of wild plants and planting them in fields. They invented **irrigation** systems, digging ditches and canals to move water from rivers to fields where crops could be grown.

Agriculture also changed the ways people interacted with each other. Because people who farmed stayed in one area, they began to live in larger groups. In addition, some animals, such as pigs, couldn't be herded from place to place. By about 9000 B.C., people began to live in permanent villages. Because farming made food more plentiful, populations increased. Small villages eventually grew into cities.

The History of Southwest and Central Asia • 85

Cultural Kaleidoscope
Nonindustrial

Peoples Even in today's modern world, some people live in ways similar to those of Late Stone Age people. For example, the Yanomamo of Brazil's rain forest live as subsistence farmers and hunters. Yanomamo farmers grow plantains and bananas. They supplement their diets with nuts, seed pods, and mushrooms. Their meat comes from a variety of game animals, including the anaconda, a huge snake that they hunt with bows and poisoned arrows. Most Yanomamo live in small villages. The Yanomamo had no contact with outsiders until the late 1940s.

Activity: Have students conduct research on nonindustrial societies in today's world. Students could choose among indigenous peoples of New Guinea, the Amazon rain forest, parts of Africa, or other places. Ask students to concentrate on the skills and knowledge that help the people live in their particular environments.

◄**Map Answer**

barley, grapes, wheat

LEVEL 2: (Suggested time: 30 min.) Have students create time lines that show what scientists believe to be the progress of humans from the appearance of *Homo sapiens* between 400,000 and 410,000 years ago up to the time that the first cities appeared about 5,000 years ago. On their time lines, have students list the developments and achievements of early humans.

LEVEL 3: Have students combine their time lines into one and reproduce it on a long piece of butcher paper. Ask students to illustrate the time line as if it were a cave painting. Refer them to the illustration of the cave paint-

ings of Lascaux on the previous page. You may want to provide additional resources and allocate extra time for this activity.

➤**ASSIGNMENT:** Tell students that agriculture, one of the most important achievements of early humans, affects all aspects of our daily lives. Have each student write a paragraph that tells how agriculture affects him or her personally each day. (Example: Our breakfast cereal is made from grains grown by farmers. Many of the clothes we wear are made of cotton.)

Cultural Kaleidoscope
Inca Farming

Practices Agriculture began long ago in South America also. Scientific examination of organic material in the soil shows that people farmed the Andes region of Peru intensively from about 2000 B.C. to A.D. 100. When the region's climate cooled, farming declined, and soil erosion increased.

About A.D. 1230, the climate warmed, and the Inca took over the area. Archaeological evidence suggests that the Inca may have used sophisticated soil conservation techniques. They built a long canal to irrigate fields, terraced the hillsides to grow crops, and planted alder trees that helped curb soil erosion. After the Spanish conquest of Peru, the terraces deteriorated. Today, the alder trees are found only in a few remote ravines.

Activity: Have students conduct research on ancient farming practices developed at various sites around the world and report their findings to the class.

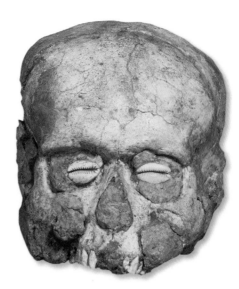

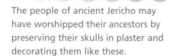

The people of ancient Jericho may have worshipped their ancestors by preserving their skulls in plaster and decorating them like these.

In towns and cities, people shared new ideas and methods of doing things. Historians think that the first cities were built some 10,000 years ago. Jericho, the world's oldest known city, developed around 8000 B.C. on the Jordan River in Southwest Asia. About 3,000 people lived in Jericho at this time. The people of Jericho grew wheat and barley and built a massive stone wall around their city.

Because of the ways it changed people's lives, agriculture and the domestication of animals were enormously important. In fact, learning how to grow food prepared the way for a new chapter in the story of human life—the story of civilization.

✓ **READING CHECK:** (*Summarizing*) How did agriculture change how people lived? As farmers they didn't have to migrate to hunt for food.

The Beginnings of Civilization

Historians describe civilizations as having four basic features. First, a civilization is made up of people living in an organized society, not simply as a loosely connected group. Second, people are able to produce more food than they need to survive. Third, they live in towns or cities with some form of government. And fourth, there is a **division of labor**. This means that people perform specific, different jobs.

Agriculture and Civilization How did the development of agriculture affect the growth of civilization? Before agriculture, people spent almost all of their time finding food. When a group of people could produce more than it needed to survive, some people didn't have to grow food at all. They could develop other skills, such as making pottery or cloth. Then they could trade these goods or even services for food or other needs.

86 • Chapter 4

Teaching Objective 2

LEVEL 1: (Suggested time: 30 min) Have students list the four main characteristics shared by civilizations (organized society, produce extra food, live in towns and cities with governments, practice division of labor). Ask each student to write a short paragraph explaining how each characteristic relates to the development of civilization. (Answers will vary but should note that organized society allows for cooperation and the development of government, laws, and customs; surplus food allows time for activities besides survival; government helps ensure order; and division of labor allows people to do different jobs.) **ESOL**

LEVELS 2 AND 3: (Suggested time: 10 min) Have students complete the Level 1 activity. Then ask students to identify two more accomplishments characteristic of civilizations (a calendar and some form of writing). Have students work in pairs to draw two-column charts with one of these characteristics at the top of each column. Then ask students to list the reasons why each characteristic contributes to a civilization. (Examples: A calendar told people when to plant crops and when to expect rain; writing allowed people to keep records and communicate more easily.) Lead a discussion about the significance of calendars and writing in our civilization. **COOPERATIVE LEARNING**

Trade and Cities Once people began to trade, they had to deal with each other in more complex ways. Disagreements arose, creating a need for laws. Governments developed to fill that need. Government officials made laws and made sure they were obeyed. In addition, religious leaders taught people what they should and shouldn't do. During this time in human history, religion and government were closely connected. In fact, leaders often had both political and religious power.

When people traded, they went where they could exchange goods with other people. Many of these places were along rivers or seacoasts because people often traveled by water. Some of these places grew into cities where people exchanged ideas along with products. Over time, city dwellers built palaces, temples, and other public buildings.

The Development of Writing Trade in ancient times, like business today, required record-keeping. Written languages may have developed from this need. The invention of writing dates back to about 3000 B.C. in Southwest Asia. Farmers also needed to keep track of seasonal cycles. They had to know when it was time to plant new crops and when they could expect rain. Over time, they developed calendars.

Once they had writing and calendars, people began to keep written records of events. **History**, which is the written record of human civilization, had begun.

✔ **READING CHECK:** (*Identifying Cause and Effect*) How did trade lead to the development of writing? Written records were needed to produce and exchange goods.

River Valley Civilizations

Human civilization began in four different river valleys. Each of these regions provided rich soil and access to water for crops.

▼

Linking Past to Present

Another Benefit of Rivers The development of travel by water has stimulated the growth of trade. Throughout history, water travel has usually been cheaper and faster than travel overland. As a result, goods transported by water are usually cheaper than those that must come by land from far away.

Activity: Have students conduct research to determine the relative costs of sending a 50-pound package to a distant city by water and overland.

Teaching Objective 3

ALL LEVELS: (Suggested time: 20 min) Ask students to imagine that they are members of a farming community searching for a new home. Ask students what two features they would require in a new location (rich, fertile soil and water for their crops). Then call on volunteers to explain briefly why the earliest civilizations developed in river valleys. Have them locate the four river valleys where civilization began on the world map in the textbook's atlas. You may want to extend the activity by leading a discussion about what hazards these river valleys may have posed, in contrast to their advantages. (Possible answers: exposure to invasion, floods)

CLOSE

Call on volunteers to discuss how the illustrations in this section reflect the development and achievements of early humans.

REVIEW, ASSESS, RETEACH

Have students complete the Section Review. Then have pairs of students create a set of 10 question-and-answer flash cards about early humans and the birth of civilization. Pairs of students can then quiz each other with their cards. Then have students complete Daily Quiz 4.1.
ESOL, COOPERATIVE LEARNING

Answers to Section 1 Review

Define For definitions, see the glossary and index.

Reading for the Main Idea

1. Possible answers: Humans used stone tools 2.5 million years ago; humans created art 40,000 years ago. **(NGS 17)**

2. People traded the goods they made and the services they offered for food or other goods they needed. **(NGS 11)**

3. Water and fertile soil were necessary for farming. **(NGS 5)**

Critical Thinking

4. Disagreements arising from trade created the need for law and order.

Organizing What You Know

5. Outer ovals—people live in an organized society; able to produce more food than they need to survive; live in towns or cities with a government; practice division of labor

Visual Record Answer ▶

placed weights in one side of a balancing scale and goods for sale in the other to measure the amount of the goods

---

The people of the Indus Valley traded with other civilizations including Mesopotamia. These weights were used to weigh goods for sale such as wheat, rice, and cotton.

Interpreting the Visual Record **How do you think a merchant used these weights?**

River Valley Civilizations

Now let's return to the history of Southwest and Central Asia. The earliest civilization in these areas arose along the Tigris and Euphrates (yooh-FRAY-teez) Rivers in Southwest Asia. Called Mesopotamia, which means "between the rivers," this area was in present-day Iraq. Civilizations also developed in three other places. All four were river valleys. In the Nile River valley, Egyptian civilization developed. The first civilization of India was centered on the Indus River. Early Chinese civilization began in the valley of the Huang, or Yellow, River. (See the map on the previous page.)

These four river valleys had fertile soil for farming and water for irrigation. Because the people there had to work together to build irrigation and flood control systems, government developed further. The valley dwellers also learned how to make metal tools and weapons. First they used bronze, then iron. Eventually, the valley peoples developed advanced civilizations. In addition, all of them wrote down information about themselves. Thus, these civilizations mark the beginning of human history.

✓ **READING CHECK:** (**Drawing Inferences**) How did physical geography influence the beginnings of civilization? River valleys provided fertile soil and water for farming.

Homework Practice Online
Keyword: SK5 HP4

Define and explain: hominids, prehistory, nomads, land bridges, irrigation, division of labor, history

Reading for the Main Idea

1. (*Human Systems*) What are some important discoveries that scientists have made about life in prehistoric times?

2. (*Human Systems*) How did the division of labor lead to the development of trade?

3. (*Environment and Society*) Why did early civilizations develop around river valleys?

Critical Thinking

4. Identifying Cause and Effect How did the needs of early civilizations lead to the development of government?

Organizing What You Know

5. Summarizing Copy the following graphic organizer. Use it to describe the traits of civilizations.

What Is Civilization?

Have students complete Main Idea Activity S1. Then have students copy the headings and subheadings in the section. Ask them to write sentences stating the main ideas for each heading and subheading. **ESOL**

EXTEND

Invite interested students to conduct research about scientists who study ancient hominid and human remains, the methods they use, and the information they gather. Students may research "Lucy"—the female hominid who lived some 3 million years ago—whose skeletal remains were discovered by Donald Johanson in Ethiopia in 1974. Others may conduct research on the findings of Mary and Louis Leakey in Tanzania in the late 1970s. Encourage students to supplement their reports with graphics and illustrations. Have students present their findings to the class. **BLOCK SCHEDULING**

Section 2 — Mesopotamia and the Fertile Crescent

Read to Discover

1. What skills did the Sumerians develop?
2. What were some features of other civilizations of Mesopotamia and the Fertile Crescent?
3. What was Persian rule like?

Vocabulary

Fertile Crescent
ziggurats
pictographs
cuneiform
Hanging Gardens
provinces

People

Sumerians
Babylonians
Hammurabi
Hittites
Persians
Darius I

Places

Babylon

Reading Strategy

READING ORGANIZER Before you read, draw a circle in the center of a sheet of paper. Label the circle Fertile Crescent Groups. Draw six rays out from the circle and draw circles at the end of each ray. Label the outer circles Sumerians, Babylonians, Hittites, Assyrians, Chaldeans, and Persians. As you read, write what you learn about each group of people next to each circle.

The Fertile Crescent, c. 3000 B.C.

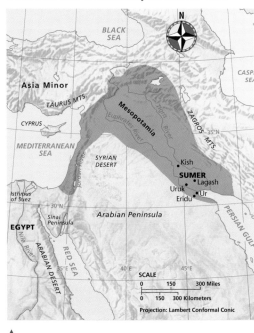

The world's earliest civilizations began in the Fertile Crescent. The waters of the Tigris, Euphrates, and Jordan Rivers allowed these civilizations to thrive.

The Fertile Crescent

A strip of fertile land begins along the Jordan River and curves through Southwest Asia to the Persian Gulf. The Tigris and the Euphrates (yooh-FRAY-teez) Rivers flow through Mesopotamia, the eastern part of the region. Because the land is good for farming, the area is called the **Fertile Crescent**.

The Tigris-Euphrates valley lies on a wide, flat plain. As a result, the rivers often flooded in the past.

The Land By 8000 B.C., farmers had begun to grow crops in the region. In time they learned to control river flooding and to irrigate their fields. Early residents worked together to build canals and dikes. They used these skills to irrigate their fields and return floodwaters to the rivers. A new civilization developed as a result of their cooperation.

Although the area's wide plain had good farmland, the flat topography allowed a problem to develop. No mountains or other natural barriers protected the area's borders from invasion. As a result, conquerors would often sweep in and take over the region.

Section 2

Objectives

1. Identify what skills the Sumerians developed.
2. Describe some features of other civilizations of Mesopotamia and the Fertile Crescent.
3. Explore what Persian rule was like.

FOCUS

Bellringer

Copy these instructions onto the chalkboard: *Look at the map on the first page of Section 2. You have probably seen this same region on news reports and in newspapers in recent years. What are some of the present-day countries of this area?* (Students will probably recognize the area as containing Israel, Turkey, Saudi Arabia, and Iraq.) Point out that although the region has certain advantages, such as three major rivers, it has also been the scene of conflict over the centuries.

Building Vocabulary

Write the vocabulary terms on the board and have students find their definitions. Point out that **ziggurat** is from the ancient Assyrian language—not one from which English has received many words. In contrast, many of our words come from Latin, including **cuneiform**, which comes from a Latin word for "wedge." Explain that cuneiform writing was done with a wedge-shaped stick that was pressed into clay.

SECTION 2 RESOURCES

Reproducibles
◆ Lecture Notes, Section 2
◆ Block Scheduling Handbook, Chapter 4
◆ Know It Notes S2
◆ Biography Activity: Darius I

Technology
◆ One-Stop Planner CD-ROM, Lesson 4.2
◆ Geography and Cultures Visual Resources 72
◆ Homework Practice Online
◆ HRW Go Site

Review, Reinforcement, and Assessment Resources
◆ Daily Quiz 4.2
◆ Main Idea Activity S2
◆ Chapter Summaries and Review
◆ English Audio Summary 4.2
◆ Spanish Audio Summary 4.2

EYE ON EARTH

Flatlanders Geographically, the Fertile Crescent is readily accessible from almost all directions. The mountains to the north and east have many valleys and natural passes. Unlike the Sahara in Africa, the desert to the west and south is easy to cross, as are the many rivers in the area. Thus, the Sumerians had few natural boundaries to protect their cities and farmland from invasion by nomadic peoples.

Critical Thinking: How might Mesopotamia's lack of natural boundaries have been an advantage also?

Answer: Although Mesopotamia was vulnerable to invasion, the Sumerians were able to reach the areas around it to engage in trade, exchange ideas, or invade their neighbors.

The Sumerians Historians say that the Sumerians developed the first civilization in the Fertile Crescent. They lived in an area called Sumer, in the southern part of Mesopotamia. Most Sumerians were farmers. When they could grow extra food, some people could become artisans and traders.

The Sumerians developed many technical skills. They were probably the first people to use wheeled vehicles. They also used a machine called a potter's wheel, which allowed workers to make high-quality bowls and jars. Sumerian builders were very advanced. To worship their gods, they built great temples, known as **ziggurats**. The ziggurats were shaped like pyramids and set upon heavy bases. Because the surrounding land was flat, people could see the temples from miles around. The ziggurats were both religious and governmental centers.

The Sumerians' greatest achievement was the world's first writing system. At first, people sent messages using small pictures, called pictographs, drawn on clay tablets. However, drawing these **pictographs** took too much time. So, the Sumerians simplified the pictures, until the marks no longer looked like the objects they represented. Over time, some of these simplified pictures stood for sounds, not objects. In this way, the first letters were created. To form the letters, a Sumerian writer would press the end of a triangular stick into soft clay. The stick formed wedge-shaped marks on the clay. This form of writing became known as **cuneiform** (kyoo-NEE-uh-fawrm).

✓ **READING CHECK:** (*Finding the Main Idea*) What was the Sumerians' greatest achievement? the world's first writing system

This ziggurat was built in about 2100 B.C. in what is now Iraq. When the ziggurat was first constructed, additional layers would have risen above those that remain. The Sumerians may have built ziggurats as bridges between heaven and Earth.

Interpreting the Visual Record How do you think visitors reacted when they first saw a ziggurat?

Visual Record Answer ▶

Visitors were probably very impressed by their first views of a ziggurat.

90 • Chapter 4

TEACH

Teaching Objective 1

ALL LEVELS: (Suggested time: 15 min.) Copy the following graphic organizer onto the chalkboard, omitting the blue answers. Have students work in pairs to fill it in with information about the Sumerians' accomplishments. Then lead a discussion about processes that are made easier or how societies can be helped by the development of a writing system. (Examples: keeping business records, writing down laws so that everyone knows what they are, recording instructions for later generations on how to perform various tasks, writing down historical events so that people can learn from them, and so on.) **ESOL, COOPERATIVE LEARNING,** [LS] **VISUAL-SPATIAL**

- first people to use wheeled vehicles
- potter's wheel—high-quality bowls and jars
- **Sumerians**
- first writing system—developed from pictographs into cuneiform
- ziggurats—pyramids set on heavy bases, both religious and government centers

A Flood of Invaders

Eventually, the Sumerians were conquered. Hundreds of years later the Babylonians (bab-l-LOHN-ee-uhnz) took over the same area. The culture is named for its beautiful city, Babylon, on the southern Euphrates River.

The Babylonians In some ways, the Babylonian and Sumerian civilizations were similar. The people were farmers, artisans, and traders. The Babylonians were even better merchants than the Sumerians. Babylonian traders went beyond the Fertile Crescent—all the way to Egypt and India.

The greatest Babylonian king was Hammurabi (ham-uh-RAHB-ee). In the 1790s B.C., he conquered most of the Tigris-Euphrates valley. Hammurabi was not only a powerful military leader but also an outstanding lawmaker. He put together a set of laws governing many aspects of daily life. The collection is known as the Code of Hammurabi. The code included the idea of "an eye for an eye." For example, if a poorly built house fell on and killed the owner, the builder was killed as a punishment. Penalties weren't equal, however. So, a slave may have suffered a worse punishment than a rich man for the same crime. Still, the code was an improvement on ancient customs. No longer could people take the law into their own hands.

The Hittites Babylon fell to invaders around 1600 B.C. The first of these conquerors were the Hittites (HIT-yts). They came from what is now southeastern Turkey.

The Hittites had two major skills that helped them conquer their enemies. They built chariots and used them well in battle. In addition, they were among the first people to make iron weapons. They learned to use heat to separate the metal from iron ore. Iron tools, such as a better plow, helped the Hittites in peacetime also.

BIOGRAPHY

Hammurabi
(died c. 1750 B.C.)

As king of Babylon in the 1700s B.C., Hammurabi collected 282 laws, known as the Code of Hammurabi. The code was one of the world's first sets of written laws. Hammurabi's laws dealt with family matters, trade, agriculture, and criminal acts.

The code ends with a blessing for people who obey the laws and curses for those who do not. Inscribed on a large plaque, the code survives today. It is in the Louvre Museum in Paris. *What activities did the Code of Hammurabi address?*

Cultural Kaleidoscope
Hittite Religion A Hittite king was also his kingdom's chief priest. On occasion, a king would even hurry home from a military campaign to perform religious duties.

When a Hittite king died he supposedly became a god. The Hittites also had a custom of adopting the gods of their conquered subjects. As a result, the number of Hittite gods continued to grow. At the height of their power, the Hittites may have worshipped more than 600 gods. Arinna the sun goddess was the most powerful of the deities, while Tarhunnas the weather god stood at her side.

Critical Thinking: Why do you think the Hittites adopted the gods of their conquered subjects?

Answer: Students may suggest that the Hittites wanted to win some acceptance from the peoples they conquered.

The ruins of an ancient Hittite city in present-day Turkey reflects the impressive building skills of the Hittites. This entrance is known as the Lion Gate for its sculptures of lions that guarded the city.

◀

◀**Biography Answer**

family matters, trade, agriculture, and criminal acts

The History of Southwest and Central Asia • 91

Teaching Objective 2

LEVEL 1: (Suggested time: 45 min.) Organize the class into four groups—for the Babylonians, Hittites, Assyrians, and Chaldeans. Supply art and craft materials. Have each group create a movie poster for an action movie about its assigned culture. You may also want to have groups create storyboards for trailers for their movies. Students may also develop characters and storylines for them. **ESOL, COOPERATIVE LEARNING, LS VISUAL-SPATIAL**

LEVEL 2: (Suggested time: 30 min.) Have each student write a paragraph or brief essay to fill in and complete these statements: "I would have liked to visit Mesopotamia and the Fertile Crescent while the _____ were in power because _____. I would not have liked to visit Mesopotamia and the Fertile Crescent while the _____ were in power because _____." Then call on volunteers to read their paragraphs or essays to the class. **LS VERBAL-LINGUISTIC**

USING ILLUSTRATIONS

The Hanging Gardens of Babylon Focus students' attention on the illustration on this page. Invite students to talk about what it might have been like to have such gardens in one's palace.

Point out that over the centuries many artists have depicted the gardens, and in many different ways—some of them quite fanciful. Lead a discussion about why the Hanging Gardens of Babylon may have caught the imagination of artists so forcefully. (Possible answers: Factors that may have contributed to the gardens' fascination could include their growing many floors above the ground, the contrast of lush vegetation in the middle of a desert, or the romantic story about the king who wanted to make his queen happy.)

The Hanging Gardens of Babylon were included in the Seven Wonders of the World, but no traces of the gardens remain today. However, written accounts of the gardens describe the terraces irrigated by the Euphrates River. This painting shows one artist's idea about how the gardens may have looked.

▼

The Assyrians Next on the scene were the Assyrians, who swooped down from northern Mesopotamia. Their army was fearsome. It was organized into regular units, led by professional officers, and equipped with iron weapons. The Assyrian army was able to conquer an empire that stretched all the way to Egypt.

Assyrians ruled by terror. They used cruel punishments on those who dared to get in their way. Sometimes when they had conquered a people, they carried all of them off to a different land. These methods made many enemies, of course. In the 600s B.C. the Assyrians lost their empire.

The Chaldeans As the Assyrian Empire crumbled, the Chaldeans took over their lands. Under their king Nebuchadnezzar (neb-uh-kuhd-NEZ-uhr), Babylon again became a great city. Its most famous feature were its **Hanging Gardens**. These were actually lush gardens built on rooftops. Water pumped from the Euphrates River kept the gardens green. According to legend, the king ordered the gardens be planted for his wife. She missed the green hills of her homeland.

The Chaldeans were expert astronomers, making careful records of the movement of stars and planets. They also excelled at mathematics. The Chaldeans developed the idea of square roots along with many other basic mathematical concepts.

✓ **READING CHECK:** *Summarizing* What were the names of four other major Mesopotamian civilizations? Babylonians, Hittites, Assyrians, Chaldeans

92 • Chapter 4

Teaching Objective 3

LEVEL 1: (Suggested time: 30 min.) Ask students to imagine that they are Persian soldiers like the one whose picture appears on the next page. Have each student write a letter home to friends or family in the voice of the soldier. Encourage students to include details about Persian civilization in their letters. **LS** INTRAPERSONAL

LEVEL 2: (Suggested time: 30 min.) Organize the class into pairs and supply encyclopedias or other research materials. Point out that the Persians interacted with some other cultures that students have studied or will study. For example, the ancient Greeks fought a series of wars with the Persians. The Greeks, then, had their own views of Persian civilization. Have each pair of students examine research materials to find other peoples' opinions of the Persians and to compare those opinions with the text information. Call on volunteers to share what they have found with the class. **COOPERATIVE LEARNING, LS** LOGICAL-MATHEMATICAL

The Persians

Another civilization, however, would outshine those that had come before it. A people called the Persians spread out from Iran. In 539 B.C. they conquered Babylon. Little by little, Persian rulers took over all the lands between India and southeastern Europe. Their empire became the largest the world had ever seen. King Darius I was one of its most powerful rulers.

Persian Rule The Persian Empire was divided into large areas called **provinces**. Darius named a governor to rule each one. Darius also used spies called "the king's eyes and ears" to report on the governors. He wanted to make sure they stayed loyal to him. The provinces had to pay heavy taxes to Darius and supply soldiers for his army.

A huge system of well-built roads made this system work. Spies, along with messengers, soldiers, and traders, could move around the empire easily. By changing horses at stations along the way, fast riders could cover about 1,700 miles in nine days.

Persian Law Because it was so large, many different peoples with different customs lived within the empire. In general, the Persians allowed people to keep their own religions, languages, and even local laws. For example, women of old Babylon had more rights than women in Iran. A system of Persian laws, however, applied to everybody. Government officials made sure the judges were fair and didn't take bribes. In fact, justice and fairness were very important to Persian society.

✓ **READING CHECK:** (*Analyzing Information*) Why was Persian rule successful? spies, huge system of well-built roads, system of laws and justice

▲
A highly skilled army helped expand and maintain the Persian Empire. Archers like this one belonged to an elite unit called the "10,000 immortals."

Section Review 2

Define or identify: Fertile Crescent, Sumerians, ziggurats, pictographs, cuneiform, Babylonians, Hammurabi, Hittites, Hanging Gardens, Persians, Darius I, provinces

Reading for the Main Idea

1. (*Finding the Main Idea*) What were the Sumerians' main achievements?

2. (*Summarizing*) What are some lasting contributions made by the peoples of Southwest Asia?

Critical Thinking

3. **Making Generalizations** How did Mesopotamia's physical geography affect its history?

4. **Comparing and Contrasting** How did Assyrian rule compare to Persian rule?

Organizing What You Know

5. **Time Line** Copy the following time line onto a large piece of paper. Fill in as many events as you can.

3000 B.C.   2000 B.C.   1000 B.C.   A.D. 1
    2500 B.C.   1500 B.C.   500 B.C.

go.hrw.com **Homework Practice Online** Keyword: SK5 HP4

Answers to Section 2 Review

Define or identify For definitions and identifications, see the glossary and index.

Reading for the Main Idea

1. use of wheeled vehicles, potter's wheel, ziggurats, world's first writing system

2. in addition to the Sumerian achievements, Hammurabi's Code, chariots, iron, astronomy, mathematical concepts, government organization of the Persians, Persian law

Critical Thinking

3. The flat land was excellent for agriculture, but it lacked natural barriers to invasion.

4. The Persians organized their empire carefully and were concerned about justice and fairness. In contrast, the Assyrians ruled by terror. **(NGS 13)**

Organizing What You Know

5. 8000 B.C.—farming established in the region; 1790s B.C.—Hammurabi conquered most of the Tigris-Euphrates valley; 1600 B.C.—Babylon fell to invaders; 600s B.C.—Assyrians lost their empire; 539 B.C.—Persians conquered Babylon.

CLOSE

Lead a brief class discussion about possible reasons why the Code of Hammurabi allowed different punishments for the same crime.

REVIEW, ASSESS, RETEACH

Have students complete the Section Review. Then have students choose one of the civilizations discussed in the section and write three statements about it. These statements should begin "I come from a civilization that....," or "In my civilization..." Have students play a who-am-I game using the statements. Then have students complete Daily Quiz 4.2.

Have students complete Main Idea Activity S2. Then have students work in pairs to create graphic organizers using the section's content.
ESOL, COOPERATIVE LEARNING

EXTEND

Have interested students conduct research on the looting of ancient artifacts from Iraqi museums and archaeological sites during the 2003 war in Iraq and the significance of those artifacts to the cultures they represented.

Section 3 Land of Three Faiths

Read to Discover
1. How did Judaism develop in Southwest Asia?
2. How did the life of Jesus lead to the development of Christianity?
3. Who was Muhammad, and what did he teach?

Vocabulary
Judaism
Exodus
Ten Commandments
monotheism
Torah
Gospels
disciples
Resurrection

Christianity
New Testament
Qur'an
Five Pillars of Islam

Places
Palestine
Jerusalem
Mecca

People
Hebrews
Abraham
Moses
Jesus
Saul of Tarsus
Muhammad
Muslims

Reading Strategy

FOLDNOTES: TRI-FOLD Create a **Tri-Fold** FoldNote described in the Appendix. Label one column Judaism, another Christianity, and the third Islam. As you read this section, write what you learn about each religion on the FoldNote.

Judaism

You have read how many civilizations developed in the Fertile Crescent and nearby lands in Southwest Asia. The region was also the birthplace of three religions—Judaism, Christianity, and Islam. All three grew into worldwide religions with many millions of followers.

Floor tiles from an ancient synagogue in Israel form an image of a Jewish menorah. This seven-branched candleholder is a symbol of Judaism and used during the celebration of Hanukkah.

Out of Sumer The oldest of the three faiths is **Judaism**. It developed among a people called the Hebrews, who lived in the grasslands of the Fertile Crescent. Much of what we know about the Hebrews comes from their own writings. These writings later were the basis for the Bible. According to these accounts, the founder of the Hebrews was a shepherd from Sumer named Abraham.

Perhaps in about 2000 B.C., Abraham led his family to the area called Palestine. The Bible tells that God commanded Abraham to move there. If Abraham obeyed this command, God promised him a new nation. This agreement would give birth to the nation of Israel. Abraham's descendants lived in Israel for many years. Eventually, the Hebrews went to Egypt. The Egyptians made them slaves. According to tradition, a leader named Moses led them out of Egypt. They went northeast in search of the "promised land." Today, Jews still celebrate the **Exodus**, the escape from slavery in Egypt.

Section 3

Objectives
1. Trace how Judaism developed in Southwest Asia.
2. Explore how the life of Jesus led to the development of Christianity.
3. Clarify who Muhammad was and what he taught.

FOCUS

Bellringer

Copy the following instructions onto the chalkboard: *What are some ways that religious beliefs are affecting world events?* Discuss responses. (Students may note terrorist acts based on religious beliefs, humanitarian aid by faith-based organizations, religious aspects of various social issues, or other examples.) Point out that study of the world's religions is essential to understanding history—both ancient and modern.

Building Vocabulary

Write the vocabulary terms on the chalkboard and have students read their definitions. Then write *Judaism, Christianity,* and *Islam* on the board. Ask students to come to the board and write the vocabulary terms under the religion to which they relate.

Moses Character Trait: Responsibility

According to the Bible, Moses accepted the responsibility for getting the Hebrews released from slavery and bringing them to a faraway promised land. The task required that he lead them across the Red Sea and through a desert. Although the Hebrews found their promised land, Moses died before he could reach it.

Moses is an important figure in three of the world's great religions. The words of Moses lived on and helped shape the Jewish faith. He is also revered by Christians and Muslims.

How may a sense of responsibility have aided Moses throughout the journey?

BIOGRAPHY

Judaism's Beginnings The Bible tells that during the journey, Moses brought the **Ten Commandments** to his people. These were laws given to him by the Hebrew god Yahweh (YAH-way). They stressed the importance of worshipping God. The commandments also taught people to honor their parents and how to live together in peace. For example, they shouldn't lie, steal, or kill. When the Hebrews agreed to follow the Ten Commandments, they accepted God's rule. The agreement to live by God's laws in return for his protection was called a covenant.

Over time, the Hebrews' basic ideas about God changed. At first, they thought of Yahweh as one god among other gods. Later they saw him as the only God. We call this idea **monotheism**. With the change to monotheism, the religion we know today as Judaism truly began.

The Torah and Mosaic Law The teachings of Moses were written down in five books, known as the **Torah**. The Hebrew word Torah means "to show the way," or "to teach." The law of Moses, or Mosaic law, included the Ten Commandments along with laws written later. Jewish synagogues keep a copy of the Torah on handwritten scrolls of parchment.

Mosaic law valued human life more than did older laws. Mosaic law also guided Hebrews' daily lives. The laws said that the Hebrews must not work on the Sabbath, the seventh day of each week. The Sabbath was considered a day of worship and rest. The laws set down other rules, such as which foods Jews could eat. Jews believe that keeping these laws is part of the covenant that the Hebrews made with God centuries ago. Belief in God and their covenant has helped the Jews endure through many hardships.

By the late 900s B.C., Israel was split in two. The northern kingdom remained Israel, with Samaria as its capital. The southern kingdom became Judah, with Jerusalem as its capital.

▼

The Founding of Israel, c. 900s B.C.

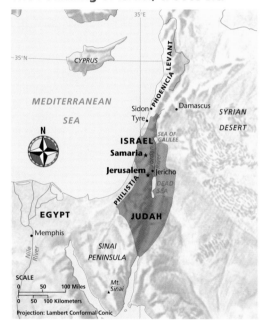

SCALE
0   50   100 Miles
0 50 100 Kilometers
Projection: Lambert Conformal Conic

✓ **READING CHECK:** *Analyzing Information* How did Judaism change over time? The Hebrews' ideas about Yahweh changed to monotheism.

The History of Southwest and Central Asia • 95

TEACH

Teaching Objective 1

LEVEL 1: (Suggested time: 15 min.) Write this statement on the chalkboard: *Judaism was not founded by a single individual, but developed gradually over time.* Have students write a paragraph expanding on the statement. (Students should note that Abraham and Moses were among the people important to the history of Judaism. They should also observe that the Hebrews' concept of God changed over time.)

LS VERBAL-LINGUISTIC

LEVELS 2 AND 3: (Suggested time: 45 min.) Provide research materials for this activity. Note that information on the subject matter is available in both religious and secular sources.

Have students work in pairs or groups to conduct research on men and women whose stories are told in the Old Testament. Examples include Noah, Cain and Abel, Joshua, Judith and Holofernes, Samson and Delilah, Samuel, Solomon, Saul, David, Ruth and Naomi, and Job. Ask students to report on their subjects, along with information on what lessons or principles the stories illustrate. For example, the story of Job emphasizes patience and faith in the face of adversity. **COOPERATIVE LEARNING**

Across the Curriculum
LITERATURE

Sources for the Life of Jesus The first four books of the New Testament, the Gospels, are the main sources for information about the life of Jesus. These books are attributed to Matthew, Mark, Luke, and John. The first three agree closely with each other. The fourth, John, is quite different from the others in many details.

Non-Christian writers also mention Jesus, but not in great detail. The Roman writers Tacitus, Suetonius, and Pliny the Younger all refer to Jesus. A Jewish writer named Josephus—or Joseph ben Matthias—also records something about Jesus.

Activity: Have interested students compare the various sources for historical information about Jesus.

Visual Record Answer ▶

Answers will vary, but may include the cross, halo, and palm branches.

This mosaic above the entrance to an Italian mausoleum is an example of early Christian art. Jesus shown as a shepherd taking care of sheep is a common Christian symbol.

Interpreting the Visual Record What other symbols do you see in the picture?

▶

Christianity

To study the next religion, we look again to Judaism and a time about 2,000 years ago. Not all Jews held exactly the same beliefs. Some Jews wanted to rebel against the Romans, who had conquered their ancient land. Others believed a Messiah, or spiritual leader, would save them from all enemies. Long before, Jewish holy men called prophets had said that the Messiah would come some day.

Birth and Life of Jesus of Nazareth As you can see, these were troubled times. Into this setting a boy was born in Bethlehem to a poor young woman and her carpenter husband. The boy Jesus grew up in Nazareth as a faithful Jew.

Most of what we know about Jesus comes from the first four books of the New Testament in the Christian Bible. These books, known as the **Gospels**, tell that Jesus studied the writings of Jewish prophets. Eventually, Jesus began to preach. A small group of followers called **disciples** helped spread his message. Jesus told the people who gathered around him that God would judge humanity. To prepare, people should ask God to forgive them for having sinned.

Jesus had two basic commandments for his followers. They should love God above all else and love others as much as they loved themselves. He also said that people should be humble and kind. His message of love and forgiveness drew large crowds.

Death and Resurrection The authorities didn't like the fact that Jesus was so popular. Some leaders thought that Jesus was putting himself above religious and civil law. Finally, the authorities in Jerusalem decided that Jesus was a serious problem and had to be executed.

According to the Gospels, the Romans crucified Jesus. That is, he was nailed to a wooden cross and left there to die. The Gospels report that after Jesus died on the cross he was buried, but rose from the dead three days later. This event was the **Resurrection**. After living

96 • Chapter 4

Teaching Objective 2

LEVEL 2: (Suggested time: 20 min.) Tell students that Jesus is reported to have drawn many people to him at an event called The Sermon on the Mount. In this sermon, among many other messages, Jesus preached about the importance of working for peace; being meek, merciful, and pure in heart; and seeking righteousness. Have each student write a diary entry as if he or she had been present for the sermon. Students may choose to be a follower of Jesus, a Roman soldier, a Jew who is unconvinced by the words of Jesus, or another role. Note that additional information on The Sermon on the Mount is available in both religious and secular sources.
LS INTRAPERSONAL

LEVEL 3: Provide research materials and outline maps of the eastern Mediterranean region. Have students work in groups to map the journeys of Paul and to summarize his activities while on those travels. Note that information on the subject matter is available in both religious and secular sources. **COOPERATIVE LEARNING**

The Spread of Christianity

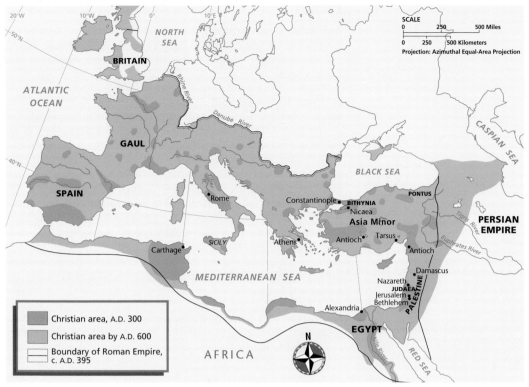

SCALE
0   250   500 Miles
0   250   500 Kilometers
Projection: Azimuthal Equal-Area Projection

Christian area, A.D. 300
Christian area by A.D. 600
Boundary of Roman Empire, c. A.D. 395

among his disciples for 40 days, Jesus rose into heaven. The disciples believed that these events showed that Jesus was indeed the Messiah. They called him Jesus Christ. Christos was the Greek word for Messiah. From this word we get the name for the new faith, **Christianity**.

A New Faith The early Christians taught that because Jesus died for them and conquered death, all people could be saved. That is, everyone's sins could be forgiven, and they could live again after death.

At first, the disciples preached only to other Jews. One Jew, Saul of Tarsus, preached the Christian message to non-Jews too. Saul, also called Paul, said that people didn't have to be Jews in order to be Christians. Paul traveled throughout the eastern Mediterranean area preaching. His encouraging letters to Christian communities make up a large portion of the **New Testament**. This part of the Bible tells the stories of Jesus, his followers, and later Christian ideas. Christians around the world base their faith on the message of the New Testament.

▲ From its beginnings in Judea, in some 300 years Christianity spread across the Roman Empire and beyond. Some of the Roman emperors persecuted Christians. Constantine was the first emperor to embrace the faith—in the early A.D. 300s.

Interpreting the Map What are some of the cities where Christianity was well established by the end of the A.D. 300s?

READING CHECK: *Finding the Main Idea* On what event did early Christians base their preaching? the Resurrection of Jesus

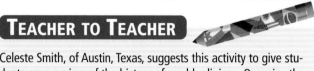

DAILY LIFE

Prayer Rugs The use of prayer rugs developed many years after the death of Muhammad. Muslims often use them to cover the ground on which they worship. Prayer rugs are usually 2 to 4 feet wide and 4 to 8 feet long. They may be decorated with religious designs or prayers in beautiful Arabic script.

Islamic art generally does not include images of humans or animals. Therefore, prayer rugs are characterized by rich colors and detailed geometric patterns. These decorations always include the arched *mihrab,* or prayer niche, that is pointed toward Mecca when the rug is in use.

In this photo, Iraqi Muslims kneel to pray. Devout Muslims pray five times a day while facing Mecca, the holy city of Islam. At the proper times, a person called a muezzin calls the faithful to prayer from a high tower called a minaret.

▼

Islam

Both Judaism and Christianity teach that there is only one God. **Islam**, the third of the great religions that developed in Southwest Asia, is also monotheistic. It began farther to the southeast, in what is now Saudi Arabia.

A Voice in the Desert In the A.D. 600s, Arabia didn't have a central government. Instead, Arab clans often fought for wealth and power. Most Arabs worshipped many gods and goddesses. One of the places where they worshipped their gods was in the town of Mecca.

A young businessman named Muhammad often left Mecca's crowded streets to pray in a desert cave. One day, according to Islamic belief, Muhammad heard a voice cut through the cave's silence. The voice was that of an angel. It ordered Muhammad to tell about the glories of Allah—"God" in Arabic. Over the next 22 years, Muhammad received hundreds of messages. Muhammad and his early followers memorized or wrote down all of Allah's messages. After Muhammad's death, his followers put together all of these messages in one book called the **Qur'an**. This holy book of Islam is written in Arabic and contains 114 chapters.

Muhammad's Message Muhammad began with only two basic ideas. First, there was only one God. Second, everyone who believed in God had to follow his laws. Believers then formed a special community. Members of this community were supposed to help each other.

These ideas weren't popular. Merchants made money off of the people who came to Mecca to worship the old gods. They didn't want Arabs to believe in only one god. Clan leaders didn't like the idea of one big community. They feared they would lose power. Mecca's rulers started to threaten Muhammad. Finally, in 622, Muhammad and his followers fled about 200 miles to the town of Medina. This event is called the *hijrah* (hi-JY-ruh), or "flight." It came to mark the beginning of the Islamic calendar. After many years of fighting, Mecca finally welcomed Muhammad back to the city.

Teaching Objective 3

LEVEL 1: (Suggested time: 15 min.) Copy the following graphic organizer onto the chalkboard, omitting the blue answers. Have students complete it to review events in the life of Muhammad according to Islamic tradition and the spread of Islam. Students' graphic organizers will vary.
ESOL, [LS] **VISUAL-SPATIAL**

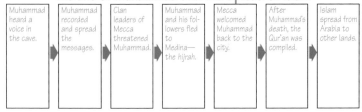

The Life of Muhammad and the Spread of Islam

| Muhammad heard a voice in the cave. | Muhammad recorded and spread the messages. | Clan leaders of Mecca threatened Muhammad. | Muhammad and his followers fled to Medina—the hijrah. | Mecca welcomed Muhammad back to the city. | After Muhammad's death, the Qur'an was compiled. | Islam spread from Arabia to other lands. |

LEVEL 2: (Suggested time: 30 min.) Have students create name poems of *Muhammad* or other names or concepts related to Islam. To create a name poem, have each student write the word or name down the page and then add a word, phrase, or sentence horizontally that begins with the first letter of the original word and provides information about it. For example, for the "M" in "Muhammad," a student may write "Medina was where he fled during the *hijrah*." Then have students decorate their name poems with geometric and plant designs, since early Islamic tradition required that art not show animals or people. [LS] **VISUAL-SPATIAL**

The Five Pillars At Muhammad's death, the basis for a new religion had been laid. Followers of Islam, called Muslims, were to follow five rules. They are called the **Five Pillars of Islam**. The Five Pillars order Muslims to: (1) Say that there is only one God, and that Muhammad is God's prophet; (2) Pray five times a day toward Mecca; (3) Help the poor; (4) Fast during the holy month of Ramadan; and (5) Go on a pilgrimage to Mecca.

Other rules apply also. Muslims are not supposed to drink alcohol or eat pork. Although Muslim men may have four wives, they must treat each wife with respect. Many other rules appear in the Qur'an. They include rules about inheriting property and the treatment of slaves.

Muslims believe that people who obey God's rules go to a paradise when they die. The Qur'an describes it as a beautiful garden full of wonderful things, like fine food. Those who did not obey God would burn in fire forever.

We have seen that three religions began in Southwest Asia. Of these, Islam became the most widespread in the region. In fact, within a hundred years of Muhammad's death, Islam stretched from the Atlantic Ocean to India. You will learn how that happened in the next section.

✓ **READING CHECK:** *Identifying Cause and Effect*
Why did Mecca's rulers reject Muhammad's message at first?
Merchants made money off of the people who came to Mecca to worship the old gods. Clan leaders feared they would lose power if people formed one big community.

In the courtyard of the Great Mosque in Mecca stands a shrine called the Kaaba. Each year, millions of Muslims travel to Mecca during the hajj, or pilgrimage, and circle the Kaaba seven times. Muslims consider the site the most sacred place on Earth.

▼

Homework Practice Online
Keyword: SK5 HP4

Define or identify: Judaism, Hebrews, Abraham, Moses, Exodus, Ten Commandments, monotheism, Torah, Jesus, Gospels, disciples, Resurrection, Christianity, Saul of Tarsus, New Testament, Islam, Muhammad, Qur'an, Muslims, Five Pillars of Islam

Reading for the Main Idea

1. *Places and Regions* What role does Mosaic law play in Judaism?
2. *Places and Regions* How did Saul of Tarsus affect early Christianity?

Critical Thinking

3. **Drawing Inferences and Conclusions** Which of the Five Pillars of Islam is related to how Muslims should treat other people?

4. **Drawing Inferences and Conclusions** What are features that Judaism, Christianity, and Islam have in common?

Organizing What You Know

5. **Summarizing** Copy the graphic organizer below. Use it to describe the main beliefs of Judaism, Christianity, and Islam.

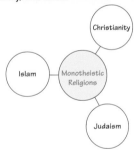

The History of Southwest and Central Asia • 99

Answers to Section 3 Review

Define or identify For definitions and identifications, see the glossary and index.

Reading for the Main Idea

1. central role, because they contain teachings of Moses, the Ten Commandments, and Jewish laws **(NGS 10)**
2. said that non-Jews could become Christians, spread Christianity throughout the eastern Mediterranean world

Critical Thinking

3. the third pillar, about requiring that Muslims help the poor
4. Answers will vary but should include that all are monotheistic and require a virtuous life of their followers. **(NGS 10)**

Organizing What You Know

5. Use the section content to fill in the graphic organizer.

CLOSE

Remind students that all three of the religions covered in this section are monotheistic. Challenge students to note the roles that these faiths will play in events as students continue their studies of the Eastern Hemisphere.

REVIEW, ASSESS, RETEACH

Have students complete the Section Review. Then have students write down important names, places, vocabulary terms, and ideas covered in the section and describe their significance.

Have students complete Daily Quiz S3. Then have students work in pairs to re-read the section to each other, pausing to discuss material that poses difficulty. **COOPERATIVE LEARNING**

EXTEND

Have interested students conduct research on minority sects or divisions of the three religions. Some of these divisions had many followers long ago but have faded into history. Others still have many adherents. For example, some students may want to learn more about the Nestorian Church, which is an ancient Persian form of Christianity that claims some 175,000 followers. **BLOCK SCHEDULING**

Section 4 Empires in Southwest and Central Asia

Read to Discover
1. How did Islam spread to become a large empire?
2. What other rulers took over Southwest and Central Asia?

Vocabulary
caliph
mosques
shah

People
Abbasids
Caliph Harun ar-Rashid
Mongols
Genghis Khan
Ottoman Turks
Suleiman
Babur the Tiger

Places
Baghdad

Reading Strategy

TAKING NOTES Use the headings in this section to create an outline. As you read this section, write what you learn about Southwest and Central Asia under each heading.

The Muslim Empire

After the death of Muhammad, Abu Bakr became Islam's first caliph, or successor, in A.D. 632.

Muhammad's followers formed an army that fought for control of Arabia. By the time of his death in 632, they had taken over most of the peninsula. A new problem arose, however. Muhammad's followers couldn't agree on who should be the leader. They broke into two groups over who should be **caliph** (KAY-luhf), which means "deputy."

Muhammad had not named anyone to take over his leadership role. He did have a daughter, Fatima. Some of Muhammad's followers thought the caliph should be a descendant of Fatima and her husband Ali. Another group thought that any Muslim could become caliph. The first group eventually became known as the Shia. People in the second group were called the Sunni. This division still plays a big role in modern politics in Southwest Asia.

Spreading the Word Although the conflict was bitter and bloody, the division didn't slow the growth of Islam. One reason lay with a policy begun by 'Umar (OO-mahr), one of Muhammad's closest friends. People could get money if they or family members signed up to serve in the military. The armies grew huge and powerful as a result. Mighty Persia fell to them by 642. The armies pushed south and west. By 750, Muslim forces had conquered the Arabian Peninsula, North Africa, and Spain.

100 • **Chapter 4**

Section 4

Objectives
1. Show how Islam spread to become a large empire.
2. Describe other rulers who took over Southwest and Central Asia.

FOCUS

Bellringer

Copy this passage onto the chalkboard: *You learned in the last section that Islam eventually extended from the Atlantic Ocean to India. How do you think this was accomplished?* (Students may suggest willing conversion, forced conversion, military conquest, or other methods.) Tell students they will learn how Islam spread and how other empires took control of Southwest and Central Asia in this section.

Building Vocabulary

Write the vocabulary terms on the chalkboard and call on volunteers to read their definitions aloud. Point out that **caliph** and **mosques** come from the Arabic language and the **shah** is from Persian.

The Spread of Islam

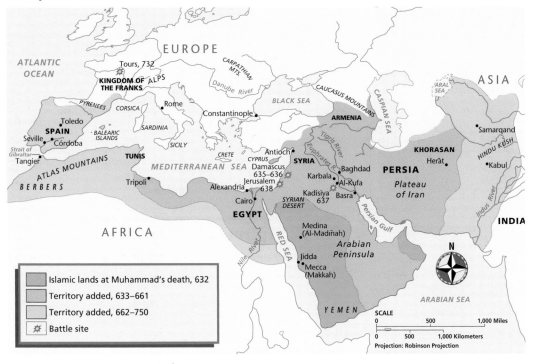

Many of the conquered people chose to become Muslims. Others did not. The Qur'an had given special protection to Jews, Christians, and other people who had written religious texts. They were called People of the Book. These protected peoples had to pay higher taxes than Muslims. In general, though, the taxes weren't a heavy burden.

Abbasid Rule Meanwhile, conflict within the Muslim leadership continued. For a time, a clan that had fought against Muhammad in Mecca was in power. Later, a new group that claimed descent from Muhammad's uncle 'Abbas took over the leadership. They were called the Abbasids. Abbasid rule reached its height under Caliph Harun ar-Rashid (huh-ROON ahr-rah-SHEED). Under Harun's rule industries in metalwork, paper, and cloth developed. He supported musicians and poets. However, Harun had the power of life and death over his subjects and often used that power. Stories tell that Harun would leave his palace in disguise with his executioner at his side.

Baghdad, on the Tigris River, was Harun's capital. It became a center of learning, with a fine university. It was a beautiful busy city at the center of a vast trade network. Among the goods that flowed through Baghdad were carpets, silks, rubies, peacocks, horses, and medicines. By the middle of the 1000s, however, invasions by nomadic tribes and crop failures caused Baghdad to decline.

In the 100 years following Muhammad's death, Islam spread quickly. Muslim Arabs conquered many other peoples, uniting them within Islam.

Interpreting the Map How far west had Islam spread by A.D. 662?

Across the Curriculum
LITERATURE

The *Thousand and One Nights* One of the world's most famous collections of stories was written down about a thousand years ago. Although the stories were first written in Arabic, they also have connections in India, Iran, Iraq, Egypt, Turkey, and possibly Greece.

The *Thousand and One Nights*, also known as *Arabian Nights*, are said to be stories told by a beautiful young woman to save her own life. According to the basic plot, a king hated all women, after having been betrayed by his wife. So, each day he would marry and kill a new wife. The number of women in the kingdom was gradually exhausted. Finally, the vizier's daughter Sheherazade was picked as the unlucky next wife. She had a plan, however. Every evening she told her husband a new story, but would save the ending for the next night. Sheherazade's stories were so entertaining that the troubled king gave up his wicked ways. Sheherazade's tales comprise the *Thousand and One Nights.*

◄**Map Answer**

all the way to the Atlantic Ocean coasts of Spain and North Africa

TEACH

Teaching Objective 1

ALL LEVELS: (Suggested time: 15 min.) Lead a class discussion about the origin of the split between Sunni and Shia Muslims. (Shia—The caliph should be a descendant of Muhammad's daughter Fatima and her husband; Sunni—Any Muslim could become the caliph.) Point out that this division still plays a big role in political events in Southwest Asia and elsewhere in the Islamic world. You may want to challenge students to examine newspapers for stories that mention Sunni and Shia Muslims. **ESOL**

LEVEL 2: (Suggested time: 30 min.) Ask students to imagine that they are historians living in Spain, North Africa, or what is now Pakistan in the year A.D. 750. They have been asked to write a new introduction to update a history of the Mediterranean world published in A.D. 500. Have students write their introductions to summarize what happened in the Mediterranean world in the 250 years between the publication of the two editions.
LS VERBAL-LINGUISTIC

A Soldier's Life Horses were absolutely essential to the spread and success of the Mongol Empire. The Mongol soldier spent his life in the saddle. When the army was on the move, the Mongols could even sleep while riding. At one time in Hungary, the Mongol cavalry traveled 270 miles in only three days. The Mongols also used iron stirrups and powerful compound bows that could be used effectively from the saddle.

Critical Thinking: Ask students what advantages excellent horsemanship gave the Mongols.

Answer: Students should mention better mobility and versatility as soldiers.

The interior of the Great Mosque in Córdoba, Spain, shows the lasting beauty of Moorish architecture. A cathedral was built within the mosque after Christians took back the city.

Interpreting the Visual Record Why do you think arches are important in certain building designs?

Visual Record Answers ▶

They can hold up heavy loads and leave interior spaces open.

use and style of bows and arrows, styles of human and horse armor, use of musical instruments on the battlefield

▶

This illustration from the 1200s shows a Mongol battle.

Interpreting the Visual Record What may this picture tell us about Mongol armor and weapons?

102 • Chapter 4

Muslim Civilization The Muslim Empire grew rich from trade with other parts of the world. To help manage the huge empire's economy, banking developed. Banks had both central and branch offices. Bankers even worked with letters of credit, similar to today's checks.

The Muslim Empire had many accomplishments. Centers of learning like Córdoba and Toledo in Spain attracted scholars from around the world. Muslim doctors were highly skilled. They even performed eye surgery! Geographers drew remarkably accurate maps. Mathematicians introduced the number system we use today to Europe. Throughout the Islamic world, architects built beautiful houses of worship called **mosques**.

✓ **READING CHECK:** (*Finding the Main Idea*) How far did the Muslim Empire reach? the Arabian Peninsula, North Africa, and Spain

Later Empires

In the 1200s, a new threat faced Islam. From far to the east came the Mongols, a fierce non-Muslim tribe of nomads. The Mongols were skilled warriors who fought on horseback. Under Genghis Khan and his descendants, the Mongols conquered a huge empire. It reached from Korea in the east to what is now Hungary in Europe. The ancient lands of Mesopotamia and Persia fell into Mongol hands. In 1258 the Mongols killed the last Abbasid caliph and destroyed Baghdad. Later, the region's Mongol rulers converted to Islam. Fights between Mongols broke out, though. The Mongol Empire in Southwest and Central Asia fell apart.

Teaching Objective 2

ALL LEVELS: (Suggested time: 15 min.) Copy the following graphic organizer onto the chalkboard, omitting the blue answers. Have students complete it to distinguish among the four later empires covered in this section. Point out that only the Mongols were non-Muslims, but later Mongol rulers converted to Islam. Then lead a discussion about which empire probably left the least lasting impression on the region. (Students may reply that the Mongols, being nomads, may have built few great monuments and, therefore, didn't leave a lasting impression.)

ESOL, LS **VISUAL-SPATIAL**

Four Empires of Southwest and Central Asia

Mongols	Ottomans	Safavids	Mughals
• skilled warriors on horseback	• 1300s—captured most of Turkey	• much of Iran	• northern India in 1500s
• huge empire under Genghis Khan and descendants	• named for Osman	• began 1500, when Shia ruler conquered Persia	• first leader—Babur the Tiger
• Korea to Hungary	• 1453—took Constantinople	• ruler—shah	• 1600s—Shah Jahan and the Taj Mahal
• 1258—killed caliph and destroyed Baghdad	• 1500s—grew under Suleiman	• built on trade	• 1700s—Great Britain taking over Mughal lands
• converted to Islam	• improved courts, built mosques, schools, hospitals, bridges	• capital—Esfahan	
• broke apart because of fights between Mongols	• southeastern Europe, western Asia, northern Africa	• collapsed by 1736	

Over the centuries other peoples and rulers came to power in parts of Southwest and Central Asia. Although these rulers came from different ethnic groups, they were all Muslims.

The Ottomans During the 1300s, a group of Muslim warriors captured most of what is now Turkey. They were called the Ottoman Turks after their ancestor Osman. In 1453, the Ottomans took the Christian city of Constantinople and made it their capital. The Ottoman Empire continued to grow in the 1500s under the leadership of Suleiman (soo-lay-MAHN). Suleiman's people called him "the Lawgiver" because he improved the court system and issued new laws. He also built mosques, schools, hospitals, bridges, and other public works. Under Suleiman, the Ottomans ruled much of southeastern Europe, western Asia, and northern Africa. Although it slowly lost power, the empire lasted until 1922.

The Safavids Another Muslim empire, the Safavid Empire, included much of what is now Iran. It began about 1500 when a Shia Muslim ruler conquered Persia. He took the title **shah**, an ancient Persian word for "king." The Safavids built their wealth on trade. Their capital, Esfahan, was one of the world's most beautiful cities. The Safavid Empire collapsed by 1736.

The Mughals The Mughal Empire was founded in northern India in the 1500s. Its first leader was a Mongol leader called Babur the Tiger. One of the most famous Mughal rulers was Shah Jahan, who built the famous Taj Mahal in the mid-1600s. Soon after his reign, however, the Mughal Empire began to crumble. In the 1700s, Great Britain began taking over Mughal lands.

✓ **READING CHECK: Summarizing** What were the four empires that followed the Muslim Empire in Southwest and Central Asia? Mongols, Ottomans, Safavids, and Mughals

▲
The Safavids built this mosque in Persia in the 1600s. A mosque is a place for worship and a symbol of Islam.

Interpreting the Visual Record What material appears to decorate the dome of the mosque and the minarets alongside?

go.hrw.com **Homework Practice Online**
Keyword: SK5 HP4

Section Review 4

Define or identify: caliph, Abbasids, Caliph Harun al-Rashid, mosques, Mongols, Genghis Khan, Ottoman Turks, Suleiman, shah, Babur the Tiger

Reading for the Main Idea

1. (*Places and Regions*) What caused the split between the Shia and the Sunni?

2. (*Places and Regions*) What areas did the Muslim Empire include?

Critical Thinking

3. **Summarizing** What were some accomplishments of the Muslim Empire?

4. **Analyzing Information** Why do you think the Muslims treated those they called People of the Book with some respect?

Organizing What You Know

5. **Categorizing** Copy the following graphic organizer. Use it to identify the people and features of these Southwest and Central Asian empires.

Empire	People	Features
Mongol		
Ottoman		
Safavid		
Mughal		

The History of Southwest and Central Asia • 103

Answers to Section 4 Review

Define or identify For definitions and identifications, see the glossary and index.

Reading for the Main Idea

1. the question of who would succeed Muhammad as leader (**NGS 10**)

2. extended from the Atlantic coast of North Africa to India and included most of Spain

Critical Thinking

3. banking, centers of learning, medicine, eye surgery, geography, mathematics, beautiful houses of worship

4. Possible answer: Like Muslims, People of the Book based their beliefs on texts considered sacred messages.

Organizing What You Know

5. People: Mongol—non-Muslim nomads; Ottoman—Muslim warriors in Turkey; Safavid—Muslims in Iran; Mughals—Muslims in northern India; Features—See the graphic organizer answers on the previous page for the features.

◀ **Visual Record Answer**

glazed tile

CLOSE

Baghdad's most glorious era is the setting for some of the tales in a classic collection—the *Thousand and One Nights.* Aladdin, Sinbad, and Ali Baba are among the stories' favorite characters. Read a story to the students from the collection. You may want to have students draw pictures of the action while you read.

REVIEW, ASSESS, RETEACH

Have students complete the Section Review. Then have students work in pairs to write four fill-in-the-blank questions about the section's content. Then have students complete Daily Quiz 4.4.

Have students complete Main Idea Activity S4. Then have students work in pairs to create flowcharts of events covered in the section. **ESOL, COOPERATIVE LEARNING, LS VISUAL-SPATIAL**

EXTEND

Have interested students conduct research on cities and monuments built by the Ottoman, Safavid, and Mughal Empires. Students should prepare illustrated reports for the class. **BLOCK SCHEDULING**

Define and Identify
For definitions and identifications, see the glossary and index.

Review the Main Ideas

16. people living in an organized society, producing more food than they need to survive, living in towns or cities with some form of government, with division of labor

17. Agriculture produced enough food that people didn't have to spend all their time finding food, so they developed other skills.

18. wheeled vehicles, potter's wheel, ziggurats, writing system

19. through terror

20. Answers will vary but should include that all are monotheistic and require a virtuous life of their followers. **(NGS 10)**

21. his Resurrection **(NGS 10)**

22. banking, centers of learning, medicine, eye surgery, geography, mathematics, beautiful houses of worship

23. They were skilled warriors who fought on horseback.

Think Critically

24. allowed them to hunt, make clothing, create art, and develop many other skills

25. They could keep records of the past and make plans for the future.

26. Moses led them out of Egypt.

27. over who can be caliph

28. Muslim armies grew huge and powerful because people could share in the empire's wealth if they signed up to serve in the military.

CHAPTER 4 Review and Practice

Define and Identify
Identify each of the following:

1. hominid
2. land bridges
3. irrigation
4. Sumerians
5. Fertile Crescent
6. Persians
7. cuneiform
8. Judaism
9. Abraham
10. Christianity
11. Jesus
12. Muhammad
13. mosques
14. Genghis Khan
15. Ottoman Turks

Review the Main Ideas

16. What are the four characteristics of civilization?

17. How did the development of agriculture lead to the growth of villages and towns?

18. What were some of the Sumerians' achievements?

19. How did the Assyrians rule?

20. What do Judaism, Christianity, and Islam have in common?

21. What event convinced Jesus' followers that he was the Messiah?

22. What were some achievements of the Islamic Empire?

23. How were the Mongols able to conquer so much territory?

Think Critically

24. Drawing Conclusions Why is the ability to make and use tools an important step in human development?

25. Drawing Inferences Why are the developments of a calendar, a system of counting, and a system of writing so important to a civilization?

26. Analyzing Information According to tradition, how did the Jews escape slavery in Egypt?

27. Contrasting On what issue do the Sunni and the Shia disagree?

28. Evaluating How did the Muslim Empire become so powerful?

Map Activity

29. Identify the places marked on the map.
Sumer
Mesopotamia
Palestine
Arabia
Baghdad

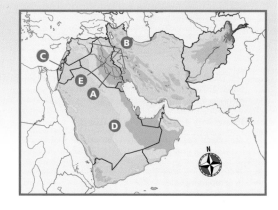

Map Activity
29. A. Sumer
B. Mesopotamia
C. Palestine
D. Arabia
E. Baghdad

Writing Activity

Imagine that you are a merchant who comes to Mesopotamia to do business. Write a diary entry about what you see both in the cities and in the countryside. First, choose a time period in which to set your "visit." Then review which culture controlled the area at the time and what life was like during that time. You may want to pay particular attention to the technologies that you see demonstrated and how those technologies affect your business deals. For example, how might the Persian road system have affected your ability to bring goods to market? Use the illustrations in the chapter to help you add detail to your diary entry.

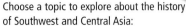

internet connect

Internet Activity: go.hrw.com
KEYWORD: SK5 GT4

Choose a topic to explore about the history of Southwest and Central Asia:
- Learn more about the development of writing.
- Explore the Persian Empire.
- Trace the spread of the Mongol Empire.

Social Studies Skills Practice

Interpreting Maps

Study the following map about trade routes from Mesopotamia. Then answer the questions.

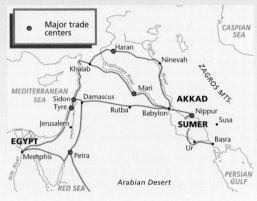

1. What role did the Tigris and Euphrates play in trade?
2. According to this map, how far west did the trade routes from Mesopotamia extend?
3. Why do you think there were no routes through the Arabian Desert?
4. What major trade center was located in Sumer?

Analyzing Primary Sources

Read the following passage from the Code of Hammurabi. Then answer the questions.

"If any one open his ditches to water his crop, but is careless, and the water flood the field of his neighbor, then he shall pay his neighbor corn for his loss. . . . If a man let in the water, and the water overflow the plantation of his neighbor, he shall pay ten gur *of corn for every ten* gan *of land."*

1. What is the main purpose of this portion of the Code of Hammurabi?
2. Based on your knowledge of ancient civilizations, why would this issue be important?
3. Based on your understanding of this quote, what do you think a *gur* and a *gan* are?
4. Does the punishment in the code seem just and fair? Why or why not?

Writing Activity

Students' diary entries should accurately reflect historical data in the chapter and include the correct technologies for the chosen era. Use Rubric 40, Writing to Describe, to evaluate student work.

Interpreting Maps

1. essential for trade, to avoid going though the deserts
2. Memphis, Egypt
3. not enough water to support the people and animals in a caravan
4. Nippur

Analyzing Primary Sources

1. to set a punishment for flooding a neighbor's field
2. Irrigation allowed for the crop surpluses that made these civilizations possible.
3. *gur*—unit of weight; *gan*—unit of measure for measuring land
4. Answers will vary, with some students calling it just because it provides compensation for destroyed property. Others may feel it is excessive punishment for something that could happen accidentally.

CHAPTER 4 — REVIEW AND ASSESSMENT RESOURCES

Reproducible
- Readings in World Geography, History, and Culture 50
- Critical Thinking Activity 50
- Vocabulary Activity 50

Technology
- Chapter 4 Test Generator (on the One-Stop Planner)

- HRW Go site
- Audio CD Program, Chapter 4

Reinforcement
- Chapter 4 Review and Practice
- Chapter Summaries and Review
- Chapter 4 Test

- Chapter 4 Test for English Language Learners and Special-Needs Students

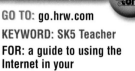

internet connect

GO TO: go.hrw.com
KEYWORD: SK5 Teacher
FOR: a guide to using the Internet in your classroom

The Eastern Mediterranean
Chapter Resource Manager

Objectives	Pacing Guide	Reproducible Resources
SECTION 1 **Physical Geography** (pp. 107–09) 1. Identify the main physical features of the eastern Mediterranean. 2. Identify the climate types of the region. 3. Identify the natural resources found in this area.	**Regular** .5 day Lecture Notes, Section 1 **Block Scheduling** .5 day *Block Scheduling Handbook, Chapter 5*	**RS** Know It Notes S1 **RS** Graphic Organizer 5 **ELL** Main Idea Activity S1
SECTION 2 **Turkey** (pp. 110–13) 1. Describe the history of the area that is now Turkey. 2. Describe the government and economy of Turkey. 3. Describe how Turkish society is divided.	**Regular** 1 day Lecture Notes, Section 2 **Block Scheduling** .5 day *Block Scheduling Handbook, Chapter 5*	**RS** Know It Notes S2 **E** Cultures of the World Activity 5 **E** Biography Activity: Mustafa Kemal **ELL** Main Idea Activity S2
SECTION 3 **Israel and the Occupied Territories** (pp. 114–17) 1. Describe the early history of Israel. 2. Describe modern Israel. 3. Describe the conflict over the Occupied Territories.	**Regular** 1 day Lecture Notes, Section 3 **Block Scheduling** .5 day *Block Scheduling Handbook, Chapter 5*	**RS** Know It Notes S3 **SM** Geography for Life Activity 5 **IC** Interdisciplinary Activities for the Middle Grades 22 **SM** Map Activity 5 **ELL** Main Idea Activity S3
SECTION 4 **Syria, Lebanon, and Jordan** (pp. 118–21) 1. Describe the government and economy of Syria. 2. Describe how Lebanese society is divided. 3. Identify the events that have shaped the history of Jordan.	**Regular** 1 day Lecture Notes, Section 4 **Block Scheduling** .5 day *Block Scheduling Handbook, Chapter 5*	**RS** Know It Notes S4 **ELL** Main Idea Activity S4

Chapter Resource Key

RS Reading Support

IC Interdisciplinary Connections

E Enrichment

SM Skills Mastery

A Assessment

REV Review

ELL Reinforcement and English Language Learners and English for Speakers of Other Languages (ESOL)

 Transparencies

 CD–ROM

 Music

 Video

 go. hrw .com Internet

 Holt Presentation Maker Using Microsoft® PowerPoint®

 One-Stop Planner CD–ROM

See the *One-Stop Planner* for a complete list of additional resources for students and teachers.

One-Stop Planner CD–ROM

It's easy to plan lessons, select resources, and print out materials for your students when you use the *One-Stop Planner CD–ROM with Test Generator.*

Technology Resources	Review, Reinforcement, and Assessment Resources
One-Stop Planner CD–ROM, Lesson 5.1	ELL Main Idea Activity S1
ARGWorld CD–ROM	REV Section 1 Review
Geography and Cultures Visual Resources with Teaching Activities 37–41	A Daily Quiz 5.1
Homework Practice Online	REV Chapter Summaries and Review
HRW Go site	ELL English Audio Summary 5.1
	ELL Spanish Audio Summary 5.1
One-Stop Planner CD–ROM, Lesson 5.2	ELL Main Idea Activity S2
ARGWorld CD–ROM	REV Section 2 Review
Homework Practice Online	A Daily Quiz 5.2
HRW Go site	REV Chapter Summaries and Review
	ELL English Audio Summary 5.2
	ELL Spanish Audio Summary 5.2
One-Stop Planner CD–ROM, Lesson 5.3	ELL Main Idea Activity S3
ARGWorld CD–ROM	REV Section 3 Review
Music of the World Audio CD Program, Selection 12	A Daily Quiz 5.3
Homework Practice Online	REV Chapter Summaries and Review
HRW Go site	ELL English Audio Summary 5.3
	ELL Spanish Audio Summary 5.3
One-Stop Planner CD–ROM, Lesson 5.4	ELL Main Idea Activity S4
ARGWorld CD–ROM	REV Section 4 Review
Homework Practice Online	A Daily Quiz 5.4
HRW Go site	REV Chapter Summaries and Review
	ELL English Audio Summary 5.4
	ELL Spanish Audio Summary 5.4

internet connect

HRW ONLINE RESOURCES

GO TO: go.hrw.com
Then type in a keyword.

TEACHER HOME PAGE
KEYWORD: SK5 TEACHER

CHAPTER INTERNET ACTIVITIES
KEYWORD: SK5 GT5

Choose an activity to:
• visit the Dead Sea.
• compare Israeli and Arab foods.
• travel to historic Jerusalem.

CHAPTER ENRICHMENT LINKS
KEYWORD: SK5 CH5

CHAPTER MAPS
KEYWORD: SK5 MAPS5

ONLINE ASSESSMENT
Homework Practice
KEYWORD: SK5 HP5
Standardized Test Prep Online
KEYWORD: SK5 STP5
Rubrics
KEYWORD: SS Rubrics

COUNTRY INFORMATION
KEYWORD: SK5 Almanac

CONTENT UPDATES
KEYWORD: SS Content Updates

HOLT PRESENTATION MAKER
KEYWORD: SK5 PPT5

ONLINE READING SUPPORT
KEYWORD: SS Strategies

CURRENT EVENTS
KEYWORD: S5 Current Events

Meeting Individual Needs

Ability Levels

Level 1 Basic-level activities designed for all students encountering new material

Level 2 Intermediate-level activities designed for average students

Level 3 Challenging activities designed for honors and gifted-and-talented students

ESOL Activities that address the needs of students with Limited English Proficiency

Chapter Review and Assessment

IC	Interdisciplinary Activities for the Middle Grades 24	A	Unit 5 Test
E	Readings in World Geography, History, and Culture 50, 51, and 52		Chapter 5 Test Generator (on the One-Stop Planner)
SM	Critical Thinking Activity 5		Audio CD Program, Chapter 5
REV	Chapter 5 Review and Practice	A	Chapter 5 Test for English Language Learners and Special-Needs Students
REV	Chapter Summaries and Review	A	Unit 5 Test for English Language Learners and Special-Needs Students
ELL	Vocabulary Activity 5		
A	Chapter 5 Test		HRW Go Site

The Eastern Mediterranean
Previewing Chapter Resources

Holt Online Learning

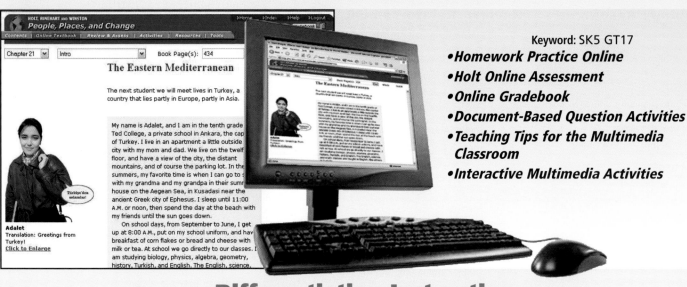

Chapter 21 | Intro | Book Page(s): 434

The Eastern Mediterranean

The next student we will meet lives in Turkey, a country that lies partly in Europe, partly in Asia.

My name is Adalet, and I am in the tenth grade at Ted College, a private school in Ankara, the capital of Turkey. I live in an apartment a little outside the city with my mom and dad. We live on the twelfth floor, and have a view of the city, the distant mountains, and of course the parking lot. In the summers, my favorite time is when I can go to stay with my grandma and my grandpa in their summer house on the Aegean Sea, in Kusadasi near the ancient Greek city of Ephesus. I sleep until 11:00 A.M. or noon, then spend the day at the beach with my friends until the sun goes down.

On school days, from September to June, I get up at 8:00 A.M., put on my school uniform, and have breakfast of corn flakes or bread and cheese with milk or tea. At school we go directly to our classes. I am studying biology, physics, algebra, geometry, history, Turkish, and English. The English, science,

Adalet
Türkiye'den selamlar!
Translation: Greetings from Turkey!
Click to Enlarge

Keyword: SK5 GT17

- *Homework Practice Online*
- *Holt Online Assessment*
- *Online Gradebook*
- *Document-Based Question Activities*
- *Teaching Tips for the Multimedia Classroom*
- *Interactive Multimedia Activities*

Differentiating Instruction

Reading and Writing Support

◄ Graphic Organizer Activity
- Vocabulary Activity
- Chapter Summary and Review
- Know It Notes
- Audio CD

Active Learning

◄ Block Scheduling Handbook
- Cultures of the World Activity
- Interdisciplinary Activity
- Map Activity
- Critical Thinking Activity 21
- Music of the World CD: Music from an Israeli Yeshira

Primary Sources and Advanced Learners

- Geography for Life Activity: What Future for Jerusalem?
◄ Map Activity: Israel: Struggles for Land
- Readings in World Geography, History and Culture:
  - 50 The Islamic City
  - 51 The Bedouin Way
  - 52 Visit to a Kibbutz

Assessment Program

◄ Daily Quizzes S1–4
- Chapter Test
- Chapter Test for English Language Learners and Special-Needs Students

Spanish and ESOL

- Vocabulary Activity
- Main Idea Activities for English Language Learners and Special-Needs Students
- Chapter Summary and Review
- Spanish Audio Summary
- Know It Notes S1–4
◄ Chapter Test for English Language Learners and Special-Needs Students

Special Education Modifications

Your **I.D.E.A. Works! CD-ROM** will provide modified versions of the following teaching materials:

- Guided Reading Strategies S1–4
- Vocabulary Activity
◄ Main Idea Activities S1–4
- Daily Quizzes S1–4
- Chapter 5 Test
- Flash cards of chapter vocabulary terms

Teacher Resources

Books for Teachers

Gilbert, Martin. *The Atlas of Jewish History.* William Morrow & Co., 1993.

Seal, Jeremy. *A Fez of the Heart: Travels around Turkey in Search of a Hat.* Harvest Books, 1996.

Water for the Future: The West Bank and Gaza Strip, Israel, and Jordan. National Academy Press, 1999.

Books for Students

Marston, Elsa. *Lebanon: New Light in an Ancient Land.* Discovering Our Heritage. Dillon Press, 1994. History, culture, religion, and politics of a beautiful but troubled country.

Pilbeam, Mavis, and John Malam. *Mesopotamia and the Fertile Crescent.* Looking Back. Raintree/Steck-Vaughn, 1999. Addresses many aspects of the lives of the region's diverse inhabitants, including government, art, religion, and the impact of war on everyday life.

Schami, Rafik. Trans. Rika Lesser. *A Hand Full of Stars.* Puffin, 1992. Daily life of a Syrian teenager who wants to be a journalist.

Waldman, Neil. *The Never-Ending Greenness.* William Morrow & Co. (Library), 1997. Israel's reforestation efforts through the eyes of an old immigrant. **SHELTERED ENGLISH**

Multimedia Materials

Golda Meir: A Profile. Video, 26 min. Lucerne Media.

People and Places: Israel. Video, 22 min. AIMS Media.

Turkey. Video, 47 min. Lonely Planet.

Videos and CDs

Videos

- *CNN. Presents Geography: Yesterday and Today, Segment 21 Jordan's Water Crisis*
- *ARG World*

Holt Researcher

http://researcher.hrw.com

- *Solomon*
- *David*
- *Meir, Golda*
- *Turkey*
- *Syria*
- *Jordan*
- *Israel*
- *Lebanon*
- *Cyprus*

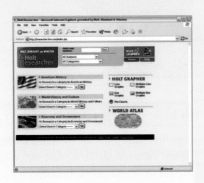

Transparency Packages

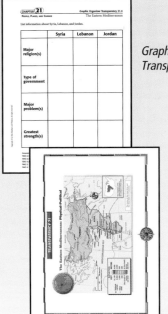

Graphic Organizer Transparencies 5.1–4

Geography and Cultures Visual Resources Transparencies 66–70

71 The Eastern Mediterranean: Physical-Political

Map Activities Transparency 05 Israel: Struggles for Land

The Eastern Mediterranean

The next student we will meet lives in Turkey, a country that lies partly in Europe, partly in Asia.

WHY IT MATTERS

You might point out these reasons why we should know more about the eastern Mediterranean region.

▸ The eastern Mediterranean region is a geographical, economic, and cultural crossroads. The region has made many contributions to world civilization. It has also been the scene of conflict over the years.

▸ Judaism and Christianity began in the region. Both faiths have affected American culture.

▸ The United States has been a supporter of Israel since its creation. This policy has contributed to anti-American feelings and actions among some Arabs.

My name is Adalet, and I am in the tenth grade at Ted College, a private school in Ankara, the capital of Turkey. I live in an apartment a little outside the city with my mom and dad. We live on the twelfth floor, and have a view of the city, the distant mountains, and of course the parking lot. In the summers, my favorite time is when I can go to stay with my grandma and my grandpa in their summer house on the Aegean Sea, in Kusadasi near the ancient Greek city of Ephesus. I sleep until 11:00 A.M. or noon, then spend the day at the beach with my friends until the sun goes down.

On school days, from September to June, I get up at 8:00 A.M., put on my school uniform, and have breakfast of corn flakes or bread and cheese with milk or tea. At school we go directly to our classes. I am studying biology, physics, algebra, geometry, history, Turkish, and English. The English, science, and math classes are taught in English, the others in Turkish.

Türkiye'den selamlar!

Translation: Greetings from Turkey!

CHAPTER PROJECT

Have students draw and embellish a map of Jerusalem showing the sacred sites of the three major religions. Students should write appropriate captions for each site that explain the relationship between the religious ideas about the site and the culture of the region.

STARTING THE CHAPTER

Copy the names of the countries of the eastern Mediterranean region—*Turkey, Lebanon, Syria, Jordan,* and *Israel*—onto the chalkboard, leaving several inches of space between the countries' names. Ask students to respond by sharing facts that they know about a particular country. (Students may mention that part of Turkey is in both Asia and Europe. They may also mention that the modern state of Israel was created after World War II, or that Lebanon was torn apart by ethnic and religious conflicts. Other responses are also possible.) Write each response under the name of the appropriate country. Tell students that they will learn more about the eastern Mediterranean region in this chapter.

Section 1 Physical Geography

Read to Discover

1. What are the main physical features of the eastern Mediterranean?
2. What are the climate types of the region?
3. What natural resources are found in this area?

Vocabulary

phosphates
asphalt

Places

Dardanelles
Bosporus
Sea of Marmara
Jordan River
Dead Sea

Syrian Desert
Negev

Reading Strategy

BRAINSTORMING Write the letters of the alphabet down a sheet of paper. With a partner, brainstorm what you already know about the eastern Mediterranean region. List your ideas next to as many letters as possible.

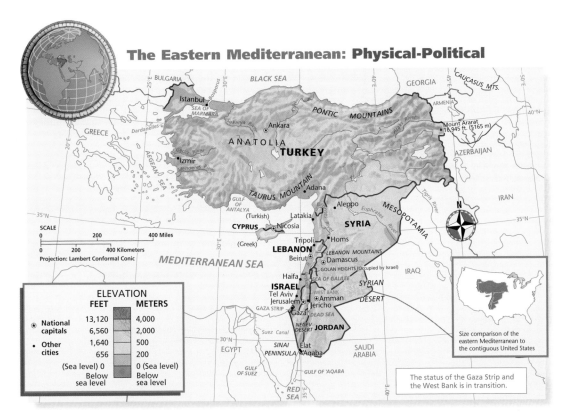

The Eastern Mediterranean: Physical-Political

ELEVATION		
	FEET	METERS
⊛ National capitals	13,120	4,000
	6,560	2,000
• Other cities	1,640	500
	656	200
	(Sea level) 0	0 (Sea level)
	Below sea level	Below sea level

SCALE
0   200   400 Miles
0   200   400 Kilometers
Projection: Lambert Conformal Conic

Size comparison of the eastern Mediterranean to the contiguous United States

The status of the Gaza Strip and the West Bank is in transition.

The Eastern Mediterranean • 107

SECTION 1 RESOURCES

Reproducible
◆ Lecture Notes, Section 1
◆ Block Scheduling Handbook, Chapter 5
◆ Know It Notes S1
◆ Graphic Organizer 5

Technology
◆ One-Stop Planner CD–ROM, Lesson 5.1
◆ Homework Practice Online
◆ Geography and Cultures Visual Resources with Teaching Activities 37–41
◆ HRW Go site

Reinforcement, Review, and Assessment
◆ Section 1 Review
◆ Daily Quiz 5.1
◆ Main Idea Activity S1
◆ Chapter Summaries and Review
◆ English Audio Summary 5.1
◆ Spanish Audio Summary 5.1

Section 1

Objectives

1. Identify the main physical features of the eastern Mediterranean.
2. Describe the climate types of this region.
3. List this region's natural resources.

FOCUS

Bellringer

Copy the following instructions onto the chalkboard: *Look at the map on this page. Write down all the intersections you see occurring in the eastern Mediterranean.* Discuss student responses. (Students should note the intersection of continents as well as countries.) Tell students that in Section 1 they will learn more about the eastern Mediterranean.

Using the Physical-Political Map

Have students examine the map on this page. Call attention to the shapes of the countries and the region's landforms. Point out that the region has few natural boundaries. Tell students that they will learn how the borders of the eastern Mediterranean countries changed several times during the 1900s as a result of political events.

EYE ON EARTH

The Negev Restored One of the desert climate areas of this region is the Negev. By the 1960s many native species that roamed the Negev during biblical times had become endangered or extinct. Conservationists launched programs to protect and reintroduce wildlife.

Today, three fourths of the Negev have been designated as nature preserves. Visitors can see foxes, gazelles, hyenas, ostriches, wolves, and zebras. The onager, a type of donkey, and the oryx, a type of antelope, have also returned to the Negev. With more prey available, the leopard again prowls the Negev. Because it is at the top of the desert's food chain, the leopard's return shows that the full range of the area's wildlife is being restored.

Activity: Have students use pictures of the Negev's animals to create a travel poster for the region.

**GO TO: go.hrw.com
KEYWORD: SJ5 CH5
FOR: Web sites about the Negev**

Visual Record Answer ▶

possible answer: connects the Black Sea area and Russia to the Mediterranean world

Our Amazing Planet

The Dead Sea, which covers an area of just 394 square miles (1,020 sq km), contains approximately 12.7 billion tons of salt. Each year the Jordan River deposits 850,000 additional tons.

Istanbul lies on both sides of the waterway known as the Bosporus. This waterway divides Europe from Asia.

Interpreting the Visual Record

(Movement) Why do you think the Bosporus would be an important crossroads of trade?

▼

108 Chapter 5

Physical Features

The countries of the eastern Mediterranean are Turkey, Lebanon, Syria, Jordan, and Israel. In addition to its own territory, Israel controls areas known as the Occupied Territories. These include the West Bank, the Gaza Strip, and the Golan Heights.

On Two Continents The eastern Mediterranean region straddles two continents. A small part of Turkey lies on Europe's Balkan Peninsula. This area consists of rolling plains and hills. A narrow waterway, made up of the Dardanelles (dahrd-uhn-ELZ), the Bosporus (BAHS-puh-ruhs), and the Sea of Marmara (MAHR-muh-ruh), separates Europe from Asia. The larger, Asian part of Turkey is mostly plateaus and highlands.

Hills, Valleys, and Plains Heading south from Turkey and into Syria, we cross a narrow plain. The Euphrates River, fed by precipitation in Turkey's eastern mountains, flows southeast through this plain. Farther south are more hills and plateaus. Two main ridges run north-south. One runs from southwestern Syria through western Jordan. The other, closer to the coast, runs through Lebanon, Israel, and the West Bank. The Jordan River valley separates these two ridges. A narrow coastal plain rims the region along its seacoasts. In western Turkey the coastal plain is wider.

River and Sea The Jordan River begins in Syria and flows south. Israel and the West Bank lie on the west side of the river. The country of Jordan lies on the east side. The Jordan River flows into the Dead Sea. This unusual body of water is the lowest point on any continent—1,312 feet (400 m) below sea level. It is so salty that swimmers cannot sink in it.

✓ READING CHECK: (*Places and Regions*) What are the region's main physical features? Rolling plains; hills; narrow waterway of Dardanelles, Bosporus, and Sea of Marmara; plains; Euphrates River; Jordan River; Dead Sea

Climate

Dry climates are the rule in most of this region. However, there are important variations. Turkey's Black Sea coast and the Mediterranean coast all the way to Israel have a Mediterranean climate. Central Syria

---

TEACH

Teaching Objectives 1–3

ALL LEVELS: (Suggested time: 30 min.) Copy the graphic organizer onto the chalkboard, omitting the blue answers. Use it to help students learn about the physical features, climate types, and resources of the eastern Mediterranean region. Have students copy the organizer into their notebooks and complete it. **ESOL,** **LS** **VISUAL-SPATIAL**

THE EASTERN MEDITERRANEAN		
Physical Features	Climate Types	Resources
Balkan Peninsula, Dardanelles, Bosporus, Sea of Marmara, Euphrates River, Jordan River, Dead Sea, Syrian Desert, Negev	Mediterranean, desert, humid subtropical	limited farmland and pastureland, sulfur, mercury, phosphates, asphalt

and lands farther south have a desert climate. A small area of northeastern Turkey has a humid subtropical climate.

The Syrian Desert covers much of Syria and Jordan. It usually receives less than five inches (12.7 cm) of rainfall a year. Another desert, the Negev (NE-gev), lies in southern Israel.

✓ **READING CHECK:** (*Places and Regions*) What are the climates of the eastern Mediterranean? *Mediterranean, desert, humid subtropical*

Resources

Unlike nearby countries in Southwest Asia, the countries of the eastern Mediterranean do not have large oil reserves. The people of this region make their living from the land in other ways.

Limited Farming Commercial farming is possible only where rain or irrigation provides enough water. Subsistence farming and livestock herding are common in drier areas. Desert areas support a few nomadic herders.

Mineral Resources Many minerals, including sulfur, mercury, and copper, are found in the region. **Phosphates**—mineral salts containing the element phosphorus—are produced in Syria, Jordan, and Israel. Phosphates are used to make fertilizers. The area also exports **asphalt**—the dark tarlike material used to pave streets. The Dead Sea is a source of mineral salts.

✓ **READING CHECK:** (*Places and Regions*) What natural resources are found in this area? *Minerals, including sulfur, mercury, copper, phosphates, asphalt*

A shepherd in eastern Turkey watches his sheep.

Interpreting the Visual Record

(*Human-Environment Interaction*) **Why is livestock herding common in many parts of the eastern Mediterranean region?**

▼

Homework Practice Online

Keyword: SK5 HP5

Section Review 1

Define and explain: phosphates, asphalt

Working with Sketch Maps On a map of the eastern Mediterranean that you draw or that your teacher provides, label the following: Dardanelles, Bosporus, Sea of Marmara, Jordan River, Dead Sea, Syrian Desert, and the Negev.

Reading for the Main Idea

1. (*Places and Regions*) What country lies on two continents?

2. (*Places and Regions*) What are the most common climates of the region?

3. (*Places and Regions*) How do geographic factors affect the economic activities of the region?

Critical Thinking

4. **Drawing Inferences and Conclusions** How do you think the Dead Sea got its name?

Organizing What You Know

5. **Categorizing** Copy the following graphic organizer. Use it to list the major landforms and bodies of water of each region.

Country/ territory	Landforms and bodies of water

The Eastern Mediterranean • 109

CLOSE

Remind students that this region is at the intersection of three continents—Asia, Europe, and Africa. Ask students to describe the possible economic and cultural consequences of living in such a region. (Students might mention trade and cultural exchanges or geopolitical struggles for control over a strategically important region.)

REVIEW, ASSESS, RETEACH

Have students complete the Section Review. Then have students work in groups of three to create eight matching questions that relate each country to its corresponding landforms, climates, or natural features. Finally, have students complete Daily Quiz 5.1. **COOPERATIVE LEARNING**

Have students complete Main Idea Activity S1. Then organize students into small groups. Have each group create a map for one of the eastern Mediterranean countries. Each map should identify the main physical features, climate types, and resources of the assigned country. **COOPERATIVE LEARNING, ESOL,** [LS] **VISUAL-SPATIAL**

EXTEND

Have interested students conduct research on the cedars of Lebanon and how deforestation changed the country's landscape. **BLOCK SCHEDULING**

Section 2 · Turkey

Read to Discover

1. What is the history of the area that is now Turkey?
2. What kind of government and economy does Turkey have?
3. How is Turkish society divided?

Vocabulary
secular

Places
Ankara
Istanbul

People
Kemal Atatürk

Reading Strategy

FOLDNOTES: LAYERED BOOK Create the FoldNote titled **Layered Book** described in the Appendix. Label the book Turkey. Label the pages with these geography themes: Location and Place, Human-Environment Interaction, Movement, and Region. As you read, write what you learn about Turkey that supports the themes.

Place Ottoman monarchs lived in the Topkapi Palace built in 1462.

History

Turkey, except for the small part that lies in Europe, makes up a region called Asia Minor. In ancient times this area was part of the Hittite and Persian Empires. In the 330s B.C. Alexander the Great conquered Asia Minor. Later it became part of the Roman Empire. Byzantium, renamed Constantinople, was one of the most important cities of the empire. After the fall of Rome, Constantinople became the capital of the Byzantine Empire.

In the A.D. 1000s the Seljuk Turks invaded Asia Minor. The Seljuks were a nomadic people from Central Asia who had converted to Islam. In 1453 another Turkish people, the Ottoman Turks, captured the city of Constantinople. They made it the capital of their Islamic empire.

Ottoman Empire During the 1500s and 1600s the Ottoman Empire was very powerful. It controlled territory in North Africa, Southwest Asia, and southeastern Europe. In the 1700s and 1800s the empire gradually weakened.

In World War I the Ottoman Empire fought on the losing side. When the war ended, the Ottomans lost all their territory outside of what is now Turkey. Greece even invaded western Asia Minor in an attempt to take more land. However, the Turkish army pushed out the invaders. Military officers

---

Section 2

Objectives

1. Discuss the history of the area that is now Turkey.
2. Describe Turkey's government and economy.
3. Identify the divisions in Turkish society.

FOCUS

Bellringer

Copy the following instructions onto the chalkboard: *Write down any images, words, or facts associated with the country of Turkey that come to mind.* Discuss student responses. (Students might mention Turkish baths, recent earthquakes, or Turkey's role in regional conflicts.) Tell students that in Section 2 they will learn more about Turkey.

Building Vocabulary

Write the term **secular** on the chalkboard. Have a volunteer read the definition aloud from the glossary. Ask students how this word may apply to American society. (Students may mention that the separation of church and state is a principle of the U.S. Constitution.)

◄
A boy holds a Turkish national flag during celebrations on Republic Day. A banner behind him shows Atatürk, the founder of modern Turkey.

then took over the government. Their leader was a war hero, Mustafa Kemal. He later adopted the name Kemal Atatürk, which means "father of the Turks." He formally dissolved the Ottoman Empire and created the nation of Turkey. He made the new country a democracy and moved the capital to Ankara. Constantinople was renamed Istanbul in 1930.

Modern Turkey Atatürk wanted to modernize Turkey. He believed that to be strong Turkey had to westernize. He banned the fez, the traditional hat of Turkish men, and required that they wear European-style hats. The Latin alphabet replaced the Arabic one. The European calendar and metric system replaced Islamic ones. Women were encouraged to vote, work, and hold office. New laws made it illegal for women to wear veils.

✓ READING CHECK:　(Human Systems)　What is the history of what is now Turkey? Asia Minor conquered by Alexander the Great; later part of Roman, Byzantine Empires; invaded by Seljuk Turks, Ottoman Turks; empire lost; Mustafa Kemal took over government

Government and Economy

Today, Turkey has a legislature called the National Assembly. A president and a prime minister share executive power. The Turkish military has taken over the government three times. However, each time it has returned power to civilian hands.

Although most of its people are Muslim, Turkey is a **secular** state. This means that religion is kept separate from government. For example, the religion of Islam allows a man to have up to four wives. However, by Turkish law a man is permitted to have just one wife. In recent years Islamic political parties have attempted to increase Islam's role in Turkish society.

Turkish women harvest grapes.
Interpreting the Visual Record　(Place)
What kind of climate do Turkey's coastal plains have?
▼

The Eastern Mediterranean　111

National Geography Standard 13
Earthquakes, Cooperation, and Conflict A major challenge facing the Turkish government is rebuilding areas hit by a devastating earthquake. On August 17, 1999, the worst earthquake in 60 years struck Turkey. The quake measured 7.4 on the Richter scale, and the trembling was felt 180 miles (340 km) away. The quake actually pushed parts of Turkey several feet westward.

The death toll had reached more than 18,000 within a week. Countries around the world contributed to the recovery effort. Greece, Turkey's old adversary, was the first country to fly food and medicine to the victims. The two countries had had their last military confrontation only three years earlier.

Activity: Have students conduct research and report on earthquakes in Turkey.

🖳 **internet** connect
GO TO: **go.hrw.com**
KEYWORD: **SJ5 CH5**
FOR: **Web sites about modern earthquakes**

◄**Visual Record Answer**

a Mediterranean climate

TEACH

Teaching Objective 1
ALL LEVELS: (Suggested time: 20 min.) Copy the following graphic organizer, omitting the blue answers. Use it to help students understand the significance of individuals or groups on the history of this area. **ESOL**

EVENTS AND ERAS IN TURKISH HISTORY

| Alexander the Great conquers the area | ⇨ | Seljuk Turks invade | ⇨ | Ottoman Turks invade and establish an empire | ⇨ | Kemal Atatürk gains power and establishes modern Turkey |

Teaching Objective 2
ALL LEVELS: (Suggested time: 30 min.) Have students write letters to Kemal Atatürk to tell him about the legacy of his work, as shown in Turkey's government and economy. (Students' letters should mention that Turkey is a secular country with a democratic government; the military has taken control of Turkey's government three times but has restored civilian control each time; Turkey's economy has a mix of traditional and modern industries.) Ask volunteers to read their letters to the class.
LS VERBAL-LINGUISTIC

GLOBAL PERSPECTIVES

Kurds and Kurdistan One of the many ethnic groups of Turkey are the Kurds. Kurds make up about 20 percent of Turkey's population. Their ancient homeland, often called Kurdistan, includes southeastern Turkey and parts of northeastern Syria, northern Iraq, and western Iran. The Kurds speak languages unrelated to Turkish. Their traditional way of life is nomadic. National borders that were drawn after World War I disrupted the nomadic routes of the Kurds.

Many Kurds in all four countries want an independent state. By the late 1990s, a Kurdish rebellion in Turkey had cost at least 30,000 lives. The leader of Turkey's Kurdish rebels, Abdullah Ocalan, is serving a life sentence for treason.

Activity: Have students locate the area known as Kurdistan on an outline map of Southwest Asia.

Connecting to Literature
Answers
1. because the large number of people made too much noise
2. for all the people who died in the flood

CONNECTING TO *Literature*

Statue of Gilgamesh

Gilgamesh is the hero of this ancient story that was popular all over Southwest Asia. In this passage Utnapishtim (oot-nuh-peesh-tuhm), whom the gods have given everlasting life, tells Gilgamesh about surviving a great flood.

Epic of Gilgamesh

"In those days . . . the people multiplied, the world bellowed like a wild bull, and the great god was aroused by the clamor[1]. Enlil (en-LIL) heard the clamor and he said to the gods in council, 'The uproar of mankind is intolerable[2] and sleep is no longer possible by reason of the babel[3].' So the gods agreed to exterminate[4] mankind. Enlil did this, but Ea (AY-uh) because of his oath warned me in a dream. . . . 'Tear down your house, I say, and build a boat. . . . then take up into the boat the seed of all living creatures.'

Utnapishtim does as he is told. He builds a boat and fills it with supplies, his family, and animals. Then terrible rains come and flood Earth.

"When the seventh day dawned the storm from the south subsided, the sea grew calm, the flood was stilled; I looked at the face of the world and there was silence, all mankind was turned to clay. . . . I opened a hatch and the light fell on my face. Then I bowed low, I sat down and I wept, . . . for on every side was the waste of water."

Analyzing Primary Sources
1. Why did the god bring the flood?
2. Why does Utnapishtim cry?

Vocabulary   [1]clamor: noise   [2]intolerable: not bearable   [3]babel: confusing noise   [4]exterminate: kill off

Turkey's economy includes modern factories as well as village farming and craft making. The most important industries are clothing, chemicals, and oil processing. About 40 percent of Turkey's labor force works in agriculture. Grains, cotton, sugar beets, and hazelnuts are major crops. The Turkish economy has grown rapidly in recent years, but inflation is a problem. Large numbers of Turks have left Turkey in search of better jobs. By 2001, an estimated 1.2 million Turks were working abroad to earn higher wages.

In the 1990s Turkey began building dams on the Tigris and Euphrates Rivers. These will provide electricity and irrigation water. However, the dams have caused concern for Syria and Iraq. They are disturbed that another country controls the sources of their water.

✓ **READING CHECK:** (*Human Systems*) What kind of government and economy does Turkey have? Secular state with legislature and a shared executive; modern industrial, agricultural

Teaching Objective 3

LEVELS 1 AND 2: (Suggested time: 25 min.) Tell students to imagine that they are foreign-exchange students living in Turkey. Then pair students and have each pair write a postcard to a friend or family member that describes the cultural and political divisions in Turkish society. (Postcards should mention the Kurdish desire for independence, the split between the urban middle class and villagers with a more traditional outlook, and political divisions between secularists and Islamists.) Ask volunteers to read their postcards to the class. **ESOL, COOPERATIVE LEARNING**

LEVEL 3: (Suggested time: 30 min.) Tell students to imagine that they are Turks. Then pair students and have each pair write a dialogue about the divisions in Turkish society. Have volunteers perform their dialogues for the class. **LS INTERPERSONAL**

►**ASSIGNMENT:** To help students learn more about Turkey's history, have them conduct research on some aspect of Turkish economic, political, or cultural history. Then have students prepare short oral reports to present their findings to the class.

People and Culture

Turkey has more than 68 million people. Ethnic Turks make up 80 percent of the population. Kurds are the largest minority. They are about 20 percent of the population. Since ancient times the Kurds have lived in what is today southeastern Turkey. Kurds also live in nearby parts of Iran, Iraq, and Syria. In the 1980s and 1990s some Kurds fought for independence from Turkey. The Turkish government has used military force against this rebellion.

Kemal Atatürk's changes created a cultural split between Turkey's urban middle class and rural villagers. The lifestyle and attitudes of middle-class Turks have much in common with those of middle-class Europeans. Most Turks, though, are more traditional. Islam influences their attitudes on matters such as the role of women. This cultural division is a factor in Turkish politics.

Turkish cooking is much like that of the rest of the Mediterranean region. It features olives, vegetables, cheese, yogurt, and bread. Shish kebab—grilled meat on a skewer—is a favorite Turkish dish.

✓ **READING CHECK:** (**Human Systems**) What are the divisions in Turkish society?
Kurds; cultural, between urban and rural people ▶

(**Place**) Crowds pass through a square near the University of Istanbul. Different styles of dress reflect the diverse attitudes that exist in Turkey today.

Section Review 2

Define or identify: Kemal Atatürk, secular

Working with Sketch Maps On the map you created in Section 1, label Ankara and Istanbul. What are the advantages of Istanbul's location?

Reading for the Main Idea

1. (**Human Systems**) How did Atatürk try to modernize Turkey?

2. (**Human Systems**) What foods are popular in Turkish cooking?

Homework Practice Online
Keyword: SK5 HP5

Critical Thinking

3. **Finding the Main Idea** Why were some Turks unhappy with changes brought about by Atatürk?

4. **Analyzing Information** Why is the Turkish government building dams on the Tigris and Euphrates Rivers? How will this affect countries downriver?

Organizing What You Know

5. **Sequencing** Create a time line listing major events in Turkey's history. List major people, groups, invasions, empires, and changes in government.

|———————————————————|
400 B.C.   A.D. 2000

The Eastern Mediterranean • 113

CLOSE

Tell students that Turkey has become a major international tourist destination. Ask students to explain the physical or cultural attractions that might draw tourists to Turkey.

Have students complete Main Idea Activity S2. Then have students write newspaper headlines for stories about events in Turkish history and the country's current situation. **ESOL**

REVIEW, ASSESS, RETEACH

Have students complete the Section Review. Then organize students into groups of four. Have each group write 10 multiple-choice questions about the section. Then have students complete Daily Quiz 5.2.
COOPERATIVE LEARNING, LS **VERBAL-LINGUISTIC**

EXTEND

Have interested students conduct research on the history of the Turkish-Greek conflict over Cyprus. Tell students to also consider the current state of relations between Greece and Turkey. Have students create a time line to present their findings. **BLOCK SCHEDULING**

Section 3 — Israel and the Occupied Territories

Read to Discover
1. What was the early history of Israel like?
2. What is modern Israel like?
3. What is the conflict over the Occupied Territories?

Vocabulary
Diaspora
Zionism

Places
Jerusalem
Gaza Strip
Golan Heights
West Bank
Tel Aviv

Reading Strategy

TAKING NOTES Before you read, write the main ideas down the left side of a sheet of paper. As you read this section, write what you learn about Israel next to the main ideas.

Place The ancient port of Caesarea lies on the coast of Israel. It was the regional capital during the time of Roman control. Today the harbor structure is partly underwater.

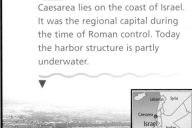

Ancient Israel

The Hebrews, the ancestors of the Jews, first established the kingdom of Israel about 3,000 years ago. It covered roughly the same area as the modern State of Israel. In the 60s B.C. the Roman Empire conquered the region, which they called Palestine. After a series of Jewish revolts, the Romans forced most Jews to leave the region. This scattering of the Jewish population is known as the **Diaspora**.

During the era of Roman control, a Jewish man named Jesus began preaching. Jesus taught that faith and love were more important than Judaism's many laws. His teachings particularly appealed to the poor and powerless. Both Roman and Jewish rulers saw Jesus as dangerous. Jesus was tried and executed by the Roman authorities. His followers believe he rose from the dead. Christianity—Jesus's teachings and the belief in his resurrection—spread through the Roman Empire. In time, Christianity became the most common religion of the Mediterranean region.

Arabs conquered Palestine in the mid-600s. From the 1000s to the 1200s, European armies launched a series of invasions called the Crusades. Crusaders captured Jerusalem in 1099. In time the Crusaders were pushed out of the area altogether. From the 1500s to World War I, Palestine was part of the Ottoman Empire. At the end of the war, it came under British control.

✔ **READING CHECK:** *Human Systems* What significant events occurred in the early history of the area of Israel?
Kingdom of Israel established 3,000 years ago; 60s B.C., conquered by Roman Empires; Christianity developed; mid-600s, conquered by Arabs, 1500s to World War I, Ottoman Empire control

114 · Chapter 5

Section 3

Objectives
1. Recount the early history of Israel.
2. Describe what modern Israel is like.
3. Explain the conflict over the Occupied Territories.

FOCUS

Bellringer

Copy the following instructions onto the chalkboard: *Write down three or four things that you have heard about the country of Israel.* Compile a list of students' responses on the chalkboard. Tell students that the United States has political, cultural, and religious ties with Israel. Inform them that in Section 3 they will learn more about Israel and the Occupied Territories.

Building Vocabulary

Write the terms **Diaspora** and **Zionism** on the chalkboard. Have volunteers read aloud the definitions from the glossary. Point out to students that the words *Diaspora* and *Zionism* refer to two movements that occurred during different periods in history—the first to the dispersal of the Jewish population of ancient Israel, the second to the creation of a Jewish homeland in modern Israel.

FOCUS ON CULTURE

Dialing for Peace

"Hello Peace!" is the name of a popular phone service in Israel, the West Bank, and Gaza. This free service gives Israelis and Palestinians the rare chance to talk directly to each other. The service's organizers hope it will lead to a better understanding between the two cultures. For example, a 20-year-old Palestinian man named Sammy used the service to chat with an Israeli soldier. After the soldier explained to Sammy that he felt bad about guarding Palestinian neighborhoods, Sammy said, "Now I know they do care. And now I have hope that there can be peace." By keeping the lines of communication open, the "Hello Peace" organizers are bringing new hope to the region.

In what other ways could groups in conflict ease tensions?

Modern Israel

In the late 1800s a movement called **Zionism** began among European Jews. Zionism called for Jews to establish a country or community in Palestine. Tens of thousands of Jews moved to the area.

After World War II, the United Nations recommended dividing Palestine into Arab and Jewish states. Jewish leaders declared the independent state of Israel. Armies from surrounding Arab countries invaded Israel. The Israelis defeated the Arabs.

Many Palestinians fled to other Arab states, particularly to Jordan and Lebanon. Some used terrorist attacks to strike at Israel. Israel and its Arab neighbors also fought wars in 1956, 1967, and 1973.

Government and Economy Israel has a prime minister and a parliament, called the Knesset. There are two major political parties and many smaller parties.

Israel has built a strong military for protection from the Arab countries around it. Terrorist attacks have also occurred. At age 18 most Israeli men and women must serve in the military.

▲
Thousands of devout Jews gather for prayer during Passover at the Western Wall. This wall is all that survives from an ancient temple complex.

▲ **Focus on Culture Answer**

Answers will vary, but students may mention arts and cultural exchanges, small group meetings, or other possibilities.

TEACH

Teaching Objectives 1–2

ALL LEVELS: (Suggested time: 40 min.) Lead a discussion about events in the early history of Israel. (Students should mention the ancient kingdom of Israel, Roman rule and the Diaspora, the spread of Christianity, the Arab conquest of Palestine, the Crusades, and Ottoman rule in Palestine.) Then copy the following graphic organizer onto the chalkboard, omitting the blue answers. Use it to help students learn about modern Israel. **ESOL**

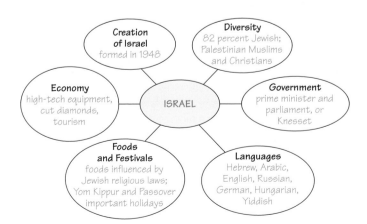

Creation of Israel
formed in 1948

Diversity
82 percent Jewish;
Palestinian Muslims
and Christians

Economy
high-tech equipment,
cut diamonds,
tourism

ISRAEL

Government
prime minister and
parliament, or
Knesset

Foods
and Festivals
foods influenced by
Jewish religious laws;
Yom Kippur and Passover
important holidays

Languages
Hebrew, Arabic,
English, Russian,
German, Hungarian,
Yiddish

Dead Sea in a Glass Along with Jerusalem, the Dead Sea is a major tourist attraction for Israel. The Dead Sea is 51 miles (82 km) long. It is fed by the Jordan River, but it has no outlet to the sea. When the freshwater that comes in evaporates, it leaves behind a rich concentrate of minerals and salts. No wildlife can live in the salty water, which is so buoyant that swimmers cannot sink in it.

There are several resorts on the Dead Sea's shores. The sea's black mud is said to improve the complexion, and many people claim the water relieves their aching joints.

Activity: Have students research the mineral and salt content of the Dead Sea. As closely as possible, reproduce the sea's water in a glass.

The West Bank in Transition

Control of West Bank:
- Israeli
- Palestinian civil, Israeli security
- Palestinian before 2003
- Palestinian, 2003
- City of Jerusalem

The Gaza Strip is densely populated and has few natural resources. Israel captured this territory from Egypt in 1967.

Israel has a modern, diverse economy. Items like high-technology equipment and cut diamonds are important exports. Tourism is a major industry. Israel's lack of water limits farming. However, using highly efficient irrigation, Israel has successfully increased food production. It imports grain but exports citrus fruit and eggs.

Languages and Diversity Israel's population includes Jews from all parts of the world. Both Hebrew and Arabic are official languages. When they arrive in Israel, many Jews speak English, Russian, German, Hungarian, Yiddish, or Arabic. The government provides classes to help them learn Hebrew.

About 82 percent of Israel's population is Jewish. The rest of it is mostly Arab. About three fourths of these are Muslim. The rest are Christian.

Food and Festivals Israeli food is influenced by Jewish religious laws. Jews are forbidden to eat pork and shellfish. They also cannot eat meat and milk products at the same meal. The country's food is as diverse as the population. Eastern European dishes are popular, as are Southwest Asian foods.

For Jews, Saturday is a holy day. Yom Kippur, the most important Jewish holiday, is celebrated in October. Passover, in the spring, celebrates the Hebrews' escape from captivity in Egypt. During Passover, people eat matzo (MAHT-suh), a special bread without yeast.

✓ **READING CHECK:** (*Human Systems*) What are modern Israel's government, economy, and culture like?

Gov.—prime minister, parliament; econ.—modern, diverse; culture—Jews, Palestinians, Muslims, Christians

The Occupied Territories

In 1967 Israel captured the Gaza Strip, the Golan Heights, and the West Bank. These are sometimes called the Occupied Territories.

Disputed Land The Gaza Strip is a small, crowded piece of coastal land. More than a million Palestinians live there. The area has almost no resources. The Golan Heights is a hilly area on the Syrian

Marcia Caldwell of Austin, Texas, suggests the following activity to help students learn about Israel and the Occupied Territories: Organize students into small groups and distribute one poster-board cube with eight-inch-wide faces to each group. Have students affix images and phrases that relate to the six essential elements of geography on the faces of the cube. You may wish to direct students to newspapers, magazines, and the Internet as they search for pertinent images and phrases. Hang the completed cubes from the ceiling around the classroom.

Teaching Objective 3

ALL LEVELS: (Suggested time: 30 min.) Pair students and have each pair draw and color a map showing Israel after the statehood declaration and today, with the Israeli-occupied territories. Then have each pair write a paragraph analyzing the conflicts in the area. You may want to challenge students to propose solutions for the area's problems.
ESOL, COOPERATIVE LEARNING

border. In 1981 Israel formally declared the Golan Heights part of Israel. Syria still claims this territory.

The West Bank is the largest of the occupied areas, with a population of about 2.2 million. Since Israel took control of the West Bank, more than 187,000 Jews have moved into settlements there. The Palestinians consider this an invasion of their land. This has caused tension and violence between Arabs and Israelis.

Israel annexed East Jerusalem in 1980. Even before this, the Israeli government had moved the capital from Tel Aviv to Jerusalem. Most foreign countries have chosen not to recognize this transfer. The Palestinians still claim East Jerusalem as their rightful capital.

Control of Jerusalem is a difficult and often emotional question for Jews, Muslims, and Christians. The city contains sites that are holy to all three religions.

The Future of the Territories In the 1990s Israel agreed to turn over parts of the Occupied Territories to the Palestinians. In return, the Palestinian leadership—the Palestinian Authority—agreed to work for peace. Parts of the Gaza Strip and West Bank have been transferred to the Palestinian Authority. More areas of the West Bank are expected to be handed over in the future.

The future of the peace process is uncertain. Some Palestinian groups have continued to commit acts of terrorism. Some Jewish groups believe for religious reasons that Israel must not give up the West Bank. Other Israelis fear they would be open to attack if they withdrew from the territories.

✓ **READING CHECK:** (Human Systems) Why have the Occupied Territories been a source of conflict?

Jews, Muslims, and Christians all have religious ties to Jerusalem.

Muslim women gather to pray at the Dome of the Rock in Jerusalem.

Section Review 3

Define and explain: Diaspora, Zionism

Working with Sketch Maps On the map you created in Section 2, label Jerusalem, Gaza Strip, Golan Heights, West Bank, and Tel Aviv.

Reading for the Main Idea

1. (Environment and Society) How has technology allowed Israel to increase its food production?

2. (Human Systems) What historical factors helped create a culturally diverse region in Israel?

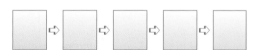

Homework Practice Online Keyword: SK5 HP5

Critical Thinking

3. **Finding the Main Idea** How do political boundaries in Israel create conflicts?

4. **Summarizing** What are some difficult issues involved in the Israeli-Palestinian peace process?

Organizing What You Know

5. **Sequencing** Copy the following graphic organizer. Use it to list the sequence of events that led to the formation of modern Israel.

☐ ⇨ ☐ ⇨ ☐ ⇨ ☐ ⇨ ☐

The Eastern Mediterranean • 117

Answers to Section 3 Review

Define For definitions, see the glossary.

Working with Sketch Maps Maps will vary, but listed places should be labeled accurately.

Reading for the Main Idea

1. through water from irrigation **(NGS 14)**

2. When it was created, people moved to Israel from countries around the world. **(NGS 9)**

Critical Thinking

3. They cut across cultural lines, and each feels entitled to the land. **(NGS 13)**

4. occupation of the Gaza Strip, Golan Heights, and West Bank; new settlements in the West Bank; annexation of East Jerusalem; Israeli government's moving to Jerusalem; control of Jerusalem

Organizing What You Know

5. Hebrews form ancient kingdom of Israel; Romans expel Jews in the Diaspora; Zionist movement begins; tens of thousands of Jews move to area; British control ends in 1948, and Jews establish State of Israel

CLOSE

Have students summarize the role Israel plays in world politics as well as its role as a religious center. Ask them to speculate how Israel's role might change in the future.

REVIEW, ASSESS, RETEACH

Have students complete the Section Review. Then pair students and have each pair create five true-or-false questions about Israel. Have pairs exchange questions with other pairs and quiz each other. Then have students complete Daily Quiz 5.3. **COOPERATIVE LEARNING**

Have students complete Main Idea Activity S3. Then create an outline for the section on the chalkboard using the subheads and have volunteers fill it in. **ESOL**

EXTEND

Have interested students conduct research on the significance of certain Jewish religious holidays and observances, such as Yom Kippur and Rosh Hashanah. Then have students create posters showing how these holidays are observed. **BLOCK SCHEDULING**

Section 4 — Syria, Lebanon, and Jordan

Read to Discover
1. What kind of government and economy does Syria have?
2. How is Lebanese society divided?
3. What events have shaped the history of Jordan?

Vocabulary
mandate

Places
Damascus
Beirut
Amman

People
Hafiz al-Hassad
King Hussein

Reading Strategy

FOLDNOTES: DOUBLE-DOOR   Create a FoldNote titled **Double-Door** described in the Appendix. Write Syria, Lebanon, and Jordan on the upper flap. Label the three sections Syria, Lebanon, and Jordan. As you read, write what you learn about each country.

Syria

The capital of Syria, Damascus, is believed to be the oldest continuously inhabited city in the world. For centuries it was a leading regional trade center. Syria became part of the Ottoman Empire in the 1500s. After World War I, France controlled Syria as a **mandate**. Mandates were former territories of the defeated nations of World War I. They were placed under the control of the winning countries after the war. Syria finally became independent in the 1940s.

Politics and Economy From 1971 to 2000, the Syrian government was led by Hafiz al-Assad. Assad increased the size of Syria's military. He wanted to match Israel's military strength and protect his rule from his enemies within Syria. Assad's son, Bashar, was elected president after his father's death in 2000.

Syria's government owns the country's oil refineries, larger electrical plants, railroads, and some factories. Syria's key manufactured goods are textiles, food products, and chemicals. Agriculture remains important.

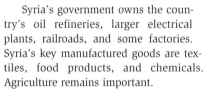

Place Roman columns still stand in the ancient city of Apamea, Syria.

Section 4

Objectives
1. Describe Syria's government and economy.
2. Discuss the divisions in Lebanese society.
3. Recount events that have shaped Jordan's history.

FOCUS

Bellringer

Copy the following instructions onto the chalkboard: *Imagine that our school is made up of three distinct groups that have different languages, different religions, different loyalties, and different customs. What do you think our most difficult challenge would be?* Then have students discuss what links or separates cultures and societies. Tell them that this is the system that exists in Lebanon today. Tell students that in Section 4 they will learn more about Lebanon and its neighbors.

Building Vocabulary

Write the term **mandate** on the chalkboard. Ask students to suggest possible definitions. (Some may suggest that a mandate is a law or guideline.) Tell students that the word *mandate* also refers to a system of governing former colonies.

An Ancient Settlement
Jubayl, formerly known as Byblos, is one of the oldest continuously inhabited cities in the world. The city lies just north of Beirut, Lebanon. It was a fishing village about 7,000 years ago. Later, the town became an important port from which cedar wood and oil were shipped to Egypt. During the 900s B.C. it was the main city in Phoenicia, a region that included present-day Lebanon.

Byblos was invaded several times. Today, the visitor can see many remnants of its long history, including Egyptian temples, a Roman amphitheater, and a castle built during the Crusades.

Activity: Have students find Jubayl in an atlas. Call on volunteers to point out possible routes that would have connected the city to Egypt and Rome. Lead a discussion about the advantages and disadvantages that the city's location presented.

Syria has only small deposits of oil and natural gas. It is rich in limestone, basalt, and phosphates.

People Syria's population of more than 17 million is about 90 percent Arab. The other 10 percent includes Kurds and Armenians. About 74 percent of Syrians are Sunni Muslim. Another 16 percent are Alawites and Druze, members of small branches of Islam. About 10 percent of Syrians are Christian. There are also small Jewish communities in some cities.

✔ **READING CHECK:** (*Places and Regions*) How is Syria's economy organized?
Economy—mostly command, agricultural

Lebanon

Lebanon is a small, mountainous country on the Mediterranean coast. It is home to several different groups of people. At times these different groups have fought each other.

History and People During the Ottoman period many religious and ethnic minority groups settled in Lebanon. After World War I Lebanon, along with Syria, became a French mandate. Lebanon finally gained independence in the 1940s.

The Lebanese are overwhelmingly Arab, but they are divided by religion. Most Lebanese are either Muslim or Christian. Each of those groups is divided into several smaller groups. Muslims are divided into Sunni, Shia, and Druze. The Maronites are the largest of the Christian groups in Lebanon. At the time of independence, there were slightly more Christians than Muslims. Over time, however, Muslims became the majority.

▲
People must drill for water in dry areas of Syria.
Interpreting the Visual Record
(*Human-Environment Interaction*)
Judging from this photo, how has technology affected the lifestyle of people in desert areas?

▲
This photograph from the early 1900s shows a tall cedar tree in the mountains of northern Lebanon. Lebanon's cedars have long been a symbol of the country.

The Eastern Mediterranean • 119

▲ **Visual Record Answer**
provided modern transportation and mobile drilling equipment

TEACH

Teaching Objective 1
ALL LEVELS: (Suggested time: 20 min.) Have each student write five headlines for articles discussing features of Syria's government and economy. (Headlines should mention that Syria was ruled by one person—Hafiz al-Assad—until 2001; Assad increased the size of Syria's military; the government owns many of the country's utilities and industries; Syria's most important goods are textiles, food products and chemicals; agriculture remains a key part of the economy; or that Syria has limestone, basalt, and phosphates.)
LS VERBAL-LINGUISTIC, INTRAPERSONAL

Teaching Objective 2
LEVEL 1: (Suggested time: 40 min.) Pair students and have each pair create a graphic organizer to represent the divisions in Lebanese society. Then lead a discussion about possible ways in which such differences may be resolved through political means. **ESOL, COOPERATIVE LEARNING**

LEVELS 2 and 3: (Suggested time: 20 min.) Have students write a speech addressing the divisions in Lebanon's society. Call on volunteers to deliver their speeches. Speeches should offer possible political solutions.
LS AUDITORY-MUSICAL

FOOD FESTIVAL

Luscious Latkes Latkes are potato pancakes that are traditionally eaten during the Jewish holiday of Hanukkah.

This recipe serves five to six people. First, grate three or four medium potatoes. Squeeze any excess water from the grated potatoes. Then grate one small onion and mix into the potatoes. Mix in one egg, 2 to 3 tbs. flour, and salt and pepper to taste. Form into patties and fry in a well-oiled skillet until both sides are golden-brown. Place the latkes on a paper towel to drain the excess oil. Serve them with apple sauce or sour cream.

▲
A vendor in Beirut sells postcards of what the city looked like before it was scarred by war.

Interpreting the Visual Record What were the effects of the civil war in Lebanon?

▲
The city of Petra in Jordan dates back more than 2,000 years. This building was carved out of the sandstone cliff.

Visual Record Answer ▶

Beirut badly damaged, Lebanon's economy hurt

Civil War For some decades after independence, Christian and Muslim politicians managed to share power. A complex system assigned certain government positions to different religious groups. For example, the president was always a Maronite. However, over time this cooperation broke down. The poorest group, the Shia, grew rapidly but were not given additional power. Tensions mounted. Adding to the divisions between Lebanese was the presence of hundreds of thousands of Palestinian refugees living in Lebanon. Ethnic and religious groups armed themselves, and in the 1970s fighting broke out. Warfare between Lebanese groups lasted until 1990. Tens of thousands of people died, and the capital, Beirut, was badly damaged.

During the 1990s Lebanon's economy slowly recovered from the civil war. The refining of crude oil brought in by pipeline is a leading industry. Other industries include food processing, textiles, cement, chemicals, and jewelry making. Lebanese farmers produce tobacco, fruit, grains, and vegetables.

✓ **READING CHECK:** (**Human Systems**) What is causing divisions in Lebanese society? **Conflict between Christians, Muslims; Palestinian refugees**

Jordan

Jordan's short history has been full of conflict. Great Britain drew its borders, and Jordan's royal family is actually from Arabia. The country has few resources and several powerful neighbors. In addition, most of its people think of another country as their homeland. Yet Jordan has survived.

History and Government The country of Jordan (called Transjordan until 1949) was created from Ottoman territory following World War I. The British controlled the area as a mandate. They established an Arabian prince named Abdullah as the monarch of the new country. Abdullah had helped the British in World War I, but he had been driven out of Saudi Arabia. In the 1940s the country became fully independent. After the creation of Israel and the war of 1948, Jordan annexed the Arab lands of the West Bank.

At the time of its independence, Jordan's population was small. Most Jordanians lived a nomadic or seminomadic life. After each of the Arab-Israeli wars of 1948 and 1967, hundreds of thousands of Palestinian Arab refugees came to live in Jordan. These immigrants strained Jordan's resources. In addition, a cultural division arose between the Palestinians and the "original" Jordanian Arabs. After 1967 Palestinians actually made up a majority of Jordan's people.

From 1952 to 1999 Jordan was ruled by King Hussein. Most observers, both inside and outside Jordan, considered him one of the

Teaching Objective 3

ALL LEVELS: (Suggested time: 25 min.) Copy the graphic organizer at right onto the chalkboard, omitting the blue answers. Use it to help students describe the history of Jordan. Organize the class into groups of three and have each group complete the organizer. In each group one student should identify important events in Jordan's history, another student should summarize these events, and the last student should comment on the significance and importance of each event. Have groups present their organizers to the class. **ESOL, COOPERATIVE LEARNING**

JORDAN'S HISTORY

Event	Summary	Significance
borders established	Great Britain drew borders after WWI	foreign influence in creation of country
monarchy established	Abdullah named as monarch	British ally named to rule country
independence	full independence gained in 1940s	independence from foreign rule
war of 1948	war with Israel	annexed Arab lands of the West Bank
Arab-Israeli wars	wars between Arab nations and Israel	Palestinian refugees immigrate to Jordan
rule of Hussein	King Hussein rules from 1952 to 1999	considered one of the best rulers of region

King Hussein (1935–1999) **Character Trait: Kindness**

On his 18th birthday, Hussein ibn Talal was crowned king of Jordan. King Hussein is known to Jordanians as "The Humane King" for the ways he improved living conditions in Jordan. He also developed economic opportunities for Jordanians and built new highways across the country. Throughout his reign, Hussein also made many attempts to bring about peace in the Middle East. In 1994, he signed a peace treaty with Israel.

Why is Hussein known as "The Humane King"?

best rulers in the region. Hussein's popularity allowed him to begin some democratic reforms in the 1980s and 1990s. Today, the division between Palestinian and Jordanian Arabs causes less conflict.

Economy and Resources Jordan is a poor country with limited resources. The country does produce phosphates, cement, and potash. Tourism and banking are becoming important industries. Jordan depends on economic aid from the oil-rich Arab nations and the United States. Amman, the capital, is Jordan's only large city.

Jordanian farmers raise fruits and vegetables in the Jordan River valley, using irrigation. Some highland areas receive enough winter rainfall to grow grains. Raising sheep and goats is an important source of income. However, overgrazing has caused soil erosion. A crucial resource issue for Jordan is its shortage of water.

✓ **READING CHECK:** (*Human Systems*) How did King Hussein affect Jordan's history? He was considered by many to be one of the best rulers in the region and enacted democratic reforms.

Homework Practice Online
Keyword: SK5 HP5

Define or identify: mandate, Hafiz al-Hassad, King Hussein

Working with Sketch Maps On the map you created in Section 3, label Damascus, Beirut, and Amman.

Reading for the Main Idea
1. (*Human Systems*) How did Hafiz al-Assad affect Syria?
2. (*Human Systems*) What divisions led to conflict in Lebanon?
3. (*Places and Regions*) Which of the countries discussed in this section does not border the Mediterranean Sea?

Critical Thinking
4. **Finding the Main Idea** How have foreign countries influenced Jordan?

Organizing What You Know
5. **Categorizing** Use the graphic organizer to gather information about Syria, Lebanon, and Jordan.

	Syria	Lebanon	Jordan
Major religion(s)			
Type of government			
Major problem(s)			
Greatest strength(s)			

The Eastern Mediterranean • 121

Answers to Section 4 Review

Define or identify For definition and identifications, see the glossary and index.

Working with Sketch Maps Maps will vary, but listed places should be located accurately.

Reading for the Main Idea
1. ruled from 1971 to 2000 and increased the size of the military (**NGS 12**)
2. religious and political divisions between Christians and Muslims (**NGS 13**)
3. Jordan (**NGS 4**)

Critical Thinking
4. drew its borders, established its monarchy, immigrated there, and provided economic aid

Organizing What You Know
5. Answers should reflect information from the section.

▲ **Biography Answer**

for improving living conditions for Jordanians

Ask for volunteers to complete the following sentence: The most important challenge facing Syria, Jordan, or Lebanon is ___. Discuss answers.

REVIEW, ASSESS, RETEACH

Have students complete the Section Review. Then organize the class into three groups. Have each group represent one of the countries in this section and lead the class in a discussion on challenges facing its assigned country. Then have students complete Daily Quiz 5.4.
COOPERATIVE LEARNING

Have students complete Main Idea Activity S4. Have students use handwritten headlines, magazine pictures, newspaper articles, and their own drawings to create a collage that answers the Read to Discover questions.
ESOL, LS VISUAL-SPATIAL

EXTEND

Have interested students conduct research on King Hussein and Jordan's political role in this region. Have students include how Jordan was affected by his death. **BLOCK SCHEDULING**

Define and Identify

For definitions and identifications, see the glossary and index.

Review the Main Ideas

10. Euphrates and Jordan rivers

11. lowest point on any continent, so salty that swimmers cannot sink in it; produces mineral salts

12. sulfur, mercury, copper, phosphates, asphalt

13. Europe, Asia, Africa

14. Because it fought on the losing side, it lost all territory outside Turkey. After military officers took over the government, Mustafa Kemal formally dissolved the Ottoman Empire.

15. Turkey now has a national assembly, its economy includes modern factories, and it is a secular state.

16. Judaism, Christianity, and Islam

17. Hebrews, Roman Empire, Arabs, European Crusaders, Ottoman Empire, Great Britain

18. Palestinians consider the movement of many Jews into the Occupied Territories as an invasion of their land. (NGS 13)

19. They are divided by religion. (NGS 13)

Think Critically

20. to move it farther into Turkey and to separate it from the site of the Ottoman Empire's capital

21. People of different backgrounds have moved to Israel, making it culturally diverse.

22. It receives little rainfall, and countries depend on rivers for water. One country can dam a river that flows into another country, reducing the flow of water into the country downstream. (NGS 13)

23. Jordan's resources were strained and a cultural division arose.

24. The assignment of certain government positions to certain religious groups caused tension between the groups.

Review and Practice

Define and Identify

Identify each of the following:

1. phosphates
2. asphalt
3. Kemal Atatürk
4. secular
5. Diaspora
6. Zionism
7. mandate
8. Hafiz al-Hassad
9. King Hussein

Review the Main Ideas

10. What are the region's main rivers? Where do they flow?

11. What makes the Dead Sea an unusual body of water? What are its commercial uses?

12. What mineral resources are located in the eastern Mediterranean?

13. People and customs from what three continents have influenced the eastern Mediterranean region?

14. How did the Ottoman Empire come to an end?

15. How has westernization changed Turkey's government, economy, and culture?

16. What three major religions have holy sites in Jerusalem?

17. What cultures have ruled the lands now called Israel and the Occupied Territories?

18. What is the conflict over the Occupied Territories?

19. What issue divides the Arabs of Lebanon?

Think Critically

20. Drawing Inferences and Conclusions Why do you think Atatürk moved Turkey's capital from Istanbul to Ankara?

21. Finding the Main Idea How has human migration to Israel affected its population?

22. Analyzing Information Why is conflict over dams in this region so important?

23. Analyzing Information How did refugees from Palestine affect Jordan?

24. Drawing Inferences and Conclusions Why did attempts to balance religious groups' participation in Lebanon's government fail?

Map Activity

25. On a separate sheet of paper, match the letters on the map with their correct labels.

Dardanelles	Negev
Bosporus	Istanbul
Sea of Marmara	Tel Aviv
Jordan River	Jerusalem
Dead Sea	Damascus

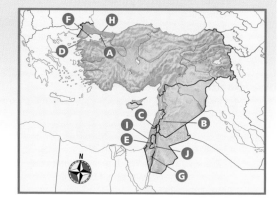

Map Activity

25. A. Istanbul
B. Damascus
C. Jordan River
D. Dardanelles
E. Jerusalem
F. Sea of Marmara
G. Negev
H. Bosporus
I. Tel Aviv
J. Dead Sea

Writing Activity

Imagine that your family is about to travel to the eastern Mediterranean for a vacation. Your parents have asked you to help plan the trip. Write about the places you would like to visit and the reasons you would find them interesting. Be sure to use standard grammar, spelling, sentence structure, and punctuation.

internet connect

Internet Activity: go.hrw.com
KEYWORD: SK5 GT5

Choose a topic to explore about the eastern Mediterranean:
- Visit the Dead Sea.
- Compare Israeli and Arab foods.
- Travel to historic Jerusalem.

Social Studies Skills Practice

Interpreting Charts

Study the following chart and answer the questions.

Projected Growth of Turkey's Kurdish Population			
Year	Total Population of Turkey (in millions)	Kurdish Population in Turkey (in millions)	Percentage of Turkish Population that is Kurdish
1990	56.7	13.7	24.1
2000	65.9	18.7	28.4
2020	87.5	32.3	36.9
2050	105.8	47.0	44.4

Source: Mehrdad R. Izady, *The Kurds: A Concise Handbook,* 1992

1. In what year will the Kurds make up the greatest percentage of the Turkish population?
2. What prediction can you make about Kurdish population growth?
3. Which group appears to have a higher birthrate? the Kurds or the overall Turkish population?
4. Based on this chart and your knowledge of the region, what might result from the continued growth of the Kurdish population?

Analyzing Primary Sources

Read the following passage from a 2003 newspaper article about the Dead Sea. Then answer the questions.

"In less than 50 years, the lowest point on earth has dropped even lower—from 1,294 feet below sea level to 1,360 feet. . . . The Dead Sea's only sources of water are sparse rainfall—less than 3 inches a year—and the Jordan River. But Israel and Jordan have diverted so much of the river's flow for agricultural use that the Dead Sea gets just 10 percent of the water it once did. At the same time, the sea's own waters are being sucked out by Israeli and Arab companies that extract the potassium and other minerals . . . The result? The level of the Dead Sea is dropping by more than 3 feet per year."

1. By how many feet has the Dead Sea dropped in the past 50 years?
2. What is the Dead Sea's only source for water?
3. What two factors are causing the level of the Dead Sea to drop?
4. At the current rate, how much lower will the Dead Sea be in 10 years?

Writing Activity
Answers will vary, but information included should be consistent with written material. Students should include sites from the area as well as reasons for visiting the sites. Use Rubric 37, Writing Assignments, to evaluate student work.

Interpreting Charts
1. 2050
2. It will grow both in size and as a percentage of the Turkish population.
3. The Kurdish birth rate is higher than the overall Turkish rate.
4. The Kurds may continue to demand independence, and violence may result.

Analyzing Primary Sources
1. from 1,294 feet below sea level to 1,360 feet below, a total of 66 feet
2. sparse rainfall and the Jordan River
3. Jordan River supplies less water because its water is used for agriculture; Dead Sea water is removed by companies seeking minerals.
4. more than 30 feet lower

CHAPTER 5

REVIEW AND ASSESSMENT RESOURCES

Reproducible
- Readings in World Geography, History, and Culture 50, 51, and 52
- Critical Thinking Activity 5
- Vocabulary Activity 5

Technology
- Chapter 5 Test Generator (on the One-Stop Planner)

- Audio CD Program, Chapter 5
- HRW Go site

Reinforcement, Review, and Assessment
- Chapter 5 Review
- Chapter Summaries and Review
- Chapter 5 Test

- Chapter 5 Test for English Language Learners and Special-Needs Students
- Unit 2 Test
- Unit 2 Test for English Language Learners and Special-Needs Students

internet connect

GO TO: go.hrw.com
KEYWORD: SJ5 Teacher
FOR: a guide to using the Internet in your classroom

CHAPTER 6

The Arabian Peninsula, Iraq, Iran, and Afghanistan

Chapter Resource Manager

Objectives	Pacing Guide	Reproducible Resources
SECTION 1		
Physical Geography (pp. 125–27) **1.** Identify the major physical features of the region. **2.** Describe the climates found in this region. **3.** Identify the region's important resources.	**Regular** .5 day Lecture Notes, Section 1 **Block Scheduling** .5 day Block Scheduling Handbook, Chapter 6	**RS** Know It Notes S1 **IC** Interdisciplinary Activities for the Middle Grades 21, 23 **ELL** Main Idea Activity S1
SECTION 2		
The Arabian Peninsula (pp. 128–35) **1.** Describe what Saudi Arabia's history, government, and people are like. **2.** Identify the kinds of government and economy the other countries of the Arabian Peninsula have.	**Regular** 2.5 days Lecture Notes, Section 2 **Block Scheduling** .5 day Block Scheduling Handbook, Chapter 6	**RS** Know It Notes S2 **RS** Graphic Organizer 6 **E** Cultures of the World Activity 5 **E** Creative Strategies for Teaching World Geography, Lessons 14 and 15 **SM** Geography for Life Activity 6 **SM** Map Activity 6 **ELL** Main Idea Activity S2
SECTION 3		
Iraq (pp. 136–38) **1.** Identify the key events in Iraq's history. **2.** Describe Iraq's government and economy. **3.** Describe the makeup of Iraq's population.	**Regular** 1 day Lecture Notes, Section 3 **Block Scheduling** .5 day Block Scheduling Handbook, Chapter 6	**RS** Know It Notes S3 **E** Environmental and Global Issues Activity 5 **ELL** Main Idea Activity S3
SECTION 4		
Iran and Afghanistan (pp. 139–41) **1.** Identify some important events in Iran's history. **2.** Describe what Iran's government and people are like. **3.** Describe the problems Afghanistan faces today.	**Regular** 1 day Lecture Notes, Section 4 **Block Scheduling** .5 day Block Scheduling Handbook, Chapter 6	**RS** Know It Notes S4 **E** Biography Avtivity: Jalal ad-Din Rumi **ELL** Main Idea Activity S4

Chapter Resource Key

RS Reading Support
IC Interdisciplinary Connections
E Enrichment
SM Skills Mastery
A Assessment
REV Review

ELL Reinforcement and English Language Learners and English for Speakers of Other Languages (ESOL)
 Transparencies
 CD–ROM

 Music
 Video
 Internet
 Holt Presentation Maker Using Microsoft® PowerPoint®

 One-Stop Planner CD–ROM

See the **One-Stop Planner** for a complete list of additional resources for students and teachers.

One-Stop Planner CD–ROM

It's easy to plan lessons, select resources, and print out materials for your students when you use the *One-Stop Planner CD–ROM with Test Generator.*

Technology Resources	Review, Reinforcement, and Assessment Resources	
One-Stop Planner CD–ROM, Lesson 6.1 *ARGWorld* CD–ROM Geography and Cultures Visual Resources with Teaching Activities 37–41 Homework Practice Online HRW Go site	**ELL**	Main Idea Activity S1
	REV	Section 1 Review
	A	Daily Quiz 6.1
	REV	Chapter Summaries and Review
	ELL	English Audio Summary 6.1
	ELL	Spanish Audio Summary 6.1
One-Stop Planner CD–ROM, Lesson 6.2 *ARGWorld* CD–ROM Homework Practice Online HRW Go site	**ELL**	Main Idea Activity S2
	REV	Section 2 Review
	A	Daily Quiz 6.2
	REV	Chapter Summaries and Review
	ELL	English Audio Summary 6.2
	ELL	Spanish Audio Summary 6.2
One-Stop Planner CD–ROM, Lesson 6.3 *ARGWorld* CD–ROM Homework Practice Online HRW Go site	**ELL**	Main Idea Activity S3
	REV	Section 3 Review
	A	Daily Quiz 6.3
	REV	Chapter Summaries and Review
	ELL	English Audio Summary 6.3
	ELL	Spanish Audio Summary 6.3
One-Stop Planner CD–ROM, Lesson 6.4 *ARGWorld* CD–ROM Music of the World Audio CD Program, Selection 11 Homework Practice Online HRW Go site	**ELL**	Main Idea Activity S4
	REV	Section 4 Review
	A	Daily Quiz 6.4
	REV	Chapter Summaries and Review
	ELL	English Audio Summary 6.4
	ELL	Spanish Audio Summary 6.4

internet connect

HRW ONLINE RESOURCES

<u>GO TO:</u> go.hrw.com
Then type in a keyword.

TEACHER HOME PAGE
 KEYWORD: SK5 TEACHER

CHAPTER INTERNET ACTIVITIES
 KEYWORD: SK5 GT6

Choose an activity to:
• visit Mesopotamia.
• discover the importance of camels.
• see Arabian arts and crafts.

CHAPTER ENRICHMENT LINKS
 KEYWORD: SK5 CH6

CHAPTER MAPS
 KEYWORD: SK5 MAPS6

ONLINE ASSESSMENT
Homework Practice
 KEYWORD: SK5 HP6
 Standardized Test Prep Online
 KEYWORD: SK5 STP6
 Rubrics
 KEYWORD: SS Rubrics

COUNTRY INFORMATION
 KEYWORD: SK5 Almanac

CONTENT UPDATES
 KEYWORD: SS Content Updates

HOLT PRESENTATION MAKER
 KEYWORD: SK5 PPT6

ONLINE READING SUPPORT
 KEYWORD: SS Strategies

CURRENT EVENTS
 KEYWORD: S5 Current Events

Meeting Individual Needs

Ability Levels

Level 1 Basic-level activities designed for all students encountering new material

Level 2 Intermediate-level activities designed for average students

Level 3 Challenging activities designed for honors and gifted-and-talented students

ESOL Activities that address the needs of students with Limited English Proficiency

Chapter Review and Assessment

IC	Interdisciplinary Activities for the Middle Grades 24	**ELL**	Vocabulary Activity 6
		A	Chapter 6 Test
E	Readings in World Geography, History, and Culture 47, 48, and 49		Chapter 6 Test Generator (on the One-Stop Planner)
		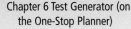	Audio CD Program, Chapter 6
SM	Critical Thinking Activity 6	**A**	Chapter 6 Test for English Language Learners and Special-Needs Students
REV	Chapter 6 Review and Practice		
REV	Chapter Summaries and Review		HRW Go Site

123B

The Arabian Peninsula, Iraq, Iran, and Afghanistan

Holt Online Learning

Previewing Chapter Resources

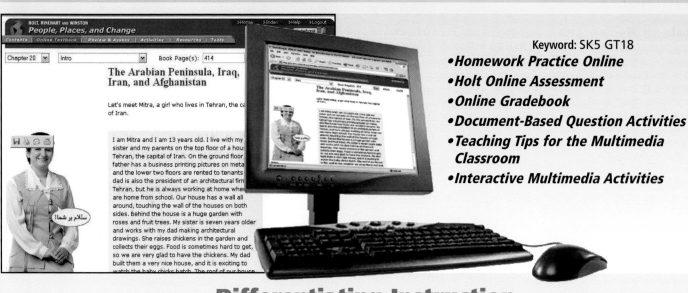

Keyword: SK5 GT18

- *Homework Practice Online*
- *Holt Online Assessment*
- *Online Gradebook*
- *Document-Based Question Activities*
- *Teaching Tips for the Multimedia Classroom*
- *Interactive Multimedia Activities*

Differentiating Instruction

Reading and Writing Support

◀ *Graphic Organizer Activity: Islam and the Arab Peninsula*
- *Vocabulary Activity*
- *Chapter Summary and Review*
- *Know It Notes*
- *Audio CD*

Active Learning

◀ *Block Scheduling Handbook*
- *Cultures of the World Activity*
- *Interdisciplinary Activity*
- *Map Activity*
- *Critical Thinking Activity 20*
- *Music of the World CD: Classical Music of Iran*

Primary Sources and Advanced Learners

- *Geography for Life Activity: The Hajj*
◀ *Map Activity: Islam*
- *Readings in World Geography, History and Culture:*
  - *47 People of the Empty Quater*
  - *48 Change Comes to Iran*
  - *49 Exploring a Souk*

Assessment Program

- *Daily Quizzes S1–4*
◀ *Chapter Test*
- *Chapter Test for English Language Learners and Special-Needs Students*

Spanish and ESOL

- *Vocabulary Activity*
◀ *Main Idea Activities for English Language Learners and Special-Needs Students*
- *Chapter Summary and Review*
- *Spanish Audio Summary*
- *Know It Notes S1–4*
- *Chapter Test for English Language Learners and Special-Needs Students*

Special Education Modifications

Your **I.D.E.A. Works! CD-ROM** will provide modified versions of the following teaching materials:

◀ *Guided Reading Strategies S1–4*
- *Vocabulary Activity*
- *Main Idea Activities S1–4*
- *Daily Quizzes S1–4*
- *Chapter 6 Test*
- *Flash cards of chapter vocabulary terms*

Teacher Resources

Books for Teachers

Abdelkarim, Abbas, ed. *Change and Development in the Gulf.* St. Martin's Press, 1999.

El-Sanabary, Nagat. *Education in the Arab Gulf States and the Arab World.* Garland Publications, 1992.

Mackey, Sandra. *The Iranians: Persia, Islam, and the Soul of a Nation.* Plume Book, 1998.

Books for Students

Foster, Leila Merrell. *The Story of the Persian Gulf War.* Cornerstones of Freedom. Children's Press, 1991. Causes and events of the 1991 conflict.

Lyle, Garry. *Iran* Major World Nations. Chelsea House Publishers, 1997. History, geography, culture, religion, and people of the Islamic republic.

McCarthy, Kevin. *Saudi Arabia: A Desert Kingdom.* Dillon Press, 1997. Examines traditional Saudi society and the country's transition from poverty to wealth, among other topics.

Heide, Florence Parry, and Judith Heide Gilliland. *The House of Wisdom.* DK Ink, 1999. Fictional story of Ishaq, who lives in Baghdad in the 800s.
SHELTERED ENGLISH

Multimedia Materials

Iraq: Cradle of Civilization. (Video, 29 min.) Films for the Humanities and Sciences.

Middle East: Ancient Civilizations to the Present. CD–ROM with Labpack. Educational Software Institute.

Saudi Arabia: Kingdom of Black Gold. (Video, 29 min.) Films for the Humanities and Sciences.

Videos and CDs

Videos

- **CNN** *Presents Geography: Yesterday and Today, Segment 22 Kuwait—Restoring the Environment*
- **CNN** *Presents World Cultures: Yesterday and Today, Segments 9 and 33*
- *ARG World*

Holt Researcher

http://researcher.hrw.com

- *League of Arab States (also known as the Arab League)*
- *Organization of Petroleum Exporting Countries (OPEC)*
- *Iran-Iraq War*
- *Abbas the Great*
- *Hammurabi*
- *Muhammad*
- *Afghanistan*
- *Iran*
- *Iraq*
- *Kuwait*
- *Saudi Arabia*
- *Yemen*
- *Oman*

Transparency Packages

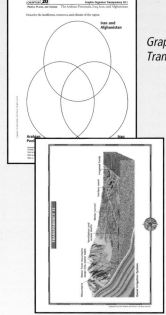

Graphic Organizer Transparencies 6.1–4

Geography and Cultures Visual Resources Transparencies 66–70

72 The Arabian Peninsula, Iraq, Iran, and Afghanistan: Physical-Political

73 Qanat Irrigatin System

74 Nomadic Encampment

Map Activities Transparency 06 Islam

WHY IT MATTERS

Tell students that there are many reasons why they should know more about the Arabian Peninsula, Iraq, Iran, and Afghanistan.

▶ The world's first urban civilization, Sumer, developed in what is now Iraq. The mighty Persian Empire ruled the area later. These civilizations have left behind great works of art, architecture, and literature.

▶ This region contains most of the world's known oil reserves.

▶ The U.S. military has been involved in the region. For example, U.S. forces invaded Iraq in 2003.

▶ This region is the cradle of Islam. Islam is the fastest-growing religion in the United States.

The Arabian Peninsula, Iraq, Iran, and Afghanistan

Let's meet Mitra, a girl who lives in Tehran, the capital of Iran.

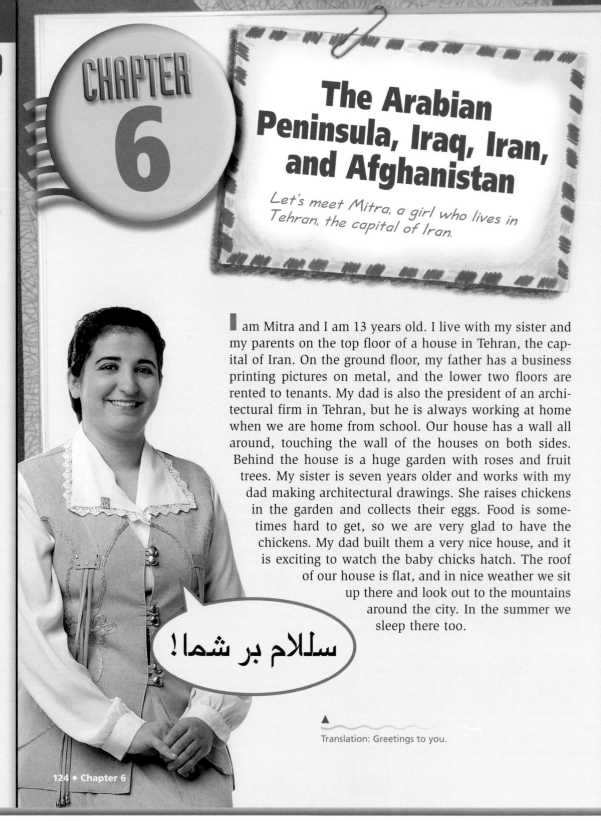

I am Mitra and I am 13 years old. I live with my sister and my parents on the top floor of a house in Tehran, the capital of Iran. On the ground floor, my father has a business printing pictures on metal, and the lower two floors are rented to tenants. My dad is also the president of an architectural firm in Tehran, but he is always working at home when we are home from school. Our house has a wall all around, touching the wall of the houses on both sides. Behind the house is a huge garden with roses and fruit trees. My sister is seven years older and works with my dad making architectural drawings. She raises chickens in the garden and collects their eggs. Food is sometimes hard to get, so we are very glad to have the chickens. My dad built them a very nice house, and it is exciting to watch the baby chicks hatch. The roof of our house is flat, and in nice weather we sit up there and look out to the mountains around the city. In the summer we sleep there too.

سلام بر شما!

Translation: Greetings to you.

124 • Chapter 6

CHAPTER PROJECT

Have students conduct research on the conventions of Islamic art. Then have them create a "name poem" of an important person, place, or term associated with Southwest Asia and decorate it in Islamic style, with plant forms and geometric patterns. A name poem arranges the letters of the name vertically, then for each letter provides a phrase that pertains to the poem's subject and that begins with the letter.

STARTING THE CHAPTER

Copy the following headings onto the chalkboard: *What I know about Southwest Asia* and *What I want to know about Southwest Asia*. Ask volunteers to compile lists under the headings. If most of the items in the first column relate to oil or political unrest, point out that there is much more to learn about the region. Tell students that they will learn about the history, economy, and cultures of the Arabian Peninsula, Iraq, Iran, and Afghanistan in this chapter.

Section 1 Physical Geography

Read to Discover

1. What are the major physical features of the region?
2. What climates are found in this region?
3. What are the region's important resources?

Vocabulary

exotic rivers
wadis
fossil water

Places

Persian Gulf
Arabian Peninsula
Red Sea
Arabian Sea
Tigris River

Euphrates River
Elburz Mountains
Zagros Mountains
Hindu Kush
Rub' al-Khali

Reading Strategy

READING ORGANIZER Create a three-column chart. Title the first column Arabian Peninsula, the second column Tigris-Euphrates plain, and the third column Mountains and Plateaus. As you read this section, list the countries and characteristics found in each region.

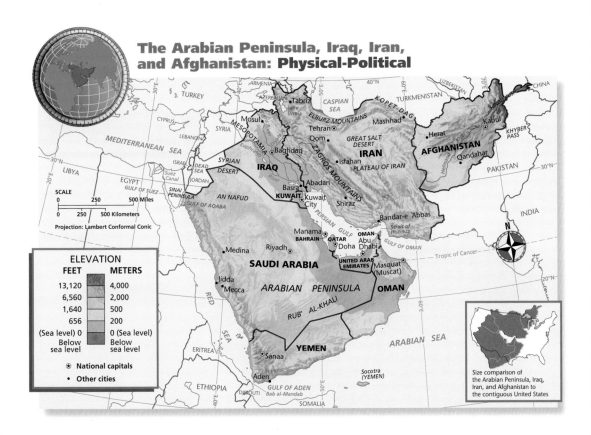

The Arabian Peninsula, Iraq, Iran, and Afghanistan: Physical-Political

ELEVATION
FEET / METERS
13,120 / 4,000
6,560 / 2,000
1,640 / 500
656 / 200
(Sea level) 0 / 0 (Sea level)
Below sea level / Below sea level

⊛ National capitals
• Other cities

SCALE
0 250 500 Miles
0 250 500 Kilometers
Projection: Lambert Conformal Conic

Size comparison of the Arabian Peninsula, Iraq, Iran, and Afghanistan to the contiguous United States

The Arabian Peninsula, Iraq, Iran, and Afghanistan • 125

SECTION 1 RESOURCES

Reproducible
- Lecture Notes, Section 1
- Block Scheduling Handbook, Chapter 6
- Know It Notes S1
- Interdisciplinary Activities for the Middle Grades 21, 23

Technology
- One-Stop Planner CD–ROM, Lesson 6.1
- Homework Practice Online
- Geography and Cultures Visual Resources with Teaching Activities 37–41
- HRW Go site

Reinforcement, Review, and Assessment
- Section 1 Review
- Daily Quiz 6.1
- Main Idea Activity S1
- Chapter Summaries and Review
- English Audio Summary 6.1
- Spanish Audio Summary 6.1

Section 1

Objectives

1. Name the major physical features of this region.
2. List the climates found in this region.
3. Identify the region's important resources.

FOCUS

Bellringer

Copy the following instructions onto the chalkboard: *Make a list of adjectives to describe sand—what it looks like, feels like, where you find it, what it does, and so on.* Discuss responses. Tell students that in Section 1 they will learn about a region with one of the great sand deserts of the world.

Using the Physical-Political Map

Have students examine the map on this page. Call on volunteers to name the major bodies of water in the region, and to point out the Strait of Hormuz and the Bab al-Mandab. Ask why some or all of the region's bodies of water might be of strategic or economic importance. Then ask what countries border these bodies of water, and how they might be able to use their locations to their advantage in the region or in the world.

The Arabian Peninsula, Iraq, Iran, and Afghanistan 125

EYE ON EARTH

The Ghost of a River

Satellite images have detected traces of an ancient river that apparently flowed from the Hejaz Mountains of western Saudi Arabia eastward across the desert, forming a large delta that once covered what is now Kuwait. The river, which may have been three miles wide in places, probably dates to a relatively wet period that occurred between 5,000 and 11,000 years ago. Similar discoveries in North Africa have yielded new sources of groundwater. That possibility exists for the ancient Saudi Arabian river also.

Critical Thinking: How may the use of satellite imagery to locate a new water source affect this region?

Answer: Answers will vary but could include new settlements or greater crop production.

📶 internet connect

GO TO: go.hrw.com
KEYWORD: SK5 CH6
FOR: Web sites about the Arabian Peninsula, Iraq, Iran, and Afghanistan

Physical Features

The 10 countries of this region are laid out like a semicircle, with the Persian Gulf in the center. They are Saudi Arabia, Kuwait (koo-WAYT), Bahrain (bah-RAYN), Qatar (KAH-tuhr), the United Arab Emirates (E-muh-ruhts), Oman (oh-MAHN), Yemen (YE-muhn), Iraq (i-RAHK), Iran (i-RAN), and Afghanistan (af-GA-nuh-stan).

This area can be divided into three landform regions. The Arabian Peninsula is a large rectangular area. The Red Sea, Gulf of Aden, Arabian Sea, and Persian Gulf border the peninsula. North of the Arabian Peninsula is the plain of the Tigris (TY-gruhs) and Euphrates (yooh-FRAY-teez) Rivers. In ancient times, this area was called Mesopotamia (me-suh-puh-TAY-mee-uh), or the "land between the rivers." East of this plain is a region of mountains and plateaus. It stretches through Iran and Afghanistan.

The surface of the Arabian Peninsula rises gradually as one moves westward from the Persian Gulf. The highest point is in the southwest, in the mountains of Yemen.

North of the Arabian Peninsula is a low, flat plain. It runs from the Persian Gulf into northern Iraq. The Tigris and Euphrates Rivers flow across this plain. They are what are known as **exotic rivers**. Exotic rivers begin in humid regions and then flow through dry areas.

East of this low plain the land climbs sharply. Most of Iran is a plateau bordered by mountains. The Elburz (el-BOOHRZ) Mountains and Kopet-Dag range lie in the north. The Zagros (ZA-gruhs) Mountains lie in the southwest. Afghanistan includes many mountain ranges, such as the towering Hindu Kush range.

✔ **READING CHECK:** (*Places and Regions*) What are the major physical features of this area? Arabian Peninsula, plain of the Tigris and Euphrates Rivers, mountains of Yemen, Elburz Mountains, Kopet-Dag, Hindu Kush

Climate

Most of Southwest Asia has a desert climate. A nearly constant high-pressure system in the atmosphere causes this climate. Some areas—mostly high plateaus and the region's edges—do get winter rains or snow. These areas generally have steppe climates. Some mountain peaks receive more than 50 inches (130 cm) of rain per year.

Cold nighttime temperatures and extremely hot days help break rock into sand in Saudi Arabia's Rub' al-Khali, or "empty quarter."

Interpreting the Visual Record How do you think wind affects these sand dunes?

▼

Visual Record Answer ▶

changes their shape and size

TEACH

Teaching Objectives 1–2

ALL LEVELS: (Suggested time: 20 min.) Copy the following graphic organizer onto the chalkboard, omitting the blue answers. Have students use the map and the text to complete the organizer. **ESOL**

Physical Geography of the Region

Rivers	Mountains	Bodies of water	Deserts	Climate types
Tigris Euphrates	Elburz Kopet-Dag Zagros Hindu Kush	Persian Gulf Red Sea Arabian Sea	Great Salt Rub'al-Khali An Nafud	desert steppe

Teaching Objective 3

ALL LEVELS: (Suggested time: 45 min.) Organize the class into groups. Have each group create a visual presentation about the oil industry in Southwest Asia by collecting from magazines and other sources pictures of oil rigs, supertankers, refineries, oil ministers at OPEC meetings, and so on. Then have a student from each group present the group's work to the class. Finally, refer students to the land use and resources map in the Unit Atlas. Have students use the map to compare land use and resources of the Arabian Peninsula with land use and resources elsewhere in the region. **ESOL, COOPERATIVE LEARNING**

The desert can be both very hot and very cold. In summer, afternoon temperatures can reach 129°F (54°C). During the night, however, the temperature may drop quickly. Temperatures sometimes dip below freezing during winter nights.

The Rub' al-Khali (ROOB ahl-KAH-lee), or "empty quarter," of southern Saudi Arabia is the largest sand desert in the world. In northern Saudi Arabia is the An Nafud (ahn nah-FOOD), another desert.

✓ **READING CHECK:** (*Places and Regions*) What are the climates of this region? desert, steppe

Resources

Water is an important resource everywhere, but in this region it is crucial. Many desert regions are visited only by nomads and their animal herds. In many places, springs or wells provide water. Nomads sometimes get water by digging shallow wells into dry streambeds called **wadis**. Wells built with modern technology can reach water deep underground. The groundwater in these wells is often **fossil water**. Fossil water is water that is not being replaced by rainfall. Wells that pump fossil water will eventually run dry.

Other than water, oil is the region's most important mineral resource. Most of the oilfields are located near the shores of the Persian Gulf. The countries of the region are not rich in resources other than oil. Iran is an exception, with deposits of many metals.

✓ **READING CHECK:** (*Places and Regions*) What are the region's important resources? water, oil, metals in Iran

Human-Environment Interaction Beneath the Red Sea lie many valuable resources, such as oil, sulfur, and metal deposits.

▼

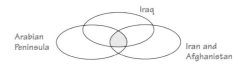

go.hrw.com **Homework Practice Online**
Keyword: SK5 HP6

Section Review 1

Define and explain: exotic rivers, wadis, fossil water

Working with Sketch Maps On a map of the Arabian Peninsula, Iraq, Iran, and Afghanistan that you draw or that your teacher provides, label the following: Persian Gulf, Arabian Peninsula, Red Sea, Arabian Sea, Tigris River, Euphrates River, Elburz Mountains, Zagros Mountains, Hindu Kush, and Rub' al-Khali.

Reading for the Main Idea
1. (*Places and Regions*) Why do you think Mesopotamia was important in ancient times?
2. (*Places and Regions*) What is the region's climate?

Critical Thinking
3. **Drawing Inferences and Conclusions** Why do you think the Persian Gulf is important to international trade?
4. **Drawing Inferences and Conclusions** What settlement pattern might you find in this region?

Organizing What You Know
5. **Summarizing** Copy the following graphic organizer. Use it to list as many details of landforms, resources, and climate as you can. Place them in the correct part of the diagram.

Iraq
Arabian Peninsula
Iran and Afghanistan

The Arabian Peninsula, Iraq, Iran, and Afghanistan • 127

Answers to Section 1 Review

Define For definitions, see the glossary.

Working with Sketch Maps Maps will vary, but listed places should be labeled in their approximate locations.

Reading for the Main Idea
1. fertile, well-watered area **(NGS 4)**
2. desert or steppe **(NGS 4)**

Critical Thinking
3. large oilfields near its shores, used for transport of oil in tankers
4. widely scattered settlements, because they need to be near water sources

Organizing What You Know
5. Students' answers should describe landforms, resources, and climate. They may mention that all three regions have a desert climate, oil, and limited water supplies.

CLOSE

Tell students that what we now call Southwest Asia has also been known as the Middle East. Ask students to speculate why that term is now used less often. Explain that *Middle East* described the region from a European perspective, in terms of the region's physical relationship to Europe.

REVIEW, ASSESS, RETEACH

Have students complete the Section Review. Then have each student use the physical-political map of the region and the text to write two matching questions that connect countries to physical features, climates, or resources. Collect the questions and quiz the class. Then have students complete Daily Quiz 6.1.

Have students complete Main Idea Activity S1. Then have students draw storyboards for a trailer advertising a documentary film about the region's physical geography. **ESOL,** **LS** **VISUAL-SPATIAL**

EXTEND

Have interested students conduct research on camels, including the physiological characteristics that suit them to the desert, the history of their use by humans, and their current role in Arab life. Then have students create an advertisement describing the benefits of owning a camel.
BLOCK SCHEDULING

Section 2 The Arabian Peninsula

Read to Discover

1. What are Saudi Arabia's history, government, and people like?
2. What kinds of government and economy do the other countries of the Arabian Peninsula have?

Vocabulary
Muslims
caliph
Sunni
Shia
Qur'an
OPEC

Places
Mecca
Riyadh

People
Muhammad

Reading Strategy

FOLDNOTE: TRI-FOLD Create the FoldNote titled **Tri-Fold** described in the Appendix. Write what you know about the Arabian Peninsula in the column labeled "Know." Then write what you want to know in the column labeled "Want." As you read the section, write what you learn in the column labeled "Learn."

Place) Non-Muslims are not allowed to enter Mecca, Islam's holiest city.

128 • Chapter 6

Saudi Arabia

Saudi Arabia is by far the largest country of the Arabian Peninsula. Although the kingdom of Saudi Arabia was not created until the 1930s, the region has long been an important cultural center.

Islam The history of the Arabian Peninsula is closely linked to Islam. This religion was founded by Muhammad, a merchant from the Arabian town of Mecca. Around A.D. 610 he had a vision that he had been named a prophet by Allah, or God. Arab armies and merchants carried Muhammad's teachings to new areas. Islam spread quickly across North Africa, much of Asia, and parts of Europe. Followers of Islam are called **Muslims**. Islam provides a set of rules to guide human behavior.

The Islamic world was originally ruled by a religious and political leader called a **caliph**. Gradually this area broke up into several empires. There are also religious divisions within Islam. Followers of the largest branch of Islam are called **Sunni**. Followers of the second-largest branch of Islam are called **Shia**. In the late 600s

---

Section 2

Objectives

1. Describe Saudi Arabia's history, government, and people.
2. Review the kinds of government and economy found in other nations of the Arabian Peninsula.

FOCUS

Bellringer

Copy the following instructions onto the chalkboard: *Look at the photo on this page. What do you think is happening in this city?* Discuss responses. Tell students that people go to Mecca on a pilgrimage, or a journey to a sacred place. Making the journey is an important duty for people who follow Islam, one of the world's major religions. Tell students that in Section 2 they will learn more about Islam and about the region where it began.

Building Vocabulary

Write the vocabulary terms **Muslims, caliph, Sunni, Shia, Qur'an,** and **OPEC** on the chalkboard. Have volunteers look up the definitions in the glossary, read them aloud, and then use them in a sentence. Point out that these terms refer to either Islam or the oil economy, both of which are important to societies of the Arabian Peninsula.

these two groups disagreed over who should lead the Islamic world. There are many smaller groups within Islam as well.

Islamic culture helps to unite Muslims around the world. For example, all Muslims learn Arabic to read the **Qur'an**, the holy book of Islam. Muslims are also expected to visit Mecca at least once. These practices and many others help make Muslims part of a global community.

Government and Economy In the 1920s a local ruler from the Saud family of central Arabia conquered his neighbors and in 1932 created the kingdom of Saudi Arabia. Members of the Saud family have ruled the country ever since. Riyadh, a city near the center of the country, became the capital.

Saudi Arabia is a monarchy with no written constitution or elected legislature. Most government officials are relatives of the king. The king may ask members of his family, Islamic scholars, and tribal leaders for advice on important decisions.

For some time, Saudi Arabia and the United States have had a close relationship. Both countries have strategic military and economic interests in the region. Saudi Arabia purchases U.S. weapons, such as fighter planes. In 1990, when Iraq invaded Kuwait, the Saudi government allowed U.S. military forces to operate from Saudi Arabia. However, the September 11 terrorist attacks strained the relationship because most of the hijackers were from Saudi Arabia.

Oil and related industries are the most important part of the Saudi economy. Saudi Arabia has the world's largest reserves of oil. It is also the world's leading exporter of oil. Saudi Arabia is a leader of the Organization of Petroleum Exporting Countries, or **OPEC**. The members of OPEC try to influence the price of oil on world markets.

Opened in 1986, this causeway links Saudi Arabia to Bahrain.
Interpreting the Visual Record Why are modern transportation systems important to a country's economy?

The Arabian Peninsula, Iraq, Iran, and Afghanistan • 129

TEACH

Teaching Objective 1

LEVEL 1: (Suggested time: 25 min.) Copy the graphic organizer onto the chalkboard, omitting the blue answers. Have students fill in the four boxes with details about each topic. Students may provide more details than those supplied. Then lead a class discussion on how Islam and oil relate to various aspects of Saudi Arabian society today.
ESOL, LS VISUAL-SPATIAL

Saudi Arabia's History, Government, and Economy

History of Islam	Political Developments
A.D. 610—Muhammad reports his vision. Islam spreads. late 600s—Sunni and Shia Muslims disagree about leadership of Islam.	1920s—Local ruler conquers neighbors, creates kingdom of Saudi Arabia in 1932. King rules with advice of others. Saudi Arabia and United States establish close relationship.

Traditional Economy	Oil Industry
Barley, dates, fruits, millet, vegetables, and wheat are traditional crops. Nomads kept sheep, goats, horses, and camels.	1930s—oil discovered in Saudi Arabia. Country becomes world's leading oil exporter. Oil becomes most important part of economy and pays for desalination plants.

The Arabian Peninsula, Iraq, Iran, and Afghanistan   129

EYE ON EARTH

Hidden Desert Danger

Sabchat is the Arabic word used to describe a slushy, salty, flat area that lies just above the water table. There are many in the desert areas of Qatar and Saudi Arabia.

A *sabchat* forms when the wind blows away the sand and soil down to the water table. Silt, clay, and salts accumulate. A crust forms on the surface. The crust may be a thick armorlike layer of salt or a thin layer over quicksand. A thin sheet of sand may drift over a *sabchat*, hiding it from view.

This aerial view shows how fossil water has converted desert land near Riyadh into farmers' fields. Each circular plot has a water source at its center.

internet connect

GO TO: go.hrw.com

KEYWORD: SK5 CH6

FOR: Web sites about *sabchat* and deserts

Our Amazing Planet

A *sabchat* is a thick, slushy deposit of sand, silt, mud, and salt found in coastal Saudi Arabia. A *sabchat* can trap people and animals who do not see it in time.

Oil was discovered in Saudi Arabia in the 1930s. Before then farming and herding had been the main economic activities. Crops included barley, dates, fruits, millet, vegetables, and wheat. Nomads kept herds of sheep, goats, horses, and camels.

Like other oil-rich states in the region, Saudi Arabia has tried to increase its food production. Because freshwater is scarce, desalination plants remove the salt from seawater. This water is then used in farming. Income from oil allows the Saudi government to pay for this expensive process. Even so, Saudi Arabia imports much of its food.

People and Customs Nearly all Saudis are ethnic Arabs and speak Arabic. About 85 percent are Sunni. The rest are Shia. Most Saudis now live in cities, and a sizable middle class has developed. The Saudi government provides free health care and education to its citizens.

Some 65 percent of Saudi Arabia's workers are from other countries, including Yemen and Pakistan. Unemployment is very high among young Saudis. One reason is the very high population growth rate. More than 40 percent of Saudis are younger than 15. Another reason is that many young Saudis study religion instead of the technical subjects their economy requires.

Saudi laws and customs limit women's activities. For example, a woman rarely appears in public without her husband or a male relative. Women may not drive cars. However, women may make up two thirds of the country's Internet users.

Islam is an important part of Saudi Arabia's culture. Muslims pray five times each day. Friday is their holy day. Because Islam encourages modesty, Saudi clothing keeps arms and legs covered. Men traditionally wear a loose, ankle-length shirt. They often wear a cotton headdress held in place with a cord. These styles are practical in the desert, giving protection from sun, wind, and dust. Saudi women usually wear a black cloak and veil in public.

Saudi Arabia has several Islamic holidays. One of the most important is 'Id al-Fitr, a feast ending the month of Ramadan. During Ramadan, Muslims do not eat or drink anything between dawn and sunset. Saudis may attend huge dinner parties after sundown, however.

✓ **READING CHECK:** (*Human Systems*) What is significant about Saudi Arabia's history, government, and people? history—linked to Islam; government—monarchy with no constitution; people—mostly Sunni, city dwellers, follow Islamic practices

Other Countries of the Arabian Peninsula

Six small coastal countries share the Arabian Peninsula with Saudi Arabia. All are heavily dependent on oil. All but Yemen are monarchies, and each is overwhelmingly Islamic. Oil is a major part of each country's economy. However, possession of differing amounts of oil has made some countries much richer than others.

LEVELS 2 AND 3: (Suggested time: 30 min.) Tell students to imagine that they lived in Mecca in the A.D. 650s and that they found a time machine in the desert that brought them forward in time to the present. Have students write a monologue about their experiences in the present day in which they reflect on how much life in Saudi Arabia has changed. Ask them to record observations about history, the government, economy, and people.
LS INTRAPERSONAL

Teaching Objective 2

LEVEL 1: (Suggested time: 20 min.) Pair students and have pairs list the six other countries of the Arabian Peninsula in their notebooks. Ask them to designate each country with an **M** if it is a monarchy, an **E** if the government is elected, an **O** if oil is an important part of the economy, and an **N** if new industries are starting to play a major role in the economy.
COOPERATIVE LEARNING

LEVELS 2 AND 3: (Suggested time: 30 min.) Have students write letters to an advice column for a newspaper in one of the six smaller countries of the Arabian Peninsula. The issues of oil wealth, the presence of foreign workers, or limitation of political rights are possible topics for their letters.
LS VERBAL-LINGUISTIC

CONNECTING TO Math

Muslim Contributions to Mathematics

Muslim astronomers in the 1500s

During the early centuries of the Middle Ages, European art, literature, and science declined. However, during this same period Islamic civilization, stretching from Spain to the borders of China, was flowering. Muslim scholars made important advances in art, literature, medicine, and mathematics.

The system of numerals we call Arabic, including the use of the zero, was first created in India. However, it was Muslim thinkers who introduced that system to Europe. They also developed algebra, geometry, and trigonometry. In fact, words like *algebra* and *algorithm* come from Arabic words.

Other Muslims advanced the study of astronomy and physics. Arab geographers calculated distances between cities, longitudes and latitudes, and the direction from one city to another. Muslims developed the first solution for cubic equations. They also defined ratios and used mathematics to explain the rainbow.

Understanding What You Read

1. Where did the Arabic system of numerals originate, and how did it get to Europe?
2. How did Muslim scholars contribute to our knowledge of geography?

Kuwait The country of Kuwait was established in the mid-1700s. Trade and fishing were once the main economic activities there. Oil, which was discovered in the 1930s, has made Kuwait very rich. The Iraqi invasion of 1990 caused massive destruction.

As in Saudi Arabia, a royal family dominates politics in Kuwait. In 1992, however, Kuwait held elections for a legislature. Less than 15 percent of Kuwait's population were given the right to vote. These people were all men from well-established families.

Bahrain and Qatar Bahrain is a group of small islands in the western Persian Gulf. It is a constitutional monarchy headed by a ruling royal family and a legislature. These islands have been a center for trade since ancient times. In 1986 a 15.5 mile (25 km) bridge was completed that connects Bahrain to Saudi Arabia, making movement between the two countries easier.

Across the Curriculum
TECHNOLOGY

Cell Phones in Southwest Asia Cellular phones are very popular in Southwest Asia. The phones are status symbols. They are also convenient.

The widespread use of cellular phones is also partly due to the religious conservatism of Southwest Asia. In Kuwait, some young men contrive to meet young women by driving around with two cellular phones. When they see a likely prospect, they toss one of the phones to her, then use the other to call her.

Discussion: Lead a discussion about cell phone use and Kuwaiti culture. Then compare cell phone use in the United States with usage in Kuwait.

Connecting to Math
Answers
1. India; brought to Europe by Muslim thinkers
2. figured distances between cities, longitudes and latitudes, and the direction from one city to another

---

Teaching Objectives 1–2

LEVEL 1: (Suggested time: 15 min.) Prepare in advance slips of paper on which you have written roles for various individuals of the Arabian Peninsula. Here are some examples: a caliph of the 600s, a member of Saudi Arabia's royal family, a Saudi Islamic scholar, a general in the United States army stationed in Saudi Arabia, a foreign worker, a nomadic herder, an emir of the UAE, or a member of Yemen's government. Prepare a role for each student. You may need to repeat some. Have students draw a slip from a hat and create a sentence that gives a clue to their identity. Call on volunteers to read their sentences. Ask other students to attempt to identify the role of each speaker and explain his or her significance.

LEVEL 2: (Suggested time: 30 min.) Organize students into groups. Have each group use the roles from the Level 1 activity to create a conversation that those people might have if they were all invited to the same dinner party. **COOPERATIVE LEARNING**

LEVEL 3: Have students use the Level 2 activity and library resources to create a written plan for the entire dinner party, including a menu of local dishes, a program of entertainment, and proper etiquette for the occasion. You may need to schedule extra time for this activity. **LS INTERPERSONAL**

HUMAN SYSTEMS

Through Yemeni Windows

Note the distinctive architecture in the photo on the opposite page. In Sanaa, Yemen's capital, some houses still have windows made of alabaster. The Arabic word for *alabaster* translates into English as "moonstone." Although you cannot see through it, alabaster allows a soft light to enter a room.

To make the windows, alabaster was mined by hand and then cut into slabs 1/2 to a full centimeter thick. Although beautiful from inside and out, alabaster darkens and cracks with age. Because alabaster needs to be replaced as often as every five years, glass is much cheaper.

Activity: Have students conduct further research on Yemeni architecture and building techniques. Have students build scale models of particular examples.

Chart Answer ▲

Yemen

Visual Record Answer ▶

Students may suggest that religious law requires the separation.

The Arabian Peninsula

Country	Population/ Growth Rate	Life Expectancy	Literacy Rate	Per Capita GDP
Bahrain	667,238 / 1.6%	71, male / 76, female	89%	$14,000
Kuwait	2,183,161 / 3.3%	76, male / 78, female	85%	$15,000
Oman	2,807,125 / 3.4%	70, male / 74, female	76%	$8,300
Qatar	817,052 / 2.9%	71, male / 76, female	83%	$21,500
Saudi Arabia	24,293,844 / 3.3%	67, male / 71, female	79%	$10,500
United Arab Emirates	2,484,818 / 1.6%	72, male / 77, female	78%	$22,000
Yemen	19,349,881 / 3.4%	59, male / 63, female	50%	$840
United States	290,342,554 / 0.9%	74, male / 80, female	97%	$37,600

Source: Central Intelligence Agency, *The World Factbook 2003*

Interpreting the Chart Which country has the lowest standard of living?

Oil was discovered in Bahrain in the 1930s, creating wealth for the country. However, by the 1990s this oil was starting to run out, and banking and tourism are now becoming important to the economy. Bahrain also refines crude oil imported from nearby Saudi Arabia.

Qatar occupies a small peninsula in the Persian Gulf. Like Bahrain, Qatar is ruled by a powerful monarch. In the 1990s, Qatar's ruler announced a plan to make the country more democratic. He also ended censorship of Qatari newspapers and television.

Qatar's economy used to be based on pearl fishing. Today Qatar relies on oil and huge natural gas reserves for its income.

The United Arab Emirates The United Arab Emirates, or UAE, consists of seven tiny kingdoms. They are ruled by emirs. This country also has great reserves of oil and natural gas. Profits from these resources have created a modern, comfortable lifestyle for the people of the UAE. The government has also worked to build up other industries.

Like Saudi Arabia and many of the small Persian Gulf countries, the UAE depends on foreign workers. In the UAE, foreign workers outnumber citizens.

Oman Oman is located just outside the mouth of the Persian Gulf. The country is slightly smaller than Kansas. In ancient times, Oman was a major trade center for merchants traveling the Indian Ocean. Today, Oman's economy is heavily dependent on oil. However, Oman does not have the oil wealth of Kuwait or the UAE. Therefore, the government, ruled by the Al Bu Sa'id family, is attempting to create new industries.

◀

Kindergarten students in the United Arab Emirates kneel to pray.

Interpreting the Visual Record *Place* For what cultural reason do you think these girls and boys are seated in separate rows?

132 Chapter 6

▶**ASSIGNMENT:** Have students use library resources to conduct research on Islamic practices and holidays, including Ramadan and the annual arrival of Muslim pilgrims in Mecca. Tell students to examine and explain the significance of these practices.

TEACHER TO TEACHER

Sandra Rojas of Commerce City, Colorado, suggests the following activity to help students learn about the Arabian Peninsula: On a large sheet of paper draw a wall map of the Arabian Peninsula with the region's political boundaries marked. Organize the class into seven groups and assign each group one of the countries of the Arabian Peninsula. Have each group locate information on the economy, culture, and government of its country. Then have members from each group copy the information about their country onto the wall map. Use different colored markers for each country. Display the wall map while students complete the chapter.

Yemen Yemen is located on the southern corner of the Arabian Peninsula. It borders the Red Sea and the Gulf of Aden. Yemen was formed in 1990 by the joining of North Yemen and South Yemen. The country has an elected government and several political parties. However, political corruption and internal conflicts have threatened this young democracy.

In ancient times, farmers in this area used very advanced methods of irrigation and farming. Yemen was famous for its coffee. Today, Yemen is the poorest country on the Arabian Peninsula. Oil was not discovered there until the 1980s. It now generates a major part of the national income.

✓ **READING CHECK:** (*Human Systems*) How are the governments and economies of the countries of the Arabian Peninsula organized? All but Yemen are monarchies. Oil is a major part of the economies.

(*Place*) An important part of Yemen's culture is its distinctive architecture, which features tall buildings and carved wooden windows.

Homework Practice Online
Keyword: SK5 HP6

Define and explain: Muhammad, Muslims, caliph, Sunni, Shia, Qur'an, OPEC

Working with Sketch Maps On the map you created in Section 1, label Mecca and Riyadh. Why is Riyadh's location more suitable than Mecca's to be the capital city of Saudi Arabia?

Reading for the Main Idea

1. (*Places and Regions*) What kind of government does Saudi Arabia have?

2. (*Environment and Society*) What role does oil play in the economies of small countries on the Arabian Peninsula?

Critical Thinking

3. **Drawing Inferences and Conclusions** How might trips to Mecca help create a sense of community among Muslims?

4. **Drawing Inferences and Conclusions** Why would a country like Saudi Arabia or the United Arab Emirates bring in large numbers of foreign workers?

Organizing What You Know

5. **Comparing** Copy the following graphic organizer. Use it to list these countries' locations, governments, and economies. Place them in the appropriate part of the chart.

	Location	Government	Economy
Saudi Arabia			
Kuwait			
Bahrain			
Qatar			
UAE			
Oman			
Yemen			

Answers to Section 2 Review

Define or identify For definitions and identifications, see the glossary and index.

Working with Sketch Maps Riyadh is more centrally located.

Reading for the Main Idea

1. monarchy (NGS 4)

2. most important export (NGS 15)

Critical Thinking

3. They might bring people together for a common reason.

4. needed for work in oil industry

Organizing What You Know

5. S. Arabia—Arabian Peninsula, monarchy, oil; Kuwait—between S. Arabia and Iraq, monarchy, oil; Bahrain—Persian Gulf islands, monarchy, oil, banking, tourism; Qatar—peninsula on Persian Gulf, monarchy, oil and gas; UAE—on Persian Gulf, monarchy, oil and gas; Oman—on Arabian Sea, monarchy, oil; Yemen—on Arabian Peninsula, elected government, farming and oil

CLOSE

Ask students to describe the characteristics of monarchy as a form of government. Elicit opinions as to which form students would expect to be more responsive to public opinion—democracy or monarchy?

REVIEW, ASSESS, RETEACH

Have students complete the Section Review. Then have them work in groups to reread the section silently and then discuss it among themselves. Then have students complete Daily Quiz 6.2. **COOPERATIVE LEARNING**

Have students complete Main Idea Activity S2. Organize students into groups. Assign each group one of the countries covered in this section. Have each group devise symbols for its country's government and economy and make a flag incorporating the symbols. **ESOL, COOPERATIVE LEARNING**

EXTEND

Have interested students conduct research on the OPEC oil embargo of 1973. Have them use their findings to write a report explaining both the immediate and long-term economic effects of the embargo on Southwest Asia and the United States. **BLOCK SCHEDULING**

HISTORICAL GEOGRAPHY

Oil and Azerbaijan The Persian Gulf region is not the only place to have been transformed by oil wealth. At the beginning of the 1900s, prior to the discovery of oil in Saudi Arabia, Azerbaijan produced half of the world's oil. As a result, Baku, the capital of Azerbaijan, developed into a beautiful, prosperous city. Wealthy European industrialists left behind palatial mansions and lush parks.

Recent estimates suggest that more oil exists in the region. Some believe as much as 200 billion barrels worth of oil may still be found under the Caspian Sea near Baku. In 1994 several international oil companies signed an agreement to begin drilling in the area.

Activity: Have students conduct research on the history of the Baku oil fields. Then have students predict how Baku might be affected if indeed more oil is found under the Caspian Sea. How might the architecture, transportation, education, communications, and political influence of the region be changed?

➤ This Case Study feature addresses National Geography Standards 9, 11, 12, and 16.

CASE STUDY

SAUDI ARABIA: HOW OIL HAS CHANGED A COUNTRY

At the beginning of the 1900s, Saudi Arabia was a poor country. Most people followed traditional ways of life and lived by herding animals, farming, or fishing. There were few good roads or transportation systems, and health care was poor.

Major Oil Fields in Saudi Arabia

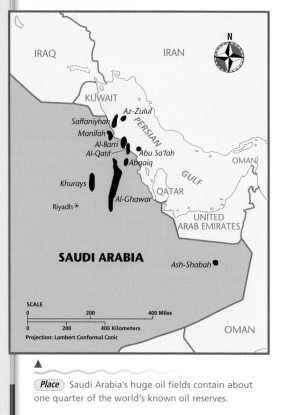

Place Saudi Arabia's huge oil fields contain about one quarter of the world's known oil reserves.

Then, in the mid-1930s, oil was discovered in Saudi Arabia. Soon, even larger oil reserves were found. Eventually it was learned that Saudi Arabia had the largest oil reserves in the world. Most of the country's oil reserves are located in eastern Saudi Arabia along the Persian Gulf coast. The Al-Ghawar oil field, discovered in 1948, is the largest in the world. In addition to this field, Saudi Arabia has at least nine other major oil fields. The discovery of these huge oil reserves changed Saudi Arabia's economy and society.

Rising income from oil exports gave Saudi Arabia's government more and more money to invest. New airports, apartments, communications systems, oil pipelines, and roads were built. In 1960 Saudi Arabia had about 1,000 miles (1,600 km) of roads. By 1997 it had about 91,000 miles (145,600 km). Saudi Arabia's cities grew as people left small villages. These changes helped modernize Saudi Arabia's economy.

Saudi society was also affected. The standard of living rose, and people had more money to spend on goods. Foreign companies began to open stores and restaurants in Saudi Arabia. New schools were built throughout the country, and education became available to all citizens. The literacy rate increased from about 3 percent to about 63 percent. Thousands of Saudis traveled to other countries, and many new universities were opened. Health care also improved.

As Saudi Arabia's economy grew, many foreign workers came to the country to work. In the early 2000s foreign workers made up about 25 percent of Saudi Arabia's population. These workers included people from Yemen, Egypt, Palestine, Syria, Iraq, South Korea, and the Philippines. Americans and Europeans also went to Saudi Arabia to work in the oil industry.

The development of the oil industry greatly increased Saudi Arabia's importance in the world. In 1960 Saudi Arabia was a founding member of

CASE STUDY

Setting the Scene

It is difficult to underestimate the importance of oil in the world today. Every day more than 70 million barrels of oil are shipped from producers to consumers by a complex system of tankers and pipelines. The discovery and exploitation of oil resources can have a dramatic effect on a country's economy and role in international politics. A good example of such an economic and political transformation is Saudi Arabia. In less than 100 years, it has progressed from being one of the world's poorest countries to one of the richest. This is the direct result of the discovery and exploitation of its oil resources. Petroleum accounts for 90 percent of Saudi Arabia's exports. This newfound wealth has had far-reaching implications for Saudi Arabia's people.

Building a Case

After students have read "Saudi Arabia: How Oil Has Changed a Country," engage them in a discussion by asking the following questions. What was life like for most Saudis before the discovery of oil? (They herded animals, farmed and fished.) When was oil discovered? (In the mid-1930s) How did oil wealth affect education in Saudi Arabia? (New schools and universities were built. More people had access to education, and the literacy rate improved.) How did the oil industry change the population of Saudi Arabia? (Resulted in the presence of foreign workers, including Yemeni, Egyptians, Palestinians, Syrians, and others) How did oil wealth change Saudi Arabia's relations with other countries? (OPEC gave it greater influence over international affairs. Its military power increased. Foreign aid donations increased.)

◀ (Movement) Oil is refined in eastern Saudi Arabia. Then it is pumped into ships and exported to countries around the world.

Understanding What You Read

Answers

1. The people of the region depended primarily on herding animals, farming, and fishing. Few roads existed. Health care was poor. Literacy rates were lower.

2. New infrastructure like roads, airports, schools, and communications facilities has been built. The standard of living rose and literacy rates have improved. Foreign workers have become a significant portion of the population.

the Organization of Petroleum Exporting Countries (OPEC). Members of OPEC try to influence the price of oil on the world market. Saudi Arabia's huge oil reserves make it one of OPEC's most powerful member countries.

The Saudi government has also bought military equipment from the United States and other countries. This military strength has increased Saudi Arabia's importance in the Persian Gulf region. Since 1991, Saudi Arabia has given large sums to countries that sided with it against Iraq in the Persian Gulf War. Egypt, Turkey, and Syria have especially benefited from this aid.

Today, Saudi Arabia is a wealthy country. This wealth has come almost entirely from the sale of oil. Saudi Arabia is currently the world's leading oil exporter. Oil provides about 90 percent of the government's export earnings. Saudi Arabia exports oil to Japan, the United States, South Korea, and many other countries.

◀ (Movement) Since the mid-1960s Saudi Arabia has expanded its transportation network. A modern road system now connects many parts of the country.

Understanding What You Read

1. What was Saudi Arabia like before oil was discovered there?

2. How has oil changed Saudi Arabia's economy and society?

Drawing Conclusions

Ask students to consider the future prospects of Saudi Arabia. Emphasize that oil is a limited resource and will not provide a source of wealth indefinitely. Some facts to consider: the world's estimated oil reserves are being used up. If current rates of consumption continue, shortages will occur in the mid-2000s. Point out that many of the investments the Saudis are making will have long term benefits—specifically improved education, communication, and transportation systems. Explain that agricultural development is very important to the Saudi government. Major irrigation projects financed by oil profits were constructed in the 1970s to decrease dependence on imported food. From 1976 to 1993, the amount of culti vated land increased so much that Saudi Arabia had become a food exporter by the mid-1990s.

Going Further: Think Critically

The discovery of precious metals can also have a major impact on a region. Gold, diamonds, and silver have all had significant impacts on different parts of the world. Provide students with a global map of mineral resources and one of the following: a set of encyclopedias, a computer with access to the Internet, or an almanac that includes brief country descriptions. Then organize them into groups and have them answer the following questions:
• What countries have deposits of diamonds, gold, and silver?
• When were these resources discovered?
• How did the discovery of resources affect settlement of the area?
• How much of the country's economy is based on these resources?

Section 3 Iraq

Read to Discover

1. What were the key events in Iraq's history?

2. What are Iraq's government and economy like?

3. What is the makeup of Iraq's population?

Vocabulary
embargo

Places
Baghdad

Reading Strategy

TAKING NOTES Draw a large triangle on a sheet of paper. Draw two lines across the triangle to create three sections. As you read, write details about Iraq's history in the lower part of the triangle. Write details about its government and economy in the middle of the triangle. Finally, write the details about its people in the top part of the triangle.

Before March 2003, murals and posters of Saddam Hussein were found throughout Baghdad, Iraq's capital.

136 ● Chapter 6

History

The history of Mesopotamia, an ancient region in Iraq, stretches back to some of the world's first civilizations. The Sumerian, Babylonian, and Assyrian cultures arose there. The Persians conquered Mesopotamia in the 500s B.C. Alexander the Great made it part of his empire in 331 B.C. In the A.D. 600s Arabs conquered Mesopotamia, and the people gradually converted to Islam.

Mesopotamia became part of the Ottoman Empire in the 1500s. During World War I Great Britain took over the region. The British set up a kingdom of Iraq in 1932 and placed a pro-British ruler in power. In the 1950s a group of Iraqi army officers overthrew this government.

After several more changes in government, the Ba'ath (BAH-ahth) Party took power in 1968. A Ba'ath leader named Saddam Hussein became the president and leader of the armed forces. He was a harsh ruler. Saddam controlled the press, restricted personal freedoms, and killed an unknown number of political enemies.

In 1980 Iraq invaded Iran. Saddam Hussein hoped to take advantage of the confusion following the Iranian Revolution. The Iranians fought back, however, and the Iran-Iraq War dragged on until 1988. Casualties were high on both sides. Both countries' economies were damaged.

In 1990, Iraq invaded Kuwait, a small oil-rich country. This event shocked Western leaders. They were also concerned that Iraq would control such a large share of the world's oil. In addition, Iraq had weapons of mass destruction (WMDs), including chemical and biological weapons. An alliance of countries, led by the United States and Great Britain, soon forced the Iraqis out of Kuwait. This 1991 event was called the Persian Gulf War. Saddam remained in power, however.

Section 3

Objectives

1. Relate the key events in Iraq's history.

2. Examine Iraq's government and economy.

3. Describe the makeup of Iraq's population.

FOCUS

Bellringer

Copy the following questions onto the chalkboard: *Do you know any military personnel who have fought in Iraq? What have you heard about his or her experiences there?* Discuss responses. Tell students that the United States and Iraq went to war in 1990 and 2003 and that in Section 3 they will learn more about Iraq's history and culture.

Building Vocabulary

Write the vocabulary term **embargo** on the chalkboard. Ask a volunteer to read aloud the definition from the text or glossary. Point out the Spanish derivation of the word; it contains "bar" from *barra*, which means a bar that can be put across something. Ask students to discuss the relationship between the word history and the definition.

Because he would not accept all the UN's terms for peace, the UN placed an **embargo**, or limit on trade, on Iraq. As a result, Iraq's economy suffered.

✓ **READING CHECK:** (*Human Systems*) What are some key events in Iraq's history? 1932—creation, 1950s—overthrow of pro-British ruler, 1968—Ba'ath to power, 1970s—Saddam Hussein to power, 1980—war with Iran, 1990–91—invasion of Kuwait and Persian Gulf War

Iraq Today

Shortly after the fighting stopped, Saddam faced two rebellions. He brutally put down uprisings of Shia Muslims in the south and of Kurds in the north. The UN forced Saddam to end all military activity in the Kurdish area of northern Iraq. The UN also required that Iraq allow inspectors into the country to make sure he had destroyed the WMDs. Iraq failed to cooperate completely with the UN and armed conflict continued off and on.

In the meantime, the events of September 11, 2001 had created new tensions. The U.S. government believed Iraq aided terrorists. In March 2003, U.S. forces began attacking Iraqi targets. Within a few weeks Saddam's government fell. The United States then began the long, difficult process of rebuilding the country.

One of the main goals of U.S. officials was creating a stable, democratic country. Another was repairing Iraq's oil industry. Before the war with Iran, Iraq was the world's second-largest oil exporter. Time will tell if Iraq can again be a major oil producer.

Oil isn't Iraq's only resource. From earliest times its wide plains have produced many food crops. Irrigation from the Tigris and Euphrates Rivers allows farmers to grow barley, cotton, rice, vegetables, wheat, dates, and other fruits.

✓ **READING CHECK:** (*Environment and Society*) What happened to Iraq's oil industry? damaged by years of warfare

In March 2003, war left much of Baghdad without electricity and water. Some restaurants, however, stayed open by cooking with propane gas on the city's sidewalks. ◄

Our Amazing Planet

Dust storms occur throughout Iraq and can rise to several thousand feet above the ground. These storms often happen during the summer. Five or six usually strike central Iraq in July, the worst month.

Cultural Kaleidoscope

The Ma'dan Iraq's wars and irrigation projects on the Tigris and Euphrates Rivers have affected the Ma'dan, also known as the Marsh Arabs.

The Ma'dan are an ancient people who occupy the marshy land just north of where the rivers meet. They do little farming. Instead, they fish and raise water buffalo. They cut river reeds to build their homes and furniture. The Ma'dan also harvest cereal grains and date palms. To get around they use canoe-like boats.

The previous Iraqi government has built dams upriver. Because the rivers no longer flow freely, the marsh has been reduced to mud in some places. Fish and bird habitats have been destroyed.

Activity: Refer to the photo of the Ma'dan settlement on the following page. Have students point out ways the Ma'dan way of life appears to differ from that of city or desert dwellers.

☑ **internet** connect

GO TO: **go.hrw.com**
KEYWORD: **SK5 CH6**
FOR: **Web sites about the Ma'dan**

The Arabian Peninsula, Iraq, Iran, and Afghanistan • 137

TEACH

Teaching Objective 1
ALL LEVELS: (Suggested time: 15 min.) Have students list the various cultures and key events that have shaped Iraq's history from the Sumerians to the conflict that began in 2003. **ESOL**

Teaching Objective 2
ALL LEVELS: (Suggested time: 15 min.) List *Government* and *Economy* as column heads on the chalkboard. Have volunteers list as many terms as they can under each column to describe Iraq. **ESOL**

Teaching Objective 3
ALL LEVELS: (Suggested time: 20 min.) Copy the following graphic organizer. Have students complete and color it to show the makeup of Iraq's population. What religion do most Iraqis practice? (Islam) **ESOL**

Iraq's Population

small minority groups

Kurds

Arabs

Answers to Section 3 Review

Define For definition, see the glossary.

Working with Sketch Maps Most of Iraq's population is concentrated around the plains of the Tigris and Euphrates River Valleys because of water resources.

Reading for the Main Idea

1. Sumerians, Babylonians, Assyrians, Arabs, the Ottoman Empire, and the British **(NGS 13)**

2. dictatorship—Saddam Hussein maintains a large army and secret police force **(NGS 12)**

Critical Thinking

3. to prevent Iraq from conquering its neighbors and to protect the region's oil resources

4. They have damaged the economy and resulted in limits being placed on the country's oil exports. **(NGS 13)**

Organizing What You Know

5. Answers should include the Arab conquest of Mesopotamia (A.D. 600s), occupation by the Ottoman Empire (1500s) and the British (during World War I), the Ba'ath Party takeover (1968), the Iran war (1980–88), and the Persian Gulf War (1990–91).

Place The Ma'dan are a minority people who live in Iraq's southern marshes. Saddam's government drained part of the marshes, putting the Ma'dan way of life in danger.

People

More than 75 percent of the population are Arabs. Some 15 to 20 percent are Kurds, and the rest belong to small minority groups. Nearly all Iraqis are Muslim. About two thirds of Iraqis are Shia. Saddam and his supporters, however, were Sunnis. Under Saddam, the government often conflicted with Shia leaders.

After decades of harsh government and warfare Iraq's future remains uncertain. Rebuilding schools, hospitals, roads, and other basic structures may take years. Creating a free and prosperous society may be an even bigger challenge.

✓ **READING CHECK:** *Human Systems* What challenges face Iraqis?
uncertain future; rebuilding schools, hospitals, roads, and a free and prosperous society

Homework Practice Online
go.hrw.com
Keyword: SK5 HP6

Section Review 3

Define and explain: embargo

Working with Sketch Maps On the map you created in Section 2, label Baghdad. Where would you expect most of Iraq's population to be concentrated? Why?

Reading for the Main Idea

1. *Human Systems* What are some different groups that have controlled Mesopotamia?

2. *Human Systems* What was Iraq's government like under Saddam Hussein?

Critical Thinking

3. **Finding the Main Idea** Why did several countries force Iraqi troops out of Kuwait?

4. **Analyzing Information** How have recent wars affected Iraq's economy?

Organizing What You Know

5. **Sequencing** Create a time line tracing the history of the area now known as Iraq. List events from the Arab conquest to 2003.

A.D. 600s ——————————————— 2003

138 • Chapter 6

CLOSE

Ask students what they have heard on the news or read in the newspaper lately about daily life in Iraq. You may want to skim the morning paper in advance to supply a discussion topic.

REVIEW, ASSESS, RETEACH

Have students complete the Section Review. Then have them write four multiple-choice questions about the section. Collect the questions and quiz the class orally. Then have students complete Daily Quiz 6.3.

Have students complete Main Idea Activity S3. Have students work in groups to create flowcharts or other graphic displays that depict the answers to the Read to Discover questions.
ESOL, COOPERATIVE LEARNING, LS **VISUAL-SPATIAL**

EXTEND

Have interested students conduct research on the environmental devastation caused by war in Iraq. Have them share their findings with the class in the form of posters or dioramas. **BLOCK SCHEDULING**

Section 4 Iran and Afghanistan

Read to Discover

1. What were some important events in Iran's history?
2. What are Iran's government and people like?
3. What problems does Afghanistan face today?

Vocabulary
shah
theocracy

Places
Tehran
Khyber Pass
Kabul

People
Shirin Ebadi

Reading Strategy

READING ORGANIZER Before you read, draw two large overlapping circles on a sheet of paper. As you read, write what you learn about Iran in one circle. Then write what you learn about Afghanistan in the other circle. Where the circles overlap, write the characteristics that the countries share.

Iran

Iran is a large country with a large population, rich history, and valuable natural resources. A revolution in 1979 made Islam the guiding force in Iran's government.

History The Persian Empire, established in the 500s B.C., was centered in what is now Iran. It was the greatest empire of its time and was an important center of learning. In the 300s B.C. Alexander the Great conquered the Persian Empire. In the A.D. 600s Arabs invaded the region and established Islam. Persian cultural and scientific contributions became elements of Islamic civilization. Later, different peoples ruled the region, including the Mongols and the Safavids.

Human-Environment Interaction In the dry climates of Iran and Afghanistan, some farmers use an ancient irrigation method. Runoff from mountains moves through tunnels, called *qanats* (kuh-NAHTS), to fields. The Taliban destroyed some *qanats* in Afganistan.

Qanat Irrigation System

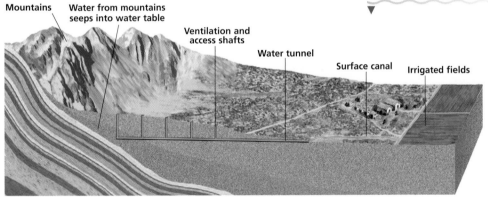

Mountains
Water from mountains seeps into water table
Ventilation and access shafts
Water tunnel
Surface canal
Irrigated fields

SECTION 4 RESOURCES

Reproducible
◆ Lecture Notes, Section 4
◆ Know It Notes S4
◆ Biography Activity: Rumi

Technology
◆ One-Stop Planner CD–ROM, Lesson 6.4
◆ Music of the World Audio CD Program, Selection 11
◆ Homework Practice Online
◆ HRW Go site

Reinforcement, Review, and Assessment
◆ Section 4 Review
◆ Daily Quiz 6.4
◆ Main Idea Activity S4
◆ Chapter Summaries and Review
◆ English Audio Summary 6.4
◆ Spanish Audio Summary 6.4

Section 4

Objectives

1. List some of the important events in Iran's history.
2. Describe Iran's government and people.
3. Identify problems that Afghanistan faces today.

FOCUS

Bellringer

Copy these instructions onto the chalkboard: *Look at the diagram on this page. How does this system seem to compare to the irrigation system indicated in the aerial photo in Section 2? Do you think one system may be more efficient than the other?* Discuss responses. Tell students that the *qanat* system is used in Iran and that in Section 4 they will learn more about Iran.

Building Vocabulary

Write the key terms **shah** and **theocracy** on the chalkboard. Call on volunteers to locate the word histories in a dictionary and read them to the class. Lead a discussion comparing theocracy and democracy.

FOOD FESTIVAL

Fit for a Persian Princess

This Persian apple dessert uses rose water or orange-flower water—typical Southwest Asian ingredients—for flavoring. Both are available at gourmet and specialty food shops.

Peel and cut up 3 medium apples. Place the apples in a blender with 2½ tbs sugar, 2 tbs lemon juice, 1 tbs rose or orange-flower water, and a pinch of salt. Process 20 to 30 seconds, until coarsely chopped.

Biography Answer ▲

by working to improve the lives of women, children, and refugees

BIOGRAPHY

Shirin Ebadi
(1947–)

Character Trait: Respect

Iranians hoping for more democratic reforms were encouraged in 2003 by Shirin Ebadi's receiving the Nobel Peace Prize. Ebadi is a lawyer, judge, and author. However, her work improving human rights in Iran has at times made her unpopular with the country's authorities. Ebadi's special interests include better conditions for women, children, and refugees.

How does Shirin Ebadi show respect towards others?

During New Year celebrations, Iranians grow or buy fresh grass to symbolize spring and life.

▼

140 • Chapter 6

In 1921 an Iranian military officer took power and encouraged reform. He claimed the old Persian title of **shah**, or king. In 1941 the Shah's son took control. He was an ally of the United States and Britain and tried to modernize Iran. His programs were unpopular, however, and in 1979 he was overthrown.

Iran's new government set up an Islamic republic. Soon afterward, relations with the United States broke down. A mob of students attacked the U.S. Embassy in Iran's capital, Tehran, in November 1979. They took Americans hostage with the approval of Iran's government. More than 50 Americans were held by force for a year. The Iranian Revolution itself was soon followed by a long, destructive war with Iraq beginning in 1980.

Government and Economy Iran is a **theocracy**—a government ruled by religious leaders. The country has an elected president and legislature. An expert on Islamic law is the supreme leader, however.

Iran's government has supported many hard-line policies. For example, the country's government has called for the destruction of the state of Israel. Iran has also supported terrorist groups in other countries. However, in the 2000s some signs indicated that Iran was trying to make democratic reforms.

Iran has the fifth-largest oil reserves in the world. Oil is its main industry. Iran is a member of OPEC. Iran's other industries include construction, food processing, and the production of beautiful woven carpets. About one third of Iran's workforce is employed in agriculture.

People and Customs Iran has a population of about 68 million—one of the largest in Southwest Asia. It is also quite diverse. Ethnic Persians make up a slight majority. Other groups include ethnic Azerbaijanis, Kurds, Arabs, and Turkomans. Persian is the official language. Almost all Iranians speak Persian, although some speak it as a second language. The region's other languages include several Kurdish dialects, some Turkic languages, and Arabic.

The Shia branch of Islam is Iran's official religion. About 90 percent of Iranians are Shia. About 10 percent of Iran's residents are Sunni Muslim. The rest are Christian, Jewish, or practice other religions.

In addition to the Islamic holy days, Iranians celebrate Nauruz—the Persian New Year. They also recognize the anniversary of the Iranian Revolution on February 11. Iranian food features rice, bread, vegetables, fruits, and lamb. Strong tea is a popular drink among many Iranians.

✓ **READING CHECK:** (*Human Systems*) What are Iraq's government and people like? Theocracy with an elected president and legislature; supreme leader is Islamic law expert; diverse population; Persian most commonly spoken language; Shia branch of Islam is official religion

---

TEACH

Teaching Objective 1

ALL LEVELS: (Suggested time: 30 min.) Copy the following graphic organizer onto the chalkboard, omitting the blue answers. Have students add notes to the time line to identify key events in Iran's history. **ESOL**

Teaching Objective 2

ALL LEVELS: (Suggested time: 20 min.) Lead a discussion in which students compare Iran's current government and people to the government and people of other Southwest Asian countries.

Teaching Objective 3

ALL LEVELS: (Suggested time: 30 min.) Have students write a brief news report stating the problems that Afghanistan faces today.

Key Events in Iran's History

Persian Empire established	Persian Empire conquered by Alexander the Great	Arab invasion of the region and establishment of Islam	Shah in power	Shah overthrown by Islamic republic	Beginning of war with Iraq
500s B.C.	300s B.C.	A.D. 600s	1921	1979	1980

Afghanistan

Afghanistan is a landlocked country of high mountains and fertile valleys. Merchants, warriors, and missionaries have long used the Khyber (KY-buhr) Pass to reach India. This narrow passage through the Hindu Kush lies between Afghanistan and Pakistan.

History and People In 1979 the Soviet Union sent troops into Afghanistan to help the communist government there in a civil war. This led to a long war between Soviet troops and Afghan rebels. The Soviets left in 1989, and an alliance of Afghan groups took power. Turmoil continued, and in the mid-1990s a radical Muslim group known as the Taliban arose. Its leaders took over most of the country, including the capital, Kabul. The Taliban ruled Afghanistan strictly. For example, they forced women to wear veils and to stop working outside the home.

In 2001 Taliban officials came into conflict with the United States. Investigation of terrorist attacks on September 11 on Washington, D.C., and New York City led to terrorist Osama bin Laden and his al Qaeda network, based in Afghanistan. U.S. and British forces then attacked Taliban and al Qaeda targets and toppled the Taliban government.

The long period of war has damaged Afghanistan's industry, trade, and transportation systems. Farming and herding are the most important economic activities now.

Afghans belong to many different ethnic groups. The most numerous are the Pashtun, Tajik, Hazara, and Uzbek. Almost all Afghans are Muslims, and about 84 percent are Sunni.

✓ **READING CHECK:** (**Human Systems**) What are some of the challenges Afghanistan faces today? *Damaged economy, political conflict*

Iran and Afghanistan

COUNTRY	POPULATION/ GROWTH RATE	LIFE EXPECTANCY	LITERACY RATE	PER CAPITA GDP
Afghanistan	28,717,213 3.4%	47, male 46, female	36%	$700
Iran	68,278,826 1.1%	69, male 71, female	79%	$6,800
United States	290,342,554 0.9%	74, male 80, female	97%	$37,600

Source: Central Intelligence Agency, *The World Factbook 2003*

Interpreting the Chart How many times greater is the U.S. per capita GDP than Afghanistan's?

Define or identify: Shirin Ebadi, shah, theocracy

Working with Sketch Maps On the map you created in Section 3, label Tehran, Khyber Pass, and Kabul. What physical features do Tehran and Kabul have in common?

Reading for the Main Idea

1. (**Places and Regions**) What ethnic and religious groups live in Iran?

2. (**Human Systems**) How have Afghanistan's recent wars affected the country?

Critical Thinking

3. **Making Generalizations and Predictions** What challenges might the Iranian government face in the future?

4. **Drawing Inferences and Conclusions** How might Afghanistan's political problems be affected by its rugged physical geography?

Organizing What You Know

5. **Sequencing** Copy the following graphic organizer. Use it to show the main events in Iran in recent decades.

Homework Practice Online go.hrw.com Keyword: SK5 HP6

The Arabian Peninsula, Iraq, Iran, and Afghanistan • 141

Answers to Section 4 Review

Define or identify For definition or identification, see the glossary and index.

Working with Sketch Maps Tehran and Kabul are both located in high desert plateaus.

Reading for the Main Idea

1. ethnic Persians, ethnic Azerbaijanis, Kurds, Arabs, Turkmans; Shia, Sunni Muslims, Christians, and Jews **(NGS 4)**

2. damaged industry, trade, and transportation **(NGS 13)**

Critical Thinking

3. Students should note possible internal problems between the government and religious leaders and problems with foreign countries because of Iran's support of terrorist organizations.

4. The country's geography makes it difficult to organize and rule people. **(NGS 15)**

Organizing What You Know

5. shah gains power; Islamic republic overthrows shah; U.S. Embassy attacked in Tehran; American hostages captured; war with Iraq

▲ **Chart Answer**

almost 54 times greater

CLOSE

Remind students that Iran and Afghanistan have both affected U.S. history. Ask students to identify events in U.S. history that were linked to these two countries.

REVIEW, ASSESS, RETEACH

Have students complete the Section Review. Then pair students and have pairs quiz each other on terms, places, and dates from the section. Then have students complete Daily Quiz 6.4. Then have students design official seals for Iran and Afghanistan, including information from the section.

ESOL, COOPERATIVE LEARNING

EXTEND

Have interested students conduct research on Zoroastrianism and Baha'i, two religions that originated in Iran. Ask them to compare and contrast the basic beliefs of the two religions to other major religions.

BLOCK SCHEDULING

Define and Identify

For definitions and identifications, see the glossary and index.

Review the Main Ideas

13. Arabian Peninsula, plains of Tigris and Euphrates Rivers, mountains and plateaus (NGS 4)

14. mainly desert and steppe

15. oil (NGS 4)

16. Saudi Arabia, Iraq, Iran, Kuwait, Qatar, UAE, Oman, Yemen (NGS 4)

17. Qatar (NGS 4)

18. Persian

19. They were concerned that Iraq would control such a large share of the world's oil, and because Iraq had weapons of mass destruction.

20. Shia Muslims and Kurds

21. Arabs

22. tension between countries, disrupted governments, caused internal problems (NGS 4)

23. the Taliban

Think Critically

24. Economies are hurt when oil prices fall.

25. the region's desert climate and lack of water

26. Answers will vary but should indicate an understanding of the political and economic situation of Iran and the region.

27. to protect independent countries and oil supplies in the area and to defeat terrorist networks

28. rebuilding schools, hospitals, roads, and other basic structures; creating a free and prosperous society

Review and Practice

Define and Identify

Identify each of the following:

1. exotic rivers
2. wadis
3. fossil water
4. Muslims
5. Muhammad
6. Sunni
7. Shia
8. Qur'an
9. OPEC
10. embargo
11. theocracy
12. Shirin Ebadi

Review the Main Ideas

13. What are the three landform regions that make up this part of Southwest Asia?

14. What is the climate in Southwest Asia like?

15. What is the most important resource of this region?

16. Which countries in this area have large reserves of oil?

17. Which small country has some of the largest natural gas reserves in the world?

18. What language is widely spoken in Iran?

19. Why were Western leaders concerned when Iraq invaded Kuwait?

20. What two groups in Iraq rebelled against Saddam Hussein's regime?

21. What ethnic group do most Iraqis belong to?

22. How have wars affected politics in this region?

23. What group ruled Afghanistan after the Soviets left the country?

Think Critically

24. Drawing Inferences and Conclusions Why might it be dangerous for these countries' economies to be almost entirely dependent on the sale of oil?

25. Summarizing Some of the countries of Southwest Asia are trying to increase crop production. What environmental factors might make this difficult?

26. Drawing Inferences and Conclusions How might Iran's recent history have been different if the 1979 revolution had not taken place?

27. Finding the Main Idea Why has the United States become involved in the politics of this region?

28. Summarizing What are the main goals to rebuilding Iraq?

Map Activity

29. On a separate sheet of paper, match the letters on the map with their correct labels.

Persian Gulf
Tigris River
Euphrates River
Hindu Kush
Mecca

Riyadh
Baghdad
Tehran
Khyber Pass
Kabul

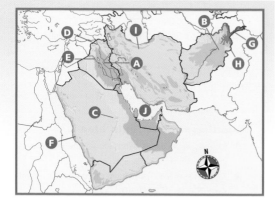

Map Activity

29. A. Baghdad

B. Kabul

C. Riyadh

D. Tigris River

E. Euphrates River

F. Mecca

G. Hindu Kush

H. Khyber Pass

I. Tehran

J. Persian Gulf

Writing Activity

Imagine that you have been asked to write a description of travel conditions in one of the following countries: Afghanistan, Iran, Iraq, or Saudi Arabia. Use your textbook, the library, and the Internet to research your country. Then write a few paragraphs about its climate, attractions, and cultural events.

internet connect

Internet Activity: **go.hrw.com**
KEYWORD: **SK5 GT6**

Choose a topic to explore about the Arabian Peninsula, Iraq, Iran, and Afghanistan:
- Visit Mesopotamia.
- Discover the importance of camels.
- See Arabian arts and crafts.

Social Studies Skills Practice

Interpreting Graphs

In the countries you learned about in this chapter, education for women is often limited. Study the following graph and answer the questions.

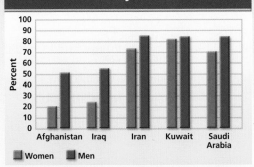

Literacy Rates

Source: Central Intelligence Agency, *World Factbook 2003*

1. Which countries have the highest literacy rates for women?
2. What can you tell about the education of women in Afghanistan and Iraq?
3. Which country has nearly the same number of literate men and women?

Analyzing Primary Sources

In this chapter, you have learned that Iran is a theocracy. However, Iran's president Mohammad Khatami hopes to move the country towards democracy. Read the following quote from Khatami and answer the questions.

"Our constitution explicitly states that absolute power belongs to God and it is God that has made man the ruler of his fate. Nothing and no one can take this right away from humans. This is a view of Islam which results in a system based on the rule of the people, a free system, a democratic one, and a system based on the rule of laws which themselves have been accepted and approved by the people.

We believe our country has suffered . . . from dependence on foreigners. Therefore, the kind of Islam that we offer is the kind . . . that leads us to independence."

Source: *New York Times*, November 10, 2001

1. According to Iran's constitution, who has absolute power?
2. What does Khatami claim Iran has suffered from?
3. According to Khatami, what will lead Iran towards independence?

Writing Activity
Answers will vary depending on the country each student selects. Paragraphs should include information about climate, interesting sites, cultural events, and other information that might be useful for a travel brochure. Encourage students to add pictures or illustrations to their brochure. Use Rubric 42, Writing to Inform, to evaluate student work.

Interpreting Graphs
1. Afghanistan and Iraq
2. Education for women is not readily available and lags far behind education for men.
3. Kuwait

Analyzing Primary Sources
1. God
2. dependence on foreigners
3. Islam

The Arabian Peninsula, Iraq, Iran, and Afghanistan • 143

CHAPTER 6

REVIEW AND ASSESSMENT RESOURCES

Reproducible
- Readings in World Geography, History, and Culture 47, 48, and 49
- Critical Thinking Activity 6
- Vocabulary Activity 6

Technology
- Chapter 6 Test Generator (on the One-Stop Planner)
- Audio CD Program, Chapter 6
- HRW Go site

Reinforcement, Review, and Assessment
- Chapter Review and Practice
- Chapter Summaries and Review
- Chapter 6 Test
- Chapter 6 Test for English Language Learners and Special-Needs Students

internet connect

GO TO: **go.hrw.com**
KEYWORD: **SK5 Teacher**
FOR: a guide to using the Internet in your classroom

Central Asia
Chapter Resource Manager

Objectives	Pacing Guide	Reproducible Resources
SECTION 1 **Physical Geography** (pp. 145–46) 1. Identify the main landforms and climates of Central Asia. 2. Identify the resources that are important to Central Asia.	**Regular** .5 day Lecture Notes, Section 1 **Block Scheduling** .5 day *Block Scheduling Handbook, Chapter 7*	**RS** Know It Notes S1 **SM** Geography for Life Activity 7 **SM** Map Activity 7 **ELL** Main Idea Activity S1
SECTION 2 **History and Culture** (pp. 147–50) 1. Describe how trade and invasions affected the history of Central Asia. 2. Describe political and economic conditions in Central Asia today.	**Regular** 1 day Lecture Notes, Section 2 **Block Scheduling** .5 day *Block Scheduling Handbook, Chapter 7*	**RS** Know It Notes S2 **RS** Graphic Organizer 7 **E** Cultures of the World Activity 4 **E** Biography Activity: Makhtumkuli **ELL** Main Idea Activity S2
SECTION 3 **The Countries of Central Asia** (pp. 151–53) 1. Identify aspects of culture in Kazakhstan. 2. Describe Kyrgyz culture. 3. Explain politics in Tajikistan. 4. Identify art forms in Turkmenistan. 5. Descrube Uzbekistan's population.	**Regular** 1 day Lecture Notes, Section 3 **Block Scheduling** .5 day *Block Scheduling Handbook, Chapter 7*	**RS** Know It Notes S3 **E** Biography Activity: Makhtumkuli **ELL** Main Idea Activity S3

Chapter Resource Key

RS Reading Support

IC Interdisciplinary Connections

E Enrichment

SM Skills Mastery

A Assessment

REV Review

ELL Reinforcement and English Language Learners and English for Speakers of Other Languages (ESOL)

 Transparencies

 CD–ROM

 Music

Video

  Internet

 Holt Presentation Maker Using Microsoft® PowerPoint®

 One-Stop Planner CD–ROM

See the *One-Stop Planner* for a complete list of additional resources for students and teachers.

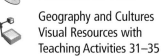

One-Stop Planner CD–ROM

It's easy to plan lessons, select resources, and print out materials for your students when you use the *One-Stop Planner CD–ROM with Test Generator.*

internet connect

HRW ONLINE RESOURCES

GO TO: go.hrw.com
Then type in a keyword.

TEACHER HOME PAGE
   KEYWORD: SK5 TEACHER

CHAPTER INTERNET ACTIVITIES
   KEYWORD: SK5 GT7

Choose an activity to:
- study the climate of Central Asia.
- travel along the historic Silk Road.
- learn about nomads and caravans.

CHAPTER ENRICHMENT LINKS
   KEYWORD: SK5 CH7

CHAPTER MAPS
   KEYWORD: SK5 MAPS7

ONLINE ASSESSMENT
Homework Practice
   KEYWORD: SK5 HP7
   Standardized Test Prep Online
   KEYWORD: SK5 STP7
   Rubrics
   KEYWORD: SS Rubrics

COUNTRY INFORMATION
   KEYWORD: SK5 Almanac

CONTENT UPDATES
   KEYWORD: SS Content Updates

HOLT PRESENTATION MAKER
   KEYWORD: SK5 PPT7

ONLINE READING SUPPORT
   KEYWORD: SS Strategies

CURRENT EVENTS
   KEYWORD: S5 Current Events

Technology Resources

- One-Stop Planner CD–ROM, Lesson 7.1
- *ARGWorld* CD–ROM
- Geography and Cultures Visual Resources with Teaching Activities 31–35
- Homework Practice Online
- HRW Go site

- One-Stop Planner CD–ROM, Lesson 7.2
- *ARGWorld* CD–ROM
- Music of the World Audio CD Program, Selection 10
- Homework Practice Online
- HRW Go site

- One-Stop Planner CD–ROM, Lesson 7.3
- *ARGWorld* CD–ROM
- Homework Practice Online
- HRW Go site

Review, Reinforcement, and Assessment Resources

ELL	Main Idea Activity S1
REV	Section 1 Review
A	Daily Quiz 7.1
REV	Chapter Summaries and Review
ELL	English Audio Summary 7.1
ELL	Spanish Audio Summary 7.1

ELL	Main Idea Activity S2
REV	Section 2 Review
A	Daily Quiz 7.2
REV	Chapter Summaries and Review
ELL	English Audio Summary 7.2
ELL	Spanish Audio Summary 7.2

ELL	Main Idea Activity S3
REV	Section 3 Review
A	Daily Quiz 7.3
REV	Chapter Summaries and Review
ELL	English Audio Summary 7.3
ELL	Spanish Audio Summary 7.3

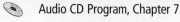

Chapter Review and Assessment

IC	Interdisciplinary Activity for the Middle Grades 19
E	Readings in World Geography, History, and Culture 46
SM	Critical Thinking Activity 7
REV	Chapter 7 Review and Practice
REV	Chapter Summaries and Review
ELL	Vocabulary Activity 7
A	Chapter 7 Test
A	Unit 2 Test
	Chapter 7 Test Generator (on the One-Stop Planner)
	Audio CD Program, Chapter 7
A	Chapter 7 Test for English Language Learners and Special-Needs Students
A	Unit 2 Test for English Language Learners and Special-Needs Students
	HRW Go Site

Meeting Individual Needs

Ability Levels

Level 1 Basic-level activities designed for all students encountering new material

Level 2 Intermediate-level activities designed for average students

Level 3 Challenging activities designed for honors and gifted-and-talented students

ESOL Activities that address the needs of students with Limited English Proficiency

Central Asia
Previewing Chapter Resources

Holt Online Learning

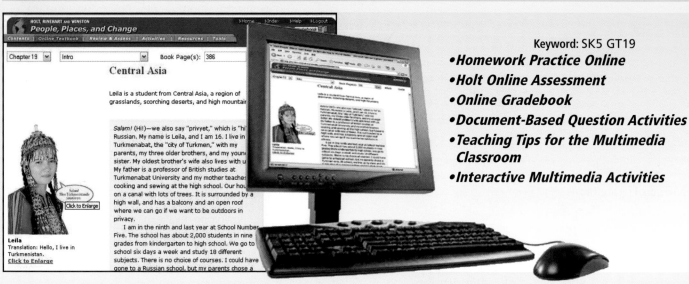

Keyword: SK5 GT19

- *Homework Practice Online*
- *Holt Online Assessment*
- *Online Gradebook*
- *Document-Based Question Activities*
- *Teaching Tips for the Multimedia Classroom*
- *Interactive Multimedia Activities*

Differentiating Instruction

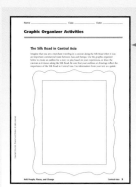

Reading and Writing Support

◀ *Graphic Organizer Activity*
- *Vocabulary Activity*
- *Chapter Summary and Review*
- *Know It Notes*
- *Audio CD*

Active Learning

- *Block Scheduling Handbook*
- *Cultures of the World Activity*
- *Interdisciplinary Activity*
- *Map Activity*
◀ *Critical Thinking Activity 19*
- *Music of the World Audio CD: Music of Kyrgyzstan*

Primary Sources and Advanced Learners

- *Geography for Life Activity: Environmenttal Crises in the Aral Sea Basin*
◀ *Map Activity: The Vanishing Aral Sea*
- *Readings in World Geography, History and Culture:*
  - *45 Life in the Mahalla*
  - *46 Exploring Central Asia*

Assessment Program

◀ *Daily Quizzes S1–3*
- *Chapter Test*
- *Chapter Test for English Language Learners and Special-Needs Students*

Spanish and ESOL

◀ *Vocabulary Activity*
- *Main Idea Activities for English Language Learners and Special-Needs Students*
- *Chapter Summary and Review*
- *Spanish Audio Summary*
- *Know It Notes S1–3*
- *Chapter Test for English Language Learners and Special-Needs Students*

Special Education Modifications

Your **I.D.E.A. Works! CD-ROM** will provide modified versions of the following teaching materials:

- *Guided Reading Strategies S1–3*
- *Vocabulary Activity*
◀ *Main Idea Activities S1–3*
- *Daily Quizzes S1–3*
- *Chapter 7 Test*
- *Flash cards of chapter vocabulary terms*

Teacher Resources

Books for Teachers

Minahan, James. *Miniature Empires: A Historical Dictionary of the Newly Independent States.* Greenwood Publishing Group, Inc., 1998.

O'Bannon, George W. *From Desert and Oasis: Arts of the People of Central Asia.* University of Georgia Press, 1998.

Ruffin, M. Holt, Daniel C. Waugh, and S. Frederick Starr, eds. *Civil Society in Central Asia.* University of Washington Press, 1999.

Books for Students

Gilchrist, Cherry. *Stories from the Silk Road.* Barefoot Books, 1999. Stories of the culture, history, and folklore along the ancient trade route. **SHELTERED ENGLISH**

Polo, Marco. *The Travels of Marco Polo.* Wordsworth Editions, Ltd., 1997. Marco Polo and his journey to China and India.

Schneider, Mical. *Between the Dragon and the Eagle (Adventures in Time Books).* Carolrhoda Books, 1997. The story of a journey of a single bolt of blue silk that traveled from China to Rome 2,000 years ago.

Thomas, Paul. *The Central Asian States: Tajikistan, Uzbekistan, Kyrgyzstan, Turkmenistan (Former Soviet States).* Millbrook Press, 1992. History, development, current status, and possible future of the four countries. **SHELTERED ENGLISH**

Multimedia Materials

Central Asia: Kyrgystan and Uzbekistan. Video, 47 min. Lonely Planet.

Hundred Thousand Fools of God: Musical Travels in Central Asia. Audio CD with book. Indiana University Press.

The Silk Road. CD–ROM. DNA Media, Inc.

Videos and CDs

Videos

- **CNN** *Presents Geography: Yesterday and Today, Segment 20 Dateline Kazalchstan*
- **CNN** *Presents World Cultures: Yesterday and Today, Segment 19 The Silk Road*
- *ARG World*

Holt Researcher
http://researcher.hrw.com

- *Kazakhstan*
- *Turkmenistan*
- *Uzbekistan*
- *Tajikistan*
- *Kyrgyzstan*

Transparency Packages

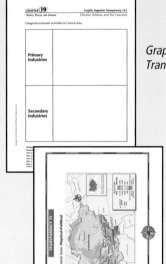

Graphic Organizer Transparencies 7.1–3

Geography and Cultures Visual Resources Transparencies 66–70
75 Central Asia: Physical-Political

Map Activities Transparency 07 The Vanishing Aral Sea

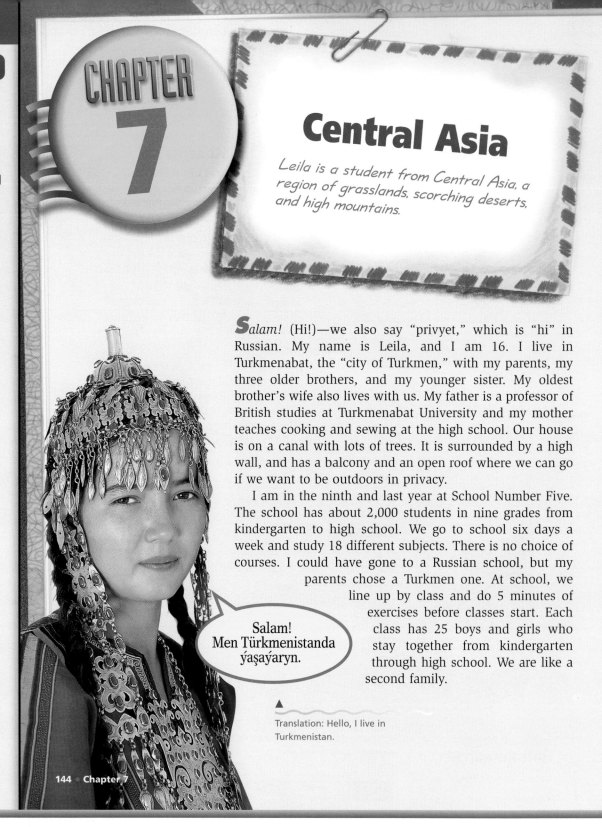

CHAPTER 7

Central Asia

Leila is a student from Central Asia, a region of grasslands, scorching deserts, and high mountains.

Salam! (Hi!)—we also say "privyet," which is "hi" in Russian. My name is Leila, and I am 16. I live in Turkmenabat, the "city of Turkmen," with my parents, my three older brothers, and my younger sister. My oldest brother's wife also lives with us. My father is a professor of British studies at Turkmenabat University and my mother teaches cooking and sewing at the high school. Our house is on a canal with lots of trees. It is surrounded by a high wall, and has a balcony and an open roof where we can go if we want to be outdoors in privacy.

I am in the ninth and last year at School Number Five. The school has about 2,000 students in nine grades from kindergarten to high school. We go to school six days a week and study 18 different subjects. There is no choice of courses. I could have gone to a Russian school, but my parents chose a Turkmen one. At school, we line up by class and do 5 minutes of exercises before classes start. Each class has 25 boys and girls who stay together from kindergarten through high school. We are like a second family.

Salam! Men Türkmenistanda ýaşaýaryn.

Translation: Hello, I live in Turkmenistan.

144 • Chapter 7

Section 1 Physical Geography

Read to Discover

1. What are the main landforms and climates of Central Asia?

2. What resources are important to Central Asia?

Vocabulary

landlocked
oasis

Places

Pamirs
Tian Shan
Aral Sea
Kara-Kum

Kyzyl Kum
Syr Dar'ya
Amu Dar'ya
Fergana Valley

Reading Strategy

FOLDNOTES: TWO-PANEL FLIP CHART Create the FoldNote titled **Two-Panel Flip Chart** described in the Appendix. Label one panel Landforms and Climates. Label the other panel Resources. As you read this section, write what you learn beneath each panel.

Central Asia: Physical-Political

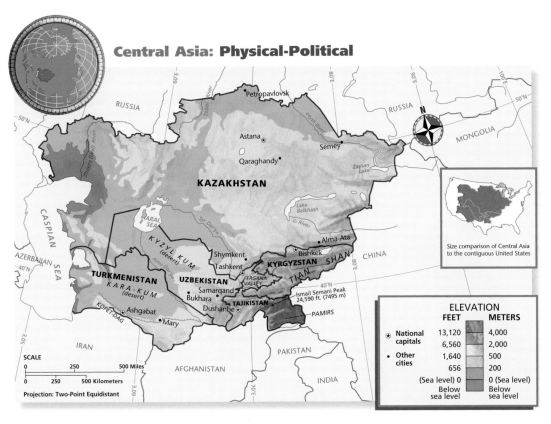

Size comparison of Central Asia to the contiguous United States

ELEVATION

	FEET	METERS
⊛ National capitals	13,120	4,000
	6,560	2,000
• Other cities	1,640	500
	656	200
(Sea level) 0		0 (Sea level)
Below sea level		Below sea level

SCALE
0   250   500 Miles
0   250   500 Kilometers
Projection: Two-Point Equidistant

Central Asia • 145

Section 1

Objectives

1. Identify the main landforms and climates of Central Asia.

2. Describe the resources that are important to Central Asia.

FOCUS

Bellringer

Copy the following instructions onto the chalkboard: *Look at the map on this page. Estimate the distance between Semey and Tashkent. How many major cities are there between Semey and Mary?* Have students share their responses. (The distance is about 750 miles. There is one city—Bukhara.) Then ask what this information tells us about the urban density of Kazakhstan. (Students might suggest that Kazakhstan has a low urban density.) Tell students that in Section 1 they will learn more about the physical geography of Central Asia.

Using the Physical-Political Map

Have students examine the map on this page. Ask volunteers to describe the boundaries of the Central Asian countries and to name the nations that border the region. (Afghanistan, China, Iran, and Russia) Ask students why Russia may want to stay on good terms with the countries of Central Asia. (Possible answer: to maintain a buffer zone between itself and other countries)

EYE ON EARTH

Potential Problem in the Pamirs Lake Sarez in eastern Tajikistan was created in 1911 when a massive earthquake caused part of a mountain to collapse, blocking the Murgab River. Today the lake stretches about 37 miles (60 km) behind the dam created by the landslide. Downstream, waters of the Murgab flow into the Pyandzh River which becomes the Amu Dar'ya.

If another earthquake were to cause the dam to collapse, a huge wall of water would destroy entire villages and threaten the lives of thousands of people. The dam's isolation in the Pamirs and the poverty of Central Asian countries make it difficult to find a solution to this potentially disastrous problem.

Discussion: Ask students to consider how wealthy nations could help Central Asian and other poor countries meet the challenges posed by problems such as Lake Sarez.

internet connect

GO TO: go.hrw.com
KEYWORD: SK5 CH7
FOR: Web sites about the Pamirs

Visual Record Answer ▶

Their heavy fur coats protect them from the cold.

▶ Mountain climbers make camp before attempting to scale a peak in the Pamirs.

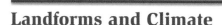

Our Amazing Planet

With temperatures above 122°F (50°C), it is not surprising that the creatures that live in the Kara-Kum are a tough group. Over a thousand species live there, including cobras, scorpions, tarantulas, and monitor lizards. These lizards can grow to more than 5 feet (1.5 m) long.

Lynxes can still be found in the mountains of Central Asia.

Interpreting the Visual Record How are these lynxes well suited to the environment in which they live?

Landforms and Climate

This huge, **landlocked** region is to the east of the Caspian Sea. Landlocked means the region does not border an ocean. The region lies north of the Pamirs (puh-MIRZ) and Tian Shan (TYEN SHAHN) mountain ranges.

Diverse Landforms As the name suggests, Central Asia lies in the middle of the largest continent. Plains and low plateaus cover much of this area. Around the Caspian Sea the land is as low as 95 feet (29 m) below sea level. However, the region includes high mountain ranges along the borders with China and Afghanistan.

Arid Lands Central Asia is a region of mainly steppe, desert, and highland climates. Summers are hot, with a short growing season. Winters are cold. Rainfall is sparse. However, north of the Aral (AR-uhl) Sea rainfall is heavy enough for steppe vegetation. Here farmers can grow crops using rain, rather than irrigation, as their water source. South and east of the Aral Sea lie two deserts. One is the Kara-Kum (kahr-uh-KOOM) in Turkmenistan. The other is the Kyzyl Kum (ki-ZIL KOOM) in Uzbekistan and Kazakhstan. Both deserts contain several **oasis** settlements where a spring or well provides water.

✓ **READING CHECK:** *Places and Regions* What are the landforms and climates of Central Asia? Plains, low plateaus, high mountain ranges; steppe, desert, highland

Resources

The main water sources in southern Central Asia are the Syr Dar'ya (sir duhr-YAH) and Amu Dar'ya (uh-MOO duhr-YAH) rivers. These rivers flow down from the Pamirs and then across dry plains. Farmers have used them for irrigation for thousands of years. When it first flows down from the mountains, the Syr Dar'ya passes through the

146 Chapter 7

TEACH

Teaching Objectives 1–2

ALL LEVELS: (Suggested time: 20 min.) Copy the following graphic organizer onto the chalkboard, omitting the blue answers. Use it to help students identify the main landforms, climates, and resources of Central Asia. Pair students and have each pair complete the organizer.
ESOL, COOPERATIVE LEARNING

THE PHYSICAL GEOGRAPHY OF CENTRAL ASIA

Landforms	mountains—the Pamirs, and Tian Shan; plains; low plateaus; deserts—Kara-Kum and Kyzyl Kum
Climates	steppe, desert, and highland
Resources	water—Syr Dar'ya and Amu Dar'ya; the Fergana Valley; oil, gas, gold, copper, uranium, zinc, lead, and coal

▶**ASSIGNMENT:** Have students write a short story about an adventure in the mountains or deserts of Central Asia. Ask them to use elements in the Section 1 illustrations and Our Amazing Planet as ideas for the plot.

Fergana Valley. This large valley is divided among Uzbekistan, Kyrgyzstan, and Tajikistan. As the river flows toward the Aral Sea, irrigated fields line its banks.

During the Soviet period, the region's population grew rapidly. Also, the Soviets encouraged farmers to grow cotton. This crop grows well in Central Asia's sunny climate. However, growing cotton uses a lot of water. Increased use of water has caused the Aral Sea to shrink.

A Dying Sea Today, almost no water from the Syr Dar'ya or Amu Dar'ya reaches the Aral Sea. The rivers' waters are used up by human activity. The effect on the Aral Sea has been devastating. It has lost more than 75 percent of its water since 1960. By 2003 it had shrunk to two smaller seas divided by a desert. Towns that were once fishing ports are now dozens of miles from the shore. Winds sweep the dry seafloor, blowing dust, salt, and pesticides hundreds of miles.

Mineral Resources The Central Asian countries' best economic opportunity is in their fossil fuels. Uzbekistan, Kazakhstan, and Turkmenistan all have huge oil and natural gas reserves. However, transporting the oil and gas to other countries is a problem. Economic and political turmoil in some surrounding countries has made it difficult to build pipelines.

Several Central Asian countries are also rich in other minerals. They have deposits of gold, copper, uranium, zinc, and lead. Kazakhstan has vast amounts of coal. Rivers in Kyrgyzstan and Tajikistan could be used to create hydroelectric power.

This boat sits rusting on what was once part of the Aral Sea. The sea's once thriving fishing industry has been destroyed.

▼

✓ READING CHECK: *Environment and Society* How has human activity affected the Aral Sea? It has used up the water from the rivers that used to flow into the sea and had depleted the sea's water.

Section Review 1

Define and explain: landlocked, oasis

Working with Sketch Maps On a map of Central Asia that you draw or that your teacher provides, label the following: Pamirs, Tian Shan, Aral Sea, Kara-Kum, Kyzyl Kum, Syr Dar'ya, Amu Dar'ya, and Fergana Valley.

Reading for the Main Idea
1. *Environment and Society* What has caused the drying up of the Aral Sea?
2. *Places and Regions* What mineral resources does Central Asia have?

go.hrw.com **Homework Practice Online**
Keyword: SK5 HP7

Critical Thinking
3. **Analyzing Information** Why did the Soviets encourage Central Asian farmers to grow cotton?
4. **Finding the Main Idea** What factors make it hard for the Central Asian countries to export oil and gas?

Organizing What You Know
5. **Sequencing** Copy the following graphic organizer. Use it to describe the courses of the Syr Dar'ya and Amu Dar'ya, including human activities that use water.

Melting snows in the Pamirs ⇨ ⇨ Aral Sea

Central Asia • 147

Answers to Section 1 Review

Define For definitions, see the glossary.

Working with Sketch Maps Maps will vary, but listed places should be labeled in their approximate location.

Reading for the Main Idea
1. The rivers' waters are used up by human activity upstream. (NGS 14)
2. oil, natural gas, gold, copper, uranium, zinc, lead, and coal (NGS 4)

Critical Thinking
3. probably because cotton grows well in Central Asia
4. Economic and political turmoil in some surrounding countries has made it difficult to build pipelines in the region.

Organizing What You Know
5. irrigation of crops (NGS 4)

CLOSE

Tell students that the mountains in Kyrgyzstan, particularly the Tian Shan—also known as the Celestial Mountains—are considered by some to be as beautiful as the mountains in Nepal and Switzerland. Have students share memories and impressions of mountains they have visited.

Have students complete Main Idea Activity S1. Then have students draw storyboards for a television commercial attempting to attract tourists to Central Asia. Commercials should highlight the region's landscape, climate, and resources. **ESOL,** LS **VISUAL-SPATIAL**

REVIEW, ASSESS, RETEACH

Have students complete the Section Review. Then organize students into triads. Have each triad write eight matching questions that link landforms, climate, or natural resources to a particular country in Central Asia. Have groups exchange their questions and answer them. Then have students complete Daily Quiz 7.1. **COOPERATIVE LEARNING**

EXTEND

Tell students about the Torugart Pass, an overland route from Bishkek, Kyrgyzstan, through the Tian Shan to China. The pass was until recently closed to international travelers. Have interested students conduct research on and map the overland trade routes to China. **BLOCK SCHEDULING**

Visual Record Answer ▶

mosques and minarets

Section 2 History and Culture

Read to Discover

1. How did trade and invasions affect the history of Central Asia?
2. What are political and economic conditions like in Central Asia today?

Vocabulary
nomads
caravans

Reading Strategy

READING ORGANIZER Before you read, draw three large boxes on a sheet of paper. Label the first box Trade. Label the second box Invasions and the Soviet Era. Finally, label the third box Today. As you read this section, write what you learn about the history and culture of Central Asia in the boxes.

Bukhara, in Uzbekistan, was once a powerful and wealthy trading center of Central Asia.

Interpreting the Visual Record (*Place*)
What architectural features can you see that distinguish Bukhara as an Islamic city?

▼

History

For centuries, Central Asians have made a living by raising horses, cattle, sheep, and goats. Many of these herders lived as **nomads**, people who often move from place to place. Other people became farmers around rivers and oases.

Trade At one time, the best land route between China and the eastern Mediterranean ran through Central Asia. Merchants traveled in large groups, called **caravans**, for protection. The goods they carried included silk and spices. As a result, this route came to be called the Silk Road. Cities along the road became centers of wealth and culture.

Central Asia's situation changed after Europeans discovered they could sail to East Asia through the Indian Ocean. As a result, trade through Central Asia declined. The region became isolated and poor.

148   Chapter 7

Section 2

Objectives

1. Explain how trade and invasions affected Central Asia's history.
2. Describe the political and economic conditions in Central Asia today.

FOCUS

Bellringer

Copy the following instructions onto the chalkboard: *Write down three things about life as a nomad. Use knowledge you may have of the Plains Indians, touring performers, migrant workers, and so on.* Discuss responses. Tell students that in Section 2 they will learn more about the nomadic peoples of Central Asia.

Building Vocabulary

Write the vocabulary terms **nomads** and **caravans** on the chalkboard. Have volunteers read aloud the definitions from the text's glossary. Tell students that the word *nomad* comes from the Greek language and that the word *caravan* is Persian in origin. Point out that Greece and Persia are two of the major cultural influences on Central Asia.

CONNECTING TO History

Silk processing in modern Uzbekistan

The Silk Road

The Silk Road stretched 5,000 miles (8,000 km) across Central Asia from China to the Mediterranean Sea. Along this route passed merchants, armies, and diplomats. These people forged links between East and West.

The facts of the Silk Road are still wrapped in mystery. Chinese trade and military expeditions probably began moving into Central Asia in the 100s B.C. Chinese trade goods soon were making their way to eastern Mediterranean ports.

Over the next several centuries, trade in silk, spices, jewels, and other luxury goods increased. Great caravans of camels and oxcarts traveled the Silk Road in both directions. They crossed the harsh deserts and mountains of Central Asia. Cities like Samarqand and Bukhara grew rich from the trade. In the process, ideas and technology also moved between Europe and Asia.

Travel along the Silk Road was hazardous. Bandits often robbed the caravans. Some travelers lost their way in the desert and died. In addition, religious and political turmoil occasionally disrupted travel.

Understanding What You Read
1. What was the Silk Road?
2. Why was the Silk Road important?

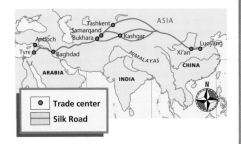

Invasions and the Soviet Era
About A.D. 500, Turkic-speaking nomads from northern Asia spread through Central Asia. In the 700s Arab armies took over much of the region, bringing Islam. In the 1200s the armies of Mongol leaders conquered Central Asia. Later, another Turkic people, the Uzbeks, took over parts of the region. In the 1800s the Russian Empire conquered Central Asia.

After the Russian Revolution, the Soviet government set up five republics in Central Asia. The Soviets encouraged ethnic Russians to move to this area and made the nomads settle on collective ranches or farms. Religion was discouraged. Russian became the language of government and business. The government set up schools and hospitals. Women were allowed to work outside the home.

✓ **READING CHECK:** (*Human Systems*) What type of government system did the five republics set up by the Soviet Union have? One in which the government controlled many aspects of life

Central Asia • 149

Culture and Music
A Central Asian

Hero An epic poem celebrates the achievements of Manas, a legendary hero of Kyrgyzstan. The poem follows Kyrgyz conflicts with other peoples and emphasizes the Kyrgyz struggle for independence. It also provides information about Kyrgyz daily life. At more than 500,000 lines, *Manas* is the longest poem in the world. Parts of *Manas* date back more than 1,000 years. Specially trained performers called *manaschi* go into a trance before they recite parts of *Manas* for audiences.

Discussion: Attila the Hun was another conqueror from Central Asia who is praised in his homeland but not elsewhere. For a Kyrgyz song that mourns the death of Attila play Selection 10 on the Music of the World Audio CD Program. Use the text and questions in the Teacher's Guide.

Connecting to History
Answers
1. a trade route linking China to the Mediterranean Sea
2. linked East and West; helped ideas move between Europe and Asia

---

TEACH

Teaching Objectives 1–2
ALL LEVELS: (Suggested time: 20 min.) Copy the following graphic organizer onto the chalkboard, omitting the blue answers. Use it to help students understand how trade and invasions affected Central Asia's history and its current political and economic conditions. Have volunteers fill in the organizer on the chalkboard. Tell students to copy the organizer into their notebooks. **ESOL,** **LS** **VISUAL-SPATIAL**

Central Asia's History and Current Conditions

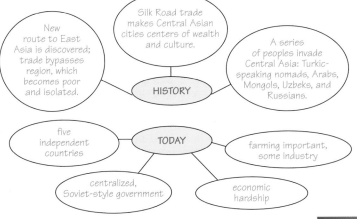

Answers to Section 2 Review

Define For definitions, see the glossary.

Working with Sketch Maps Places should be labeled in their approximate locations.

Reading for the Main Idea

1. farming, herding, trading **(NGS 14)**

2. Possible answers: Turkic-speaking nomads, Arab armies, Mongols, Uzbeks, the Russian Empire **(NGS 13)**

3. Soviets set up five republics, made nomads settle on collective ranches or farms, discouraged religion, made Russian official language, established schools. **(NGS 12)**

Critical Thinking

4. reaction against long Soviet rule; desire to be more Western **(NGS 10)**

Organizing What You Know

5. primary—growing crops, mining metals, raising livestock, drilling for oil; secondary—making cloth, food products, chemicals from oil; manufacturing tractors **(NGS 4)**

Visual Record Answer ▶

Students might mention the desks or the students' uniforms.

▲
A Kyrgyz teacher conducts class.

Interpreting the Visual Record How is this class similar to yours?

Central Asia Today

The five republics became independent countries when the Soviet Union broke up in 1991. All have strong economic ties to Russia. Ethnic Russians still live in every country in the region. However, all five countries are switching from the Cyrillic alphabet to the Latin alphabet. The Cyrillic alphabet had been imposed on them by the Soviet Union. The Latin alphabet is used in most Western European languages, including English, and in Turkey.

Government All of these new countries have declared themselves to be democracies. However, they are not very free or democratic. Each is ruled by a strong central government that limits opposition and criticism.

Economy Some of the Central Asian countries have oil and gas reserves that may someday make them rich. For now, though, all are suffering economic hardship. Causes of the hardships include outdated equipment, lack of funds, and poor transportation links.

Farming is important in the Central Asian economies. Crops include cotton, wheat, barley, fruits, vegetables, almonds, tobacco, and rice. Central Asians raise cattle, sheep, horses, goats, and camels. They also raise silkworms to make silk thread.

Industry in Central Asia includes food processing, wool textiles, mining, and oil drilling. Oil-rich Turkmenistan and Kazakhstan also process oil into other products. Kazakhstan and Uzbekistan make heavy equipment such as tractors.

✔ **READING CHECK:** (*Human Systems*) How do political freedoms in the region compare to those of the United States? Citizens' criticism of or opposition to the government is limited, whereas in the United States people can speak freely.

go.hrw.com

Homework Practice Online

Keyword: SK5 HP7

Section Review 2

Define and explain: nomads, caravans

Working with Sketch Maps On the map you created in Section 1, draw and label the five Central Asian countries.

Reading for the Main Idea

1. (*Environment and Society*) How have the people of Central Asia made a living over the centuries?

2. (*Human Systems*) What are four groups that invaded Central Asia?

3. (*Human Systems*) How did Soviet rule change Central Asia?

Critical Thinking

4. **Drawing Inferences and Conclusions** What does the switch to the Latin alphabet suggest about the Central Asian countries?

Organizing What You Know

5. **Categorizing** Copy the following graphic organizer. Use it to categorize economic activities in Central Asia. Place the following items in the chart: making cloth, growing crops, mining metals, making food products, raising livestock, making chemicals from oil, drilling for oil, and manufacturing tractors.

Primary industries	Secondary industries

CLOSE

Have students examine the section again to identify the different time periods discussed. Then have them determine when in Central Asia's history they would choose to live. Discuss responses.

Have students complete Main Idea Activity S2. Then have students suggest designs for commemorative stamps for each political, cultural, and economic period in Central Asia's history. **ESOL**

REVIEW, ASSESS, RETEACH

Have students complete the Section Review. Then organize them into groups of four. Have each group write eight true/false questions about the section. Have groups exchange their questions and answer them. Then have students complete Daily Quiz 7.2. **COOPERATIVE LEARNING**

EXTEND

Have interested students create a plan for a family of four—two parents and two children—to live as nomads in the United States today. Remind them to consider how the family will make its living, how the children will be educated, what provisions the family will need, and where it will go. **BLOCK SCHEDULING**

Section 3 The Countries of Central Asia

Read to Discover

1. What are some important aspects of culture in Kazakhstan?
2. How does Kyrgyz culture reflect nomadic traditions?
3. Why have politics in Tajikistan in recent years been marked by violence?
4. What are two important art forms in Turkmenistan?
5. How is Uzbekistan's population significant?

Vocabulary
yurt
mosques

Places
Tashkent
Samarqand

Reading Strategy

READING ORGANIZER Draw a circle in the center of a sheet of paper. Label the circle Central Asian Countries. Draw five lines from the circle. Then, draw a small circle at the end of each line. Label the five circles Kazakhstan, Kyrgyzstan, Tajikistan, Turkmenistan, and Uzbekistan. As you read this section, write what you learn about each country next to each circle.

Kazakhstan

Of the Central Asian nations, Kazakhstan was the first to be conquered by Russia. Russian influence remains strong there. About one third of Kazakhstan's people are ethnic Russians. Kazakh and Russian are both official languages. Many ethnic Kazakhs grow up speaking Russian at home and have to learn Kazakh in school.

Kazakhstanis celebrate the New Year twice—on January 1 and again on Nauruz, the start of the Persian calendar's year. Nauruz falls on the spring equinox.

Food in Central Asia combines influences from Southwest Asia and China. Rice, yogurt, and grilled meat are common ingredients. One Kazakh specialty is smoked horsemeat sausage with cold noodles.

✓ **READING CHECK:** *Human Systems* How has Kazakhstan been influenced by Russia? *Was first to be conquered by Russia: about one third of the people are ethnic Russians; Russian is commonly spoken*

Kyrgyzstan

Kyrgyzstan has many mountains, and the people live mostly in valleys. People in the southern part of the country generally share cultural ties with Uzbekistan. People in northern areas are more linked to nomadic cultures and to Kazakhstan.

A woman in Uzbekistan grills meat on skewers.
▼

Central Asia 151

Section 3

Objectives

1. Identify some important aspects of culture in Kazakhstan.
2. Explain how Kyrgyz culture reflects nomadic traditions.
3. Discuss the political violence of recent years in Tajikistan.
4. Describe two important art forms in Turkmenistan.
5. Analyze how Uzbekistan's population is significant.

FOCUS

Bellringer

Copy the following instructions onto the chalkboard: *Imagine that a student from Central Asia has joined our class for the next year. Write down four customs or other facets of our lives you believe that he or she should see or experience.* Ask volunteers to share their lists with the class. Tell students that in Section 3 they will learn more about the individual countries of Central Asia.

Building Vocabulary

Write the vocabulary terms **yurt** and **mosques** on the chalkboard. Have volunteers locate and read aloud the definitions from the text's glossary. Ask students to suggest structures they have seen or heard of with similar shapes or functions. (Possible answers: yurt—tepee, trailer; mosques—churches, temples, synagogues)

FOOD FESTIVAL

Salad from Central Asia
Here is an easy recipe for Kazakh rice salad. You may want to ask students to contribute the ingredients. Then mix up the salad in class. This recipe serves six. Double or triple it to serve everyone.

Combine these ingredients in a large bowl: 1 c. cooked brown rice, cold; 1 c. cooked buckwheat, cold; ½ c. dates, chopped; 3 cloves garlic, minced; 2 tbs. fresh ginger, minced; ¾ c. cashews or almonds, crushed; ½ c. rice wine vinegar; ½ c. extra virgin olive oil; ¾ c. fresh cilantro, chopped.

The word *kyrgyz* means "forty clans." Clan membership is still important in Krygyz social, political, and economic life. Many Kyrgyz men wear black and white felt hats that show their clan status.

Nomadic traditions are still important to many Kyrgyz. The **yurt** is a movable round house of wool felt mats over a wood frame. Today the yurt is a symbol of the nomadic heritage. Even people who live in cities may put up yurts for weddings and funerals.

✓ **READING CHECK:** *Human Systems* In what ways do the Kyrgyz continue traditions of their past? By emphasizing clan membership and constructing yurts

Tajikistan

In the mid-1990s Tajikistan experienced a civil war. The Soviet-style government fought against a mixed group of reformers, some of whom demanded democracy. Others called for government by Islamic law. A peace agreement was signed in 1996, but tensions remain high.

The other major Central Asian languages are related to Turkish. However, the Tajik language is related to Persian. Tajiks consider the great literature written in Persian to be part of their cultural heritage.

✓ **READING CHECK:** *Human Systems* What has happened in politics in recent years in Tajikistan? In the mid-1990s there was a civil war between reformers and Soviet-style government; tensions remain high.

Turkmenistan

The major first language of Turkmenistan is Turkmen. In 1993 Turkmenistan adopted English, rather than Russian, as its second official language. However, some schools teach in Russian, Uzbek, or Kazakh.

Islam has experienced a revival in Central Asia since the breakup of the Soviet Union. Many new **mosques**, or Islamic houses of worship, are being built and old ones are being restored. Donations from other Islamic countries, such as Saudi Arabia and Iran, have helped

Turkoman women display carpets. Central Asian carpets are famous for their imaginative patterns, bright colors, and expert artistry.

Interpreting the Visual Record
Movement Why were carpets suited to the nomadic way of life?

Visual Record Answer ▶

Carpets can be transported to any location.

152 • Chapter 7

TEACH

Teaching Objectives 1–5

ALL LEVELS: (Suggested time: 30 min.) Copy the following graphic organizer onto the chalkboard, omitting the blue answers. Point out to students that each circle represents one of the Central Asian countries. The lines indicate that the countries have much in common. Refer students to the Read to Discover questions. Call on students to suggest phrases that answer the questions and that highlight the countries' distinct traits. Write the phrases in the circles. **ESOL**

Distinctive Traits of Central Asian Countries

Kazakhstan
- Russian influence strong
- Kazakh and Russian official languages
- combined influences in food

Turkmenistan
- English—second official language
- Islamic principles taught in schools
- important art forms—carpets, poetry

Kyrgyzstan
- in north—linked to nomadic cultures
- clan membership still important
- black and white felt hats to show class status
- yurts—movable round houses

Tajikistan
- civil war in mid-1990s: Soviet-style government against reformers
- language related to Persian
- Persian literature part of heritage

Uzbekistan
- largest population in Central Asia
- Uzbek—official language
- Tashkent and Samarkand—Silk Road cities
- traditional art—embroidering with gold

these efforts. The government of Turkmenistan supports this revival and has ordered schools to teach Islamic principles. However, like the other states in the region, Turkmenistan's government views Islam with some caution. It does not want Islam to become a political movement.

Historically, the nomadic life required that all possessions be portable. Decorative carpets were the essential furniture of a nomad's home. They are still perhaps the most famous artistic craft of Turkmenistan. Like others in Central Asia, the people of Turkmenistan also have an ancient tradition of poetry.

✓ **READING CHECK:** (*Human Systems*) What are two forms of art in Turkmenistan, and how do they reflect its cultural traditions? Decorative carpets, poetry; ancient forms of artistic expression

Uzbekistan

Uzbekistan has the largest population of the Central Asian countries— about 24 million people. Uzbek is the official language. People are required to study Uzbek to be eligible for citizenship.

Tashkent and Samarqand are ancient Silk Road cities in Uzbekistan. They are famous for their mosques and Islamic monuments. Uzbeks are also known for their art of embroidering fabric with gold.

✓ **READING CHECK:** (*Human Systems*) What is one of an Uzbekistan citizen's responsibilities? To study the Uzbek language

Central Asia

COUNTRY	POPULATION/ GROWTH RATE	LIFE EXPECTANCY	LITERACY RATE	PER CAPITA GDP
Kazakhstan	16,763,795 .02%	58, male 69, female	98%	$7,200
Kyrgyzstan	4,892,808 1.5%	59, male 68, female	97%	$2,900
Tajikistan	6,863,752 2.1%	61, male 67, female	99%	$1,300
Turkmenistan	4,775,544 1.8%	57, male 65, female	98%	$6,700
Uzbekistan	25,981,647 1.6%	60, male 68, female	99%	$2,600
United States	290,342,554 0.9%	74, male 80, female	97%	$37,600

Source: Central Intelligence Agency, *The World Factbook 2003*

Interpreting the Chart Which country has the lowest per capita GDP in the region?

Homework Practice Online
Keyword: SK5 HP7

Section Review 3

Define and explain: yurt, mosques

Working with Sketch Maps On the map you created in Section 2, label Tashkent and Samarqand.

Reading for the Main Idea

1. (*Places and Regions*) In which Central Asian nation is the influence of Russia strongest? Why is this true?

2. (*Human Systems*) What were the two sides in Tajikistan's civil war fighting for?

3. (*Human Systems*) What is the role of Islam in the region today?

Critical Thinking

4. **Finding the Main Idea** What are two customs or artistic crafts of modern Central Asia that are connected to the nomadic lifestyle?

Organizing What You Know

5. **Contrasting** Copy the following graphic organizer. Use it to describe the conditions in Central Asia during the Soviet era and today.

	Soviet era	Today
Type of government		
Official language		
Alphabet		
Government attitude toward Islam		

Central Asia • 153

Answers to Section 3 Review

Define For definitions, see the glossary.

Working with Sketch Maps Maps should correctly depict the locations of the two cities.

Reading for the Main Idea

1. Kazakhstan; about one third of people there are ethnic Russians **(NGS 4)**

2. type of government— Soviet-style or reform **(NGS 13)**

3. It has experienced a revival. **(NGS 10)**

Critical Thinking

4. Answers might include yurts, carpets.

Organizing What You Know

5. Soviet—communist; Russian; Cyrillic; Islam discouraged; today—so-called democracies but actually centralized, Soviet-style; in some places, Russian and local language, like Kazakh; Latin; government supports revival

▲ **Chart Answer**

Tajikistan

CLOSE

Ask students whether they can note any similarities between cultural practices in the United States and those in Central Asia.

REVIEW, ASSESS, RETEACH

Have students complete the Section Review. Then organize students into groups of four. Have each group write five multiple-choice questions about the section. Have groups trade questions and then answer them. Then have students complete Daily Quiz 7.3. **COOPERATIVE LEARNING**

Have students complete Main Idea Activity S3. Then have students design flags for each Central Asian nation, including symbols for peoples, customs, and religion. **ESOL,** **LS** **VISUAL-SPATIAL**

EXTEND

Have interested students conduct research on the resurgence of barter as a means of doing business in the Central Asian republics. Have students develop their own barter system for basic goods. **BLOCK SCHEDULING**

HISTORICAL GEOGRAPHY

Hutu and Tutsi An example of a recent conflict between farmers and nomads is the fighting between the Hutu and Tutsi in eastern Africa. The Hutu first settled the area that is now Rwanda and Burundi from about 500 B.C. to the year 1000. Hutu life centered on small-scale agriculture. During the 1300s and 1400s the Tutsi entered the region. They were pastoral nomads who depended on large herds of big-horned cattle. The Tutsi soon gained control over the area, gave up their nomadic lifestyle and became "lords" over Hutu farmers. Despite their small numbers, the Tutsi dominated the Hutu economically and politically for almost 600 years. In the late 1990s violence erupted between the Hutu and the Tutsi. In 1994 the United Nations sent peacekeepers to stabilize the region.

Activity: Have students conduct research on the current relationship between the Hutu and the Tutsi. Ask students to find out how successful UN forces were at bringing peace to the region. Have students report their findings in the form of a newsmagazine article.

➤ This Case Study feature addresses National Geography Standards 3, 4, 8, 9, and 15.

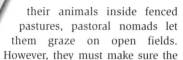

CASE STUDY

KAZAKHS: PASTORAL NOMADS OF CENTRAL ASIA

Nomads are people who move around from place to place during the year. Nomads usually move when the seasons change so that they will have enough food to eat. Herding, hunting, gathering, and fishing are all ways that different nomadic groups get their food.

Nomads that herd animals are called pastoral nomads. Their way of life depends on the seasonal movement of their herds. Pastoral nomads may herd cattle, horses, sheep, goats, yaks, reindeer, camels, or other animals. Instead of keeping their animals inside fenced pastures, pastoral nomads let them graze on open fields. However, they must make sure the animals do not overgraze and damage the pastureland. To do this, they keep their animals moving throughout the year. Some pastoral nomads live in steppe or desert environments. These nomads often have to move their animals very long distances between winter and summer pastures.

The Kazakhs of Central Asia are an example of a pastoral nomadic group. They have herded horses, sheep, goats, and cattle for hundreds of years. Because they move so much, the Kazakhs do not have permanent homes. They bring their homes with them when they travel to new places.

A Kazakh nomad keeps a watchful eye over a herd of horses.
▼

CASE STUDY

Setting the Scene

In areas like Central Asia where climate and soil are not favorable for agricultural development, pastoral nomadism is a lifestyle that allows people to feed themselves. The Kazakhs have traditionally supported themselves by raising camels, cattle, horses, and sheep. In order to feed their herds and to ensure that fresh pastures are always available, the Kazakhs have developed a complex seasonal migration system. This migratory lifestyle is reflected in the kinds of homes they build—yurts. During the Soviet rule of Kazakhstan, new systems of agriculture requiring fixed settlements were introduced into the area. These farms became obstacles to the seasonal movement of animals.

Building a Case

After students have read the case study, ask them the following questions: Who are pastoral nomads? (people who move around during the year to maintain herds of livestock) What are some of the animals that pastoral nomads herd? (cattle, horses, sheep, goats, yaks, reindeer, and camels) Why must animals in desert regions be kept moving throughout the year? (to prevent overgrazing and provide fresh grass shoots) How far do some Kazakh families move in a year? (500 miles or 805 km) How do the kinds of houses built by Kazahks reflect their nomadic lifestyle? (Yurts are impermanent structures that are designed to be easily moved.)

◀ **Movement** Yurts are carefully stitched together by hand. When it is time to move to new pastures, they are carried from place to place on horseback or on small wagons.

The Kazakhs live in tent-like structures called yurts. Yurts are circular structures made of bent poles covered with thick felt. Yurts can be easily taken apart and moved. They are perfect homes for the Kazakhs' nomadic lifestyle.

During the year, a Kazakh family may move its herds of sheep, horses, and cattle as far as 500 miles (805 km). For one Kazakh family, each year is divided into four different parts. The family spends the first part of the year in winter grazing areas. Then, in early spring, they move to areas with fresh grass shoots. When these spring grasses are gone, the family moves their animals to summer pastures. In the fall, the animals are kept for six weeks in autumn pastures. Finally, the herds are taken back to their winter pastures. Each year, the cycle is repeated.

The nomadic lifestyle of the Kazakhs has changed, however. In the early 1800s people from Russia and eastern Europe began to move into the region. These people were farmers. They started planting crops in areas that the Kazakhs used for pasture. This made it more difficult for the Kazakhs to move their animals during the year. Later, when Kazakhstan was part of the Soviet Union, government officials encouraged the Kazakhs to settle in villages and cities. Many Kazakhs still move their animals during the year. However, tending crops has also become an important way to get food.

Seasonal Movement of a Kazakh Family

Elevation (in feet) — 0, 2,000, 4,000, 6,000
Distance (in miles) — 20, 40, 60, 80, 100, 120, 140

summer, spring, fall, winter, river

▲ During the year, a Kazakh family may move its herds to several different pasture areas as the seasons change.

Interpreting the Graph Why do you think animals are moved to higher elevations during the summer and to lower elevations during the winter?

Understanding What You Read

1. Why do some pastoral nomads have to travel such great distances?

2. How has the nomadic lifestyle of the Kazakhs changed during the last 100 years?

Drawing Conclusions

Focus discussion on the challenges confronted by the pastoral nomads in Kazakhstan. Ask students when Russians and eastern Europeans began settling the area. (late 1800s) How was their food production system different? (They were farmers, not herders.) How did this system conflict with the nomadic way of life? (It blocked access to pasturelands.) Here is some additional information to share with students: Between 1906 and 1912, Russian settlers established more than 500,000 farms. Many Kazakhs were displaced. In the 1950s and 1960s Soviet officials tried to settle the remaining nomads and expand cultivation. Some 60 percent of Kazakhstan's pasture lands were planted with crops. Today, 84 percent of pastures are devoted to cattle and sheep. Point out that this suggests the area may be more suited to herding than farming.

Going Further: Thinking Critically

The Kazakhs are only one example of nomads. Other examples include the Inuit of the Arctic, Plains Indians of North America, !Kung of the Kalahari Desert, Ona of Tierra del Fuego, Fulani of West Africa, Bedouins of the Arabian Desert, Masai of East Africa, Chukchi of Siberia, Lapps of Finland, and Tuareg of the Sahara. Have students work in small groups to conduct research on a nomadic group. Ask them to answer these questions: What is the people's main food source? What are the climate and soil like where they live? What environmental pressures do they experience? What kind of houses do they build? Have they had conflicts with settled farming peoples? If so, what were the issues? What was the outcome? You may want to have each group create a puppet show to present its findings.

Define and Identify
For definitions, see the glossary.

Review the Main Ideas
7. steppe, desert, and highland

8. Much of the fishing industry has been destroyed, and dust from the sea floor endangers people's health. (NGS 4)

9. a trade route that linked East Asia to Mediterranean ports

10. Europeans discovered they could sail to East Asia through the Indian Ocean.

11. nomads forced to settle on collective ranches and farms, religion discouraged, Russian language used for government and business, schools and hospitals set up, women allowed to work outside the home

12. declared to be democracies; but freedoms, opposition, and criticism still limited by strong central governments (NGS 13)

13. cotton, wheat, barley, fruits, vegetables, almonds, tobacco, rice, silk, wool textiles, oil products, heavy equipment

14. Kazakhstan

15. civil war between the Soviet-style government against reformers

16. supports the revival and has ordered schools to teach Islamic principles, but doesn't want Islam to become a political movement

17. Russian, Kazakh, Tajik language, Turkmen, English, Uzbek (NGS 10)

18. Uzbekistan (NGS 9)

Think Critically
19. Soviets imposed Russian, Cyrillic alphabet on Central Asia; after Soviet collapse, some nations returned to local languages, adopted Latin alphabet.

Review and Practice

Define and Identify
Identify each of the following:

1. landlocked
2. oasis
3. nomads
4. caravans
5. yurt
6. mosques

Review the Main Ideas

7. What types of climates are most common in Central Asia?

8. What problems have resulted from the shrinking of the Aral Sea?

9. What was the Silk Road?

10. Why did trade through Central Asia decline?

11. How did Soviet rule change Central Asians' way of life?

12. What are the Central Asian governments like?

13. What are some of Central Asia's main crops and products?

14. Which of the Central Asian countries still has a strong Russian presence?

15. What happened in the mid-1990s in Tajikistan?

16. How has the government of Turkmenistan responded to the revival of Islam?

17. What are some of the languages spoken in Central Asia?

18. Which of the region's countries has the largest population?

Think Critically

19. Summarizing How have politics influenced language and the alphabet used in Central Asia?

20. Finding the Main Idea How do the artistic crafts of Central Asia reflect the nomadic lifestyle?

21. Analyzing Information Why did the Soviets encourage cotton farming in the region? What were the environmental consequences?

22. Finding the Main Idea What obstacles are making it hard for the Central Asian countries to export their oil?

23. Summarizing What are some reasons the Central Asian countries have experienced slow economic growth since independence? How are they trying to improve the situation?

Map Activity

24. On a separate sheet of paper, match the letters on the map with their correct labels.

Caspian Sea	Kara-Kum
Pamirs	Kyzyl Kum
Tian Shan	Tashkent
Aral Sea	Samarqand

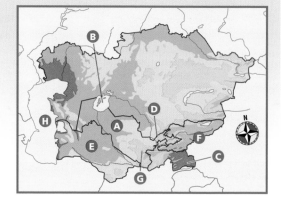

20. Answers may vary, but carpets and yurts—two art forms—can be moved around.

21. because a growing population needed more cotton; caused the Aral Sea to shrink

22. economic, political turmoil has made it difficult to build pipelines

23. outdated equipment, lack of funds, poor transportation links; some nations are trying to diversify their economic products.

Map Activity
24. A. Kyzyl Kum
B. Aral Sea
C. Pamirs
D. Tashkent
E. Kara-Kum
F. Tian Shan
G. Samarqand
H. Caspian Sea

Writing Activity

Imagine that you are a caravan trader traveling along the Silk Road during the 1200s. Write a journal entry describing your journey from the Mediterranean Sea through Central Asia. You may want to describe the landscape, other people that you meet, or dangers that you face. Be sure to use standard grammar, spelling, sentence structure, and punctuation.

internet connect

Internet Activity: **go.hrw.com**
KEYWORD: **SK5 GT7**

Choose a topic to explore about Central Asia:
- Study the climate of Central Asia.
- Travel along the historic Silk Road.
- Learn about nomads and caravans.

Social Studies Skills Practice

Interpreting Charts

Study the following chart and then answer the questions.

Rural and Urban Population in Central Asia, 1989–1992		
Country	**Urban Population**	**Rural Population**
Kazakhstan	9,610,000	7,120,000
Kyrgyzstan	1,680,000	2,770,000
Tajikistan	1,660,000	3,440,000
Turkmenistan	1,590,000	1,930,000
Uzbekistan	8,040,000	11,770,000

Source: Federal Research Division, Library of Congress

1. Which country had the largest urban population? The smallest?
2. Which country had the largest rural population? The smallest?
3. Which country's urban population was larger than its rural population?
4. Which country had urban and rural populations that were roughly the same size?

Analyzing Primary Sources

Read the following quote from Mrs. B. Ospanova, a citizen of Kazakhstan. Then answer the questions.

"I am glad that the republic is independent. My husband and I feel more liberated. Earlier we lived from salary to salary, the flat [apartment] was small, we stood in turn for a car during 20 years. But another times came and my husband organized his own small-scale business. We bought a big flat, a car and gave education to our children. Is it bad? Work and you will have everything. I, for example, have no nostalgia for Soviet times."

1. What problems with the Soviet-era economy does Mrs. Ospanova discuss?
2. What new business opportunity became available after independence?
3. How has life changed for the Ospanova family since independence?
4. What does Mrs. Ospanova identify as the key to success in Kazakhstan?

Writing Activity

Information could include difficult travel due to unfamiliar terrain, varied climate, warring factions. Use Rubric 15, Journals, to evaluate work.

Interpreting Charts

1. Kazakhstan; Turkmenistan
2. Uzbekistan; Turkmenistan
3. Kazakhstan
4. Turkmenistan

Analyzing Primary Sources

1. living from salary to salary, living in a small apartment, having to wait 20 years for a car
2. opportunity to own a small business
3. They have bought a big apartment and a car and have provided education for their children.
4. work

REVIEW AND ASSESSMENT RESOURCES

Reproducible
- Readings in World Geography, History, and Culture 45 and 46
- Critical Thinking Activity 7
- Vocabulary Activity 7

Technology
- Chapter 7 Test Generator (on the One-Stop Planner)

- HRW Go site
- Audio CD Program, Chapter 7

Reinforcement, Review, and Assessment
- Chapter 7 Review and Practice
- Chapter Summaries and Review
- Chapter 7 Test

- Chapter 7 Test for English Language Learners and Special-Needs Students
- Unit 4 Test
- Unit 4 Test for English Language Learners and Special-Needs Students

internet connect

GO TO: **go.hrw.com**
KEYWORD: **SK5 Teacher**
FOR: a guide to using the Internet in your classroom

GEOGRAPHY SIDELIGHT

Many Central Asians have been working to restore the practice of Islam in their region. These efforts have been met with a certain amount of governmental resistance. In order to limit the power of Islamic political movements, some governments in the region have imposed restrictions on Muslims. For example, some Islamic-based political groups have been banned. Even the wearing of long beards, which can symbolize adherence to fundamentalist Islamic beliefs, has been outlawed in some areas.

Kazakhstan, Kyrgyzstan, and Turkmenistan are viewed as less politically vulnerable to Islamic fundamentalist movements. Russian cultural influences are more widespread in these three countries than in Uzbekistan and Tajikistan. In addition to being geographically close to Iran and Afghanistan—countries where Islamic political movements have been very powerful—Uzbekistan and Tajikistan have well-established Islamic institutions.

Critical Thinking: What is the relationship of Islam to Central Asian countries?

Answer: Many people have tried to increase its influence, while governments have tried to limit it.

➤ **This Focus On Culture feature addresses National Geography Standards 3, 5, 10, and 13.**

Differences and Connections

In this textbook the countries of Africa are grouped together. This has been done to emphasize the region's connections. Yet any region as large as Africa has important differences from place to place. East Africa is different from West Africa, and West Africa is different from North Africa. This is also true of other large regions. In South America, for example, Brazil is different from Argentina in many important ways.

North Africa and Southwest Asia One subregion of Africa that geographers often include in another region is North Africa. These geographers see more connections between North Africa and Southwest Asia than between North Africa and the rest of the continent. For example, in both areas Arabic is the main language. The major religion is Islam. Political issues also tie North Africa to its eastern neighbors, as does physical geography. The countries of North Africa and Southwest

▲
The Muhammad Ali Mosque is one of many beautiful places of worship for Muslims in Cairo, Egypt. Although various religions, including Judaism and Christianity, are practiced in North Africa and Southwest Asia, most people in the two regions are Muslim.

Asia are part of a vast desert region. These countries face common issues such as water conservation and water management.

The African Continent There are also many reasons for placing North Africa in a region with the rest of Africa. People in Africa share some important historical, cultural, and economic ties. For example, ancient Egyptians had close contact with other peoples in Africa. In turn, cultures south of the Sahara contributed to the development of Egypt's great Nile Valley civilizations. Farther west, Mediterranean peoples have long traded with West African kingdoms south of the Sahara. Such contact helped spread

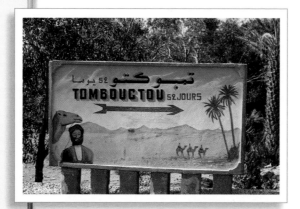

◀
This sign in Morocco is in both Arabic and French. Arabic is spoken throughout North Africa and many parts of Southwest Asia.

FOCUS ON CULTURE

Recalling Concepts

Review with students what they learned in the preceding unit about the political and economic relationships between the countries of Central Asia and the former Soviet Union. (Students should mention that these countries were Soviet republics, that the economies of these countries were part of the Soviet economy, and that the Soviet Union set up schools and hospitals and made Russian the language of government and business.) Point out that these countries were part of the Soviet Union for approximately 70 years. Remind students that the cultural and ethnic differences between the people of these countries and of Russia contributed to the drive by Central Asians to gain independence from the Soviet Union. On a wall map show students the relative location of Kazakhstan, Uzbekistan, Turkmenistan, Azerbaijan, Kyrgyzstan, and Tajikistan between Russia and the countries of Southwest Asia.

Regional Links

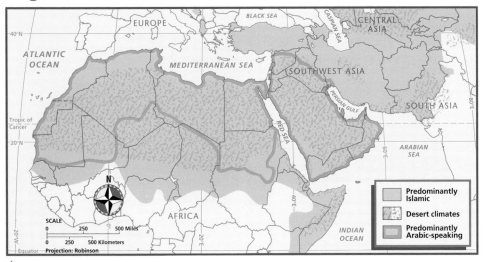

Language, religion, and climate are some of the ties between North Africa and Southwest Asia. Arabic speakers, Muslims, and desert climates are dominant throughout much of the two regions and in parts of the surrounding transition zones.

Islam among the peoples of North Africa and the rest of the continent. Today, there are mosques as far south as Nigeria and Tanzania.

North Africa also has political connections to the rest of Africa. Many African countries face similar political and economic challenges. In part, these issues arise from their shared colonial history. To resolve some of these issues, the countries of North Africa are working with other African countries. They have formed associations such as the Organization of African Unity.

Transition Zones There are many differences and connections between North Africa and the rest of the continent. Perhaps they are most evident in a band of countries that lie just south of the Sahara. These countries stretch from Mauritania in the west to Ethiopia and Sudan in the east. They form a transition zone. In other words, they resemble both North Africa and Africa south of the

Sahara. In Chad and Sudan, for example, strong political and cultural differences separate north and south. The northern regions of these countries are tied closely to North Africa. The southern regions of these countries are tied closely to African countries to the south.

North Africa and the countries in the transition zone have important connections to two major world regions. Which region they are placed in depends on the geographer's point of view. Understanding the differences among countries and their connections to other areas of the world is important. It is more important than deciding where on a map a region begins or ends.

Understanding What You Read

1. What ties are there between North Africa and Southwest Asia?
2. What ties are there between North Africa and the rest of the African continent?

Understanding What You Read

Answers
1. economic—Central Asia exported cotton and oil to Soviet territories and imported Soviet manufactured goods; cultural—Soviet Union strongly influenced culture of Central Asia, and many Central Asians learned how to speak Russian
2. because Turkey's business leaders are trying to expand their industries into Central Asia; because of expanded air travel, roads, and rail lines; because of the resurgence of Islam; and because of common reaction against Western culture

Going Further: Thinking Critically

Direct students' attention to the map on this page. Have them name the countries that share each language group. Then ask the following questions: What language is common in a very small area of Southwest Asia and Central Asia? (Greek) What is the main language group of Central Asia? (Turkic) What language groups are most common in Southwest Asia? (Iranic and Semitic) Then organize the class into three groups and assign each group one of the three dominant language groups. Have each group conduct research on the history of the language group in Central Asia or Southwest Asia.

PRACTICING
THE SKILL

1. Students should describe a local environmental problem fully. They should relate the environmental problem to their community.

2. Students should present options for solving the problem.

3. Students should list advantages and disadvantages of options.

4. Students should choose an option, create a plan with the option, explain their plan, and present it.

Visual Record Answer ▶

Possible answer: by containing the oil within a flexible barrier and removing it manually from the surface

➤ **This GeoSkills feature addresses National Geography Standards 4 and 14.**

Building Skills for Life: Interpreting the Past

Both people and places are a product of the past. Therefore, understanding the geography of past times is important. It gives us a more complete understanding of the world today.

History and geography can hardly be separated. All historical events have to happen somewhere. These events are affected by local geography. For example, wheat and barley were domesticated in an area of Southwest Asia called the Fertile Crescent. This region received enough rainfall for these crops to grow.

Geographers who specialize in studying the past are called historical geographers. Historical geographers are interested in where things used to be and how they developed. They also try to understand how people's beliefs and values influenced historical events. In other words, why did people do what they did?

All geographers must be skilled at interpreting the past. Cultural geographers might study how old buildings and houses reflect earlier times. Physical geographers may need to reconstruct past landscapes. For example,

▲ Ancient ruins in Petra, Jordan, can provide clues to the region's past.

many rivers have changed their course. Understanding where a river used to flow could help explain its present course.

In your study of geography, think about how a place's history has shaped the way it is today. Look for clues that can tell you about its past. Ask yourself how people may have thought about a place in earlier times. No matter where you are, the evidence of the past is all around!

THE SKILL

1. Look at some of the buildings in your community. How old do you think they are? Do some look older than others? Can you describe how building styles in your community have changed over time? Why do you think styles have changed?

2. Analyze an important historical event that occurred in your state. What happened? Where did it happen? How was the event influenced by local geography?

3. Interpret the settlement history of your state or community. When was it settled? What attracted people to it? How do you think they felt about the place at the time?

160 • **Unit 2 GeoSkills**

GeoSkills

Going Further: Thinking Critically

Have students investigate ways in which their peers are involved in environmental movements. Organize students into groups. Have each group find an example of young people's activism in environmental issues. Students may select an individual or an organization to profile. If a group has selected an individual, ask its members to prepare a résumé for that person. If a group selected an organization, ask its members to prepare a brochure about the organization. Have students include answers to as many of the following questions as possible:

• What is the individual's or organization's main goal?
• Did a certain specific incident or issue inspire the activist(s) to get involved?

• How might other students become involved in this effort?
• Are there aspects of the work done by the organization or individual that might appeal especially to young people?
• How is work done by the organization or individual publicized?
• What is the most important accomplishment achieved so far by the individual or organization?

Have each group present its work to the class.

HANDS on GEOGRAPHY

One way to interpret the past is by studying old travel accounts. They often have detailed information about the people, places, and daily life of past times.

One famous travel account describes the journeys of Ibn Battuta. Ibn Battuta was one of the greatest travelers in history. During the mid-1300s he traveled about 75,000 miles (120,700 km) throughout parts of Asia and Africa. Near the end of his travels, he gave a long account of the many places he visited. This account is a valuable historical document today.

The following passage is taken from Ibn Battuta's travel account. In this passage, Ibn Battuta is visiting the Sultan of Birgi, a town in what is now western Turkey. Read the passage, and then answer the Lab Report questions.

> *In the course of this audience the sultan asked me this question: "Have you ever seen a stone that fell from the sky?" I replied, "I have never seen one, nor ever heard tell of one." "Well," he said, "a stone did fall from the sky outside this town of ours," and then called some men and told them to bring the stone. They brought in a great black stone, very hard and with a glitter in it—I reckoned its weight to amount to a hundredweight. The sultan ordered the stonebreakers to be summoned, and four of them came and on his command to strike it they beat upon it as one man four times with iron hammers, but made no impression on it. I was astonished at this phenomenon, and he ordered it to be taken back to its place.*

▲ This painting shows Ibn Battuta during his travels in the mid-1300s.

Lab Report

1. What did the "stone that fell from the sky" look like? What do you think it was?

2. Why do you think Ibn Battuta was "astonished" by what he saw?

3. What can this story tell us about the historical geography of this region?

Answers

1. The environmental problems in Chelyabinsk caused many deaths and health problems, including birth defects and cancer.

2. Students might suggest cleaning up the nuclear waste in Chelyabinsk and the Techa River. Students may also suggest further evacuating the area until it is safe for people to live there.

3. Physical geographic studies can help locate sources of pollution and demonstrate the effects of pollution on air, land, soil, and water. Cultural geographic studies can show the effects of pollution on people. These studies can propose ways to prevent similar problems in the future.

internet connect

GO TO: go.hrw.com
KEYWORD: SK5 CH14
FOR: Web sites about children and pollution

Central Asia 161

Holding back the desert in Morocco

UNIT 3

Africa

Cape Town, South Africa

162   Unit 3

USING THE ILLUSTRATIONS

Direct students' attention to the photographs on these pages. Point out the Masai men in the center. The Masai are a nomadic people of East Africa. Their high-jumping dance may go on for hours. Masai dancing, game parks, and beautiful scenery attract tourists to Kenya. Ask students how the photo of the Masai dancers contrasts with the photo of Cape Town. (Possible answer: contrast of traditional rural culture and modern urban culture) Emphasize that Africa's cultures are very diverse, ranging from ways of life that are almost unchanged over many centuries to those that are influenced by the latest styles and technologies.

Focus attention on the photo at the top of this page. Tell students that the Sahara has spread over large tracts of land in northern and western Africa, turning grasslands into desert. Ask what the man in the photo is doing to stop or slow the process (building fences to keep sand from covering the land). Point out that low-technology efforts like this can be very effective and that one person can make a big difference in solving environmental problems.

Point out the woman using the microscope. Tell students that African medical personnel face many challenges, including a shortage of equipment.

A Physician in Sierra Leone

Dr. James Li went to Africa fresh out of medical school to work as a general practice physician. Here he describes what it was like to work at a hospital in Sierra Leone. **WHAT DO YOU THINK?** *What might Dr. Li's patients think about health care in the United States?*

Malaria, tuberculosis, and leprosy were widespread in our hospital population. We often saw patients who had walked over 100 miles for treatment. None of the patients in our area had access to clean water. Phone lines installed by the British had been cut down and the copper wires melted to make cooking pots. Our hospital was in the remote jungle, about six hours by dirt road from the nearest major city. It had 140 beds. In the clinic, we saw several hundred other patients each day. Food for the staff and patients was grown on the hospital grounds.

I came to love the people who were our patients, particularly the very young and the very old. In the midst of shortages, I met people who lived happily and suffered the tragedies of utter poverty with a dignity that would have failed me. These reflections fill me with a strange combination of awe, sadness, humility, and excitement.

Hospital in Butare, Rwanda

Masai dancers, Kenya

Giraffe

Understanding Primary Sources

1. What were conditions like at Dr. Li's hospital?
2. How does Dr. Li describe the culture of Sierra Leone?

MORE FROM THE FIELD

Tuberculosis (TB) causes about 3 million deaths worldwide each year. It spreads through the air and infects the lungs. In recent years, doctors in the United States are seeing many TB cases that are resistant to drug therapy.

Malaria is primarily a tropical disease. It kills some 1.5 to 2.7 million people each year. Children under five are most vulnerable. More than 90 percent of malaria cases and the great majority of malaria deaths occur in tropical Africa. One basic method for preventing malaria is to eliminate the *Anopheles* mosquito, which transmits the disease. Draining marshes, swamps, and stagnant pools eliminates the mosquito's breeding places.

Activity: Have students create a world map showing areas with a high malaria risk. Discuss ways that individuals can eliminate standing water in their communities.

Understanding Primary Sources
Answers
1. busy, cut off from conveniences
2. resilient—they lived happily and suffered the tragedies of poverty with dignity

Africa 163

CHAPTERS

PEOPLE IN THE PROFILE

Note that the elevation profile crosses Africa just north of Mount Kenya. Known locally as Kirinyaga (meaning "Mountain of Whiteness"), Mount Kenya is the second-highest mountain in Africa. Mount Kenya is home to the Kikuyu people who farm the fertile lower slopes of the mountain.

The Kikuyu have played a significant role in Kenya's history. By the end of the 1800s, most of Africa had been colonized by European countries. The Kikuyu were the first ethnic group in Kenya to fight for independence from Britain. They started the Mau Mau rebellion, which in the 1950s advocated violent resistance to British rule. During the revolt, thousands of Kikuyu rebels were killed and many more were put into detention camps in an attempt by the British to stop the uprising. Despite these efforts, the Mau Mau rebellion sparked the Kenyan independence movement.

Jomo Kenyatta, the first prime minister and president of Kenya, was a member of the Kikuyu people. The Kikuyu continued to play a major role in Kenya's political system throughout Kenyatta's rule.

Critical Thinking: How did the Kikuyu fight British rule?

Answer: by starting the Mau Mau rebellion

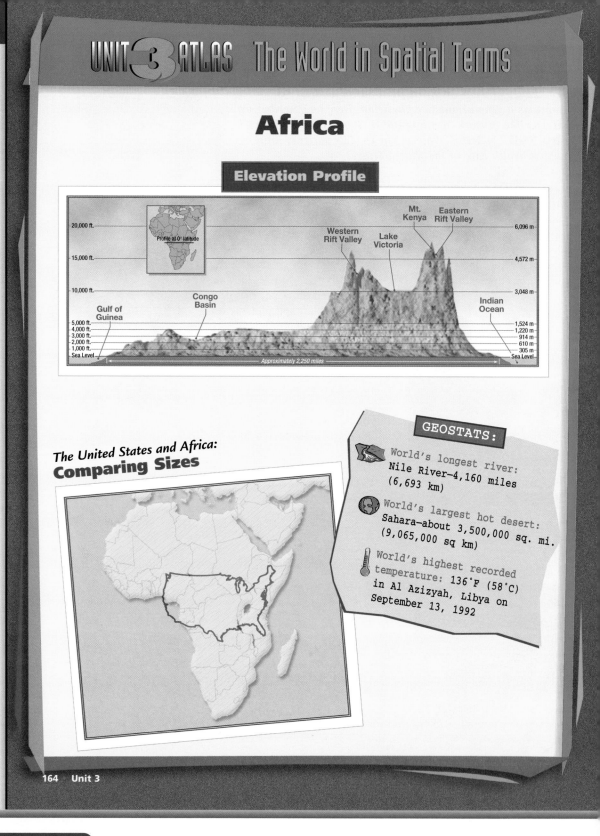

UNIT 3 ATLAS The World in Spatial Terms

Africa

Elevation Profile

Profile at 0° latitude

20,000 ft. — 6,096 m
15,000 ft. — 4,572 m
10,000 ft. — 3,048 m

Western Rift Valley
Lake Victoria
Mt. Kenya
Eastern Rift Valley

Gulf of Guinea
Congo Basin
Indian Ocean

5,000 ft.
4,000 ft.
3,000 ft.
2,000 ft.
1,000 ft.
Sea Level

1,524 m
1,220 m
914 m
610 m
305 m
Sea Level

Approximately 2,250 miles

The United States and Africa:
Comparing Sizes

GEOSTATS:

World's longest river: Nile River—4,160 miles (6,693 km)

World's largest hot desert: Sahara—about 3,500,000 sq. mi. (9,065,000 sq km)

World's highest recorded temperature: 136°F (58°C) in Al Aziyah, Libya on September 13, 1992

OVERVIEW

In this unit, students will learn that Africa's physical and human geography are extremely diverse. The continent contains the world's largest desert (the Sahara) and the longest river (the Nile). There are snowcapped mountains that border vast plains. In the tropics are dense rain forests.

Africa's human mosaic is equally varied. Hundreds of different ethnic groups speak numerous languages. Archaeological digs in East Africa have unearthed remains indicating that the earliest humans lived there. Wealthy, sophisticated king-doms developed in many regions. Later, European merchants arrived, and the international slave trade began. The

slave trade left a tragic legacy. European colonizers were next to arrive. Europeans often ignored the ancient political and cultural divisions among the people. The negative effects of colonialism are still being felt.

Today, Africa faces the future with advantages and disadvantages. Desertification and high birth-rates are widespread problems. Millions of Africans live in poverty. However, the continent has rich undeveloped resources. More African governments are responding to their citizens' needs.

Africa: Physical

UNIT 3 ATLAS

Map of Africa: Physical

EUROPE

40°N

30°N

Strait of Gibraltar

ATLAS MOUNTAINS

MOROCCO

TUNISIA

MEDITERRANEAN SEA

Suez Canal

ISTHMUS OF SUEZ

SOUTHWEST ASIA

40°E

50°E

40°N

Canary Islands (SPAIN)

WESTERN SAHARA (Sovereignty disputed)

Tropic of Cancer

ALGERIA

LIBYA

GULF OF SUEZ

EGYPT

ARABIAN DESERT

Aswan High Dam

Tropic of Cancer

S A H A R A

AHAGGAR MOUNTAINS

LIBYAN DESERT

NUBIAN DESERT

RED SEA

30°N

20°N

CAPE VERDE

MAURITANIA

MALI

NIGER

CHAD

Nile R.

White Nile

ERITREA

GULF OF ADEN

20°N

Senegal R.

Niger River

CHAD BASIN

Lake Chad

S A H E L

SUDAN

SUDAN BASIN

DJIBOUTI

GAMBIA

SENEGAL

GUINEA-BISSAU

GUINEA

SIERRA LEONE

LIBERIA

FOUTA DJALLON

BURKINA FASO

BENIN

TOGO

NIGERIA

GHANA

Benue River

CENTRAL AFRICAN REPUBLIC

CAMEROON

Ubangi R.

Bomu R.

Uele River

Blue Nile

ETHIOPIA

ETHIOPIAN HIGHLANDS

EASTERN RIFT VALLEY

SOMALIA

10°N

GULF OF GUINEA

EQUATORIAL GUINEA

SÃO TOMÉ AND PRÍNCIPE

REPUBLIC OF THE CONGO

CONGO BASIN

Congo River

UGANDA

Lake Victoria

KENYA

Equator

GABON

DEMOCRATIC REPUBLIC OF THE CONGO

RWANDA

BURUNDI

Kasai R.

SERENGETI PLAIN

Kilimanjaro 19,341 ft. (5895 m)

WESTERN RIFT VALLEY

TANZANIA

Lake Tanganyika

Zanzibar

INDIAN OCEAN

SEYCHELLES

Equator

ATLANTIC OCEAN

CABINDA (ANGOLA)

KATANGA PLATEAU

Lake Malawi (Nyasa)

COMOROS

10°S

ANGOLA

Zambezi R.

Victoria Falls

ZAMBIA

MALAWI

MADAGASCAR

MAURITIUS

NAMIBIA

NAMIB DESERT

ZIMBABWE

BOTSWANA

KALAHARI DESERT

MOZAMBIQUE

Mozambique Channel

Tropic of Capricorn

SWAZILAND

SOUTH AFRICA

LESOTHO

Orange R.

DRAKENSBERG MOUNTAINS

SCALE

0   500   1000 Miles

0   500   1000 Kilometers

Projection: Azimuthal Equal Area

30°S

ELEVATION

FEET	METERS
13,120	4,000
6,560	2,000
1,640	500
656	200
(Sea level) 0	0 (Sea level)
Below sea level	Below sea level

N

---

1. (Region) Which region of Africa has the highest mountains? Which country appears to have the largest number of high mountains?

2. (Place) Which countries have areas that lie below sea level? Where is the highest point in Africa?

Critical Thinking

3. (Region) Which North African mountains might create a rain-shadow effect?

4. (Region) Compare this map to the **climate map** of the region. Which areas might have tropical rain forests?

Africa • 165

Physical Map

Answers

1. eastern; Ethiopia

2. Algeria, Tunisia, Egypt, Ethiopia, Djibouti; Tanzania

Critical Thinking

3. Atlas Mountains

4. areas with humid tropical climates, such as the Congo Basin, the east coast of Madagascar, and the coasts of Sierra Leone and Liberia

---

USING THE PHYSICAL MAP

As students examine the **physical map** on this page, tell the class that Africa is the second-largest continent. Then ask students what bodies of water surround Africa (Mediterranean Sea, Atlantic Ocean, Gulf of Guinea, Indian Ocean, Gulf of Aden, Red Sea). Africa has great rivers and deserts. Ask students to identify some of each (deserts: Sahara, Kalahari, Namib; rivers: Nile, Niger, Congo, Zambezi, Orange).

Point out that across most of Africa the major landforms are plateaus and basins. You may want to review the definitions of these terms. Call on a volunteer to identify the major basins (Chad Basin, Sudan Basin, Congo Basin). Then ask students where the region's largest plateau is located (southern Africa).

PEOPLE IN THE PROFILE

Your Classroom Time Line

These are the major dates and time periods for this unit. Have students enter them on the time line you created earlier. You may want to watch for these dates as students progress through the unit.

c.* 3200 B.C. The northern Nile River area unites into one Egyptian kingdom.

c. 2000 B.C. The great pyramids at Giza are built for Egyptian rulers.

1500–1000 B.C. Egyptians carve tombs into the sides of cliffs.

332 B.C. Alexander the Great founds Alexandria, Egypt.

A.D. 300s Christianity is adopted in Ethiopia.

*c. stands for *circa* and means "about."

Political Map

Answers

1. Lesotho
2. Equatorial Guinea
3. Madagascar; Cape Verde, São Tomé and Príncipe, Mauritius, Comoros, Seychelles

Critical Thinking

4. makes trade and communication easier; also, large settlements farther south limited by the Sahara

Africa: Political

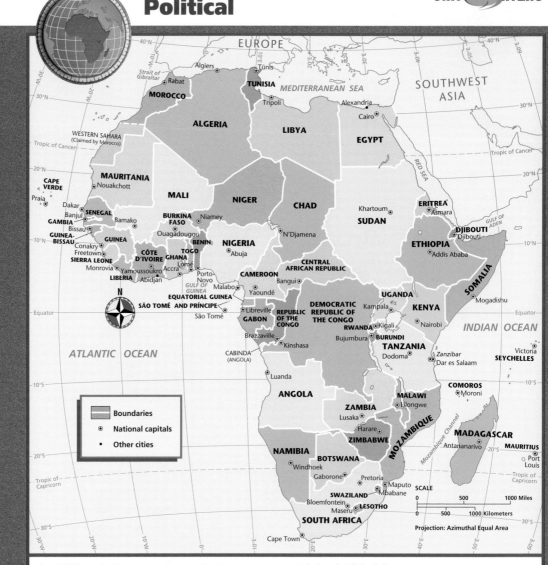

1. **Place** Which country is completely surrounded by another country?

2. **Location** Which country lies mostly on the mainland but has its capital on an island?

3. **Place** What is the largest African island country? What are the other island countries?

Critical Thinking

4. **Human-Environment Interaction** Compare this map to the **climate map** of the region. Why do you think the capitals of Algeria, Tunisia, and Libya all lie on the Mediterranean Sea?

166 • Unit 3

USING THE POLITICAL MAP

Focus students' attention on the **political map** of Africa. Call on a volunteer to identify all the mainland countries that have a seacoast while others name the landlocked countries they border. You may want to review the meaning of *landlocked*. Ask students to find the mainland country that is divided into two parts—one large and one very small (Angola). Then ask them to name the largest country in Africa (Sudan).

Have students compare this map to the **physical, climate,** and **population maps** of the continent. Ask students which of the region's boundaries appear to be unrelated to physical features (straight lines in northern and southern Africa). Then ask students to identify one reason that these

boundaries may have been drawn in this way. (They are in dry, sparsely populated areas where there are no rivers or other major physical features to serve as natural boundaries.)

ONLINE ATLAS
GO TO: go.hrw.com
KEYWORD: SK5 MapsU3

Africa: Climate

UNIT 3 ATLAS

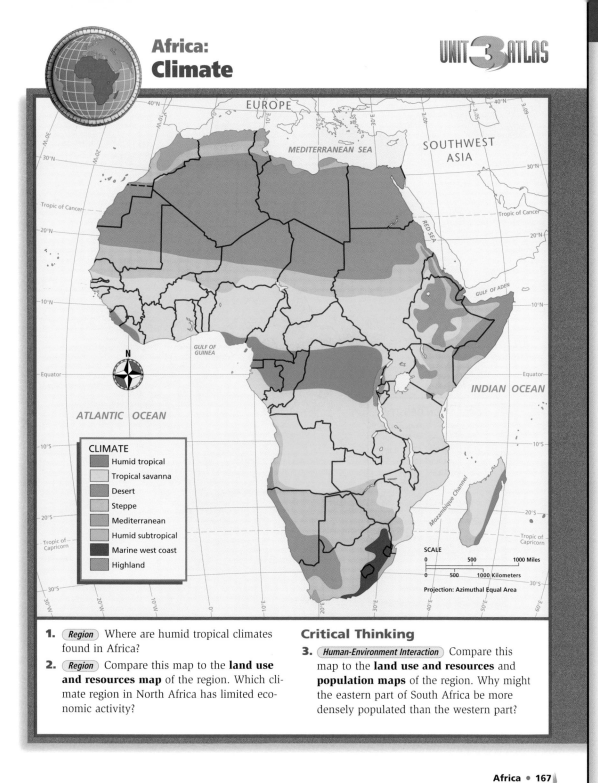

CLIMATE
- Humid tropical
- Tropical savanna
- Desert
- Steppe
- Mediterranean
- Humid subtropical
- Marine west coast
- Highland

SCALE
0   500   1000 Miles
0   500   1000 Kilometers
Projection: Azimuthal Equal Area

EUROPE

MEDITERRANEAN SEA

SOUTHWEST ASIA

RED SEA

GULF OF ADEN

GULF OF GUINEA

ATLANTIC OCEAN

INDIAN OCEAN

Mozambique Channel

Tropic of Cancer

Equator

Tropic of Capricorn

1. **Region** Where are humid tropical climates found in Africa?

2. **Region** Compare this map to the **land use and resources map** of the region. Which climate region in North Africa has limited economic activity?

Critical Thinking

3. **Human-Environment Interaction** Compare this map to the **land use and resources** and **population maps** of the region. Why might the eastern part of South Africa be more densely populated than the western part?

Africa • 167

Your Classroom Time Line (continued)

late 600s–early 700s Arab armies conquer Egypt and North Africa.

c. 800s Kingdom of Ghana rises to power.

1300s Mansa Mūsā, king of Mali, wins fame for his wealth and wise rule.

1500s The Portuguese set up their first settlements on the East African coast.

1600s The demand for slave labor in the American colonies increases.

1652 The Dutch set up a trade station at Cape Town.

1800s Great Britain takes over southern Africa's Cape Colony.

1820s Americans create the territory of Liberia.

1833 British ban slavery in their empire.

Climate Map

Answers

1. parts of central Africa, small part of coastal western Africa, east coast of Madagascar

2. desert

Critical Thinking

3. pleasant climate and plentiful resources

USING THE CLIMATE MAP

Have students review the **climate map** of Africa on this page and identify the climate region that most resembles their own local climate. Have students compare the latitude of their location with that of the corresponding African climate. Then ask students to write statements relating climate and latitude. (Examples: Latitude affects climate. Places in low latitudes generally have a hot climate. Those in middle latitudes have a temperate climate. Places in high latitudes generally have a cold climate.)

Then have students compare this map to the **physical map**. Ask them which countries have a highland climate region although they are on the equator or within 10 degrees of the equator(Democratic Republic of the Congo, Uganda, Rwanda, Burundi, Kenya, Ethiopia). Then ask students how altitude affects climate. (Higher altitudes create milder climates, even at very low latitudes.)

Africa: Population

Your Classroom Time Line (continued)

1860s French build the Suez Canal.

1860s Dutch discover diamonds in the northern Cape Colony.

1886 Gold is discovered in Transvaal, southern Africa.

1899 The Boers and the British in southern Africa engage in warfare.

1912 Europeans control all of North Africa.

1912 The African National Congress (ANC) is formed.

1922 Egypt gains limited independence.

1936–41 Italy annexes Ethiopia.

late 1940s South Africa establishes apartheid.

internet connect

ONLINE ATLAS
GO TO: go.hrw.com
KEYWORD: SK5 MapsU3

Population Map

Answers
1. Egypt; Nile River

2. Kinshasa and Johannesburg

Critical Thinking
3. Either too much or too little rain can limit human activity.

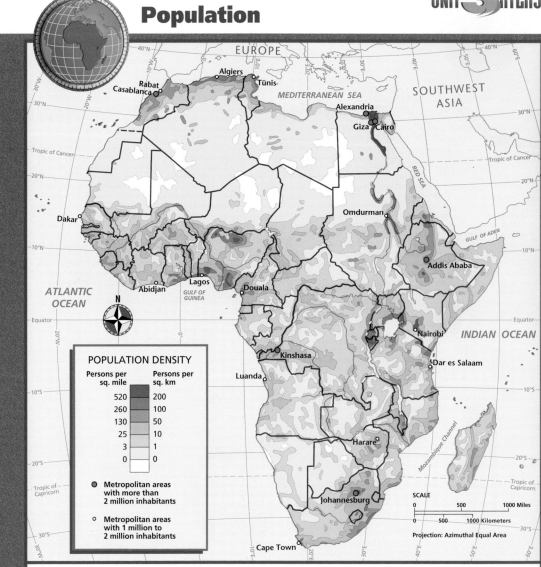

POPULATION DENSITY

Persons per sq. mile	Persons per sq. km
520	200
260	100
130	50
25	10
3	1
0	0

● Metropolitan areas with more than 2 million inhabitants

○ Metropolitan areas with 1 million to 2 million inhabitants

SCALE
0 — 500 — 1000 Miles
0 — 500 — 1000 Kilometers
Projection: Azimuthal Equal Area

1. (Place) Which country has the most cities with more than 2 million people? Compare this map to the **physical map** of the region. Which river flows through or near these cities?

2. (Place) What are the two largest African cities shown south of the equator?

Critical Thinking

3. (Human-Environment Interaction) Compare this map to the **climate map** of the region. Notice that both the humid tropical climate region in central Africa and the desert regions in the north and south are areas of low population density. What is one conclusion you might draw from this?

USING THE POPULATION MAP

Have students examine the **population map** of Africa on this page and identify relative locations of the areas with the highest population density. (Examples: near the Gulf of Guinea, in the far northeast, near the lake in East Africa, in the far southeast) List student responses on the chalkboard. Then ask students to compare this map to the **political map** of the continent. Ask volunteers to identify the countries that correspond to the areas of high population density and to write the countries' names next to the relative location descriptions on the chalkboard.

Africa: Land Use and Resources

UNIT **3** ATLAS

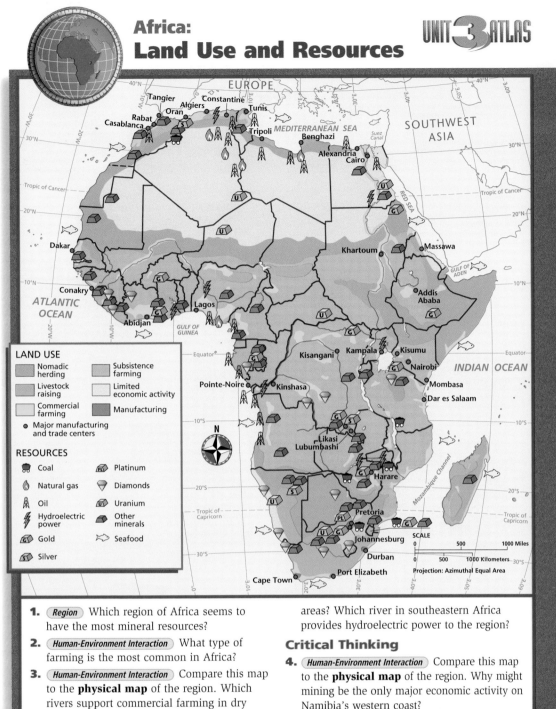

LAND USE

- Nomadic herding
- Livestock raising
- Commercial farming
- Subsistence farming
- Limited economic activity
- Manufacturing
- ● Major manufacturing and trade centers

RESOURCES

- Coal
- Natural gas
- Oil
- Hydroelectric power
- Gold
- Silver
- Platinum
- Diamonds
- Uranium
- Other minerals
- Seafood

SCALE
0   500   1000 Miles
0   500   1000 Kilometers
Projection: Azimuthal Equal Area

Your Classroom Time Line (continued)

1950s–60s Many African countries gain their independence.

1964 Nelson Mandela is sentenced to life in prison.

1969 Mu'ammar al-Gadhafi takes over Libya.

1979 Egypt signs a peace treaty with Israel.

1980s Millions of Ethiopians suffer from famine.

1990s Severe drought hits Somalia.

1990 Nelson Mandela is released from prison.

1994 Nelson Mandela is elected president of South Africa.

2000 Zimbabwean war veterans spearhead occupation of white-owned farms.

2003 Former Ugandan dictator Idi Amin dies in Saudi Arabia.

2004 Prime Minister Tony Blair visits Libya.

1. **Region** Which region of Africa seems to have the most mineral resources?

2. **Human-Environment Interaction** What type of farming is the most common in Africa?

3. **Human-Environment Interaction** Compare this map to the **physical map** of the region. Which rivers support commercial farming in dry areas? Which river in southeastern Africa provides hydroelectric power to the region?

Critical Thinking

4. **Human-Environment Interaction** Compare this map to the **physical map** of the region. Why might mining be the only major economic activity on Namibia's western coast?

Africa • 169

Land Use and Resources Map

Answers
1. southeastern
2. subsistence farming
3. Niger and Nile Rivers; Zambezi River

Critical Thinking
4. The Namib Desert limits agricultural activity.

USING THE LAND USE AND RESOURCES MAP

Focus students' attention on the **land use and resources map** on this page. Call on volunteers for general statements about the distribution of resources. (Examples: Resources are not distributed evenly. Most of the oil and gas industry is in northern Africa. Some countries have very few resources.)

Have students compare this map to the **physical map**. Ask them which countries have no manufacturing centers, precious metals, or other minerals (Mali, Chad, Somalia) and what economic activities these countries depend on instead (nomadic herding, subsistence farming, small amounts of commercial farming and livestock raising).

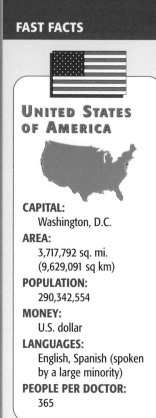

UNITED STATES OF AMERICA

CAPITAL:
Washington, D.C.

AREA:
3,717,792 sq. mi.
(9,629,091 sq km)

POPULATION:
290,342,554

MONEY:
U.S. dollar

LANGUAGES:
English, Spanish (spoken by a large minority)

PEOPLE PER DOCTOR:
365

Fast FACTS

Africa

ALGERIA
CAPITAL:
Algiers
AREA:
919,590 sq. mi.
(2,381,740 sq km)
POPULATION:
32,818,500
MONEY:
Algerian dinar
LANGUAGES:
Arabic (official), French, Berber
PEOPLE PER DOCTOR:
1,066

BURKINA FASO
CAPITAL:
Ouagadougou
AREA:
105,869 sq. mi.
(274,200 sq km)
POPULATION:
13,228,460
MONEY:
CFAF*
LANGUAGES:
French (official), ethnic languages
PEOPLE PER DOCTOR:
27,158

ANGOLA
CAPITAL:
Luanda
AREA:
481,351 sq. mi.
(1,246,700 sq km)
POPULATION:
10,766,471
MONEY:
kwanza
LANGUAGES:
Portuguese (official), Bantu languages
PEOPLE PER DOCTOR:
data not available

BURUNDI
CAPITAL:
Bujumbura
AREA:
10,745 sq. mi.
(27,830 sq km)
POPULATION:
6,096,156
MONEY:
Burundi franc
LANGUAGES:
Kirundi (official), French (official), Swahili
PEOPLE PER DOCTOR:
16,667

BENIN
CAPITAL:
Porto-Novo
AREA:
43,483 sq. mi.
(112,620 sq km)
POPULATION:
7,041,490
MONEY:
CFAF*
LANGUAGES:
French (official), Fon, Yoruba, other ethnic languages
PEOPLE PER DOCTOR:
14,216

CAMEROON
CAPITAL:
Yaoundé
AREA:
183,567 sq. mi.
(475,440 sq km)
POPULATION:
15,746,179
MONEY:
CFAF*
LANGUAGES:
English (official), French (official), 24 ethnic language groups
PEOPLE PER DOCTOR:
14,286

BOTSWANA
CAPITAL:
Gaborone
AREA:
231,803 sq. mi.
(600,370 sq km)
POPULATION:
1,573,267
MONEY:
pula
LANGUAGES:
English (official), Setswana
PEOPLE PER DOCTOR:
4,395

CAPE VERDE
CAPITAL:
Praia
AREA:
1,557 sq. mi. (4,033 sq km)
POPULATION:
412,137
MONEY:
Cape Verdean escudo
LANGUAGES:
Portuguese, Crioulo
PEOPLE PER DOCTOR:
3,448

*Communaute Financiere Africaine franc

Countries not drawn to scale.

FAST FACTS ACTIVITIES

LEVEL 1: (Suggested time: 30 min.) Ask students to study the Fast Facts feature on African countries and to suggest some ways that European colonization has affected African countries. (Possible answers: In many of the countries a European language is an official language. Many countries use money derived from European currency.) Have students write a paragraph explaining their suggestions, citing facts to support them. In particular, students should note the widespread use of the Communaute Financiere Africaine franc (CFAF) and include their thoughts on what this indicates about colonial power.

LEVEL 2: (Suggested time: 40 min.) Direct students' attention to the figures that describe the number of people per doctor. Ask students to explain why they think this data is not available for many African countries (Possible answers: Many of these countries are experiencing economic, political, or social tensions, and the governments are not stable enough to gather the information. Africa's physical geography—rivers, jungles, mountains, deserts—may make data collection difficult.)

UNIT 3 ATLAS

UNIT 3 ASSESSMENT RESOURCES

Reproducible
- Unit 3 Test
- Unit 3 Test for English Language Learners and Special-Needs Students

CENTRAL AFRICAN REPUBLIC

CAPITAL: Bangui

AREA:
240,534 sq. mi.
(622,984 sq km)

POPULATION: 3,683,538

MONEY: CFAF*

LANGUAGES: French (official), Sangho (national language), tribal languages

PEOPLE PER DOCTOR: 18,660

CONGO, REPUBLIC OF THE

CAPITAL: Brazzaville

AREA:
132,046 sq. mi.
(342,000 sq km)

POPULATION: 2,954,258

MONEY: CFAF*

LANGUAGES:
French (official), Lingala, Monokutuba

PEOPLE PER DOCTOR: 3,704

CHAD

CAPITAL:
N'Djamena

AREA:
495,752 sq. mi.
(1,284,000 sq km)

POPULATION:
9,253,493

MONEY:
CFAF*

LANGUAGES:
French (official), Arabic (official), Sara and Sango

PEOPLE PER DOCTOR: 27,765

CÔTE D'IVOIRE

CAPITAL:
Yamoussoukro

AREA:
124,502 sq. mi.
(322,460 sq km)

POPULATION: 16,962,491

MONEY: CFAF*

LANGUAGES:
French (official), Dioula, ethnic languages

PEOPLE PER DOCTOR:
data not available

COMOROS

CAPITAL:
Moroni

AREA:
838 sq. mi.
(2,170 sq km)

POPULATION:
632,948

MONEY:
Comoran franc

LANGUAGES:
Arabic (official), French (official), Comoran

PEOPLE PER DOCTOR:
10,000

DJIBOUTI

CAPITAL:
Djibouti

AREA:
8,494 sq. mi.
(22,000 sq km)

POPULATION:
457,130

MONEY:
Djiboutian franc

LANGUAGES:
French (official), Arabic (official), Somali, Afar

PEOPLE PER DOCTOR:
5,000

CONGO, DEMOCRATIC REPUBLIC OF THE

CAPITAL:
Kinshasa

AREA:
905,563 sq. mi.
(2,345,410 sq km)

POPULATION:
56,625,039

MONEY:
Congolese franc

LANGUAGES:
French (official), Lingala, Kingwana, Kikongo, Tshiluba

PEOPLE PER DOCTOR:
data not available

EGYPT

CAPITAL:
Cairo

AREA:
386,660 sq. mi.
(1,001,450 sq km)

POPULATION:
74,718,797

MONEY:
Egyptian pound

LANGUAGES:
Arabic (official), English, French

PEOPLE PER DOCTOR:
472

Sources: Central Intelligence Agency, *The World Factbook 2003; United Nations Development Programme: Health Profile,* pop. figures are 2003 estimates.

Africa • 171

internet connect

ONLINE ATLAS
GO TO: go.hrw.com
KEYWORD: SK5 FACTSU3

Highlights of Country Statistics
- *CIA World Factbook*
- Library of Congress country studies
- Flags of the world

FAST FACTS ACTIVITIES

Create a bar graph on the chalkboard, listing figures in increments of 5,000 (starting at 0) through 50,000 along the y-axis (the vertical axis). These figures represent people. Title the graph People per Doctor in African Countries. Add a bar for the United States, which has about 365 people per doctor. (Point out that the figure for the United States is so low compared to many of the other countries that the representation of it is barely visible on the graph.) Then select students to come to the chalkboard and create and label a bar for each country. Continue until all the countries with available data, or a representative sample, have been placed on the graph.

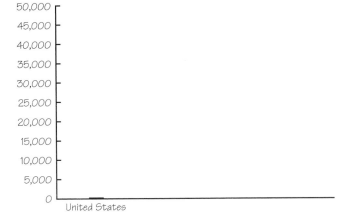

People per Doctor in African Countries

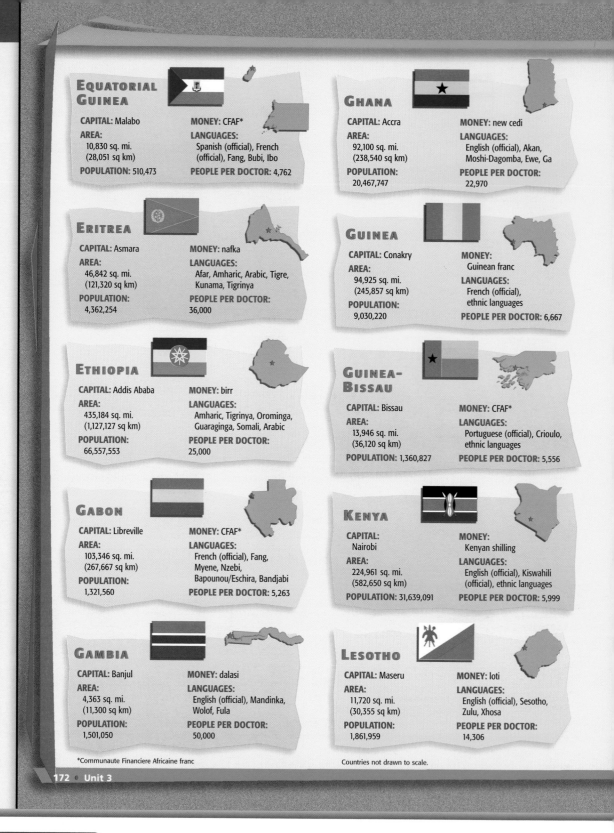

EQUATORIAL GUINEA

CAPITAL: Malabo

AREA:
10,830 sq. mi.
(28,051 sq km)

POPULATION: 510,473

MONEY: CFAF*

LANGUAGES:
Spanish (official), French (official), Fang, Bubi, Ibo

PEOPLE PER DOCTOR: 4,762

ERITREA

CAPITAL: Asmara

AREA:
46,842 sq. mi.
(121,320 sq km)

POPULATION:
4,362,254

MONEY: nafka

LANGUAGES:
Afar, Amharic, Arabic, Tigre, Kunama, Tigrinya

PEOPLE PER DOCTOR:
36,000

ETHIOPIA

CAPITAL: Addis Ababa

AREA:
435,184 sq. mi.
(1,127,127 sq km)

POPULATION:
66,557,553

MONEY: birr

LANGUAGES:
Amharic, Tigrinya, Orominga, Guaraginga, Somali, Arabic

PEOPLE PER DOCTOR:
25,000

GABON

CAPITAL: Libreville

AREA:
103,346 sq. mi.
(267,667 sq km)

POPULATION:
1,321,560

MONEY: CFAF*

LANGUAGES:
French (official), Fang, Myene, Nzebi, Bapounou/Eschira, Bandjabi

PEOPLE PER DOCTOR: 5,263

GAMBIA

CAPITAL: Banjul

AREA:
4,363 sq. mi.
(11,300 sq km)

POPULATION:
1,501,050

MONEY: dalasi

LANGUAGES:
English (official), Mandinka, Wolof, Fula

PEOPLE PER DOCTOR:
50,000

GHANA

CAPITAL: Accra

AREA:
92,100 sq. mi.
(238,540 sq km)

POPULATION:
20,467,747

MONEY: new cedi

LANGUAGES:
English (official), Akan, Moshi-Dagomba, Ewe, Ga

PEOPLE PER DOCTOR:
22,970

GUINEA

CAPITAL: Conakry

AREA:
94,925 sq. mi.
(245,857 sq km)

POPULATION:
9,030,220

MONEY:
Guinean franc

LANGUAGES:
French (official), ethnic languages

PEOPLE PER DOCTOR: 6,667

GUINEA-BISSAU

CAPITAL: Bissau

AREA:
13,946 sq. mi.
(36,120 sq km)

POPULATION: 1,360,827

MONEY: CFAF*

LANGUAGES:
Portuguese (official), Crioulo, ethnic languages

PEOPLE PER DOCTOR: 5,556

KENYA

CAPITAL:
Nairobi

AREA:
224,961 sq. mi.
(582,650 sq km)

POPULATION: 31,639,091

MONEY:
Kenyan shilling

LANGUAGES:
English (official), Kiswahili (official), ethnic languages

PEOPLE PER DOCTOR: 5,999

LESOTHO

CAPITAL: Maseru

AREA:
11,720 sq. mi.
(30,355 sq km)

POPULATION:
1,861,959

MONEY: loti

LANGUAGES:
English (official), Sesotho, Zulu, Xhosa

PEOPLE PER DOCTOR:
14,306

*Communaute Financiere Africaine franc

Countries not drawn to scale.

FAST FACTS ACTIVITIES

Discuss the trends displayed in the graph. (Sample questions: Which countries have the highest number of people per doctor? Which countries have the lowest number? Where do most of the countries fall on the graph?) Invite students to offer possible explanations for the trends. Ask them how the number of doctors might affect public health in Africa.

LEVEL 3: (Suggested time: 45 min.) Have the students work in small groups to prepare for a debate. Have half of the groups prepare arguments to support using a single language throughout Africa. Ask the other groups to prepare arguments maintaining the wide variety of languages and dialects. Have students include a theory that explains how so many languages and dialects developed as well as the possible effects of linguistic diversity. You may want to stage the debate as if it took place at the United Nations.

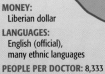

LIBERIA

CAPITAL: Monrovia

AREA:
43,000 sq. mi.
(111,370 sq km)

POPULATION:
3,317,176

MONEY:
Liberian dollar

LANGUAGES:
English (official),
many ethnic languages

PEOPLE PER DOCTOR: 8,333

LIBYA

CAPITAL: Tripoli

AREA:
679,358 sq. mi.
(1,759,540 sq km)

POPULATION:
5,499,074

MONEY: Libyan dinar

LANGUAGES:
Arabic, Italian, English

PEOPLE PER DOCTOR:
data not available

MADAGASCAR

CAPITAL: Antananarivo

AREA:
226,656 sq. mi.
(587,040 sq km)

POPULATION:
16,979,744

MONEY:
Malagasy franc

LANGUAGES:
French (official),
Malagasy (official)

PEOPLE PER DOCTOR: 4,167

MALAWI

CAPITAL: Lilongwe

AREA:
45,745 sq. mi.
(118,480 sq km)

POPULATION:
11,651,239

MONEY:
Malawian kwacha

LANGUAGES: English (official),
Chichewa (official), many
ethnic languages

PEOPLE PER DOCTOR: 50,000

MALI

CAPITAL: Bamako

AREA:
478,764 sq. mi.
(1,240,000 sq km)

POPULATION: 11,626,219

MONEY: CFAF*

LANGUAGES:
French (official), Bambara,
many ethnic languages

PEOPLE PER DOCTOR: 25,000

UNIT 3 ATLAS

MAURITANIA

CAPITAL: Nouakchott

AREA:
397,953 sq. mi.
(1,030,700 sq km)

POPULATION:
2,912,584

MONEY:
ouguiya

LANGUAGES:
Hassaniya Arabic (official),
Wolof (official), Pulaar,
Soninke, French

PEOPLE PER DOCTOR: 11,085

MAURITIUS

CAPITAL:
Port Louis

AREA:
718 sq. mi.
(1,860 sq km)

POPULATION:
1,210,447

MONEY:
Mauritian rupee

LANGUAGES:
English (official), Creole,
French, Hindi, Urdu, Hakka,
Bhojpuri

PEOPLE PER DOCTOR: 1,182

MOROCCO

CAPITAL:
Rabat

AREA:
172,413 sq. mi.
(446,550 sq km)

POPULATION:
31,689,265

MONEY:
Moroccan dirham

LANGUAGES:
Arabic (official), Berber,
French

PEOPLE PER DOCTOR: 2,923

MOZAMBIQUE

CAPITAL:
Maputo

AREA:
304,494 sq. mi.
(801,590 sq km)

POPULATION:
17,479,266

MONEY:
metical

LANGUAGES:
Portuguese (official), ethnic
languages

PEOPLE PER DOCTOR:
131,991

Sources: Central Intelligence Agency, *The World Factbook 2003; United Nations Development Programme: Health Profile,* pop. figures are 2003 estimates.

NAMIBIA

CAPITAL:
Windhoek

AREA:
318,694 sq. mi.
(825,418 sq km)

POPULATION:
1,927,447

MONEY:
Namibian dollar, South African rand

LANGUAGES:
English (official), Afrikaans, German, Oshivambo, Herero, Nama

PEOPLE PER DOCTOR: 4,594

NIGER

CAPITAL: Niamey

AREA:
489,189 sq. mi.
(1,267,000 sq km)

POPULATION:
11,058,590

MONEY: CFAF*

LANGUAGES:
French (official), Hausa, Djerma

PEOPLE PER DOCTOR:
35,141

NIGERIA

CAPITAL: Abuja

AREA:
356,667 sq. mi.
(923,768 sq km)

POPULATION:
133,881,703

MONEY:
naira

LANGUAGES:
English (official), Hausa, Yoruba, Ibo, Fulani

PEOPLE PER DOCTOR: 4,496

RWANDA

CAPITAL:
Kigali

AREA:
10,169 sq. mi.
(26,338 sq km)

POPULATION:
7,810,056

MONEY:
Rwandan franc

LANGUAGES:
Kinyarwanda (official), French (official), English (official), Kiswahili

PEOPLE PER DOCTOR: 50,000

SÃO TOMÉ AND PRÍNCIPE

CAPITAL: São Tomé

AREA:
386 sq. mi. (1,001 sq km)

POPULATION:
175,883

MONEY:
dobra

LANGUAGES:
Portuguese (official)

PEOPLE PER DOCTOR: 3,125

SENEGAL

CAPITAL: Dakar

AREA:
75,749 sq. mi.
(196,190 sq km)

POPULATION: 10,580,307

MONEY: CFAF*

LANGUAGES:
French (official), Wolof, Pulaar, Diola, Mandinka

PEOPLE PER DOCTOR: 14,285

SEYCHELLES

CAPITAL:
Victoria

AREA:
176 sq. mi. (455 sq km)

POPULATION: 80,469

MONEY:
Seychelles rupee

LANGUAGES: English (official), French (official), Creole

PEOPLE PER DOCTOR: 906

SIERRA LEONE

CAPITAL: Freetown

AREA:
27,699 sq. mi. (71,740 sq km)

POPULATION: 5,732,681

MONEY: leone

LANGUAGES:
English (official), Mende, Temne, Krio

PEOPLE PER DOCTOR: 10,832

SOMALIA

CAPITAL:
Mogadishu

AREA:
246,199 sq. mi.
(637,657 sq km)

POPULATION:
8,025,190

MONEY:
Somali shilling

LANGUAGES:
Somali (official), Arabic, Italian, English

PEOPLE PER DOCTOR:
data not available

SOUTH AFRICA

CAPITALS: Pretoria, Cape Town, Bloemfontein

AREA:
471,008 sq. mi.
(1,219,912 sq km)

POPULATION: 42,768,678

MONEY: rand

LANGUAGES: 11 official languages, including Afrikaans, English, Ndebele, Pedi, Sotho, Swazi, Tsonga, Tswana, Venda, Xhosa, Zulu

PEOPLE PER DOCTOR: 1,742

*Communaute Financiere Africaine franc

Countries not drawn to scale.

SUDAN

CAPITAL: Khartoum

AREA:
967,493 sq. mi.
(2,505,810 sq km)

POPULATION:
38,114,160

MONEY:
Sudanese dinar

LANGUAGES: Arabic (official), Nubian, Ta Bedawie, English, many ethnic languages

PEOPLE PER DOCTOR: 11,300

SWAZILAND

CAPITAL: Mbabane

AREA:
6,704 sq. mi. (17,363 sq km)

POPULATION:
1,161,219

MONEY: lilangeni

LANGUAGES:
English (official), siSwati

PEOPLE PER DOCTOR:
data not available

TANZANIA

CAPITALS:
Dar es Salaam and Dodoma

AREA:
364,898 sq. mi.
(945,087 sq km)

POPULATION:
35,922,454

MONEY:
Tanzanian shilling

LANGUAGES:
Kiswahili (official), English (official), Arabic, many ethnic languages

PEOPLE PER DOCTOR: 20,511

TOGO

CAPITAL: Lomé

AREA:
21,925 sq. mi.
(56,785 sq km)

POPULATION: 5,429,299

MONEY: CFAF*

LANGUAGES:
French (official), Ewe, Mina, Kabye, Dagomba

PEOPLE PER DOCTOR: 16,667

TUNISIA

CAPITAL:
Tunis

AREA:
63,170 sq. mi.
(163,610 sq km)

POPULATION: 9,924,742

MONEY:
Tunisian dinar

LANGUAGES:
Arabic (official), French

PEOPLE PER DOCTOR:
1,640

UGANDA

CAPITAL:
Kampala

AREA:
91,135 sq. mi.
(236,040 sq km)

POPULATION:
25,632,794

MONEY:
Ugandan shilling

LANGUAGES:
English (official), Luganda, Swahili, Arabic

PEOPLE PER DOCTOR:
25,000

ZAMBIA

CAPITAL:
Lusaka

AREA:
290,584 sq. mi.
(752,614 sq km)

POPULATION:
10,307,333

MONEY:
Zambian kwacha

LANGUAGES:
English (official), Bemba, Kaonda, Lozi, Lunda, Luvale, many ethnic languages

PEOPLE PER DOCTOR: 10,917

ZIMBABWE

CAPITAL:
Harare

AREA:
150,803 sq. mi.
(390,580 sq km)

POPULATION: 12,576,742

MONEY:
Zimbabwean dollar

LANGUAGES:
English (official), Shona, Sindebele

PEOPLE PER DOCTOR: 6,909

internet connect

COUNTRY STATISTICS
GO TO: go.hrw.com
KEYWORD: SK5 FACTSU3
FOR: more facts about Africa

Sources: Central Intelligence Agency, *The World Factbook 2003;* United Nations Development *Programme: Health Profile;* pop. figures are 2003 estimates.

CHAPTER 8

Africa's History

Chapter Resource Manager

Objectives	Pacing Guide	Reproducible Resources
SECTION 1		
Ancient Egypt 1. Explain why the Nile was an important river to the Egyptians. 2. Identify some of the achievements of the Egyptians. 3. Analyze the basis of Egyptian religion. 4. Explore the great kingdoms developed along the Nile south of Egypt.	**Regular** 3 days Lecture Notes, Section 1 **Block Scheduling** 1.5 days *Block Scheduling Handbook, Chapter 8*	**RS** Know it Notes S1 **RS** Graphic Organizer 8 **SM** Critical Thinking Activity 22 **SM** Map Activity 22 **ELL** Main Idea Activity S1
SECTION 2		
Early Sub-Saharan Africa 1. Explain how historians study cultures that left no written records. 2. Clarify how trade affected the growth of kingdoms in Sub-Saharan Africa.	**Regular** .5 day Lecture Notes, Section 2 **Block Scheduling** .5 day *Block Scheduling Handbook, Chapter 8*	**RS** Know It Notes S2 **E** Readings in World Geography, History, and Culture: Readings 57, 66 **ELL** Main Idea Activity S2
SECTION 3		
Imperialism in Africa 1. Analyze the effects that imperialism had on Africa. 2. Explain why European nations wanted colonies in Africa.	**Regular** 1 day Lecture Notes, Section 3 **Block Scheduling** .5 day *Block Scheduling Handbook, Chapter 8*	**RS** Know It Notes S3 **E** Readings in World Geography, History, and Culture: Reading 60 **E** Biography Activity: Menelik II **ELL** Main Idea Activity S3
SECTION 4		
Nationalist Movements in Africa 1. Show how World War I increased feelings of nationalism in Africa. 2. Explain what made South Africa different from the rest of Africa. 3. Analyze some results of independence for African countries.	**Regular** 1 day Lecture Notes, Section 4 **Block Scheduling** .5 day *Block Scheduling Handbook, Chapter 8*	**RS** Know It Notes S4 **E** Biography Activities: Naguib Mahfouz, Kofi Annan **ELL** Main Idea Activity S4

Chapter Resource Key

RS Reading Support

IC Interdisciplinary Connections

E Enrichment

SM Skills Mastery

A Assessment

REV Review

ELL Reinforcement and English Language Learners and English for Speakers of Other Languages (ESOL)

 Transparencies

 CD–ROM

 Music

 Video

 go. hrw .com Internet

 Holt Presentation Maker Using Microsoft® PowerPoint®

 One-Stop Planner CD–ROM

See the *One-Stop Planner* for a complete list of additional resources for students and teachers.

One-Stop Planner CD–ROM

It's easy to plan lessons, select resources, and print out materials for your students when you use the *One-Stop Planner CD–ROM with Test Generator.*

Technology Resources	Review, Reinforcement, and Assessment Resources	
One-Stop Planner CD-ROM, Lesson 8.1 Geography and Cultures Visual Resources 81 *ARGWorld* CD–ROM Homework Practice Online HRW Go site	ELL	Main Idea Activity S1
	REV	Section 1 Review
	A	Daily Quiz 8.1
	REV	Chapter Summaries and Review
	ELL	English Audio Summary 8.1
	ELL	Spanish Audio Summary 8.1
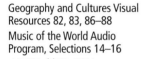 One-Stop Planner CD-ROM, Lesson 8.2 Geography and Cultures Visual Resources 82, 83, 86–88 Music of the World Audio Program, Selections 14–16 *ARGWorld* CD–ROM Homework Practice Online HRW Go site	ELL	Main Idea Activity S2
	REV	Section 2 Review
	A	Daily Quiz 8.2
	REV	Chapter Summaries and Review
	ELL	English Audio Summary 8.2
	ELL	Spanish Audio Summary 8.2
One-Stop Planner CD-ROM, Lesson 8.3 Geography and Cultures Visual Resources 81, 82, 86–88 *ARGWorld* CD–ROM Homework Practice Online HRW Go site	ELL	Main Idea Activity S3
	REV	Section 3 Review
	A	Daily Quiz 8.3
	REV	Chapter Summaries and Review
	ELL	English Audio Summary 8.3
	ELL	Spanish Audio Summary 8.3
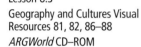 One-Stop Planner CD-ROM, Lesson 8.4 Geography and Cultures Visual Resources 81, 82, 86–88 *ARGWorld* CD–ROM Homework Practice Online HRW Go site	ELL	Main Idea Activity S4
	REV	Section 4 Review
	A	Daily Quiz 8.4
	REV	Chapter Summaries and Review
	ELL	English Audio Summary 8.4
	ELL	Spanish Audio Summary 8.4

Meeting Individual Needs

Ability Levels

Level 1 Basic-level activities designed for all students encountering new material

Level 2 Intermediate-level activities designed for average students

Level 3 Challenging activities designed for honors and gifted-and-talented students

ESOL Activities that address the needs of students with Limited English Proficiency

internet connect

HRW ONLINE RESOURCES

GO TO: go.hrw.com
Then type in a keyword.

TEACHER HOMEPAGE
KEYWORD: SK5 TEACHER

CHAPTER INTERNET ACTIVITIES
KEYWORD: SK5 GT8

Choose an activity to:
- learn more about ancient Egypt.
- write a report about the trading states of Sub-Saharan Africa.
- write a biography of a figure in Africa's history.

CHAPTER ENRICHMENT LINKS
KEYWORD: SK5 CH8

CHAPTER MAPS
KEYWORDS: SK5 MAPS8

ONLINE ASSESSMENT
Homework Practice
KEYWORD: SK5 HP8
Standardized Test Prep Online
KEYWORD: SK5 STP8
Rubrics
KEYWORD: SS Rubrics

COUNTRY INFORMATION
KEYWORD: SK5 Almanac

CONTENT UPDATES
KEYWORD: SS Contents Updates

HOLT PRESENTATION MAKER
KEYWORD: SK5 PPT8

ONLINE READING SUPPORT
KEYWORD: SS Strategies

CURRENT EVENTS
KEYWORD: SS Current Events

Chapter Review and Assessment

E	Readings in World Geography, History, and Culture 57, 60, 66
SM	Critical Thinking Activity 8
REV	Chapter 8 Review and Practice
REV	Chapter Summaries and Review
ELL	Vocabulary Activity 8
A	Chapter 8 Test
A	Chapter 8 Test Generator (on the One-Stop Planner)
	Audio CD program, Chapter 8
A	Chapter 8 Test for English Language Learners and Special Needs Students
	HRW Go site

175B

Africa's History
Previewing Chapter Resources

Holt Online Learning

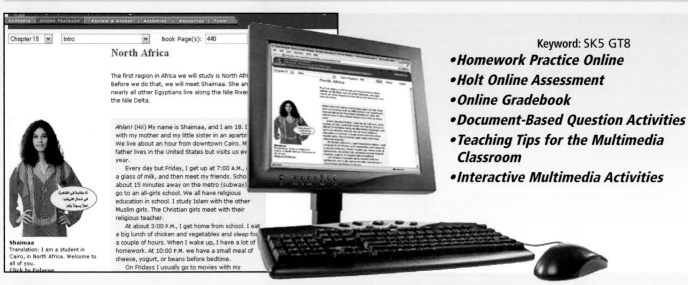

Keyword: SK5 GT8

- *Homework Practice Online*
- *Holt Online Assessment*
- *Online Gradebook*
- *Document-Based Question Activities*
- *Teaching Tips for the Multimedia Classroom*
- *Interactive Multimedia Activities*

Differentiating Instruction

Reading and Writing Support
◀ Graphic Organizer Activity
- *Vocabulary Activity*
- *Chapter Summary and Review*
- *Know-It Notes S1–4*
- *Audio CD*

Active Learning
- *Block Scheduling Handbook*
- *Cultures of the World Activity*
- *Interdisciplinary Activity*
- *Map Activity*
◀ Critical Thinking Activity: The Geometry of Ancient Egypt's Pyramids

Primary Sources and Advanced Learners
◀ Map Activity: Ancient North Africa
- *Readings in World Geography, History and Culture:*
  - *57 Leo Africanus: Description of Timbuktu (1526)*
  - *60 The Kikuyu Meet Europeans*
  - *66 The Moors of Mozambique*

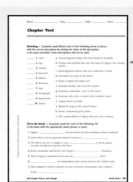

Assessment Program
- *Daily Quizzes S1–4*
◀ Chapter Test
- *Chapter Test for English Language Learners and Special-Needs Students*

Spanish and ESOL
- *Vocabulary Activity*
- *Main Idea Activities for English Language Learners and Special-Needs Students*
- *Chapter Summary and Review*
- *Spanish Audio Summary*
◀ Know-It Notes S1–4
- *Chapter Test for English Language Learners and Special-Needs Students*

Special Education Modifications
Your **I.D.E.A. Works! CD-ROM** will provide modified versions of the following teaching materials:
- *Guided Reading Strategies S1–4*
- *Vocabulary Activity*
- *Main Idea Activities S1–4*
◀ Daily Quizzes S1–4
- *Chapter 8 Test*
- *Flash cards of chapter vocabulary terms*

Teacher Resources

Books for Teachers

Baines, John, and Jaromir Malek. *Cultural Atlas of Ancient Egypt.* Checkmark Books, 2000.

Iliffe, John. *Africans: The History of a Continent.* Cambridge University Press, 1995.

Fyle, C. Magbaily. *Introduction to the History of African Civilization: Colonial and Post-Colonial Africa.* Rowman & Littlefield, 2001.

Mandela, Nelson. *Long Walk to Freedom.* Back Bay Books, 1995.

Books for Students

Broida, Marian, and Gary Beckman. *Ancient Egyptians and Their Neighbors: An Activity Guide.* Chicago Review Press, 1999. Includes writing and math activities and instructions for making pyramids, costumes, jewelry, and recipes.

McGraw, Eloise. *Mara, Daughter of the Nile.* Puffin, 1999. Adventures of an Egyptian slave girl who acts as a spy in the royal palace of Thebes during Queen Hatshepsut's reign. Fiction.

Washington, Donna L. *A Pride of African Tales.* Amistad Press, 2003. Illustrated collection of African folktales from different regions of Africa.

Mathabane, Mark. *Kaffir Boy: The True Story of a Black Youth's Coming of Age in Apartheid South Africa.* Free Press, 1998.

Multimedia Materials

Mummies and The Wonders of Ancient Egypt. Video, A & E Entertainment.

Africa: The Story of a Continent. Video, Home Vision Entertainment.

Mandela and de Klerk. Video, Hallmark Home Entertainment.

Videos and CDs

Videos

- **CNN** *Presents World Cultures: Yesterday and Today, Segment 2 Restoring the Sphinx*
- *ARG World*

Holt Researcher

http://researcher.hrw.com

- *African Caravan Routes*
- *African Trade*
- *Two Views of Africa*
- *Africa in 1750*
- *Colonialism in Africa*
- *Cities of Africa*
- *Growth of the Byzantine Empire*
- *Africa*

Transparency Packages

Geography and Cultures Visual Resources Transparencies
76 Africa: Physical
83 Terracotta Portrait Head

Map Activities Transparency Ancient North Africa

Here are some reasons why students should find the history of Africa interesting:

▶ The monuments and artworks created by the Egyptians and their neighbors thousands of years ago continue to fascinate us.

▶ The great trading kingdoms of Sub-Saharan Africa are not well known in the West, but their accomplishments are impressive.

▶ Events of the colonial era continue to affect present-day politics in Africa.

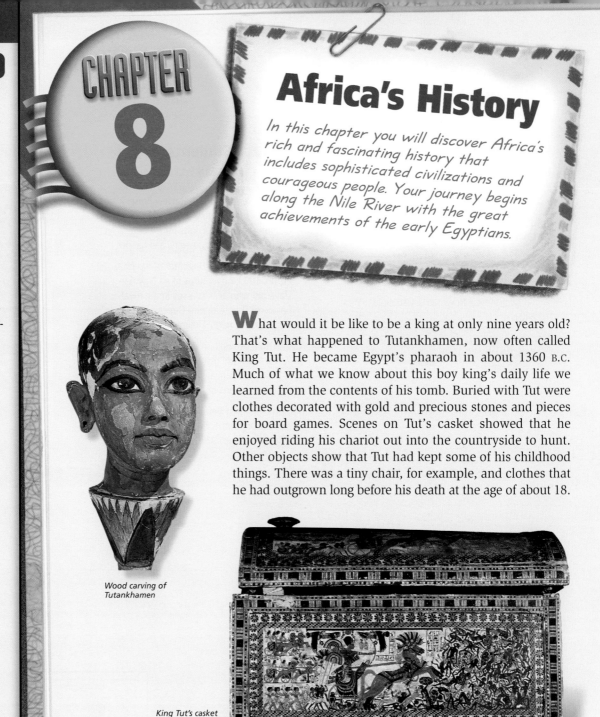

CHAPTER 8

Africa's History

In this chapter you will discover Africa's rich and fascinating history that includes sophisticated civilizations and courageous people. Your journey begins along the Nile River with the great achievements of the early Egyptians.

What would it be like to be a king at only nine years old? That's what happened to Tutankhamen, now often called King Tut. He became Egypt's pharaoh in about 1360 B.C. Much of what we know about this boy king's daily life we learned from the contents of his tomb. Buried with Tut were clothes decorated with gold and precious stones and pieces for board games. Scenes on Tut's casket showed that he enjoyed riding his chariot out into the countryside to hunt. Other objects show that Tut had kept some of his childhood things. There was a tiny chair, for example, and clothes that he had outgrown long before his death at the age of about 18.

Wood carving of Tutankhamen

King Tut's casket

CHAPTER PROJECT

Have students create models of ancient monuments of Africa—either as the ruins appear now, or as the structures were originally built. Possibilities include Egyptian pyramids, the Great Sphinx, the pyramids of Meroë, and Great Zimbabwe, among others. Students should attach information about the monument—when it was built and by whom, construction methods, religious significance, and so on. Photograph models and place the photos in student portfolios, along with the textual information.

STARTING THE CHAPTER

Call on a volunteer to read aloud the story about Tutankhamen on this page. Point out that Tut had been king of Egypt for several years already when he was the students' age. What would that have been like? As king, Tutankhamen would have eaten the finest food, worn the nicest clothes, and had practically every wish fulfilled. Yet, the small items found in his grave may indicate that he missed his childhood. In addition, Tut's death is still a mystery. Some evidence indicates that he was murdered while still a teen. Ask students to comment on the saying "It's good to be king" in light of Tut's story. Tell students they will learn more about the Egyptians and many other Africans in this chapter.

Section 1 Ancient Egypt

Get Ready to Read

1. Why was the Nile an important river to the Egyptians?

2. What were some of the achievements of the Egyptians?

3. What was Egyptian religion based on?

4. What great kingdoms developed along the Nile south of Egypt?

Vocabulary
dynasty
pharaohs
pyramids
sphinxes
hieroglyphics
papyrus
Rosetta Stone
mummification

Places
Nile River
Red Sea
Giza
Kush
Aksum

People
Ramses II
Imhotep
Hatshepsut
King 'Ezana

Reading Strategy

FOLDNOTES: PYRAMID Create a **Pyramid** FoldNote as described in the Appendix. As you read, write what you learn about Egyptians on one triangle, Kush on another triangle, and Aksum on the third triangle.

The Nile Valley

Early Egyptians lived along the Nile River. At about 4,160 miles (6,693 km) long, the Nile is the world's longest river. As the Nile flooded each spring, the waters spread fine soil over the river's banks. This process supported plentiful crops of wheat and barley. It also created a very fertile area that cut right through the Sahara, the world's largest desert. Without the Nile and its annual flood, Egypt would not exist. As a result, Egypt is often called the Gift of the Nile.

The Nile Valley offered other advantages also. The river flows south to north, which made it possible for early residents to sail to the Mediterranean Sea. East and west of the Nile, deserts and the Red Sea provided early civilizations natural protection from invaders. The Isthmus of Suez, a land bridge between Africa and Asia, allowed trade between early Egyptians and their neighbors.

Government and Society Over hundreds of years, the rich Nile River valley supported the development of two kingdoms with distinct cultures. Around 3100 B.C., King Menes united them and founded a **dynasty**, a family line of rulers that passes power from one generation to the next. In later years, these rulers were called **pharaohs**. The pharaohs controlled the government completely. They also served as judges, high priests, and generals of the armies.

The Kingdom of Egypt around 1450 B.C.

▲

Interpreting the Map **Into which body of water does the Nile River flow?**

Section 1 Resources

Reproducibles
◆ Lecture Notes, Section 1
◆ Block Scheduling Handbook, Chapter 8
◆ Know It Notes S1
◆ Map Activity 22
◆ Critical Thinking Activity 22

Technology
◆ One-Stop Planner CD-ROM, Lesson 8.1
◆ Geography and Cultures Visual Resources 81
◆ Homework Practice Online
◆ HRW Go Site

Review, Reinforcement, and Assessment Resources
◆ Section 1 Review
◆ Daily Quiz 8.1
◆ Main Idea Activity S1
◆ Chapter Summaries and Review
◆ English Audio Summary 8.1
◆ Spanish Audio Summary 8.1

◀ **Map Answer**

Mediterranean Sea

Africa's History • 177

Section 1

1. Explain why the Nile was an important river to the Egyptians.

2. Identify some of the achievements of the Egyptians.

3. Analyze the basis of Egyptian religion.

4. Explore the great kingdoms developed along the Nile south of Egypt.

Focus

Bellringer

Copy the following question onto the chalkboard: *What are some things you associate with ancient Egypt?* (Possible answers: pyramids, the Sphinx, pharaohs, Cleopatra, mummies, and so on) Point out that ancient Egypt was one of the world's first civilizations and one of the greatest of all time. Students will learn more about the Egyptians in Section 1.

Building Vocabulary

Write the vocabulary terms on the chalkboard. Call on volunteers to locate and read their definitions. Point out that **dynasty** is derived from a Greek word meaning "lordship" or "rule." **Pharaohs** comes from an Egyptian word for "great house." **Hieroglyphics** comes from two Greek words—*hiero* means "sacred," and *glyphein* means "to carve." Ask students how these roots are reflected in the meanings of each word.

GLOBAL PERSPECTIVES

Ramses II in the Middle East During the early part of his reign, Ramses fought to regain territory in Africa and the Middle East that Egypt had held earlier. His main enemies were the Hittites, a powerful people of Asia Minor. Ramses waged a long war against the Hittites. The major battle was fought in 1274 at Kadesh, in what is now northern Syria. Ramses hailed it as a great triumph. In 1258 B.C. a treaty declared that the contested land would be divided. In addition, Ramses agreed to marry the daughter of the Hittite king.

Activity: Have students locate Kadesh on a historical atlas. Point out the distance that the Egyptians had to travel to fight the battle.

Egyptian society was divided into two classes. Priests, scribes, and government officials formed the upper class. Peasants and farmers formed the lower class. Some also had to serve in the military. During the months that their fields were flooded, the farmers worked on building projects such as canals or the pyramids. You will read more about these projects on the following pages.

During the time of the pharaohs, Egypt's contact with other lands grew through conquest and trade. By about 1085 B.C., Egypt had expanded into what are now Syria, Israel, and Libya. The Egyptians traded with peoples throughout Southwest Asia and North Africa.

Egypt's Later History In the 1200s B.C., Ramses II, also known as Ramses the Great, ruled Egypt. Ramses was considered great for his military leadership and the massive monuments he had built during his reign. Ramses the Great was Egypt's last strong leader. After his rule, attacks from foreign peoples, including the Phoenicians, the Persians, and the Greeks, weakened Egypt. By the 500s B.C., Greeks, Romans and eastern Mediterranean peoples settled in the region. As a result, Egypt was no longer ruled by Egyptians.

✓ **READING CHECK:** (*Main Idea*) What role did the Nile play in the creation of early Egyptian civilization? Annual floods produced fine soil that supported plentiful crops.

Along the west bank of the Nile at Giza, Egyptians built enormous pyramids to honor their kings. Each of the millions of limestone blocks that make up the pyramids weighs an average of 2.5 tons.

178 Chapter 8

TEACH

Teaching Objective 1

ALL LEVELS: (Suggested time: 10 min.) Point out that among the features a civilization needs to thrive are reliable supplies of food and water, ways to defend itself, and transportation methods. Ask students how Egypt's geography supplied all four of these. (The Nile's annual flood spread soil over farmers' fields and irrigated them at the same time, making raising food relatively easy. The river itself supplied water. Since it flows south to north, but winds blow north to south, the Nile makes transportation easy. The deserts east and west of the Nile provided natural protection from enemies.) Then lead a discussion on Egypt's government and history.

LEVEL 1: (Suggested time: 10 min.) Copy the following graphic organizer onto the chalkboard, omitting the blue answers. Have students work in pairs to fill in the organizer with a description of the class structure of ancient Egypt. Tell each pair of students to fill in each section by identifying the people who belonged to each class. Call on volunteers to share their organizers with the class. **ESOL, COOPERATIVE LEARNING**

Egyptian Achievements

In addition to their architectural achievements, Egyptians developed a writing system that used pictures and symbols we call **hieroglyphics**. More than 600 signs, pictures, and symbols represented different words and sounds. The Egyptians wrote on stone or a paperlike material called **papyrus** made from the inner stalk of the reedlike papyrus plant. Egyptian officials recorded many important events and details about daily life on papyrus.

Scholars can read Egyptian hieroglyphics today because of a discovery in 1799. A French soldier found a large stone in the Egyptian village of Rosetta. Known as the **Rosetta Stone**, this stone had writings carved in Greek, hieroglyphics, and an Egyptian writing style called demotic. When scholars realized that the three passages were of the same text, they used the Greek text to translate the hieroglyphics. Now scholars can read and understand other hieroglyphic texts.

Egyptians also developed an accurate 365-day calendar similar to the one we use today. This calendar had 12 months of 30 days each. The remaining five days were holidays. To keep track of years, they counted the years of a pharaoh's reign. For example, they might refer to the first, second, or tenth years of the reign of a certain pharaoh. Egyptians also used a number system based on 10, and they understood both fractions and geometry.

Pyramids Built as tombs for the pharaohs over 4,000 years ago, the Egyptian **pyramids** are still some of the most magnificent structures in the world. Most of these huge stone monuments were built along the west bank of the Nile. The most famous Egyptian pyramids are located at Giza, near Cairo. Built around 2600 B.C., the Great Pyramid was the tomb of the pharaoh Khufu. See the Connecting to Technology feature in the next chapter for more information on how pyramids were built.

One of the most talented pyramid architects was Imhotep. He designed the famous step pyramid of King Djoser, an early Egyptian ruler. Imhotep was not only a brilliant architect but also a great healer and writer.

Egyptian Hieroglyphics

Hieroglyph	English Meaning	Hieroglyph	English Meaning
	heart		rain
	to cry		to make an offer
	to fly		to sail upstream
	tree		to go

▲

The Egyptians developed one of the world's first writing systems. Hieroglyphic writing used pictures, or hieroglyphs, to represent objects and sounds.

ENVIRONMENT AND SOCIETY

Sailing the Nile Living along the Nile, the Egyptians were among the earliest developers of river transportation. An image on a pot from about 3200 B.C. shows that Egyptians were already using sails to travel on the Nile. Early boats floated downriver. Then their captains could raise a sail and be carried back upstream by the wind, which blows most often from the north. Rafts and barges carried goods up and down the Nile. Ferries traveled across the river and along the canals.

Critical Thinking: How may the geography of the Nile Valley and the development of water transportation have contributed to the rise of a unified government in Egypt?

Answer: The use of boats for transportation would have enabled a leader to impose authority on places along the river. This would probably have helped a leader dominate the entire population of Egypt.

Hatshepsut (ruled c. 1490–1468 B.C.)

One of Egypt's most remarkable pharaohs was a woman. Hatshepsut reigned during a time of peace and prosperity. She is perhaps best known for increasing Egyptian trade. Among the items she received from faraway lands were gold, precious woods, baboons, and living trees. In addition, Hatshepsut sponsored great building projects, several of which still stand. *What did Hatshepsut accomplish as pharoah?*

BIOGRAPHY

◀**Biography Answer**

increased trade, sponsored great building projects

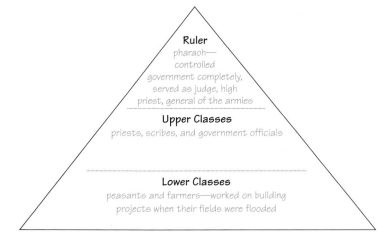

Ruler
pharaoh—controlled government completely, served as judge, high priest, general of the armies

Upper Classes
priests, scribes, and government officials

Lower Classes
peasants and farmers—worked on building projects when their fields were flooded

LEVEL 2: (Suggested time: 45 min.) Have students create time lines of Egyptian history on butcher paper. Provide research materials for more information about Ramses the Great—in particular about Abu Simbel, a huge monument that bears four images of Ramses. Have students retain their time lines and illustrate them as they learn more about ancient Egypt. **ESOL,** LS **VISUAL-SPATIAL**

Teaching Objective 2

LEVEL 1: (Suggested time: 15 min.) Have students work in pairs to create diagrams or charts detailing Egyptian achievements related to writing, paper, the calendar, pyramids, sphinxes, and temples. **COOPERATIVE LEARNING,** LS **VISUAL-SPATIAL**

Linking Past to Present

The Great Sphinx Theories swirl about the Great Sphinx like the desert sands in a gale-force wind. Several of the stories and theories originated with the Greeks, who were fascinated with Egyptian culture. One modern proposal claims that erosion marks in the limestone from which the statue was carved prove that it is much older than most historians say.

One thing that is certain is that soldiers have used the Sphinx for target practice. In the process, they knocked chunks from the nose and beard. Some say Turks did the damage, while others blame Napoléon's troops.

Activity: Ask students to find myths and stories surrounding the Great Sphinx and share them with the rest of the class.

History Close-Up Answer ▶

Some students may say that it is gloomy because so much of Egyptian religion was connected to the afterlife. Others may say that the color and liveliness of the paintings show that the Egyptians loved life so much that they wanted to live forever.

The Great Sphinx The Egyptians are also known for building sculptures called **sphinxes**. A sphinx is a monster that has a lion's body and a human head. The most famous Egyptian sphinx is the Great Sphinx, which stands near the pyramids at Giza. Carved from a solid block of bedrock in the 2500s B.C., the head of the Great Sphinx is probably a likeness of the pharaoh Khafre. His tomb lies in one of Giza's pyramids. The sphinx's body stretches about 170 feet long and stands 66 feet tall.

Temples Sphinxes also stood guard in front of temples. Egyptians built enormous temples to their gods. The interior of Egyptian temples housed large statues representing different gods. However, only the king and some priests were allowed inside the temples. Common people had to pray outside.

To honor the gods, priests cared for the temple's statues with offerings of food twice a day. The priests also dressed the statues in linen clothing and fine jewelry. At the main temple in Karnak, the public could only see the temple's statues during a festival held each year. At this time, priests escorted the statues of three gods down the Nile to the temple at Luxor. During the elaborate parade, people sang hymns and danced in celebration of the gods.

✓ **READING CHECK:** (*Summarizing*) What were some achievements of the early Egyptians?
writing system, pyramids, sphinxes, and temples

History Close-Up

Karnak's Great Temple Sunlight reveals the brilliantly painted inner hall of Karnak's Great Temple in this illustrated re-creation. The temple's massive columns tower about 70 feet above a parade of priests and royal attendants leaving the temple during an annual festival. Royal attendants carry the sacred statues of the temple's gods in a miniature golden ship. The images and hieroglyphics on the walls and columns celebrate the lives of two kings—Ramses II and his father Seti I. **Does Karnak's Great Temple appear gloomy or cheerful? How might the temple's appearance reflect the Egyptians belief in life after death? Defend your answer.**

LEVEL 2: (Suggested time: 20 min.) Review the achievements of ancient Egypt. Then have each student write a paragraph or brief essay to answer this question: *If you had lived in ancient Egypt, in which achievement would you have liked to take part?* Students should provide reasons for their choices. **LS INTRAPERSONAL**

LEVEL 3: (Suggested time: 30 min.) Point out to students that some of the symbols used in Egyptian hieroglyphics resembled the objects they represented. For example, the symbol for *eat* might show a person with a hand held to his mouth. Challenge students to create hieroglyphic characters for some common English words. Then have each student write a story or paragraph about Egypt using these characters in place of the words they represent. Have students exchange papers and attempt to decipher the hieroglyphics they have received. Then lead a discussion about Egyptian hieroglyphics and the attempts by archaeologists to decipher them. **LS VERBAL-LINGUISTIC**

USING ILLUSTRATIONS

Karnak's Great Temple
Challenge students to decipher some of the scenes depicted on the temple's walls and columns. (Possibilities include the pharaohs taking part in ceremonies, pharaohs interacting with gods, a woman fixing someone's hair, and so on.) Point out the Egyptians' clothing. In what ways was it appropriate for Egypt's climate? (The clothing appears to be loose, comfortable, and made out of white cotton or linen. It would have been very appropriate for the hot climate.) Encourage students to find other details in the illustration.

Africa's History • 181

ALL LEVELS: Have students create murals that depict the many accomplishments of ancient Egyptian civilization. Challenge students to base the style of their murals on the paintings shown on the walls of Karnak's Great Temple. Point out that Egyptian art conforms to rules. For example, people are always shown in profile, but their eyes are shown as from the front. Also, the artwork lies in clear rows, or registers, that tell a story or connect to a theme. You may want to provide additional examples of Egyptian tomb or temple paintings for guidance. **LS** **VISUAL-SPATIAL**

Teaching Objective 3

ALL LEVELS: Review the basics of Egyptian religion with the class. Then, provide art and craft materials. Invite students to create their own mummies. Students could use strips of fabric or newspaper dipped into glue to wrap a doll. When the "mummy" is dry, have students paint a mask on the top of the face. **ESOL, LS KINESTHETIC**

Mummies around the World The Egyptians weren't the only people whose mummies archaeologists have found. Mummies have been unearthed in places as different as China, northern Europe, and the Peruvian Andes. Some mummies formed accidentally, through the actions of ice, dry air, or being submerged in oxygen-poor water. Other mummies, including the Egyptians, were preserved intentionally.

Activity: Have students work in groups to conduct research on mummies from Peru, China, Denmark, or other locations and present illustrated reports to the class.

No royal tomb in ancient Egypt was without a copy of the *Book of the Dead.* Egyptians believed the book was a necessary guide to the afterlife.

Interpreting the Visual Record What does this page of the book show?

Visual Record Answer ▶

Osiris weighing a person's heart against a feather

Egyptian Religion

Egyptian religion was based on the belief in an afterlife. Egyptians believed Osiris, the god of the underworld, met them in death. Death to them was simply the beginning of a new life in the next world. There were several obstacles, however, to eternal life.

The Egyptians believed their life force, or *ka,* left the body at death. A person's soul, or *ba,* did not leave the body until after burial. Then the *ba* had to pass through doorways of fire and cobras to get to the hall of judgment. There, the person's heart was weighed on a scale against a feather. The god Osiris then determined whether the person's heart was too heavy. If the heart wasn't balanced, a monster that was part lion, part hippopotamus, and part crocodile would eat the heart. On the other hand, if the person's heart was balanced, he or she earned an afterlife filled with all the pleasures they enjoyed in life.

Because the Egyptians believed the body was needed in an afterlife, they preserved their dead rulers through a process called **mummification**. To mummify a body, the Egyptians first removed the internal organs. The heart, however, was left in place. They then covered the body with substances to dry it out. The body was then rubbed with ointment and wrapped in linen. They placed a mask over the head and shoulders and placed the mummy in a coffin. Sometimes, this coffin was placed inside two other coffins. The mummy's internal organs were dried and placed inside four different jars.

In addition to the mummy, the tomb also housed many items that the person might need on the afterlife journey, including clothes, food, jewelry, tools, and weapons. Scenes of the dead ruler making offerings to the gods decorated the tomb's walls. To protect the body, sculpted or painted figures of servants also lined the walls. To help guide a person into the afterlife, a copy of the *Book of the Dead* was placed in the tomb. Written on rolls of papyrus, the book included maps and magic spells that provided protection for the person's soul.

✓ **READING CHECK:**

Finding the Main Idea Why did Egyptians mummify their dead rulers? They believed the body was needed in an afterlife.

LEVEL 2: Organize the class into groups and provide groups with extra research materials. Ask each group to conduct research on a particular Egyptian god. Students should find pictures of how the Egyptians portrayed the god, what role the god had in mythology, and any particular myths about the god. Some of the gods are Osiris, Isis, Amun, Thoth, Ptah, Anubis, Maat, Hathor, Re, Seth, and Bastet. Have students present illustrated oral reports to the class. **COOPERATIVE LEARNING**

▶**ASSIGNMENT:** Have students write diary entries as if they were observers or participants in the mummification of a great pharaoh. Entries should include reflections on the basics of Egyptian religion.

Kush and Aksum

Two great ancient kingdoms developed along the Nile River south of Egypt. The first was Kush. It was eventually conquered by Aksum, its neighbor to the southeast.

Kush Kush was probably founded around 2000 B.C. By about 1500 B.C., however, it was conquered by Egypt. Egypt ruled Kush for many years. The two countries were never completely unified, however, and Kush remained largely free from Egyptian control. In the 700s B.C., Kush invaded and conquered Egypt. The kings of Kush ruled Egypt for about 50 years. In the 600s B.C., invasions by groups from Southwest Asia weakened the kingdom. Kush survived, however, and became a powerful kingdom again.

The people of Kush were mostly traders. They traveled along the Nile to trade goods and ideas with Egypt. Because of this trade, Kush's culture was in many ways similar to Egypt's. Kush also lay along the trade routes between the Red Sea and the Nile. Caravans traveling between these two areas passed through Kush. This allowed the kingdom to become a rich trading center. The Kushites built huge pyramids and temples. They made beautiful pottery and jewelry. They also developed a written form of their language.

Kush and Aksum

Map showing MEDITERRANEAN SEA, EGYPT (Memphis, Thebes), Nile River, NUBIAN DESERT, NUBIA (Karmah, Napata, Meroë), SUDAN, Blue Nile, Atbara R., RED SEA, Arabian Peninsula, Adulis, Aksum, Gulf of Aden, ETHIOPIA, ETHIOPIAN HIGHLANDS

Legend:
- Kush, c. 500 B.C.
- Aksum, c. A.D. 400

Scale: 0 — 300 — 600 Miles / 0 — 300 — 600 Kilometers
Azimuthal Equal-Area Projection

Interpreting the Map On what river would goods from Kush be sent to Egypt?

The Lion Temple was built by the people of Kush.

Interpreting the Visual Record What are some features that this temple shares with Karnak's Great Temple?

Africa's History • 183

Teaching Objective 4

ALL LEVELS: (Suggested time: 15 min.) Copy the following graphic organizer onto the chalkboard, omitting the blue answers. Have students complete it to review the features of Kush and Aksum. Ask students to fill in the central bar with the basic fact that connects the two kingdoms. Then have students work in pairs to create time lines of Kush and Axum.

ESOL, LS VISUAL-SPATIAL

Kush
probably founded around 2000 b.c., conquered and ruled by Egypt, then conquered and ruled Egypt, weakened by invasions but became powerful again, traded along Nile and Red Sea, built pyramids and temples, made pottery and jewelry, developed written language

two great kingdoms south of Egypt

Aksum
in Ethiopean Highlands, traded along Nile and Red Sea, conquered Kush, became Christian under King 'Ezana, declined because of soil exhaustion and competition for trade

Answers to Section 1 Review

Define or identify For definitions and identifications, see the glossary and index.

Reading for the Main Idea

1. floods provided fine soil for farming; transportation, safe area between deserts

2. hieroglyphics, calendar, number system based on 10 and other mathematical principles, pyramids, sphinxes, temples

Critical Thinking

3. so they could enjoy those things in the afterlife **(NGS 10)**

4. similar—both dependant on trade along Nile and Red Sea; different—Kush's culture more similar to Egypt's, Aksum became Christian

Organizing What You Know

5. See the section content for events of 2600 B.C., 2500s B.C., 1085 B.C., 1500 B.C., 1200s B.C., 700s B.C., 600s B.C., 500s B.C., A.D. 100s, A.D. 350, A.D. 300s, and the A.D. 500s.

Visual Record Answer ▶

a door

▲

The people of Aksum carved massive stelae like this one from solid blocks of stone. These monuments were erected on a royal burial ground and are thought to represent buildings as high as 13 stories.

Interpreting the Visual Record What is represented at the bottom of this stela?

Aksum Aksum lay in a hilly area called the Ethiopian Highlands. Like Kush, Aksum controlled trade routes between the Red Sea and the Nile. In addition, Aksum lay on trade routes between the Red Sea and central Africa. By the A.D. 100s, Aksum had grown into a major trading kingdom. Two hundred years later, it had also become a strong military power. In about A.D. 350, Aksum conquered Kush.

At the time of its conquest of Kush, Aksum was ruled by King 'Ezana. He was a strong leader who led other rulers in the area. While he was king, 'Ezana became a Christian. He made Christianity the official religion of Aksum. The form of Christianity that 'Ezana followed included some local traditions, customs, and beliefs. This practice made it popular with other people throughout the region. Christianity slowly became a powerful influence in East Africa.

From the A.D. 300s to the 600s, Aksum continued to grow rich from trade. By this time, it controlled nearly all the trade on the western shore of the Red Sea. In the late A.D. 500s, however, Aksum began to decline for several reasons. One reason may have been soil exhaustion. Farmers had been growing crops in this region for hundreds of years. Over time, it probably became more difficult for farmers to produce enough food to support the population.

Increased competition for trade also hurt Aksum. By the 700s, the Persian Empire had taken over much of the trade along the Red Sea. Muslim traders from the north also took business away from Aksum. Faced with these new trading empires, Aksum slowly lost most of its economic and political power.

✔ **READING CHECK:** (*Contrasting*) How was the form of Christianity practiced in Aksum different from Christianity as practiced elsewhere? included some local traditions, customs, and beliefs

go.hrw.com **Homework Practice Online**

Keyword: SK5 HP8

Section Review 1

Define or identify: dynasty, pharoahs, Ramses II, hieroglyphics, papyrus, Rosetta Stone, pyramids, Imhotep, Hatshepsut, sphinxes, mummification, King 'Ezana

Reading for the Main Idea

1. (*Environment and Society*) How was the Nile River important to the Egyptians?

2. (*Human Systems*) What are some of the achievements of Egyptian civilization?

Critical Thinking

3. **Making Generalizations** Why did the Egyptians bury dead rulers in tombs filled with material goods?

4. **Comparing and Contrasting** In what ways was civilization in Kush similar to and different from civilization in Aksum?

Organizing What You Know

5. **Sequencing** Copy the following time line. Fill in as many events as you can.

3000 B.C.	2000 B.C.	1000 B.C.	A.D. 1 A.D. 500
2500 B.C.	1500 B.C.	500 B.C.	

CLOSE

Lead a brief discussion about what sights and sounds students would like to have experienced in ancient Egypt, Kush, or Aksum.

REVIEW, ASSESS, RETEACH

Have students complete the Section Review. Then have students write down what they think are the two most important facts in each subsection of Section 1. Then have students complete Daily Quiz 8.1.

Have students complete Main Idea Activity S1. Then have each student write five true-false statements over the section material. Call on volunteers to read their statements. As a class, convert each false statement into a true one. **LS INTERPERSONAL**

EXTEND

Have interested students conduct research on "Egyptomania"—the fascination with all things Egyptian that has affected interior design, fashion, movies, toys, jewelry, and many other fields. This fascination was particularly widespread following the discovery in 1922 of Tutankhamen's tomb. **BLOCK SCHEDULING**

Section 2 — Early Sub-Saharan Africa

Read to Discover

1. How do historians study cultures that left no written records?
2. How did trade affect the growth of kingdoms in Sub-Saharan Africa?

Vocabulary

oral history

Places

Swahili States
Zimbabwe
Ghana
Mali
Timbuktu

People

Mansa Musa

Reading Strategy

FOLDNOTES: TRI-FOLD Create a **Tri-Fold** FoldNote as described in the Appendix. Label the columns East Africa, Zimbabwe, and West Africa. As you read, write what you learn about these trading states in each column.

Ancient Sub-Saharan Africa

Egypt was the first kingdom to develop in Africa, but it was not the only one. South of the vast desert called the Sahara, many different cultures developed. In time some of these groups established city-states, kingdoms, and even empires. It is sometimes difficult, however, for historians to study the earliest African civilizations.

Language One reason for this difficulty is the absence of written records. Historians therefore must find other ways to study early cultures. One common method is the study of **oral history**, spoken information passed from one generation to the next.

These oral traditions are often contained in stories or songs. Many of the stories tell about great kings and heroes from the past. Other stories included animals playing tricks on each other, which usually ended in an important lesson. Many cultures of ancient Sub-Saharan Africa had an official storyteller who memorized these stories. Storytellers used different voices and facial expressions to express emotion as they spoke. They entertained large audiences with their performances. In some parts of Africa storytellers are still performing today. Scholars today study these tales to learn about Africa's past.

The modern languages of Africa can also provide clues about the continent's history. Scholars have tried to figure out which African languages are related. This is often a clue that cultures have had

The Yoruba were skilled artisans. This life-sized head of a king was sculpted from bronze. The vertical lines on the face may represent ritual scarring.

Africa's History • 185

SECTION 2 RESOURCES

Reproducibles
- Lecture Notes, Section 2
- Block Scheduling Handbook, Chapter 8
- Know It Notes S2
- Readings in World Geography, History, and Culture, Readings 57, 66

Technology
- One-Stop Planner CD-ROM, Lesson 8.2
- Geography and Cultures Visual Resources 82, 83, 86–88
- Music of the World Audio CD Program, Selection 14–16
- Homework Practice Online
- HRW Go Site

Review, Reinforcement, and Assessment Resources
- Section 2 Review
- Daily Quiz 8.2
- Main Idea Activity S2
- Chapter Summaries and Review
- English Audio Summary 8.2
- Spanish Audio Summary 8.2

Section 2

Objectives

1. Explain how historians study cultures that left no written records.
2. Clarify how trade affected the growth of kingdoms in Sub-Saharan Africa.

FOCUS

Bellringer

Copy the following question onto the board: *What geographical features may help trade and travel flourish in a region?* (Possible answers: rivers, seas, natural resources, lack of natural barriers such as mountains) Discuss responses. Point out that in Africa, kingdoms arose in places that had these very features. Tell students that in this section they will learn more about the kingdoms of ancient Africa.

Building Vocabulary

Write **oral history** on the chalkboard and have students read its definition from the glossary. Remind students that many civilizations existed for centuries before they developed written languages. The histories of these people were passed on from one generation to the next in spoken form. Challenge students to think of oral traditions that are passed along in their own cultures.

COOPERATIVE LEARNING

Oral Histories Organize the class into groups, and assign a present-day Sub-Saharan people to each group. Examples include Yoruba, Hausa, Ibo, and many others. Ask each group to conduct research on its people's history and culture. Groups should prepare oral presentations in which they take turns playing the people's storyteller to relate the information to the class.

▶

Many houses built in Africa today are similar to those built in ancient times.
Interpreting the Visual Record From what materials are traditional houses like this made?

contact with each other in the past. Some African languages are related to languages spoken in other parts of the world. Scholars have learned from this that early Africans had contact with people from distant lands. Other evidence suggests the same thing. Bananas, for example, have been popular in Africa for a long time, but the banana tree is not native to Africa. Early traders must have brought the plant from Asia.

Life in Early Africa There is much historians do not know about life in ancient Sub-Saharan Africa. However, they have pieced together a picture of life in the region. Across most of the continent, life was centered around small villages. Usually, all of the people in a village were related to each other. These relationships helped tie the village together. Older members of a community were often its leaders. Everyone in the village respected and obeyed them. Women played many roles in early African societies. They were responsible for farming. In addition, people in some societies traced their family lines through their mothers.

Life was very similar in many villages across Africa. Most people were involved in farming, herding, or fishing. Basic agricultural practices did not vary much from place to place. Most people in early Africa also had similar religious beliefs. They believed that spirits, including the spirits of their ancestors, were all around. They also believed in many gods who controlled nature and human activities.

✓ **READING CHECK:** (*Summarizing*) What do historians study to learn about ancient Africa? oral histories, languages, plants

Visual Record Answer ▶

wood, grasses, other natural materials

Teaching Objective 1

LEVELS 1 AND 2: (Suggested time: 15 min.) Copy the following graphic organizer onto the chalkboard, omitting the blue answers. Ask students to copy it into their notebooks. Then pair students and have the pairs fill in the chart with information about how historians study early African civilizations. Lead a discussion about how these methods are used to study cultures and periods in which there was no written language.
ESOL, COOPERATIVE LEARNING, [LS] **VISUAL-SPATIAL**

STUDYING EARLY AFRICAN SOCIETIES	
Historians study . . .	to learn about . . .
oral histories	tales of kings and heroes from the past
modern languages	other cultures with which the society had contact
trade goods	parts of the world with which the society traded

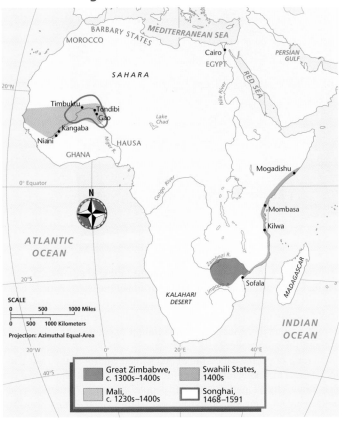

African Trading States, c. A.D. 1230–1591

SCALE
0   500   1000 Miles
0   500   1000 Kilometers
Projection: Azimuthal Equal-Area

Great Zimbabwe,
c. 1300s–1400s

Mali,
c. 1230s–1400s

Swahili States,
1400s

Songhai,
1468–1591

◄ Great wealth from trade helped develop several powerful states throughout Africa. In the east, the Swahili States and Great Zimbabwe traded goods with peoples across the Indian Ocean. In the west, an almost endless supply of gold and salt gave rise to the kingdoms of Mali and Songhai.

Interpreting the Map What trading advantage did the Swahili States have in their location?

The Trading States

Egypt, Kush, and Aksum were the largest kingdoms in ancient Africa. Like these kingdoms, most of the civilizations of Sub-Saharan Africa were great traders. Across the continent, trade connected Africa with other civilizations.

East Africa Along the coast of East Africa, dozens of small city-states appeared. The earliest such city-states, like Mogadishu (moh-guh-DEE-shoo) and Mombasa, were located in the northern part of the region. Eventually city-states like these lined most of the eastern coast of Africa. They controlled trade in the Indian Ocean. They sold gold, ivory, hides, and tortoise shells to traders from around the world. They also sold slaves. In exchange, these traders brought weapons and porcelain to Africa.

Eventually a new culture arose out of this trade. A new language, called Swahili, developed. It was an African language, but it also included many words from Arabic. For this reason, the city-states of East Africa are sometimes called the Swahili States.

▲ Sailing vessels called dhows were used by Swahili traders to cross the Indian Ocean. These vessels are still in use today.

Africa's History • 187

◄ **Map Answer**

a long coastline on the Indian Ocean, access to both the Middle East and East Asia

Teaching Objective 2

LEVEL 3: (Suggested time: 15 min.) On the chalkboard, write the word *good*. Ask students if they know the words for *good* in Spanish, French, or Italian. Write the translated words on the board. (Spanish—*bueno;* Italian—*buono;* French—*bon*) Help students find similarities among the words and discuss why the words are similar. (They all come from the Latin word *bonus,* which means "good." Spain, Italy, and France were once part of the Roman Empire, where Latin was spoken.) Explain that analyzing modern languages can sometimes reveal clues about relationships between ancient cultures. Point out that historians have studied African languages in this way to learn about early cultures in Africa.
LS VERBAL-LINGUISTIC

ALL LEVELS: (Suggested time: 30 min.) On the chalkboard, list the kingdoms covered in this section: the Swahili States, Zimbabwe, Ghana, Mali, and Songhai. Have students work in pairs to discuss the role that trade played for each one of these kingdoms. Then lead a discussion to review the information. **LS INTERPERSONAL**

National Geography Standard 12

African Coasts and Settlement Early cities and states of West Africa were primarily inland, and the region's coast remained relatively unsettled. Prevailing northerly winds made sailing off the West African Coast difficult.

The East African coast, in contrast, promoted sea-borne activities and settlement. The monsoon winds and Indian Ocean currents aided traders in sailing there.

Critical Thinking Ask students how these geographical differences may affect technological development.

Answer Students may answer that technological advances in the west may focus on herding and farming. Advances in the east may focus on boats and sailing.

▶

These ruins of the Great Zimbabwe fortress near Masvingo, Zimbabwe, reveal the past glory of a trading empire.

Interpreting the Visual Record What do these ruins reveal about the region's natural resources?

Zimbabwe Later traders built settlements farther south. By A.D. 900, gold had been discovered in the interior of southeastern Africa. This gold was shipped to the coast on the Zambezi River. The discovery of gold greatly increased trade along the Indian Ocean because many peoples wanted it. African kingdoms fought to control the sources of gold and the gold trade.

A group of people called the Shona gained control of the region in the 1200s. Their kingdom was centered around Great Zimbabwe, a huge stone city of perhaps 10,000 people or more. *Zimbabwe* is a Shona word that means "stone houses." From Great Zimbabwe, the Shona controlled the gold trade out of southeastern Africa. Great Zimbabwe's builders used local granite to create the rectangular blocks that formed the city's stone structures. A circular stone wall that reaches up to 36 feet in height is the largest structure at Great Zimbabwe. Within this stone enclosure, local traders exchanged gold for porcelain, glass beads, and other goods with traders from China and India. Great Zimbabwe was abandoned during the 1400s.

West Africa In West Africa, trade centered on the Atlantic Ocean. Many trading societies developed between the Atlantic and Lake Chad. The most powerful trading societies in this region were those that controlled trade routes across the Sahara. Traders from the north brought salt across the desert in exchange for gold from West Africa. Cities grew up along these trade routes.

The first of the great West African trading kingdoms was Ghana. It began as a trading village in what is now Mauritania. Gold trade made the kings of Ghana rich and powerful. They built strong armies and conquered new lands. Eventually, however, Ghana declined. In about A.D. 1235, a neighboring people conquered Ghana. They set up a new empire called Mali.

CLOSE

LEVELS 2 AND 3: (Suggested time: 45 min.) Organize students into groups and have each group design an illustrated cover for a magazine called *Ancient Africa* that will feature the trading states of East Africa, Zimbabwe, or West Africa. Then have groups write short summaries of articles that could be included in an issue of the magazine. Topics may include history, trade, arts, architecture, or geography. **COOPERATIVE LEARNING, LS VISUAL-SPATIAL**

If possible, download an image of a $50 note of Zimbabwe's currency from the Internet to show to the class. The bill has an illustration of the ruins of Great Zimbabwe on it. Ask students what this may indicate about the importance of the site to the people of the country today. (Great Zimbabwe is a source of pride for Zimbabwe's people and is an important symbol of the country's past.)

Mansa Musa (died 1332)

Mansa Musa was famous not just because he supported education and the arts. He was also very wealthy. When he went on a pilgrimage to Mecca, 500 slaves carrying gold rods walked in front of him. Mansa Musa gave away so much gold while in Egypt that the precious metal lost much of its value.

Why would gold go down in value when it is plentiful?

Mali covered all of the area that had been Ghana. It also included new lands to the north and west. Mali reached the height of its power in the early 1300s under a ruler named Mansa Musa. He was a strong supporter of education and the arts. During his reign, the city of Timbuktu became an important center of learning and trade. People came from as far away as Egypt and Arabia to study at the university there. After Mansa Musa died, Mali began to weaken. In 1468, rebels captured Timbuktu. They set up a new kingdom called Songhai.

Songhai was a powerful trading kingdom. It was centered on the city of Gao, a key trade center on the Niger River. By this time the Niger had become an important trade route. The kings of Songhai encouraged Islamic study at the university in Timbuktu. This helped Timbuktu remain an important cultural and trade center. Goods from Europe, India, and China were exchanged there. Timbuktu also remained a center of learning. Books sold for very high prices in the markets there. Songhai remained a powerful state until 1591. In that year, it was conquered by Morocco.

✓ **READING CHECK:** (*Identifying Cause and Effect*) What led to the development of strong kingdoms in West Africa? **trade with merchants from across the Sahara**

Homework Practice Online
Keyword: SK5 HP8

Section Review 2

Define or Identify: oral history, Mansa Musa

Reading for the Main Idea

1. (*Human Systems*) What do scholars study to learn about early African civilizations?

2. (*Human Systems*) What were some items traded by early African trading kingdoms?

3. (*Human Systems*) What East African culture developed as a result of trade?

Critical Thinking

4. **Drawing Inferences and Conclusions** Why were some of the civilizations of Sub-Saharan Africa located on or near the coast?

Organizing What You Know

5. **Comparing and Contrasting** Copy the following chart. Use it to name and describe the trading kingdoms of early Sub-Saharan Africa.

State	Location in Africa	Features

Africa's History • 189

Answers to Section 2 Review

Define or identify For definition and identification, see the glossary and index.

Reading for the Main Idea

1. oral history, languages, trade goods (NGS 17)

2. gold, ivory, hides, tortoise shells, slaves (NGS 10)

3. the Swahili States

Critical Thinking

4. trade routes generally over water instead of over land; easier to ship goods (NGS 11)

Organizing What You Know

5. Swahili States—east coast; traded across Indian Ocean; Great Zimbabwe—interior southeast Africa; created by Shona, traded gold, built fortresses; Ghana—West Africa; traded with merchants from across Sahara; powerful army; Mali—West Africa; conquered Ghana, built Timbuktu; Songhai—on Niger River; powerful traders, made Timbuktu a center of learning

◀**Biography Answer**

When something is plentiful it is no longer rare, so the price goes down.

REVIEW, ASSESS, RETEACH

Have students complete the Section Review. Then have each student write three trivia questions based on the text. Have students answer each other's questions. Then have students complete Daily Quiz 8.2 **ESOL**

Have students complete Main Idea Activity S2. Then have students imagine that they are television producers. Ask students to write brief scripts for an educational special program about the history of Sub-Saharan Africa. **LS VERBAL-LINGUISTIC**

EXTEND

Have interested students conduct research on the folklore of the regions studied in this section and write a retelling of one of the tales they discover. Encourage students to include illustrations and to present their stories to the class. **BLOCK SCHEDULING**

SECTION 3 RESOURCES

Reproducibles
- Lecture Notes, Section 3
- Block Scheduling Handbook, Chapter 8
- Know It Notes S3
- Readings in World Geography, History, and Culture, Reading 60
- Biography Activity: Menelik II

Technology
- One-Stop Planner CD-ROM, Lesson 8.3
- Geography and Cultures Visual Resources 81, 82, 86–88
- Homework Practice Online
- HRW Go Site

Review, Reinforcement, and Assessment Resources
- Section 3 Review
- Daily Quiz 8.3
- Main Idea Activity S3
- Chapter Summaries and Review
- English Audio Summary 8.3
- Spanish Audio Summary 8.3

Section 3 Imperialism in Africa

Read to Discover
1. What effects did imperialism have on Africa?
2. Why did European nations want colonies in Africa?

Vocabulary
imperialism
nationalism

People
Samory Touré

Reading Strategy

READING ORGANIZER Draw a circle in the center of a sheet of paper. Label the circle *Imperialism*. Draw three rays from the circle. Then draw a circle at the end of each ray. Label the three rays Nationalism in Europe, Modern Technology, and Partition of Africa. As you read this section, write what you learn about imperialism in each circle.

▲ This cartoon was created after Cecil Rhodes, a British imperialist, announced he wanted to build a railroad from Egypt to South Africa. Rhodes believed a railroad would help Great Britain control more territory in Africa.

European Imperialism

Between 1870 and 1914, many European countries tried to control much of Africa. Using a practice called **imperialism**, they tried to dominate other countries' government, trade, and culture. Beginning in the early 1800s, most European nations ended their participation in the slave trade. Instead of slaves, they focused on trading products such as gold, ivory, and rubber. To get these goods, Europeans believed they needed to dominate regions of Africa rich in these natural resources.

Nationalism in Europe In addition to economic reasons, imperialism was also caused by the desire of European nations to expand their empires. In the 1800s, many small European states unified to form larger nations. In the process, a new sense of national pride called **nationalism** was created. These new nations fought for power and control of land and resources.

Modern Technology Imperialism in Africa would not have been possible without new weapons and advances in transportation and medicine. These changes were the result of the Industrial Revolution in Europe during the 1800s. Discovery of a treatment to control malaria, for example, made it possible for Europeans to live in tropical regions.

By the 1880s, steam replaced wind as a source of power for warships. However, ships could only carry about two weeks' worth of coal.

Section 3

Objectives
1. Analyze the effects that imperialism had on Africa.
2. Explain why European nations wanted colonies in Africa.

FOCUS

Bellringer

Copy these instructions onto the chalkboard: *Look at the cartoon on the first page of Section 3. What does it mean? How do you think Europeans of the late 1800s reacted to this drawing?* Discuss responses. Students will learn more about the attitudes reflected in the cartoon in this section.

Building Vocabulary

Write the vocabulary terms on the chalkboard and have students read their definitions. Point out that **imperialism** is based on the word *empire,* and *imperialism* involves the building of an empire. Point out that **nationalism** is a complicated idea. Sometimes nationalism is about gaining independence. However, nationalism may also be about caring only for one's own country's interests, even when it hurts other people or other countries. The second definition applies in this case.

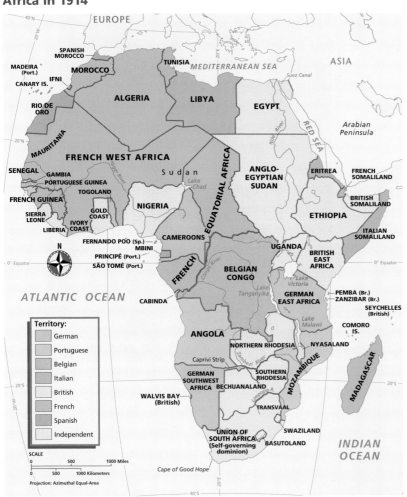

USING ILLUSTRATIONS

The Map of Africa Have students examine the map on this page and compare it to the modern map of Africa in this unit's atlas. Ask: What are some of the modern countries that were part of French West Africa? (part of Morocco, Mauritania, Mali, Niger, Burkina Faso, Côte d'Ivoire, Chad) Which imperial power dominated northeast Africa? (the British) Which two imperial powers appear to have controlled the largest amounts of territory? (the British and French) Which power had only one large colony? (the Belgians) Invite students to craft their own questions about the map.

As a result, ports where ships could stop to resupply coal were needed. Along the African coast, such ports became so valuable that colonies grew around them. Settlers and the military provided some protection to the ships.

Partition of Africa The competition between European nations for land in Africa was fierce. To lessen this tension, countries held a conference in Berlin, Germany, in 1884–85. There European leaders came to an agreement that there had to be settlers living in each European colony. If a colony did not have any settlers, it could not exist. Second, they agreed that a nation had to get approval from other nations to claim new territory. Finally, they decided that nations had to end slavery in their colonies.

▲

By about 1914, most major European countries had colonies throughout Africa.

Interpreting the Map Which African nation was not a European colony?

◀ **Map Answer**

Liberia and Ethiopia

Africa's History • 191

TEACH

Teaching Objectives 1–2

LEVEL 1: (Suggested time: 20 min.) Copy the following graphic organizer onto the chalkboard, omitting the blue answers. Have students work in pairs to complete it. Then lead a discussion about whether or not industrialization had made imperialism practically inevitable and how the abuses of imperialism could have been avoided. **ESOL, INTERPERSONAL**

IMPERIALISM IN AFRICA	
Causes	**Results**
• desire for gold, ivory, rubber	• new roads and railroads built in Africa
• desire to expand empires	• new crops and farming methods
• nationalism	• European medicine
• treatment of malaria	• resistance by Africans who did not want Europeans telling them how to live
• steamships' need for coal	

HUMAN SYSTEMS

Zulu Resistance More often than not, European troops won their battles with the native Africans. There was at least one dramatic exception.

At the battle of Isandhlwana in South Africa, the British assumed that modern artillery and the well-trained British soldiers would easily defeat Zulu warriors. Thus when they set out to attack the Zulu forces, the British troops didn't reinforce their camp. A force of 20,000 Zulu warriors overran the camp, killed most of the 1,700 men there, and stole the British supplies. It was a significant victory. The Zulu warriors went from Isandhlwana to nearby Rorke's Drift, where the British put up a stronger defense. The few British survivors from the earlier battle had been able to warn the Rorke's Drift forces.

Critical Thinking: Why may the British have made such a serious blunder at Isandhlwana?

Answer: Student may suggest that the British were convinced that they were superior, so they underestimated the Zulu military strength and tactical skills.

Visual Record Answer ▶

Possible answers: grief, frustration

▶

In the late 1900s, Samory Touré resisted French colonialism in his native Guinea by creating his own army. Touré also tried to create a kingdom in West Africa, but was later captured by the French.

Interpreting the Visual Record **What emotion is Touré expressing in this portrait?**

Between 1885 and 1914, almost all of Africa was divided between Belgium, France, Great Britain, Germany, Spain, Italy, and Portugal. Only Ethiopia and Liberia remained independent. Former slaves from the United States went to Africa and settled in Liberia which became an independent nation in 1847. In drawing boundaries throughout Africa, Europeans did not consider the African peoples living there. Africans already had their own political and cultural boundaries. Many kingdoms and states that had already been established were divided by the Europeans.

✓ READING CHECK: (*Human Systems*) Why did European nations colonize Africa? to control Africa's natural resources such as gold, ivory, and rubber

African Resistance

During the period of European imperialism, new roads and railroads were built throughout Africa. Europeans introduced new crops and new ways of farming. European medicine helped save and improve the lives of Africans. But even though European imperialism did benefit some Africans, most objected to European rule. Many Africans did

LEVELS 2 AND 3: (Suggested time: 30 min.) Complete the Level 1 graphic organizer and discussion. Then have students imagine that they are either European government officials in favor of imperialism or Africans who are resisting European imperialism. Ask students to create editorial cartoons expressing the viewpoints of either side. **LS** **VISUAL-SPATIAL**

TEACHER TO TEACHER

Susan Walker of Beaufort, South Carolina, recommends this activity to familiarize students with the issues surrounding imperialism in Africa. Have students work in groups to imagine a European colony in Africa called Cowabunga. Each group should compile a set of rules for the colony as if they were the colony's founders, including guidelines for getting along with the African people. Groups should assume that the colony's administration includes both advocates and critics of imperialism. Ask students to write scenarios for a range of situations that may arise in Cowabunga and to solve the problems they encounter realistically.

not want Europeans telling them how to live. Ethnic groups throughout Africa resisted adopting European culture. Africans wanted to keep their own cultures and religions.

As Europeans continued to dominate Africans, wars erupted between Africans and Europeans. Even though Africans did not have rifles like the Europeans, they fought fiercely. In southern Africa, the Zulu fought against a British invasion of their land. The Zulu defeated the British in the first war in 1879. However, the British invaded Zululand again several months later and defeated the Zulu. A war correspondent described the Zulu's courage by writing, "Their noble ardour (determination) could not endure in the face of . . . civilized warfare."

A major resistance against European imperialism, however, came from a military leader in Guinea named Samory Touré. He fought the French for 15 years. Touré proclaimed himself king, and his empire was the largest in West Africa. In 1898, the French captured Touré and defeated his army.

Many Africans resisted the attempt by Europeans to change their way of life. Some African leaders, however, cooperated with the Europeans. For example, in 1892, a king in northern Ghana signed a free trade treaty with Great Britain. The French hoped Africans living in their colonies would adopt French culture. Most Europeans, however, did not think Africans should be treated equally.

✓ **READING CHECK:** (**Human Systems**) In what ways did Africans resist European imperialism? resisted adopting European culture; fought Europeans in armed conflicts

▲
This drawing from about 1875 shows a Zulu warrior with shield, spears, and traditional dress.

Homework Practice Online
Keyword: SK5 HP8

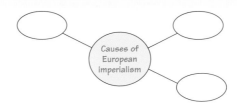

Define or identify: imperialism, nationalism, Samory Touré

Reading for the Main Idea

1. (**Places and Regions**) What region of Africa was colonized by the British?

2. (**Human Systems**) In what ways did Africans resist European imperialism?

Critical Thinking

3. **Finding the Main Idea** Why did Africans resist European imperialism?

4. **Analyzing Information** Why did Europeans draw political boundaries in Africa?

Organizing What You Know

5. **Summarizing** Copy the following graphic organizer. Use it to list three causes of European imperialism in Africa.

Causes of European imperialism

Africa's History • 193

Answers to Section 3 Review

Define or identify For definitions and identifications, see the glossary and index.

Reading for the Main Idea

1. northeastern Africa, southern Africa, some colonies in western Africa **(NGS 4)**

2. resisted adopting European culture, armed conflict

Critical Thinking

3. They did not want Europeans telling them how to live.

4. to lessen the tension between European powers

Organizing What You Know

5. desire for products such as gold, ivory, and rubber; nationalism, needs created by modern technology

CLOSE

Lead a brief class discussion about use of the phrase "civilized warfare" by the war correspondent reporting on Zulu resistance. Is the phrase an oxymoron?

REVIEW, ASSESS, RETEACH

Have students complete the Section Review. Then have students work in pairs to debate the benefits and costs of imperialism in Africa. Then have students complete Daily Quiz 8.3.

Have students complete Main Idea Activity S3. Then ask each student to make a list of important names and places from the section. Call on volunteers to state the significance of each one while other class members record what they say. **ESOL, LS INTERPERSONAL**

EXTEND

Have interested students read and analyze "The White Man's Burden" a poem by Rudyard Kipling about imperialism. Ask students to present the poem to the class, along with a discussion of how Kipling's attitudes reflected those of other Europeans.

Visual Record Answer ▶

to control the region's resources, such as rubber

Section 4 Nationalist Movements

Read to Discover
1. How did World War I increase feelings of nationalism in Africa?
2. What made South Africa different from the rest of Africa?
3. What were some results of independence for African countries?

Vocabulary
boycotted
apartheid

People
Nelson Mandela
Wole Soyinka

Reading Strategy

TAKING NOTES Use the headings in this section to create an outline. As you read about nationalist movements in Africa, write what you learn beneath each heading.

▲
A French colonist directs African workers on a rubber plantation in French Equatorial Africa in the 1940s.

Interpreting the Visual Record Why did the French want to control this region of Africa?

Beginnings of Nationalism in Africa

Until the years following World War I, European countries controlled nearly all of Africa. Europe's African colonies gained access to better health care, more effective farming methods, and improved roads and railroads. The people who lived in these colonies, however, had few rights. They played little part in running their countries, and their cultures were usually not respected by the colonial rulers.

Around the end of the war, the people in these colonies began to express resentment over European control. Many Africans did not want to continue working for low wages on land owned by European colonists. As a result, many Africans moved to cities to find better work. There they organized workers' associations and protested unfair treatment by colonial governments. They developed more pride in their own cultures and national identities. These feelings of nationalism led to demands for self-rule. By the 1930s many colonies in Africa were calling for independence.

✓ **READING CHECK:** *Summarizing* Why did many colonies in Africa want to become independent? people had few rights; no part in running their countries; cultures not respected

194 • Chapter 8

Section 4

Objectives

1. Show how World War I increased feelings of nationalism in Africa.
2. Explain what made South Africa different from the rest of Africa.
3. Analyze some results of independence for African countries.

FOCUS

 Bellringer

Copy the following passage onto the chalkboard: *What do you know about recent events in Africa? Write a few sentences to describe some of the events.* Discuss student responses. Point out that many African countries were controlled by European powers until the mid-1900s. In some places this colonial history continues to influence events. Tell students they will learn more about Africa in the 1900s in this section.

Building Vocabulary

Write the vocabulary terms on the chalkboard and have students read their definitions. Point out that **boycotted** is derived from the name of Charles Boycott, an English landowner in Ireland whose Irish tenants took nonviolent action against him in the 1880s. Ask them how this relates to the meaning of *boycotted*. The point out that **apartheid** is from the Afrikaans language spoken in South Africa. It means "apartness."

African Nationalism

Most African countries did not actually become independent until after World War II. African soldiers who had fought in British and French armies during the war had been exposed to new ideas. They probably learned about European political systems from their fellow soldiers. When they returned home, they brought some new ideas with them. Some began to protest against racism and political oppression.

These protests were linked to a worldwide movement called Pan-Africanism. The movement was begun by people of African descent living in Britain, the United States, and the West Indies. They wanted cultural unity and equality for everyone of African heritage. Members of the Pan-African movement wanted two things. First, they sought to end European control over Africa. They also wanted Africa to become a homeland for all people of African descent. Despite these efforts, however, it took many years for most African colonies to gain independence. In some countries the people were able to achieve their goals peacefully. In others, however, the fight for independence became an armed struggle.

▲

The Organization of African Unity (OAU), whose flag is seen here, grew out of the Pan-African movement in the 1960s. In 2002, the OAU changed its name to the African Union.

Ghana gained independence from Great Britain in 1957.
Interpreting the Visual Record How are these women celebrating their independence from colonial rule?

▼

Africa's History · 195

TEACH

Teaching Objectives 1–2

LEVEL 1: (Suggested time: 25 min.) Organize the class into groups and assign each group one of the African colonies whose independence movement is described in this chapter. Then have each group create a poster that illustrates one aspect of that country's experience. Display the posters around the classroom. **ESOL,** [LS] **VISUAL-SPATIAL**

LEVEL 2: (Suggested time: 20 min.) Have students imagine they are African soldiers fighting in the British army during World War I. Have them write a short letter home describing how life among Europeans is different from life in a European colony. Direct students to mention particular ideas they may have picked up from their fellow soldiers. Call on volunteers to share their letters with the class. [LS] **VERBAL-LINGUISTIC**

FOOD FESTIVAL

A Pharaoh's Feast The Nile River and the wetlands alongside it provided a wide range of food-stuffs to the Egyptians. The royal families ate very well. Tomb excavations tell us that among the foods on the pharaohs' tables were quail, pigeon stew, beef ribs, stewed figs, fresh berries, and cheese. Eel, perch, and carp were among the fish that swam in the Nile and that the Egyptians caught for the table. Hunters brought down antelope and gazelle. Tomb reliefs show workers smoking bees from their hives so they could collect the honey.

Have students conduct research on the foods of ancient Egypt and mimic a banquet that may have been set before a pharaoh.

Visual Record Answer ▶

Possible answer: concentrate on building the future instead of punishing people for past actions

British Colonies The first British African colony to gain independence was the Gold Coast. Protestors staged demonstrations and **boycotted**, or refused to buy, British goods. Finally in 1957 the British agreed to let the people of the Gold Coast choose their own government. The people voted for independence. The Gold Coast became the independent nation of Ghana. Other British colonies followed this example. The colonies that became Kenya, Malawi, Nigeria, and Zambia all won their independence by the 1960s. Zimbabwe became independent in 1980.

Other Colonies By 1962 France had granted independence to nearly all of its African colonies. Other European countries were not as quick to give up their colonies. Belgium gave up any claim to its Congo colony—which later became the Democratic Republic of the Congo—after violence broke out in 1959. Portugal also refused to free its colonies until after bloody civil wars. Angola, the last Portuguese colony in Africa, won its independence in 1975.

South Africa The independent Union of South Africa was created in 1910. However, from the beginning, its government had been controlled by the descendants of British and Dutch settlers. White South Africans enforced a policy of **apartheid**. This was a system of laws that denied black South Africans any political rights. Many South Africans—both black and white—protested apartheid laws. Some protests turned violent, and others were violently put down. Many people were killed. Black leaders like Nelson Mandela were thrown into prison. Other countries around the world also disapproved of apartheid policies. Some of these countries refused to trade or have any dealings with South Africa.

Things changed in the 1990s. South Africa banned apartheid. Nelson Mandela was freed from prison and was elected president in 1994. Mandela and his government worked to establish a new government based on equality for all South Africans.

✓ **READING CHECK:** (*Contrasting*) How was South Africa different from other African countries? developed a policy of apartheid

◀ Nelson Mandela called on the people of South Africa to "heal the wounds of the past."

Interpreting the Visual Record What do you think the phrase "heal the wounds of the past" means?

Teaching Objective 3

ALL LEVELS: (Suggested time: 10 min.) Copy the following graphic organizer onto the chalkboard, omitting the blue answers. Have students complete it as a class. **ESOL,** **LS** **VISUAL-SPATIAL**

INDEPENDENT AFRICA

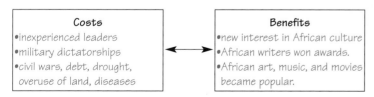

Costs	Benefits
•inexperienced leaders	•new interest in African culture
•military dictatorships	•African writers won awards.
•civil wars, debt, drought, overuse of land, diseases	•African art, music, and movies became popular.

LEVELS 2 AND 3: (Suggested time: 45 min.) Tell students to imagine that they have just been elected to lead newly independent African countries. Ask them to think about what changes they may make to their countries and their governments to assure better futures for their people. Have each student write a short campaign speech expressing his or her ideas. Encourage students to note problems that their countries may have faced as colonies before they achieved independence. **LS** **VERBAL-LINGUISTIC**

Life in Independent Africa

Independence did not solve all of the problems of the former African colonies. In addition, new challenges faced the newly independent countries. At the same time, however, people around the world developed a new interest in Africa and its cultures.

Challenges Many political leaders of the new African countries were inexperienced. If they were unable to improve conditions in their countries, military leaders sometimes took control. Many African countries were run by military dictatorships through the late 1900s. Civil wars broke out between ethnic groups in some countries. Thousands of people died. Many countries also fell into debt. Crops failed due to droughts and the overuse of land, and millions more people died. Diseases like malaria and AIDS have also killed many Africans.

Cultural Revival As demands for independence in Africa grew, people around the world developed an interest in African culture. Writers like Nigeria's Wole Soyinka and Chinua Achebe won awards for their stories about African life. African music and art became more popular around the world. Also, African directors such as Senegal's Ousmane Sembene made movies that were appreciated in many countries.

✓ **READING CHECK:** (*Summarizing*) How did life in Africa change after independence? **new challenges for independent countries; worldwide interest in African culture**

▲
Beginning in the early 1900s, African art was recognized outside of Africa. The expressive style of African artists influenced artists throughout the world including Spanish painter Pablo Picasso.

Homework Practice Online
Keyword: SK5 HP8

Section Review 4

Define or Identify: boycotted, apartheid, Nelson Mandela, Wole Soyinka

Reading for the Main Idea
1. (Human Systems) How did World War I lead to the growth of nationalism in Africa?
2. (Human Systems) What were some features of life in independent Africa?

Critical Thinking
3. **Drawing Inferences and Conclusions** How did other countries influence South Africa's decision to end apartheid?

4. **Analyzing** How did boycotting British goods affect the Gold Coast's struggle for independence?

Organizing What You Know
5. **Identifying Cause and Effect** Copy the following graphic organizer. Use it to describe the process that led to the growth of nationalism in and independence for former African colonies.

Answers to Section 4 Review

Define or identify For definitions and identifications, see the glossary and index.

Reading for the Main Idea
1. African soldiers who fought in the war were exposed to new ideas. **(NGS 13)**

2. political instability, crop failure, disease, cultural revival **(NGS 10)**

Critical Thinking
3. They refused to trade or have any dealings with South Africa. **(NGS 13)**
4. It led to success for the struggle for independence.

Organizing What You Know
5. Answers will vary but should mention African soldiers returning from World War I, the beginnings of nationalist movements, the demand for self-rule, and the granting of independence.

CLOSE

Draw students' attention to the mask on this page. Ask students to analyze the appeal that this style of art may have for people of other cultures.

REVIEW, ASSESS, RETEACH

Have students complete the Section Review. Then have students work in pairs to create outlines of the section. Then have students complete Daily Quiz 8.4.

Have students complete Main Idea Activity S4. The have students work in small groups to discuss the map in Section 3 in terms of the independence movements covered in this section.

EXTEND

Have interested students locate and bring to class selections of the music of the anti-apartheid movement. Beautiful multi-part singing was a common feature of anti-apartheid demonstrations. **BLOCK SCHEDULING**

CHAPTER 8 REVIEW

Define and Identify
For definitions and identifications, see the glossary and index.

Review the Main Ideas
13. to be tombs for pharaohs

14. Soil exhaustion caused a food shortage and the Persians took control of Aksum's trade.

15. Swahili

16. It was made of stone. (NGS 16)

17. new weapons, cure for malaria, advances in transportation

18. The colony needed settlers, approval from other nations for new territory, and an end to their slave trade.

19. to end European control and make Africa a homeland for people of African descent

20. Gold Coast

Thinking Critically
21. to preserve their bodies for an afterlife (NGS 10)

22. Their location on the coast was ideal for trade and resulted in the exchange of different cultures and languages.

23. Life was centered around small villages and most people farmed, herded, or fished. (NGS 10)

24. Africans resisted European imperialism because they wanted to defend their land and traditional ways of life.

25. Political leaders of some African countries were inexperienced, civil wars broke out, and drought caused widespread hunger.

Review and Practice

Define and Identify
Identify each of the following:

1. pharaohs
2. pyramids
3. hieroglyphics
4. mummification
5. Imhotep
6. oral history
7. Mansa Musa
8. imperialism
9. nationalism
10. Samory Touré
11. apartheid
12. Nelson Mandela

Review the Main Ideas
13. Why did the Egyptians build pyramids?

14. Why did the kingdom of Aksum decline?

15. What language is a combination of an African language and Arabic?

16. What was a unique feature of Great Zimbabwe?

17. What factors made imperialism possible?

18. What was necessary before a European country could claim a colony in Africa?

19. What did supporters of Pan-Africanism want in Africa?

20. Which British colony in Africa was the first to achieve independence?

Thinking Critically
21. Summarizing Why did ancient Egyptians mummify their dead rulers?

22. Analyzing Information How do you think the location of the Swahili States affected the creation of a new culture in East Africa?

23. Finding the Main Idea What was life like in ancient Sub-Saharan Africa?

24. Drawing Inferences and Conclusions Why do you think Africans resisted European imperialism?

25. Analyzing Information What were some challenges African countries faced after independence?

Map Activity
26. Identify the places marked on the map.
Egypt
Nile River
Red Sea
Kush
Swahili States
Great Zimbabwe

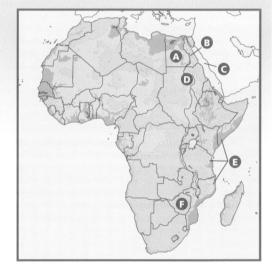

Map Activity
26. A. Egypt

B. Nile River

C. Red Sea

D. Kush

E. Swahili States

F. Great Zimbabwe

Writing Activities

Imagine that you are a reporter for a newspaper in South Africa in the 1990s. Write a news story about the protests you witness and what the protesters hope to achieve. Think about who you would interview and what questions you would ask. Be sure to use standard grammar, spelling, sentence structure, and punctuation.

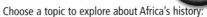

☑ internet connect ▤▤▤

Internet Activity: **go.hrw.com**
KEYWORD: **SK5 GT8**

Choose a topic to explore about Africa's history:
• Learn more about ancient Egypt.
• Write a report about the trading states of Sub-Saharan Africa.
• Write a biography of a figure in Africa's history.

Social Studies Skills Practice

Interpreting Maps

Study the following map of Indian Ocean trade routes. Then answer the questions.

Indian Ocean Trade Routes

INDIA
ARABIA
AFRICA
Equator
SWAHILI COAST
INDIAN OCEAN

→ Trade route
⇝ Monsoon winds

1. Based on your knowledge of physical geography, how did traders sail easily back and forth across the Indian Ocean?
2. What regions outside Africa did East Africans trade with?
3. How do you think trade influenced the lives of East Africans?

Analyzing Primary Sources

Read the following passage from "The Great Hymn to the Aten," an early Egyptian hymn to the sun god Aten. Then answer the questions.

Your rays nurse all fields.
When you shine they live, they grow for you;
You made the seasons to foster all that you made,
Winter to cool them, heat that they taste you.
You made the far sky to shine therein,
To behold all that you made;
You alone, shining in your form of living Aten,
Risen, radiant, distant, near.
You made millions of forms from yourself alone,
Towns, villages, fields, the river's course;
All eyes observe you upon them,
For you are the Aten of daytime on high . . .

1. What is the subject of this hymn?
2. Why do you think an early Egyptian wrote this hymn?
3. What did the early Egyptians believe the god Aten was responsible for making?
4. From reading this passage, do you think religion was a central part of Egyptian life? Why or why not?

Africa's History • 199

Writing Activity

News stories and questions will vary but should display understanding of the chapter contents. Use Rubric 23, Newspapers, to evaluate student writing.

Interpreting Maps

1. They used the monsoon winds.
2. Arabia and India
3. Students may mention acculturation, noting that Arab traders contributed to the development of Swahili culture in East Africa.

Analyzing Primary Sources

1. the sun and its importance to crop growth
2. to ensure a good harvest
3. seasons, towns, villages, fields, the river's course
4. Most students will say that religion was a central part of Egyptian life, because the god Aten is credited with controlling many aspects of existence.

CHAPTER 8

REVIEW AND ASSESSMENT RESOURCES

Reproducible
◆ Readings in World Geography, History, and Culture 57, 60, 66
◆ Critical Thinking Activity 8
◆ Vocabulary Activity 8

Technology
◆ Chapter 8 Test Generator (on the One-Stop Planner)

◆ HRW Go site
◆ Audio CD Program, Chapter 8

Reinforcement, Review, and Assessment
◆ Chapter 8 Review and Practice
◆ Chapter Summaries and Review

◆ Chapter 8 Test
◆ Chapter 8 Test for English Language Learners and Special-Needs Students

☑ internet connect ▤

GO TO: **go.hrw.com**
KEYWORD: **SK5 Teacher**
FOR: a guide to using the Internet in your classroom

North Africa
Chapter Resource Manager

Objectives	Pacing Guide	Reproducible Resources
SECTION 1		
Physical Geography (pp. 201–04) 1. Identify the major physical features of North Africa. 2. Identify the climates, plants, and wildlife found in North Africa. 3. Identify North Africa's major resources.	**Regular** 1 day Lecture Notes, Section 1 **Block Scheduling** .5 day *Block Scheduling Handbook, Chapter 9*	**RS** Know It Notes S1 **SM** Geography for Life Activity 9 **E** Lab Activity for Geography and Earth Science, Hands-On 4 **ELL** Main Idea Activity S1
SECTION 2		
History and Culture (pp. 205–11) 1. Identify the major events in the history of North Africa. 2. Identify some important facts about the people and culture of North Africa.	**Regular** 1 day Lecture Notes, Section 2 **Block Scheduling** .5 day *Block Scheduling Handbook, Chapter 9*	**RS** Know It Notes S2 **RS** Graphic Organizer 9 **E** Cultures of the World Activity 6 **E** Creative Strategies for Teaching World Geography, Lessons 14, 15, and 16 **IC** Interdisciplinary Activity for the Middle Grades 26, 27 **SM** Map Activity 9 **ELL** Main Idea Activity S2
SECTION 3		
Egypt Today (pp. 212–14) 1. Describe what the people and cities of Egypt are like today. 2. Identify Egypt's important economic activities. 3. Identify the challenges Egypt faces today.	**Regular** .5 day Lecture Notes, Section 3 **Block Scheduling** .5 day *Block Scheduling Handbook, Chapter 9*	**RS** Know It Notes S3 **E** Biography Activity: Anwar al-Sadat **ELL** Main Idea Activity S3
SECTION 4		
Libya, Tunisia, Algeria, and Morocco (pp. 215–17) 1. Describe what the region's people and cities are like today. 2. Identify the countries' important economic activities. 3. Identify the challenges the countries face today.	**Regular** 1 day Lecture Notes, Section 4 **Block Scheduling** .5 day *Block Scheduling Handbook, Chapter 9*	**RS** Know It Notes S4 **ELL** Main Idea Activity S4

Chapter Resource Key

RS	Reading Support	**ELL**	Reinforcement and English Language Learners and English for Speakers of Other Languages (ESOL)	Internet	
IC	Interdisciplinary Connections			Holt Presentation Maker Using Microsoft® PowerPoint®	
E	Enrichment				
SM	Skills Mastery		Transparencies		
A	Assessment		CD–ROM		
REV	Review		Music		
			Video		

  One-Stop Planner CD–ROM

See the *One-Stop Planner* for a complete list of additional resources for students and teachers.

One-Stop Planner CD–ROM

It's easy to plan lessons, select resources, and print out materials for your students when you use the *One-Stop Planner CD–ROM with Test Generator.*

☑ internet connect

HRW ONLINE RESOURCES

__GO TO: go.hrw.com__
Then type in a keyword.

TEACHER HOME PAGE
  KEYWORD: SK5 TEACHER

CHAPTER INTERNET ACTIVITIES
  KEYWORD: SK5 GT9

Choose an activity to:
• journey through the Sahara.
• examine the rich history of North Africa.
• practice using Arabic calligraphy.

CHAPTER ENRICHMENT LINKS
  KEYWORD: SK5 CH9

CHAPTER MAPS
  KEYWORD: SK5 MAPS9

ONLINE ASSESSMENT
Homework Practice
  KEYWORD: SK5 HP9
  Standardized Test Prep Online
  KEYWORD: SK5 STP9
  Rubrics
  KEYWORD: SS Rubrics

COUNTRY INFORMATION
  KEYWORD: SK5 Almanac

CONTENT UPDATES
  KEYWORD: SS Content Updates

HOLT PRESENTATION MAKER
  KEYWORD: SK5 PPT9

ONLINE READING SUPPORT
  KEYWORD: SS Strategies

CURRENT EVENTS
  KEYWORD: S5 Current Events

Technology Resources

- One-Stop Planner CD–ROM, Lesson 9.1
- Geography and Cultures Visual Resources with Teaching Activities 43–41
- *ARGWorld* CD–ROM
- Homework Practice Online
- HRW Go site

- One-Stop Planner CD–ROM, Lesson 9.2
- *ARGWorld* CD–ROM
- Homework Practice Online
- HRW Go site

- One-Stop Planner CD–ROM, Lesson 9.3
- *ARGWorld* CD–ROM
- Homework Practice Online
- HRW Go site

- One-Stop Planner CD–ROM, Lesson 9.4
- *ARGWorld* CD–ROM
- Music of the World Audio CD Program, Selection 13
- Homework Practice Online
- HRW Go site

Review, Reinforcement, and Assessment Resources

ELL	Main Idea Activity S1
REV	Section 1 Review
A	Daily Quiz 9.1
REV	Chapter Summaries and Review
ELL	English Audio Summary 9.1
ELL	Spanish Audio Summary 9.1

ELL	Main Idea Activity S2
REV	Section 2 Review
A	Daily Quiz 9.2
REV	Chapter Summaries and Review
ELL	English Audio Summary 9.2
ELL	Spanish Audio Summary 9.2

ELL	Main Idea Activity S3
REV	Section 3 Review
A	Daily Quiz 9.3
REV	Chapter Summaries and Review
ELL	English Audio Summary 9.3
ELL	Spanish Audio Summary 9.3

ELL	Main Idea Activity S4
REV	Section 4 Review
A	Daily Quiz 9.4
REV	Chapter Summaries and Review
ELL	English Audio Summary 9.4
ELL	Spanish Audio Summary 9.4

Meeting Individual Needs

Ability Levels

Level 1 Basic-level activities designed for all students encountering new material

Level 2 Intermediate-level activities designed for average students

Level 3 Challenging activities designed for honors and gifted-and-talented students

ESOL Activities that address the needs of students with Limited English Proficiency

Chapter Review and Assessment

E	Readings in World Geography, History, and Culture 53 and 54
SM	Critical Thinking Activity 9
REV	Chapter 9 Review and Practice
REV	Chapter Summaries and Review
ELL	Vocabulary Activity 9
A	Chapter 9 Test
	Chapter 9 Test Generator (on the One-Stop Planner)
	Audio CD Program, Chapter 9
A	Chapter 9 Test for English Language Learners and Special-Needs Students
	HRW Go Site

North Africa
Previewing Chapter Resources

Holt Online Learning

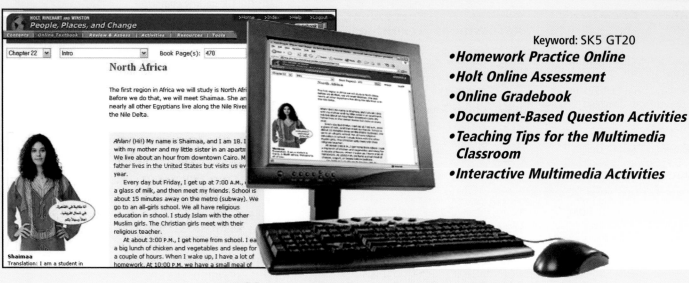

Keyword: SK5 GT20

- *Homework Practice Online*
- *Holt Online Assessment*
- *Online Gradebook*
- *Document-Based Question Activities*
- *Teaching Tips for the Multimedia Classroom*
- *Interactive Multimedia Activities*

Differentiating Instruction

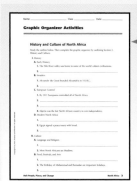

Reading and Writing Support
◄ Graphic Organizer Activity
- *Vocabulary Activity*
- *Chapter Summary and Review*
- *Know It Notes*
- *Audio CD*

Active Learning
- *Block Scheduling Handbook*
- *Cultures of the World Activity*
- *Interdisciplinary Activity*
- ◄ *Map Activity*
- *Critical Thinking Activity 22*
- *Music of the World CD: Islamic Devotional Music of Morocco*

Primary Sources and Advanced Learners
◄ Geography for Life Activity: The Camel
- *Map Activity: Ancient North Africa*
- *Readings in World Geography, History and Culture:*
  - *53 Moroccans Confront Their Future*
  - *54 Egypt's Threatened Nile Delta*

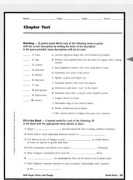

Assessment Program
- *Daily Quizzes S1–4*
- ◄ *Chapter Test*
- *Chapter Test for English Language Learners and Special-Needs Students*

Spanish and ESOL
- *Vocabulary Activity*
- ◄ *Main Idea Activities for English Language Learners and Special-Needs Students*
- *Chapter Summary and Review*
- *Spanish Audio Summary*
- *Know It Notes S1–4*
- *Chapter Test for English Language Learners and Special-Needs Students*

Special Education Modifications
Your **I.D.E.A. Works! CD-ROM** will provide modified versions of the following teaching materials:
- ◄ *Guided Reading Strategies S1–4*
- *Vocabulary Activity*
- *Main Idea Activities S1–4*
- *Daily Quizzes S1–4*
- *Chapter 9 Test*
- *Flash cards of chapter vocabulary terms*

Teacher Resources

Books for Teachers

Fromentin, Eugene. *Between Sea and Sahara: An Algerian Journal.* Ohio University Press, 2000.

Layachi, Azzedine, ed. *Economic Crisis and Political Change in North Africa.* Praeger Pub Text, 1998.

The Middle East and North Africa 2000. Europa Publications, 2000.

Zoubir, Yahia H., ed., and William B. Quandt. *North Africa in Transition: State, Society, and Economic Transformation in the 1990s.* University Press of Florida, 1999.

Books for Students

Heide, Florence Parry. *The Day of Ahmed's Secret.* William Morrow & Co., 1990. Follows Ahmed through the streets of modern Cairo as he delivers butane from his donkey cart. **SHELTERED ENGLISH**

Raskin, Lawrie, and Deborah Pearson. *52 Days by Camel: My Sahara Adventure.* Annick Press, 1999. Throwing snowballs in the Sahara, getting caught in a sandstorm, and other real-life adventures on a trip across the Sahara.

Scoones, Simon. *The Sahara and Its People.* Raintree/Steck-Vaughn, 1997. The environment and lifestyles found in the vast and numerous regions of the Sahara.

Multimedia Materials

Africa North. CD–ROM. World Class.

Ancient Egyptian Civilization. Labpack. AIMS Media.

Saving the Sphinx. (Video, 60 min.) Lucerne Media.

Videos and CDs

Videos

- **CNN** *Presents Geography: Yesterday and Today, Segment 23 Cairo—Selling the Suburbs*
- **CNN** *Presents World Cultures: Yesterday and Today, Segment 22 Restoring the Sphinx*
- *ARG World*

Holt Researcher

http://researcher.hrw.com

- *Organization of African Unity (OAU)*
- *Africa*
- *Ramses II*
- *Barbary Coast*
- *Colonialism in Africa*
- *Morocco*
- *Algeria*
- *Tunisia*
- *Libya*
- *Egypt*

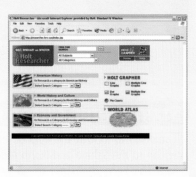

Transparency Packages

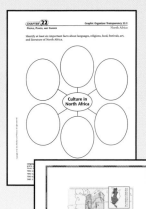

Graphic Organizer Transparencies 9.1–4

Geography and Cultures Visual Resources Transparencies 76–80

81 North Africa: Physical-Political

Map Activities Transparency 09 Ancient North Africa

CHAPTER 9

WHY IT MATTERS

You may want to emphasize the importance of learning about North Africa by sharing these points with your students:

▶ Egypt, Morocco, and Tunisia help maintain peace in the region.

▶ Events in the oil-producing region of North Africa can affect the price of gas and oil in the United States.

▶ North African countries have produced beautiful architecture, textiles, music, literature, and foods that many Americans enjoy.

▶ The ancient Egyptians produced many magnificent monuments, cultural artifacts, and technological achievements. Ancient Egyptian artifacts can be viewed in museums across the United States.

North Africa

The first region in Africa we will study is North Africa. Before we do that, we will meet Shaimaa. She and nearly all other Egyptians live along the Nile River or in the Nile Delta.

Ahlan! (Hi!) My name is Shaimaa, and I am 18. I live with my mother and my little sister in an apartment. We live about an hour from downtown Cairo. My father lives in the United States but visits us every year.

Every day but Friday, I get up at 7:00 A.M., drink a glass of milk, and then meet my friends. School is about 15 minutes away on the metro (subway). We go to an all-girls school. We all have religious education in school. I study Islam with the other Muslim girls. The Christian girls meet with their religious teacher.

At about 3:00 P.M., I get home from school. I eat a big lunch of chicken and vegetables and sleep for a couple of hours. When I wake up, I have a lot of homework. At 10:00 P.M. we have a small meal of cheese, yogurt, or beans before bedtime.

On Fridays I usually go to movies with my girlfriends and walk along the Nile. Sometimes I stay home and listen to music.

أنا طالبة في القاهرة,
في شمال افريقيا.
أهلاً وسهلاً بكم

Translation: I am a student in Cairo, in North Africa. Welcome to all of you.

CHAPTER PROJECT

Have five groups of students conduct research on one of the five basic types of dunes. Provide students with sand and a large rectangular pan and have each group make a model of the dune. Groups should then write a summary of how their dune types are formed. Ask each group to present its model and summary to the other groups. Photograph the dune models and summaries and place them in students' portfolios.

STARTING THE CHAPTER

Tell students to look at the map on the following page, and direct their attention to the Sahara and North Africa's borders. Tell students that the Sahara has been compared to an ocean, and that camels have been referred to as "ships of the desert." Ask students to speculate why such comparisons might have been made. (The Sahara is vast, as is an ocean; also, camels are a major mode of transportation in the desert, as ships are a major mode of transportation in the ocean.) Then ask students to describe the southern borders of the North African countries. (The borders are unusually straight.) Tell students that borders in North Africa were drawn by Great Britain and France, which colonized the region. Tell students that they will learn more about the countries of North Africa in this chapter.

Section 1 Physical Geography

Read to Discover

1. What are the major physical features of North Africa?
2. What climates, plants, and wildlife are found in North Africa?
3. What are North Africa's major resources?

Vocabulary

ergs
regs
depressions
silt

Places

Red Sea
Mediterranean Sea
Sahara
Nile River
Sinai Peninsula
Ahaggar Mountains

Atlas Mountains
Qattara Depression
Nile Delta
Lake Nasser
Suez Canal

Reading Strategy

USING PRIOR KNOWLEDGE On a sheet of paper write the word Know on the left side. Write Learn on the right side. Look at the physical-political map of North Africa. What do you know about this region? Write your answers on the left side of the paper. As you read the section, write what you learn on the right side.

North Africa: Physical-Political

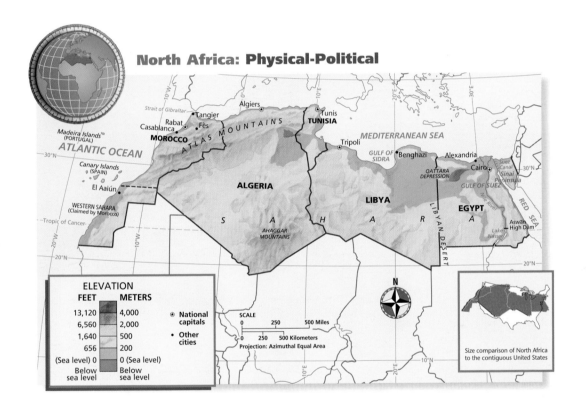

ELEVATION

FEET	METERS
13,120	4,000
6,560	2,000
1,640	500
656	200
(Sea level) 0	0 (Sea level)
Below sea level	Below sea level

⊛ National capitals
• Other cities

SCALE
0   250   500 Miles
0   250   500 Kilometers
Projection: Azimuthal Equal Area

Size comparison of North Africa to the contiguous United States

North Africa • 201

Section 1

Objectives

1. Identify the major physical features of North Africa.
2. Describe the climate, plants, and wildlife found in North Africa.
3. Identify the major resources of North Africa.

Focus

Bellringer

Copy the following instructions onto the chalkboard: *Recall the hottest summer temperatures you have experienced. How do you change your daily routine on hot summer days? Imagine what adjustments you would have to make in North Africa, where summer temperatures commonly rise higher than 120°F.* Tell students to respond in writing, and ask volunteers to share their responses with the class. Then tell students that in Section 1 they will learn more about the physical geography of North Africa.

Using the Physical-Political Map

Have students examine the map on this page and locate the five countries of the region (Morocco, Algeria, Tunisia, Libya, Egypt). Have them name the mountain ranges (Atlas, Ahaggar). Have them estimate the distance between Tripoli and the Ahaggar Mountains (800 miles). Then have them find a similar distance on the map of their own region and compare the terrains.

Across the Curriculum

SCIENCE

The Sahara The Sahara has not always been as dry as it is in modern times. Neolithic petroglyphs show pictures of giant buffalo, elephant, rhinoceros, and hippopotamus in areas now too dry for such animals to survive. Some scientists think that the Sahara dried up around 4000 B.C.

Critical Thinking: What, in addition to climate changes, could account for the extinction of these animals from this region?

Answer: Students might suggest that overhunting or human destruction of the animals' habitat could have caused their extinction.

internet connect

GO TO: go.hrw.com
KEYWORD: SK5 CH9
FOR: Web sites about the Sahara

Visual Record Answer ▶

Trees draw water from the oasis.

internet connect

GO TO: go.hrw.com
KEYWORD: SK5 CH9
FOR: Web sites about North Africa

Oases like this one in Algeria are scattered throughout the vast Sahara.

Interpreting the Visual Record How do these trees survive in the desert's harsh, dry climate?

▼

Physical Features

North Africa includes Morocco, Algeria, Tunisia, Libya, and Egypt. The region stretches from the Atlantic Ocean to the Red Sea. Off the northern coast is the Mediterranean Sea. In the south is the Sahara (suh-HAR-uh), a vast desert. The region also has mountains, the northern Nile River valley, and the Sinai (SY-ny) Peninsula.

The Sahara The huge Sahara covers most of North Africa and stretches southward. The name *Sahara* comes from the Arabic word for "desert." The Sahara is the largest desert in the world. It is so big that nearly all of the United States would fit into it.

Large areas of this very dry region have few people or none at all. Great "seas" of sand dunes called **ergs** cover about a quarter of the desert. Much of the rest of the Sahara is made up of broad, windswept gravel plains. These gravel plains are called **regs**.

Mountains Do you think of deserts as flat regions? Well, the Sahara is not flat. Some sand dunes and ridges rise as high as 1,000 feet (305 m). The Sahara also has mountain ranges. For example, the Ahaggar (uh-HAH-guhr) Mountains are located in the central Sahara. Their highest peak is 9,842 feet (3,000 m). The Atlas Mountains on the northwestern side of the Sahara are higher. Mountains there rise to 13,671 feet (4,167 m).

There also are very low areas in the Sahara. These low areas are called **depressions**. The Qattara (kuh-TAHR-uh) Depression in western Egypt is 440 feet (134 m) below sea level. Other low areas often have large, dry lake beds. Water from rare rain storms collects there.

TEACH

Teaching Objective 1

ALL LEVELS: (Suggested time: 10 min.) Provide each student with an outline map of the region. Have students identify the locations of physical features and label them on their maps. Tell students to create a key explaining the meanings of any symbols. **ESOL,** LS **VISUAL-SPATIAL**

Teaching Objective 2

ALL LEVELS: (Suggested time: 20 min.) Organize the class into three groups and assign each group a climate type found in North Africa. Give each group a sheet of butcher paper or poster board, an outline map of the region, colored pencils or markers, and a glue stick. Have each group use the materials to create a chart that shows the location of their climate type and the plants and animals found in the area. Instruct the groups to also describe their climate types in words or pictures. Have a representative from each group present the group's poster to the class.
ESOL, COOPERATIVE LEARNING, LS **KINESTHETIC**

The Nile The world's longest river, the Nile, flows northward through the eastern Sahara. The Nile empties into the Mediterranean Sea. It is formed by the union of two rivers, the Blue Nile and the White Nile. They meet in Sudan, south of Egypt.

The Nile River valley is like a long oasis in the desert. Water from the Nile irrigates surrounding farmland. The Nile fans out near the Mediterranean Sea, forming a large river delta. About 99 percent of Egypt's population lives in the Nile River valley and the Nile Delta.

For centuries rain far to the south caused annual floods along the northern Nile that left rich **silt** in surrounding fields. Silt is finely ground soil good for growing crops. The Aswan High Dam, which was completed in 1971, was built to control flooding. Water trapped by the dam formed Lake Nasser in southern Egypt. However, the dam also traps silt, preventing it from being carried downriver. Today Egypt's farmers must use fertilizers to enrich the soil.

The Sinai and Suez Canal East of the Nile is the triangular Sinai Peninsula. Barren, rocky mountains and desert cover the Sinai. Between the Sinai and the rest of Egypt is the Suez Canal. The canal was built by the French in the 1860s. It is a strategic waterway that connects the Mediterranean Sea with the Red Sea.

✓ **READING CHECK:** *Places and Regions* What are the major physical features of North Africa? *Sahara, mountains, Nile River valley, Sinai Peninsula*

Climate, Vegetation, and Animals

There are three main climates in North Africa. A desert climate covers most of the region. Temperatures range from mild to very hot. How hot can it get? Temperatures as high as 136°F (58°C) have been recorded in Libya! However, the humidity is very low. As a result, temperatures can drop quickly after sunset.

Water from the Nile River irrigates rich farmlands along the river and in its delta. You can clearly see the Nile Delta in the satellite photograph. The irrigated farmlands of the delta are shown in red.

Interpreting the Visual Record
(Human-Environment Interaction)
Why do you think most Egyptians live near the Nile River?

Our Amazing Planet

The Arabian camel has long been used for transportation in the Sahara. It can store water in the fat of its hump. Camels have survived for more than two weeks without drinking.

North Africa • 203

National Geography Standard 14
Dam Pros and Cons
Although the Aswān High Dam controls the flooding of the Nile River, stores water for use, and provides hydroelectric power, it also has had a negative impact on the region. In addition to the loss of fertile soil, critics cite the incursion of saltwater from the Mediterranean Sea into the Nile Delta and a reduction in the number of fish along the delta shore as problems that have been caused by the dam.

Critical Thinking: In addition to the benefits of the dam that were mentioned in the passage, why might a dam-construction project be popular in a country?

Answer: Answers will vary, but students might mention the jobs that would be created by such a project or the excitement generated by a large public-works project.

◄ **Visual Record Answer**
access to fertile soil and water for irrigation, industry, and drinking

Teaching Objective 3
ALL LEVELS: (Suggested time: 15 min.) To help students learn about the resources of North Africa copy the following graphic organizer onto the chalkboard, omitting the connecting lines. Tell students to copy the organizer into their notebooks. Have each student complete the graphic organizer by connecting each box to the appropriate area or areas. Ask volunteers to share their answers with the class. **ESOL**

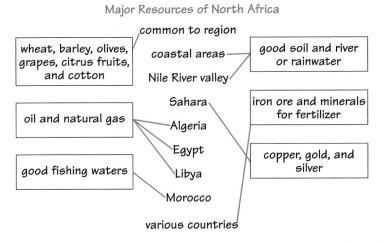

Major Resources of North Africa

Answers to Section 1 Review

Define For definitions, see the glossary.

Working with Sketch Maps Maps will vary, but listed places should be labeled in their approximate locations. Aswān High Dam created Lake Nasser.

Reading for the Main Idea

1. the Ahaggar and the Atlas Mountains (NGS 4)

2. the Sinai Peninsula (NGS 4)

3. It flooded and left deposits of fertile silt. (NGS 15)

Critical Thinking

4. likely to be near water sources

Organizing What You Know

5. climates—desert, Mediterranean, steppe; plants and animals—grasses, small shrubs, trees, insects, snails, small reptiles, gazelles, hyenas, baboons, foxes, weasels; resources—good soil and water sources in coastal areas, fishing off the Atlantic coast, oil and gas, iron ore and minerals for fertilizers, copper, gold, and silver

In some areas there has been no rain for many years. However, rare storms can cause flash floods. In places these floods as well as high winds have carved bare rock surfaces out of the land. Storms of sand and dust can also be severe.

Hardy plants and animals live in the desert. Grasses, small shrubs, and even trees grow where there is enough water. Usually this is in oases. Gazelles, hyenas, baboons, foxes, and weasels are among the region's mammals.

Much of the northern coast west of Egypt has a Mediterranean climate. Winters there are mild and moist. Summers are hot and dry. Plant life includes grasses, shrubs, and even a few forests in the Atlas Mountains. Areas between the Mediterranean climate and the Sahara have a steppe climate. Shrubs and grasses grow there.

✔ **READING CHECK:** (*Physical Systems*) How does climate affect the plants and wildlife of North Africa? It determines what lives in a region: desert—hardy plants and animals, more wildlife in oases; Mediterranean—grasses, shrubs, forests; steppe—shrubs, grasses.

Olives like these in Morocco are an important agricultural product in North Africa. Olives and olive oil are common ingredients in many foods around the Mediterranean.

▼

Resources

Good soils and rain or river water aid farming in coastal areas and the Nile River valley. Common crops are wheat, barley, olives, grapes, citrus fruits, and cotton. The region also has good fishing waters.

Oil and gas are important resources, particularly for Libya, Algeria, and Egypt. Morocco mines iron ore and minerals used to make fertilizers. The Sahara has minerals such as copper, gold, and silver.

✔ **READING CHECK:** (*Physical Systems*) What are North Africa's major resources? Good soils, river water, oil, gas, iron ore; minerals

go.hrw.com **Homework Practice Online**
Keyword: SK5 HP9

Section Review 1

Define and explain: ergs, regs, depressions, silt

Working with Sketch Maps On a map of North Africa that you draw or that your teacher provides, label the following: Red Sea, Mediterranean Sea, Sahara, Nile River, Sinai Peninsula, Ahaggar Mountains, Atlas Mountains, Qattara Depression, Nile Delta, Lake Nasser, and the Suez Canal. In a box in the margin, identify the dam that created Lake Nasser.

Reading for the Main Idea

1. (*Places and Regions*) What two mountain ranges are found in North Africa?

2. (*Places and Regions*) What part of Egypt is east of the Suez Canal?

3. (*Environment and Society*) How did the Nile affect farming in the river valley?

Critical Thinking

4. **Drawing Inferences and Conclusions** Where would you expect to find most of North Africa's major cities?

Organizing What You Know

5. **Summarizing** Use this graphic organizer to describe the physical features of North Africa.

Climates	Plants and Animals	Resources

CLOSE

Ask a student to point out one of the major landforms and a climate zone of North Africa on a wall map. Lead a discussion on how the landforms and climates of this region may affect the lives of people who live there.

REVIEW, ASSESS, RETEACH

Have students complete the Section Review. Then organize students into groups and distribute five index cards to each group. Have each group create five where-am-I questions and swap its cards with the other groups. Then have students complete Daily Quiz 9.1. **COOPERATIVE LEARNING**

EXTEND

Have interested students conduct research on Nile River navigation throughout history. Ask them to find information on any or all of these topics: (1) ancient and modern boat construction, (2) prevailing winds, (3) effect of the rapids on navigation, and (4) income generated by modern tourist cruises. Have students present the results of their research as a written report or illustrated poster. **BLOCK SCHEDULING**

Section 2 History and Culture

Read to Discover

1. What are the major events in the history of North Africa?
2. What are some important facts about the people and culture of North Africa?

Vocabulary
pharaohs
hieroglyphs
Bedouins

Places
Alexandria
Cairo
Fès
Western Sahara

People
Alexander the Great
Naguib Mahfouz

Reading Strategy

FOLDNOTES: TWO-PANEL FLIP CHART Create the FoldNote titled **Two-Panel Flip Chart** described in the Appendix. Label one flap History and the other flap Culture. As you read the section, write what you learn about each topic beneath its flap.

History

The Nile River valley was home to some of the world's oldest civilizations. Sometime after 3200 B.C. lands along the northern Nile were united into one Egyptian kingdom.

The early Egyptians used water from the Nile to grow wheat, barley, and other crops. They also built great stone pyramids and other monuments. Egyptian **pharaohs**, or kings, were buried in the pyramids. How did the Egyptians build these huge monuments? See Connecting to Technology on the next page.

The Egyptians also traded with people from other places. To identify themselves and their goods, the Egyptians used **hieroglyphs** (HY-ruh-glifs). Hieroglyphs are pictures and symbols that stand for ideas or words. They were the basis for Egypt's first writing system.

West of Egypt were people who spoke what are called Berber languages. These people herded sheep and other livestock. They also grew wheat and barley in the Atlas Mountains and along the coast.

Invaders Because of North Africa's long coastline, the region was open to invaders over the centuries. Those invaders included people from the eastern Mediterranean, Greeks, and Romans. For example, one invader was the Macedonian king Alexander the Great. He founded the city of Alexandria in Egypt in 332 B.C. This city became an important seaport and trading center on the Mediterranean coast.

Beginning in the A.D. 600s, Arab armies from Southwest Asia swept across North Africa. They brought the Arabic language and Islam to the

▲
The tombs of early Egyptian pharoahs were decorated with paintings, crafts, and treasures. You can see hieroglyphs across the top of this wall painting.

North Africa • 205

Linking Past to Present

The Necropolis at Bahariya In 1999, archae-ologists announced the discovery three years earlier of the largest mummy burial site ever found in Egypt. Located at the Bahariya Oasis, 230 miles from the Giza pyramids, the site contained evidence dating it from the 300s B.C. to the A.D. 100s. This site was undisturbed by grave robbers and contained large numbers of gold artifacts.

Activity: Have students con-duct research on and then pre-sent a news broadcast about one of the major archaeological dis-coveries such as the tomb of King Tutankhamen or the burial site at the Bahariya Oasis.

Connecting to Technology
Answers
1. pyramids, tombs, and stone temples; to show the power of Egyptian rulers
2. The Egyptians rolled blocks of stone on logs and hauled them up ramps.

internet connect

GO TO: go.hrw.com
KEYWORD: SK5 CH9
FOR: Web sites about
Egyptian mummies

CONNECTING TO Technology

BUILDING THE PYRAMIDS

The monuments of ancient Egypt are among the wonders of the world. They are thousands of years old. These pyramids, temples, and other structures reflect the power of Egyptian rulers and the skills of Egyptian engineers.

The most famous of Egypt's monuments are the huge stone pyramids at Giza near Cairo. The pyramids there were built more than 4,000 years ago as tombs for Egyptian pharaohs. The largest structure is the Great Pyramid. At its base the pyramid's sides are each about 755 feet (230 m) long. The pyramid rises nearly 500 feet (152 m) above the desert floor.

How did the Egyptians build the pyramids? Workers cut large blocks of stone far away and rolled them on logs to the Nile. From there the blocks were moved on barges. At the building site, the Egyptians finished carving the blocks. Then they built dirt and brick ramps alongside the pyramids. They hauled the blocks up the ramps.

The average weight of each of the 2.3 million blocks in the Great Pyramid is 2.5 tons (2.25 metric tons). Building the Great Pyramid prob-ably required from 10,000 to 30,000 workers. They finished the job in about 20 years, but the pyramid still stands thousands of years later.

Understanding What You Read
1. What kinds of monuments did the Egyptians build?
2. How did the Egyptians make up for not having wheeled vehicles?

206 • Chapter 9

TEACH

Teaching Objective 1
LEVEL 1: (Suggested time: 20 min.) Copy the following chart onto the chalkboard, omitting the blue answers. Organize the class into four groups. Assign one group Ancient North Africa, another group Invaders, the third European Control, and the last group Modern North Africa. Have groups compile information about significant groups in each category and put it in the chart. **ESOL, COOPERATIVE LEARNING**

History of North Africa

Ancient North Africa	Invaders	European Control	Modern North Africa
Egyptian kingdom united c. 3200 B.C.; Egyptians farmed, built pyramids, developed trade, used hieroglyphs; Berbers lived west of Egypt, herded livestock, grew wheat and barley	Greeks, Romans; Alexander the Great—founded Alexandria; Arabs beginning in A.D. 600s—brought Arabic and Islam	control began in 1800s, completed by 1912; Italy—Libya; Spain—northern Morocco; France—rest of Morocco, Tunisia, Algeria; Great Britain—Egypt; all independent by 1962	building strong ties with other Arab countries; several wars against Israel; 1979, Egypt became first Arab nation to sign peace treaty with Israel; 1976, Morocco took over Western Sahara

region. Today most North Africans are Muslim and speak Arabic. Under Muslim rule, North African cities became major centers of learning, trade, and craft making. These cities included Cairo in Egypt and Fès in Morocco.

European Control In the 1800s European countries began to take over the region. By 1912 they controlled all of North Africa. In that year Italy captured Libya from the Ottoman Empire. Spain already controlled northern Morocco. France ruled the rest of Morocco as well as Tunisia and Algeria. Egypt was under British control.

Egypt gained limited independence in 1922. The British kept military bases there and maintained control of the Suez Canal until 1956. During World War II the region was a major battleground. After the war, North Africans pushed for independence. Libya, Morocco, and Tunisia each won independence in the 1950s.

Algeria was the last North African country to win independence. Many French citizens had moved to the country. They considered Algeria part of France. Algeria finally won independence in 1962, after a long, bitter war. Most French residents of Algeria then moved to France.

Modern North Africa Since independence, the countries of North Africa have tried to build stronger ties with other Arab countries. For example, Egypt led other Arab countries in several wars against Israel. However, in 1979 Egypt signed a peace treaty with Israel.

In 1976 Morocco took over the former Spanish colony of Western Sahara. Western Saharan rebels have been trying to win independence from Morocco since then.

✓ **READING CHECK:** (*Places and Regions*) What were some major events in the history of North Africa? Invasions by Mediterranean peoples, Greeks, Romans, Arab armies; control by European countries; independence

▲
The ruins of an old Roman amphitheater remain in Alexandria, Egypt.

The inset photograph shows the beautiful doors of the royal palace in Fès, Morocco.

▼

HUMAN SYSTEMS

Small Start for a Big War France's colonial presence in Algeria began in 1830 when the French king invaded the country in hopes of gaining popularity at home. He had found his excuse to attack Algeria three years earlier when the country's ruler struck the French consul with a fly whisk during a meeting. Algeria remained under French control until the Algerian War brought independence in 1962.

Independence came at a heavy price. Some 10,000 French soldiers and more than 100,000 Algerians were killed during the fighting. In addition, many villages were destroyed and some 2,000,000 peasants had to be relocated.

Activity: Have students create charts to categorize and list examples of French influence in Algeria.

LEVELS 2 AND 3: (Suggested time: 45 min.) Organize students into four groups. Assign each group one of the following time periods: Ancient North Africa, Invaders, European Control, or Modern North Africa. Have each group prepare a time line of main events for its time period and write an essay assessing the significance of the individuals involved in the events. Once groups have finished their work, have one student from each group present his or her group's time lines to the class and discuss the significance of the events. **COOPERATIVE LEARNING**

Teaching Objective 2

LEVEL 1: (Suggested time: 20 min.) Draw two large circles on a piece of butcher paper. Divide one circle into six equal parts and cut it into six wedges. Organize the class into six groups and assign each group a topic: language, religion, food, festivals, art, and literature. Have each group write or draw pictures illustrating information about its topic on its wedge. Then have students glue their wedges onto the circle. **ESOL, COOPERATIVE LEARNING, LS KINESTHETIC**

LEVELS 2 AND 3: (Suggested time: 25 min.) Have each student complete the Level 1 lesson. Then have students select one of the wedges created in the Level 1 activity and write a short poem based on the images from the wedge. **LS VERBAL-LINGUISTIC**

Culture and Music

The Berbers The Berbers, Morocco's original people, call themselves Amazigh, or "free and noble men." Their culture is distinct from Moroccan Arab culture. For instance, Berber women have more personal freedom. Although most Berbers are Muslims, others are Christians or Jews.

Many Berbers feel that Arab culture treats them unfairly. One example of this occurs when the Berbers register their children on official records. They find that non-Arab names like Jurgurtha and Messina are not allowed. In addition, schools hold classes in Arabic, not the main Berber language, Tamazight. As a result, many Berber children who speak no Arabic drop out of school.

Discussion: Moroccan music has absorbed Berber influences, including the use of bagpipes and a type of oboe. For an example of Moroccan music, play Selection 13 on the Music of the World Audio CD Program. Use the text and questions in the Teacher's Guide.

Visual Record Answer ▶

The agricultural products are varied.

▲ The floor of the beautiful Muhammad Ali mosque in Cairo is covered with carpet. Muslim men kneel and bow with their faces to the ground to pray.

A variety of vegetables and meat surround a large serving of couscous.

Interpreting the Visual Record What does this food tell you about agricultural products of the region?

▼

Culture

As you have read, the histories of the North African countries have much in common. You will also find many cultural similarities among those countries.

Language and Religion Egyptians, Berbers, and **Bedouins** make up nearly all of Egypt's population. Bedouins are nomadic herders who travel throughout deserts of Egypt and Southwest Asia. Most people in the countries to the west are of mixed Arab and Berber ancestry. Arabic is the major language. Some people speak Berber languages.

Most ethnic Europeans left North Africa after the region's countries became independent. However, French, Italian, and English still are spoken in many areas.

Most North Africans are Muslims. Of the region's countries, Egypt has the largest number of non-Muslims. About 6 percent of Egyptians are Christians or practice other religions.

Food and Festivals What kind of food would you eat on a trip to North Africa? Grains, vegetables, fruits, and nuts are common there. Many meals include couscous (KOOS-koos). Couscous is made from wheat and looks like small pellets of pasta. It is steamed over boiling water or soup. Often it is served with vegetables or meat, butter, and olive oil. Some people mix their couscous with a fiery hot sauce called *harissa*.

A popular dish in Egypt is *fuul*. It is made from fava beans mashed with olive oil, salt, pepper, garlic, and lemons. The combination is then served with hard-boiled eggs and bread.

Important holidays in North Africa include the birthday of the prophet of Islam, Muhammad. The birthday is marked

208 • **Chapter 9**

TEACHER TO TEACHER

Wendy Mason of San Marcos, Texas, suggests the following activity to help students learn about North African history and culture: Pair students and have them prepare a storyboard for a slide show presentation on North African history and culture. Have pairs draw their storyboards on large sheets of poster board and present them to the class. After all the pairs have presented their storyboards, lead a class discussion on combining ideas from all the storyboards to make one class storyboard.

►ASSIGNMENT: Have students select a topic for a documentary film on North Africa and then prepare a movie poster to advertise the documentary. Encourage students to consider the region's history, languages, customs, interesting sites, and culture when choosing their documentary topics. Also encourage students to cut out pictures or to add illustrations to their posters for added interest.

with lights, parades, and special sweets of honey, nuts, and sugar. During the holy month of Ramadan, Muslims abstain from food and drink during the day.

Art and Literature North Africa has long been known for its beautiful architecture, wood carving, and other crafts. Women weave a variety of textiles. Among these are beautiful carpets that feature geometric designs and bright colors.

The region has also produced important writers and artists. For example, Egyptian poetry and other writing date back thousands of years. One of Egypt's most famous writers is Naguib Mahfouz. In 1988 he became the first Arab writer to win the Nobel Prize in literature. Egypt also has a growing movie industry. Egyptian films in Arabic have become popular throughout Southwest Asia and North Africa.

Many North Africans also enjoy popular music based on singing and poetry. The musical scale there has many more notes than are common in Western music. As a result, North African tunes seem to wail or waver. Musicians often use instruments such as the three-stringed *sintir* of Morocco.

▲
This Algerian woman and her daughter are using a loom to weave a rug. The loom allows a rug maker to weave horizontal and vertical threads together.

✓ **READING CHECK:** (*Human Systems*) What are some important facts about the people and culture of North Africa? Arabic major language; Islam major religion; Ramadan major holiday; architecture, arts and crafts, literature major contributions to world

Section Review 2

Define or identify: pharaohs, hieroglyphs, Alexander the Great, Bedouins, Naguib Mahfouz

Working with Sketch Maps On the map you drew in Section 1, label Alexandria, Cairo, Fès, and Western Sahara. In a box in the margin, identify the country that claims Western Sahara.

Reading for the Main Idea

1. (*Places and Regions*) What early civilization thrived along the northern Nile River about 3200 B.C.?

2. (*Human Systems*) How did Islam and the Arabic language come to North Africa?

3. (*Human Systems*) Which European countries controlled countries in North Africa by 1912?

go.hrw.com
Homework Practice Online
Keyword: SK5 HP9

Critical Thinking

4. Drawing Inferences and Conclusions Look at the world map in the textbook's Atlas. Why do you think the Suez Canal is an important waterway for world shipping?

Organizing What You Know

5. Summarizing Copy the following graphic organizer. Use it to identify at least six important facts about the languages, religions, food, festivals, art, and literature of North Africa.

Culture in North Africa

North Africa • 209

Answers to Section 2 Review

Define or identify For definitions and identifications, see the glossary and index.

Working with Sketch Maps Alexandria, Cairo, Fès, and Western Sahara should be located accurately. Morocco claims Western Sahara.

Reading for the Main Idea

1. the Egyptians (NGS 4)

2. Arabic armies (NGS 9)

3. Italy—Libya; Spain—northern Morocco; France—rest of Morocco, Algeria, and Tunisia; Great Britain—Egypt (NGS 13)

Critical Thinking

4. provides a water route between the Indian Ocean and the Mediterranean Sea

Organizing What You Know

5. languages—Arabic, Berber, French, Italian, English; religions—Islam, Christianity, others; food—couscous and other grains, vegetables, fruit, nuts; festivals—Muhammad's birthday, Ramadan; art—architecture, wood carvings, weaving, music; literature—long tradition of poetry (NGS 10)

CLOSE

Ask students to give examples of the importance of the Nile River to Egyptians in the past and today. (Students might note the location of temples and cities, transportation, source of drinking water and irrigation, and so on.) Point out that the Nile made Egypt a magnet for traders, travelers, and invaders.

REVIEW, ASSESS, RETEACH

Have students complete the Section Review. Next, have students prepare crossword puzzles about North Africa. When the puzzles are completed, photocopy them and let each student work a puzzle created by another student. Then have students complete Daily Quiz 9.2.

Have students complete Main Idea Activity S2. Then organize students into three groups and have each group create a large outline map of North Africa on butcher paper. Using the outline map as a base, have the groups create collages from pictures that illustrate information about North Africa. **ESOL, COOPERATIVE LEARNING,** LS **VISUAL-SPATIAL**

EXTEND

Have students research and explain the significance of the major holidays of Islam, including Ramadan. Ask them to describe the origins of the holidays and how they are recognized in a written report. **COOPERATIVE LEARNING, BLOCK SCHEDULING**

GEOGRAPHY SIDELIGHT

Sahara Rock Art Throughout the Sahara, thousands of paintings and engravings decorate caves and cliff overhangs. Stone-age peoples created these works of art when the region's climate was much wetter than it is today. Fertile grassland supported large populations of animals. The rock art shows images of giraffes, crocodiles, and hippopotamuses. Some paintings show strange human figures with large round heads. Scholars believe these images may represent floating spirits.

Activity: Have students conduct research on rock art in other places around the world. Ask students to compare the art from various regions for differences and similarities. Students should also attempt to learn what the art says about the people who created it.

COULD YOU SURVIVE THE SAHARA?

A Land of Sun and Sand

Despite scorching heat, blinding sandstorms, scorpions, poisonous snakes, and death by starvation or thirst, people have traveled across the desert sands of the Sahara for centuries. Groups of merchants, or caravans, still travel together in the desert for protection. These merchants trade mostly in salt, or "white gold." However, water is the most important resource needed to survive the Sahara. Travelers must find a source of water every few days, or they will perish in temperatures of more than 130 degrees!

SURVIVAL CHALLENGE

You are an archaeologist working at a dig near Lake Chad. You want to find the ruins of Garama, the main city of an ancient warrior people known as the Garamantes. The city's location, in southern Libya, is not on your map. You do have a list of riddles that guided traders north during the height of the Garamantian Empire. Each riddle will lead you to the next source of water. A caravan is leaving soon for Tripoli, so jump on a camel and set out on your adventure! Remember—to survive today's environment, you'll have to solve riddles about the ancient environment. How may looking at the region's geography today shed light on its past?

Throughout the Sahara, traders travel great distances in camel caravans like this one.

210   Chapter 9

Survival Challenge Activity

Have students read the list of riddles titled "The Way to Garama" and examine the map. By answering each riddle, students should find their way to the wells along the route and survive their trip across the Sahara. Starting near Lake Chad, ask what the evidence of "long necks" could tell us about the Sahara's past geography. (Rock art showing giraffes tells us that if the area could support vegetation, the climate was much wetter.) Now move on from the well near the rock art. Where did three ancient rivers flow? Remind students that wadis are dry streambeds. What does the presence of wadis tell us about the Sahara's past geography? (Wadis show that rivers have flowed there.) From the well north of the wadis, what feature used to be a lake, and to what does "white gold" refer? (The salt flat

was a lake. Traders called salt "white gold" because it was a valuable trade item.) What does the presence of a salt flat tell us about the Sahara's past geography? (Lakes were more plentiful in the Sahara's past when the region was wetter.) Proceeding from the last well, where would one find shade in the desert? (at an oasis) What may the presence of an oasis tell us about the Sahara's past? (This oasis is a remnant of the vegetation that was there when the region was wetter.) The next clue leads our travelers to an ancient irrigation system. However, if the climate had been much wetter in the past, why was such a system necessary to the Garamantes? (The climate had become much drier over the centuries. The Garamantes had to irrigate with fossil water from underground aquifers.)

Land of Change

The Sahara was not always a desert. About 8000 B.C. the region was a grassland. Stone age peoples who lived in this environment fished in large lakes and hunted giraffes, elephants, and zebras. Early peoples engraved pictures of these animals on rock walls.

By about 500 B.C. the Garamantes were powerful in the Sahara. Even though the Sahara was by this time much drier, the Garamantes grew crops. By digging miles of irrigation canals, the Garamantes tapped into billions of gallons of fossil water. From what you have learned about the importance of water in the desert, what may have caused the Garamantian civilization to decline? How do you think peoples today survive in dry environments? Can you predict what might happen to them in the future?

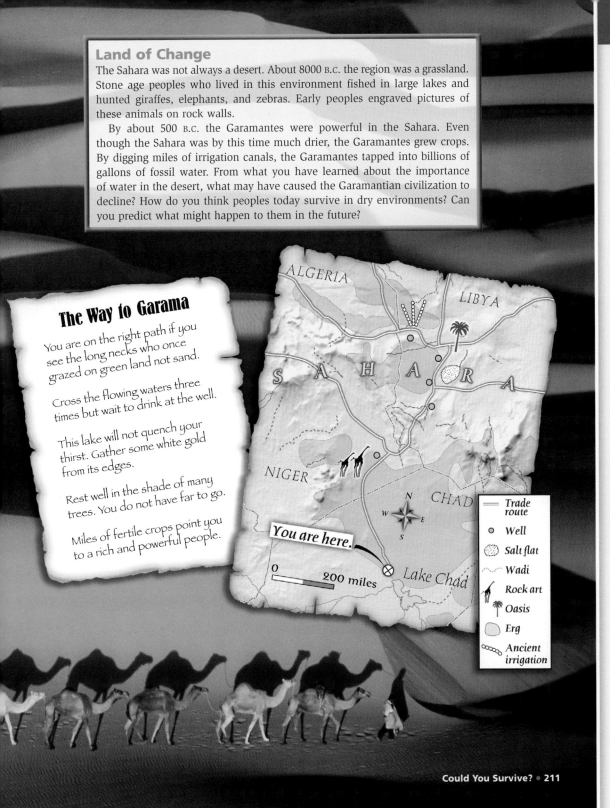

The Way to Garama

You are on the right path if you see the long necks who once grazed on green land not sand.

Cross the flowing waters three times but wait to drink at the well.

This lake will not quench your thirst. Gather some white gold from its edges.

Rest well in the shade of many trees. You do not have far to go.

Miles of fertile crops point you to a rich and powerful people.

You are here.

0   200 miles

	Trade route
⊙	Well
⬭	Salt flat
⌁	Wadi
𓃒	Rock art
🌴	Oasis
⬭	Erg
∞∞	Ancient irrigation

Could You Survive? • 211

Going Further: Thinking Critically

Students have already learned the importance of water in an arid climate like the Sahara. Point out Lake Chad on the map. One of Africa's largest lakes, Lake Chad is shrinking. Overgrazing has reduced the amount of vegetation that surrounds the lake. This loss of vegetation has, in turn, caused the region's climate to become drier. Annual monsoon rains provided most of the lake's water in the past. However, since the 1960s, the region has experienced a series of droughts. Without the rains, the region started to undergo a process of desertification—soils lose their fertility and ability to support plant life.

Lead a discussion about what effect Lake Chad's decline may have on the region's physical and human geography. Point out that the population of the region is increasing. What may happen if the lake dries up completely? (With a growing population, demand for water will increase. The Sahara will expand farther south and people will no longer be able to live in the region.)

➤ **This Could You Survive? feature addresses National Geography Standards 10, 11, 17, and 18.**

Land of Change Activity

Explain to students that the Garamantes used an irrigation system called *foggaras* to extract fossil water from underground aquifers. Remind students that fossil water is groundwater that is not replaced by rain water. To build the *foggaras*, slaves dug deep shafts into aquifers. A series of underground tunnels linked the shafts. By using fossil water from the Sahara region for more than 600 years, the Garamantes extracted a total of some 30 billion gallons of water. How may using this nonrenewable resource have led to the decline of Garamantian civilization? (Possible answer: The Garamantes extracted all of the fossil water that was available to them. When the aquifer was depleted the civilization collapsed.)

Some people living in North Africa today also rely on fossil water for their survival. The world's largest fossil water reserve—the Nubian aquifer—lies beneath most of Egypt, Libya, and Chad. In 1991, Libya began building a network of tunnels to extract millions of gallons of water from this aquifer. Today, this "human-made river" delivers water to Libya's coastal cities. What are the risks involved in using fossil water? Why are people willing to take these risks? (Fossil water is not a renewable resource, and it will eventually run out. People living in arid regions feel they have no choice but to use fossil water because it is their only water source.)

Section 3 Egypt Today

Read to Discover
1. What are the people and cities of Egypt like today?
2. What are Egypt's important economic activities?
3. What challenges does Egypt face today?

Vocabulary
fellahin

Places
Egypt
Cairo
Alexandria

People
Anwar Sadat

Reading Strategy

FOLDNOTES: LAYERED BOOK Create the FoldNote titled **Layered Book** described in the Appendix. Write Egypt Today on the top tab. Label the other tabs People and Cities, Economy, and Challenges. As you read this section, write what you learn about each topic above each label.

People and Cities

Egypt is North Africa's most populous country. More than 74 million people live there.

Rural Egypt More than half of all Egyptians live in small villages and other rural areas. Most rural Egyptians are farmers called **fellahin** (fel-uh-HEEN). They own very small plots of land. Most fellahin also work large farms owned by powerful families. Many also depend on money sent home by family members working abroad. Many Egyptians work in Europe or oil-rich countries in Southwest Asia.

Cities Egypt's capital and largest city is Cairo. More than 10 million people live there. Millions more live in surrounding cities.

Place A muezzin (moo-E-zuhn) calls Muslims to prayer in Cairo. A muezzin often makes his calls from the door or the minaret, or tower, of a mosque. His calls—or recordings played through speakers—can be heard throughout Islamic communities five times daily.

Section 3

Objectives
1. Describe the people and cities of Egypt today.
2. List Egypt's important economic activities.
3. Identify the challenges that Egypt faces today.

FOCUS

Bellringer
Copy the following instructions onto the chalkboard: *Imagine what it would be like to live in a country with cities thousands of years old. What might be the benefits and drawbacks of living in such a country?* Tell students to respond in writing. Ask volunteers to share their responses with the class. (Students might mention that such a country would have many antiquities and sites of historical interest or that streets and lanes might be narrow.) Tell students that in Section 3 they will learn that Egypt is a modern nation with ties to the ancient world.

Building Vocabulary
Write the vocabulary term **fellahin** on the chalkboard. Ask a volunteer to find and read aloud the word's definition and origin (Arabic) from the dictionary. Then ask students to describe where they think most fellahin might live (near the Nile River and the Nile Delta).

◄

Place Tourist ships sit on the Nile River in Luxor. Tourists visit the ruins of a beautiful temple built there more than 2,300 years ago. These and other historical sites make tourism an important part of Egypt's economy.

Cairo was founded more than 1,000 years ago along the Nile. Its location at the southern end of the delta helped it grow. The city lies along old trading routes between Asia and Europe. Later it was connected by railroad to Mediterranean ports and the Suez Canal.

Today Cairo is a mixture of modern buildings and small, mud-brick houses. People continue to move there from rural areas. Many live in makeshift housing. Traffic and pollution are serious problems.

Alexandria has more than 4 million people. It is located in the Nile Delta along the Mediterranean coast. The city is a major seaport and home to many industries.

✔ **READING CHECK:** *Places and Regions* What are Egypt's people and cities like today? More than half of the people live in rural areas; cities are congested and heavily populated, with both modern and traditional architecture

Economy

To provide for its growing population, Egypt is working to expand its industries. Textiles, tourism, and oil are three of the most important industries. The Suez Canal is another source of income. Ships pay tolls to pass through it. Ships use the canal to avoid long trips around southern Africa. This makes the canal one of the world's busiest waterways.

About 30 percent of Egyptian workers are farmers. A warm, sunny climate and water for irrigation make the Nile Delta ideal for growing cotton. Farmlands along the Nile River are used for growing vegetables, grain, and fruit.

✔ **READING CHECK:** *Places and Regions* How does the Suez Canal affect Egypt's economy? Provides income from tolls

Our Amazing Planet

Fish is an important food for people living along the Nile. One fish, the giant Nile perch, can grow to a weight of 300 pounds (136 kg).

Egypt

COUNTRY	POPULATION/ GROWTH RATE	LIFE EXPECTANCY	LITERACY RATE	PER CAPITA GDP
Egypt	74,718,797 1.9%	68, male 73, female	58%	$3,900
United States	290,342,554 0.9%	74, male 80, female	97%	$37,600

Source: Central Intelligence Agency, *The World Factbook 2003*

Interpreting the Chart How does the growth rate of Egypt compare to that of the United States?

Linking Past to Present

Luxor The Temple of Luxor is made up of courtyards, halls, and chambers surrounded by rows of gigantic columns. The columns are shaped to resemble papyrus plants topped by buds.

Construction of the temple complex was begun by the pharaoh Amenhotep III, although there may have been an earlier temple on this spot. Several succeeding pharaohs added to the structure. Later still, a shrine to Alexander the Great was added. A Roman legion made its headquarters inside this temple. Christian churches and a mosque were built on different parts of the site.

Today Luxor is one of Egypt's major tourist attractions. In addition to the popular Nile River cruises, visitors can reach Luxor by train or airplane.

Activity: Have interested students research the Temple of Luxor and prepare maps of the complex as it might have looked during different periods of history.

◄**Chart Answer**

It is higher.

Answers to Section 3 Review

Define For definitions, see the glossary.

Working with Sketch Maps Egypt should be labeled in its approximate location. Cairo is the capital of Egypt.

Reading for the Main Idea

1. Some people want an Islamic government, which would mean fewer freedoms. **(NGS 9)**

2. textiles, tourism, oil, shipping through the Suez Canal, cotton, vegetables, grain, and fruit **(NGS 4, 11)**

Critical Thinking

3. for access to water for irrigation and travel

4. Its location at the southern end of the Nile Delta helped it grow through trade. **(NGS 12)**

Organizing What You Know

5. Answers should include the challenges of farming, crowded cities, health issues, literacy rate, and debates over Egypt's role in the world and the influence of Islam in the country's government.

Biography Answer ▶

negotiated peace between Egypt and Israel

BIOGRAPHY

Anwar Sadat
(1918–1981)

Character Trait: Cooperation

As Egypt's president for 11 years, Anwar Sadat was best known for negotiating peace between Egypt and Israel. During his historic visit to Israel in 1977, Sadat acknowledged Israel's existence and called for the return of Palestinian land. In 1978, Sadat received the Nobel Peace Prize along with Israel's Prime Minister Menachem Begin for both of their efforts in achieving peace. Three years later, however, an extremist group who opposed peace with Israel assassinated Sadat.

How did President Sadat cooperate with Israel?

Challenges

Egypt faces important challenges today. For example, the country's farmland is limited to the Nile River valley and delta. To keep the land productive, farmers must use more and more fertilizer. This can be expensive. In addition, overwatering has been a problem. It has brought to the surface salts that are harmful to crops. These problems and a rapidly growing population have forced Egypt to import much of its food.

In addition, Egyptians are divided over their country's role in the world. Many want their country to remain a leader among Arab countries. However, others want their government to focus more on improving life for Egyptians at home.

Many Egyptians live in severe poverty. Many do not have clean water for cooking or washing. The spread of disease in crowded cities is also a problem. In addition, about half of Egyptians cannot read and write. Still, Egypt's government has made progress. Today Egyptians live longer and are much healthier than 50 years ago.

Another challenge facing Egyptians is the debate over the role of Islam in the country. Some Muslims want to shape the country's government and society along Islamic principles. However, some Egyptians worry that such a change would mean fewer personal freedoms. Some supporters of an Islamic government have turned to violence to advance their cause. Attacks on tourists in the 1990s were particularly worrisome. A loss of tourism would hurt Egypt's economy.

✓ **READING CHECK:** *Places and Regions* What are some of the challenges Egypt faces today? Necessity of importing food due to the expense of fertilizer and from overwatering, division over country's role in the world; severe poverty, disease, illiteracy; role of Islam, violence

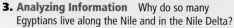

Homework Practice Online
Keyword: SK5 HP9

Section Review 3

Define or identify: fellahin, Anwar Sadat

Working with Sketch Maps On the map you drew in Section 2, label Egypt, Cairo, and Alexandria. Identify the capital of Egypt.

Reading for the Main Idea

1. *Human Systems* What is the relationship between religion and culture in Egypt today?

2. *Places and Regions* What industries and crops are important to Egypt's economy?

Critical Thinking

3. **Analyzing Information** Why do so many Egyptians live along the Nile and in the Nile Delta?

4. **Finding the Main Idea** How has Cairo's location shaped its development?

Organizing What You Know

5. **Summarizing** Copy the following graphic organizer. Use it to describe some of the challenges facing Egypt today.

Challenges

CLOSE

Have students recall the challenges faced by Egypt today. Then have them compare the challenges facing Egypt with the challenges faced by the United States. Ask students if both countries can deal with similar challenges in the same way. Have volunteers justify and explain their answers.

REVIEW, ASSESS, RETEACH

Have students complete the Section Review. Then have them work in pairs to write five questions about modern Egypt on index cards, placing the answers on the reverse side. When students have finished, have each pair exchange cards with another pair and answer the questions. Then have students complete Daily Quiz 9.3. **COOPERATIVE LEARNING**

Have students complete Main Idea Activity S3. Then organize students into four groups and assign each group Cities, People, Economy, or Challenges. Have groups use their textbooks to list information about their assigned topics. Then share the findings in class. **ESOL, COOPERATIVE LEARNING**

EXTEND

Have interested students conduct research on life in Egypt today and create a print or multimedia presentation outlining daily life in either a rural or urban setting. Have students share their presentations with the class. **BLOCK SCHEDULING**

Section 4 Libya, Tunisia, Algeria, and Morocco

Read to Discover

1. What are the region's people and cities like today?
2. What are the countries' important economic activities?
3. What challenges do the countries face today?

Vocabulary

Casbah
souks
free port
dictator

Places

Libya
Tunisia
Algeria
Morocco
Tripoli
Benghazi
Algiers
Casablanca
Rabat
Tunis
Strait of Gibraltar

People

Mu 'ammar al-Gadhafi

Reading Strategy

READING ORGANIZER Create a five-column chart on a sheet of paper. Label the columns Country, People, Cities, Economy, and Challenges. In the Country column, write Libya, Tunisia, Algeria, and Morocco, skipping several lines between them. As you read the section, write what you learn about each country in the appropriate column.

SECTION 4 RESOURCES

Reproducible
◆ Lecture Notes, Section 4
◆ Know It Notes S4

Technology
◆ One-Stop Planner CD–ROM, Lesson 9.4
◆ Homework Practice Online
◆ HRW Go site

Reinforcement, Review, and Assessment
◆ Section 4 Review
◆ Daily Quiz 9.4
◆ Main Idea Activity S4
◆ Chapter Summaries and Review
◆ English Audio Summary 9.4
◆ Spanish Audio Summary 9.4

People and Cities

Western Libya, Tunisia, Algeria, and Morocco are often called the Maghreb (MUH-gruhb). This Arabic word means "west" or "the direction of the setting sun." Most of the Maghreb is covered by the Sahara. There you will find sandy plains and rocky uplands. Cities and farmland are located in narrow coastal strips of land. These strips lie between the Atlantic and Mediterranean coasts in the north and the Sahara and Atlas Mountains farther inland.

Libya is almost completely desert. Fertile land is limited to small areas along the coast. Cities and most of the population are found in those coastal areas. Libya is the most urbanized country in the region. More than 85 percent of Libya's more than 5 million people live in cities. The largest cities are Benghazi and the capital, Tripoli.

Algiers is a large city and is Algeria's capital. The central part of Algiers is a maze of winding alleys and tall walls. This old district is called the **Casbah**. The Casbah is basically an old fortress. **Souks**, or marketplaces, are found there today. The centers of other North African cities also have Casbahs.

Other large cities include Casablanca and Rabat in Morocco and Tunis in Tunisia. Another Moroccan city, Tangier, overlooks the Strait of Gibraltar. This beautiful city was once a Spanish territory. Today tourists can take a quick ferry ride from Spain across the strait to Tangier, a **free port**. A free port is a city in which almost no taxes are placed on goods sold there.

▲ With a backdrop of brightly colored mosaics, Moroccan boys enjoy a day in Tangier's Casbah.

✓ **READING CHECK:** (*Places and Regions*) What geographic factors explain the region's population patterns? The region is mostly desert, and the cities and farmland are therefore located along the coast.

North Africa • 215

Section 4

Objectives

1. Describe the region's people and cities today.
2. List the countries' important economic activities.
3. Identify the challenges the countries face today.

FOCUS

Bellringer

Write the name of your town, city, or regional center on the chalkboard. Then copy the following instructions onto the chalkboard: *Identify old and new neighborhoods or districts in the community. What resources helped create the new features?* Tell students to respond in writing. Then tell students that in Section 4 they will learn how Libya, Tunisia, Algeria, and Morocco also display contrasts between old and new.

Building Vocabulary

Write **Casbah**, **souks**, and **free port** on the chalkboard. Explain that a Casbah is the old district of a city that served as a fortress, a souk is a marketplace usually found within the Casbah, and a free port is a city with few taxes placed on goods. Tell students that all of these terms are important to understanding the economy of this region. Then have a student look up **dictator** in the glossary. Mention that one of the countries of North Africa is ruled by a dictator.

Crazy for Couscous Explain to students that preparing couscous from scratch is very time consuming. Therefore, many people use packaged couscous. It can be prepared for serving in a variety of ways. For instance, steamed couscous can be served as a dessert when topped with raisins, sugar, and cinnamon.

Purchase and prepare a package of couscous according to the directions. Prepare two separate batches of couscous, one as described above and one as described in Section 2.

Chart Answer

Morocco

Libya, Tunisia, Algeria, and Morocco

Country	Population/ Growth Rate	Life Expectancy	Literacy Rate	Per Capita GDP
Algeria	32,818,500 1.65%	69, male 72, female	70%	$5,300
Libya	5,499,074 2.4%	74, male 78, female	83%	$7,600
Morocco	31,689,265 1.6%	68, male 72, female	52%	$3,900
Tunisia	9,924,742 1.7%	74, male 76, female	74%	$6,500
United States	290,342,554 0.9%	74, male 80, female	97%	$37,600

Source: Central Intelligence Agency, *The World Factbook 2003*

Interpreting the Chart Which country is the least economically developed?

Place Marrakech (muh-RAH-kish) is a popular tourist resort in central Morocco. It sits in the foothills of the Atlas Mountains.

▼

Economy

Oil, mining, and tourism are important industries in these countries. Oil is the most important resource, particularly in Libya and Algeria. Money from oil pays for schools, health care, other social programs, and military equipment. The region's countries also have large deposits of natural gas, iron ore, and lead.

Morocco is the only North African country with little oil. However, the country is an important producer and exporter of fertilizer.

About 20 percent of the workers in Libya, Tunisia, and Algeria are farmers. In Morocco farmers make up about half of the labor force. North Africa's farmers grow and export wheat, other grains, olives, fruits, and nuts. However, the region's desert climate and poor soils limit farming, particularly in Libya. Libya imports most of its food.

The Maghreb countries have close economic relationships with European countries. This is partly because of old colonial ties between North Africa and Europe. In addition, European countries are located nearby, lying just across the Mediterranean Sea. Formal agreements between North African countries and the European Union (EU) also have helped trade. Today about 80 percent of Tunisia's trade is with EU countries. The largest trade partners of Algeria, Libya, and Morocco are also EU members. Many European tourists visit North Africa.

✓ **READING CHECK:** *Places and Regions* How does the oil industry affect Libya's and Algeria's schools, health care, and other social programs? provides money to fund them

---

TEACH

Teaching Objectives 1–3

ALL LEVELS: (Suggested time: 30 min.) Copy the following graphic organizer onto the chalkboard, omitting the blue answers. Use it to help students learn about the people, cities, economic activities, and today's challenges that characterize Libya, Tunisia, Algeria, and Morocco by having the class supply the missing information. **ESOL**

Features of the Maghreb

People	most people live in the narrow coastal region between Atlantic and Mediterranean coasts in north and Sahara and Atlas Mountains farther inland
Cities	cities located in narrow coastal region; Libya most urbanized; largest cities are Algiers (Algeria), Tripoli and Benghazi (Libya), Casablanca and Rabat (Morocco), Tunis (Tunisia); Tangier (Morocco) is a free port
Economic Activities	oil, mining, tourism, natural gas, iron ore, lead, fertilizer, farming, trade
Today's Challenges	need for more economic and political freedom; dictatorship in Libya; deciding role of Islam in government

Challenges

The countries of the Maghreb have made much progress in health and education. However, important challenges remain. Among these challenges is the need for more economic freedom. Each of these countries has had elements of a command economy, in which government owns and operates industry. However, in recent years the region's governments have moved to loosen that control. They have sold some government-owned businesses. They have also taken other steps to help private industry grow.

Political freedoms are limited for many North Africans. Many have little say in their governments. For example, since 1969 Libya has been ruled by a **dictator**, Mu'ammar al-Gadhafi. A dictator is someone who rules a country with complete power. Gadhafi has supported bombing, kidnapping, and other acts of violence against Israel and Israel's supporters. As a result, countries have limited their economic relationships with Libya.

As in Egypt, another challenge is conflict over the role of Islam in society. For example, in Algeria some groups want a government based on Islamic principles and laws. In 1992 the government canceled elections that many believed would be won by Islamic groups. Violence between Algeria's government and some Islamic groups has claimed thousands of lives since then.

✓ **READING CHECK:** (*Places and Regions*) What are some of the challenges the region's countries face today? *Economic and political freedom; conflict over Islam's role*

These Islamic students at a religious school in Libya are reciting verses from the Qur'an. Religious education is important in this mostly Islamic region.

▼

Section Review 4

Define or identify: Casbah, souks, free port, dictator, Mu'ammar al-Gadhafi

Working with Sketch Maps On the map you created in Section 3, label Libya, Tunisia, Algeria, Morocco, Tripoli, Benghazi, Algiers, Casablanca, Rabat, Tunis, and the Strait of Gibraltar. In a box in the margin, identify the national capitals of the region's countries.

Reading for the Main Idea

1. (*Places and Regions*) What are the old, central districts of many North African cities like?

2. (*Places and Regions*) What type of economy have these nations had, and how is this changing?

Homework Practice Online
Keyword: SK5 HP9

Critical Thinking

3. **Finding the Main Idea** Where are the region's farms and most of its people found today? Why?

4. **Analyzing Information** How are the political rights of North Africans different from those of people in the United States?

Organizing What You Know

5. **Summarizing** Copy the following graphic organizer. Use it to list industries, resources, farm products, and trade partners of the Maghreb countries.

Industries	
Resources	
Farm products	
Trade partners	

North Africa • 217

Answers to Section 4 Review

Define or identify For definitions and identifications, see the glossary and index.

Working with Sketch Maps The capitals are Libya—Tripoli; Algeria—Algiers; Morocco—Rabat; and Tunisia—Tunis.

Reading for the Main Idea

1. They include a Casbah and a souk. **(NGS 4)**

2. command; governments have moved to loosen their control **(NGS 12)**

Critical Thinking

3. along the coast; to be closer to water and away from the desert

4. Political rights of North Africans are limited, and people have little say in their governments, whereas in the United States people enjoy the right to vote and participate in the political process.

Organizing What You Know

5. industries—oil, mining, tourism, and fertilizer; resources—oil, natural gas, iron ore, and lead; farm products—wheat and other grains, olives, fruits, and nuts; trade partners—European countries **(NGS 4)**

CLOSE

Tell students that the Casbah of Algiers has been used as a metaphor for the Algerian nation. Then lead a class discussion about why certain sites or monuments might become symbols or metaphors for a nation.

REVIEW, ASSESS, RETEACH

Have students complete the Section Review. Discuss the review in class. Then have students complete Daily Quiz 9.4.

Then organize students into four groups and assign each group one of the following topics: People, Places, Products, or Challenges in Libya, Tunisia, Algeria, and Morocco. Distribute poster board to the groups, and have each group create a graphic organizer to present information related to its topic. **ESOL, COOPERATIVE LEARNING**

EXTEND

Have interested students conduct research on the colonial history of Libya, Tunisia, Algeria, or Morocco. Have students use their findings to create an annotated time line for one of the four countries.
BLOCK SCHEDULING

Define and Identify
For definitions and identifications, see the glossary and index.

Review the Main Ideas
17. The Sahara covers most of the region and settlement is limited to coastal areas. (NGS 4)

18. desert, Mediterranean, and steppe (NGS 4)

19. They considered Algeria part of France.

20. the birthday of Muhammad, the holy month of Ramadan (NGS 10)

21. Cairo

22. farming-related issues, rapidly growing population, health and literacy issue, its role as an Arab country, and the role of Islam in the country (NGS 18)

23. textiles, tourism, oil, mining, fertilizer

24. Libya (NGS 4)

25. because of old colonial ties between North Africa and Europe

Think Critically
26. The harsh desert climate has caused settlements to be located near water sources.

27. to be near water sources

28. as a shipping route from the Mediterranean Sea to the Indian Ocean

29. Debate over the role of Islam in government has sometimes caused internal conflict; conflict with Israel has sometimes strained international relations.

30. political tensions, lack of adequate water resources, and problems related to population growth

---

Review and Practice

Define and Identify
Identify each of the following:

1. ergs
2. regs
3. depressions
4. silt
5. pharaohs
6. hieroglyphs
7. Alexander the Great
8. Naguib Mahfouz
9. Bedouins
10. fellahin
11. Anwar Sadat
12. Casbah
13. souks
14. free port
15. dictator
16. Mu'ammar al-Gadhafi

Review the Main Ideas

17. How does geography affect settlement patterns in North Africa?

18. What are North Africa's main climates?

19. Why did many French citizens move to Algeria before 1962?

20. What are some important holidays in North Africa?

21. Which Egyptian city lies along old trading routes and was founded more than 1,000 years ago?

22. What are some important challenges facing Egypt today?

23. What are the most important industries in North Africa?

24. Which is the most urbanized country in North Africa?

25. Why do the Maghreb countries have close economic relationships with European countries?

Think Critically

26. Finding the Main Idea How do you think the Sahara has influenced settlement in the region?

27. Finding the Main Idea Why are most of North Africa's cities and population located in coastal areas?

28. Analyzing Information Why is the Suez Canal important to world trade?

29. Finding the Main Idea In what way has Islam influenced politics in North Africa?

30. Making Generalizations and Predictions Based on what you have read, what kinds of challenges do you think North Africans will face in coming decades? Explain your answer.

Map Activity

31. On a separate sheet of paper, match the letters on the map with their correct labels.

Sinai Peninsula	Western Sahara
Ahaggar Mountains	Tripoli
Atlas Mountains	Algiers
Nile Delta	Casablanca
Cairo	Strait of Gibraltar

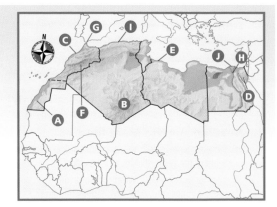

Map Activity
31. A. Western Sahara
B. Ahaggar Mountains
C. Casablanca
D. Sinai Peninsula
E. Tripoli
F. Atlas Mountains
G. Strait of Gibraltar
H. Cairo
I. Algiers
J. Nile Delta

Writing Activity

Imagine that you are a Bedouin teenager in the Sahara. Write a one-paragraph journal entry about a typical day in your life. How do you cope with the desert heat? What is it like living without a permanent home? What religion do you practice? What do you eat? Use the library and other resources to help you. Be sure to use standard grammar, spelling, sentence structure, and punctuation.

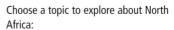

internet connect

Internet Activity: **go.hrw.com**
KEYWORD: SK5 GT9

Choose a topic to explore about North Africa:

- Journey through the Sahara.
- Examine the rich history of North Africa.
- Practice using Arabic calligraphy.

Social Studies Skills Practice

Analyzing Graphs

Arable land is land that is suitable for farming. Study the following chart of the percentages of arable land in North Africa. Then answer the questions.

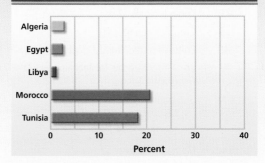

Arable Land in North Africa

(Bar chart showing percent of arable land by country: Algeria, Egypt, Libya, Morocco, Tunisia; x-axis labeled "Percent" from 0 to 40)

1. Which country has the least land suitable for growing crops?
2. Which country has the most land suitable for growing crops?
3. Overall, do the countries of North Africa have good land for farming? Explain your answer.
4. What can you determine about the region's climate and soils from these numbers?

Analyzing Primary Sources

Read the following excerpt from Egyptian writer Naguib Mahfouz's acceptance speech after he was awarded the Nobel Prize for Literature. Then answer the questions.

"This man coming from the third world, how did he find the peace of mind to write stories? You are perfectly right. I come from a world labouring under the burden of debts whose paying back exposes it to starvation or very close to it. . . . Fortunately, art is generous and sympathetic. In the same way that it dwells with the happy ones it does not desert the wretched [unhappy]. It offers both alike the convenient means for expressing what swells up in their [heart]."

1. According to Mahfouz, what purpose does writing serve?
2. Does Mahfouz feel that everyone can become writers? Why?
3. What does Mahfouz mean when he says he comes from the third world?
4. According to Mahfouz, how are third-world countries burdened?

Writing Activity

Answers will vary, but the information included should be consistent with text material. Students should respond to the various questions as well as demonstrate an understanding of the Bedouin culture and lifestyle. Use Rubric 15, Journals, to evaluate student work.

Interpreting Graphs

1. Libya
2. Morocco
3. No, the chart indicates that most of the land is not suited for farming. Only two of the countries have near 20 percent arable land, and the other countries have much smaller percentages.
4. not a great deal, since the suitability of land for farming can be determined by several factors

Analyzing Primary Sources

1. It provides a means of expression.
2. yes, because "art is generous and sympathetic."
3. from a country that is neither part of the wealthy Western democratic countries, nor was part of the old Soviet Empire

CHAPTER 9 REVIEW AND ASSESSMENT RESOURCES

Reproducible

- Readings in World Geography, History, and Culture 53 and 54
- Critical Thinking Activity 9
- Vocabulary Activity 9

Technology

- Chapter 9 Test Generator (on the One-Stop Planner)
- Audio CD Program, Chapter 9
- HRW Go site

Reinforcement, Review, and Assessment

- Chapter 9 Review and Practice
- Chapter Summaries and Review
- Chapter 9 Test
- Chapter 9 Test for English Language Learners and Special-Needs Students

internet connect

GO TO: **go.hrw.com**
KEYWORD: SK5 Teacher
FOR: a guide to using the Internet in your classroom

Objectives	Pacing Guide	Reproducible Resources
SECTION 1		
Physical Geography (pp. 221–23)	**Regular**	**RS** Know It Notes S1
1. Identify the landforms and climates found in West Africa.	.5 day	**ELL** Main Idea Activity S1
2. Explain why the Niger River is important to the region.	Lecture Notes, Section 1	
3. Identify the resources of West Africa.	**Block Scheduling**	
	.5 day	
	Block Scheduling Handbook, Chapter 10	
SECTION 2		
History and Culture (pp. 224–28)	**Regular**	**RS** Know It Notes S2
1. Identify the great African kingdoms that once ruled the region.	1 day	**RS** Graphic Organizer 10
2. Explain how contact with Europeans affected West Africa.	Lecture Notes, Section 2	**E** Cultures of the World Activity 6
3. Identify the challenges the governments of the region face.	**Block Scheduling**	**E** Creative Strategies for Teaching World Geography, Lesson 16
4. Identify some features of West African culture.	.5 day	**SM** Geography for Life Activity 23
	Block Scheduling Handbook, Chapter 10	**IC** Interdisciplinary Activities for the Middle Grades 26, 27, 28
		ELL Main Idea Activity S2
SECTION 3		
The Sahel Countries (pp. 229–31)	**Regular**	**RS** Know It Notes S3
1. Describe what Mauritania, Mali, and Niger are like today.	.5 day	**SM** Map Activity 10
2. Describe the challenges Chad and Burkina Faso face.	Lecture Notes, Section 3	**ELL** Main Idea Activity S3
	Block Scheduling	
	.5 day	
	Block Scheduling Handbook, Chapter 10	
SECTION 4		
The Coastal Countries (pp. 232–35)	**Regular**	**RS** Know It Notes S4
1. Describe what life in Nigeria is like today.	1 day	**SM** Map Activity 10
2. Identify some economic challenges the other countries of the region face.	Lecture Notes, Section 4	**E** Biography Activity: Wole Soyinka
	Block Scheduling	**ELL** Main Idea Activity S4
	.5 day	
	Block Scheduling Handbook, Chapter 10	

Chapter Resource Key

RS Reading Support

IC Interdisciplinary Connections

E Enrichment

SM Skills Mastery

A Assessment

REV Review

ELL Reinforcement and English Language Learners and English for Speakers of Other Languages (ESOL)

 Transparencies

 CD-ROM

 Music

 Video

 go.hrw.com Internet

Holt Presentation Maker Using Microsoft® PowerPoint®

 One-Stop Planner CD–ROM

See the *One-Stop Planner* for a complete list of additional resources for students and teachers.

One-Stop Planner CD–ROM

It's easy to plan lessons, select resources, and print out materials for your students when you use the *One-Stop Planner CD–ROM with Test Generator.*

Technology Resources	Review, Reinforcement, and Assessment Resources	
One-Stop Planner CD–ROM, Lesson 10.1	ELL	Main Idea Activity S1
Our Environment CD–ROM/ Seek and Tell/People Affecting Nature	REV	Section 1 Review
ARGWorld CD–ROM	A	Daily Quiz 10.1
Geography and Cultures Visual Resources with Teaching Activities 43–48	REV	Chapter Summaries and Review
Homework Practice Online	ELL	English Audio Summary 10.1
HRW Go site	ELL	Spanish Audio Summary 10.1
One-Stop Planner CD–ROM, Lesson 10.2	ELL	Main Idea Activity S2
ARGWorld CD–ROM	REV	Section 2 Review
Homework Practice Online	A	Daily Quiz 10.2
HRW Go site	REV	Chapter Summaries and Review
	ELL	English Audio Summary 10.2
	ELL	Spanish Audio Summary 10.2
One-Stop Planner CD–ROM, Lesson 10.3	ELL	Main Idea Activity S3
ARGWorld CD–ROM	REV	Section 3 Review
Homework Practice Online	A	Daily Quiz 10.3
HRW Go site	REV	Chapter Summaries and Review
	ELL	English Audio Summary 10.3
	ELL	Spanish Audio Summary 10.3
One-Stop Planner CD–ROM, Lesson 10.4	ELL	Main Idea Activity S4
ARGWorld CD–ROM	REV	Section 4 Review
Music of the World Audio CD Program, Selection 14	A	Daily Quiz 10.4
Homework Practice Online	REV	Chapter Summaries and Review
HRW Go site	ELL	English Audio Summary 10.4
	ELL	Spanish Audio Summary 10.4

internet connect

HRW ONLINE RESOURCES

GO TO: go.hrw.com
Then type in a keyword.

TEACHER HOME PAGE
KEYWORD: SK5 TEACHER

CHAPTER INTERNET ACTIVITIES
KEYWORD: SK5 GT10

Choose an activity to:
• find out about giant baobab trees.
• meet the people of West Africa.
• learn about the history of the slave trade.

CHAPTER ENRICHMENT LINKS
KEYWORD: SK5 CH10

CHAPTER MAPS
KEYWORD: SK5 MAPS10

ONLINE ASSESSMENT
Homework Practice
KEYWORD: SK5 HP10
Standardized Test Prep Online
KEYWORD: SK5 STP10
Rubrics
KEYWORD: SS Rubrics

COUNTRY INFORMATION
KEYWORD: SK5 Almanac

CONTENT UPDATES
KEYWORD: SS Content Updates

HOLT PRESENTATION MAKER
KEYWORD: SK5 PPT10

ONLINE READING SUPPORT
KEYWORD: SS Strategies

CURRENT EVENTS
KEYWORD: S5 Current Events

Meeting Individual Needs

Ability Levels

Level 1 Basic-level activities designed for all students encountering new material

Level 2 Intermediate-level activities designed for average students

Level 3 Challenging activities designed for honors and gifted-and-talented students

ESOL Activities that address the needs of students with Limited English Proficiency

Chapter Review and Assessment

E	Readings in World Geography, History, and Culture 55, 56, and 57	A	Chapter 10 Test
SM	Critical Thinking Activity 10		Chapter 10 Test Generator (on the One-Stop Planner)
REV	Chapter 10 Review and Practice		Audio CD Program, Chapter 10
REV	Chapter Summaries and Review	A	Chapter 10 Test for English Language Learners and Special-Needs Students
ELL	Vocabulary Activity 10		HRW Go Site

West Africa
Previewing Chapter Resources

Holt Online Learning

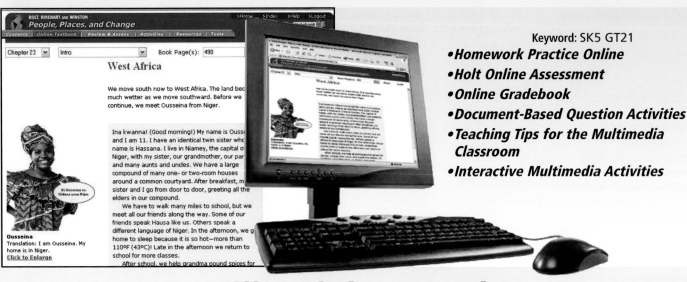

Keyword: SK5 GT21

- *Homework Practice Online*
- *Holt Online Assessment*
- *Online Gradebook*
- *Document-Based Question Activities*
- *Teaching Tips for the Multimedia Classroom*
- *Interactive Multimedia Activities*

Differentiating Instruction

Reading and Writing Support

- *Graphic Organizer Activity*
- ◀ *Vocabulary Activity*
- *Chapter Summary and Review*
- *Know It Notes*
- *Audio CD*

Active Learning

- *Block Scheduling Handbook*
- *Cultures of the World Activity*
- *Interdisciplinary Activity*
- *Map Activity*
- ◀ *Critical Thinking Activity 23*
- *Music of the World CD: Music of Ghana*

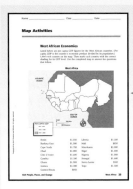

Primary Sources and Advanced Learners

- *Geography for Life Activity: Patterns of West African Migration*
- ◀ *Map Activity: West African Economies*
- *Readings in World Geography, History and Culture:*
  - *56 Travels in the Sahara*
  - *57 Leo Africans: Description of Timbuktu (1526)*

Assessment Program

- ◀ *Daily Quizzes S1–4*
- *Chapter Test*
- *Chapter Test for English Language Learners and Special-Needs Students*

Spanish and ESOL

- *Vocabulary Activity*
- *Main Idea Activities for English Language Learners and Special-Needs Students*
- *Chapter Summary and Review*
- *Spanish Audio Summary*
- *Know It Notes S1–4*
- ◀ *Chapter Test for English Language Learners and Special-Needs Students*

Special Education Modifications

Your **I.D.E.A. Works! CD-ROM** will provide modified versions of the following teaching materials:

- ◀ *Guided Reading Strategies S1–4*
- *Vocabulary Activity*
- *Main Idea Activities S1–4*
- *Daily Quizzes S1–4*
- *Chapter 10 Test*
- *Flash cards of chapter vocabulary terms*

Teacher Resources

Books for Teachers

Adams, W. M., A. S. Goudie, and A. R. Orme, eds. *The Physical Geography of Africa*. Oxford Regional Environments. Oxford University Press, 1996.

Chilson, Peter. *Riding the Demon: On the Road in West Africa*. University of Georgia Press, 1999.

Onwumechili, Chuka. *African Democratization and Military Coups*. Praeger, 1998.

Books for Students

Binns, Tony and Robert Bowden. *West Africa, Country Fact Files*. Raintree/Steck-Vaughn, 1998. Geography, natural resources, economics, and the environment.

Haskins, Jim, and Kathleen Benson. *African Beginnings*. Lothrop, 1998. Examines ancient African kingdoms, including Nubia, Ghana, Mali, Songhay, and Kongo.
SHELTERED ENGLISH

Koslow, Philip. *Centuries of Greatness: The West African Kingdoms 750–1900*. Chelsea House, 1994. Beginning with Ghana, traces early African kingdoms and their cultures.

Onyefulu, Ifeoma. *Grandfather's Work: A Traditional Healer in Nigeria*. Millbrook, 1999. A child describes work of his grandfather, the village healer.

Multimedia Materials

Africa Inspirer. CD–ROM with Labpack. Educational Software Institute.

Africa: Sierra Leone, Ghana, Kenya. Video, 26 min. Films for the Humanities and Sciences.

West Africa: Benin, Mali and Burkina Faso. Video, 47 min. Lonely Planet.

Videos and CDs

Videos

- **CNN** *Presents Geography: Yesterday and Today, Segment 24 The Women of Nigeria*
- *ARG World*

Holt Researcher

http://researcher.hrw.com

- *Organization of African Unity (OAU)*
- *Africa*
- *Colonialism in Africa*
- *Azikiwe, Nnamdi*
- *Nigeria*
- *Niger*
- *Chad*
- *Sierra Leone*
- *Liberia*
- *Ghana*

Transparency Packages

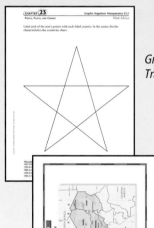

Graphic Organizer Transparencies 10.1–4

Geography and Cultures Visual Resources Transparencies 76–80
82 West Africa: Physical Political
83 Terracotta Portrait Head
84 Cacao: From Field to Consumer

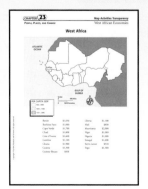

Map Activities Transparency 10 West African Economies

CHAPTER 10

West Africa

We move south now to West Africa. The land becomes much wetter as we move southward. Before we continue, we meet Ousseina from Niger.

Ina kwanna! (Good morning!) My name is Ousseina, and I am 11. I have an identical twin sister whose name is Hassana. I live in Niamey, the capital of Niger, with my sister, our grandmother, our parents, and many aunts and uncles. We have a large compound of many one- or two-room houses around a common courtyard. After breakfast, my sister and I go from door to door, greeting all the elders in our compound.

We have to walk many miles to school, but we meet all our friends along the way. Some of our friends speak Hausa like us. Others speak a different language of Niger. In the afternoon, we go home to sleep because it is so hot—more than 110°F (43°C)! Late in the afternoon we return to school for more classes.

After school, we help grandma pound spices for dinner, sweep the room, and wash the dishes. At bedtime, grandma tells us stories and sings.

Ni Ousseina ce. Gidana yana Nijar.

Translation: I am Ousseina. My home is in Niger.

220 Chapter 10

CHAPTER PROJECT

Have students select a country of West Africa and use the six essential elements of geography to make an illustrated brochure about the country. Instruct students to create six panels for their brochures—one for each of the elements.

STARTING THE CHAPTER

Hold up a jar of peanut butter. Ask students to name as many products as they can that are made from peanuts (candy, cookies, oil for cooking). Point out that peanuts originated in Africa, that they were brought from there to our continent, and that in the 1900s they replaced cotton as the main crop grown on many southern farms. Tell students that they will learn about West Africa, where peanuts are an important crop, in this chapter.

Section 1 Physical Geography

Read to Discover

1. What landforms and climates are found in West Africa?
2. Why is the Niger River important to the region?
3. What resources does West Africa have?

Vocabulary

zonal
Sahel
harmattan
tsetse fly
bauxite

Places

Sahara
Sahel
Niger River
Gulf of Guinea

Reading Strategy

READING ORGANIZER Create a spider map by drawing a circle on a sheet of paper. Label the circle West Africa. Create legs for Landforms, Climate, Niger River, and Resources. As you read the section, write what you learn beneath each leg.

West Africa: Physical-Political

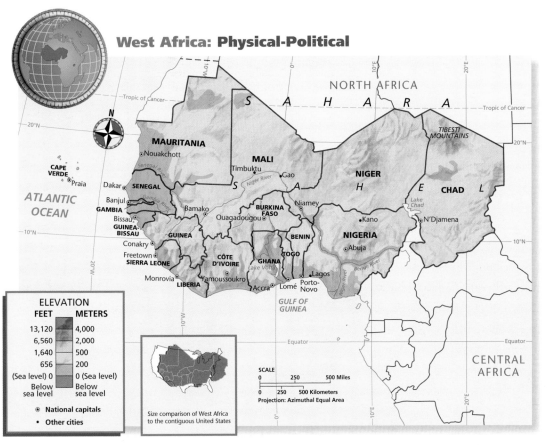

ELEVATION

FEET	METERS
13,120	4,000
6,560	2,000
1,640	500
656	200
(Sea level) 0	0 (Sea level)
Below sea level	Below sea level

⊛ National capitals
• Other cities

SCALE
0   250   500 Miles
0 250 500 Kilometers
Projection: Azimuthal Equal Area

Size comparison of West Africa to the contiguous United States

West Africa • 221

Section 1

Objectives

1. Describe the landforms and climates found in West Africa.
2. Explain the importance of the Niger River to the region.
3. Identify the resources found in West Africa.

FOCUS

Bellringer

Copy the following instructions onto the chalkboard: *List two ways that deserts may spread into non-desert areas. Discuss responses.* (Possible answers: drought, overgrazing grasses, cutting trees, destroying plant life, changing climate) Explain that plants and trees help hold soil in place. When vegetation is removed or dies and no rain falls, the topsoil blows away, causing deserts to spread. Tell students that in Section 1 they will learn more about the physical geography of West Africa, including how the desert is growing in the region.

Using the Physical-Political Map

Have students examine the map on this page. Call on volunteers to name the Sahel countries (Mauritania, Mali, Niger, Burkina Faso, and Chad) and the coastal countries (Senegal, Gambia, Guinea-Bissau, Guinea, Sierra Leone, Liberia, Côte d'Ivoire, Ghana, Togo, Benin, and Nigeria). Tell students that the Sahara is expanding into the Sahel countries. Have students discuss problems the encroaching desert may pose for the people of those countries and, in turn, for people in the coastal countries.

GO TO: go.hrw.com
KEYWORD: SK5 CH10
FOR: Web sites about
West Africa

ENVIRONMENT AND SOCIETY

The Tsetse Fly Found only in Africa near the equator, the tsetse fly transmits a parasite to humans by biting them. The parasite causes the deadly illness trypanosomiasis (tri-pa-nuh-suh-MY-uh-suhs), also known as sleeping sickness. Early symptoms include high fever, weakness, and headache. As the disease progresses, the parasite invades the central nervous system. Eventually, the patient may lapse into a coma and die.

Medical treatment for trypanosomiasis requires hospitalization. Protection can help prevent tsetse fly bites and includes wearing khaki or olive-colored long pants and long-sleeved shirts and using a bednet at night.

Activity: Have students conduct research on other insects that transmit disease in tropical areas.

internet connect

GO TO: go.hrw.com
KEYWORD: SK5 CH10
FOR: Web sites about
the tsetse fly

Visual Record Answer ▶

Farmers carry water in inexpensive containers, rather than through an expensive irrigation system.

Landforms and Climate

West Africa is largely a region of plains. There are low mountains in the southwest and high mountains in the northeast. Four major climate types stretch from east to west in bands or zones. Therefore, geographers say the region's climates are **zonal**.

The Sahara The northernmost parts of the region lie within the Sahara, the first climate zone. The Sahara is the world's largest desert. It stretches across northern Africa from the Atlantic Ocean to the Red Sea. Large areas of this dry climate zone have few or no people.

The Sahel South of the Sahara is a region of dry grasslands called the **Sahel** (sah-HEL). This second climate zone has a steppe climate. Rainfall varies greatly from year to year. In some years it never rains. During winter a dry, dusty wind called the **harmattan** (hahr-muh-TAN) blows south from the Sahara.

During the late 1960s a drought began in the Sahel. Crops failed for several years, and there was not enough grass for the herds. Animals overgrazed the land, and people cut the few large trees for firewood. Wind blew away fertile soil, and the Sahara expanded southward. Without plants for food, many animals and people died. Recent years have been rainier, and life has improved.

The Savanna Farther south is the savanna zone. It contains good soil, thick grass, and scattered tall trees. Farmers can do well when the rains come regularly. However, the region is home to a dangerous insect. The **tsetse** (TSET-see) **fly** carries sleeping sickness, a deadly disease. Although insecticides can help control the flies, they are too expensive for most people to buy.

The Coast and Forest The fourth climate zone lies along the Atlantic and Gulf of Guinea coasts. Many of West Africa's largest cities lie in this coastal zone. You will find a wet, humid tropical climate there. Plentiful rain supports tropical rain forests. However, many trees

Farmers use river water to irrigate onion fields in central Mali. Farming can be difficult in the dry Sahel.

Interpreting the Visual Record

Human-Environment Interaction How do you think economic factors have affected the use of technology in bringing water to the fields?

TEACH

Teaching Objective 1

ALL LEVELS: (Suggested time: 20 min.) Copy the following graphic organizer onto the chalkboard, omitting the blue answers. Use it to help students describe West Africa's zones. **ESOL**, **LS** VISUAL-SPATIAL

Teaching Objectives 2–3

ALL LEVELS: (Suggested time: 10 min.) Ask students to look at the chapter map and locate the cities that lie within Mali and Niger. Then ask students what the cities have in common. (They are inland and on the Niger River.) Then have students list the resources found in West Africa. Ask them to name the country whose resources became more valuable in the 1900s (Nigeria). **ESOL**

Zones of West Africa

CLIMATE ZONE	DESCRIPTION
Sahara	largest desert
Sahel	dry grasslands with steppe climate
savanna	good soil, thick grass, scattered trees
coast and forest	wet humid tropical climate, rain forests

have been cut to make room for growing populations. As a result, environmental damage is a serious problem.

✓ **READING CHECK:** (*Places and Regions*) What are the region's landforms and climate zones? plains, mountains, desert, grasslands, forests; desert, steppe, savanna, humid tropical

The Niger River

The most important river in West Africa is the Niger (NY-juhr). The Niger River starts in low mountains just 150 miles (241 km) from the Atlantic Ocean. It flows eastward and southward for 2,600 miles (4,183 km) and empties into the Gulf of Guinea.

The Niger brings life-giving water to West Africa. In the Sahel it divides into a network of channels, swamps, and lakes. This network is known as the inland delta. The Niger's true delta on the Gulf of Guinea is very wide. Half of Nigeria's coastline consists of the delta.

✓ **READING CHECK:** (*Environment and Society*) Why is the Niger River important to West Africa? It sustains life in West Africa.

▲
The hippopotamus is just one of the many animal species living in the Niger region. Hippopotamuses are good swimmers and can stay underwater for as long as six minutes.

Resources

West Africa's mineral riches include diamonds, gold, iron ore, manganese, and **bauxite**. Bauxite is the main source of aluminum. Nigeria is a major exporter of oil. In fact, oil and related products make up about 95 percent of that country's exports.

✓ **READING CHECK:** (*Places and Regions*) What are some of the region's resources? Minerals—diamonds, gold, iron ore, manganese, and bauxite; oil and oil products

Section Review 1

Define and explain: zonal, Sahel, harmattan, tsetse fly, bauxite

Working with Sketch Maps On a map of West Africa, label the following: Sahara, Niger River, and Gulf of Guinea.

Reading for the Main Idea

1. (*Physical Systems*) What effect has drought had on West Africa's vegetation?

2. (*Places and Regions*) What natural resources are found in West Africa?

3. (*Places and Regions*) What is West Africa's most important river? Describe its two delta regions.

go.hrw.com **Homework Practice Online** Keyword: SK5 HP10

Critical Thinking

4. **Making Generalizations and Predictions** Where in the region would you expect to find the densest populations? Why?

Organizing What You Know

5. **Summarizing** Copy the following graphic organizer. Use it to list and describe the region's climate zones.

Zones	Characteristics

West Africa • 223

Section 2 History and Culture

Read to Discover
1. What great African kingdoms once ruled the region?
2. How did contact with Europeans affect West Africa?
3. What challenges do the region's governments face?
4. What are some features of West African culture?

Vocabulary
archaeology
oral history
animism

Places
Timbuktu

People
Mansa Musa

Reading Strategy

READING ORGANIZER Before you read, draw eight boxes down the center of a sheet of paper. As you read this section, write what you learn in the boxes to create a chain of events in the history of West Africa.

West Africa's History

Much of what we know about West Africa's early history is based on **archaeology**. Archaeology is the study of the remains and ruins of past cultures. **Oral history**—spoken information passed down from person to person through generations—offers other clues.

Great Kingdoms Ancient artifacts suggest that the earliest trading towns developed in the Niger's inland delta. Traders brought dates and salt from the desert. People from the Sahel sold animals and hides. Other trade goods were grains, fish, kola and other tropical nuts, and metals, such as gold. (Much later, kola nuts provided the flavor for cola drinks.) This trade helped African kingdoms grow. One of the earliest West African kingdoms, Ghana (GAH-nuh), had become rich and powerful by about A.D. 800.

 Place These early West African cliff paintings illustrate features from a ceremonial ritual for young people.

Section 2

Objectives
1. Describe the great kingdoms that once ruled the region.
2. Analyze how European contact affected West Africa.
3. Identify the challenges faced by the region's governments.
4. Describe some features of West African culture.

FOCUS

Bellringer

Copy the following question onto the chalkboard: *What are three objects from our culture that might be found in later years by archaeologists?* Discuss responses. Then have volunteers state what those artifacts might tell future researchers about our culture. Tell students that in Section 2 they will learn that objects found in West Africa tell us much about the region's cultural history.

Building Vocabulary

Write the vocabulary terms on the chalkboard. Call on volunteers to read the definitions of **archaeology** and **oral history**. Point out that the suffix *-ism* usually refers to a system of beliefs and that **animism** refers to a system of beliefs based on the idea that natural objects, such as water, plants, or animals, have spirits.

Some 200 years later, North African merchants began crossing the Sahara to trade in Ghana. These merchants introduced Islam to West Africa. In time, Islam became the main religion practiced in the Sahel.

Later Ghana fell to Muslim warriors from Morocco. The Muslim empire of Mali (MAH-lee) replaced the kingdom of Ghana. Mali stretched from the Niger's inland delta to the Atlantic coast. Mansa Musa was king of Mali during the early 1300s. Famous for his wealth and wise rule, Mansa Musa supported artists, poets, and scholars.

The kingdom of Songhay (SAWNG-hy) came to power as Mali declined. With a university, mosques, and more than 100 schools, the Songhay city of Timbuktu was a cultural center. By about 1600, however, Moroccan invasions had weakened the kingdom.

Forested areas south of the Sahel were also home to great civilizations. In what is now Nigeria, wealthy kings were buried with brass sculptures and other treasures.

✓ **READING CHECK:** (*Human Systems*) What are some of the great African kingdoms that once ruled the region? Ghana, Mali, Songhay

The Slave Trade During the 1440s Portuguese explorers began sailing along the west coast of Africa. The Europeans called it the Gold Coast for the gold they bought there. Once they could buy gold where it was mined, the Europeans stopped buying it from Arab traders. As a result, the trans-Sahara trade and the great trade cities faded.

For a while, both Europeans and Africans profited from trade with each other. However, by the 1600s the demand for labor in Europe's American colonies changed everything. European traders met this demand by selling enslaved Africans to colonists. The slave trade was very profitable for these traders.

The slave trade had devastating effects on West African communities. Families were broken up when members were kidnapped and enslaved. Many Africans died on the voyage to the Americas. Most who survived were sent to the West Indies or Brazil. The slave trade finally ended in the 1800s. By then millions of Africans had been forced from their homes.

Colonial Era and Independence In the late 1800s, many European countries competed for colonies in West Africa. France claimed most of the region's northwest. Britain, Germany, and Portugal seized the rest.

In all of West Africa only tiny Liberia remained independent. Americans had founded it in the 1820s as a home for freed slaves. Sierra Leone, a British colony, also became a home for freed slaves.

We might think that salt is common and cheap, but it was precious to the traders of the Sahara. At one time it was worth its weight in gold.

Place There are many reminders of the slave trade and its effects on West Africans. Performers here reenact the treatment of enslaved Africans in an old slave house in Dakar, Senegal.

Too Much Gold? Mansa Musa, emperor of Mali, made a pilgrimage to Mecca in 1324. It was this journey that displayed Mali's incredible wealth to other countries.

Some 60,000 retainers accompanied the emperor. Included were 12,000 slaves, all dressed in brocade and silk. Mansa Musa rode on horseback behind 500 slaves, each bearing a staff decorated with gold. Each of the 80 camels in the baggage train carried 300 pounds of gold.

Mansa Musa spent so much gold in Cairo that the market was flooded with it, causing a decline in gold prices that lasted at least 12 years.

Critical Thinking: Why may spending so much gold reduce its value?

Answer: Students may say that the more there is of a product, the lower its value.

internet connect

GO TO: go.hrw.com
KEYWORD: SK5 CH10
FOR: Web sites about Mansa Musa

West Africa • 225

TEACH

Teaching Objectives 1–2
ALL LEVELS: (Suggested time: 30 min.) Copy the following graphic organizer onto the chalkboard, omitting the blue answers. For each footprint have students suggest a phrase to describe a step in West Africa's history. **ESOL**

Teaching Objective 3
LEVEL 1: (Suggested time: 10 min.) Have students list as many challenges facing West African governments as possible. (Students might mention civil wars and military rulers, high birthrates, crowded cities, unemployment, and lack of education.) Then ask students to suggest possible solutions for each problem listed. Discuss responses as a class. **ESOL,** **LS** **INTERPERSONAL**

Linking Past to Present

Liberia As opposition to slavery took hold in the early 1800s, agents from the U.S. government and two officers from the American Colonization Society received permission from African chiefs to allow freed slaves from the United States to settle at the mouth of the Mesurado River. From 1822 to 1865, American freed slaves settled there.

Critical Thinking: Why do you think freed slaves wanted to settle in Liberia?

Answer: They had originally come from Africa and may have wished to return there. In addition, the freed slaves may have felt that they didn't face a promising future in the United States.

Some Europeans moved to West Africa to run the colonies. They built roads, bridges, and railroads. Teachers and missionaries set up Christian churches and schools. After World War II, Africans increasingly worked for independence. Most of the colonies gained independence during the 1950s and 1960s. Portugal, the last European country to give up its West African colonies, did so in 1974.

✔ **READING CHECK:** (*Human Systems*) What impact did contact with Europeans have on West Africa? began the slave trade, which devastated West African communities

Challenges

Independence brought a new set of challenges to the region. The borders that the Europeans had drawn ignored human geography. Sometimes borders separated members of one ethnic group. Other borders grouped together peoples that did not get along. As a result, many West Africans were more loyal to their ethnic groups than to their new countries. In addition, too few people had been trained to run the new governments. Dictators took control in many countries. Unrest and military rulers still trouble the region. Some countries have made progress, however. For example, in 1996 Chad created its first democratic constitution.

The governments of West African countries have several difficult problems in common. Birthrates are high. As a result, more and more people must make a living from the small amount of fertile land. In addition, many people are moving to already crowded cities even though urban jobs are few. These countries must also find ways to educate more of their people. Many families cannot afford to send their children to school.

✔ **READING CHECK:** (*Places and Regions*) What are three challenges the region faces? Political boundaries cut across culture regions, causing ethnic conflict and civil war; land cannot support large populations; lack of education is caused by poverty.

(**Place**) A roadside market provides a glimpse of crowded Lagos, Nigeria's largest city. More than 10 million people live in and around Lagos. Overcrowded cities are a problem throughout much of the region.

▼

LEVELS 2 AND 3: (Suggested time: 45 min.) Have students complete the Level 1 exercise for this objective. Then ask students to use their list and other resources to prepare a newspaper commentary on West Africa's challenges. (LS) **VERBAL-LINGUISTIC**

Teaching Objective 4

LEVEL 1: (Suggested time: 30 min.) Organize students into four groups. Assign each group one of the following culturally influenced characteristics of West African life: languages, religion, clothing, or housing. Have each group draw examples of those characteristics on slips of colored paper and create a collage by pasting their examples onto a piece of posterboard. **ESOL, COOPERATIVE LEARNING,** (LS) **KINESTHETIC**

LEVELS 2 AND 3: (Suggested time: 45 min.) Organize students into groups and have each group develop an illustrated cover for a magazine about West African culture. Then have all group members write one-paragraph summaries of articles that could be included in the magazine. Article subjects might include languages, religions, clothing and housing. **COOPERATIVE LEARNING**

➤**ASSIGNMENT:** Have students imagine they are exchange students living in West Africa. Ask students to write a letter to a friend comparing life in West Africa to life back home.

CONNECTING TO Literature

Marriage Is a Private Affair
by Chinua Achebe

Chinua Achebe was born in an Ibo village in Nigeria in 1930. Many of his writings explore the changes colonialism brought to Africa. They also look at the conflict between old and new ways. In this story, Achebe looks at different views a father and son have about marriage.

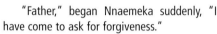

A Nigerian church carving

"Father," began Nnaemeka suddenly, "I have come to ask for forgiveness."

"Forgiveness? For what, my son?" he asked in amazement.

"It's about this marriage question."

"Which marriage question?"

"I can't—we must—I mean it is impossible for me to marry Nweke's daughter."

"Impossible? Why?" asked his father.

"I don't love her."

"Nobody said you did. Why should you?" he asked.

"Marriage today is different . . ."

"Look here, my son," interrupted his father, "nothing is different. What one looks for in a wife are a good character and a Christian background."

Nnaemeka saw there was no hope along the present line of argument.

"Moreover," he said. "I am engaged to marry another girl who has all of Ugoye's good qualities, and who . . ."

His father did not believe his ears. "What did you say?" he asked slowly and disconcertingly[1]. . . .

"Whose daughter is she, anyway?"

"She is Nene Atang."

"What!" All the mildness was gone again. "Did you say Neneataga, what does that mean?"

"Nene Atang from Calabar. She is the only girl I can marry." This was a very rash reply and Nnaemeka expected the storm to burst.

Analyzing Primary Sources

1. What universal theme does the passage illustrate?

2. Why do you think the father and son disagree about marriage?

Vocabulary [1]disconcertingly: disturbingly

Across the Curriculum
MUSIC
Hubert Ogunde

Hubert Ogunde was an influential African writer. This Nigerian playwright, actor, theater manager, and musician pioneered Nigerian folk opera. His works often used satire to comment on colonization, political strife, and government corruption. Ogunde sketched the operas' plots and wrote down and rehearsed the songs but had the performers improvise the dialogue. His plays influenced urban pop culture in West Africa.

Activity: Have students compare this type of performance with television programs in the United States and explain the similarities and differences.

Connecting to Literature
Answers

1. the relationship between love and marriage

2. The father believes in traditional marriages, while the son believes in a modern approach to marriage.

TEACHER TO TEACHER

Cindy Herring of Round Rock, Texas, suggests the following activity. Organize students into groups and give each group a sheet of butcher paper and art supplies. Have each group develop an illustrated time line for a designated period in West African history. Illustrations may be drawn or cut out of magazines. Combine all the groups' time lines to form one large time line.

CLOSE

Refer students to the feature on this page. Lead a discussion about how the father's ideas about marriage compare to most Americans' ideas.

REVIEW, ASSESS, RETEACH

Have students complete the Section Review. Then organize students into four groups and give each group five index cards. Assign each group one of the following topics: great kingdoms; the slave trade; the colonial era and independence; and progress and challenges. Have each group write five questions about its topic on one side of each card and the answers on the other side. Have groups exchange cards and quiz each other. Then have students complete Daily Quiz 10.2. **COOPERATIVE LEARNING**

Answers to Section 2 Review

Define or identify For definitions and identification, see the glossary and index.

Working with Sketch Maps Timbuktu should be labeled in its approximate location. Timbuktu was important because it was a cultural center.

Reading for the Main Idea

1. Many West Africans died, and millions were forced from their homes as a result of the slave trade. **(NGS 9)**
2. the Sahel; in the southern region **(NGS 10)**

Critical Thinking

3. Students may suggest that people with shared histories and challenges are more likely to understand each others' point of view.
4. lack of wood or other building materials

Organizing What You Know

5. Possible answers include: military rulers, high birthrates, overcrowded cities, and lack of affordable education

▲

(**Place**) These homes in Burkina Faso are made of a mixture of mud, water, and cow dung. Trees are scarce in the Sahel and savanna zones. As a result, there is little wood for construction. Women are responsible for painting and decorating the walls of the homes.

Culture

Hundreds of ethnic groups exist in West Africa today. Hundreds of languages are spoken in the region. In some areas, using the colonial languages of French or English helps people from different groups communicate. West African languages that many people share, such as Fula and Hausa, also aid communication.

Religion The traditional religions of West Africa have often been forms of **animism**. Animism is the belief that bodies of water, animals, trees, and other natural objects have spirits. Animists also honor the memories of ancestors. In some isolated areas animism still forms the basis of most religious practices. Today most people of the Sahel practice Islam. Farther south live many Christians.

Clothing and Homes Some West Africans, particularly in cities, wear Western-style clothing. Others wear traditional robes, pants, blouses, and skirts. These are often made from colorful patterned cotton fabric. Because of the warm climate, most clothing is loose and flowing. Many women wear beautiful folded and wrapped headdresses. In the desert men often wear turbans. Both men and women may use veils to protect their faces from blowing sand.

Rural homes are small and simple. Many homes in the Sahel and savanna zones are circular. Straw or tin roofs sit atop mud, mud-brick, or straw huts. However, in cities you will find some modern buildings.

✓ **READING CHECK:** (*Human Systems*) What are some features of West African culture? Hundreds of ethnic groups and languages; animism; Western-style and traditional clothing; traditional and modern architecture

Homework Practice Online
go.hrw.com
Keyword: SK5 HP10

Section Review 2

Define or identify: archaeology, oral history, Mansa Musa, animism

Working with Sketch Maps On the map you created in Section 1, label Timbuktu. What made Timbuktu an important Songhay city?

Reading for the Main Idea

1. (*Human Systems*) How did European contact affect West Africa's people?
2. (*Human Systems*) Where in West Africa are Islam and Christianity practiced?

Critical Thinking

3. **Drawing Inferences and Conclusions** How might shared histories and challenges lead to more cooperation among the region's countries?
4. **Drawing Inferences and Conclusions** Why do you think mud bricks are used in West Africa?

Organizing What You Know

5. **Summarizing** Use the following graphic organizer to summarize challenges facing West Africa.

West Africa

Have students complete Main Idea Activity S2. Then have students draw an outline map of the region on butcher paper. Have them create a map key that depicts symbols for products traded in West Africa. Then have students draw or glue symbols on the map in the appropriate areas. Display and discuss the map. **ESOL,** **LS** **VISUAL-SPATIAL**

EXTEND

Have interested students conduct research on French influences that remain in West Africa's languages, architecture, art, music, government, or literature. Have students show and explain the influence in the form of posters, collages, or graphic organizers. **BLOCK SCHEDULING**

Section 3   The Sahel Countries

Read to Discover

1. What are Mauritania, Mali, and Niger like today?
2. What challenges do Chad and Burkina Faso face?

Vocabulary

millet
sorghum
malaria
staple

Places

Nouakchott
Senegal River
Gao
Tibesti Mountains
Lake Chad
Ouagadougou

People

Moors

Reading Strategy

READING ORGANIZER   Draw a three-column chart on a sheet of paper. Label the columns Country, Economic Activities, and Challenges. As you read this section, list each country and what you learn about their economic activities and challenges.

SECTION 3 RESOURCES

Reproducible
◆ Lecture Notes, Section 3
◆ Know It Notes S3
◆ Map Activity 10

Technology
◆ One-Stop Planner CD–ROM, Lesson 10.3
◆ Homework Practice Online
◆ HRW Go site

Reinforcement, Review, and Assessment
◆ Section 3 Review
◆ Daily Quiz 10.3
◆ Main Idea Activity S3
◆ Chapter Summaries and Review
◆ English Audio Summary 10.3
◆ Spanish Audio Summary 10.3

Mauritania, Mali, and Niger

Most of the people in these three large countries are Muslim. Mauritania, in fact, has laws based on Islam. These countries are also former French colonies, and French influence remains. In Mali and Niger, the official language is French. However, the people there speak more than 60 different local languages.

Today, drought and the expanding desert make feeding the people in these countries difficult. In the Sahel nomads depend on their herds of cattle, goats, and camels. In the savanna regions farmers grow **millet** and **sorghum**. These grain crops can usually survive drought.

Mauritania Many Mauritanians are Moors, people of mixed Arab and Berber origin. They speak Arabic. In the past, Moors enslaved some of the black Africans. Today, tension between the two groups continues.

Women carry goods for sale in a market in central Mali. Much of Mali's economic activity takes place in the Niger River's inland delta.

Interpreting the Visual Record

(*Human-Environment Interaction*) Why is Mali's economic activity centered around the inland delta?

West Africa • 229

◄ **Visual Record Answer**

because most of the country is desert with few resources

Section 3

Objectives

1. Describe modern Mauritania, Mali, and Niger.
2. Analyze challenges facing Chad and Burkina Faso.

FOCUS

Bellringer

Copy the following question onto the chalkboard: *What could you do to survive if all your community's sources of water—wells, lakes, rivers, aquifers, pipelines—were going dry?* Discuss responses. Point out that this is happening in parts of the Sahel countries. Explain to students that in Section 3 they will find out more about the causes and results of the region's water shortages.

Building Vocabulary

Write the vocabulary terms on the chalkboard and call on volunteers to read the definitions aloud. Tell students that **millet** and **sorghum** are examples of **staple** grain crops grown in the Sahel and that **malaria** is a disease spread by mosquitoes.

National Geography Standard 15

The Devastation of Drought The economies of countries of the Sahel, such as Niger, fluctuate with the weather. When there are periods of ample rainfall, the land can support as many as 10 million cattle, sheep, and goats. However, the droughts of the 1970s and 1980s destroyed all but 1 million animals, bringing famine to the country.

Activity: Have students suggest other countries whose economies are linked to weather conditions.

Chart Answer ▶

Mali, Nigeria

(Region) Mud and other local materials were used to build many mosques in the Sahel. This mosque is located in Djenné [je-NAY], Mali. The majority of people living in the Sahel are Muslims.

Our Amazing Planet

The Tuareg (TWAH-reg) people of the Sahara and Sahel pound powdered blue dye into their flowing robes. They do this rather than dip the fabric in precious water. The blue powder wears off onto the skin, where it may help hold in moisture.

The Sahel Countries

COUNTRY	POPULATION/ GROWTH RATE	LIFE EXPECTANCY	LITERACY RATE	PER CAPITA GDP
Burkina Faso	13,228,460 / 2.6%	43, male / 45, female	27%	$1,080
Chad	9,253,493 / 3.1%	46, male / 50, female	48%	$1,100
Mali	11,626,219 / 3%	44, male / 46, female	46%	$860
Mauritania	2,912,584 / 2.9%	49, male / 54, female	41%	$1,900
Niger	11,058,590 / 2.7%	42, male / 42, female	17%	$830
United States	290,342,554 / 0.9%	74, male / 80, female	97%	$37,600

Source: Central Intelligence Agency, *The World Factbook 2003*

Interpreting the Chart Based on the numbers in the chart, which two countries in the region are the least economically developed?

230 • Chapter 10

Most Mauritanians were once nomadic herders. Today, the expanding Sahara has crowded more than half of the nomads into the cities. Just 40 years ago, Nouakchott (nooh-AHK-shaht), Mauritania's capital, was a small village. More than 700,000 people live there now. About half of the population lives in shacks at the city's edges.

Throughout the country, people are very poor. Only in the far south, near the Senegal River, can farmers raise crops. Fishing in the Atlantic Ocean is another source of income.

Mali To the east of Mauritania lies landlocked Mali. The Sahara covers much of northern Mali. In the south lies a wetter farming region. About 80 percent of Mali's people fish or farm along the Niger River. Cotton is the country's main export. Timbuktu and Gao (GOW), ancient trading cities, continue to attract tourists.

Health conditions in Mali are poor. **Malaria**, a disease spread by mosquitoes, is a major cause of death among children.

Niger The Niger River flows through just the southwestern corner of landlocked Niger. Only about 3 percent of Niger's land is good for farming. All of the country's farmland lies along the Niger River and near the Nigerian border. Much of the rest of Niger lies within the Sahara. Farmers raise cotton, peanuts, beans, peas, and rice. Millet and sorghum are two of the region's **staple**, or main, food crops. The grains are cooked like oatmeal. Nomads in the desert region depend on the dairy products they get from their herds for food.

✓ **READING CHECK:** *Places and Regions* What is it like to live in Mauritania, Mali, and Niger? **People are generally poor farmers and herders; most are Muslim and speak French. Life is often difficult because of drought and the expanding desert.**

TEACH

Teaching Objectives 1–2

ALL LEVELS: (Suggested time: 35 min.) Copy the following graphic organizer onto the chalkboard, omitting the blue answers. Use it to help students describe the Sahel countries. Have students complete the organizer. Then ask students to create their own graphic organizer to depict the challenges facing Chad and Burkina Faso. Lead a discussion in which students compare all five of the Sahel countries. **ESOL,** LS **VISUAL-SPATIAL**

The Sahel Countries

Country	Climate	Crops	Economy	Challenges
Mauritania	desert	(no specific crops listed)	farming, fishing, herding	poverty, tensions, expanding desert
Mali	desert	cotton	fishing, farming, tourism	malaria, poverty
Niger	desert	cotton, sorghum, peanuts, peas, rice, millet	farming, herding	poverty, expanding desert

Chad and Burkina Faso

Drought has also affected the former French colonies of Chad and Burkina Faso (boohr-KEE-nuh FAH-soh). These countries are among the world's poorest and least developed. Most people farm or raise cattle.

Chad Chad is located in the center of Africa. The Tibesti Mountains in northern Chad rise above the Sahara. Lake Chad is in the south. Not long ago, the lake had a healthy fishing industry. It even supplied water to several other countries. However, drought has evaporated much of the lake's water. At one time, Lake Chad had shrunk to just one third its size in 1950.

The future may be better for Chad. A civil war ended in the 1990s. Also, oil reserves now being explored may help the economy.

Burkina Faso This country's name means "land of the honest people." Most of its people follow traditional religions. The country has thin soil and few mineral resources. Few trees remain in or near the capital, Ouagadougou (wah-gah-DOO-goo). They have been cut for firewood and building material. Jobs in the city are also scarce. To support their families many young men work in other countries. However, foreign aid and investment are starting to help the economy.

✓ **READING CHECK:** (*Places and Regions*) What are the challenges facing Chad and Burkina Faso? drought, poverty, underdevelopment; scarcity of natural resources in Burkina Faso has led to economic problems

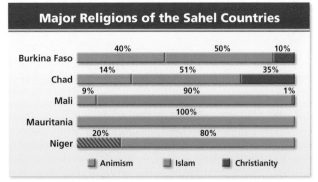

Major Religions of the Sahel Countries

Country		
Burkina Faso	40%	50%	10%
Chad	14%	51%	35%
Mali	9%	90%	1%
Mauritania	100%		
Niger	20%	80%	

■ Animism   ■ Islam   ■ Christianity

Source: Central Intelligence Agency, *The World Factbook 2003*

▲
Although most people in the Sahel are Muslim, some practice forms of animism and Christianity.

Interpreting the Graph (*Place*) Which country's population is entirely Muslim? Which countries have significant numbers of Christians?

Homework Practice Online
Keyword: SK5 HP10

Section Review 3

Define or identify: millet, sorghum, Moors, malaria, staple

Working with Sketch Maps On the map you created in Section 2, draw the boundaries of Mauritania, Mali, Niger, Chad, and Burkina Faso. Then label Nouakchott, Senegal River, Gao, Tibesti Mountains, Lake Chad, and Ouagadougou. In a box in the margin, describe what has happened to Lake Chad in recent decades.

Reading for the Main Idea

1. (*Places and Regions*) Why has Nouakchott grown so rapidly?

2. (*Places and Regions*) Which European language is most common in the Sahel countries? Why?

Critical Thinking

3. **Drawing Inferences and Conclusions** How do the typical foods of Niger relate to the country's water resources?

4. **Comparing** What do Chad and Burkina Faso have in common with the other Sahel countries?

Organizing What You Know

5. **Comparing** Copy the following graphic organizer. Label each of the star's points with one of the Section 3 countries. In the center, list characteristics the countries share.

West Africa • 231

Section 3 Review

Answers to Section 3 Review

Define or identify For definitions or identification, see the glossary and index.

Working with Sketch Maps Places should be labeled in their approximate locations. Lake Chad has shrunk.

Reading for the Main Idea

1. The expanding Sahara has crowded nomads into Nouakchott. **(NGS 4)**

2. French; France controlled the Sahel countries as colonies. **(NGS 4)**

Critical Thinking

3. Farmers grow food crops in areas where there is enough water. Nomads in dry areas rely on products from their herds.

4. similar climate, colonial background, religions, economic activities

Organizing What You Know

5. five points—Burkina Faso, Chad, Mali, Mauritania, Niger; possible for center—Sahel climate zone, farming, low literacy rate, former French colonies, hurt by droughts

◄ **Graph Answer**

Mauritania; Burkina Faso and Chad

CLOSE

Refer to the photo of the Djenné mosque on the previous page. Challenge students to suggest possible steps in the building's construction.

REVIEW, ASSESS, RETEACH

Have students complete the Section Review. Then have students choose one of the section's countries and write three statements about their country. Have students play a where-am-I game using the statements. Then assign one of the Sahel countries to each of five groups. Have groups create mobiles depicting characteristics of their country. **ESOL, COOPERATIVE LEARNING**

EXTEND

Have interested students conduct research on the Tuareg and other nomadic peoples of the Sahel countries and describe their cultures in a report. Tell them to include information about the relationships between these cultures and their artforms and/or music. **BLOCK SCHEDULING**

Section 4 — The Coastal Countries

Read to Discover
1. What is life in Nigeria like today?
2. What economic challenges do the region's other countries face?

Vocabulary
secede
griots
cacao

Places
Abuja
Lagos
Dakar
Monrovia
Lake Volta

People
Wole Soyinka

Reading Strategy

FOLDNOTES: TRI-FOLD Create a **Tri-Fold** FoldNote as described in the Appendix. Write what you know about West Africa's coastal countries in the column labeled "Know." Then, write what you want to know in the column labeled "Want." As you read the chapter, write what you learn about each country in the column labeled "Learn."

▲
The faces of Nigeria are very young. About 45 percent of all Nigerians are younger than 15 years old. Only about 22 percent of all Americans are that young.

Nigeria

The largest country along West Africa's coast is Nigeria. With more than 130 million people, it has Africa's largest population.

Nigeria's People Nigeria was once an important British colony. Like many other colonies, Nigeria's borders included many ethnic groups. Today, a great variety of ethnic groups live in Nigeria. The Yoruba, Fula, Hausa, and Ibo are four of the largest ethnic groups. More than 200 languages are spoken there.

Nigeria's ethnic groups have not always gotten along. In the 1960s the Ibo tried to **secede**. That is, they tried to break away from Nigeria and form their own country. They called it Biafra (bee-AF-ruh). However, the Ibo lost the bloody war that followed.

Avoiding ethnic conflicts has continued to be an issue in Nigeria. It was important in choosing a site for a new Nigerian capital in the late 1970s. Leaders chose Abuja (ah-BOO-jah) because it was centrally located in an area of low population density.

Nigeria's Economy Nigeria has some of the continent's richest natural resources. Oil is the country's most important resource. Major oil fields are located in the Niger River delta and just off the coast. Oil accounts for 95 percent of the country's export earnings. Nigeria also

Section 4

Objectives
1. Describe life in Nigeria today.
2. Identify the economic challenges faced by other coastal West African countries.

FOCUS

 Bellringer

Copy the following instructions onto the chalkboard: *Look at the flags on the Fast Facts pages. Write down why you think Liberia's flag looks the way it does.* Discuss responses. Remind students that Liberia was founded as a home for freed slaves from the United States. Liberia's flag was based on the American flag. Tell students they will learn more about Liberia and the other coastal countries of West Africa in Section 4.

Building Vocabulary

Write the vocabulary terms on the chalkboard. Ask students if they know a person who tells really interesting stories. Point out that **griots** are storytellers who pass on the histories of peoples of Senegal and Gambia. Tell them that the seeds of the **cacao** tree are used to make chocolate and that to **secede** means to break away to form another country, an action that often leads to war.

Human-Environment Interaction
Oil drilling rigs like this one are common in areas of southern Nigeria. Oil accounts for about 20 percent of Nigeria's GDP.

---

has good roads and railroads. Lagos (LAY-gahs), the former capital, is the country's largest city. The city is a busy seaport and trade center.

Although the country has rich resources, many Nigerians are poor. A major cause of the poverty there is a high birthrate. Nigeria can no longer feed its growing population without importing food. Another cause is the economy's dependence on oil. When prices are low, the whole country suffers. A third cause of Nigeria's poverty is a history of bad government. Corrupt government officials have used their positions to enrich themselves.

✓ **READING CHECK:** *Places and Regions* What are Nigeria's people and economy like today? many ethnic groups, languages; frequent ethnic conflict; economy based on oil; poverty is a problem

Other Coastal Countries

Several small West African countries lie along the Atlantic Ocean and the Gulf of Guinea. They are struggling to develop their economies.

Senegal and Gambia Senegal (se-ni-GAWL) wraps around Gambia (GAM-bee-uh). The odd border was created by French and British diplomats. Senegal, a former French colony, is larger and richer than Gambia, a former British colony. Dakar (dah-KAHR) is Senegal's capital and an important seaport and manufacturing center. Senegal and Gambia have many similarities. Peanuts are their most important crop. Common foods include chicken stew and fish with a peanut sauce. Tourism is growing slowly.

Place The headdresses and patterned clothing worn by these women in Dakar are common in Senegal.

West Africa • 233

HUMAN SYSTEMS

French and British Control
Senegal and part of Gambia were once part of the Wolof Empire. They came under separate rule when Europeans colonized the area. Both France and Great Britain established posts in the 1600s. The British and French fought at various times for control of the Gambia River and its trade. In the early 1800s the British gained control of the river basin, while the French maintained their hold on Senegal.

The two European powers ruled their colonies differently. The French colonizers of Senegal exerted direct control over the colony. They sought to assimilate the Senegalese into a French way of life. This practice proved effective only in the cities. In contrast, the British controlled their colony indirectly through Gambian rulers.

Discussion: Lead a class discussion about how differences in colonial rule might affect modern life in Senegal and Gambia.

🖪 **internet** connect
GO TO: go.hrw.com
KEYWORD: SK5 CH10
FOR: Web sites about Senegal or Gambia

TEACH

Teaching Objective 1

ALL LEVELS: (Suggested time: 20 min.) Copy the following graphic organizer onto the chalkboard, omitting the blue answers. Use it to help students describe modern Nigeria. Organize the class into two groups. Have one group find positive aspects of modern Nigeria. Have the second find challenges faced by modern Nigeria. Have volunteers from each group write their information on the organizer.
ESOL, COOPERATIVE LEARNING

Positive Aspects

oil, good railroads and roads, centrally located capital

NIGERIA

Challenges

corruption in government, ethnic tension, high birthrate, economic dependency on oil

FOOD FESTIVAL

Okra and Yams Explain that okra and yams are West African foods used in the United States.

Okra can be served pickled, boiled, sautéed, or fried and is used to thicken and flavor gumbos and stews. Point out that yams are often confused with sweet potatoes, but the two are from different plant species. Sweet potatoes can be substituted in most recipes that call for yams. Have students research recipes for okra and yams and bring samples to class for everyone to taste.

FOCUS ON CULTURE

The Ashanti of Ghana

Festivals and ceremonies help the Ashanti people of Ghana keep their heritage of royal grandeur alive. The Ashanti observe the Akwasidae ceremony every six weeks. On this occasion, the Ashanti king emerges from his palace to receive the respect of his people. It is quite a sight. The king, wearing heavy gold ornaments, rides beneath immense colorful umbrellas. Drummers, dancers, musicians, and singers accompany the procession.

What does the king do during the Akwasidae ceremony?

Many of the people speak a language called Wolof (WOH-lawf). **Griots** (GREE-ohz) are important to the Wolof-speakers and other West Africans. Griots are storytellers who pass on the oral histories of their tribes or peoples. Sometimes the griots combine music with their stories, which may take hours or days to tell. Wolof women wear complex hairstyles and gold jewelry.

Guinea, Guinea-Bissau, and Cape Verde Guinea's main natural resource is a huge supply of bauxite. Its small neighbor to the east, Guinea-Bissau (GI-nee bi-SOW), has undeveloped mineral resources. Cape Verde (KAYP VUHRD) is a group of volcanic islands in the Atlantic. It is West Africa's only island country. Farming and fishing bring in the most money there.

Liberia and Sierra Leone Liberia is Africa's oldest republic. Monrovia, Liberia's capital, was named for U.S. president James Monroe. The freed American slaves who settled Liberia and their

Focus on Culture Answer ▲

The king emerges from his palace and leads a procession.

▶
Flowers color the countryside on Santa Antão island in Cape Verde. However, farming can be difficult because droughts are common in the island country.

Teaching Objective 2

LEVEL 1: (Suggested time: 40 min.) Organize the class into eleven groups and assign each group one of the region's countries. Have each group fold a piece of paper lengthwise and crosswise, creating four boxes. Have groups fill in each box with the following information on economic development for their assigned country: per capita GDP, literacy rate, major economic resources, economic challenges, possible solutions to challenges. You may want to provide encyclopedias or other library resources so that students can add detail.
ESOL, COOPERATIVE LEARNING, LS KINESTHETIC

LEVELS 2 AND 3: (Suggested time: 45 min.) Have students work in pairs to write stories about economic challenges in one of the coastal countries. Then ask them to convert their stories into rhyming poems, such as griots might perform. Have them recite their tales to the class. Allow students to use notes or cue cards.
COOPERATIVE LEARNING, LS AUDITORY-MUSICAL

descendants lived in coastal towns. They often clashed with the Africans already living there. Those Africans and their descendants were usually poorer and lived in rural areas. In the 1980s conflicts led to a bitter civil war. Sierra Leone (lee-OHN) has also experienced violent civil war. The fighting has wrecked the country's economy. Now, both Liberia and Sierra Leone must rebuild. They do have natural resources on which to build stronger economies. Liberia produces rubber and iron ore. Sierra Leone exports diamonds.

Ghana and Côte d'Ivoire The countries of Ghana and Côte d'Ivoire (koht-dee-VWAHR) have rich natural resources. Those resources may help them build strong economies. Ghana is named for the ancient kingdom, although the kingdom was northwest of the modern country. Ghana has one of the largest human-made lakes in the world—Lake Volta. Gold, timber, and **cacao** (kuh-KOW) are major products. Cocoa and chocolate are made from the seeds of the cacao tree. The tree came originally from Mexico and Central America.

Côte d'Ivoire is a former French colony whose name means "Ivory Coast" in English. It is a world leader in cacao and coffee exports. Côte d'Ivoire also boasts Africa's largest Christian church building.

Togo and Benin Unstable governments have troubled both Togo and Benin (buh-NEEN) since independence. Both have experienced periods of military rule. Their fragile economies have contributed to their unstable and sometimes violent politics. These long, narrow countries are poor. The people depend on farming and herding for income. Palm tree products, cacao, and coffee are the main crops in Togo and Benin.

✓ READING CHECK: (*Places and Regions*) What are characteristics of the economies of the coastal countries? Senegal, Gambia—some manufacturing, peanuts, tourism; Guinea, Guinea-Bissau—minerals; Cape Verde—farming, fishing; Liberia—rubber, iron ore; Sierra Leone—diamonds; Ghana—gold, timber, cacao; Côrte d'Ivoire—cacao, coffee, Togo, Benin—farming, herding

BIOGRAPHY

Wole Soyinka
(1934–)

Character Trait: Integrity

As the first black African to receive the Nobel Prize for Literature, Wole Soyinka is considered one of Africa's greatest writers. Some of Soyinka's works are based on his tribe, the Yoruba. His plays also include African dance and music. During the Nigerian civil war in the 1960s, Soyinka was jailed for 22 months for speaking out against the fighting. After his release from prison, he taught playwriting at Nigerian universities.

How did Wole Soyinka show integrity?

Homework Practice Online
go.hrw.com
Keyword: SK5 HP10

Section Review 4

Define or identify: secede, griots, cacao, Wole Soyinka

Working with Sketch Maps On the map that you drew in Section 3, draw the boundaries for the coastal countries. Label Abuja, Lagos, Dakar, Monrovia, and Lake Volta. In a box in the margin, identify the largest and most populous country on West Africa's coast.

Reading for the Main Idea

1. (*Places and Regions*) How is Cape Verde different from the other countries in the region?

2. (*Places and Regions*) What is Nigeria's most important natural resource? Why?

Critical Thinking

3. **Finding the Main Idea** Why must Liberia and Sierra Leone rebuild their economies?

4. **Analyzing Information** Why was choosing a new capital important to Nigeria's future?

Organizing What You Know

5. **Summarizing** Copy the following graphic organizer. Use it to list three main causes of poverty in Nigeria today.

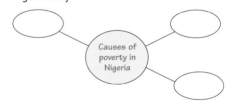

Causes of poverty in Nigeria

Answers to Section 4 Review

Define or identify For definitions or identifications, see the glossary and index.

Working with Sketch Maps Maps will vary, but listed places should be labeled in their approximate locations. The largest and most populous country on West Africa's coast is Nigeria.

Reading for the Main Idea

1. West Africa's only island nation (NGS 4)

2. oil; makes up 95 percent of Nigeria's exports

Critical Thinking

3. Civil wars disrupted both countries. (NGS 18)

4. to help avoid further ethnic conflict

Organizing What You Know

5. Possible answers: high birthrate, economic dependence on oil, government corruption

▲ **Biography Answer**

He spoke out against the fighting in the middle of a civil war.

CLOSE

Focus students' attention on the photo of the Lagos roadside market in Section 2. Ask students to suggest why shopping at this market may be important for cultural as well as economic reasons. (Possible answers: opportunity to socialize, meet friends, exchange news)

REVIEW, ASSESS, RETEACH

Have students complete the Section Review. Then organize students into groups and have each group create a crossword puzzle about the coastal countries of West Africa. Photocopy the puzzles and have groups exchange and complete them. Then have students complete Daily Quiz 10.4.

COOPERATIVE LEARNING, LS VISUAL-SPATIAL

EXTEND

Have interested students conduct research and report on the artistic traditions of West Africa's coastal countries. Examples include terra cotta heads from the Nok civilization, bronze heads created in the Ife kingdom, and sculptures made by people of Benin in brass, bronze, and ivory.

BLOCK SCHEDULING

Define and Identify

For definitions and identifications, see the glossary and index.

Review the Main Ideas

18. Sahara, Sahel, savanna, and coast and forest (NGS 4)

19. The inland delta consists of swamps, channels, and lakes, while the true delta is wide and located on the coast. (NGS 4)

20. with merchants from North Africa (NGS 9)

21. Families were broken up and many Africans died on the voyage to the Americas.

22. Possible answers: caused crops to fail, forced nomads into cities, dried up sources of water. (NGS 15)

23. Islam

24. oil (NGS 15)

25. Liberia was founded in the 1820s by the United States as a home for freed slaves.

Think Critically

26. Possible answers: crowded with new arrivals from areas struck by drought, near water sources, and in better climate

27. Early trade brought Islam and increased the power and wealth of the kingdoms. European trade caused a decline in Saharan trade and introduced the slave trade.

28. Possible answers: language, religion, clothing, and buildings

29. European colonizers ignored ethnic rivalries when they drew Africa's borders

30. Liberia was founded for freed American slaves rather than as a European colony.

Review and Practice

Define and Identify

Identify each of the following:

1. zonal
2. Sahel
3. harmattan
4. tsetse fly
5. bauxite
6. archaeology
7. oral history
8. Mansa Musa
9. animism
10. millet
11. sorghum
12. malaria
13. staple
14. secede
15. griots
16. cacao
17. Wole Soyinka

Review the Main Ideas

18. What are the four climate zones of West Africa?

19. How do the Niger River's two delta regions differ?

20. How did Islam come to West Africa?

21. What were the effects of the slave trade on West African communities?

22. How has drought affected the countries of the Sahel?

23. What religion do most people in the Sahel practice?

24. On what natural resource does Nigeria's economy depend?

25. How did the United States influence the development of Liberia?

Think Critically

26. Drawing Inferences and Conclusions Why are many of West Africa's largest cities located in the coastal and forest zone?

27. Finding the Main Idea What role did trade play in the early West African kingdoms and later European colonies in the region?

28. Analyzing Information What are three cultural features of West Africa influenced by Europeans?

29. Drawing Inferences and Conclusions How have borders set by European colonial powers led to conflicts such as Nigeria's war in Biafra in the late 1960s?

30. Contrasting How is Liberia's history different from that of other West African countries?

Map Activity

31. On a separate sheet of paper, match the letters on the map with their correct labels.

Niger River
Gulf of Guinea
Timbuktu
Nouakchott
Senegal River
Tibesti Mountains
Lake Chad
Abuja
Lagos
Lake Volta

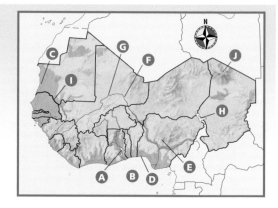

Map Activity

31. A. Lake Volta

B. Gulf of Guinea

C. Nouakchott

D. Lagos

E. Abuja

F. Niger River

G. Timbuktu

H. Lake Chad

I. Senegal River

J. Tibesti Mountains

Writing Activity

Imagine that you are an economic adviser to a West African country of your choice. Use print resources to prepare a short economic report for your country's leader. Identify the country's important natural resources and what can be done with them. In addition, describe economic advantages or disadvantages of the country's climate, location, and physical features. Be sure to use standard grammar, spelling, sentence structure, and punctuation.

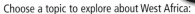

internet connect

Internet Activity: go.hrw.com
KEYWORD: SK5 GT10

Choose a topic to explore about West Africa:
• Find out about giant baobab trees.
• Meet the people of West Africa.
• Learn about the history of the slave trade.

Social Studies Skills Practice

Interpreting Graphs

Today, Nigeria relies on crude oil production for much of its wealth. However, during the 1980s the country's oil industry experienced many ups and downs. Study the graph and answer the questions.

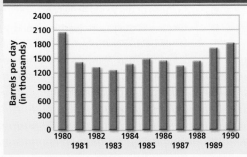

Nigeria's Crude Oil Production, 1980–1990

Barrels per day (in thousands)

Source: Energy Information Administration

1. In what year did Nigeria produce the least amount of oil?

2. In what years did Nigeria produce more than 1.5 million barrels per day?

3. By approximately how much did oil production decline between 1980 and 1981?

4. Did Nigeria's oil production between 1988 and 1990 increase or decrease?

Analyzing Primary Sources

Read the following description of the kingdom of Ghana in the 1060s by the Arab geographer Al Bakri. Then answer the questions.

"The city of Ghana consists of two towns lying in a plain. One of these towns is inhabited by Muslims. It is large and possesses twelve mosques in one of which the people assemble for the Friday prayer . . . Around the town are wells of sweet water from which they drink and near which they grow vegetables. The land between the two towns is covered with houses. The houses of the inhabitants are made of stone and acacia wood. The king has a palace and a number of dome-shaped dwellings, the whole surrounded by an enclosure like the defensive wall of a city."

1. What resource may have determined the location of the two towns?

2. Why do you think the houses were made of stone and acacia wood?

3. Why were mosques in only one town within the kingdom of Ghana?

4. What is a unique feature of the king's palace?

West Africa • 237

Writing Activity

Information should be consistent with text material. Students should identify all the elements that relate to their country's economy. Use Rubric 42, Writing to Inform, to evaluate student work.

Interpreting Graphs

1. 1983
2. 1980, 1989, and 1990
3. 600,000
4. Oil production increased.

Analyzing Primary Sources

1. water
2. Those were the plentiful resources of the region.
3. The people in one town were Muslim and the people in the other town were not.
4. It includes several dome-shaped buildings and is surrounded by a wall.

CHAPTER 10 **REVIEW AND ASSESSMENT RESOURCES**

Reproducible
◆ Readings in World Geography, History, and Culture 55, 56, and 57
◆ Critical Thinking Activity 10
◆ Vocabulary Activity 10

Technology
◆ Chapter 10 Test Generator (on the One-Stop Planner)
◆ Audio CD Program, Chapter 10
◆ HRW Go site

Reinforcement, Review, and Assessment
◆ Chapter 10 Review and Practice
◆ Chapter Summaries and Review
◆ Chapter 10 Test
◆ Chapter 10 Test for English Language Learners and Special-Needs Students

internet connect

GO TO: go.hrw.com
KEYWORD: SK5 Teacher
FOR: a guide to using the Internet in your classroom

CHAPTER 11

East Africa
Chapter Resource Manager

Objectives	Pacing Guide	Reproducible Resources
SECTION 1 **Physical Geography** (pp. 239–41) 1. Identify the major landforms of East Africa. 2. Identify the rivers and lakes that are important in this region. 3. Identify East Africa's climate types and natural resources.	**Regular** .5 day Lecture Notes, Section 1 **Block Scheduling** .5 day *Block Scheduling Handbook, Chapter 11*	**RS** Know It Notes S1 **SM** Geography for Life Activity 24 **ELL** Main Idea Activity S1
SECTION 2 **History and Culture** (pp. 242–44) 1. Identify the important events and developments that have influenced the history of East Africa. 2. Describe the culture of East Africa.	**Regular** .5 day Lecture Notes, Section 2 **Block Scheduling** .5 day *Block Scheduling Handbook, Chapter 11*	**RS** Know It Notes S2 **RS** Graphic Organizer 11 **E** Cultures of the World Activity 6 **E** Creative Strategies for Teaching World Geography, Lesson 16 **IC** Interdisciplinary Activities for the Middle Grades 26, 27, 28 **E** Biography Activity: Menelik II **ELL** Main Idea Activity S2
SECTION 3 **The Countries of East Africa** (pp. 245–48) 1. Explain why settlers come to Kenya. 2. Describe how Tanzania was created. 3. Describe Rwanda and Burundi. 4. Describe Uganda. 5. Identify the physical features of Sudan.	**Regular** 1 day Lecture Notes, Section 3 **Block Scheduling** .5 day *Block Scheduling Handbook, Chapter 11*	**RS** Know It Notes S3 **E** Creative Strategies for Teaching World Geography, Lesson 17 **SM** Map Activity 11 **ELL** Main Idea Activity S3
SECTION 4 **The Horn of Africa** (pp. 249–51) 1. Identify the main physical features of Ethiopia. 2. Describe Eritrea. 3. Explain what Somalia is like. 4. Identify the physical and cultural characteristics of Djibouti.	**Regular** .5 day Lecture Notes, Section 4 **Block Scheduling** .5 day *Block Scheduling Handbook, Chapter 11*	**RS** Know It Notes S4 **E** Biography Activity: Menelik II **ELL** Main Idea Activity S4

Chapter Resource Key

RS Reading Support
IC Interdisciplinary Connections
E Enrichment
SM Skills Mastery
A Assessment
REV Review

ELL Reinforcement and English Language Learners and English for Speakers of Other Languages (ESOL)
 Transparencies
 CD–ROM

 Music
 Video
 Internet
 Holt Presentation Maker Using Microsoft® PowerPoint®

 One-Stop Planner CD–ROM

See the *One-Stop Planner* for a complete list of additional resources for students and teachers.

One-Stop Planner CD–ROM

It's easy to plan lessons, select resources, and print out materials for your students when you use the *One-Stop Planner CD–ROM with Test Generator.*

Technology Resources	Review, Reinforcement, and Assessment Resources

One-Stop Planner CD–ROM, Lesson 11.1
  Earth: Forces and Formations CD–ROM/Seek and Tell/Forces and Processes
  Geography and Cultures Visual Resources with Teaching Activities 43–47
  ARGWorld CD–ROM
  Homework Practice Online
 HRW Go site
	ELL Main Idea Activity S1
	 REV Section 1 Review
	 A Daily Quiz 11.1
	 REV Chapter Summaries and Review
	 ELL English Audio Summary 11.1
	 ELL Spanish Audio Summary 11.1

One-Stop Planner CD–ROM, Lesson 11.2
  ARGWorld CD–ROM
  Music of the World Audio CD Program, Selection 15
  Homework Practice Online
 HRW Go site
	ELL Main Idea Activity S2
	 REV Section 2 Review
	 A Daily Quiz 11.2
	 REV Chapter Summaries and Review
	 ELL English Audio Summary 11.2
	 ELL Spanish Audio Summary 11.2

One-Stop Planner CD–ROM, Lesson 11.3
  ARGWorld CD–ROM
  Music of the World Audio CD Program, Selection 15
     Homework Practice Online
 HRW Go site
	ELL Main Idea Activity S3
	 REV Section 3 Review
	 A Daily Quiz 11.3
	 REV Chapter Summaries and Review
	 ELL English Audio Summary 11.3
	 ELL Spanish Audio Summary 11.3

One-Stop Planner CD–ROM, Lesson 11.4 *ARGWorld* CD–ROM Homework Practice Online HRW Go site	**ELL** Main Idea Activity S4 **REV** Section 4 Review **A** Daily Quiz 11.4 **REV** Chapter Summaries and Review **ELL** English Audio Summary 11.4 **ELL** Spanish Audio Summary 11.4

internet connect

HRW ONLINE RESOURCES

GO TO: go.hrw.com
Then type in a keyword.

TEACHER HOME PAGE
KEYWORD: SK5 TEACHER

CHAPTER INTERNET ACTIVITIES
KEYWORD: SK5 GT11

Choose an activity to:
• hike Mount Kilimanjaro.
• learn about cultural groups in East Africa.
• travel back to ancient Nubian kingdoms.

CHAPTER ENRICHMENT LINKS
KEYWORD: SK5 CH11

CHAPTER MAPS
KEYWORD: SK5 MAPS11

ONLINE ASSESSMENT
Homework Practice
KEYWORD: SK5 HP11
Standardized Test Prep Online
KEYWORD: SK5 STP11
Rubrics
KEYWORD: SS Rubrics

COUNTRY INFORMATION
KEYWORD: SK5 Almanac

CONTENT UPDATES
KEYWORD: SS Content Updates

HOLT PRESENTATION MAKER
KEYWORD: SK5 PPT11

ONLINE READING SUPPORT
KEYWORD: SS Strategies

CURRENT EVENTS
KEYWORD: S5 Current Events

Chapter Review and Assessment

E	Readings in World Geography, History, and Culture 58, 59, and 60	**A**	Chapter 11 Test
SM	Critical Thinking Activity 11	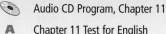	Chapter 11 Test Generator (on the One-Stop Planner)
REV	Chapter 11 Review and Practice		Audio CD Program, Chapter 11
REV	Chapter Summaries and Review	**A**	Chapter 11 Test for English Language Learners and Special-Needs Students
ELL	Vocabulary Activity 11		HRW Go Site

Meeting Individual Needs

Ability Levels

Level 1 Basic-level activities designed for all students encountering new material

Level 2 Intermediate-level activities designed for average students

Level 3 Challenging activities designed for honors and gifted-and-talented students

ESOL Activities that address the needs of students with Limited English Proficiency

East Africa
Previewing Chapter Resources

Holt Online Learning

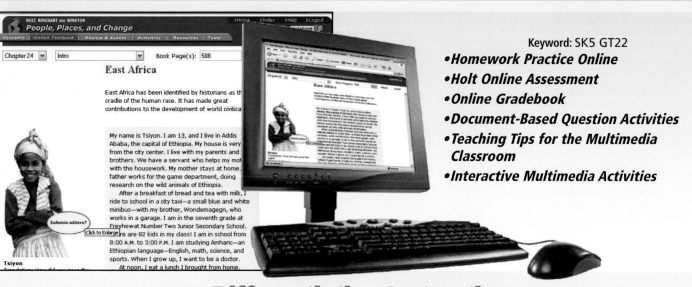

Keyword: SK5 GT22

- *Homework Practice Online*
- *Holt Online Assessment*
- *Online Gradebook*
- *Document-Based Question Activities*
- *Teaching Tips for the Multimedia Classroom*
- *Interactive Multimedia Activities*

Differentiating Instruction

Reading and Writing Support

◄ *Graphic Organizer Activity*
- *Vocabulary Activity*
- *Chapter Summary and Review*
- *Know It Notes*
- *Audio CD*

Active Learning

- *Block Scheduling Handbook*
- *Cultures of the World Activity*
- *Interdisciplinary Activity*
- *Map Activity*
◄ *Critical Thinking Activity 24*
- *Music of the World Audio CD: Masai Music of Kenya*

Primary Sources and Advanced Learners

- *Geography for Life Activity: Lake Victoria*
◄ *Map Activity: The Serengeti*
- *Readings in World Geography, History and Culture:*
  - *58 Government by Magic Spell*
  - *59 Along the Great Rift*
  - *60 The Kikuyn Meet Europeans*

Assessment Program

- *Daily Quizzes S1–4*
- *Chapter Test*
◄ *Chapter Test for English Language Learners and Special-Needs Students*

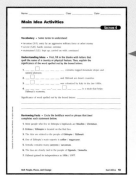

Spanish and ESOL

- *Vocabulary Activity*
◄ *Main Idea Activities for English Language Learners and Special-Needs Students*
- *Chapter Summary and Review*
- *Spanish Audio Summary*
- *Know It Notes S1–4*
- *Chapter Test for English Language Learners and Special-Needs Students*

Special Education Modifications

Your **I.D.E.A. Works! CD-ROM** will provide modified versions of the following teaching materials:

◄ *Guided Reading Strategies S1–4*
- *Vocabulary Activity*
- *Main Idea Activities S1–4*
- *Daily Quizzes S1–4*
- *Chapter 11 Test*
- *Flash cards of chapter vocabulary terms*

Teacher Resources

Books for Teachers

Gourevitch, Philip. *We Wish to Inform You that Tomorrow We Will Be Killed with Our Families: Stories from Rwanda.* Farrar, Strauss, and Giroux, 1998.

Huxley, Elspeth. *The Flame Trees of Thika.* Penguin, 2000.

Lumumba-Kasongo, Tukumbi. *The Dynamics of Economic and Political Relations Between Africa and Foreign Powers.* Praeger, 1999.

Books for Students

Lewin, Ted, and Betsy Lewin. *Gorilla Walk.* Lothrop, 1999. Recounts a journey to southern Uganda to view mountain gorillas.

Mann, Kenny. *Zenj, Buganda: East Africa.* African Kingdoms of the Past. Dillon Press, 1996. History, legends, and life of indigenous and immigrant peoples of ancient Zenj and Buganda.

Sayre, April Pulley. *If You Should Hear a Honey Guide.* Houghton Mifflin, 1995. Shows close connection between people and animals living in the East African bush. **SHELTERED ENGLISH**

Wilkes, Sybella. *One Day We Had to Run: Refugee Children Tell Their Stories in Words and Paintings.* Millbrook Press Trade, 1995. Stories of children from Somalia, Sudan, and Ethiopia who faced many dangers before reaching safety in Kenya.

Multimedia Materials

Africa—South of the Sahara: How Do People Use Their Environment? Video, 15 min. Agency for Instructional Technology.

East Africa: Tanzania and Zanzibar. Video, 47 min. Lonely Planet.

Swinging Safari Explore and Print. CD–ROM National Geographic Society.

Videos and CDs

Videos

- **CNN.** *Presents Geography: Yesterday and Today, Segment 25 The Nairobi National Park*
- **CNN.** *Presents World Cultures: Yesterday and Today, Segment 32 A Kenyan Reggae Festival*
- *ARG World*

Holt Researcher

http://researcher.hrw.com

- *Organization of African Unity (OAU)*
- *Africa*
- *Colonialism in Africa*
- *Ali, Sonni*
- *Kenyatta, Jomo*
- *Muhammad Ahmad*
- *Sudan*
- *Ethiopia*
- *Somalia*
- *Kenya*
- *Rwanda*

Transparency Packages

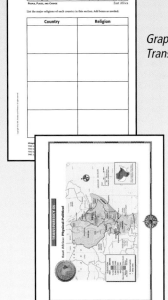

Graphic Organizer Transparencies 11.1–4

Geography and Cultures Visual Resources Transparencies 76–80
86 East Africa: Physical-Political

Map Activities Transparency 11 The Serengeti

Point out to students that there are many reasons why they should know more about East Africa. Here are some of them:

- Many scientists believe the human species has its origins in East Africa. Some of the most important fossil remains of humans come from the Olduvai Gorge in Tanzania.
- The region contains wildlife not found elsewhere. This wildlife is of interest to people around the world.
- Events in the region have influenced the foreign policy of the United States, including the use of armed forces and economic aid.

CHAPTER 11

East Africa

East Africa has been identified by historians as the cradle of the human race. It has made great contributions to the development of world civilization.

My name is Tsiyon. I am 13, and I live in Addis Ababa, the capital of Ethiopia. My house is very far from the city center. I live with my parents and my brothers. We have a servant who helps my mother with the housework. My mother stays at home. My father works for the game department, doing research on the wild animals of Ethiopia.

After a breakfast of bread and tea with milk, I ride to school in a city taxi—a small blue and white minibus—with my brother, Wondemagegn, who works in a garage. I am in the seventh grade at Freyhewat Number Two Junior Secondary School. There are 82 kids in my class! I am in school from 8:00 A.M. to 3:00 P.M. I am studying Amharic—an Ethiopian language—English, math, science, and sports. When I grow up, I want to be a doctor.

At noon, I eat a lunch I brought from home. When I get home, I help my mother sweep the house. Then I watch television. In the evenings, I do my homework.

Indemin adderu?

Translation: How did you pass the night?

238 Chapter 11

CHAPTER PROJECT

Have students create dioramas of East Africa's remarkable ecosystems, such as the Sudd, the Serengeti, Lake Nakuru, or Kilimanjaro. Have them depict physical features, vegetation, animal life, and whatever makes the place unique. Photograph dioramas for placing in student portfolios.

STARTING THE CHAPTER

Have students imagine that they are going on safari in Africa. Ask them to imagine what kinds of animals they may see. (Possible answers: elephants, lions, zebras, wildebeests, hippopotamuses, rhinoceroses) What kinds of scenery may they see? (Possible answers: grasslands, mountains in the distance, unusual trees, dry areas, villages with mud-walled houses with grass roofs) Tell them that this is the view many people have of Africa, but it applies most appropriately to parts of East Africa. Tell students they will learn about East Africa in this chapter.

Section 1 Physical Geography

Read to Discover

1. What are the major landforms of East Africa?
2. Which rivers and lakes are important in this region?
3. What are East Africa's climate types and natural resources?

Vocabulary

rifts

Places

Great Rift Valley
Mount Kilimanjaro
Lake Victoria
White Nile
Blue Nile

Reading Strategy

FOLDNOTES: DOUBLE-DOOR Create the FoldNote titled **Double-Door** described in the Appendix. Label the top flap "Rivers and Lakes" and the bottom flap "Climate and Resources." Label the paper beneath the top flap "Rift Valleys" and the paper beneath the lower flap "Mountains and Plains." Then write what you learn about each topic under each label.

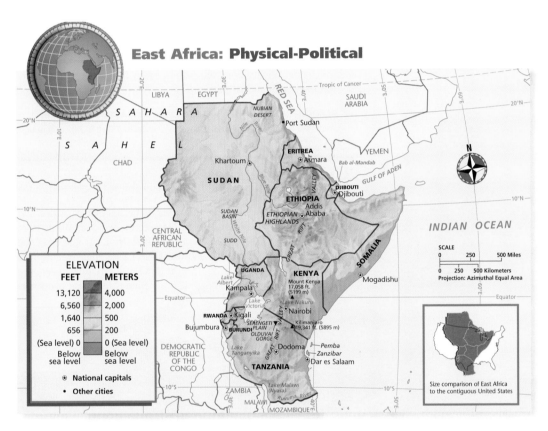

East Africa: Physical-Political

East Africa • 239

SECTION 1 RESOURCES

Reproducible
◆ Lecture Notes, Section 1
◆ Block Scheduling Handbook, Chapter 11
◆ Know It Notes S1
◆ Geography for Life Activity 24

Technology
◆ One-Stop Planner CD–ROM, Lesson 11.1
◆ Homework Practice Online
◆ Geography and Cultures Visual Resources with Teaching Activities 43–47
◆ Earth: Forces and Formations CD–ROM/Seek and Tell/Forces and Processes
◆ HRW Go site

Reinforcement, Review, and Assessment
◆ Section 1 Review
◆ Daily Quiz 11.1
◆ Main Idea Activity S1
◆ Chapter Summaries and Review
◆ English Audio Summary 11.1
◆ Spanish Audio Summary 11.1

Section 1

Objectives

1. Describe the major landforms of East Africa.
2. Identify the important rivers and lakes in this region.
3. Describe the climate types and natural resources of East Africa.

FOCUS

Bellringer

Copy the following instructions onto the chalkboard: *Look at the map at the beginning of the chapter and notice the lakes. Why do you think the lakes form a chain?* Discuss responses. Tell students that they are looking at surface evidence of East Africa's rift system. Explain to students that in Section 1 they will learn more about the physical geography of East Africa.

Using the Physical-Political Map

Have students examine the map on this page. Then have them describe the location of the Great Rift Valley (runs north through Tanzania up to Eritrea). Have students explain the effect East Africa's location may have on climate patterns in the region (wet tropical on the coast, dry in the north and west away from the coast). How may highland areas affect climate? (cooler temperatures, affecting rainfall)

EYE ON EARTH

Cichlids in Trouble

Scientists studying Lake Victoria's origins have concluded that its 300 species of cichlids, which are brightly colored fish, have evolved just in the last 12,000 years.

However, the number of cichlids is dwindling. Because of overfishing, habitat loss, and the introduction to the lake of Nile perch, which feed on the cichlids, the number of cichlids has dropped. Because cichlids feed on algae, their destruction contributes to an increase in algae in the lake, which clouds the water and makes it difficult for the fish to find their brightly colored mates.

Our Amazing Planet

Baobab (BOW-bab) trees are one of the few kinds of trees on the African savanna. It is also one of the largest trees in the world. It can grow as large as 30 feet (9 m) in diameter and to a height of 60 feet (18 m). The trunks are often used to store water or as temporary shelters.

internet connect

GO TO: go.hrw.com
KEYWORD: SK5 CH11
FOR: Web sites about Lake Victoria

The Land

East Africa is a land of high plains and plateaus. In the north, deserts and dry grasslands define the landscape. In the southwest, large lakes dot the plateaus. In the east, sandy beaches and beautiful coral reefs run along the coast. East Africa's most striking features are its great **rifts**. They cut from north to south across the region. Rifts are long, deep valleys with mountains or plateaus on either side. Rifts form when Earth's tectonic plates move away from each other.

The Rift Valleys Deep beneath East Africa's surface, Earth's mantle is churning. This movement causes the land to arch and split along the rift valleys. If you look at the Great Rift Valley from the air, it looks like a giant scar. The Great Rift Valley is made up of two rifts—the eastern rift and the western rift. The rift walls are usually a series of steep cliffs. These cliffs drop an average of about 9,000 feet (2,743 m) to the valley floor. The eastern rift begins north of the Red Sea. The rift continues south through Eritrea (er-uh-TREE-uh) and Ethiopia (ee-thee-OH-pee-uh) into southern Tanzania (tan-zuh-NEE-uh). The western rift extends from Lake Albert in the north to Lake Malawi (mah-LAH-wee), also known as Lake Nyasa, in the south.

Mountains and Plains East Africa also has many volcanic mountains. Mount Kilimanjaro (ki-luh-muhn-JAHR-oh), at 19,341 feet (5,895 m), is Africa's tallest mountain. Although this part of Africa is along the equator, the mountain is so high that snow covers its two volcanic cones. Plains along the eastern rift in Tanzania and Kenya are home to famous national parks.

✔ **READING CHECK:** (*Places and Regions*) What are the major landforms of East Africa? High plains, plateaus, deserts, grasslands, beaches, rifts, mountains

This is a crater rim view of Mount Kilimanjaro. Another name for this volcano is Kilima Njaro—"shining mountain" in Swahili.

Rivers and Lakes

East Africa is the site of a number of rivers and large lakes. The Nile is the world's longest river. It begins in East Africa and flows north to the Mediterranean Sea. Water from small streams collects in Lake Victoria, the source of the White Nile. Waters from Ethiopia's highlands form the Blue Nile. These two rivers

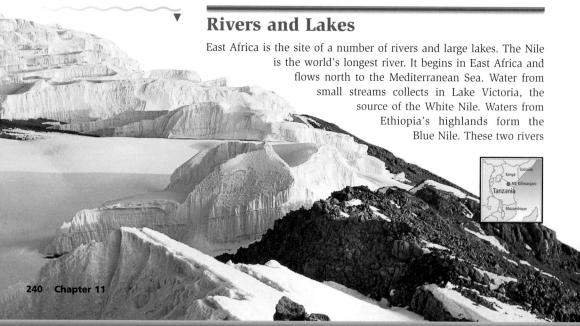

TEACH

Teaching Objectives 1–2

ALL LEVELS: (Suggested time: 20 min.) Copy the following graphic organizer onto the chalkboard, omitting the blue answers. Assign each of four groups one of the following topics: the Great Rift Valley, mountains and plains, rivers, or lakes. Have each group use the text and the map to find names or characteristics of the topic. Ask members from each group to come up to the chalkboard and fill in the organizer.
ESOL, COOPERATIVE LEARNING, LS VISUAL-SPATIAL

Teaching Objective 3

ALL LEVELS: (Suggested time: 30 min.) Have students sketch an outline map of East Africa. Then ask them to label the climate zones and shade them in different colors. Then have students list the natural resources found in the region. **ESOL**

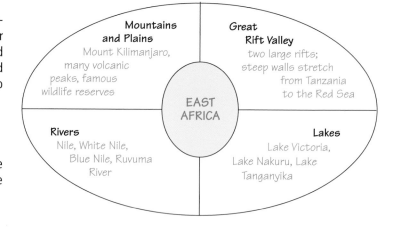

Mountains and Plains
Mount Kilimanjaro, many volcanic peaks, famous wildlife reserves

Great Rift Valley
two large rifts; steep walls stretch from Tanzania to the Red Sea

EAST AFRICA

Rivers
Nile, White Nile, Blue Nile, Ruvuma River

Lakes
Lake Victoria, Lake Nakuru, Lake Tanganyika

meet at Khartoum, Sudan, to create the mighty Nile. The Nile provides a narrow, fertile lifeline through Sudan by providing irrigation in the desert.

Lake Victoria is Africa's largest lake in area, but it is shallow. Along the western rift is a chain of great lakes. Many of the lakes along the drier eastern rift are quite different. Heat from Earth's interior makes some of these eastern lakes so hot that no human can swim in them. Others, like Lake Nakuru, are too salty for most fish. However, algae in Lake Nakuru provides food for more than a million flamingos.

✓ **READING CHECK:** (*Places and Regions*) Which rivers and lakes are most important in this region? The Nile, Lake Victoria, Lake Nakuru

▲

Lake Nakuru is known in part for the many flamingos that gather there.

Climate and Resources

Northern Sudan and the northeast coast have desert and steppe climates. The climate changes to tropical savanna as you travel south. However, the greatest climate changes occur along the sides of the rift valleys. The rift floors are dry, with grasslands and thorn shrubs. In contrast, the surrounding plateaus and mountains have a humid highland climate and dense forests. Rain falls at the high elevations, but the valleys are in rain shadows.

Most East Africans are farmers or herders. However, the region does have mineral resources such as coal, copper, diamonds, gold, iron ore, and lead.

✓ **READING CHECK:** (*Places and Regions*) What are East Africa's climate types and natural resources? desert, steppe, tropical savanna, humid highland; coal, copper, diamonds, gold, iron ore, lead

Section Review 1

Define and explain: rifts

Working with Sketch Maps On a map of East Africa that you draw or that your teacher provides, label the following: Great Rift Valley, Mount Kilimanjaro, Lake Victoria, White Nile, and Blue Nile. How do the mountains help support the river systems?

Reading for the Main Idea

1. (*Places and Regions*) What are the major landforms of East Africa?

2. (*Places and Regions*) Which rivers and lakes are located in this part of Africa?

3. (*Physical Systems*) Why are volcanic mountains found in parts of East Africa?

Homework Practice Online
Keyword: SK5 HP11

Critical Thinking

4. **Drawing Inferences and Conclusions** How do you think the climate types found in East Africa influence what grows there?

Organizing What You Know

5. **Summarizing** Copy the following graphic organizer. Use it to describe what you know about East Africa's physical geography.

	Vegetation	Climates
Coasts		
Rift Valleys		
Plateaus/mountains		

East Africa • 241

CLOSE

Point out the relationships between landforms and climates types found in East Africa. Describe how tectonic forces act upon landforms and bodies of water. Then have students recall other places in the world where tectonic forces act upon landforms.

REVIEW, ASSESS, RETEACH

Have students complete Main Idea Activity S1. Then have students choose one of the lines of latitude marked on the physical-political map of East Africa. Ask students to write a description of the landforms, bodies of water, climates, and resources they would encounter if they made a journey from the coast of the Red Sea or Indian Ocean west along that line of latitude. **ESOL**

EXTEND

Have students investigate the search for the origins of the Blue Nile and White Nile. Instruct them to pay particular attention to the difficulties imposed on the explorers by the region's physical geography. **BLOCK SCHEDULING**

Section 2 East Africa's History and Culture

Read to Discover

1. What important events and developments influenced the history of East Africa?
2. What is the culture of East Africa like?

Vocabulary
Swahili

People
Amanirenus

Reading Strategy

TAKING NOTES Use the headings in this section to create an outline. As you read the section, write what you learn about East Africa's history and culture beneath each heading.

History

Several early civilizations developed at the site known as Meroë, near where the branches of the Nile come together. These civilizations had their own forms of writing. Each controlled a major trade route. East Africans traded ivory and gold, among other things.

This statue depicts a prince from the early Nubian civilization of northern Sudan.

Christianity and Islam Like Egypt, Ethiopia was an early center of Christianity. In the A.D. 500s Christianity spread into neighboring Nubia, which is now part of Egypt and Sudan. In Nubia, Christian kingdoms lasted until about 1500. Ethiopia still has a large Christian population today.

Arab armies conquered Egypt and North Africa by about A.D. 700. However, these armies were not able to keep control of East Africa. Gradually, Arabic-speaking nomads spread into northern Sudan from Egypt. They brought their Islamic faith with them. At the same time, Islam spread to the coastal region of what is now Somalia. Christianity is believed to have been introduced in Ethiopia as early as the A.D. 300s. Christian kingdoms, particularly in Ethiopia, have fought wars with Muslim leaders. Religion continues to be a source of conflict in this East African region.

The Slave Trade The east coast slave trade dates back more than 1,000 years. Most slaves went to Islamic countries in Africa and Asia. The Portuguese had begun setting up forts and settlements on the East African coast by the early 1500s. At first, the Europeans made little

Section 2

Objectives

1. Describe the important events and developments that influenced the history of East Africa.
2. Analyze the culture of East Africa.

FOCUS

Bellringer

Copy the following passage onto the chalkboard: *Karibu! Hujambo? is a common greeting in East Africa. What do you think it means?* Discuss responses. (The greeting means Welcome! How are you?) Tell students that in Section 2 they will learn more about the culture and history of East Africa.

Building Vocabulary

Write **Swahili** on the chalkboard. Explain to students that the phrase in the previous activity is in the Swahili language. Swahili is one of many features of the diverse culture of East Africa.

National Geography Standard 10

Trade and Cultural Diffusion Trade networks have connected East Africa to other regions for centuries. These trade links apparently extended as far as China. For example, an East African tomb from the 1700s includes Ming dynasty porcelain as part of its decoration. The island of Zanzibar, as a market for trade goods, was also a point from which the Islamic religion and the Swahili language were introduced into Africa's interior.

Swahili is a good example of the kind of cultural diffusion that characterizes East Africa. The Swahili language is the result of the mixing of Arabic with African languages. Swahili also refers to the new culture that emerged in East Africa.

Critical Thinking: How might trade foster cultural change?

Answer: Students may say that along with goods, foreign merchants would introduce new ideas.

Kings and nobles of Meroë were buried in these pyramids.

effort to move into the interior. However, in the late 1700s the East African island of Zanzibar became an international slave-trading center. Later, plantations like those of the Americas were set up with slave labor to grow cloves and sugarcane.

Africa Divided In the mid-1800s European adventurers traveled into the African interior searching for the source of the Nile. Here they found rich lands well suited for agriculture. In the 1880s the European powers divided up most of the continent. Most of Africa's modern borders resulted from this process. Control over much of East Africa went to the British. Germany colonized Tanzania, Rwanda, and Burundi. After World War I, with the defeat of Germany, the British took over Tanzania. Belgium gained control of Rwanda and Burundi.

Conflict Within East Africa, just Kenya was settled by large numbers of Europeans. The colonial rulers usually controlled their countries through African deputies. Many of these deputies were traditional chiefs, who often favored their own peoples. This tended to strengthen ethnic rivalries. These ethnic divisions have made it hard for governments to create feelings of national identity.

Independence Ethiopia was never colonized. Its mountains provided natural protection, and its peoples and emperors resisted colonization. It was, however, annexed by Italy from 1936 to 1941. Most East African countries were granted independence by European colonizers in the early 1960s. More recently, East Africa has become headquarters for some international companies and organizations.

✔ **READING CHECK:** (*Human Systems*) Which European countries influenced the history of East Africa? Portugal, Britain, Germany, Belgium, Italy

BIOGRAPHY

Amanirenus
(lived 20s B.C.)

Early in East Africa's history, women often ruled in the region. Those who ruled Kush used the title "Candace." Amanirenus was one of them. She led her army against invading Romans in 24 B.C. Both she and the Romans claimed that they won the fight. The Kushites were able to remove the head from a statue of Augustus Caesar. They put it under the temple stairs so everyone who entered could step on the foreigner who threatened their land.

What symbol did the Kushites use to express their pride in their land?

◄ **Biography Answer**

putting the head from a statue of Augustus Caesar under the stairs

East Africa • 243

TEACH

Teaching Objective 1

ALL LEVELS: (Suggested time: 20 min.) Copy the following graphic organizer onto the chalkboard, omitting the blue answers. Organize students into three groups to find information about one of the following influences: religion, the slave trade, or colonization. Have members from each group fill in the appropriate part of the organizer. Then have students speculate on how these historical factors or events have influenced the region's culture today. **ESOL, COOPERATIVE LEARNING**

EAST AFRICA'S HISTORY		
Religion	Trade	Colonization
• Arabic-speaking nomads spread Islamic faith	• slaves traded to Arabia	• Great Britain
	• Portuguese start European slave trade	• Germany
• Christianity from Ethiopian kingdoms		• Italy annexed Ethiopia

Teaching Objective 2

ALL LEVELS: (Suggested time: 20 min.) Pair students and have pairs compose poems or riddles about the culture of East Africa. Call on volunteers to read their compositions aloud. **LS AUDITORY-MUSICAL**

East Africa 243

Answers to Section 2 Review

Define or identify For definitions and identifications, see the glossary and index.

Working with Sketch Maps Maps will vary, but bodies of water should be highlighted in their approximate locations. Early civilizations settled there because of the good climate and environment.

Reading for the Main Idea

1. Portugal, Great Britain, and Germany (NGS 9)

2. Christianity and Islam (NGS 10)

Critical Thinking

3. ethnic conflicts, such as that between the Tutsi and the Hutu in Rwanda; religious conflicts

4. Swahili may unify people who also speak other languages.

Organizing What You Know

5. A.D. 400—Sudan conquered and Christianity introduced; 700—Arab nomads introduce Islam; early 1500s—Portuguese establish settlements; 1700s—European slave trade begins; late 1800s—European colonization; early 1960s—independence; 1990s—ethnic conflicts

▲
Afar nomads stop for rest in a desert region of northern Ethiopia.

Culture

East Africa has the world's longest history of human settlement. Gradually, the region developed the continent's greatest diversity of people and ways of life. The **Swahili** language is widely spoken in East Africa. This Bantu language has been greatly influenced by Arabic. In fact, the word Swahili comes from the Arabic word meaning "on the coast."

East Africa shares many challenges with other African regions. One challenge is that populations are growing faster than the economies that support them. Many jobless people have crowded into the cities. Another challenge is religious and ethnic conflict. Such conflict and other political problems have slowed economic progress. Often a country's wealth is spent on weapons rather than helping people.

The ethnic conflicts have roots in the region's history. Colonial borders drawn by Europeans often lumped different ethnic groups into one country. Differences between groups have led to conflict in some countries since independence.

The worst ethnic conflict has been in Rwanda and Burundi. Thousands of Tutsi were killed by the Hutu in Rwanda in the 1990s. There also has been fighting between Muslims and Christians in the northern part of the region.

✓ **READING CHECK:** (*Human Systems*) What conflicts have occurred between groups in East Africa? ethnic conflicts, such as that between Tutsi and Hutu in Rwanda, and religious conflicts

go. hrw .com **Homework Practice Online**
Keyword: SK5 HP11

Define or identify: Amanirenus, Swahili

Working with Sketch Maps On the map you created in Section 1, highlight the location of the bodies of water you labeled. Why do you think early civilizations settled near these bodies of water?

Reading for the Main Idea

1. (*Human Systems*) Which European countries influenced the history of this area?

2. (*Human Systems*) What are the main religions practiced in East Africa?

Critical Thinking

3. **Finding the Main Idea** What conflicts have occurred because of political boundary lines?

4. **Drawing Inferences and Conclusions** Why might Swahili be a particularly important language in East Africa?

Organizing What You Know

5. **Sequencing** Create a time line listing historical events in East Africa from the A.D. 400s to the 1990s. Be sure to include the adoption of Christianity, the slave trade, exploration, colonial rule, independence, and ethnic conflict.

A.D. 400 ———————————— 1990s

CLOSE

Play Selection 15 from the Music of the World Audio CD Program for students. It is a song of the Masai warriors of Kenya. Point out the Masai dancers in the photos of this unit's opening pages. Challenge students to listen to the music and imagine these same men dancing to the song.

REVIEW, ASSESS, RETEACH

Have students complete the Section Review. Then have pairs of students organize the challenges of East Africa into economic, political, religious, and ethnic areas. Have them identify a historical influence that led to each challenge. Then have students complete Daily Quiz 11.2.

Have students complete Main Idea Activity S2. Then have them draw a time line on a piece of butcher paper. Assign groups of students periods in East African history and have them draw or find pictures to illustrate events. Have students glue their pictures to the time line. Display and discuss the time line. **ESOL,** LS

EXTEND

Have interested students conduct research on the history of Christianity in Ethiopia. Have them pay particular attention to the churches of Lalibela, which were hewn out of solid rock, starting at ground level. Allow students to present their findings in an illustrated report. **BLOCK SCHEDULING**

Section 3 The Countries of East Africa

Read to Discover

1. Why did settlers come to Kenya?
2. How was Tanzania created?
3. What are Rwanda and Burundi like?
4. What is Uganda like?
5. What are the physical features of Sudan?

Vocabulary
gorge

Places
Kenya
Tanzania
Rwanda
Burundi
Uganda
Sudan

People
Kikuyu
Tutsi
Hutu

Reading Strategy

READING ORGANIZER Before you read, draw a circle in the center of a sheet of paper. Label the circle East African Countries. Draw five rays from the circle. Draw a circle at the end of each ray. Label the circles Kenya, Tanzania, Rwanda and Burundi, Uganda, and Sudan. As you read the section, write what you learn about the countries beside each circle.

Kenya

Kenya's first cities were founded along the coast of the Indian Ocean by Arab traders. Beginning in the 1500s Portugal controlled this coast for about 200 years. Arabs then recaptured it.

During the 1800s British merchants began trading on the coast. They built a railway from Mombasa to Lake Victoria. British settlers then came to take advantage of the fertile highlands. People from India and Pakistan also came to work on the Europeans' farms. Many of the local people, particularly the Kikuyu, moved out of their traditional areas. They became farmworkers or took jobs in the cities. After World War II many Africans protested British colonial rule. There were peaceful demonstrations as well as violent ones.

One conflict was over land. The British and the Kikuyu viewed land differently. The British considered land a sign of personal wealth, power, and property. The Kikuyu saw land as a source of food rather than something to be bought or sold. This caused conflict because the British wanted the land. Kenya gained independence from Britain in the 1960s, and its government has been quite stable ever since.

Kenya is a popular tourist destination. Tourism is a major source of income for the country. Kenya's greatest challenge is its rapidly increasing population. There is no empty farmland left in most areas. Much of Kenya has been set aside as national parkland.

Movement As in the rest of Africa, Europeans once ruled colonies in East Africa. Fort Jesus, founded in 1593 by the Portuguese, is a national monument in Kenya.

East Africa • 245

Section 3

Objectives

1. Explain why settlers came to Kenya.
2. Describe how Tanzania was created.
3. Explain what Rwanda and Burundi are like.
4. Explain what Uganda is like.
5. Describe the physical features of Sudan.

FOCUS

 Bellringer

Copy the following instructions onto the chalkboard: *Look at the chart of statistics on the next page. Write down one statement about the African countries listed that you can conclude from the chart.* Discuss responses. (Possible answers: Burundi has the lowest literacy note. Kenya has the lowest population growth rate. Sudan has the highest per capita GDP.) Tell students that in Section 3 they will learn more about the countries of East Africa.

Building Vocabulary

Ask students to describe a canyon. Then have students visualize a narrow canyon with steep sides. Explain to students that they have just visualized a **gorge**. Tell students that a gorge is one of the major landforms of East Africa. Have volunteers explain what they know about the kinds of physical processes that create canyons and gorges.

East Africa 245

EYE ON EARTH

Serengeti Food Chain

The Serengeti Plain provides a good example of a complex food chain. The plain's grasses and other plants are the chain's foundation. Termites, ants, and other insects eat the plants and serve as food for birds and small carnivores. Large herbivorous animals such as wildebeests, zebras, gazelles, and giraffes also feed on the plants. Big predators, including lions, leopards, and cheetahs, feed on the small and large plant-eating animals. Vultures, hyenas, and other scavengers eat what they leave. Beetles help scour the bones.

Wildebeests are a particularly interesting link in the Serengeti food chain. During the dry season they migrate north to greener fields. Thousands of animals go on the run, thundering across the plains. Lions and other predators follow, preying on slow or sick animals that cannot keep up with the herd.

Activity: Have students diagram the food chains described.

Chart Answer ▲

Burundi

East Africa

COUNTRY	POPULATION/ GROWTH RATE	LIFE EXPECTANCY	LITERACY RATE	PER CAPITA GDP
Burundi	6,096,156 2.2%	42, male 44, female	52%	$600
Kenya	31,639,091 1.3%	45, male 45, female	85%	$1,020
Rwanda	7,810,056 1.8%	38, male 40, female	70%	$1,200
Sudan	38,114,160 2.7%	56, male 58, female	61%	$1,420
Tanzania	35,922,454 1.7%	43, male 46, female	78%	$630
Uganda	25,632,794 2.9%	43, male 46, female	70%	$1,260
United States	290,342,554 0.9%	74, male 80, female	97%	$37,600

Source: Central Intelligence Agency, *The World Factbook 2003*

Interpreting the Chart **Which country has the lowest literacy rate?**

These giraffe feed on the tree-studded grasslands of the Serengeti. This reserve was opened in 1974 and is Kenya's most famous and popular animal reserve.

▼

Many people would like to farm these lands. If the national parks are converted to farmland, however, African wildlife would be endangered. In addition, the tourism industry would likely suffer.

✔ **READING CHECK:** (*Human Systems*) Why did settlers come to Kenya? for trade, land

Tanzania

South of Kenya is the large country of Tanzania. It was created in the 1960s when Tanganyika and the island of Zanzibar united. Today many tourists come to explore numerous national parks and Mount Kilimanjaro. The mountain's southern slopes are a rich agricultural region that provides coffee and tea for exports. Also in Tanzania is the Serengeti Plain. On this plain, herds of antelope and zebras still migrate freely, following the rains. Nearby is a famous archaeological site, Olduvai Gorge. A **gorge** is a narrow, steep-walled canyon. Evidence of some of the earliest humanlike fossils have been found in Olduvai Gorge.

Tanzania is a country of mainly poor subsistence farmers. Poor soils and limited technology have restricted productivity. This country has minerals, particularly gold and diamonds. Although the Tanzanian government has tried to make the country more self-sufficient, it has not yet succeeded.

✔ **READING CHECK:** (*Places and Regions*) How was the country of Tanzania created? when Tanganyika and Zanzibar united

246 • Chapter 11

TEACH

Teaching Objective 1

ALL LEVELS: (Suggested time: 30 min.) Have students design a mural that identifies the various groups that settled in Kenya and explains the reasons why they came. Ask students to refer to Section 2 for details. (Murals should depict these groups: Arabs—trade, slaves; Portuguese—trade, slaves; British—farming; Indians and Pakistanis—farm work)

ESOL, LS **VISUAL-SPATIAL**

Teaching Objective 2

ALL LEVELS: (Suggested time: 10 min.) Have students write a brief news report on the creation of Tanzania. Students should mention how and when Tanzania was created as well as some of the physical features found in that country and how they have influenced its economic development.

➤**ASSIGNMENT:** Ask students to imagine that they are explorers traveling through East Africa. Have them write three journal entries about the experience. Entries should include a description of the physical features as well as the people and customs of the area. LS **VERBAL-LINGUISTIC**

CONNECTING TO *Science*

Olduvai Gorge, Tanzania

Many scientists believe the human species has its origins in Africa. Archaeologists there have discovered fossil remains of humans and humanlike animals several million years old. Some of the most important finds have occurred at a site known as Olduvai Gorge.

Located in Tanzania, Olduvai is a steep-sided canyon some 30 miles (48 km) long. It is up to 300 feet (90 m) deep. The exposed sides of this gorge contain fossil deposits estimated to be more than 4 million years old. Along with the fossils, scientists found stone tools and the remains of numerous humanlike animals.

Archaeologists Louis and Mary Leakey played a key role in uncovering Olduvai's secrets. In 1931 Louis Leakey found remains of ancient tools and bones in the gorge. Then in 1959 Mary Leakey found the skeleton of an *Australopithecus*, the first humanlike creature to walk upright. Several years later, the Leakeys found the remains of a more advanced species. The new find was known as *Homo habilis*. The species could make stone tools.

These discoveries helped provide some of the missing links between humans and their ancestors. Today archaeological work at Olduvai Gorge continues to add to our understanding of human origins.

Understanding What You Read

1. What is Olduvai Gorge?
2. What part has Olduvai played in the search for human origins?

Layers of Discovery

Tectonic activity of the Olduvai Gorge area created conditions that were good for both the preservation of ancient remains and for their eventual discovery.

The Olduvai fossil beds were laid down in a lake basin. Frequent changes in the lake's levels and ashfalls from volcanoes buried remains quickly, preserving them. Volcanic action and sedimentation created seven major layers. Then relatively constant fault movements and volcanic action cut through the layers of rock and sediment that had accumulated over the millennia. Flowing water further exposed the layers and skeletal remains they contained.

Activity: Have students draw diagrams to depict how skeletal remains were preserved and then exposed in Olduvai Gorge. Call on students to explain their diagrams to the class.

Connecting to Science
Answers

1. a steep-sided canyon in Tanzania
2. Remains of ancient tools and skeletons were found in the exposed sides of the canyon.

Rwanda and Burundi

These two countries in fertile highlands were once German colonies. After World War I the Belgians ruled them. In the 1960s, after they gained independence, they were divided into two countries. Both countries are mostly populated by two ethnic groups—the Tutsi and the Hutu. Violence between the groups has killed thousands. Rwanda and Burundi have the densest rural settlement in Africa. Foreign aid has helped improve farming and health care.

Red colobus monkeys of Zanzibar eat charcoal, which absorbs poisons in the fruit-tree leaves the monkeys sometimes eat.

✓ **READING CHECK:** (*Human Systems*) Why did the creation of Rwanda and Burundi create conflict? Political boundaries were drawn across cultural lines, leading to fighting between the Hutu and the Tutsi.

East Africa • 247

Teaching Objectives 3–5

ALL LEVELS: (Suggested time: 15 min.) Copy the following graphic organizer onto the chalkboard, omitting the blue answers, to help students compare Rwanda, Burundi, Uganda, and Sudan. Then lead a discussion about the causes of the challenges and possible solutions for them. **ESOL**

	Physical Features	Challenges
Rwanda	fertile highland	violence between ethnic groups
Burundi	fertile highland	violence between Tutsi and Hutu
Uganda	fertile plateau	violent dictatorship, collapsed economy
Sudan	Sahara, dry savannas, the Sudd	conflicts between Arab and traditionally African cultures

TEACHER TO TEACHER

Susan Walker of Beaufort, South Carolina, suggests the following activity to help students learn about the discoveries at Olduvai Gorge: Have students conduct research on the discoveries and how they were found in the rock layers. Then have them construct a scale model of the site, using modeling clay or salt-flour dough tinted different shades to depict the seven major layers. Have students place small objects in the clay to stand for artifacts and fossils. Finally, demonstrate how tectonic action and erosion exposed the remains by cutting and lifting parts of the clay "landscape."

Answers to Section 3 Review

Define or identify For definitions and identifications, see the glossary and index.

Working with Sketch Maps Maps will vary, but listed places should be labeled accurately. The agriculturally fertile countries are located in different climate zones than the others.

Reading for the Main Idea
1. good farmland, refuge for wildlife, important tourist destination **(NGS 4)**
2. Kenya's wildlife refuges, Mount Kilimanjaro, the Serengeti Plain, and the Olduvai Gorge **(NGS 4)**

Critical Thinking
3. provides a water supply and makes it possible to farm
4. has taken thousands of lives, limited foreign investment, and slowed economic development **(NGS 13)**

Organizing What You Know
5. Kenya—fertile farmland, growing population; Tanzania—gold and diamonds, limited farming productivity; Rwanda and Burundi—fertile land, ethnic conflicts; Uganda—fertile farmland, collapsed economy; Sudan—minerals and oil, civil wars and religious conflicts

Uganda

Uganda, another site of an ancient empire, is found on the plateau north and west of Lake Victoria. Economic progress has been slow. Foreign investment stopped as a result of a violent dictatorship. In the 1970s the country's economy collapsed. Limited peace and democracy were achieved in the late 1980s.

✓ **READING CHECK:** (*Human Systems*) What is Uganda like today? relatively peaceful and democratic

Sudan

Sudan is Africa's largest country. It has three physical regions. The Sahara makes up the northern half of the country. Dry savannas extend across the country's center. Much of southern Sudan is taken up by a swamp called the Sudd. Sudan is mainly an agricultural country, but it is also developing some of its mineral resources. Oil reserves have not yet been developed.

Modern Sudanese culture shows influences of Arab and traditionally African cultures. Arab Muslims make up about 70 percent of the population and have political power. They dominate northern Sudan. Khartoum, the capital, is located in this area. During the last several decades there was a civil war between northern Muslims and southerners who practice Christianity or traditional African religions.

✓ **READING CHECK:** (*Human Systems*) What conflict has been occurring in Sudan? civil war between different religious groups

▲ Alfred Louis Sargent created this engraving of Khartoum, Sudan, in the 1800s.

go.hrw.com **Homework Practice Online**
Keyword: SK5 HP11

Section Review 3

Define or identify: Kikuyu, gorge, Tutsi, Hutu

Working with Sketch Maps On the map you created in Section 2, label Kenya, Tanzania, Rwanda, Burundi, Uganda, and Sudan. Why are some of the countries of this region agriculturally fertile while others are not?

Reading for the Main Idea
1. (*Places and Regions*) What makes the highlands of Kenya important?
2. (*Places and Regions*) Which areas of East Africa are tourist attractions?

Critical Thinking
3. **Making Generalizations and Predictions** How might irrigation help a region's economic development?
4. **Finding the Main Idea** How has unrest hurt Rwanda and some other East African countries?

Organizing What You Know
5. **Summarizing** Copy the following graphic organizer. Use it to list each country in this section. In one column list resources important to its development, and in the next column list obstacles that could prevent the country's economic success.

Country	Resources	Obstacles

248 • Chapter 11

CLOSE

Tell students that the locations and landforms of East African countries greatly affected their history and the challenges they face today. Have students summarize the region's challenges. (Possible answers: lack of resources, political unrest, ethnic conflict, religious conflict, economic development)

REVIEW, ASSESS, RETEACH

Have students complete the Section Review. Then have each student write a short-answer question for each of the six countries in Section 3. Collect the questions and use them to quiz the class orally.

Have students complete Main Idea Activity S3. Then draw an outline map of this region on butcher paper. Organize students into five groups and assign each group a country. Have students write the resources and challenges of their assigned country on small slips of paper. Have students label the countries and glue their strips of paper onto the map. **ESOL, COOPERATIVE LEARNING**

EXTEND

Have interested students investigate wildlife conservation programs in East Africa. Ask them to concentrate on government efforts to balance economic progress, tourism, and conservation. **BLOCK SCHEDULING**

Section 4 The Horn of Africa

Read to Discover

1. What are the main physical features of Ethiopia?
2. What is Eritrea like?
3. What is Somalia like?
4. What are the physical and cultural characteristics of Djibouti?

Vocabulary

droughts

Places

Ethiopia
Eritrea
Somalia
Djibouti
Bab al-Mandab

People

Somali

Reading Strategy

READING ORGANIZER Before you read, draw a large square on a sheet of paper. Draw a vertical line down the center of the square. Draw a horizontal line across the center of the square. Label the boxes Ethiopia, Eritrea, Somalia, and Djibouti. As you read the section write details about each country in its box.

Ethiopia

Ethiopia is one of the world's poorest countries. The rugged mountain slopes and upland plateaus have rich volcanic soil. Agriculture is Ethiopia's chief economic activity. It exports coffee, livestock, and oilseeds. However, during the last 30 years the region has experienced serious **droughts**. Droughts are periods when little rain falls and crops are damaged. Drought, combined with war and ineffective government policies, caused the starvation of several million people in the 1980s.

Except for a time when Ethiopia was at war with Italy, the Ethiopian highlands have never been under foreign rule. The mountains protected the interior of the country from invasion. Most of the highland people are Christian, while most of the lowland people are Muslim.

✔ **READING CHECK:** *Places and Regions* What physical features are found in Ethiopia? mountains, plateaus

As Afar nomads in Ethiopia move their encampment, they are continually challenged by the environment.

Interpreting the Visual Record

Movement **How important are these camels for the Afar? What purpose do they serve?**

East Africa ◆ 249

SECTION 4 RESOURCES

Reproducible
◆ Lecture Notes, Section 4
◆ Know It Notes S4
◆ Biography Activity: Menelik II

Technology
◆ One-Stop Planner CD–ROM, Lesson 11.4
◆ Homework Practice Online
◆ HRW Go site

Reinforcement, Review, and Assessment
◆ Section 4 Review
◆ Daily Quiz 11.4
◆ Main Idea Activity S4
◆ Chapter Summaries and Review
◆ English Audio Summary 11.4
◆ Spanish Audio Summary 11.4

◀ **Visual Record Answer**

probably very important, because they make survival in the harsh environment possible

---

Section 4

Objectives

1. Describe the main physical features of Ethiopia.
2. Describe what Eritrea is like.
3. Explain what Somalia is like.
4. Explain the physical and cultural characteristics of Djibouti.

FOCUS

Bellringer

Copy the following instructions onto the chalkboard: *Look at the photos in Section 4 and read the captions. Write down one question that you have about what you see in the photos.* Discuss responses. Ask students to keep their questions handy and try to answer them as they read Section 4. Tell students they will learn more about the countries that occupy the Horn of Africa in Section 4.

Building Vocabulary

Ask students what is the longest period without rain that they can remember. Discuss responses. Tell students a **drought** is a period of little rain. Mention that droughts have affected many people who live in the Horn of Africa.

FOOD FESTIVAL

Food, Platter, or Both?

The staple of Ethiopian cuisine is a large sourdough pancake called *injera*.

Ethiopians place *injera* directly on the table and pour spicy stew onto the *injera*. Diners then break off a piece of the bread with the right hand and use it to scoop up bits of stew. Have students bring stew and use pita bread as the *injera*. Students can scoop up bits of stew with the pieces of bread. Or, challenge students to locate recipes for *injera*, make it at home, and bring samples to class. In Ethiopia, *injera* is made with a grain called teff. Since teff is hard to find in the United States, students may experiment with substituting buckwheat. Recipes for *injera* using buckwheat are available on the Internet.

Chart Answer

Djibouti; highest literacy rate and per capital GDP

Visual Record Answer

Possible answers: arches, domes, minarets

COUNTRY	POPULATION/ GROWTH RATE	LIFE EXPECTANCY	LITERACY RATE	PER CAPITA GDP
Djibouti	457,130 2.1%	42, male 44, female	68%	$1,300
Eritrea	4,362,254 1.3%	51, male 55, female	59%	$740
Ethiopia	66,557,553 1.9%	40, male 42, female	43%	$750
Somalia	8,025,190 3.4%	45, male 49, female	38%	$550
United States	290,342,554 0.9%	74, male 80, female	97%	$37,600

The Horn of Africa

Source: Central Intelligence Agency, *The World Factbook 2003*

Interpreting the Chart Which country in the region has the highest level of economic development, and why?

The main mosque, Khulafa el Rashidin, was built in 1937 with Italian Carrara marble in Asmara, Eritrea.

Interpreting the Visual Record What architectural elements of this building have you seen in other regions you have studied?

Eritrea

Eritrea, located on the Red Sea, was once part of Ethiopia. In the late 1800s the Italians made this area a colony. In the 1960s it became an Ethiopian province. After years of war, Eritrea broke away from Ethiopia in 1993. The economy has slowly improved since then. The population is made up of Muslims and Christians.

✓ **READING CHECK:** *Places and Regions* What is Eritrea like today? improved economy; population made up of Muslims and Christians

Somalia

Somalia is a land of deserts and dry savannas. Most Somalis are nomadic herders. Livestock and bananas are the main exports. Somalia is less diverse than most other African countries. Most residents of Somalia are members of the Somali people. Most Somali share the same culture, religion (Islam), language (Somali), and way of life (herding). Somalia has been troubled by civil war. In the 1990s widespread starvation caused by the war and a severe drought attracted international attention. The United Nations sent aid and troops to the country. U.S. troops were sent to Somalia to assist with this operation.

✓ **READING CHECK:** *Environment and Society* How have drought and conflict affected Somalia? caused widespread starvation

250 Chapter 11

TEACH

Teaching Objectives 1–4

ALL LEVELS: (Suggested time: 25 min.) Copy the following graphic organizer onto the chalkboard, omitting the blue answers. Have students copy and complete it. Then ask for volunteers to provide answers for the graphic on the chalkboard. Use the completed graphic organizer to discuss similarities and differences among these societies. **ESOL**

Country	Location or Physical Features	Key Characteristics
Ethiopia	on Red Sea, mountains and plateaus	agricultural, poor, suffered droughts
Eritrea	on Red Sea	independent since 1993, improving economy
Somalia	deserts and dry savannas	mainly herders, less diverse culture, troubled by civil war and drought
Djibouti	on Bab al-Mandab, partly below sea level	independent since 1977, port provides income, depends on Ethiopian agriculture

Djibouti

Djibouti is a small desert country. It lies on the Bab al-Mandab. This is the narrow strait that connects the Red Sea and the Indian Ocean. The strait lies along a major shipping route. This has helped Djibouti's economy. In the 1860s Djibouti came under French control. It gained independence in 1977. The French government still contributes economic and military support to the country. Its port, which serves landlocked Ethiopia, is a major source of income. Djibouti is heavily dependent on food imports.

The people of Djibouti include the Issa and the Afar. The Issa are closely tied to the people of Somalia. The Afar are related to the people of Ethiopia. Members of both groups are Muslim. Somalia and Ethiopia have both wanted to control Djibouti. So far the country has maintained its independence.

✓ **READING CHECK:** (*Places and Regions*) What are Djibouti's physical and cultural features? **desert country on a strait; Issa and Afar peoples**

Djibouti's Lake Assal has one of the lowest surface levels on the planet. It lies 515 feet (157 m) below sea level. The only way to reach this area is by use of a four-wheel drive vehicle.

Section Review 4

Define or identify: droughts, Somali

Working with Sketch Maps On the map you created in Section 3, label Ethiopia, Eritrea, Somalia, Djibouti, and Bab al-Mandab. What physical features help the economies of the region?

Reading for the Main Idea

1. (*Places and Regions*) What physical features have helped protect Ethiopia from foreign invasion?
2. (*Places and Regions*) What country was part of Ethiopia until it broke away in 1993?

Homework Practice Online
Keyword: SK5 HP11

Critical Thinking

3. **Drawing Inferences and Conclusions** Why do you think France remains interested in Djibouti?
4. **Finding the Main Idea** Why have foreign aid agencies been involved in East Africa?

Organizing What You Know

5. **Analyzing Information** Copy the following graphic organizer. Use it to show the major religions of these countries. Add boxes as needed.

Country	Religion

East Africa • 251

Answers to Section 4 Review

Define or identify For definitions and identifications, see the glossary and index.

Working with Sketch Maps Maps will vary, but listed places should be labeled in their approximate locations. The rich volcanic soil of Ethiopia and the proximity of the Indian Ocean help some of the economies.

Reading for the Main Idea
1. mountains
   (NGS 4)
2. Eritrea **(NGS 4)**

Critical Thinking
3. Djibouti's location on the Bab al-Mandab strait makes it important.
4. Massive droughts and civil wars have prompted foreign aid.

Organizing What You Know
5. Ethiopia—Christianity and Islam; Eritrea—Christianity and Islam; Somalia—Islam; Djibouti—Islam

---

CLOSE

Lead a discussion about the roles the United States has played or could play in this region.

REVIEW, ASSESS, RETEACH

Have students complete the Section Review. Organize the class into small groups. Have each group create a 10-term crossword puzzle about the Horn of Africa. Photocopy the puzzles and have groups exchange and complete them. Then have students complete Daily Quiz 11.4.
COOPERATIVE LEARNING

EXTEND

Have interested students examine the roles that strategic waterways, such as the Bab al-Mandab, have had on the history and economic development of countries where they are located. Tell them to compare the Bab al-Mandab, the Strait of Hormuz, and the Strait of Gibraltar and present their findings in chart form. **BLOCK SCHEDULING**

Define and Identify
For definitions, see the glossary and index.

Review the Main Ideas
7. fertile land, coal, copper, diamonds, and iron ore (NGS 4)

8. movement of two tectonic plates away from each other (NGS 7)

9. Ethiopia's mountains provided natural protection, and its peoples and emperors resisted colonization.

10. tourism

11. center for the international slave trade

12. poor soil in some areas and limited technology

13. They all controlled Kenya at one time or another, affecting Kenya's history, language, development, and culture.

14. The British saw land as a sign of wealth, power and property. The Kikuyu saw land as a source of food.

15. Hutu and Tutsi

16. Droughts caused millions to starve, but foreign countries sent aid. (NGS 15)

17. the Bab al-Mandab, which lies along a major shipping route that connects the Red Sea and the Indian Ocean

Think Critically
18. provided trade routes and the location of ancient civilizations

19. Unstable governments and constant fighting have kept many foreign investors away. (NGS 18)

20. Students should note the limiting factors of the region's physical features and the distribution of water and other natural resources.

Review and Practice

Define and Identify
Identify each of the following:
1. rifts
2. Swahili
3. Kikuyu
4. gorge
5. droughts
6. Somali

Review the Main Ideas
7. What are East Africa's main natural resources?
8. What caused the formation of the Great Rift Valley of East Africa?
9. Why didn't Europeans ever colonize Ethiopia?
10. What is a major source of income for Kenya?
11. What was the island of Zanzibar known for in the late 1700s?
12. What factors have slowed Tanzania's economic growth?
13. How have Arabs, Portuguese, the British, and the Kikuyu affected Kenya?
14. How did the British and Kikuyu view land differently?
15. What two ethnic groups live mostly in Rwanda and Burundi?

16. How have droughts in the Horn of Africa affected its people and their relationship with the rest of the world?
17. What landform in Djibouti has helped the country's economy?

Think Critically
18. **Finding the Main Idea** What is the significance of the Nile River in this region's human history?
19. **Analyzing Information** Why are foreign investors hesitant to invest in many countries of this region?
20. **Summarizing** Why do most East Africans make their living by farming and herding?
21. **Making Generalizations and Predictions** What problems have resulted in part from the boundary lines drawn by European powers, and how might the countries of East Africa overcome these problems?
22. **Analyzing Information** How has Ethiopia avoided falling under foreign rule for most of its history?

Map Activity
23. On a separate sheet of paper, match the letters on the map with their correct labels.

Great Rift Valley	White Nile
Mount Kilimanjaro	Blue Nile
Lake Victoria	Bab al-Mandab

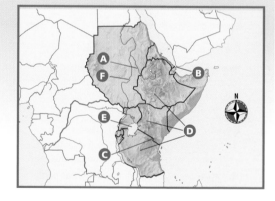

21. ethnic conflict; students might mention either allowing ethnic groups to relocate to be united or changing political boundaries to unite ethnic groups.

22. The mountains protected the interior from invasion.

Map Activity
23. **A.** Blue Nile
B. Bab al-Mandab
C. Mount Kilimanjaro
D. Great Rift Valley
E. Lake Victoria
F. White Nile

Writing Activity

Imagine that you have been awarded an all-expenses-paid vacation to East Africa. Write a letter to your travel agent explaining what you want to do on your trip. List and describe physical features you want to see and African wildlife and historical sites you would like to explore. Be sure to use standard grammar, spelling, sentence structure, and punctuation.

internet connect

Internet Activity: go.hrw.com
KEYWORD: SK5 GT11

Choose a topic to explore about East Africa:
- Hike Mount Kilimanjaro.
- Learn about cultural groups in East Africa.
- Travel back to ancient Nubian kingdoms.

Social Studies Skills Practice

Interpreting Charts

You have read about the role of religion in the history and culture of East Africa. Study the following chart and answer the questions below.

Religion in East Africa

Country	Christian	Muslim	Indigenous
Burundi	67%	10%	23%
Kenya	78%	10%	10%
Rwanda	94%	5%	0.1%
Sudan	5%	70%	25%
Tanzania (mainland)	30%	35%	35%
Uganda	66%	16%	18%

Source: Central Intelligence Agency, *The World Factbook 2003*

1. Where is Christianity most heavily practiced?
2. Where is Islam most heavily practiced?
3. Indigenous religions are practiced the least in which country?
4. Which two countries have the most similar patterns of religious diversity?

Analyzing Primary Sources

In "The Snows of Kilimanjaro," a short story written by Ernest Hemingway in 1938, a couple travels on safari to East Africa. Read the following passage that describes their view of the region's landscape from a small airplane. Then answer the questions.

"Then they were over the first hills and the wildebeeste were trailing up them, and then they were over the mountains with sudden depths of green-rising forest and the solid bamboo slopes, and then the heavy forest again, sculptured into peaks and hollows until they crossed, and hills sloped down and then another plain, hot now, and purple brown, bumpy with heat . . ."

1. How does an aerial view give you a sense of the region's physical geography?
2. What types of landforms, vegetation, and wildlife are described?
3. From this passage, what can you tell about the climate of the region?
4. How does the landscape described in this passage differ from other areas of East Africa?

East Africa • 253

CHAPTER 11 REVIEW

Writing Activity

Answers will vary, but the information included should be consistent with text material. Students' itineraries should include physical features found in the region, historical sites, and African wildlife. Use Rubric 42, Writing to Inform, to evaluate student work.

Interpreting Charts

1. Rwanda
2. Sudan
3. Rwanda
4. Burundi and Uganda

Analyzing Primary Sources

1. shows the landscape's diversity, which would not be so easily apparent from a slow journey on land
2. hills, mountains, plains; forest, bamboo, dry vegetation; wildebeeste
3. diverse, from humid forests to dry plains
4. Some other large areas of Africa, such as much of the Sahara, include only one type of landscape.

CHAPTER 11 REVIEW AND ASSESSMENT RESOURCES

Reproducible
- Readings in World Geography, History, and Culture 58, 59, and 60
- Critical Thinking Activity 11
- Vocabulary Activity 11

Technology
- Chapter 11 Test Generator (on the One-Stop Planner)
- HRW Go site
- Audio CD Program, Chapter 11

Reinforcement, Review, and Assessment
- Chapter 11 Review and Practice
- Chapter Summaries and Review
- Chapter 11 Test
- Chapter 11 Test for English Language Learners and Special-Needs Students

internet connect

GO TO: go.hrw.com
KEYWORD: SK5 Teacher
FOR: a guide to using the Internet in your classroom

Central Africa
Chapter Resource Manager

Objectives	Pacing Guide	Reproducible Resources
SECTION 1 **Physical Geography** (pp. 255–57) 1. Identify the major physical features of central Africa. 2. Identify the climates, plants, and animals found in the region. 3. Identify the major natural resources of central Africa.	**Regular** .5 day Lecture Notes, Section 1 **Block Scheduling** .5 day *Block Scheduling Handbook, Chapter 12*	**RS** Know It Notes S1 **SM** Map Activity 12 **ELL** Main Idea Activity S1
SECTION 2 **History and Culture** (pp. 258–61) 1. Describe the history of central Africa and the challenges people there face today. 2. Describe the people and cultures of central Africa.	**Regular** 1 day Lecture Notes, Section 2 **Block Scheduling** .5 day *Block Scheduling Handbook, Chapter 12*	**RS** Know It Notes S2 **RS** Graphic Organizer 12 **E** Cultures of the World Activity 6 **E** Creative Strategies for Teaching World Geography, Lesson 16 **IC** Interdisciplinary Activities for the Middle Grades 26, 27, 28 **E** Biography Activity: Patrice Lumumba **ELL** Main Idea Activity S2
SECTION 3 **The Democratic Republic of the Congo** (pp. 262–64) 1. Describe the history of the Democratic Republic of the Congo. 2. Describe the people and culture of the country. 3. Describe the economy of the country.	**Regular** 1 day Lecture Notes, Section 3 **Block Scheduling** .5 day *Block Scheduling Handbook, Chapter 12*	**RS** Know It Notes S3 **SM** Geography for Life Activity 25 **E** Biography Activity: Patrice Lumumba **ELL** Main Idea Activity S3
SECTION 4 **The Other Central African Countries** (pp. 265–67) 1. Describe the people and economies of the northern central African countries. 2. Describe the people and economies of the southern central African countries.	**Regular** .5 day Lecture Notes, Section 4 **Block Scheduling** .5 day *Block Scheduling Handbook, Chapter 12*	**RS** Know It Notes S4 **ELL** Main Idea Activity S2

Chapter Resource Key

RS   Reading Support

IC   Interdisciplinary Connections

E   Enrichment

SM   Skills Mastery

A   Assessment

REV   Review

ELL   Reinforcement and English Language Learners and English for Speakers of Other Languages (ESOL)

 Transparencies

 CD–ROM

 Music

 Video

 Internet

 Holt Presentation Maker Using Microsoft® PowerPoint®

 One-Stop Planner CD–ROM

See the *One-Stop Planner* for a complete list of additional resources for students and teachers.

One-Stop Planner CD–ROM

It's easy to plan lessons, select resources, and print out materials for your students when you use the *One-Stop Planner CD–ROM with Test Generator.*

Technology Resources	Review, Reinforcement, and Assessment Resources	
One-Stop Planner CD–ROM, Lesson 12.1	ELL	Main Idea Activity S1
Geography and Cultures Visual Resources with Teaching Activities 43–47	REV	Section 1 Review
	A	Daily Quiz 12.1
ARGWorld CD–ROM	REV	Chapter Summaries and Review
Homework Practice Online	ELL	English Audio Summary 12.1
HRW Go site	ELL	Spanish Audio Summary 12.1
One-Stop Planner CD–ROM, Lesson 12.2	ELL	Main Idea Activity S2
ARGWorld CD–ROM	REV	Section 2 Review
Homework Practice Online	A	Daily Quiz 12.2
	REV	Chapter Summaries and Review
HRW Go site	ELL	English Audio Summary 12.2
	ELL	Spanish Audio Summary 12.2
One-Stop Planner CD–ROM, Lesson 12.3	ELL	Main Idea Activity S3
ARGWorld CD–ROM	REV	Section 3 Review
Homework Practice Online	A	Daily Quiz 12.3
	REV	Chapter Summaries and Review
HRW Go site	ELL	English Audio Summary 12.3
	ELL	Spanish Audio Summary 12.3
One-Stop Planner CD–ROM, Lesson 12.4	ELL	Main Idea Activity S4
ARGWorld CD–ROM	REV	Section 4 Review
Homework Practice Online	A	Daily Quiz 12.4
	REV	Chapter Summaries and Review
HRW Go site	ELL	English Audio Summary 12.4
	ELL	Spanish Audio Summary 12.4

✓ internet connect

HRW ONLINE RESOURCES

GO TO: go.hrw.com
Then type in a keyword.

TEACHER HOME PAGE
KEYWORD: SK5 TEACHER

CHAPTER INTERNET ACTIVITIES
KEYWORD: SK5 GT12

Choose an activity to:
• identify threats to the Congo Basin.
• visit the people of central Africa.
• learn the importance of African cloth.

CHAPTER ENRICHMENT LINKS
KEYWORD: SK5 CH12

CHAPTER MAPS
KEYWORD: SK5 MAPS12

ONLINE ASSESSMENT
Homework Practice
KEYWORD: SK5 HP12
Standardized Test Prep Online
KEYWORD: SK5 STP12
Rubrics
KEYWORD: SS Rubrics

COUNTRY INFORMATION
KEYWORD: SK5 Almanac

CONTENT UPDATES
KEYWORD: SS Content Updates

HOLT PRESENTATION MAKER
KEYWORD: SK5 PPT12

ONLINE READING SUPPORT
KEYWORD: SS Strategies

CURRENT EVENTS
KEYWORD: S5 Current Events

Meeting Individual Needs

Ability Levels

Level 1 Basic-level activities designed for all students encountering new material

Level 2 Intermediate-level activities designed for average students

Level 3 Challenging activities designed for honors and gifted-and-talented students

ESOL Activities that address the needs of students with Limited English Proficiency

Chapter Review and Assessment

E	Readings in World Geography, History, and Culture 61, 62, and 63
SM	Critical Thinking Activity 12
REV	Chapter 12 Review and Practice
REV	Chapter Summaries and Review
ELL	Vocabulary Activity 12
A	Chapter 12 Test
	Chapter 12 Test Generator (on the One-Stop Planner)
	Audio CD Program, Chapter 12
A	Chapter 12 Test for English Language Learners and Special-Needs Students
	HRW Go Site

Central Africa
Previewing Chapter Resources
Holt Online Learning

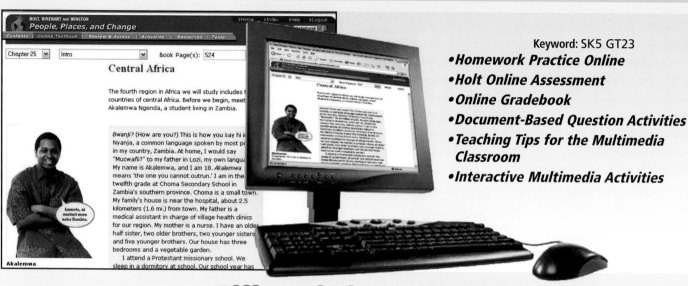

HOLT, RINEHART AND WINSTON
People, Places, and Change

Contents | Online Textbook | Review & Assess | Activities | Resources | Tools

Chapter 25 ▼ | Intro ▼ | Book Page(s): 524

Central Africa

The fourth region in Africa we will study includes the countries of central Africa. Before we begin, meet Akalemwa Ngenda, a student living in Zambia.

Bwanji? (How are you?) This is how you say hi in Nyanja, a common language spoken by most people in my country, Zambia. At home, I would say "Mucwañi?" to my father in Lozi, my own language. My name is Akalemwa, and I am 18. *Akalemwa* means 'the one you cannot outrun.' I am in the twelfth grade at Choma Secondary School in Zambia's southern province. Choma is a small town. My family's house is near the hospital, about 2.5 kilometers (1.6 mi.) from town. My father is a medical assistant in charge of village health clinics for our region. My mother is a nurse. I have an older half sister, two older brothers, two younger sisters, and five younger brothers. Our house has three bedrooms and a vegetable garden.

I attend a Protestant missionary school. We sleep in a dormitory at school. Our school year has

Akalemwa

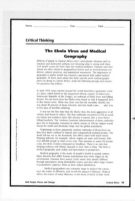

Keyword: SK5 GT23

- *Homework Practice Online*
- *Holt Online Assessment*
- *Online Gradebook*
- *Document-Based Question Activities*
- *Teaching Tips for the Multimedia Classroom*
- *Interactive Multimedia Activities*

Differentiating Instruction

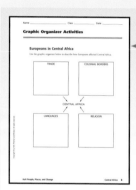

Reading and Writing Support

◀ Graphic Organizer Activity
- *Vocabulary Activity*
- *Chapter Summary and Review*
- *Know It Notes*
- *Audio CD*

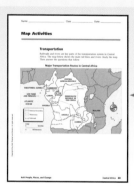

Primary Sources and Advanced Learners

- *Geography for Life Activity: Conservation of Forest Resources*
◀ Map Activity: Transportation
- *Readings in World Geography, History and Culture:*
  - *61 Shopping from Salaula*
  - *62 Lifeline of a Nation*
  - *63 Encounters with Pygmies*

Spanish and ESOL

- *Vocabulary Activity*
◀ Main Idea Activities for English Language Learners and Special-Needs Students
- *Chapter Summary and Review*
- *Spanish Audio Summary*
- *Know It Notes S1–4*
- *Chapter Test for English Language Learners and Special-Needs Students*

Active Learning

- *Block Scheduling Handbook*
- *Cultures of the World Activity*
- *Interdisciplinary Activity*
- *Map Activity*
◀ Critical Thinking Activity 25

Assessment Program

◀ Daily Quizzes S1–4
- *Chapter Test*
- *Chapter Test for English Language Learners and Special-Needs Students*

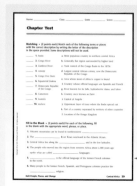

Special Education Modifications

Your **I.D.E.A. Works! CD-ROM** will provide modified versions of the following teaching materials:
- *Guided Reading Strategies S1–4*
- *Vocabulary Activity*
- *Main Idea Activities S1–4*
- *Daily Quizzes S1–4*
◀ Chapter 12 Test
- *Flash cards of chapter vocabulary terms*

Teacher Resources

Books for Teachers

Hochschild, Adam. *King Leopold's Ghost.* Houghton Mifflin Company, 1998.

Matthiessen, Peter. *African Silences.* Vintage Books, 1992.

Winslow, Philip C. *Sowing the Dragon's Teeth: Land Mines and the Global Legacy of War.* Beacon Press, 1998.

Books for Students

Laure, Jason. *Zambia.* Enchantment of the World. Children's Press, 1989. Geography, climate, history, people, industry, and culture.

Mutwa, Credo Vusa'Mazulu. *Indaba, My Children.* Grove Press, 1999. Collection of African myths and folktales.

Siy, Alexandra. *The Efe: People of the Ituri Rain Forest.* Global Villages. Dillon Press, 1993. Culture and history of a people threatened by the industrial world.

Stanley, Sanna. *Monkey Sunday: A Story from a Congolese Village.* Farrar, Strauss & Giroux, 1998. Thanksgiving celebration interrupted by local animals.
SHELTERED ENGLISH

Multimedia Materials

Africa Trail. CD–ROM. Queue, Inc.

Destination Cameroon. Video, 20 min. Educational Video Network.

Zambia: A Copper Miner's Family. Video, 20 min. Films for the Humanities and Sciences

---

Videos and CDs

Videos

- *CNN Presents Geography: Yesterday and Today, Segment 26 The Medicine Tree*
- *ARG World*

Holt Researcher

http://researcher.hrw.com

- *Organization of African Unity (OAU)*
- *Africa*
- *Colonialism in Africa*
- *New Imperialism*
- *Democratic Republic of the Congo*
- *Republic of the Congo*
- *Cameroon*
- *Angola*

Transparency Packages

Graphic Organizer Transparencies 12.1–4

Geography and Cultures Visual Resources Transparencies 76–80
87 Central Africa: Physical-Political

Map Activities Transparency 12 Transportation

There are many reasons why students in the United States should know about the geography of central Africa:

▶ Events in the region have affected U.S. foreign policy in recent decades.

▶ The region contains rich deposits of minerals that are useful to people around the world.

▶ Central Africa is home to many plant and animal species found nowhere else.

▶ The tropical rain forest of central Africa plays a significant role in influencing the world's climate.

CHAPTER 12

Central Africa

The fourth region in Africa we will study includes the 10 countries of central Africa. Before we begin, meet Akalemwa Ngenda, a student living in Zambia.

Lumela, ni muituti mwa naha Zambia.

Translation: Hi, I am a student in Zambia.

Bwanji? (How are you?) This is how you say hi in Nyanja, a common language spoken by most people in my country, Zambia. At home, I would say "Mucwañi?" to my father in Lozi, my own language. My name is Akalemwa, and I am 18. *Akalemwa* means "the one you cannot outrun." I am in the twelfth grade at Choma Secondary School in Zambia's southern province. Choma is a small town. My family's house is near the hospital, about 2.5 kilometers (1.6 mi.) from town. My father is a medical assistant in charge of village health clinics for our region. My mother is a nurse. I have an older half sister, two older brothers, two younger sisters, and five younger brothers. Our house has three bedrooms and a vegetable garden. I attend a Protestant missionary school. We sleep in a dormitory at school. Our school year has three three-month terms, starting in January. We have a month vacation after each one. I want to be a doctor, so I am studying math, physics, chemistry, biology, English, and geography.

CHAPTER PROJECT

Have students plan a festival to highlight and celebrate the musical styles of central Africa, including makossa and soukous. Ask them to obtain recordings of the music and explain the music's importance in the region. Place programs, photographs, or recordings in portfolios.

STARTING THE CHAPTER

Distribute green paper to students. Have them cut a heart shape out of the paper. Explain that they are going to study the heart of Africa. Ask students to speculate about why green was the color chosen. (The region contains dense rain forests and jungles.) Tell them that the region has other climate and vegetation types as well as tropical rain forests. Ask what colors they might choose for a tropical savanna climate and forested highlands. Instruct students to keep their green hearts for a later activity. Tell students they will learn more about central Africa in this chapter.

Section 1 Physical Geography

Read to Discover

1. What are the major physical features of central Africa?
2. What climates, plants, and animals are found in the region?
3. What major natural resources does central Africa have?

Vocabulary

basin
canopy
copper belt
periodic markets

Places

Congo Basin
Western Rift Valley
Lake Tanganyika
Lake Malawi
Congo River
Zambezi River

Reading Strategy

VISUALIZING INFORMATION Look at the pictures in this section. What do they show you about Central Africa? Write your answers on a sheet of paper. As you read this section, write down the new information you learn.

SECTION 1 RESOURCES

Reproducible
- Lecture Notes, Section 1
- Block Scheduling Handbook, Chapter 12
- Know It Notes S1
- Map Activity 12

Technology
- One-Stop Planner CD–ROM, Lesson 12.1
- Homework Practice Online
- Geography and Cultures Visual Resources with Teaching Activities 43–47
- HRW Go site

Reinforcement, Review, and Assessment
- Section 1 Review
- Daily Quiz 12.1
- Main Idea Activity S1
- Chapter Summaries and Review
- English Audio Summary 12.1
- Spanish Audio Summary 12.1

Central Africa: Physical-Political

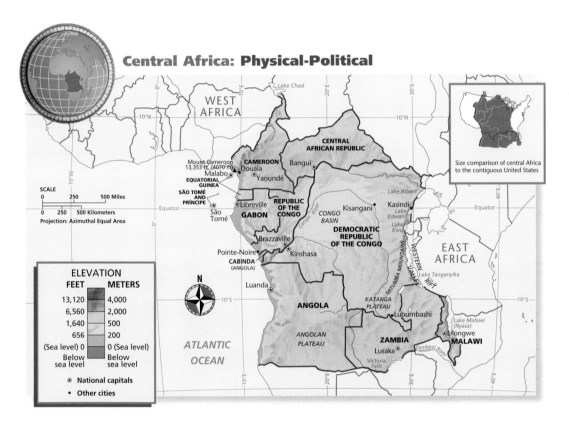

Size comparison of central Africa to the contiguous United States

SCALE
0   250   500 Miles
0   250   500 Kilometers
Projection: Azimuthal Equal Area

ELEVATION
FEET	METERS
13,120	4,000
6,560	2,000
1,640	500
656	200
(Sea level) 0	0 (Sea level)
Below sea level	Below sea level

⊛ National capitals
• Other cities

Central Africa • 255

Section 1

Objectives

1. Identify the major physical features of central Africa.
2. Describe the climates, plants, and animals found in the region.
3. Identify the major natural resources of central Africa.

FOCUS

Bellringer

Copy the following instructions onto the chalkboard: *Look at the physical-political map of central Africa. Work with a partner to select a country, a landform, and a river on the map. Then describe the relative locations of the items you and your partner selected.* Allow students time to write their responses. Discuss the relative locations students provide. Then tell students that in Section 1 they will learn more about the importance of the features they described.

Using the Physical-Political Map

Have students examine the map on this page. Ask them to describe the main physical features of the region. Their descriptions should include rivers, plains, and mountains. Draw students' attention to the Congo River, which is a vital transportation route of central Africa.

EYE ON EARTH

The ITC The climate of central Africa is affected by a belt of converging trade winds that encircle Earth near the equator. Known as the Intertropical Convergence Zone, this belt shifts north and south seasonally as our planet's position relative to the Sun changes during Earth's annual revolution.

Unstable moist tropical air is forced upward where it is cooled and condensed to produce heavy rainfall. In July and August this rainfall occurs mainly in the northern part of central Africa. Then the zone shifts southward, and as a result the southern regions receive the most rain in January and February. In March, it shifts northward again. Altitude, ocean currents, and proximity to the sea also influence the amount of rainfall specific regions receive.

Critical Thinking: Have students look at this chapter's physical-political map. Ask students where in Angola the Intertropical Convergence Zone would bring the least rain.

Answer: southwestern Angola

Our Amazing Planet

One of the Congo River's most common animals is the crocodile. This sharp-toothed reptile can grow to about 20 feet (6 m) in length. It swims by sweeping its long tail from side to side.

Location Local people call Victoria Falls *Mosi-oa-Tunya,* which means "the smoke that thunders." The Zambezi River plunges 355 feet (108 m) over a cliff between Zambia and Zimbabwe.

Physical Features

Central Africa stretches southward from Cameroon and the Central African Republic to Angola and Zambia. The Atlantic Ocean lies off the western coast.

Think of the region as a big soup bowl with a wide rim. Near the middle of the bowl is the Congo Basin. A **basin** is a generally flat region surrounded by higher land such as mountains and plateaus.

In northwestern Cameroon are volcanic mountains. The highest is 13,353 feet (4,070 m). Central Africa's highest mountains lie along the Western Rift Valley. Some of these snow-capped mountains rise to more than 16,700 feet (5,090 m). The Western Rift Valley stretches southeastward from the Democratic Republic of the Congo. Lake Tanganyika (tan-guhn-KEE-kuh) and Lake Malawi are found there.

Two major river systems drain the region. In the north the Congo River flows westward to the Atlantic Ocean. Hundreds of smaller rivers flow into the Congo. In the south the Zambezi (zam-BEE-zee) River flows eastward to the Indian Ocean. The Zambezi is famous for its great falls, hydroelectric dams, and lakes.

✓ **READING CHECK:** Places and Regions What are the major physical features of central Africa? Congo Basin, volcanic mountains, Western Rift Valley, Lake Tanganyika, Lake Malawi, Congo River, Zambezi River

Climates, Plants, and Animals

Central Africa lies along the equator and in the low latitudes. The Congo Basin and much of the Atlantic coast have a humid tropical climate. It is wet and warm all year. This climate supports a large, dense tropical rain forest.

The many different kinds of trees in the tropical rain forest form a complete **canopy**. This is the uppermost layer of the trees where the limbs spread out. Leaves block sunlight to the ground below.

Small antelopes, hyenas, elephants, and okapis live in the rain forest region. The okapi is a short-legged relative of the giraffe. Many insects also live in the forest. However, few other plants or creatures

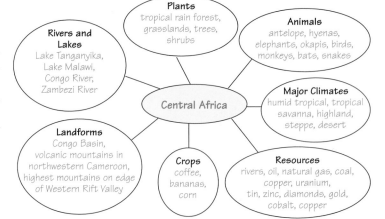

TEACH

Teaching Objectives 1–3

ALL LEVELS: (Suggested time: 20 min.) Copy the following graphic organizer onto the chalkboard, omitting the blue answers. Use it to help students describe central Africa's physical geography. Call on volunteers to fill in the ovals with appropriate words and phrases for each category. Have students use this unit's atlas also. **ESOL,** **LS** **VISUAL-SPATIAL**

Central Africa

Plants: tropical rain forest, grasslands, trees, shrubs

Animals: antelope, hyenas, elephants, okapis, birds, monkeys, bats, snakes

Rivers and Lakes: Lake Tanganyika, Lake Malawi, Congo River, Zambezi River

Major Climates: humid tropical, tropical savanna, highland, steppe, desert

Landforms: Congo Basin, volcanic mountains in northwestern Cameroon, highest mountains on edge of Western Rift Valley

Crops: coffee, bananas, corn

Resources: rivers, oil, natural gas, coal, copper, uranium, tin, zinc, diamonds, gold, cobalt, copper live on the forest floor. This is because little sunlight shines through the canopy. Many animals live in the trees. They include birds, monkeys, bats, and snakes. Large areas of the tropical rain forest are being cleared rapidly for farming and timber. This threatens the plants, animals, and people who live there.

North and south of the Congo Basin are large areas with a tropical savanna climate. Those areas are warm all year, but they have distinct dry and wet seasons. There are grasslands, scattered trees, and shrubs. Only in the high eastern mountains is there a highland climate. Dry steppe and even desert climates are found in the far south.

✓ **READING CHECK:** (Places and Regions) What are the region's climates, plants, and animals? humid tropical, tropical savanna, highland, steppe, desert; tropical rain forest, grasslands, trees, shrubs; antelopes, hyenas, elephants, okapis, birds, monkeys, insects, bats, snakes

Resources

Central Africa's rivers are among the region's most important natural resources. They are used for travel, trade, and producing hydroelectricity. Other energy resources are oil, natural gas, and coal.

Central Africa has many minerals, including copper, uranium, tin, zinc, diamonds, gold, and cobalt. Most of Africa's copper is found in an area called the **copper belt**, which includes northern Zambia and the southern Democratic Republic of the Congo.

Central African countries have mostly traditional economies. Most people in central Africa are subsistence farmers. However, an increasing number of farmers are growing crops for sale. Common crops include coffee, bananas, and corn. In rural areas, people trade their products in **periodic markets**. A periodic market is an open-air trading market. It is set up regularly at a crossroads or in a town.

✓ **READING CHECK:** (Places and Regions) What is central Africa's most important natural resource, and why? rivers; support travel, trade, and produce hydroelectricity

▲
Elephants have created a network of trails and clearings throughout the tropical rain forest. Many animals will gather at forest clearings.

Homework Practice Online
Keyword: SK5 HP12

Section Review 1

Define and explain: basin, canopy, copper belt, periodic markets

Working with Sketch Maps On a map of central Africa that you draw or that your teacher provides, label the following: Congo Basin, Western Rift Valley, Lake Tanganyika, Lake Malawi, Congo River, and Zambezi River. In a box in the margin, describe the location of the highest mountains.

Reading for the Main Idea

1. (Places and Regions) What major landforms and rivers are found in the region?

2. (Physical Systems) Why do few plants and animals live on the floor of the tropical rain forest?

3. (Places and Regions) For the most part, what type of economy do central African countries have?

Critical Thinking

4. Making Generalizations and Predictions How might central Africa become a rich region?

Organizing What You Know

5. Summarizing Copy the following graphic organizer. Use it to describe the region's climates, plants and animals, and major resources.

Climates	Plants and Animals	Resources

Central Africa • 257

Answers to Section 1 Review

Define For definitions, see the glossary.

Working with Sketch Maps Maps will vary, but listed places should be labeled in their approximate locations. The highest mountains lie along the edge of the Western Rift Valley.

Reading for the Main Idea

1. Congo Basin, volcanic mountains, edge of Western Rift Valley, Congo and Zambezi Rivers **(NGS 4)**

2. Sunlight does not get through the canopy. **(NGS 8)**

3. traditional **(NGS 4)**

Critical Thinking

4. It has rich resources, particularly metals, minerals, and oil. **(NGS 18)**

Organizing What You Know

5. Climates—humid tropical, tropical savanna, highland, steppe, desert; Plants and Animals—antelope, hyenas, elephants, okapis, birds, monkeys, bats, snakes, insects; Resources—rivers, oil, natural gas, coal, copper, uranium, tin, zinc, diamonds, gold, cobalt **(NGS 4)**

CLOSE

Refer to the photo of Victoria Falls on the previous page. Ask students what a local person might tell them about the falls. (Possible answers: how far away the sound can be heard, stories about people who have fallen over the falls)

REVIEW, ASSESS, RETEACH

Have students complete the Section Review. Then pair students and have pairs draw symbols on their green hearts to represent vegetation types, landforms, climates, animals, and resources of central Africa. Have students create a key for their hearts. Then have students complete Daily Quiz 12.1. **COOPERATIVE LEARNING**

Have students complete Main Idea Activity S1. Then organize students into three groups. Have each group outline information on physical features; climates, plants, and animals; or resources. **ESOL**

EXTEND

Have interested students conduct research on the Congo Basin and design covers for a book about the area. **BLOCK SCHEDULING**

Section 2 History and Culture

Read to Discover
1. What is the history of central Africa, and what challenges do the people there face today?
2. What are the people and cultures of central Africa like?

Vocabulary
ivory
dialects

Places
Brazzaville
Kinshasa

Reading Strategy

READING ORGANIZER Before you read, create a spider map. Draw a circle. Label the circle History and Culture. Draw seven legs and label them Early History, Modern Central Africa, Challenges, Peoples and Languages, Religion, Food, and The Arts. As you read the section, write what you learn about these topics next to each leg.

History

This carved mask was created by a Bantu-speaking people called the Fang. Most live in Cameroon, Equatorial Guinea, and Gabon. Their ancestors moved there in the 1800s.

Early humans lived in central Africa many thousands of years ago. They had different languages and cultures. About 2,000 years ago new peoples began to move into the region from western Africa. Those new peoples spoke what are called Bantu languages. Today, Bantu languages are common in most of the region.

Early History Several early Bantu-speaking kingdoms formed in central Africa. Among the most important was the Kongo Kingdom. It was located around the mouth of the Congo River. The Kongo and other central Africans traded with peoples in western and eastern Africa.

Some of the early kingdoms used slaves. In the late 1400s, Europeans came to the region. They began to trade with some African kingdoms for slaves. The Europeans took many enslaved Africans to the Americas. Europeans also wanted the region's forest products and other resources, such as **ivory**. Ivory is a cream-colored material that comes from elephant tusks. It is used in making fine furniture, jewelry, and crafts.

Some African kingdoms became richer by trading with Europeans. However, all were gradually weakened or destroyed by the Europeans. European countries divided all of central Africa into colonies in the late 1800s. The colonial powers were France, the United Kingdom, Belgium, Germany, Spain, and Portugal.

The Europeans drew colonial borders that ignored the homelands of central Africa's ethnic groups. Many groups were lumped together in colonies. These groups spoke different languages and had different

258 • **Chapter 12**

Section 2

Objectives
1. Analyze the history of central Africa, and discuss the challenges the people there face today.
2. Describe the people and cultures of central Africa.

FOCUS

Bellringer

Copy this question onto the chalkboard: *What type of economy might you expect to find in a region with fertile farmland, rich mineral deposits, and a mighty river system?* Discuss responses. (Possible answer: a prosperous region) Tell students that although central Africa has many natural resources, most of its people are poor. Point out that the region's history may provide some clues to why the region is not wealthy today. Explain to students that in Section 2 they will learn more about central Africa's history and culture.

Building Vocabulary

Write the vocabulary terms on the chalkboard. Call on volunteers to find the definitions in a dictionary and read them aloud. Explain that elephant tusks are made of **ivory**. Because elephants are killed for their tusks, it is now illegal to import ivory into the United States. Point out that a **dialect** is usually associated with a certain geographic region. You may want to lead a discussion about how some people in different parts of the United States speak different dialects of English. However, simply using one or two words differently does not create a different dialect.

ways of life. These differences resulted in conflicts, particularly after the colonies won independence.

Modern Central Africa African colonies did not gain independence until after World War II. The largest central African colony was the Belgian Congo. It is now the Democratic Republic of the Congo. That country won independence in 1960. Angola won independence from Portugal in 1975. It was the last European colony in central Africa.

Independence for some African countries came after bloody wars. After independence, fighting between some ethnic groups continued within the new countries. The region also became a battleground in the Cold War. The United States and the Soviet Union supported their allies in small wars throughout Africa. The region's wars killed many people and caused great damage. Some fighting continues off and on in the region.

Challenges Today Ending these wars is one of central Africa's many challenges today. The region's countries must also develop their natural resources more effectively. This would help the many poor people who live there. Another great challenge is stopping the spread of diseases such as malaria and AIDS. These diseases are killing millions of people and leaving many orphans.

✓ **READING CHECK:** (*Human Systems*) What role did Europeans play in central Africa's history? initially traded with kingdoms, then colonized central Africa, dividing it up without regard to ethnic boundaries

Culture

Today, about 100 million people live in central Africa. They belong to many different ethnic groups with varying customs.

In 1986 a cloud of carbon dioxide killed many people and animals near Cameroon's Lake Nyos. The lake is located in the center of a volcanic mountain. An earthquake may have allowed the gas to escape from deep in the lake.

Zambian women are grinding wheat to prepare it for cooking. They are using rods called pestles. The container is called a mortar. This technique is used for grinding many ingredients.

Central Africa 259

TEACH

Teaching Objective 1

LEVEL 1: (Suggested time: 20 min.) Copy the following graphic organizer onto the chalkboard, omitting the blue answers. Use it to help students understand central Africa's history and the challenges that exist there today. Have students copy the organizer into their notebooks and break down the history of central Africa into nine steps. Ask them to concentrate on how past events have played a part in creating the challenges the region faces today. Then complete the organizer as a class. **ESOL**

Major Steps in Central Africa's History

Step 1: West Africans moved into central Africa 2,000 years ago.

Step 2: Bantu-speaking kingdoms were set up and began trading with western and eastern Africa.

Step 3: Early African kingdoms used slaves.

Step 4: Europeans arrived and traded for slaves.

Step 5: European countries ignored ethnic groups when dividing Africa into colonies.

Step 6: African colonies gained independence.

Step 7: Ethnic differences caused problems.

Step 8: The United States and Soviet Union supported African allies in wars.

Step 9: Wars prevented development of natural resources and cooperation to prevent diseases.

GLOBAL PERSPECTIVES

The Island of Bioko

Although Spanish and French are now the official languages of Equatorial Guinea, Portugal was the first European country to control the area.

Equatorial Guinea lies chiefly on the African mainland and includes the island of Bioko, which was sighted by the Portuguese in about 1472. Portugal controlled the area until 1778, when it ceded the land to Spain. The Spanish withdrew after a yellow fever outbreak. The British, who outlawed the slave trade in 1807, took control. The Royal Navy used the island's strategic location in its efforts to stop slave traders.

Later, Spain regained control of Bioko. In 1959, Africans of Spanish Guinea gained the same rights as Spaniards. The country became independent in 1968.

Activity: Have students conduct research on the region's history and have them write ships' logs to describe the experiences of Portuguese, Spanish, and British sailors at Bioko.

Connecting to History
Answers

1. areas that are now part of Nigeria and Cameroon
2. brought new ways for growing food, used tools of iron, brought Bantu languages

CONNECTING TO History

A headrest from early Luanda, a Bantu kingdom

BANTU LANGUAGES

About 2,000 years ago, the movement of groups of people began to change Africa. Traders, farmers, and other people moved across the southern third of Africa. Experts believe these people came from areas that are now part of Nigeria and Cameroon. Their movement across Africa lasted many centuries. During this period new languages developed. We call them Bantu languages. The grammar and root sounds of the different Bantu languages remain similar.

Some Bantu speakers moved southward along the Atlantic coast. Others moved eastward to Kenya and then turned southward. Over time they reached the tip of southern Africa. The Bantu speakers mixed with peoples who already lived in these lands.

The migration of Bantu speakers had important effects on African life. They brought new ways for growing food. They used tools made of iron, which others also began to use. The Bantu-speakers of course brought their languages. Today, many Africans speak Swahili, Zulu, and other Bantu languages.

Understanding What You Read

1. (Movement) From where did the Bantu peoples come?
2. (Movement) How did their movement shape Africa?

Peoples and Languages As you have read, many central Africans speak Bantu languages. However, those languages can be very different from each other. In fact, hundreds of different languages and **dialects** are spoken in the region. A dialect is a variation of a language.

Many people in the region speak African languages in everyday life. However, the official languages of the central African countries are European. French is the official language of the former French colonies in the north. It is also the official language of the Democratic Republic of the Congo. English is the official language in Zambia and Malawi. Portuguese is spoken in Angola and the island country of São Tomé and Príncipe. Spanish and French are the official languages of tiny Equatorial Guinea.

Religion Many people in the former French, Spanish, and Portuguese colonies are Roman Catholic. Protestant Christianity is most common in former British colonies. Many people practice traditional African religions. In some cases Christian and African practices have been combined.

260 • Chapter 12

TEACHER TO TEACHER

Jean Eldredge of Altamonte Springs, Florida, suggests this activity. Have students label lines of latitude and longitude—from 40°N to 40°S and 20°W to about 55°E—on a blank sheet of paper. Then have students draw an outline of Africa onto their grid. Then instruct them to fill in borders and physical features of the central African countries.

Teaching Objective 2

ALL LEVELS: (Suggested time: 30 min.) Draw a large circle on a piece of white butcher paper. Cut the circle into quarters. Organize the class into four groups. Assign each group one of the following topics: languages, religion, food, or arts. Give each group a quarter of the paper circle and colored markers. Have students write or draw information about their topic on their paper. Instruct them to use different colors to show how culture traits spread, if known. For example, they might use brown for Muslim influences, blue for French, and so on. Tape completed quarters together to create a cultural kaleidoscope of central Africa. **ESOL, COOPERATIVE LEARNING,** LS **KINESTHETIC**

Human-Environment Interaction These Cameroon juju dancers are calling attention to the destruction of the tropical rain forest. Note the headpieces that represent some of the forest's animals.

Many Muslims live near the mostly Muslim countries of the Sahel in the north. Zambia also has many Muslims as well as Hindus. The Hindus are the descendants of immigrants from southern Asia.

Food In most central African countries, corn, rice, grains, and fish are common foods. In the tropical rain forest, plantains, cassava, and various roots are important foods. For example, in Cameroon you might eat a dish called *fufu. Fufu,* a thick, pasty ball of mashed cassava, yams, or plantains, is served with chicken, fish, or a beef gravy.

The Arts *Makossa* dance music from Cameroon has become popular throughout Africa. It can be played with various instruments, including guitars and electric keyboards. The cities of Brazzaville and Kinshasa on the Congo River are the home of *soukous* music.

The region is also famous for carved masks, sculpture, and beautiful cotton gowns. The gowns are dyed in bright colors. They often show pictures that represent things important to the wearer.

Region The *likembe*, or thumb piano, was invented in the lower Congo region. Today its music is heard in many African countries.

✓ **READING CHECK:** Human Systems What are some characteristics of the people and culture of central Africa? Bantu and European languages spoken; Christianity and traditional African religions practiced; traditional music, carved masks, sculpture, cotton gowns are important arts

Section Review 2

Define and explain: ivory, dialects

Working with Sketch Maps On the map you created in Section 1, label Brazzaville and Kinshasa.

Reading for the Main Idea

1. (Human Systems) Why are many languages that are spoken today in central Africa related?

2. (Human Systems) What have been some of the causes of wars in central Africa?

3. (Human Systems) What arts are popular in the region?

Critical Thinking

4. **Finding the Main Idea** How did Europeans influence the culture of the region?

Organizing What You Know

5. **Summarizing** Copy the following graphic organizer. Use it to identify central Africa's challenges.

go.hrw.com
Homework Practice Online
Keyword: SK5 HP12

Central Africa • 261

Section 2 Review

Answers to Section 2 Review

Define For definitions, see the glossary.

Working with Sketch Maps Brazzaville and Kinshasa should be located accurately.

Reading for the Main Idea

1. related to languages spread by Bantu speakers long ago **(NGS 9)**

2. fight for independence, ethnic troubles, Cold War rivalries **(NGS 13)**

3. *makossa* music, *soukous* music, carved masks, sculpture, cotton gowns **(NGS 10)**

Critical Thinking

4. brought European languages, religions; separated some ethnic groups, lumped others together into colonies

Organizing What You Know

5. ending wars, developing resources more efficiently, stopping spread of diseases such as malaria and AIDS

CLOSE

Have interested students use the steps from the Teaching Objective 1 activity to write song lyrics describing the region's history.

REVIEW, ASSESS, RETEACH

Have students complete the Section Review. Then pair students. Have each student use material in Section 2 to prepare a five-word crossword puzzle. Ask the pairs to exchange and solve each other's puzzles. Then have students complete Daily Quiz 12.2. **COOPERATIVE LEARNING**

Have students complete Main Idea Activity S2. Assign the following topics to groups: history, challenges, languages and religions, and food and the arts. Have each group draw information in appropriate places on an outline map of central Africa. Display and discuss the map. **ESOL, COOPERATIVE LEARNING**

EXTEND

Have students conduct research on Jinga Mbande, a woman who fought against the Portuguese colonialists in Angola in the 1600s. A good source is *The Warrior Queens*, by Antonia Frasier. You may want to have students report their findings in the form of a eulogy—a speech given upon a famous person's death. **BLOCK SCHEDULING**

Central Africa 261

Section 3 The Democratic Republic of the Congo

Read to Discover
1. What is the history of the Democratic Republic of the Congo?
2. What are the people and culture of the country like?
3. What is the economy of the country like?

Vocabulary
civil war

Places
Lubumbashi

People
Mobutu Sese Seko

Reading Strategy

READING ORGANIZER Before you read, draw a circle in the center of a sheet of paper. Label the circle Democratic Republic of the Congo. Draw three rays from the circle. Draw a circle at the end of each ray. Label the circles History, People, and Economy. As you read this section, write what you learn about these topics next to each circle.

A dancer performs in a coming-of-age ceremony for young people. Many such African traditions have survived the period of colonial rule by Europeans.

262   Chapter 12

History

Portuguese sailors made contact with the Kongo Kingdom in 1482. Over time the slave trade and other problems weakened the Kongo and other African kingdoms.

A Belgian Colony In the 1870s King Leopold II of Belgium took control of the Congo Basin. The king ruled the Congo Free State as his personal colony until 1908. His soldiers treated the Africans harshly. They forced people to work in mines and on plantations. These policies brought international criticism.

The Belgian government took control of the colony from the king in 1908. Many Belgian businesses and people moved there. They mined copper and other resources. The giant colony won independence from tiny Belgium in 1960.

A New Country Many Belgians fled the country after 1960. There were few teachers, doctors, and other professionals left in the former colony. In addition, people from different areas and ethnic groups fought each other. These problems were partly to blame for keeping the country poor.

A dictator, who later changed his name to Mobutu Sese Seko, came to power in 1965. He was an ally of the United States during the Cold War. Mobutu changed the country's name to Zaire in 1971. During his rule, the country suffered from economic problems and government corruption.

Section 3

Objectives
1. Recount the history of the Democratic Republic of the Congo.
2. Describe the people and culture of the country.
3. Analyze the economy of the country.

FOCUS

Bellringer

Copy this information onto the chalkboard: *All of these names are for the same country: Congo Free State, Belgian Congo, Republic of the Congo, Zaire, and the Democratic Republic of the Congo. What can you conclude from this country's many name changes?* Discuss students' responses. (Possible answers: changes in government, instability) Tell students the country has indeed had a troubled history. Explain to students that in Section 3 they will learn more about the history and culture of the Democratic Republic of the Congo.

Building Vocabulary

Write **civil war** on the chalkboard. Call on a volunteer to read the definition. Ask students why the phrase might be considered an oxymoron, or two words in a term that seem to contradict each other. (The word *civil* can mean "polite." Wars are not polite.)

A new government took over in 1997 after a **civil war**. A civil war is a war between two or more groups within a country. The new government changed the country's name to the Democratic Republic of the Congo. However, fighting between ethnic groups has continued.

✓ READING CHECK: (*Human Systems*) What has the history of the Democratic Republic of the Congo been like? filled with numerous conflicts

The Democratic Republic of the Congo

COUNTRY	POPULATION/ GROWTH RATE	LIFE EXPECTANCY	LITERACY RATE	PER CAPITA GDP
Democratic Republic of the Congo	53,625,039 2.9%	47, male 51, female	65%	$600
United States	290,342,554 0.9%	74, male 80, female	97%	$37,600

Source: Central Intelligence Agency, *The World Factbook 2003*

The People

More than 50 million people live in the Democratic Republic of the Congo today. The population is very diverse. It is divided among more than 200 ethnic groups. The Kongo people are among the largest groups. These groups speak many different languages, but the official language is French. About half of the country's people are Roman Catholic. Protestant Christians, Muslims, and people who practice traditional African religions also live in the country.

More than 4 million people live in Kinshasa, the capital and largest city. Kinshasa is a river port located along the Congo River near the Atlantic coast. The crowded city has some modern buildings. However, most of the city consists of poor slums.

✓ READING CHECK: (*Human Systems*) What are the people and culture of the Democratic Republic of the Congo like? diverse, many different languages spoken, half Roman Catholic

Human-Environment Interaction

A family sells charcoal along a road in the northern Democratic Republic of the Congo. Charcoal is a major fuel source. In many rural areas there is no electricity.

▼

Central Africa 263

TEACH

Teaching Objective 1
ALL LEVELS: (Suggested time: 20 min.) Copy the following graphic organizer onto the chalkboard, omitting the blue answers. Use it to help students describe historical actions taken and the results of these actions in the history of the Democratic Republic of the Congo. Call on volunteers to describe results from the causes listed. Encourage students to refer to Section 2 for more information on regional history. **ESOL**

History of the Democratic Republic of the Congo

Portuguese contact → Slave trade weakened kingdoms.
Leopold II treated people harshly. → international criticism
Belgian government took control. → Belgians moved there for business.
Congo gained independence in 1960. → Many Belgian professionals left.
Few professionals, many problems → Country stayed very poor.
Mobutu Sese Seko in power → economic problems, corruption
Civil war erupted. → New government took over.

Answers to Section 3 Review

Define or identify For definition and identification, see the glossary and index.

Working with Sketch Maps Lubumbashi should be located accurately. Most of the area's copper is shipped through Lubumbashi.

Reading for the Main Idea

1. Belgium (NGS 4)
2. few professionals, ethnic fighting, poverty (NGS 4)

Critical Thinking

3. more than 200 ethnic groups, many different languages and religions; Kongo people
4. would allow resources to be shipped more efficiently; educated citizens might bring greater economic development

Organizing What You Know

5. 1482—Portuguese make contact with Kongo Kingdom; 1870s—Leopold II takes control of Congo Basin; 1908—Belgian government takes control; 1960—independence; 1965—Mobutu takes power; 1971—changed to Zaire; 1997—Mobutu loses power after civil war

The Congo River lies in the distance in this photograph of Kinshasa.

The Economy

The Democratic Republic of the Congo is a treasure chest of minerals and tropical resources. For example, the south is part of central Africa's rich copper belt. Much of the copper from the area is shipped through the city of Lubumbashi (loo-boom-BAH-shee). The country also has gold, diamonds, and cobalt. The country's tropical rain forest also supplies wood, food, rubber, and other products.

However, the country's people are very poor. Most people live in rural areas. They must farm and trade for food. Civil war, bad government, and crime have scared many foreign businesses away. As a result, the country's rich resources have helped few of its people.

For the economy to improve, the country needs peace and a stable government. Schools must be improved and better health care provided. The country also must repair and expand roads and railways. If its challenges are met, the country's resources can make the future brighter.

✓ **READING CHECK:** *Environment and Society* How might the economy of the country improve? If government, schools, health care, and transportation networks improve, the country could take advantage of its rich resources.

Homework Practice Online
Keyword: SK5 HP12

Section Review 3

Define or identify: Mobutu Sese Seko, civil war

Working with Sketch Maps On the map you created in Section 2, label the Democratic Republic of the Congo and Lubumbashi. Why is Lubumbashi economically important?

Reading for the Main Idea

1. (*Places and Regions*) What European country ruled what is now the Democratic Republic of the Congo as a colony until 1960?

2. (*Places and Regions*) What were some problems the country faced after independence?

Critical Thinking

3. **Finding the Main Idea** In what ways is the Democractic Republic of the Congo a culturally diverse country? What ethnic group is among the largest?

4. **Drawing Inferences and Conclusions** How might better schools and transportation help the country's economy?

Organizing What You Know

5. **Sequencing** Copy the following time line. Use it to identify important groups and individuals in the history of the present-day Democratic Republic of the Congo.

1482 — 2000

Teaching Objectives 2–3

ALL LEVELS: (Suggested time: 30 min.) Assign one group the topic People and the other Economy. Have each group create a mobile from cardboard, wire hangers, and string about its topic as it relates to the Democratic Republic of the Congo. **LS KINESTHETIC**

CLOSE

Ask students to think of uses for the country's major resources. Provide encyclopedias for students to look up unfamiliar resources, such as cobalt.

REVIEW, ASSESS, RETEACH

Have students complete the Section Review. Then have students outline the section. Then have students complete Daily Quiz 12.3.

Have students complete Main Idea Activity S3. Then have students create illustrated travel guides for the Democratic Republic of the Congo, including information on history, the people, cities, and the economy. **ESOL**

EXTEND

Ask students to prepare proposals for developing the country's natural resources. Have them present their proposals on storyboards for a slide show for government officials. **BLOCK SCHEDULING**

Section 4 — The Other Central African Countries

Read to Discover

1. What are the people and economies of the northern central African countries like?
2. What are the people and economies of the southern central African countries like?

Vocabulary

exclave

Places

Douala
Yaoundé
Luanda

SECTION 4 RESOURCES

Reproducible
◆ Lecture Notes, Section 4
◆ Know It Notes S4

Technology
◆ One-Stop Planner CD–ROM, Lesson 12.4
◆ Homework Practice Online
◆ HRW Go site

Reinforcement, Review, and Assessment
◆ Section 4 Review
◆ Daily Quiz 12.4
◆ Main Idea Activity S4
◆ Chapter Summaries and Review
◆ English Audio Summary 12.4
◆ Spanish Audio Summary 12.4

Reading Strategy

FOLDNOTES: TWO-PANEL FLIP CHART Create the FoldNote **Two-Panel Flip Chart.** Label one flap Northern Central Africa and the other flap Southern Central Africa. As you read this section, write what you learn about these regions beneath each flap.

Northern Central Africa

Six countries make up northern central Africa. Four are Cameroon, the Central African Republic, Gabon, and the Republic of the Congo. They gained independence from France in 1960. Cameroon had been a German colony until after World War I. Tiny Equatorial Guinea gained independence from Spain in 1968. The island country of São Tomé and Príncipe won independence from Portugal in 1975.

The People Cameroon is by far the most populous country in this region. About 15.8 million people live there. The Central African Republic has the second-largest population, with 3.5 million. Tiny São Tomé and Príncipe has only about 165,000 people.

A large variety of ethnic groups are found in northern central Africa. Many people are moving from rural areas to cities to search for jobs. Governments are struggling to provide basic services in those crowded cities.

Douala (doo-AH-lah) and Yaoundé (yown-DAY) in Cameroon are the largest cities. Each has more than 1 million people. Douala is an important seaport on the Atlantic coast. Yaoundé is Cameroon's capital. Brazzaville, the capital of the Republic of the Congo, also has 1 million people. The city is a major Congo River port.

The Economy Most of the area's countries are very poor. Most people are farmers. Gabon has the strongest economy in central

Region Although the region's cities are growing rapidly, most people still live in rural areas. This small village is located in northern Cameroon. As in much of rural Africa, several buildings make up a family's home.

▼

Central Africa 265

Section 4

Objectives

1. Describe the people and economies of the northern central African countries.
2. Describe the people and economies of the southern central African countries.

FOCUS

Bellringer

Copy this question onto the chalkboard: *What are some physical challenges you might face if you lived close to the equator?* Allow students time to write their answers. Discuss responses. (Possible answers: heat, humidity, insects) Point out that central Africa lies near the equator. Tell students that in Section 4 they will learn more about how the location and other physical factors affect people's lives in the other countries of central Africa.

Building Vocabulary

Write **exclave** on the chalkboard. Tell students that the prefix *ex-* usually means "out of." The words *excavate* and *exclude* are examples. Explain that an exclave is a part of a country that is separated by territory of other countries. Ask students if the United States has an exclave (Alaska).

FOOD FESTIVAL

Are You a *Fufu* Fan?

Central African cooks serve *fufu* with meat dishes that have a gravy, like we might serve mashed potatoes. Here is an instant, Americanized version of *fufu*.

Bring six cups of water to a boil in a large pot. Add two cups each of instant mashed potato flakes and tapioca. Using a strong wooden spoon, stir constantly for 10 to 15 minutes. If the *fufu* is thinner than mashed potatoes, add more of the dry ingredients. The *fufu* should be very thick. Shape into balls and serve immediately. *Fufu* is eaten by tearing off a small handful and using it to scoop up the meat and sauce.

Chart Answer

São Tomé and Príncipe, Cameroon

Northern Central Africa

Country	Population/ Growth Rate	Life Expectancy	Literacy Rate	Per Capita GDP
Cameroon	15,746,179 2.0%	47, male 49, female	79%	$1,700
Central African Republic	3,683,538 1.6%	40, male 43, female	51%	$1,300
Congo, Republic of the	2,954,258 1.5%	49, male 51, female	84%	$900
Equatorial Guinea	510,473 2.5%	53, male 57, female	86%	$2,700
Gabon	1,321,560 2.5%	55, male 58, female	63%	$5,700
São Tomé and Príncipe	175,883 3.2%	64, male 67, female	79%	$1,200
United States	290,342,554 0.9%	74, male 80, female	97%	$37,600

Source: Central Intelligence Agency, *The World Factbook 2003*

Interpreting the Chart Which country in the region has the smallest population? the largest?

Africa. More than half of the value of its economy comes from the oil industry. Oil is important in Cameroon as well as in the Republic of the Congo.

The mighty Congo River is also a vital trade and transportation route. As a result, it plays a major role in the region's economy. Many of the region's goods and farm products are shipped down river to Brazzaville. Brazzaville lies across the Congo River from Kinshasa. From Brazzaville, goods are shipped by railroad to a port on the Atlantic coast.

✓ **READING CHECK:** (Human Systems) What are the people and economies of northern central Africa like? Large variety of ethnic groups; mostly poor farming nations; oil important in Gabon, Cameroon, and Democratic Republic of the Congo

Southern Central Africa

Zambia, Malawi, and Angola make up the southern part of central Africa. The British gave Zambia and Malawi independence in 1964. Angola won independence from Portugal in 1975.

The People The populations of the three southern countries are nearly the same size. They range from about 10 million in Zambia to more than 11 million in Malawi. Angola and Zambia are much larger in area than Malawi. Large parts of Angola and Zambia have few people. Most people in the region live in rural areas. They grow crops and herd cattle and goats.

(Movement) Riverboats carry the king of Zambia's Lozi people to a dryland home during the flooding season. This event is an annual ritual for the Lozi, who live in western Zambia. As in other central African countries, many different ethnic groups live in Zambia.

TEACH

Teaching Objectives 1–2

ALL LEVELS: (Suggested time: 20 min.) Copy the following graphic organizer onto the chalkboard, omitting the blue answers. Use it to help students describe the region's people and economies. Ask students to copy it into their notebooks and to fill in the name of the country best described by the phrase. **ESOL**

Central Africa's People and Economies

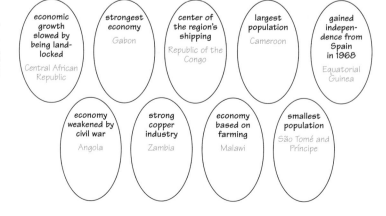

economic growth slowed by being landlocked — Central African Republic

strongest economy — Gabon

center of the region's shipping — Republic of the Congo

largest population — Cameroon

gained independence from Spain in 1968 — Equatorial Guinea

economy weakened by civil war — Angola

strong copper industry — Zambia

economy based on farming — Malawi

smallest population — São Tomé and Príncipe

Angola's capital, Luanda, is the southern region's largest city. More than 2 million people live there. Seen from the sea, Luanda looks like a modern city. The city has many high-rise buildings and factories. Unfortunately, Luanda and its people have suffered from poverty and years of war. Rebels fought the Portuguese in the 1960s and early 1970s. After independence, the country plunged into civil war. Fighting continued off and on until 2002. Many people have been killed or injured by land mines.

The Economy In peacetime, the future of Angola could be bright. There are many places with fertile soils. The country has large deposits of diamonds and oil. The oil is found offshore north of Luanda and in the exclave of Cabinda. An **exclave** is part of a country that is separated by territory of other countries. Cabinda is separated from the rest of Angola by the Democratic Republic of the Congo.

Much of Zambia's income comes from rich copper mines. However, 85 percent of Zambia's workers are farmers. Most of the country's energy comes from hydroelectric dams and power plants along rivers.

About 75 percent of Malawi's people live in rural areas. Nearly all of them are farmers. The building of factories and industries has been slow. Aid from other countries and religious missionaries has been important to the economy.

Southern Central Africa

COUNTRY	POPULATION/ GROWTH RATE	LIFE EXPECTANCY	LITERACY RATE	PER CAPITA GDP
Angola	10,766,471 1.2%	36, male 38, female	42%	$1,600
Malawi	11,651,239 2.2%	37, male 38, female	62%	$670
Zambia	10,307,333 1.5%	37, male 38, female	80%	$890
United States	290,342,554 0.9%	74, male 80, female	97%	$37,600

Source: Central Intelligence Agency, *The World Factbook 2003*

Interpreting the Chart Which country in the region has the highest literacy rate?

✔ **READING CHECK:** (*Human Systems*) What are the people and economies of the southern central African countries like? mostly rural dwellers who farm and herd; Angola— economy hurt by conflict, large supply of diamonds and oil; Zambia—copper mining, farming; Malawi—farming, foreign aid

go. hrw .com **Homework Practice Online**
Keyword: SK5 HP12

Section Review 4

Define and explain: exclave

Working with Sketch Maps On the map you created in Section 3, label the countries of northern and southern central Africa, and Douala, Yaoundé, and Luanda. In a box in the margin, describe Luanda.

Reading for the Main Idea

1. (*Places and Regions*) Which country has the strongest economy in central Africa?

2. (*Environment and Society*) What significance does oil have in the economies of many countries in the region?

3. (*Human Systems*) What has happened in Angola since that country won its independence?

Critical Thinking

4. **Analyzing Information** Why is Brazzaville important to the region's economy?

Organizing What You Know

5. **Summarizing** Copy the following graphic organizer. Divide it into nine rows below the headings. Use it to list the countries discussed in this section. Then identify the European country that colonized each central African country. Finally, list the date each country won independence.

Country	European colonial ruler	Year of independence

Central Africa • 267

WORKSHEET ►**ASSIGNMENT:** Have students create a new flag for one of the countries of central Africa, using text information to choose relevant colors and symbols. Ask students to write a paragraph explaining the colors and symbols.

CLOSE

Lead a class discussion on how living in the exclave of Cabinda may affect daily life.

REVIEW, ASSESS, RETEACH

Have students complete the Section Review. Then have each student write a one-sentence description for one of the countries in Section 4 for a where-am-I game. Call on students to read their descriptions and ask others to identify the country. Then have students complete Daily Quiz 12.4.

Have students complete Main Idea Activity S4. Then have students create a chart that identifies the major challenges facing central Africa by country. **ESOL**

EXTEND

Have students conduct research on the copper industry. Ask them to report their results on illustrated posters. **BLOCK SCHEDULING**

Define and Identify

For definitions and identification, see the glossary and index.

Review the Main Ideas

10. Congo, Zambezi (NGS 4)
11. edge of the Western Rift Valley
12. mostly traditional economies
13. migration of Bantu speakers from western Africa (NGS 9)
14. war, development of natural resources, and stopping the spread of disease (NGS 18)
15. Roman Catholicism, Protestant Christianity, Islam, traditional African religions (NGS 10)
16. France, United Kingdom, Belgium, Portugal, Spain (NGS 13)
17. Oil economy has made it the strongest economy in the region. (NGS 15)
18. from hydroelectric dams and power plants along rivers

Think Critically

19. Because little sunlight reaches the forest floor, few plants provide food or shelter for the animals.
20. ethnic groups with rivalries lumped together in colonies; other ethnic groups divided
21. made them important shipping ports for regional goods
22. common languages in countries where many ethnic languages are spoken; helpful in business and government as language bridge between groups
23. Cold War rivalries drew the United States and Soviet Union into the area's small regional wars and made them worse.

Review and Practice

Define and Identify

Identify each of the following:

1. basin
2. canopy
3. copper belt
4. periodic markets
5. ivory
6. dialects
7. civil war
8. Mobutu Sese Seko
9. exclave

Review the Main Ideas

10. What two river systems are most important in central Africa?
11. Where are central Africa's highest mountains found?
12. What types of economies do central African countries practice?
13. How were the Bantu languages introduced to central Africa?
14. What challenges are the countries of central Africa facing today?
15. What religions are practiced by people in the Democratic Republic of the Congo?
16. What European countries once colonized central Africa?
17. How important has oil been to Gabon's economy?
18. How does Zambia get their energy?

Think Critically

19. **Drawing Inferences and Conclusions** Why do few large animals live on the floor of central Africa's tropical rain forests?
20. **Finding the Main Idea** How have borders drawn by European colonial powers contributed to ethnic conflicts in central Africa?
21. **Analyzing Information** How have their locations on major rivers or near important natural resources aided the growth of cities such as Brazzaville and Lubumbashi?
22. **Drawing Inferences and Conclusions** Why do you think European languages are still the official languages in the countries of central Africa?
23. **Finding the Main Idea** How did the Cold War contribute to problems in central Africa?

Map Activity

24. On a separate sheet of paper, match the letters on the map with their correct labels.

Congo Basin	Zambezi River
Western Rift Valley	Kinshasa
Lake Tanganyika	Lubumbashi
Lake Malawi	Douala
Congo River	Luanda

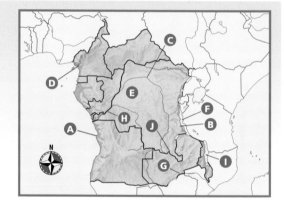

Map Activity

24. **A.** Luanda
B. Western Rift Valley
C. Congo River
D. Douala
E. Congo Basin
F. Lake Tanganyika
G. Zambezi River
H. Kinshasa
I. Lake Malawi
J. Lubumbashi

Writing Activity

Imagine that you have been hired to write a magazine article describing challenges facing central Africans. Write a descriptive headline and a brief summary for your proposed article. The article should cover the region's economic, political, and health challenges. Be sure to use standard grammar, spelling, sentence structure, and punctuation.

internet connect

Internet Activity: go.hrw.com
KEYWORD: SK5 GT12

Choose a topic to explore about central Africa:
- Identify threats to the Congo Basin.
- Visit the people of central Africa.
- Learn the importance of African cloth.

Social Studies Skills Practice

Interpreting Maps

Study the map of the Democratic Republic of Congo below. Then answer the questions.

Civil War in the Democratic Republic of Congo, 1998

CAMEROON
REPUBLIC OF THE CONGO
Congo River
GABON
DEMOCRATIC REPUBLIC OF CONGO
Brazzaville
Kinshasa
ATLANTIC OCEAN

Areas of government control
Areas of rebel control

1. What is the main idea of this map?
2. Which group controlled most of eastern Democratic Republic of Congo?
3. Which group controlled the Democratic Republic of Congo's capital?
4. Based on what you know about the region, why would control of Kinshasa be important?

Analyzing Primary Sources

Read the following quote from Werner Vansant, a humanitarian aid worker in the Democratic Republic of Congo during the 1998–2002 civil war. Then answer the questions.

"This is not a war of troops fighting against troops. It's a war against civil society, where infrastructures are destroyed and looted, all medicines stolen from health posts, key people like nurses are killed in villages, and agricultural fields are destroyed. So people have no food, no medical care, they don't get treated . . . They hide in the jungle for weeks and get malnourished, sick, weaker and weaker. Sometimes you see people coming out of the bush in terrible, terrible conditions, without clothes and without anything. Those are the victims of this war."

1. Why does Vansant think this civil war is different from other wars?
2. What goods and services do people in the Democratic Republic of Congo lack because of the war?
3. How did ordinary people respond to the crisis caused by the war?
4. Why does Vansant call people who are not fighting "the victims of the war"?

Central Africa • 269

Writing Activity

Paragraphs will vary, but should be consistent with text material. Students should include economic, political, and health challenges in their paragraphs. Use Rubric 42, Writing to Inform, to evaluate student work.

Interpreting Maps

1. to show areas held by the two sides during the civil war in the Democratic Republic of Congo in 1998
2. the rebels
3. the government
4. It is on the Congo River, so control of Kinshasa could affect the flow of food and other essential supplies. By affecting international trade, control of Kinshasa could also affect the economy of the whole country.

Analyzing Primary Sources

1. It's not a war of troops against troops; he sees it as a "war against civil society."
2. medical care, medicine, food
3. tried to hide from the fighting
4. because they suffer from the disruptions caused by the fighting

---

CHAPTER 12

REVIEW AND ASSESSMENT RESOURCES

Reproducible
- Readings in World Geography, History, and Culture 61, 62, and 63
- Critical Thinking Activity 12
- Vocabulary Activity 12

Technology
- Chapter 12 Test Generator (on the One-Stop Planner)
- Audio CD Program, Chapter 12
- HRW Go site

Reinforcement, Review, and Assessment
- Chapter 12 Review and Practice
- Chapter Summaries and Review
- Chapter 12 Test
- Chapter 12 Test for English Language Learners and Special-Needs Students

internet connect

GO TO: go.hrw.com
KEYWORD: SK5 Teacher
FOR: a guide to using the Internet in your classroom

CHAPTER 13

Southern Africa
Chapter Resource Manager

Objectives	Pacing Guide	Reproducible Resources
SECTION 1 **Physical Geography** (pp. 271–73) 1. Identify the major physical features and climates of southern Africa. 2. Identify the resources found in the region.	**Regular** .5 day Lecture Notes, Section 1 **Block Scheduling** .5 day *Block Scheduling Handbook, Chapter 13*	**RS** Know It Notes S1 **ELL** Main Idea Activity S1
SECTION 2 **Southern Africa's History and Culture** (pp. 274–77) 1. Describe what the early history of southern Africa was like. 2. Describe how Europeans gained control of southern Africa, and what changes this caused.	**Regular** 1 day Lecture Notes, Section 2 **Block Scheduling** .5 day *Block Scheduling Handbook, Chapter 13*	**RS** Know It Notes S2 **RS** Graphic Organizer 13 **E** Cultures of the World Activity 6 **E** Creative Strategies for Teaching World Geography, Lesson 16 **SM** Geography for Life Activity 26 **IC** Interdisciplinary Activities for the Middle Grades 26, 27, 28 **E** Biography Activity: Nelson Mandela **ELL** Main Idea Activity S2
SECTION 3 **South Africa Today** (pp. 278–81) 1. Describe South Africa's policy of apartheid. 2. Identify the factors that led to the end of apartheid. 3. Describe what South Africa's economy is like. 4. Describe South Africa's prospects for the future.	**Regular** 1 day Lecture Notes, Section 3 **Block Scheduling** .5 day *Block Scheduling Handbook, Chapter 13*	**RS** Know It Notes S3 **E** Biography Activity: Nelson Mandela **ELL** Main Idea Activity S3
SECTION 4 **The Other Southern Africa Countries** (pp. 282–85) 1. Identify the groups that have influenced Namibia's culture. 2. Identify the factors that have helped Botswana's economy. 3. Describe Zimbabwe's economy. 4. Explain why Mozambique has remained so poor. 5. Identify the events that have marked Madagascar's recent history.	**Regular** 1 day Lecture Notes, Section 4 **Block Scheduling** .5 day *Block Scheduling Handbook, Chapter 13*	**RS** Know It Notes S4 **SM** Map Activity 13 **ELL** Main Idea Activity S4

Chapter Resource Key

RS	Reading Support	**ELL**	Reinforcement and English Language Learners and English for Speakers of Other Languages (ESOL)		Music
IC	Interdisciplinary Connections				Video
E	Enrichment				Internet
SM	Skills Mastery		Transparencies		Holt Presentation Maker Using Microsoft® PowerPoint®
A	Assessment		CD–ROM		
REV	Review				

 One-Stop Planner CD–ROM

See the *One-Stop Planner* for a complete list of additional resources for students and teachers.

269A

One-Stop Planner CD–ROM

It's easy to plan lessons, select resources, and print out materials for your students when you use the *One-Stop Planner CD–ROM with Test Generator.*

internet connect

HRW ONLINE RESOURCES

<u>GO TO: go.hrw.com</u>
Then type in a keyword.

TEACHER HOME PAGE
KEYWORD: SK5 TEACHER

CHAPTER INTERNET ACTIVITIES
KEYWORD: SK5 GT13

Choose an activity to:
• explore the Namib Desert.
• go on a South African safari.
• investigate apartheid.

CHAPTER ENRICHMENT LINKS
KEYWORD: SK5 CH13

CHAPTER MAPS
KEYWORD: SK5 MAPS13

ONLINE ASSESSMENT
Homework Practice
KEYWORD: SK5 HP13
Standardized Test Prep Online
KEYWORD: SK5 STP13
Rubrics
KEYWORD: SS Rubrics

COUNTRY INFORMATION
KEYWORD: SK5 Almanac

CONTENT UPDATES
KEYWORD: SS Content Updates

HOLT PRESENTATION MAKER
KEYWORD: SK5 PPT13

ONLINE READING SUPPORT
KEYWORD: SS Strategies

CURRENT EVENTS
KEYWORD: S5 Current Events

Technology Resources

 One-Stop Planner CD–ROM, Lesson 13.1

 Geography and Cultures Visual Resources with Teaching Activities 43–47

 ARGWorld CD–ROM

Homework Practice Online

HRW Go site

 One-Stop Planner CD–ROM, Lesson 13.2

 ARGWorld CD–ROM

Music of the World Audio CD Program, Selection 16

Homework Practice Online

HRW Go site

 One-Stop Planner CD–ROM, Lesson 13.3

 ARGWorld CD–ROM

Homework Practice Online

HRW Go site

 One-Stop Planner CD–ROM, Lesson 13.4

ARGWorld CD–ROM

Music of the World Audio CD Program, Selection 16

Homework Practice Online

HRW Go site

Review, Reinforcement, and Assessment Resources

ELL	Main Idea Activity S1
REV	Section 1 Review
A	Daily Quiz 13.1
REV	Chapter Summaries and Review
ELL	English Audio Summary 13.1
ELL	Spanish Audio Summary 13.1

ELL	Main Idea Activity S2
REV	Section 2 Review
A	Daily Quiz 13.2
REV	Chapter Summaries and Review
ELL	English Audio Summary 13.2
ELL	Spanish Audio Summary 13.2

ELL	Main Idea Activity S3
REV	Section 3 Review
A	Daily Quiz 13.3
REV	Chapter Summaries and Review
ELL	English Audio Summary 13.3
ELL	Spanish Audio Summary 13.3

ELL	Main Idea Activity S4
REV	Section 4 Review
A	Daily Quiz 13.4
REV	Chapter Summaries and Review
ELL	English Audio Summary 13.4
ELL	Spanish Audio Summary 13.4

Meeting Individual Needs

Ability Levels

Level 1 Basic-level activities designed for all students encountering new material

Level 2 Intermediate-level activities designed for average students

Level 3 Challenging activities designed for honors and gifted-and-talented students

ESOL Activities that address the needs of students with Limited English Proficiency

Chapter Review and Assessment

E	Readings in World Geography, History, and Culture 64, 65, and 66		Chapter 13 Test Generator (on the One-Stop Planner)
SM	Critical Thinking Activity 13		Audio CD Program, Chapter 13
REV	Chapter 13 Review and Practice	A	Chapter 13 Test for English Language Learners and Special-Needs Students
REV	Chapter Summaries and Review		
ELL	Vocabulary Activity 13	A	Unit 3 Test for English Language Learners and Special-Needs Students
A	Chapter 13 Test		
A	Unit 3 Test		HRW Go Site

Southern Africa
Previewing Chapter Resources

Holt Online Learning

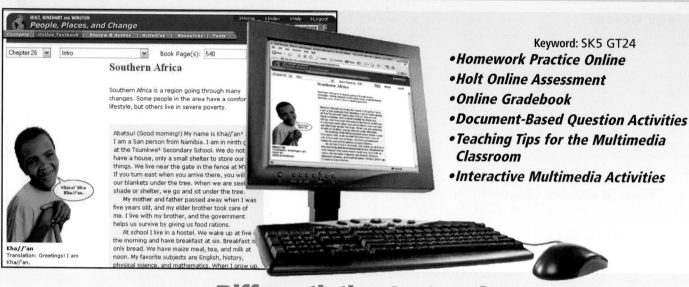

Keyword: SK5 GT24

- *Homework Practice Online*
- *Holt Online Assessment*
- *Online Gradebook*
- *Document-Based Question Activities*
- *Teaching Tips for the Multimedia Classroom*
- *Interactive Multimedia Activities*

Differentiating Instruction

Reading and Writing Support

◄ Graphic Organizer Activity
- *Vocabulary Activity*
- *Chapter Summary and Review*
- *Know It Notes*
- *Audio CD*

Active Learning

- *Block Scheduling Handbook*
- *Cultures of the World Activity*
- *Interdisciplinary Activity*
- *Map Activity*
◄ *Critical Thinking Activity 26*
- *Music of the World CD: Music of Madagascar*

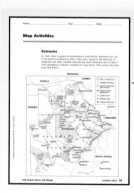

Primary Sources and Advanced Learners

- *Geography for Life Activity: Apartheid*
◄ *Map Activity: Botswana*
- *Readings in World Geography, History and Culture:*
  - *64 Namibia's Skeleton Coast*
  - *65 Experiencing Apartheid*
  - *66 Moors or Mazambique*

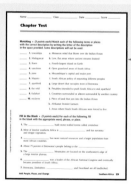

Assessment Program

- *Daily Quizzes S1–4*
◄ *Chapter Test*
- *Chapter Test for English Language Learners and Special-Needs Students*

Spanish and ESOL

- *Vocabulary Activity*
◄ *Main Idea Activities for English Language Learners and Special-Needs Students*
- *Chapter Summary and Review*
- *Spanish Audio Summary*
- *Know It Notes S1–4*
- *Chapter Test for English Language Learners and Special-Needs Students*

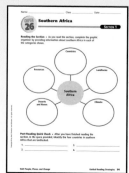

Special Education Modifications

Your **I.D.E.A. Works!** CD-ROM will provide modified versions of the following teaching materials:

◄ *Guided Reading Strategies S1–4*
- *Vocabulary Activity*
- *Main Idea Activities S1–4*
- *Daily Quizzes S1–4*
- *Chapter 13 Test*
- *Flash cards of chapter vocabulary terms*

Teacher Resources

Books for Teachers

Bechky, Alan. *Adventuring in Southern Africa: Botswana, Zimbabwe, Zambia, Malawi, Namibia, South Africa, Swaziland, Lesotho,* Sierra Club Books, 1997.

Frankel, Glenn. *Rivonia's Children:* Three Families and the Cost of Conscience in White South Africa. Farrar, Straus and Giroux, 1999.

Murphy, Dervla. *South from the Limpopo: Travels through South Africa.* Overlook Press, 1999.

Samatar, Abdi Ismail. *An African Miracle: State and Class Leadership and Colonial Legacy in Botswana Development.* Heinemann, 1999.

Books for Students

McKee, Tim. *No More Strangers Now: Young Voices from a New South Africa.* DK Pub., 1998. Twelve South African teens' diverse experiences under apartheid.

Stein, R. Conrad. *Cape Town.* Chelsea House, 1999. Physical aspects, history, social life, and customs of the legislative capital.
SHELTERED ENGLISH

Watson, Lyall, and Keith West (illustrator). *Warriors, Warthogs and Wisdom: An African Childhood.* Kingfisher Books, 1997. A white South African's experience growing up during the 1940s, including adventures with his best friend, a Zulu chief.

Multimedia Materials

Nelson Mandela: A Journey to Freedom. Video, 50 min. PBS.

Strike: The Story of a South African Boy. Video, 19 min. AIMS Media.

Wild Africa 2: Okavango, Chobe, Makgadikgadi. CD–ROM. Sumeria

Videos and CDs

Videos

- *CNN. Presents Geography: Yesterday and Today, Segment 27 Mining in South Africa*
- *CNN. Presents World Cultures: Yesterday and Today, Segment 24 The Farms of Zimbabwe*
- *ARG World*

Holt Researcher

http://researcher.hrw.com

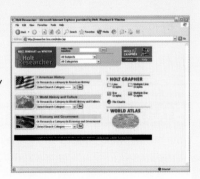

- *Mandela, Nelson*
- *Organization of African Unity (OAU)*
- *Africa*
- *Colonialism in Africa*
- *Tutu, Desmond*
- *Africa in 1750*
- *South Africa*
- *Madagascar*
- *Zimbabwe*
- *Mozambique*

Transparency Packages

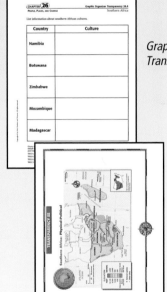

Graphic Organizer Transparencies 13.1–4

Geography and Cultures Visual Resources Transparencies 76–80
88 Southern Africa: Physical-Political

Map Activities Transparency 13 Botswana

CHAPTER 13

Southern Africa

Southern Africa is a region going through many changes. Some people in the area have a comfortable lifestyle, but others live in severe poverty.

*A*batsu! (Good morning!) My name is Kha//'an[1] and I am a San person from Namibia. I am in ninth grade at the Tsumkwe[2] Secondary School. We do not have a house, only a small shelter to store our things. We live near the gate in the fence at M'Kata. If you turn east when you arrive there, you will see our blankets under the tree. When we are seeking shade or shelter, we go and sit under the tree.

My mother and father passed away when I was five years old, and my elder brother took care of me. I live with my brother, and the government helps us survive by giving us food rations.

At school I live in a hostel. We wake up at five in the morning and have breakfast at six. Breakfast is only bread. We have maize meal, tea, and milk at noon. My favorite subjects are English, history, physical science, and mathematics. When I grow up, I want to be a doctor.

=Xai-o![3] Mi o Kha//'an.

Translation: Greetings! I am Kha//'an.

[1] The "//" is a click made by clucking the tongue at the sides of the mouth.
[2] The "k" in Tsumkwe is another kind of click. It is made by placing the tongue on the roof of the mouth and bringing it down with a "pop."
[3] The = is a click made by placing the tip of the tongue on the ridge behind the upper front teeth and bringing it down with a "pop."

270 • Chapter 13

Section 1 — Physical Geography

Read to Discover

1. What are the major physical features and climates of southern Africa?
2. What resources are found in the region?

Vocabulary

enclaves
the veld
pans

Places

Drakensberg
Inyanga Mountains
Cape of Good Hope
Kalahari Desert
Namib Desert
Orange River
Aughrabies Falls
Limpopo River

Reading Strategy

FOLDNOTES: LAYERED BOOK — Create the FoldNote titled **Layered Book** described in the Appendix. Label the layers of the book Countries, Landforms, Climates, and Resources. As you read this section, write what you learn about each topic in the appropriate layer of the book.

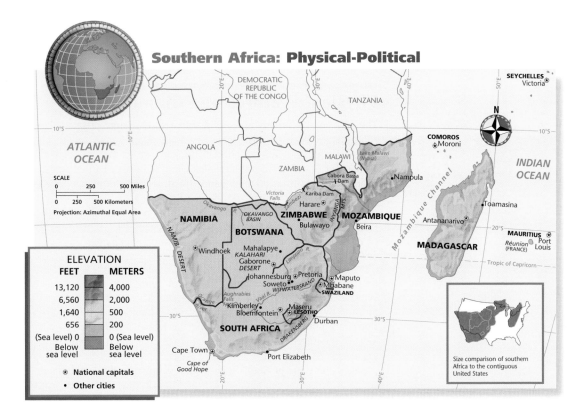

Southern Africa: Physical-Political

DEMOCRATIC REPUBLIC OF THE CONGO
SEYCHELLES
Victoria
TANZANIA
ATLANTIC OCEAN
ANGOLA
COMOROS
Moroni
MALAWI
Lake Malawi (Nyasa)
ZAMBIA
INDIAN OCEAN
Cabora Bassa Dam
Nampula
Victoria Falls
Kariba Dam
Harare
Toamasina
NAMIBIA
OKAVANGO BASIN
ZIMBABWE
MOZAMBIQUE
Antananarivo
Okavango
Bulawayo
Beira
MADAGASCAR
MAURITIUS
Réunion (FRANCE)
Port Louis
BOTSWANA
Windhoek
Mahalapye
KALAHARI DESERT
Gaborone
Johannesburg
Pretoria
Maputo
Soweto
Mbabane
SWAZILAND
Tropic of Capricorn
NAMIB DESERT
Aughrabies Falls
Vaal R.
WITWATERSRAND
Kimberley
Maseru
LESOTHO
Bloemfontein
Durban
SOUTH AFRICA
Orange River
DRAKENSBERG
Cape Town
Port Elizabeth
Cape of Good Hope

SCALE
0   250   500 Miles
0   250   500 Kilometers
Projection: Azimuthal Equal Area

ELEVATION

FEET	METERS
13,120	4,000
6,560	2,000
1,640	500
656	200
(Sea level) 0	0 (Sea level)
Below sea level	Below sea level

⊛ National capitals
• Other cities

Size comparison of southern Africa to the contiguous United States

---

Section 1

SECTION 1 RESOURCES

Reproducible
- Lecture Notes, Section 1
- Block Scheduling Handbook, Chapter 13
- Know It Notes S1

Technology
- One-Stop Planner CD–ROM, Lesson 13.1
- Homework Practice Online
- Geography and Cultures Visual Resources with Teaching Activities 43–47
- HRW Go site

Reinforcement, Review, and Assessment
- Section 1 Review
- Daily Quiz 13.1
- Main Idea Activity S1
- Chapter Summaries and Review
- English Audio Summary 13.1
- Spanish Audio Summary 13.1

Objectives

1. Identify the major physical features and climates of southern Africa.
2. Describe the resources found in the region.

FOCUS

Bellringer

Copy the following questions onto the chalkboard: *What are some possible advantages of living on a peninsula between two oceans? What are some possible disadvantages?* Have students respond in writing. Discuss students' answers. Then tell students that for many centuries southern Africa's location and resources have made the region attractive to outsiders. Tell students that in Section 1 they will learn more about the physical geography of southern Africa.

Using the Physical-Political Map

Have students examine the map on this page. Then ask students to describe the relative location of southern Africa in terms of its natural boundaries. (south of the Zambezi River, west of the Indian Ocean, east of the Atlantic Ocean) Then have students use the map to identify the region's landforms. (island, cape, deserts, escarpment, mountains, peninsula)

The Drakensberg range rises sharply in eastern South Africa.

internet connect

GO TO: go.hrw.com
KEYWORD: SK5 CH13
FOR: Web sites about the Namib Desert

Our Amazing Planet

*D*rakensberg means "dragon mountain" in the Afrikaans language. The Zulu, one of the peoples of the region, call it Kwathlamba, meaning "barrier of pointed spears" or "piled-up rocks."

Countries of the Region

Lining southern Africa's coasts are Namibia (nuh-MI-bee-uh), South Africa, and Mozambique (moh-zahm-BEEK). Botswana (bawt-SWAH-nah), Zimbabwe (zim-BAH-bway), and the two tiny countries of Lesotho (luh-SOH-toh) and Swaziland (SWAH-zee-land) are all land-locked. Lesotho and Swaziland are **enclaves**—countries surrounded or almost surrounded by another country. Madagascar (ma-duh-GAS-kuhr), off the east coast, is the world's fourth-largest island.

Physical Features and Climate

The surface of southern Africa is dominated by a large plateau. The southeastern edge of this plateau is a mountain range called the Drakensberg (DRAH-kuhnz-buhrk). The steep peaks rise as high as 11,425 feet (3,482 m) from the plains along the coast. Farther north, another mountain range, the Inyanga (in-YANG-guh) Mountains, forms the plateau's eastern edge.

The open grassland areas of South Africa are known as **the veld** (VELT). Kruger National Park covers 7,523 square miles (19,485 sq km) of the veld. The park contains lions, leopards, elephants, rhinoceroses, hippos, baboons, and antelope.

Climate The region's climates range from desert to cool uplands. Winds carry moisture from the Indian Ocean. These winds are forced upward by the Drakensberg and Inyanga Mountains. The eastern slopes are rainy, but climates are drier farther inland and westward. Most of the interior of southern Africa is semiarid and has steppe and savanna vegetation.

Near the Cape of Good Hope, winter rains and summer drought create a Mediterranean climate. Off the Cape, storms and rough seas are common.

272 • Chapter 13

SOUTHERN AFRICA'S PHYSICAL GEOGRAPHY

COUNTRIES	LANDFORMS	CLIMATES	BODIES OF WATER	RESOURCES
South Africa, Namibia, Botswana, Zimbabwe, Mozambique, Madagascar, Swaziland, and Lesotho	large plateau, the veld, the Drakensberg, Inyanga Mountains, Kalahari Desert, and Namib Desert	desert, semi-arid, steppe, savanna, Mediterranean	Orange River, Aughrabies Falls, Limpopo River	gold, diamonds, platinum, copper, uranium, coal, and iron ore

Deserts and Rivers In the central and western parts of the region, savanna and steppe give way to two major deserts. The Kalahari (ka-luh-hahr-ee) occupies most of Botswana. Here ancient streams have drained into low, flat areas, or **pans**. Minerals left behind when the water evaporated form a glittering white layer.

The Namib (NAH-mib) Desert lies along the Atlantic coast. Inland, the Namib blends into the Kalahari and steppe. Almost no rain falls, but at night fog rolls in from the ocean. Some plants and animals survive by using the fog as a source of water.

Southern Africa has some of the world's most spectacular rivers and waterfalls. The Orange River passes through the Aughrabies (oh-KRAH-bees) Falls as it flows to the Atlantic. When the water is highest, the Aughrabies Falls are several miles wide. The water tumbles down 19 separate waterfalls. The Limpopo (lim-POH-poh) River is the region's other major river. It flows into the Indian Ocean.

✓ **READING CHECK:** (*Places and Regions*) What are southern Africa's physical features and climate? plateau, Drakensberg mountain range, the veld, rivers, waterfalls; desert, cool uplands, semiarid with steppe and savanna

Resources

vegetation, Mediterranean

Southern Africa is very rich in mineral resources. Gold, diamonds, platinum, copper, uranium, coal, and iron ore are all found in the region. Where rain is plentiful or irrigation is possible, farmers can grow a wide range of crops. Ranchers raise livestock on the high plains. Some nomadic herders still live in desert areas.

✓ **READING CHECK:** (*Places and Regions*) What are the main resources of southern Africa? minerals—gold, diamonds, platinum, copper, uranium, coal, iron ore; farmland

internet connect

GO TO: go.hrw.com
KEYWORD: SK5 CH13
FOR: Web sites about southern Africa

The Orange River flows down the spectacular Aughrabies Falls. The falls are near the Namibian border in northwestern South Africa.

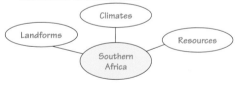

go.hrw.com **Homework Practice Online**
Keyword: SK5 HP13

Section Review 1

Define and explain: enclaves, the veld, pans

Working with Sketch Maps On a map of southern Africa that you draw or that your teacher provides, label the following: Drakensberg, Inyanga Mountains, Cape of Good Hope, Kalahari Desert, Namib Desert, Orange River, Aughrabies Falls, and Limpopo River. The Orange River forms part of the border between what two countries?

Reading for the Main Idea

1. (*Places and Regions*) What are the major landforms of southern Africa?

2. (*Places and Regions*) What are the main natural resources of the region?

3. (*Physical Systems*) How do physical processes affect southern Africa's climate?

Critical Thinking

4. **Drawing Inferences and Conclusions** How do you think the climate off the Cape of Good Hope has affected shipping in the area?

Organizing What You Know

5. **Summarizing** Copy the following graphic organizer. Use it to list the landforms, climates, and resources of southern Africa.

Climates
Landforms
Resources
Southern Africa

Southern Africa • 273

Answers to Section 1 Review

Define For definitions, see the glossary.

Working with Sketch Maps Maps will vary, but listed places should be labeled in their approximate locations. The Orange River forms the border between Namibia and South Africa.

Reading for the Main Idea

1. large plateau, the Drakensberg, the Inyanga Mountains, and the veld **(NGS 4)**

2. gold, diamonds, platinum, copper, uranium, and iron ore **(NGS 4)**

3. The Drakensburg forces moisture from the Indian Ocean upward and causes the eastern slopes to be rainy, while climates are drier farther inland. **(NGS 7)**

Critical Thinking

4. limited shipping because of rough seas

Organizing What You Know

5. landforms—large plateau, the Drakensberg, the Inyanga Mountains, and the veld; climates—desert, semiarid, steppe, savanna, and Mediterranean; resources—gold, diamonds, platinum, copper, uranium, iron ore, farmland, and ranchland

CLOSE

Remind students that the location and resources of the region attracted people from other parts of the world and continue to affect the region's economy, politics, and culture. Ask students to identify some of the resources of the region and explain how location and resources affect the economy of the region.

REVIEW, ASSESS, RETEACH

Have students complete the Section Review. Then tell each student to write four multiple-choice questions based on the information in this section. Pair students and have them take turns asking each other their questions. Then have students complete Daily Quiz 13.1. **COOPERATIVE LEARNING**

Have students complete Main Idea Activity S1. Then have groups create wall maps of the region with symbols for physical features, natural resources, and climate types. Display the maps.
ESOL, COOPERATIVE LEARNING

EXTEND

Until the 1800s, millions of quaggas—zebra-like animals—roamed the veld of South Africa. The last captive quagga died in 1883. Have interested students conduct research on efforts by South African scientists to bring back the quagga by tracing their DNA from zebras. Have students record their findings in a written report. **BLOCK SCHEDULING**

Visual Record Answer ▶

may have depended on hunting for survival

Section 2 Southern Africa's History and Culture

Read to Discover

1. What was the early history of southern Africa like?
2. How did Europeans gain control of southern Africa, and what changes did this cause?

Vocabulary
Boers

Places
Cape Town

Reading Strategy

TAKING NOTES Use the headings in this section to create an outline. As you read the section, write what you learn beneath each heading.

▲
Ancient rock art of southern Africa often includes hunters and animals.
Interpreting the Visual Record What do these images suggest about the people who made them?

Early History

Southern Africa's landscape and climate have influenced the region's history. For example, monsoon winds blow from the Indian Ocean to southern Africa from November to February. From May to September the wind blows the other way, from Africa to Asia. Ancient ships used these winds to make regular trading voyages between the two continents.

The Khoisan Some of the oldest human fossils have been found in southern Africa. By about 18,000 B.C., groups of hunter-gatherers were living throughout the mainland region. They left distinctive paintings of people and animals on rock surfaces. Some descendants of these people still live in certain desert regions. They speak languages of the Khoisan language family, which share unusual "click" sounds. However, most Khoisan people were absorbed into groups that moved into the region later.

Bantu Migrations Some 1,500–2,000 years ago a different group of people spread from central Africa into southern Africa. They spoke another family of languages known as Bantu. Today, most southern Africans speak one of the more than 200 Bantu languages. Scholars believe the early Bantu people introduced the use of iron to make tools. The Bantu are also thought to have introduced cattle herding to the region.

Section 2

Objectives

1. Describe the early history of southern Africa.
2. Explain how Europeans gained control of the region, and identify the changes this caused.

FOCUS

Bellringer

Copy the following question onto the chalkboard: *How might the physical geography of southern Africa have affected its history?* Allow for students to respond in writing. Discuss students' responses. Students might mention that the abundant resources and the location of southern Africa may have attracted foreigners. Tell students that in Section 2 they will learn more about the history and culture of southern Africa.

Building Vocabulary

Write the vocabulary term on the chalkboard. Explain that **Boers** is the name given to descendants of the original white Dutch colonial settlers of South Africa who first settled there in the 1600s.

Shona and Swahili By about A.D. 1000 one Bantu group, the Shona, had built an empire. It included much of what is now Zimbabwe and Mozambique. They farmed, raised cattle, and traded gold with other groups on the coast. They also constructed stone-walled towns called zimbabwe. The largest town, now called Great Zimbabwe, may have had 10,000 to 20,000 residents. Great Zimbabwe was abandoned in the 1400s.

Among Great Zimbabwe's trading partners were the Swahili-speaking people of the east coast. These were Africans who had adopted Islam and many Arab customs by the A.D. 1100s. The Swahili-speakers were sailors and traders. Archaeologists have found Chinese porcelain at Great Zimbabwe. This suggests that Africa and East Asia were connected by an Indian Ocean trade network.

Madagascar Madagascar's early history is quite different from the rest of southern Africa. Madagascar's first settlers came from Asia, rather than Africa, about A.D. 700. The island's culture shows the influence of both Africa and Asia. Malagasy, Madagascar's official language, is related to languages spoken in Indonesia. Malagasy also includes many words from the Bantu language family.

Mozambique In the early 1500s the Portuguese set up forts in Mozambique. They hoped to take over the region's gold trade from the Swahili-speakers and Arabs. The Portuguese also established large estates along the Zambezi River that used slave labor. In the 1700s and 1800s Mozambique became an important part of the slave trade. Africans were captured there and sent as slaves to Brazil and other parts of the world.

✓ **READING CHECK:** (*Human Systems*) What were some key events in the early history of southern Africa? 1,500-2,000 years ago—Bantu migrations; A.D. 1000—Shona empire; A.D. 700—Asian settlers reach Madagascar; 1500—Portuguese build forts in Mozambique; 1700s and 1800s—Mozambique important to slave trade

▲
People fish with nets in the Indian Ocean. Fishing is an important industry in Mozambique and Madagascar.

The Portuguese built this prison in Mozambique in the 1800s.

Interpreting the Visual Record
(*Movement*) **How might this architecture reflect European influences?**
◄

Southern Africa • 275

EYE ON EARTH

Leaping Lemurs! Along with a unique early history, Madagascar has unique wildlife. The island has an estimated 200,000 species of plants and animals, three fourths of which are not found anywhere else in the world.

Among the animals unique to the island is the lemur, a suborder of primates that has both nocturnal and diurnal species. One lemur active during the day is the indri, which has rounded ears and soft black and white fur. Its appearance resembles a cross between a teddy bear and a panda. It has extraordinary gymnastic ability and is able to propel backwards nearly 30 feet (10 m), flipping in midair to land face forward.

The indri and other species are endangered by deforestation, which has reduced the original forest by 90 percent. Species of plants that may hold cures for human diseases are also endangered.

◄**Visual Record Answer**

Students should mention the turret and other features that look like a European castle.

TEACH

Teaching Objective 1

LEVELS 1 AND 2: (Suggested time: 30 min.) Copy the following graphic organizer onto the chalkboard, omitting the blue answers. Organize the class into three groups. Assign the first group Khoisan and Bantu, the second Shona and Swahili, and the third Asians and Portuguese. Have each group find information about how, when, or where each group arrived, and the cultural changes each brought. **ESOL, COOPERATIVE LEARNING**

GROUP	HOW, WHEN, WHERE	CULTURAL CHANGES
Khoisan	hunter-gatherers, 18,000 B.C., throughout mainland	Khoisan language family, rock paintings
Bantu	spread from central Africa, 1,500–2,000 years ago, southern Africa	Bantu language family, use of iron, cattle herding
Shona	built an empire, A.D. 1000, Zimbabwe and Mozambique	farmed, raised cattle, traded gold
Swahili	sailors and traders, A.D. 1100, east coast	adopted Islam and Arab customs, traded with East Asia
Asians	settled on island, A.D. 700, Madagascar	Asian and African influences, language related to Indonesia
Portuguese	traders, early 1500s, Mozambique	set up forts, slave use and trade

Linking Past to Present

Shaka Zulu

Shaka (c. 1787–1828), the powerful founder of the Zulu Empire, was a legendary figure even in his own time. An imposing 6'3" warrior, Shaka gained his authority to rule mainly through the fear he inspired. He engaged the small Zulu clan—one of hundreds in southern Africa—in a series of tribal wars that resulted in the Zulu becoming the dominant group in the region.

Shaka Zulu has not been forgotten. He has become a symbol of Zulu strength and greatness. He also plays a role in popular culture. For example, the singing group Ladysmith Black Mambazo released an album under the name *Shaka Zulu*. Tourists can visit Shakaland, a cultural village in South Africa, to learn about Zulu traditions.

Critical Thinking: How is Shaka's popularity reflected in South African culture today?

Answer: Ladysmith Black Mambazo's album is named *Shaka Zulu;* Shakaland is a tourist site.

internet connect

GO TO: go.hrw.com
KEYWORD: SK5 CH13
FOR: Web sites about Zulu

In this painting, British ships sail past the Cape of Good Hope. The distinctively shaped Table Mountain is visible in the distance.

Our Amazing Planet

Much of southern Africa was a malaria zone. Quinine, a medicine made from a South American tree, could combat malaria. Using this medicine, Europeans were able to move into lowland areas where malaria was common.

In this 1935 photograph, elephant tusks and rhino horns are inspected in a London warehouse.

276 Chapter 13

The Dutch, British, and Portuguese in South Africa

The land around the Cape of Good Hope lacked the gold and copper of the Zambezi Valley. However, it had a Mediterranean climate. It also was free of the mosquitoes and tsetse flies that spread tropical diseases. In 1652 the Dutch set up a trade station at a natural harbor near the Cape. This small colony would eventually become known as Cape Town. It provided supplies to Dutch ships sailing between the Dutch East Indies and Europe. The Dutch brought in slaves to work in the colony. Some were Malays from Southeast Asia. Others were Africans bought at slave markets in other parts of Africa.

Afrikaners and Afrikaans The main language spoken in the colony was Dutch. Over time, Khoisan, Bantu, and Malay words were added, creating a new language called Afrikaans. White descendants of the original colonists are called Afrikaners. Some European men married Khoisan or Malay women. People descended from Malays, Khoisan, or a mixture of these with Europeans are called Coloureds.

A British Colony Afrikaner frontier farmers called **Boers** gradually spread out from the original colony. Then, in the early 1800s, Great Britain took over the area of the Cape. The Boers resisted the British colonial government. Many Boers packed all their belongings into wagons and moved farther east and north. This movement was called the Great Trek.

At about the same time, a Bantu-speaking group, the Zulu, became a powerful fighting force. They conquered the surrounding African peoples, creating their own empire. When the Boers moved into the northern plains, they entered Zulu territory. The two sides clashed over control of the land. Eventually the Zulu were challenged by the British and defeated after a series of battles.

LEVEL 3: (Suggested time: 25 min.) Have students write a report on an archaeological study of southern Africa. Students should list artifacts and fossils that represent the various groups and how they influenced southern Africa's early history. Each artifact or fossil should also include where it was found and its approximate age. (cave paintings dating back to 18,000 B.C. to represent the Khoisan; iron tools 1,500–2,000 years old to represent the Bantu; gold and Chinese porcelain from A.D. 1000 in Zimbabwe and Mozambique to represent the Shona; guns and European tools from the early 1500s in Mozambique to represent the Portuguese)

Teaching Objective 2

ALL LEVELS: (Suggested time: 45 min.) Organize students into five groups. Assign each group one of Section 2's subsections, starting after "The Dutch, British, and Portuguese in South Africa." Give each group a large sheet of paper and have the group design a mural for its section. Combine each group's designs into one large mural and display it in the classroom. Discuss the finished product.

ESOL, COOPERATIVE LEARNING, LS **VISUAL-SPATIAL**

Trade in Slaves and Ivory The British banned slavery in their empire in 1833. The Portuguese colonies of Angola and Mozambique remained as Africa's main slave markets. The slave trade eventually ended in the late 1800s. African trade began to focus on ivory—the tusks of elephants. Hunters wiped out the entire elephant population in some parts of southern Africa.

Diamonds, Gold, and Colonies In the 1860s diamonds were discovered in the northern part of the Cape Colony. In 1886 gold was discovered in the Transvaal, an area controlled by the Boers. Thousands of British and others came to South Africa. Railroads were built to connect the interior with the coast.

As the British moved north from the Cape Colony, some Boers moved into what is now Botswana. Afraid that the Boers would take over his country, Botswana's ruler asked for British protection. In 1885 Botswana (then known as Bechuanaland) came under British control. What is now Namibia became German Southwest Africa—a German colony. In 1889 what is now Zimbabwe came under control of the British South Africa Company as part of Rhodesia. It became a self-governing British colony in 1923.

South Africa In 1899 tensions over land and mineral wealth led to war between the Boers and the British. The Boers were greatly outnumbered, but held off the British army for three years. In the end the Boers were defeated. Their territory was added to the British colony of South Africa. In 1920, following Germany's defeat in World War I, Namibia was placed under South Africa's control.

✔ **READING CHECK:** (**Human Systems**) How did Europeans gain control of southern Africa, and what changes did this cause? initially founded colonies, then spread out, conquering native peoples militarily; European groups struggled for control over area, established trade in slaves, ivory and minerals

▲
This old steam train still operates in South Africa. The British built this and other railroads during the colonial period.

Interpreting the Visual Record
(Movement) Why did the Europeans connect the interior with the coast?

Section Review 2

Define and explain: Boers

Working with Sketch Maps On the map you created in Section 1, label Cape Town. What were the advantages of Cape Town's location?

Reading for the Main Idea
1. (**Human Systems**) How did the Bantu affect the history of southern Africa?
2. (**Human Systems**) How do archaeologists believe Chinese porcelain came to Great Zimbabwe?

Critical Thinking
3. **Finding the Main Idea** How did the slave trade affect southern Africa?
4. **Analyzing Information** What European groups settled in southern Africa? How did these groups interact with each other?

Organizing What You Know
5. **Sequencing** Copy the following time line. Use it to mark important events in the history of southern Africa from 18,000 B.C. to 1920.

18,000 B.C. ——————————————— 1920

go.hrw.com **Homework Practice Online**
Keyword: SK5 HP13

Southern Africa • 277

CLOSE

Call on volunteers to name all the outside groups that entered the area, how and why they arrived, the areas they controlled, and the cultural impact of their presence.

REVIEW, ASSESS, RETEACH

Have students complete the Section Review. Have each student prepare three "Who Am I?" questions covering the groups discussed in the text. Collect questions and use them to review. Then have students complete Daily Quiz 13.2.

Have students complete Main Idea Activity S2. Create an outline of the important information presented in the section on the chalkboard. Leave some parts of the outline blank and have students provide the missing information. Then have all students copy the outline for use as a study reference. **ESOL**

EXTEND

Have interested students conduct research on the Great Trek of the Boers. Ask students to use their research to write and illustrate descriptions of what the journey may have been like. **BLOCK SCHEDULING**

Biography Answer ▶

by working to improve the government and living conditions for all South Africans

Section 3 South Africa Today

Read to Discover
1. What was South Africa's policy of apartheid?
2. What factors led to the end of apartheid?
3. What is South Africa's economy like?
4. What are South Africa's prospects for the future?

Vocabulary
apartheid
townships
sanctions

Places
Witwatersrand
Johannesburg
Durban
Port Elizabeth

People
Nelson Mandela
Desmond Tutu

Reading Strategy

READING ORGANIZER Before you read this section, draw a large circle on a sheet of paper. Draw a vertical line and a horizontal line across the center of the circle. Label the parts Racial Divisions, Pressure against South Africa, Economy, and Future. As you read this section, write what you learn in each part of the circle.

BIOGRAPHY

Nelson Mandela
(1918–   )

Character Trait: Citizenship

Because he protested against apartheid, Nelson Mandela was imprisoned for 26 years. In 1990, however, South Africa's President de Klerk released Mandela from prison. Mandela and de Klerk shared the Nobel Peace Prize in 1993. One year later, Mandela became South Africa's first black president. He wrote a new constitution and worked to improve the living conditions of black South Africans.

How did Nelson Mandela show citizenship?

Racial Divisions

In the early 1900s South Africa's government, which was dominated by Afrikaners, became increasingly racist. Some black South Africans opposed the government. They formed the African National Congress (ANC) in 1912 to defend their rights. However, the trend toward racial division and inequality continued.

After World War II South Africa became an independent country. The South African government set up a policy of separation for its different peoples. This policy was called **apartheid**, meaning "apartness." The government divided people into three groups: whites, coloureds and Asians, and blacks—the overwhelming majority. Coloureds and Asians were only allowed to live in certain areas. Each African tribe or group was given its own rural "homeland."

The whites owned most of the good farmland. They also owned the mines and other natural resources. Black Africans had no rights in white areas. Blacks' land, housing, and health care were poor compared to those for whites. Education for blacks was limited, and classes were often taught in Afrikaans. Coloureds' facilities were poor but slightly better than those for blacks. People who protested these rules were sent to prison. One of those imprisoned was a lawyer named Nelson Mandela, a leader of the ANC.

Many blacks found work in white-owned industries, mines, shops, and farms. They had to live in separate areas called **townships**. These were often crowded clusters of tiny homes. They were far from the jobs in the cities and mines.

✓ **READING CHECK:** (*Human Systems*) What was apartheid?
South African government policy of separating its different peoples

Section 3

Objectives
1. Describe South Africa's policy of apartheid.
2. Identify the factors that led to the end of apartheid.
3. Describe South Africa's economy.
4. Analyze South Africa's prospects for the future.

FOCUS

 Bellringer

Copy the following questions onto the chalkboard: *Would you like to visit South Africa? Why or why not?* Have students respond in writing. Explain that for decades most U.S. citizens did not travel to South Africa because of the way the government treated a majority of its people. Now that the government has changed, tourists from the United States are enjoying South Africa's many attractions. Tell students that in Section 3 they will learn more about apartheid and South Africa.

Building Vocabulary

Have students look at the first half of the word **apartheid** (apart). What can they conclude about the word's meaning? In Dutch, *-heid* is similar to the English suffix *-hood,* meaning a "condition" or "quality." Therefore, apartheid is the condition of being apart or separate. Tell students that **townships** and **sanctions** are terms that can be related to apartheid.

In townships like Kayalitsha, black workers lived in crude shacks.

Interpreting the Visual Record How did the apartheid system affect the roles and responsibilities of South Africans?

Pressure against South Africa

Many people around the world objected to South Africa's apartheid laws. Some countries banned trade with South Africa. Some companies in the United States and Europe refused to invest their money in South Africa. Many international scientific and sports organizations refused to include South Africans in their meetings and competitions. These penalties, called **sanctions**, were intended to force South Africa to end apartheid.

South Africa and Its Neighbors During the 1960s, 1970s, and 1980s other countries in southern Africa gained their independence from colonial rule. British colonists in Rhodesia protested Britain's decision to grant independence. They declared their own white-dominated republic in 1970. This break resulted in years of violence and civil war. Finally the white government agreed to hold elections. They turned the country over to the black majority. The new government renamed the country Zimbabwe.

Mozambique was granted independence in 1975 after 10 years of war against Portuguese rule. However, rebels backed by Rhodesia and South Africa plunged Mozambique into another long war. Despite violent resistance, Namibia continued to be ruled by South Africa until independence in 1990.

The End of Apartheid As other countries in southern Africa gained independence, South Africa became more and more isolated. Protest within the country increased. The government outlawed the ANC. Many ANC members were jailed or forced to leave the country.

Southern Africa • 279

Southern Africa 279

GLOBAL PERSPECTIVES

A Low-Tech Solution As South Africa works to improve its economy, one industry is making changes throughout Africa. A radio invented in Great Britain may provide people in countries with little electricity and no money for batteries the ability to receive information on everything from health to election news. Operated by windup springs that provide power, the radios are manufactured in South Africa and are sufficiently inexpensive that people in many developing countries can afford them. The company that manufactures the radio also makes windup flashlights. The company provides jobs and produces useful products for sale in developing countries.

Activity: Have students prepare a radio show about the daily life of American students that could be broadcast to students in a developing country.

Biography Answer

using nonviolent protest and economic pressure to gain freedom for black South Africans

BIOGRAPHY

Desmond Tutu
(1931–)

Character Trait: Integrity

Black South Africans struggling for equality found an able leader in Desmond Mpilo Tutu. Educated in South Africa and England, Tutu worked his way up into the highest levels of the Anglican church. So, people around the world listened when he spoke out against apartheid. Tutu emphasized using nonviolent protest and economic pressure to gain freedom for black South Africans. In 1984, Tutu received the Nobel Peace Prize for his efforts to end apartheid peacefully.

What makes Desmond Tutu a man of integrity?

These are uncut, or rough, diamonds. Diamonds are the hardest mineral. This makes them useful for certain types of cutting and drilling.

Antiapartheid protesters turned increasingly to violence. South African forces attacked suspected rebel bases in neighboring countries like Botswana and Zimbabwe.

Finally, in the late 1980s South Africa began to move away from the apartheid system. In 1990 the government released Nelson Mandela from prison. Mandela was elected president in 1994 after all South Africans were given the right to vote.

Today all races have equal rights in South Africa. Public schools and universities are open to all, as are hospitals and transportation. However, economic equality has been slow in coming. White South Africans are still wealthier than the vast majority of black South Africans. Also, divisions between different black ethnic groups have caused new tensions. Still, South Africans now hope for a better future.

READING CHECK: (*Human Systems*) Why and how did South Africa do away with apartheid? Sanctions, isolation brought pressure; released Mandela, allowed equal rights, multi racial elections

South Africa's Economy

South Africa's government is trying to create jobs and better conditions for black workers and farmers. However, South Africa's mineral wealth and industries are still mostly owned by white people. Even officials who favor reform are afraid that too-rapid change will weaken the economy. They fear it will drive educated and wealthy whites to leave the country. The government has avoided taking white-owned farmland to divide among black farmers.

South Africa's energy resources include coal and hydroelectric power. Rich uranium mines provide fuel for nuclear power plants. In addition to gold and diamonds, mineral resources include copper, platinum, iron ore, and chromium.

The Witwatersrand region around Johannesburg is the continent's largest industrial area. South African and foreign companies build computers, cars, televisions, and many other products needed for modern life. The major port is Durban on the Indian Ocean coast. Cape Town and Port Elizabeth are other important ports.

READING CHECK: (*Human Systems*) How has apartheid continued to affect South Africa's economy today? Mineral wealth, industries, and farmland are mostly owned by whites.

South Africa's Future

South Africa has more resources and industry than most African countries but faces severe problems. It must begin to deliver equal education and economic opportunities to the entire population.

TEACH

Teaching Objective 3

ALL LEVELS: (Suggested time: 10 min.) Copy the following graphic organizer onto the chalkboard, omitting the blue answers. Have students complete it to help them understand South Africa's economy. **ESOL**

SOUTH AFRICA'S ECONOMY		
Resources	Industries	Concerns
coal, hydroelectric power, uranium, gold, diamonds, copper, platinum, iron ore, and chromium	computers, cars, televisions, and other products needed for modern life	better working conditions for black workers and farmers, most mineral wealth and industries still owned by whites

Teaching Objective 4

LEVEL 1: (Suggested time: 20 min.) Pair students and have each pair develop an agenda for a conference about South Africa's future. The agenda should address challenges facing South Africa as well as opportunities for the future. **ESOL, COOPERATIVE LEARNING**

LEVELS 2 AND 3: (Suggested time: 25 min.) Have students draft a campaign speech for a presidential candidate in South Africa. Speeches should address challenges facing the country, possible solutions to those challenges, and the country's prospects for the future. Have volunteers read their speeches aloud to the class. **LS AUDITORY-MUSICAL**

Place Cape Town has grown into a large industrial city. In this photograph, the harbor is visible beyond the tall buildings of the business district.

New problems have arisen since the end of apartheid. Crime has increased in the large cities. Also, South Africa, like the rest of the region, is facing a terrible AIDS epidemic.

There are 11 official languages in South Africa, although English is used in most areas. South Africa produces fine wines from the region around Cape Town. It has a unique cooking style combining Dutch, Malay, and African foods. The country also has a lively tradition of literature and the arts. Today, traditional ethnic designs are used in clothing, lamps, linens, and other products. These are sold to tourists and locals alike.

✓ READING CHECK: (Places and Regions) What are the challenges faced by South Africa?
unequal education and economic opportunities, crime, AIDS

South Africa

COUNTRY	POPULATION/ GROWTH RATE	LIFE EXPECTANCY	LITERACY RATE	PER CAPITA GDP
South Africa	42,768,678 0.3%	47, male 46, female	86%	$10,000
United States	290,342,554 0.9%	74, male 80, female	97%	$37,600

Source: Central Intelligence Agency, *The World Factbook 2003*

Interpreting the Chart **What is South Africa's per capita GDP?**

Homework Practice Online
Keyword: SK5 HP13

Define or identify: apartheid, Nelson Mandela, townships, sanctions, Desmond Tutu

Working with Sketch Maps On the map you created in Section 2, label Witwatersrand, Johannesburg, Durban, and Port Elizabeth.

Reading for the Main Idea
1. (Human Systems) What was the system of apartheid, and how did it affect the roles and responsibilities of South Africans?
2. (Human Systems) How did people around the world protest apartheid?

3. (Places and Regions) What challenges remain for South Africa?

Critical Thinking
4. **Analyzing Information** Why is South Africa the continent's most economically developed country?

Organizing What You Know
5. **Summarizing** Use this graphic organizer to list information about life in South Africa during apartheid and since the system ended.

During apartheid	Since apartheid ended

Southern Africa • 281

Section 3 Review

Answers to Section 3 Review

Define or identify For definitions and identifications, see the glossary and index.

Working with Sketch Maps Maps will vary, but listed places should be labeled in their approximate locations.

Reading for the Main Idea
1. a system of racial segregation; limited power to whites **(NGS 13)**
2. by banning trade with South Africa, refusing to invest money in South Africa, refusing South Africa's admission to meetings and competitions **(NGS 12)**
3. lack of equal education and economic opportunities for all races, increased crime rate, and an AIDS epidemic **(NGS 4)**

Critical Thinking
4. energy/mineral resources, developed industries, and important ports **(NGS 18)**

Organizing What You Know
5. apartheid—whites owned most natural resources, Black Africans had no rights in white areas, were forced to live in townships with poor facilities; since the end of apartheid—all races have equal rights, political prisoners freed

▲ **Chart Answer**

$10,000

CLOSE

Remind students that the end of apartheid in South Africa offers hope and challenges for the future. Ask students to identify some of the hopes for South Africa's future.

REVIEW, ASSESS, RETEACH

Have students complete the Section Review. Have students create crossword puzzles about South Africa. Photocopy the puzzles and have students exchange and complete them. Then have students complete Daily Quiz 13.3.
LS VERBAL-LINGUISTIC

Have students complete Main Idea Activity S3. Organize students into four groups. Assign the first group Apartheid, the second End of Apartheid, the third South Africa's Economy, and the fourth Challenges. Have each group use pictures and text from magazines to create a collage of information about its topic. Display and discuss the collages. **ESOL, COOPERATIVE LEARNING**

EXTEND

Have interested students conduct research on the African National Congress and make a scrapbook depicting important events in the organization's history. Display the scrapbooks in the classroom. **BLOCK SCHEDULING**

Visual Record Answer ▶

lack of resources and the encroachment of modern society into their region

Section 4 The Other Southern African Countries

Read to Discover

1. What groups have influenced Namibia's culture?
2. What factors have helped Botswana's economy?
3. What is Zimbabwe's economy like?
4. Why has Mozambique remained so poor?
5. What events have marked Madagascar's recent history?

Vocabulary

Organization of African Unity (OAU)

Places

Windhoek
Gaborone
Harare
Maputo

Reading Strategy

READING ORGANIZER Before you read, create a three-column chart on a sheet of paper. Label the columns Country, Resources, and Challenges. Then list each country covered in this section in the Country column. As you read this section, write what you learn about the resources and challenges of each country.

A San grandmother and child drink water from an ostrich egg. The San people traditionally lived by hunting and gathering. However, just a few live this way today.

Interpreting the Visual Record

Human-Environment Interaction **What factors do you think might lead many San people to give up their traditional way of life?**

▼

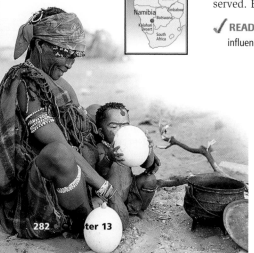

282   ter 13

Namibia

Most Namibians live in the savannas of the north or in the cooler central highlands. Windhoek, the capital, is located in these highlands. About 6 percent of the population is white, mainly of German descent. The rest of the population is divided among several different ethnic groups. Most Namibians are Christian. English is the official language. However, schooling was in Afrikaans until recently.

At independence in 1990, white farmers held most of the productive land. Most of Namibia's income comes from the mining of diamonds, copper, lead, zinc, and uranium. Fishing in the Atlantic Ocean and sheep ranching are also important sources of income.

Namibian culture shows many different influences. In many rocky areas, ancient rock engravings and paintings of the Khoisan are preserved. Beer and pastries reflect the period of German colonization.

✓ **READING CHECK:** *Human Systems* What are Namibia's cultural influences? white people of German descent; many other different cultures, including ancient Khoisan peoples

Botswana

Botswana is a large, landlocked, semiarid country. Thanks to mineral resources and stable political conditions, Botswana is one of Africa's success stories. Cattle ranching and mining of copper and diamonds are the principal economic activities. Recently, international companies have set up factories here. A new capital,

Section 4

Objectives

1. Identify the groups that influenced Namibia's culture.
2. Describe the factors that have helped Botswana's economy.
3. Describe Zimbabwe's economy.
4. Explain why Mozambique remains poor.
5. Describe the events that marked Madagascar's recent history.

FOCUS

Bellringer

Copy the following instruction and question onto the chalkboard: *Look at the physical-political map in Section 1. What physical features might affect the economic and political conditions in Namibia, Botswana, Zimbabwe, Mozambique, and Madagascar?* Have students respond in writing. (possible answers: deserts, some are landlocked, isolated island) Tell students that in Section 4 they will learn more about these southern African countries.

Building Vocabulary

Write the vocabulary term on the chalkboard. Ask students why a country might join the **Organization of African Unity**. Explain to students that this organization tries to promote cooperation between African countries.

Gaborone, was built after independence. Like the other countries of the region, Botswana belongs to the **Organization of African Unity (OAU)**. The OAU, founded in 1963, tries to promote cooperation between African countries.

Botswana's population is less than 1.6 million. About 79 percent belong to a single ethnic group, the Tswana. Most of the population live in the savanna and steppe areas of the east and south. The San and other minority groups mostly live in the northern swamps and the Kalahari Desert. About 15 percent of Botswana's people are Christian. The rest follow traditional African religions.

Botswana's major river, the Okavango, flows from Angola into a huge basin. The swamps of this basin are home to elephants, crocodiles, antelope, lions, hyenas, and other animals. Many tourists travel to Botswana to see these wild animals in their habitat.

Traditional crafts of Botswana include ostrich-eggshell beadwork and woven baskets with complex designs. People there also produce colorful wool tapestries and rugs.

☑ **READING CHECK:** (*Places and Regions*) Why might Botswana be considered a success story? because it has had a stable political conditions, has made good use of its resources, and has attracted foreign investment

▲
The Okavango River spreads out to form a large swampy area. Dense vegetation allows only small boats to move through the narrow channels.

Zimbabwe

Zimbabwe's capital is Harare. Zimbabwe gained independence in 1980. Since then, the country has struggled to create a more equal distribution of land and wealth. White residents make up less than 1 percent of the population. However, they still own most of the large farms and ranches.

Zimbabwe exports tobacco, corn, sugar, and beef. It now manufactures many everyday items, including shoes, batteries, and radios. Exports of gold, copper, chrome, nickel, and tin are also important to Zimbabwe's economy.

The AIDS epidemic threatens to kill hundreds of thousands of Zimbabwe's people, leaving many orphans behind. These effects will make economic growth harder. Other diseases such as malaria and tuberculosis are often deadly. There are also tensions between the majority Shona people and the minority Ndebele.

Artists in Zimbabwe have revived the tradition of stone sculpture found at Great Zimbabwe. Some of the larger pieces are among the most striking examples of modern art in the world.

☑ **READING CHECK:** (*Places and Regions*) What is Zimbabwe's economy like? exports agricultural products, minerals; manufactures everyday items

Other Southern African Countries

COUNTRY	POPULATION/ GROWTH RATE	LIFE EXPECTANCY	LITERACY RATE	PER CAPITA GDP
Botswana	1,573,267 0.5%	32, male 32, female	79%	$9,500
Madagascar	16,979,744 3%	53, male 58, female	69%	$760
Mozambique	17,479,266 0.8%	31, male 32, female	48%	$1,000
Namibia	1,927,447 1.4%	44, male 41, female	84%	$6,900
Zimbabwe	12,576,742 0.2%	40, male 38, female	90%	$2,400
United States	290,342,554 0.9%	74, male 80, female	97%	$37,600

Source: Central Intelligence Agency, *The World Factbook 2003*

Interpreting the Chart **Which countries are the least economically developed in the region?**

Southern Africa • 283

Culture and Music
Ancestors and Beliefs

Members of Zimbabwe's largest ethnic group, the Shona, believe that the god Mwari is active in their daily lives, including in politics. In fact, some say that Mwari approved an 1896 rebellion against white settlement. Mwari is said to speak through a woman who goes into a trance before delivering a message. When, in turn, Shona want to approach Mwari, they must do so by calling on ancestral spirits. Many Shona combine traditional and Christian beliefs.

Discussion: Other peoples of southern Africa also try to communicate with their ancestors. To hear a ceremony from Madagascar for calling ancestral spirits, play Selection 16 on the Music of the World Audio CD Program. Use the text and questions in the Teacher's Guide.

◀ **Chart Answer**

Madagascar, Mozambique, Zimbabwe

TEACH

Teaching Objective 1
ALL LEVELS: (Suggested time: 25 min.) Pair students and have each pair design a magazine cover for an issue featuring Namibian culture. Display covers around the room. **ESOL, COOPERATIVE LEARNING**

Teaching Objectives 2–3
ALL LEVELS: (Suggested time: 30 min.) Pair students and have them write an essay that compares and contrasts the economies of Botswana and Zimbabwe. Essays should include what factors helped make the economies successful. **ESOL, COOPERATIVE LEARNING**

 ►**ASSIGNMENT:** Tell students to imagine that they are traveling through southern Africa. Have them write journal entries describing each country they visit. Entries should mention such items as economy, culture, language, and challenges.

FOOD FESTIVAL

A Picnic Safari Have students prepare a southern Africa food safari. Serve fruit in a vanilla-sugar syrup topped with lichee nuts (Madagascar), Portuguese cheese and black olives (Mozambique), and mealie bread (South Africa).

Here is a recipe for mealie bread: 2 c. biscuit mix, 1 c. canned creamed corn, 2 tbs sugar, 1 egg, 1/2 c. milk. Mix and spread in 9 in. baking pan. Spread 2 oz. melted butter over mixture. Bake in a 400° oven for 20 min. You will find that mealie bread is something like corn pudding.

Connecting to History
Answers

1. by European participants at a conference in Berlin
2. divided some ethnic groups into separate colonies and combined other groups that were hostile to each other

CONNECTING TO History

In 1884–85, representatives of Europe's colonial countries met in Berlin. These countries included Belgium, France, Germany, Great Britain, Italy, Portugal, and Spain. Each was conquering areas in Africa. Their claims to territory were beginning to overlap. Leaders began to worry that a rivalry in Africa might trigger a war in Europe.

The Berlin conference was called to agree to boundaries for these African colonies. No Africans were invited to the conference. The European representatives divided up Africa among themselves. The new borders sometimes followed physical features, such as lakes and mountains. Many simply followed straight lines of latitude or longitude. Often people from the same ethnic group were separated by the new borders. In other places, ethnic groups hostile to each other were grouped together.

Most of the European colonies in Africa became independent after 1960. However, the leaders of the new African countries have

AFRICA'S BORDERS

Cartoon of France and Britain dividing Africa

mostly avoided drawing new boundary lines. So these countries still struggle with the borders they inherited from the Berlin Conference. These borders have made it hard for many African countries to build national loyalty among their citizens.

Understanding What You Read

1. How were Africa's borders established?
2. What consequences have these borders had for modern Africa?

Mozambique

Mozambique is one of the world's poorest countries. Its economy was badly damaged by civil war after independence from Portugal. Today, Mozambique's ports of Maputo—the capital—and Beira once again ship many products from interior Africa. The taxes collected on these shipments are an important source of revenue. Energy sources include coal and new hydroelectric dams on the Zambezi River. Plantations grow cotton, cashews, sugar, and tea.

Most of Mozambique's people belong to various Bantu ethnic groups. Each group has its own language. However, the country's official language is Portuguese. About 30 percent of the people are Christian, and 20 percent are Muslim.

284 • Chapter 13

Teaching Objective 4

LEVEL 1: (Suggested time: 15 min.) Have students write a letter home as if they were exchange students in Mozambique. Letters should describe the causes of the country's poverty and explain what the country is doing to try to solve its economic challenges. **ESOL,** **LS** **VERBAL-LINGUISTIC**

LEVELS 2 AND 3: (Suggested time: 25 min.) Have students write scripts for an oral presentation on Mozambique. Presentations should state why Mozambique is a poor country as well as offer suggestions for rebuilding its economy. Have volunteers present their information to the class.
LS **AUDITORY-MUSICAL**

Teaching Objective 5

ALL LEVELS: (Suggested time: 20 min.) Copy the following graphic organizer onto the chalkboard, omitting the blue answers. Have students complete the time line to document recent events in Madagascar's history.
ESOL

MADAGASCAR'S HISTORY

1800s	early 1990s		1996
French colony	rule of socialist dictator ends	period of democracy	former dictator voted back into power

Mozambique is famous for its fiery pepper or *peri-perri* sauces. They are often served on shrimp and rice.

✓ **READING CHECK:** (*Places and Regions*) What factor limited Mozambique's economic development? **civil war**

Madagascar

Madagascar is a former French colony. It was ruled by a socialist dictator until the early 1990s. At that point the people demanded a new political system. The optimism that came with democracy faded as the new leaders struggled with poverty. Surprisingly, in 1996 the people voted the former dictator back into power.

Nearly all of Madagascar's people are still very poor. There is little industry. Most of the country's income comes from exports of coffee, sugar, vanilla, and cloves. Most of the people depend on subsistence farming.

Madagascar has many animals found nowhere else. This is because the island has been separated from the African mainland for millions of years. Some 40 species of lemurs, relatives of apes, live only on this island. However, destruction of the rain forests threatens many of Madagascar's animals with extinction.

Malagasy and French are spoken throughout Madagascar. About 52 percent of the people follow traditional African religions. Some 41 percent are Christian, and about 7 percent are Muslim.

✓ **READING CHECK:** (*Places and Regions*) What has Madagascar's recent history been like? **People voted former dictator into power, people are poor, little industry**

▲
Remnants of French culture can still be seen in Madagascar.

Interpreting the Visual Record
(*Movement*) Which of these vendors' foods suggests a connection to French culture?

[go.hrw.com] **Homework Practice Online**
Keyword: SK5 HP13

Section Review 4

Define and explain: Organization of African Unity (OAU)

Working with Sketch Maps On the map you created in Section 3, label Windhoek, Gaborone, Harare, and Maputo. Which cities are located on the plateau of the southern African interior?

Reading for the Main Idea

1. (*Human Systems*) How have diseases affected Zimbabwe's people and economy?

2. (*Human Systems*) How did civil war affect Mozambique?

3. (*Environment and Society*) What minerals does Namibia have, and how do they affect its economy?

Critical Thinking

4. **Drawing Inferences and Conclusions** How do you think the fact that Botswana's population is almost entirely of a single ethnic group has affected its politics?

Organizing What You Know

5. **Summarizing** Copy the following graphic organizer. Use it to list information about southern African cultures.

Country	Culture
Namibia	
Botswana	
Zimbabwe	
Mozambique	
Madagascar	

Southern Africa • 285

Answers to Section 4 Review

Define For definition, see the glossary.

Working with Sketch Maps Windhoek, Gaborone, and Harare are located on the plateau.

Reading for the Main Idea

1. threaten to kill thousands and leave many orphans, and make economic growth harder (**NGS 9**)

2. slowed economic development (**NGS 13**)

3. diamonds, copper, lead, zinc, uranium; provide money through mining and sale of the minerals (**NGS 4**)

Critical Thinking

4. Students might suggest that Botswana has not experienced as much ethnic political conflict as other southern African countries.

Organizing What You Know

5. Charts should include information from the section.

◀ **Visual Record Answer**

the long loaves of bread

CLOSE

Have students identify how location and climate have created challenges for southern Africa and suggest possible solutions to these challenges.

REVIEW, ASSESS, RETEACH

Have students complete the Section Review. Then organize students into five groups. Assign each group a southern African country and have its members write six questions and answers on index cards about their country. Have groups exchange cards and quiz each other. Then have students complete Daily Quiz 13.4. **COOPERATIVE LEARNING**

Have students complete Main Idea Activity S4. Pair students and have them develop a chart that compares the economies of all the countries of southern Africa. **ESOL, COOPERATIVE LEARNING**

EXTEND

Have interested students create dioramas of the Namib Desert or the Kalahari Desert. They should display the landforms, plant and animal life, economic activities, and the presence of mineral resources. **BLOCK SCHEDULING**

Define and Identify

For definitions and identifications, see the glossary and index.

Review the Main Ideas

11. Lesotho and Swaziland

12. The Kalahari has pans and mineral deposits. The Namib Desert receives almost no rain, but a night fog provides water for some plants and animals. (NGS 4)

13. mineral resources, including gold, diamonds, platinum, coal, uranium, copper, and iron ore

14. by means of monsoon winds that blow across the Indian Ocean (NGS 15)

15. the Bantu language family, use of iron, and cattle herding (NGS 9)

16. Gold, diamonds, copper, platinum, iron ore, and chromium contribute to its wealth. (NGS 15)

17. the tradition of stone sculpture

18. because the island has been separated from the African mainland for millions of years

19. whites, Coloureds and Asians, and Blacks; Blacks (NGS 9)

Think Critically

20. on the eastern coast; good climate and soil for farming

21. economic isolation from other countries; increased protests

22. white descendants of original Dutch colonists who challenged British rule

23. unstable governments, lack of industry, ethnic conflicts, and disease

24. encouraged many Europeans to settle there and establish colonies

CHAPTER 13 Review and Practice

Define and Identify

Identify each of the following:

1. enclaves
2. the veld
3. pans
4. Boers
5. apartheid
6. Nelson Mandela
7. townships
8. sanctions
9. Desmond Tutu
10. Organization of African Unity (OAU)

Review the Main Ideas

11. What two South African countries are enclaves?

12. What are southern Africa's two deserts like?

13. What natural resources are very plentiful in southern Africa?

14. How did traders travel between Africa and Asia?

15. What did the original Bantu migrants bring to southern Africa?

16. How have mineral resources affected South Africa?

17. What form of art have artists in Zimbabwe revived?

18. Why are some animals found only in Madagascar?

19. What three racial groups were defined and separated by apartheid? Which group made up the majority of the population?

Think Critically

20. Drawing Inferences and Conclusions In what parts of southern Africa do you think most farming takes place? Why?

21. Analyzing Information What finally motivated the South African government to end the apartheid system?

22. Summarizing Who were the Afrikaners, and what role did they play in the history of southern Africa?

23. Summarizing What factors have slowed the economic development of the countries in this region?

24. Finding the Main Idea How did the discovery of diamonds and gold affect the settlement of Europeans in southern Africa?

Map Activity

25. On a separate sheet of paper, match the letters on the map with their correct labels.

Drakensberg	Kalahari Desert
Inyanga Mountains	Namib Desert
	Orange River
Cape of Good Hope	Limpopo River
	Harare

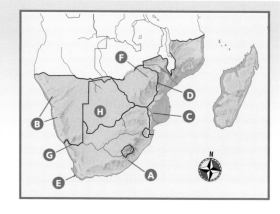

Map Activity

25. A. Drakensberg
B. Namib Desert
C. Limpopo River
D. Inyanga Mountains
E. Cape of Good Hope
F. Harare
G. Orange River
H. Kalahari Desert

Writing Activity

Write a brief essay in which you compare and contrast Botswana and Mozambique. How are the physical features of these two countries similar or different? How do these features affect the economies of Botswana and Mozambique? What are the major industries? Be sure to use standard grammar, spelling, sentence structure, and punctuation.

internet connect

Internet Activity: **go.hrw.com**
KEYWORD: **SK5 GT13**

Choose a topic to explore about southern Africa:

- Explore the Namib Desert.
- Go on a South African safari.
- Investigate apartheid.

Writing Activity

Student essays should describe the physical features, economies, and major industries of the two countries. Use Rubric 9, Comparing and Contrasting, to evaluate student work.

Analyzing Charts

1. about 20 percent
2. Botswana
3. Madagascar
4. yes, because large percentages of the adult population are infected

Analyzing Primary Sources

1. apartheid
2. democracy
3. a society in which all persons live together in harmony and with equal opportunity
4. He may have feared that other means would be unsuccessful.

Social Studies Skills Practice

Analyzing Charts

Many people in southern Africa carry the HIV virus that causes the disease called AIDS. Study the following chart and then answer the questions.

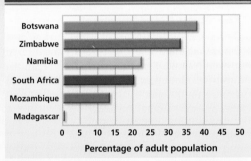

Adult Rate of HIV/AIDS

Percentage of adult population

Source: Central Intelligence Agency, *The World Factbook 2003*

1. What percentage of South Africa's adult population has HIV/AIDS?
2. Which country has the highest adult rate of HIV/AIDS?
3. Which country has the lowest adult rate of HIV/AIDS?
4. Based on the information in this chart, is AIDS a significant problem in most of southern Africa? Explain your answer.

Analyzing Primary Sources

On April 20, 1964, Nelson Mandela spoke at the opening of his trial. Read the following excerpt from his speech. Then answer the questions.

"I have fought against white domination [control], and I have fought against black domination. I have cherished the ideal of a democratic and free society in which all persons live together in harmony and with equal opportunities. It is an ideal which I hope to live for and to achieve. But if needs be, it is an ideal for which I am prepared to die."

1. What South African policy was Nelson Mandela fighting to abolish?
2. What type of government does Nelson Mandela cherish?
3. What are Nelson Mandela's goals?
4. Why might Mandela feel he must be prepared to die for his beliefs?

Southern Africa • 287

CHAPTER 13

REVIEW AND ASSESSMENT RESOURCES

Reproducible

- Readings in World Geography, History, and Culture 64, 65, and 66
- Critical Thinking Activity 13
- Vocabulary Activity 13

Technology

- Chapter 13 Test Generator (on the One-Stop Planner)

- HRW Go site
- Audio CD Program, Chapter 13

Reinforcement Review, and Assessment

- Chapter 13 Review and Practice
- Chapter Summaries and Review
- Chapter 13 Test

- Chapter 13 Test for English Language Learners and Special-Needs Students
- Unit 6 Test
- Unit 6 Test for English Language Learners and Special-Needs Students

internet connect

GO TO: **go.hrw.com**
KEYWORD: **SK5 Teacher**
FOR: a guide to using the Internet in your classroom

GEOGRAPHY SIDELIGHT

In a country where women often do not participate in public life, Wangari Maathai is an exception. She holds a doctorate from the University of Nairobi and has received international recognition for her environmental activism.

In the late 1980s Maathai again acted on behalf of the environment. The major political party had wanted to build a skyscraper in a popular open space in downtown Nairobi. Maathai protested that it is as important to leave some land undeveloped for people as it is to preserve land for animals. She also protested the high cost of developing the area. The money was to be borrowed from foreign banks. Maathai protested that any more borrowed money should go to feeding, educating, and helping Kenya's people.

In early 1999 Maathai and several supporters were severely beaten when they tried to plant trees in a forest on Nairobi's outskirts.

Critical Thinking: How has Wangari Maathai worked to protect the environment?

Answer: She protested the development of a space in downtown Nairobi, saying that the money should be used for the people.

➤ **This Focus On Environment feature addresses National Geography Standards 4, 13, 14, and 16.**

FOCUS ON ENVIRONMENT

Kenya's Tree Planters

Twenty million young trees scattered throughout Kenya offer new hope to farmers and families. The trees were planted by women who farm these lands. "We are planting trees to ensure our own survival," says Wangari Maathai. She is the founder of Kenya's Green Belt Movement.

Deforestation

Like many other developing countries, Kenya is a country of farmers and herders. The most productive farmlands are in the highlands. This area was once green with trees and plants. Over the past century, however, much of this land has been cleared. Today, less than 10 percent of the original forests remain. Many trees were cut for firewood, which people use for cooking.

Without tree roots to hold the soil in place, the land eroded. The land was losing its fertility.

Farmers moved to the savannas in search of better land.

Wangari Maathai recognized what was happening. "When I would visit the village where I was born," she says, "I saw whole forests had been cleared for cultivation and timber. People were moving onto hilly slopes and riverbeds and marginal areas that were only bush when I was a child." Maathai was shocked to find children suffering from malnutrition. People were no longer eating foods such as beans and corn. Instead, they were eating refined foods such as rice. They were doing this because these foods need less cooking—and thus less firewood.

The Green Belt Movement

On June 5, 1977, in honor of World Environment Day, Maathai and a few supporters planted seven trees in Nairobi, Kenya's capital. Thus began the Green Belt Movement. This movement then spread through the Kenyan highlands and captured people's attention around the world.

From the beginning, Maathai knew that the success of her efforts depended mainly on women. In Kenya, men tend cash crops such as coffee and cotton. Women collect firewood and grow corn, beans, and other food crops. It is the women who grow the food their families eat. The women were the first to see the connection between poor soil and famine.

◄
Human-Environment Interaction Many of the trees in Kenya's highlands have been cleared for crops.

FOCUS ON ENVIRONMENT

Solving Local Problems

After students have read the feature, ask if they were inspired by Wangari Maathai's story. Begin a class discussion about ways that individuals can be effective agents for change in their communities. Encourage students to talk about people they may know who address local problems as Maathai has done. Ask students to consider why Maathai's program was successful. (The people who were directly affected by the problem of soil erosion were encouraged to participate directly in the solution.)

The movement's workers encouraged women in Kenya to plant trees. They pointed out that women would not have to walk miles to collect firewood. They would have wood available nearby for fires, fences, and buildings. If the tree seedlings survived, the women would also be paid a small sum of money.

First, a few small nurseries were started to give out free seedlings. The nurseries are staffed by local women who are paid for their work. Nurseries also train and pay local people known as Green Belt Rangers. The Rangers visit farms, check on seedlings, and offer advice.

Before long, nurseries were appearing in communities throughout the highlands. Kenyan women talked to friends and neighbors about the benefits of planting trees. Neighbors encouraged Esther Wairimu to plant seedlings. Five years later, her fields were surrounded by mango, blue gum, and other trees. "I have learned that a tree… is life," she says.

Today, the advantages of planting trees are clear. Farmers now have fuel and shade. Even more important, the soil is being protected from

▲

(*Human-Environment Interaction*) Workers from the Green Belt Movement teach schoolchildren in Kenya how to care for tree seedlings.

erosion. The number of Green Belt nurseries has grown to about 5,000. Most are run by women.

Expanding the Movement

Maathai believes that local people must work together to protect the environment. She stresses that the Green Belt Movement relies on farmers. The movement receives little government support. Most of the money comes from small personal donations.

Now Maathai dreams of spreading her movement to other African countries. "We must never lose hope…," she says. "One person *can* make a difference."

Wangari Maathai (right) has encouraged Kenyan women to plant millions of trees. Women are paid for the seedlings they plant that survive.

▼

Going Further: Thinking Critically

Point out that the feature emphasizes the geography element of environment and society. Ask students to draw a before-and-after picture that illustrates how the interaction between environment and society was both harmful and beneficial to Kenya (harmful: people cleared the forests to obtain firewood, causing soil erosion; beneficial: people planted trees to restore the soil and water supply). Ask students if they think such problems can be avoided in the future. Why or why not? How might the problems be avoided?

PRACTICING
THE SKILL

1. Students should describe an ecosystem in their region and note how the plants and animals that live there depend on each other for survival.

2. Students might suggest that the disappearance of one group would seriously affect the well-being of other groups.

3. Students might suggest that construction or pollution have affected ecosystems in their community. Students will probably note that some plants and animals are disappearing as a result of pressures from human activities.

Geo SKILLS

Building Skills for Life: Understanding Ecosystems

The plants and animals in an area, together with the nonliving parts of their environment, form an ecosystem. An important thing to remember about ecosystems is that each part is interconnected.

Life on Earth depends on the energy and nutrients flowing through ecosystems. Energy and nutrients move between plants, animals, and soils through food chains and food webs.

Most ecosystems involve three groups of organisms: producers, consumers, and decomposers. Producers make their own food. Plants are producers. They make food by combining carbon dioxide, nutrients from the soil, sunlight, and water. Consumers are unable to make food. They have to get food from producers or from other consumers. Humans are consumers. We eat plants (producers) and animals (consumers). Decomposers get food from dead organisms and wastes. Bacteria and fungi are decomposers.

Elephants have adapted to the ecosystem of Africa's Namib Desert.

▼

Like all forms of life, humans depend on ecosystems for survival. Knowing how ecosystems work helps us understand how we are connected to both living and nonliving things. It can also help us manage, protect, and use our environments wisely.

THE SKILL

1. Describe an ecosystem in the region where you live. What plants and animals live there? How are they connected?

2. Make a table showing some of the producers, consumers, and decomposers in an ecosystem. What do you think would happen if one of these groups suddenly disappeared?

3. Try to identify some ways that human activities have changed ecosystems in your community. Have some plants or animals disappeared?

GEO SKILLS

Going Further: Thinking Critically

Ask students to identify an organism that is endangered or approaching extinction and to conduct research on the ecosystem in which their chosen organism lives. Then ask them to write an essay explaining the role of their organism in its ecosystem and how the disappearance of that organism would affect the ecosystem. Finally, have each student draw two diagrams—one that illustrates the organism's ecosystem and another that shows what the ecosystem would be like if the organism disappeared.

You may want to have students concentrate on plants or animals often viewed as unattractive or a nuisance. For example, some people do not like snakes or bats, and many species of both animals are endangered. They are as important to their ecosystems as koalas, tigers, or giant pandas are to theirs. If you choose this option, have students create a public awareness campaign that highlights the entire ecosystem's health. You might also ask students to create a mascot for the campaign to enhance the image of the species.

HANDS on GEOGRAPHY

Like all organisms, lions are part of an ecosystem. Lions survive by killing and eating other animals, such as zebras and gazelles. After lions have killed an animal, they eat their fill. Then other animals such as vultures and hyenas eat what is left.

The lion itself is food for other organisms. Small animals like ticks, fleas, and mosquitoes drink the lion's blood. The lion's waste serves as food for organisms that live in the soil. When the lion dies, it will be eaten by other animals.

How does the lion fit into its ecosystem? You can answer this question by drawing a connections web. These guidelines will help you get started.

1. Draw a picture of a lion.

2. Think of interactions that lions have with other parts of their environment.

3. Include these interactions in your drawing. For example, lions eat zebras, so you could add a zebra to your drawing.

4. Draw lines connecting the lion to other parts of its environment. For example, you could draw a line connecting the lion and the zebra.

5. Be sure to extend the connections to include nonliving parts of the environment as well. For example, lions eat

zebras, zebras eat grass, and grass depends on sunlight.

6. Continue making connections on your diagram. When you are done, answer the Lab Report questions.

Lab Report

1. Label the producers, consumers, and decomposers on your connections web. To which group do lions belong?

2. How are lions dependent on nonliving parts of their environment?

3. Imagine there are no more lions. How do you think the ecosystem shown in your connections web would be affected?

Lab Report

Answers

1. Students' webs should be clearly labeled and should identify lions as consumers.

2. Lions are indirectly dependent on nonliving parts of the environment, such as sunlight. Sunlight helps grass grow. Zebras eat the grass. Lions eat the zebras.

3. Students should demonstrate how the disappearance of lions could cause overpopulation and eventual starvation for the zebras. The vultures and hyenas may also be adversely affected. Also, insects and small organisms in the soil would have less food.

Southern Africa 291

UNIT OBJECTIVES

1. Describe how landforms, climate, and water resources affect the way people live in South Asia.

2. Identify the natural resources of South Asia, and link them to the region's economic development.

3. Trace the history of South Asia, and identify the interactions through time of the region's cultural groups.

4. Analyze the social and environmental challenges facing the nations of South Asia.

5. Interpret special-purpose maps for insight into how the people of South Asia adapt to geographical differences within the region.

UNIT 4

South Asia

CHAPTER 14
India

CHAPTER 15
India's Neighbors

Swayambhunath Stupa, Kathmandu, Nepal

Karakoram Range, Pakistan

292 • Unit 4

USING THE ILLUSTRATIONS

Direct students' attention to the photos on these pages. Point out the Karakoram Range on a wall map. The Karakorams are part of a mountain system that includes the Himalayas.

Note the small photo of the Bengal tiger. You may want to direct students' attention to the Focus On Environment feature at the end of this unit. It describes efforts to save the dwindling tiger population of South Asia.

Point out the polo players at an elephant festival. Polo, a sport that involves hitting a ball with a long-handled mallet, is traditionally played on horseback. In South Asia there are indeed polo matches played while riding elephants.

The girls in the center photo are from Rajasthan. You may want to locate a map of India that shows the individual states and have students find Rajasthan in the northwestern part of the country.

Finally, point out Swayambhunath Stupa. One may avoid the tongue-twisting name by using its other name, the Monkey Temple, which refers to the many monkeys that live there.

A Scholar in India

Emily K. Bloch coordinates educational programs at the South Asia Outreach center at the University of Chicago. Her special area of interest is South Asian children's literature. Here she describes the many types of transportation she has used in India. **WHAT DO YOU THINK?** *Which type of transportation would you enjoy the most?*

In my travels throughout India, I've had the good fortune to ride on a variety of vehicles. I've ridden in buses and cycle-rickshaws, taxis and three-wheeled scooters, on a motorcycle through Calcutta and on the crossbar of a bicycle. I rode in a howdah [seat] on the back of an elephant in a wildlife sanctuary. I even had an uncomfortable, but very welcome, lift in a bullock cart.

But my favorite mode of travel is also one of the most popular in India— riding the great trains. The railway, with more than 1.5 million employees, is the largest employer in the world. It has nearly 40,000 miles of track. Eleven thousand trains, connecting more than 7,000 stations, carry about 12 million people daily. Though the luxury of the princely rail lines beckons, and the first-class cars provide food and bed-linens, I love the crowded, second-class, wooden-benches experience and look forward to my next journey side by side with my fellow Indian and foreign travelers.

Women in festival dress, Rajasthan, India

Polo players at elephant festival, Jaipur, India

Understanding Primary Sources

1. What do Emily Bloch's transportation experiences illustrate about the use of technology in India?

2. Which method of travel does Emily Bloch prefer? Why?

White Bengal tiger

South Asia **293**

MORE FROM THE FIELD

As a British colony, India was a land where more than 1,000 languages were spoken. Society was further divided by religion and the caste system.

Construction of the railroads, which began in the 1850s, helped unite India politically and economically. The railroads provided a way for India's agricultural products and natural resources to reach the port cities and thus to reach world markets.

Critical Thinking: How did railroads affect Indian economic development?

Answer: provided a way to get products to port cities and world markets

Understanding Primary Sources
Answers

1. The many types of transportation indicate that there is a wide range in the use of technology in India, and that economic factors probably determine what type of transportation people in India use.

2. riding the trains; seems to provide a closer relation-ship with the people of India

CHAPTERS

14 **India**
explores the geography and cultural diversity of the largest country in South Asia. It also describes the serious economic and environmental challenges facing India.

15 **India's Neighbors**
profiles the six countries that surround India: Pakistan, Nepal, Bhutan, Bangladesh, Sri Lanka, and the Maldives.

PEOPLE IN THE PROFILE

Note that the elevation profile crosses the eastern part of India that is almost cut off from the rest of the country. Assam is one of the states in the area.

About two thirds of the state's working population is involved in agriculture. Festivals in Assam are important social and cultural events. Not surprisingly, the three chief nonreligious festivals, called Bihu, are related to agriculture. The Bohag Bihu—also known as the Rongali Bihu—takes place in April and celebrates the new year, the arrival of spring, and the beginning of the planting season. The Bohag Bihu lasts for several days. One of its main attractions is dancing.

The Magh Bihu in mid-January is a harvest festival. Feasting is its key activity. The third main festival is the Kangali Bihu, which is held in October. *Kangali* means "poor," and this festival occurs at a time of the year when most people have already consumed most of their stored food grains.

Critical Thinking: How does Assam's dependence on agriculture influence its celebrations?

Answer: Festivals are based on agriculture and celebrate it with dancing and feasting.

South Asia

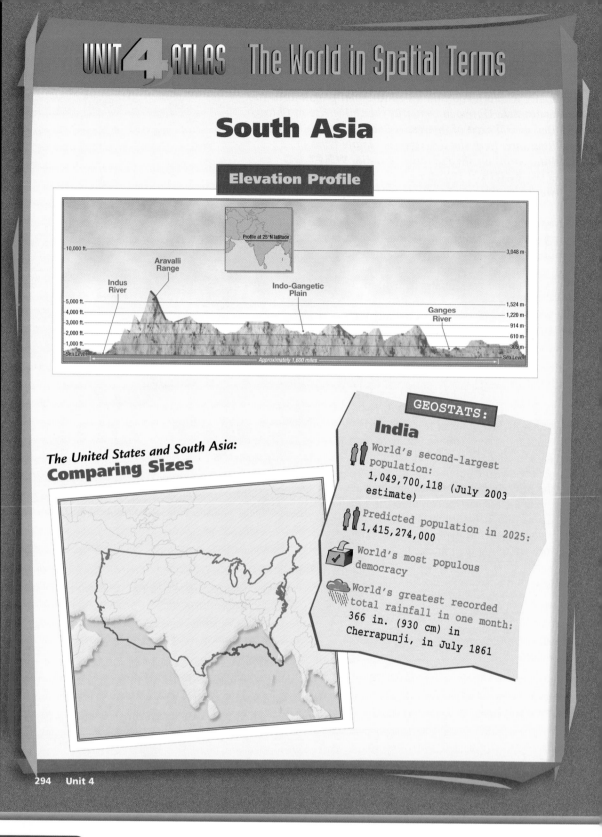

Elevation Profile

Profile at 25°N latitude

10,000 ft. — 3,048 m

Aravalli Range

Indus River

Indo-Gangetic Plain

5,000 ft. — 1,524 m
4,000 ft. — 1,220 m
3,000 ft. —
2,000 ft. —
1,000 ft. —
Sea Level

Ganges River

914 m
610 m
305 m
Sea Level

Approximately 1,600 miles

The United States and South Asia:
Comparing Sizes

GEOSTATS:

India

World's second-largest population: 1,049,700,118 (July 2003 estimate)

Predicted population in 2025: 1,415,274,000

World's most populous democracy

World's greatest recorded total rainfall in one month: 366 in. (930 cm) in Cherrapunji, in July 1861

OVERVIEW

In this unit, students will learn about the geographic and cultural contrasts of South Asia, one of the most densely populated regions on Earth.

The Indian Subcontinent is separated from the rest of Asia by the highest mountains in the world. The Himalayas drop to the fertile Gangetic Plain. Plateau and desert lands lie to the south and west. Climate patterns are greatly influenced by monsoon winds that bring wet and dry seasons to much of the region.

India dominates the subcontinent. With more than 1 billion people, it is the world's most populous democracy. It is a land of stunning contrasts—from nuclear technology and a strong computer industry to subsistence farming and homeless city-dwellers. Ancient customs sometimes clash with modern trends. Conflicts between India and its neighbors over territory increase political tensions.

The surrounding countries also face the difficult tasks of feeding their growing populations and of developing their economies while protecting the environment.

South Asia: Physical

UNIT 4 ATLAS

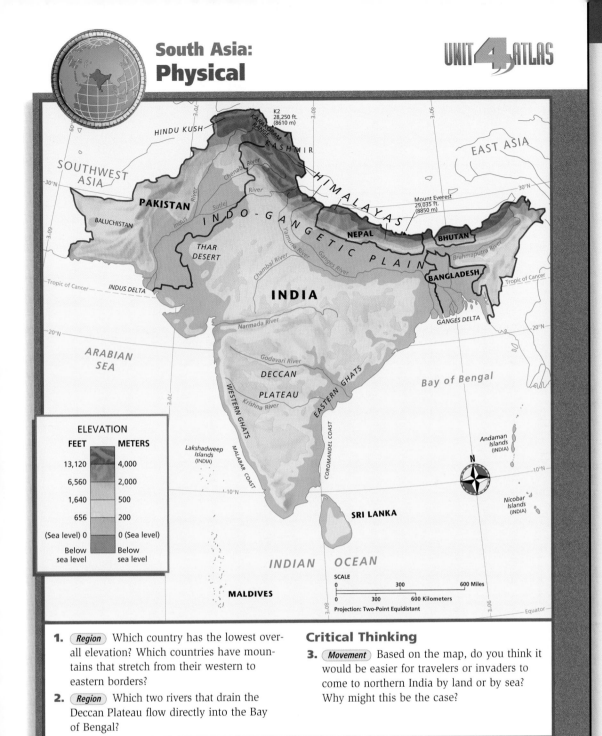

ELEVATION

FEET	METERS
13,120	4,000
6,560	2,000
1,640	500
656	200
(Sea level) 0	0 (Sea level)
Below sea level	Below sea level

SCALE
0 ⸻ 300 ⸻ 600 Miles
0 ⸻ 300 ⸻ 600 Kilometers
Projection: Two-Point Equidistant

1. (Region) Which country has the lowest overall elevation? Which countries have mountains that stretch from their western to eastern borders?

2. (Region) Which two rivers that drain the Deccan Plateau flow directly into the Bay of Bengal?

Critical Thinking

3. (Movement) Based on the map, do you think it would be easier for travelers or invaders to come to northern India by land or by sea? Why might this be the case?

South Asia • 295

Physical Map

Answers
1. Bangladesh; Nepal, Bhutan

2. Godavari and Krishna Rivers

Critical Thinking
3. by sea; because they could more easily sail up the rivers than cross the mountain ranges

---

USING THE PHYSICAL MAP

Have students examine the **physical map** on this page and identify South Asia's three major landform regions. (Students should name the Himalayas, the Gangetic Plain, and the Deccan Plateau.) Then call on a student to describe the courses of the three main rivers that flow from the Himalayas—the Indus, the Ganges, and the Brahmaputra.

Call on a volunteer to identify the two mountain ranges that are part of the Himalayas (Hindu Kush, Karakoram Range).

Your Classroom Time Line

These are the major dates and time periods for this unit. Have students enter them on the time line you created earlier. You may want to watch for these dates as students progress through the unit.

c. 2500 B.C. Civilization develops in the Indus River valley.

c. 1750 B.C. Indo-Aryans move into northern India.

c. 1500 B.C. The Indus civilization disappears.

c. 500 B.C. Siddhartha Gautama establishes Buddhism.

A.D. 1000 Muslim armies begin raiding northwestern India.

*c. stands for *circa* and means "about."

Political Map
Answers

1. Maldives and Sri Lanka; Sri Lanka

2. Bangladesh

3. Nepal and Bhutan

Critical Thinking

4. Students might suggest that the physical separation between the two territories may have fostered Bangladeshis' psychological sense of separation from Pakistan.

South Asia: Political

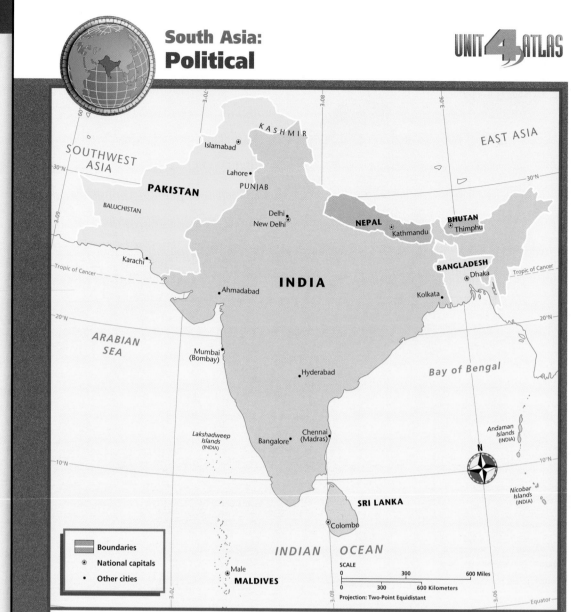

Map legend:
- Boundaries
- ⊛ National capitals
- • Other cities

SCALE
0 — 300 — 600 Miles
0 — 300 — 600 Kilometers
Projection: Two-Point Equidistant

Labels on map: KASHMIR, SOUTHWEST ASIA, Islamabad, Lahore, PAKISTAN, PUNJAB, BALUCHISTAN, Karachi, Delhi, New Delhi, NEPAL, Kathmandu, BHUTAN, Thimphu, EAST ASIA, BANGLADESH, Dhaka, Tropic of Cancer, Ahmadabad, INDIA, Kolkata, ARABIAN SEA, Mumbai (Bombay), Hyderabad, Bay of Bengal, Lakshadweep Islands (INDIA), Bangalore, Chennai (Madras), Andaman Islands (INDIA), Nicobar Islands (INDIA), SRI LANKA, Colombo, INDIAN OCEAN, Male, MALDIVES, Equator

1. (*Place*) What are the region's two island countries? Which is larger?

2. (*Location*) Which country is almost completely surrounded by India?

3. (*Region*) Compare this map to the **physical map**. Which small countries might be called the "Mountain Kingdoms?"

Critical Thinking

4. (*Location*) Bangladesh was once part of Pakistan. What role do you think Bangladesh's location may have played in its drive for independence?

USING THE POLITICAL MAP

 While students examine the **political map** of South Asia on this page, ask what is unusual about the boundary of India. (Students should note that a small part of the country connects with the remainder by a narrow strip of land.) Call on a volunteer to suggest why part of the region known as Kashmir is in Pakistan and part is in India. (The region is claimed by both countries.)

internet connect

ONLINE ATLAS
GO TO: go.hrw.com
KEYWORD: SK5 MapsU4
FOR: Web links to online maps of the region

South Asia: Climate

UNIT **4** ATLAS

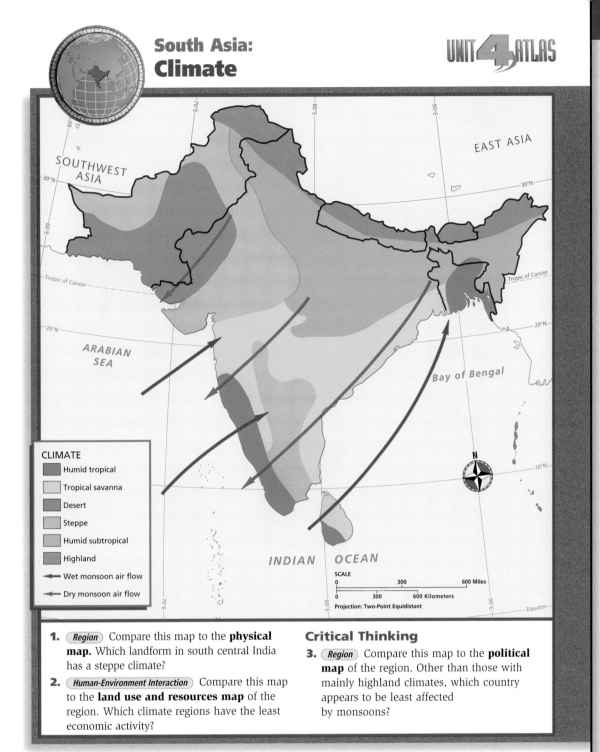

CLIMATE
- Humid tropical
- Tropical savanna
- Desert
- Steppe
- Humid subtropical
- Highland
- ← Wet monsoon air flow
- ← Dry monsoon air flow

SOUTHWEST ASIA

EAST ASIA

ARABIAN SEA

Bay of Bengal

INDIAN OCEAN

Tropic of Cancer

Tropic of Cancer

Equator

SCALE
0   300   600 Miles
0   300   600 Kilometers
Projection: Two-Point Equidistant

1. (Region) Compare this map to the **physical map.** Which landform in south central India has a steppe climate?

2. (Human-Environment Interaction) Compare this map to the **land use and resources map** of the region. Which climate regions have the least economic activity?

Critical Thinking

3. (Region) Compare this map to the **political map** of the region. Other than those with mainly highland climates, which country appears to be least affected by monsoons?

South Asia • 297

Your Classroom Time Line, (continued)

A.D. **1200s** A Muslim kingdom is established at Delhi.

1400s Sikhism begins.

1505 The Portuguese establish a trading post in Sri Lanka.

early 1500s The Mughal Empire comes to power.

1600s The English East India Company wins rights to trade in the Mughal Empire.

1700s–1800s The British slowly take control of India.

1700s The British receive Sri Lanka from the Dutch.

1857 Indian sepoys revolt against the British.

1885 Nationalists create the Indian National Congress.

1947 The British divide their Indian colony into India and Pakistan.

1948 Sri Lanka gains its independence from Britain.

1953 Tenzing Norgay and Sir Edmund Hillary reach the summit of Mount Everest.

Climate Map

Answers
1. Deccan Plateau
2. highland and desert climates

Critical Thinking
3. Pakistan

USING THE CLIMATE MAP

Have students look closely at the **climate map** on this page and compare it to the **physical map** of the region. Ask students the following questions: What is the dominant climate in Pakistan? (desert) Which country in the region has mostly humid tropical and humid subtropical climates?(Bangladesh) Which island country has tropical savanna and humid tropical climates? (Sri Lanka) What low mountain range appears to catch much of the rain from the wet monsoon? (Western Ghats)

Your Classroom Time Line,
(continued)

1971 East Pakistan breaks away from West Pakistan, forming independent Bangladesh.

1984 The Indian government uses force to defeat Sikh rebels.

1990 Muslim separatist groups begin campaign of violence in Kashmir.

1998 India carries out nuclear tests.

1999 General Pervez Musharraf leads a military takeover of Pakistan.

2000 India marks birth of its billionth citizen.

2003 Pakistan and India agree to a cease-fire in Kashmir.

2004 Nepal joins the World Trade Organization (WTO).

☑ internet connect

ONLINE ATLAS
GO TO: go.hrw.com
KEYWORD: SK5 MapsU4
FOR: Web links to online maps of the region

Population Map

Answers
1. Kolkata
2. Indo-Gangetic Plain

Critical Thinking
3. dry climates and few other resources

South Asia:
Population

POPULATION DENSITY

Persons per sq. mile	Persons per sq. km
520	200
260	100
130	50
25	10
3	1
0	0

● Metropolitan areas with more than 2 million inhabitants

○ Metropolitan areas with 1 million to 2 million inhabitants

SCALE
0   300   600 Miles
0   300   600 Kilometers
Projection: Two-Point Equidistant

1. (Location) Compare this map to the **physical map**. Which large Indian city is located on the Ganges Delta?

2. (Region) Compare this map to the **physical map** of the region. What is the name of the large densely populated area in the northeastern part of the region?

Critical Thinking

3. (Human-Environment Interaction) Compare this map to the **climate** and **land use and resources maps**. Why do you think few people live along the western and eastern edges of Pakistan?

USING THE POPULATION MAP

As students examine the **population map** on this page, ask them to write a general statement about the population pattern in South Asia. (Example: South Asia is a densely populated region with many large cities.)

Have students compare this map to the **physical map**. Call on a volunteer to identify the country with more than 520 people per square mile throughout most of its area. (Bangladesh) What desert area has more than 260 residents per square mile? (a narrow strip of land in southern Pakistan) What physical feature makes this dense population possible? *(the Indus River)*

South Asia:
Land Use and Resources

UNIT 4 ATLAS

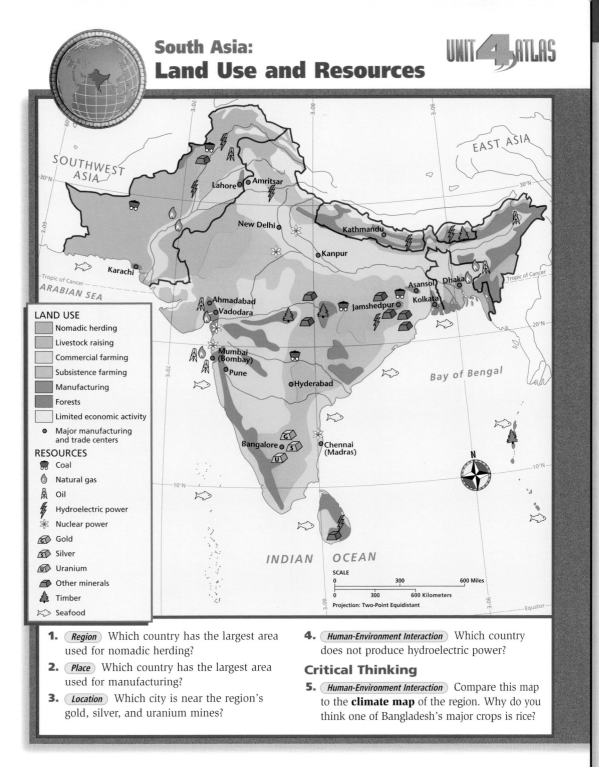

LAND USE
- Nomadic herding
- Livestock raising
- Commercial farming
- Subsistence farming
- Manufacturing
- Forests
- Limited economic activity
- ● Major manufacturing and trade centers

RESOURCES
- Coal
- Natural gas
- Oil
- Hydroelectric power
- Nuclear power
- G Gold
- S Silver
- U Uranium
- Other minerals
- Timber
- Seafood

SCALE
0 — 300 — 600 Miles
0 — 300 — 600 Kilometers
Projection: Two-Point Equidistant

1. (Region) Which country has the largest area used for nomadic herding?

2. (Place) Which country has the largest area used for manufacturing?

3. (Location) Which city is near the region's gold, silver, and uranium mines?

4. (Human-Environment Interaction) Which country does not produce hydroelectric power?

Critical Thinking

5. (Human-Environment Interaction) Compare this map to the **climate map** of the region. Why do you think one of Bangladesh's major crops is rice?

South Asia • 299

Land Use and Resources Map
Answers
1. Pakistan
2. India
3. Bangalore
4. Bangladesh
Critical Thinking
5. The country's wet, warm climate is good for growing rice.

USING THE LAND USE AND RESOURCES MAP

Focus students' attention on the **land use and resources map** on this page. Then ask students to answer the following questions: Which types of land use are most widespread in the region? (commercial farming, subsistence farming) Where is India's largest manufacturing and trade region? (on the Arabian Sea) Which cities are in that region? (Ahmadabad, Vadodara, Mumbai, and Pune)

Have students compare this map to the **physical map** of South Asia. Call on a volunteer to identify where in India timber is harvested and which river may be used to transport the timber to manufacturing centers (northern edge of the Deccan Plateau; Narmada River).

UNITED STATES OF AMERICA

CAPITAL:
Washington, D.C.

AREA:
3,717,792 sq. mi.
(9,629,091 sq km)

POPULATION:
290,342,554

MONEY:
U.S. dollar

LANGUAGES:
English, Spanish (spoken by a large minority)

ARABLE LAND:
19 percent

South Asia

BANGLADESH

CAPITAL:
Dhaka

AREA:
55,598 sq. mi.
(144,000 sq km)

POPULATION:
138,448,210

MONEY:
taka

LANGUAGES:
Bangla (official), English

ARABLE LAND:
73 percent

BHUTAN

CAPITAL:
Thimphu

AREA:
18,147 sq. mi.
(47,000 sq km)

POPULATION:
2,139,549

MONEY:
ngultrum, Indian rupee

LANGUAGES:
Dzongkha

ARABLE LAND:
2 percent

Crystal clear waters in the Maldives

INDIA

CAPITAL:
New Delhi

AREA:
1,269,338 sq. mi.
(3,287,590 sq km)

POPULATION:
1,049,700,118

MONEY: Indian rupee

LANGUAGES:
Hindi (official), English (associate official), 14 other official languages, many ethnic languages

ARABLE LAND: 56 percent

MALDIVES

CAPITAL:
Male

AREA:
116 sq. mi.
(300 sq km)

POPULATION:
329,684

MONEY:
rufiyaa

LANGUAGES:
Maldivian Dhivehi, English

ARABLE LAND:
10 percent

Countries not drawn to scale.

internet connect

ONLINE ATLAS
GO TO: go.hrw.com
KEYWORD: SK3 MapsU5
FOR: Web links to online maps of the region

FAST FACTS ACTIVITIES

LEVEL 1: (Suggested time: 30 min.) Provide students with a copy of the following table. Explain that imports are goods bought from other countries and that exports are goods sold to other countries. Ask students which two South Asian countries import more than twice as much as they export (Maldives and Nepal). If students do not know the term, point out that this type of imbalance is called a trade deficit. Then ask students what effect a trade deficit might have on a country's economy. (A trade deficit generally weakens a country's economy.)

Imports and Exports of South Asia

	Imports	Exports
Bangladesh	$8.5 billion	$6.2 billion
Bhutan	$196 million	$154 million
India	$53.8 billion	$44.5 billion
Maldives	$395 million	$110 million
Nepal	$1.6 billion	$720 million
Pakistan	$11.1 billion	$9.8 billion
Sri Lanka	$5.4 billion	$4.6 billion
United States	$1.17 trillion	$687 billion

Source: *The World Almanac and Book of Facts, 2003*

Buddhist monks in Kandy, Sri Lanka

UNIT 4 ATLAS

UNIT 4 ASSESSMENT RESOURCES

Reproducible
- Unit 4 Test
- Unit 4 Test for English Language Learners and Special-Needs Students

NEPAL

CAPITAL:
Kathmandu

AREA:
54,363 sq. mi.
(140,800 sq km)

POPULATION:
26,469,569

MONEY:
Nepalese rupee

LANGUAGES:
Nepali (official), other ethnic languages

ARABLE LAND:
17 percent

SRI LANKA

CAPITAL: Colombo

AREA:
25,332 sq. mi.
(65,610 sq km)

POPULATION:
19,742,439

MONEY:
Sri Lankan rupee

LANGUAGES:
Sinhala, Tamil, English

ARABLE LAND:
14 percent

internet connect

COUNTRY STATISTICS
GO TO: go.hrw.com
KEYWORD: SK5 FactsU4
FOR: more facts about South Asia

PAKISTAN

CAPITAL:
Islamabad

AREA:
310,401 sq. mi.
(803,940 sq km)

POPULATION:
150,694,740

MONEY:
Pakistani rupee

LANGUAGES:
Punjabi, Sindhi, Siraiki, Pashtu, Urdu (official), Balochi, Hindko, Brahui, English, many ethnic languages

ARABLE LAND:
27 percent

Sources: Central Intelligence Agency, *The World Factbook 2003;*
The World Almanac and Book of Facts 2003; pop. figures are 2003 estimates.

internet connect

COUNTRY STATISTICS
GO TO: go.hrw.com
KEYWORD: SK5 MapsU4

Highlights of Country Statistics
Links to online country statistics for South Asia include:
- *CIA World Factbook*
- Library of Congress country studies
- Flags of the world

301

FAST FACTS ACTIVITIES

LEVEL 2: (Suggested time: 40 min.) Call attention to the percentage of arable land listed for each country in the Fast Facts feature. Remind students that arable land is land suitable for growing crops. Refer students to this unit's atlas, to note the landform and climatic conditions of the South Asian countries. Have students write a paragraph about the correlations between the type of landforms, climate, and the percent of arable land. Ask them to provide specific examples to support their reasoning.

LEVEL 3: (Suggested time: 45 min.) Have students work in groups to prepare news bulletins for a South Asian country. Coverage may include weather, economic outlook, and other stories. Encourage students to use the Fast Facts feature, this unit's atlas, and information throughout the unit in their reports. (Example: "Welcome to Bangladesh Nightly News. Earlier today, the annual monsoon season kicked off to a roaring start, drenching the capital city of Dhaka. In economic news, economists predict that the taka's value will soon change as imports again surpass exports, climbing past the $8.5 billion mark.")

CHAPTER 14

India
Chapter Resource Manager

Objectives	Pacing Guide	Reproducible Resources
SECTION 1 **Physical Geography** (pp. 303–05) **1.** Identify the main landform regions of India. **2.** Identify the major rivers in India. **3.** Identify the climate types of India. **4.** Identify the natural resources of India.	**Regular** .5 day Lecture Notes, Section 1 **Block Scheduling** .5 day *Block Scheduling Handbook, Chapter 14*	**RS** Know It Notes S1 **ELL** Main Idea Activity S1
SECTION 2 **India's History** (pp. 306–11) **1.** Identify the outside groups that affected India's history. **2.** Describe the Mughal Empire. **3.** Describe how Great Britain gained control of India. **4.** Describe why India was divided when it became independent.	**Regular** 2 days Lecture Notes, Section 2 **Block Scheduling** .5 day *Block Scheduling Handbook, Chapter 14*	**RS** Know It Notes S2 **RS** Graphic Organizer 14 **E** Cultures of the World Activity 8 **E** Creative Strategies for Teaching World Geography, Lessons 20 and 21 **SM** Geography for Life Activity 30 **IC** Interdisciplinary Activities for the Middle Grades 33, 34, 35 **E** Biography Activity: Mohandas Gandhi **SM** Map Activity 14 **ELL** Main Idea Activity S2
SECTION 3 **India Today** (pp. 312–17) **1.** Identify the four major religions that originated in India. **2.** Explain the caste system. **3.** Identify the languages that are important in India. **4.** Describe the government and economy of India.	**Regular** 2 days Lecture Notes, Section 3 **Block Scheduling** .5 day *Block Scheduling Handbook, Chapter 14*	**RS** Know It Notes S3 **E** Biography Activity: Mohandas Gandhi **ELL** Main Idea Activity S3

Chapter Resource Key

RS Reading Support
IC Interdisciplinary Connections
E Enrichment
SM Skills Mastery
A Assessment
REV Review

ELL Reinforcement and English Language Learners and English for Speakers of Other Languages (ESOL)

 Transparencies

 CD–ROM

 Music

 Video

 go.hrw.com Internet

 Holt Presentation Maker Using Microsoft® PowerPoint®

 One-Stop Planner CD–ROM

See the *One-Stop Planner* for a complete list of additional resources for students and teachers.

One-Stop Planner CD–ROM

It's easy to plan lessons, select resources, and print out materials for your students when you use the *One-Stop Planner CD–ROM with Test Generator.*

HRW ONLINE RESOURCES

<u>GO TO: go.hrw.com</u>
Then type in a keyword.

TEACHER HOME PAGE
  KEYWORD: SK5 TEACHER

CHAPTER INTERNET ACTIVITIES
  KEYWORD: SK5 GT14

Choose an activity to:
• tour the regions of India.
• travel to ancient India.
• learn about Mohandas Gandhi.

CHAPTER ENRICHMENT LINKS
  KEYWORD: SK5 CH14

CHAPTER MAPS
  KEYWORD: SK5 MAPS14

ONLINE ASSESSMENT
Homework Practice
  KEYWORD: SK5 HP14
  Standardized Test Prep Online
  KEYWORD: SK5 STP14
  Rubrics
  KEYWORD: SS Rubrics

COUNTRY INFORMATION
  KEYWORD: SK5 Almanac

CONTENT UPDATES
  KEYWORD: SS Content Updates

HOLT PRESENTATION MAKER
  KEYWORD: SK5 PPT14

ONLINE READING SUPPORT
  KEYWORD: SS Strategies

CURRENT EVENTS
  KEYWORD: S5 Current Events

Technology Resources

 One-Stop Planner CD–ROM, Lesson 14.1

 Geography and Cultures Visual Resources with Teaching Activities 55–60

 ARGWorld CD–ROM

 Homework Practice Online
HRW Go site

 One-Stop Planner CD–ROM, Lesson 14.2

 ARGWorld CD–ROM

Music of the World Audio CD Program, Selection 17

Homework Practice Online
HRW Go site

 One-Stop Planner CD–ROM, Lesson 14.3

 ARGWorld CD–ROM

Homework Practice Online
HRW Go site

Review, Reinforcement, and Assessment Resources

ELL	Main Idea Activity S1
REV	Section 1 Review
A	Daily Quiz 14.1
REV	Chapter Summaries and Review
ELL	English Audio Summary 14.1
ELL	Spanish Audio Summary 14.1

ELL	Main Idea Activity S2
REV	Section 2 Review
A	Daily Quiz 14.2
REV	Chapter Summaries and Review
ELL	English Audio Summary 14.2
ELL	Spanish Audio Summary 14.2

ELL	Main Idea Activity S3
REV	Section 3 Review
A	Daily Quiz 14.3
REV	Chapter Summaries and Review
ELL	English Audio Summary 14.3
ELL	Spanish Audio Summary 14.3

Meeting Individual Needs

Ability Levels

Level 1 Basic-level activities designed for all students encountering new material

Level 2 Intermediate-level activities designed for average students

Level 3 Challenging activities designed for honors and gifted-and-talented students

ESOL Activities that address the needs of students with Limited English Proficiency

Chapter Review and Assessment

E	Readings in World Geography, History, and Culture 75 and 76	**A**	Chapter 14 Test
			Chapter 14 Test Generator (on the One-Stop Planner)
SM	Critical Thinking Activity 14		Audio CD Program, Chapter 14
REV	Chapter 14 Review and Practice	**A**	Chapter 14 Test for English Language Learners and
REV	Chapter Summaries and Review		Special-Needs Students
ELL	Vocabulary Activity 14		HRW Go Site

CHAPTER 14

India

Previewing Chapter Resources

Holt Online Learning

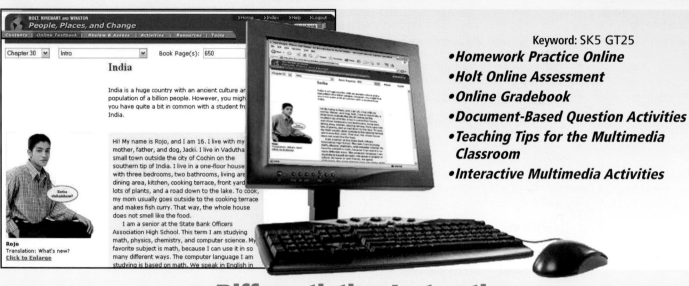

Keyword: SK5 GT25

- **Homework Practice Online**
- **Holt Online Assessment**
- **Online Gradebook**
- **Document-Based Question Activities**
- **Teaching Tips for the Multimedia Classroom**
- **Interactive Multimedia Activities**

Differentiating Instruction

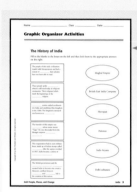

Reading and Writing Support

◄ Graphic Organizer Activity
- Vocabulary Activity
- Chapter Summary and Review
- Know It Notes
- Audio CD 6.1–4

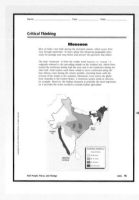

Active Learning

- Block Scheduling Handbook
- Cultures of the World Activity
- Interdisciplinary Activity
- Map Activity
◄ Critical Thinking Activity 30
- Music of the World CD: Ragas of India

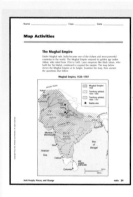

Primary Sources and Advanced Learners

- Geography for Life Activity: Mapping India's Historical Capital Cities
◄ Map Activity: The Mughal Empire
- Readings in World Geography, History and Culture:
  - 75 Bombay: City of Hope
  - 76 A Village Comes Into Its Own

Assessment Program

◄ Daily Quizzes S1–3
- Chapter Test
- Chapter Test for English Language Learners and Special-Needs Students

Spanish and ESOL

- Vocabulary Activity
◄ Main Idea Activities for English Language Learners and Special-Needs Students
- Chapter Summary and Review
- Spanish Audio Summary
- Know It Notes S1–3
- Chapter Test for English Language Learners and Special-Needs Students

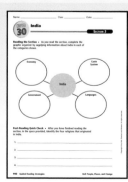

Special Education Modifications

Your **I.D.E.A. Works! CD-ROM** will provide modified versions of the following teaching materials:

◄ Guided Reading Strategies S1–3
- Vocabulary Activity
- Main Idea Activities S1–3
- Daily Quizzes S1–3
- Chapter 14 Test
- Flash cards of chapter vocabulary terms

Teacher Resources

Books for Teachers

Gadgil, Madhav, and Ramachandra Guha. *This Fissured Land: An Ecological History of India.* University of California Press, 1993.

Klass, Morton. *Caste: The Emergence of the South Asian Social System.* South Asia Books, 1998.

Yogananda, Paramhansa. *Autobiography of a Yogi.* Crystal Clarity Publications, 1999.

Books for Students

Das, Prodeepta. *I Is for India.* Silver Burdett, 1996. An alphabetical listing of historical and cultural information on India.

Krishnaswami, Uma. *Shower of Gold: Girls and Women in the Stories of India.* Shoe String/Linnet, 1999. Tales, folklore, fables, and legends based on the lives of real women.

Pollard, Michael. *The Ganges.* Great Rivers. Marshall Cavendish, 1997. Traces the river's course, describing its physical features, history, and importance.
SHELTERED ENGLISH

Rose, Deborah Lee. *The People Who Hugged the Trees: An Environmental Folk Tale.* Roberts Rinehart, 1994. Combines environmental protection, Indian geography, and conflict resolution.

Multimedia Materials

Ancient India. Transparency Kit. Glencoe.

Art and Architecture of India. Video, 75 min. Alarion Press.

The Dynasty: The Nehru-Gandhi Story. Video, 180 min. PBS.

Videos and CDs

Videos

- **CNN** *Presents Geography: Yesterday and Today, Segment 32 Indian Pop Music*
- **CNN** *Presents World Cultures: Yesterday and Today, Segment 3 The Sacred Ganges; Segment 10 Mother Teresa*
- *ARG World*

Holt Researcher

http://researcher.hrw.com

- *Gandhi, Mohandas*
- *Indo-Aryan Migration into India*
- *Chandragupta Maurya*
- *Mahal, Mumtaz*
- *Mother Teresa of Calcutta*
- *Nationalist Violence in India*
- *India*

Transparency Packages

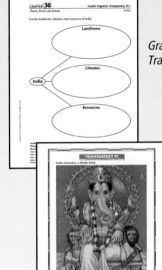

Graphic Organizer Transparencies 14.1–3

Geography and Cultures Visual Resources Transparencies 89–93
94 India: Physical-Political
95 Ganesh, A Hindu Deity

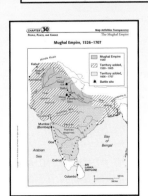

Map Activities Transparency 14 The Mughal Empire

There are many reasons why American students should know more about India.

▶ India is projected to become the world's most populous country within the next generation.

▶ India is one of the world's nuclear powers.

▶ It is essential to the future health of the world's economy that India, one of the world's poorest countries, continues to make economic progress.

▶ Many Indians and Indian-Americans now live and work in the United States.

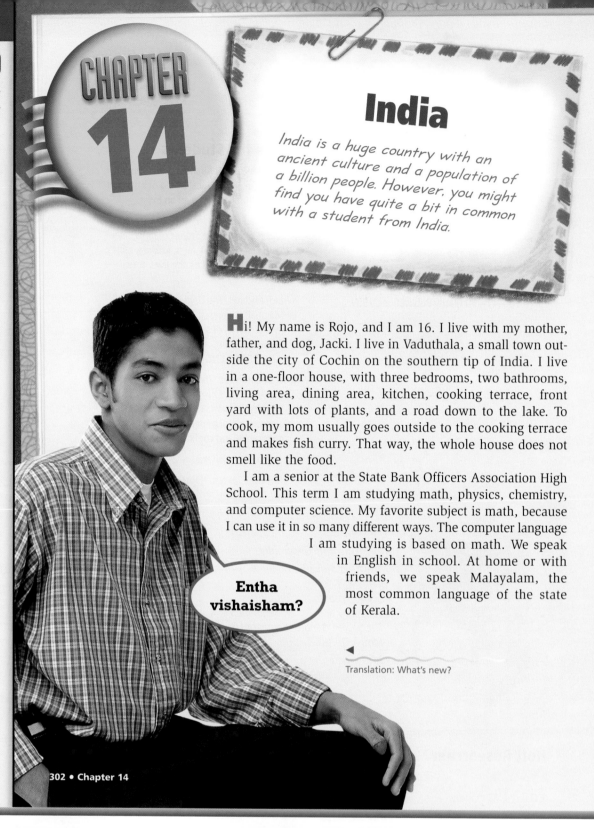

CHAPTER 14

India

India is a huge country with an ancient culture and a population of a billion people. However, you might find you have quite a bit in common with a student from India.

Hi! My name is Rojo, and I am 16. I live with my mother, father, and dog, Jacki. I live in Vaduthala, a small town outside the city of Cochin on the southern tip of India. I live in a one-floor house, with three bedrooms, two bathrooms, living area, dining area, kitchen, cooking terrace, front yard with lots of plants, and a road down to the lake. To cook, my mom usually goes outside to the cooking terrace and makes fish curry. That way, the whole house does not smell like the food.

I am a senior at the State Bank Officers Association High School. This term I am studying math, physics, chemistry, and computer science. My favorite subject is math, because I can use it in so many different ways. The computer language I am studying is based on math. We speak in English in school. At home or with friends, we speak Malayalam, the most common language of the state of Kerala.

Entha vishaisham?

◀ Translation: What's new?

302 • Chapter 14

CHAPTER PROJECT

Have students use the six essential elements of geography to create clothes-hanger mobiles about India. You may wish to refresh students' memories about the six elements. Display students' mobiles around the classroom. Then remove the hangers to place mobiles in students' portfolios.

STARTING THE CHAPTER

Ask students to think of images, places, or scenes that they associate with India. (Students might mention elephants, mountains, the Taj Mahal, cobras, or other images.) Tell students that India is undergoing rapid economic changes and that it is the site of a thriving software industry. Tell students that India also makes more movies than any other country in the world. Tell students they will learn that India is a mix of ancient and modern, urban and rural, rich and poor in this chapter.

Section 1 Physical Geography

Read to Discover

1. What are the three main landform regions of India?
2. What are the major rivers in India?
3. What climate types does India have?
4. What natural resources does India have?

Reading Strategy

READING ORGANIZER Before you read, create a spider map. Draw a circle in the center of a sheet of paper. Create four legs that you label Landforms, Rivers, Climate, and Resources. As you read this section, list what you learn about each topic beneath each leg.

Vocabulary

teak

Places

Gangetic Plain	Ganges River
Deccan	Bay of Bengal
Eastern Ghats	Brahmaputra River
Western Ghats	Thar Desert

SECTION 1 RESOURCES

Reproducible
- Lecture Notes, Section 1
- Block Scheduling Handbook, Chapter 14
- Know It Notes S1

Technology
- One-Stop Planner CD–ROM, Lesson 14.1
- Homework Practice Online
- Geography and Cultures Visual Resources with Teaching Activities 55–60
- HRW Go site

Reinforcement, Review, and Assessment
- Section 1 Review
- Daily Quiz 14.1
- Main Idea Activity S1
- Chapter Summaries and Review
- English Audio Summary 14.1
- Spanish Audio Summary 14.1

India: Physical-Political

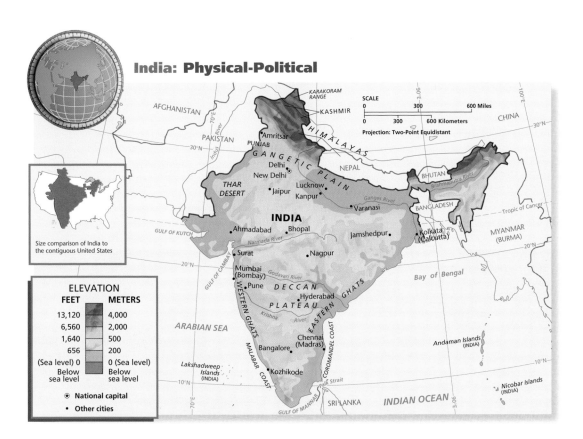

Size comparison of India to the contiguous United States

ELEVATION

FEET	METERS
13,120	4,000
6,560	2,000
1,640	500
656	200
(Sea level) 0	0 (Sea level)
Below sea level	Below sea level

⊛ National capital
• Other cities

India • 303

Section 1

Objectives

1. Identify the three main landform regions of India.
2. List the major rivers in India.
3. Describe India's climate types.
4. Discuss India's natural resources.

FOCUS

Bellringer

Copy the following instruction and question onto the chalkboard: *Examine the physical-political map in Section 1. What natural boundaries separate India from other countries?* Allow students to respond in writing. Students might suggest the Himalayan Mountains, the Thar Desert, the Arabian Sea, and the Bay of Bengal. Tell students that in Section 1 they will learn more about the physical geography of India.

Using the Physical-Political Map

Have students examine the map on this page. Have students name the major bodies of water that border India. Then ask them to name and describe the location of major landforms. Note the variety of landforms and elevations in India. Ask students where they think population is most heavily concentrated and why. (Possible answers: on the Gangetic Plain and along rivers, because of the availability of water)

India 303

internet connect

GO TO: go.hrw.com
KEYWORD: SK5 CH14
FOR: Web sites about India

DAILY LIFE

Questions of Purity and Pollution Many Hindus believe that in Varanasi, a Hindu holy city, the waters of the Ganges River can wash away sickness and sin. Religious pilgrims travel to Varanasi to bathe in the river. Also, some Hindus wish to be cremated on the banks of the Ganges. They believe that they will be freed from an endless cycle of rebirths.

Unfortunately, the Ganges River is highly polluted. Sewage and industrial waste contaminate the river. In addition, the dead bodies of people who cannot afford to be cremated are dumped into the river. However, local residents continue to use the river for doing laundry, bathing, or washing their hair. Some devoted Hindus refuse to believe that the holy river could be polluted. Since the mid-1980s environmental groups have worked to clean up the Ganges.

Critical Thinking: How has human activity changed the Ganges?

Answer: Sewage and industrial waste and dead bodies pollute the river.

Visual Record Answer ▶

It is a very fertile area for farmland.

A farmer plows rice fields in northern India. The Himalayas rise in the distance.

Interpreting the Visual Record
Human-Environment Interaction Why do so many of India's people live on the Gangetic Plain?

▼

Landforms

India has three main landform regions: the Himalayas, the Gangetic (gan-JE-tik) Plain, and the Deccan (DE-kuhn). The Himalayas run along the country's northern border and were created when two tectonic plates collided and pushed Earth's crust up.

The vast Gangetic Plain lies to the south of the Himalayas. It stretches about 1,500 miles (2,415 km) across northern India. About half of India's population lives there.

South of the Gangetic Plain is the triangular peninsula known as the Deccan. Most of its area is a plateau, which is divided by many hills and valleys. The plateau's edges are defined by the Eastern Ghats (GAWTS) and Western Ghats. These low mountain ranges separate the plateau's eastern and western edges from narrow coastal plains.

✓ **READING CHECK:** (*Places and Regions*) What are the three main landform regions of India? Himalayas, Gangetic Plain, Deccan

Rivers

India's most important river, the Ganges (GAN-jeez), begins on the southern slopes of the Himalayas. It then flows southeastward across northern India. It spreads into a huge delta before flowing into the Bay of Bengal. Hindus call the Ganges the "Mother River" and consider it sacred. Rich silt left by the Ganges has made the Gangetic Plain India's farming heartland.

The Brahmaputra (brahm-uh-POO-truh) River starts in the Plateau of Tibet. It flows through the far northeastern corner of India. From there the Brahmaputra flows southward through Bangladesh, where it empties into the Ganges Delta. The Narmada (nuhr-MUH-duh), Godavari (go-DAH-vuh-ree), and Krishna (KRISH-nuh) Rivers drain the Deccan. A large irrigation project along the Narmada River is under construction. It will include more than 40 branch canals.

✓ **READING CHECK:** (*Places and Regions*) What are India's most important rivers? Ganges, Brahmaputra, Narmada, Godavari, Krishna

304 Chapter 14

TEACH

Teaching Objectives 1–3

ALL LEVELS: (Suggested time: 30 min.) Have each student draw a simple map of India. Then have each student label and shade in different colors the three main landform regions of India, draw the four major rivers in blue, and then label the country's climate regions. (Students should label the Gangetic Plain, the Deccan, and the Himalayas; they should draw and identify the Narmada, Ganges, Godavari, and Krishna Rivers; they should also label the highland, humid tropical, tropical savanna, and steppe climates in the appropriate places.) Ask volunteers to share their maps with the class. **ESOL,** LS **KINESTHETIC**

Teaching Objective 4

ALL LEVELS: (Suggested time: 10 min.) Copy the following graphic organizer onto the chalkboard, omitting the blue answers. Use it to help students identify India's natural resources. Ask volunteers to share their answers. **ESOL,** LS **VISUAL-SPATIAL**

India's Natural Resources	
Mineral and Other Resources	Agricultural and Other Resources
iron ore, bauxite, uranium, coal, oil deposits, and gemstones	fertile farmlands and forests

Climate

India has a variety of climate types. Areas in the Himalayas have high-land climates with snow and glaciers. The Thar Desert near the border with Pakistan is hot and dry year-round. The Gangetic Plain has a humid tropical climate. Farther south in the Deccan there are tropical savanna and steppe climates.

Seasonal winds—monsoons—bring moist air from the Indian Ocean in summer. In winter the wind brings dry air from the Asian interior. The timing of the monsoons is very important to farmers in India. If the summer rains come too soon or too late, food production suffers.

✓ **READING CHECK:** (*Places and Regions*) What are India's climates?
highland, desert, humid tropical, tropoical savanna, steppe

Resources

India's fertile farmlands are important to its economy. Most of India's people work in agriculture. The country also produces cash crops for export. These include cashew nuts, cotton, jute, spices, sugarcane, tea, and tobacco.

Large deposits of iron ore, bauxite, uranium, and coal are among India's mineral resources. There are some oil reserves, but not enough to meet the country's needs. Gemstones are a valuable export.

India's forests are an important resource, as well as home to wildlife. **Teak**, one of the most valuable types of wood, grows in India and Southeast Asia. Teak is very strong and durable and is used to make ships and furniture.

✓ **READING CHECK:** (*Places and Regions*) What are India's natural resources?
fertile soil, minerals, some oil, forests

Our Amazing Planet

The city of Cherrapunji (cher-uh-POOHN-jee), in northeastern India, holds the world's record for rainfall in one year: almost 87 feet (26.5 m)!

Homework Practice Online
Keyword: SK5 HP14

Section Review 1

Define and explain: teak

Working with Sketch Maps On a map of India that you draw or that your teacher provides, label the following: Gangetic Plain, Deccan, Eastern Ghats, Western Ghats, Ganges River, Bay of Bengal, Brahmaputra River, and Thar Desert. How would you describe the relative location of India?

Reading for the Main Idea

1. (*Places and Regions*) What is the main mountain range of India?

2. (*Places and Regions*) What are some of India's most important cash crops? What type of wood is a valuable forest product?

Critical Thinking

3. Making Generalizations and Predictions What do you think happens to India's crops if the monsoon rains come too soon? too late?

4. Summarizing How does the Ganges affect economic activities in India?

Organizing What You Know

5. Summarizing Copy the following graphic organizer. Use it to list the landforms, climates, and resources of India.

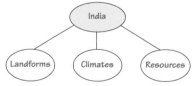

India • 305

Answers to Section 1 Review

Define For definition, see the glossary.

Working with Sketch Maps Maps will vary, but listed places should be labeled in their approximate locations. India's relative location is in southern Asia.

Reading for the Main Idea
1. the Himalayas (NGS 4)
2. cashew nuts, cotton, sugarcane, jute, spices, tea, and tobacco; teak (NGS 4)

Critical Thinking
3. Crops get rain too early and fail; crops dry up and fail. (NGS 7)
4. enriches the Gangetic Plain, makes it India's farming heartland

Organizing What You Know
5. landforms—the Himalayas, the Gangetic Plain, and the Deccan; climates—highland, desert, humid tropical, savanna, and steppe; resources—farmland, iron ore, bauxite, uranium, coal, oil deposits, gemstones, forests, and teak

CLOSE

Locate weather information on your area in a local newspaper to find the average annual rainfall. Ask students to compare this amount with the world record recorded in Cherrapunji, India, listed on this page in the Our Amazing Planet feature. Lead a discussion on how life in your area would change if you received the same amount of rain as Cherrapunji.

REVIEW, ASSESS, RETEACH

Have students complete the Section Review. Then pair students and have each pair write eight quiz questions about the landforms, bodies of water, climate types, and resources of India. Have each pair exchange its quiz with another pair and complete the quiz it receives. Then have students complete Daily Quiz 14.1. **COOPERATIVE LEARNING**

Have students complete Main Idea Activity S1. Then trace a wall map of India. Have each of three groups label one of the following: landform regions, climate types and regions, or natural resources. **ESOL, COOPERATIVE LEARNING**

EXTEND

Have interested students conduct research on Indian mythology associated with either the Ganges or Brahmaputra Rivers. Have students present an oral report summarizing the myth as well as a visual illustration of some aspect of the myth. **BLOCK SCHEDULING**

India 305

Visual Record Answer ▶

by the uniform size of the bricks and the straight rows of buildings

Section 2 India's History

Read to Discover

1. What outside groups affected India's history?
2. What was the Mughal Empire like?
3. How did Great Britain gain control of India?
4. Why was India divided when it became independent?

Vocabulary	Places	People
Sanskrit	Delhi	Harappans
sepoys	Kolkata	Akbar
boycott	Mumbai	Mohandas Gandhi

Reading Strategy

READING ORGANIZER Before you read, draw four large boxes down a sheet of paper. As you read this section, write what you learn in the boxes to create a chain of events in India's history.

Mohenjo Daro was one of the largest cities of the Harappan civilization.

Interpreting the Visual Record How might you tell from this photo that Harappan cities were well planned?

▼

Early Indian Civilizations

The first urban civilization on the Indian Subcontinent was centered around the Indus River valley. Its territory was mainly in present-day Pakistan but also extended into India. Scholars call this the Harappan civilization after one of its cities, Harappa. By about 2500 B.C. the people of this civilization were living in large, well-planned cities. Scholars believe the Harappans traded by sea with the peoples of Mesopotamia. The Harappans had a system of writing, but scholars have not been able to read it. As a result, very little is known about Harappan religion and customs.

306   Chapter 14

Section 2

Objectives

1. Identify the outside groups that have affected India's history.
2. Describe the Mughal Empire.
3. Explain how Great Britain gained control of India.
4. Discuss why India was divided when it became independent.

FOCUS

Bellringer

Copy the following question onto the chalkboard: *How might the physical boundaries of India have affected its history?* Have students respond in writing and discuss answers. Students might suggest that before technological advances permitted long sea voyages, India would have been protected from invasion. Tell students that in Section 2 they will learn more about the history and culture of India.

Building Vocabulary

Copy the vocabulary terms, **Sanskrit**, **sepoys**, and **boycott**, onto the chalkboard. Explain that Sanskrit is an ancient language that is used today for Hindu religious rituals. Sepoys were local Indian soldiers commanded by British officers. A boycott, or refusal to buy certain goods in protest, was an important tactic used by Indians against their British colonial rulers.

The Indo-Aryans By about 1500 B.C. a new group of people had come into northern India. Scholars call these people Indo-Aryans. Their language was an early form of **Sanskrit**. Sanskrit is still used in India in religious ceremonies.

The Indo-Aryans took control of northern India. These new arrivals mixed with Indian groups that were already living there. Their religious beliefs and customs mixed as well, forming the beginnings of the Hindu religion.

Hills and mountains prevented the Indo-Aryans from conquering southern India. However, Sanskrit and other Indo-Aryan cultural traits spread to the south.

The Coming of Islam About A.D. 1000, Muslim armies began raiding northwestern India. In the early 1200s a Muslim kingdom was established at Delhi. Because the monarch was known as a sultan, this kingdom was called the Delhi sultanate. The Delhi sultanate eventually gained control over most of northern India. It also became a leading center of Islamic art, culture, and science. Most Indians, however, kept their own religions and did not convert to Islam.

Over the next two centuries the Delhi sultanate expanded into the Deccan. However, in the early 1500s a new invasion from Central Asia swept into India. This new conquest marked the beginning of the Mughal (MOO-guhl) Empire.

✓ **READING CHECK:** *Human Systems* How did outside groups affect early Indian history? *Indo-Aryans—brought Sanskrit, formed beginnings of Hindu religion; Muslim armies—formed Deli sultanate; Central Asians—conquered Delhi sultanate, established Mughal Empire*

The Mughal Empire

The founder of the Mughal Empire was Babur, whose name meant "the Tiger." Babur was descended from Mongol emperor Genghis Khan. He was not only a brilliant general, but also a gifted poet. Babur defeated the last sultan of Delhi and took over most of northern India. After his death, however, Babur's lands were divided among his sons. They fought each other for years.

Babur's grandson, Akbar, finally emerged to reunite the Mughal Empire. He recaptured northern India and then expanded his empire into central India. Akbar was a good ruler as well as a successful conqueror. He reorganized the government and the tax system to make them more efficient. The fertile farmland and large population of the Gangetic Plain made the Mughal Empire rich. It quickly became one of the most powerful states in the world. The reign of Akbar and his successors was a golden age of architecture, painting, and poetry.

◄ **Place** This carved-lion pillar comes from Sarnath, an ancient city in northern India. The pillar was created in the 200s B.C. and is now the state emblem of India.

▲ This illustration is from a book of the life of Babur, the first Mughal emperor. It shows Babur surrounded by servants and nobles.

Across the Curriculum
LITERATURE

Sanskrit Sanskrit is one of the two classical languages of India. The other classical language is Tamil, a South Indian language that belongs to the Dravidian family of languages. Many ancient works of literature are written in both languages; however, only Tamil continues to be widely spoken today. Sanskrit is used mainly for Hindu religious rituals and ceremonies.

Unlike many languages, Sanskrit was formally developed by grammarians. These scholars created a broad set of rules for Sanskrit's usage. The grammarian Panini, who lived about 400 B.C., wrote the most famous set of rules for Sanskrit.

Many works of Indian literature were written in Sanskrit. Famous Sanskrit works include the *Ramayana* and the *Mahabharatha*, which are known around the world. Both are epic poems that examine themes such as loyalty, duty, and love.

Activity: Have students find and read an epic poem, such as the *Iliad, Song of Roland,* or *Beowulf.* Then lead a class discussion on what information these epics provide about the cultures in which they were created.

TEACH

Teaching Objective 1

ALL LEVELS: (Suggested time: 15 min.) Copy the following graphic organizer onto the chalkboard, omitting the blue answers. Use it to help students identify various groups that affected India's history. Have each student complete the organizer by filling in the names of the outside and inside groups identified in the section. Have each student also provide a short description of how each outside group affected India's history. Ask volunteers to share their answers with the class. **ESOL**

Groups That Affected India's History

OUTSIDE GROUPS
- Indo-Aryans had brought their language and religious beliefs by about 1500 B.C.
- First Muslim armies came about A.D. 1000 and later established Delhi sultanate.
- Invaders from central Asia came in early 1500s and established Mughal Empire.
- British started arriving in 1600s and colonized India.

INSIDE GROUP
- Harappans

Across the Curriculum
LITERATURE

Arundhati Roy Indian writers have gained attention recently. Many Indian novelists write in the English language, which allows a wide audience to read their work. The popularity of Indian novels may also be explained by the rise of a new, global culture.

One Indian writer who has gained fame is Arundhati Roy. Her novel, *The God of Small Things,* won England's top book prize in 1997. Among other issues, Roy's novel deals with violence and discrimination against lower-caste Indians. Despite the praise Roy's work received, some Indians were angry about things she wrote in her novel. Roy's book attracted a lawsuit in India.

Critical Thinking: What might the disputes involving Roy's book indicate about the importance people place on literature?

Connecting to Literature
Answers
1. tree-shaded, steep
2. Manja's descriptions might have related to the journey's difficulty, the fear of robbers, or his own physical exertion.

CONNECTING TO *Literature*

Indian writer R.K. Narayan's My Days: A Memoir *describes the author's childhood in the early 1900s. In the following passage Narayan recalls traveling from boarding school to his parents' new home. At that time, travel was complicated and sometimes dangerous.*

At the proper time, I was awakened and put into a huge mat-covered wagon drawn by a pair of bullocks; I sat on a bed of straw covered over with a carpet; a stalwart[1] peon[2] from Hassan high school was seated beside the driver. Manja was his name . . . Part of the way as we traveled along, Manja got off and walked ahead of the caravan, carrying a staff menacingly. Some spots in that jungle and mountain country were well-known retreats of highway robbers; one form of protection was to travel in a closely moving caravan with Manja waving a staff at the head of the column, uttering blood-curdling challenges. That was enough to keep off robbers in those days.

We passed along miles and miles of tree-shaded highway, gigantic mango and blueberry trees and lantana[3] shrubs in multicolored bloom stretching away endlessly. A couple of times the bullocks were rested beside a pond or a well. The road wound up and down steep slopes—the sort of country I had never known before. . . . The overpowering smell of straw in the wagon and the slow pace of the bullocks with their bells jingling made me drowsy . . . After hours of tossing on straw, we came to a bungalow[4] set in a ten-acre field. [It was my parents' new home.] . . . The moment I was received into the fold at the trellised ivy-covered porch, I totally ignored Manja, and never looked in his direction, while he carried my baggage in.

Analyzing Primary Sources
1. What are some of the words the author uses to describe the countryside?
2. How do you think Manja's description of this journey might be different from the author's?

A bullock cart and a double-decker bus in India

Vocabulary   [1]stalwart: strong and reliable   [2]peon: a menial laborer   [3]lantana: shrub with colorful flowers   [4]bungalow: one-story house with low roof that originated in Bengal, India

Teaching Objective 2

LEVEL 1: (Suggested time: 20 min.) Pair students and have each pair create a bulleted list of the Mughal Empire's achievements. (Lists should mention the efficient government and tax system; the wealth gained from farmland and the empire's large population; the flowering of architecture, painting, and poetry; and religious tolerance.) Ask volunteers to share and discuss their lists with the class. Compile a master list of features on the chalkboard and have students copy the list into their notes.
ESOL, COOPERATIVE LEARNING, LS VERBAL-LINGUISTIC

LEVELS 2 AND 3: (Suggested time: 20 min.) Tell students to imagine that they are editors who must write a summary for a book jacket. Then have each student write a short summary to describe achievements of the Mughal Empire. Ask volunteers to read their summaries to the class.

➤**ASSIGNMENT:** Have each student create a collage to represent various achievements of the Mughal Empire. Display students' collages around the classroom.

Place The Taj Mahal is one of the most famous buildings in the world.

The ruling Mughals were Muslim, but Islam remained a minority religion in India. Most people continued to practice Hinduism. Akbar himself was tolerant and curious about other religions. He invited religious scholars and priests—including Christians, Hindus, Jains, and Muslims—to his court. He even watched them debate.

Akbar's grandson, Shah Jahan, is remembered for the impressive buildings and monuments he had built. These include the famous Taj Mahal. This grand building contains the tomb of Shah Jahan's beloved wife, Mumtaz Mahal.

In the 1600s and 1700s the Mughal Empire slowly grew weaker. Wars in the Deccan and revolts in many parts of the empire drained Mughal resources. At about this time, Europeans became an important force in Indian history.

✓ **READING CHECK:** (*Human Systems*) What was the Mughal Empire like?
powerful, efficient government; many artistic achievements

The British

During the 1700s and 1800s the British slowly took control of India. At first this was done by the English East India Company. This company won rights to trade in the Mughal Empire in the 1600s. The East India Company first took control of small trading posts. Later the British gained more Indian territory.

Company Rule As the Mughal Empire grew weaker, the British East India Company expanded its political power. The company also built up its own military force. This army was made up mostly of

Construction of the Taj Mahal began in 1631 and was not completed until 1653. Almost 20,000 people worked on the building.

Cultural Kaleidoscope
The Sepoy Mutiny
The British rulers of India attempted to change traditional Hindu and Muslim social customs. These changes contributed to rising discontent before the Indian Mutiny.

The rebellion began when British officers ordered sepoys to load cartridges into new rifles. The sepoys were ordered to bite off the ends of cartridges rumored to be lubricated with cow and pig fat. Because Muslims are barred from eating pigs and Hindus are barred from eating cows, many Indian soldiers refused to load their guns. As punishment, they were chained and put into prison. This provoked the rebellion's outbreak.

A large section of the civilian population supported the sepoys. Although the British put down the rebellion, they began to take Indian opinions into account when making laws for India.

Critical Thinking: What does the cartridge incident indicate about British attitudes toward Indian culture?

Answer: Students may say they appeared to be either ignorant of or insensitive to Indian cultures.

India • 309

Teaching Objective 3
ALL LEVELS: (Suggested time: 30 min.) Pair students and have each pair create a flowchart on posterboard to show how Great Britain gained control of India. (Flowcharts should show that first they took control of small trading posts; then they gained larger pieces of territory; they used local Indian soldiers in their army; and they backed one Indian ruler against another; by the mid-1850s they controlled more than half of India.) Ask volunteers to display and explain their flowcharts to the class.
ESOL, COOPERATIVE LEARNING

TEACHER TO TEACHER

Jim Corley of Durant, Oklahoma, suggests the following activity to help students understand the history of India: Organize the class into four groups. Have one group conduct research on early civilizations that affected India. Have the second group conduct research on the Mughal Empire. Have the third group conduct research on Great Britain's control of India. The final group should conduct research on India's independence. Have each group use its information to create an illustrated presentation. Have each group present its illustrations, and lead a class discussion on each subject.

Linking Past to Present

Gandhi Gandhi's political philosophy, based on truth, love, and nonviolence, was revolutionary. Dr. Martin Luther King Jr. adopted Gandhi's tactics of nonviolent protest as part of the U.S. civil rights movement. Today, organizers of a wide variety of movements continue to use Gandhi's methods.

Critical Thinking: How has Gandhi's political message remained important today?

Answer: His tactics of nonviolent protest are used around the world.

Biography Answer ▲

by maintaining a nonviolent approach to protest

▲
In September 1857, British and loyal Sikh troops stormed the gate of Delhi, defended by rebel sepoys.

BIOGRAPHY

Mohandas Gandhi
(1869–1948)

Character Trait: Integrity

Gandhi practiced nonviolence in his struggle for Indian independence and the rights of India's lowest classes. Civil rights leaders in the United States and other countries have adopted Gandhi's nonviolent methods.

Among Gandhi's campaigns was a protest on the salt tax. To avoid having to buy salt and pay the tax, Gandhi and thousands of followers walked 200 miles to make salt from seawater.

Although he lived peacefully, violence took Gandhi's life. A radical Hindu who thought Gandhi was too kind to Muslims assassinated him.

How did Gandhi show integrity?

sepoys, Indian troops commanded by British officers. The British used the strategy of backing one Indian ruler against another in exchange for cooperation. By the mid-1800s the company controlled more than half of India. The rest was divided into small states ruled by local princes.

The British changed the Indian economy to benefit British industry. India produced raw materials, including cotton, indigo—a natural dye—and jute. These materials were then shipped to Britain for use in British factories. Spices, sugar, tea, and wheat were also grown in India for export. Railroads were built to ship the raw materials to Calcutta (now Kolkata), Bombay (now Mumbai), and other port cities. India also became a market for British manufactured goods. Indians, who had woven cotton cloth for centuries, were now forced to buy British cloth.

The Indian Mutiny British rule angered and frightened many Indians. In 1857, the sepoy troops revolted. They killed their British officers and other British residents. The violence spread across northern India. Large numbers of British troops were rushed to India. In the end the British crushed the rebellion.

The Indian Mutiny convinced the British government to abolish the British East India Company. The British government began to rule India directly, and India became a British colony.

Anti-British Protest During the late 1800s Indian nationalism took a different form. Educated, middle-class Indians led this movement. In 1885 these Indian nationalists created the Indian National Congress to organize their protests. At first they did not demand independence. Instead, they asked only for fairer treatment, such as a greater share of government jobs. The British refused even these moderate demands.

After World War I more and more Indians began demanding the end of British rule. A lawyer named Mohandas K. Gandhi became the most important leader of this Indian independence movement.

Gandhi and Nonviolence Gandhi reached out to the millions of Indian peasants. He used a strategy of nonviolent mass protest. He called for Indians to peacefully refuse to cooperate with the British. Gandhi led protest marches and urged Indians to **boycott**, or refuse to buy, British goods. Many times the police used violence against marchers. When the British jailed Gandhi, he went on hunger strikes. Gandhi's determination and self-sacrifice attracted many followers. Pressure grew on Britain to leave India.

✓ **READING CHECK:** (*Human Systems*) What role did the British play in India?
They slowly took control in the 1700s and 1800s; after the Indian Mutiny the British government took complete control and ruled the country as a colony.

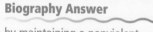

Teaching Objective 4

LEVEL 1: (Suggested time: 25 min.) Tell students that Muslims were a minority in India prior to Indian independence. Pair students and tell one student in each pair to imagine that he or she is a member of the Indian National Congress. Tell the other student to imagine that he or she is a Muslim who would like a separate Muslim state. Then have each pair write a short dialogue in which both partners explain their positions. Ask students to perform their dialogues for the class. **ESOL,** **LS INTERPERSONAL**

LEVELS 2 AND 3: (Suggested time: 20 min.) Have each student write a short poem to explain the partition of India. Ask volunteers to recite their poems for the class. **LS AUDITORY-MUSICAL**

Independence and Division

After World War II the British government decided to give India independence. The British government and the Indian National Congress wanted India to become one country. However, India's Muslims demanded a separate Muslim state. Anger and fear grew between Hindus and Muslims. India seemed on the verge of civil war.

Finally, in 1947 the British divided their Indian colony into two independent countries, India and Pakistan. India was mostly Hindu. Pakistan, which then included what is today Bangladesh, was mostly Muslim. However, the new boundary left millions of Hindus in Pakistan and millions of Muslims in India. Masses of people rushed to cross the border. Hundreds of thousands were killed in rioting and panic.

▲
Movement In the chaotic days of August 1947, millions of people left their homes to cross the new border between India and Pakistan. These Muslims are preparing to leave New Delhi by train.

✓ **READING CHECK:** *Places and Regions* Why was India divided when it became independent? **Muslims and Hindus were in conflict, and India seemed on the verge of civil war.**

Section Review 2

Define or identify: Harappans, Sanskrit, Akbar, sepoys, Mohandas Gandhi, boycott

Working with Sketch Maps On the map you created in Section 1, label Delhi, Kolkata, and Mumbai. What bodies of water are important to each of these cities?

Reading for the Main Idea

1. *Human Systems* What made the Mughal Empire one of the most powerful states in the world?

2. *Human Systems* How did the British East India Company gain control of most of India?

3. *Human Systems* Who was the most important leader of the Indian independence movement, and what was his strategy?

Critical Thinking

4. **Finding the Main Idea** Why was the British colony of India divided into two countries?

Organizing What You Know

5. **Sequencing** Copy the following time line. Use it to mark important events in Indian history from 2500 B.C. to A.D. 1947.

2500 B.C.   A.D. 1947

go.hrw.com **Homework Practice Online** Keyword: SK5 HP14

India • 311

Section 2 Review

Answers to Section 2 Review

Define or identify For definitions and identifications, see the glossary and index.

Working with Sketch Maps The Ganges River is important to Delhi, the Bay of Bengal and Ganges River are important to Kolkata, and the Arabian Sea is important to Mumbai.

Reading for the Main Idea

1. reorganized, efficient government and tax system; the Gangetic Plain's fertile farmland and large population **(NGS 12)**

2. took control of small trading posts; gained larger pieces of territory; used Indian soldiers; and backed Indian rulers against each other

3. Mohandas K. Gandhi; nonviolent protest

Critical Thinking

4. Muslims demanded a separate state, and tensions grew between Hindus and Muslims.

Organizing What You Know

5. Use Section 2 to construct the time line.

CLOSE

Have students identify and summarize the cultural, political, and economic influences of outside groups on India.

REVIEW, ASSESS, RETEACH

Have students complete the Section Review. Then pair students. Have each student within the pair create a four-question multiple-choice quiz based on the information discussed in this section. Have students within the pair take turns quizzing each other. Then have students complete Daily Quiz 14.2. **COOPERATIVE LEARNING**

Have students complete Main Idea Activity S2. Then organize the class into four groups. Assign the first the Harappan civilization, the second the Indo-Aryans, the third the Muslims and Mughals, and the fourth the British. Have each group find a lasting influence or influences of each of the groups. Ask each group to share its ideas with the class. **ESOL, COOPERATIVE LEARNING**

EXTEND

Encourage interested students to conduct research on tensions in India between Hindus and Muslims by reading newsmagazines and newspapers from recent years. Ask students to try to discover the sources of tension, the ways groups have expressed their frustrations, and the methods used by political leaders to handle these conflicts. **BLOCK SCHEDULING**

India **311**

Section 3 India Today

Read to Discover
1. What four major religions originated in India?
2. What is the caste system?
3. What languages are important in India?
4. What kind of government does India have, and what is India's economy like?

Vocabulary
reincarnation
dharma
karma
nirvana
caste system
Dalits
green revolution

People
Siddhartha Gautama
Mother Teresa

Places
Kashmir

Reading Strategy

FOLDNOTES: FOUR-CORNER FOLD Create the FoldNote titled **Four-Corner Fold** described in the Appendix. Label the flaps Religions, Castes, Languages, and Government and Economy. As you read this section, write what you learn beneath each flap.

Religions of India

Religion is an important part of Indian culture. Four major religions—Hinduism, Buddhism, Jainism, and Sikhism—originated in India. Christianity and Islam, both of which originated elsewhere, also have millions of followers in India. About 81 percent of India's people are Hindu. About 12 percent of Indians are Muslim, and 2.3 percent are Christian. Around 2 percent are Sikh, and 2.5 percent are Buddhist, Jain, Parsi, or followers of another religion. Remember that 1 percent of India's population is about 10 million people!

Hinduism Hinduism is one of the oldest religions in the world. It is a combination of the beliefs of the Indo-Aryans, who arrived in India in around 1750 B.C., and those of earlier Indian peoples. Hindus worship many gods. Hinduism teaches that all gods and all living beings are part of a single spirit called Brahma.

According to Hinduism, when people die their souls are reborn in new bodies. This process is called **reincarnation**. Every time a person is reborn, he or she must fulfill a moral duty, called **dharma**. A person's dharma depends upon the position he or she is born into. Hindus believe that people's actions during their lifetime have moral consequences, or **karma**, that affect how they will be reborn the next time. A person with good karma may be reborn as a person of higher status. A person with bad karma may be reborn with lower status, or as an animal or insect. People who in

 Place Cows mingle with pedestrians and bicyclists in the street of an Indian town.

312   Chapter 14

Section 3

Objectives
1. Identify the four major religions that originated in India.
2. Explain the caste system.
3. Identify the languages that are important in India.
4. Describe what kind of government India has and discuss India's economy.

FOCUS

Bellringer

Copy the following instructions onto the chalkboard: *India's population is predicted to reach 1.7 billion in 2050. Compile a list of problems facing a poor country with a large and growing population.* Discuss responses. (Students might mention shortages of food, medical supplies, and housing, or the possibility of group conflicts over resources.) Tell students that in Section 3 they will learn more about India today.

Building Vocabulary

Copy the following vocabulary terms onto the chalkboard: **reincarnation**, **karma**, **nirvana**, **caste system**, **Dalits**, and **green revolution**. Ask students if they are familiar with any of the terms and if so, which ones. Then ask volunteers to read the terms' definitions aloud from the glossary.

each of their lifetimes fulfill their dharma may eventually break the cycle of birth and rebirth. They become one with Brahma.

Hinduism also teaches a special respect for certain plants and animals. Cows are considered sacred and are protected. Hindus do not eat beef. Even today, cows can be seen roaming cities and villages. Monkeys and some snakes are also sacred. The most sacred river is the Ganges, where millions of Hindus make a religious pilgrimage every year.

Hindus build temples for their gods and honor them with festivals at least once a year. Festivals may involve religious ceremonies, dance, and music. During the annual new year celebration, called Diwali, Hindus exchange gifts and set off fireworks.

Buddhism The founder of Buddhism, Siddhartha Gautama (sid-DAHR-tuh GOW-tuh-muh), was born a Hindu about 563 B.C. As a son of a prince, he lived a luxurious life. At age 29, Gautama left his palace and set out to learn about hunger, disease, and death.

For six years he searched for the truth. One day Gautama suddenly had a feeling of enlightenment—a state of calm and understanding. He then developed the main principles of Buddhism—the Four Noble Truths. Among these was the belief that all human life contains suffering and sadness and that desire causes suffering. By rejecting desire, people could achieve **nirvana**, or perfect peace.

Gautama rejected many of the beliefs of Hinduism, particularly that goodness and one's position in life were inherited. He also believed that priests should practice good conduct, nonviolence, and poverty.

Gautama spread his philosophy far and wide until his death about 483 B.C. His followers call him the Buddha, or "the Enlightened One." Eventually, Buddhism spread to many other parts of Asia. Buddhism is no longer widely practice in India. However, the religion is very important in Sri Lanka, China, Japan, and Southeast Asia.

▲ The Buddha is often depicted in poses of meditation.

FOCUS ON CULTURE

An Elephant-Headed God

One of the most beloved Hindu gods is Ganesh, who has the head of an elephant. Ganesh is called the Remover of Obstacles. To ensure their success, important events, such as weddings, begin with the worship of Ganesh. During Ganesh Chaturthi, a festival that honors him, Indians bring statues of Ganesh into their homes and later dip them in the sea or a river.

How do Hindus honor Ganesh?

DAILY LIFE

Indian Festivals India's diverse religious communities provide many opportunities for festivals. Muslims celebrate 'Id al-Fitr and Mohurrum. Sikhs celebrate Guru Nanak Jayanti, Jains celebrate Mahavir Jayanti, Buddhists celebrate Buddha's birthday, and Christians celebrate Christmas.

Some Hindu festivals revolve around birthday celebrations for Hindu gods. Hindu celebrations combine religious ceremonies, processions, music, dances, and feasting. One festival, Diwali, takes place in October. It honors the goddess Laksmi and is celebrated through feasting, worship, ceremonial lights, and fireworks. Tiny oil lamps are lit to outline every house and hut. Navaratri, a nine-day festival, is celebrated throughout India but activities differ according to the region.

☑ **internet** connect

GO TO: **go.hrw.com**
KEYWORD: **SK5 CH14**
FOR: **Web sites about festivals of India**

▲ **Focus on Culture Answer**

by starting special events by worshipping him and dipping his image in the sea or a river

---

TEACH

Teaching Objective 1

ALL LEVELS: (Suggested time: 15 min.) Copy the following graphic organizer onto the chalkboard, omitting the blue answers. Use it to help students identify four major religions that originated in India. Pair students and have each pair complete the organizer by filling in the names of the religions along with short descriptions of the religions' central beliefs or aspects of the religions' histories. Ask volunteers to share their answers with the class. **ESOL, COOPERATIVE LEARNING**

Facts About Indian Religions

Buddhism—
• Founded by Siddhartha Gautama, the Buddha
• By not lying, stealing, or being greedy, people can reach nirvana.

Jainism—
• All things in nature have souls.
• Reject all forms of violence against living things

Sikhism—
• Founded in the late 1400s
• Combines elements of Hinduism and Islam

Hinduism—
• Belief in reincarnation and karma
• Gods include Vishnu, Brahma, and Siva.
• All gods and living beings are part of one spirit.

HUMAN SYSTEMS

The Golden Temple The majority of Sikhs live in the state of Punjab, where their religion originated. The Harmandir Sahib, or Golden Temple as it is more commonly known, is the religion's holiest site. The temple was built in the early 1600s under the leadership of the Sikhs' fifth guru.

The Sikhs have defended their temple against various invaders. Although it has been destroyed many times, Sikhs have rebuilt the temple each time. The front of the temple is covered with a thin layer of gold. Visitors enter the temple by walking across a marble causeway, which crosses a lake.

▲ A Sikh guards the Golden Temple, the center of the Sikh religion, in Amritsar, India. Sikh men can be recognized by their beards and special turbans.

Interpreting the Visual Record (Place)
Do you know of any other religious or cultural groups whose members have a distinctive way of dressing?

Many Dalits, like this woman in Goa, still perform jobs that Indians consider dirty or impure.
▼

Visual Record Answer ▲

Answers will vary. Students may mention Hasidic Jews, the Amish, or some Muslim women.

Jainism Jainism was founded at about the same time as Buddhism. It teaches that all things in nature—animals, plants, and stones—have souls. Jains reject all forms of violence against any living thing. They are strict vegetarians. Some even cover their noses with cloth to avoid breathing in insects and thus killing them.

Jains make up only a small minority. However, they have made many contributions to Indian art, mathematics, and literature.

Sikhism Sikhism was founded in the late 1400s. It combines elements of Hinduism and Islam. Members of this religion are called Sikhs. Traditionally, many Sikh men have become soldiers. They continue to play an important role in India's army.

Most Sikhs live in the state of Punjab in northern India. Some Sikhs want to break away from India and form an independent country. The Indian government has refused to allow this, and violent clashes have resulted.

✔ **READING CHECK:** (**Human Systems**) What four religions originated in India?
Hinduism, Buddhism, Jainism, Sikhism

Castes

Another key feature of Indian society is the **caste system**. Castes are groups of people whose birth determines their position in society. The castes are ranked in status, from highest to lowest. People from a

Teaching Objective 2

LEVEL 1: (Suggested time: 20 min.) Tell students that although caste has diminished somewhat in importance, it is still a feature of Indian society. Call on volunteers to describe the caste system in their own words. Conclude by leading a discussion about why abolishing a traditional social system such as the caste system is so difficult. **LS** **INTERPERSONAL**

LEVELS 2 AND 3: (Suggested time: 40 min.) Ask each student to write a short essay about the features of the caste system and why it might be so difficult to abolish a traditional social system like the caste system. Ask volunteers to read their essays to the class. **LS** **VERBAL-LINGUISTIC**

➤**ASSIGNMENT:** Ask students to conduct further research on the caste system in India today. Tell students to concentrate on specific examples of government programs to help lower-caste Indians, the progress that lower-caste Indians have made, and the challenges that they still face. Have students prepare oral reports to present their findings.

higher caste cannot marry or even touch people of lower castes. The people at the bottom, called **Dalits**, do work that higher castes consider unclean. They wash and cremate dead bodies, process cow hides into leather goods, and sweep up trash.

Gandhi tried to improve people's attitudes toward the Dalits. He called them "Children of God." After independence, the Indian government officially ended the caste system. However, it is still a strong force in Indian society. The government also tried to improve economic conditions for the Dalits. Today some Dalits are educated and have good jobs. The majority, though, are still poor.

✔ **READING CHECK:** (*Human Systems*) How does the caste system create conflict in Indian society? separates society, keeps some people poor

Languages

India's people speak an amazing number of different languages. There are 24 languages with a million or more speakers, plus hundreds of other languages. Hindi is the main language of about 30 percent of the people, mostly in northern India. In 1965 it became the official national language. However, the states of southern India have resisted the push to adopt Hindi. English is still commonly used in government, business, and higher education throughout India.

✔ **READING CHECK:** (*Human Systems*) What languages are important in India? Hindi, English, and 22 others

Government and Economy

India has made a great deal of economic progress since gaining independence, but the country remains poor. Rapid population growth strains the country's resources, and the divisions among India's people make it difficult to govern.

Government India is ruled by a democratic government. With more than 1 billion people, the country is the world's largest democracy. The structure of the government is based on Britain's parliamentary system. However, as in the United States, India's central government shares power with state governments.

Indian politics have sometimes been marked by violence and assassinations. The government used force to defeat Sikh rebels in 1984. There have also been outbreaks of

BIOGRAPHY

Mother Teresa
(1910–1997)

Character Trait: Kindness

Mother Teresa dedicated her life to helping people. She is best known for founding a mission for the sick and homeless in Kolkata. In 1979, Mother Teresa accepted the Nobel Peace Prize in honor of the millions of people she dedicated her life to caring for. Today, Mother Teresa's example of kindness toward the needy continues around the world at 4,500 missions she created.

How did Mother Teresa show kindness to others?

Place Parliament House, New Delhi, is the home of India's legislative branch.

Cultural Kaleidoscope
Government and Diversity The Indian parliament consists of the president and two houses. The Lok Sabha is the lower house of parliament, and the Rajya Sabha is the upper house. The position of president in India is largely ceremonial—the prime minister wields the real power.

Much of India's constitution was built on laws enacted during British rule. However, the diversity of India's population has created unique challenges for the government. India's constitution is one of the longest in the world. Its 395 articles, numerous schedules, and more than 70 amendments affect the country's government all the way to the local level.

Discussion: Why may India's constitution be so long and detailed?

▲ **Biography Answer**

by helping sick and homeless people

India • 315

Teaching Objective 3

LEVEL 1: (Suggested time: 40 min.) Have the class brainstorm the challenges that linguistic diversity would present to a country. Then pair students and have each pair draw a comic strip to show the role of languages in Indian society. Ask students to display and explain their comic strips to the class. **ESOL, COOPERATIVE LEARNING**

LEVEL 2: (Suggested time: 30 min.) Lead a class discussion about why linguistic diversity may present challenges to a country. Then have each student create a poster to show how language divides Indian society. Ask volunteers to present and explain their posters to the class. **LS VISUAL-SPATIAL**

LEVEL 3: (Suggested time: 30 min.) Have each student write a short poem about the different languages that are important in Indian society, and the challenges that linguistic diversity might present in India. Ask volunteers to recite their poems for the class. **LS AUDITORY-MUSICAL**

FOOD FESTIVAL

Tandoori Cooking A tandoor is a clay oven used in India to cook meat that has been marinated in a mixture of plain yogurt, lemon juice, ginger, garlic, cloves, cumin, coriander, hot peppers, and turmeric. Marinade ingredients may vary. The meat can be served with rice and chutney or sliced and served on bread with mayonnaise flavored with mint, cilantro, chili, onion, and vinegar. Many Indian dishes contain blends of herbs, spices, fruits, nuts, grains, and yogurt.

Challenge students to prepare tandoori recipes and share the results with the class.

▲
India has stationed large numbers of troops in Kashmir.

(Human-Environment Interaction)
Peppers are harvested in northern India.
▼

violence between Hindus and Muslims. In 1992 a mob of Hindus tore down a mosque that stood on a Hindu holy site. Riots broke out in many parts of India as a result.

India's border with Pakistan has been in dispute since 1947. Both countries claim a mountainous region called Kashmir. Before India gained independence, Kashmir was ruled by a Hindu prince. Most of its people were Muslim, however. India and Pakistan have fought over Kashmir several times. Today, both countries have nuclear weapons, making the prospect of a future war even more frightening.

Economy India's economy is a mixture of the traditional and the modern. In thousands of villages, farmers work the fields just as they have for centuries. At the same time, modern factories and high-tech service industries demonstrate India's potential for wealth. However, the country still does not have enough good roads and telecommunications systems.

Close to 60 percent of India's workforce are farmers. Farming makes up 25 percent of India's GDP. Most farmers work on small farms less than 2.5 acres (1 hectare) in size. Many grow barely enough to feed themselves and their families. In recent years, the government has worked to promote commercial farming.

India's leading crops include rice, wheat, cotton, tea, sugarcane, and jute. Cattle and water buffalo are raised to pull plows and to provide milk.

316   Chapter 14

Teaching Objective 4

LEVELS 1 AND 2: (Suggested time: 30 min.) Have each student create a chart on India's government and economy. Then ask students to discuss how India's government and economy compare to that of the United States. **ESOL**

LEVEL 3: (Suggested time: 40 min.) Ask each student to create a collage to represent the important features of India's government and economy. Ask volunteers to display and explain the different elements of their collages to the class. **LS KINESTHETIC**

Beginning in the 1960s, the Indian government started agricultural programs known as the **green revolution**. This effort encouraged farmers to adopt more modern methods. It promoted greater use of fertilizers, pesticides, and new varieties of wheat and rice. Crop yields increased. In years with good weather, India is self-sufficient in food and can export farm products.

India is considered a developing country. However, its economy is large enough to rank among the world's top 10 industrial countries. India's industries include textiles, jewelry, cars, bicycles, oil products, chemicals, food processing, and electronics.

India's moviemaking industry is one of the world's largest. Mumbai is a major moviemaking center. Movies are an incredibly popular form of entertainment, as millions of Indians cannot read. Many Indian movie stars have gone into politics. Indian movies have a distinctive style. They usually feature music and dancing and often draw on themes from Indian myths. Indian movies are popular in many other countries as well.

India now has a large, well-educated middle class. These people have enough money for luxuries like cable television and personal computers. Some Indians are very rich. Yet the majority of Indians are still poor.

✓ **READING CHECK:** (*Places and Regions*) What are India's government and economy like? government—limited, parliamentary democracy; economy—mix of traditional and market, among the 10 largest in the world

▲ Red-hot steel is poured into molds in a foundry near Kolkata.

Interpreting the Visual Record **Which of India's industries might use the steel produced here?**

Homework Practice Online
Keyword: SK5 HP14

Section Review 3

Define or identify: reincarnation, dharma, karma, Siddhartha Gautama, nirvana, caste system, Dalits, Mother Teresa, green revolution

Working with Sketch Maps On the map that you created in Section 2, label the Kashmir region of India. What other country claims Kashmir?

Reading for the Main Idea

1. (*Human Systems*) What are the main religions practiced in India? Which religion has the largest number of followers?

2. (*Environment and Society*) How did India's government increase agricultural output in the 1960s?

Critical Thinking

3. **Drawing Inferences and Conclusions** Why might India's government find it difficult to improve the economic situation of the Dalits?

4. **Finding the Main Idea** Why are movies such a popular form of entertainment in India?

Organizing What You Know

5. **Categorizing** Copy the following graphic organizer. Use it to list the leading crops and industries of India.

Leading crops	Leading industries

India • 317

Answers to Section 3 Review

Define or identify For definitions and identifications, see the glossary and index.

Working with Sketch Maps Kashmir should be located accurately. Pakistan claims Kashmir.

Reading for the Main Idea

1. Hinduism, Islam, Christianity, Sikhism, Buddhism, Jainism; Hinduism (**NGS 10**)

2. by instituting practices including greater use of fertilizer and pesticides and encouraging farmers to grow new varieties of wheat and rice (**NGS 14**)

Critical Thinking

3. The majority are poor, and caste prejudice still exists in Indian society. (**NGS 18**)

4. because millions of Indians cannot read

Organizing What You Know

5. crops—rice, wheat, cotton, tea, sugarcane, and jute; industries—moviemaking, textiles, jewelry, cars, bicycles, oil products, chemicals, food processing, and electronics

◄ **Visual Record Answer**

manufacturing cars or bicycles

CLOSE

Ask students to recount facts about India's religions, government, and economy.

REVIEW, ASSESS, RETEACH

Have students complete the Section Review. Then have students write one question on each of the following topics: religion and caste system, languages, government, and economy. Collect students' questions and use them to quiz the class. Then have students complete Daily Quiz 14.3.

Have students complete Main Idea Activity S3. Then organize students into three groups and assign each a section of the chapter. Have each group prepare an outline of its section and present the outline to the class. **ESOL, COOPERATIVE LEARNING**

EXTEND

Have interested students conduct research on Lakshmi Bai, the Rani of Jhansi, who led rebels against British troops during the Indian Mutiny, and on Phoolan Devi, whose life became the subject of the film *Bandit Queen*. They might compare and contrast the lives of these two women to more traditional Indian women's roles. **BLOCK SCHEDULING**

Define and Identify

For definitions and identifications, see the glossary and index.

Review the Main Ideas

15. Two tectonic plates collided and pushed up Earth's crust. **(NGS4)**

16. Hindus consider the Ganges sacred and call it "Mother River."

17. Farmers depend on summer winds from the Indian Ocean to bring rain.

18. the Harrapan civilization **(NGS 9)**

19. the Indo-Aryans **(NGS 9)**

20. the British **SS.A.2.3.6**

21. anger over British rule

22. reincarnation—human soul is reborn many times in different bodies; karma—a person's actions create a positive or negative force **(NGS 10)**

23. religion, caste, and language **(NGS 10)**

24. 24 major languages plus hundreds more

Think Critically

25. Southern Indian states have resisted adopting Hindi. **(NGS 9)**

26. They are used for textiles, jewelry, cars, bicycles, oil products, chemicals, and food processing.

27. encouraged farmers to change their methods of farming through new technology and crops; increased crop yields and exports

28. The empire was very powerful, and Akbar and his successors sponsored architecture, painting, and poetry. They also promoted religious tolerance.

29. might bring more income to the country **(NGS 18)**

Review and Practice

Define and Identify

Identify each of the following:

1. teak
2. Sanskrit
3. sepoys
4. boycott
5. reincarnation
6. karma
7. nirvana

8. caste system
9. Dalits
10. green revolution
11. Harappans
12. Mohandas Gandhi
13. Siddhartha Gautama
14. Mother Teresa

Review the Main Ideas

15. How were the Himalayas formed?

16. What is unique about the Ganges River?

17. Why are monsoons important to Indian farmers?

18. What was the first urban civilization on the Indian Subcontinent?

19. Who brought Sanskrit to India?

20. Who slowly took control of India after the Mughal Empire weakened?

21. What caused the Indian Mutiny of 1857?

22. What are the Hindu ideas of reincarnation and karma?

23. What factors divide Indian society?

24. How many languages are spoken in India?

Think Critically

25. Drawing Inferences and Conclusions Why do you think Hindi has not become the language of all of India?

26. Summarizing How do India's natural resources affect its economy?

27. Finding the Main Idea How did the Indian government's promotion of new farming technology affect India's farming culture?

28. Drawing Inferences and Conclusions Why do you think the Mughal Empire under Akbar and his successors was considered a "golden age"?

29. Drawing Inferences and Conclusions How might the growth of a well-educated, high-tech workforce affect India's economy?

Map Activity

30. On a separate sheet of paper, match the letters on the map with their correct labels.

Himalayas
Gangetic Plain
Deccan
Eastern Ghats
Western Ghats

Ganges River
Brahmaputra River
Thar Desert

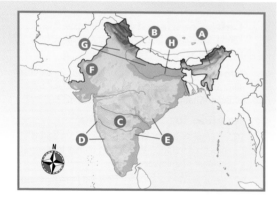

Map Activity

30. A. Brahmaputra River

B. Himalayas

C. Deccan

D. Western Ghats

E. Eastern Ghats

F. Thar Desert

G. Gangetic Plain

H. Ganges River

Writing Activity

Write a one- to two-page report about how religion influences life in India. List and describe India's major religions, then write about how they relate to politics, border disputes, social classes, daily life, languages, the economy, and so on. Be sure to use standard grammar, spelling, sentence structure, and punctuation.

internet connect

Internet Activity: **go.hrw.com**
KEYWORD: **SK5 GT14**

Choose a topic to explore about India:
- Tour the regions of India.
- Travel to ancient India.
- Learn about Mohandas Gandhi.

Writing Activity

Reports will vary, but the information included should be consistent with text material. Use Rubric 42, Writing to Inform, to evaluate student work.

Interpreting Maps

1. Maharashtra
2. Orissa, Andhra Pradesh
3. Delhi
4. Uttaranchal, Uttar Pradesh, Bihar, West Bengal, Sikkim

Analyzing Primary Sources

1. Violence does not solve problems.
2. He is a nonviolent man
3. He worked toward India's independence by leading nonviolent protests against the British government.
4. Gandhi believed that love would triumph eventually.

Social Studies Skills Practice

Interpreting Maps

India is divided into 28 states and 7 territories. Study the map and then answer the questions.

The States and Territories of India

1. In which state is Mumbai located?
2. If you were traveling from Kolkata to Chennai, which states would you travel through?
3. Which state or territory shares the same name as a major city in India?
4. Which states and territories border Nepal?

Analyzing Primary Sources

Using what you have learned about Gandhi, read the following quotes. Then answer the questions.

"I object to violence because when it appears to do good, the good is only temporary; the evil it does is permanent."

"An eye for an eye makes the whole world blind."

"Whether humanity will consciously follow the law of love, I do not know. But that need not disturb me. The law will work just as the law of gravitation works, whether we accept it or not."

1. What is the main idea of these statements?
2. What can you learn about Gandhi by reading these quotes?
3. How do these statements relate to Gandhi's role in achieving independence for India?
4. What is Gandhi's opinion about the "law of love"?

India • 319

REVIEW AND ASSESSMENT RESOURCES

Reproducible
- Readings in World Geography, History, and Culture 75 and 76
- Critical Thinking Activity 14
- Vocabulary Activity 14

Technology
- Chapter 14 Test Generator (on the One-Stop Planner)
- Audio CD Program, Chapter 14
- HRW Go site

Reinforcement, Review, and Assessment
- Chapter 14 Review and Practice
- Chapter Summaries and Review
- Chapter 14 Test
- Chapter 14 Test for English Language Learners and Special-Needs Students

internet connect

GO TO: **go.hrw.com**
KEYWORD: **SK5 Teacher**
FOR: a guide to using the Internet in your classroom

Objectives	Pacing Guide	Reproducible Resources
SECTION 1 **Physical Geography** (pp. 321–23) 1. Identify the major physical features located in the Indian Perimeter. 2. Identify the climates and natural resources found in the region. 3. Describe the physical features of the island countries.	**Regular** .5 day Lecture Notes, Section 1 **Block Scheduling** .5 day *Block Scheduling Handbook, Chapter 15*	**RS** Know It Notes S1 **SM** Geography for Life Activity 31 **E** Lab Activity for Geography and Earth Science, Demonstration 10 **ELL** Main Idea Activity S1
SECTION 2 **Pakistan and Bangladesh** (pp. 324–27) 1. Describe the history of Pakistan. 2. Identify some features of Pakistan's culture. 3. Describe the history of Bangladesh. 4. Identify the challenges that face Bangladesh today.	**Regular** 1 day Lecture Notes, Section 2 **Block Scheduling** .5 day *Block Scheduling Handbook, Chapter 15*	**RS** Know It Notes S2 **RS** Graphic Organizer 15 **E** Cultures of the World Activity 8 **IC** Interdisciplinary Activities for the Middle Grades 33, 34, 35 **ELL** Main Idea Activity S2
SECTION 3 **The Himalayan and Island Countries** (pp. 330–35) 1. Identify some important features of Nepal. 2. Describe how Bhutan developed over time. 3. Describe what Sri Lanka is like. 4. Identify some economic activities of the Maldives.	**Regular** 2 days Lecture Notes, Section 3 **Block Scheduling** .5 day *Block Scheduling Handbook, Chapter 15*	**RS** Know It Notes S3 **IC** Interdisciplinary Activities for the Middle Grades 33, 34, 35 **SM** Map Activity 15 **E** Biography Activity: Tenzing Norgay **ELL** Main Idea Activity S3

Chapter Resource Key

RS	Reading Support	**ELL**	Reinforcement and English Language Learners and English for Speakers of Other Languages (ESOL)	Internet	
IC	Interdisciplinary Connections			Holt Presentation Maker Using Microsoft® PowerPoint®	
E	Enrichment				
SM	Skills Mastery		Transparencies		
A	Assessment		CD–ROM		
REV	Review		Music		
			Video		

One-Stop Planner CD–ROM

See the *One-Stop Planner* for a complete list of additional resources for students and teachers.

One-Stop Planner CD–ROM

It's easy to plan lessons, select resources, and print out materials for your students when you use the *One-Stop Planner CD–ROM with Test Generator.*

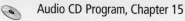

internet connect

HRW ONLINE RESOURCES

<u>GO TO:</u> go.hrw.com
Then type in a keyword.

TEACHER HOME PAGE
  KEYWORD: SK5 TEACHER

CHAPTER INTERNET ACTIVITIES
  KEYWORD: SK5 GT15

Choose an activity to:
• climb the Himalayas.
• learn about Sri Lanka's history.
• visit the regions of Pakistan.

CHAPTER ENRICHMENT LINKS
  KEYWORD: SK5 CH15

CHAPTER MAPS
  KEYWORD: SK5 MAPS15

ONLINE ASSESSMENT
Homework Practice
  KEYWORD: SK5 HP15
  Standardized Test Prep Online
  KEYWORD: SK5 STP15
  Rubrics
  KEYWORD: SS Rubrics

COUNTRY INFORMATION
  KEYWORD: SK5 Almanac

CONTENT UPDATES
  KEYWORD: SS Content Updates

HOLT PRESENTATION MAKER
  KEYWORD: SK5 PPT15

ONLINE READING SUPPORT
  KEYWORD: SS Strategies

CURRENT EVENTS
  KEYWORD: S5 Current Events

Technology Resources

- One-Stop Planner CD–ROM, Lesson 15.1
- Geography and Cultures Visual Resources with Teaching Activities 55–59
- *ARGWorld* CD–ROM
- Homework Practice Online
- HRW Go site

- One-Stop Planner CD–ROM, Lesson 15.2
- Earth: Forces and Formations CD–ROM/Seek and Tell/Forces and Processes
- *ARGWorld* CD–ROM
- Homework Practice Online
- HRW Go site

- One-Stop Planner CD–ROM, Lesson 15.3
- *ARGWorld* CD–ROM
- Music of the World Audio CD Program, Selection 18
- Homework Practice Online
- HRW Go site

Review, Reinforcement, and Assessment Resources

ELL	Main Idea Activity S1
REV	Section 1 Review
A	Daily Quiz 15.1
REV	Chapter Summaries and Review
ELL	English Audio Summary 15.1
ELL	Spanish Audio Summary 15.1

ELL	Main Idea Activity S2
REV	Section 2 Review
A	Daily Quiz 15.2
REV	Chapter Summaries and Review
ELL	English Audio Summary 15.2
ELL	Spanish Audio Summary 15.2

ELL	Main Idea Activity S3
REV	Section 3 Review
A	Daily Quiz 15.3
REV	Chapter Summaries and Review
ELL	English Audio Summary 15.3
ELL	Spanish Audio Summary 15.3

Meeting Individual Needs

Ability Levels

Level 1 Basic-level activities designed for all students encountering new material

Level 2 Intermediate-level activities designed for average students

Level 3 Challenging activities designed for honors and gifted-and-talented students

ESOL Activities that address the needs of students with Limited English Proficiency

Chapter Review and Assessment

E	Readings in World Geography, History, and Culture 77 and 78
SM	Critical Thinking Activity 15
REV	Chapter 15 Review and Practice
REV	Chapter Summaries and Review
ELL	Vocabulary Activity 15
A	Chapter 15 Test
A	Unit 4 Test
	Chapter 15 Test Generator (on the One-Stop Planner)
	Audio CD Program, Chapter 15
A	Chapter 15 Test for English Language Learners and Special-Needs Students
A	Unit 4 Test for English Language Learners and Special-Needs Students
	HRW Go Site

CHAPTER 15

India's Neighbors

Previewing Chapter Resources

Holt Online Learning

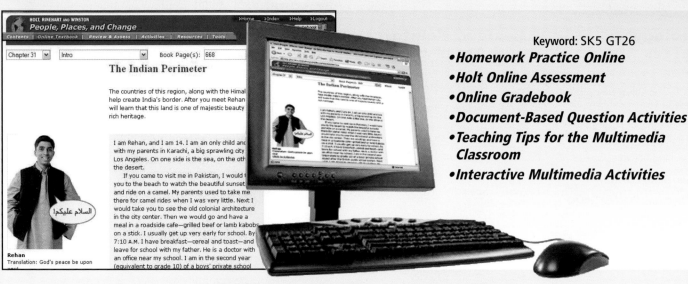

Keyword: SK5 GT26

- *Homework Practice Online*
- *Holt Online Assessment*
- *Online Gradebook*
- *Document-Based Question Activities*
- *Teaching Tips for the Multimedia Classroom*
- *Interactive Multimedia Activities*

Differentiating Instruction

Reading and Writing Support

◄ *Graphic Organizer Activity*
- *Vocabulary Activity*
- *Chapter Summary and Review*
- *Know It Notes*
- *Audio CD*

Active Learning

- *Block Scheduling Handbook*
- *Cultures of the World Activity*
- *Interdisciplinary Activity*
◄ *Map Activity*
- *Critical Thinking Activity 31*
- *Music of the World CD: Music of the Himalayas*

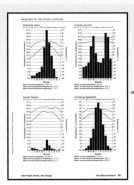

Primary Sources and Advanced Learners

- *Geography for Life Activity: Climates of India's Neighbors*
◄ *Map Activity: Sri Lanka*
- *Readings in World Geography, History and Culture:*
  - *77 Getting Married in Pakistan*
  - *78 The Water of Life*

Assessment Program

◄ *Daily Quizzes S1–3*
- *Chapter Test*
- *Chapter Test for English Language Learners and Special-Needs Students*

Spanish and ESOL

- *Vocabulary Activity*
- *Main Idea Activities for English Language Learners and Special-Needs Students*
- *Chapter Summary and Review*
- *Spanish Audio Summary*
- *Know It Notes S1–3*
◄ *Chapter Test for English Language Learners and Special-Needs Students*

Special Education Modifications

Your **I.D.E.A. Works! CD-ROM** will provide modified versions of the following teaching materials:

- *Guided Reading Strategies S1–3*
- *Vocabulary Activity*
◄ *Main Idea Activities S1–3*
- *Daily Quizzes S1–3*
- *Chapter 15 Test*
- *Flash cards of chapter vocabulary terms*

Teacher Resources

Books for Teachers

Bernstein, Jeremy. *In the Himalayas: Journeys through Nepal, Tibet, and Bhutan.* The Lyons Press, 1996.

Fleming, Peter. *News from Tartary: A Journey from Peking to Kashmir.* Northwestern University Press, 1999.

Zeppa, Jamie. *Beyond the Sky and the Earth: A Journey into Bhutan.* Macmillan General Books, 1999.

Books for Students

Brace, Steve. *Bangladesh.* Economically Developing Countries. Thomson Learning, 1995. Text, charts, maps, and photographs describe the country's physical geography and economic development.

Coburn, Broughton. Everest: *Mountain Without Mercy.* National Geographic Society, 1997. Chronicles the blizzard and rescue expedition of May 1996.

Cumming, David. *Bangladesh.* Country Fact Files. Raintree/Steck-Vaughn, 1999. The country's geography, natural resources, economics, and the environment.

Khan, Eaniqa, and Rob Unwin. *Pakistan.* Country Insights. Raintree/Steck-Vaughn, 1998. City and village life.
SHELTERED ENGLISH

Multimedia Materials

Mount Everest. Video, 160 min. PBS.

The Living Edens: Bhutan, the Last Shangra La. Video, 60 min. PBS.

Up to the Himalayas. CD–ROM. DNA Multimedia.

Videos and CDs

Videos

- *CNN. Presents Geography: Yesterday and Today, Segment 33 The Tengboche Monastery*
- *ARG World*

Holt Researcher

http://researcher.hrw.com

- *Gautama, Siddhartha*
- *Pakistan*
- *Population and Population Projections—Asia*
- *Asian Economies*
- *Nepal*
- *Bangladesh*

Transparency Packages

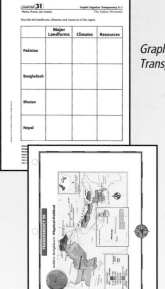

Graphic Organizer Transparencies 15.1–3

Geography and Cultures Visual Resources Transparencies 89–93
96 India's Neighbors: Physical-Political

Map Activities Transparency 15 Sir Lanka

CHAPTER 15

WHY IT MATTERS

You may wish to point out to students that there are many reasons why we should know more about India's neighbor.

▶ These countries contain many sites of historical and cultural interest as well as spectacular landscapes.

▶ Pakistan and India have developed nuclear weapons. Consequently, political developments in the region may gain global significance.

▶ Some countries of the region are very poor and have rapidly growing populations. Developing the potential of these populations and establishing economic stability can benefit the world economy.

India's Neighbors

The countries of this region, along with the Himalayas, help create India's border. After you meet Rehan you will learn that this land is one of majestic beauty with a rich heritage.

I am Rehan, and I am 14. I am an only child and live with my parents in Karachi, a big sprawling city like Los Angeles. On one side is the sea, on the other is the desert.

If you came to visit me in Pakistan, I would take you to the beach to watch the beautiful sunsets and ride on a camel. My parents used to take me there for camel rides when I was very little. Next I would take you to see the old colonial architecture in the city center. Then we would go and have a meal in a roadside cafe—grilled beef or lamb kabobs on a stick. I usually get up very early for school. By 7:10 A.M. I have breakfast—cereal and toast—and leave for school with my father. He is a doctor with an office near my school. I am in the second year (equivalent to grade 10) of a boys' private school styled after the British public school system.

Next year, I am going to America with my mother. My parents want me to have a chance to go to a world-class university.

السلام عليكم!

Translation: God's peace be upon you!

320 • Chapter 15

CHAPTER PROJECT

Organize students into two groups. Have all students conduct research on tourism in South Asia. Then tell one group to prepare arguments in favor of tourism in Pakistan, Bangladesh, Nepal, or Bhutan. Have the other group prepare arguments against tourism. Allow students to prepare. Then conduct the debate, acting as the moderator. Have students place their notes for the debate in their portfolios.

STARTING THE CHAPTER

Provide small jars containing some of the aromatic spices used in the cuisines of the countries bordering India. Possibilities include asafetida, black pepper, cardamom, cloves, coriander, cumin, fennel, and tumeric. (Most of these are available from supermarkets.) Allow students to pass the jars around and smell the spices. Ask them what images the scents bring to mind. Discuss responses. (Students might mention busy markets, caravans, or other images.) Point out that cooks in the region grind their own spices and create their own unique spice mixtures. Tell students that they will learn more about the history, cultures, and foods of India's neighbors in this chapter.

Section 1 — Physical Geography

Read to Discover

1. What major physical features are located in the Indian Perimeter?
2. What climates and natural resources are found in this region?
3. What are the physical features of the island countries?

Vocabulary
cyclones
storm surges

Places
Brahmaputra River
Ganges River
Himalayas
Mount Everest
Tarai
Karakoram Range
Hindu Kush
Khyber Pass
Indus River
Thar Desert

Reading Strategy

VISUALIZING INFORMATION Before you read, look at the map and pictures in this section. What environmental challenges do you think the people living in this region could face? Write your answers on a sheet of paper under the name of each country: Pakistan, Bangladesh, Bhutan, and Nepal.

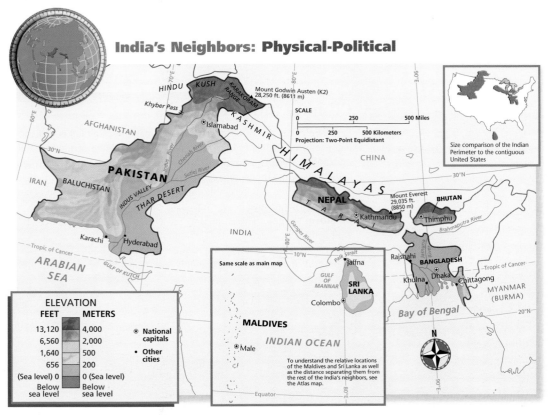

India's Neighbors: Physical-Political

SCALE
0 250 500 Miles
0 250 500 Kilometers
Projection: Two-Point Equidistant

Mount Godwin Austen (K2) 28,250 ft. (8611 m)

Mount Everest 29,035 ft. (8850 m)

Size comparison of the Indian Perimeter to the contiguous United States

HINDU KUSH
Khyber Pass
KARAKORAM RANGE
AFGHANISTAN
Islamabad
KASHMIR
CHINA
IRAN
BALUCHISTAN
PAKISTAN
Indus Valley
Chenab River
Sutlej River
THAR DESERT
HIMALAYAS
NEPAL
Kathmandu
TARAI
BHUTAN
Thimphu
Brahmaputra River
INDIA
Ganges River
Karachi
Hyderabad
Tropic of Cancer
ARABIAN SEA
GULF OF KUTCH
Rajshahi
BANGLADESH
Khulna Dhaka Chittagong
Tropic of Cancer
MYANMAR (BURMA)
Bay of Bengal
30°N
30°N
20°N

Same scale as main map
10°N
Palk Strait
Jaffna
GULF OF MANNAR
SRI LANKA
Colombo
MALDIVES
INDIAN OCEAN
Male
Equator

To understand the relative locations of the Maldives and Sri Lanka as well as the distance separating them from the rest of the India's neighbors, see the Atlas map.

ELEVATION
FEET	METERS
13,120	4,000
6,560	2,000
1,640	500
656	200
(Sea level) 0	0 (Sea level)
Below sea level	Below sea level

⊛ National capitals
• Other cities

Section 1

Objectives

1. Identify the major physical features of the countries neighboring India.
2. Discuss the climates and natural resources found in this region.
3. Name the physical features of the island countries.

FOCUS

Bellringer

Copy the following instructions onto the chalkboard: *In 1998 Bangladesh suffered from flooding so severe that two thirds of the land was under water. Use the physical and climate maps in this unit's atlas to list factors that might have contributed to the flooding.* Discuss responses. (Students might mention low elevation, proximity to rivers, or heavy rains.) Tell students that in Section 1 they will learn more about how the region's physical geography contributes to flooding in Bangladesh. They will also learn about

the physical geography of other countries in the region in Section 1.

Using the Physical-Political Map

Have students examine the map on this page. Then ask students to name all of the mainland region's countries. (Pakistan, Nepal, Bhutan, and Bangladesh) Then ask students to locate the island countries. (Sri Lanka and the Maldives) Conclude by discussing the ways in which India may dominate this region may.

National Geography Standard 13

Cooperation, Conflict, and a Glacier The Siachen Glacier in the Karakoram Range bears the distinction of being the world's highest battlefield. Since 1984, Indian and Pakistani troops have fought for control of the strip of inhospitable land 47 miles (76 km) long. Each country is afraid that the other will gain control of this previously unclaimed glacier.

Thus far, very few soldiers on either side have been killed by hostile fire. Temperatures on the glacier can drop to −40°C (−40°F), and some troops are stationed as high as 22,000 feet (6,706 m) above sea level. The punishing elevation, weather, and terrain have caused majority of the casualties.

Activity: Have students conduct additional research on military conflicts between India and Pakistan. Ask them to concentrate on the causes of the conflicts and possible solutions.

Visual Record Answer ▶

by allowing farmers to grow more crops in a limited space

---

internet connect

GO TO: go.hrw.com
KEYWORD: SK5 CH15
FOR: Web sites about India's Neighbors

Terraced fields in the mountains of Nepal allow farmers to increase their production of millet and corn.

Interpreting the Visual Record

(Human-Environment Interaction) How can terracing lead to increased crop production?

322 • Chapter 15

Physical Features

The broad delta formed by the Brahmaputra (brahm-uh-POO-truh) and Ganges (GAN-jeez) Rivers covers most of Bangladesh. Some 200 rivers and streams crisscross this eastern part of the Indian Subcontinent. These numerous waterways, the low elevation of the land, and heavy monsoon rains combine to bring frequent floods to Bangladesh. Although these floods cause great damage, they leave behind a layer of fertile soil.

North of Bangladesh is Bhutan. This tiny country lies high in the mountain range known as the Himalayas (hi-muh-LAY-uhz). To the west is Nepal. The Himalayas occupy some 75 percent of Nepal's land area. Mount Everest, Earth's highest mountain, is located on Nepal's border with China. The Tarai (tuh-RY) is a low plain along Nepal's southern border. It is the country's main farming area. West of the Himalayas is the Karakoram (kah-rah-KOHR-oohm) Range. To the west the Karakorams merge into another mountain range, the Hindu Kush.

On Pakistan's western border is the Khyber (KY-buhr) Pass. For centuries, invaders and traders have traveled through this high mountain pass to India. East of the Khyber Pass is the Indus River. The Indus Valley lies mostly to the east of the river. This valley is Pakistan's main farming region and its most heavily populated area. East of these fertile lands is the Thar (TAHR) Desert, or the Great Indian Desert. A barren, hilly, and dry plateau in western Pakistan joins the plateaus of Iran.

✔ **READING CHECK:** (*Places and Regions*) What are the major physical features of this region? delta, rivers, streams, Himalayas, Khyber Pass, Indus Valley, deserts

Climate and Resources

Bangladesh has one of the world's wettest climates. Rainfall is generally more than 60 inches (127 to 152 cm) each year. Most of the rain falls from June to October, during the wet summer monsoon. In the early and late weeks of the monsoon, **cyclones** sweep in from the Bay of Bengal. These violent storms resemble the hurricanes of the Caribbean. They bring high winds and heavy rain. Cyclones are often accompanied by **storm surges**. These are huge waves of water that are whipped up by fierce winds. The summer monsoon brings hot, wet weather to the lowland areas of Bhutan and Nepal. In the mountains, climates are generally

---

TEACH

Teaching Objectives 1–2

ALL LEVELS: (Suggested time: 20 min.) Pair students and have each pair create a mock Web page that lists the physical features, climate types, and natural resources of Pakistan, Nepal, Bangladesh, and Bhutan. Display Web pages around the classroom. **ESOL, COOPERATIVE LEARNING,** LS **VISUAL-SPATIAL**

Teaching Objective 3

ALL LEVELS: (Suggested time: 10 min.) Copy the following graphic organizer onto the chalkboard, omitting the blue answers. Have each student complete the organizer. Ask volunteers to share their answers with the class. **ESOL**

Physical Features of the Island Countries

SRI LANKA
• plains in northern half and coastal areas
• mountains and hills in south-central part

MALDIVES
• group of about 1,200 tiny islands
• elevation of 6 feet or less above sea level

much cooler. Much of Pakistan has a desert climate, receiving less than 10 inches (25 cm) of rain each year. Summer temperatures can reach as high as 120°F (49°C).

Bangladesh's most important resource is its fertile farmland. About 15 percent of Bangladesh is forested, so it has some timber supplies. However, severe deforestation and soil erosion have plagued the region, particularly in Nepal. Bhutan and Nepal have farmland in low-land areas. Both countries have some minerals, but few are mined. Pakistan has large natural gas reserves but limited oil supplies. It has to import oil to meet its energy needs. Pakistan's other natural resources include coal, limestone, and salt.

✓ **READING CHECK:** (*Places and Regions*) What are the natural resources of the region? Fertile farmland, timber, some minerals, natural gas

The Island Countries

India's neighbors also include Sri Lanka and the Maldives. Sri Lanka is a large island located just off the southeastern tip of India. Plains cover most of the island's northern half and coastal areas. Mountains and hills rise in the south-central part of the island.

About 1,200 tiny tropical islands in the Indian Ocean make up the Maldives. The island group stretches from south of India to the equator. Only about 200 of the islands are inhabited. None rises more than 6 feet (1.8 m) above sea level.

✓ **READING CHECK:** (*Places and Regions*) What are the physical features of the island countries? Plains, mountains, hills, low elevation

In May 1997 a cyclone and storm surges devastated Bangladesh. More than 1.5 million people were left homeless.

Homework Practice Online
Keyword: SK5 HP15

Section Review 1

Define and explain: cyclones, storm surges

Working with Sketch Maps On a map of India and India's Neighbors that you draw or that your teacher provides, label the following: Brahmaputra River, Ganges River, Himalayas, Mount Everest, Tarai, Karakoram Range, Hindu Kush, Khyber Pass, Indus River, and Thar Desert. Where is Earth's highest mountain located? What plains area is Nepal's main farming region?

Reading for the Main Idea

1. (*Places and Regions*) Why has the Khyber Pass been important in the history of Pakistan and India?

2. (*Places and Regions*) How have erosion and defor-estation affected the region? Which country has been most affected by these problems?

3. (*Places and Regions*) What island countries are found in the region? How are they different from each other?

Critical Thinking

4. **Drawing Inferences and Conclusions** How do you think climate affects life in Pakistan and Bangladesh?

Organizing What You Know

5. **Summarizing** Copy the following graphic orga-nizer. Use it to describe the landforms, climates, and resources of the region.

	Major Landforms	Climates	Resources
Pakistan			
Bangladesh			
Bhutan			
Nepal			

India's Neighbors • 323

Section 1 Review

Answers to Section 1 Review

Define For definitions, see the glossary.

Working with Sketch Maps Places should be labeled in their approximate locations. The mountain is on Nepal's bor-der with China; the Tarai is the farming area.

Reading for the Main Idea

1. used for centuries for access into Indian interior **(NGS 4)**

2. depleted available timber and fertile soil; Nepal **(NGS 4)**

3. Sri Lanka—large island; plains, mountains, hills; Maldives—about 1,200 tiny flat tropical islands **(NGS 4)**

Critical Thinking

4. Possible answer: by determin-ing when crops can be planted **(NGS 15)**

Organizing What You Know

5. Pakistan—Hindu Kush, Karakoram Range, Indus Valley, Thar Desert; desert; natural gas, coal, limestone, salt; Bangladesh—delta of Brahmaputra and Ganges Rivers; wet; farmland and for-est; Bhutan—Himalayas; hot and wet, cool; farmland; Nepal—Himalayas, Mount Everest, Tarai; hot and wet, cool; farmland

CLOSE

Read descriptions of or list geographic features of the countries mentioned in Section 1. Have students identify the country described.

REVIEW, ASSESS, RETEACH

Have students complete the Section Review. Then organize students into small groups and have each group write five matching questions about each country's physical geography. Have groups quiz other groups with the questions they have prepared. Then have students complete Daily Quiz 15.1. **COOPERATIVE LEARNING**

Have students complete Main Idea Activity S1. Then have students design their own graphic organizers to depict answers to the Read to Discover questions. **ESOL,** **LS** **VISUAL-SPATIAL**

EXTEND

Have interested students conduct research on one of the invasions that occurred through the Khyber Pass. Have each student give a short presen-tation about his or her chosen event. Ask students to use maps or other visual resources in their presentations. **BLOCK SCHEDULING**

Section 2 Pakistan and Bangladesh

Read to Discover

1. What is the history of Pakistan?
2. What are some features of Pakistan's culture?
3. What is the history of Bangladesh?
4. What challenges face Bangladesh today?

Vocabulary
cholera

Places
Pakistan
Bangladesh
Karachi
Lahore
Islamabad
Dhaka

People
Muhammad Yunus

Reading Strategy

READING ORGANIZER Create a four-column chart. Label the columns Country, History, Population, and Culture. As you read this section, write what you learn about Pakistan and Bangladesh on your chart.

▲
These tombs in Pakistan were built in the 1500s–1700s. Women's graves had floral carvings. Horses and swords decorated men's tombs.

Pakistan's History

An ancient civilization developed in the Indus River valley about 2500 B.C. Ruins of cities show that this was a large and well-organized society. The cause of the disappearance of this civilization about 1500 B.C. remains a mystery.

Over time the fertile Indus River valley was inhabited and conquered by many different groups. It has been part of the empires of Persia, Alexander the Great, and the Mughals. About A.D. 1000 Turkish invaders established Islam in the area. Islam has been the main religion there ever since.

In the early 1600s merchants from England formed the English East India Company to increase the spice trade. It later became known as the British East India Company. Although trade was only moderately successful, the company established England's power in India. It was not until 1947 that India gained independence.

Upon independence, India became two countries. The division into two countries was based on religion. India was mostly Hindu. East and West Pakistan were inhabited mainly by Muslims. Although East Pakistan and West Pakistan were mostly Muslim, they had other cultural differences. These differences led East Pakistan to break away in 1971. It became known as Bangladesh.

✓ **READING CHECK:** (*Human Systems*) What was Pakistan's early history like?
early civilizations in Indus valley; Turkish invaders established Islam; British dominated India; Indian independence and division in 1947

Section 2

Objectives

1. Discuss Pakistan's history.
2. Describe some features of Pakistan's culture.
3. Discuss Bangladesh's history.
4. Identify challenges facing Bangladesh today.

FOCUS

Bellringer

Copy the following passage onto the chalkboard: *How would you learn about the thoughts and emotions of people who lived long ago if you could not read their language? Think about what other things might serve as clues about a civilization.* Discuss responses. Tell students that there was an advanced civilization in the Indus Valley whose language we cannot read. Tell students that in Section 2 they will learn about the history and culture of Pakistan and Bangladesh.

Building Vocabulary

Write the term cholera on the chalkboard. Have a volunteer read aloud the term's definition from the dictionary. Point out that cholera has claimed many lives in South Asia. In fact, cholera is blamed for at least 370,000 deaths in India alone during the period of 1898 to 1907.

Pakistan Today

Pakistan's population is 97 percent Muslim. The country has many different languages and ethnic groups. A small number of Christians, Buddhists, and Hindus also live in Pakistan. Urdu is Pakistan's official language. However, less than 10 percent of the population speak it as their primary language. Many upper-class Pakistanis speak English.

Population Pakistan has the world's sixth largest population. The cities contain about a third of that population. The largest are the port city of Karachi (kuh-RAH-chee), Lahore (luh-HOHR), and the capital, Islamabad. Like the rest of the region, Pakistan is experiencing rapid population growth. In fact, the Indian Subcontinent accounted for about 30 percent of the world's population growth in the late 1990s. How does Pakistan support so many people? The Indus River valley has one of the world's largest irrigation systems. It allows the country to grow enough food for the large population. However, overall economic progress has been slow.

Culture In Pakistan a woman joins her husband's family at marriage. Marriages are usually arranged by parents. The young woman's parents often pay a large amount of money to the young man's family.

Pakistan celebrates many of the same Islamic festivals as other Southwest Asian countries. Festival meals are similar to those of Iran in their emphasis on rice, the region's staple food. Meals also include the grilled meat of chickens, goats, and sheep, as well as delicious breads. Pakistani foods feature strong spices and flavors.

✓ **READING CHECK:** *Human Systems* What is the culture of Pakistan like?
Arranged marriages, Islamic traditions spicy foods

Pakistan and Bangladesh

Country	Population/ Growth Rate	Life Expectancy	Literacy Rate	Per Capita GDP
Bangladesh	138,448,210 2.1%	61, male 61, female	43%	$1,700
Pakistan	150,694,740 2.1%	61, male 63, female	45%	$2,100
United States	290,342,554 0.9%	74, male 80, female	97%	$37,600

Source: Central Intelligence Agency, *The World Factbook 2003*

Interpreting the Chart Which country in the region has a larger population?

Place Pakistan's flag symbolizes the country's commitment to Islam and the Islamic world. The crescent and star are symbols of Islam. The vertical white stripe represents religious minorities.
▼

India's Neighbors • 325

TEACH

Teaching Objectives 1 and 3
ALL LEVELS: (Suggested time: 20 min.) Pair students and have each pair create an annotated and forked time line that shows the common history of Pakistan and Bangladesh as well as their separate histories. Encourage students to plot the dates on their time lines accurately. Ask volunteers to explain their time lines to the class. **ESOL, COOPERATIVE LEARNING, LS LOGICAL-MATHEMATICAL**

Teaching Objective 2
LEVEL 1: (Suggested time: 45 min.) Pair students and have each pair create a collage to represent features of Pakistani culture. Have volunteers discuss their collages with the class.
ESOL, COOPERATIVE LEARNING, LS KINESTHETIC

Across the Curriculum
TECHNOLOGY
Small Loans, Big Results

The Grameen Bank provides small loans to the poorest people in Bangladesh. Loan recipients use the money to purchase supplies or equipment needed for operating a small business. For example, one recipient might buy a sewing machine for a home tailoring business.

One Grameen program sells mobile telephones to individuals in small villages that have no other modern communications equipment. The owner then sells—for a small fee—access to the phone to other members of the community. The program's goal is to provide telephone service to 100 million people in nearly 70,000 villages.

▲

(**Place**) Multan is a commercial and industrial center with several colleges and a university. The city came under Muslim control in the A.D. 700s.

Bangladesh's History

Bangladesh is part of a region known as Bengal. Bengal's many rivers are used for transporting goods. This is one reason why the area was important to Europeans in the 1500s. From the 1500s through the 1700s, the Mughal Empire combined Islam and regional Indian traditions to create a distinctive culture in this region. Eventually, the Mughal Empire weakened. The British East India Company then expanded its control over the area.

Because the British East India Company was so powerful, it could control what was traded. Therefore, British goods came into the region, but few goods other than rice and jute were exported. With a decline in trade, industry suffered. As a result, the region's economy became more agricultural in the 1800s. As you learned earlier, East Pakistan became the independent country of Bangladesh in 1971.

✓ **READING CHECK:** (*Places and Regions*) What has Bangladesh's history been like? British East India Company controlled trade and limited exports, so industry suffered and made the country more agricultural.

Bangladesh Today

Unlike other South Asian countries, Bangladesh has only one main ethnic group—the Bengalis. They make up 98 percent of the population. Social standing is based mostly on wealth and influence rather than on heredity or caste. Muslims may move up or down in status. Even among the country's Hindus, caste has much less importance than it does in India.

LEVELS 2 AND 3: (Suggested time: 30 min.) Tell students to imagine that they are social scientists who are writing a book about Pakistan's culture. Then have each student write an outline for the book. Ask volunteers to share their outlines with the class. **LS VERBAL-LINGUISTIC**

Teaching Objective 4

ALL LEVELS: (Suggested time: 15 min.) Copy the graphic organizer onto the chalkboard, omitting the blue answers. Have students complete the organizer. Use it to help students learn about the challenges facing Bangladesh. Then challenge students to draw lines between those shown to depict how some of the challenges are connected. (For example, flooding can spread disease.) **ESOL**

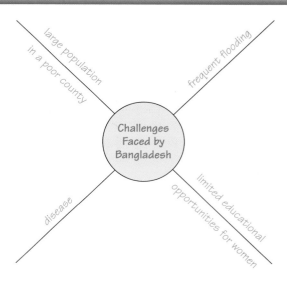

large population in a poor county

frequent flooding

Challenges Faced by Bangladesh

disease

limited educational opportunities for women

Population Bangladesh is about the same size as Wisconsin. However, it has a population nearly half the size of the entire U.S. population. Only 24 percent of Bangladesh's population lives in cities. The country's capital and largest city is Dhaka (DA-kuh). Cities and rural areas are densely populated. On average in Bangladesh there are 2,580 people per square mile (670/sq km).

Flooding and disease are two of the country's biggest challenges. Occasional violent tropical cyclones bring huge storm surges on shore. In addition, runoff from heavy rains in the distant Himalayas causes extensive flooding. When the land is flooded, sewage often washes into the water. As a result, Bangladesh has often suffered from epidemics of diseases like **cholera**. Cholera is a severe intestinal infection.

Culture Family life in Bangladesh is different from that in Pakistan. For example, many Bangladeshi women keep close ties to their own families after marriage. However, as in other South Asian countries, marriages are arranged by parents. Most couples typically do not know each other prior to their wedding.

More girls are going to secondary schools and universities than ever. Even so, the literacy rate for women remains just about half that of men. Bangladesh's official language, Bengali (Bangla), is the language spoken in schools. The country celebrates Islam's main festivals with feasts that feature fish and rice.

✓ **READING CHECK:** (*Places and Regions*) What are some challenges that Bangladesh faces today? flooding, disease

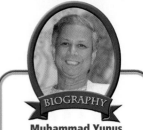

BIOGRAPHY

Muhammad Yunus
(1940–)

Character Trait: Fairness

With a dream to eliminate world poverty, Muhammad Yunus founded a bank in his native Bangladesh. Since then, Yunus' Grameen Bank has lent over 3 billion dollars to poor Bangladeshis. In addition to giving out loans, Grameen Bank also teaches people how to use their money effectively. Through his fair treatment of the poor, Yunus continues to give millions an opportunity for a better future.

How does Muhammad Yunus show fairness towards poor people?

go.hrw.com
Homework Practice Online
Keyword: SK5 HP15

Section Review 2

Define or identify: cholera, Muhammad Yunus

Working with Sketch Maps On the map you created in Section 1, label Pakistan, Bangladesh, Karachi, Lahore, Islamabad, and Dhaka. What does the name of Pakistan's capital indicate about the country's dominant religion?

Reading for the Main Idea

1. (*Places and Regions*) Why were East and West Pakistan separated from India in 1947? When did East and West Pakistan split into two independent countries?

2. (*Environment and Society*) What technology allows Pakistan to grow enough food for its large population? How?

3. (*Environment and Society*) What climatic condition contributes to the high disease rate in Bangladesh? How?

Critical Thinking

4. **Contrasting/Comparing** How are marriage and married life in Pakistan different from marriage and married life in Bangladesh? How are they similar?

Organizing What You Know

5. **Comparing/Contrasting** Copy the following graphic organizer. Use it to compare and contrast Pakistan and Bangladesh.

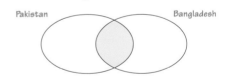

Pakistan   Bangladesh

Answers to Section 2 Review

Define or identify For definition and identification, see the glossary and index.

Working with Sketch Maps The name *Islamabad* indicates the importance of Islam.

Reading for the Main Idea

1. British division of India into predominantly Muslim and Hindu areas; 1971 **(NGS 4)**

2. irrigation of the Indus Valley **(NGS 14)**

3. cyclones; result in flooding, washing sewage into water supply **(NGS 15)**

Critical Thinking

4. Pakistani women join their husbands' families at marriage. Bangladeshi women keep close ties to their own families. However, in both countries most marriages are arranged.

Organizing What You Know

5. Pakistan—many languages and ethnic groups, desert climate; Bangladesh—Bengali ethnic group, flooding; in common—predominantly Muslim countries with similar cultural heritage, large populations, high rates of illiteracy

◀ **Biography Answer**

by giving them the chance to borrow money

CLOSE

List six of the historical events discussed in Section 2 on the chalkboard, but organize the events out of chronological order. Call on volunteers to arrange the events in the correct order.

REVIEW, ASSESS, RETEACH

Have students complete the Section Review. Then organize students into small groups and have each group write an outline of the section. Have groups share their outlines with the class. Then have students complete Daily Quiz 15.2.

Have students complete Main Idea Activity S2. Then organize students into small groups and have each group create an illustrated magazine cover, including story titles, for either Pakistan or Bangladesh. Have groups present their magazine covers to the class.
ESOL, COOPERATIVE LEARNING

EXTEND

Have interested students conduct research on Mohenjo Daro or Harappa, two significant Indus civilization sites, and focus on the street plan, construction techniques and materials, or the social organization of either city. Students should also compare the ancient cities to modern cities.
BLOCK SCHEDULING

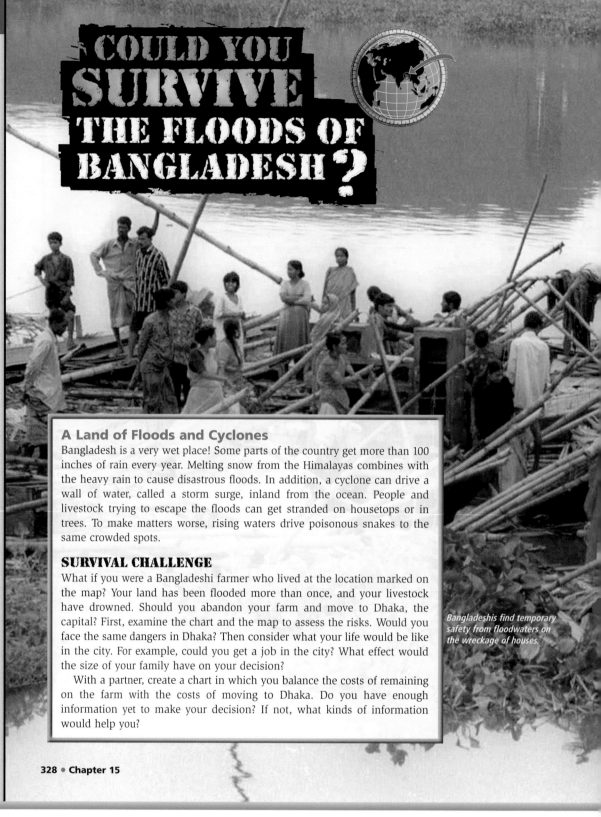

COULD YOU SURVIVE THE FLOODS OF BANGLADESH?

More Dangers for Bangladesh Bangladeshis face other dangers besides floods. What may have been the world's deadliest tornado struck several cities in 1989, killing about 1,300 people. Bangladesh also holds the record for heaviest hailstones—balls of ice weighing more than two pounds. These monster hailstones killed dozens of people. In addition, ground-water containing arsenic threatens the health of Bangladeshis. (For more information on this problem, see the Environment and Society side wrap feature in Section 2 of Chapter 2.)

Finally, focus attention on the area on the feature's map labeled "Subject to salt build-up." Farming in this area is difficult because the salt can severely limit crop yields. In addition, Bangladeshis who venture into the coastal mangrove forest in the Sundarbans area risk meeting one of the forest's many tigers.

internet connect

GO TO: go.hrw.com
KEYWORD: SK5 CH15
FOR: more information on weather extremes.

A Land of Floods and Cyclones

Bangladesh is a very wet place! Some parts of the country get more than 100 inches of rain every year. Melting snow from the Himalayas combines with the heavy rain to cause disastrous floods. In addition, a cyclone can drive a wall of water, called a storm surge, inland from the ocean. People and livestock trying to escape the floods can get stranded on housetops or in trees. To make matters worse, rising waters drive poisonous snakes to the same crowded spots.

SURVIVAL CHALLENGE

What if you were a Bangladeshi farmer who lived at the location marked on the map? Your land has been flooded more than once, and your livestock have drowned. Should you abandon your farm and move to Dhaka, the capital? First, examine the chart and the map to assess the risks. Would you face the same dangers in Dhaka? Then consider what your life would be like in the city. For example, could you get a job in the city? What effect would the size of your family have on your decision?

With a partner, create a chart in which you balance the costs of remaining on the farm with the costs of moving to Dhaka. Do you have enough information yet to make your decision? If not, what kinds of information would help you?

Bangladeshis find temporary safety from floodwaters on the wreckage of houses.

Survival Challenge Activity

To help students create their charts, discuss the concept of "push" and "pull" factors in migration. The reasons a farmer would want to leave the countryside would be the "push" factors. Those that would draw a farmer to the city are the "pull" factors.

Threat of floods would be a "push" factor. Have students examine the chart and map to determine if Dhaka experiences flooding. (It's on the edge of a "high or seldom flooded land" area, but it was flooded in 1998.) So, moving to Dhaka wouldn't eliminate the threat of flooding completely. However, some of Dhaka's sturdier buildings have stood since the 1600s. In the countryside, many people die when high winds collapse their flimsy houses onto them. Ask students where basic survival may be easier. (If one could find a sturdy and affordable place to live in Dhaka, basic survival may be easier there.)

What else may work as a "pull" factor? For example, how easily may one get work in Dhaka? Bangladesh has little industry, so factory jobs for unskilled workers are limited. Even for educated people, unemployment is high. If the farmer had a large family, job opportunities may be limited for the spouse and children.

Call on students to defend their decisions to stay or leave their farms. (Students may note that they would want more information about life in Dhaka or predictions about future floods before making a decision.)

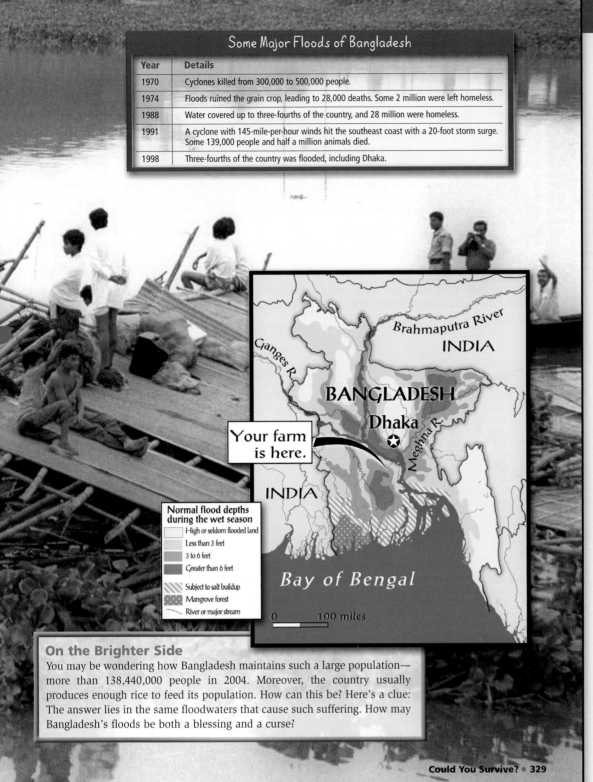

Some Major Floods of Bangladesh

Year	Details
1970	Cyclones killed from 300,000 to 500,000 people.
1974	Floods ruined the grain crop, leading to 28,000 deaths. Some 2 million were left homeless.
1988	Water covered up to three-fourths of the country, and 28 million were homeless.
1991	A cyclone with 145-mile-per-hour winds hit the southeast coast with a 20-foot storm surge. Some 139,000 people and half a million animals died.
1998	Three-fourths of the country was flooded, including Dhaka.

Your farm is here.

Normal flood depths during the wet season

High or seldom flooded land

Less than 3 feet

3 to 6 feet

Greater than 6 feet

Subject to salt buildup

Mangrove forest

River or major stream

0   100 miles

Brahmaputra River

INDIA

Ganges R.

BANGLADESH

Dhaka

Meghna R.

INDIA

Bay of Bengal

On the Brighter Side

You may be wondering how Bangladesh maintains such a large population—more than 138,440,000 people in 2004. Moreover, the country usually produces enough rice to feed its population. How can this be? Here's a clue: The answer lies in the same floodwaters that cause such suffering. How may Bangladesh's floods be both a blessing and a curse?

Going Further: Thinking Critically

Bangladesh lies at the mercy of several rivers, all of which begin in other countries. First, point out the sources of these rivers on a detailed physical map of Bangladesh and the surrounding region: Surma River (India), Ganges River (Nepal), and Brahmaputra (China). As a result, Bangladesh has limited power over regulating these rivers.

Near Bangladesh's western border lies the Indian town of Farakka, where a dam called the Farakka Barrage spans the Ganges River. The dam has caused tension between Bangladesh and India because it reduces the river's flow to areas that need the river's water.

Activity: Organize the class into teams to represent Bangladesh and India. Have the teams conduct research on the Farakka Barrage and other river-related conflicts that trouble the two countries. Then stage a conference at which the two sides air their grievances and compromise on solutions.

➤ This Could You Survive? feature addresses National Geography Standards 1, 9, 12, and 18.

On the Brighter Side Activity

Remind students that the rivers of Bangladesh bring rich silt down from the mountains. As a result, the soil is so fertile that farmers can raise three rice crops per year. In addition, floods carry fish to areas where they can breed. Fish are an important source of protein. So, life in the countryside has some advantages. If farmers decide to stay there, how could they protect themselves from danger?

Ask students what else they or the government could do to reduce flood casualties. (Students may suggest better evacuation procedures, but with so much land under water, there are few safe places left. Others may suggest

shelters.) In fact, the Bangladeshi government has built more than 1,200 shelters in low-lying areas where people and their livestock can get above the floodwaters.

Are there other ways besides farming to make a living in the countryside? Encourage students to review the text's information on Bangladesh for clues. (Students may decide that getting a micro-loan and starting a small business would allow them to avoid some of the worst hazards of flooding. They wouldn't have to depend so heavily on land or livestock.)

Section 3 The Himalayan and Island Countries

Read to Discover

1. What are some important features of Nepal?
2. How has Bhutan developed over time?
3. What is Sri Lanka like?
4. What are some economic activities of the Maldives?

Vocabulary

stupas
graphite
atolls

Places

Nepal
Kathmandu
Bhutan
Thimphu
Sri Lanka
Colombo

Maldives
Male

People

Tenzing Norgay

Reading Strategy

FOLDNOTES: LAYERED BOOK Create the FoldNote titled **Layered Book** described in the Appendix. Label the top layer Nepal. Label the other layers Bhutan, Sri Lanka, and the Maldives. As you read this section, write what you learn about each country above its label.

Place A temple to the Hindu god Krishna can be seen from Durban Square in Patan, near Kathmandu, Nepal. The pillar in the square honors Krishna's companion, Garuda.

Nepal

Nepal's history is linked to the early civilizations of northern India. Nepal shared its languages, culture, and economic base with peoples to the south. It was probably in Nepal that Gautama, the Buddha, was born about 563 B.C. Some of the oldest monuments to the Buddha are **stupas** in Nepal. They date back to before 300 B.C. Stupas are mounds of earth or stones covering the ashes of the Buddha or relics of Buddhist saints. Like India, Nepal adopted Buddhism at first but was mostly Hindu by A.D. 1200. About 90 percent of Nepal's people are now Hindus.

The British never formally ruled Nepal. Their army did defeat the Nepalese army in the early 1800s. As a result, the British took away the territories claimed by Nepal and sent an official to maintain indirect control. The British later recognized Nepal's independence. Nepal now is a constitutional monarchy with a king and elected parliament.

One of Nepal's ethnic groups is the Sherpa. The Sherpa guide and serve as porters for Himalayan expeditions. Tenzing Norgay, a Sherpa, and Sir Edmund Hillary, an explorer from New Zealand, climbed Mount Everest in 1953. They were the first to reach the summit.

✔ **READING CHECK:** *Places and Regions* What has the history of Nepal been like? linked to early northern Indian civilizations; believed to be the birthplace of the Buddha; indirectly controlled by the British; gained independence and is now a constitutional monarchy

Section 3

Objectives

1. Describe some important features of Nepal.
2. Explain how Bhutan has developed.
3. Discuss what Sri Lanka is like.
4. Identify some economic activities of the Maldives.

FOCUS

🎧 Bellringer

Copy the following questions onto the chalkboard: *What is the highest mountain in the world? What would it be like to climb that mountain?* Discuss responses. (Mount Everest is the highest mountain. Students' descriptions will vary.) Point out that many tourists come to Nepal to view Mount Everest. Tell students that in Section 3 they will learn more about the Himalayan countries, Nepal and Bhutan. They will also learn about the island countries, Sri Lanka and the Maldives.

Building Vocabulary

Write the terms **stupas**, **graphite**, and **atolls** on the chalkboard. Ask volunteers to look up the terms and their origins in a dictionary and to read them aloud to the class. Tell students that the terms *stupa* and *atoll* originated in the region and that they describe cultural and physical phenomena that are not found in Europe.

CONNECTING TO Technology

The world's highest peak, Mount Everest, sits on the border between China and Nepal. At 29,035 feet (8,850 m), it is one of the world's greatest mountaineering challenges.

After many failed attempts, two climbers—Edmund Hillary and Tenzing Norgay—finally reached the summit in 1953. One factor in their success was the use of advanced equipment. This equipment included special boots, oxygen bottles, and radio gear. Since then, technology has continued to play a key role in efforts to scale the Himalayas.

CLIMBING MOUNT EVEREST

Today's climbers use a wide range of sophisticated gear. This gear includes everything from space-age mountaineering clothes to remote sensors and satellite-tracking devices. Even so, climbing Everest remains very dangerous. In the 1990s more than 50 climbers lost their lives trying to scale the peak. Now scientists are testing new medical technologies on Mount Everest in hopes of preventing such tragedies in the future.

A joint project of the National Aeronautics and Space Administration (NASA) and Yale University has been analyzing the effects of high-altitude climbing on the human body. In 1998 this project sent a team of climbers up Mount Everest wearing "bio-packs." These packs included high-tech devices to monitor heart rate, blood oxygen, and other vital signs. This data was transmitted instantly to a base camp on Everest. There doctors could analyze the results. Scientists believe that this kind of "telemedicine" will help save lives in other extreme environments, including outer space.

Understanding What You Read

1. How do climbers use technology on Mount Everest?
2. How might climbers benefit from the use of new medical technology?

Sir Edmund Hillary (left) and Tenzing Norgay (right)

Nepal Today

Like other countries of the region, Nepal's economy is based on agriculture. More than 80 percent of the people make a living from farming. Most are subsistence farmers. The best farmland is found on the Tarai—Nepal's "breadbasket." Farmers there grow such crops as rice, other grains, and sugarcane. In the hills north of the Tarai, farmers grow fruits, grains, and vegetables. Kathmandu (kat-man-DOO), Nepal's capital and largest city, is located in this central region. For the most part, the Himalayan region is not good for

Culture and Music

Art of Nepal's Monks and Nuns In Nepal, monks and nuns maintain ancient Buddhist practices, including traditional rituals and art forms. Among the arts they practice is the creation of mandalas, which are circular designs with symbolic meaning, made with colored sand. Creating a sand mandala takes several days of precise work. When complete, the mandala's creators destroy it to show that life, like the beautiful work of art, does not last.

Activity: Have students conduct research for pictures of mandalas. For the sound of a Buddhist ritual, listen to Selection 18 on the Music of the World Audio CD Program. Use the text and questions in the Teacher's Guide.

Connecting to Technology
Answers
1. They use specialized equipment for mountaineering.
2. It might save the lives of injured climbers.

TEACH

Teaching Objective 1

ALL LEVELS: (Suggested time: 15 min.) Copy the following graphic organizer onto the chalkboard, omitting the blue answers. Use it to help students identify the important features of Nepal. Have each student complete the organizer by filling in information about Nepal's culture, history, and economy. Ask volunteers to share their answers with the class. **ESOL**

Important Features of Nepal

CULTURE
- shares cultural heritage with India
- predominantly Hindu
- Buddhist legacy remains.

HISTORY
- birthplace of Buddha
- indirectly controlled by British
- independent country with unstable multi-party system

ECONOMY
- agrarian economy
- few industries
- tourism important but has led to environmental damage

Nepal Today

National Geography Standard 6:
Bhutan by Another Name

Bhutan's natural boundaries—dense forests and mountains—have helped keep it isolated. Little is known about the early history of Bhutan. Bhutanese call their country Druk-yul, which means "the land of the thunder dragon." The name *Bhutan* is used only in the country's English-language communication.

Discussion: What may Bhutan's traditional name suggest about the way the Bhutanese view their country?

▲
Human-Environment Interaction
Nepalese women are experts at winnowing grain. Winnowing is the process of separating chaff from grain by fanning.

Place Folk dancers in traditional dress perform near Thimphu, Bhutan.
▼

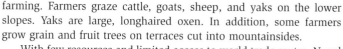

farming. Farmers graze cattle, goats, sheep, and yaks on the lower slopes. Yaks are large, longhaired oxen. In addition, some farmers grow grain and fruit trees on terraces cut into mountainsides.

With few resources and limited access to world trade routes, Nepal has developed few industries. Most of its industries are based on farm products, such as jute. Jute is a plant fiber that is used in making twine. Tourism is one of the fastest-growing and most important industries in Nepal. Tourists like to hike and climb in the mountains.

Tourism brings in much-needed income to Nepal. However, the constant stream of hikers and climbers threatens the country's environment. How? Many visitors leave behind trash. Also, their need for firewood contributes to deforestation and soil erosion. This problem is worsened as Nepalese clear woodland for farming and for wood for fuel. In response, Nepal's government has restricted access by visitors to some of the most affected areas.

✓ **READING CHECK:** (*Places and Regions*) What is Nepal like? agricultural; tourism and important industry but threatens environment, as do deforestation and erosion

Bhutan

Little is known about the early history of Bhutan. Buddhism was practiced there as early as the A.D. 600s. Most of the people are of Tibetan origin and are Buddhist. In the 1600s a Tibetan monk helped organize Bhutan as a unified state. Then in the late 1700s the East India Company's business dealings increased British influence.

Bhutan, although very isolated, was under Indian control during British rule over that country.

TEACH

Teaching Objective 2

LEVEL 1: (Suggested time: 15 min.) Pair students and have each pair compile a bulleted list that describes the history, culture, and economy of Bhutan. Ask volunteers to read their lists to the class. **ESOL, COOPERATIVE LEARNING**

LEVEL 2: (Suggested time: 30 min.) Have students use their lists from the Level 1 activity to write a short poem that describes Bhutan. Ask volunteers to recite their poems. **COOPERATIVE LEARNING,** 🄻🄢 **AUDITORY-MUSICAL**

TEACHER TO TEACHER

Joanne Sadler of Buffalo, New York, suggests the following activity to help students learn about the countries neighboring India: Tell students to imagine that they are foreign exchange students who have been living in Nepal, Bhutan, Sri Lanka, or the Maldives for the past year. Have each student write a short article for your newspaper's travel section that describes life in that country today as well as aspects of the country's culture and history. Ask volunteers to read their letters to the class.

Bhutan's ruler, or maharaja, declared a constitutional monarchy in 1969.

✓ **READING CHECK:** (*Places and Regions*) What has the history of Bhutan been like? isolated; under Indian control; constitutional monarchy established in 1969

Bhutan Today

Until the mid-1970s, the government of Bhutan followed a policy of near total isolation. Even today, the country's international ties are somewhat limited.

Much of Bhutan's economy is traditional. More than 90 percent of the people make a living as subsistence farmers. Most grow rice, wheat, corn, and potatoes in fertile valleys and on mountainside terraces. A few grow fruits and spices for export. On mountain pastures, farmers raise cattle, goats, sheep, and yaks. Thimphu (thim-POO) is Bhutan's capital.

Timber and hydroelectricity are among Bhutan's most important resources. The country sells both to India, its main trading partner. Tourism is also a source of income for Bhutan. However, the government limits the number of visitors. By restricting tourism, the government hopes to protect Bhutan's way of life from outside influences and environmental damage.

✓ **READING CHECK:** (*Places and Regions*) What is Bhutan like today? limited international ties, traditional economy, limited tourism

Sri Lanka

When Buddhism swept over India between the 400s and 200s B.C., Buddhist missionaries came to Sri Lanka. From Sri Lanka, traders spread Buddhism eastward to what are now Thailand and Indonesia. About 74 percent of Sri Lankans today belong to the Sinhalese ethnic group, and most are Buddhists. Sri Lanka has many dome-shaped stupas honoring the Buddha. Many are shaded by trees said to have been grown from cuttings of the original bo tree. It is believed the Buddha achieved enlightenment under this tree.

Throughout its history, Sri Lanka has been largely independent from India. In the 1500s the Portuguese established a trading post on the island. They were overthrown by the Dutch. The Dutch turned over Sri Lanka, then known as Ceylon, to the British in the late 1700s. The British granted independence in 1948. The new government made Sinhalese the official language and promoted Buddhism. An Indian and Hindu minority group, the Tamils, protested. Fighting between Tamils and the government has killed many people.

✓ **READING CHECK:** (*Places and Regions*) How have Europeans played a role in Sri Lanka's history? Portuguese—established a trading post in the 1500s; Dutch—overthrew Portuguese and turned over to Ceylon to British in the late 1700s; British—granted independence in 1948

Himalayan and Island Countries

COUNTRY	POPULATION/ GROWTH RATE	LIFE EXPECTANCY	LITERACY RATE	PER CAPITA GDP
Bhutan	2,139,549 2.1%	53, male 53, female	42%	$1,300
Maldives	329,684 3.0%	62, male 64, female	97%	$3,900
Nepal	26,469,569 2.3%	59, male 58, female	45%	$1,400
Sri Lanka	19,742,439 0.9%	70, male 75, female	90%	$3,700
United States	290,342,554 0.9%	74, male 80, female	97%	$37,600

Source: Central Intelligence Agency, *The World Factbook 2003*

Interpreting the Chart Which country has the lowest literacy rate?

▲ (*Place*) Buddhist monks prepare to pray at the top of Adam's Peak. The "yellow" robe is a symbol of Buddhism. The color of the robe varies according to the dye used.

India's Neighbors • 333

COOPERATIVE LEARNING

Biogeography in the Himalayas Bhutan and Nepal are known for their biological richness. The Himalayas have prevented plant species from spreading northward from India and southward from China. Botanists have estimated that there are at least 6,500 species of flowering plants in Nepal.

There may be even more species in Bhutan, partly because the country has cold and warm climate regions within a small area. Also, the country's isolation has saved it from mass deforestation. There are conifers, oaks, maples, laurels, and magnolias unique to Bhutan.

Organize students into six groups and assign each group one of the following topics: Nepal's climates, Nepal's plant life, Nepal's animal life, Bhutan's climates, Bhutan's plant life, or Bhutan's animal life. Have groups conduct research on their topic. Then have the groups use their findings to create murals that depict the connections among climates, plant life, and animal life for the two countries. Have students create two murals—one for each country.

▲ **Chart Answer**

Bhutan

Teaching Objective 3

LEVEL 1: (Suggested time: 20 min.) Pair students and have each student create a graphic organizer to present information about Sri Lanka's history, culture, and economy. Ask volunteers to present their organizers to the class. **COOPERATIVE LEARNING**

LEVELS 2 AND 3: (Suggested time: 30 min.) Tell students to imagine that they must write an encyclopedia entry about Sri Lanka. Have each student write a short entry describing Sri Lanka's history, culture, and economy. Ask students to include information from the photos and photo captions in their entries. Ask volunteers to read their entries to the class.
LS VERBAL-LINGUISTIC

FOOD FESTIVAL

Homemade Ice Cream from Pakistan Banana ice cream is a popular dessert in Pakistan. To prepare ice cream for six, combine four ripe bananas and a 14-ounce can of sweetened condensed milk in a large bowl. Whisk in ¾ cup of whipping cream. Pour the banana mixture into a cake pan. Cover the pan and freeze until the mixture is softly set, stirring it occasionally. Transfer the mixture to a large bowl. Using an electric mixer, beat the ice cream until it is fluffy. Return the ice cream to the pan and cover and freeze it until firm, about six hours.

(**Place**) The Dalada Maligawa (Temple of the Tooth) houses the sacred tooth of Buddha. Pilgrims come to pay respect to the Tooth Relic during daily ceremonies.

Human-Environment Interaction
Semiprecious stones such as the sapphire, ruby, cat's eye, topaz, and garnet are mined in Sri Lanka.

334 • Chapter 15

Sri Lanka Today

Caste determines how Sri Lankans behave toward one another. As in India, many Sri Lankans believe associating with a member of a lower caste brings bad karma. Bad karma forces a person to undergo endless reincarnations, or rebirths. It also prevents him or her from finding nirvana, or spiritual release.

Sri Lanka has several features in common with the countries of the mainland. First, it is a mainly rural country. Less than 25 percent of Sri Lankans live in cities. Second, about 38 percent of Sri Lankans make a living from farming. They grow rice, fruits, and vegetables. Sri Lankan farmers also grow coconuts, rubber, and tea for export. Sri Lanka has a number of industries. They include food processing, textiles and apparel, telecommunications, insurance, and banking.

Mining is another important economic activity in Sri Lanka. The main resources mined are graphite and precious gems. Sri Lanka leads the world in **graphite** exports. Graphite is a form of carbon used in pencils and many other products. Recently, manufacturing—particularly of textiles and clothing—has grown in importance. Many textile and clothing factories are found in Colombo, the capital of Sri Lanka. Located on the west coast, Colombo is the country's largest city. It is also its most important commercial center and seaport. Sri Lanka's economy has grown in recent years. However, continuing ethnic conflicts between the Sinhalese majority and the Tamil minority threaten the country's progress.

✓ **READING CHECK:** (*Places and Regions*) What is Sri Lanka like today?
caste system; mainly rural; some industry, mining; ethnic conflict

Teaching Objective 4

LEVEL 1: (Suggested time: 20 min.) Pair students and have each pair create a collage to show the main economic activities in the Maldives. Ask each pair to present its collage. **ESOL, COOPERATIVE LEARNING**

LEVELS 2 AND 3: (Suggested time: 20 min.) Pair students and have each pair write a song about the main economic activities in the Maldives and their relations to the country's physical geography. Ask volunteers to sing their songs for the class. **COOPERATIVE LEARNING**

►**ASSIGNMENT:** Have each student create a map of the Maldives and use symbols to represent the main economic activities of the islands. Students should also create a key to explain their symbols. Display students' maps around the classroom.

The Maldives

The Maldives were originally settled by Buddhists from Sri Lanka. Today the main religion is Islam. Education includes traditional teachings of the Qur'an. However, there are no colleges or universities.

The Maldives consists of 19 **atolls**. An atoll is a ring of coral surrounding a body of water called a lagoon. These atolls sit atop an ancient submerged volcanic plateau. Altogether, the islands cover about 115 square miles (298 sq km). The largest island, Male (MAH-lay), is home to about one fourth of the population. A city by the same name serves as the country's capital. Only about 25 percent of the people live in cities.

Tourism is the Maldives largest industry. Fishing, particularly of tuna, is another of the country's chief economic activities. Exports of fresh, dried, frozen, and canned fish account for about half the country's income. Breadfruit—a fruit that resembles bread when baked—and coconuts are the Maldives' main food crops. Most other food must be imported. A small clothing industry and boatbuilding and repair are other sources of income for this island country.

✓ **READING CHECK:** (*Environment and Society*) What geographic factors affect the economic activities of the Maldives?
Good soil, ocean waters contribute to fishing and farming.

These fishers are working together to corral fish in large nets.

Interpreting the Visual Record
(*Human-Environment Interaction*) Why must so many people be involved in catching fish in this way?

Homework Practice Online
Keyword: SK5 HP15

Section Review 3

Define or identify: stupas, Tenzing Norgay, graphite, atolls

Working with Sketch Maps On the map you created in Section 2, label Nepal, Kathmandu, Bhutan, Thimphu, Sri Lanka, Colombo, Maldives, and Male.

Reading for the Main Idea

1. (*Environment and Society*) How have the people of Nepal used the lower slopes of the Himalayas?
2. (*Human Systems*) How does the caste system affect social interaction in Sri Lanka?
3. (*Places and Regions*) What are the major economic activities of the Maldives?

Critical Thinking

4. **Comparing** In what ways have the cultures, people, and histories of India and the countries in this section been linked?

Organizing What You Know

5. **Categorizing** Copy the following graphic organizer. Use it to list the benefits and drawbacks of tourism in Nepal and Bhutan.

Tourism in Nepal and Bhutan
Benefits | Drawbacks

India's Neighbors • 335

Section 3 Review

Answers to Section 3 Review

Define or identify For definitions and identification, see the glossary and index.

Working with Sketch Maps Maps will vary, but listed places should be labeled in their approximate locations.

Reading for the Main Idea

1. by grazing animals on the land and raising crops on terraces cut into hillsides **(NGS 14)**
2. keeps people from associating with those of lower castes **(NGS 10)**
3. fishing and the processing of fish **(NGS 4)**

Critical Thinking

4. Students' should discuss cultural, military, political, and religious links.

Organizing What You Know

5. Benefits—brings income; Drawbacks—results in environmental damage

◄ **Visual Record Answer**

net's size and the absence of machinery

CLOSE

Ask students to recall what they have learned about global warming. Then ask students how the Maldives may be affected by global warming. (Rising water levels could threaten the Maldives, which lie at a low elevation.)

Have students complete Main Idea Activity S3. Then have students design commemorative stamps for Nepal, Bhutan, Sri Lanka, or the Maldives. **ESOL,** **LS** **VISUAL-SPATIAL**

REVIEW, ASSESS, RETEACH

Have students complete the Section Review. Then pair students and have each pair use the Section 3 vocabulary terms and places to create a hidden-word puzzle. Have pairs solve and discuss other pairs' puzzles. Then have students complete Daily Quiz 15.3. **COOPERATIVE LEARNING**

EXTEND

Have interested students conduct research on Anuradhapura, a town in Sri Lanka that for hundreds of years was the capital of the Sinhalese kings. It is sacred to Buddhists as the site where the ruler converted to Buddhism. Ask students to create a poster about Anuradhapura's history and cultural attractions. **BLOCK SCHEDULING**

Define and Identify
For definitions and identifications, see the glossary and index.

Review the Main Ideas

9. the Ganges and Jamuna rivers (NGS 4)

10. Mount Everest

11. wet summer monsoon and cyclones

12. Pakistan, Bangladesh, and the Maldives; Sri Lanka and Bhutan; Nepal (NGS 9)

13. Bangladesh—woman often keeps close ties to her own family after marriage; Pakistan—woman joins husband's family, arranged marriage, parents pay large amount of money

14. seafood, textiles, timber, and hydroelectric power (NGS 4)

15. few resources and limited access to world trade routes; farm products, such as jute

16. to lessen outside influence and environmental damage

17. Colombo contains textile and clothing manufacturing industries and is a seaport.

18. atolls (NGS 4)

Think Critically

19. The pass has allowed several groups to invade and conquer it.

20. brought income; environmental damage (NGS 13)

21. initiated British colonization of the region

22. rural; economies based on agriculture

23. Pakistan and Bangladesh were created originally as West and East Pakistan because the people there were mainly Muslims, in contrast to the Indian population, which was mainly Hindu.

Review and Practice

Define and Identify
Identify each of the following:

1. cyclones
2. storm surges
3. cholera
4. Muhammad Yunus
5. stupas
6. Tenzing Norgay
7. graphite
8. atolls

Review the Main Ideas

9. What two rivers are important to Bangladesh?

10. What mountain is located on Nepal's border with China?

11. What brings so much rain to Bangladesh?

12. Which three of India's Neighbors are dominated by Islam? Which two are primarily Buddhist? Which one is populated mostly by Hindus?

13. How is married life for women in Bangladesh different from married life in Pakistan?

14. What are some important resources of India's Neighbors?

15. Why have so few industries developed in Nepal? What are some of Nepal's industries?

16. Why does the government of Bhutan limit tourism?

17. Why is Colombo, Sri Lanka an important commercial center?

18. What kinds of islands make up the Maldives?

Think Critically

19. **Drawing Inferences and Conclusions** What role do you think the Khyber Pass might have played in the history of this region?

20. **Finding the Main Idea** How has tourism benefited countries in the region? What problems has it caused?

21. **Analyzing Information** How did the British East India Company affect the history of this region?

22. **Analyzing Information** Is the population of India's Neighbors mostly rural or mostly urban? Explain your answer.

23. **Drawing Inferences and Conclusions** How has religion played a role in shaping the region's borders?

Map Activity

24. On a separate sheet of paper, match the letters on the map with their correct labels.

Brahmaputra River	Hindu Kush
Ganges River	Khyber Pass
Himalayas	Indus River
Tarai	Thar Desert

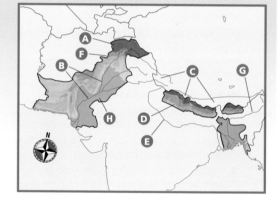

Map Activity

24. **A.** Hindu Kush

    B. Indus River

    C. Himalayas

    D. Tarai

    E. Ganges River

    F. Khyber Pass

    G. Brahmaputra River

    H. Thar Desert

Writing Activity

Imagine that you are moving to one of India's Neighbors. In which country would you choose to live? State your choice and explain your reasons in two or three paragraphs. Explain how landforms, climate, culture, and economy influenced your decision. Be sure to use standard grammar, spelling, sentence structure, and punctuation.

internet connect

Internet Activity: go.hrw.com
KEYWORD: SK5 GT15

Choose a topic to explore about India's Neighbors.
- Climb the Himalayas.
- Learn about Sri Lanka's history.
- Visit the regions of Pakistan.

Social Studies Skills Practice

Interpreting Cartoons

Study the cartoon about Mount Everest below. Then answer the questions.

WHY ARE WE PICKING ALL THIS TRASH UP?

BECAUSE IT'S THERE.

©2000 Paul Dlugokencky (www.aDailyCartoon.com) for APS News

Source: ©2000 Paul Dlugokencky

1. What problem does this cartoon highlight?
2. How does this cartoonist show that the problem is a major one?
3. Why do you think there is trash on Mount Everest?
4. Who does the cartoonist believe should be responsible for responding to the trash problem?

Analyzing Primary Sources

Read the following quote from Sheika Hasina, who was the prime minister of Bangladesh at the time of this 2000 interview. Then answer the questions.

"We're trying to create an environment that will help us participate in globalization. . . . In 1996, Bangladesh, a country with 120 million people, had only 200,000 phones. We've undertaken major expansion and introduced cellular phones. We've withdrawn taxes on computers, all of which we import. . . . We've started computer schools to create more skilled workers. We now have more than 50 Internet service providers."

Source: *Los Angeles Times*

1. What issue does this quote focus on?
2. What is Bangladesh doing to create skilled workers?
3. What changes does Sheika Hasina see as the key to improving Bangladesh?
4. How might withdrawing taxes on computers promote economic development?

Writing Activity

Answers will vary, but the information included should be consistent with text material. Each student should explain his or her choice by relating how landforms, climate, culture, and economy influenced the choice. Use Rubric 37, Writing Assignments, to evaluate student work.

Interpreting Cartoons

1. littering by tourists and climbers
2. The trash pile is as large as a mountain.
3. Climbers leave trash behind rather than increasing their loads.
4. climbers and tourists themselves

Analyzing Primary Sources

1. the increasing use of technology and economic development in Bangladesh
2. creating computer schools to train skilled workers
3. introducing high-tech tools such as computers, cellular phones, and internet access
4. Without taxes, businesses can buy computers at a lower cost.

CHAPTER 15

REVIEW AND ASSESSMENT RESOURCES

Reproducible
- Readings in World Geography, History, and Culture 77 and 78
- Critical Thinking Activity 15
- Vocabulary Activity 15

Technology
- Chapter 15 Test Generator (on the One-Stop Planner)

- Audio CD Program, Chapter 15
- HRW Go site

Reinforcement, Review, and Assessment
- Chapter Review and Practice
- Chapter Summaries and Review
- Chapter 15 Test

- Chapter 15 Test for English Language Learners and Special-Needs Students
- Unit 8 Test
- Unit 8 Test for English Language Learners and Special-Needs Students

internet connect

GO TO: go.hrw.com
KEYWORD: SK5 Teacher
FOR: a guide to using the Internet in your classroom

Saving Tigers

The Sundarbans is an area of thick forest and swamps on the coast of the Indian Ocean. As part of the Ganges Delta, it spans the India-Bangladesh border. The Sundarbans is one of the most important protected tiger habitats in South Asia.

People who live in the Sundarbans area would prefer not to enter the forest, for fear of tiger attacks. They take the risk, however, to fish and gather wood or honey.

Several ingenious methods have been used to combat human-eating tigers. Life-sized dummies rigged with car batteries have been placed in the forest. The dummy emits a mild electric shock upon contact, thereby training tigers to fear humans. Local people also wear government-issued face masks on the backs of their heads when they enter the forest. Tigers usually attack from the back, so the mask confuses the animals. It appears, however, that the Sundarbans tigers may have figured out the trick.

Critical Thinking: How have people in the Sundarbans area tried to prevent tiger attacks?

Answer: by training the tigers through the use of dummies and face masks

➤ This Focus On Environment feature addresses National Geography Standards 4, 14, 15, and 18.

The Tiger

In the early 1800s India's tiger population was very large. By 1900, hunters had reduced the tiger population to about 40,000. To protect these tigers, India's British rulers placed strict limits on hunting them. Laws against illegal hunting were strictly enforced. After India won its independence in 1947, the hunting laws were often ignored, however. As a result, fewer than 2,000 tigers remained in India by 1972.

Why Are Tigers Endangered?

Unfortunately, laws have not kept people from hunting tigers. Tiger bones are used in traditional Chinese medicines. The bones are in high demand. International treaties now make it illegal to sell any part of an endangered species. However, the international trade in tiger bones continues.

Loss of habitat also threatens tiger survival. India's population has about doubled in the last 50 years. More land is now farmed to feed these additional people. As a result, many forests where tigers lived have been cleared for farming. As tiger habitat has decreased, so has the number of tigers.

International Efforts to Save the Tiger

Many people realized that tigers would not survive in the wild without protection. As a result, several international organizations and governments are working to ensure the tiger's future.

India's Project Tiger In 1973 the Indian government took steps to try to save its remaining tigers. With support from the World Wildlife Fund, nine tiger reserves were created as part of Project Tiger. By 2003, 27 reserves had been set up throughout India.

Each reserve has a core area. No one can enter this area without a park ranger. The core area is surrounded by a buffer zone. People can use land in these zones in ways that do not harm the environment.

Once on the verge of extinction, tigers have rebounded in India due largely to Project Tiger.

▼

FOCUS ON ENVIRONMENT

Solving Problems

Tell students to imagine that they are Indian farmers living near a wildlife preserve. They are meeting to find a solution that will allow their villages to survive and grow while protecting the tigers and their habitat. Have students create a list of their specific concerns. (Possible answers: the need for farmland and firewood, protection against attacks by tigers) Then have them suggest ways of addressing these concerns. Write students' suggestions on the chalkboard. Then have students examine each suggestion's consequences for the tigers and reject any that do not also help protect the animals. Then have students work in pairs to refine the remaining solution(s) into a written proposal.

Realm of the Tiger

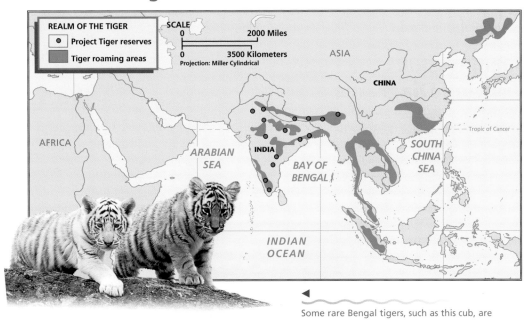

REALM OF THE TIGER
- Project Tiger reserves
- Tiger roaming areas

SCALE
0 — 2000 Miles
0 — 3500 Kilometers
Projection: Miller Cylindrical

ASIA
CHINA
INDIA
ARABIAN SEA
BAY OF BENGAL
SOUTH CHINA SEA
INDIAN OCEAN
AFRICA
— Tropic of Cancer —

◄ Some rare Bengal tigers, such as this cub, are white. In the last 100 years, only about a dozen white tigers have been seen in the wild.

Some conservationists are reaching out to nearby villagers. Villagers have often felt that tigers are being protected at their expense. The conservationists want to show that tiger reserves can also help villagers. One organization has introduced new types of water buffalo that need very little grazing land. To boost the local economy, it has helped women sell their handicrafts in urban areas. The Global Environment Facility and the World Bank also helped. They spent about $10 million to aid villages around India's Ranthambhore National Park.

China's Year of the Tiger Despite these efforts, the number of tigers remains low. In 1998, the Chinese Year of the Tiger, conservationists in Hong Kong tried a new approach. They started an advertising campaign to remind people how important tigers are in traditional Chinese culture. The advertisements showed children dressed in clothes with popular tiger designs. The advertise-

ments read, "They protect your children; who will protect them?" Chinese conservationists hope their campaign will encourage people to stop using medicines made with tiger bones. They also hope it will encourage people to join the fight to save the world's tigers.

Your Turn

Imagine you are planning a worldwide campaign to save tigers in the wild. Write a short report that explains your plan and answers the following questions:

1. How would the Project Tiger reserves and the Chinese advertising campaign fit into your plan?

2. Do you think it is more important to save tiger habitat or to keep people from hunting them? why?

Understanding What You Read

Answers

1. Students' reports should express a reasonable link between the Project Tiger reserves and the Chinese advertising campaign and the student's plan.

2. Students should support their answers.

🔲 **internet** connect

CHAPTER WEB LINKS
GO TO: go.hrw.com
KEYWORD: SK5 CH15

FOR: Web sites about tigers

Going Further: Thinking Critically

There are many endangered species in the United States. Have students contact your state's wildlife agency or conservation organizations for information on endangered species in your area. Then have students examine how local attitudes toward the species may affect its prospects. Organize the class into two groups—one to propose an advertising campaign to influence attitudes and the other to plan on-site conservation efforts. Then have the groups work together to make certain the plans they have devised comprise a coordinated effort.

PRACTICING THE SKILL

1. Students' answers should describe their chosen diagram and discuss why it is difficult or easy to understand.

2. You may want to refer students to the photo of a sailing ship in Chapter 3. Students' answers should address each of the steps for drawing a diagram.

3. Students' answers should address each of the steps for drawing a diagram. Diagrams might show the rocks in place at the top of the mountain, breaking off, and creating the landslide.

➤ This GeoSkills feature addresses National Geography Standards 1 and 7.

GeoSKILLS

Building Skills for Life: Drawing Diagrams

Diagrams are drawings that explain how things work or fit together. They can be helpful in many different situations. For example, suppose you bought a bicycle and had to put it together. How would you do it? The easiest way would be to follow a diagram.

The goal of a diagram is to explain something. Diagrams are not intended to show exactly how something looks in real life. Diagrams should be easy to understand, neat, and simple.

In geography, diagrams are often used to show how different things are related. Physical geographers use diagrams to explain how sea and land breezes develop or how volcanoes form. Cultural geographers use diagrams to show settlement patterns and housing styles.

You can draw diagrams too. To draw a diagram, first decide exactly what you want it to show. Choose a short, descriptive title. Plan your diagram by making a quick sketch. How many drawings will you need? How will you arrange them? Then carefully draw your diagram. Label the important features. Use colors, patterns, and symbols if you need to. Use a ruler for straight lines and write the title at the top. Then add a short caption at the bottom that explains your diagram.

Sea and Land Breezes

As warm air rises, it creates an area of low pressure over the land.

The cool air moves toward the land, producing a sea breeze.

Cool air

Air over the water is cooler and creates an area of high pressure.

Air over land is cooler and creates an area of high pressure.

The cool air moves toward the water, producing a land breeze.

Air over the water is warmer and creates an area of low pressure.

Breezes from the ocean cool the warmer land surface during the day. At night, cooler land surface breezes blow toward the ocean.

PRACTICING THE SKILL

1. Choose a diagram from a book, magazine, or newspaper. Write a short paragraph about the diagram. What does it show? Is it clear and easy to understand? why or why not?

2. Draw a diagram that shows how wind moves a sailboat through water.

3. Draw a diagram that shows how rocks can break off a mountain and cause a landslide.

GEOSKILLS

Going Further: Thinking Critically

Organize the class into small groups. Prepare in advance slips of paper naming everyday skills that young children may not yet have mastered but at which your students are adept. Possibilities include riding a bicycle, programming a VCR, loading a dishwasher, changing a lightbulb, assembling a triple-decker sandwich, or scoring a soccer goal. Prepare one skill for each group. Ask each group to draw a skill from a hat. Allow groups to trade their assigned skills if they wish. Then have groups use the steps described in Building Skills for Life: Drawing Diagrams to draw a diagram that shows how to complete the task. Then have the groups exchange their diagrams and challenge them to improve another group's diagram. Finally, return the diagrams to the groups that created them and ask the students to summarize what they learned from the activity.

HANDS on

GEOGRAPHY

The Himalayas are the highest mountains on Earth. Nine of the ten highest peaks in the world are located there. The Himalayas have 110 peaks that rise above 24,000 feet (7,315 m).

How did the Himalayas get to be so high? When were they formed? Drawing a diagram is one way to show how the Himalayas became the world's highest mountains.

Read the paragraph below. It describes how and when the Himalayas formed. Use this information to draw a diagram showing how the Himalayas became the world's highest mountains.

The Himalayas were formed long ago by the movement of Earth's tectonic plates. About 180 million years ago, the Indo-Australian plate broke off from the ancient supercontinent Gondwana and began moving north. This plate included what is now the Indian Subcontinent. About 50 million years ago, the Indo-Australian plate collided with the Eurasian plate and was forced under it. As the Indo-Australian plate was pulled under the Eurasian plate, the Himalayas began to rise. They grew slowly at first. Then, about 30 million years ago, the Himalayas began rising faster. However, they did not become the highest mountains in the world until about 500,000 years ago. The Himalayas are still rising today.

Mountain peaks rise above the clouds in the world's highest mountains.

Lab Report

1. Is your diagram clear and easy to understand? Show your diagram to another person to see if he or she can easily understand it.

2. Did you use colors or symbols in your diagram? why or why not?

3. By drawing a diagram of the Himalayas, did you learn something about diagrams in general? What did you learn?

Lab Report

Answers

1. Students should share their diagrams and discuss whether they are easy to understand.

2. Students should explain the use of colors and symbols in their diagrams.

3. Students might suggest that they learned more about the amount of skill and thought that a good diagram requires.

Unit 4 Hands On 341

UNIT OBJECTIVES

1. Describe how climate and landforms affect the way people live in East and Southeast Asia.

2. Identify the political, economic, social, and cultural characteristics of East and Southeast Asia.

3. Explain the importance of East and Southeast Asia as a major region of the world.

4. Understand links among the physical geography, historical geography, and cultural geography of East and Southeast Asia.

5. Interpret special-purpose maps to analyze relationships among climate, population patterns, and economic resources in East and Southeast Asia.

UNIT 5

East and Southeast Asia

CHAPTER 16
China, Mongolia, and Taiwan

CHAPTER 17
Japan and the Koreas

CHAPTER 18
Southeast Asia

Shwedagon Pagoda, Yangon, Myanmar

Rice paddies near Guilin, China

342 Unit 5

USING THE ILLUSTRATIONS

Direct students' attention to the photographs on these pages. Have them select the photo that may portray a nomadic way of life (the Mongolian man outside his home). Ask what led them to this conclusion. (Possible answer: The house appears temporary or movable.) Then inquire which photo shows a settled way of life and why students chose it (rice farmer; shows agriculture). Ask how the Chinese farmer's field compares to farmland students have seen in the United States. (Possible answers: The plants are in standing water. There are no distinct rows.) Ask what con-

clusions students can draw from this. (Rice farming requires plenty of water. Much work is done by hand.)

Point out the Shwedagon Pagoda, a Buddhist shrine in Myanmar. The solid brick structure is covered with gold. It is more than 300 feet (90 m) tall.

Finally, ask students to look at the people in the center photo. They are dressed for the Festival of the Ages parade held every year in October in Kyoto, Japan. The procession illustrates clothing styles from the 700s through the 1800s. Thousands of costumed people join the parade.

A Peace Corps Volunteer in Mongolia

Matt Heller served as a Peace Corps volunteer in Mongolia. He worked as an English teacher and coordinated a greenhouse reconstruction project. **WHAT DO YOU THINK?** *What kinds of changes would you have to make in your life to live in Mongolia?*

I've been a Peace Corps volunteer in Mongolia for eighteen months. I live in a *ger*, a tent with a small wood stove in the center. It is strong and practical, perfect for a nomadic herder. I, however, am an English teacher in a small school in rural Mongolia. *Ger* life is hard. It makes twenty-year-olds look thirty-five. It makes your soul hard.

Mongolians are very proud of their history. Once, while sitting on the train going from Ulaanbaatar to my own town, Bor-Undur, a Mongolian pointed to his arm and said, "In here is the blood of Genghis Khan. Beware." There is no argument to that statement. I responded, "Yes, older brother (a respectful title addressed to elders), your country is beautiful. Mongolians are lucky."

Along with many other things, I'm learning how Mongolians live. In the steppe there is very little snow, only biting wind and dust. It gets as cold as –50 degrees, not counting the wind chill factor. If I leave tea in a mug, it will freeze by morning. I've broken three mugs that way.

A Mongolian outside his home

Festival of Ages parade, Kyoto, Japan

Understanding Primary Sources

1. What conclusion does Matt Heller make about Mongolians and their past?
2. How does Matt Heller describe the climate in Mongolia?

Giant panda

East and Southeast Asia • 343

MORE FROM THE FIELD

Genghis Khan was a conqueror who unified nomadic Mongolian tribes and then, in the early 1200s, extended his power across Asia all the way to the Black Sea. His fast-moving cavalry relied on hardy ponies that needed no feed other than the grass of the steppe. Mare's milk was a staple food. The Mongols' *gers*, or yurts, were made of horsehair. In fact, the Mongols were so dependent on their horses that their country was said to be "the back of a horse."

Activity: Have students conduct research on nomadic Mongolians of today. Ask them to compare the role of horses in modern Mongolian society to the role they played in Genghis Khan's day. Then have them work in groups to compose song lyrics that relate their research results.

Understanding Primary Sources
Answers
1. proud of and closely connected to their past
2. cold, windy, dry, dusty

CHAPTERS

16 **China, Mongolia, and Taiwan**
explains the physical geography, history, and culture of these three countries.

17 **Japan and the Koreas**
describes the geography and interrelated histories and cultures of Japan, North Korea, and South Korea.

18 **Southeast Asia**
examines the physical and human geography of the five mainland countries (Vietnam, Laos, Cambodia, Thailand, Myanmar) and the five island countries (Malaysia, Singapore, Brunei, Indonesia, Philippines).

PEOPLE IN THE PROFILE

Note that the elevation profile crosses the Plateau of Tibet, which has an average elevation of over 15,000 feet (4,570 m). People who travel to Tibet from low-lying areas can suffer or even die from altitude sickness if they do not take time to become acclimated.

How are the Tibetans able to live at such high altitudes? Recent studies suggest that their metabolism has adapted in response to the lack of oxygen. It appears that the hearts and brains of those living in Tibet's mountains use glucose and oxygen differently than people who live at low elevations. Also, they have developed enzymes that process oxygen more efficiently. Some scientists who have compared the Quechua of the Andes to the Sherpa of Tibet found that the Sherpa had adapted more fully to high altitudes because, as a people, they have been in Tibet at least 10,000 years longer than the Quechua have been in Peru.

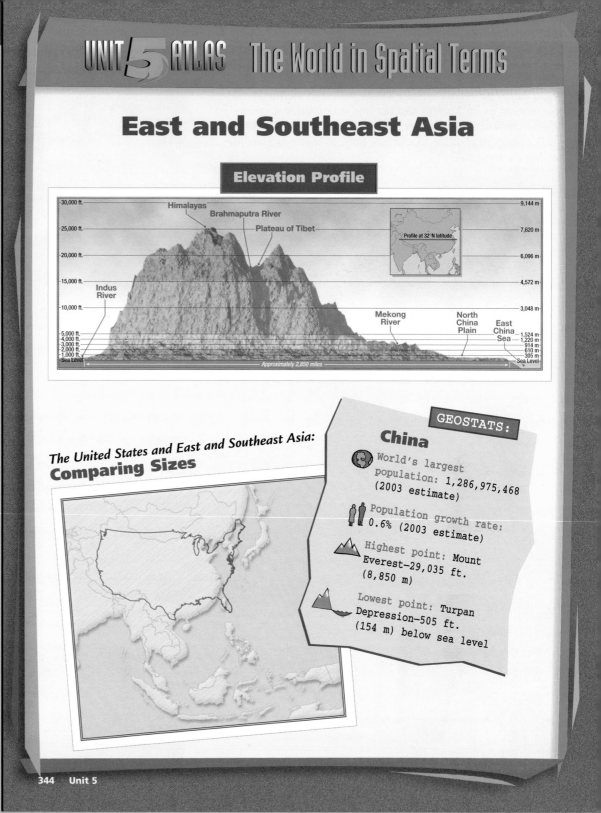

UNIT 5 ATLAS   The World in Spatial Terms

East and Southeast Asia

Elevation Profile

The United States and East and Southeast Asia:
Comparing Sizes

GEOSTATS:

China

World's largest population: 1,286,975,468 (2003 estimate)

Population growth rate: 0.6% (2003 estimate)

Highest point: Mount Everest—29,035 ft. (8,850 m)

Lowest point: Turpan Depression—505 ft. (154 m) below sea level

OVERVIEW

This unit introduces students to East and Southeast Asia. The region stretches from Myanmar (also called Burma) in the west to Japan in the northeast. Russia lies to the north and the Indian Subcontinent to the southwest. The Indian Ocean is at the southern edge, and the Pacific Ocean is at the eastern edge.

Because it includes such a vast area, the region exhibits an equally wide range of landforms, climate types, economies, and cultures. People who live much as their ancestors did thousands of years ago contrast with busy workers crowding the sidewalks of dynamic modern cities. In all, approximately one third of the world's population lives in this region.

Although only a small percentage of the region's huge land area is suitable for farming, most of the people there are involved in agriculture. Industry continues to gain in importance, however.

East and Southeast Asia:
Physical

UNIT 5 ATLAS

☐ **internet** connect

ONLINE ATLAS
GO TO: go.hrw.com
KEYWORD: SK5 MapsU5
FOR: Web links to online maps of the region

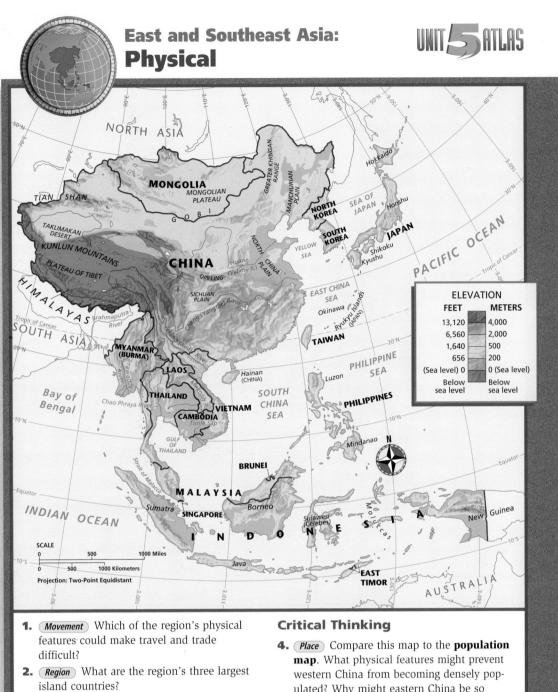

ELEVATION

FEET		METERS
13,120		4,000
6,560		2,000
1,640		500
656		200
(Sea level) 0		0 (Sea level)
Below sea level		Below sea level

SCALE
0   500   1000 Miles
0   500   1000 Kilometers
Projection: Two-Point Equidistant

1. (*Movement*) Which of the region's physical features could make travel and trade difficult?

2. (*Region*) What are the region's three largest island countries?

3. (*Location*) Which countries have territory on the mainland and on islands?

Critical Thinking

4. (*Place*) Compare this map to the **population map**. What physical features might prevent western China from becoming densely populated? Why might eastern China be so densely populated?

East and Southeast Asia • 345

Physical Map
Answers
1. large expanses of water, high mountains, vast deserts
2. Indonesia, Japan, Philippines
3. China, Malaysia

Critical Thinking
4. mountains and deserts; presence of rivers, wide plains

USING THE PHYSICAL MAP

Call on a volunteer to describe the landforms of China and Mongolia. Then have students examine the **political map** on the next page and draw conclusions about the connections between China's landforms and the building of the Great Wall. (This area lacks natural barriers to movement from the north, and rulers wanted to protect the North China Plain from invasions by the people of the Mongolian Plateau.) Point out to students that the Philippines, Japan, and Indonesia are on the Pacific Ring of Fire. Then remind them of the volcanic activity that occurs along the edges of the tectonic plates.

Your Classroom Time Line

These are the major dates and time periods for this unit. Have students enter them on the time line you created earlier. You may want to watch for these dates as students progress through the unit.

c.* 5000 B.C. Rice farming develops near the Chang River.

c. 2000 B.C. Chinese living in the Huang valley form kingdoms.

551 B.C. Confucius is born.

200s B.C. The Great Wall of China is completed.

206 B.C.–A.D. 220 The Han dynasty rules China.

108 B.C. Chinese invade Korea.

by A.D. 100 Buddhism reaches China from India.

600s Tibet's Potala Palace is built.

early 900s The Koryo dynasty rises to power in Korea.

*c. stands for *circa* and means "about."

Political Map

Answers
1. Mongolia
2. Laos; Mongolia

Critical Thinking
3. Himalayas; Mekong River, river between North Korea and China

East and Southeast Asia: Political

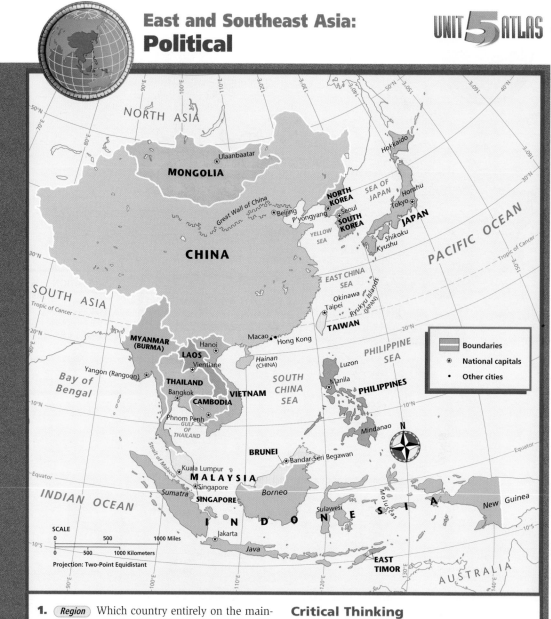

Boundaries
⊛ National capitals
• Other cities

SCALE
0   500   1000 Miles
0   500   1000 Kilometers
Projection: Two-Point Equidistant

1. **Region** Which country entirely on the mainland shares a border with just one of the region's other countries?

2. **Location** What is the only landlocked country in Southeast Asia? Which country in East Asia is landlocked?

Critical Thinking

3. **Region** Compare this map to the **physical map** of the region. Which physical feature forms the border of southwestern China? Which other physical features form natural borders in the region?

USING THE POLITICAL MAP

As students examine the **political map** on this page, have them name the largest country on the map (China) and the smallest (Singapore). Call on volunteers to name the mainland countries (Mongolia, China, North Korea, South Korea, Myanmar, Thailand, Laos, Vietnam, Cambodia, part of Malaysia) and the island countries (Japan, Taiwan, Philippines, Indonesia, Singapore, Brunei, part of Malaysia). Then ask students which of the mainland countries has the largest number of international borders (China).

internet connect

ONLINE ATLAS
GO TO: go.hrw.com
KEYWORD: SK5 MapsU5

East and Southeast Asia: Climate

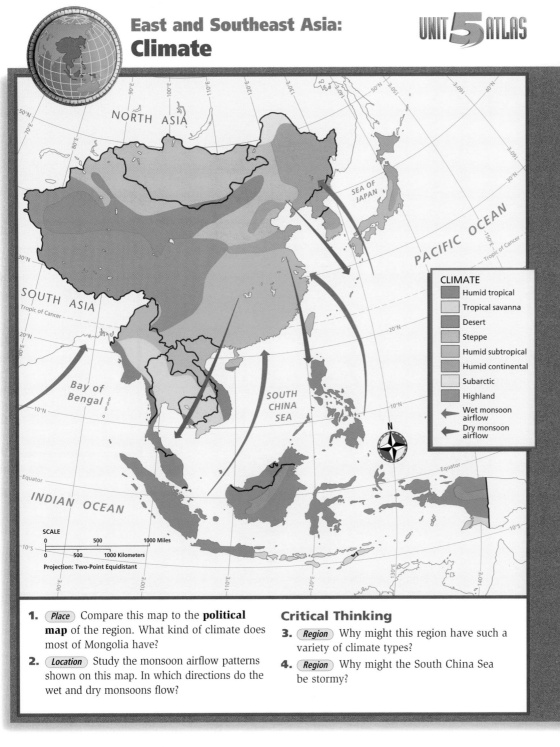

CLIMATE
- Humid tropical
- Tropical savanna
- Desert
- Steppe
- Humid subtropical
- Humid continental
- Subarctic
- Highland
- ← Wet monsoon airflow
- ← Dry monsoon airflow

SCALE
0   500   1000 Miles
0   500   1000 Kilometers
Projection: Two-Point Equidistant

UNIT 5 ATLAS

Your Classroom Time Line (continued)

1279–1368 Mongols rule China.

late 1200s Marco Polo visits China.

1368–1644 The Ming dynasty rules China.

1500s Europeans begin establishing colonies in Southeast Asia.

1644–1912 The Manchu dynasty rules China.

1853 Commodore Matthew Perry's ships sail into Tokyo Bay.

1895 Japan defeats China in the Sino-Japanese War.

1898 The United States wins the Philippines from Spain.

1910 Japan annexes Korea.

1912 Sun Yat-sen establishes the Republic of China.

1930s Japanese soldiers invade Manchuria and China.

1941 Japan attacks Pearl Harbor; United States declares war on Japan.

1. **(Place)** Compare this map to the **political map** of the region. What kind of climate does most of Mongolia have?

2. **(Location)** Study the monsoon airflow patterns shown on this map. In which directions do the wet and dry monsoons flow?

Critical Thinking

3. **(Region)** Why might this region have such a variety of climate types?

4. **(Region)** Why might the South China Sea be stormy?

Climate Map

Answers

1. steppe

2. wet—south to north; dry—north to south

Critical Thinking

3. wide variety of latitudes, landforms, and elevations

4. warm climate, monsoon winds

USING THE CLIMATE MAP

As students examine the **climate map** on this page, point out that the region stretches from 50° north of the equator to 10° south. Ask students what effect this wide latitude range would be likely to have on the climate of the region (a wide range of climate types). Have them discuss the extremes of the region's climates, which range from subarctic to humid tropical. Have students identify other countries that lie as far north as Mongolia (such as Canada) and as far south as Indonesia (such as Brazil).

Your Classroom Time Line (continued)

1945 World War II ends.

1946 Philippines gains its independence.

1949 Mao Zedong establishes the communist People's Republic of China.

1948 Korea divides into two countries.

early 1950s Korean War is fought.

1960s–70s The United States fights in the Vietnam War.

1966–76 Mao Zedong implements the Cultural Revolution in China.

1989 Chinese troops kill protesters in Tiananmen Square.

1997 British return control of Hong Kong to China.

1999 Macao is returned to China.

internet connect

ONLINE ATLAS
GO TO: **go.hrw.com**
KEYWORD: **SK5 MapsU5**

Population Map

Answers

1. more than 520 persons per square mile (200 per sq km)

2. Taklimakan Desert

Critical Thinking

3. located at the mouths of rivers

East and Southeast Asia: Population

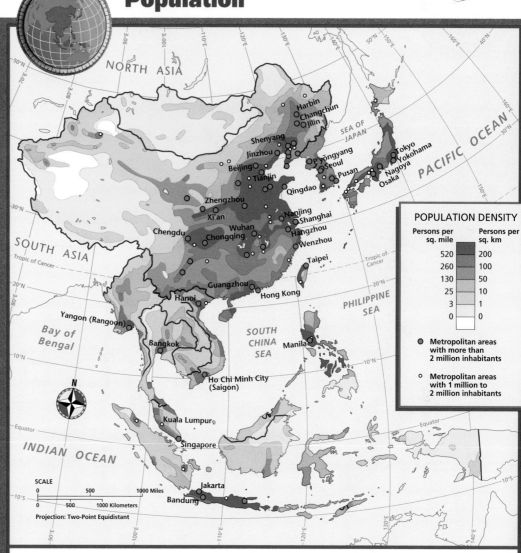

POPULATION DENSITY

Persons per sq. mile		Persons per sq. km
520		200
260		100
130		50
25		10
3		1
0		0

● Metropolitan areas with more than 2 million inhabitants

○ Metropolitan areas with 1 million to 2 million inhabitants

SCALE
0   500   1000 Miles
0   500   1000 Kilometers
Projection: Two-Point Equidistant

1. (*Place*) What is the population density in the area between Shanghai and Beijing?

2. (*Region*) Compare this map to the **physical map** of the region. Which physical features help explain the low population density in western China?

Critical Thinking

3. (*Human-Environment Interaction*) Compare this map to the **physical map** of the region. Which physical features help explain the high population densities near Bangkok, Ho Chi Minh City, and Yangon (Rangoon)?

USING THE POPULATION MAP

As students examine the **population map**, ask which countries do not have metropolitan areas with more than 2 million inhabitants (Brunei, Cambodia, Laos, Mongolia). Then ask which country has low population density throughout its entire area (Mongolia). Have students compare the **population map** with the **physical** and **political maps** on previous pages. Ask which sea might be the most at risk for pollution by agricultural and urban runoff (Yellow Sea).

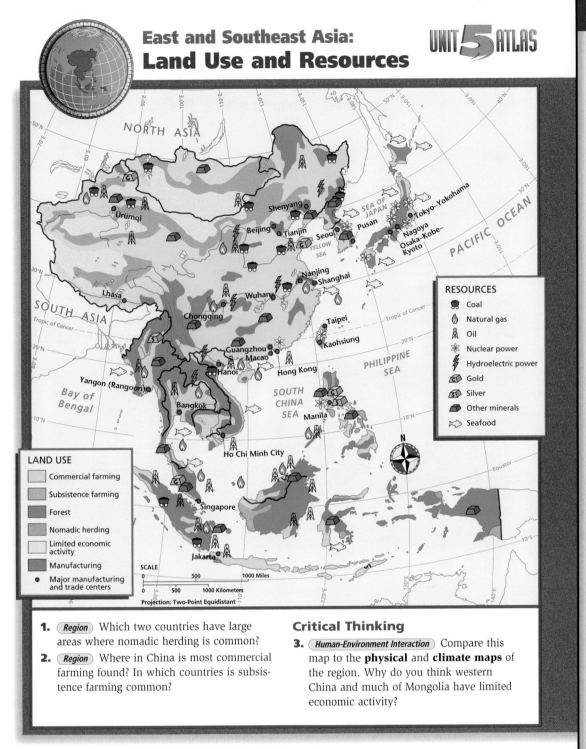

East and Southeast Asia:
Land Use and Resources

UNIT 5 ATLAS

RESOURCES

🝳	Coal
🝔	Natural gas
🝚	Oil
✳	Nuclear power
⚡	Hydroelectric power
Ⓖ	Gold
Ⓢ	Silver
🝳	Other minerals
🗋	Seafood

LAND USE

	Commercial farming
	Subsistence farming
	Forest
	Nomadic herding
	Limited economic activity
	Manufacturing
●	Major manufacturing and trade centers

SCALE
0   500   1000 Miles
0   500   1000 Kilometers
Projection: Two-Point Equidistant

1. (Region) Which two countries have large areas where nomadic herding is common?

2. (Region) Where in China is most commercial farming found? In which countries is subsistence farming common?

Critical Thinking

3. (Human-Environment Interaction) Compare this map to the **physical** and **climate maps** of the region. Why do you think western China and much of Mongolia have limited economic activity?

Your Classroom Time Line (continued)

2001 North Korea says it is grappling with the worst spring drought of its history.

2002 Terrorist bomb attack on Bali in Indonesia kills 202 people, most of them tourists. Another bomb explodes near the U.S. consulate.

2003 China and Hong Kong are hit by the SARS virus.

2003 China launches its first manned spacecraft.

Land Use and Resources Map

Answers

1. China and Mongolia

2. eastern and northeastern regions; China, all the other countries except Brunei, Singapore, and Japan

Critical Thinking

3. harsh desert climate, mountains

USING THE LAND USE AND RESOURCES MAP

As students examine the **land use and resources map** on this page, point out that most residents of the region are involved in agriculture. Ask students which type of agriculture is practiced in the most densely populated areas (commercial farming). Then ask which types of economic activities are practiced in Mongolia (nomadic herding) and in the island countries along the equator (forestry).

UNITED STATES OF AMERICA

CAPITAL:
Washington, D.C.

AREA:
3,717,792 sq. mi.
(9,629,091 sq km)

POPULATION:
281,421,906

MONEY:
U.S. dollar

LANGUAGES:
English, Spanish (spoken by a large minority)

INTERNET USERS:
165.75 million (2002)

East and Southeast Asia

BRUNEI

CAPITAL:
Bandar Seri Begawan

AREA:
2,228 sq. mi. (5,770 sq km)

POPULATION:
358,098

MONEY:
Bruneian dollar

LANGUAGES:
Malay (official), English, Chinese

NUMBER OF INTERNET USERS: 35,000

JAPAN

CAPITAL:
Tokyo

AREA:
145,882 sq. mi.
(377,835 sq km)

POPULATION:
127,214,499

MONEY:
yen

LANGUAGES:
Japanese

NUMBER OF INTERNET USERS:
56,000,000

CAMBODIA

CAPITAL:
Phnom Penh

AREA:
69,900 sq. mi.
(181,040 sq km)

POPULATION:
13,124,764

MONEY:
riel

LANGUAGES:
Khmer (official), French

NUMBER OF INTERNET USERS: 10,000

LAOS

CAPITAL:
Vientiane

AREA:
91,428 sq. mi.
(236,800 sq km)

POPULATION:
5,921,545

MONEY:
kip

LANGUAGES:
Lao (official), French, English, ethnic languages

NUMBER OF INTERNET USERS: 10,000

CHINA

CAPITAL:
Beijing

AREA:
3,705,386 sq. mi.
(9,596,960 sq km)

POPULATION:
1,286,975,468

MONEY:
yuan

LANGUAGES:
Mandarin, Yue, other forms of Chinese

NUMBER OF INTERNET USERS: 45,800,000

MALAYSIA

CAPITAL:
Kuala Lumpur

AREA:
127,316 sq. mi.
(329,750 sq km)

POPULATION:
23,092,940

MONEY:
ringgit

LANGUAGES: Bahasa Melayu (official), English, Chinese dialects, ethnic languages

NUMBER OF INTERNET USERS: 5,700,000

INDONESIA

CAPITAL:
Jakarta

AREA:
741,096 sq. mi.
(1,919,440 sq km)

POPULATION:
234,893,453

MONEY:
Indonesian rupiah

LANGUAGES:
Bahasa Indonesia (official), English, Dutch, Javanese

NUMBER OF INTERNET USERS: 4,400,000

MONGOLIA

CAPITAL:
Ulaanbaatar

AREA:
604,247 sq. mi.
(1,565,000 sq km)

POPULATION:
2,712,315

MONEY:
togrog/tugrik

LANGUAGES:
Khalkha Mongol, Turkic, Russian

NUMBER OF INTERNET USERS: 40,000

Countries not drawn to scale.

FAST FACTS ACTIVITIES

LEVEL 1: (Suggested time: 20 min.) Have students calculate the number of Internet users per person in an industrialized country such as Japan, Taiwan, or South Korea and a nonindustrialized country such as Myanmar, Cambodia, or Mongolia. (Students should divide the number of Internet users by the number of people.) Ask students to write a sentence or two describing the relationship between industrialization and television ownership.

LEVEL 2: (Suggested time: 45 min.) Have students use the accompanying table to calculate the actual number of people aged 14 and younger in the countries of East and Southeast Asia. Then have them create a chart that shows the number of people from 0 to 14 years old in the countries of East and Southeast Asia. Have students use the chart in the chapter on Japan and the Koreas comparing the populations of Japan and the United States as a model, but have students use one figure for every 500,000 people.

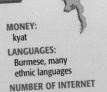

MYANMAR
(Burma)

CAPITAL:
Yangon (Rangoon)

AREA:
261,969 sq. mi.
(678,500 sq km)

POPULATION:
42,510,537

MONEY:
kyat

LANGUAGES:
Burmese, many
ethnic languages

**NUMBER OF INTERNET
USERS:** 10,000

UNIT 5 ASSESSMENT RESOURCES
Reproducible
◆ Unit 5 Test
◆ Unit 5 Test for English Language Learners and Special-Needs Students

SOUTH KOREA

CAPITAL:
Seoul

AREA:
38,023 sq. mi.
(98,480 sq km)

POPULATION: 48,289,037

MONEY:
South Korean won

LANGUAGES:
Korean, English

**NUMBER OF INTERNET
USERS:** 25,600,000

NORTH KOREA

CAPITAL:
P'yŏngyang

AREA:
46,540 sq. mi.
(120,540 sq km)

POPULATION:
22,466,481

MONEY:
North Korean won

LANGUAGES:
Korean

**NUMBER OF INTERNET
USERS:** not available

TAIWAN

CAPITAL:
Taipei

AREA:
13,892 sq. mi.
(35,980 sq km)

POPULATION:
22,548,000

MONEY:
New Taiwan
dollar

LANGUAGES: Mandarin,
Taiwanese (Min), Hakka
dialects

**NUMBER OF INTERNET
USERS:** 10,100,000

PHILIPPINES

CAPITAL:
Manila

AREA:
115,830 sq. mi.
(300,000 sq km)

POPULATION:
84,619,974

MONEY:
Philippine peso

LANGUAGES:
Filipino, English

**NUMBER OF INTERNET
USERS:** 4,500,000

THAILAND

CAPITAL:
Bangkok

AREA:
198,455 sq. mi.
(514,000 sq km)

POPULATION: 64,265,276

MONEY:
baht

LANGUAGES: Thai, English,
ethnic languages

**NUMBER OF INTERNET
USERS:** 1,200,000

VIETNAM

CAPITAL:
Hanoi

AREA:
127,243 sq. mi.
(329,560 sq km)

POPULATION:
81,624,716

MONEY:
dong

LANGUAGES: Vietnamese
(official), Chinese,
English, French,
Khmer, ethnic languages

**NUMBER OF INTERNET
USERS:** 409,000

SINGAPORE

CAPITAL:
Singapore

AREA:
250 sq. mi. (648 sq km)

POPULATION:
4,608,595

MONEY:
Singapore dollar

LANGUAGES:
Chinese, Malay, Tamil,
English

**NUMBER OF INTERNET
USERS:** 2,310,000

internet connect
COUNTRY STATISTICS
GO TO: go.hrw.com
KEYWORD: SK5 FactsU5
FOR: more facts about East
and Southeast Asia

Sources: Central Intelligence Agency, *The World Factbook 2003;* Taipei Economic and Cultural Representative Office, figures are 2003 estimates.

East and Southeast Asia 351

internet connect
COUNTRY STATISTICS
GO TO: **go.hrw.com**
KEYWORD: **SK5 Facts U5**

**Highlights
of Country
Statistics**
• *CIA World Factbook*
• Library of Congress
country studies
• Flags of the world

PERCENTAGE OF POPULATION AGED 0–14

Brunei	30	Myanmar	28
Cambodia	39	(Burma)	
China	23	North Korea	25
Indonesia	30	Philippines	36
Japan	14	Singapore	17
Laos	42	South Korea	21
Malaysia	34	Taiwan	20
Mongolia	31	Thailand	24
		Vietnam	30

Source: Central Intelligence Agency, *The World Factbook 2003*

FAST FACTS ACTIVITIES

LEVEL 3: (Suggested time: 45 min.) Have students use the historical and economic information in this unit to write an essay that explains the population differences illustrated in the accompanying table. Encourage them to use supplemental resources.

CHAPTER 16

China, Mongolia, and Taiwan
Chapter Resource Manager

Objectives	Pacing Guide	Reproducible Resources
SECTION 1 **Physical Geography** (pp. 353–56) 1. Identify the physical features of China, Mongolia, and Taiwan. 2. Identify the types of climate found in China, Mongolia, and Taiwan. 3. Identify the natural resources of China, Mongolia, and Taiwan.	**Regular** 1 day Lecture Notes, Section 1 **Block Scheduling** .5 day *Block Scheduling Handbook, Chapter 16*	**RS** Know It Notes S1 **E** Lab Activity for Geography and Earth Science, Hands-On 1 **ELL** Main Idea Activity S1
SECTION 2 **China's History and Culture** (pp. 357–63) 1. Identify the major events in the history of China. 2. Name some features of China's culture.	**Regular** 2 days Lecture Notes, Section 2 **Block Scheduling** .5 day *Block Scheduling Handbook, Chapter 16*	**RS** Know It Notes S2 **RS** Graphic Organizer 16 **E** Cultures of the World Activity 7 **E** Creative Strategies for Teaching World Geography, Lesson 18 **SM** Geography for Life Activity 27 **IC** Interdisciplinary Activities for the Middle Grades 29, 30, 31 **E** Biography Activity: Genghis Khan **SM** Map Activity 16 **ELL** Main Idea Activity S2
SECTION 3 **China Today** (pp. 364–67) 1. Describe where most of China's people live. 2. Identify the major cities in China and what they are like. 3. Describe China's economy. 4. Identify the challenges that China faces.	**Regular** 1 day Lecture Notes, Section 3 **Block Scheduling** .5 day *Block Scheduling Handbook, Chapter 16*	**RS** Know It Notes S3 **ELL** Main Idea Activity S3
SECTION 4 **Mongolian and Taiwan** (pp. 368–71) 1. Describe how Mongolia's culture developed. 2. Describe Taiwan's culture.	**Regular** 1 day Lecture Notes, Section 4 **Block Scheduling** .5 day *Block Scheduling Handbook, Chapter 16*	**RS** Know It Notes S4 **E** Cultures of the World Activity 7 **E** Creative Strategies for Teaching World Geography, Lesson 18 **E** Biography Activity: Genghis Khan **ELL** Main Idea Activity S4

Chapter Resource Key

RS Reading Support
IC Interdisciplinary Connections
E Enrichment
SM Skills Mastery
A Assessment
REV Review

ELL Reinforcement and English Language Learners and English for Speakers of Other Languages (ESOL)
 Transparencies
 CD–ROM

 Music
 Video
 Internet
 Holt Presentation Maker Using Microsoft® PowerPoint®

  One-Stop Planner CD–ROM

See the ***One-Stop Planner*** for a complete list of additional resources for students and teachers.

One-Stop Planner CD–ROM

It's easy to plan lessons, select resources, and print out materials for your students when you use the *One-Stop Planner CD–ROM with Test Generator.*

Technology Resources	Review, Reinforcement, and Assessment Resources	

One-Stop Planner CD–ROM, Lesson 16.1
  Geography and Cultures Visual Resources with Teaching Activities 49–54
  ARGWorld CD–ROM
  Homework Practice Online
 HRW Go site
	ELL Main Idea Activity S1
	 REV Section 1 Review
	 A Daily Quiz 16.1
	 REV Chapter Summaries and Review
	 ELL English Audio Summary 16.1
	 ELL Spanish Audio Summary 16.1	

One-Stop Planner CD–ROM, Lesson 16.2 *ARGWorld* CD–ROM Music of the World Audio CD Program, Selection 19 Homework Practice Online HRW Go site	**ELL** Main Idea Activity S2 **REV** Section 2 Review **A** Daily Quiz 16.2 **REV** Chapter Summaries and Review **ELL** English Audio Summary 16.2 **ELL** Spanish Audio Summary 16.2	
One-Stop Planner CD–ROM, Lesson 16.3 *ARGWorld* CD–ROM Homework Practice Online HRW Go site	**ELL** Main Idea Activity S3 **REV** Section 3 Review **A** Daily Quiz 16.3 **REV** Chapter Summaries and Review **ELL** English Audio Summary 16.3 **ELL** Spanish Audio Summary 16.3	
One-Stop Planner CD–ROM, Lesson 16.4 *ARGWorld* CD–ROM Homework Practice Online HRW Go site	**ELL** Main Idea Activity S4 **REV** Section 4 Review **A** Daily Quiz 16.4 **REV** Chapter Summaries and Review **ELL** English Audio Summary 16.4 **ELL** Spanish Audio Summary 16.4	

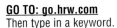

HRW ONLINE RESOURCES

GO TO: go.hrw.com
Then type in a keyword.

TEACHER HOME PAGE
  KEYWORD: SK5 TEACHER

CHAPTER INTERNET ACTIVITIES
  KEYWORD: SK5 GT16

Choose an activity to:
• follow the Great Wall of China.
• visit the land of Genghis Khan.
• see the artistic treasures of China.

CHAPTER ENRICHMENT LINKS
  KEYWORD: SK5 CH16

CHAPTER MAPS
  KEYWORD: SK5 MAPS16

ONLINE ASSESSMENT
Homework Practice
  KEYWORD: SK5 HP16
  Standardized Test Prep Online
  KEYWORD: SK5 STP16
  Rubrics
  KEYWORD: SS Rubrics

COUNTRY INFORMATION
  KEYWORD: SK5 Almanac

CONTENT UPDATES
  KEYWORD: SS Content Updates

HOLT PRESENTATION MAKER
  KEYWORD: SK5 PPT16

ONLINE READING SUPPORT
  KEYWORD: SS Strategies

CURRENT EVENTS
  KEYWORD: S5 Current Events

Meeting Individual Needs

Ability Levels

Level 1 Basic-level activities designed for all students encountering new material

Level 2 Intermediate-level activities designed for average students

Level 3 Challenging activities designed for honors and gifted-and-talented students

ESOL Activities that address the needs of students with Limited English Proficiency

Chapter Review and Assessment

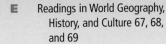
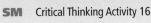

E	Readings in World Geography, History, and Culture 67, 68, and 69	**A**	Chapter 16 Test
SM	Critical Thinking Activity 16		Chapter 16 Test Generator (on the One-Stop Planner)
REV	Chapter 16 Review and Practice		Audio CD Program, Chapter 16
REV	Chapter Summaries and Review	**A**	Chapter 16 Test for English Language Learners and Special-Needs Students
ELL	Vocabulary Activity 16		HRW Go Site

351B

China, Mongolia, and Taiwan

Previewing Chapter Resources

Holt Online Learning

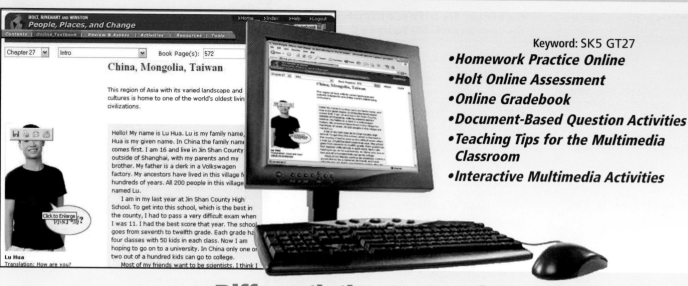

Keyword: SK5 GT27

- *Homework Practice Online*
- *Holt Online Assessment*
- *Online Gradebook*
- *Document-Based Question Activities*
- *Teaching Tips for the Multimedia Classroom*
- *Interactive Multimedia Activities*

Differentiating Instruction

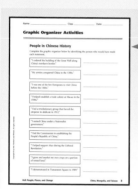

Reading and Writing Support

◀ Graphic Organizer Activity
- *Vocabulary Activity*
- *Chapter Summary and Review*
- *Know It Notes*
- *Audio CD*

Active Learning

- *Block Scheduling Handbook*
- *Cultures of the World Activity*
- *Interdisciplinary Activity*
- ◀ *Map Activity*
- *Critical Thinking Activity 27*
- *Music of the World CD: Music of the* Gugin

Primary Sources and Advanced Learners

◀ Geography for Life Activity: Feng Shui
- *Map Activity: Ancient China*
- *Readings in World Geography, History and Culture:*
  - *67 How Dragaon Pond Got Its Name*
  - *68 China's Coming Great Flood*
  - *69 Democracy Comes to Taiwan*

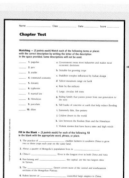

Assessment Program

- *Daily Quizzes S1–4*
- ◀ *Chapter Test*
- *Chapter Test for English Language Learners and Special-Needs Students*

Spanish and ESOL

- *Vocabulary Activity*
- ◀ *Main Idea Activities for English Language Learners and Special-Needs Students*
- *Chapter Summary and Review*
- *Spanish Audio Summary*
- *Know It Notes S1–4*
- *Chapter Test for English Language Learners and Special-Needs Students*

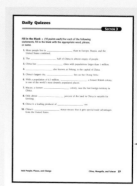

Special Education Modifications

Your **I.D.E.A. Works! CD-ROM** will provide modified versions of the following teaching materials:
- *Guided Reading Strategies S1–4*
- *Vocabulary Activity*
- *Main Idea Activities S1–4*
- ◀ *Daily Quizzes S1–4*
- *Chapter 16 Test*
- *Flash cards of chapter vocabulary terms*

Teacher Resources

Books for Teachers

Dutton, Michael, ed. *Streetlife China.* Cambridge University Press, 1998.

Qing, Dai, John G. Thibodeau, and Philip B. Williams, eds. *The River Dragon Has Come!: The Three Gorges Dam and the Fate of China's Yangtze River and Its People.* M.E. Sharpe, 1998.

Spence, Jonathan D. *The Chan's Great Continent: China in Western Minds.* W. W. Norton, 1998.

Books for Students

Baldwin, Robert F. *Daily Life in Ancient and Modern Beijing.* Runestone Press, 1999. Chronology of the customs, culture, history, and traditions of Beijing.

Namioka, Lensey. *Ties That Bind, Ties That Break.* Delacorte Press, 1999. Novel about a Chinese girl during a time of dramatic cultural and political transitions.

Reynolds, Jan. *Mongolia: Vanishing Cultures.* Harcourt Brace, 1994. Daily life of two nomadic boys in Mongolia.

Yu, Ling. *A Family in Taiwan.* Lerner Publications, 1990. Life in Taipei as seen through the eyes of a 12-year-old girl.
SHELTERED ENGLISH

Multimedia Materials

Astonishing Asia. CD–ROM. National School Products CD–ROM Software.

Chinese Art and Architecture. Video, 55 min. Alarion Press.

East Asia Global Studies. CD–ROM. Worldview Software.

Videos and CDs

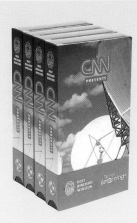

Videos

- **CNN** *Presents Geography: Yesterday and Today, Segment 28 The Yangtze River Dam*
- **CNN** *Presents World Cultures: Yesterday and Today, Segments 4, 12, 19*
- *ARG World*

Holt Researcher

http://researcher.hrw.com

- *Confucius*
- *Jiang Qing*
- *Laozi*
- *Mao Zedong*
- *Shi Huangdi*
- *Wu-ti*
- *Empress Wu*
- *China*
- *Taiwan*
- *China's Urban Centers*

Transparency Packages

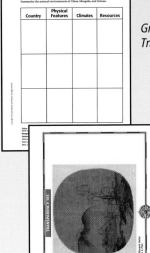

Graphic Organizer Transparencies 16.1–4

Geography and Cultures Visual Resources Transparencies 97–101

102 China, Mongolia, and Taiwan: Physical-Political

103 Landscape on a Fan

104 Tea: From Plantation to Consumer

Map Activities Transparency 16 Ancient China

WHY IT MATTERS

There are many reasons why American students should know more about China, Mongolia, and Taiwan. Here are a few:

▶ Americans buy many goods that were produced in China and Taiwan; these countries are important trading partners of the United States.

▶ China has the largest population of any country.

▶ China's strategic location and its status as a nuclear power influence the foreign policy of the United States.

▶ Mongolia and China have shaped world history, and China has made important cultural and technological contributions to the world.

CHAPTER 16

China, Mongolia, and Taiwan

This region of Asia with its varied landscape and cultures is home to one of the world's oldest living civilizations.

Hello! My name is Lu Hua. Lu is my family name, and Hua is my given name. In China the family name comes first. I am 16 and live in Jin Shan County, outside of Shanghai, with my parents and my brother. My father is a clerk in a Volkswagen factory. My ancestors have lived in this village for hundreds of years. All 200 people in this village are named Lu.

I am in my last year at Jin Shan County High School. To get into this school, which is the best in the county, I had to pass a very difficult exam when I was 11. I had the best score that year. The school goes from seventh to twelfth grade. Each grade has four classes with 50 kids in each class. Now I am hoping to go on to a university. In China only one or two out of a hundred kids can go to college.

Most of my friends want to be scientists. I think I would like to be a diplomat, to travel, and have adventures. My family are common people, though, not Chinese Communist Party members, so I may not get into the diplomatic college.

你好嗎?

Translation: How are you?

352 ● Chapter 16

CHAPTER PROJECT

Obtain several abacuses from an Asian import shop. Invite an expert to demonstrate basic addition and subtraction on an abacus. On a sheet of paper, have students devise math problems that can be solved using an abacus. Have students solve the problems with the abacuses and write down the correct answers. After students exchange problems and solve them, use the answer key to check students' solutions. Put papers and answer keys in portfolios.

STARTING THE CHAPTER

Hold up a compass, a porcelain object, and a piece of paper. Tell students to describe in writing the importance of each object for human civilization. (Students may mention that the compass made possible wide-ranging exploration, that porcelain has functional and decorative value, and that paper has enabled people to communicate and reproduce their ideas.) Ask students to speculate on the origins of each item. If students are unaware of the objects' origins, tell them that they are based on Chinese innovations. Tell students that in this chapter they will learn about other contributions to world culture made by the people of China, Mongolia, and Taiwan.

Section 1 Physical Geography

Read to Discover

1. What are the physical features of China, Mongolia, and Taiwan?
2. What types of climate are found in China, Mongolia, and Taiwan?
3. What natural resources do China, Mongolia, and Taiwan have?

Vocabulary

dikes
arable

Places

Himalayas
Mount Everest
Kunlun Mountains
Tian Shan
Plateau of Tibet
Taklimakan Desert
Tarim Basin
Gobi
North China Plain
Huang River
Chang River
Sichuan (Red) Basin
Xi River

Reading Strategy

USING VISUAL INFORMATION Look at the map and photographs in this section. Where do you think most of China's population lives? What challenges do the people of Mongolia and Taiwan face? Write your answers on a sheet of paper. As you read this section, correct your predictions and add more details.

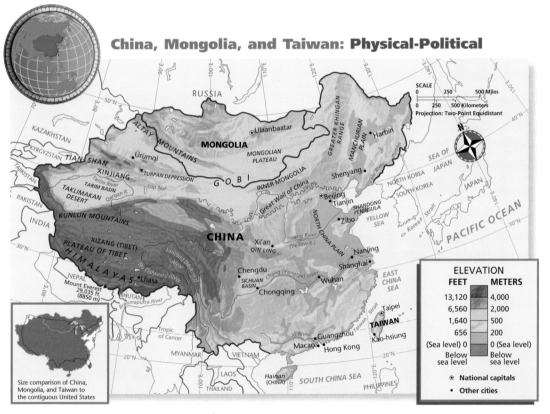

China, Mongolia, and Taiwan: Physical-Political

China, Mongolia, and Taiwan • 353

SECTION 1 RESOURCES

Reproducible
- Lecture Notes, Section 1
- Block Scheduling Handbook, Chapter 16
- Know It Notes S1
- Lab Activity for Geography and Earth Science, Hands-On 1

Technology
- One-Stop Planner CD–ROM, Lesson 16.1
- Homework Practice Online
- Geography and Cultures Visual Resources with Teaching Activities 49–54
- HRW Go site

Reinforcement, Review, and Assessment
- Section 1 Review
- Daily Quiz 16.1
- Main Idea Activity S1
- Chapter Summaries and Review
- English Audio Summary 16.1
- Spanish Audio Summary 16.1

Section 1

Objectives

1. Identify the physical features of China, Mongolia, and Taiwan.
2. Describe the types of climate found in China, Mongolia, and Taiwan.
3. List the natural resources of China, Mongolia, and Taiwan.

FOCUS

Bellringer

Display examples of traditional Chinese ink-on-paper landscape painting. (Find examples in art history texts and books on China.) Ask students what they can learn about China's physical geography by looking at the paintings. Tell students that China has a wide range of landforms and climates, as the paintings indicate. Tell students they will learn more about the physical geography of China, Mongolia, and Taiwan in this chapter.

Using the Physical-Political Map

Have students examine the map on this page. Ask volunteers to locate the mountain ranges, plains, plateaus, and rivers. Then ask a volunteer to identify the physical features that one would encounter if traveling directly from Lhasa to Harbin and from Guangzhou to Ulaanbaatar.

China, Mongolia, and Taiwan 353

Linking Past to Present

A Legendary Desert In his writings, Marco Polo described mirages experienced by travelers crossing the Taklimakan Desert. *Taklimakan* is a Turkic word meaning "enter and you will not come out."

Activity: Have students conduct research on the Taklimakan Desert and write a folktale about how it received its name.

▲
These snow-covered mountains are in the Wolong Nature Reserve in central China.

Interpreting the Visual Record

(Region) **What climate types would you expect to find in this area of the reserve?**

🖥 **internet** connect

GO TO: go.hrw.com
KEYWORD: SK5 CH16
FOR: Web sites about China, Mongolia, and Taiwan

Visual Record Answer ▲

highland climates

Physical Features

China has some of the world's tallest mountains, driest deserts, and longest rivers. Mongolia (mahn-GOHL-yuh) is China's neighbor to the north. It is a large, rugged, landlocked country. Burning hot summers and bitter cold winters are common there. In contrast, Taiwan (TY-WAHN) is a green tropical island just off the coast of mainland China.

Mountains The towering Himalayas (hi-muh-LAY-uhz), the world's tallest mountain range, run along China's southwestern border. Mount Everest lies in the Himalayas on China's border with Nepal. At 29,035 feet (8,850 m), it is the world's tallest mountain. If you move north from the Himalayas, you will find several other mountain ranges. These are the Kunlun Mountains (KOON-LOON), the Tian Shan (TYEN SHAHN), and the Altay Mountains (al-TY). To the east, on Mongolia's eastern border with China, you will see the Greater Khingan (KING-AHN) Range.

Mountains stretch the length of Taiwan and cover the eastern half of the island. In some places, the mountains end in steep cliffs at the edge of the Pacific Ocean. To the west of the mountains is a fertile coastal plain.

Plateaus, Basins, and Deserts Isolated plateaus and basins separate the region's mountain ranges. The huge Plateau of Tibet lies between the Himalayas and the Kunlun Mountains. With an average elevation of 16,000 feet (4,877 m), it is the world's highest plateau. The Taklimakan (tah-kluh-muh-KAHN) Desert is a huge expanse of sand. It occupies the central part of the Tarim (DAH-REEM) Basin in western China. In the northeastern corner of the basin, the Turpan (toohr-PAHN) Depression drops about 505 feet (154 m) below sea level.

TEACH

Teaching Objective 1

LEVEL 1: (Suggested time: 45 min.) Organize the class into small groups. Provide students with a large piece of cardboard, construction paper, markers, modeling clay, glue, and scissors. Have each group prepare a large, three-dimensional outline map of the region that includes the major landforms and rivers. Display maps around the classroom.
ESOL, COOPERATIVE LEARNING, LS **KINESTHETIC**

LEVELS 2 AND 3: (Suggested time: 15 min.) Tell students that some ancient Chinese maps have north and south reversed, with north at the bottom of the page. Call volunteers to the chalkboard to sketch outline maps of China, Taiwan, and Mongolia in this configuration. Ask other volunteers to draw in the major landforms and rivers. Ask other students to participate by providing any necessary hints and guidance to students at the chalkboard. You may wish to provide students with colored chalk.
LS **KINESTHETIC**

The Mongolian Plateau covers most of the country of Mongolia. The Gobi (GOH-bee) takes up much of the central and southeastern sections of the plateau. The Gobi is the coldest desert in the world and covers more than 500,000 square miles (1,295,000 sq km). Much of the Gobi is gravel and bare rock.

Plains China and Mongolia have few areas of lowlands made up of coastal and river floodplains. However, these fertile plains support the major population centers. Millions of people live in the North China Plain. It is the largest plain in China and is crossed by major rivers.

Rivers The river known as the Huang (HWAHNG) rises on the eastern edge of the Plateau of Tibet. It flows eastward through the North China Plain and empties into the Yellow Sea. It takes its name, which means "yellow river," from the yellowish mud it carries. Winds carry loess, a yellowish-brown soil, from the Gobi to northern China. The Huang picks up the loess as the river flows through the region. On its way to the sea the river dumps the loess, raising the river bottom. This can lead to flooding. Floodwaters deposit a layer of rich silt that is good for farming but also cause great damage and loss of life. As a result, the Huang has long been known as China's Sorrow. The Chinese have tried to control the Huang by building **dikes**. These high banks of earth or concrete help reduce flooding.

The Chang (CHAHNG), or Yangtze (YAHNG-TSE), River also rises in the Plateau of Tibet. It flows eastward for 3,434 miles (5,525 km) across central China through the fertile Sichuan (SEE-CHWAHN), or Red, Basin. The Chang is China's—and Asia's—longest river. In fact, its name means "long river." The Chang is one of China's most important transportation routes. It is connected to the Huang by the world's oldest and longest canal system, the Grand Canal. The Xi (SHEE) River is southern China's most important river and transportation route.

✓ **READING CHECK:** (*Places and Regions*) What are the major physical features of this region? mountains, plateaus, basins, deserts, plains, rivers

Climate

China, Mongolia, and Taiwan are part of a huge region with several different climates. China's precipitation varies. The southeastern coastal region is the country's most humid area. As you move northwestward the climate becomes steadily drier. The extreme northwest has a true desert climate.

Seasonal monsoon winds greatly affect the climate of the region's southern and eastern parts. In winter, winds from Central Asia bring dry, cool-to-cold weather to eastern

Our Amazing Planet

China has greater potential for hydroelectric power than any other country in the world. When completed in 2009, the Three Gorges Dam on the Chang River will be the world's largest dam.

The Gobi is the world's third-largest desert. Herders ride Bactrian camels.

Interpreting the Visual Record (*Place*)
What characteristics of a desert environment can be seen in this photo?

▼

China, Mongolia, and Taiwan **355**

HUMAN SYSTEMS

A Very Grand Canal
The Grand Canal, which links Beijing and Hangzhou, is more than 1,000 miles (1,609 km) long. Construction on the canal may have begun as long ago as the 300s B.C. The Sui dynasty rebuilt this oldest section during the A.D. 600s, and each succeeding dynasty expanded the canal until the Mongols completed it in the 1200s. The canal provided an important transportation and communication link between cities and outlying lands of the empire. In 1958 the Chinese government began work to straighten, dredge, and widen the canal to allow larger vessels to pass through.

Critical Thinking: What influence might the Grand Canal have on China's economy?

Answer: considerable influence, because it was essential for trade across the huge country

◄**Visual Record Answer**
bare ground, no vegetation

Teaching Objective 2
ALL LEVELS: (Suggested time: 10 min.) Copy the following graphic organizer onto the chalkboard, omitting the blue answers. Have each student complete the chart by filling in the climate regions of China, Mongolia, and Taiwan and their corresponding climate types. Ask volunteers to share their answers with the class. Then ask students where they think most of China's population may live (eastern half) and why (enough rainfall for growing crops).

Region	Climate Type
Southeastern coastal region	Humid and wet
Northwest	Dry
Extreme northwest	Desert

Teaching Objective 3
ALL LEVELS: (Suggested time: 20 min.) Organize the class into small groups. Provide each group with an outline map of the region. Have each group create a map key with symbols to represent the various resources found in each country. Tell students to draw the symbols on the maps in appropriate places. Display and discuss student maps.
ESOL, COOPERATIVE LEARNING, [LS] **VISUAL-SPATIAL**

China, Mongolia, and Taiwan

Answers to Section 1 Review

Define For definitions, see the glossary.

Working with Sketch Maps
The North China Plain and coastal plains of Taiwan are the most fertile areas.

Reading for the Main Idea

1. Plateau of Tibet between the Himalayas and the Kunlun Mountains; Mount Everest; on China's border with Nepal **(NGS 4)**

2. Huang, Chang, Xi River; it often floods **(NGS 15)**

3. Gobi and Taklimakan Deserts **(NGS 4)**

Critical Thinking

4. latitude, ocean currents, high mountains, large interior, and monsoons **(NGS 7)**

Organizing What You Know

5. China—Himalayas, Kunlun Mountains, Tian Shan, Altay Mountains, Plateau of Tibet, Tarim Basin, Turpan Depression, North China Plain; from tropical to desert; gold, iron ore, lead, salt, zinc, uranium, coal, oil; Mongolia—Mongolian Plateau, Khingan Range; hot summers, cold winters, desert; coal, oil, iron ore, and copper; Taiwan—mountains and coastal plains; tropical; arable land **(NGS 4)**

Chart Answer

Mongolia

COUNTRY	POPULATION/ GROWTH RATE	LIFE EXPECTANCY	LITERACY RATE	PER CAPITA GDP
China	1,286,975,468 0.6%	70, male 74, female	86%	$4,400
Mongolia	2,712,315 1.4%	61, male 66, female	99%	$1,840
Taiwan	22,548,000 0.8%	74, male 80, female	94%	$17,400
United States	281,421,906 0.9%	74, male 80, female	97%	$36,200

China, Mongolia, and Taiwan

Source: Central Intelligence Agency, *The World Factbook 2003*

Interpreting the Chart Which country has the fastest rate of population growth?

This bronze vessel dates to the A.D. 1000s. Found in a tomb, it is just over a foot long (30 cm) and is covered with detailed animal designs.

Asia. In summer, winds from the Pacific bring warm, wet air. This creates hot, rainy summers. Typhoons sometimes hit the coastal areas during the summer and fall. Typhoons are violent storms with high winds and heavy rains similar to hurricanes. They often bring flooding and cause a great deal of damage.

✓ **READING CHECK:** *Places and Regions* What are the climates of China, Mongolia, and Taiwan like?
varied with humid, dry, and desert regions

Resources

China has a wide range of mineral resources. These include gold, iron ore, lead, salt, uranium, and zinc, as well as energy resources such as coal and oil. China has greater coal reserves than any other country. At the present rate of use, these reserves will last another 1,000 years. China also produces enough oil to meet most of its own needs.

Mongolia has deposits of coal, copper, gold, iron ore, and oil. Taiwan's most important natural resource is its **arable** land, or land that is suitable for growing crops.

✓ **READING CHECK:** *Places and Regions* What are the region's resources?
gold, iron ore, lead, salt, uranium, zinc, coal, copper, oil, arable land

Homework Practice Online
go.hrw.com
Keyword: SK5 HP16

Section Review 1

Define and explain: dikes, arable

Working with Sketch Maps On a map of China, Mongolia, and Taiwan that you draw or that your teacher provides, label the following: the Himalayas, Mount Everest, Kunlun Mountains, Tian Shan, Plateau of Tibet, Taklimakan Desert, Tarim Basin, Gobi, North China Plain, Huang River, Chang River, Sichuan Basin, and Xi River. Where do you think the most fertile areas of the region are located?

Reading for the Main Idea

1. *Places and Regions* What and where is the world's largest plateau? What is the world's tallest mountain? Where is it located?

2. *Environment and Society* What are three major rivers in eastern and southern China? How does the Huang affect China's people?

3. *Places and Regions* What is the region's driest area?

Critical Thinking

4. **Drawing Inferences and Conclusions** What do you think might be the major factors that influence this region's climate?

Organizing What You Know

5. **Summarizing** Summarize the natural environments of China, Mongolia, and Taiwan.

Country	Physical Features	Climates	Resources

CLOSE

Tell students that in 1999 the official figure for Mount Everest's elevation was revised. Scientists operated Global Positioning System satellite equipment at the mountain's top to determine that the peak is about seven feet higher than the previous official measurement, which had been made in 1954. The mountain's official elevation is now 29,035 feet (8,850 m).

REVIEW, ASSESS, RETEACH

Have students complete the Section Review. Then pair students and have each pair create six flashcards for a where-am-I game. Students should describe a climate region or geographic feature on the front of each card and write the answer on the back. Have pairs exchange cards with other pairs and answer the other pairs' questions. Then have students complete Daily Quiz 16.1. **COOPERATIVE LEARNING**

Have students complete Main Idea Activity S1. Then organize students into small groups and have each group create an outline of the section. **ESOL, COOPERATIVE LEARNING**

EXTEND

Have interested students conduct research on the typhoons that hit China's coastal areas. Students should investigate how typhoons are formed and how they affect China. **BLOCK SCHEDULING**

Section 2 China's History and Culture

Read to Discover

1. What are some of the major events in the history of China?
2. What are some features of China's culture?

Vocabulary

emperor
dynasty
porcelain
martial law
pagodas

Places

China
Great Wall

People

Confucius
Genghis Khan
Sun Yat-sen
Mao Zedong
Dalai Lama

Reading Strategy

USING PRIOR KNOWLEDGE Before you read this section, list information you already know about China's history and culture. Compare your list with a partner. As you read this section, add more information to your list. Then compare your completed list with your partner's list.

History

Farmers have cultivated rice in southern China for some 7,000 years. Warm, wet weather made the region ideal for growing rice. Rice remains one of the region's main sources of food. Farmers in drier northern China grew a grain called millet and other crops. The early Chinese also grew hemp for fiber for clothing and spun silk from the cocoons of silkworms. Various cultures developed, particularly along the region's rivers.

The Qin Dynasty and the Great Wall Beginning about 2000 B.C. northern Chinese living in the Huang valley formed kingdoms. As Chinese civilization began to develop, peoples from various regions organized into large states. Each state was governed by an **emperor**—a ruler of a large empire. An emperor is often a member of a **dynasty**. A dynasty is a ruling family that passes power from one generation to the next. Beginning in about 500 B.C., the Chinese began building earthen

Place The Great Wall of China, including its branches and curves, stretches more than 2,000 miles (3,218 km).

China, Mongolia, and Taiwan 357

Section 2

Objectives

1. Identify some of the major events in the history of China.
2. Discuss some features of China's culture.

Focus

Bellringer

Copy the following passage onto the chalkboard: *Chinese artisans from various eras created impressive objects. Look at the photographs in this section. What may they tell you about China's history and culture?* Discuss responses. Tell students that in Section 2 they will learn about China's history and culture.

Building Vocabulary

Copy the vocabulary terms—**emperor, dynasty, porcelain, martial law,** and **pagodas**—onto the chalkboard. Have volunteers read the terms' definitions aloud. Point out that a dynasty can also be any family or group that maintains great power, wealth, or position for several generations. Ask students to give examples of real-life or fictional dynasties that fit either or both meanings. (Example: a basketball team that wins the championship for several years in a row)

Reproducible
◆ Lecture Notes, Section 2
◆ Graphic Organizer 16
◆ Geography for Life Activity 16
◆ Creative Strategies for Teaching World Geography, Lesson 18
◆ Interdisciplinary Activities for the Middle Grades 29, 30, 31
◆ Map Activity 16
◆ Biography Activity: Genghis Khan

Technology
◆ Music of the World Audio CD Program, Selection 19
◆ Homework Practice Online
◆ HRW Go site

Reinforcement, Review, and Assessment
◆ Section 2 Review
◆ Chapter Summaries and Review
◆ English Audio Summary 16.2
◆ Spanish Audio Summary 16.2

DAILY LIFE

Working for the Government The Chinese civil service system, created during the Qin dynasty, helped maintain stability within the empire for more than 2,000 years. People who scored well on certain examinations were chosen for the civil service. These civil servants helped carry out imperial laws and keep records. Other countries used the Chinese civil service system as a model when creating their own civil services.

These government servants became known as mandarins. The word *mandarin* has Spanish, Portuguese, Malay, and Sanskrit roots. It eventually referred both to the officials and the dialect they spoke. Today the country's official language is Mandarin Chinese.

Critical Thinking: Why might mandarins have so greatly influenced language in China?

Answer: Students may suggest that because government business was conducted in Mandarin, it became important for people to know the dialect.

Biography Answer ▶

by arguing for a different system of government

Archaeologists have discovered 6,000 of these uniquely crafted soldiers near Xi'an.

BIOGRAPHY

Confucius
(c. 551 B.C.–479? B.C.)

The philosopher's real name was K'ung Ch'iu or K'ung Fu-tzu ("Master K'ung"). We know him by the Latin version of his name—Confucius.

Few details about the life of Confucius are certain. We do know he was born about 551 B.C. in eastern China. It was a time troubled by warfare and wicked rulers. In response, Confucius argued for a different system of behavior and government. His ideas have shaped Chinese society for centuries.

How did Confucius influence Chinese society?

358 • **Chapter 16**

walls hundreds of miles long. These walls separated the kingdoms from the northern nomads and from each other. Records show that the first emperor of the Qin, also spelled Ch'in (CHIN), dynasty ordered the building of the Great Wall along China's northern border. People began to connect the sections of walls about 200 B.C.

The Qin dynasty is well known for its contributions to China's culture. It left behind many historical artifacts. For example, when the first emperor died, he was buried with thousands of life-sized warriors and horses made of clay. You might wonder why someone would want their tomb filled with clay figures. It was an ancient Chinese funeral tradition to bury masters with clay soldiers for protection. Since the Qin emperor had made many enemies during his life, he wanted protection after his death.

During the Qin dynasty the Chinese used a writing system to record their history. This system was similar to the one used in China today. China's name also dates from this time period. In Chinese, China means "Qin kingdom" or "middle kingdom." This name may refer to the Chinese belief that China was the center, or middle, of the world.

The Han Dynasty The Han dynasty came after the Qin dynasty. From the 200s B.C. to the A.D. 200s, the Han dynasty expanded its kingdom southward. The Han also extended the Great Wall westward to protect the Silk Road. This road was originally used by trading caravans taking silk and other Chinese goods to regions west of China. During the Han dynasty the Chinese invented the compass, which aided travel. The dynasties that followed the Han made China even more powerful. The Chinese continued to make important contributions to society. Later contributions include paper and **porcelain** (POHR-suh-luhn), a type of very fine pottery.

TEACH

Teaching Objective 1

LEVEL 1: (Suggested time: 40 min.) Organize the class into eight groups. Assign each group one of the following topics: Ancient China, Qin dynasty, Han dynasty, Mongols, Ming dynasty and the Manchu, the Republics, Mao, and Post-Mao. Have groups illustrate on large, unlined notecards the events occurring during their assigned time period. Create a time line on the chalkboard or on butcher paper. Then have each group attach its notecard in the appropriate place to create a pictorial time line of events in Chinese history. (The time line should include: Ancient China—rice, hemp, silk, and forma-

tion of kingdoms; Qin dynasty—Great Wall, written history, artifacts, and country's name; Han dynasty—expansion of kingdom; extension of Great Wall, compass, paper, and porcelain; Mongols—conquest of China; Ming dynasty and the Manchu—overthrow of Mongols, strengthened Great Wall, development of Chinese culture, control by the Qing dynasty; Republics—overthrow of Qing dynasty, Japanese invasion of China; Mao—People's Republic of China, Cultural Revolution; post-Mao—Tiananmen Square protest, free market reforms.) **ESOL, COOPERATIVE LEARNING**

Mongols, Ming Dynasty, and the Manchu In the 1200s Mongol armies led by Genghis Khan conquered China. *Khan* is a title that means "ruler." The Mongols were feared and known for spreading terror throughout the region. Their use of horses added to their military advantage.

Within 100 years the Ming dynasty seized control of China. After several battles with the Mongols, the Ming emperors closed China to outsiders. These emperors strengthened the Great Wall and focused on the development of their own culture.

In the 1600s a group called the Manchu began expanding from their home in Manchuria. Manchuria is located in far northeastern China. The Manchus conquered Inner Mongolia, Korea, and all of northern China. Led by the Qing (CHING) dynasty, the Manchu controlled China for more than 260 years. The dynasty's strong government slowly weakened, however, and was overthrown in the early 1900s.

Outside Influences Marco Polo was one of the few Europeans to visit China before the 1500s. Europeans reached China by following the Silk Road. None came by sea before the 1500s. In the 1500s Portuguese sailors established a trade colony at Macao (muh-KOW) in south China. French and British sailors and traders followed. The Chinese believed that foreigners had little to offer other than silver in return for Chinese porcelain, silk, and tea. Even so, Europeans introduced crops like corn, hot chili peppers, peanuts, potatoes, sweet potatoes, and tobacco. By the 1800s the European countries wanted to control China's trade. A series of conflicts caused China to lose some of its independence. For example, during this period the British acquired Hong Kong. The British, Germans, and French also forced China to open additional ports. China did not regain total independence until the mid-1900s.

The Republics of China In 1912 a revolutionary group led by Sun Yat-sen (SOOHN YAHT-SUHN) forced the last emperor to abdicate, or give up power. This group formed the first Republic of China. Mongolia and Tibet each declared their independence.

After Sun Yat-sen's death the revolutionaries split into two groups, the Nationalists and the Communists. A military leader named Chiang Kai-shek (chang ky-SHEK) united China under a Nationalist government. The Communists opposed him, and a civil war began. During

The Catalan Atlas from the 1300s shows Marco Polo's family traveling by camel caravan.

Interpreting the Visual Record

(*Movement*) What kind of information might this atlas provide?

▼

This time line reviews major events in China's rich history. The last Chinese dynasty was overthrown in 1912.

Interpreting the Time Line

What events have shaped China's government in the 1900s?

▼

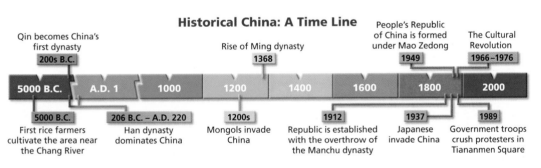

Historical China: A Time Line

Qin becomes China's first dynasty
200s B.C.

Rise of Ming dynasty
1368

People's Republic of China is formed under Mao Zedong
1949

The Cultural Revolution
1966–1976

| 5000 B.C. | A.D. 1 | 1000 | 1200 | 1400 | 1600 | 1800 | 2000 |

5000 B.C.
First rice farmers cultivate the area near the Chang River

206 B.C. – A.D. 220
Han dynasty dominates China

1200s
Mongols invade China

1912
Republic is established with the overthrow of the Manchu dynasty

1937
Japanese invade China

1989
Government troops crush protesters in Tiananmen Square

China, Mongolia, and Taiwan • 359

LEVEL 2: (Suggested time: 15 min.) Tell students to imagine that newspaper reporters have been around since ancient times. Pair students and assign each pair a period of Chinese history. Then have each pair use the time line in this section to write three or four headlines to describe the major events of its assigned period. Ask volunteers to read their headlines to the class. **COOPERATIVE LEARNING,** LS **VERBAL-LINGUISTIC**

LEVEL 3: (Suggested time: 45 min.) Pair students and assign each pair one period of Chinese history. Tell one student in each pair to imagine that he or she is a reporter, and tell the other student to imagine that he or she is a historian. Have each pair write a transcript of an interview, including questions and answers, about its assigned historical period. Have students conduct their interviews for the class. LS **INTERPERSONAL**

Linking Past to Present

Famine in China

A great famine in China began in 1958 despite a record grain crop. There were many reasons for the famine. The government had set very high targets for grain production. Feeling pressured, government-run farms provided exaggerated estimates of their grain harvests. As a result, the government sent large amounts of grain to the cities. Some rural people were left to starve.

Also, the government had sent many farmers to work in factories. With fewer farmers working in the fields, grain production dropped.

The Chinese famine ended in 1962. Today, the food supply in China is much larger than it was during the 1960s. Furthermore, because Chinese farmers hold much larger grain stocks than they once did, the chances of another rural famine have decreased greatly.

Activity: Have students write essays explaining how the famine illustrates the need for limiting the power of government.

Biography Answer

widespread starvation

BIOGRAPHY

Mao Zedong
(1893–1976)

Mao Zedong founded a new country—the People's Republic of China. His policies, however, created disasters for his country's people.

Early in his career, Mao and 90,000 followers set off on a 6,000-mile walk to establish a new headquarters. Half of the group didn't survive the trip. Later, his economic program, The Great Leap Forward, brought widespread starvation. Some 20 million died. Mao's Cultural Revolution was supposed to make China an ideal Communist society. Instead, the country was damaged and many people were killed.

What was the result of Mao's Great Leap Forward?

Place The Potala Palace in Tibet was built in the A.D. 600s. Today, it has more than 1,000 rooms and is used for religious and political events.

World War II both groups fought the Japanese. The Communists finally defeated the Nationalists in 1949. Led by Mao Zedong (MOW ZUH-DOOHNG), the Communists set up the People's Republic of China. Mao's version of communism is known as Maoism. Only one political party—the Communist Party—was allowed.

Chiang Kai-shek and his Nationalists retreated to Taiwan. There they created a government for what they called the Republic of China. This government maintained its control through **martial law**, or military rule, for many years.

Mao's China Under Mao the government took over the country's economy. His government seized private land and organized it into large, government-run farms. Factories were also put under state control. The central government decided the amount and type of food grown on a farm. It also regulated the production of factory goods, owned all housing, and decided where people should live. Sometimes families were separated or forced to relocate. Women were given equal status and assigned equal work duties. Religious worship was prohibited. Despite the efforts to organize the economy, there were planning errors. In the 1960s a famine killed about 30 million people.

In 1966 Mao began a movement called the Cultural Revolution. The Revolution was an attempt to make everyone live a peasant way of life. Followers of Mao were known as Red Guards. They closed schools and universities. Millions of people were sent to the countryside to work in the fields. Opponents were imprisoned or executed.

►**ASSIGNMENT:** Have each student locate a news article about current events in China. Ask each student to write a brief summary of his or her chosen article. Then have volunteers read their summaries to the class. Hold a question-and-answer session to review the material.

Teaching Objective 2

LEVEL 1: (Suggested time: 20 min.) Copy the following graphic organizer onto the chalkboard, omitting the blue answers. Pair students and ask each pair to complete the organizer. Ask volunteers to share their answers with the class. **ESOL, COOPERATIVE LEARNING,** LS **VISUAL-SPATIAL**

Features of Chinese Culture

Lifestyle
- Education highly valued
- One-child policy
- Government control of newspapers and telephone system
- Varied regional cuisines

Values and Beliefs
- Taoism—emphasizes path that agrees with nature and avoidance of everyday concerns
- Confucianism—respect for parents and rulers; parents and rulers act with justice
- Buddhism—search for truth, knowledge, and enlightenment

Languages
- Seven major Chinese dialects
- Mandarin the official language

Tibet Bordering the Himalayas in southwest China, the territory of Tibet is sometimes called the "Roof of the World." About two million people live in Tibet today. Tibetans see themselves as a separate nation and consider Lhasa their capital. However, Tibet is officially a part of China. The Chinese government wants Tibetans to be Chinese. In addition, China does not want Tibetans to practice their traditional Buddhist culture. For example, during China's Cultural Revolution, Chinese troops destroyed thousands of Buddhist monasteries. Many religious writings and art were demolished.

Tibetans trace their history back to the A.D. 500s when Tibet began as a Buddhist nation. In the 1400s, a religious leader called the Dalai Lama ruled Tibet. Since then 14 men have served as Dalai Lama. After a violent uprising against China in 1959, the 14th Dalai Lama sought exile in India where he lives today. In 1989, the Dalai Lama received the Nobel Peace Prize for his nonviolent protest against Chinese occupation of Tibet.

✓ **READING CHECK:** (**Human Systems**) What are some major events in China's history? dynasties, republics, establishment of communist government, cultural revolution, death of Mao, Tiananmen Square

Culture

About 92 percent of China's population consider themselves Han Chinese. Almost everyone can speak one of the seven major Chinese dialects. Mandarin Chinese is the official language and the most common.

Values and Beliefs Several philosophies and religions began in China. Taoism (TOW-i-zuhm), or Daoism (DOW-i-zuhm), is an ancient Chinese religion. Taoists believe that humans should try to follow a path that agrees with nature and avoids everyday concerns. The word *dào* means "the path." Each object or natural feature is thought to have its own god or spirit that may reward good deeds or bring bad luck.

The teachings of Confucius also have been important to Chinese culture. Confucius was a philosopher who lived from 551 to 479 B.C. His teachings stressed the importance of family. Confucius believed that children should

The Chinese New Year is also called the Lunar New Year. This is because the cycles of the moon are the basis for the Chinese calendar.

Interpreting the Visual Record

(*Place*) What object are parade participants carrying? What does it resemble?

◀ **Visual Record Answer**

a large puppet; a dragon

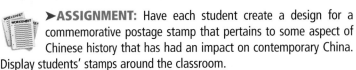

China, Mongolia, and Taiwan **361**

LEVEL 2: (Suggested time: 20 min.) Have each student create a collage that illustrates the impact of traditional Chinese culture, including languages, values and beliefs, on the modern Chinese lifestyle. Ask volunteers to present and explain their collages to the class. **LS KINESTHETIC**

LEVEL 3: (Suggested time: 20 min.) Tell students to imagine that they are foreign exchange students who are living in China. Have each student write a letter to a friend or family member back home to describe various features of Chinese culture, including languages, values and beliefs, and the modern Chinese lifestyle. Ask volunteers to read their letters to the class. **LS VERBAL-LINGUISTIC**

➤**ASSIGNMENT:** Have each student create a design for a commemorative postage stamp that pertains to some aspect of Chinese history that has had an impact on contemporary China. Display students' stamps around the classroom.

➤**ASSIGNMENT:** Tell students to imagine that they are Chinese university students living during the Cultural Revolution. Have each student write two or three journal entries to describe Mao's actions during the Revolution and the consequences for the Chinese people.

Across the Curriculum
LITERATURE

Women's Writing Hundreds of years ago, women in southern Hunan province developed a form of writing known as *nüshu*, or "women's writing." Women invented *nüshu* as a secret script. It enabled women to communicate with each other. *Nüshu* gave women a way to share stories, poems, and letters about their lives. *Nüshu* also allowed women to express ideas that challenged male control of society. Most women who read and wrote *nüshu* were unable to read and write Chinese script.

The Chinese government suppressed the use of *nüshu* during the 1960s. Most women are now educated to read and write Chinese but not *nüshu*. Researchers believe that only two women in rural villages still use *nüshu*. They fear that the language will soon be lost forever.

Discussion: Lead a class discussion on how *nüshu* was related to male control of society.

Connecting to Literature
Answers

1. written by a follower of Confucius, whose teachings stressed the importance of family

2. to encourage children to take care of their parents

CONNECTING TO *Literature*

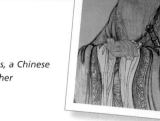

Confucius, a Chinese philosopher

This Chinese tale comes from the Hsiao Ching, *or* Book of Filial Piety—*which means "devotion to parents." A student of a follower of Confucius is believed to have written it about 400 B.C. This story encourages children to protect their parents.*

A Loving Son

Wu Meng was eight years old and very dutiful to his parents. His family was so poor that they could not afford to furnish their beds with mosquito-curtains. Every summer night thousands of mosquitoes attacked them, feasting upon their flesh and blood.

Wu Meng looked at his tired parents asleep on their bed as thousands of mosquitoes fiercely attacked them. Wu saw them sucking his parents' blood, which caused his heart to grieve.

To protect his parents, Wu decided that he would not drive the mosquitoes away from himself. Lying on the bed, he threw off his clothes, and soon feeling the pain of the mosquito attacks, he cried: "I have no fear of you, nor have you any reason to fear me. Although I have a fan, I will not use it, nor will I strike you with my hand. I will lie very quietly and let you gorge to the full." Such was his love for his parents!

Analyzing Primary Sources
1. How does this tale reflect traditional Chinese philosophical beliefs?
2. Why do you think the author of the *Hsiao Ching* wrote this story?

respect their parents and subjects should respect their ruler. He believed people should treat those under their control justly and argued that state power should be used to improve people's lives.

The religion called Buddhism also has been important in China. It was founded by an Indian prince, Siddhartha Gautama. Gautama was born in Nepal about 563 B.C. He decided to search for truth and knowledge. Enlightenment—peace and a sense of being one with the universe—came to him while he was sitting under a Bo or Bodhi tree. As a result, he was given the name Buddha, which means "awakened or enlightened one." Buddhism reached China from India about A.D. 100. It became the country's main religion between the 300s and 500s. Indian architecture also became popular in China. Chinese **pagodas**, or Buddhist temples, are based on Indian designs. Pagodas have an upward-curving roof. Some pagodas are 15 stories tall.

TEACHER TO TEACHER

Marcia Caldwell of Austin, Texas, suggests the following activity to help students understand Chinese philosophy: First, tell students that in ancient Chinese thought there are two complementary forces contained in all things—Yin and Yang. Yin is conceived of as Earth, female, dark, passive, and yielding. It is associated with the moon, winter, even numbers, valleys and streams, the tiger, the color orange, and a broken line. Yang is conceived of as the Sun, male, light, active, and forceful. It is associated with odd numbers, mountains, summer, the dragon, the color blue, and an unbroken line. According to the belief, as one of the principles increases the other decreases. This interaction is believed to describe the actual processes of the universe; their remaining in balance is essential to universal harmony.

Have students write down the qualities associated with each principle. Provide students with a large representation of the Yin-Yang symbol. See the example at right. Lead a discussion about how the two sides of the symbol balance and interconnect.

Tell students to use their lists as inspiration for a topic for a poem. Then have them brainstorm with a partner to choose words associated with both the Yin and Yang aspects of the topic. Instruct them to write the words on the correct sides of the symbol and incorporate the words into a brief poem, which they write below the symbol. Finally, invite students to illustrate their poems.

Yin

Yang

Lifeways Chinese culture highly values education. Chinese children are required to attend nine years of school. However, just 1 to 2 percent of students pass the difficult entrance exams to get into a university.

The Chinese government tries to control many aspects of everyday life. For example, parents are allowed to have just one child. This is because the government is trying to slow population growth.

The government also controls the newspapers and telephone system. This allows it to limit the flow of information and ideas. Satellite TV, the Internet, and e-mail are becoming more widespread, however. This makes it more difficult for the government to control communication between individuals.

Chinese food varies widely from region to region. Food in Beijing is heavily salted and flavored with garlic and cilantro. Sichuan-style cooking features hot pepper sauces. Cantonese cooking was introduced to the United States by immigrants from Guangzhou (GWAHNG-JOH).

Traditional Chinese medicine stresses herbal products and harmony with the universe. People around the world have used acupuncture. This therapy involves inserting fine needles into specific parts of the body for pain relief. Many Chinese herbal remedies have been used by American drug companies as the basis for modern medicines.

China has rich literary traditions. Painting, porcelain, sculpture, and carving of ivory, stone, and wood are also popular. Performing arts emphasize traditional folktales and stories shown in dances or operas with elaborate costumes.

✔ **READING CHECK:** (**Human Systems**) What is China's culture like?
beliefs include Taoism, Confucianism, Buddhism; education important; government controlled society; rich traditions

▲

For more than 200 years the Beijing Opera, or Peking Opera, has been recognized worldwide for its artistic contributions. Originally performed for the royal family, it is now viewed by the public and is aired on Chinese television and radio stations.

Homework Practice Online
Keyword: SK5 HP16

Section Review 2

Define or identify: emperor, dynasty, Confucius, porcelain, Genghis Khan, Sun Yat-sen, Mao Zedong, martial law, Dalai Lama, pagodas

Working with Sketch Maps On the map you created in Section 1, label China and the Great Wall. Why do you think the Chinese chose to build the Great Wall where they did?

Reading for the Main Idea

1. (**Human Systems**) What contributions did the Qin and Han dynasties make to Chinese history?

2. (**Human Systems**) How did Mao's rule change China?

3. (**Human Systems**) How has China changed since Mao's death in 1976?

Critical Thinking

4. **Summarizing** What are three philosophies or religions that have been important in China? Describe them.

Organizing What You Know

5. **Summarizing** Copy the following graphic organizer. Use it to describe the Ming and the Manchu.

Ming Dynasty	Manchu

China, Mongolia, and Taiwan • 363

Answers to Section 2 Review

Define or identify For definitions and identifications, see the glossary and index.

Working with Sketch Maps The north was more vulnerable.

Reading for the Main Idea

1. Qin—built Great Wall, kept history, and gave the country its name; Han—expanded kingdom; extended Great Wall; invented compass, paper, and porcelain **(NGS 12)**

2. government took control of property, housing, jobs; gave women equal status; one-child families; suppressed religion **(NGS 12)**

3. modernized government, turned over parts of the economy to private interests **(NGS 12)**

Critical Thinking

4. Taoism—follow a path that agrees with nature and avoids everyday concerns; Confucianism—respect for elders and rulers; Buddhism—becoming one with the universe

Organizing What You Know

5. Ming—overthrew Mongols, strengthened Great Wall, focused on Chinese culture; Manchu—from Manchuria, conquered large area, strong government

CLOSE

Draw five or more large squares on the chalkboard. Ask volunteers to sketch each box something they might see if they visited China today. Discuss the historical or cultural significance of each sketch.

REVIEW, ASSESS, RETEACH

Have students complete the Section Review. Then have each student write two quiz questions pertaining to the information in Section 2. Collect the questions and use them to quiz the class orally. Then have students complete Daily Quiz 16.2.

Have students complete Main Idea Activity S2. Then organize students into four groups—one for each of these topics: Dynasties, Outside Influences, Republics of China, and Culture. Have each group create a poster about its assigned topic. Have students present their posters to the class. **ESOL, COOPERATIVE LEARNING,** **LS VISUAL-SPATIAL**

EXTEND

Have interested students conduct research on the Chinese origins of papermaking and wood-block printing. Have students write a report to discuss their findings. You may also want them to use potatoes to create their own "wood blocks." Ask volunteers to share their reports with the class. **BLOCK SCHEDULING**

Chart Answer ▶

150,000,000 people

Section 3 — China Today

Read to Discover

1. Where do most of China's people live?
2. What are the major cities in China, and what are they like?
3. What is China's economy like?
4. What challenges does China face?

Vocabulary

command economy
multiple cropping
most-favored-nation status

Places

Shanghai   Beijing
Nanjing   Hong Kong
Wuhan   Macao
Chongqing

Reading Strategy

READING ORGANIZER Before you read this section, create a concept map. Draw a circle in the center of a sheet of paper. Label the circle China Today. Draw four lines coming out of the circle. Then draw a circle at the end of each line. Label the circles Population, Cities, Economy, and Challenges. As you read, write what you learn about each topic beside its circle.

China's Population

China has the largest population in the world—some 1.28 billion people. That number is equal to about 20 percent of the world's population. More people live in China than in all of Europe, Russia, and the United States combined. China's population is growing rapidly—by about 11 million each year. Some years ago, China's leaders took steps to bring the growth rate under control. They encouraged people to delay getting married and starting families. The government also tried to limit couples to one child.

China's population is not evenly distributed across the land. The western half of the country, which is mostly desert and mountain ranges, is almost empty. Just 10 percent of China's people live there. The rest are crowded into the country's eastern half. In fact, more people live in the North China Plain than in the entire United States. However, this region is only about the size of Texas. Most Chinese live in the countryside. Even so, China has 40 cities with populations greater than 1 million.

✓ **READING CHECK:** (Human Systems) Where do most of China's people live?
in the eastern half of the country

COMPARING POPULATIONS

China and the United States

China

United States

👤 = 150,000,000 people

Source: Central Intelligence Agency, *The World Factbook 2003*

Interpreting the Chart How many people does one figure on the chart represent?

China's Cities

Studying China's physical features helps explain why its residents live where they do. By locating rivers and river valleys, we can see where millions of people could best survive.

Several of China's most important cities are located on the Chang River. Shanghai, the country's largest city, lies on the Chang Delta. It serves as China's leading industrial center and is the major seaport.

364 • Chapter 16

Section 3

Objectives

1. Explain where most of China's people live.
2. Identify the major cities of China, and describe what they are like.
3. Discuss China's economy.
4. Describe the challenges China faces.

FOCUS

Bellringer

Copy the following instructions onto the chalkboard: *Compile a list of three or four things that you know about China's population, cities, or economy.* Discuss responses. (Students may mention that China is the world's most populous country, that China's cities are crowded and rapidly modernizing, or that China's economy is growing rapidly.) **Tell** students that in Section 3 they will learn more about life in China today.

Building Vocabulary

Copy the following vocabulary terms onto the chalkboard: **command economy, multiple cropping,** and **most-favored-nation status**. Ask students to examine the terms and then define any parts of the terms with which they are familiar. (Students may know the meanings of *command, multiple, economy,* and *most-favored*.) Have volunteers read the terms and their definitions aloud from the section's text or glossary.

Using the map in Section 1, follow the course of the Chang River inland. Locate the cities of Nanjing and Wuhan (WOO-HAHN). These two industrial centers were built around iron-ore and coal mines. If you continue to follow the river upstream, you will reach Chongqing (CHOOHNG-CHING), located in the Sichuan Basin. It is one of the few large cities in China's interior. Guangzhou, located at the mouth of the Xi River, is southern China's largest city. Long famous as a trading center, it was known in the West as Canton. Today Guangzhou is one of China's major industrial cities.

Beijing, also known as Peking, is China's capital. It was built more than 3,000 years ago as a trading center. Beijing is the largest city in northern China and is well known for its cultural heritage.

Southeast of Guangzhou is Hong Kong. With a population of 6.5 million, Hong Kong is one of the world's most densely populated places. It is only half as large as Rhode Island, but has more than seven times as many people. Hong Kong is China's major southern seaport and is a center for banking, international trade, and tourism.

The British occupied the island of Hong Kong in the 1830s. In the late 1800s Hong Kong was leased to the British for 99 years. The lease ran out in 1997, and the British left. Hong Kong then became a special administrative region of China. Hong Kong has some political independence and is allowed to maintain its free-market economy. Macao, a nearby port city, was once a Portuguese colony. At the end of 1999, it was returned to China.

✓ **READING CHECK:** (*Places and Regions*) What are the major cities of China? **Shanghai, Nanjing, Wuhan, Chongqing, Guangzhou, Beijing, Hong Kong**

EYE ON EARTH

Wildlife in Hong Kong?
Although it is a large, crowded city, Hong Kong is home to more than a bustling economy. On hiking trails through the many parks, visitors may spot monkeys, some of the many birds that live there, or some of the 390 native tree species.

Some 40 percent of Hong Kong's land is protected from development. It is too late for some animals, such as tigers, that have been crowded out. The South China red fox is among the few carnivores that still live in Hong Kong. Pollution from increased development poses a threat to the remaining wildlife.

Conservation efforts are underway in Hong Kong. Local environmental groups are working to survey the remaining wildlife and to promote environmental awareness.

Activity: Have students conduct research on how protecting the environment affects economic development. Have students present their findings to the class

Towering skyscrapers mark Shanghai's constantly changing skyline.

Interpreting the Visual Record (*Place*)
How can you tell this city is growing rapidly?

▼

China, Mongolia, and Taiwan 365

◄ **Visual Record Answer**

several buildings under construction, buildings crowded together

TEACH

Teaching Objectives 1–2

All LEVELS: (Suggested time: 20 min.) First, discuss how settlement patterns in China are related to geographic factors by reviewing the population map in this unit's atlas. (The population is concentrated in China's eastern half because deserts and mountains dominate the western half.) Then copy the following graphic organizer onto the chalkboard, omitting the blue answers. Have students complete the organizer by identifying and describing China's major cities. Ask volunteers to share their answers with the class. Finally, point out that most of the cities are in eastern China. **ESOL**

Eastern China
- Beijing—China's capital, largest city in northern China
- Nanjing—iron-ore and coal mines
- Shanghai—China's largest city, leading industrial center and a major seaport, much new construction
- Wuhan—iron-ore and coal mines
- Guangzhou—southern China's largest city, major industrial city
- Hong Kong—former British colony that maintains free-market economy, densely populated, a major seaport, major banking center, commerce, and tourism
- Macao—former Portuguese colony, port

Interior
- Chongqing—one of few large cities in China's interior

ENVIRONMENT AND SOCIETY

Three Gorges, Many Issues

In the 1990s the Chinese government began construction of a gigantic dam on the Chang River. The Three Gorges Dam, scheduled for completion in 2009, will create a reservoir hundreds of miles long. It will flood two cities, more than 100 towns, and almost 2,000 villages. This project has forced more than 1 million people to relocate.

The plan is to control the flooding of the river and to produce needed electric power. The government hopes that the dam will attract commerce to China's interior and that it will help modernize the country's economy.

Opponents of the project fear the loss of farmland, the potential pollution, and the loss of hundreds of historical sites. Wildlife is also threatened. For example, the habitat of the river dolphin will be destroyed. Only about 100 individuals of this rare species are left.

Activity: Have students conduct further research on the Three Gorges Dam. Then have students discuss the different points of view regarding the dam's effect on China.

Visual Record Answer ▶

plentiful water, human labor, and animal power

China's Economy

When the Chinese Communists took power in 1949 they set up a **command economy**. In this type of economy, the government owns most industries and makes most economic decisions. It set almost all production goals, prices, and wages.

Industry The Communists took over an economy that was based almost entirely on farming. Soon the Communist government introduced programs to build industry. Today, China is an industrial giant. It produces everything from satellites and rockets to toys.

In the late 1970s the government began to introduce elements of free enterprise. Now farmers can grow and market their own crops on part of their rented land. Many state-run factories are being closed or turned over to private industries. Millions of Chinese have started small businesses. A few Chinese have become wealthy. Some business owners can afford to build private homes and to buy cars and computers. However, most Chinese are poor.

Agriculture Only about 10 percent of China's land is good for farming. Nevertheless, China is a world leader in the production of many crops and can meet most of its food needs. China's huge workforce makes this possible. More than 50 percent of Chinese workers are farmers. Having many farmers means the land can be intensively worked to produce high yields. Farmers have also increased production by cutting terraces into hillsides to create new farmland.

China is divided between rice-growing and wheat-growing regions. The divide lies midway between the Huang and the Chang River. To the south, rice is the main crop. Here the warm wet weather makes **multiple cropping** possible. Multiple cropping means that two or three crops are raised each year on the same land. This practice makes southern China more prosperous than northern China.

✓ **READING CHECK:** (*Human Systems*) What kind of economy does China have? command, with some elements of free enterprise

Models of rice fields like these have been found in Han dynasty tombs.
Interpreting the Visual Record
(*Human-Environment Interaction*) What resources appear to be necessary for growing rice in this region?

▼

366 ● Chapter 16

Teaching Objective 3

ALL LEVELS: (Suggested time: 20 min.) Remind students of the concepts of command, traditional, and market economy. Then organize students into groups. Have each group create a poster comparing the U.S. economic system to that of China. (Posters should note that China has a command economy with some elements of free enterprise, and that the United States has a mostly market, free-enterprise system.) Ask groups to present their posters to the class and to explain the benefits of the U.S. free enterprise system. **COOPERATIVE LEARNING,** 🔲 **LOGICAL-MATHEMATICAL**

Teaching Objective 4

ALL LEVELS: (Suggested time: 20 min.) Organize the class into two large groups. Tell one group that it is responsible for reporting the economic progress that China has made in recent decades. Tell the other group to list the challenges that China still faces. (One group should mention that China has progressed by increasing its standard of living, by expanding industrial production, and by instituting economic freedoms; the other group should mention that China is still relatively poor, that it faces environmental problems, that its most-favored-nation status is in jeopardy, and that it still has not instituted political reforms.) **COOPERATIVE LEARNING**

China's Government

After Mao's death in 1976, the new Chinese communist leadership admitted some past mistakes. It tried to modernize the government.

Although the government has allowed individuals some economic freedom, it restricts political and religious freedom. In 1989 the Chinese army was called in to attack pro-democracy student demonstrators in Tiananmen Square in Beijing (BAY-JING). Many students were injured or killed. Other rebellions among China's ethnic minorities, particularly in Tibet, have been crushed.

✓ **READING CHECK:** (*Human Systems*) What freedoms does China's government restrict? pollution, lack of political reforms, trade status threatened by poor human rights record

Future Challenges

China has enjoyed remarkable economic success in recent years. China's drive to industrialize has caused major problems. For example, the air and water are badly polluted by factory wastes.

Another challenge involves the government's unwillingness to match the new economic freedoms with political reforms. China's human rights record has affected its economic relations with other countries. The U.S. government has considered canceling China's **most-favored-nation status** several times. Countries with this status get special trade advantages from the United States. China's economic future might depend on its government's willingness to accept political reforms.

✓ **READING CHECK:** (*Human Systems*) What challenges does China face? relatively poor, polluted; poor human rights record threatens free trade status

By the mid-1990s clothing, electrical equipment, footwear, textiles, and other consumer goods were among China's leading exports. Employees of the Bei Bei Shoe Factory glue soles on by hand on an assembly line in Shanghai.

Section Review 3

Define and explain: command economy, multiple cropping, most-favored-nation status

Working with Sketch Maps On the map you created in Section 2, label Shanghai, Nanjing, Wuhan, Chongqing, Beijing, Hong Kong, and Macao. In the margin of your map, draw a box for each city. List the characteristics of each city in its box.

Reading for the Main Idea

1. (*Places and Regions*) Where do most people in China live? Why?

2. (*Places and Regions*) Along which rivers are several of China's most important cities located? Why?

3. (*Environment and Society*) What farming practices have allowed the Chinese to increase production?

Homework Practice Online Keyword: SK5 HP16

Critical Thinking

4. **Finding the Main Idea** How has the Chinese government changed its economic policies since the late 1970s? What has been the impact of these changes?

Organizing What You Know

5. **Summarizing** Copy the following graphic organizer. Use it to describe the kinds of challenges facing China today. Identify specific environmental, political, and economic challenges.

Challenges

China, Mongolia, and Taiwan • 367

Answers to Section 3 Review

Define For definitions, see the glossary.

Working with Sketch Maps Maps will vary, but listed places should be labeled in their approximate locations. Students may list any of several characteristics.

Reading for the Main Idea

1. in the eastern half; because the western half is mostly desert and mountain ranges **(NGS 4)**

2. Chang and Xi Rivers serve as ports and trading centers **(NGS 4)**

3. cutting terraces into hillsides; practicing multiple cropping **(NGS 14)**

Critical Thinking

4. introduced elements of free enterprise; improved standard of living and rise to status as industrial giant

Organizing What You Know

5. environmental—polluted air and water; political—poor human rights record; economic—relatively poor, most-favored-nation status in jeopardy **(NGS 18)**

CLOSE

Based on the information presented in this section, ask students to predict what news stories they might read about in the next few years related to China's population, cities, economy, and government.

REVIEW, ASSESS, RETEACH

Have students complete the Section Review. Then pair students and have pairs reread the section and discuss it among themselves. Then have students complete Daily Quiz 16.3. **COOPERATIVE LEARNING**

Have students complete Main Idea Activity S3. Then ask them to create a map of China. Have groups cut out figures to represent population, major cities, the economy, and challenges facing China. Paste their information onto the map. **ESOL, COOPERATIVE LEARNING**

EXTEND

Have students create an annotated time line of Hong Kong's history. Have students write a caption explaining how aspects of its history are reflected in modern Hong Kong society. **BLOCK SCHEDULING**

Section 4 Mongolia and Taiwan

Read to Discover
1. How has Mongolia's culture developed?
2. What is Taiwan's culture like?

Vocabulary
gers

Places
Mongolia
Ulaanbaatar
Taiwan
Kao-hsiung
Taipei

People
Chiang Kai-shek

Reading Strategy

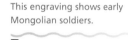

FOLDNOTES: TWO-PANEL FLIP CHART Create a **Two-Panel Flip Chart** as described in the Appendix. Label one of the flaps Mongolia and the other flap Taiwan. As you read this section, write what you learn about each country beneath its flap.

Mongolia

Mongolia is home to the Mongol people and has a fascinating history. You will learn of invaders and conquests and a culture that prizes horses.

Mongolia's History Today when people discuss the world's leading countries, they do not mention Mongolia. However, 700 years ago Mongolia was perhaps the greatest power in the world. Led by Genghis Khan, the Mongols conquered much of Asia, including China. Later leaders continued the conquests, building the greatest empire the world had seen. The Mongol Empire reached its height in the late 1200s.

It stretched from Europe's Danube River in the west to the Pacific Ocean in the east. Over time, however, the empire declined. In the late 1600s Mongolia fell under the rule of China.

In 1911, with Russian support, Mongolia declared its independence from China. Communists took control of the country 13 years later and established the Mongolian People's Republic. The country then came under the influence of the Soviet Union. Mongolia became particularly dependent on the Soviet Union for economic aid. This aid ended when the Soviet Union collapsed

This engraving shows early Mongolian soldiers.
▼

368 • Chapter 16

Section 4

Objectives
1. Recount how Mongolia's culture has developed.
2. Describe Taiwan's culture.

FOCUS

 Bellringer

Copy the following instructions onto the chalkboard: *Look at the photos in Section 4 and read the captions. What can the photos tell you about differences in the physical and human geography of Mongolia and Taiwan?* Discuss responses. (Possible answers: Mongolia is flatter and drier than Taiwan. Herding is common in Mongolia, but probably not common in Taiwan.) Tell students that Mongolia and Taiwan are indeed very different and that they will learn about these places in Section 4.

Building Vocabulary

Draw students' attention to the photograph of *gers* in this section. Explain that they are Mongolian homes. Ask students what this photograph tells them about Mongolian life. (Students may mention that *gers* are not fixed to the ground and can be moved fairly easily. Students may conclude that Mongolians shift locations quite often.)

◀

(Movement) Nomads of Mongolia live in *gers* like those shown here.

in the early 1990s. Since then, Mongolians have struggled to build a democratic government and a free-market economy.

Mongolia's Culture Despite years of Communist rule and recent Western influence, the Mongolian way of life remains quite traditional. Many people still follow a nomadic lifestyle. They live as herders, driving their animals across Mongolia's vast grasslands. They make their homes in **gers** (GUHRZ). These are large, circular felt tents that are easy to raise, dismantle, and move.

Since most people live as herders, horses play an important role in Mongolian life. Mongolian children learn to ride when they are very young—often before they are even five years old. In Mongolia, the most powerful piece in the game of chess is the horse, not the queen.

Mongolia Today Mongolia is a large country—slightly larger than Alaska. Its population numbers just over 2.7 million. Some 25 percent of Mongolians live in Ulaanbaatar (oo-lahn-BAH-tawr), the capital city. Ulaanbaatar is also Mongolia's main industrial and commercial center. Mongolia's other cities are quite small. Not one has a population greater than 100,000.

✔ **READING CHECK:** (*Human Systems*) What are some elements of Mongolian culture? traditional, nomadic lifestyle; people living in *gers* and herding animals

Taiwan

For many years the island of Taiwan was known in the West as Formosa. This name came from Portuguese sailors who visited the island in the late 1500s. They thought the island was so lovely that they called it *Ilha Formosa*, or "beautiful island."

In the Gobi, temperatures can range from -40°F (-40°C) in January to 113°F (45°C) in July. Some areas of this desert receive little more than 2 inches (5 cm) of rain each year.

EYE ON EARTH

A Rare Bird of Mongolia
Mongolia is the home of a much sought-after falcon, the saker. Valued by Genghis Khan for their hunting abilities, sakers are still prized for their speed and agility.

There is a limited legal trade in the birds for research purchases. There is also an illegal trade; falconers from the Arab states will pay up to $200,000 for a saker. As a result of its popularity, the falcon's survival is in doubt. Illegal trading of sakers has caused the bird to become endangered in the wild.

Activity: Have students conduct research on the illegal international trade in endangered species. Ask students to use their findings to create maps showing the sources, routes, and destinations of the trade. The maps should also show which species are targeted.

TEACH

Teaching Objective 1

LEVEL 1: (Suggested time: 30 min.) Pair students and have each pair create a collage to represent elements of Mongolia's culture. Display students' collages around the classroom. **ESOL, COOPERATIVE LEARNING,** **LS KINESTHETIC**

LEVELS 2 AND 3: (Suggested time: 20 min.) Have each student write a short poem about Mongolia's culture. Ask volunteers to recite their poems to the class. **LS AUDITORY-MUSICAL**

►**ASSIGNMENT:** Tell students to imagine that for six months they will live with Mongolian nomads. Their hosts herd livestock from horseback and live in *gers*. Each student's luggage may weigh no more than 30 pounds. Have students gather information on the weight of each item they might take and then consider the consequences of choosing some items but not others. Encourage students to take Mongolia's climate and culture into account. Then have students create their lists and discuss which are the most important items.

FOOD FESTIVAL

Chinese Almond Cakes

Have students make these cakes for a New Year's celebration.

Sift together 2½ c. all-purpose flour and ¾ tsp baking powder. Blend in 1 c. shortening and 1½ c. sugar. Stir in ¼ tsp almond extract, 2 Tbs beaten egg and 1 Tbs water. Knead dough and let stand for 5 minutes. Then form dough into 1½ inch balls. Flatten balls into cake-like shapes. Press an almond into each cake. (You will need about 30 almonds.) Bake on greased baking sheets in a 375° oven for 5 minutes. Reduce heat to 300° and bake for 8–10 minutes more, or until golden.

Chiang Kai-shek served in the Japanese army before returning to China to help overthrow the Manchu dynasty. He was head of the Nationalist government in China for 20 years, then moved with his followers to Taiwan.

Region Taiwan has good farmlands, but the island's eastern half is mountainous.

Taiwan's History The Chinese began settling Taiwan in the A.D. 600s. Some 600 years later the Japanese took control of eastern Taiwan. The search for spices brought European traders to Taiwan. The Dutch, Portuguese, and Spanish all tried to set up bases there. However, raiders from mainland China drove out these Europeans in the mid-1600s.

The struggle among the Chinese, Japanese, and Europeans for control of Taiwan continued until the late 1800s. In 1895 a treaty between the Chinese and the Japanese gave Taiwan to Japan. The Japanese then tried to force their way of life on the people of Taiwan. The Taiwanese rebelled against these efforts, but their revolts were crushed by the Japanese military.

After Japan's surrender at the end of World War II in 1945, China once again took command of Taiwan. In 1949 Mao Zedong established the People's Republic of China in mainland China. Chiang Kai-shek and the Nationalist Chinese government fled to Taiwan. The Nationalist government controlled Taiwan through martial law for decades. In recent years, however, the government has expanded democratic rights. China still claims that Taiwan is a province of China—not an independent country.

Taiwan's Culture Taiwan's history is reflected in its culture. Its population is about 85 percent native Taiwanese. They are descendants of people who migrated from China to Taiwan over hundreds of years. Chinese ways dominate Taiwan's culture. However, some building styles and certain foods reflect Japanese influences. European and American practices and customs have strongly influenced Taiwan's way of life in recent years. This is particularly true in the cities.

370 Chapter 16

Teaching Objective 2

ALL LEVELS: (Suggested time: 15 min.) Copy the following graphic organizer onto the chalkboard, omitting the blue answers. Have students complete the organizer by filling in facts about Taiwan's culture. Ask volunteers to share their answers with the class. **ESOL**

LEVELS 2 AND 3: (Suggested time: 45 min.) Draw a series of seven footsteps on the chalkboard and label each foot with a date in Taiwan's history. Ask volunteers to recount what happened at each step in Taiwan's history and to write the correct responses into the footsteps. Have students copy the footsteps and events into their notes. Then have students consult library resources to find details about how these events affected Taiwan's culture. **LS VISUAL-SPATIAL**

Taiwan Today Taiwan has a modern, industrial economy and a population of about 22 million. These people live on an island the size of Delaware and Maryland combined. Most people live on the western coastal plain of Taiwan. Population densities there can reach higher than 2,700 per square mile (1,042 per sq km). Taiwan's two largest cities, Kao-hsiung (KOW-SHYOOHNG) and Taipei (TY-PAY), are located on the coastal plain. Taipei is the capital city. It faces serious overcrowding and environmental problems. The thousands of cars, motorcycles, and trucks that clog Taipei's streets each day cause severe air pollution.

In the early 1950s Taiwan's economy was still largely based on agriculture. Today, however, only about 8 percent of workers make a living as farmers. Even so, Taiwan still produces enough rice—the country's chief food crop—to feed all of its people. Taiwan's farmers also grow fruits, sugarcane, tea, and vegetables.

Taiwan now has one of Asia's most successful economies. It is a world leader in the production and export of computers and sports equipment.

▲
Taipei, Taiwan, was founded in the 1700s and has developed into an important city for overseas trade.

✓ **READING CHECK:** (**Human Systems**) What are some elements of the culture of Taiwan? 85 percent native Taiwanese; Chinese influence dominant; Japanese influence in some building styles and foods; some European and American customs

Define or identify: *gers,* Chiang Kai-shek

Working with Sketch Maps On the map you created in Section 3, label Mongolia, Ulaanbaatar, Taiwan, Kao-hsiung, and Taipei. In the border of your map, draw a box for each city. Describe each city in its box. How has the history of each city played a part in its growth?

Reading for the Main Idea

1. (**Human Systems**) How do most people earn a living in Mongolia?
2. (**Human Systems**) Write a brief outline of the significant individuals or groups that have influenced Taiwan's history.

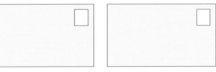

Homework Practice Online
Keyword: SK5 HP16

3. (**Human Systems**) How has Taiwan's economy changed since the early 1950s?

Critical Thinking

4. **Analyzing Information** What are some problems Taiwan faces today?

Organizing What You Know

5. **Summarizing** Copy the following graphic organizer. Use it to design and write two postcards to a friend describing life in Mongolia. In your postcards, note how life follows traditional patterns yet is also undergoing changes.

China, Mongolia, and Taiwan • 371

Section 4 Review

Answers to Section 4 Review

Define or identify For definition and identification, see the glossary and index.

Working with Sketch Maps Ulaanbaatar—capital of Mongolia, 25 percent of population, commerce and industry; Taipei—capital of Taiwan, overcrowded and polluted, on coastal plain

Reading for the Main Idea

1. by herding animals (NGS 12)
2. Chinese settle in 600s; Japanese control in 1100s; Chinese raiders drive out Europeans in 1600s; treaty gives Japanese control in 1895; China gets control after WWII; Chiang Kai-shek and nationalists flee to Taiwan (NGS 13)
3. changed from agriculture to industry (NGS 12)

Critical Thinking

4. overcrowding and pollution

Organizing What You Know

5. Postcards will vary but information should be consistent with text material.

CLOSE

Tell students to imagine that Mongolia and Taiwan are redesigning their flags. Ask students what symbols Mongolia and Taiwan might use on a newly designed flag. Have students explain their responses.

REVIEW, ASSESS, RETEACH

Have students complete the Section Review. Then pair students and have each pair create a graphic organizer to present important facts about the culture and history of Mongolia and Taiwan. Have students present their organizers to the class. Then have students complete Daily Quiz 16.4. **COOPERATIVE LEARNING, LS VISUAL-SPATIAL**

Have students complete Main Idea S4. Then ask each student to write down one fact about Mongolia and one fact about Taiwan. Collect the facts and review them with the class. **ESOL**

EXTEND

Have interested students conduct research on the conquests of Genghis Khan. Have students use their findings to create a short oral report about the Mongolian Empire under Genghis Khan and a map showing the extent of the empire. **BLOCK SCHEDULING**

Define and Identify
For definitions and identifications, see the glossary and index.

Review the Main Ideas
18. isolated plateaus and basins (NGS 4)

19. carries loess, a yellowish-brown soil (NGS 4)

20. ordered construction of the Great Wall (NGS 14)

21. an attempt to make everyone live a peasant way of life

22. former British colony, has some political independence, is allowed to maintain its free-market economy

23. farm

24. Mongolia (NGS 13)

25. computers and sports equipment (NGS 11)

Think Critically
26. They had to travel overland, which entailed a long, difficult journey.

27. Cultural isolation might have continued.

28. It imposed the peasant's lifestyle on people and resulted in the closing of schools, people being sent to the countryside to work, and the imprisonment of opponents.

29. Electronic media make information from other countries available to the Chinese people. This free flow of information could threaten communist control.

30. Most people are descendants of Chinese immigrants, so Chinese is dominant. Other cultural features reflect Japanese, American, and European influences.

CHAPTER 16 Review and Practice

Define and Identify
Identify each of the following:

1. dikes
2. arable
3. emperor
4. Confucius
5. dynasty
6. porcelain
7. Genghis Khan
8. Sun Yat-sen
9. martial law
10. Mao Zedong
11. Dalai Lama
12. pagodas
13. command economy
14. multiple cropping
15. most-favored-nation status
16. *gers*
17. Chiang Kai-shek

Review the Main Ideas

18. What physical features separate this region's mountain ranges?

19. Why is the Huang called the Yellow River?

20. What idea did the first emperor of the Qin dynasty have that greatly affected the landscape of China?

21. What was the purpose of the Cultural Revolution in China?

22. How does Hong Kong differ from the rest of China?

23. What do more than 50 percent of China's workers do for a living?

24. What country discussed in this chapter once ruled a vast empire that stretched into Europe?

25. What are Taiwan's leading exports?

Think Critically

26. Drawing Inferences and Conclusions Why do you think so few Europeans reached China before the 1500s?

27. Drawing Inferences and Conclusions How might Chinese history have been different if Europeans had not forced trade upon the Chinese?

28. Finding the Main Idea What was the Cultural Revolution and how did it affect life in China?

29. Making Generalizations and Predictions In what ways does modern technology threaten the Chinese government's ability to control the flow of information in the country? What changes might the free flow of information bring to China?

30. Analyzing Information How is Taiwan's history reflected in the island's culture today?

Map Activity

31. On a separate sheet of paper, match the letters on the map with their correct labels.

Mount Everest
Plateau of Tibet
North China Plain
Huang River

Chang River
Great Wall
Shanghai
Hong Kong
Ulaanbaatar

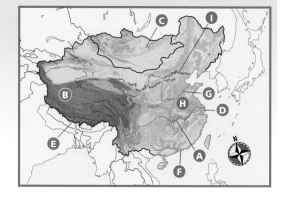

Map Activity
31. A. Chang River

B. Plateau of Tibet

C. Ulaanbaatar

D. Shanghai

E. Mount Everest

F. Hong Kong

G. Huang He

H. North China Plain

I. Great Wall

Writing Activity

Imagine that you are a Chinese university professor. Using the time line in section 2, the text, and other sources, write a brief lesson plan on China's history. You may want to include some visuals, such as photographs of artifacts, in your lesson plan. Be sure to use standard grammar, spelling, sentence structure, and punctuation.

internet connect

Internet Activity: go.hrw.com
KEYWORD: SK5 GT16

Choose a topic to explore about China, Mongolia, and Taiwan:
- Follow the Great Wall of China.
- Visit the land of Genghis Khan.
- See the artistic treasures of China.

Social Studies Skills Practice

Interpreting Graphs

Study the following graph and answer the questions.

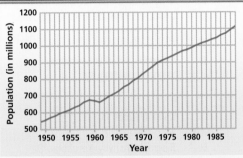

Total Population of China, 1949–1989

Population (in millions) vs. Year (1950–1985)

Source: *The Cambridge Handbook of Contemporary China*, 1991

1. What was the total population of China in 1950?
2. During what period did the population decline?
3. In what year did the population reach one billion?
4. How much did the population grow between 1965 and 1985?

Analyzing Primary Sources

Read the following passage from a 1993 U.S. State Department publication on Mongolia. Then answer the questions.

"As a result of rapid urbanization and industrial growth policies under the communist regime, Mongolia's deteriorating environment has become a major concern. The burning of soft coal coupled with thousands of factories in Ulaanbaatar has resulted in severely polluted air. Deforestation, overgrazed pastures, and . . . by plowing up more virgin land has increased soil erosion. The government responded by . . . increasing publicity on environmental issues."

1. What are the two main causes of environmental problems in Mongolia?
2. What is the result of burning coal in Mongolia?
3. How has agricultural development affected the environment?
4. How might publicity help solve the problem of environmental damage?

China, Mongolia, and Taiwan • 373

Writing Activity

Lesson plans will vary but should be consistent with text material. Use Rubric 40, Writing to Describe, to evaluate student work.

Interpreting Graphs

1. about 550 million
2. 1959–61
3. 1981
4. from about 730 million to more than 1050 million, or just over 1 billion

Analyzing Primary Sources

1. burning of soft coal, thousands of factories
2. severely polluted air
3. Overgrazing pastures and plowing virgin soil has increased soil erosion.
4. Publicity may educate the public about issues related to environmental damage.

CHAPTER 16 · REVIEW AND ASSESSMENT RESOURCES

Reproducible
- Readings in World Geography, History, and Culture 67, 68, and 69
- Critical Thinking Activity 16
- Vocabulary Activity 16

Technology
- Chapter 16 Test Generator (on the One-Stop Planner)
- Audio CD Program, Chapter 16
- HRW Go site

Reinforcement, Review, and Assessment
- Chapter 16 Review and Practice
- Chapter Summaries and Review
- Chapter 16 Test
- Chapter 16 Test for English Language Learners and Special-Needs Students

internet connect

GO TO: go.hrw.com
KEYWORD: SK5 Teacher
FOR: a guide to using the Internet in your classroom

CHAPTER 17

Japan and the Koreas
Chapter Resource Manager

Objectives	Pacing Guide	Reproducible Resources
SECTION 1 **Physical Geography** (pp. 375–78) 1. Identify the physical features of Japan and Korea. 2. Identify the natural resources of the region. 3. Identify the climate types of the region.	**Regular** 1 day Lecture Notes, Section 1 **Block Scheduling** .5 day *Block Scheduling Handbook, Chapter 17*	**RS** Know It Notes S1 **E** Lab Activities for Geography and Earth Science, Demonstrations 5, 6, 7 **ELL** Main Idea Activity S1
SECTION 2 **The History and Culture of Japan** (pp. 379–81) 1. Describe Japan's early history and culture. 2. Describe the modernization of Japan.	**Regular** 1 day Lecture Notes, Section 2 **Block Scheduling** .5 day *Block Scheduling Handbook, Chapter 17*	**RS** Know It Notes S2 **RS** Graphic Organizer 17 **E** Creative Strategies for Teaching World Geography, Lesson 18, 19 **E** Cultures of the World Activity 7 **E** Biography Activity: Kenzaburo Oe **ELL** Main Idea Activity S2
SECTION 3 **Japan Today** (pp. 382–86) 1. Describe where most Japanese live. 2. Describe what most Japanese cities are like. 3. Describe life in Japan. 4. Describe how the Japanese economy has developed.	**Regular** 1 day Lecture Notes, Section 3 **Block Scheduling** .5 day *Block Scheduling Handbook, Chapter 17*	**RS** Know It Notes S3 **SM** Map Activity 17 **E** Biography Activity: Kenzaburo Oe **ELL** Main Idea Activity S3
SECTION 4 **The History and Culture of the Koreas** (pp. 387–89) 1. Explain what Korea's ancient history was like. 2. Identify the major events of Korea's early modern period. 3. Describe the division of Korea and its effects.	**Regular** .5 day Lecture Notes, Section 4 **Block Scheduling** .5 day *Block Scheduling Handbook, Chapter 17*	**RS** Know It Notes S4 **IC** Interdisciplinary Activities for the Middle Grades 29, 30, 31 **ELL** Main Idea Activity S4
SECTION 5 **South and North Korea Today** (pp. 390–93) 1. Describe South Korea's government and society. 2. Describe South Korea's economy. 3. Describe North Korea. 4. Describe how North Korea's government has affected the country's development.	**Regular** 1 day Lecture Notes, Section 5 **Block Scheduling** .5 day *Block Scheduling Handbook, Chapter 17*	**RS** Know It Notes S5 **SM** Geography for Life Activity 28 **ELL** Main Idea Activity S5

Chapter Resource Key

RS	Reading Support	**ELL**	Reinforcement and English Language Learners and English for Speakers of Other Languages (ESOL)		Music
IC	Interdisciplinary Connections				Video
E	Enrichment				Internet
SM	Skills Mastery		Transparencies		Holt Presentation Maker Using Microsoft® PowerPoint®
A	Assessment		CD–ROM		
REV	Review				

 One-Stop Planner CD–ROM

See the *One-Stop Planner* for a complete list of additional resources for students and teachers.

One-Stop Planner CD–ROM

It's easy to plan lessons, select resources, and print out materials for your students when you use the *One-Stop Planner CD–ROM with Test Generator.*

♪ internet connect

HRW ONLINE RESOURCES

GO TO: go.hrw.com
Then type in a keyword.

TEACHER HOME PAGE
KEYWORD: SK5 TEACHER

CHAPTER INTERNET ACTIVITIES
KEYWORD: SK5 GT17

Choose an activity to:
• investigate volcanoes.
• visit Japan and the Koreas.
• compare your school to a Japanese school.

CHAPTER ENRICHMENT LINKS
KEYWORD: SK5 CH17

CHAPTER MAPS
KEYWORD: SK5 MAPS17

ONLINE ASSESSMENT
Homework Practice
KEYWORD: SK5 HP17
Standardized Test Prep Online
KEYWORD: SK5 STP17
Rubrics
KEYWORD: SS Rubrics

COUNTRY INFORMATION
KEYWORD: SK5 Almanac

CONTENT UPDATES
KEYWORD: SS Content Updates

HOLT PRESENTATION MAKER
KEYWORD: SK5 PPT17

ONLINE READING SUPPORT
KEYWORD: SS Strategies

CURRENT EVENTS
KEYWORD: S5 Current Events

Technology Resources

 One-Stop Planner CD–ROM, Lesson 17.1
 ARGWorld CD–ROM
Geography and Cultures Visual Resources with Teaching Activities 49–52
Homework Practice Online
HRW Go site

 One-Stop Planner CD–ROM, Lesson 17.2
ARGWorld CD–ROM
Music of the World Audio CD Program: Selection 20
Homework Practice Online
HRW Go site

 One-Stop Planner CD–ROM, Lesson 17.3
ARGWorld CD–ROM
Homework Practice Online
HRW Go site

 One-Stop Planner CD–ROM, Lesson 17.4
ARGWorld CD–ROM
Homework Practice Online
HRW Go site

 One-Stop Planner CD–ROM, Lesson 17.5
ARGWorld CD–ROM
Homework Practice Online
HRW Go site

Review, Reinforcement, and Assessment Resources

ELL	Main Idea Activity S1
REV	Section 1 Review
A	Daily Quiz 17.1
REV	Chapter Summaries and Review
ELL	English Audio Summary 17.1
ELL	Spanish Audio Summary 17.1

ELL	Main Idea Activity S2
REV	Section 2 Review
A	Daily Quiz 17.2
REV	Chapter Summaries and Review
ELL	English Audio Summary 17.2
ELL	Spanish Audio Summary 17.2

ELL	Main Idea Activity S3
REV	Section 3 Review
A	Daily Quiz 17.3
REV	Chapter Summaries and Review
ELL	English Audio Summary 17.3
ELL	Spanish Audio Summary 17.3

ELL	Main Idea Activity S4
REV	Section 4 Review
A	Daily Quiz 17.4
REV	Chapter Summaries and Review
ELL	English Audio Summary 17.4
ELL	Spanish Audio Summary 17.4

ELL	Main Idea Activity S5
REV	Section 5 Review
A	Daily Quiz 17.5
REV	Chapter Summaries and Review
ELL	English Audio Summary 17.5
ELL	Spanish Audio Summary 17.5

Chapter Review and Assessment

E	Readings in World Geography, History, and Culture 70 and 71	A	Chapter 17 Test
SM	Critical Thinking Activity 17		Chapter 17 Test Generator (on the One-Stop Planner)
REV	Chapter 17 Review and Practice		Audio CD Program, Chapter 17
REV	Chapter Summaries and Review	A	Chapter 17 Test for English Language Learners and Special-Needs Students
ELL	Vocabulary Activity 17		HRW Go Site

Meeting Individual Needs

Ability Levels

Level 1 Basic-level activities designed for all students encountering new material

Level 2 Intermediate-level activities designed for average students

Level 3 Challenging activities designed for honors and gifted-and-talented students

ESOL Activities that address the needs of students with Limited English Proficiency

CHAPTER 17
Japan and the Koreas
Previewing Chapter Resources

Holt Online Learning

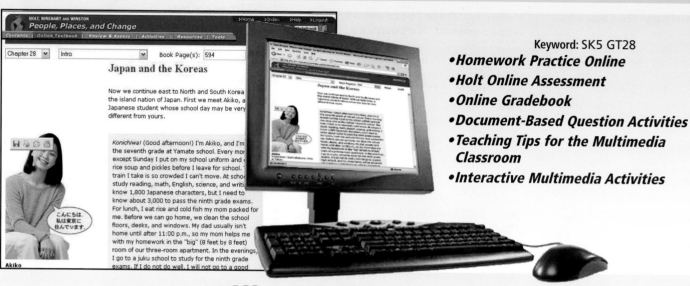

Keyword: SK5 GT28

- *Homework Practice Online*
- *Holt Online Assessment*
- *Online Gradebook*
- *Document-Based Question Activities*
- *Teaching Tips for the Multimedia Classroom*
- *Interactive Multimedia Activities*

Differentiating Instruction

Reading and Writing Support
◄ Graphic Organizer Activity
- *Vocabulary Activity*
- *Chapter Summary and Review*
- *Know It Notes*
- *Audio CD*

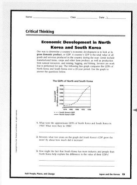

Active Learning
- *Block Scheduling Handbook*
- *Cultures of the World Activity*
- *Interdisciplinary Activity*
- *Map Activity*
◄ Critical Thinking Activity 28
- *Music of the World CD: The One-Stringed Ichigenkin*

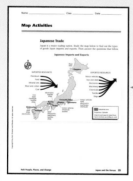

Primary Sources and Advanced Learners
- *Geography for Life Activity: Can Korea Be United Successfully?*
◄ Map Activity: Japanese Trade
- *Readings in World Geography, History and Culture:*
  - *70 the Talisman*
  - *71 North Korea on the Edge*

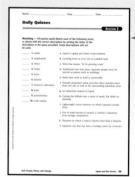

Assessment Program
◄ Daily Quizzes S1–5
- *Chapter Test*
- *Chapter Test for English Language Learners and Special-Needs Students*

Spanish and ESOL
- *Vocabulary Activity*
◄ Main Idea Activities for English Language Learners and Special-Needs Students
- *Chapter Summary and Review*
- *Spanish Audio Summary*
- *Know It Notes S1–5*
- *Chapter Test for English Language Learners and Special-Needs Students*

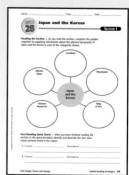

Special Education Modifications
Your I.D.E.A. Works! CD-ROM will provide modified versions of the following teaching materials:
◄ Guided Reading Strategies S1–5
- *Vocabulary Activity*
- *Main Idea Activities S1–5*
- *Daily Quizzes S1–5*
- *Chapter 17 Test*
- *Flash cards of chapter vocabulary terms*

Teacher Resources

Books for Teachers

Ashburne, John Frederick. *The Best of Kansai: Kyoto, Osaka, Kobe.* Charles E. Tuttle, 1998.

Lie, John. *Han Unbound: The Political Economy of South Korea.* Stanford University Press, 1998.

Morton, W. Scott. *Japan: Its History and Culture.* McGraw-Hill, 1994.

Books for Students

Buck, Pearl S. *The Big Wave.* Harpercrest, 1973. After his village and family are swept away by a tsunami, Jiya learns to live with danger. **SHELTERED ENGLISH**

Galvin, Irene Flum. *Japan: A Modern Land with Ancient Roots.* Exploring Cultures of the World. Marshall Cavendish, 1996.

Park, Frances, and Ginger Park. *My Freedom Trip.* Boyds Mills Press, 1998. True story of a North Korean girl's escape to South Korea. **SHELTERED ENGLISH**

Ross, Stewart. *Causes and Consequences of the Rise of Japan and the Pacific Rim.* Causes and Consequences. Raintree/Steck-Vaughn, 1995. Explains the sudden growth of regional economies in the region.

Multimedia Materials

Japan 2000. CD–ROM. Films for the Humanities and Sciences.

Japanese Art and Architecture. Video kit, 75 min. Alarion Press.

USA Wars: Korea. CD–ROM. Quanta Press.

Videos and CDs

Videos

- **CNN** *Presents Geography: Yesterday and Today, Segment 29 The Tokyo Grave Crisis*
- **CNN** *Presents World Cultures: Yesterday and Today, Segment 28 Japan's Royal Family*
- *ARG World*

Holt Researcher

http://researcher.hrw.com

- *Hideyoshi, Toyotomi*
- *Ieyasu, Tokugawa*
- *Nobunaga, Odo*
- *Japan*
- *Japan Invades Manchuria*
- *South Korea*
- *North Korea*

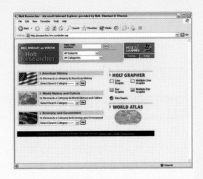

Transparency Packages

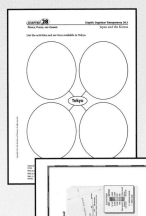

Graphic Organizer Transparencies 17.1–4

Geography and Cultures Visual Resources Transparencies 97–101

105 Japan and the Koreas: Physical-Political

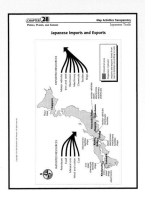

Map Activities Transparency 17 Japanese Trade

WHY IT MATTERS

You may wish to point out that there are many reasons why we should know more about Japan and the Koreas.

▶ The region's economies are directly linked with ours.

▶ North Korea has developed nuclear power.

▶ During World War II the United States and Japan were enemies. Since then Japan has been an ally. Occasionally trade or environmental issues threaten the relationship.

▶ Japanese and Korean culture offer a wealth of literature, art, philosophy, music, crafts, foods, and other traditions.

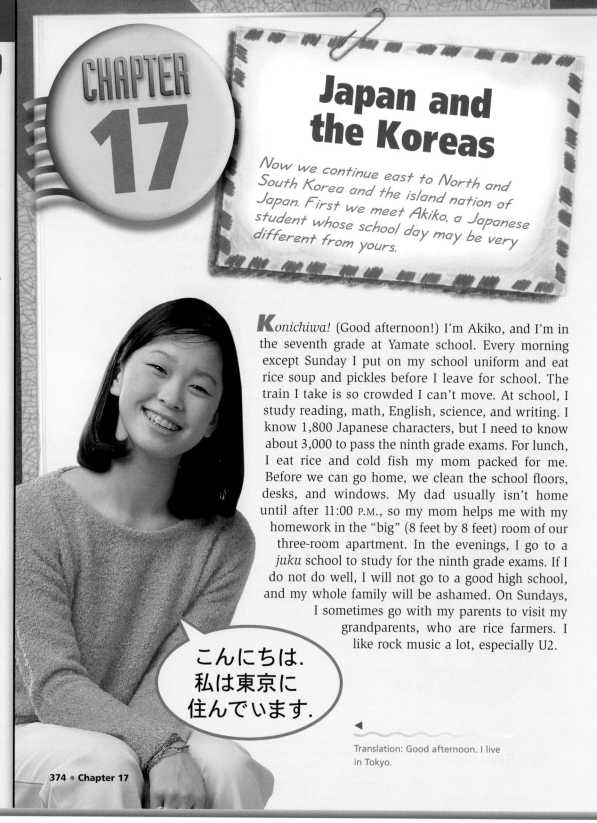

CHAPTER 17

Japan and the Koreas

Now we continue east to North and South Korea and the island nation of Japan. First we meet Akiko, a Japanese student whose school day may be very different from yours.

Konichiwa! (Good afternoon!) I'm Akiko, and I'm in the seventh grade at Yamate school. Every morning except Sunday I put on my school uniform and eat rice soup and pickles before I leave for school. The train I take is so crowded I can't move. At school, I study reading, math, English, science, and writing. I know 1,800 Japanese characters, but I need to know about 3,000 to pass the ninth grade exams. For lunch, I eat rice and cold fish my mom packed for me. Before we can go home, we clean the school floors, desks, and windows. My dad usually isn't home until after 11:00 P.M., so my mom helps me with my homework in the "big" (8 feet by 8 feet) room of our three-room apartment. In the evenings, I go to a *juku* school to study for the ninth grade exams. If I do not do well, I will not go to a good high school, and my whole family will be ashamed. On Sundays, I sometimes go with my parents to visit my grandparents, who are rice farmers. I like rock music a lot, especially U2.

こんにちは。
私は東京に
住んでいます。

Translation: Good afternoon. I live in Tokyo.

374 • Chapter 17

CHAPTER PROJECT

Have students make models or dioramas of a typical Japanese or Korean home, including features of everyday life, such as furniture. Take photographs of the dioramas for inclusion in student portfolios.

STARTING THE CHAPTER

Create two columns on the chalkboard. Label them *What you already know about Japan and the Koreas* and *What you want to know about Japan and the Koreas*. Call on volunteers to offer items for both categories. Tell students that while studying this chapter they will be able to check their knowledge and add to it by filling the gaps they have mentioned. Add that Japan, North Korea, and South Korea affect the economy and security of countries around the world, including the United States. Tell students they will learn more about the connections among Japan, the Koreas, and the United States in this chapter.

Section 1 Physical Geography

Read to Discover

1. What are the physical features of Japan and the Koreas?
2. What natural resources does the region have?
3. Which climate types are found in the region?

Vocabulary

tsunamis
Oyashio Current
Japan Current

Places

Korean Peninsula
Sea of Japan
Hokkaido

Honshu
Shikoku
Kyushu

Reading Strategy

FOLDNOTES: DOUBLE-DOOR Create a **Double-Door** FoldNote as described in the Appendix. Label the outer flaps Japan and the Koreas. As you read this section, write what you learn about the physical features, resources, and climate of Japan in the center section, North Korea in the top section, and South Korea in the bottom section.

Japan and the Koreas: Physical-Political

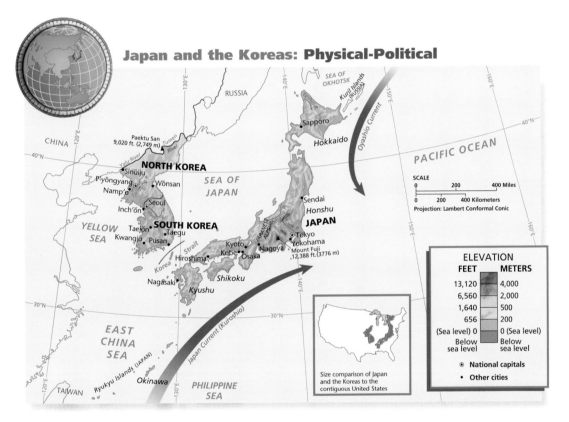

SECTION 1 RESOURCES

Reproducible
◆ Lecture Notes, Section 1
◆ Block Scheduling Handbook, Chapter 17
◆ Know It Notes S1
◆ Lab Activities for Geography and Earth Science, Demonstrations 5, 6, 7

Technology
◆ One-Stop Planner CD–ROM, Lesson 17.1
◆ Homework Practice Online
◆ Geography and Cultures Visual Resources with Teaching Activities 49-52
◆ HRW Go site

Reinforcement, Review, and Assessment
◆ Section 1 Review
◆ Daily Quiz 17.1
◆ Main Idea Activity S1
◆ Chapter Summaries and Review
◆ English Audio Summary 17.1
◆ Spanish Audio Summary 17.1

Section 1

Objectives

1. Describe the physical features of Japan and the Koreas.
2. Identify the region's natural resources.
3. Describe the climate types found in the region.

FOCUS

Bellringer

Copy the following instructions onto the chalkboard: *Look at the photo of the bullet train and Mount Fuji on the next page. What do you think Mount Fuji's shape can tell us about how it was formed? Write down your ideas.* Discuss responses. Then tell the students that Fuji's conical shape indicates that it is a volcano and that volcanoes and earthquakes have affected life in Japan. Tectonic events are rare in the Koreas, however. Tell students that in Section 1 they will learn more about the region's physical geography.

Using the Physical-Political Map

Have students examine the map on this page. Ask volunteers to name the principal landforms that Japan, North Korea, and South Korea occupy and the bodies of water that surround them. Then, comparing the latitude of these countries to the East Coast of the United States, have students predict their climates. Point out the Oyashio and Japan Currents. Ask students to speculate on how these currents affect Japan's climate.

ENVIRONMENT AND SOCIETY

Parks in Peril Climbing Mount Fuji is a popular activity in Japan. The ascent has long been a pilgrimage for Japanese Buddhists, who regard the peak as sacred. Now recreational climbers can drive halfway up the mountain and walk the rest of the way. The rising numbers of automobile tourists and climbers, however, are creating significant problems with erosion, garbage, pollution, and traffic.

Activity: Have students research U.S. national parks that are threatened by their own popularity. (Examples: Yellowstone, Grand Canyon, Yosemite) Ask them to compare those problems with Mount Fuji's. How are the issues similar or different?

The world's largest crab lives off the southeastern coast of Japan. The giant spider crab can grow larger than 12 feet (3.6 m) across (from claw to claw). It can also weigh more than 40 pounds (18 kg)!

A *shinkansen*, or bullet train, speeds past Mount Fuji. This Hiroshima-to-Kokura train travels at an average 162.3 mph (261.8 kmh) but has a maximum speed of 186 mph (300 kmh).

Interpreting the Visual Record (Place) **What physical features might make building railroads in this region of Japan difficult?**

Visual Record Answer ►

mountains

Physical Features

The Korean Peninsula extends southward about 600 miles (965 km) from mainland Asia. The peninsula is relatively close to southern Japan.

The Korean Peninsula is about the same size as Utah. It contains two countries, North Korea and South Korea. The Yalu and Tumen Rivers separate North Korea from China. The Tumen River also forms a short border with Russia. Off the coast of the Korean Peninsula lie more than 3,500 islands.

The Sea of Japan separates Japan from the Eurasian mainland. The narrow Korea Strait lies between South Korea and the island country of Japan. No place in Japan is more than 90 miles (145 km) from the sea. Japan is about the size of California. It is made up of four large islands called the home islands. The country also includes more than 3,000 smaller islands. The home islands from north to south are Hokkaido (hoh-KY-doh), Honshu (HAWN-shoo), Shikoku (shee-KOH-koo), and Kyushu (KYOO-shoo). South of the home islands are Japan's Ryukyu (ree-YOO-kyoo) Islands. Okinawa is the largest of these islands. Fewer than half of the Ryukyus are inhabited.

Mountains Rugged and heavily forested mountains are a common sight in the landscape of this region. Mountains cover about 75 percent of Japan. Many of Japan's mountains were formed by volcanic activity. The country's longest mountain range, the Japanese Alps, forms a volcanic spine through Honshu. The small amount of plains in these countries is found along the coasts and river valleys.

The Ring of Fire Japan lies along the Pacific Ring of Fire—a region of volcanic activity and earthquakes. Under Japan the dense

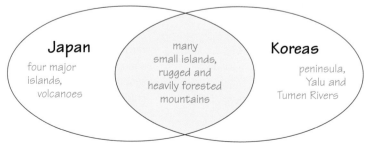

TEACH

Teaching Objective 1

ALL LEVELS: (Suggested time: 15 min.) Copy the following graphic organizer onto the chalkboard, omitting the blue answers. Use it to help students create lists of the physical features of Japan and the Koreas. Call on students to come to the chalkboard and fill in words and phrases to describe the features. In the center, have them list features the countries have in common. **ESOL,** **LS** **INTERPERSONAL**

Physical Features of Japan and the Koreas

Japan
four major islands, volcanoes

many small islands, rugged and heavily forested mountains

Koreas
peninsula, Yalu and Tumen Rivers

Pacific plate dives beneath the lighter Eurasian and Philippine plates. This subduction zone borders the Pacific side of the Japanese islands, forming the Japan Trench. This is one of the deepest places on the ocean floor. The movement of one tectonic plate below another builds up tension in Earth's crust. The Eurasian plate buckles and pushes up, creating mountains and fractures in the crust. Magma flows up through these fractures. Where magma rises to the surface, it forms volcanoes. Today, Japan has about 40 active volcanoes. Mount Fuji (FOO-jee), Japan's highest peak, is an inactive volcano.

Because Japan lies along a subduction zone, earthquakes are also common. As many as 1,500 occur every year. Most are minor quakes. In 1995, however, an earthquake killed more than 5,000 people in Kobe.

Underwater earthquakes sometimes create huge waves called **tsunamis** (tsooh-NAH-mees). These dangerous waves can travel hundreds of miles per hour. They can also be as tall as a 10-story building when they reach shore. In 1993 a tsunami caused terrible destruction when it struck the coast of Hokkaido.

Unlike Japan, the Korean Peninsula is not located in a subduction zone. As a result, it has no active volcanoes and is dominated by eroded mountains. Earthquakes are quite rare.

✓ READING CHECK: (*Places and Regions*) What are the physical features of Japan and the Koreas? Korean Peninsula, Yula and Yumen Rivers, mountains, volcanoes, Japan Trench

Natural Resources

Except for North Korea, the region is not rich in natural resources. It has no oil or natural gas. The Korean Peninsula's mountainous terrain and rivers, however, are good for producing hydroelectric power. North Korea also has iron ore, copper, zinc, lead, and coal.

Japan lies near one of the world's best fisheries. East of Japan the cool **Oyashio** (oh-YAH-shee-oh) **Current** dives beneath the warm, less dense **Japan Current**. The cool water scours the bottom, bringing nutrients to the surface. Fish can find plentiful food to eat in this rich marine environment.

✓ READING CHECK: (*Places and Regions*) What are the region's natural resources? rivers for hydroelectric power; iron ore, copper, zinc, lead, coal in North Korea; fishing

▲ Every hour an artificial volcano erupts at Ocean Dome, the world's largest indoor beach, at Miyazaki, Japan.

Across the Curriculum
SCIENCE
The Great Kanto Earthquake Just as they were preparing for lunch on September 1, 1923, Yokohama residents were rocked by an earthquake that may have lasted 10 full minutes. More than 800 aftershocks would follow. The devastation was unimaginable—not just from the tremors but also from the fires and the thousands of landslides unleashed by the quake. In one enclosed location alone, about 40,000 people perished by fire. Not surprisingly, the quake also created a tsunami, but it caused relatively little damage. Some 143,000 people were killed. About 694,000 houses were damaged or destroyed.

Activity: Have students conduct research on how scientists analyzed the Kanto earthquake in an effort to save lives the next time the earth shook. Have them create models that show some of the innovations in building codes.

☑ internet connect
GO TO: go.hrw.com
KEYWORD: SK5 CH17
FOR: Web sites about earthquakes

Teaching Objective 2
LEVEL 1: (Suggested time: 20 min.) Have students create an illustration for the cover of a book about Japan's natural resources. Instruct them to show what they know about those resources in the illustration. Display the book covers. **ESOL,** ⓛ **VISUAL-SPATIAL**

LEVELS 2 AND 3: (Suggested time: 30 min.) Have students write a title and subtitle for their book from the Level 1 activity. Then have them write a summary paragraph that might appear in an advertisement for the book. ⓛ **VERBAL-LINGUISTIC**

Teaching Objective 3
ALL LEVELS: (Suggested time: 30 min.) Assign each of five groups one of these locations: northern Hokkaido, mouth of the Yalu River, Okinawa, Seoul, or Tokyo. Have each group write weather reports for typical summer and winter days for their locales. **COOPERATIVE LEARNING**

CLOSE
Call on a volunteer to pick random spots on a wall map of Japan and the Koreas. Ask the class to suggest ways that physical features, volcanic activity, vegetation, or climate in those places would affect their daily lives if they lived there.

Answers to Section 1 Review

Define For definitions, see the glossary.

Working with Sketch Maps Korean rivers produce hydroelectric power. Japan relies on the sea for fish.

Reading for the Main Idea

1. Japan has volcanoes and frequent earthquakes. **(NGS 7)**

2. Oyashio Current—keeps northern coastal areas cool in summer; Japan Current—warms southern Japan **(NGS 7)**

Critical Thinking

3. People who live on the coastal plains use resources from the sea.

4. rely on imports, trade

Organizing What You Know

5. Japan—mountains, volcanoes, coastal plains; few resources; humid continental, humid subtropical; South Korea—mountains, coastal plains; few resources; humid subtropical; North Korea—mountains, coastal plains; iron ore, copper, zinc, lead, coal; humid continental

Visual Record Answer ▶

Walls trap water in fields.

Climate

The Koreas and Japan each have two climate regions. Hokkaido, northern Honshu, and the northern part of the Korean Peninsula have a humid continental climate. The Oyashio Current keeps areas near the coast of northern Japan cool in summer. Winters are long and cold, and the growing season is short. The rest of the Korean Peninsula and Japan have a humid subtropical climate. Winters are mild. Summers are hot and humid. The Japan Current, which flows northward from the tropical North Pacific, warms southern Japan. This part of the region experiences heavy rains and typhoons during the summer. Some areas receive up to 80 inches (203 cm) of rain each year.

✓ **READING CHECK:**
Places and Regions What is the region's climate?

humid continental, humid subtropical

◀
Terracing creates more arable land for South Korean farmers.

Interpreting the Visual Record
Human-Environment Interaction
How do the terraces here hold water?

go.hrw.com **Homework Practice Online**
Keyword: SK5 HP17

Section Review 1

Define and explain: tsunamis, Oyashio Current, Japan Current

Working with Sketch Maps On a map of Japan and the Koreas that you draw or that your teacher provides, label the following: the Korean Peninsula, Sea of Japan, Hokkaido, Honshu, Shikoku, and Kyushu. On what physical features might Japan and the Koreas depend for their economies?

Reading for the Main Idea

1. **Physical Systems** How has Japan's location in a subduction zone made it different from the Koreas?

2. **Physical Systems** How do ocean currents affect the climates of Japan?

Critical Thinking

3. **Drawing Inferences and Conclusions** How do you think residents are affected by this region's mountainous terrain and the nearness of the sea?

4. **Making Generalizations and Predictions** What can you predict about South Korea's and Japan's economies?

Organizing What You Know

5. **Summarizing** List the landforms, natural resources, and climates of Japan, North Korea, and South Korea.

	Landforms	Resources	Climate
Japan			
South Korea			
North Korea			

REVIEW, ASSESS, RETEACH

Have students complete the Section Review. Then pair students. Have each student create four multiple-choice questions based on the information in Section 1. Have pairs exchange and complete each other's quizzes. Then have students complete Daily Quiz 17.1. **COOPERATIVE LEARNING**

Have students complete Main Idea Activity S1. Then organize them into three groups. Have each group create a wall map of the region. Ask one group to create symbols for physical features, the second symbols for natural resources, and the third symbols for climate types. Have the groups draw or glue the symbols onto their maps in the correct areas. **ESOL**

EXTEND

Have interested students conduct research on the connections between the physical geography of the region and how its landscape, plants, and animals are portrayed in traditional arts, such as pottery, paintings on silk, lacquerware, and embroidery on silk. Ask students to match natural design elements with the species or places they portray. **BLOCK SCHEDULING**

Section 2 The History and Culture of Japan

Read to Discover
1. What was Japan's early history and culture like?
2. How did the modernization of Japan take place?

Vocabulary
Shintoism
shamans
samurai
shogun
Diet

People
Murasaki Shikibu

Reading Strategy
FOLDNOTES: KEY-TERM FOLD Create a **Key-Term Fold** FoldNote as described in the Appendix. Then write a vocabulary term from the section on each tab. Under each tab, write the definition of the term.

Early Japan

Japan's first inhabitants came from central Asia thousands of years ago. Rice farming was introduced to Japan from China and Korea about 300 B.C. As the population increased, farmers irrigated new land for growing rice. They also built dikes and canals to channel water into the rice paddies. Local chieftains organized the workers and controlled the flow of water. This control allowed the chieftains to extend their political power over larger areas.

Religion The earliest known religion of Japan, **Shintoism**, centers around the *kami*. *Kami* are spirits of natural places, sacred animals, and ancestors. Many of Japan's mountains and rivers are sacred in Shintoism. **Shamans**, or priests who communicated with the spirits, made the *kami*'s wishes known.

Buddhism and Confucianism were later introduced from China. Buddhist shrines were often located next to older *kami* shrines. Today, as in the past, most Japanese practice Shintoism and Buddhism. As you learned in an earlier chapter, the principles of Confucianism include respect for elders, parents, and rulers.

▲
Todaiji Temple in Nara, Japan, contains the largest wooden hall in the world and a statue of Buddha that is more than 48 feet (15 m) tall.

Interpreting the Visual Record (*Place*)
What interesting features do you see in this building's architecture?

Japan and the Koreas • 379

Section 2 Resources

Reproducible
◆ Lecture Notes, Section 2
◆ Know It Notes S2
◆ Graphic Organizer 17
◆ Creative Strategies for Teaching World Geography, Lessons 18, 19
◆ Cultures of the World Activity 7
◆ Biography Activity: Kenzaburo Oe

Technology
◆ One-Stop Planner CD–ROM, Lesson 17.2
◆ Music of the World Audio CD Program, Selection 20
◆ Homework Practice Online
◆ HRW Go site

Reinforcement, Review, and Assessment
◆ Section 2 Review
◆ Daily Quiz 17.2
◆ Main Idea Activity S2
◆ Chapter Summaries and Review
◆ English Audio Summary 17.2
◆ Spanish Audio Summary 17.2

◀ **Visual Record Answer**

large roofs, wide doors, decorations

Section 2

Objectives
1. Describe Japan's early history and culture.
2. Examine how the modernization of Japan took place.

Focus

Bellringer

Copy the following question and instruction onto the chalkboard: *How could living on an island make life both easier and more difficult?* Discuss responses. Point out that its island location has given Japan both advantages and disadvantages. Ask students to refer to their lists as they study the history and culture of Japan. Tell students that in Section 2 they will learn about early Japan and learn how modern Japan was created.

Building Vocabulary

Write the key terms on the chalkboard. Call on volunteers to find and read their definitions aloud. Point out that **Shintoism** is based on the Japanese word *Shinto*. **Samurai** and **shogun** are Japanese words. **Diet** comes from a Middle English word for "day's journey" or "day for meeting." (The Japanese word for the Diet is *Kokkai*.) Ask a volunteer to relate the meaning of *Diet* to the word's history. Ask a student to propose another context in which we might use the word **shamans**. (Possible answer: Modern religious leaders may be labeled as shamans in news reports.)

Across the Curriculum
ART

The Japanese Influence In the late 1700s Chinese art was very popular with Europeans. As a result, people were prepared to appreciate new forms of Asian arts when Japanese wood-block prints started arriving in Europe. These colorful pictures of outdoor scenes and city life were packed around the china dishes exported to Europe. Hokusai (1760–1849) and Hiroshige (1797–1858) were two of the most successful printmakers.

The clean lines, balanced design, and subject matter appealed to many European artists, particularly in the late 1800s. Many of them either tried to copy the Japanese style or included aspects of it in their work. Vincent van Gogh and James A. McNeill Whistler are two notable examples.

Connecting to Art

Answers
1. China
2. left off the roofs

Biography Answer ▶

Because she was educated and lived at court, she probably had an easier life than most Japanese women.

CONNECTING TO Art

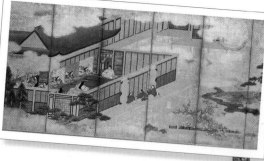

A Japanese scroll painting showing a scene from The Tale of Genji.

Japanese Scroll Paintings

Beginning in the 1100s and 1200s Japanese artists created beautifully detailed ink paintings on paper scrolls. This form of art originated in China where artists painted mostly mountain landscapes. In Japan, however, scroll paintings told stories. The themes of many scroll paintings included Buddhist teachings and historical subjects.

Many Japanese scrolls were as long as 30 feet and included text. In these paintings, artists purposely left the roofs off of buildings so they could show the interiors.

Understanding What You Read
1. Where did scroll painting originate?
2. How did Japanese artists show the interior of buildings?

BIOGRAPHY
Murasaki Shikibu
(c. 978–c. 1026)

The women who lived at a Japanese emperor's court were educated in many areas. One of the women, Murasaki Shikibu, wrote the world's first novel—*The Tale of Genji*. The book describes court life in about A.D. 1000.

How might Murasaki Shikibu's life have compared with that of most Japanese women?

The Shoguns In the A.D. 700s Japan began to develop a political system of its own. Many small feudal domains were each ruled by a lord. **Samurai** (SA-muh-ry) were warriors who served the lords. Rivalries were put aside when a foreign threat appeared. For example, the feudal domains united against the Mongols in the 1200s. Later, power shifted from the emperor to a **shogun**. The word *shogun* means "great general" and is the highest rank for a warrior.

In the mid-1500s, Portuguese traders arrived in Japan. Spanish missionaries followed, introducing Christianity to Japan. Europeans were later forced to leave. Japanese leaders feared that foreign ideas might undermine Japanese society. Japan remained cut off from the Western world until the mid-1850s.

✓ **READING CHECK:** (**Human Systems**) What was early Japan like? controlled by chieftains; Shintoism developed; Buddhism and Confucianism introduced from China; feudal domains developed; cut off from Western world until mid-1850s

380 • Chapter 17

TEACH

Teaching Objectives 1–2
ALL LEVELS: (Suggested time: 20 min.) Copy the following graphic organizer onto the chalkboard, omitting the blue answers. Use it to help students describe early and modern Japan. Ask students to copy the organizer and fill it in with the main events and features of Japan's early and modern periods. **ESOL,** **LS** **VISUAL-SPATIAL**

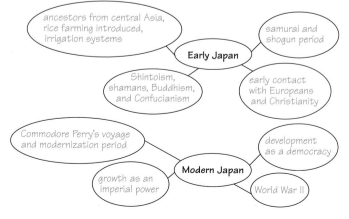

Early and Modern Japan

Modern Japan

In 1853 U.S. commodore Matthew Perry's warships sailed into Tokyo Bay. Perry displayed U.S. naval power and brought gifts that showed the wonders of American technology. Perry's arrival convinced the Japanese that they needed to become as politically strong as the Americans and Europeans. In the 1860s Japan began to industrialize and modernize its educational, legal, and governmental systems.

An Imperial Power Japan needed resources in order to industrialize. As a result, it began to expand its empire around 1900. Japan annexed, or took control of, Korea in 1910. Japan also took over northeastern China and its supply of coal and iron ore. Japan continued to expand in Asia during the late 1930s.

World War II During World War II Japan was an ally of Germany and Italy. Japan brought the United States into the war in 1941 by attacking the U.S. naval base at Pearl Harbor, Hawaii. Japan conquered much of Southeast Asia and many Pacific islands before being defeated by U.S. and Allied forces in 1945. With the end of World War II Japan lost its empire.

Government After World War II the United States occupied Japan until 1952. With U.S. aid, Japan began to rebuild into a major world industrial power. Japan also established a democratic government. Today, Japan is a constitutional monarchy with several political parties. The government is made up of the **Diet** (DY-uht)—an elected legislature—and a prime minister. Japan's emperor remains a symbol of the nation, but he has no political power.

▲

(**Movement**) Commodore Matthew Perry arrives in Japan in 1853.

✓ **READING CHECK:** (*Places and Regions*) How did Japan modernize? result of American contact, Japan industrialized and modernized its institutions; expanded its empire.

Section Review 2

Define or identify: Shintoism, shamans, Murasaki Shikibu, samurai, shogun, Diet

Working with Sketch Maps On the map you created in Section 1, label China and Korea. In a box in the margin, identify the body of water that separates Korea from Japan. Why do you think China and Korea had a strong influence on Japan's culture and history?

Reading for the Main Idea

1. (*Human Systems*) What religions have been practiced in Japan, and from where did they come?

2. (*Places and Regions*) Why did Japan decide to trade with the United States and Europe?

Critical Thinking

3. **Finding the Main Idea** How and why did rice farming develop in Japan?

4. **Analyzing Information** What influences do the principles of Confucianism have on the Japanese?

Organizing What You Know

5. **Sequencing** Copy the following graphic organizer. Use it to show important developments in modern Japanese history from the 1850s to today.

[ ] ⇨ [ ] ⇨ [ ] ⇨ [ ] ⇨ [ ]

Homework Practice Online
go.hrw.com
Keyword: SK5 HP17

Japan and the Koreas • 381

Answers to Section 2 Review

Define or identify For definitions and identifications, see the glossary and index.

Working with Sketch Maps China and the Sea of Japan should be located accurately. China and Korea were close to Japan and had well-developed cultures.

Reading for the Main Idea

1. Shintoism—early Japanese religion; Buddhism and Confucianism—introduced from China **(NGS 9)**

2. U.S. military power and industry convinced Japanese they needed to become strong **(NGS 4)**

Critical Thinking

3. introduced from China and Korea around 300 B.C.; irrigation of new land to feed increased population; dikes built to channel water

4. respect for elders, parents, and rulers

Organizing What You Know

5. Commodore Perry's visit convinced Japan to trade with the West; Japan began to industrialize and modernize; Japan expanded throughout Korea, northeastern China, and Asia; Japan fought and lost World War II; Japan rebuilt as an industrialized, democratic country.

CLOSE

Tell students that among the gifts that Commodore Perry brought with him to Japan were a scale-model train, telescope, clocks, telegraph transmitter, and three lifeboats. Ask them to consider what the Japanese may have thought of these items. Ask students what products from a previously unknown land would convince them to trade with that country and why.

REVIEW, ASSESS, RETEACH

Have students complete the Section Review. Then organize the class into pairs. Have each student create five who-am-I questions based on the section's information about individuals and groups. Have students take turns asking each other their questions. Then have students complete Daily Quiz 17.2. **COOPERATIVE LEARNING**

Have students complete Main Idea Activity S2. Then have students use information from the text and class notes to create an illustrated time line depicting the major events of Japanese history. **ESOL**

EXTEND

Have interested students imagine they are foreign correspondents assigned to Japan in the 1860s. Ask them to write newspaper articles describing the conditions and experiences of the modernization period, conducting additional research as needed. Have students share their articles with the class. **BLOCK SCHEDULING**

Section 3 Japan Today

Read to Discover
1. Where do most Japanese live?
2. What are the major Japanese cities like?
3. What is life in Japan like?
4. How has the Japanese economy developed?

Vocabulary
megalopolis
kimonos
futon
intensive cultivation
work ethic
protectionism
trade surplus

Places
Inland Sea
Osaka
Tokyo
Kobe
Kyoto

Reading Strategy

FOLDNOTES: TRI-FOLD Create a **Tri-Fold** FoldNote as described in the Appendix. Write what you know about Japan in the column labeled "Know." Then write what you want to know in the column labeled "Want." As you read the section, write what you learn about Japan in the column labeled "Learn."

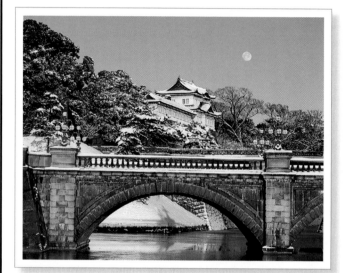

▲ Beyond Tokyo's Nijubashi Bridge is the Imperial Palace, the home of the emperor.

Where People Live

Japan is one of the world's most densely populated countries. It is slightly smaller than California but has nearly four times as many people! There are an average of 863 people per square mile (333/sq km). However, Japan is very mountainous. Within its area of livable land, population density averages 7,680 people per square mile (2,964/sq km).

Most people live on the small coastal plains, particularly along the Pacific and the Inland Sea. Japan's major cities and farms compete for space on these narrow coastal plains. Only about 11 percent of Japan's land is arable, or fit for growing crops.

The Japanese have reclaimed land from the sea and rivers. In some places, they have built dikes to block off the water. They have drained the land behind the dikes so it could be used for farming or housing. They have even built artificial islands. The airport near Osaka, for example, was built on an artificial island in the early 1990s.

✔ **READING CHECK:** (*Human Systems*) Where do most people in Japan live?
on the small coastal plains, particularly along the Pacific and Inland Sea

---

Section 3

Objectives
1. Describe where most Japanese live.
2. Analyze the characteristics of Japan's major cities.
3. Describe what life is like in Japan.
4. Explain how the Japanese economy has developed.

FOCUS

 ### Bellringer

Copy this haiku and these instructions onto the chalkboard:

If I could bundle
Fuji's breezes back to town . . .
*What a souvenir!**

How do you think the poet feels about the city? Write down your ideas. Discuss responses. Tell students haiku are Japanese poems that contain 17 syllables. They are arranged in three lines with five syllables in the first and last lines and seven in the middle. Haiku do not rhyme. Many haiku are about nature. In this example from Matsuo Basho, the poet captures his feelings in just a few words. Tell students that they will try writing their own haiku about Japanese city life. Then tell students that in Section 3 they will learn more about life in Japan today.

translated by Peter Beilenson and Harry Behn

Japan's Cities

Japan's cities, like major cities everywhere, are busy, noisy, and very crowded. Almost 30 million people live within 20 miles of the Imperial Palace in Tokyo. This densely populated area forms a **megalopolis**. A megalopolis is a giant urban area that often includes more than one city as well as the surrounding suburban areas. Yokohama is Japan's major seaport.

Most of Tokyo was built recently. An earthquake in 1923 and bombings during World War II destroyed most of the old buildings.

Tokyo is the capital and the center of government. Japan's banking, communications, and education are also centered here. Tokyo is densely populated, and land is scarce. As a result, Tokyo's real estate prices are among the world's highest.

Tokyo's Ginza shopping district is the largest in the world. Some department stores sell houses and cars and provide dental care. They also offer classes on how to properly wear **kimonos**—traditional robes—and to arrange flowers.

High rents in Ginza and elsewhere in Tokyo encourage the creative use of space. Tall buildings line the streets. However, shops are also found below the streets in the subway stations. Another way the Japanese have found to maximize space is the "capsule hotel." The guests in these hotels sleep in compartments too small to stand in upright. Businesspeople often stay in these hotels rather than commuting the long distances to their homes.

So many people commute to and from Tokyo that space on the trains must also be maximized. During peak travel periods, commuters are crammed into cars. They are helped by workers hired to push as many people into the trains as possible.

Another megalopolis in Japan is located in the Kansai region. It has three major cities: Osaka (oh-SAH-kah), Kobe (KOH-bay), and Kyoto (KYOH-toh). Industrial Osaka has been a trading center for centuries. Kobe is an important seaport. Kyoto was Japan's capital for more than 1,000 years.

busy, noisy, crowded, expensive; space is limited and thus is maximized

✓ **READING CHECK:**

Places and Regions What is life like in Japan's major cities?

	Japan			
COUNTRY	POPULATION/ GROWTH RATE	LIFE EXPECTANCY	LITERACY RATE	PER CAPITA GDP
Japan	127,214,499 0.1%	78, male 84, female	99%	$28,000
United States	290,342,554 0.9%	74, male 80, female	97%	$37,600

Source: Central Intelligence Agency, *The World Factbook 2003*

Interpreting the Chart (Place) **How does life expectancy in Japan compare to that of the United States?**

Japanese workers stay focused on their responsibilities on an electronics production line.
▼

GO TO: go.hrw.com
KEYWORD: SK5 CH17
FOR: Web sites about Tokyo

National Geography Standard 2

Tokyo Addresses In Tokyo only the major streets are named. Many city addresses are determined by dividing the city into wards and other districts. A ward is divided into sections, which in turn are further divided into subdivisions. Each block of each subdivision is numbered, as is each house on a block. The houses are numbered in the order they were built, not in consecutive order. Japan's residents identify an address by using a system that gives numbers for the block, house, and subdivision, and names for the section and ward.

Here is a fictional address: 3–1–2 Yamabuki, Chiyoda-ku. That address means "subdivision 3, block 1, house 2, in the Yamabuki section of Chiyoda ward."

Activity: Have students sketch maps to show how local addresses are created. Ask them to compare their maps to the Japanese model and describe the differences.

🖵 **internet** connect

▲ **Chart Answer**

It is higher.

Building Vocabulary

Have students find the key terms and their definitions in the text. Then create two columns on the chalkboard, one titled Daily Life and the other titled Economy. Have students assign each of the terms to one of the columns. (**Kimonos** and **futon** relate to daily life. The remaining terms relate to the economy.)

TEACH

Teaching Objective 1

ALL LEVELS: (Suggested time: 15 min.) Organize the class into five groups. Assign each group a different set of places to use as the end points of an elevation profile, such as Nagasaki to Hiroshima. (See the elevation profile at the beginning of this unit for an example.) Have the students draw the cross sections and label the locations of cities, mountains, and coastal plains. Ask them also to write a sentence to summarize where on the elevation profile the population is concentrated (on the coastal plains).
ESOL, COOPERATIVE LEARNING

Culture and Music
Living National Treasures of Japan

Although the Japanese create cutting-edge modern inventions, they also cherish ancient arts, crafts, and techniques. These range from dyeing fabric and making clay pots to operating puppets and playing the flute. The most talented artisans and performers who keep these ancient skills alive receive the title Living National Treasure, or *ningen kokuho,* from the Japanese government. About 70 people hold the title at a time. The government pays the *ningen kokuho* a generous pension for the rest of their lives.

Discussion: Several musicians are among the *ningen kokuho.* To hear traditional music of a one-stringed Japanese instrument called the *ichigenkin,* listen to Selection 20 on the Music of the World Audio CD Program. Use the text and questions in the Teacher's Guide.

Visual Record Answer ▶

It is in Japanese; otherwise it is very similiar.

Location The port of Kobe is located in the central part of the Japanese islands.

▲
Japanese and American all-star baseball teams compete in Yokohama.

Interpreting the Visual Record Place
How is this scoreboard different from one in the United States?

Life in Japan

Japan is a very homogeneous nation. In other words, almost everyone—more than 99 percent of the population—is ethnically Japanese and shares a common language and culture. Japanese society has traditionally been dominated by men, but this is changing. More Japanese women have jobs today than in the past, but most women are still expected to be dutiful wives and mothers. Many quit their jobs when they marry.

Many Japanese families live in suburbs, where housing is cheaper. As a result, many Japanese spend as much as three hours commuting to and from work.

Because land is so scarce, most Japanese homes do not have large yards. Most homes are also smaller than typical American homes. Rooms are usually used for more than one purpose. For example, a living room may also serve as a bedroom. During the day, people sit on cushions at low tables. At night, they sleep on the floor on a **futon** (FOO-tahn)—a lightweight cotton mattress. In the morning they put the mattress away, and the bedroom becomes a living room again.

For most occasions, people wear Western-style clothing. Many Japanese wear kimonos at festivals and weddings. Listening to music and playing video games are popular leisure activities. Baseball, golf, and skiing are also popular. On festival days, families may gather to enjoy the cherry blossoms or visit a local shrine or temple. They might also watch the ancient sport of sumo wrestling or traditional dramas on television. Many Japanese enjoy traditional arts such as the tea ceremony, flower arranging, growing dwarf potted trees called bonsai, and kite flying.

✓ **READING CHECK:** Human Systems What is life like in Japan? more than 99 percent of the people are ethnically Japanese, share a common language and culture; many families live in suburbs; homes are smaller than American homes; people wear Western-style clothing, enjoy sports, traditional arts

384 • **Chapter 17**

Teaching Objective 2

LEVELS 2 AND 3: (Suggested time: 30 min.) Review the characteristics of haiku. Ask students to use the lists they created for the Level 1 activity to write a haiku that describes some aspect of life in a large Japanese city. Call on volunteers to read their poems aloud. **LS** **VERBAL-LINGUISTIC**

Teaching Objective 3

ALL LEVELS: (Suggested time: 30 min.) Have students work in pairs to conduct interviews for a television program to be called A Day in the Life of the Japanese People. **COOPERATIVE LEARNING**

TEACHER TO TEACHER

Celeste Smith of Austin, Texas, suggests the following activity to help students learn about life in Japan. Have students work in groups to create collages that summarize home life in Japanese cities. Collages may include pictures from magazines, newspapers, drawings, and pieces of fabric. Have students include pictures of Japanese homes, gardens, products, celebrations, families, and anything else students find relevant. Ask students to tell what the illustrations depict. Display the collages.

Japan's Economy

Japan has few natural resources. It therefore imports many of the raw materials it uses to run its industries. Oil is one key material that Japan must import. The country produces about one third of its energy through nuclear power.

The sea is an important source of food. Japan has the world's largest fishing industry. It also imports fish from all over the world. Fish is a major part of the Japanese diet. In fact, Tokyo's largest fish market sells about 5 million pounds of seafood each day. The average Japanese eats more than 100 pounds of fish each year. In contrast, the average American eats less than 5 pounds each year.

Agriculture Most Japanese farms are located on Honshu. Many farmers own their land and live in small villages. Farms in Japan are much smaller than those in the United States. The average Japanese farm is about 2.5 acres (1 hectare). Most American farms are about 150 times larger. Japan's shortage of land means that there is little pastureland for livestock. Meat is a luxury. The Japanese get most of their protein from fish and soybeans.

Farmers make the most of their land by terracing the hillsides. This means cutting the hillside into a series of small flat fields. The terraces look like broad stair steps. The terraces give farmers more room to grow crops. Japanese farmers use **intensive cultivation**—the practice of growing food on every bit of available land. Even so, Japan must import about two thirds of its food.

Farmers are encouraged to stay on the land and to grow as much rice as possible. However, many farms are too small to be profitable. To solve this problem, the Japanese government buys the rice crop. The price is set high enough to allow farmers to support their families. The government then resells it at the same price. Because this price is much higher than the world market price, the government restricts rice imports.

Seeds of the tea plant were first brought to Japan about A.D. 800. Tea is now an important product of southern Japan. Top-quality teas are harvested by hand only. Workers pick just the tender young leaves at the plant's tip.

Interpreting the Visual Record

(*Human-Environment Interaction*)

How might using machines for harvesting leaves affect the quality of the tea?

▼

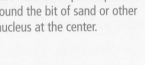

ENVIRONMENT AND SOCIETY

Pearls from Japan
Cultured pearls are among the many products from Japanese seas. The world's best-known pearl producer, Mikimoto, is located at Ago Bay in southern Japan. In 1893, Kokichi Mikimoto discovered that carefully tended oysters could grow nearly perfect pearls around an implanted nucleus. The process takes three to six years. Westerners at first believed that Mikimoto's cultured pearls were fakes, but the technique eventually gained widespread acceptance. Japanese underwater pearl farms now yield about 70 tons (63 metric tons) of pearls each year, despite pollution problems and competition from rapidly expanding Chinese producers.

Critical Thinking: How might people have first discovered the pearl creation process?

Answer: They may have found pearls in different stages in oysters they were eating. They may also have cut a pearl open and found the bit of sand or other nucleus at the center.

◄**Visual Record Answer**

may reduce the quality, because machines are unable to select only the young, tender leaves

---

➤**ASSIGNMENT:** Have students design flags or banners that might be displayed in a parade celebrating Japanese farming.

Teaching Objective 4

ALL LEVELS: (Suggested time: 15 min.) Copy the following graphic organizer onto the chalkboard, omitting the blue answers. Use it to help students describe Japan's economy. Lead a discussion about Japan's dependence on imported raw materials, oil, and food and the importance of its fishing industry. Then call on students to fill in the bulleted lines with the main features of Japan's economy.

Japan's Economy

Agriculture	Industry	Global Market
• most farms on Honshu	• automobiles, televisions, cameras, CD players	• trade surplus created by protectionism
• small farms	• work ethic	• objections from other countries
• terraced hillsides an example of intensive cultivation	• good employer-employee relations	• competition from other Asian countries
• government price supports for rice, limits on rice imports	• investment in other countries	

Answers to Section 3 Review

Define For definitions, see the glossary.

Working with Sketch Maps The cities are large, busy, noisy, crowded, and part of a megalopolis.

Reading for the Main Idea

1. little land for farming, so dikes are built and land is reclaimed from the sea **(NGS 15)**

2. imports raw materials for industries **(NGS 11)**

Critical Thinking

3. Western clothing, music, video games, baseball, golf, skiing

4. because many countries have a trade deficit with Japan

Organizing What You Know

5. Imperial Palace, part of megalopolis, center of government, banking, communications, education, Ginza. Paragraphs will vary. **(NGS 12)**

▲ A worker in this Japanese automobile factory does his job with the help of a robot.

Industry Japan imports most of its raw resources. These resources are then used to make goods to sell in other countries. For example, Japan is known for its high-quality automobiles. Japan also makes televisions, cameras, and compact disc players.

There are many reasons for Japan's economic success. Most Japanese have a strong **work ethic**. This is the belief that work in itself is worthwhile. Most Japanese work for large companies and respect their leaders. In return, employers look after workers' needs. They offer job security, exercise classes, and other benefits.

The Japanese have also benefited from investments in other countries. For example, some Japanese companies have built automobile factories in the United States. Other Japanese companies have invested in the American entertainment and real estate industries.

Japan and the Global Market Japan's economy depends on trade. In the past the government set up trade barriers to protect Japan's industries from foreign competition. This practice is called **protectionism**. This has helped Japan build up a huge **trade surplus**. A trade surplus means that a nation exports more than it imports. Other countries have objected to Japan's trade practices. Some countries have even set up barriers against Japanese goods. As a result, Japan has eased some trade barriers.

Japan has other economic problems, too. Some Asian countries that pay lower wages are able to produce goods more cheaply than Japan. The most important problem Japan—and Asia—faced in the 1990s was an economic slowdown. It threatened the country's prosperity. Japan is now in a recovery and slow-growth period.

✓ **READING CHECK:** (*Human Systems*) How have Japan's leaders tried to protect the nation's economy? by setting up trade barriers to protect Japan's industries and built up a trade surplus

go.
hrw
.com
Homework Practice Online
Keyword: SK5 HP17

Section Review 3

Define and explain: megalopolis, kimonos, futon, intensive cultivation, work ethic, protectionism, trade surplus

Working with Sketch Maps On the map you created in Section 2, label Inland Sea, Osaka, Tokyo, Kobe, and Kyoto. Draw a box in the margin of your map. What do the cities have in common? Write your answer in the margin box.

Reading for the Main Idea

1. (*Environment and Society*) How does Japan's physical geography affect farming?

2. (*Human Systems*) How has Japan developed its industries without plentiful raw materials?

Critical Thinking

3. **Drawing Inferences and Conclusions** In what ways do the daily lives of the Japanese reflect influences of Western culture?

4. **Drawing Inferences and Conclusions** Why do you suppose other countries might be concerned about Japan's surplus?

Organizing What You Know

5. **Summarizing** Copy the following graphic organizer. Use it to list the activities and services available in Tokyo.

Tokyo

386 • Chapter 17

CLOSE

Ask students to imagine that they have recently moved to Japan. What would they include in letters to friends in the United States? How is Japanese daily life different from American daily life?

REVIEW, ASSESS, RETEACH

Have students complete the Section Review. Then organize them into groups. Assign each group one of the section's main topics. Ask them to write three sentences to summarize their topic's main points and read their sentences to the class. Then have students complete Daily Quiz 17.3. **COOPERATIVE LEARNING**

Have students complete Main Idea Activity S3. Then create an outline on the chalkboard of the most important information from the section. Leave some of the categories blank and have students fill in the missing information. **ESOL**

EXTEND

Organize students into groups. Assign one of Japan's political parties to each group. Have students use additional resources to write a brief history explaining the significance of the assigned political party. Then stage a debate between two "party leaders" that allows them to share the information with the class. **COOPERATIVE LEARNING, BLOCK SCHEDULING**

Section 4 — The History and Culture of the Koreas

Read to Discover

1. What was Korea's ancient history like?
2. What were the major events of Korea's early modern period?
3. Why was Korea divided after World War II, and what were the effects of the division?

Vocabulary

demilitarized zone

Places

North Korea
South Korea

Reading Strategy

TAKING NOTES Use the headings in this section to create an outline. As you read, write what you learn about the history and culture of the Koreas under each heading.

Section 4 Resources

Reproducible
◆ Lecture Notes, Section 4
◆ Know It Notes S4
◆ Interdisciplinary Activities for the Middle Grades 29, 30, 31

Technology
◆ One-Stop Planner CD–ROM, Lesson 17.4
◆ Homework Practice Online
◆ HRW Go site

Reinforcement, Review, and Assessment
◆ Section 4 Review
◆ Daily Quiz 17.4
◆ Main Idea Activity S4
◆ Chapter Summaries and Review
◆ English Audio Summary 17.4
◆ Spanish Audio Summary 17.4

Ancient Korea

Korea's earliest inhabitants were nomadic hunters from north and central Asia. About 1500 B.C. they adopted rice farming, which had been introduced from China. Then, in 108 B.C., the Chinese invaded Korea. This invasion marked the beginning of a long period of Chinese influence on Korean culture. The Chinese introduced their system of writing and their system of examinations for government jobs. They also introduced Buddhism and Confucianism to Korea.

Korea's original religion—shamanism—continued to be practiced, along with the newer traditions introduced from China. According to shamanism, natural places and ancestors have spirits. Many mountains are particularly sacred to Koreans. Shamanism is still practiced in South Korea.

Over the centuries, Korean tribes eventually recaptured most of the peninsula. In the A.D. 600s the kingdom of Silla (SI-luh) united the peninsula. Korea's golden age began. Korea became known in Asia for its architecture, painting, ceramics, and fine jewelry.

▲ A weaver demonstrates his craft near Seoul.

◀ This celadon vase is from the A.D. 1000s.

Japan and the Koreas • 387

Section 4

Objectives

1. Describe Korea's ancient history.
2. Analyze the major events of Korea's early modern period.
3. Explain the history and results of Korea's division after World War II.

FOCUS

Bellringer

Copy the following instructions onto the chalkboard: *Work with a partner to make a folding fan from a sheet of paper. Illustrate it with scenes reflecting natural environments.* Ask volunteers to display their fans. Then tell students that fans have long been part of Korean life in the summer. Artists painted views of waterfalls, mountains, and other scenes on them. Tell students that in Section 4 they will learn more about Korean culture and history.

Building Vocabulary

Write the term **demilitarized zone** on the board and circle the prefix *de-*. Explain that *de-* means "removal" or "reversal." When *de-* is added to *militarized*, *demilitarized* means "the removal of the military." Point out Korea's demilitarized zone on a map and explain that no troops are allowed in this area. Ask students what other words they know using *de-* that carry the meaning of removal. (Possible answers: deice, deport, derail)

Across the Curriculum
LITERATURE

Pansori Many Koreans enjoy traditional folk tales. The most famous of these is a kind of ballad called a *pansori*, which is often chanted to the beat of drums. One of the best-known *pansori* is the Tale of Sim Chong, a story about a devoted daughter who was willing to sacrifice herself in order to restore her blind father's eyesight. This tale, like many other Korean folk tales, reinforces the Confucian value of duty to the family.

A film made recently in South Korea recounts an ancient tale of cruelty, true love, and perseverance from Korea's dynastic era. The story is told in *pansori* form so the audience is immersed in both Korean history and culture.

Discussion: Lead a discussion about which stories teach traditional values to American children. Students may mention stories like Aesop's fable about the tortoise and the hare (perseverance), the tale of George Washington and the cherry tree (honesty), or others.

Heavy fencing and explosives have kept people out of the demilitarized zone for decades. As a result, this land has provided a safe home for rare animal and plant species. Some scientists hope that in the future the DMZ can be set aside as a nature preserve, which would attract tourists while protecting the wildlife.

During the Silla period Korea began using the results of examinations to award government jobs. Generally only boys who were sons of noblemen could take the examinations. People from the lower classes could not rise to important positions by studying and passing the examinations, as they could in China.

By the early 900s a new kingdom had taken power. The modern name of Korea comes from this kingdom's name, Koryo. During the Koryo dynasty, Korean artisans invented the first movable metal type. During the following dynasty, scholars developed the Hangul (HAHN-gool) alphabet, which was officially adopted in 1446. Hangul was much easier to use with the Korean language than Chinese characters had been. Because Hangul had only 24 symbols, it was easier to learn. It had previously been necessary to memorize about 20,000 Chinese characters to read the Buddhist scriptures.

✓ **READING CHECK:** (**Human Systems**) How did the Chinese influence Korea's ancient history? They invaded the region and influenced Korean culture.

Early Modern Korea

By the early 1600s China again controlled Korea. For 300 years Korea remained under Chinese control. Closed off to most other outsiders, Korea became known as the Hermit Kingdom. During this period, Catholicism was introduced into Korea through missionaries in China. Korea's Christian community was sometimes persecuted and remained small until the mid-1900s.

In the mid-1890s Japan defeated China in the Sino-Japanese War. This cleared the way for Japan to annex Korea in 1910. The Japanese ruled harshly. They took over the Korean government and many businesses and farms. Koreans were forced to take Japanese names, and

388 • Chapter 17

TEACH

Teaching Objectives 1–2
ALL LEVELS: (Suggested time: 45 min.) Have the students create storyboards for key scenes in an imaginary television special entitled "Korea through Good Times and Bad." **LS VISUAL-SPATIAL**

Teaching Objective 3
ALL LEVELS: (Suggested time: 15 min.) Copy the following graphic organizer onto the chalkboard, omitting the blue answers. Use it to list five items for each category. **ESOL**

Korea before World War II	Korea after World War II
1. many influences, invasion from China	1. U.S. and Soviet troops remained after war
2. shamanism, newer religious traditions from north	2. Soviets helped communists take over north
3. Silla, Koryo periods—many accomplishments	3. invasion of South Korea by North Korea
4. invasion by China, Hermit Kingdom period	4. UN and Chinese troops sent in, Korean War
5. invasion by Japan	5. truce and creation of DMZ

Japanese was taught in the schools. Japan ruled Korea until the end of World War II.

✓ **READING CHECK:** *Places and Regions* What were some major events in Korea's early modern period? 1600s—controlled by China, Catholicism introduced; 1910—Japan annexed Korea and ruled it harshly until the end of World War II

A Divided Korea

At the end of World War II, U.S. and Soviet troops oversaw the Japanese departure from Korea. Because the Soviets wanted communism to spread to other countries, they helped Communist leaders take power in the north. The United States backed a democratic government in the south. The United Nations hoped that the Koreas would reunite. However, the United States and the Soviet Union could not agree on a plan. In 1948 South Korea officially became the Republic of Korea. North Korea became the Democratic People's Republic of Korea led by Korean Communist dictator Kim Il Sung.

In 1950 North Korea tried to unify the country by invading South Korea, resulting in the Korean War. The United Nations sent troops—mostly U.S.—to defend South Korea. Communist China sent forces to North Korea. A truce was declared in 1953, but Korea remains divided. The border between North Korea and South Korea is a strip of land roughly 2.4 miles (4 km) wide called the **demilitarized zone** (DMZ). This buffer zone separates the two countries. A total of about 1 million U.S., South Korean, and North Korean soldiers patrol the DMZ. It is the world's most heavily guarded border.

In 2000, the leaders of both Koreas met to discuss the future. Also, families that had been separated for decades were briefly reunited. However, the two Koreas have not agreed on terms of reunification.

✓ **READING CHECK:** *Places and Regions* What were some events in Korea's history after World War II? U.S. and Soviet troops oversaw Japanese departure, influence caused the division of Korea; 1950—North invaded South, UN sent troops for the South's defense; truce declared in 1953, but country remains divided

Our Amazing Planet

Casting bronze bells is an ancient Korean craft. The largest bell in South Korea, completed in A.D. 771, is more than 12 feet (3.6 m) tall and weighs about 25 tons (110,000 kg). When struck, it is said that the bell's tone can be heard 40 miles (64 km) away.

Section Review 4

Define and explain: demilitarized zone

Working with Sketch Maps On the map you created in Section 3, label North Korea and South Korea. In the margin, draw a box and include in it information that explains the significance of the DMZ. When was it established?

Reading for the Main Idea
1. *Human Systems* What were some of the accomplishments of the early Koreans before about 1600? What dynasty gave Korea its name?

2. *Human Systems* What long-lasting effect did the Korean War have on the Korean Peninsula?

Critical Thinking
3. **Analyzing Information** How has the Korean Peninsula been influenced by other countries?
4. **Making Generalizations and Predictions** What might be preventing North Korea and South Korea from reuniting?

Organizing What You Know
5. **Sequencing** Copy the following time line. Use it to list the important events of Korean history from 1500 B.C. through the 1500s.

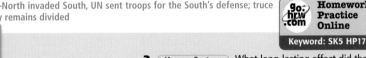
1500 B.C.   1500s

go.hrw.com **Homework Practice Online** Keyword: SK5 HP17

Japan and the Koreas • 389

Section 4 Review

Answers to Section 4 Review

Define For definition, see the glossary.

Working with Sketch Maps The DMZ prevents people and goods from crossing the border between North and South Korea. It was established after the Korean War.

Reading for the Main Idea
1. architecture, painting, ceramics, jewelry, movable metal type, Hangul alphabet; Koryo (NGS 9)
2. physical, economic, and political division

Critical Thinking
3. China—origin of writing and political systems, religion; Japan—conquered Korea, forced Koreans to take Japanese names and speak Japanese
4. possible answer: philosophical and political differences

Organizing What You Know
5. 1500 B.C.—adoption of rice farming; 108 B.C.—Chinese invade; A.D. 600—kingdom of Silla and golden age begins; 900—Koryo dynasty begins; 1446—Hangul adopted

CLOSE

Remind students that a Korean king directed the development of the Hangul alphabet. Lead a discussion on what steps students would take to design a new alphabet for the English language.

REVIEW, ASSESS, RETEACH

Have students complete the Section Review. Then organize the class into pairs. Have each student write a fill-in-the-blank question from each of the text subsections. Ask students to trade papers and answer each other's questions. Then have students complete Daily Quiz 17.4. **COOPERATIVE LEARNING, LS VERBAL-LINGUISTIC**

Have students complete Main Idea Activity S4. Then have them create a sequential-step diagram that describes Korea's history. Have students fill in the major events and add details about Korean culture. **ESOL**

EXTEND

Have interested students conduct research on the traditional dress, or *hanbok*, of Korea. You may want to have them create a poster describing *hanbok* and illustrating it using fabric scraps. More ambitious students may want to construct doll-sized examples. **BLOCK SCHEDULING**

Chart Answer ▶

It is much lower.

Section 5 · South and North Korea Today

Read to Discover
1. What are South Korea's government and society like?
2. What is South Korea's economy like?
3. What is North Korea like?
4. How has North Korea's government affected the country's development?

Vocabulary
entrepreneurs
chaebol
kimchi
famine

Places
Seoul
Pusan
P'yongyang

People
Kim Il Sung

Reading Strategy

READING ORGANIZER Create a spider map by drawing a circle on a sheet of paper. Label the circle South and North Korea Today. Create legs for People and Government, Society, and Economy. As you read the section, write what you learn about each country beneath each leg.

South Korea's People and Government

South Korea is densely populated. There are 1,197 people per square mile (462/sq km). Most people live in the narrow, fertile plain along the western coast of the Korean Peninsula. Travel in the peninsula's mountainous interior is difficult, so few people live there. South Korea's population is growing slowly, at about the same rate as in most industrialized countries.

South Korea's Cities Because South Korea is densely populated, space is a luxury—just as it is in Japan. Most South Koreans live in small apartments in crowded cities. Seoul (SOHL) is the country's capital and largest city. The government, the economy, and the educational system are centered there. After the Korean War, the population exploded because refugees flocked to Seoul seeking work and housing. By 1994 the city had nearly 11 million residents. Today, Seoul is one of the world's most densely populated cities. It has some 7,000 people per square mile (2,703/sq km).

South Korea's second-largest city is Pusan (POO-sahn). This major seaport and industrial center lies on the southern coast. Pusan also has an important fishing industry.

The rapid growth of South Korea's cities has brought problems. Housing is expensive. The many factories, cars, and coal-fired heating systems sometimes cause dangerous levels of air pollution. Industrial waste has also polluted the water.

Interpreting the Chart **How does North Korea's per capita GDP compare to that of South Korea?**

North Korea and South Korea

Country	Population/ Growth Rate	Life Expectancy	Literacy Rate	Per Capita GDP
North Korea	22,466,481 1.1%	68, male 74, female	99%	$1,000
South Korea	48,289,037 0.7%	72, male 79, female	98%	$19,400
United States	290,342,554 0.9%	74, male 80, female	97%	$37,600

Source: Central Intelligence Agency, *The World Factbook 2003*

Section 5

Objectives
1. Describe South Korea's government and society.
2. Analyze South Korea's economy.
3. Describe North Korea.
4. Explain how the government has affected North Korea's development.

FOCUS

Bellringer

Copy this scenario onto the chalkboard: *Imagine that you live in what used to be one country, but it has been divided into two countries by war. Your friends and family live in the other section, but you cannot visit them. Write a paragraph that you might include in a diary if you lived in this place.* Discuss responses. Compare the diary entries to Korea's situation. Tell students that in Section 5 they will learn more about the impact of division on Korea.

Building Vocabulary

Write the key terms on the chalkboard. Have students read the definitions in the text. You may want to read aloud the recipe for **kimchi** from Food Festival or the sidebar feature on the next page that mentions the Kimchi Festival. If possible, bring a sample to class. Discuss if or how Korean *chaebol* compare to any American business relationships with which students are familiar. You may want to ask students about news reports they have seen about **famine** in other countries.

Postwar Government South Korea is technically a democracy, but it was run by military dictators until the late 1980s. More recently, South Korea introduced a multiparty democratic government. The government controls economic development but does not own businesses and property.

✓ **READING CHECK:** (*Human Systems*) What kind of government does South Korea have? a multiparty democracy

South Korean Society

Like Japan's, South Korea's population is homogeneous. Most Koreans complete high school. About half go on to some form of higher education. Women are beginning to hold important jobs.

Traditional Families Most Koreans marry someone they meet through their parents. Most families still value sons. This is because only a son can take over the family name. Only a son can lead the ceremonies to honor the family's ancestors. Some couples who do not have a son adopt a boy with the same family name. This is not too difficult because there are few family names in Korea.

Religion Today, Christianity is the most common religion, followed closely by Buddhism. Whatever their religion, most Koreans take part in ceremonies to honor their ancestors. Most also follow Confucian values. Many Koreans still ask shamans for personal advice.

✓ **READING CHECK:** (*Human Systems*) What is South Korea's society like? homogenous, well educated, male dominated

This view looks out over the busy harbor of Pusan. Travelers can take a ferry from Pusan across the Korean Strait to Japan.

Interpreting the Visual Record
(*Movement*) **How does this photo show the importance of shipping to this region's economy?**

National Geography Standard 10

Fun Festivals Visitors to South Korea can enjoy a wide range of festivals. Among the many activities featured at various festivals are snowboarding, ice sculpting, bull riding, making paper, catching fireflies, flying kites, designing jewelry, and guessing the weight of raw fish.

In October the city of Kwangju hosts the annual four-day Kimchi Festival. Festival organizers hope to attract tourists and educate the world about kimchi. The event begins with an opening ceremony and a parade. At the display area visitors can taste, buy, or just look at all kinds of kimchi dishes. There are several competitions, with a special category for foreigners.

Discussion: Ask students what food festivals are held in your area and how they reflect the region's culture. What other foods are typical of your region?

◀ **Visual Record Answer**
Many large ships are docked.

TEACH

Teaching Objective 1
LEVEL 1: (Suggested time: 15 min.) Have students list the main points they would include in a newspaper entitled *South Korea—Then and Now.*
ESOL, 🔲 **VERBAL-LINGUISTIC**

LEVELS 2 AND 3: (Suggested time: 45 min.) Have students use the lists they created for the Level 1 activity to write and illustrate their story.
🔲 **VISUAL-SPATIAL**

Teaching Objective 2
ALL LEVELS: (Suggested time: 15 min.) Copy the following graphic organizer onto the chalkboard, omitting the blue answers. Use it to help students describe how agriculture and industry are part of South Korea's economy. **ESOL**

```
                    Economy
```

Industry	Agriculture
many businesses run by families or chaebol	less than 20 percent of land can be farmed
nuclear power encouraged by government	must import food
high-technology industry, electronic goods, steel, shipbuilding, automobiles, textiles	small farms along western and southern coasts
economic slowdown and recovery	much work done by hand
	rice, Chinese cabbage, soybeans

Kimchi There are countless recipes for kimchi, a favorite Korean condiment. Here is one version. First, wash and drain 2 pounds of cabbage and cut into pieces. Sprinkle with 2 tbs salt and let stand for 4 hours. Press out liquid. Mix in 1½ tbs minced onion, 1 tsp minced garlic, ⅔ tsp minced ginger, and ½–1 tbs crushed red pepper. Place mixture in large glass jar with a tight-fitting lid. Refrigerate for 4 days. Koreans serve kimchi as a relish at almost every meal.

This is one of many statues of Kim Il Sung in P'yŏngyang. He led North Korea from the end of World War II until his death in 1994. Although dead, Kim Il Sung was declared the "Eternal President" of North Korea in 1998.

392

South Korea's Economy

After the war, South Korea industrialized quickly, and its market economy grew. By the 1990s it had become one of the strongest economies in Asia.

Industry Koreans' strong sense of family often carries over into work. Large groups of relatives may become **entrepreneurs**. This means they use their money and talents to start and manage a business. Businesses are sometimes linked through family and personal ties into huge industrial groups called *chaebol*.

The government has encouraged the use of nuclear power. It also has encouraged the growth of high-technology industries. These industries make electronic goods for export. Other important industries are steel, shipbuilding, automobiles, and textiles. In the late 1990s South Korea, like many other Asian countries, experienced an economic slowdown. It is now making a rapid recovery.

Agriculture South Korea has the peninsula's richest agricultural land. However, less than 20 percent of the land can be farmed. The shortage of land means that South Korea must import about half of its food.

Most South Korean farms are small and lie along the western and southern coasts. The rugged terrain makes using heavy machinery difficult. As a result, farmers must do much of their work by hand and with small tractors. Since the late 1980s there has been a shortage of farmworkers.

Farmers grow rice on about half their land. Other important crops are Chinese cabbage and soybeans. Soybeans are used to make soy sauce and tofu, or bean curd. Chinese cabbage that has been spiced and pickled is called **kimchi**. This is Korea's national dish.

✓ **READING CHECK:** (*Places and Regions*) What is South Korea's economy like? industrialized, with high-technology industries, as well as steel, shipbuilding, automobiles, and textiles

North Korea's People and Government

North Korea's Communist Party controls the government. Kim Il Sung's son, Kim Jong Il, took over leadership in 1998 and continued his father's strict policies.

For years, North Korea had ties mostly with other Communist countries. Since the Soviet Union's breakup, North Korea has been largely isolated from the rest of the world. In addition, many countries are worried about North Korea's ability to make nuclear weapons. In 2002 North Korea announced plans to restart a nuclear reactor. Just a year later, the government said it had enough materials to build six nuclear bombs. Negotiations have not solved the crisis.

Like South Korea and Japan, North Korea has a homogeneous population. However, North Korea is not as densely populated as South Korea.

Teaching Objectives 3–4
ALL LEVELS: (Suggested time: 45 min.) Have students present skits that portray life in North Korea and how the government's control of the economy affects the people. **ESOL, LS AUDITORY-MUSICAL**

Teaching Objectives 1–4
LEVEL 1: (Suggested time: 30 min.) Have students create an outline that includes information for a Web site about North Korea or South Korea. Ask students to include a basic map and titles for the main links. **ESOL**

LEVELS 2 AND 3: (Suggested time: 30 min.) Have students imagine that they are veterans of the Korean War living in either North Korea or South Korea. Then ask them to write letters that compare pre- and postwar history, politics, and living conditions. Ask volunteers from each "side" to read their letters to the class. **LS VERBAL-LINGUISTIC**

The capital of North Korea is P'yŏngyang (pyuhng-YANG). More than 3 million people live there. North Korea's only university is in P'yŏngyang. Few private cars are on the city streets. Most residents use buses or the subway system to get around. At night, many streets are dark because the city frequently experiences shortages of electricity.

✓ **READING CHECK:** (*Places and Regions*) What is North Korea like? homogenous population; Communist; shortages of electricity in cities

North Korea's Economy

North Korea has a command economy. This means that the central government plans the economy and controls what is produced. The government also owns all the land and housing and controls access to jobs.

North Korea's best farmland is along the west coast. Only 14 percent of North Korea's land can be farmed. Most of this land is owned by the state. It is farmed by cooperatives—groups of farmers who work the land together. Some people have small gardens to grow food for themselves or to sell at local markets.

North Korea does not produce enough food to feed its people. It lost its main source of food and fertilizer when the Soviet Union collapsed. Poor harvests in the mid-1990s made the situation worse. **Famine**, or severe food shortages, resulted. The government's hostility toward the West made getting aid difficult. Thousands starved.

North Korea is rich in mineral resources. It has also developed a nuclear power industry. North Korea makes machinery, iron, and steel. However, its factories use outdated technology.

✓ **READING CHECK:** (*Human Systems*) How has North Korea's government affected the country's economic development? It has limited its modernization because it owns all industry and controls access to jobs.

▲ Rice farming requires large amounts of human energy for transplanting, weeding, and harvesting. These farmers are planting seedlings.

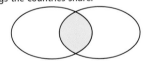

go.
hrw
.com
Homework Practice Online
Keyword: SK5 HP17

Section Review 5

Define or identify: entrepreneurs, *chaebol*, Kim Il Sung, kimchi, famine

Working with Sketch Maps On the map you created in Section 4, label Seoul, Pusan, and P'yŏngyang. Why do you think these cities remain important? Write your answer in a box in the margin.

Reading for the Main Idea

1. (*Places and Regions*) How did South Korea's cities change after the Korean War?

2. (*Environment and Society*) How does North Korea's physical geography affect its farmers?

3. (*Places and Regions*) What kind of economies do North and South Korea have, and how are they different?

Critical Thinking

4. **Finding the Main Idea** How have entrepreneurs affected South Korea's economy?

Organizing What You Know

5. **Sequencing** List characteristics of the government, industry, and agriculture of North and South Korea since World War II. Where the circles overlap, list things the countries share.

Japan and the Koreas • 393

Answers to Section 5 Review

Define For definitions, see the glossary.

Working with Sketch Maps They are located on waterways and are important for trade.

Reading for the Main Idea

1. rapid growth, pollution, housing shortage **(NGS 4)**

2. best farmland along west coast, only 14 percent can be farmed **(NGS 15)**

3. South Korea—market, industrialized, modern; North Korea—command, government-owned factories, old machinery **(NGS 4)**

Critical Thinking

4. use money and talents to start a business; businesses are sometimes linked in a *chaebol*

Organizing What You Know

5. North—communist, industry undeveloped, farming by cooperatives; South—democratic, industrialized, much farm work done by hand; both—farming on coasts, import food, nuclear power

CLOSE

Challenge students to imagine that they are members of a committee called New Ideas for a New Millennium. The committee was created to propose steps to move North and South Korea closer to reunification. Brainstorm suggestions.

REVIEW, ASSESS, RETEACH

Have students complete the Section Review. Ask students to suggest phrases or sentences that describe either North or South Korea. Then have students complete Daily Quiz 17.5.

Have students complete Main Idea Activity for S5. Then organize the class into groups. Give each a sheet of newsprint with two columns headed North Korea and South Korea. Have each student add a fact to each column until all the basic information in the section has been covered. **ESOL, COOPERATIVE LEARNING**

EXTEND

Have interested students conduct research on aspects of the Korean War, such as important personalities or battles. Some may research the U.S. Army's medical service during the war and compare their findings with how it was portrayed in the television program *M*A*S*H.* **BLOCK SCHEDULING**

Define and Identify

For definitions and identifications, see the glossary and index.

Review the Main Ideas

17. islands, mountains, volcanoes, coastal plain; peninsula, mountains, coastal plain (NGS 4)

18. Both have two climate regions—humid continental in the north and humid subtropical in the south.

19. rule by emperors and shoguns

20. because Japan was expanding its empire in Asia and because Japan had attacked the U.S. naval base at Pearl Harbor, Hawaii (NGS 13)

21. fishing; oil

22. because Japan has set up barriers to protect Japan's industries from foreign competition (NGS 11)

23. rice farming, writing system, system of examinations for government jobs, Buddhism, and Confucianism (NGS 10)

24. serves as a buffer zone separating North and South Korea; world's most heavily guarded border

25. because only a son can take over the family name and lead ceremonies to honor the family's ancestors

26. controlled by the Communist Party, isolation from the rest of the world, shortages of electricity and food (NGS 18)

Think Critically

27. Mountainous interiors forced settlement on coastal plains.

28. Japan—many islands, volcanoes and earthquakes are common; Koreas—peninsula, no volcanoes, earthquakes are rare

29. irrigated land to grow rice, built dikes and canals

30. Possible answer: It grew so large that it began to spread and join other large cities nearby.

31. North Korea—command economy run by government, produces some machinery, iron, steel, but lags behind in high-quality goods; South Korea—highly industrialized market economy, produces quality export goods

CHAPTER 17 Review and Practice

Define and Identify

Identify each of the following:

1. tsunamis
2. shamans
3. Murasaki Shikibu
4. samurai
5. shogun
6. Diet
7. kimonos
8. intensive cultivation
9. work ethic
10. protectionism
11. trade surplus
12. entrepreneurs
13. *chaebol*
14. Kim Il Sung
15. kimchi
16. famine

Review the Main Ideas

17. What are the main geographic features of Japan and the Koreas?

18. How are the climates of Japan and South Korea similar?

19. What kind of political system did Japan have early in its history?

20. Why did the United States go to war against Japan in 1941?

21. Japan leads the world in which industry? What key material must it import?

22. Why have other countries objected to Japan's trade practices?

23. What contributions did the Chinese make to ancient Korea?

24. What purpose does the demilitarized zone serve? What makes it unique?

25. Why are sons valued in South Korean families?

26. What are some problems that face North Koreans?

Think Critically

27. Analyzing Information How have geographic features affected where people live in Japan and the Korean Peninsula?

28. Contrasting What physical features make Japan different from the Koreas? Create a chart to organize your answer.

29. Finding the Main Idea How have the Japanese changed the physical landscape to meet their needs?

30. Analyzing Information How has Tokyo developed into a megalopolis?

31. Contrasting How do the economies and governments of North and South Korea differ?

Map Activity

32. On a separate sheet of paper, match the letters on the map with their correct labels.

Hokkaido	Tokyo
Honshu	Seoul
Shikoku	P'yŏngyang
Kyushu	

Map Activity

32. **A.** P'yŏngyang
  B. Shikoku
  C. Seoul
  D. Hokkaido
  E. Kyushu
  F. Honshu
  G. Tokyo

Writing Activity

Imagine that you are traveling in Japan, North Korea, or South Korea. Write a one-page letter to a friend describing the places you have visited and an adventure you have had during your stay. Be sure to use standard grammar, spelling, sentence structure, and punctuation.

internet connect

Internet Activity: **go.hrw.com**
KEYWORD: **SK5 GT17**

Choose a topic to explore Japan and the Koreas:
- Investigate volcanoes.
- Visit Japan and the Koreas.
- Compare your school to a Japanese school.

Social Studies Skills Practice

Interpreting Political Cartoons

In this chapter you have learned that North Korea caused concern among many countries with its nuclear weapons program. Study the following political cartoon that addresses the relationship between President Bush and Kim Jong Il. Then answer the questions.

Source: Daryl Cagle, Slate.com

1. What is the main idea of this cartoon?
2. Which character represents President Bush?
3. What is Kim Jong Il's character holding?
4. What is Kim Jong Il preventing President Bush from doing?

Analyzing Primary Sources

Read the following passage about young Samurai warriors from *Bushido, the Warrior's Code* by Inazo Nitobe. Then answer the questions.

"The stereotype of Spartan courage and of ignoring pain was indoctrinated [taught] into the children from the time of their birth. The fledgling samurai with an empty stomach knew it was a disgrace to feel the pangs [pains] of hunger. During training they were subjected to periods of deprivation [withholding] of food and exposure to extreme cold. Endurance was the hallmark of a successful novice [beginner]."

1. When did Samurai training begin for future warriors?
2. What was life like for a young samurai?
3. Why would it be a disgrace to feel hungry?
4. How might this kind of training aid a warrior in battle?

Japan and the Koreas • 395

Writing Activity

Answers will vary, but the information included should be consistent with text material. Use Rubric 40, Writing to Describe, to evaluate student work.

Interpreting Political Cartoons

1. Kim Jong Il's continued trickery regarding its nuclear weapons program
2. the one on the left
3. a nuclear weapon
4. possible answer: limiting North Korea's nuclear weapons development program

Analyzing Primary Sources

1. in childhood
2. challenging, difficult, uncomfortable
3. They were taught to ignore pain.
4. by allowing him to focus on the larger fight despite personal discomfort

---

REVIEW AND ASSESSMENT RESOURCES

Reproducible
- Readings in World Geography, History, and Culture 70 and 71
- Critical Thinking Activity 17
- Vocabulary Activity 17

Technology
- Chapter 17 Test Generator (on the One-Stop Planner)
- Audio CD Program, Chapter 17
- HRW Go site

Reinforcement, Review, and Assessment
- Chapter 17 Review and Practice
- Chapter Summaries and Review

- Chapter 17 Test
- Unit 5 Test
- Chapter 17 Test for English Language Learners and Special-Needs Students
- Unit 5 Test for English Language Learners and Special-Needs Students

internet connect

GO TO: **go.hrw.com**
KEYWORD: **SK5 Teacher**
FOR: **a guide to using the Internet in your classroom**

Objectives

Reproducible Resources

Objectives	Pacing Guide	Reproducible Resources		
SECTION 1				
Physical Geography (pp. 397–99) 1. Identify the major physical features of Southeast Asia. 2. Identify the climates, vegetation, and wildlife found in the region. 3. Identify the resources found in Southeast Asia.	**Regular** .5 day Lecture Notes, Section 1 **Block Scheduling** .5 day *Block Scheduling Handbook, Chapter 18*	RS	Know It Notes S1	
		ELL	Main Idea Activity S1	
SECTION 2				
History and Culture (pp. 400–03) 1. Identify some important events in the history of Southeast Asia. 2. Describe what the people and culture of Southeast Asia are like today.	**Regular** 1 day Lecture Notes, Section 2 **Block Scheduling** .5 day *Block Scheduling Handbook, Chapter 18*	RS	Know It Notes S2	
		RS	Graphic Organizer 18	
		E	Cultures of the World Activity 7	
		E	Creative Strategies for Teaching World Geography, Lesson 18	
		SM	Geography for Life Activity 29	
		IC	Interdisciplinary Activities for the Middle Grades 29, 30	
		SM	Map Activity 18	
		ELL	Main Idea Activity S2	
SECTION 3				
Mainland Southeast Asia Today (pp. 404–06) 1. Identify where people in the mainland countries live today. 2. Describe the economies of the main.land countries.	**Regular** .5 day Lecture Notes, Section 3 **Block Scheduling** .5 day *Block Scheduling Handbook, Chapter 18*	RS	Know It Notes S3	
		IC	Interdisciplinary Activity for the Middle Grades 31	
		ELL	Main Idea Activity S3	
		E	Biography Activity: Aung San Suu Kyi	
SECTION 4				
Island Southeast Asia Today (pp. 407–11) 1. Identify the major cities of the island countries. 2. Describe the economies of island countries.	**Regular** 1 day Lecture Notes, Section 4 **Block Scheduling** .5 day *Block Scheduling Handbook, Chapter 18*	RS	Know It Notes S4	
		IC	Interdisciplinary Activity for the Middle Grades 31	
		ELL	Main Idea Activity S4	

Chapter Resource Key

RS	Reading Support	**ELL**	Reinforcement and English Language Learners and English for Speakers of Other Languages (ESOL)
IC	Interdisciplinary Connections		
E	Enrichment		
SM	Skills Mastery		Transparencies
A	Assessment		CD–ROM
REV	Review		

 Music

 Video

 Internet

Holt Presentation Maker Using Microsoft® PowerPoint®

  One-Stop Planner CD–ROM

See the *One-Stop Planner* for a complete list of additional resources for students and teachers.

One-Stop Planner CD–ROM

It's easy to plan lessons, select resources, and print out materials for your students when you use the *One-Stop Planner CD–ROM with Test Generator.*

Technology Resources

  One-Stop Planner CD–ROM, Lesson 18.1

  Geography and Cultures Visual Resources with Teaching Activities 49–53

  ARGWorld CD–ROM

  Homework Practice Online

    HRW Go site

  One-Stop Planner CD–ROM, Lesson 18.2

  ARGWorld CD–ROM

  Music of the World Audio CD Program, Selection 21

    Homework Practice Online

    HRW Go site

  One-Stop Planner CD–ROM, Lesson 18.3

  ARGWorld CD–ROM

    Homework Practice Online

    HRW Go site

  One-Stop Planner CD–ROM, Lesson 18.4

  ARGWorld CD–ROM

  Music of the World Audio CD Program, Selection 22

    Homework Practice Online

    HRW Go site

Review, Reinforcement, and Assessment Resources

ELL	Main Idea Activity S1
REV	Section 1 Review
A	Daily Quiz 18.1
REV	Chapter Summaries and Review
ELL	English Audio Summary 18.1
ELL	Spanish Audio Summary 18.1

ELL	Main Idea Activity S2
REV	Section 2 Review
A	Daily Quiz 18.2
REV	Chapter Summaries and Review
ELL	English Audio Summary 18.2
ELL	Spanish Audio Summary 18.2

ELL	Main Idea Activity S3
REV	Section 3 Review
A	Daily Quiz 18.3
REV	Chapter Summaries and Review
ELL	English Audio Summary 18.3
ELL	Spanish Audio Summary 18.3

ELL	Main Idea Activity S4
REV	Section 4 Review, p. 631
A	Daily Quiz 18.4
REV	Chapter Summaries and Review
ELL	English Audio Summary 18.4
ELL	Spanish Audio Summary 18.4

HRW ONLINE RESOURCES

GO TO: go.hrw.com
Then type in a keyword.

TEACHER HOME PAGE
KEYWORD: SK5 TEACHER

CHAPTER INTERNET ACTIVITIES
KEYWORD: SK5 GT18

Choose an activity to:
• explore an Indonesian rain forest.
• learn about shadow puppets.
• see the buildings of Southeast Asia.

CHAPTER ENRICHMENT LINKS
  KEYWORD: SK5 CH18

CHAPTER MAPS
  KEYWORD: SK5 MAPS18

ONLINE ASSESSMENT
Homework Practice
  KEYWORD: SK5 HP18
  Standardized Test Prep Online
  KEYWORD: SK5 STP18
  Rubrics
  KEYWORD: SS Rubrics

COUNTRY INFORMATION
  KEYWORD: SK5 Almanac

CONTENT UPDATES
  KEYWORD: SS Content Updates

HOLT PRESENTATION MAKER
  KEYWORD: SK5 PPT18

ONLINE READING SUPPORT
  KEYWORD: SS Strategies

CURRENT EVENTS
  KEYWORD: S5 Current Events

Meeting Individual Needs

Ability Levels

Level 1 Basic-level activities designed for all students encountering new material

Level 2 Intermediate-level activities designed for average students

Level 3 Challenging activities designed for honors and gifted-and-talented students

ESOL Activities that address the needs of students with Limited English Proficiency

Chapter Review and Assessment

E	Readings in World Geography, History, and Culture 72, 73, and 74
SM	Critical Thinking Activity 18
REV	Chapter 18 Review and Practice
REV	Chapter Summaries and Review
ELL	Vocabulary Activity 18
A	Chapter 18 Test
A	Unit 5 Test

 Chapter 18 Test Generator (on the One-Stop Planner)

 Audio CD Program, Chapter 18

A Chapter 18 Test for English Language Learners and Special-Needs Students

A Unit 5 Test for English Language Learners and Special-Needs Students

 HRW Go Site

CHAPTER 18

Southeast Asia

Previewing Chapter Resources

Holt Online Learning

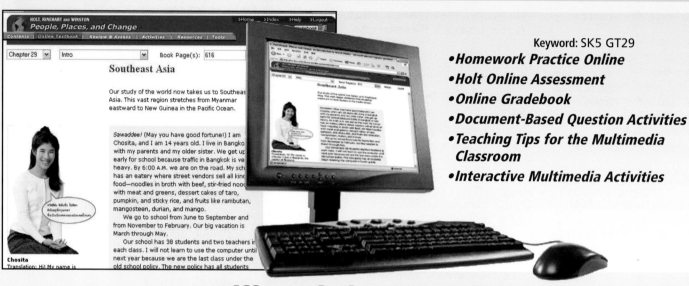

Keyword: SK5 GT29

- *Homework Practice Online*
- *Holt Online Assessment*
- *Online Gradebook*
- *Document-Based Question Activities*
- *Teaching Tips for the Multimedia Classroom*
- *Interactive Multimedia Activities*

Differentiating Instruction

Reading and Writing Support

◀ Graphic Organizer Activity
- *Vocabulary Activity*
- *Chapter Summary and Review*
- *Know It Notes*
- *Audio CD*

Active Learning

- *Block Scheduling Handbook*
- *Cultures of the World Activity*
- *Interdisciplinary Activity*
- Map Activity ◀
- *Critical Thinking Activity 29*
- *Music of the World CD 20–21*

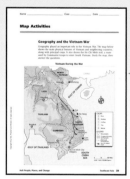

Primary Sources and Advanced Learners

- *Geography for Life Activity: Sacred Buildings*
- Map Activity: Geography and the Vietnam War ◀
- *Readings in World Geography, History and Culture:*
  - *72 Life in Rural Thailand*
  - *73 Chicken Industry*
  - *74 Escaping from Vietnam*

Assessment Program

- *Daily Quizzes S1–4*
- Chapter Test ◀
- *Chapter Test for English Language Learners and Special-Needs Students*

Spanish and ESOL

- *Vocabulary Activity*
- Main Idea Activities for English Language Learners and Special-Needs Students ◀
- *Chapter Summary and Review*
- *Spanish Audio Summary*
- *Know It Notes S1–4*
- *Chapter Test for English Language Learners and Special-Needs Students*

Special Education Modifications

Your I.D.E.A. Works! CD-ROM will provide modified versions of the following teaching materials:

◀ Guided Reading Strategies S1–4
- *Vocabulary Activity*
- *Main Idea Activities S1–4*
- *Daily Quizzes S1–4*
- *Chapter 18 Test*
- *Flash cards of chapter vocabulary terms*

Teacher Resources

Books for Teachers

Daws, Gavin, and Marty Fujita. *Archipelago: Islands of Indonesia.* University of California Press, 1999.

Murray, Geoffrey, and Audrey Perera. *Singapore: The Global City-State.* St. Martin's Press, 1996.

Wang, Gung Wu. *China and Southeast Asia: Myths, Threats, and Culture.* World Scientific Publishing Co., 1999.

Books for Students

Cheneviere, Alain, and Lisa Davidson (photographer). *Pak in Indonesia (My Future).* Lerner Publications Company, 1996. Story of a young bull driver and the culture, geography, and economy of his country.

Rawson, Philip S. *The Art of Southeast Asia: Cambodia, Vietnam, Thailand, Laos, Burma, Java, Bali (World of Art).* Thames & Hudson, 1999.

Stewart, Whitney. *Aung San Suu Kyi: Fearless Voice of Burma (Newsmakers Biographies).* Lerner Publications Company, 1997. Biography of the Burmese leader who won the Nobel Peace Prize in 1991 while under house arrest.

Viesti, Joseph F., and Diane Hall (contributor). *Celebrate! in Southeast Asia.* William Morrow & Co. (Library), 1996. Describes a variety of celebrations in Southeast Asia. **SHELTERED ENGLISH**

Multimedia Materials

Asia Alive. CD–ROM. MediaAlive.

Asia: Laos, Cambodia, Vietnam. Video, 28 min. Films for the Humanities and Sciences.

Southeast Asia: How Does Change Occur? Video, 15 min. Agency for Instructional Technology.

Videos and CDs

Videos

- **CNN** *Presents Geography: Yesterday and Today, Segment 30 The Highway to Propserity*
- *ARG World*

Holt Researcher

http://researcher.hrw.com

- *Association of Southeast Asian Nations (ASEAN)*
- *Suu Kyi, Aung San*
- *Hayslip, Le Ly*
- *Aquino, Corazon*
- *Southeast Asian Treaty Organization (SEATO)*
- *Ho Chi Minh*
- *Mongkut*
- *Vietnam*
- *Malaysia*

Transparency Packages

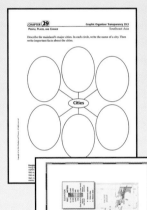

Graphic Organizer Transparencies 18.1–4

Geography and Cultures Visual Resources Transparencies 97–101
106 Southeast Asia: Physical-Political

Map Activities Transparency 18 Geography and the Vietnam War

WHY IT MATTERS

You may want to reinforce students' interest in Southeast Asia by pointing out these concepts:

▸ The economies of some Pacific Rim countries are so fast-growing they have been called the tigers. The tigers have many trade links to the United States.

▸ The Vietnam War has affected the American consciousness. Our experiences there continue to affect U.S. policies.

▸ The struggle of East Timor to win independence from Indonesia required the assistance of the UN.

CHAPTER 18

Southeast Asia

Our study of the world now takes us to Southeast Asia. This vast region stretches from Myanmar eastward to New Guinea in the Pacific Ocean.

Sawaddee! (May you have good fortune!) I am Chosita, and I am 14 years old. I live in Bangkok with my parents and my older sister. We get up early for school because traffic in Bangkok is very heavy. By 6:00 A.M. we are on the road. My school has an eatery where street vendors sell all kinds of food—noodles in broth with beef, stir-fried noodles with meat and greens, dessert cakes of taro, pumpkin, and sticky rice, and fruits like rambutan, mangosteen, durian, and mango.

We go to school from June to September and from November to February. Our big vacation is March through May.

Our school has 38 students and two teachers in each class. I will not learn to use the computer until next year because we are the last class under the old school policy. The new policy has all students begin learning the computer in fourth grade.

สวัสดีค่ะ ดิฉันชื่อ โชสิตา ดิฉันอยู่ที่กรุงเทพฯ ซึ่งเป็นเมืองหลวงของประเทศไทยค่ะ

▲
Translation: Hi! My name is Chosita. I live in Bangkok, the capital of Thailand.

CHAPTER PROJECT

In Indonesia, puppet theater is often used to convey ethical messages and commentary. Have students make puppets and present a skit about an ethical dilemma. Place a copy of the script and a photograph of the puppet in students' portfolios.

STARTING THE CHAPTER

Locate Southeast Asia's mainland and islands on a wall map. Point out that the region lies between India and China, on the Indochina Peninsula. Explain to students how this location has influenced Southeast Asia throughout history. (colonization, the spread of various languages, religions, and customs, etc.) Then call attention to the region's location between the Pacific and Indian Oceans. Use this information as a springboard for helping students focus on the physical, economic, and political characteristics of Southeast Asia.

Section 1 Physical Geography

Read to Discover
1. What are the major physical features of Southeast Asia?
2. What climates, vegetation, and wildlife are found in the region?
3. What resources does Southeast Asia have?

Vocabulary
mainland
archipelagos

Places
Indochina Peninsula
Malay Peninsula
New Guinea
Malay Archipelago
Philippines
Irian Jaya
Borneo
Java
Sumatra
Mekong River

Reading Strategy
MNEMONIC DEVICE Write the letters to the words Tropical down a sheet of paper. As you read this section, use each letter to write what you learn about the physical geography of Southeast Asia.

Southeast Asia: Physical-Political

ELEVATION		
FEET		METERS
13,120		4,000
6,560		2,000
1,640		500
656		200
(Sea level) 0		0 (Sea level)
Below sea level		Below sea level

⊛ National capitals
• Other cities
▫ Historic sites

Size comparison of Southeast Asia to the contiguous United States

Southeast Asia • 397

SECTION 1 RESOURCES
Reproducible
- Lecture Notes, Section 1
- Block Scheduling Handbook, Chapter 18
- Know It Notes S1

Technology
- One-Stop Planner CD–ROM, Lesson 18.1
- Homework Practice Online
- Geography and Cultures Visual Resources with Teaching Activities 49–53
- HRW Go site

Reinforcement, Review, and Assessment
- Section 1 Review
- Daily Quiz 18.1
- Main Idea Activity S1
- Chapter Summaries and Review
- English Audio Summary 18.1
- Spanish Audio Summary 18.1

Section 1

Objectives
1. Identify the major physical features of Southeast Asia.
2. Describe the climates, vegetation, and wildlife of Southeast Asia.
3. Name the resources found in Southeast Asia.

FOCUS

Bellringer
Copy the following instructions onto the chalkboard: *Look at the photos and map in this section. What do they tell you about the physical geography of Southeast Asia?* Have students write their answers. Discuss their responses. Ask students to keep what they have written at hand so they can compare their original impressions with what they learn as they progress through the section. Tell students that in Section 1 they will learn more about the physical geography of Southeast Asia.

Using the Physical-Political Map
Have students examine the map on this page. Then ask students to locate the various countries of mainland and island Southeast Asia. Call on volunteers to identify a peninsula (the Indochina or Malay Peninsula) and a delta (Irrawaddy, Chao Phraya, Mekong, or Hong). Point out to students the difference in size between Singapore and Brunei and the other countries. (Singapore and Brunei are much smaller.)

Southeast Asia 397

EYE ON EARTH

Way Up and Way Down
Climbing high mountains is often considered one of the greatest challenges to human adventurers. However, Low's Gully in Malaysia presents a different kind of challenge. This steep ravine on the island of Borneo is about 8,600 feet (2,600 m) deep. Above it rises Mount Kinabalu, the highest mountain in Southeast Asia.

Adventurers who want to descend to the floor of Low's Gully must first climb about three quarters of the way up Mount Kinabalu. The descent then takes them down narrow cracks and steep granite cliffs. Dense vegetation and frequent flash floods near the gully's floor provide more challenges.

Activity: Have students write a scene for the script of an action movie in which two characters descend into Low's Gully.

Visual Record Answer ▶

They may be flooded and become submerged by rising river waters.

internet connect

GO TO: go.hrw.com
KEYWORD: SK5 CH18
FOR: Web sites about
Southeast Asia

The Mekong River flows through a floodplain along the border between Thailand and Laos.

Interpreting the Visual Record What might happen to low islands and surrounding areas during the wet monsoon?

Physical Features

Southeast Asia is made up of two peninsulas and two large island groups. The Indochina and Malay (muh-LAY) Peninsulas lie on the Asian **mainland**. A mainland is a region's main landmass. The two large groups of islands, or **archipelagos** (ahr-kuh-PE-luh-gohs), lie between the mainland and New Guinea. They are the Malay Archipelago—made up mostly of Indonesia—and the Philippines. The Philippines are sometimes considered part of the Malay Archipelago. Western New Guinea is called Irian Jaya. It is part of Indonesia.

Landforms Southeast Asia's highest mountains are on the mainland in northern Myanmar (MYAHN-mahr). Mountain ranges fan out southward into Thailand (TY-land), Laos (LOWS), and Vietnam (vee-ET-NAHM). Between the mountains are low plateaus and river floodplains. The floodplains are rich farmlands.

Some of the large islands also have high mountains. Those islands include Borneo, Java, Sumatra, New Guinea, and some in the Philippines. They are part of the Pacific Ring of Fire. Earthquakes and volcanic eruptions often shake this part of the world.

Rivers Five major river systems drain the mainland. Many people and the largest cities are found near these rivers. The greatest river is the Mekong (MAY-KAWNG). The Mekong River flows southeast from China to southern Vietnam. You will read about the other rivers later in this chapter.

✓ **READING CHECK:** (*Places and Regions*) What are Southeast Asia's major physical features? Peninsulas, islands, mountain ranges, plateaus, river floodplains, river systems

Climate Vegetation, and Wildlife

The warm temperatures of this tropical region generally do not change much during the year. However, northern and mountain areas tend to be cooler.

TEACH

Teaching Objectives 1–3
ALL LEVELS: (Suggested time: 20 min.) Copy the following graphic organizer onto the chalkboard, omitting the blue answers. Call on students to provide words and phrases to describe the physical features, climates, vegetation and wildlife, and resources of the mainland and island regions of Southeast Asia. **ESOL,** LS **VISUAL-SPATIAL**

SOUTHEAST ASIA

Physical Features	Climates	Vegetation and Wildlife	Resources
Indochina and Malay Peninsulas, Malay Archipelago, the Philippine Islands, five major river systems, and some mountains	tropical, with seasonal monsoons	rain forest, rhinoceroses, orangutans, tigers, and elephants	forests, rich farmland, tin, iron ore, oil, gas

Much of the rainfall on the mainland is seasonal. Wet monsoon winds from nearby warm oceans bring heavy rains in the summer. Dry monsoons from the northeast bring drier weather in winter. Most of the islands are wet all year. Typhoons bring heavy rains and powerful winds to the island countries.

The region's tropical rain forests are home to many kinds of plants and animals. About 40,000 kinds of flowering plants grow in Indonesia alone. Rhinoceroses, orangutans, tigers, and elephants also live in the region. However, many of these plants and animals are endangered. Southeast Asia's rain forests are being cleared for farmland, tropical wood, and mining.

◄ *Orangutan* is a Malaysian word for "man of the forest." These apes once lived in jungles throughout much of Southeast Asia. Hunting by humans has thinned the orangutan population in much of the region. Most orangutans today live on Borneo and Sumatra.

✔ **READING CHECK:** (*Places and Regions*) What are the region's climates, vegetation, and wildlife like?
Tropical; tropical rain forests; many different plants and animals, some endangered

Resources

Southeast Asia's rain forests produce valuable wood and other products. Thailand, Indonesia, and Malaysia (muh-LAY-zhuh) are the world's largest producers of natural rubber. The rubber tree is native to South America. However, it grows well in Southeast Asia's tropical climates.

Rich volcanic soils, floodplains, and tropical climates are good for farming. Abundant water and good soils in river deltas are ideal for growing rice. Coconuts, palm oil, sugarcane, coffee, and spices are also key products. Countries here also mine tin, iron ore, oil, and gas.

✔ **READING CHECK:** (*Places and Regions*) What are the region's important resources? rain forests, rich soils, abundant water, tin, iron ore, oil, gas

Homework Practice Online
Keyword: SK5 HP18

Section Review 1

Define and explain: mainland, archipelagos

Working with Sketch Maps On a map of Southeast Asia that your teacher provides or that you draw, label the following: Indochina Peninsula, Malay Peninsula, New Guinea, Malay Archipelago, Philippines, Irian Jaya, Borneo, Java, Sumatra, and the Mekong River. In a box in the margin, describe the Mekong River.

Reading for the Main Idea

1. (*Places and Regions*) Where are the region's highest mountains?

2. (*Places and Regions*) Where are large cities found?

3. (*Places and Regions*) Which countries are the world's largest producers of natural rubber?

Critical Thinking

4. Making Generalizations and Predictions What do you think might happen to the region's wildlife if much of the tropical rain forests continue to be destroyed?

Organizing What You Know

5. Summarizing Copy the following graphic organizer. Use it to describe the region's climates, vegetation and wildlife, and resources.

Climates	Vegetation and wildlife	Resources

Southeast Asia • 399

Answers to Section 1 Review

Define For definitions, see the glossary.

Working with Sketch Maps Maps will vary, but the listed places should be labeled in their approximate locations.

Reading for the Main Idea

1. northern Myanmar **(NGS 4)**

2. on or near the region's five major rivers **(NGS 4)**

3. Thailand, Indonesia, Malaysia **(NGS 4)**

Critical Thinking

4. Much wildlife will die and disappear as habitat is destroyed. **(NGS 18)**

Organizing What You Know

5. climates—tropical wet and dry seasons on mainland, most islands wet all year; vegetation and wildlife—tropical rain forest, many kinds of plants, trees, and animals, including rhinos, orangutans, tigers, elephants; resources—forests, good farmland, tin, iron ore, oil, gas

CLOSE

Ask students to identify items they are familiar with that utilize Southeast Asian products such as coconuts, sugarcane, and rubber. (Examples include candy bars, soft drinks, or bicycle tires.)

REVIEW, ASSESS, RETEACH

Have students complete the Section Review and use the map and text to create four true-or-false questions for the region's physical features, climate, wildlife and vegetation, and resources. Have students quiz a partner using their questions. Then have students complete Daily Quiz 18.1. **COOPERATIVE LEARNING**

Have students complete Main Idea Activity S1. Then organize the class into groups. Have each group design graphics and text for a Web site providing information about the physical features, climate, wildlife, and resources of Southeast Asia. **ESOL, COOPERATIVE LEARNING**

EXTEND

Have interested students conduct research on volcanic eruptions and earthquakes in the Pacific Ring of Fire during the 1900s. Have them mark affected areas on a map and use it as a visual aid in a short oral presentation to the class. **BLOCK SCHEDULING**

History Close-Up Answer ▶

possible answer: that it was wealthy, well-organized, and could call on many workers to complete a huge project

Section 2 History and Culture

Read to Discover
1. What are some important events in the history of Southeast Asia?
2. What are the people and culture of Southeast Asia like today?

Vocabulary
refugees

Places
Angkor
Cambodia
Thailand
Vietnam
Laos

Indonesia
Malaysia
Timor
Myanmar
Singapore

Reading Strategy
TAKING NOTES Use the headings in this section to create an outline. As you read, write what you learn about the history and culture of Southeast Asia beneath each heading.

History Close-Up

Angkor Wat The magnificent stone towers of Angkor Wat rise from the Southeast Asian rain forest in this illustrated re-creation set in the early A.D. 1100s. Hindu priests are shown entering the temple where they will make offerings to statues of Hindu gods. To the Khmer, Angkor Wat was the center of the universe. The temple's towers symbolized mythical mountains. Reservoirs of water surrounding the temple represented the oceans. **What do you think this illustration says about Khmer society?**

History

Southeast Asia was home to some of the world's earliest human settlements. Over time many peoples moved there from China and India. The Khmer (kuh-MER) developed the most advanced of the region's early societies. The Khmer Empire was based in Angkor in what is now Cambodia (kam-BOH-dee-uh). It controlled a large area from the early A.D. 800s to the mid-1200s.

Colonial Era Europeans began to establish colonies in Southeast Asia in the 1500s. By the end of the 1800s, the Portuguese, British, Dutch, French, and Spanish controlled most of the region. The United States won control of the Philippines from Spain after the Spanish-American War in 1898. Just Siam (sy-AM), now called Thailand, remained independent.

Japan invaded and occupied most of Southeast Asia during World War II. After Japan was defeated in 1945, the United States granted the Philippines independence a year later. European countries tried to

400 • Chapter 18

Section 2

Objectives
1. Analyze important events in the history of Southeast Asia.
2. Describe the people and culture of Southeast Asia today.

FOCUS

Bellringer

Copy the following instructions onto the chalkboard: *Why may it be difficult for countries made up of many islands to maintain a peaceful union? Why may having many islands be beneficial? Write down two possible answers for each question.* Allow students time to write their responses. Discuss students' answers. Tell students that in Section 2 they will learn more about the people and cultures of Southeast Asia.

Building Vocabulary

Write the key term **refugees** on the chalkboard. Point out to students that *refuge,* the root of the word, means "a safe place." Select a volunteer to locate and read aloud the meaning of *refugees.* Point out the relationship between the meaning of *refugees* and the meaning of *refuge.*

regain control of their colonies in the region. Some Southeast Asians decided to fight for independence. One of the bloodiest wars was in French Indochina. The French finally left in 1954. Their former colonies of Vietnam, Laos, and Cambodia became independent. By the mid-1960s, European rule had ended in most of the region.

Modern Era Unfortunately, fighting did not end in some countries when the Europeans left. Vietnam split into two countries. In the 1960s the United States sent troops to defend South Vietnam against communist North Vietnam. Civil wars also raged in Laos and Cambodia. In 1975, communist forces took power in all the countries. As communism continued to spread throughout the region, North and South Vietnam were then united into one country.

The region's wars caused terrible destruction. Millions died, including more than 50,000 Americans. About 1 million Vietnamese **refugees** tried to escape the communist takeover in South Vietnam. Refugees are people who flee their own country, usually for economic or political reasons. Many refugees from the region came to the United States.

In Cambodia more than 1 million people died under a cruel communist government. That government ruled from 1975 to 1978. Then Vietnam invaded Cambodia in 1978, sparking another conflict. That war continued off and on until the mid-1990s. Many Cambodian refugees fled to Thailand.

Communists and other groups also fought against governments in the Philippines, Indonesia, and Malaysia. In 1975 Indonesia invaded the former Portuguese

Linking Past to Present
The Khmer Rouge and Refugees

In the 1970s the Khmer Rouge regime in Cambodia attempted to establish an agrarian society based on Marxism. Its leaders' strategy included the systematic destruction of both the traditional rural culture and the Western-influenced culture of the country's cities. More than 1 million Cambodians died during the four years of Khmer Rouge domination.

Thousands of people fled Cambodia attempting to escape the regime. Many eventually made it to the United States after spending years in Thailand's refugee camps.

Continued political unrest in the 1980s resulted in the migration of more than 500,000 additional Cambodians to Thailand. Many of these refugees eventually settled elsewhere, such as in France or in the United States.

Discussion: Lead a class discussion that addresses the following questions: Under what conditions would you seek refuge in another country? Do you feel other countries have a responsibility toward people seeking refuge? Why or why not? If so, to what extent?

Southeast Asia • 401

TEACH

Teaching Objective 1

LEVEL 1: (Suggested time: 20 min.) Copy the following graphic organizer onto the chalkboard, omitting the blue answers. Ask students to fill it in to show the progression of influences on Southeast Asia. **ESOL**

INFLUENCES ON SOUTHEAST ASIA

Settlers from China and India → Khmer Empire → Europeans → Various governments (communist, democratic, etc.)

LEVELS 2 AND 3: (Suggested time: 45 min.) Give students an outline map of Southeast Asia. Have students create a symbol for each of the influences identified in the graphic organizer in the previous activity. Have students connect their symbols with arrows to demonstrate the directions from which each influence advanced. Then have students present a brief oral report to the class on the history of movements to Southeast Asia, using their map as a visual aid.

GLOBAL PERSPECTIVES

The Era of Smoke

Political unrest in East Timor was not the only challenge facing Indonesia in the late 1990s. In 1997 uncontrolled fires began burning in parts of Indonesia, destroying up to 17,600 square miles (45,580 sq km) of forest. Smog settled over Borneo and Sumatra, in what is known there as "the era of smoke."

Government regulations to prevent fires went unenforced. For example, some logging practices resulted in dry and flammable tracts of forest, and plantation owners regularly burned land to clear it.

The problem has continued into the 2000s. Some environmental organizations have begun to pressure Indonesia to enforce the laws more strictly. The government has threatened to revoke logging licenses if the fires continue.

Activity: Have students conduct research on the 1997 fires in Indonesia.

internet connect

GO TO: **go.hrw.com**
KEYWORD: **SK5 CH18**
FOR: **Web sites about current events in Indonesia**

colony of East Timor. The East Timorese demanded independence. However, the Indonesian military kept a tight grip on the region. The people of East Timor voted for independence in 1999. East Timor then plunged again into violence. The United Nations sent troops to restore peace and manage the area before independence was achieved.

Governments The region's countries have had different kinds of governments. Many have been ruled by dictators. Some countries, such as the Philippines and Indonesia, now have governments elected by the people.

In other countries, the people still have little say in their government. For example, Myanmar is ruled by a military government. That government has jailed and even killed its opponents. Vietnam and Laos are still ruled by Communist governments. Only recently have Indonesians been allowed to vote in free elections. In some countries, such as Singapore, the same party always wins elections.

✓ **READING CHECK:** (*Places and Regions*) What were some key events in Southeast Asian history? 1500s—Europeans established colonies and began to control regions; World War II—Japan invaded; mid 1960s—European rule had mostly ended, Vietnam War, civil wars in Laos and Cambodia

Culture

The populations of most countries in Southeast Asia are very diverse. This is because many different peoples have moved to the area over time. Today, for example, nearly 70 percent of the people in Myanmar are Burmese. However, Chinese, Asian Indians, and many other ethnic groups also live there.

(**Place**) The Shwedagon Pagoda is a beautiful Buddhist shrine in Yangon, Myanmar. Pagodas are important parts of a Buddhist temple complex.

402 • Chapter 18

Teaching Objective 2

LEVEL 1: (Suggested time: 30 min.) Call students' attention to the characteristics of the people and cultures of Southeast Asia that are discussed throughout this section. Call on students to take turns reading aloud the parts of the section that describe these attributes of human geography, while a volunteer lists them on the chalkboard.
ESOL, LS **AUDITORY-MUSICAL**

LEVEL 2: (Suggested time: 25 min.) Have each student design a cover for a magazine titled *Southeast Asia Today*. Students' covers should reflect the information covered in this section. Encourage students to use drawings and pictures as well as a variety of type sizes to distinguish items of greater and lesser interest. LS **VISUAL-SPATIAL**

LEVEL 3: (Suggested time: 30 min.) Have students write an article for a magazine titled *Southeast Asia Today*. Encourage students to relate the region's history and culture to life there today. LS **VERBAL-LINGUISTIC**

Many ethnic Chinese live in the largest cities of most Southeast Asian countries. In Singapore they are a majority of the population—more than 75 percent. Singapore is a tiny country at the tip of the Malay Peninsula.

Languages and Religions The peoples of Southeast Asia speak many different languages. For example, in the former Dutch colony of Indonesia, most people speak Bahasa Indonesia. However, Javanese, other local dialects, English, and Dutch are also spoken there. European and Chinese languages are spoken in many other countries.

In addition, Indians, Chinese, Arab traders, and Europeans brought different religions to the region. For example, Hinduism is practiced in the region's Indian communities. However, Buddhism is the most common religion in the mainland countries today. Islam is the major religion in Malaysia, Brunei, and Indonesia. In fact, Indonesia has the largest Islamic population in the world. Nearly 90 percent of its more than 234 million people are Muslim.

Christians are a minority in most of the former European colonies. However, more than 80 percent of people in the Philippines, a former Spanish colony, are Roman Catholic.

Food Southeast Asian foods have been influenced by Chinese, South Asian, and European cooking styles. There are many spicy, mild, and sweet varieties. Rice is the most important food in nearly all of the countries. It is served with many other foods and spices, such as curries and chili peppers. Coconut is also important. It is served as a separate dish or used as an ingredient in other foods.

Women in Laos sprinkle water on Buddhist monks during a New Year festival. This custom symbolizes the washing away of the old year.
Interpreting the Visual Record
What kinds of clothes are the monks wearing?

✔ **READING CHECK:** (*Human Systems*) How have migration and cultural borrowing influenced the region's culture? great cultural diversity, many languages spoken; religions practiced; foods reflect influence of many different regions

go.hrw.com
Homework Practice Online
Keyword: SK5 HP18

Section Review 2

Define and explain: refugees

Working with Sketch Maps On the map you created in Section 1, label the region's countries, Angkor, and Timor. In a box in the margin, describe the recent history of East Timor.

Reading for the Main Idea

1. (*Places and Regions*) What was the Khmer Empire?
2. (*Human Systems*) How did Europeans influence the region's history and culture?

Critical Thinking

3. **Drawing Inferences and Conclusions** Why do you think European countries wanted to regain their Southeast Asian colonies following World War II?
4. **Finding the Main Idea** What religion is most common in the mainland countries? in the island countries?

Organizing What You Know

5. **Sequencing** Copy the following time line. Use it to identify important people, years, periods, and events in Southeast Asia's history.

```
+----------------------------------------------+
A.D. 800                                    2000
```

Southeast Asia • 403

Section 3 Mainland Southeast Asia Today

Read to Discover
1. Where do people in the mainland countries live today?
2. What are the economies of the mainland countries like?

Vocabulary
klongs

Places
Bangkok
Yangon
Hanoi
Ho Chi Minh City
Chao Phraya River
Irrawaddy River
Hong (Red) River
Vientiane
Phnom Penh

People
Aung San Suu Kyi

Reading Strategy

READING ORGANIZER Before you read this section, draw a large five-pointed star on a sheet of paper. As you read, write what you learn about Vietnam, Laos, Cambodia, Thailand, and Myanmar in the space created by the points. In the center, write the characteristics all the countries share.

People and Cities

Most mainland Southeast Asians today live in rural areas. Many are farmers in fertile river valleys and deltas. Fewer people live in remote hill and mountain villages.

However, the region's cities have been growing rapidly. People are moving to urban areas to look for work. The cities have many businesses, services, and opportunities that are not found in rural areas. Many of the cities today are crowded, smoggy, and noisy.

Look at the chapter map. You will find that the largest cities are located along major rivers. Location near rivers places these cities near important rice-growing areas. Access to rivers also makes them key

A Vietnamese man sells incense sticks in Ho Chi Minh City.

404 Chapter 18

Section 3

Objectives
1. Identify the areas where mainland Southeast Asians live.
2. Describe the economies of the mainland countries.

FOCUS

Bellringer
Copy the following question and instruction onto the chalkboard: *Would you rather live in a rural area or in the city? Write your answer and a few sentences explaining why in your notebook.* Allow students time to write their responses. Explain to students that most mainland Southeast Asians live in rural areas. Tell students that in Section 3 they will learn more about where people of mainland Southeast Asia live.

Building Vocabulary
Write the term **klongs** on the chalkboard. Ask a volunteer to locate the term and to read aloud its definition. Point out that *klongs* is a Thai word. Then ask students to suggest words we use in English to describe the same thing. (Possible answers: canal, waterway, aqueduct, drainpipe, sewer tunnel)

shipping centers for farm and factory products. The largest cities are Bangkok, Yangon, Hanoi, and Ho Chi Minh City.

Bangkok The mainland's largest city is Bangkok, Thailand's capital. Bangkok lies near the mouth of the Chao Phraya (chow PRY-uh) River. More than 7 million people live there. Much of Bangkok is connected by **klongs**, or canals. The klongs are used for transportation and for selling and shipping goods. They also drain water from the city.

Other Cities The region's second-largest city is Yangon, formerly known as Rangoon. It is Myanmar's capital and major seaport. The city is located in the Irrawaddy River delta on the coast of the Andaman Sea. To the east, Vietnam's largest cities are also located in major river deltas. The capital, Hanoi (ha-NOY), is located in the Hong (Red) River delta in the north. Ho Chi Minh City is located in the Mekong River delta in the south. Ho Chi Minh City was once known as Saigon and was South Vietnam's capital. Today it is an important seaport and business center with more than 4.6 million people.

▲ **Movement** Boat traffic can be heavy along Bangkok's *klongs*. These canals have been part of the city's transportation system for centuries.

✓ **READING CHECK:** (*Places and Regions*) Where do most people in mainland Southeast Asia live today and why? mostly in rural areas; because many are farmers and need access to fertile river valleys and deltas

Economy

War, bad governments, and other problems have slowed progress in most of the mainland countries. However, rich resources could make the future brighter for the people there.

Vietnam Vietnam's economy has been slowly recovering since the end of the war in 1975. In recent years, the Communist government has begun moving from a command economy to a more market-oriented one. Some people are now allowed to own private businesses. Most Vietnamese remain farmers.

Most of Vietnam's factories, coal, oil, and other resources are in the north. The Hong and Mekong River deltas are major farming areas. Rice is the most important crop and food. In many places it is planted twice each year.

Mainland Southeast Asia

Country	Population/ Growth Rate	Life Expectancy	Literacy Rate	Per Capita GDP
Cambodia	13,124,764 1.8%	55, male 60, female	70%	$1,500
Laos	9,921,545 2.5%	52, male 66, female	53%	$1,700
Myanmar	42,510,537 0.5%	54, male 57, female	83%	$1,500
Thailand	64,265,276 0.9%	71, male 73, female	96%	$6,900
Vietnam	81,624,716 1.3%	67, male 72, female	94%	$2,250
United States	290,342,554 0.9%	74, male 80, female	97%	$37,600

Source: Central Intelligence Agency, *The World Factbook 2003*

Interpreting the Chart According to the data in the chart, which country in the region is the most economically developed?

EYE ON EARTH

Let's Go to Laos!
Until recently, very little was known about Laos. The country's geography and politics largely isolated it from the outside world. However, in recent years the Communist government has been trying to attract foreign travelers to boost Laos's economy. As a result, more tourists are visiting the country.

Some visitors journey to a lovely valley hidden deep in the forest. The only way to reach the valley is by sailing along Hin Boun River, which flows into the valley through a cave about 6 miles (10 km) long. Other tourists prefer to visit cultural sites, such as the Pak Ou caves. Visitors to the caves find thousands of Buddha statues that were moved there more than 400 years ago to protect them from invaders.

Activity: Have students conduct research on the Internet for information on interesting sites in Laos. Then have students create travel fliers featuring them.

☑ **internet** connect

GO TO: **go.hrw.com**
KEYWORD: **SK5 CH18**
FOR: **Web sites about traveling to Laos**

◄ **Chart Answer**

Thailand

TEACH

Teaching Objective 1
ALL LEVELS: (Suggested time: 20 min.) Copy the following graphic organizer onto the chalkboard, omitting the blue answers. Have students list descriptions of life in mainland Southeast Asia. **ESOL**

Teaching Objective 2
ALL LEVELS: (Suggested time: 30 min.) Before class, prepare large cutouts of Vietnam, Laos, Cambodia, Thailand, and Myanmar. Do not label them. Organize the class into five groups and give each group one of the cutouts. Have each group identify its country and list three facts about its economy on the cutout. Then allow groups to assemble their cutouts to configure a map of Southeast Asia. Each group should report its facts to the class while placing its cutout on the chalkboard.
ESOL, COOPERATIVE LEARNING

Rural Life	Both	Urban Life
• in remote hill and mountain villages • most people live here	• near major rivers • near rice-growing areas	• has businesses • crowded, smoggy, noisy • important shipping areas

Answers to Section 3 Review

Define For definition and identification, see the glossary and index.

Working with Sketch Maps region's largest city, Bangkok, is Thailand's capital; lies near mouth of Chao Phraya River; connected by *klongs*

Reading for the Main Idea

1. rural areas, particularly in fertile river valleys and deltas; because most are farmers **(NGS 4)**

2. to look for work **(NGS 9)**

3. Thailand; because of its rich natural resources **(NGS 4)**

Critical Thinking

4. war, nondemocratic governments, and other political problems **(NGS 18)**

Organizing What You Know

5. Bangkok—mainland's largest city, *klongs;* Yangon—Myanmar's capital, major seaport; Hanoi—Vietnam's capital, in Hong Delta; Ho Chi Minh City—formerly Saigon, important seaport and business center, Mekong Delta; Vientiane—Laos's capital; Phnom Penh—Cambodia's capital, in southern rice-growing area

Biography Answer ▶

by refusing to give up her fight for democracy, even when punished

---

BIOGRAPHY

Aung San Suu Kyi
(1945–)

Character Trait: Integrity

As a human rights advocate in her native Myanmar, Aung San Suu Kyi has dedicated her life to improving the lives of her people. In 1990, Myanmar's military government refused to give up power when Suu Kyi's party won control of the country's parliament. For her opposition to military rule, the government has placed Suu Kyi under house arrest several times. In 1991, she was awarded the Nobel Peace Prize for her efforts to bring democracy to Myanmar. Today, Suu Kyi continues to fight for democratic reform and free elections.

How has Aung San Suu Kyi shown integrity?

Laos This mountainous, landlocked country has few good roads, no railroads, and few telephones and televisions. Only some cities have electricity. The economy is mostly traditional—most people are subsistence farmers. They produce just enough food for themselves and their families. The Communist government in Vientiane (vyen-TYAHN), the capital, has also recently begun allowing more economic freedom.

Cambodia Economic progress in Cambodia has been particularly slow because of war and political problems. Agriculture is the most important part of the economy. The capital and largest city, Phnom Penh (puh-NAWM PEN), is located along the Mekong River. It lies in Cambodia's southern rice-growing area.

Thailand Thailand's economy has had problems but is the strongest of the mainland countries. This is partly because Thailand has rich resources. These resources include timber, natural rubber, seafood, rice, many minerals, and gems. Factories produce computers and electronics. Many Thai operate small businesses. Tourism is also important.

Myanmar This former British colony is also called Burma. It gained independence in 1948 and was officially renamed Myanmar in 1989. It has rich resources, including copper, tin, iron ore, timber, rubber, and oil. However, a harsh military government has limited political freedom. This has slowed economic progress.

✓ **READING CHECK:** (*Places and Regions*) What are the mainland economies like?

some moving from traditional or command to market; all suffering from problems, including war, political problems

go.hrw.com **Homework Practice Online**
Keyword: SK5 HP18

Section Review 3

Define or identify: *klongs*, Aung San Suu Kyi

Working with Sketch Maps On the map you created in Section 2, label Bangkok, Yangon, Hanoi, Ho Chi Minh City, Chao Phraya River, Irrawaddy River, Hong (Red) River, Vientiane, and Phnom Penh. Describe the mainland's largest city.

Reading for the Main Idea

1. (*Places and Regions*) Where do most mainland Southeast Asians live and why?

2. (*Human Systems*) Why are many people moving to cities?

3. (*Places and Regions*) Which country has the strongest economy and why?

Critical Thinking

4. **Finding the Main Idea** What kinds of problems appear to have slowed economic progress in the region?

Organizing What You Know

5. **Summarizing** Copy the following graphic organizer. Use it to describe the mainland's major cities. In each of its six circles, write the name of a city. In the circles, write important facts about the cities.

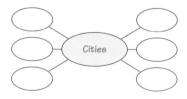

Cities

CLOSE

Take a poll: Would students rather live in rural or urban areas of Southeast Asia? Why? Compare students' answers with the initial preferences indicated in the section opener.

REVIEW, ASSESS, RETEACH

Have students complete the Section Review. Then have students imagine they are writing a letter to a pen pal in mainland Southeast Asia. Have them ask questions that address the main ideas of the section. Then have students trade their letters with a partner and answer their partner's questions. **COOPERATIVE LEARNING, [LS] VERBAL-LINGUISTIC**

Have students complete Main Idea Activity S3. Then have students write three facts related to the Read to Discover questions at the beginning of the section. When complete, select volunteers to share their facts with the class. **ESOL**

EXTEND

Have interested students conduct research on King Mongkut of Thailand, who kept Thailand from being colonized. Then have them compare what they have learned to any of the movies, plays, or books about him and share their findings with the class. **BLOCK SCHEDULING**

Section 4 Island Southeast Asia Today

Read to Discover
1. What are the major cities of the island countries?
2. What are the economies of the island countries like?

Vocabulary
kampongs
sultan

Places
Jakarta   Luzon
Manila   Bali
Kuala Lumpur

Reading Strategy

READING ORGANIZER Before you read, create a chart with three columns. Label the columns Country, Major City, and Resources. As you read this section, write what you learn about Indonesia, the Philippines, Singapore, Malaysia, and Brunei on your chart.

SECTION 4 RESOURCES

Reproducible
- Lecture Notes, Section 4
- Know It Notes S4
- Interdisciplinary Activity for the Middle Grades 31

Technology
- One-Stop Planner CD–ROM Lesson 18.4
- Music of the World Audio CD Program, Selection 22
- Homework Practice Online
- HRW Go site

Reinforcement, Review, and Assessment
- Daily Quiz 18.4
- Main Idea Activity S4
- English Audio Summary 18.4
- Spanish Audio Summary 18.4

People and Cities

Indonesia is the largest of the island countries and the world's fourth-most-populous country. The country's more than 17,000 islands were known as the Dutch East Indies until 1949. Malaysia, Singapore, and Brunei were British colonies. The British granted independence to Malaysia in 1963. Singapore split from Malaysia in 1965. In 1984 Brunei became the region's last European colony to gain independence. As you have read, the Philippines gained independence from the United States in 1946. More than 7,000 islands make up that country.

Many people live in rural areas in the island countries. However, the island countries are more urbanized than the mainland countries. As on the mainland, many people are moving to cities in search of jobs. One country, Singapore, is simply a large city on a small island.

Modern skyscrapers tower over colonial-era buildings in Singapore. The city has one of the world's busiest ports.

Interpreting the Visual Record *Place*
What does Singapore's architecture tell you about its economy and culture?

▼

Southeast Asia • 407

◄ **Visual Record Answer**
good economy, modern western influence

Section 4

Objectives
1. Name the major cities of the island countries of Southeast Asia.
2. Describe the economies of the island countries of Southeast Asia.

FOCUS

Bellringer
Copy the following instructions onto the chalkboard: *Indonesia's national motto is "The many are one." Write the reasons you think this is appropriate for a country comprised of more than 7,000 individual islands.* Allow students to write their responses. Lead a discussion based on students' answers. Tell students that in Section 4 they will learn more about the people and culture of Indonesia and the other island countries of Southeast Asia.

Building Vocabulary
Write **kampongs** and **sultan** on the chalkboard and have volunteers locate and read the definitions. Then have students write sentences using the words. Select volunteers to share their sentences with the class.

DAILY LIFE

Watch Your Step!

Singapore's very strict government is devoted to preserving order. Visitors must follow the rules carefully, or they will be punished. Some punishable offenses include driving without a seatbelt, smuggling chewing gum into the country, and not flushing toilets in public buildings. In addition to paying a fine, people caught littering must undergo counseling.

Because Singapore's government operates much like an efficiently run corporation, the country has been referred to as a nation-corporation. For the tourist willing to follow the rules, Singapore offers a wide range of attractions, from lively festivals and parades to a nighttime cable-car ride down a mountain. There are also many dining options. The city's low crime rate helps make Singapore a popular tourist destination.

Connecting to Art

Answers

1. in ancient societies, including Greece, Rome, China, and India
2. lasts all night, is accompanied by the traditional music of Java

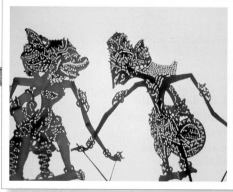

Wayang puppets

Puppetry is an art form with roots in ancient civilizations, including Greece, Rome, China, and India. On the Indonesian island of Java, one of the world's great puppet traditions is known as *wayang*. This shadow puppet theater still entertains audiences.

Wayang puppets are beautiful works of art. The puppets are made from thin sheets of painted leather. They are pierced with holes so that light can shine through them. Then they are mounted on sticks. The performance takes place behind a screen. A light source is placed behind the puppets. The puppet's shadows fall on the screen and are visible to the audience on the other side.

Wayang performances tell stories from the *Ramayana* and the *Mahabharata*. These are two long poems of the Hindu religion. Hinduism came to Java from India hundreds of years ago. The puppets play the parts of gods, heroes, and villains. A performance usually lasts all night and includes the traditional music of Java. The music is played by an orchestra that includes gongs and other traditional instruments.

Over the years, *wayang* artists have developed other types of puppets. Some puppets are wooden forms. A new generation of artists is even creating computerized stories for *wayang* theater.

Understanding What You Read
1. Where did puppetry originate?
2. What is a *wayang* performance like?

Jakarta The region's largest city is Jakarta, Indonesia's capital. More than 11 million people live there. It is located on Java, which is by far Indonesia's most populous island. Many Indonesians live in **kampongs** around Jakarta. A kampong is a traditional village. It has also become the term for the crowded slums around large cities.

Singapore If you traveled from Jakarta to Singapore, you would find two very different cities. Singapore is one of the most modern and cleanest cities in the world. Crime rates also are very low. How has Singapore accomplished this?

Its government is very strict. For example, fines for littering are stiff. People caught transporting illegal drugs can be executed. The government even bans chewing gum and certain movies and music.

TEACH

Teaching Objective 1

LEVEL 1: (Suggested time: 20 min.) Copy the following graphic organizer onto the chalkboard, omitting the blue answers. Use it to help students identify major cities and to list at least one feature of each city. **ESOL**

MAJOR CITY	IMPORTANT FEATURE
Jakarta	largest city, many kampongs
Singapore	modern, clean, low crime rate, strict laws
Manila	capital of Philippines, major seaport
Kuala Lumpur	Malaysia's capital, cultural and business center

LEVELS 2 AND 3: Singapore is a colonial city. The region's other major cities also have been affected by colonialism. Organize students into four groups. Assign each of the groups Singapore, Jakarta, Manila, or Kuala Lumpur. Have groups conduct research on how colonizers affected the assigned city's development. Then have groups conduct a panel discussion to compare their results. You may want to allow extra time for this activity. **COOPERATIVE LEARNING**

Is the lack of some individual freedoms a good trade-off for less crime, a clean city, and a strong economy? Some people in Singapore say yes. Others believe Singapore can be just as successful with less government control.

Other Cities The region's other large cities include Manila and Kuala Lumpur. More than 10 million people live in Manila, the capital of the Philippines. The city is a major seaport and industrial center on Luzon. Luzon is the country's largest and most populated island.

Kuala Lumpur is Malaysia's capital as well as its cultural, business, and transportation center. It is a modern city with two of the world's tallest buildings, the twin Petronas Towers.

✓ **READING CHECK:** *Places and Regions* What are some of the major cities of the island countries?

Jakarta, Singapore, Manila, Kuala Lumpur

Economy

The economies of the island countries grew rapidly until the mid-1990s. Then economic and political problems slowed growth for a while. However, rich resources are helping the economies there to recover. In addition, wages and labor costs are low in many of the countries. This means that companies there can manufacture many products more cheaply for export.

Indonesia Europeans once called Indonesia the Spice Islands because of its cinnamon, pepper, and nutmeg. Today, its rich resources include natural rubber, oil, natural gas, and timber. Indonesia also has good farmlands for rice and other crops. Busy factories turn out clothing, electronics, and furniture. Some islands, such as Bali, are popular with tourists.

Island Southeast Asia

Country	Population/ Growth Rate	Life Expectancy	Literacy Rate	Per Capita GDP
Brunei	358,098 / 2.1%	71, male / 76, female	92%	$18,600
Indonesia	234,893,453 / 1.5%	66, male / 71, female	88%	$3,100
Malaysia	23,092,940 / 1.8%	69, male / 74, female	89%	$9,300
Philippines	84,619,974 / 1.9%	66, male / 72, female	96%	$4,200
Singapore	4,608,595 / 1.7%	77, male / 83, female	93%	$24,000
United States	290,342,554 / 0.9%	74, male / 80, female	97%	$37,600

Source: Central Intelligence Agency, *The World Factbook 2003*

Interpreting the Chart According to the chart, which country's economic development is closest to that of the United States?

Human-Environment Interaction
Farming is an important economic activity in the Philippines. In mountain areas, farmers plant rice and other crops in terraced fields. These flat terraces hold water and slow erosion along mountainsides.

Southeast Asia • 409

Teaching Objective 2

LEVEL 1: (Suggested time: 30 min.) Organize the class into five groups and assign each group one of the following countries: Indonesia, the Philippines, Singapore, Malaysia, or Brunei. Have each group prepare a list of facts about the economy of its country. When complete, have students compare the economic organization of the nations.
ESOL COOPERATIVE LEARNING

LEVELS 2 AND 3: (Suggested time: 30 min.) Organize the class into groups of five and assign each group one of the countries in this section. Have each group categorize each fact compiled in the Level 1 lesson that pertains to its assigned country as positive or negative. Then have each group write a public service announcement accentuating positive aspects and downplaying negative circumstances of its country's economic situation. Have groups present their announcement to the class, then discuss the techniques each group used to make its country's economy seem bright.
COOPERATIVE LEARNING

FOOD FESTIVAL

Cha Thai (Thai Iced Tea)

Here is a refreshing version of iced tea from Thailand. Place 8 decaffeinated black tea bags in a teapot. Pour 4 cups boiling water over the tea. Let steep for 5 minutes. Fill four 10 oz. glasses with ice cubes; then fill two thirds full with tea. Into each glass, stir 2 tbs evaporated milk and a dash of ground cinnamon. Sweeten to taste. Note that this recipe serves four. Be prepared to increase the recipe's proportions to serve your entire class.

Dancers attract tourists to the island of Bali. Indonesia has many different dance styles. This *Barong* dancer uses her hands, arms, and eyes to tell a traditional story.

Electronics and technology products are increasingly important to the region's economies. This Filipino is working at a semiconductor manufacturing plant.

Large areas of Indonesia's tropical rain forests are often burned for farming. Smoke from the fires can spread for hundreds of miles. The smoke sometimes blots out sunlight, smothering cities in haze.

The Philippines The Philippines is mostly an agricultural country today. A big problem is the gap between rich and poor Filipinos. A few very rich Filipinos control most of the land and industries. Most farmers are poor and own no land.

The economy has improved in recent years. Companies sell many electronics and clothing products to overseas customers, particularly in the United States. The country also has rich resources, including tropical forests, copper, gold, silver, and oil. Farmers grow sugarcane, rice, corn, coconuts, and tropical fruits.

Singapore Singapore is by far the most economically developed country in all of Southeast Asia. The British founded the city at the tip of the Malay Peninsula in 1819. This location along major shipping routes helped make Singapore rich. Goods are stored there before they are shipped to their final stop. In addition, many foreign companies have opened banks, offices, and high-technology industries there.

Malaysia Malaysia is made up of two parts. The largest part lies on the southern Malay Peninsula. The second part lies on the northern portion of Borneo. Well-educated workers and rich resources make Malaysia's future look bright. The country produces natural rubber, electronics, automobiles, oil, and timber. The government is trying to attract more high-technology companies to the country. Malaysia is also the world's leading producer of palm oil.

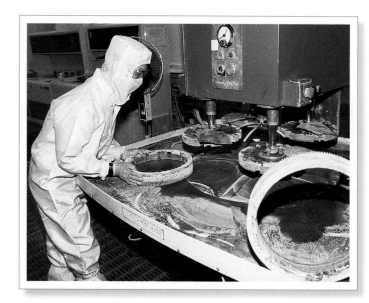

►**ASSIGNMENT:** Have students prepare for an interview for the position of economic adviser to one of the countries in the Southeast Asian islands. Students should research and describe how the factors of production have influenced the country's economic history and recommend steps for improving the economy. Have students write notes to use for interviews in which they demonstrate their expertise.

TEACHER TO TEACHER

Sandra Rojas of Commerce City, Colorado, suggests this activity to help students learn about the islands of Southeast Asia. Have each student conduct research as if he or she were planning a trip around the Southeast Asian islands. Explain to students that they should plan as if they were going to stay with local people. They should, therefore, study local customs. Students should prepare a presentation for the class in which they show their intended route on a map and display drawings and pictures that show the sights they intend to see. They should also describe how they might adjust their ways of dressing, eating, or socializing in order to fit in with their host families.

Brunei Large deposits of oil have made Brunei rich. This small country on the island of Borneo is ruled by a sultan. A sultan is the supreme ruler of a Muslim country. Brunei shares the island of Borneo with Indonesia and Malaysia.

✔ READING CHECK: (Places and Regions) How do rich resources affect the economies of the island countries?

They are helping countries regain the prosperity of the mid-1990s.

▲
Human-Environment Interaction
This beautiful mosque in Brunei's capital reflects the country's oil wealth. Money from oil and natural gas production pays for many social services there.

Section Review 4

Define and explain: kampongs, sultan

Working with Sketch Maps On the map you created in Section 3, label Jakarta, Manila, Kuala Lumpur, Luzon, and Bali. In a box in the margin, identify the most heavily populated islands in Indonesia and the Philippines.

Reading for the Main Idea

1. (Places and Regions) What is the region's largest city? What is the importance of Manila and Kuala Lumpur to their countries?

2. (Places and Regions) Why was Indonesia once called the Spice Islands? What European country once controlled nearly all of Indonesia?

Homework Practice Online
Keyword: SK5 HP18

Critical Thinking

3. **Analyzing Information** Some Singaporeans say that limiting some individual freedoms is a good trade-off for less crime and a better economy. Do you agree? Why or why not?

4. **Comparing/Contrasting** How have Singapore and Brunei become rich countries?

Organizing What You Know

5. **Summarizing** Copy the following graphic organizer. Use it to list the nine Southeast Asian countries that are former European colonies. Next to each country's name, write the name of the European country that once controlled it.

Southeast Asian country	European colonial power

Southeast Asia • 411

Answers to Section 4 Review

Define For definitions, see the glossary.

Working with Sketch Maps Java and Luzon are the most heavily populated islands.

Reading for the Main Idea

1. Jakarta; capital cities, centers of industry, commerce, and transportation (NGS 4)

2. because of the many spices there; the Netherlands (NGS 4)

Critical Thinking

3. Answers will vary, but students should demonstrate knowledge of the government's strict policies.

4. Singapore—located on major shipping route, home to many foreign companies; Brunei—oil companies

Organizing What You Know

5. Cambodia, Laos, Vietnam—France; Brunei, Malaysia, Myanmar, Singapore—Britain; Indonesia—the Netherlands (East Timor—Portugal); Philippines—Spain, then United States; Thailand—independent

CLOSE

Ask each student to write down one reason why it is important to know about each of the island groups of Southeast Asia. Call on students to share their responses. Compile students' answers on the chalkboard.

Have students complete Main Idea Activity S4. Then have students draw and label pictures to illustrate important facts about the people, cities, and economies of the Southeast Asian islands. **ESOL**

REVIEW, ASSESS, RETEACH

Have students complete the Section Review. Then have students examine the illustrations in the section. Ask students to write a question about each illustration. Collect the questions and use them to lead a class discussion about the section. Then have students complete Daily Quiz 18.4.

EXTEND

Focus students' attention on the photo of the *Barong* dancer in this section. Have interested students conduct research on traditional music and dance styles of Bali and how they relate to Balinese society. Ask students to learn a basic dance using hand, arm, and eye movements and demonstrate it to the class. **BLOCK SCHEDULING,** **LS KINESTHETIC**

HISTORICAL GEOGRAPHY

Pribumi and *Keturunan*

As the colonial presence of the Dutch and Portuguese suggests, Indonesia has been a place where foreigners have mixed with the local people. Indonesians have terms to distinguish between indigenous people *(pribumi)* and outsiders *(keturunan)*. Before the Dutch and Portuguese arrived, Arab traders introduced Islam to the region. As a result, about 88 percent of the Indonesian people are Muslim. Hinduism and Buddhism were introduced even earlier.

More recently, an influx of Chinese immigrants has arrived, further complicating the ethnic mosaic of Indonesia. There may be as many as 6 million Chinese Indonesians. They are engaged heavily in commerce and are generally more prosperous than their fellow citizens. In 1998 this disparity in wealth led to some anti-Chinese demonstrations.

Activity: List in chronological order the arrival of each of the outside groups mentioned above. What enduring cultural elements did they contribute to Indonesia's culture?

➤ This Case Study Feature addresses National Geography Standards 5, 10, and 15.

CASE STUDY

MULTIETHNIC INDONESIA

Indonesia is a multiethnic country—a country with many different ethnic groups. The national motto of Indonesia is *Bhinneka Tunggal Ika,* which means "the many are one." This motto comes from the many different ethnic groups that live there.

More than 300 different ethnic groups live in Indonesia. Most of these groups speak their own language and have their own way of life. No single ethnic group holds a majority. The largest are the Javanese, Sundanese, Madurese, and Coastal Malays. The country also has many smaller ethnic groups, such as the Dayaks and the Balinese. Why does Indonesia have so many different ethnic groups? Part of the answer lies in the country's diverse physical geography.

Indonesia is a very large country. It is made up of more than 17,000 islands. About 228 million people live on these islands. Indonesia's islands, mountains, and dense rain forests have served as boundaries between different ethnic groups. Many small ethnic groups lived in isolation and had very little contact with other peoples. Over time, these groups developed their own cultures, languages, and ways of life.

The modern country of Indonesia has its roots in the early 1600s. About this time, Dutch traders built forts in the area. They wanted to protect the trade routes used by Dutch ships to transport spices and other goods. The Dutch remained an important force in the region until Indonesia became independent in 1949. The long history of

Movement Most Indonesians are related to the peoples of East Asia. However, in the eastern islands, most people are of Melanesian origin. Over the centuries, many Arabs, Indians, and Europeans have added to the country's ethnic diversity.

▼

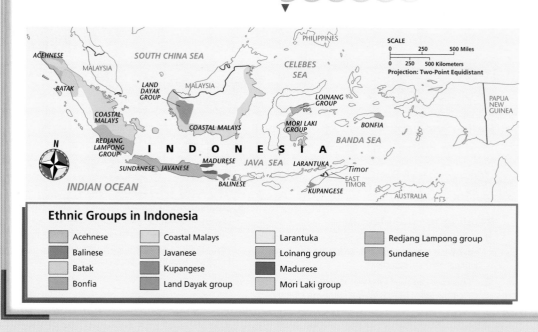

Ethnic Groups in Indonesia

- Acehnese
- Balinese
- Batak
- Bonfia
- Coastal Malays
- Javanese
- Kupangese
- Land Dayak group
- Larantuka
- Loinang group
- Madurese
- Mori Laki group
- Redjang Lampong group
- Sundanese

CASE STUDY

Setting the Scene

Indonesia is a good example of how physical and cultural factors can affect ethnic diversity. Because Indonesia is comprised of many different islands, physical isolation has resulted in many different ethnic groups. Of the more than 17,000 islands that make up Indonesia, at least 6,000 are inhabited. Cultural factors, such as language and a shared colonial history, have a unifying rather than a fragmenting effect. These factors are used by the central government to promote a national identity. The ongoing turmoil in East Timor, which erupted into violence in 1999, illustrates the difficulties the central government faces.

Building a Case

Have students read "Multiethnic Indonesia." Then conduct a classroom discussion about the multiethnic character of Indonesia. Use the following questions to guide the discussion: How many different ethnic groups are there in Indonesia? (more than 300) What are some of the larger ethnic groups? (Javanese, Sundanese, Madurese, and Coastal Malays) Now look at a detailed map of Indonesia. Show students that each of the ethnic groups listed in the text corresponds to an island (e.g., Javanese: Java; Balinese: Bali, and so on). Point out that island isolation leads to the development of different ethnic groups over time. How many different islands are there in Indonesia? (more than 17,000) Suggest that many unrecognized groups might exist.

◄ Place The Balinese are one of Indonesia's many ethnic groups. Unlike most other Indonesians, Hinduism is their main religion.

Dutch control helped unify the islands into the modern country of Indonesia.

In addition to this shared past, several other factors have helped unify Indonesia. For example, Indonesia's government has promoted the country's official language, Bahasa Indonesia. Although most Indonesians speak more than one language, Bahasa Indonesia is used in schools and government. The use of this language has been an important force in uniting the country. The government has also tried to develop a common Indonesian culture. It has promoted national holiday celebrations, education, popular art, and television and radio programs.

A shared history, a common education system, and an official language help give isolated ethnic groups an Indonesian identity. However, the country's multiethnic society still faces some important challenges. In certain parts of Indonesia, people want independence. For example, in 1999 people in East Timor voted for independence from Indonesia. This caused a great deal of unrest. Most people there supported the vote, but others did not. When some groups rioted, many Timorese left the area for their own safety. The Acehnese, an ethnic group on the island of Sumatra, have also been seeking independence.

Ethnic Groups in Indonesia

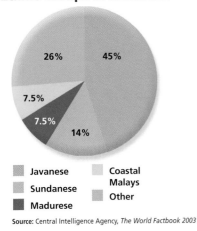

45%
26%
7.5%
7.5%
14%

- Javanese
- Sundanese
- Madurese
- Coastal Malays
- Other

Source: Central Intelligence Agency, *The World Factbook 2003*

Understanding What You Read

1. How diverse is Indonesia's society? What has helped to promote cooperation among the different ethnic groups that live in the country?

2. What are some important challenges facing Indonesia today?

Drawing Conclusions

Shift the discussion to focus on how such a diverse nation binds itself together. Highlight the role of the government in uniting the mosaic of peoples. What has the government done to foster a national identity in Indonesia? (It has promoted a common language, common education system, and national celebrations.) Point out as well that it has attempted to block regional autonomy. How has a shared history helped create an Indonesian identity? (There is a long history of Dutch control of Indonesia dating back to the 1600s.) Point out that the island of Timor was settled and controlled by the Portuguese—not the Dutch. Suggest that having had a different colonizer contributed to a desire on the part of the Timorese for independence.

Going Further: Thinking Critically

The Pacific has many islands spread out over a large area. Organize the students into small groups and provide each group with an atlas. Have students answer the following questions:
- How many islands belong to France? the United States? What other countries have possessions in the Pacific?
- How many independent countries can you find?
- If you were drawing national boundaries based only on the groupings of islands regardless of colonial history, how might the national boundaries be different?
- How might the colonizing nations and the physical geography have influenced the number of different ethnic groups in the Pacific?

Define and Identify

For definitions and identifications, see the glossary and index.

Review the Main Ideas

8. Indochina and Malay Peninsulas, Malay Archipelago, and the Philippines (NGS 4)

9. northern Myanmar (NGS 4)

10. tin and iron ore

11. the Khmer

12. war, undemocratic governments, political problems (NGS 4)

13. coal and oil (NGS 4)

14. through their colonies in the region (NGS 9)

15. more urbanized than the mainland

16. Traders, invaders, and other people have brought different cultures, including languages.

Think Critically

17. located near major rice-growing areas, good locations for shipping goods (NGS 12)

18. European, Chinese, and Indian

19. Philippines—United States granted independence in 1946; Vietnam—long war that ended in 1954 pushed French out

20. mainland—wet and dry seasons; islands—dry throughout year; typhoons, earthquakes, volcanic eruptions

21. Labor costs are low, keeping manufacturing costs low and exporting less expensive.

Review and Practice

Define and Identify

Identify each of the following:

1. mainland
2. archipelagos
3. refugees
4. *klongs*
5. Aung San Suu Kyi
6. kampongs
7. sultan

Review the Main Ideas

8. What peninsulas and archipelagos make up Southeast Asia?

9. Where will you find the highest mountains in Southeast Asia?

10. What mineral resources are found in Southeast Asia?

11. Which early society in Southeast Asia was based in Angkor?

12. What factors have slowed economic progress in mainland Southeast Asia?

13. What resources are important to the economy of Vietnam?

14. How did European countries influence Southeast Asia?

15. What is a common feature of the island countries in Southeast Asia?

16. Why do you think so many languages are spoken in Southeast Asia?

Think Critically

17. Drawing Inferences and Conclusions Why are some cities located near river deltas so large?

18. Finding the Main Idea What outside cultures have strongly influenced the development of Southeast Asian culture?

19. Analyzing Information How did the Philippines and Vietnam gain independence?

20. Finding the Main Idea How do the climates of mainland countries differ from those in the island countries? What natural disasters are a danger in the region?

21. Analyzing Information How do labor costs affect the island countries' economies?

Map Activity

22. On a separate sheet of paper, match the letters on the map with their correct labels.

Indochina Peninsula	Mekong River
Malay Peninsula	Timor
Malay Archipelago and the Philippines	Bangkok
Irian Jaya	Jakarta
Borneo	Manila

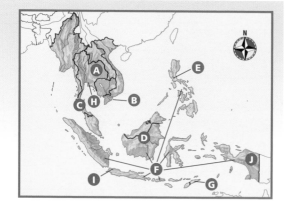

Map Activity

22. A. Indochina Peninsula

B. Mekong River

C. Malay Peninsula

D. Borneo

E. Manila

F. Malay Archipelago and the Philippines

G. Timor

H. Bangkok

I. Jakarta

J. Irian Jaya

Writing Activity

Imagine that you are an economic adviser for a poor Southeast Asian country. Write a one-paragraph summary explaining how some countries in the region built stronger economies. Use the report to suggest policies your chosen country might adopt to build its economy. Be sure to use standard grammar, spelling, sentence structure, and punctuation.

☑ internet connect

Internet Activity: go.hrw.com
KEYWORD: SK5 GT18

Choose a topic to explore about Southeast Asia:

- Explore an Indonesian rain forest.
- Learn about shadow puppets.
- See buildings of Southeast Asia.

Writing Activity

Check to see that students have included accurate information; most students will have focused on the strategies used to achieve Singapore's and Thailand's economic success. Details should be consistent with text information. Use Rubric 43, Writing to Persuade, to evaluate student work.

Interpreting Graphs

1. defense, education, health, and social welfare
2. health and social welfare
3. defense; social welfare
4. went from almost 50 percent to 35 percent

Analyzing Primary Sources

1. the sale of goods brought into the country illegally
2. used the army to seize smuggled goods
3. Myanmar has long borders with both India and Thailand.
4. North Korea

Social Studies Skills Practice

Interpreting Graphs

Study the graph below. Then answer the questions.

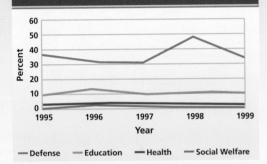

Government Spending in Myanmar

Source: International Monetary Fund

1. What four areas of government spending are shown in the graph?
2. In what two areas did government spending stay about the same?
3. In what area did the government spend the most? the least?
4. What percentage of government spending was devoted to defense during the period 1998–99?

Analyzing Primary Sources

Read the following quote by Cristina Pantoja-Hidalgo, a Filipino journalist who lived in Myanmar in the 1980s. Then answer the questions.

"Everything was available through the black market . . . But all these were underground. For example, if you owned a video shop, it was quite possible that the army would swoop upon you and would confiscate all your tapes. Burma is not as isolated as North Korea where the government is really efficient about keeping controls. The Burmese government cannot control the black market because of the common borders between India and Thailand . . . Thus, there's a great deal of smuggling."

1. What does Pantoja-Hidalgo mean by the term "black market"?
2. How did the government try to stop the black market?
3. Why was the government unable to control smuggling?
4. What country does Pantoja-Hidalgo say is more isolated than Burma?

CHAPTER 18 REVIEW AND ASSESSMENT RESOURCES

Reproducible
- Readings in World Geography, History, and Culture 72, 73, and 74
- Critical Thinking Activity 18
- Vocabulary Activity 18

Technology
- Chapter 18 Test Generator (on the One-Stop Planner)

- HRW Go site
- Audio CD Program, Chapter 18

Reinforcement, Review, and Assessment
- Chapter Review and Practice
- Chapter Summaries and Review

- Chapter 18 Test
- Chapter 18 Test for English Language Learners and Special-Needs Students
- Unit 7 Test
- Unit 7 Test for English Language Learners and Special-Needs Students

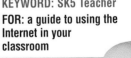

☑ internet connect

GO TO: go.hrw.com
KEYWORD: SK5 Teacher
FOR: a guide to using the Internet in your classroom

GEOGRAPHY SIDELIGHT

The islands of Indonesia are home to a vast variety of wildlife. Many of these species are endemic, or found nowhere else on Earth. For example, Komodo dragons, which can reach about 12 feet (4 m) in length, are found only on the Indonesian islands of Komodo and Rinca. To help protect these rare creatures, Indonesia has established a system of nature preserves and parks. For example, the Kulon Peninsula National Park on Java is home to the endangered Sumatran rhinoceros.

Indonesia's Mount Leuser National Park and Tanjung Puting Park are home to another endangered animal, the orangutan. Once found throughout Southeast Asia, the orangutan is now found only on the islands of Borneo and Sumatra. Indonesia's efforts to establish even more nature preserves are important steps toward protecting the country's many rare and endangered species.

Critical Thinking: How has Indonesia worked to protect its endangered species?

Answer: by establishing national parks and preserves

➤ **This Focus On Environment feature addresses National Geography Standards 4, 8, 14, and 18.**

Indonesia's Threatened Rain Forests

Why Are Rain Forests Important?
Do you know where bananas, pineapples, and oranges originally came from? Each of these plants first grew in a tropical rain forest.

Tropical rain forests are considered by many to be the most important forests in the world. It is estimated that about half of all species of plants, animals, and insects on Earth live in tropical rain forests. Rain forest trees and plants help maintain global temperatures. They also help hold rain-drenched soil in place. This prevents it from washing away and clogging rivers. About one fourth of all medicines currently found in drugstores come from tropical rain forests.

Tropical rain forests can be found in many countries along the equator and between about 20° north and south latitude. One of the largest rain forests is in Brazil's Amazon Basin. In Africa, rain forests are found in many countries, such as Gabon and the Democratic Republic of the Congo. In Southeast Asia, rain forests are found in countries such as Thailand, Vietnam, and Indonesia.

Deforestation in Indonesia Indonesia has large areas of tropical rain forest in Borneo, Sumatra, and Irian Jaya. These areas are home to many unusual species of plants and animals. For example, the largest flower in the world, the *Rafflesia arnoldii*, is found there.

Indonesia's tropical rain forests are being rapidly cut down. About 4,700 square miles (12,170 sq km) of rain forest are lost each year. This rate of deforestation is second only to Brazil's. Some people have predicted that much of Indonesia's

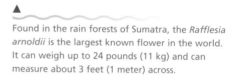

▲
Found in the rain forests of Sumatra, the *Rafflesia arnoldii* is the largest known flower in the world. It can weigh up to 24 pounds (11 kg) and can measure about 3 feet (1 meter) across.

rain forests will be gone in just 10 years. When the rain forests are cleared, animals such as the endangered orangutan do not have a home.

There are many reasons that Indonesia's tropical rain forests are being cleared. Trees from tropical rain forests produce beautiful woods. They are used to make furniture, boats, and houses. The demand for special trees and wood has made logging a profitable business. Much of

---

FOCUS ON ENVIRONMENT

Linking Local and Global Perspectives

Have students recall the problems caused by human interaction with the environment that were discussed in this Focus On Environment feature. Ask them to identify measures people in the region are taking to resolve these issues and reduce the effects of human activity on the environment. (People in Indonesia are trying to protect the rain forests by setting up parks and nature reserves that are off-limits to logging companies. Some groups are finding ways to earn a living without cutting down trees.) Then have volunteers identify international measures that are being taken to resolve these issues. (Environmental organizations are pressuring wealthy nations to stop buying wood that comes from tropical rain forests.) Lead a discussion to address the following questions: Is it important for issues such as deforestation to be resolved at both local and global levels? Why or why not? What types of issues are best addressed locally? Which are best addressed on the global level?

the logging is done by large corporations that do not replant the areas that are cut.

Deforestation in Indonesia also occurs because people need land to farm and raise animals. They also need wood for fuel. People clear the land using a method called slash-and-burn. Large trees are cut, or slashed, and left on the ground. Then the land is burned during the dry season. This clears the land of vegetation and prepares it for farming. In 1997 large areas of land in Indonesia were cleared. Huge fires burned out of control. The fires burned an area roughly the size of Denmark. Smoke filled the sky and caused some airplanes and ships to crash.

Protecting Indonesia's Rain Forests

Some people in Indonesia are trying to protect the rain forests. Parks and nature reserves have been set up that are off-limits to logging companies. Some groups are finding ways to earn money without cutting down trees. Selling fruits and nuts from the rain forest is one way. Also, international organizations such as the Rainforest Action Network are helping to protect the forests. Some environmental groups are even pressuring countries to stop buying trees that come from tropical rain forests.

▲ Much of the timber cut in Indonesia and other Southeast Asian countries is exported to Japan. Indonesia exports about 2 million tons of plywood and 145,000 tons of lumber to Japan each year.

◄ Orangutans live in the tropical rain forests of Borneo and Sumatra. Deforestation has seriously reduced their habitat. The word *orangutan* means "man of the forest."

Understanding What You Read

1. (Human-Environment Interaction) Why are Indonesia's tropical rain forests being cut down?

2. (Human-Environment Interaction) What is being done to protect Indonesia's tropical rain forests?

Understanding What You Read

Answers

1. Indonesia's tropical rain forests are being cut down to bring profit to large logging corporations, to provide land to farm or raise cattle, and to provide wood for fuel.

2. People in Indonesia are trying to protect the rain forests by setting up parks and nature reserves that are off-limits to logging companies. Some groups are finding ways to earn a living without cutting down trees. Environmental organizations are pressuring wealthy nations to stop buying trees that come from tropical rain forests.

Going Further: Thinking Critically

Have students conduct research on another Indonesian environmental story, this one with a more positive conclusion. Many Indonesian farmers have found that heavy pesticide use is much more harmful than helpful and can actually result in increased numbers of harmful insects. Through the Integrated Pest Management (IPM) program they have learned to inspect their fields carefully and use pesticides only when absolutely necessary.

Crop yields have increased. Ask students to investigate Indonesia's IPM program. Then have them create publicity materials that IPM promoters could use to begin grassroots efforts to save the country's rain forests. Have students highlight techniques and arguments that have been effective against heavy pesticide use. Ask them to determine which ones might also be effective in the struggle to save the rain forests.

PRACTICING THE SKILL

1. Students might suggest dams, highways, houses, movie theaters, office buildings, parking lots, shopping malls, streets, supermarkets, utility poles and wires, or other forms. Answers will vary according to the forms suggested.

2. Students should explain how the unique qualities of the television show or movie, such as architectural styles, are linked to the place it was filmed.

3. Students' answers should reflect the ability to read the cultural landscape in the pictures.

➤ This GeoSkills feature addresses National Geography Standards 4, 6, and 10.

Geo SKILLS

Building Skills for Life: Interpreting Cultural Landscapes

Cultural landscapes are the forms put on the land by people. For example, buildings, field patterns, and roads are all a part of cultural landscapes. Cultural landscapes show a people's way of life.

Different cultures create distinctive cultural landscapes. For example, a village in China looks very different from a village in France. By comparing how the two villages look, we can begin to see how their cultures are different.

Geographers interpret cultural landscapes. They observe a landscape, describe what they see, and try to explain how it reflects the culture of the place. This is called reading the cultural landscape.

You can read cultural landscapes too. To read a cultural landscape, start by describing what you see. What kinds of buildings are there? What are they used for? What kinds of clothing are people wearing? Then, think about how what you see relates to the place's culture. What would it be like to live there? What do people there do for fun?

Cultural landscapes tell a story. By reading and interpreting these stories, you can learn a lot about people and geography.

Place Architecture is an important part of the cultural landscape at the Black Dragon Pool in southern China.

▼

PRACTICING THE SKILL

1. Try to read the cultural landscapes of your community. What forms have people put on the land? What do they tell you about the daily life of the people who live there?

2. Watch a television show or movie and interpret the cultural landscapes you see. What is distinctive about them? How are they different from the cultural landscapes you are used to? Can you guess where the program was filmed?

3. Look carefully at the pictures in a newspaper or magazine without reading the captions. Do the pictures tell a story? Is culture a part of this story?

GEOSKILLS

Going Further: Thinking Critically

Have students imagine that they are photojournalists assigned to portray their community's culture in a photo essay for a foreign magazine. Ask students to identify at least 10 elements in their community that they feel would accurately depict their culture to a person in another country. Have students write a few sentences about each element, explaining why it should be included in the photo essay. You may wish to extend the activity by having students create an actual photo essay with their own photographs or pictures from local publications.

HANDS on GEOGRAPHY

The photographs below show two very different cultural landscapes. What can these photographs tell us about each place's culture and way of life? Look closely at each photograph and then answer the Lab Report questions.

◄ A cultural landscape in East Asia

▲ A cultural landscape in Southeast Asia

Lab Report

1. What do these two photographs show? On a separate sheet of paper, write a short description of each photograph.

2. Do these two photographs tell you something about each place's culture and way of life? On a separate sheet of paper, describe what you think the culture of these two places is like.

3. Are there some things about a place's culture that you cannot learn from just looking at a photograph? What are they? If you took a trip to these two places, what else could you learn about their cultures?

Lab Report

Answers

1. Students might note how the modern skyscrapers in the background contrast with the ancient style of the junk (boat) in the foreground. This is a photo of Hong Kong. Students should note the ornate architecture and the unusual roofline extensions in the photo from Southeast Asia. The photo depicts temporary housing for guests attending a funeral in a Toraja village in Indonesia.

2. Students might suggest that the East Asia photo depicts a modern urban culture, with some elements of older ways of life. The other photo depicts a more traditional culture.

3. Students might suggest that customs, foods, language, religion, or types of recreation are not apparent in the photos. They might learn about these things if they traveled to the places pictured.

1. Describe the landforms and climates in the Pacific world and Antarctica.
2. Identify the culture groups of the region and relate their experiences to historical events.
3. Explain the relationship of the region's resources to the economic development of Australia, New Zealand, and the Pacific Islands.
4. Identify the environmental challenges that confront the Pacific world and Antarctica.
5. Develop awareness of how events, immigration, politics, and shared goals create global connections among peoples and nations.

UNIT 6

The Pacific World and Antarctica

CHAPTER 19
Australia and New Zealand

CHAPTER 20
The Pacific Islands and Antarctica

King penguins watching photographer. Antarctica

House in Sepik River area, Papua New Guinea

Teenagers of Melbourne, Australia

420 Unit 6

USING THE ILLUSTRATIONS

Direct students' attention to the photos on these pages. Tell students that the young people in the center photo are from Melbourne, Australia. Have them locate Melbourne on a map. Ask students what they might conclude from the Australian teens' clothing and hair styles. (Possible answer: Their culture has much in common with ours.) Point out that Wellington, New Zealand, in the photo on the righthand page, appears to have some features in common with American cities. Most New Zealanders also share many culture traits with Americans.

Ask what climate extremes are represented in the small photos (very cold—Antarctica; tropical—Papua New Guinea). Ask students to suggest why the penguins do not appear to be frightened by the photographer's presence. (Possible answer: Because they seldom see humans, they are not afraid of them.) Refer back to the Papua New Guinea photo. Each village in the Sepik River area has such a house for each clan in the village. Ask students to speculate why the houses are built on stilts (to keep them above the river's floodwaters).

A Film Critic in New Zealand

David Gerstner is a film critic and lecturer from New York City. In 1999 he moved to New Zealand. He found the country was very different than he thought it would be. **WHAT DO YOU THINK?** *What do you know about New Zealand?*

First I was surprised that New Zealand has such lively cities. I had thought it was all mountains and bush. I was also surprised by the laid-back New Zealand approach to personal interaction. Celebrities, politicians, and the "common folk" have an easier time getting together. For example, I have become friends with some of New Zealand's well-known filmmakers, writers, and fashion designers—all within a year. The social playing field is more level than in the United States.

In fact, a friend and I literally ran into Jenny Shipley, who was then New Zealand's Prime Minister, on a busy street in the capital, Wellington. She was with her daughter. There were no secret service guards with them—like there would be with the U.S. president. We even had our picture taken with her! The easy-going Kiwi style of security is refreshing. However, for a New Yorker it is sometimes unsettling.

Wellington, New Zealand

Understanding Primary Sources

1. Why was David Gerstner surprised by New Zealand's cities?

2. What does this passage illustrate about New Zealand's culture?

Koalas

421

MORE FROM THE FIELD

The Maori people first came to the islands of New Zealand about 1,000 years before Captain Cook landed there in 1769. During British rule (1840–1907) conflicts arose. European settlers took most of the best land. Many Maori were displaced to the cities.

Maori culture did not die. During the 1980s Maori activism became intense. Maori people wanted their language used in education and broadcasting. They also sought compensation for natural resources that they felt had been taken from them.

Today, almost 10 percent of New Zealand's population is Maori. By law, 6 of the 120 seats in New Zealand's parliament are reserved for Maori members.

Activity: Have students conduct research on Maori society in the 2000s. You may want to have them draw editorial cartoons that express Maori concerns.

Understanding Primary Sources

Answers

1. He had thought it was all mountains and bush.

2. easy-going, laid-back approach to personal interaction

CHAPTERS

19 **Australia and New Zealand**
describes the countries' landforms, climates, water and mineral resources, unique plant and animal life, history, agriculture, industry, and population distribution.

20 **The Pacific Islands and Antarctica**
introduces the distinctive characteristics of the islands of the Pacific region and Antarctica.

UNIT 6 ATLAS The World in Spatial Terms

PEOPLE IN THE PROFILE

Note that the elevation profile follows the Tropic of Capricorn, which lies just north of Pitcairn Island. It is one of the most remote inhabited islands on Earth.

Although Polynesians lived on the island 600 years ago, it was abandoned until 1790. That year, men from the British ship *Bounty*—who had mutinied against their captain—settled on Pitcairn, along with several Tahitian men and women.

Within 10 years, all the mutineers but one, John Adams, had died. When British naval officers rediscovered Pitcairn in 1814 they were so impressed by Adams's virtues that they did not arrest him for the mutiny. Although Pitcairn's isolation was ended, the tiny population still struggled to survive. Twice the entire community moved to another island. Both times some of the settlers returned. In 1940 the sale of postage stamps began to bring in much-needed cash.

Today, Pitcairn has about 50 permanent residents. Government jobs provide the only steady employment.

Critical Thinking: How do Pitcairn's residents make a living?

Answer: mostly through government jobs

The Pacific World and Antarctica

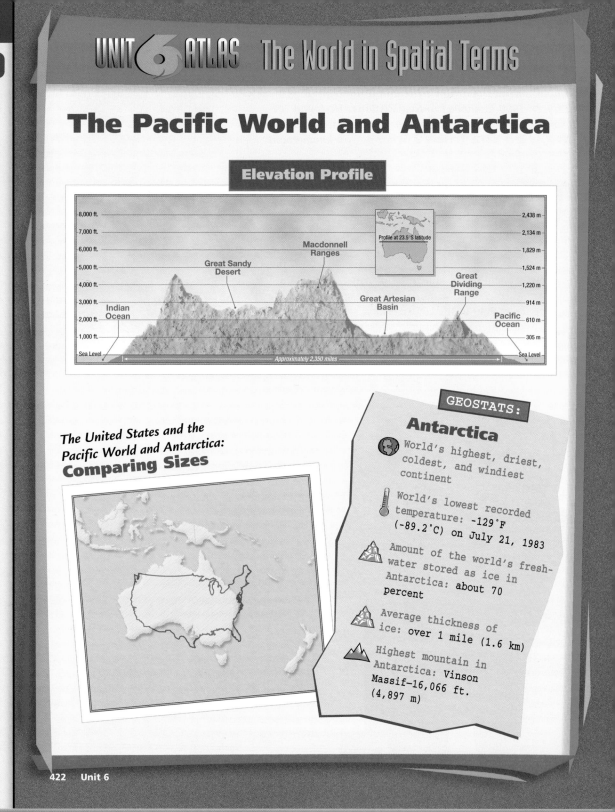

Elevation Profile

8,000 ft. — 2,438 m
7,000 ft. — 2,134 m
6,000 ft. — 1,829 m
5,000 ft. — 1,524 m
4,000 ft. — 1,220 m
3,000 ft. — 914 m
2,000 ft. — 610 m
1,000 ft. — 305 m
Sea Level — Sea Level

Profile at 23.5°S latitude

Indian Ocean
Great Sandy Desert
Macdonnell Ranges
Great Artesian Basin
Great Dividing Range
Pacific Ocean

Approximately 2,350 miles

The United States and the Pacific World and Antarctica: **Comparing Sizes**

GEOSTATS:
Antarctica

- World's highest, driest, coldest, and windiest continent
- World's lowest recorded temperature: -129°F (-89.2°C) on July 21, 1983
- Amount of the world's freshwater stored as ice in Antarctica: about 70 percent
- Average thickness of ice: over 1 mile (1.6 km)
- Highest mountain in Antarctica: Vinson Massif—16,066 ft. (4,897 m)

OVERVIEW

In this unit, students will learn about the people and geography of Australia, New Zealand, the Pacific Islands, and Antarctica.

Australia's unique ecosystems are the result of the continent's isolation. Geological activity makes New Zealand's landscape highly varied. Both countries have majority populations of British heritage and minority indigenous populations. The economies combine agriculture, manufacturing, and services. Australia and New Zealand have democratic governments. Most of the people enjoy a high standard of living.

The Pacific Islands' beauty disguises some economic difficulties. Many depend on aid from other countries.

Antarctica has too harsh an environment for permanent settlement. Several nations have established scientific research stations there.

The Pacific World and Antarctica: Physical

UNIT **6** ATLAS

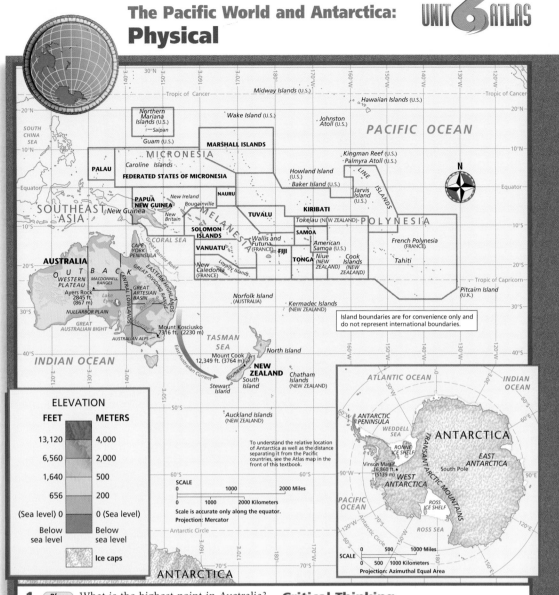

ELEVATION

FEET	METERS
13,120	4,000
6,560	2,000
1,640	500
656	200
(Sea level) 0	0 (Sea level)
Below sea level	Below sea level

Ice caps

Island boundaries are for convenience only and do not represent international boundaries.

To understand the relative location of Antarctica as well as the distance separating it from the Pacific countries, see the Atlas map in the front of this textbook.

SCALE
0   1000   2000 Miles
0   1000   2000 Kilometers
Scale is accurate only along the equator.
Projection: Mercator

SCALE
0   500   1000 Miles
0   500   1000 Kilometers
Projection: Azimuthal Equal Area

1. (Place) What is the highest point in Australia? in the region?

2. (Location) About how far apart are Guam and Tahiti? New Zealand and Australia?

3. (Region) What physical features cover most of Australia?

Critical Thinking

4. (Region) Which country is more mountainous, Australia or New Zealand?

5. (Region) Compare this map to the **climate map** of the region. Which Australian mountain range seems to cause a rain-shadow effect?

Physical Map

Answers

1. Mount Kosciusko; Vinson Massif, Antarctica

2. more than 5,000 miles (8,050 km); about 1,300 miles (2,092 km)

3. plains and plateaus

Critical Thinking

4. New Zealand

5. Great Dividing Range

USING THE PHYSICAL MAP

Have students use the scales of the main map and the inset map on this page to draw a conclusion about the relative sizes of Australia and Antarctica. (The scales are similar. Antarctica is larger than Australia.) Then have students compare the physical features of the two continents. Ask why little information about Antarctica's landforms is available from the map. (Antarctica is covered by an ice cap.) Then ask students what physical feature the continents have in common (a mountain range).

Your Classroom Time Line

These are the major dates and time periods for this unit. Have students enter them on the time line you created earlier. You may want to watch for these dates as students progress through the unit.

c.* 38,000 B.C. Aborigines move into Australia.

c. A.D. 1000 First settlers land in New Zealand.

1500s Ferdinand Magellan explores the Pacific Ocean.

1769 Captain James Cook visits New Zealand.

1770s Captain James Cook explores the Antarctic coast.

1788 British begin settling colonies in Australia.

1840 British sign a treaty with the Maori in New Zealand.

*c. stands for *circa* and means "about."

Political Map

Answers

1. Papua New Guinea; New Zealand

2. Papua New Guinea

Critical Thinking

3. Many of the island groups are not independent; they are controlled by other countries.

4. The islands of Fiji would be split.

The Pacific World and Antarctica: Political

UNIT 6 ATLAS

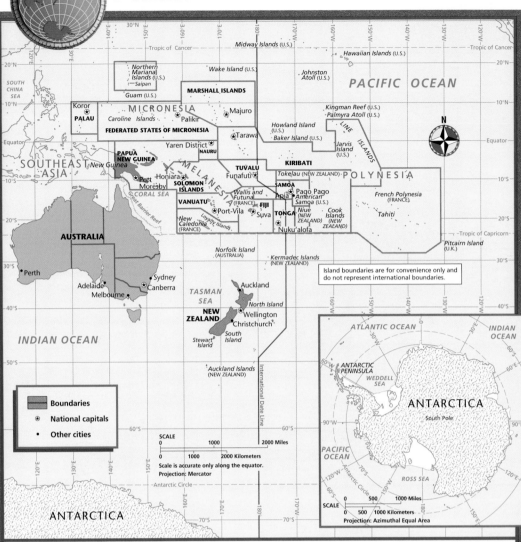

Island boundaries are for convenience only and do not represent international boundaries.

Boundaries
⊛ National capitals
• Other cities

SCALE
0 — 1000 — 2000 Miles
0 — 1000 — 2000 Kilometers
Scale is accurate only along the equator.
Projection: Mercator

SCALE
0 — 500 — 1000 Miles
0 — 500 — 1000 Kilometers
Projection: Azimuthal Equal Area

1. **Location** Which country occupies half of a large island? Which country occupies two large islands?

2. **Location** What is the only country in the region that has a land boundary with another country?

Critical Thinking

3. **Region** What is one thing you can tell about governments in the region just by looking at the map?

4. **Region** Why do you think the international date line is not a straight line?

USING THE POLITICAL MAP

Focus students' attention on the **political map** on this page. Point out that the islands of the southwestern Pacific Ocean are often grouped for convenience into three clusters. Ask students to name the groups (Melanesia, Micronesia, Polynesia). Tell the class that the prefixes in these terms refer to the dark skin of many of the people (*mela-*), the small size of the islands (*micro-*), and the large number of islands (*poly-*). Call on a volunteer to identify some of the islands within the three groups. Point out that the three terms do not relate to political boundaries.

Then ask students to name the capitals of Australia (Canberra) and New Zealand (Wellington). Call on volunteers to identify the capitals of some of the island countries.

internet connect

ONLINE ATLAS
GO TO: go.hrw.com
KEYWORD: SK5 MapsU6

The Pacific World and Antarctica: **UNIT 6 ATLAS**
Climate

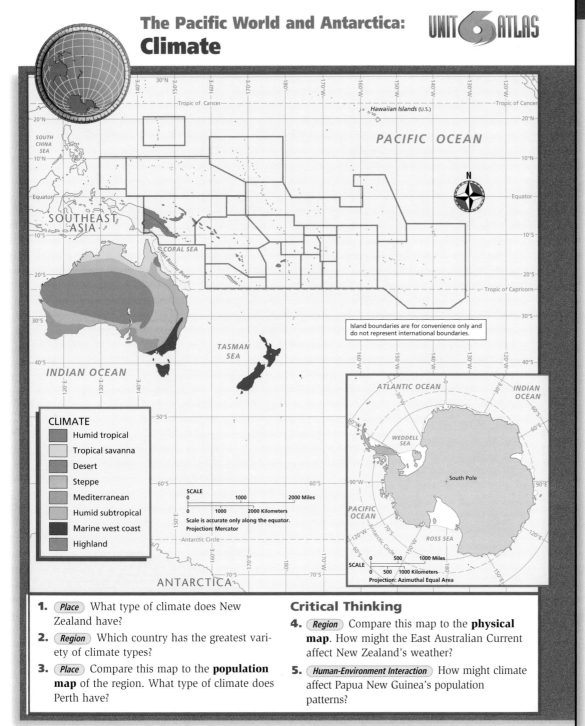

1898 The United States wins Guam from Spain.

1901 The British grant Australia its independence.

1907 New Zealand gains its independence.

1911 First expedition reaches the South Pole.

1959 Many countries sign a treaty to preserve Antarctica.

1991 An international agreement forbids mining and drilling and limits tourism in Antarctica.

CLIMATE
- Humid tropical
- Tropical savanna
- Desert
- Steppe
- Mediterranean
- Humid subtropical
- Marine west coast
- Highland

SCALE
0   1000   2000 Miles
0   1000   2000 Kilometers
Scale is accurate only along the equator.
Projection: Mercator

SCALE
0   500   1000 Miles
0   500   1000 Kilometers
Projection: Azimuthal Equal Area

Island boundaries are for convenience only and do not represent international boundaries.

1. (Place) What type of climate does New Zealand have?

2. (Region) Which country has the greatest variety of climate types?

3. (Place) Compare this map to the **population map** of the region. What type of climate does Perth have?

Critical Thinking

4. (Region) Compare this map to the **physical map**. How might the East Australian Current affect New Zealand's weather?

5. (Human-Environment Interaction) How might climate affect Papua New Guinea's population patterns?

Climate Map
Answers
1. marine west coast
2. Australia
3. Mediterranean

Critical Thinking
4. brings warm water, helps keep New Zealand's climate mild
5. Population density is probably greater on coasts where there is a humid tropical climate.

The Pacific World and Antarctica • 425

USING THE CLIMATE MAP

As students examine the **climate map** on this page, point out that all the climate types of the world are represented. Have students compare this map to the **physical map** of the region. For each climate type, call on a volunteer to describe the relative location of a place with that climate. (Examples: humid tropical—northeast coast of Papua New Guinea; tropical savanna—north coast of Australia; desert—central and western Australia) Ask which climate region includes the most land area (ice cap). Remind students that Antarctica is larger than Australia.

Your Classroom Time Line (continued)

1992 The Citizenship Act in Australia is amended to remove swearing an oath of allegiance to the British crown.

1997 Papua New Guinea suffers from prolonged drought and 1.2 million people are put at risk of starvation.

1999 New Zealand troops join UN peacekeeping force in East Timor.

2000 Australia hosts the Olympic games in Sydney.

2002 More than 90 Australians are killed in a nightclub bombing in Bali, Indonesia

internet connect

ONLINE ATLAS
GO TO: go.hrw.com
KEYWORD: SK5 MapsU6

Population Map

Answers

1. Australia

2. southeast coast

3. New Caledonia

Critical Thinking

4. Both have unpopulated areas.

The Pacific World and Antarctica: Population

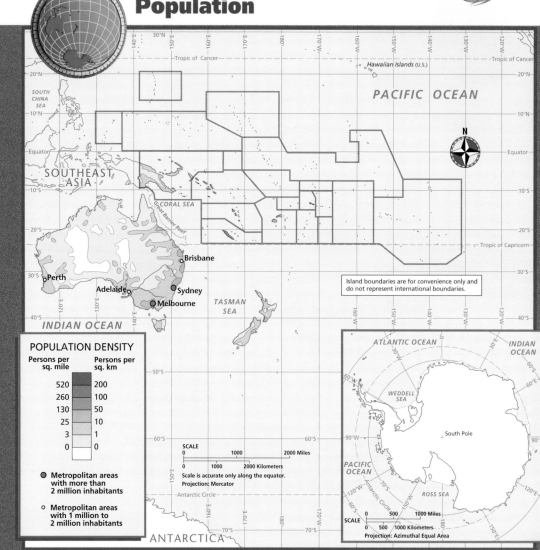

POPULATION DENSITY

Persons per sq. mile	Persons per sq. km
520	200
260	100
130	50
25	10
3	1
0	0

● Metropolitan areas with more than 2 million inhabitants

○ Metropolitan areas with 1 million to 2 million inhabitants

Island boundaries are for convenience only and do not represent international boundaries.

SCALE
Scale is accurate only along the equator.
Projection: Mercator

SCALE
Projection: Azimuthal Equal Area

1. **Place** What is the only country with cities of over 2 million people?

2. **Region** What region of Australia has the highest population density?

3. **Location** Compare this map to the **physical map**. What is the densely populated island northwest of New Zealand?

Critical Thinking

4. **Region** What large landmass has no permanent population? Why?

5. **Region** From looking at this map, what is one thing that Australia and Antarctica have in common?

USING THE POPULATION MAP

Focus students' attention on the **population map** on this page. Ask them to write a statement to summarize the region's population density. (Examples: Population density is low in the region and concentrated in a few cities. Population density is heaviest along the southeast coast of Australia.) Call on volunteers to read their sentences.

Ask students which of New Zealand's islands appears to have more people (North Island). Have students compare this map to the **physical** and **climate maps**. Then ask them why Papua New Guinea has an east-west strip of sparse population density (mountainous area with highland climate).

The Pacific World and Antarctica: Land Use and Resources

UNIT 6 ATLAS

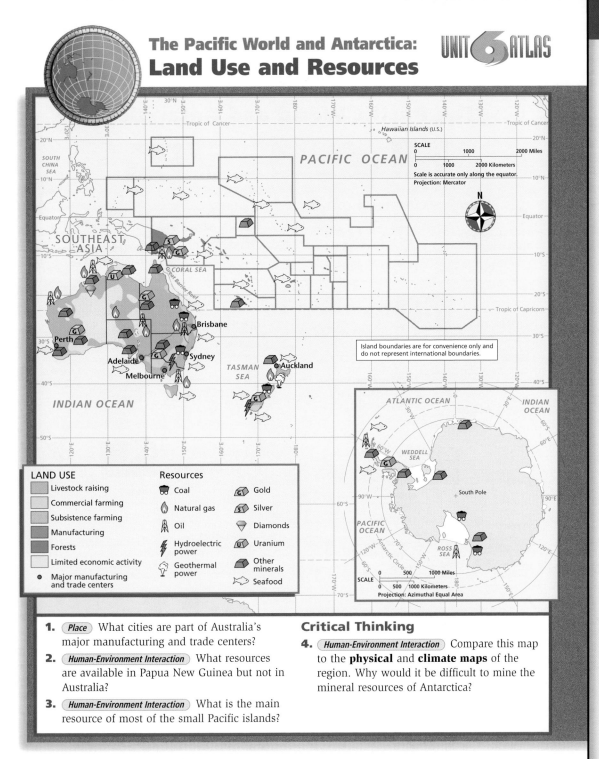

LAND USE
- Livestock raising
- Commercial farming
- Subsistence farming
- Manufacturing
- Forests
- Limited economic activity
- ● Major manufacturing and trade centers

Resources
- Coal
- Natural gas
- Oil
- Hydroelectric power
- Geothermal power
- G Gold
- S Silver
- Diamonds
- U Uranium
- Other minerals
- Seafood

Island boundaries are for convenience only and do not represent international boundaries.

1. (Place) What cities are part of Australia's major manufacturing and trade centers?

2. (Human-Environment Interaction) What resources are available in Papua New Guinea but not in Australia?

3. (Human-Environment Interaction) What is the main resource of most of the small Pacific islands?

Critical Thinking

4. (Human-Environment Interaction) Compare this map to the **physical** and **climate maps** of the region. Why would it be difficult to mine the mineral resources of Antarctica?

The Pacific World and Antarctica • 427

Land Use and Resources Map

Answers
1. Perth, Adelaide, Melbourne, Sydney, Brisbane
2. forests and silver
3. seafood

Critical Thinking
4. A harsh climate and thick ice pack would hinder mining.

USING THE LAND USE AND RESOURCES MAP

As students examine the **land use and resources map** explain that Australia's outback has been described as a storehouse of mineral wealth. Have students list the mineral resources found in Australia (coal, gold, diamonds, uranium, and other minerals). Then ask them where silver is mined (Papua New Guinea).

Have students identify the fossil fuel resources that are available in the region (coal, oil, gas). Finally, ask students which country has geothermal power (New Zealand).

UNITED STATES OF AMERICA

CAPITAL:
Washington, D.C.

AREA:
3,717,792 sq. mi.
(9,629,091 sq km)

POPULATION:
290,342,554

MONEY:
U.S. dollar

LANGUAGES:
English, Spanish (spoken by a large minority)

POPULATION AGED 0–14:
21 percent

The Pacific World and Antarctica

AUSTRALIA

CAPITAL:
Canberra
AREA:
2,967,893 sq. mi.
(7,686,850 sq km)
POPULATION:
19,731,984

MONEY:
Australian dollar
LANGUAGES:
English, ethnic languages
POPULATION AGED 0-14 YEARS:
20 percent

MARSHALL ISLANDS

CAPITAL: Majuro
AREA: 70 sq. mi. (181.3 sq km)
POPULATION: 56,429
MONEY: United States dollar

LANGUAGES:
English (official), Marshallese dialects, Japanese
POPULATION AGED 0-14 YEARS: 39 percent

FEDERATED STATES OF MICRONESIA

CAPITAL: Palikir
AREA: 271 sq. mi. (702 sq km)
POPULATION: 108,143
MONEY:
United States dollar

LANGUAGES:
English (official), Trukese, Pohnpeian, Yapese, Kosrean
POPULATION AGED 0-14 YEARS: 38 percent

NAURU

CAPITAL:
no official capital
AREA:
8 sq. mi. (21 sq km)
POPULATION:
12,570

MONEY:
Australian dollar
LANGUAGES:
Nauruan (official), English
POPULATION AGED 0-14 YEARS:
40 percent

FIJI

CAPITAL:
Suva
AREA:
7,054 sq. mi.
(18,270 sq km)
POPULATION:
868,531

MONEY:
Fijian dollar
LANGUAGES:
English (official), Fijian, Hindustani
POPULATION AGED 0-14 YEARS:
32 percent

NEW ZEALAND

CAPITAL:
Wellington
AREA:
103,737 sq. mi.
(268,680 sq km)
POPULATION:
3,951,307

MONEY:
New Zealand dollar
LANGUAGES:
English (official), Maori
POPULATION AGED 0-14 YEARS:
22 percent

KIRIBATI

CAPITAL:
Tarawa
AREA:
277 sq. mi. (717 sq km)
POPULATION:
98,549

MONEY:
Australian dollar
LANGUAGES:
English (official), I-Kiribati
POPULATION AGED 0-14 YEARS:
40 percent

PALAU

CAPITAL:
Koror
AREA:
177 sq. mi. (458 sq km)
POPULATION:
19,717
MONEY:
United States dollar

LANGUAGES:
English (official), Sonsorolese, Angaur, Japanese, Tobi, Palauan
POPULATION AGED 0-14 YEARS:
27 percent

Countries not drawn to scale.

FAST FACTS ACTIVITIES

LEVEL 1: (Suggested time: 30 min.) Refer students to the figures that show what percentage of the population is from 0 to 14 years old for countries in the Pacific world. Ask what is meant by 0 years old (newborn to age 1). Have students use these figures to create a bar graph for the countries of the Pacific world. Ask students to add the United States (21 percent) to their graphs.

Then have students write a few sentences recording their observations about the graphed figures. (Examples: Every country's figures are higher than 20 percent. A third of countries have nearly half of their population in this age group.)

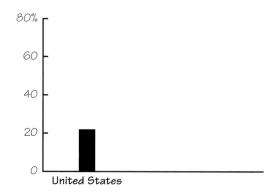

Percent of Population Aged 0–14

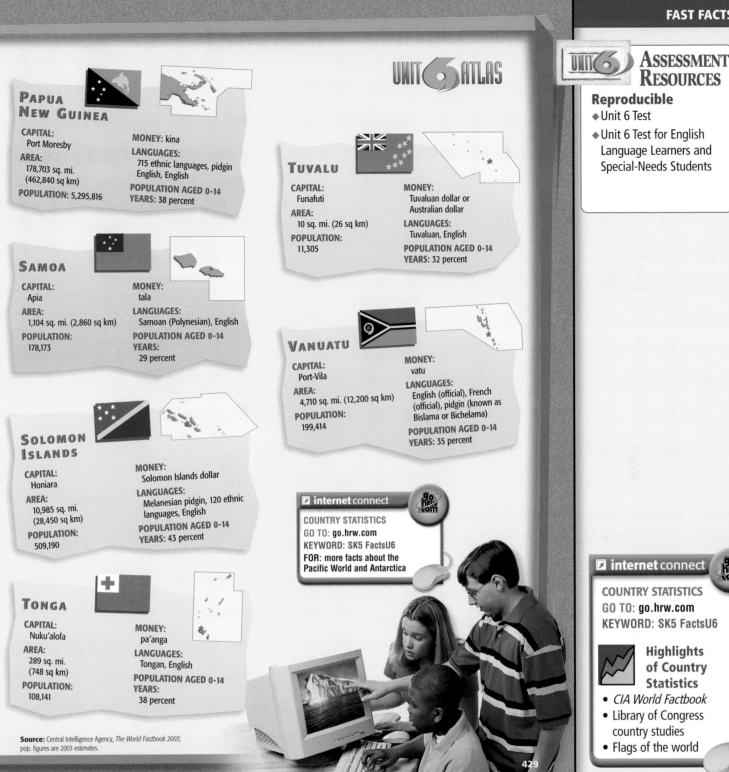

UNIT 6 ATLAS

PAPUA NEW GUINEA

CAPITAL:
Port Moresby

AREA:
178,703 sq. mi. (462,840 sq km)

POPULATION: 5,295,816

MONEY: kina

LANGUAGES:
715 ethnic languages, pidgin English, English

POPULATION AGED 0-14 YEARS: 38 percent

SAMOA

CAPITAL:
Apia

AREA:
1,104 sq. mi. (2,860 sq km)

POPULATION:
178,173

MONEY:
tala

LANGUAGES:
Samoan (Polynesian), English

POPULATION AGED 0-14 YEARS:
29 percent

SOLOMON ISLANDS

CAPITAL:
Honiara

AREA:
10,985 sq. mi. (28,450 sq km)

POPULATION:
509,190

MONEY:
Solomon Islands dollar

LANGUAGES:
Melanesian pidgin, 120 ethnic languages, English

POPULATION AGED 0-14 YEARS: 43 percent

TONGA

CAPITAL:
Nuku'alofa

AREA:
289 sq. mi. (748 sq km)

POPULATION:
108,141

MONEY:
pa'anga

LANGUAGES:
Tongan, English

POPULATION AGED 0-14 YEARS:
38 percent

TUVALU

CAPITAL:
Funafuti

AREA:
10 sq. mi. (26 sq km)

POPULATION:
11,305

MONEY:
Tuvaluan dollar or Australian dollar

LANGUAGES:
Tuvaluan, English

POPULATION AGED 0-14 YEARS: 32 percent

VANUATU

CAPITAL:
Port-Vila

AREA:
4,710 sq. mi. (12,200 sq km)

POPULATION:
199,414

MONEY:
vatu

LANGUAGES:
English (official), French (official), pidgin (known as Bislama or Bichelama)

POPULATION AGED 0-14 YEARS: 35 percent

Source: Central Intelligence Agency, *The World Factbook 2003*; pop. figures are 2003 estimates.

internet connect

COUNTRY STATISTICS
GO TO: go.hrw.com
KEYWORD: SK5 FactsU6
FOR: more facts about the Pacific World and Antarctica

internet connect

COUNTRY STATISTICS
GO TO: go.hrw.com
KEYWORD: SK5 FactsU6

Highlights of Country Statistics

• *CIA World Factbook*
• Library of Congress country studies
• Flags of the world

429

LEVEL 2: (Suggested time: 40 min.) Draw students' attention to the figures for the percentage of population that is from 0 to 14 years old. Have students write a paragraph describing the special needs of this population. (Needs may include food, shelter, child care, health care, education, supervised leisure activities, or others.)

Point out that people under 14 years old are only a few years away from childbearing and employment age. Have students write an additional paragraph explaining the possible effects that having a large segment of the population under 14 years may have on a country—particularly small island countries—such as those in the Pacific world. (Possible answers: Unemployment may rise. Population may increase beyond available housing. Greater demands on food supplies may require increased imports.)

LEVEL 3: (Suggested time: 45 min.) Ask students to imagine that they are young teens living in one of the Pacific world countries. Have them write letters to their country's leader expressing their hopes and concerns for the upcoming decade. As young teens, issues may include job and educational opportunities and others as discussed in the Level 2 activity. Encourage students to draw information from the Fast Facts feature, this unit's atlas, and the chapters to support their statements.

Australia and New Zealand

Chapter Resource Manager

Objectives	Pacing Guide	Reproducible Resources
SECTION 1		
Australia (pp. 431–37) 1. Identify Australia's natural features and resources. 2. Describe the history of Australia. 3. Describe the people and culture of Australia. 4. Describe what Australia is like today.	**Regular** 2.5 days Lecture Notes, Section 1 **Block Scheduling** .5 day *Block Scheduling Handbook, Chapter 19*	**RS** Know It Notes S1 **RS** Graphic Organizer 19 **E** Creative Strategies for Teaching World Geography, Lessons 22 and 23 **E** Environmental and Global Issues Activity 8 **SM** Geography for Life Activity 32 **IC** Interdisciplinary Activity for the Middle Grades 36 **SM** Map Activity 32 **E** Biography Activity: Truganini **ELL** Main Idea Activity S1
SECTION 2		
New Zealand (pp. 440–43) 1. Identify the natural features of New Zealand. 2. Describe the history and culture of New Zealand. 3. Describe New Zealand's cities and economy.	**Regular** 1 day Lecture Notes, Section 2 **Block Scheduling** .5 day *Block Scheduling Handbook, Chapter 19*	**RS** Know It Notes S2 **E** Cultures of the World Activity 9 **ELL** Main Idea Activity S2

Chapter Resource Key

RS	Reading Support	**ELL**	Reinforcement and English Language Learners and English for Speakers of Other Languages (ESOL)	Video
IC	Interdisciplinary Connections			Internet
E	Enrichment			Holt Presentation Maker Using Microsoft® PowerPoint®
SM	Skills Mastery		Transparencies	
A	Assessment		CD–ROM	
REV	Review		Music	

 One-Stop Planner CD–ROM

See the *One-Stop Planner* for a complete list of additional resources for students and teachers.

One-Stop Planner CD–ROM

It's easy to plan lessons, select resources, and print out materials for your students when you use the *One-Stop Planner CD–ROM with Test Generator.*

Technology Resources

 One-Stop Planner CD–ROM, Lesson 19.1

 ARGWorld CD–ROM

 Geography and Cultures Visual Resources with Teaching Activities 61–65

 Music of the World Audio CD Program, Selection 23

 Homework Practice Online

HRW Go site

 One-Stop Planner CD–ROM, Lesson 19.2

 ARGWorld CD–ROM

Homework Practice Online

HRW Go site

Review, Reinforcement, and Assessment Resources

ELL Main Idea Activity S1
REV Section 1 Review
A Daily Quiz 19.1
REV Chapter Summaries and Review
ELL English Audio Summary 19.1
ELL Spanish Audio Summary 19.1

ELL Main Idea Activity S2
REV Section 2 Review
A Daily Quiz 19.2
REV Chapter Summaries and Review
ELL English Audio Summary 19.2
ELL Spanish Audio Summary 19.2

HRW ONLINE RESOURCES

__GO TO: go.hrw.com__
Then type in a keyword.

TEACHER HOME PAGE
  KEYWORD: SK5 TEACHER

CHAPTER INTERNET ACTIVITIES
  KEYWORD: SK5 GT19

Choose an activity to:
• explore the Great Barrier Reef.
• learn about the Aborigines of Australia.
• tour New Zealand.

CHAPTER ENRICHMENT LINKS
  KEYWORD: SK5 CH19

CHAPTER MAPS
  KEYWORD: SK5 MAPS19

ONLINE ASSESSMENT
Homework Practice
  KEYWORD: SK5 HP19
  Standardized Test Prep Online
  KEYWORD: SK5 STP19
  Rubrics
  KEYWORD: SS Rubrics

COUNTRY INFORMATION
  KEYWORD: SK5 Almanac

CONTENT UPDATES
  KEYWORD: SS Content Updates

HOLT PRESENTATION MAKER
  KEYWORD: SK5 PPT19

ONLINE READING SUPPORT
  KEYWORD: SS Strategies

CURRENT EVENTS
  KEYWORD: S5 Current Events

Meeting Individual Needs

Ability Levels

Level 1 Basic-level activities designed for all students encountering new material

Level 2 Intermediate-level activities designed for average students

Level 3 Challenging activities designed for honors and gifted-and-talented students

ESOL Activities that address the needs of students with Limited English Proficiency

Chapter Review and Assessment

E Readings in World Geography, History, and Culture 79 and 80
SM Critical Thinking Activity 19
REV Chapter 19 Review and Practice
REV Chapter Summaries and Review
ELL Vocabulary Activity 19
A Chapter 19 Test
 Chapter 19 Test Generator (on the One-Stop Planner)
 Audio CD Program, Chapter 19
A Chapter 19 Test for English Language Learners and Special-Needs Students
HRW Go Site

Australia and New Zealand

Previewing Chapter Resources

Holt Online Learning

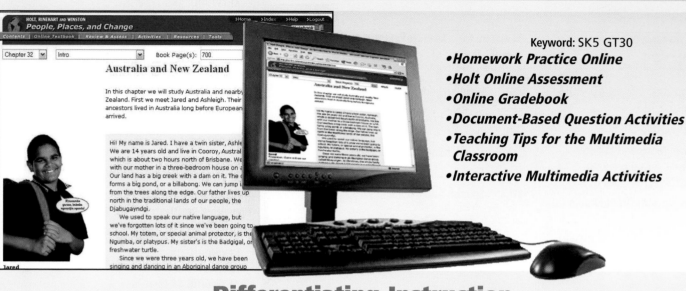

Keyword: SK5 GT30

- *Homework Practice Online*
- *Holt Online Assessment*
- *Online Gradebook*
- *Document-Based Question Activities*
- *Teaching Tips for the Multimedia Classroom*
- *Interactive Multimedia Activities*

Differentiating Instruction

Reading and Writing Support

◄ *Graphic Organizer Activity*
- *Vocabulary Activity*
- *Chapter Summary and Review*
- *Know It Notes*
- *Audio CD*

Active Learning

◄ *Block Scheduling Handbook*
- *Cultures of the World Activity*
- *Interdisciplinary Activity*
- *Map Activity*
- *Critical Thinking Activity 32*
- *Music of the World CD: Music from Northern Australia*

Primary Sources and Advanced Learners

- *Geography for Life Activity: International Air Linkages*
◄ *Map Activity: Australian Colonization*
- *Readings in World Geography, History and Culture:*
  - *79 Australia's Uncertain Future*
  - *80 Maori of New Zealand*

Assessment Program

◄ *Daily Quizzes S1–2*
- *Chapter Test*
- *Chapter Test for English Language Learners and Special-Needs Students*

Spanish and ESOL

- *Vocabulary Activity*
◄ *Main Idea Activities for English Language Learners and Special-Needs Students*
- *Chapter Summary and Review*
- *Spanish Audio Summary*
- *Know It Notes S1–2*
- *Chapter Test for English Language Learners and Special-Needs Students*

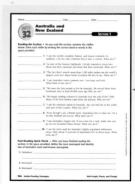

Special Education Modifications

Your **I.D.E.A. Works!** CD-ROM will provide modified versions of the following teaching materials:

◄ *Guided Reading Strategies S1–2*
- *Vocabulary Activity*
- *Main Idea Activities S1–2*
- *Daily Quizzes S1–2*
- *Chapter 19 Test*
- *Flash cards of chapter vocabulary terms*

Teacher Resources

Books for Teachers

Hoffman, Eric. *Adventuring in Australia.* Sierra Club Books, 2000.

Jefferies, Margaret. *Adventuring in New Zealand.* Sierra Club Books, 2000.

Smith, William Ramsay. *Myths and Legends of the Australian Aboriginals.* Random House, UK, 1930.

Books for Students

Darian-Smith, Kate. *The Australian Outback and Its People.* Thomson Learning, 1995. Emphasis on Aboriginal culture and its future.

Dunphy, Madeleine. *Here Is the Coral Reef.* Hyperion Books for Children, 1998. Rhyming tale about the residents of Australia's Great Barrier Reef.
SHELTERED ENGLISH

Fox, Mary Virginia. *New Zealand.* Childrens Press, 1991. Introduces the country named Land of the Long White Cloud by the Maori.

Israel, Fred L., ed. *Australia: The Unique Continent.* Chelsea House Publishers, 2000. Cultural and geographic history of the world's sixth-largest country.

Multimedia Materials

Anyplace Wild: Trekking and Climbing in New Zealand. Video, 60 min. PBS.

Australia/New Zealand. Video, 20 min. Educational Video Network.

Indigenous Australians: An Aboriginal Community Focus. CD–ROM. VEA International.

Videos and CDs

Videos

- CNN. *Presents Geography: Yesterday and Today, Segment 34 The Great Barrier Reef*
- *ARG World*

Holt Researcher

http://researcher.hrw.com

- *Australia-New Zealand-United States Security Treaty (ANZUS)*
- *Australia*
- *Australia and New Zealand*
- *New Zealand*
- *The Pacific World*

Transparency Packages

Graphic Organizer Transparencies 19.1–2

Geography and Cultures Visual Resources Transparencies 107–111

112 Australia and New Zealand: Physical-Political

Map Activities Transparency 19 Australian Colonization

You may want to reinforce interest in Australia and New Zealand by pointing out the following:

▶ Australia and New Zealand both have many rare species of plants and animals.

▶ Australia's Great Barrier Reef, the world's largest coral reef, is threatened by many aspects of modern life.

▶ Most of both countries' residents share many cultural traits with U.S. citizens.

▶ Both Australia and New Zealand are attempting to redress injustices done to native peoples and are finding ways to recognize and respect minority cultures and religions.

CHAPTER 19

Australia and New Zealand

In this chapter we will study Australia and nearby New Zealand. First we meet Jared and Ashleigh. Their ancestors lived in Australia long before Europeans arrived.

Hi! My name is Jared. I have a twin sister, Ashleigh. We are 14 years old and live in Cooroy, Australia, which is about two hours north of Brisbane. We live with our mother in a three-bedroom house on a hill. Our land has a big creek with a dam on it. The dam forms a big pond, or a billabong. We can jump into it from the trees along the edge. Our father lives up north in the traditional lands of our people, the Djabugayndgi.

We used to speak our native language, but we've forgotten lots of it since we've been going to school. My totem, or special animal protector, is the *Ngumba*, or platypus. My sister's is the *Badgigal*, or freshwater turtle.

Since we were three years old, we have been singing and dancing in an Aboriginal dance group called *Bibayungen*. At Christmas, the whole family gathers with about 1,000 people in our traditional lands for a big dance and music festival (*warrima* in our language).

Nyurramba garran, bulmba nganydjin ngunda!

Translation: Come and see our country!

430   Chapter 19

CHAPTER PROJECT

Have students conduct research on the daily lives of teens living at a sheep station in the outback. Students should focus on how the teens do schoolwork, what work they do at the station, and their entertainment options. Have students summarize their research in short reports. Then, in a class discussion, have students answer these questions: If I were moving to the Australian outback, what would I most like to take with me? What would I miss the most? Place the essays in the students' portfolios.

STARTING THE CHAPTER

Inform students that both Australia and New Zealand have many species unique to their countries. Ask students to look at the map to determine why this may be. (The region is isolated. Both countries are islands.) Ask students if they are already familiar with any animals from this region. (Possible answers: koalas, kangaroos, kiwis) Tell students they will learn more about the physical and human geography of Australia and New Zealand in this chapter.

Section 1 Australia

Read to Discover

1. What are Australia's natural features and resources?
2. What is the history of Australia?
3. What is Australia like today?

Vocabulary

artesian wells
coral reef
endemic species
marsupials
outback
rugby
bush

Places

Eastern Highlands
Central Lowlands
Western Plateau
Great Dividing Range
Tasmania
Murray-Darling Rivers
Great Artesian Basin
Great Barrier Reef
Sydney
Melbourne
Brisbane
Perth

Reading Strategy

ANTICIPATING INFORMATION Before reading, predict whether you think the following statements are true or false.

• Australia is a mountainous continent with a cool climate.
• The seasons in Australia occur at the same time of year as those in the United States.
• Australia has a very mixed population.

Check your answers while reading. Then explain why each statement is true or false.

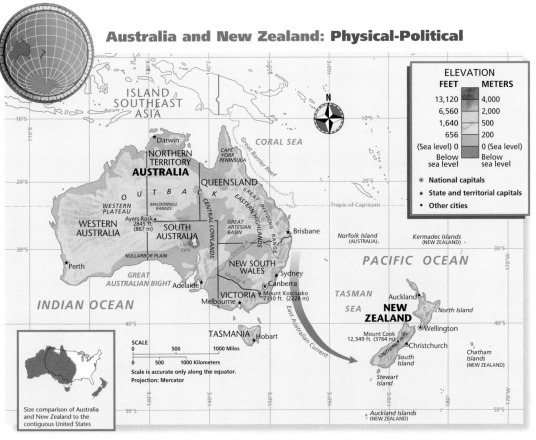

Australia and New Zealand: Physical-Political

ELEVATION		
FEET		**METERS**
13,120		4,000
6,560		2,000
1,640		500
656		200
(Sea level) 0		0 (Sea level)
Below sea level		Below sea level

⊛ National capitals
★ State and territorial capitals
• Other cities

Size comparison of Australia and New Zealand to the contiguous United States

Australia and New Zealand • 431

Section 1

Objectives

1. Identify Australia's natural features and resources.
2. Examine the history of Australia.
3. Explain what Australia is like today.

FOCUS

 ### Bellringer

Copy the following instructions onto the chalkboard: *With a partner, compile a list of several things that come to mind when you think of Australia.* When students have completed their work, invite the pairs to write their answers on the chalkboard. Discuss responses. Have students save their lists to use in the review activity at the end of the section. Tell students that in Section 1 they will learn more about Australia's physical geography, history, and culture.

Using the Physical-Political Map

Have students examine the map on this page. Then have students compare Australia's landforms with the landforms of the United States. (Australia has more desert areas, fewer rivers, and lower mountains.)

EYE ON EARTH

Explaining Australia's Monoloit Uluru-Kata Tjuta National Park is the site of Ayers Rock, a large monolith well known for its rich red color. The rusty color is caused in part by the chemical decay of minerals in the rock.

Ayers Rock has deep vertical crevices running down its sides and caves and inlets at its base. Like the red color of the rock, these formations were formed by chemical decay and sand-driven erosion.

In addition to Ayers Rock, the park has dunes reaching about 98 feet (30 m) in height and extensive sand plains. The land is valued for its rich landscape, geology, and desert ecosystems. The park management is committed to protecting its desert ecosystems.

Activity: Have students write a plan for a trip to Uluru-Kata Tjuta National Park. Tell students to plan how they would accommodate the need to preserve the park. For example, what would students do with their empty food containers?

Visual Record Answer ▶

created crevices or grooves, smooth areas

Ayers Rock in central Australia is composed of sandstone with bits of reflective minerals. The sandstone changes color as the Sun moves across the sky. At sunset Ayers Rock turns a fiery orange-red.

Ayers Rock, called Uluru by Aborigines, rises more than 1,100 feet (335 m) above the surrounding Western Plateau. It is all that is left after erosion wore away an ancient mountain.

Interpreting the Visual Record How has erosion affected Ayers Rock?
▼

Natural Features

Australia is the world's smallest, flattest, and lowest continent. In addition, it is the only country that is also a continent. The country sometimes is called the Land Down Under because it lies south of the equator. Seasons there are reversed from those north of the equator. For example, when it is winter in the United States, it is summer in Australia.

Land Australia has three main landform regions. These are the Eastern Highlands, the Central Lowlands, and the Western Plateau.

The Eastern Highlands are a system of ridges, plateaus, and valleys in the eastern part of Australia. They include the Great Dividing Range. This range stretches along the eastern coast and includes the island of Tasmania. It divides Australia's rivers into those that flow eastward and those that flow westward. Australia's one major river system, the Murray-Darling, flows westward from the range.

Australia's highest mountain is in the Great Dividing Range. It rises to just 7,310 feet (2,228 m). This tells us that Australia is very old. Erosion from wind and water has lowered the continent's mountains over millions of years.

The Central Lowlands are flatter and lower than the Eastern Highlands. The Central Lowlands include the Great Artesian Basin, Australia's largest source of underground water. **Artesian wells** dot this area. Artesian wells are those in which water rises toward the surface without being pumped. The groundwater comes from rain falling on nearby mountains. As the amount of groundwater increases, some is pushed to the surface. Much of the well water here is of poor quality, so it is used mostly for watering sheep.

TEACH

Teaching Objective 1
LEVEL 1: (Suggested time: 25 min.) Copy the following graphic organizer onto the chalkboard, omitting the blue answers. Use it to help students describe Australia's physical features and climate types. Call on students to provide words and phrases that describe the landforms, bodies of water, climates, and resources of the country. **ESOL**

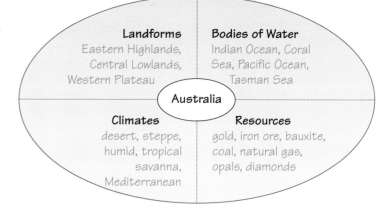

The Physical Geography of Australia

Landforms
Eastern Highlands, Central Lowlands, Western Plateau

Bodies of Water
Indian Ocean, Coral Sea, Pacific Ocean, Tasman Sea

Australia

Climates
desert, steppe, humid, tropical savanna, Mediterranean

Resources
gold, iron ore, bauxite, coal, natural gas, opals, diamonds

The Great Barrier Reef is really thousands of small reefs and tiny islands. Some rise barely above water level when the tide is low.

Pick Up Your Feet!
Australia's Great Barrier Reef, stretching more than 1,250 miles (2,000 km), is the largest structure in the world made by non-human living organisms. Hundreds of species of fish, seaweed, birds, coral, mollusks, sea snakes, and sea turtles live there.

Like all coral reefs, it is made of the skeletons of hundreds of millions of coral polyps. New polyps grow only under specific conditions. The water temperature must stay above 68°F (20°C), the coral polyps must receive sufficient sunlight, and the water must be clear and salty.

The Great Barrier Reef is very fragile. Pollution, vibrations from boats, fuel spills, and even human sweat can damage it. Coral reefs can also be damaged if people walk on them or drag diving gear over them.

Discussion: Lead a discussion addressing these questions: Should people be allowed near the reef? Why or why not? What could be done to protect this delicate ecosystem?

Farther west is the Western Plateau, which covers more than half of the continent. The treeless Nullarbor Plain stretches along the southern edge of the plateau. This plain is the flattest large area on any continent.

The Great Barrier Reef Off the northeastern coast of Australia is the Great Barrier Reef. It is the world's largest **coral reef**, stretching more than 1,250 miles (2,000 km). A coral reef is a ridge found close to shore in warm, tropical waters. It is made of rocky limestone material formed by the skeletons of tiny sea animals. You will read more about coral reefs in the next chapter.

The Great Barrier Reef and its shallow waters are home to many kinds of marine animals. They include fish, shellfish, and sea birds. Australia's government has made most of the reef a national park.

Climate Australia has been described as a desert with green edges. Dry desert and steppe climates cover most of the country. The eastern and southeastern edges and Tasmania have humid climates. Two coastal areas in the south and southwest have a Mediterranean climate. Summers there are long, dry, and sunny. Winters are mild and wet. The north has a tropical savanna climate. There monsoons bring strong wet and dry seasons.

Plants and Animals Australia has many **endemic species**. Endemic species are plants and animals that developed in one particular region of the world. Why does Australia have many endemic species? Australia has been separated from other continents for millions of years. However, over time many nonnative plants and animals have been brought to Australia. See the Case Study in this chapter.

The shallow ocean waters along Australia's northern coast are home to the deadly sea wasp jellyfish. Each jellyfish has as many as 60 tentacles that hang down six and a half feet (2 m). The venom from its sting can kill a human in less than five minutes.

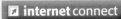

Australia and New Zealand • 433

internet connect

GO TO: go.hrw.com
KEYWORD: SK5 CH19
FOR: Web sites about the Great Barrier Reef

LEVEL 3: (Suggested time: 45 min.) Organize the class into groups. Have each group trace a map of Australia and divide it into regions as described in Section 1. Ask students to invent symbols to represent the natural features and mineral resources described in the section and to add those symbols to the appropriate regions on the map. Then have each group predict which part of the country is most important to Australia's economy.
COOPERATIVE LEARNING, LS **VISUAL-SPATIAL**

Teaching Objective 2

LEVEL 1: (Suggested time: 30 min.) Organize the class into groups. Have each group member select and illustrate an event in Australian history. Then have the group members work together to put the events in chronological order. Then have the groups check each other's work.
ESOL, COOPERATIVE LEARNING, LS **LOGICAL-MATHEMATICAL**

ENVIRONMENT AND SOCIETY

Underground Down Under
Coober Pedy is a small town in the Australian outback. The name *Coober Pedy* comes from an Aboriginal phrase meaning "white man's burrow." In fact, many of the residents of the Australian outback town live and work underground to avoid the scorching heat. Homes, shops, and a church are all carved out of the rock. Most of the world's total production of opals comes from mines in the area.

Activity: Have students work in groups to conduct research on Australian opals, including the physical processes that create opals. Then ask students to create posters showing the different types of opals. Students may use colored foil, cellophane, and tissue papers to depict the opals' colors. Display the posters around the classroom.

Connecting to Literature
Answers
1. far from other countries, winter in July
2. by calling the seas her neighbors and stating the long distances between Australia and other lands

CONNECTING TO *Literature*

Christmas on an Australian beach

THE LAND DOWN UNDER

Europeans began settling in Australia in the late 1700s. The following selection describes what settlers found in the Land Down Under. The selection comes from Christina Stead's For Love Alone, *published in 1944.*

In the part of the world Teresa came from, winter is in July, spring brides marry in September, and Christmas is consummated[1] with roast beef [and] suckling[2] pig . . . at 100 degrees in the shade, near the tall pine tree loaded with gifts and tinsel as in the old country, and old carols have rung out all through the night.

This island continent lies in the water hemisphere. On the eastern coast, the neighboring nation is Chile, though it is far, far east, Valparaiso being more than six thousand miles away in a straight line; her northern neighbors are those of the Timor Sea, the Yellow Sea; to the south is that cold, stormy sea full of earth-wide rollers, which stretches from there without land, south to the Pole.

The other world—the old world, the land [Northern] hemisphere—is far above her as it is shown on maps drawn upside-down by old-world cartographers. From that world and particularly from a scarcely noticeable island [Britain] up toward the North Pole the people came, all by steam; or their parents, all by sail. . . . Inside, over the Blue Mountains, are the plains heavy with wheat, then the endless dust, and after outcrops of silver, opal, and gold, Sahara, the salt-crusted bed of a prehistoric sea, and leafless mountain ranges. There is nothing in the interior; so people look toward the water, and above to the fixed stars and constellations which first guided men there.

Analyzing Primary Sources
1. How does life differ from that in the "old world" in Teresa's land?
2. How does the writer give the reader a sense of Australia's isolation?

[1]consummated: completed, marked, or celebrated; [2]suckling: a young mammal that is still nursing

Two of Australia's most famous native animals are the kangaroo and the koala. Both animals are **marsupials** (mahr-soo-pee-uhls). Marsupials are animals that carry their young in pouches. Eucalyptus (yoo-kuh-LIP-tuhs) is Australia's most common tree.

Minerals Australia's **outback**, or inland region, has many mineral resources such as gold, iron ore, and bauxite. Australia also has coal, natural gas, oil, and gemstones such as opals and diamonds.

✓ READING CHECK: *Places and Regions* What are the natural features of Australia? Three main landform regions; Murray-Darling river system; artesian wells; Great Barrier Reef; desert and steppe climates mostly, also humid, Mediterranean, and tropical savanna; many endemic species; mineral resources

LEVEL 2: (Suggested time: 45 min.) Pair students and have pairs conduct research and write a short script for a radio show titled *The Effects of European Settlement on Aboriginal Life.* Tell students their shows should describe Aboriginal life before and after European settlement. Have each pair produce an audiotape of its program and play the tapes to the class. **COOPERATIVE LEARNING, LS AUDITORY-MUSICAL**

LEVEL 3: (Suggested time: 45 min.) Organize the class into two groups. Have one group prepare arguments for why Australia should leave the British Commonwealth, and the other prepare arguments for why the country should remain in the Commonwealth. Ask the students to take into account the country's history of settlement and independence. Encourage students to use reference resources and then present their positions to the class. **COOPERATIVE LEARNING**

TEACHER TO TEACHER

Jean Eldredge of Altamonte Springs, Florida, suggests the following activity to help students trace the importance of wool in Australia's economy. Have students conduct research on the wool industry, starting with the annual shearing at an Australian sheep station and concluding with the wool's shipment abroad. Have students apply the six essential elements of geography to steps in the process, as appropriate. For example, for Environment and Society have students examine how the ranchers adapt to the outback's arid environment. For Human Systems, ask them to analyze how the wool gets to market.

◄ A bark painting provides a glimpse of some Aborigines' spiritual beliefs. The painting shows the path taken by a soul on its journey to another world. Traditional Aboriginal culture almost disappeared after Europeans arrived in Australia.

Aboriginal Art Draw students' attention to the illustration on this page. Aborigines of Australia have one of the oldest surviving cultures on Earth. Since they had no written language, they have traditionally used song, dance, and art to pass on knowledge and to celebrate their religion. Since ancient times the Aborigines have created rock engravings and mosaics painted on the ground. Aborigine artists now paint on canvas as well.

The artists' symbols have spiritual meanings and are handed down from one generation to the next. Wavy lines, dots, and rods all convey different ideas. Sometimes plain or concentric circles or animal tracks are also depicted.

Artists gravitate toward different styles, depending on where they live. For example, artists from Arnhem Land use many straight lines and cross-hatching. Dotted designs are common in art produced by the Aborigines of the central desert regions.

Activity: Have students try painting in the Aboriginal style using an American animal or legend as the subject matter.

History

The first humans to live in Australia were the Aborigines (a-buh-RIJ-uh-nees). They came from Southeast Asia at least 40,000 years ago. Early Aborigines hunted animals and gathered food from wild plants. They had many different languages, traditions, and customs. The arrival of Europeans changed life for the Aborigines.

European Settlers The British began settling colonies in Australia in 1788. Many of the first settlers were British prisoners, but other British settlers came, too. As the settlers built farms and ranches, they took over the Aborigines' lands. In addition, many Aborigines died of diseases brought unintentionally by the Europeans.

Independence The British granted independence to the Australian colonies in 1901. The colonies were united into one country within the British Commonwealth of Nations. Australia fought on the side of the British and other Allied forces in World Wars I and II.

Today Australia has six states and one large territory. The national capital is Canberra. Because Australia is part of the Commonwealth, the British monarch also is Australia's monarch. However, a prime minister and parliament make Australia's laws. Some Australians want their country to leave the Commonwealth and replace the monarch with an Australian president or other official.

✓ **READING CHECK:** (*Movement*) How has migration affected Australia's history? British settlers took Aborigine land and passed on diseases; led to membership in British Commonwealth

Culture

More than 90 percent of Australians today are of British or other European ancestry. Since the 1970s Asians have been moving to

States and Territories of Australia

State	Capital
New South Wales	Sydney
Victoria	Melbourne
Queensland	Brisbane
Western Australia	Perth
South Australia	Adelaide
Tasmania	Hobart

Territory	Capital
Northern Territory	Darwin
Australian Capital Territory	Canberra

Interpreting the Chart What is the capital of Tasmania?

◄**Chart Answer**

Hobart

Teaching Objective 3

ALL LEVELS: (Suggested time: 20 min.) Have students use the information presented in this section to create a pie chart depicting the ethnic diversity of the Australian population. At the bottom of their pie charts, have students write a few sentences to provide details about the significance of each group's history or culture. **LS VERBAL-LINGUISTIC**

►**ASSIGNMENT:** Have students write two paragraphs comparing and contrasting the people and culture of the United States and Australia, naming three similarities in the first paragraph and three differences in the second paragraph. Then have students write a third paragraph explaining which country would make a better home for an emigrant from a war-torn country. Students should support their answers with information presented in the first two paragraphs. Ask volunteers to read their papers to the class.

Cultural Kaleidoscope

Australia's

Cultural Mosaic Australia's ethnic composition is changing rapidly. An increasing number of the country's immigrants are from Asia. Recent immigrants have come from China, Malaysia, the Philippines, and Vietnam.

In recent years, Australia's response to migration has been a policy of multiculturalism. The aim of this approach is to maintain the integrity of each individual culture, while promoting education and awareness among all of Australia's ethnic groups.

Australian schools have adopted the use of multicultural curricula. In particular, many schools teach Asian languages and customs to students beginning in the elementary grades.

Critical Thinking: How does Australia's current multicultural policy differ from the attitudes of its first European settlers?

Answer: In contrast to Australia's current multicultural policy, the first settlers did not respect the Aborigines' culture.

Chart Answer ▶

It is higher.

▲
The Sydney Opera House opened on the city's harbor front in 1973. It is one of Australia's most well-known buildings.

Australia in growing numbers. As a result, about 7 percent of Australia's population today is ethnic Asian. Only about 1 percent of the country's people are Aborigines. Nearly all Australians speak English, but some Aborigines also speak native languages.

Religion and Holidays Most Australians are Christians. They celebrate many of the same holidays as people in the United States. However, their traditions may be different. For example, December falls during summer in Australia. Christmas there is time for a beach party, picnic, or some other outdoor activity.

Outdoor activities are popular in sunny Australia. Many people enjoy picnics, swimming, and sports. Popular sports include the British game of cricket, sailing, horse racing, surfing, and Australian Rules football. Many Australians also enjoy **rugby**. Rugby is a British game similar to football and soccer.

The Arts Music and other arts are also popular in Australia. In fact, art by Aborigines has become popular around the world. The Australian government is an important source of money for the arts. For example, the government has built many public performance halls. One of the most famous is the Opera House in Australia's largest city, Sydney.

Australia

Country	Population/ Growth Rate	Life Expectancy	Literacy Rate	Per Capita GDP
Australia	19,731,984 0.9%	77, male 83, female	100%	$27,000
United States	290,342,554 0.9%	74, male 80, female	97%	$37,600

Source: Central Intelligence Agency, *The World Factbook 2003*

Interpreting the Chart How does Australia's literacy rate compare to that of the United States?

✓ **READING CHECK:** (*Human Systems*) What are some characteristics of Australia's people?

90 percent British or European ancestry, 7 percent ethnic Asian, 1 percent Aborigine; mostly Christian

436 • Chapter 19

Teaching Objective 4

LEVEL 1: (Suggested time: 30 min.) Have students summarize Australia's strengths and the challenges facing the country today. Select volunteers to write items in a list on the chalkboard. Ask students if the United States has similar strengths or challenges. Discuss the comparisons with the class.
ESOL

LEVELS 2 AND 3: (Suggested time: 45 min.) Tell students to imagine that they are consultants who are applying for jobs to help Australia overcome one of its challenges. Students may select a challenge from the class list compiled in the Level 1 lesson. Have each student write a proposal listing several possible solutions to the selected issue. When students have finished their proposals, organize the class into groups according to the issues selected. Have members decide which of the proposed solutions would be most effective. Then have each group propose its solution to the class.
COOPERATIVE LEARNING, LS **VERBAL-LINGUISTIC**

Australia Today

About 85 percent of Australians live in and around cities. The rest live in the **bush**, or lightly populated wilderness areas. The largest cities are Sydney and Melbourne in the southeast. Brisbane, on the eastern coast, enjoys a warm, tropical climate that attracts tourists. Towns have grown around mining and ranching areas in parts of the dry, rugged outback. Large parts of the interior have few people. The seaport of Perth is the largest city in the west.

Economy Australia is a rich, economically developed country. It is a leading producer of agricultural goods such as wool, meat, and wheat. Australia supplies nearly half of the world's wool used in clothing. One of the country's most important industries is mining, particularly in the outback. Other industries include steel, heavy machines, and computers.

Challenges Australia faces important challenges. Among these is improving the economic and political status of the Aborigines. They have only recently gained back some of the rights they lost after Europeans colonized Australia. The country also must continue to build ties with Asian and Pacific countries. At one time Australia's strongest ties were with Britain. Today, its most important trading partners are much closer Asian countries and the United States. In addition, Australia must deal with the rapid growth of its cities. It also must protect native animals and the environment.

✓ **READING CHECK:** (*Places and Regions*) What is Australia's economy like?
rich, economically developed

Major Producers of Wool

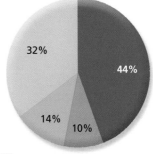

- Australia
- New Zealand
- China
- Rest of the world

Source: Based on data from The Woolmark Company

▲ Wool is produced from sheep's hair. Australia has one of the world's largest flocks of sheep.

Interpreting the Chart **What nearby country is the world's second-largest wool producer?**

Homework Practice Online
Keyword: SK5 HP19

Section Review 1

Define and explain: artesian wells, coral reef, endemic species, marsupials, outback, rugby, bush

Working with Sketch Maps On a map of Australia and New Zealand that you draw or that your teacher provides, label the following: Eastern Highlands, Central Lowlands, Western Plateau, Great Dividing Range, Tasmania, Murray-Darling Rivers, Great Artesian Basin, Great Barrier Reef, Sydney, Melbourne, Brisbane, and Perth. In a box in the margin, describe why the Great Artesian Basin is important to a dry country like Australia.

Reading for the Main Idea

1. (*Human Systems*) How has migration affected Australia's population? Which ethnic group is the largest?

2. (*Places and Regions*) What are two of Australia's most famous native marsupials?

3. (*Human Systems*) Who were the first humans to live in Australia? When did Europeans start settling there?

Critical Thinking

4. **Drawing Inferences and Conclusions** Why is building ties with Asian countries important for Australia today?

Organizing What You Know

5. **Categorizing** Copy the following graphic organizer. Use it to list Australia's climates, plants and animals, and mineral resources.

Climates	Plants and Animals	Resources

Answers to Section 1 Review

Define For definitions, see the glossary.

Working with Sketch Maps Maps will vary, but listed places should be labeled in their approximate locations. It provides water for sheep and other livestock.

Reading for the Main Idea

1. people of British and other European ancestry and Asian ancestry have moved there, leading to decline of Aborigine population; British and other European ancestry **(NGS 9)**

2. koala bear, kangaroo **(NGS 4)**
3. Aborigines; 1788 **(NGS 9)**

Critical Thinking

4. Possible answer: Trade with Asian countries is good for Australia's economy.

Organizing What You Know

5. climates—desert, steppe, humid, Mediterranean, tropical savanna; plants and animals—eucalyptus, marsupials; resources—gold, iron ore, bauxite, coal, natural gas, opals, diamonds

▲ **Chart Answer**

New Zealand

CLOSE

Call on students to answer these questions: What is a key feature of Australia's physical geography? What is a key feature of the country's human geography? Discuss responses.

REVIEW, ASSESS, RETEACH

Have students complete the Section Review. Then have students refer to the lists they made earlier of what they knew about Australia. Have students work with the same partners to correct inaccuracies and to add facts they learned in this section. Then have students complete Daily Quiz 19.1.

Then have students work in groups to prepare and perform a television commercial about Australia. **ESOL,** **COOPERATIVE LEARNING**

EXTEND

Have interested students conduct research on the Tasmanian wolf (or Tasmanian tiger, *Thylacinus cynocephalus*), a marsupial believed to have become extinct in the 1930s. Have students focus on the causes of its extinction and reasons why some people think that the animal still survives. **BLOCK SCHEDULING**

HISTORICAL GEOGRAPHY

The Eucalyptus The European settlement of Australia resulted in an exchange of species between the two continents. European botanists were very interested in the potential economic value of the new plants and animals they found in Australia. In particular, the eucalyptus tree provided a number of uses, including oils for medicine and perfume, timber, windbreaks, and ornamentation.

British botanists collected seeds and brought them back to England for cultivation. Kew Gardens near London has an excellent collection of Australian plants. Today large stands of eucalyptus can be found worldwide, from California and the Congo to Spain and Portugal.

Activity: California has recently begun an effort to remove some of its eucalyptus trees and restore native vegetation. Have students conduct research on the distribution, use, and environmental impact of eucalyptus trees.

Visual Record Answer ▶

possible answer: trampling of the river bank, which could lead to erosion

▶ **This Case Study feature addresses National Geography Standards 8, 12, and 14.**

CASE STUDY

NONNATIVE SPECIES IN AUSTRALIA

For about the last 35 million years, Australia has been separated from the other continents by oceans. During this time Australia's plants and animals developed in isolation from the rest of the world. Eventually, a unique Australian ecosystem developed. Many interesting species of plants and animals existed only in Australia. For example, kangaroos, koalas, and eucalyptus trees were all native to Australia. They were not found anywhere else in the world.

Europeans arrived in Australia in the late 1700s. They dramatically changed the natural balance that had developed over millions of years.

Europeans brought with them many new species of plants and animals. These nonnative species have had a major impact on the environment in Australia.

European settlers turned large areas of grasslands into fields for agriculture. They set up huge wheat farms in the south and southwest. They planted sugarcane fields in the northeast. These crops had never been grown in Australia. Farmers also brought nonnative animals, such as sheep, cows, and goats, into Australia. In less than 100 years, Australia had more than 100 million sheep and 8 million cows.

Cattle are herded on the island of Tasmania in Australia.

Interpreting the Visual Record Can you see how these animals are changing the environment? ▼

Introduced into Australia from Southeast Asia, water buffalo now eat food that Australia's native animals need to survive. ▶

CASE STUDY

Setting the Scene

Isolation can have a major effect on the distribution of plants and animals around the globe. Australian plant and animal life evolved to fit the continent's natural environment. Plants adapted to the low fertility of soils and gained the ability to live in a wide range of continental habitats. Marsupials filled the niches typically occupied by placental mammals on other continents. The arrival of Europeans ended the isolation of Australia's plants and animals. European settlers converted large areas of grassland into fields for agriculture and pasture. They also introduced animal species to the region that competed with Australia's native species for resources.

Building a Case

Have students read "Nonnative Species in Australia" and engage them in a discussion with the following questions: How long was Australia isolated from other continents? (35 million years) What kind of agriculture did the Europeans bring when they arrived in the late 1700s? (cattle, sheep, and goat raising; wheat and sugarcane farming) Have volunteers answer the questions at the end of the feature. Here are some additional facts to consider: About 10 percent of Australia's plants are nonnative. Introduced species threaten 64 percent of Australia's mammals, 27 percent of its birds, and 22 percent of its reptiles. More than half of Australia's endemic animal species are threatened by nonnative species.

When Europeans settled in Australia they brought with them many new plants and animals. Some of these plants and animals have become pests because they damage the environment.

Many of the nonnative species that were brought into Australia spread across the continent. Some are now considered pests. These plants and animals are seriously damaging Australia's environment. For example, camels were introduced into Australia as pack animals. Now they run wild in the desert interior. Water buffalo were introduced from Southeast Asia. They trample riverbanks, killing grasses and eroding the soil. The prickly pear cactus was introduced into Australia from the United States as a garden plant. It spread across much of the country and has been very hard to control. Cane toads were introduced in the 1930s to protect Australia's sugarcane fields from cane beetles. However, they release toxic chemicals when attacked and are now threatening native species and household pets.

Of the nonnative animals introduced into Australia, rabbits have probably been the most destructive. Brought in by hunters in the 1800s, rabbits multiplied and spread quickly. With no natural predators and lots of food, their numbers increased to about 500 million. Rabbits overgrazed Australia's grasslands and caused major soil erosion.

The introduction of nonnative species into Australia has damaged the environment in several ways. Some native species have become extinct because they could not compete with nonnative species. About 13 species of mammals and one species of bird have become extinct in Australia since the late 1700s. Many more are endangered. Nonnative species such as cows, sheep, and rabbits have caused soil erosion. These animals also consume food and water that Australia's native plants and animals need to survive. As the case of Australia shows, the introduction of nonnative species into a new environment can cause serious environmental problems.

Understanding What You Read

1. How did isolation affect Australia's ecosystem?

2. What are some of the species that Europeans brought with them to Australia? How does Australia's environment now reflect their influence?

Understanding What You Read

1. Isolation led to the development of a unique ecosystem in Australia. For example, kangaroos, koalas, and eucalyptus are native to this Australian ecosystem.

2. Europeans brought cows, goats, sheep, cane toads, camels, rabbits, and prickly pear cactus. Many of these species increased rapidly and competed with native species for resources such as food and water. Some overgrazed and caused soil erosion.

☑ **internet** connect

GO TO: **go.hrw.com**
KEYWORD: **SK5 CH19**
FOR: **Web sites about endemic species**

Drawing Conclusions

Lead a classroom discussion on the connection between soils, grasses, and animals in Australia. List each of these parts of the ecosystem on the chalkboard and have students answer the following questions:

- What was the impact of introduced species on soil? on grasses? on animals?
- How are these aspects of the natural world related to one another?
- How might changing one part of the system affect the other parts?
- Can you give examples from the text? from other sources?

Going Further: Thinking Critically

Islands are often home to rare species, which can be threatened by the introduction of new plants and animals. New Zealand, Hawaii, and Puerto Rico are just a few places where nonnative species have taken hold. Here is the percentage of nonnative species for each:

Location	Mammals	Plants	Birds	Fish
Australia	Unavailable	10%	Unavailable	13%
Hawaii	94%	47.4%	40%	76%
New Zealand	93%	46.7%	19%	53%
Puerto Rico	Unavailable	11.5%	23%	91%

Ask: How does the quantity of nonnative species in Australia compare to the other places? Why might this be so?

Section 2 New Zealand

Discover
1. What are the natural features of New Zealand?
2. What are the history and culture of New Zealand?
3. What are New Zealand's cities and economy like today?

Vocabulary
kiwi

Places
Tasman Sea
South Island
North Island
Southern Alps
Wellington
Auckland
Christchurch

Reading Strategy

TAKING NOTES Taking notes while you read will help you understand and remember the information in this section. Write down the headings in the section. As you read, fill in notes under each heading. What are the most important details under each?

Natural Features

New Zealand lies southeast of Australia across the Tasman Sea. It includes two large islands—South Island and North Island. Put together, the islands are about the size of the U.S. state of Colorado.

Land The highest mountains are the Southern Alps on South Island. These rugged, glacier-capped mountains cover the western half of the island. The highest peak reaches 12,349 feet (3,764 m). A narrow coastal plain stretches along South Island's eastern side.

North Island has three major volcanic peaks separated by a volcanic plateau. Volcanic eruptions are common. Most of the rest of North Island is covered by hills and coastal plains.

The Southern Alps stretch across much of New Zealand's South Island. New Zealand's government has established large national parks throughout the mountains.

440 • Chapter 19

Section 2

Objectives
1. Identify the natural features of New Zealand.
2. Describe the history and culture of New Zealand.
3. Explain what New Zealand's cities and economy are like today.

FOCUS

 Bellringer

Copy the following instructions onto the chalkboard: *Look at the map at the beginning of the chapter and write a short answer to this question: What would it be like to live in a country like New Zealand that is separated from other countries by hundreds of miles of ocean?* When students have finished writing, discuss their answers. Tell students that in Section 2 they will learn more about life in New Zealand.

Building Vocabulary

Write the term **kiwi** on the chalkboard. Ask a volunteer to read aloud the definition from the glossary. Inform students that this flightless bird is so deeply identified with the country that New Zealanders are often referred to as "Kiwis." Ask volunteers to suggest nicknames for Americans using a similar logic.

Autumn turns South Island's countryside golden near the city of Christchurch. New Zealand has four distinct seasons.

Climate, Wildlife, and Resources Unlike mostly dry Australia, New Zealand is humid. It has a mild marine west coast climate. Rain falls throughout the year. Winds from the west bring very heavy rain or snow to South Island's western side. The grassy plains of the drier eastern side are in a rain shadow. The north of North Island, in the lower latitudes, has a warmer, more tropical climate.

Much of New Zealand was once forested. Today, more than half is covered by pastures and farms. Sheep and other livestock graze in New Zealand's pastures. Sheep and their wool have long been important to the country's economy.

As in Australia, many animals in New Zealand are endemic species. The country's endemic species include different kinds of bats and flightless birds such as the **kiwi** (KEE-wee). The kiwi has hairlike feathers and sharp senses of smell and hearing. This bird is so linked with the country that New Zealanders are sometimes called Kiwis.

Many other species have been brought to New Zealand over time. For example, deer and trout have been introduced to provide sport for hunters and fishers.

New Zealand has fewer mineral resources than Australia. Its natural resources include gold, iron ore, natural gas, and coal.

✓ **READING CHECK:** (**Place**) What are the natural features of New Zealand?

two large islands; mountains, volcanic plateau, hills, coastal plains; many endemic species

History and Culture

New Zealand's first settlers came from other Pacific islands more than 1,000 years ago. Their descendants, the Maori (MOWR-ee), still live in New Zealand. The early settlers' main source of food was the moa—a giant, flightless bird. However, overhunting by New Zealand's early peoples wiped out the moa. The bird was extinct by the time Europeans arrived in New Zealand.

Maori traditional art, like this carved entrance arch, survived New Zealand's colonial period.

Interpreting the Visual Record What role does art play in Maori culture?

Australia and New Zealand 441

◀ **Chart Answer**

Traditional art is important in Maori culture.

Comparison of the Physical Geography of New Zealand's North Island and South Island

North Island
• three volcanic peaks separated by volcanic plateau
• hills and coastal plains
• northern area—warmer, more tropical climate

Both Islands
• marine west coast climate
• forests, pastures, farms
• endemic species
• fewer resources than Australia

South Island
• largest island
• Southern Alps—highest mountains in New Zealand
• narrow coastal plain along eastern side
• heavy rain and snow on western side
• grassy plains in rain shadow

Australia and New Zealand **441**

FOOD FESTIVAL

A Refreshing Kiwi Beverage For a New Zealand kiwi spritzer, combine 3 diced kiwifruit, 2 tbs sugar, and ½ c. orange juice in a blender. Blend until smooth. Pour ½ c. of mixture into a glass and stir in ¼ c. club soda. Note that this recipe should make approximately 4 servings. Be prepared to make more to serve your class.

▲
New Zealand's All Black Rugby Union team performs a version of the Haka (HAH-kah) before international games. The Haka is a traditional Maori dance.

▲
Mourners attend a funeral in a Maori-carved meeting house.

European Settlers A Dutch explorer in 1642 was the first European to sight New Zealand. British explorer Captain James Cook visited New Zealand in 1769. Many British settlers started to arrive after the British signed a treaty with the Maori in 1840. However, fighting broke out as British settlers took over Maori lands.

Independence The British granted New Zealand independence in 1907. Like Australia, New Zealand became a member of the British Commonwealth of Nations. New Zealanders fought alongside the British in World Wars I and II.

The government of New Zealand is led by a prime minister. An elected parliament makes the country's laws. The capital, Wellington, is located at the southern tip of North Island.

Culture Like Australia, most of New Zealand's 3.9 million people are of European ancestry. A growing number of ethnic Asians also live in the country. The Maori make up nearly 10 percent of the population. People from other Pacific islands have also come to New Zealand.

Most New Zealanders speak English. Some Maori also speak the Maori language. Most New Zealanders also are Christian. Sports, particularly rugby, are popular.

Maori culture has not disappeared. Traditional art, music, and dance remain important in Maori culture. Many Maori weddings, funerals, and other special events still are held in traditional carved houses. The Maori call these meetinghouses *whare whakairo*. Many meetinghouses are beautifully carved and decorated.

✔ **READING CHECK:** (**Human Systems**) How have conflict and cooperation affected the history of New Zealand? fighting between British and Maori initially; today, culture groups live together

---

Teaching Objectives 1–3

LEVEL 1: (Suggested time: 45 min.) Organize the class into five groups and have them make posters of the following topics about New Zealand: history and government, culture, people, natural features, and life today. Display the posters around the classroom.
ESOL, COOPERATIVE LEARNING

LEVEL 2: (Suggested time: 30 min.) Ask students to imagine that they are students in New Zealand. Have them write a letter to a friend in the United States to persuade the friend to move to New Zealand. Instruct students to discuss the country's physical geography and its cultural history as well as its cities and economy. **LS** **INTRAPERSONAL**

LEVEL 3: (Suggested time: 45 min.) Organize the class into groups. Have each group develop a front page for a New Zealand newspaper. Ask students to include information about the country's physical features and history as well as issues facing the country today using articles, cartoons, editorials, and other typical newspaper features. Then have a spokesperson from each group present his or her group's newspaper to the class.
COOPERATIVE LEARNING, LS INTERPERSONAL

New Zealand Today

Today about 75 percent of New Zealanders, including most Maori, live on North Island. Most of the country's industries and agriculture are also located there.

Cities About 85 percent of New Zealanders live in urban areas. The country's largest city and seaport, Auckland, is located in the northern part of North Island. Christchurch is South Island's largest city.

Economy New Zealand is a rich, modern country with a market economy. Its mild, moist climate helped make agriculture an important part of the economy. The country is a major producer of wool, meat, dairy products, wheat, kiwifruit, and apples.

New Zealand has become more industrialized in recent years. Factories turn out processed food, wood, paper products, clothing, and machinery. Banking, insurance, and tourism are also important industries. Australia, the United States, Japan, and the United Kingdom are the country's main trade partners.

✓ **READING CHECK:** (*Place*) What are some of New Zealand's cities, and what is its economy like?

Auckland, Christchurch; market; agricultural and industrial

Cable cars provide transportation for residents and visitors in Wellington.

New Zealand

Country	Population/ Growth Rate	Life Expectancy	Literacy Rate	Per Capita GDP
New Zealand	3,951,307 1.1%	75, male 81, female	99%	$20,200
United States	290,342,554 0.9%	74, male 80, female	97%	$37,600

Source: Central Intelligence Agency, *The World Factbook 2003*

Section Review 2

Define and explain: kiwi

Working with Sketch Maps On the map you created in Section 1, label the Tasman Sea, South Island, North Island, Southern Alps, Wellington, Auckland, and Christchurch. In a box in the margin, identify New Zealand's capital and the country's largest city.

Reading for the Main Idea

1. (*Human Systems*) From where did the ancestors of the Maori come?

2. (*Human Systems*) Describe New Zealand's economy. How has it changed in recent years?

Critical Thinking

3. Contrasting How is the physical geography of North Island different from that of South Island? Describe the physical geography of each island.

4. Drawing Inferences and Conclusions Why do you think most New Zealanders live on North Island?

Organizing What You Know

5. Summarizing Copy the following graphic organizer. Use it to list the climates, plants and animals, and resources of New Zealand.

Climates	Plants and Animals	Resources

Homework Practice Online
Keyword: SK5 HP19

Australia and New Zealand • 443

Section 2 Review

Answers to Section 2 Review

Define For definitions, see the glossary.

Working with Sketch Maps Maps will vary, but listed places should be labeled in their approximate locations. Wellington is the capital, and Auckland is the largest city.

Reading for the Main Idea

1. other Pacific islands **(NGS 9)**

2. market; agriculture is important; it has become more industrialized. **(NGS 12)**

Critical Thinking

3. North Island has volcanic peaks; South Island has glacier-capped mountains. The rest of North Island is covered by hills and coastal plains. The rest of South Island is a narrow coastal plain. **(NGS 4)**

4. Possible answer: It has a more pleasant climate.

Organizing What You Know

5. climates—marine west coast, tropical; plants and animals—wheat, sheep, kiwi, deer, trout; resources—gold, iron ore, natural gas, coal

CLOSE

Ask your students which country, Australia or New Zealand, they would prefer to visit. Have them state reasons for their preferences.

REVIEW, ASSESS, RETEACH

Have students complete the Section Review. Then have them work in groups to write multiple-choice quizzes about the section. Have groups check each other's quizzes. **COOPERATIVE LEARNING**

Have students complete Main Idea Activity S2. Then have students compile fact sheets on New Zealand's physical features, history, cities, and economy. Call on volunteers to read their fact sheets aloud. **ESOL**

EXTEND

Have interested students work in pairs to conduct research on the history of the Maori people. Instruct them to include the Maori's origins and customs. Ask them also to examine Maori political activism. Have each pair write a mock interview between an anthropologist and a Maori and present it to the class. **COOPERATIVE LEARNING, BLOCK SCHEDULING**

Define and Identify
For definitions, see the glossary and index.

Review the Main Ideas
9. Eastern Highlands, Central Lowlands, Western Plateau (**NGS 4**)

10. interior—desert, steppe; edges—humid, Mediterranean, tropical savanna (**NGS 4**)

11. volcanic plateau and peaks

12. 1788; 1840 (**NGS 9**)

13. Aborigines; Maori (**NGS 4**)

14. wool (**NGS 4**)

15. United States

Think Critically
16. possible answer: opportunity to explore a rich ecosystem

17. because of its arid climate

18. They built farms, ranches, and cities and introduced nonnative species.

19. New Zealand is more humid. Australia: desert, steppe, humid, Mediterranean, tropical savanna; New Zealand: marine west coast

20. The arts have been important to Aboriginal culture; recently the Australian government has been an important source of support for the arts.

21. by keeping the Maori language alive, practicing traditional arts, and holding special events in their carved meeting houses

Map Activity
22. A. Perth
B. Tasmania
C. Auckland
D. Great Barrier Reef
E. Central Lowlands
F. Melbourne
G. Sydney
H. Western Plateau

Review and Practice

Define and Identify
Identify each of the following:

1. artesian wells   **5.** outback

2. coral reef   **6.** rugby

3. endemic species   **7.** bush

4. marsupials   **8.** kiwi

Review the Main Ideas

9. What are the three main landform regions of Australia?

10. What are the climates of the interior and the "edges" of Australia like?

11. New Zealand's North Island is known for what type of landform?

12. When did Europeans begin to settle in Australia and New Zealand?

13. What native peoples lived in Australia and New Zealand before the arrival of Europeans?

14. Australia and New Zealand are the world's two top producers of what agricultural product?

15. What country is a major trading partner with both Australia and New Zealand?

Think Critically

16. Drawing Inferences and Conclusions Why do you think the Great Barrier Reef would interest tourists?

17. Drawing Inferences and Conclusions Why do you think Australia's interior is lightly populated?

18. Finding the Main Idea How have humans changed the natural environments of Australia and New Zealand since the arrival of Europeans?

19. Contrasting How is New Zealand's climate different from Australia's? Identify the main climates in each country.

20. Analyzing Information What role have the arts played in Australian society?

21. Drawing Inferences and Conclusions How have the Maori in New Zealand kept their traditional culture?

Map Activity
22. On a separate sheet of paper, match the letters on the map with their correct labels.

Central Lowlands   Sydney
Western Plateau   Melbourne
Tasmania   Perth
Great Barrier Reef   Auckland

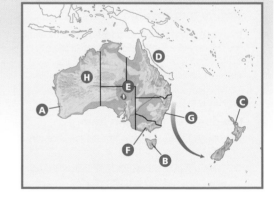

Writing Activity

Imagine that you are a European journalist in the late 1700s writing about the peoples and unique plants and animals in Australia and New Zealand. Write two paragraphs describing those peoples and endemic species. Include details that might surprise your European readers. Be sure to use standard grammar, spelling, sentence structure, and punctuation.

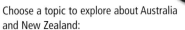

□ internet connect

Internet Activity: **go.hrw.com**
KEYWORD: SK5 GT19

Choose a topic to explore about Australia and New Zealand:
• Explore the Great Barrier Reef.
• Learn about the Aborigines of Australia.
• Tour New Zealand.

Social Studies Skills Practice

Interpreting Maps

Study the following map of some of Australia's cities. Then answer the questions.

1. What is the capital city of Australia?
2. What key characteristic can you determine about most of the cities in Australia?
3. Which city is located near the Great Barrier Reef?
4. Which city is far from a water source?

Analyzing Primary Sources

Read the following excerpt from the 1840 treaty between the Maori and the British government. Then answer the questions.

"Victoria, the Queen of England, in her concern to protect the chiefs and the subtribes of New Zealand and in her desire to preserve their chieftainship [trusteeship] and their lands and to maintain peace and good order considers it just to appoint [select] an administrator—one who will negotiate with the people of New Zealand to the end that their chiefs will agree to the Queen's government being established over all parts of this land . . ."

1. Does the treaty promise that the Maori will have an equal say in their government?
2. What will be the main role of the administrator?
3. Does the Queen express a desire to protect the Maori under her leadership? How?
4. What is the final goal of the treaty?

Writing Activity

Check to see that students have included accurate information about the region's plants and animals in the late 1700s. Details should be consistent with text information. Use Rubric 42, Writing to Inform, to evaluate student work.

Interpreting Maps

1. Canberra
2. located on or near the coast
3. Cairns
4. Alice Springs appears to be far from surface water, but the city's name indicates that springs can be found there.

Analyzing Primary Sources

1. no
2. negotiate with the people of New Zealand so that the chiefs will agree to British rule
3. includes comments about preserving the land and maintaining peace
4. to smooth the transition to British rule

REVIEW AND ASSESSMENT RESOURCES

Reproducible
◆ Readings in World Geography, History, and Culture 79 and 80
◆ Critical Thinking Activity 19
◆ Vocabulary Activity 19

Technology
◆ Chapter 19 Test Generator (on the One-Stop Planner)
◆ HRW Go site
◆ Audio CD Program, Chapter 19

Reinforcement, Review, and Assessment
◆ Chapter 19 Review and Practice
◆ Chapter Summaries and Review
◆ Chapter 19 Test
◆ Chapter 19 Test for ESOL and Special-Needs Students

□ internet connect

GO TO: **go.hrw.com**
KEYWORD: SK5 Teacher
FOR: a guide to using the Internet in your classroom

The Pacific Islands and Antarctica
Chapter Resource Manager

Objectives	Pacing Guide	Reproducible Resources
SECTION 1 **Physical Geography** (pp. 447–51) 1. Identify the physical features and resources of the Pacific Islands. 2. Identify the physical features and resources of Antarctica.	**Regular** 1.5 days Lecture Notes, Section 1 **Block Scheduling** .5 day *Block Scheduling Handbook, Chapter 20*	**RS** Know It Notes S1 **SM** Geography for Life Activity 33 **E** Lab Activities for Geography and Earth Science, Demonstrations 6 and 7 **ELL** Main Idea Activity S1
SECTION 2 **The Pacific Islands** (pp. 452–56) 1. Describe the history of the Pacific Islands. 2. Describe what the people and culture of the Pacific Islands are like. 3. Identify some challenges that Pacific Islanders face today.	**Regular** 1.5 days Lecture Notes, Section 2 **Block Scheduling** .5 day *Block Scheduling Handbook, Chapter 20*	**RS** Know It Notes S2 **RS** Graphic Organizer 20 **E** Cultures of the World Activity 9 **IC** Interdisciplinary Activities for the Middle Grades 37 **SM** Map Activity 20 **ELL** Main Idea Activity S2
SECTION 3 **Antarctica** (pp. 457–69) 1. Describe how Antarctica was explored. 2. Describe what research in Antarctica can tell us about our planet. 3. Identify the problems that threaten Antarctica's environment.	**Regular** .5 day Lecture Notes, Section 3 **Block Scheduling** .5 day *Block Scheduling Handbook, Chapter 20*	**RS** Know It Notes S3 **E** Environmental and Global Issues Activities 1 and 2 **IC** Interdisciplinary Activity for the Middle Grades 38 **E** Biography Activity: Roald Amundsen **ELL** Main Idea Activity S3

Chapter Resource Key

RS Reading Support

IC Interdisciplinary Connections

E Enrichment

SM Skills Mastery

A Assessment

REV Review

ELL Reinforcement and English Language Learners and English for Speakers of Other Languages (ESOL)

 Transparencies

 CD–ROM

 Music

 Video

 Internet

 Holt Presentation Maker Using Microsoft® PowerPoint®

 One-Stop Planner CD–ROM

See the *One-Stop Planner* for a complete list of additional resources for students and teachers.

One-Stop Planner CD–ROM

It's easy to plan lessons, select resources, and print out materials for your students when you use the *One-Stop Planner CD–ROM with Test Generator.*

Technology Resources

- One-Stop Planner CD–ROM, Lesson 20.1
- Earth: Forces and Formations CD–ROM/Seek and Tell/ Forces and Processes
- Geography and Cultures Visual Resources with Teaching Activities 61–66
- *ARGWorld* CD–ROM
- Homework Practice Online
- HRW Go site

- One-Stop Planner CD–ROM, Lesson 20.2
- *ARGWorld* CD–ROM
- Music of the World Audio CD Program, Selection 24
- Homework Practice Online
- HRW Go site

- One-Stop Planner CD–ROM, Lesson 20.3
- *ARGWorld* CD–ROM
- Homework Practice Online
- HRW Go site

Review, Reinforcement, and Assessment Resources

ELL	Main Idea Activity S1
REV	Section 1 Review
A	Daily Quiz 20.1
REV	Chapter Summaries and Review
ELL	English Audio Summary 20.1
ELL	Spanish Audio Summary 20.1

ELL	Main Idea Activity S2
REV	Section 2 Review
A	Daily Quiz 20.2
REV	Chapter Summaries and Review
ELL	English Audio Summary 20.2
ELL	Spanish Audio Summary 20.2

ELL	Main Idea Activity S3
REV	Section 3 Review
A	Daily Quiz 20.3
REV	Chapter Summaries and Review
ELL	English Audio Summary 20.3
ELL	Spanish Audio Summary 20.3

Meeting Individual Needs

Ability Levels

Level 1 Basic-level activities designed for all students encountering new material

Level 2 Intermediate-level activities designed for average students

Level 3 Challenging activities designed for honors and gifted-and-talented students

ESOL Activities that address the needs of students with Limited English Proficiency

Chapter Review and Assessment

E	Readings in World Geography, History, and Culture 81 and 82
SM	Critical Thinking Activity 20
REV	Chapter 20 Review and Practice
REV	Chapter Summaries and Review
ELL	Vocabulary Activity 20
A	Chapter 20 Test
A	Unit 6 Test
	Chapter 20 Test Generator (on the One-Stop Planner)
	Audio CD Program, Chapter 20
A	Chapter 20 Test for English Language Learners and Special-Needs Students
A	Unit 6 Test for English Language Learners and Special-Needs Students
	HRW Go Site

CHAPTER 20

The Pacific Islands and Antarctica
Previewing Chapter Resources

Holt Online Learning

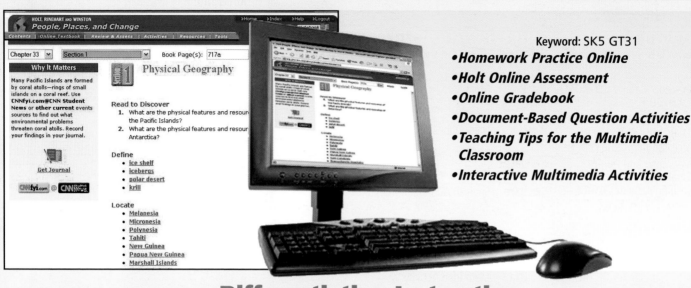

Keyword: SK5 GT31

- *Homework Practice Online*
- *Holt Online Assessment*
- *Online Gradebook*
- *Document-Based Question Activities*
- *Teaching Tips for the Multimedia Classroom*
- *Interactive Multimedia Activities*

Differentiating Instruction

Reading and Writing Support
◄ Graphic Organizer Activity
- *Vocabulary Activity*
- *Chapter Summary and Review*
- *Know It Notes*
- *Audio CD*

Active Learning
- *Block Scheduling Handbook*
- *Cultures of the World Activity*
- *Interdisciplinary Activity*
◄ Map Activity
- *Critical Thinking Activity 33*
- *Music of the World CD: Samoan Men's Choir*

Primary Sources and Advanced Learners
- *Geography for Life Activity: Diffusion Shapes the Pacific Islands*
◄ Map Activity: Pacific Island Voyages
- *Readings in World Geography, History and Culture:*
  - *81 Returning to the Rain Forest*
  - *82 Hunting Meteorites in Antarctica*

Assessment Program
◄ Daily Quizzes S1–2
- *Chapter Test*
- *Chapter Test for English Language Learners and Special-Needs Students*

Spanish and ESOL
- *Vocabulary Activity*
◄ Main Idea Activities for English Language Learners and Special-Needs Students
- *Chapter Summary and Review*
- *Spanish Audio Summary*
- *Know It Notes S1–2*
- *Chapter Test for English Language Learners and Special-Needs Students*

Special Education Modifications
Your **I.D.E.A. Works! CD-ROM** will provide modified versions of the following teaching materials:
◄ Guided Reading Strategies S1–2
- *Vocabulary Activity*
- *Main Idea Activities S1–2*
- *Daily Quizzes S1–2*
- *Chapter 20 Test*
- *Flash cards of chapter vocabulary terms*

Teacher Resources

Books for Teachers

Collier, Graham, and Patricia Collier. *Antarctic Odyssey: Endurance and Adventure in the Farthest South.* Carroll & Graf, 1999.

Finney, Ben, and Marlene Among, eds. *Voyage of Rediscovery: A Cultural Odyssey through Polynesia.* University of California Press, 1995.

Theroux, Paul. *The Happy Isles of Oceania: Paddling the Pacific.* Fawcett Books, 1993.

Books for Students

Baines, John D. *Antarctica.* Raintree/Steck-Vaughn, 1997. Discusses exploration, geography, and wildlife, as well as environmental decay.

Hermes, Jules M. *The Children of Micronesia.* Lerner Publications Company, 1995. Follows the lives of 15 children from different islands and backgrounds.
SHELTERED ENGLISH

Sperry, Armstrong. *Call It Courage.* Aladdin Paperbacks, 1990. How Mafatu, a Polynesian boy, conquered his fear of the sea.

Multimedia Materials

Heart of Antarctica. Video, 40 min. PBS.

Oceania and Antarctica. Transparency Kit. National Geographic Society.

South Pacific Oceania: The Philippines, Kiribati. Video, 22 min. Films for the Humanities and Sciences.

Videos and CDs

Videos
- CNN *Presents Geography: Yesterday and Today, Segment 35 Dateline Antarctica*
- *ARG World*

Holt Researcher
http://researcher.hrw.com
- *Papau New Guinea*
- *Pacific World and Antarctica*
- *Fiji*
- *Samoa*
- *Soloman Islands*

Transparency Packages

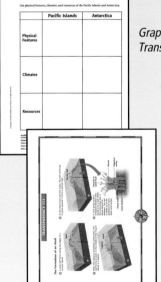

Graphic Organizer Transparencies 20.1–3

Geography and Cultures Visual Resources Transparencies 107–111
113 The Formation of an Atoll
114 The Moai of Easter Island
115 How Antarctic Ice Affects Climate

Map Activities Transparency 20 Pacific Island Voyages

445D

You may wish to point out to students these reasons for studying Pacific Islands and Antarctica:

▶ The Pacific Ocean covers about one third of Earth's surface. The Pacific Island region contains more water than land.

▶ Researchers in Antarctica have studied the rising levels of carbon dioxide in Earth's atmosphere and the thinning of the ozone layer over Antarctica. These processes may have adverse effects on Earth's climate.

▶ The natural beauty and pleasant climates of the Pacific Islands attract many tourists.

CHAPTER 20

The Pacific Islands and Antarctica

In this chapter we will study the Pacific Islands and Antarctica, two very different regions.

My name is Jean Vanessa, and I am 13 years old. I live in Vabukori, a village in Port Moresby, the capital of Papua New Guinea. My mother is a journalist. My grandmother bakes our bread in a drum oven. Sometimes we sell the bread.

My house is built on stilts. It is near the village square where we have meetings and play sports. After breakfast, I take a bus to Port Moresby Grammar School. I make my own sandwiches to take for lunch.

In my society, when you are an eldest child and a girl, and if you have younger brothers and sisters, you are your mother's helper. You have to learn to cook, clean, and take care of younger children.

My favorite holidays are Christmas and New Year's. We celebrate with feasting and singing. The villagers are divided into two groups. On Christmas Day one group cooks for the other group. They sing prophet songs about Bible stories from dawn to dusk. On New Year's Day the groups exchange roles.

Daba namona!

Translation: Good morning!

446 • Chapter 20

CHAPTER PROJECT

Have students conduct research on the explorations of the Polynesian people and build model outrigger canoes. Students should also prepare maps depicting some of the major migrations that resulted in the settlement of the Pacific Islands. Place the maps and a photograph of the model in the students' portfolios.

STARTING THE CHAPTER

Have students examine the photographs in the chapter and describe what they see. (Students are likely to describe both tropical and cold scenes.) Point out that the Pacific Island and Antarctic regions are not only very different geographically but also have been treated very differently by other nations. While international leaders have tried to preserve Antarctica's environment, Pacific Island cultures and ecosystems have sometimes suffered from international involvement. Tell students that in this chapter they will study these two very different regions.

Section 1 Physical Geography

Read to Discover
1. What are the physical features and resources of the Pacific Islands?
2. What are the physical features and resources of Antarctica?

Vocabulary
ice shelf
icebergs
polar desert
krill

Places
Melanesia
Micronesia
Polynesia
Tahiti
New Guinea
Papua New Guinea
Marshall Islands
New Caledonia
Transantarctic Mountains
Vinson Massif
Antarctic Peninsula

Reading Strategy

VISUALIZING INFORMATION Previewing the visuals in this section will help you understand the material you are about to read. What do the visuals on this page and the next two pages tell you about the regions you are studying? Write your answers on a sheet of paper.

The Formation of an Atoll

A A coral reef forms along the edges of a volcanic island.

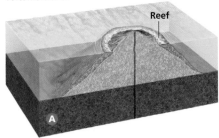
Reef

A

B As the island sinks into the ocean, the reef continues to grow upward. It forms a barrier reef.

Barrier reef

B

C When the island is completely underwater, the reef forms an atoll. In the middle of the ring of islands is a lagoon.

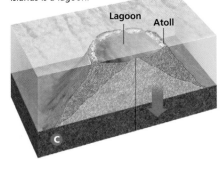
Lagoon   Atoll

C

D A coral polyp builds a limestone skeleton that bonds it to a reef. When the coral polyp dies, it leaves behind its skeleton. The reef is made up of the skeletons of many dead coral polyps.

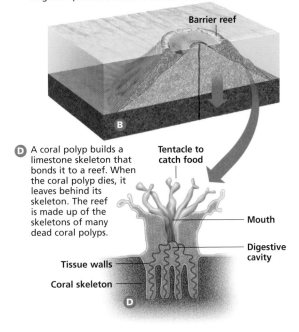
Tentacle to catch food
Mouth
Digestive cavity
Tissue walls
Coral skeleton
D

The Pacific Islands and Antarctica • 447

Section 1

Objectives
1. Describe the physical features and resources of the Pacific Islands.
2. Identify the physical features and resources of Antarctica.

FOCUS

Bellringer
Copy the following instructions onto the chalkboard: *What mental images do you form when you think of the Pacific Islands and Antarctica? Write down what you have imagined.* Allow students time to complete their responses. Then have volunteers share their images with the class. Tell students that in Section 1 they will learn more about the physical geography of these regions.

Using the Physical-Political Map
Have students examine this unit's physical and political maps. Remind students that an atoll is a ring of small islands that have formed on a coral reef surrounding a shallow lagoon. Point out that there are more than 20,000 islands in the Pacific Ocean and that many of the smaller ones are atolls.

COOPERATIVE LEARNING

Exploring New Guinea
Organize students into small groups. Tell them to imagine that they are on the staff of a travel magazine and must prepare an issue on the island of New Guinea. Students should conduct research on the natural geography of New Guinea as well as its historical geography.

Have each group prepare one feature article and one sidebar about the island to be compiled into a class magazine. Within each group, individual roles may include artist, desktop publisher, researcher, and writer.

internet connect

GO TO: go.hrw.com
KEYWORD: SK5 CH20
FOR: Web sites about New Guinea

▲

Place The airport on the left supports a healthy tourism industry in Bora-Bora, French Polynesia

The Pacific Islands

The Pacific Ocean covers more than one third of Earth's surface. East of Indonesia and the Philippines are thousands of large and small islands. These islands are divided into three regions: Melanesia, Micronesia, and Polynesia. These regions have high and low islands. Now we will look at these islands, their climates, and their resources.

High Islands There are two kinds of high islands: oceanic and continental. Oceanic high islands were formed by volcanoes rising from the sea floor. The Polynesian islands of Tahiti and Hawaii are examples of oceanic high islands. Many continental high islands also have volcanoes. However, these large islands were formed from continental rock. They lie on Australia's continental shelf. New Guinea, which is in Melanesia, is a continental high island.

New Guinea is the world's second-largest island. Only Greenland is larger. A long mountain chain stretches across the central part of New Guinea. The range's highest mountain lies in the western half of the island. It reaches an elevation of 16,535 feet (5,040 m). The western part of New Guinea is called Irian Jaya and is part of Indonesia. Papua New Guinea occupies the eastern half of the island.

Low Islands Most of the low islands are made of coral. They barely rise above sea level. Many are atolls. For example, the Marshall Islands include two parallel chains of coral atolls. The two chains are about 800 miles (1,287 km) long. The highest point is

448 • Chapter 20

TEACH

Teaching Objective 1

LEVEL 1: (Suggested time: 15 min.) Copy the following graphic organizer onto the chalkboard, omitting the blue answers. Use it to help students describe similarities and differences between the high and low islands. Call on students to fill in the organizer. **ESOL, LS VISUAL-SPATIAL**

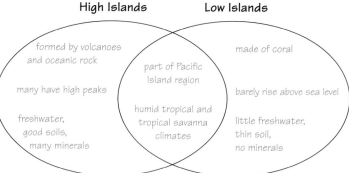

Physical Geography of the Pacific Islands

High Islands — Low Islands

formed by volcanoes and oceanic rock

many have high peaks

freshwater, good soils, many minerals

part of Pacific Island region

humid tropical and tropical savanna climates

made of coral

barely rise above sea level

little freshwater, thin soil, no minerals

just 33 feet (10 m) above sea level. Measured from the ground to their roofs, many buildings in your town are probably higher!

Climates and Plants Most of the Pacific Islands lie in the tropics and have a humid tropical climate. The temperatures are warm, and rain is common all year. New Guinea's central highland regions are cooler. Rainfall there is heavy, particularly on the southern slopes of the highlands. In some years more than 300 inches (762 cm) of rain fall there. Some islands, such as New Caledonia, have a tropical savanna climate. Rain there falls mostly in the summer.

The low islands have thin soils. These islands support few trees other than the coconut palm. However, the high islands have dense tropical rain forests. In fact, Papua New Guinea is one of the world's most densely forested countries. Many peoples living in the forests and rugged mountains of the central highlands were isolated for centuries.

Resources The islands' natural beauty and pleasant climates attract many tourists. In addition, the high islands have freshwater, good soils, and forest resources. Continental high islands also have many minerals. For example, New Guinea has copper, gold, silver, and oil. However, mining these resources is difficult in the rugged highlands and dense tropical forests.

Low islands have few resources. There is little freshwater, and thin soils limit farming. Partly because of this, low islands have smaller populations than high islands. Coconut palms and the sea are important sources of food.

✓ **READING CHECK:** (*Places and Regions*) What are the physical features and resources of the Pacific Islands? **High—formed by volcanoes or from continental rock, sometimes mountainous; low—mostly made of coral, are atolls; resources—high islands: natural beauty, freshwater, good soils, forests, some minerals; low islands: few resources, including the sea**

internet connect

GO TO: go.hrw.com
KEYWORD: SK5 CH20
FOR: Web sites about the Pacific Islands and Antarctica

(*Place*) Miners search for gold along a river in Papua New Guinea. They gently wash river water over pans to separate gold particles from less dense sand.

National Geography Standard 14

An Unwelcome Passenger
In addition to having few resources, the low island of Guam is threatened by an invasion of brown tree snakes. In the late 1950s these snakes—native to northeastern Australia, New Guinea, and nearby islands—arrived in Guam. They were probably accidentally stowed away in ship cargoes from New Guinea. The snake can easily hide itself in small spaces.

The snake has thrived on Guam because of the availability of prey and the lack of predators. By the late 1990s there were as many as 13,000 snakes per square mile in forested areas. The snake has virtually wiped out Guam's native forest birds. Several bird species—some found nowhere else in the world—have already disappeared, and many others are face extinction.

The snake has also affected humans. Guam has experienced a major power outage once every three days since 1980 because the snakes cross power lines and cause short circuits.

Discussion: Ask students the following questions: What measures could have been taken to prevent the problems caused by the brown tree snakes? What can be done now to save Guam's wildlife?

The Pacific Islands and Antarctica • 449

LEVEL 2: (Suggested time: 20 min.) Have students write paragraphs supporting the following statement: "The limitations of the low islands' physical geography have resulted in few people living there." Call on volunteers to read their paragraphs aloud to the class.

LEVEL 3: (Suggested time: 45 min.) Have students conduct research on the forests of New Guinea from the perspective of a conservationist. Call on students to present oral reports describing the flora and fauna native to the forests and advocating the preservation of these areas. **LS** **AUDITORY-MUSICAL**

Teaching Objective 2

LEVEL 1: (Suggested time: 25 min.) Pair students. Have one student in each pair use the textbook and classroom resources to list the land features and resources of Antarctica. The other student should list Antarctica's climatic and wildlife features. Then have students exchange lists with their partners and check each other's work. After discussing the lists, students can identify which of the continent's features they find most interesting and explain why to their partners. **ESOL, COOPERATIVE LEARNING**

Icebergs and Sea Level For many years scientists thought that icebergs breaking off the ice sheet of Antarctica were causing the world's ocean levels to rise. In the 1900s the sea level rose 7 inches (18 cm) and about 5.5 inches (14 cm) of that had been attributed to the breaking off of icebergs.

However, a recent study suggests that there may be other explanations. Over a five-year period researchers used satellites to measure changes in the thickness of the Antarctic ice sheet. They determined that the thickness has dropped by less than half an inch per year and that melting within the ice sheet has caused ocean levels to rise less than one inch over the last 100 years.

Scientists suggest other explanations for the rising ocean levels. These reasons include global warming, which is melting mountain glaciers and contributing to rising sea levels.

Critical Thinking: Why may scientists have thought icebergs were causing sea levels to rise?

Answer: Students might suggest that the breakaway icebergs were more immediately apparent to researchers.

Visual Record Answer ▶

wind, waves, and melting in warmer waters

▲

Huge icebergs like this one are found in the ocean waters around Antarctica. Icebergs are most numerous in the spring and summer. The warmer weather causes more ice to break away from ice sheets and glaciers.

Interpreting the Visual Record What forces do you think shaped this iceberg?

Antarctica

In the southernmost part of the world is the continent of Antarctica. This frozen land is very different from the tropical Pacific Islands.

The Land Antarctica is larger than the United States and Mexico combined. Ice covers about 98 percent of Antarctica's 5.4 million square miles (14 mil sq km). This ice sheet contains more than 90 percent of the world's ice. On average the ice sheet is more than one mile (1.6 km) thick.

The Transantarctic Mountains divide the continent into East Antarctica and West Antarctica. Antarctica's highest mountain peak is Vinson Massif. It rises to 16,864 feet (5,140 m). The continent also includes a few dry coastal valleys and the Antarctic Peninsula. (See the map of Antarctica in Focus On Environment at the end of this chapter.)

The weight of Antarctica's ice sheet causes the ice to flow slowly off the continent. When the ice reaches the coast, it forms a ledge over the water. This ledge is called an **ice shelf**. Sometimes huge chunks of ice, called **icebergs**, break away and drift into the ocean. Some of these icebergs are larger than the state of Rhode Island.

Climate and Wildlife Antarctica is the planet's coldest, driest, highest, and windiest continent. During the Southern Hemisphere's winter, the continent is hidden from the Sun. It remains in total darkness. During Antarctica's short summer, the Sun never sets.

LEVELS 2 AND 3: (Suggested time: 40 min.) Have students imagine that they are scientists conducting research on Antarctica. They have agreed to keep a journal of their discoveries and activities during their week-long stay. Students should write diary entries describing and explaining the formation of the physical features and resources of this continent and include illustrations. Have volunteers share their entries with the class.

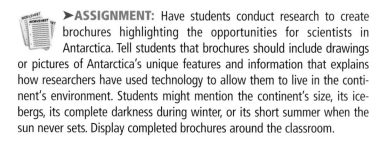

▶**ASSIGNMENT:** Have students conduct research to create brochures highlighting the opportunities for scientists in Antarctica. Tell students that brochures should include drawings or pictures of Antarctica's unique features and information that explains how researchers have used technology to allow them to live in the continent's environment. Students might mention the continent's size, its icebergs, its complete darkness during winter, or its short summer when the sun never sets. Display completed brochures around the classroom.

Antarctica's temperatures can drop below -120°F (-84°C). Less precipitation falls in this polar desert than in the Sahara in Africa. A **polar desert** is a high-latitude region that receives little precipitation. However, there is almost no evaporation or melting of ice. As a result, Antarctica's ice has built up over thousands of years.

The continent's warmest temperatures are found on the Antarctic Peninsula, which has a tundra climate. In January, during Antarctica's summer, temperatures on the coast average just below freezing.

Only tundra plant life survives in the rare ice-free areas. A few insects are the frozen land's only land animals. Antarctica has never had a permanent human population. Marine animals live in the icy waters around the continent. These animals include penguins, seals, and whales. They depend on tiny shrimplike creatures called **krill** for food.

Resources Antarctica has many mineral resources, including iron ore, gold, copper, and coal. However, there is debate over whether these resources should be mined. Some people worry that mining would harm the continent's environment. Others question whether mining in Antarctica would even be worthwhile for businesses.

✓ **READING CHECK:** (*Places and Regions*) What are the physical features and resources of Antarctica? ice sheet, mountains, limited tundra plant life, few insects, marine animals; mineral resources

The emperor penguin is one of the most common marine animals found in Antarctica. Penguins are flightless birds and are awkward on land. However, they are very good swimmers and are able to live in the icy climate.

◄

go.
hrw
.com
Homework Practice Online
Keyword: SK5 HP20

Section Review 1

Define and explain: ice shelf, icebergs, polar desert, krill

Working with Sketch Maps On maps of the Pacific Islands and Antarctica that you draw or that your teacher provides, label the following: Melanesia, Micronesia, Polynesia, Tahiti, New Guinea, Papua New Guinea, Marshall Islands, New Caledonia, Transantarctic Mountains, Vinson Massif, and Antarctic Peninsula.

Reading for the Main Idea

1. (*Places and Regions*) What kinds of islands are found in the Pacific? How were they formed?

2. (*Places and Regions*) What animal life is found in Antarctica?

3. (*Places and Regions*) Which of the Pacific Islands is the second-largest island in the world?

Critical Thinking

4. **Making Generalizations and Predictions** What might happen if people were to begin mining Antarctica's mineral deposits on a large scale?

Organizing What You Know

5. **Summarizing** Copy the following graphic organizer. Use it to list physical features, climates, and resources of the Pacific Islands and Antarctica.

	Pacific Islands	Antarctica
Physical features		
Climates		
Resources		

The Pacific Islands and Antarctica • 451

CLOSE

Ask students the following questions: Given the opportunity, would you choose to travel through the Pacific Islands in an outrigger canoe or explore Antarctica with modern equipment? On what did you base your choice?

REVIEW, ASSESS, RETEACH

Have students complete the Section Review. Then ask each student to create three multiple-choice questions for this section. Pair students and have them complete and then grade their partners' quizzes. Then have students complete Daily Quiz 20.1. **COOPERATIVE LEARNING**

Have students complete Main Idea Activity S1. Then write *high islands, low islands,* and *Antarctica* on the chalkboard. Ask students to name terms that describe the physical features and climates of each. List them under the appropriate heading. **ESOL**

EXTEND

Have interested students conduct research on the effect that global warming may be having on the low islands of the Pacific region and measures being taken to protect these islands. Have students present their findings to the class. **BLOCK SCHEDULING**

Visual Record Answer ▶

fairly accurate

Section 2 The Pacific Islands

Read to Discover
1. What is the history of the Pacific Islands?
2. What are the people and culture of the Pacific Islands like?
3. What are some challenges that Pacific Islanders face today?

Vocabulary
trust territories
Exclusive Economic Zones

Places
Guam
Northern Mariana Islands
Wake Island
French Polynesia

People
James Cook

Reading Strategy

DEVELOPING VOCABULARY   Find unfamiliar words in this section. On a sheet of paper, write down what you think they might mean. Then look the words up in a dictionary. How do the words relate to the section's topics?

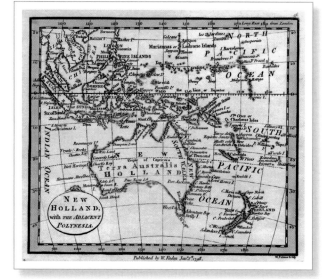

▲
This map of the South Pacific was made by a European cartographer in 1798.

Interpreting the Visual Record
Compare this map to the unit map. How accurate was this 1798 map?

452 • Chapter 20

History

Scholars believe that people began settling the Pacific Islands at least 40,000 years ago. Most early settlers came from Southeast Asia. The large islands of Melanesia were the first islands in the region settled. Over time, people moved to the islands of Micronesia and Polynesia.

Europeans in the Pacific In the early 1500s Ferdinand Magellan became the first European to explore the Pacific. In the late 1700s British captain James Cook explored the region. He visited all the main island regions of the Pacific. By the late 1800s European countries controlled most of the Pacific Islands. These European countries included France, Germany, the Netherlands, Spain, and the United Kingdom.

Modern History The Pacific Islands were battlegrounds during several wars in the colonial era. For example, the Spanish-American War of 1898 cost Spain the Philippines and Guam. They became U.S. territories after the war. Spain then sold other island territories to Germany. After World War I ended in 1918, Japan took over Germany's territories in the Pacific.

Section 2

Objectives

1. Explain the history of the Pacific Islands.
2. Describe the people and culture of the Pacific Islands.
3. Identify some of the challenges facing Pacific Islanders today.

FOCUS

 Bellringer

Copy the following instructions onto the chalkboard: *What do you think may be a benefit of living in the Pacific Islands today? What may be a challenge? Write your answers in your notebook.* Discuss student responses. Tell students that in Section 2 they will learn more about the history and challenges facing people of the Pacific Islands.

Building Vocabulary

Write the terms **trust territories** and **Exclusive Economic Zones** on the chalkboard. Have volunteers read the definitions aloud from the glossary. Then ask students to suggest possible reasons a country would want an EEZ (to ensure profit from its coastal resources) as well as how a country could enforce such a policy. (Possible answer: patrolling its coasts)

Japan conquered many other islands in World War II. The United States and its allies eventually won them back and defeated Japan. The United Nations then made some islands **trust territories**. Trust territories are areas placed under the temporary control of another country. When the territory later sets up its own government, it gains independence. U.S. trust territories included much of Micronesia.

Most of the island countries won independence in the last half of the 1900s. Australia, France, New Zealand, the United Kingdom, and the United States still have Pacific territories. U.S. territories include the Northern Mariana Islands, Guam, and Wake Island.

✓ **READING CHECK:** (*Places and Regions*) What are some events in the history of the Pacific Islands? initial settlement 40,000 years ago; 1500s—Pacific explored by Ferdinand Magellan; 1700s—explored by Captain James Cook; 1800s—islands European-controlled; battleground during several wars;1900s—independence

Culture

About 7 million people live in Melanesia, Micronesia, and Polynesia today. Check the unit map as we look more closely at each region and its people.

Melanesia Melanesia stretches from New Guinea to Fiji. It is the most populous of the three Pacific Island regions. Papua New Guinea and Fiji have the largest populations. Nearly two thirds of all Pacific Islanders live in Papua New Guinea.

Most Melanesians live in rural areas. Many homes in Melanesia and the other regions are made of timber and thatch, or straw. Papua New Guinea's capital, Port Moresby, is Melanesia's largest city. Nearly 260,000 people live there.

Melanesia's population includes ethnic Europeans and Asians, particularly Indians and Chinese. Many ethnic Asians are descended from people brought to the islands to work on colonial plantations. In Fiji, Indians make up nearly half of the population.

Either English or French is the official language on nearly all of the islands. This is a reflection of the region's colonial history. However, hundreds of local languages also are spoken there. In fact, about 700 languages are spoken in New Guinea alone. Many Papua New Guineans live in rugged, forested areas. They have had little contact with people from other areas. These isolated peoples developed their own languages.

Europeans brought Christianity to Melanesia and the other island regions. Today, most Pacific Islanders are Christian. However, some Melanesians still practice traditional local religions.

Micronesia and Polynesia Micronesia includes more than 2,000 tiny islands north of Melanesia. It stretches from Palau in the west to Kiribati in the east. Polynesia is the largest Pacific region. Its

▲ Students learn the day's lessons at a school in Papua New Guinea. Papua New Guinea's government has struggled to make education available for all students. Many countries in Micronesia and Polynesia offer schooling for students through high school.

Tok Pisin Although Papua New Guinea has slightly more than 5 million people, its residents speak more than 700 languages. There are some 6,000 languages spoken in the entire world. Most of the Papuan languages are complex and are spoken by very small groups of people.

To communicate with each other, the people of New Guinea use Tok Pisin, a language based on English. Tok Pisin is a pidgin language with a limited vocabulary. About 50,000 residents use Tok Pisin as their first language. Some 2 million more use it as their second language.

Tok Pisin plays a vital role in uniting Papuans. It is the language used most frequently in commerce and in the parliament.

Critical Thinking: Why do you think the people of Papua New Guinea speak so many different languages?

Answer: The island's physical geography and the existence of many small, isolated groups have contributed to its linguistic diversity.

The Pacific Islands and Antarctica • 453

Teaching Objective 1
ALL LEVELS: (Suggested time: 30 min.) Organize students into groups. Assign each group a significant event in the history of the Pacific Islands. Ask each group to illustrate the event and to write a caption for its illustration. Have groups display their completed pictures on the chalkboard. Ask volunteers to arrange all the events in chronological order. **ESOL, COOPERATIVE LEARNING,** 🅛🅢 **VISUAL-SPATIAL**

Teaching Objective 2
LEVEL 1: (Suggested time: 30 min.) Organize students into three groups. Assign each group one of the regions in the Pacific: Melanesia, Micronesia, or Polynesia. Have group members list aspects of the people and culture of their assigned region. Have each group present its completed list to the class. **ESOL, COOPERATIVE LEARNING**

Linking Past to Present

Tapa Cloth Early Polynesians made innovative use of available materials. They wove mats and roofs from the leaves of the coconut palm and made meals from the coconut's meat and liquid.

Early Polynesians also used tree bark to make ornamental cloth known as tapa. They pounded the bark into a feltlike cloth and decorated it with geometric designs. Polynesians used tapa for clothing, interior decoration, and bedding, among other things. Many Polynesians continue the tradition of tapa making today, and tapa craft items are important to the tourist trade.

Activity: Have students conduct research on the types of tapa cloth designs used by Polynesians. Why do they use these designs? Then have students reproduce some of the designs on paper.

Focus on Culture ▶

Answer
to make the game more relevant to their own culture

FOCUS ON CULTURE

Playing with the Rules

People of the South Pacific have made interesting changes to some European sports. Missionaries brought cricket, an English bat-and-ball game, to the Trobriand Islands east of New Guinea. The islanders changed cricket into more of a ritual. They added costumes, chants, and dances. They also changed almost all the rules. Up to 60 men play on a team. A regular cricket team has only 11 members. These huge matches may go on for weeks. A special dance and song celebrates each point. Even the game's basic movements are different. Players throw the ball as if they are throwing spears.

Pacific Islanders also enjoy other unusual sports. Outrigger canoe racing, underwater spearfishing, and coconut tree climbing are all popular sporting events.

Why do you think the Trobriand Islanders changed the rules for playing cricket?

corners at New Zealand, Hawaii, and Easter Island form a huge triangle.

The populations of most Micronesian and Polynesian islands are much smaller than those of Melanesia. However, towns on these small islands can be very crowded. Micronesia is the most urban of the Pacific Island regions. Most Polynesians live in rural areas.

As in Melanesia, ethnic Europeans and Asians live in Micronesia and Polynesia. Most people in these regions are Christian and speak either English or French. Some speak local languages or Japanese.

✓ **READING CHECK:** (**Human Systems**) What are some characteristics of the people and cultures of Melanesia, Micronesia, and Polynesia? mostly rural dwellers, ethnic Europeans and Asians, Mostly French and English-speaking, Christian

454 • Chapter 20

LEVELS 2 AND 3: (Suggested time: 45 min.) Organize students into groups of four. Have each group use drawings or pictures from magazines to write and illustrate a guidebook describing the people and culture of the Pacific Islands. Students should organize their work so that all group members have the opportunity to do both writing and illustrating.
COOPERATIVE LEARNING

Teaching Objective 3

LEVEL 1: (Suggested time: 20 min.) Copy the following graphic organizer onto the chalkboard, omitting the blue answers. Use it to help students identify challenges facing the people of the Pacific Islands. **ESOL**

Challenges Pacific Islanders Face

Economy	Environment	Culture
• Many countries import more than they export. • Many countries rely on Australia, Great Britain, Japan, the European Union, and the United Nations for economic aid.	• Nuclear tests were conducted in the region from the 1940s through the 1990s.	• Many residents fear loss of traditions and beliefs. • Modern travel and communications have introduced influences from other regions. • Residents worry about the effects of tourism, television, processed food, and alcohol.

The Pacific Islands Today

Many people imagine sunny beaches and tourists when they think of the Pacific Islands today. The islands do attract many tourists. For example, Tahiti, in French Polynesia, is a popular vacation spot. Many vacationers from South Korea and Japan enjoy visiting Guam, in Micronesia. Despite the region's healthy tourism industry, however, the Pacific countries face important challenges.

Economy The Pacific Islands are trying to build stronger economies. Tourism, agriculture, and fishing are already important there. Some countries, particularly Papua New Guinea, export valuable minerals and forest products.

Each Pacific country claims control of the fishing and seabed minerals around its islands. The 200-nautical-mile (370 km) zones they claim are called **Exclusive Economic Zones** (EEZs). Most of the world's countries also claim EEZs. A country must pay fees to fish or mine in another country's EEZ.

Natural resources should help the island economies grow. However, many Pacific countries import more products from abroad than they export. Many countries rely on the United Nations, the European Union, Great Britain, Australia, and Japan for economic aid.

Environment Many Pacific Islanders are concerned about their region's environment. Many have been angered by nuclear weapons tests conducted in the region by other countries. The United States held such tests in the islands from the 1940s to the 1960s. Radiation left some islands unsafe for people for many years. France held nuclear tests in the region until the mid-1990s.

A fisher casts his net along the coast of New Caledonia.
▶

Pacific Islands

COUNTRY	POPULATION/ GROWTH RATE	LIFE EXPECTANCY	LITERACY RATE	PER CAPITA GDP
Fiji	868,531 / 1.4%	66, male / 71, female	93%	$5,500
Kiribati	98,549 / 2.3%	57, male / 64, female	Not available	$840
Marshall Islands	56,429 / 2.3%	67, male / 71, female	93%	$1,600
Micronesia, Federated States of	108,143 / 0.4%	67, male / 70, female	89%	$2,000
Nauru	12,570 / 2.0%	58, male / 65, female	Not available	$5,000
Palau	19,717 / 1.7%	66, male / 72, female	92%	$9,000
Papua New Guinea	5,295,816 / 2.3%	62, male / 66, female	66%	$2,300
Samoa	178,173 / −0.2%	67, male / 73, female	99%	$5,600
Solomon Islands	509,190 / 3.0%	69, male / 74, female	Not available	$1,700
Tonga	108,141 / 1.9%	66, male / 71, female	99%	$2,200
Tuvalu	11,305 / 1.4%	65, male / 69, female	Not available	$1,100
Vanuatu	199,413 / 1.6%	60, male / 63, female	53%	$2,900
United States	290,342,554 / 0.9%	74, male / 80, female	97%	$37,600

Source: Central Intelligence Agency, *The World Factbook 2003*

Interpreting the Chart What is the literacy rate like in most of the Pacific Islands?

Bikini Atoll After World War II, the United States received permission from the ruler of Bikini Atoll—part of the Marshall Islands—to perform atomic weapons tests there. Residents were evacuated.

The United States set off more than 60 blasts. Most of the radioactive fallout dropped to the testing area, but some radioactive particles fell on inhabited islands.

In 1969 the U.S. military told the island's former residents that it was safe to return to Bikini. Several families then returned only to discover that their food and water were not safe to consume. Today, Bikini Atoll has been declared safe for scuba diving and fishing, but many residents still face health concerns.

Activity: Have students imagine they are post–World War II Bikini residents. Have them write letters accepting or rejecting the U.S. request to test atomic weapons on their land.

▲ **Chart Answer**

very high

LEVELS 2 AND 3: (Suggested time: 35 min.) Have students imagine that they are authors living 100 years in the future and that they have been asked to write a children's book about the challenges the Pacific Islanders faced in 2004. Students should select an issue from one of the three areas covered in the previous activity and write a paragraph summarizing the challenge and the efforts Pacific Islanders made to overcome it. Have volunteers share their paragraphs with the class. **LS VERBAL LINGUISTIC**

TEACHER TO TEACHER

Susan Walker of Beaufort, South Carolina, suggests the following activity to help students learn about the challenges facing the people of the Pacific Islands today. Have students work in groups or individually to draft a treaty for the Pacific Islands similar to the treaty drafted to protect the environment of Antarctica in 1959. Encourage students to use their textbooks as well as outside resources to complete this project.

Answers to Section 2 Review

Define For definitions and identification, see the glossary and index.

Working with Sketch Maps Maps will vary, but listed places should be labeled in their approximate locations.

Reading for the Main Idea

1. Southeast Asia; Melanesia (NGS 9)

2. France, Germany, Japan, the Netherlands, Spain, the United Kingdom, and the United States (NGS 12)

Critical Thinking

3. Many Pacific Islanders speak European languages and practice Christianity.

4. developing economies, protecting the environment, and preserving cultures (NGS 18)

Organizing What You Know

5. 1500s—Magellan explores the Pacific; late 1700s—Cook visits the Pacific Islands; late 1800s—most islands become European colonies; 1898—the Philippines and Guam become U.S. territories; 1918—Japan given German colonies; 1945—the Allies retake islands Japan had captured in World War II; late 1900s—most Pacific Islands become independent

Place This Fijian chief's home has many traditional handicrafts. Fiji's Great Council of Chiefs has influence in the country's political system and culture.

Some people who live on islands still controlled by foreign countries want independence, which has led to outbreaks of violence. This happened in the 1980s in the French territory of New Caledonia. France has agreed to give New Caledonians more control over their local government.

Culture Many Pacific Islanders are also concerned about the loss of traditional customs and beliefs. Modern travel and communications have introduced influences from other regions. Islanders worry about the cultural effects of tourism, television, processed food, and alcohol.

✓ **READING CHECK:** (*Human Systems*) What are some challenges Pacific Islanders face today? need stronger economies; face environmental dangers from nuclear testing; some conflict regarding foreign control; loss of traditional customs

Homework Practice Online
Keyword: SK5 HP20

Section Review 2

Define or identify: James Cook, trust territories, Exclusive Economic Zones

Working with Sketch Maps On the map of the Pacific Islands that you created in Section 1, label the region's countries. Then label the territories of Guam, Northern Mariana Islands, Wake Island, and French Polynesia.

Reading for the Main Idea

1. (*Human Systems*) From where did the Pacific Islands' first settlers come? Which Pacific Island region was settled first?

2. (*Human Systems*) What colonial powers once controlled most of the Pacific Islands?

Critical Thinking

3. **Finding the Main Idea** In what ways did Europeans influence the islands' cultures?

4. **Finding the Main Idea** What are some of the challenges facing Pacific Islanders today?

Organizing What You Know

5. **Sequencing** Use this time line to explain important people and events in the region's history.

1500 ———————————————— 2000

CLOSE

Ask students to answer the following question: How has colonization affected the people of the Pacific Islands?

REVIEW, ASSESS, RETEACH

Have students complete the Section Review. Then have them work in groups to write six multiple-choice questions about the information presented in this section. Have groups complete and check each other's quizzes. Then have students complete Daily Quiz 20.2.

Have students complete Main Idea Activity S2. Then organize the class into groups to compose songs about the people, history, and culture of the Pacific Islands. **ESOL, COOPERATIVE LEARNING, LS AUDITORY-MUSICAL**

EXTEND

Have interested students conduct research on Nan Madol, a ceremonial center built on 92 artificial islets within a lagoon on Pohnpei, Micronesia. As students to examine the site's history and its importance for tourism. **BLOCK SCHEDULING**

Section 3 Antarctica

Read to Discover

1. How was Antarctica explored?
2. What can research in Antarctica tell us about our planet?
3. What problems threaten Antarctica's environment?

Vocabulary
antifreeze

Places
South Pole
Ross Ice Shelf

People
Ernest Shackleton

Reading Strategy

BRAINSTORMING Brainstorm about the following topics: traveling to Antarctica, climate and conditions in Antarctica, and environmental threats to Antarctica. After brainstorming, read the section. How does your brainstorming relate to the topic? Were your thoughts about Antarctica accurate?

Early Explorers

Can you imagine a time when a large continent like Antarctica was a complete mystery? Today, orbiting satellites give us views of all of Earth's surface. Jet airliners and modern ships take people to all points on the globe. However, all of this has become possible only in the last century. For a long time, stormy ocean waters hid Antarctica from explorers. In the 1770s British explorer James Cook sighted icebergs in the waters around Antarctica. These icebergs suggested the existence of the vast, icy continent.

Other explorers followed. Some died in Antarctica's dangerous conditions while attempting to reach the South Pole and return. The huts of famous Antarctic explorers are still scattered across the continent. The first human expedition reached the South Pole in 1911.

Some countries have claimed parts of Antarctica. These countries and others agreed in 1959 to preserve the continent "for science and peace." The Antarctic Treaty of 1959 prevented more claims to the continent. It banned military activity there and set aside the whole continent for research.

✓ **READING CHECK:** (*Environment and Society*) How did the physical environment affect early efforts to explore Antarctica?

Extreme cold and stormy waters kept people from reaching the area and returning.

BIOGRAPHY

Sir Ernest Shackleton
(1874–1922)

Character Trait: Responsibility

In 1914, Ernest Shackleton and his crew of 27 men set out to be the first to cross the entire Antarctic continent. But their ship, *Endurance*, became completely frozen in ice. Using their ship's rescue boats, Shackleton and his crew sailed to a nearby deserted island. Shackleton then decided to sail another 800 miles to reach help on South Georgia Island. After surviving the dangerous journey, Shackleton then led four expeditions to rescue the rest of his crew.

What actions did Shackleton take to demonstrate responsibility?

SECTION 3 RESOURCES

Reproducible
- Lecture Notes, Section 3
- Know It Notes S3
- Environmental and Global Issues Activities 1 and 2
- Interdisciplinary Activities for the Middle Grades 38
- Biography Activity: Roald Amundsen

Technology
- One-Stop Planner CD–ROM, Lesson 20.3
- Homework Practice Online
- HRW Go site

Reinforcement, Review, and Assessment
- Daily Quiz 20.3
- Main Idea Activity S3
- Chapter Summaries and Review
- English Audio Summary 20.3
- Spanish Audio Summary 20.3

▲ **Biography Answer**

He undertook a dangerous journey to rescue his crew.

The Pacific Islands and Antarctica • 457

Section 3

Objectives

1. Describe how Antarctica was explored.
2. Explain what research in Antarctica can tell us about our planet.
3. Identify problems that threaten Antarctica's environment.

FOCUS

 Bellringer

Copy the following instructions onto the chalkboard: *Work with a partner to write five facts about Antarctica's physical geography. Try to write your facts without using your textbook.* Discuss students' answers. Then ask students to use their lists to predict some ways that Antarctica's physical geography may affect exploration and research on the continent. Tell students that in Section 3 they will learn more about exploration of and research in Antarctica.

Building Vocabulary

Write the vocabulary term **antifreeze** on the chalkboard. Draw a vertical line between *anti* and *freeze*. Have students suggest meanings for the prefix. When the correct answer (against) is given, ask volunteers to suggest meanings for the entire word. Have students check their guesses against the definition in the book.

Luau in a Can The luau, featuring a roast pig, is a traditional feast. It would be hard to duplicate a luau, but students can enjoy another Polynesian pork favorite—Spam®! During World War II, U.S. soldiers fighting in the Pacific received the canned meat product in their rations. They shared it with the local people. Spam® is still extremely popular among Pacific Islanders. Have students find and prepare Polynesian recipes using Spam® and bring samples to class to share.

Our Amazing Planet

Some of Antarctica's rocks contain bacteria and other tiny forms of life. They live in small spaces that can only be seen with a microscope. These tough survivors may be thousands of years old!

Researchers are conducting experiments in icy waters off the coast of Antarctica.
Interpreting the Visual Record What might these underwater researchers be trying to learn?

Visual Record Answer ▶

how these species survive in cold waters

Research in Antarctica

Today, researchers are the only people who live in Antarctica. They live in a number of bases or stations. U.S. stations include Palmer, on the Antarctic Peninsula, and McMurdo, on the Ross Ice Shelf. The United States also maintains a base at the South Pole. Researchers at these bases are looking for clues to Earth's past and future.

Air Pollution The researchers have made important discoveries. For example, some have studied gases trapped in old Antarctic ice. They have compared these gases with gases in Earth's atmosphere today. Their studies have shown that carbon dioxide levels in the air have risen over time. Some scientists believe high levels of carbon dioxide are responsible for global warming.

Scientists are also looking for evidence that air pollution is damaging Earth's ozone layer. The ozone layer protects living things from the harmful effects of the Sun's ultraviolet rays. Scientists have found a thinning in the ozone layer above Antarctica.

Life Other research helps us understand mysteries of life on Earth. For example, researchers have studied a kind of fish that produces a natural **antifreeze**. Antifreeze is a substance added to liquid to keep the liquid from turning to ice. Natural antifreeze in their blood protects the fish in the icy waters around Antarctica. These fish may help us understand how some animals adapt to harsh environments.

✔ **READING CHECK:** (*Environment and Society*) What can research in Antarctica tell us about our planet? information about pollution and Earth's atmosphere and about how animals adapt to environments

458 • Chapter 20

TEACH

Teaching Objectives 1–3

ALL LEVELS: (Suggested time: 20 min.) Copy the following graphic organizer onto the chalkboard, omitting the blue answers. Have students complete it to help them understand exploration, research, and environmental threats in Antarctica. **ESOL**

▶**ASSIGNMENT:** Have students use magazines, newspapers, drawings, and objects to create collages illustrating problems threatening Antarctica's environment. Encourage students to refer to the chart created in the previous exercise for ideas.

Antarctica

Exploration	Research	Environmental Threats
• James Cook sights icebergs in the waters surrounding Antarctica in the 1770s. • First expedition reaches the South Pole in 1911. • Antarctic Treaty of 1959 prevents more claims to the continent, bans military activity, and promotes research.	• Gases trapped in ice lead to conclusions that carbon dioxide levels have risen and may be responsible for global warming. • Fish with natural antifreeze help us understand how some animals adapt to harsh environments.	• There are current debates about allowing mining in the area; people fear mining will result in spills and other problems. • Researchers and tourists have left trash behind. • Oil spills have caused problems.

Cruise ships allow tourists to witness the icy beauty of Antarctica. About 10,000 tourists visit Antarctica during the summer months. A typical tourist trip lasts about two weeks. The only other economic activity in the region involves offshore fishing.

Interpreting the Visual Record

(Movement) What potential hazards do you see for ships?

Environmental Threats

Antarctica's environment is an excellent place for research. This is because humans have disturbed little of the continent. That is changing, however. As you have read, there is already debate about whether to allow mining in Antarctica. In addition, tourists and even researchers have left behind trash, polluting the local environment. Oil spills have also caused problems.

Some people fear that mining Antarctica's resources will result in other spills and problems. To prevent this, a new international agreement was reached in 1991. This agreement forbids most activities in Antarctica that do not have a scientific purpose. It bans mining and drilling and limits tourism.

✔ **READING CHECK:** (*Environment and Society*) What are some of the problems threatening Antarctica's environment? mining, tourism, pollution, oil spills

go.hrw.com **Homework Practice Online**
Keyword: SK5 HP20

Define or identify: Ernest Shackleton, antifreeze

Working with Sketch Maps On the map of Antarctica you created in Section 1, label the South Pole and Ross Ice Shelf.

Reading for the Main Idea

1. (Human Systems) Who were the first Antarctic explorers to reach the South Pole, and when did they do so?

2. (Environment and Society) What did the 1959 Antarctic Treaty do? Why do you think this kind of agreement has not been made about other places on Earth?

Critical Thinking

3. **Making Generalizations and Predictions** How might future scientific discoveries in Antarctica affect the world?

4. **Finding the Main Idea** Why did many countries in 1991 agree to ban mining and to limit tourism in Antarctica?

Organizing What You Know

5. **Summarizing** Copy the following graphic organizer. Use it to describe research in Antarctica.

Research	Purpose

The Pacific Islands and Antarctica • 459

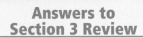
Answers to Section 3 Review

Define or identify For definitions, see the glossary and index.

Working with Sketch Maps Places should be labeled correctly.

Reading for the Main Idea

1. Amundsen, 1911; Scott, 1912 **(NGS 9)**

2. preserved Antarctica for science and peace, prevented more claims to it, banned military activity there, and set aside the whole continent for research; easier to protect Antarctica because it is uninhabited **(NGS 16)**

Critical Thinking

3. They may have environmental consequences, such as how to protect Earth's environment. **(NGS 15)**

4. because of fears that mining, other development, and tourism would pollute and otherwise disturb the environment

Organizing What You Know

5. air pollution—gases trapped in ice show rising levels of carbon dioxide; air pollution—thinning of the ozone layer; life—how life adapts to harsh environments

▲ **Visual Record Answer**

a rocky coast and floating ice

CLOSE

Tell students that young people can go to Antarctica on contract jobs to clear snow, drive machines, and so on. Ask students if they would like to go and why.

REVIEW, ASSESS, RETEACH

Have students complete the Section Review. Then organize students into three groups. Assign each group a section from the chapter. Have groups write quiz questions about the main ideas of their sections. When groups are finished have them take turns quizzing the class. Then have students complete Daily Quiz 20.3. **COOPERATIVE LEARNING**

Have students complete Main Idea Activity S3. Then have each student pretend to be a seal or a penguin. Have them write narratives from their animals' perspectives that address the Read to Discover questions. **ESOL**

EXTEND

Have interested students read Richard Byrd's *Alone*, which tells of the year he spent living alone in an Antarctic base camp. Have students write reports on the book to share with the class. **BLOCK SCHEDULING**

Define and Identify
For definitions and identifications, see the glossary and index.

Review the Main Ideas
10. Melanesia, Micronesia, Polynesia (NGS 4)

11. High islands are formed from sea-floor or continental-shelf volcanoes; low islands are formed from coral. (NGS 7)

12. because there is almost no evaporation or melting of ice (NGS 7)

13. the high islands, particularly Papua New Guinea; coconut palms (NGS 4)

14. Ferdinand Magellan and James Cook (NGS 9)

15. Japan took over Germany's territories in the Pacific and then conquered many other islands.

16. colonial influences and the isolation of peoples in a rugged, forested land

17. Micronesia

18. The 1959 Antarctic Treaty set aside the continent for peace and research and prevented more claims to Antarctica; a 1991 treaty banned mining and drilling and limits tourism. (NGS 13)

Think Critically
19. to help them develop their own economies

20. English and French are many islands' official languages, and most people are Christian.

21. Tourism could drop, with possibly severe consequences for the economy.

22. They may be concerned about losing traditional culture from outside influences. (NGS 10)

23. Pollution changes the undisturbed nature of Antarctica, making the results of research less accurate.

Review and Practice

Define and Identify
Identify each of the following:

1. ice shelf
2. icebergs
3. polar desert
4. krill
5. James Cook
6. trust territories
7. Exclusive Economic Zones
8. Ernest Shackleton
9. antifreeze

Review the Main Ideas
10. What are the three Pacific Island regions?

11. How are oceanic high islands and low islands formed?

12. Why is Antarctica covered in ice and snow even though it receives little precipitation?

13. Where are dense tropical forests found in the Pacific Islands? What trees grow on low islands?

14. Who were the first Europeans to explore the Pacific region?

15. What happened in the Pacific Islands during World War II?

16. Why are so many languages spoken by the people of Papua New Guinea?

17. Which of the Pacific Islands regions is the most urban?

18. What agreements have been made to protect Antarctica's environment?

Think Critically
19. Drawing Inferences and Conclusions Why would the Pacific Island countries want to keep their 200-nautical-mile Exclusive Economic Zones?

20. Finding the Main Idea How have Europeans influenced the languages and religions of the Pacific Islands?

21. Understanding Cause and Effect What could happen to the economies of the Pacific Islands countries if there is a sharp increase in the cost of airline tickets?

22. Drawing Inferences and Conclusions Why do you think some Pacific Islanders would not welcome the construction of a new resort even though it creates many new jobs?

23. Making Generalizations and Predictions Why would pollution threaten the value of research done in Antarctica?

Map Activity
24. Identify the places marked on the map.

Papua New Guinea
Fiji
Marshall Islands
New Caledonia
Guam
French Polynesia
Palau
Solomon Islands

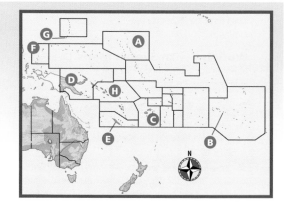

Map Activity
24. A. Marshall Islands

B. French Polynesia

C. Fiji

D. Papua New Guinea

E. New Caledonia

F. Palau

G. Guam

H. Solomon Islands

Writing Activity

Imagine that you are one of the first explorers trying to reach the South Pole. Write journal entries in which you describe what you have seen. Describe the conditions you have endured and the strategies you have used to survive. Use your textbook, the library, and the Internet to help you write your journal entries. Be sure to use standard grammar, spelling, sentence structure, and punctuation.

internet connect

Internet Activity: **go.hrw.com**
KEYWORD: **SK5 GT20**

Choose a topic to explore about the Pacific Islands and Antarctica.
- Tour the Pacific Islands.
- Explore Antarctica.
- Learn about native traditions.

Social Studies Skills Practice

Interpreting Charts

Study the chart below. Then answer the questions.

Tourism in the Pacific Islands		
Country	**Visitors in 2000**	**Visitors in 2001**
Fiji	294,070	348,014
Palau	57,732	54,111
Papua New Guinea	63,448	54,235
Samoa	87,666	88,263
Solomon Islands	5,965	3,418
Tonga	34,694	32,386
Vanuatu	57,364	53,203

Source: *The Travel Industry World Yearbook 2002*

1. Which country received the most visitors in 2000? Which received the fewest?
2. Which countries experienced an increase in visitors in 2001? Which had a decrease?
3. Which country experienced more than a 40 percent decline in the number of visitors between 2000 and 2001?
4. What event took place in 2001 that might have caused many people to stay at home rather than visit another country?

Analyzing Primary Sources

Read the following quote by explorer Captain James Cook, who described the South Pacific islands that he visited. Then answer the questions.

". . . they struck into a road leading into the Country . . . several other Roads from different parts joined into this, some equally as broad and others narrower, the most of them shaded from the Scorching Sun by fruit trees. I thought I was transported into one of the most fertile plains in Europe, here was not an inch of waste ground, the roads occupied no more space than was absolutely necessary and each fence did not take up above 4 inches and even this was not wholly lost for in many of the fences were planted fruit trees and the Cloth plant, these served as support for them . . ."

1. What can you learn about the climate from Cook's account?
2. Based on your knowledge of Cook, why do you think he compared this island to Europe?
3. What conclusions can you draw about the island's economy at the time of Cook's visit?
4. What aspect of the islanders' farms impressed Cook the most?

The Pacific Islands and Antarctica • 461

Writing Activity

Journal entries will vary, but the information included should be consistent with text material. Students should describe conditions and survival strategies. Use Rubric 15, Journals, to evaluate student work.

Interpreting Charts

1. Fiji; Solomon Islands
2. Fiji, Samoa; Palau, Papua New Guinea, Solomon Islands, Tonga, Vanuatu
3. Solomon Islands
4. the terrorist attacks of September 11, 2001

Analyzing Primary Sources

1. very hot, probably humid
2. It was the region with which he was most familiar.
3. The economy seemed to be thriving, because the fruit trees and cloth plants were plentiful.
4. how thickly planted they were and how little ground was used for fences or roads

CHAPTER 20

REVIEW AND ASSESSMENT RESOURCES

Reproducible
- Readings in World Geography, History, and Culture 81 and 82
- Critical Thinking Activity 20
- Vocabulary Activity 20

Technology
- Chapter 20 Test Generator (on the One-Stop Planner)

- HRW Go site
- Audio CD Program, Chapter 20

Reinforcement, Review, and Assessment
- Chapter 20 Review and Practice
- Chapter Summaries and Review

- Chapter 20 Test
- Unit 9 Test
- Chapter 20 Test for English Language Learners and Special-Needs Students
- Unit 9 Test for English Language Learners and Special-Needs Students

internet connect

GO TO: **go.hrw.com**
KEYWORD: **SK5 Teacher**
FOR: a guide to using the Internet in your classroom

Antarctica offers many opportunities for astronomical and space research. NASA sometimes uses the continent as a training ground for astronauts and as a laboratory for developing new technologies. One of NASA's latest projects in Antarctica is the testing of a four-wheeled robot named Nomad. This robot may someday serve as a prototype for future planetary exploration. It has successfully located meteorites in a remote area of eastern Antarctica.

This project will provide valuable information about the origins of life and help scientists fine-tune the robot for space exploration on planets with environments similar to Antarctica.

Critical Thinking: What effects might future scientific discoveries and technological innovations using the robot have?

Answer: might have both social and environmental consequences if it provides more information about the origins of life

internet connect

CHAPTER WEB LINKS
GO TO: go.hrw.com
KEYWORD: SK5 CH20
FOR: Web links about NASA in Antarctica

➤ This Focus On Environment feature addresses National Geography Standards 1, 8, 13, 14, and 18.

Preserving Antarctica

In 1912 a search party in Antarctica found the body of explorer Robert Falcon Scott. Scott had written in his diary, "Great God, what an awful place this is." He had dreamed of being the first person to reach the South Pole. However, when Scott's party arrived they found the tent and flag of Norwegian explorer Roald Amundsen. Amundsen had arrived five weeks earlier.

Almost a century later, Antarctica's modern-day explorers are research scientists. Antarctica has provided a location for international scientific research and cooperation.

A Scientific Laboratory

A wasteland to many, Antarctica is a scientific laboratory to some. Studying the continent helps scientists understand our planet. For example, the icy waters around Antarctica move north, cooling

warmer waters. This movement affects ocean currents, clouds, and weather patterns. The world's climate is also affected by Antarctic sea ice. The ice acts as a shield. It keeps Earth cool by reflecting the Sun's heat energy.

Antarctic ice also provides information about the past. Buried deep within the ice are gas bubbles that are a record of Earth's air. Scientists have compared atmospheric gases trapped in Antarctic ice with atmospheric gases of today. They learned that the use of fossil fuels has raised the amount of carbon dioxide in the air. Carbon dioxide levels are now the highest in human history.

Eyes on Antarctica

Antarctica is not owned by any single country. Some countries claim parts of Antarctica, but these claims are not recognized. In 1959 the Antarctic Treaty established Antarctica as a continent for

How Antarctic Ice Affects Climate

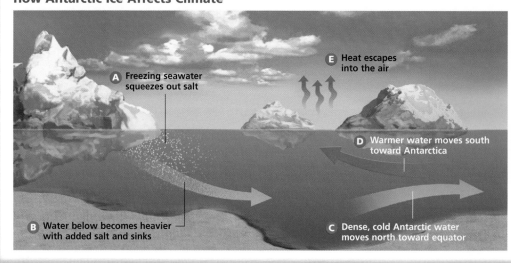

A Freezing seawater squeezes out salt

B Water below becomes heavier with added salt and sinks

C Dense, cold Antarctic water moves north toward equator

D Warmer water moves south toward Antarctica

E Heat escapes into the air

Expressing Points of View

Lead a class discussion to address the following questions: Should individual nations be allowed to claim and control Antarctica? How would these claims be verified and enforced? Should Antarctica be declared a world park on behalf of all Earth's people? How would Antarctica's neutrality be upheld? Require that students support their statements. Call on volunteers to summarize students' arguments for and against the various proposals on the chalkboard.

science and peace. The treaty was originally signed by 12 countries and was later agreed to by more than a dozen others. The Antarctic Treaty banned military activity in the region. It also made Antarctica a nuclear-free zone and encouraged scientific research.

However, the Antarctic Treaty did not cover mining rights on the continent. When Antarctica's mineral riches were discovered, some countries wanted rights to this new source of wealth. Geographers, scientists, and environmentalists also took notice. They feared that if mining took place, Antarctica's environment would suffer. In particular, they feared that a practical method of obtaining the offshore oil would be found. Antarctica's coastline and marine life could then be threatened by oil spills.

At the same time, evidence of environmental neglect at some of Antarctica's research stations appeared. Environmentalists voiced concern about scientists' careless disposal of trash and sewage. A U.S. Coast Guard captain who worked on icebreakers described pollution at McMurdo, a U.S. research station. "Trash was just rolled down the hill. . . . One of the jobs of the icebreakers was to break up the ice where the

Antarctica

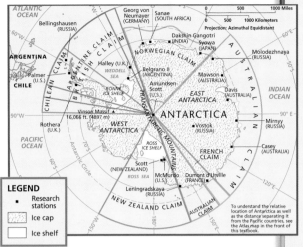

trash was and push it out to sea." In 1989, an Argentine ship ran aground in Antarctica, spilling thousands of gallons of oil. As a result, environmental concerns for the region increased.

Protecting Antarctica

In 1991, the countries that had signed the original Antarctic Treaty signed a new agreement called the Madrid Protocol. It forbids most activities on Antarctica that do not have a scientific purpose. It also bans mining and drilling and sets limits on tourism. Pollution concerns are addressed specifically.

In 50 years the agreement can be changed if enough of the signing countries agree. Then it becomes the responsibility of another generation to preserve Antarctica.

Many countries have set up research stations and bases in Antarctica, such as Argentina's Camara Base on Half Moon Island.

Your Turn

Imagine you are helping to develop the Madrid Protocol.

1. Write a short description of the provisions you want included in the treaty.

2. Be sure to explain why you think these provisions are important.

Understanding What You Read

Answers

1. Students may suggest expanding the agreement to include tourism and development of the region. Some students may suggest further limiting access to Antarctica by reducing the number of research projects allowed each year. Others may suggest keeping the agreement as it is.

2. Students should use the information available in the feature to provide reasonable support for the provisions suggested.

Focus On Environment • 463

Going Further: Thinking Critically

To help reinforce students' understanding of the geographic concept of region, have students formulate plans for Antarctica. Organize the class into four groups: research scientists, environmentalists, a mining cartel, and an international tourism company. Have each group prepare a presentation outlining their group's goals for Antarctica, its response to the Madrid Protocol, and its vision for the continent in the year 2050. Encourage students to make sketches to show how their group envisions the Antarctic region's physical, economic, and population geography in the future. Have members from each group select a spokesperson to present a report to the class.

PRACTICING THE SKILL

1. Students might suggest the need to know the physical landscape, nearby cities or towns, types of businesses, and the amount of traffic in the area.
2. Students should demonstrate knowledge of issues that affect highway construction.
3. Students should list options.
4. Students should predict consequences.
5. Students' proposals should be clearly thought out and should present different options, along with the chosen option. Presentations should include visual material.

➤ **This GeoSkills feature addresses National Geography Standards 2, 12, and 18.**

GeoSKILLS

Building Skills for Life: Making Decisions about Local Environmental Problems

Florida has named the manatee, or sea cow, its official marine mammal. The state's manatees are endangered, however. Sometimes boats hit or cut the slow-moving animals. Other dangers are pollution and fishing nets. The air-breathing animals can get tangled in the nets and drown. Some manatees get caught in underwater gates.

Imagine that you are on a committee that must decide how to protect the manatees of a coastal Florida town. How will your committee make a decision?

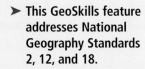

PRACTICING THE SKILL

1. **Define the problem.** First, gather information. Read printed and Internet reports. Interview environmental experts. Then narrow down the problem. For example, you may find that all the local manatee deaths were caused by boats leaving a marina.
2. **List alternatives.** Now that you have defined the problem, create possible solutions for it. Would it help to put up more signs warning boaters about the manatees? Are there ways to keep the manatees away from the marina's entrance?
3. **State the criteria.** Decide on the criteria you will use to evaluate the alternatives. For example, will you choose a plan that offers a quick solution? Is low cost more important? Maybe neither cost nor speed is as important as the solution's total success.
4. **Evaluate alternatives.** Now, evaluate your alternatives in terms of these criteria. Perhaps the committee members think that speed—doing something now!—is more important than anything else. You may find that only one plan can be started quickly.
5. **Make the decision.** Put your plan into action! Follow through and keep track of your progress. What you learn could be useful in the future.

GEOSKILLS

Going Further: Thinking Critically

Tell students to imagine that the city council in your community has just received funding for a new park. The council must decide where the park should be located and will hear proposals from various interested parties. Have students work in groups to develop a proposal to the city council for the new park's location. Have each group create a list of the considerations they think are necessary to find a location, such as where land for sale is available, and where the most potential park users live. Ask the groups to use a map of the community and any other information that might be helpful. Students should examine positive aspects of the project, such as increased recreation facilities, as well as negative ones, such as the possible loss of tax revenue if the land is removed from private hands. After each group has decided on a location, have them write a proposal for the city council. Finally, have students present their proposals to the class.

HANDS on GEOGRAPHY

Everglades National Park in southern Florida is a beautiful wilderness with many rare plants and animals. Many of those species are now threatened with extinction. Why is this happening?

Almost 1,000 people move to Florida every day! Almost 40 million people vacation in the state every year. With more people come more roads, shopping malls, and houses. Open land has also been turned into ranches, vegetable farms, and orange groves. Developments like these take away land from wilderness areas, including the Everglades. However, rare animals that live in the Everglades, such as the Florida panther, need plenty of room to survive.

Imagine that you are an expert on the Florida panther. A town at the edge of the Everglades has asked for your help in deciding whether to allow construction of a new mall there because panthers have been seen in the area. Use the decision-making process to outline a plan for your recommendation.

Lab Report

1. What kinds of information will you need to have before you can list alternatives to solve the problem?

2. Which criteria will you use?

3. How do the alternatives fit the criteria?

Answers

1. Students might suggest political leaders, transportation experts, and environmental experts and leaders.

2. Students should note that public support is typically necessary before a plan's proposals can be carried out.

3. Answers will vary. Students should support their arguments.

FOLDNOTES APPENDIX

FoldNote Instructions

Have you ever tried to study for a test or quiz but didn't know where to start? Or have you read a chapter and found that you can remember only a few ideas? Well, FoldNotes are a fun and exciting way to help you learn and remember the ideas you encounter as you read!

FoldNotes are tools that you can use to organize concepts. By focusing on a few main concepts, FoldNotes help you learn and remember how the concepts fit together. They can help you see the "big picture." Below you will find instructions for building 10 different FoldNotes.

Pyramid

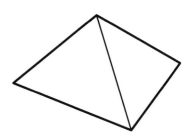

1. Place a sheet of paper in front of you. Fold the lower left-hand corner of the paper diagonally to the opposite edge of the paper.

2. Cut off the tab of paper created by the fold (at the top).

3. Open the paper so that it is a square. Fold the lower right-hand corner of the paper diagonally to the opposite corner to form a triangle.

4. Open the paper. The creases of the two folds will have created an X.

5. Using scissors, cut along one of the creases. Start from any corner, and stop at the center point to create two flaps. Use tape or glue to attach one of the flaps on top of the other flap.

Double Door

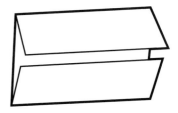

1. Fold a sheet of paper in half from the top to the bottom. Then, unfold the paper.

2. Fold the top and bottom edges of the paper to the crease.

Booklet

1. Fold a sheet of paper in half from left to right. Then, unfold the paper.

2. Fold the sheet of paper in half again from the top to the bottom. Then, unfold the paper.

3. Refold the sheet of paper in half from left to right.

4. Fold the top and bottom edges to the center crease.

5. Completely unfold the paper.

6. Refold the paper from top to bottom.

7. Using scissors, cut a slit along the center crease of the sheet from the folded edge to the creases made in step 4. Do not cut the entire sheet in half.

8. Fold the sheet of paper in half from left to right. While holding the bottom and top edges of the paper, push the bottom and top edges together so that the center collapses at the center slit. Fold the four flaps to form a four-page book.

Layered Book

1. Lay one sheet of paper on top of another sheet. Slide the top sheet up so that 2 cm of the bottom sheet is showing.

2. Hold the two sheets together, fold down the top of the two sheets so that you see four 2 cm tabs along the bottom.

3. Using a stapler, staple the top of the FoldNote.

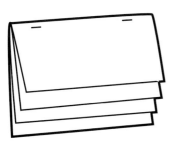

Key-Term Fold

1. Fold a sheet of lined notebook paper in half from left to right.

2. Using scissors, cut along every third line from the right edge of the paper to the center fold to make tabs.

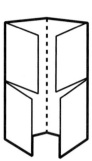

Four-Corner Fold

1. Fold a sheet of paper in half from left to right. Then, unfold the paper.

2. Fold each side of the paper to the crease in the center of the paper.

3. Fold the paper in half from the top to the bottom. Then, unfold the paper.

4. Using scissors, cut the top flap creases made in step 3 to form four flaps.

Three-Panel Flip Chart

1. Fold a piece of paper in half from the top to the bottom.

2. Fold the paper in thirds from side to side. Then, unfold the paper so that you can see the three sections.

3. From the top of the paper, cut along each of the vertical fold lines to the fold in the middle of the paper. You will now have three flaps.

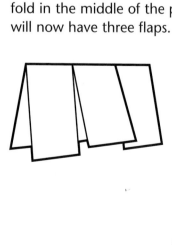

Table Fold

1. Fold a piece of paper in half from the top to the bottom. Then, fold the paper in half again.
2. Fold the paper in thirds from side to side.
3. Unfold the paper completely. Carefully trace the fold lines by using a pen or pencil.

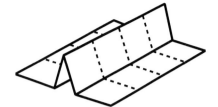

Two-Panel Flip Chart

1. Fold a piece of paper in half from the top to the bottom.
2. Fold the paper in half from side to side. Then, unfold the paper so that you can see the two sections.
3. From the top of the paper, cut along the vertical fold line to the fold in the middle of the paper. You will now have two flaps.

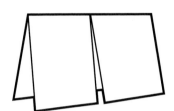

Tri-Fold

1. Fold a piece a paper in thirds from the top to the bottom.
2. Unfold the paper so that you can see the three sections. Then, turn the paper sideways so that the three sections form vertical columns.
3. Trace the fold lines by using a pen or pencil. Label the columns "Know," "Want," and "Learn."

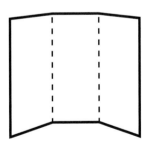

GAZETTEER

Phonetic Respelling and Pronunciation Guide

Many of the key terms in this textbook have been respelled to help you pronounce them. The letter combinations used in the respelling throughout the narrative are explained in this phonetic respelling and pronunciation guide. The guide is adapted from Merriam-Webster's Collegiate Dictionary, Tenth Edition, Merriam-Webster's Geographical Dictionary, and Merriam-Webster's Biographical Dictionary.

MARK	AS IN	RESPELLING	EXAMPLE
a	alphabet	a	*AL-fuh-bet
ā	Asia	ay	AY-zhuh
ä	cart, top	ah	KAHRT, TAHP
e	let, ten	e	LET, TEN
ē	even, leaf	ee	EE-vuhn, LEEF
i	it, tip, British	i	IT, TIP, BRIT-ish
ī	site, buy, Ohio	y	SYT, BY, oh-HY-oh
	iris	eye	EYE-ris
k	card	k	KAHRD
ō	over, rainbow	oh	OH-vuhr, RAYN-boh
ů	book, wood	ooh	BOOHK, WOOHD
ȯ	all, orchid	aw	AWL, AWR-kid
ȯi	foil, coin	oy	FOYL, KOYN
aů	out	ow	OWT
ə	cup, butter	uh	KUHP, BUHT-uhr
ü	rule, food	oo	ROOL, FOOD
yü	few	yoo	FYOO
zh	vision	zh	VIZH-uhn

*A syllable printed in small capital letters receives heavier emphasis than the other syllable(s) in a word.

A

Abu Dhabi (24°N 54°E) capital of the United Arab Emirates, 125

Abuja (ah-BOO-jah) (9°N 7°E) capital of Nigeria, 221

Accra (6°N 0°W) capital of Ghana, 221

Addis Ababa (9°N 39°E) capital of Ethiopia, 239

Afghanistan landlocked country in central Asia, 125

Africa second-largest continent; surrounded by the Atlantic Ocean, Indian Ocean, and Mediterranean Sea, A2–A3

Ahaggar Mountains mountain range in southern Algeria, 201

Alexandria (31°N 30°E) city in northern Egypt, 201

Algeria country in North Africa located between Morocco and Libya, 201

Algiers (37°N 3°E) capital of Algeria, 201

Amman (32°N 36°E) capital of Jordan, 107

Amu Dar'ya (uh-MOO duhr-YAH) river in Central Asia that drains into the Aral Sea, 145

Angkor ancient capital of the Khmer Empire in Cambodia, 397

Angola country in central Africa, 255

Ankara (40°N 33°E) capital of Turkey, 107

Antananarivo (19°S 48°E) capital of Madagascar, 271

Antarctic Circle line of latitude located at 66.5° south of the equator; parallel beyond which no sunlight shines on the June solstice (first day of winter in the Southern Hemisphere), A4–A5

Antarctic Peninsula peninsula stretching toward South America from Antarctica, A22

Antarctica continent around the South Pole, A22, 423

Apia (14°S 172°W) capital of Western Samoa, 424

Arabian Peninsula peninsula in Southwest Asia between the Red Sea and Persian Gulf, 125

Arabian Sea sea between India and the Arabian Peninsula, 125

Aral (AR-uhl) **Sea** inland sea between Kazakhstan and Uzbekistan, 145

Arctic Circle line of latitude located at 66.5° north of the equator; the parallel beyond which no sunlight shines on the December solstice (first day of winter in the Northern Hemisphere), A4–A5

Arctic Ocean ocean north of the Arctic Circle; world's fourth-largest ocean, A2–A3

Ashgabat (formerly Ashkhabad) (40°N 58°E) capital of Turkmenistan, 145

Asia world's largest continent; located between Europe and the Pacific Ocean, A3

Asmara (15°N 39°E) capital of Eritrea, 239

Astana (51°N 71°E) capital of Kazakhstan, 145

Atlantic Ocean ocean between the continents of North and South America and the continents of Europe and Africa; world's second-largest ocean, A2

Atlas Mountains African mountain range north of the Sahara, 201

Auckland (37°S 175°E) New Zealand's largest city and main seaport, 431

Aughrabies (oh-KRAH-bees) **Falls** waterfalls on the Orange River in South Africa, 271

Australia only country occupying an entire continent (also called Australia); located between the Indian Ocean and the Pacific Ocean, A3, 431

Bab al-Mandab narrow strait that connects the Red Sea with the Indian Ocean, 239

Baghdad (33°N 44°E) capital of Iraq, 101, 125

Bahrain country on the Persian Gulf in Southwest Asia, 125

Bali island in Indonesia east of Java, 397

Bamako (13°N 8°W) capital of Mali, 221

Bandar Seri Begawan (5°N 115°E) capital of Brunei, 397

Bangkok (14°N 100°E) capital and largest city of Thailand, 397

Bangladesh country in South Asia, 321

Bangui (4°N 19°E) capital of the Central African Republic, 255

Banjul (13°N 17°W) capital of Gambia, 221

Bay of Bengal body of water between India and the western coasts of Myanmar (Burma) and the Malay Peninsula, 303

Beijing (40°N 116°E) capital of China, 353

Beirut (34°N 36°E) capital of Lebanon, 107

Benghazi (32°N 20°E) major coastal city in Libya, 201

Benin (buh-NEEN) country in West Africa between Togo and Nigeria, 221

Bhutan South Asian country in the Himalayas located north of India and Bangladesh, 321

Bishkek (43°N 75°E) capital of Kyrgyzstan, 145

Bissau (12°N 16°W) capital of Guinea-Bissau, 221

Black Sea sea between Europe and Asia, A14, 107, 122

Bloemfontein judicial capital of South Africa, 271

Blue Nile East African river that flows into the Nile River in Sudan, 239

Bombay see Mumbai.

Borneo island in the Malay Archipelago in Southeast Asia, 397

Bosporus a narrow strait separating European and Asian Turkey, 107

Botswana country in southern Africa, 271

Brahmaputra River major river of South Asia that begins in the Himalayas of Tibet and merges with the Ganges River in Bangladesh, 303

Brazzaville (4°S 15°E) capital of the Republic of the Congo, 255

Brisbane (28°S 153°E) seaport and capital of Queensland, Australia, 431

Brunei (brooh-NY) country on the northern coast of Borneo in Southeast Asia, 397

Bujumbura (3°S 29°E) capital of Burundi, 239

Burkina Faso (boor-KEE-nuh FAH-soh) landlocked country in West Africa, 221

Burma see Myanmar.

Burundi landlocked country in East Africa, 239

Cairo (30°N 31°E) capital of Egypt, 201

Calcutta see Kolkata.

Cambodia country in Southeast Asia west of Vietnam, 397

Cameroon country in central Africa, *p39*, 255

Canberra (35°S 149°E) capital of Australia, 431

Cape of Good Hope cape of the southwest coast of South Africa, 271

Cape Town (34°S 18°E) major seaport city and legislative capital of South Africa, 271

Cape Verde island country in the Atlantic Ocean off the coast of West Africa, 221

Casablanca (34°N 8°W) seaport city on the western coast of Morocco, 201

Caspian Sea large inland salt lake between Europe and Asia, A16

Central African Republic landlocked country in central Africa located south of Chad, 255

Central Lowlands area of Australia between the Western Plateau and the Great Dividing Range, 431

Chad landlocked country in northern Africa, 221

Chang River major river in Central China, 353

Chao Phraya (chow-PRY-uh) **River** major river in Thailand, 397

Ghana country in West Africa, 188

Giza (30°N 31°E) Egyptian city on the west bank of the Nile, 179

Gobi desert that makes up part of the Mongolian plateau in East Africa, 353

Golan Heights hilly region in southwestern Syria occupied by Israel, 107

Great Artesian Basin Australia's largest source of underground well water; located in interior Queensland, 431

Great Barrier Reef world's largest coral reef; located off the northeastern coast of Australia, 431

Great Dividing Range mountain range of the Eastern Highlands in Australia, 431

Great Rift Valley valley system extending from eastern Africa to Southwest Asia, 239

Guam (14°N 143°E) South Pacific island and U.S. territory in Micronesia, 423

Guinea country in West Africa, 221

Guinea-Bissau (GI-nee bi-SOW) country in West Africa, 221

Gulf of Guinea part of the Atlantic Ocean south of the West African countries, 221

Hanoi (ha-NOY) (21°N 106°E) capital of Vietnam, 397

Harappa early city of the Indus River Valley, civilization of India and Pakistan, 306

Harare (18°S 31°E) capital of Zimbabwe, 271

Himalayas mountain system in Asia; world's highest mountains, 353

Hindu Kush high mountain range in northern Afghanistan, 125

Ho Chi Minh City (formerly Saigon) (11°N 107°E) major city in southern Vietnam; former capital of South Vietnam, 397

Hokkaido (hoh-KY-doh) major island in northern Japan, 377

Hong (Red) River major river that flows into the Gulf of Tonkin in Vietnam, 397

Hong Kong (22°N 115°E) former British colony in East Asia; now part of China, 353

Honiara (9°S 160°E) capital of the Solomon Islands, 424

Honshu (HAWN-shoo) largest of the four major islands of Japan, 377

Huang River (Yellow River) one of the world's longest rivers; located in northern China, 115, 353

India country in South Asia, 303

Indian Ocean world's third-largest ocean; located east of Africa, south of Asia, west of Australia, and north of Antarctica, A3

Indochina Peninsula peninsula in southeastern Asia that includes the region from Myanmar (Burma) to Vietnam, 397

Indonesia largest country in Southeast Asia; made up of more than 17,000 islands, 397

Indus River major river in Pakistan, 321

Inland Sea body of water in southern Japan between Honshu, Shikoku, and Kyushu, 377

Inyanga Mountains mountain region of Zimbabwe and Mozambique, 271

Iran country in southwestern Asia; formerly called Persia, 125

Iraq (i-RAHK) country located between Iran and Saudi Arabia, 125

Irian Jaya western part of the island of New Guinea and part of Indonesia, 397

Irrawaddy River important river in Myanmar (Burma), 397

Islamabad (34°N 73°E) capital of Pakistan, 321

Israel country in southwestern Asia, 107

Istanbul (formerly Constantinople) (41°N 29°E) largest city and leading seaport in Turkey, 107

Jakarta (6°S 107°E) capital of Indonesia, 397

Japan country in East Asia consisting of four major islands and more than 3,000 smaller islands, 377

Java major island in Indonesia, 397

Jerusalem (32°N 35°E) capital of Israel, 107

Johannesburg (26°S 28°E) city in South Africa, 271

Jordan River river in southwestern Asia that separates Israel from Syria and Jordan, 107

Jordan Southwest Asian country stretching east from the Dead Sea and Jordan River into the Arabian Desert, 107

Kabul (35°N 69°E) capital and largest city of Afghanistan, 125

Kalahari Desert dry plateau region in southern Africa, 271

Kampala (0° 32°E) capital of Uganda, 239

Kao-hsiung (23°N 120°E) Taiwan's second-largest city and major seaport, 353

Karachi (25°N 69°E) Pakistan's largest city and major seaport, 321

Karakoram Range high mountain range in northern India and Pakistan, 321

Kara-kum (kahr-uh-KOOM) desert region in Turkmenistan, 145

Kashmir mountainous region in northern India and Pakistan, 303

Kathmandu (kat-man-DOO) (28°N 85°E) capital of Nepal, 321

Kazakhstan country in Central Asia; former Soviet republic, 145

Kenya country in East Africa south of Ethiopia, 239

Khartoum (16°N 33°E) capital of Sudan, 239

Khyber Pass major mountain pass between Afghanistan and Pakistan, 125

Kigali (2°S 30°E) capital of Rwanda, 239

Kinshasa (4°S 15°E) capital of the Democratic Republic of the Congo, 255

Kiribati South Pacific country in Micronesia and Polynesia, 424

Kobe (KOH-bay) (35°N 135°E) major port city in Japan, 377

Kolkata (Calcutta) (23°N 88°E) giant industrial and seaport city in eastern India, 303

Korea peninsula on the east coast of Asia, 377

Koror capital of Palau, 424

Kuala Lumpur (3°N 102°E) capital of Malaysia, 397

Kuwait City (29°N 48°E) capital of Kuwait, 125

Kuwait country on the Persian Gulf in southwestern Asia, 125

Kyoto (KYOH-toh) (35°N 136°E) city on the island of Honshu and the ancient capital of Japan, 377

Kyrgyzstan (kir-gi-STAN) country in Central Asia; former Soviet republic, 145

Kyushu (KYOO-shoo) southernmost of Japan's main islands, 377

Kyzyl Kum (ki-zil KOOM) desert region in Uzbekistan and Kazakhstan, 145

Lagos (LAY-gahs) (6°N 3°E) former capital of Nigeria and the country's largest city, 221

Lahore (32°N 74°E) industrial city in northeastern Pakistan, 296

Lake Baikal (by-KAHL) world's deepest freshwater lake; located north of the Gobi in Russia, 321

Lake Chad shallow lake between Nigeria and Chad in western Africa, 221

Lake Malawi (also called Lake Nyasa) lake in southeastern Africa, 255

Lake Nasser artificial lake in southern Egypt created in the 1960s by the construction of the Aswan High Dam, 201

Lake Tanganyika deep lake in the Western Rift Valley in Africa, 255

Lake Victoria large lake in East Africa surrounded by Uganda, Kenya, and Tanzania, 239

Lake Volta large artificial lake in Ghana, 221

Laos landlocked country in Southeast Asia, 397

Lebanon country in Southwest Asia, 107

Lesotho country completely surrounded by South Africa, 271

Liberia country in West Africa, 221

Libreville (0° 9°E) capital of Gabon, 255

Libya country in North Africa located between Egypt and Algeria, 201

Lilongwe (14°S 34°E) capital of Malawi, 255

Limpopo River river in southern Africa forming the border between South Africa and Zimbabwe, 188

Lomé (6°N 1°E) capital of Togo, 221

Luanda (9°S 13°E) capital of Angola, 255

Lubumbashi (loo-boom-BAH-shee) (12°S 27°E) industrial city in the Democratic Republic of the Congo, 255

Luzon chief island of the Philippines, 397

Macao (22°N 113°E) former Portuguese territory in East Asia, now part of China, 353

Madagascar largest of the island countries off the eastern coast of Africa, 271

Majuro (7°N 171°E) capital of the Marshall Islands, 424

Malabo (4°N 9°E) capital of Equatorial Guinea, 255

Malawi (muh-LAH-wee) landlocked country in central Africa, 255

Malay Archipelago (ahr-kuh-PE-luh-goh) large island group off the southeastern coast of Asia including New Guinea and the islands of Malaysia, Indonesia, and the Philippines, 397

Malay Peninsula peninsula in Southeast Asia, 397

Malaysia country in Southeast Asia, 397

Maldives island country in the Indian Ocean south of India, 321

Male (5°N 72°E) capital of the Maldives, 321

Mali country in West Africa, 189

Malta island country in southern Europe located in the Mediterranean Sea between Sicily and North Africa, 222

Manama (26°N 51°E) capital of Bahrain, 125

Manila (15°N 121°E) capital of the Philippines, 397

Maputo (27°S 33°E) capital of Mozambique, 271

Marshall Islands Pacific island country in Indonesia, 424

Maseru (29°S 27°E) capital of Lesotho, 271

Masqat (Muscat) (23°N 59°E) capital of Oman, 125

Mauritania African country stretching east from the Atlantic coast into the Sahara, 221

Mauritius island country located off the coast of Africa in the Indian Ocean, 271

Mbabane (26°S 31°E) capital of Swaziland, 271

Mecca (21°N 40°E) important Islamic city in western Saudi Arabia, 98

Medina (Al Madinah) (24°N 39°E) important Islamic city north of Mecca, 125

Mediterranean Sea sea surrounded by Europe, Asia, and Africa, m377

Mekong River important river in Southeast Asia, 397

Melanesia island region in the South Pacific that stretches from New Guinea to Fiji, 423

Melbourne (38°S 145°E) capital of Victoria, Australia, 431

Micronesia island region in the South Pacific that includes the Mariana, Caroline, Marshall, and Gilbert island groups, 423

Micronesia, Federated States of island country in the western Pacific, 423

Mogadishu (2°N 45°E) capital and port city of Somalia, 239

Mongolia landlocked country in East Asia, 353

Monrovia (6°N 11°W) capital of Liberia, 221

Morocco country in North Africa south of Spain, 201

Moroni (12°S 43°E) capital of Comoros, 271

Mount Everest (28°N 87°E) world's highest peak (29,035 ft.; 8,850 m); located in the Himalayas, 353

Mount Kilimanjaro (3°S 37°E) (ki-luh-muhn-JAHR-oh) highest point in Africa (19,341 ft.; 5,895 m); located in northeast Tanzania, near Kenya border, 239

Mozambique (moh-zahm-BEEK) country in southern Africa, 271

Mumbai (Bombay) (19°S 73°E) India's largest city, 303

Murray-Darling Rivers major river system in southeastern Australia, 431

Muscat See Masqat.

Myanmar (MYAHN-mahr) (Burma) country in Southeast Asia between India, China, and Thailand, 397

N'Djamena (12°N 15°E) capital of Chad, 221

Nairobi (1°S 37°E) capital of Kenya, 239

Namib Desert Atlantic coast desert in southern Africa, 271

Namibia (nuh-MI-bee-uh) country on the Atlantic coast in southern Africa, 271

Nanjing (32°N 119°E) city along the upper Chang River in China, 353

Nauru South Pacific island country in Micronesia, 423

Negev desert region in southern Israel, 107

Nepal South Asian country located in the Himalayas, 321

New Caledonia French territory of Melanesia in the South Pacific Ocean east of Queensland, Australia, 423

New Delhi (29°N 77°E) capital of India, 303

New Guinea large island in the South Pacific Ocean north of Australia, 397

New Zealand island country located southeast of Australia, 431

Niamey (14°N 2°E) capital of Niger, 221

Nicosia (35°N 33°E) capital of Cyprus, 107

Niger (NY-juhr) country in West Africa, 221

Niger River river in West Africa, 107, 221

Nigeria country in West Africa, 221

Nile Delta region in northern Egypt where the Nile River flows into the Mediterranean Sea, 201

Nile River world's longest river (4,187 miles; 6,737 km); flows into the Mediterranean Sea in Egypt, 177, 201

Nile Valley area around the Nile River where distinct cultures developed, 177

North America continent including Canada, the United States, Mexico, Central America, and the Caribbean Islands, A2

North China Plain region of northeastern China, 353

North Island northernmost of two large continental islands of New Zealand, 431

North Korea country on the northern part of the Korean Peninsula in East Asia, 377

North Pole the northern point of Earth's axis, A22

Northern Mariana Islands U.S. commonwealth in the South Pacific, 424

Nouakchott (nooh-AHK-shaht) (18°N 16°W) capital of Mauritania, 221

Nuku'alofa capital of Tonga, 424

O

Oman country in the Arabian Peninsula; formerly known as Muscat, 125

Orange River river in southern Africa, 271

Osaka (oh-SAH-kuh) (35°N 135°E) major industrial center on Japan's southwestern Honshu island, 377

Ouagadougou (wah-gah-DOO-GOO) (12°N 2°W) capital of Burkina Faso, 221

P

P'yŏngyang (pyuhng-YANG) (39°N 126°E) capital of North Korea, 377

Pacific Ocean Earth's largest ocean; located between North and South America and Asia and Australia, A2–A3

Pakistan South Asian country located northwest of India, 321

Palau South Pacific island country in Micronesia, 424

Palikir capital of the Federated States of Micronesia, 424

Pamirs mountain area mainly in Tajikistan in Central Asia, 145

Papua New Guinea country on the eastern half of the island of New Guinea, 424

Persian Gulf body of water between Iran and the Arabian Peninsula, 125

Perth (32°S 116°E) capital of Western Australia, 431

Philippines Southeast Asian island country located north of Indonesia, 397

Phnom Penh (12°N 105°E) capital of Cambodia, 397

Plateau of Tibet high, barren plateau of western China, 353

Polynesia island region of the South Pacific that includes the Hawaiian and Line island groups, Samoa, French Polynesia, and Easter Island, 423

Port Elizabeth (34°S 26°E) seaport city in South Africa, 271

Port Louis (20°S 58°E) capital of Mauritius, 271

Port Moresby (10°S 147°E) seaport and capital of Papua New Guinea, 424

Porto-Novo (6°N 3°E) capital of Benin, 221

Port-Vila (18°S 169°E) capital of Vanuatu, 424

Praia (PRIE-uh) (15°N 24°W) capital of Cape Verde, 221

Pretoria (26°S 28°E) administrative capital of South Africa, 271

Pusan (35°N 129°E) major seaport city in southeastern South Korea, 377

Q

Qatar Persian Gulf country located on the Arabian Peninsula, 125

Qattara Depression lowland region (436 feet below sea level; 133 m) in western Egypt, 201

R

Rabat (34°N 7°W) capital of Morocco, 201

Rangoon See Yangon.

Red Sea sea between the Arabian Peninsula and northeastern Africa, 177, 125

Riyadh (25°N 47°E) capital of Saudi Arabia, 125

Ross Ice Shelf ice shelf of Antarctica, 423

Rub' al-Khali uninhabited desert area in southeastern Saudi Arabia, 125

Rwanda country in East Africa, 239

S

Sahara desert region in northern Africa, 201

Samarqand (40°N 67°E) city in southeastern Uzbekistan, 145

Samoa South Pacific island country in Polynesia, 423

Sanaa (15°N 44°E) capital of Yemen, 125

São Tomé (1°N 6°E) capital of São Tomé and Príncipe, 255

São Tomé and Príncipe island country located off the Atlantic coast of central Africa, 255

Saudi Arabia country occupying much of the Arabian Peninsula in southwestern Asia, 125

Sea of Japan body of water separating Japan from mainland Asia, 535

Sea of Marmara sea between European Turkey and the Asian peninsula of Anatolia, 107

Senegal country in West Africa, 221

Senegal River river in West Africa, 221

Seoul (38°N 127°E) capital of South Korea, 377

Seychelles island country located east of Africa in the Indian Ocean, 271

Shanghai (31°N 121°E) major seaport city in eastern China, 353

Shikoku (shee-KOH-koo) smallest of the four main islands of Japan, 377

Sichuan Basin rich agriculture and mining area along the Chang (Yangtze) River in central China, 353

Sierra Leone West African country located northwest of Liberia, 221

Sinai (SY-ny) **Peninsula** peninsula in northeastern Egypt, 201

Singapore island country located at the tip of the Malay Peninsula in Southeast Asia, 397

Solomon Islands South Pacific island country in Melanesia, 424

Somalia East African country located in the Horn of Africa, 239

South Africa country in southern Africa, 271

South Island the southern island of two main islands of New Zealand, 431

South Korea country occupying the southern half of the Korean Peninsula, 377

South Pole the southern point of Earth's axis, A22

Southern Alps mountain range in South Island, New Zealand, 431

Sri Lanka island country located south of India; formerly known as Ceylon, 321

Strait of Gibraltar (juh-BRAWL-tuhr) strait between the Iberian Peninsula and North Africa that links the Mediterranean Sea to the Atlantic Ocean, 165

Sudan East African country; largest country in Africa, 239

Suez Canal canal linking the Red Sea to the Mediterranean Sea in northeastern Egypt, 201

Sumatra large island of Indonesia, 397

Suva (19°S 178°E) capital of Fiji, 424

Swaziland country in southern Africa, 271

Sydney (34°S 151°E) largest urban area and leading seaport in Australia, 431

Syr Dar'ya (sir duhr-YAH) river draining the Pamirs in Central Asia, 145

Syria Southwest Asian country located between the Mediterranean Sea and Iraq, 107

Syrian Desert desert region covering parts of Syria, Jordan, Iraq, and northern Saudi Arabia, 107

Tahiti French South Pacific island in Polynesia, 423

Taipei (25°N 122°E) capital of Taiwan, 353

Taiwan (TY-WAHN) island country located off the southeastern coast of China, 353

Tajikistan (tah-ji-ki-STAN) country in Central Asia; former Soviet republic, 145

Taklimakan Desert desert region in western China, 353

Tanzania East African country located south of Kenya, 239

Tarai (tuh-RY) region in Nepal along the border with India, 321

Tarawa capital of Kiribati, 424

Tarim Basin arid region in western China, 353

Tashkent (41°N 69°E) capital of Uzbekistan, 145

Tasman Sea part of South Pacific Ocean between Australia and New Zealand, 431

Tasmania island state of Australia, 431

Tehran (36°N 52°E) capital of Iran, 125

Tel Aviv (tehl uh-VEEV) (32°N 35°E) largest city in Israel, 107

Thailand (TY-land) country in Southeast Asia, 397

Thar (TAHR) **Desert** sandy desert of northwestern India and eastern Pakistan; also called the Great Indian Desert, 303

Thimphu (28°N 90°E) capital of Bhutan, 321

Tian Shan (TIEN SHAHN) high mountain range separating northwestern China from Russia and some Central Asian republics, 145

Tibesti Mountains mountain group in northwest Chad, 221

Tigris River major river in southwestern Asia, 107, 125

Timbuktu (17°N 3°W) city in Mali and an ancient trading center in West Africa, 189

Togo West African country located between Ghana and Benin, 221

Tokyo (36°N 140°E) capital of Japan, 377

Tonga South Pacific island country in Polynesia, 424

Transantarctic Mountains major mountain range that divides Antarctica into East and West, 423

Tripoli (33°N 13°E) capital of Libya, 201

Tropic of Cancer parallel 23.5° north of the equator; parallel on the globe at which the Sun's most direct rays strike Earth during the June solstice (first day of summer in the Northern Hemisphere), A4–A5

Tropic of Capricorn parallel 23.5° south of the equator; parallel on the globe at which the Sun's most direct rays strike Earth during the December solstice (first day of summer in the Southern Hemisphere), A4–A5

Tunis (37°N 10°E) capital of Tunisia, 201

Tunisia country in North Africa located on the Mediterranean coast between Algeria and Libya, 201

Turkey country of the eastern Mediterranean occupying Anatolia and a corner of southeastern Europe, 107

Turkmenistan country in Central Asia; former Soviet republic, 145

Tuvalu South Pacific island country of Polynesia, 423

Uganda country in East Africa, 239
Ulaanbaatar (oo-lahn-BAH-tawr) (48°N 107°E) capital of Mongolia, 353
United Arab Emirates country located on the Arabian Peninsula, 125
Uzbekistan country in Central Asia; former Soviet republic, 145

Vanuatu South Pacific island country in Melanesia, 423
Victoria (1°S 33°E) capital of the Seychelles, 271
Vientiane (18°N 103°E) capital of Laos, 397
Vietnam country in Southeast Asia, 397
Vinson Massif (78°S 87°W) highest mountain (16,066 ft.; 4,897 m) in Antarctica, 423

Wake Island (19°N 167°E) U.S. South Pacific island territory north of the Marshall Islands, 423
Wellington (41°S 175°E) capital of New Zealand, 431
West Bank area of Palestine west of the Jordan River; occupied by Israel in 1967; political status is in transition, 107
Western Ghats (GAWTS) hills facing the Arabian Sea on the western side of the Deccan Plateau, India, 303
Western Plateau large, flat plain covering more than half of Australia, 431
Western Rift Valley westernmost of two deep troughs beginning near Lake Malawi (Lake Nyasa) in eastern Africa and continuing north into the Red Sea and then into Syria, 255

Western Sahara disputed territory in northwestern Africa; claimed by Morocco, 201
White Nile part of the Nile River system in eastern Africa, 239
Windhoek (22°S 17°E) capital of Namibia, 271
Witwatersrand (WIT-wawt-uhrz-rahnd) a range of low hills in north central South Africa, 271
Wuhan (31°N 114°E) city in south central China, 353

Xi River river in southeastern China, 353

Yamoussoukro (7°N 5°W) capital of Côte d'Ivoire, 221
Yangon (Rangoon) (17°N 96°E) capital of Myanmar (Burma), 397
Yaoundé (4°N 12°E) capital of Cameroon, 255
Yemen country located in the southwestern corner of the Arabian Peninsula, 125

Zagros Mountains mountain range of southwestern Iran, 125
Zambezi (zam-BEE-zee) **River** major river in central and southern Africa, 255
Zambia country in central Africa, 255
Zimbabwe (zim-BAH-bway) country in southern Africa, 188

GLOSSARY

Phonetic Respelling and Pronunciation Guide

Many of the key terms in this textbook have been respelled to help you pronounce them. The letter combinations used in the respelling throughout the narrative are explained in this phonetic respelling and pronunciation guide. The guide is adapted from *Merriam-Webster's Collegiate Dictionary, Tenth Edition, Merriam-Webster's Geographical Dictionary,* and *Merriam-Webster's Biographical Dictionary.*

MARK	AS IN	RESPELLING	EXAMPLE
a	alphabet	a	*AL-fuh-bet
ā	Asia	ay	AY-zhuh
ä	cart, top	ah	KAHRT, TAHP
e	let, ten	e	LET, TEN
ē	even, leaf	ee	EE-vuhn, LEEF
i	it, tip, British	i	IT, TIP, BRIT-ish
ī	site, buy, Ohio	y	SYT, BY, oh-HY-oh
	iris	eye	EYE-ris
k	card	k	KAHRD
ō	over, rainbow	oh	OH-vuhr, RAYN-boh
u̇	book, wood	ooh	BOOHK, WOOHD
ȯ	all, orchid	aw	AWL, AWR-kid
ȯi	foil, coin	oy	FOYL, KOYN
au̇	out	ow	OWT
ə	cup, butter	uh	KUHP, BUHT-uhr
ü	rule, food	oo	ROOL, FOOD
yü	few	yoo	FYOO
zh	vision	zh	VIZH-uhn

A syllable printed in small capital letters receives heavier emphasis than the other syllable(s) in a word.

A

absolute location The exact spot on Earth where something is found, often stated in latitude and longitude, **7**

acculturation The process of cultural changes that result from long-term contact with another society, **49**

acid rain A type of polluted rain, produced when pollution from smokestacks combines with water vapor, **30**

alluvial fan A fan-shaped landform created by deposits of sediment at the base of a mountain, **21**

animism A religious belief that bodies of water, animals, trees, and other natural objects have spirits, **228**

antifreeze A substance added to liquid to keep the liquid from turning to ice, **458**

apartheid The South African government policy of separation of races, which began to disappear in the 1980s, **196, 278**

aquifers Underground, water-bearing layers of rock, sand, or gravel, **26**

arable Suitable for growing crops, **355**

archaeology The study of the remains and ruins of past cultures, **224**

archipelago (ahr-kuh-PE-luh-goh) A large group of islands, **398**

artesian wells Wells in which water rises toward the surface without being pumped, **432**

asphalt The tar-like material used to pave streets, **109**

atmosphere Layer of gasses that surrounds Earth, **31**

atolls Rings of coral surrounding lagoons, **335**

axis Imaginary line that runs from the North Pole through the earth's center to the South Pole, **19**

basins Regions surrounded by mountains or other higher land, **256**

bauxite The most important aluminum ore, **223**

Bedouins Nomadic herders in the deserts of Egypt and Southwest Asia, **208**

birthrate Number of births per 1,000 people born in a year, **58**

Boers Afrikaner frontier farmers, white descendents of South Africa's original European colonists, **276**

boycotted Refused to buy, **196, 310**

bush Lightly populated wilderness areas, such as parts of Australia, **437**

cacao (kuh-KOW) A small tree on which cocoa beans grow, **235**

caliph A religious and political ruler in the Muslim world, a title which means "successor to the Prophet Muhammad," **100, 128**

canopy The uppermost layer of a forest's trees where limbs spread out and block out sunlight, **256**

caravans Groups of people who travel together for protection, **148**

cartography The art and science of mapmaking, **13**

Casbah The old fortress and central part of some North African cities, **215**

caste system A system in which people's position in society is determined by their birth into a particular caste or group, **316**

chaebol Huge industrial groups of South Korean companies, banks, and other businesses, **392**

cholera A life-threatening intestinal infection, **327**

Christianity Religion based on the teachings of Jesus, **97**

city-states Self-governing cities, such as those of ancient Africa, **187**

civil war A conflict between two or more groups within a country, **263**

civilization A highly complex culture with growing cities and economic activity, **52**

climate Weather conditions in an area over a long period of time, **32**

climatology The field of tracking Earth's larger atmospheric systems, **13**

command economy An economy in which the government owns most of the industries and makes most of the economic decisions, **56**

commercial agriculture A type of farming in which farmers produce food for sale, **52**

condensation The process by which water changes from a gas into tiny liquid droplets, **27**

copper belt A major copper-mining region of central Africa, **257**

coral reef A ridge made up of the skeletal remains of tiny sea animals and found close to shore in warm, tropical waters, **435**

Crusades A long series of battles starting in 1096 between the Christians of Europe and the Muslims to gain control of Palestine, **114**

culture A learned system of shared beliefs and ways of doing things that guide a person's daily behavior, **47**

culture region Area of the world in which people share certain culture traits, **47**

cuneiform Writing system using wedge-shaped marks on clay, **90**

currents Giant streams of ocean water that move from warm to cold or from cold to warm areas, **34**

cyclones Violent storms with high winds and heavy rain in South Asia, similar to hurricanes in the Caribbean, **322**

D

Dalits People at the bottom of the Indian caste system who do the work that is considered unclean, **315**

death rate Number of deaths per 1,000 people in a year, **58**

deforestation Destruction or loss of forest area, **39**

delta Landform created by the deposit of sediment at the mouth of a river, **21**

demilitarized zone A buffer zone that serves as a barrier separating two countries, such as North and South Korea, **389**

depressions Low areas, **202**

developing countries Countries in different stages of moving toward development, **55**

dialect A variation of a language, **260**

Diaspora The scattering of the Jewish population from Palestine under Roman rule, **114**

dictator One who rules a country with complete authority, **217**

Diet (DY-uht) Japan's elected legislature, **381**

diffusion The movement of ideas or behaviors from one cultural region to another, **9**

dikes High banks of earth or concrete built along waterfronts to help reduce flooding, **355**

disciples Small group of followers, **96**

division of labor Organization of society in which each person performs a specific job, **86**

domestication The growing of a plant or taming of an animal by a people for their own use, **51**

droughts Periods when little rain falls and crops are damaged, **249**

dynasty A ruling family that passes power from one generation to the next, **177, 357**

E

earthquakes Sudden, violent movements along a fracture in the Earth's crust, **19**

embargo A limit on trade, **137**

emigrant Person who leaves one place for another, **59**

emperor A ruler of a large empire, **357**

enclaves Countries surrounded or almost surrounded by another country, **272**

endemic species Plants and animals that developed in one particular region of the world, **433**

entrepreneurs People who use their money and talents to start a business, **392**

ergs Great "seas" of sand dunes in the Sahara, **202**

erosion The movement by water, ice, or wind of rocky materials to another location, **21**

ethnic groups Cultural groups of people who share learned beliefs and practices, **47**

ethnocentrism Seeing differences in another culture as inferior, **49**

evaporation The process by which heated water becomes water vapor and rises into the air, **27**

exclave A part of a country that is separated by territory of other countries, **267**

Exclusive Economic Zones Areas off a country's coast within which the country claims and controls all resources, **455**

Exodus Hebrews' escape from ancient Egypt, **94**

exotic rivers Rivers that begin in humid regions and then flow through dry areas, **126**

exports Products a country sells to other countries, **57**

famine A great shortage of food, **63, 393**

fault A fractured surface in Earth's crust where a mass of rock is in motion, **20**

fellahin (fel-uh-HEEN) Egyptian farmers who own very small plots of land, **212**

Five Pillars of Islam Rules Muslims follow, **99**

floodplain A landform of level ground built by sediment deposited by a river or stream, **21**

fossil water Water that is not being replaced by rainfall, **127**

free enterprise An economic system in which people, not government, decide what to make, sell, or buy, **56**

free port A city in which almost no taxes are placed on goods sold there, **215**

futon (FOO-tahn) A lightweight cotton mattress, often used in Japan, **384**

geography The study of Earth's physical and cultural features, **3**

geothermal energy A renewable energy resource produced from the heat of Earth's interior, **41**

gers (GURHZ) Large, circular tents that are easy to raise, dismantle, and move; used by nomadic herders in Mongolia, **369**

glaciers Large, slow-moving sheets or rivers of ice, **22**

global warming A slow increase in Earth's average temperature, **31**

globalization Process in which connections around the world increase and cultures around the world share similar practices, **60**

gorge A narrow, steep-walled canyon, **246**

Gospels First four books of the Christian Bible that tell about Jesus' life, **96**

graphite A form of carbon used in pencils and many other products, **334**

greenhouse effect Process by which Earth's atmosphere traps heat, **31**

green revolution A program, begun by the Indian government in the 1960s, that encouraged farmers to modernize their methods to produce more food, **317**

griots (GREE-ohz) West African storytellers who pass on the oral histories of their tribes or people, **234**

gross domestic product Value of all goods and services produced within a country, **53**

gross national product Value of all goods and services that a country produces in one year within or outside the country, **53**

groundwater Water from rainfall, rivers, lakes, and melting snow that seeps into the ground, **26**

harmattan (HAR-muh-TAN) Dry, dusty wind that blows south from the Sahara during winter, **222**

hieroglyphics (HY-ruh-glifs) Pictures and symbols used to record information in ancient Egypt, **180, 205**

history A written record of human civilization, **87**

hominid An early humanlike creature, **83**

human geography The study of people, past or present, **11**

human-environment interaction Relationship between people and the environment, **9**

humanitarian aid Medicine, food, and shelter that international relief agencies give to people in need, **63**

hurricanes Tropical storms that bring violent winds, heavy rain, and high seas, **16**

hydroelectric power A renewable energy resource produced from dams that harness the energy of falling water to power generators, **40**

icebergs Large chunks of ice that break away from glaciers and ice shelves and drift into the ocean, **450**

ice shelf A ledge of ice over coastal water, **450**

immigrant Person who arrives from another country, **59**

imperialism Control by one country over another country's government, trade, and culture, **190**

imports Products a country buys from other countries, **57**

industrialized countries Countries that rely more on industry than agriculture, **54**

intensive cultivation The practice of growing crops on every bit of available land, **385**

interdependence Depending on another country for resources or goods and services, **57**

irrigation A system of bringing water from rivers to fields through ditches and canals to water crops, **85**

ivory A cream-colored material that comes from elephant tusks and is used in making fine jewelry and handicrafts, **258**

Japan Current A warm ocean current east of Japan, **377**

Judaism Monotheistic religion that developed among the Hebrews in the Fertile Crescent, **94**

kampongs A traditional village in Indonesia; also the term for crowded slums around Indonesia's large cities, **408**

karma Among Hindus and Buddhists, the positive or negative force caused by a person's actions, **312**

kimchi Chinese cabbage that has been spiced and pickled; Korea's national dish, **392**

kimonos Traditional Japanese robes, **383**

kiwi (KEE-wee) A flightless bird in New Zealand; a name sometimes applied to New Zealanders, **441**

klongs Canals throughout Bangkok, Thailand, **405**

krill Tiny shrimplike marine animals that are an important food for larger Antarctic marine life, **451**

land bridges Strips of dry land between continents caused by sea levels dropping, **84**

landforms The shapes of land on Earth's surface, **23, 24**

landlocked Completely surrounded by land, with no direct access to the ocean, **146**

lava Magma that has broken through the crust to Earth's surface, **19**

literacy rate Percent of people who can read and write, **54**

mainland A region or country's main landmass, **398**

malaria A deadly disease spread by mosquitoes, **230**

mandate Former territories of defeated World War I countries that were placed under the control of winning countries after the war, **118**

market economy An economy in which business owners and consumers make decisions about what to make, sell, and buy, **56**

marsupials (mahr-SOO-pee-uhls) Animals that carry their young in pouches, **434**

martial law Military rule, **360**

megalopolis A giant urban area that includes a string of cities that have grown together, **383**

meteorology The field of forecasting and reporting rainfall, temperatures, and other atmospheric conditions, **13**

migration Movement of people, **59**

millet A grain crop that can survive drought, **229**

mixed economy An exchange of goods and services based on at least two other types of economic systems, **57**

monotheism Belief in only one god, **95**

mosques Islamic houses of worship, **102, 152**

most-favored-nation status A status that grants special trade advantages from the United States, **367**

movement changing locations, **6**

multicultural A mixture of different cultures within the same country or community, **47**

multiple cropping A type of agriculture in which two or three crops are raised each year on the same land, **366**

mummification Process of preserving dead bodies, **182**

Muslims Followers of Islam, **128**

nationalism The demand for self-rule and a strong feeling of loyalty to one's nation, **190**

New Testament Part of the Bible containing stories of Jesus, his followers, and later Christian ideas, **97**

nirvana Among Buddhists, the escape from the suffering of life, **313**

nomads People who often move from place to place, **83, 148**

nonrenewable resources Resources, such as coal and oil, that cannot be replaced by Earth's natural processes or that are replaced slowly, **38**

oasis A place in the desert where a spring or well provides water, **146**

OPEC Organization of Petroleum Exporting Countries, which tries to influence the price of oil on world markets, **129**

oral history Spoken information passed from one generation to the next, **185, 224**

Organization of African Unity (OAU) An organization, founded in 1963, that tries to promote cooperation among African countries, **283**

outback Australia's inland region, **434**

overpopulation More people than a region or country can self-support, **58**

Oyashio (oh-YAH-shee-oh) **Current** A cool ocean current east of Japan, **377**

ozone layer A form of oxygen in the atmosphere that helps protect Earth from harmful solar radiation, **31**

pagodas Buddhist temples, **362**

Pangaea (pan-GEE-uh) Earth's single, original super-continent from which today's continents were separated, **20**

pans Low, flat, desert areas of southern Africa into which ancient streams drained, **273**

papyrus A paper-like material made from the inner stalks of the papyrus plant, **180**

periodic markets Open-air trading markets in central Africa, **257**

perspective Point of view based on a person's experience and personal understanding, **3**

petroleum An oily liquid that can be refined into gasoline and other fuels and oils, **40**

pharaohs Ancient Egyptian kings, **177, 205**

phosphates Mineral salts containing the element phosphorus; used to make fertilizers, **109**

physical geography The study of Earth's natural landscape and physical systems, including the atmosphere, **11**

pictographs Writing system that uses small pictures to show information, **90**

place physical and human features of a specific location, **6**

plain A nearly flat area on Earth's surface, **21**

plate tectonics The theory that Earth's surface is divided into several major, slowly moving plates or pieces, **19**

polar desert A high-latitude region that receives little precipitation, **451**

popular culture Widely shared beliefs, tastes, goals, and practices, **60**

population density The average number of people living within a set area, **58**

porcelain A type of very fine pottery, **358**

precipitation The process by which water falls back to Earth, **27**

prehistory A time before written records, **83**

prevailing winds Breezes that consistently blow in the same direction over large areas of Earth, **33**

primary industries Economic activities that directly involve natural resources or raw materials, such as farming and mining, **54**

protectionism The practice of setting up trade barriers to shield industries at home from foreign competition, **386**

provinces Large areas each ruled by a governor, **93**

pyramids Huge square stone monuments with four triangular sides, **179**

quarternary industries Economic activities that include specialized skills or knowledge and work mostly with information, **54**

Qur'an The holy book of Islam, **98, 129**

race A group of people who share inherited physical or biological traits, **48**

rain shadow Dry area on the side of a mountain opposite the wind, **35**

reforestation The planting of trees in places where forests have been cut down, **39**

refugees People who flee to another country, usually for economic or political reasons, **63, 401**

regs Broad, windswept gravel plains in the Sahara, **202**

reincarnation The belief that the human soul is reborn again and again in different bodies, **312**

relative location The position of a place in relation to another place, **7**

renewable resources Materials needed and valued by people, such as soils and forests, that can be replaced by Earth's natural processes, **38**

Resurrection Christian belief that Jesus rose from the dead, **97**

rifts Long, deep valleys with mountains or plateaus on either side, **240**

Rosetta Stone Ancient rock tablet carved in Greek, Egyptian hieroglyphics, and demotic writing, **180**

rugby A game with British origins; similar to football and soccer, **436**

rural An area of open land that is often used for farming, **4**

Sahel (sah-HEL) A dry grasslands region with a steppe climate south of the Sahara, **222**

samurai (SA-muh-ry) Warriors who served Japanese lords, **380**

sanctions An economic or political penalty, such as an embargo, used by one or more countries to force another country to cease an illegal or immoral act, **279**

Sanskrit An early language form in South Asia; used as a sacred language in India today, **307**

secede To break away from a country to form another, **232**

secondary industries Economic activities that change raw materials created by primary industries into finished products, **54**

secular Kept separate from religion, as in a secular government or state, **111**

sepoys Indian troops commanded by British officers during the colonial era in India, **310**

shah An ancient Persian word for king, **103, 140**

shamans Shinto priests, **379**

Shia The second-largest branch of Islam, **128**

Shintoism The earliest known religion of Japan, **379**

shogun "Great General," the highest Japanese warrior rank, **380**

silt Finely ground soil, **203**

solar power Heat and light from the Sun, **41**

sorghum A grain crop that can survive drought, **229**

souks Marketplaces in North Africa, **215**

spatial perspective Point of view based on looking at where something is and why it is there, **3**

sphinxes Sculptures of monsters with a lion's body and a human head, **179**

staple A region or country's main food crop, **230**

storm surges Huge waves of water that are whipped up by fierce winds, particularly from cyclones, hurricanes, and other tropical storms, **322**

stupas Mounds of earth or stones covering the ashes of the Buddha or relics of Buddhist saints, **330**

subduction The movement of one of Earth's heavier tectonic plates underneath a lighter tectonic plate, **19**

subsistence agriculture A type of farming in which farmers grow just enough food to provide for themselves and their own families, **52**

sultan The supreme ruler of a Muslim country, **411**

Sunni The largest branch of Islam, **128**

Swahili A Bantu language that is widely spoken in areas of Africa, **244**

symbol A word, shape, color, flag, or other sign that stands for something else, **49**

teak A valuable type of wood; grown in India and Southeast Asia, **305**

Ten Commandments Basic laws given to Moses, **95**

terraces Horizontal ridges built into the slopes of steep hillsides to prevent soil loss and aid farming, **22**

tertiary industries Economic activities that handle goods that are ready to be sold to consumers, **54**

theocracy A government ruled by religious leaders, **140**

the veld (VELT) Open grasslands areas of South Africa, **272**

third-world countries Developing countries that lack economic opportunities, **55**

topography Shape, height, and arrangement of landforms in a certain place, **19**

Torah Five books of Moses that Jews follow, **95**

townships Special areas of crowded clusters of tiny homes for black South Africans living outside cities, **278**

trade surplus The value of exports is greater than the value of imports, **386**

tradition-based economy Exchange of goods or services based on custom and tradition, **56**

tributary Any smaller stream or river that flows into a larger stream or river, **26**

trust territories Areas placed under the temporary control of another country until they set up their own government, **453**

tsetse (TSET-see) **fly** A fly in Africa south of the Sahara that spreads sleeping sickness, a deadly disease, **222**

tsunamis (tsooh-NAH-mees) Huge waves created by undersea tectonic activity, such as earthquakes, **377**

urban An area that contains a city, **4**

wadis Dry streambeds in Southwest Asia and Africa, **127**

water cycle The circulation of water from Earth's surface to the atmosphere and back, **27**

water vapor The gaseous form of water, **27**

weather The condition of the atmosphere at a given place and time, **32**

weathering The process of breaking rocks into smaller pieces through heat, water, or other means, **20**

work ethic The belief that work in itself is worthwhile, **386**

yurt A movable round house of wool felt mats over a wood frame, **152**

ziggurats Pyramid-shaped temples built by Sumerians, **90**

Zionism The movement to establish a Jewish country or community in Palestine, **115**

zonal How climates in Africa stretch east to west in bands, **222**

SPANISH GLOSSARY

A

absolute location/posición exacta Lugar exacto de la tierra donde se localiza un punto, por lo general definido en términos de latitud y longitud, **7**

acculturation/aculturación Proceso de asimilación de una cultura a largo plazo por el contacto con otra sociedad, **49**

acid rain/lluvia ácida Tipo de lluvia contaminada que se produce cuando partículas de contaminación del aire se combinan con el vapor de agua de la atmósfera, **30**

alluvial fan/abanico aluvial Accidente geográfico en forma de abanico que se origina por la acumulación de sedimentos en la base de una montaña, **21**

animism/animismo Creencia religiosa que explica que los cuerpos de agua, los animales, los árboles y otros objetos de la naturaleza tienen un espíritu, **228**

antifreeze/anticongelante Sustancia que se agrega a un líquido para evitar que se congele, **458**

apartheid The South African government policy of separation of races, which began to disappear in the 1980s, **196, 278**

aquifers/acuíferos Capas subterráneas de roca, arena y grava en las que se almacena el agua, **26**

arable/cultivable Tierra con características que favorecen el cultivo, **355**

archaeology/arqueología Estudio de los restos de culturas pasadas, **224**

archipelago/archpiélago Grupo grande de islas, **398**

artesian wells/pozos artesianos Pozos en los que el agua sube a la superficie de la tierra sin ser impulsada por medios artificiales, **432**

asphalt/asfalto Material oscuro usado para pavimentar calles, **109**

atmosphere/atmósfera Capa de gases que rodea a la tierra, **31**

atolls/atolones Anillos de coral que se forman alrededor de las lagunas, **335**

axis/eje Línea imaginaria que corre del polo norte al polo sur, pasando por el centro de la Tierra, **19**

basins/cuencas Regiones rodeadas por montañas u otras tierras altas, **256**

bauxite/bauxita El mineral con contenido de aluminio más importante, **223**

Bedouins/beduinos Ganaderos nómadas del desierto de Egipto y el sudoeste de Asia, **208**

birthrate/índice de natalidad número de nacimientos por 1,000 personas nacidos en un año, **58**

Boers/boers agricultores africanos de raza blanca, descendientes de los primeros colonizadores europeos de Sudáfrica, **276**

boycott/boicot Rechazo de compra, **196, 310**

bush Zonas salvajes de escasa población, como ciertas regiones de Australia, **437**

cacao/cacas Árbol pequeño que produce los granos de cacao, **235**

caliph/califa Líder político y religioso del mundo musulmán, **100, 128**

canopy/dosel Capa superior de un bosque espeso en el que las ramas se entrelazan, bloqueando el paso de la luz solar, **256**

caravans/caravanas Grupos de personas que viajan juntas por razones de seguridad, **148**

cartography/cartografía Arte y ciencia de la elaboración de mapas, **13**

Casbah/casbah Antigua fortaleza y centro de las ciudades del norte de África, **215**

caste system/sistema de castas Sistema en el que la posición de una persona en la sociedad es determinada por el nivel social del grupo en el que nace, **316**

chaebol/chaebol Enormes grupos industriales formados por compañías, bancos y otros negocias en Corea del Sur, **392**

cholera/cólera Infección intestinal seria que puede provocar a muerta, **327**

Christianity/cristianismo religión basada en las enseñadas de Jesus, **97**

city-states/ciudades estado Ciudades con un sistema de autogobierno, como en la antigua África, **263**

civil war/guerra civil conflicto entre dos o más grupos dentro de un país, **503**

civilization/civilización Cultura altamente compleja con grandes ciudades y abundante actividad económica, **52**

climate/clima condiciones meteorológicas registradas en un periodo largo, **32**

climatology/climatología Registro de los sistemas atmosféricos de la Tierra, **13**

command economy/economía autoritaria Economía en la que el gobierno es propietario de la mayor parte de las industrias y toma la mayoría de las decisiones en materia de economía, **56**

commercial agriculture/agricultura comercial Tipo de agricultura cuya producción es exclusiva para la venta, **52**

condensation/condensación Proceso mediante el cual el agua cambia de estado gaseoso y forma pequeñas gotas, **27**

copper belt/región del cobre Importante región minera de producción de cobre localizada en la parte central de África, **257**

coral reef/arrecife coralino Formaciones creadas por la acumulación de los restos de animales marinos diminutos cerca de las costas en las aguas templadas de las regiones tropicales, **435**

Crusades/Cruzadas Expediciones hecas por los cristianos para recuperar la Tierra Santa de los musulmanes, **114**

culture/cultura Sistema de creencias y costumbres comunes que guía la conducta cotidiana de las personas, **47**

culture region/región cultural Región del mundo en la que se comparten ciertos rasgos culturales, **47**

currents/corrientes Enormes corrientes del océano que transportan agua tibia a las regiones frías y viceversa, **34**

cyclones/ciclones Tormentas violentas con fuertes lluvias, paracidas a los huracanes del Caribe, comunes en el sur de Asia, **322**

Dalits/dalits Personas de la clase social más baja de la India, cuyas actividades son consideradas poco salubres, **315**

death rate/índice de mortalidad número de muertes por 1,000 personas en un año, **58**

deforestation/deforestación Destrucción o pérdida de un área boscosa, **39**

deltas/deltas Formaciones creadas por la acumulación de sedimentos en las desembocadura de los ríos, **21**

demilitarized zone/zona desmilitarizada Zona de protección que sirve como barrera entre dos países en conflicto, como Corea del Norte y Corea del Sur, **389**

depressions/cavidads Zonas de elevación muy baja, **202**

developing countries/países en vaís de desarrollo países que se encuentran en alguna etapa de su proceso de desarrollo, **55**

dialect/dialecto Variación de un idioma, **260**

Diaspora/Diáspora Dispersión de la población judía que emigró de territorio palestino durante el imperio romano, **114**

dictator/dictadore Persona que ejercen total autoridad sobre un gobierno, **217**

Diet/Dieta Legislatura electa de Japón, **381**

diffusion/difusión Extensión de ideas o conducta de una región cultura a otra, **9**

dikes/diques Grandes muros de tierra o concreto construidos para contener a un cuerpo de agua y evitar inundaciones, **355**

disciples/discípulos grupo pequeño de partidarios, **96**

division of labor/división de labores Caracterísa de las civilizaciones en la cual diferentes personas realizan diferentes trabajos, **86**

domestication/domesticación Cuidado de una planta o animal para uso personal, **51**

droughts/sequías Periodos en los que los cultivos sufren daños debido a la escasez de lluvia, **249**

dynasty/dinastía Familia que gobierna y hereda el podor de generación en generación, **177, 357**

earthquakes/terremotos Movimientos repentinos y fuertes que se producen en las fisuras de la superficie de la tierra, **19**

embargo/embargo Límite impuesto a las relaciones comerciales, **137**

emigrant/emigrante persona que sale de un lugar para otro, **59**

emperor/emperador Gobernante supremo de vastos territorios, **357**

enclaves/enclaves Países rodeados en su mayor parte o en su totalidad por otro país, **272**

endemic species/especies endémicas Plantas y animales que se desarrollan en una región particular del planeta, **433**

entrepreneurs/empresarios Personas que usan su dinero y su talento para iniciar un negocio, **392**

ergs/ergs Grandes "mares" de arena formados por las dunas del desierto del Sahara, **202**

erosion/erosión Desplazamiento de agua, hielo, viento o minerales a otro lugar, **21**

ethnic groups/grupos étnicos Grupos culturales que comparten creencias y prácticas comunes, **75**

ethnocentrism/etnocentrismo ver diferencias en otra cultura como inferior, **49**

evaporation/evaporación Proceso mediante el cual el agua se convierte en vapor y se eleva en el aire, **27**

exclave/exclave Parte de un país separada por el territorio de uno o más países, **267**

Exclusive Economic Zones/zonas de exclusividad económica Zonas costeras de un país en las que éste tiene derecho a extraer y controlar los recursos existentes, **455**

Exodus/éxodo el escape de los judios de Egipto antigua, **94**

exotic rivers/ríos exóticos Ríos originados en regiones húmedas que fluyen a zonas más secas, **126**

exports/exportaciones productos que un país vende a otros paises, **57**

famine/hambruna Gran escasez de alimeno, **63, 393**

fault/falla Fractura de la superficie de la tierra que causa el movimiento de grandes masas de rocas, **20**

fellahin/fellahin agricultores egipcios dueños de pequeñas porciones de terreno, **212**

Five Pillars of Islam/cinco pilares de islam reglas que los musulmanes siguen, **99**

floodplain/llanura aluvial Especie de plataforma a nivel de la tierra, formada por la acumulación de los sedimentos de una corriente de agua, **21**

fossil water/aguas fósiles Agua que no es reemplazada por el agua de lluvia, **127**

free enterprise/libre empresa Sistema económico en el que las personas, y no el gobierno, deciden qué productos fabrican, venden y compran, **56**

free port/puerto libre Cuidad en la que casi no se aplican impuestos a los productos que allí se adquieren, **215**

futon/futón Especie de sofá ligero, también usado como cama, muy común en Japón, **384**

geography/geografía Estudio de las características físicas y culturales de la Tierra, **3**

geothermal energy/energía geotérmica Fuente energética no removable producida por el calor del interior de la tierra, **41**

gers/gers Grandes tiendas circulares que son fáciles de armar, desarmar y transportar; usadas por los ganaderos nómadas de Mongolia, **369**

glaciers/glaciares Grandes bloques de hielo que se desplazan con lenitud sobre el agua, **22**

global warming/calentamiento global Aumento lento y constante de la temperatura de la Tierra, **31**

globalization/globalización Proceso mediante el que as comunicaciones alrededor del mundo se han incrementado haciendo a las culturas más parecidas, **60**

gorge/garganta Cañón estrecho y muy profundo, **246**

Gospels/Evangelios primeros cuatro libros de la Biblia cristiana que cuenta de la vida de Jesus, **96**

graphite/grafito Tipo de carbón usado para fabricar puntas de lápices y muchos otros productos, **334**

greenhouse effect/efecto invernadero Proceso mediante el cual la atmósfera terrestre atrapa el calor de su superficie, **31**

green revolution/revolución verde Programa iniciado por el gobierno de la India en la década de 1960 para modernizar los métodos y producir mayor cantidad de alimento, **317**

griots/griots Narradores de historias de África Occidental que pasan sus tradiciones tribales de manera oral, **234**

gross domestic product/producto interno bruto Valor de todos los bienes y servicios producidos en un país, **53**

gross national product/producto nacional bruto Valor de todos los bienes y servicios producidos en un año por un país, dentro o fuera de sus límites, **53**

groundwater/agua subterránea Agua de lluvia, ríos, lagos y nieve derretida que se filtra al subsuelo, **26**

harmattan/harmattan Viento seco y polvoso que sopla con fuerza hacia el sur durante el envierno en el desierto del Sahara, **222**

hieroglyphics/jeroglificos Forma antigua de escritura con imágenes y símbolos usados para registrar información, **180, 205**

history/historia Registro escrito de la civilización humana, **87**

hominid/homínido Primera criatura similares al hombre, **83**

human-environment interaction/interacción humano-ambiente relación entre personas y el medio ambiente, **9**

humanitarian aid/ayuda humanitaria medicina, comida, y cobertizo que las agencias de ayuda internacional dan a las personas con necesidades, **63**

human geography/geografía humana estudio del pasado y presente de la humanidad, **11**

hurricanes/huracanes Tormentas tropicales con intensos vientos, fuertes lluvias y altas mareas, **16**

hydroelectric power/energía hidroeléctrica Fuente energética renovable producida en generadores impulsados por caídas de agua, **40**

icebergs/icebergs Grandes bloques de hielo que se separan de los glaciales y flotan a la deriva en el océano, **450**

ice shelf/capa de hielo Cubierta de hielo que se forma en aguas costeras, **450**

immigrant/inmigrante persona que llega de otro país, **59**

imperialism/imperialismo control por un país sobre el gobierno, comercio, y cultura de otro país, **190**

imports/importaciones productos que un país compra de otros paises, **57**

industrialized countries/paises industrializados paises que depende más en la industria que en la agricultura, **54**

intensive cultivation/cultivo intenso Cultivo de productos en cualquier terreno disponible, **385**

interdependence/interdependencia depender en otro país para recursos o productos y servicios, **57**

irrigation/riego Proceso mediante el cual el agua se hace llegar a los cultivos de manera artificial, **85**

ivory/marfil Material de color crema extraído de los colmillos de los elefantes que se usa para fabricar joyería y artículos decorativos, **258**

Japan Current/Corriente de Japón corriente oceánica de aguas tibias que fluye al este de Japón, **377**

Judaism/judaismo religón monoteística que se desarrolló entre los hebreos en semicírculo fértil, **94**

kampongs/kampongs Aldea tradicional de Indonesía; el término también se usa para referirse a las grandes poblaciones humanas establecidas en los alrededores de las ciudades de Indonesia, **408**

karma/karma Para los hinduistas y budistas, es la fuerza positiva o negativa generada por las acciones de una persona, **312**

kimchi/kimchi Especie de col china aderezada y avinagrada que se sirve como plato tradicional en Corea, **392**

kimonos/kimonos vestidos tradicionales japoneses, **383**

kiwi/kiwi Ave que no vuela, originaria de Nueva Zelanda; a veces, este término se usa para referirse a los neozelandeses, **441**

klongs/klongs Canales de Bangkok, una ciudad de Tailandia, **405**

krill/krill Animales marinos diminutos que son una importante fuente alimenticia para otras especies marinas del Océano Atlántico, **451**

land bridges/puentes de terreno Franjas de terreno seco que conecta grandes masas de tierra, **84**

landforms/accidentes geográficos Forma de la tierra en differentes partes de la superficie, **23, 24**

landlocked/sin salida al mar Zona rodeada de agua por completo y sin acceso directo al océano, **146**

lava/lava Magma que emerge del interior de la tierra por un orificio de la corteza, **19**

literacy rate/índice de alfabetismo porcentaje de personas que pueden leer y escribir, **54**

M

mainland/región continental Región donde se localiza la mayor porción de terreno de un país, **398**

malaria/malaria Enfermedad mortal que se difunde por medio de los mosquitos, **230**

mandate/mandato Territorios que formaban parte de los países derrotados en la Primera Guerra Mundial, y que pasaron a control de los países vencedores, **118**

market economy/economía de mercado Tipo de economía en la qué los consumidores ayudan a determinar qué productos se fabrican al comprar o rechazar ciertos bienes y servicios, **56**

marsupials/marsupiales Animales que transportan a sus crías en un saco, **434**

martial law/ley marcial Ley militar, **360**

megalopolis/megalópolis Enorme zona urbana que abarca una serie de ciudades que se han desarrollado juntas, **383**

meteorology/meteorología Predicción y registro de lluvias, temperaturas y otras condiciones atmosféricas, **13**

migration/migración movimiento de personas, **59**

millet/mijo Tipo de cultivo resistente a las sequías, **229**

monotheism/monoteísmo creencia en un solo dios, **95**

mosques/mezquitas Casas de adoración islámica, **102, 152**

most-favored-nation status/estatus de nación favorecida Estatus que otorga privilegios de intercambio comercial entre Estados Unidos y otros países, **367**

multicultural/multicultural Mezcla de culturas en un mismo país o comunidad, **47**

multiple cropping/cultivo múltiple Tipo de agricultura en la que se producen dos o tres cultivos cada año en las mismas tierras, **366**

mummification/momificación proceso de preservar los cuerpos de los muertos, **182**

Muslims/Musulmanes Seguidores del Islam, **128**

N

nationalism/nacionalismo Demanda de autogo-bierno y fuerte sentimiento de lealtad hacia una nación, **190**

New Testament/Testamento Nuevo parte de la Biblia que contiene historias de Jesus, sus partidarios, y ideas cristianas posteriores, **97**

nirvana/nirvana Para los budistas, es el escape de los sufrimientos de la vida, **313**

nomads/nómadas Personas que se mudan frecuentemente de un lugar a otro, **83, 148**

nonrenewable resources/recursos no renovables Recursos, como el carbón mineral y petróleo, que no pueden reemplazarse a corto plazo por medios naturales, **38**

O

oasis/oasis Lugar del desierto donde un manantial proporciona una fuente natural de agua, **146**

OPEC/OPEP Organización de países exportadores de petróleo; grupo formado para ejercer influencia en el precio de los mercados petroleros mundiales, **129**

oral history/historia oral Información oral transmitida de una persona a otra y de generación en generación, **185, 224**

Organization of African Unity (OAU)/Organización Africa Unida (OAU) Grupo fundado en 1963 para promover la cooperación entre los países africanos, **283**

outback/*Outback* (Interior) Región interior de Australia, **434**

overpopulation/superpoblación más personas que una región o un país puede mantener por sus propios medios, **58**

Oyashio Current/Corriente Oyashio Corriente de aguas frías que fluye al este de Japón, **377**

ozone/ozono Forma del oxígeno en la atmósfera que ayuda a proteger a la Tierra de los daños que produce la radiación solar, **31**

pagodas/pagodas Templos budistas, **362**

Pangaea/Pangaea Supercontinente original y único del que se separaron los continentes actuales, **201**

pans/pans Regiones desérticas del sur de África, de terreno bajo y plano, en las que desaguaban corrientes antiguas, **273**

papyrus/papiro una materia como papel hecho de la parte interna de los tallos de la planta papiro, **180**

periodic markets/mercados periódicos Mercados al aire libre en el África central, **257**

pharaohs/faraones Reyes del antiguo Egipto, **177, 205**

phosphates/fosfatos Sales minerales que contienen el elemento fósforo; se usa para hacer fertilizantes, **109**

physical geography/geografía física Estudio del paisaje natural y los sistemas físicos de la Tierra, entre ellos la atmósfera, **11**

pictographs/pictografías sistema de escribir que usa dibujos pequeños para mostrar información, **90**

plain/planicie Área casi plana de la superficie terrestre, **28**

plate tectonics/tectónica de placas Teoría de que la superficie terrestre está dividida en varias placas enormes que se mueven lentamente, **19**

polar desert/desierto polar Región de latitudes altas donde cae muy poca precipitación, **451**

population density/densidad de población Número promedio de personas que viven en una milla cuadrada o un kilómetro cuadrado, **58**

porcelain/porcelana Tipo de vajilla muy fina, **358**

precipitation/precipitación Proceso por el que el agua vuelve de regreso a la Tierra, **27**

prehistory/prehistoria Tiempo antiguo del que no se conservan registros escritos, **83**

prevailing winds/vientos predominantes brisas que sopla consistentemente en la misma dirección sobre grandes regiones de la Tierra, **33**

primary industries/industrias primarias Actividades económicas que involucran directamente recursos naturales o materia prima, tales como la agricultura y la minería, **54**

protectionism/proteccionismo Práctica de poner barreras comerciales para proteger a las industrias nacionales de la competencia de las industrias extranjeras, **386**

quaternary industries/industrias cuaternarias Actividades económicas que abarca destrezas o conocimiento especializados, y trabajan generalmente con la información, **54**

Qur'an/Corán El libro sagra do del Islam, **98, 129**

race/raza Grupo de personas que comparten características físicas o biológicas heredades, **48**

rain shadow/barrera montañosa Área seca en el sotavento de una montaña o de una cordillera, **35**

reforestation/reforestación Plantación de árboles donde los bosques han sido talados, **39**

refugees/refugiados Personas que han escapado a otro país, generalmente por razones económicas o políticas, **63, 401**

regs/regs Extensas planicies de grava azotadas por el viento, en el Sahara, **202**

reincarnation/reencarnación Creencia de que el alma humana vuelva a nacer una y otro vez en diferentes cuerpos, **312**

relative location/ubicación relativa Posición de un lugar en relación con otro, **7**

renewable resources/recursos renovables Recursos, como el suelo y los bosques, que pueden reemplazarse por medio de procesos naturales de la Tierra, **38**

Resurrection/Resurrección creencia cristiana que Jesus se levantó del muerto, **97**

rifts/hendeduras Valles largos y profundos con montañas o mesetas a cada lado, **240**

Rosetta Stone/piedra roseta tableta antigua de roca tallada en griego, jeroglíficos egipcios, y escritura demotica, **180**

rugby/rugby Juego de origen británico similar a fútbol, **436**

rural/rural Área de terreno abierto que se usa para la agricultura, **4**

Sahel/sahel Región de pastizales secos con clima estepario del Sur del Sahara, **222**

samurai/samurai Guerreros al servicio de señores japoneses, **380**

sanctions/sanciones Penalidad económica o política, como un embargo, que uno o más países usan para obligar a otro país a dejar de cometer un acto ilegal o inmoral, **279**

Sanskrit/sánscrito Idioma antiguo del Sur de Asia; en la actualidad se usa en la India como lengua sagrada en la, **307**

secede/separar Dividir un país para formar otro, **232**

secondary industries/industrias secundarias Actividades económicas que convierten en productos terminados la materia prima que producen las industrias primarias, **54**

secular/seglar Que está separado de la religión, como un gobierno o estado secular, **111**

sepoys/cipayos Tropas indias dirigidas por oficiales británicos durante el periodo colonial de la India, **310**

shah/sha Rey de Irán, **103, 140**

shamans/shaman Monje sintoísta, **379**

Shia/Shia La segunda más grande rama del Islam, **128**

Shintoism/shintoismo Religión más antigua conocida de Japón, **379**

shogun/shogún "Gran General" el más alto rango entre los guerreros japoneses, **380**

silt/cieno Tierra de granos muy finos, **203**

solar power/energía solar calor y luz del sol, **41**

sorghum/sorgo Grano de cultivo que puede sobrevivir a las sequías, **469**

souks/souks Mercados del norte de África, **215**

spatial perspective/perspectiva espacial Punto de vista basado o visto en relación con el lugar en que se encuentra un objeto, así como la razón por la que está ahí, **3**

sphinxes/esfinges esculturas de monstruos con cuerpo de leon y cabeza de humano, **179**

staple/producto básico Cultivo principal de una región o un país, **230**

storm surges/mareas de tormenta Grandes ondas de agua que se elevan por la fuerza del viento, en particular de los ciclones, huracanes y otras tormentas tropicales, **322**

stupas/stupas Montículos de tierra o piedras que cubren las cenizas del Buda o las reliquias de los santos budistas, **330**

subduction/subducción Movimiento en el que una placa tectónica terrestre más gruesa se sumerge debajo de una más delgada, **19**

subsistence agriculture/agricultura de subsistencia Tipo de agricultura en que los campesinos siembran sólo lo necesario para mantenerse a ellos mismos y a sus familias, **52**

sultan/sultán Gobernante supremo de un país musulmán, **411**

Sunni/sunita La rama más grande del Islam, **388**

Swahili/suahili Idioma bantú que se habla extensamente en África, **244**

symbol/símbolo Palabra, forma, color, estadarte o cualquier otra cosa que se use en representación de algo, **49**

teak/teca Tipo de madera preciosa que crece en la India y al sudeste de Asia, **305**

Ten Commandments/diez mandamientos reglas básicas dado a Moisés, **95**

terraces/terrazas Crestas horizontales que se construyen sobre las laderas de las colinas para prevenir la pérdida de suelo y favorecer la agricultura, **22**

tertiary industries/industrias terciarias Actividades económicas que trabajan con productos listos para vender a los consumidores, **83**

theocracy/teocracia Gobierno regido por líderes religiosos, **140**

the veld/el veld regiones de pastos altos en el sur de África, **272**

third-world countries/paises del tercer mundo paises en desarrollo que faltan oportunidades económicas, **55**

topography/topografía forma, altura y arreglo de la tierra en un cierto lugar, **19**

Torah/Tora los cinco libros de Moises que los judeos siguen, **95**

townships/municipios Regiones de multitudes de pequeñas casas apiñadas que habitan los sudafricanos de raza negra en las afueras de las ciudades, **278**

trade surplus/excedente comercial Ocurre cuando el valor de las imporaciones es mayor que el de las importaciones, **386**

tradition-based economy/economía tradicional Economía basada en las costumbres y las tradiciones, **56**

tributary/tributario Cualquier corriente pequeña o río que fluye hacia un río o una corriente más grande, **26**

trust territories/territorios bajo administración fiduciaria Regiones que están bajo el control temporal de otro país hasta que establezca su propio gobierno, **453**

tsetse fly/mosca tse tse Mosca africana del sur del Sahara que transmite el mal del sueño, una enfermedad mortal, **222**

tsunamis/tsunamis Olas muy grandes que se forman por la actividad submarina de las placas tectónicas, tales como los terremotos, **377**

urban/urbano Área en que se encuentra una ciudad, **4**

wadis/wadis Lechos secos de corrientes en el sudoeste de Asia y África, **127**

water cycle/ciclo del agua Circulación del agua del la superficie de la Tierra a la atmósfera y su regreso, **27**

water vapor/vapor de agua Estado gaseoso del agua, **27**

weather/tiempo Condiciones de la atmósfera en un tiempo y un lugar determinados, **32**

weathering/desgaste Proceso de desintegración de las rocas en pedazos pequeños por la acción del calor, el agua y otros medios, **20**

work ethic/ética laboral Creencia de que el trabajo es un mérito en sí mismo, **386**

yurt/yurta Tienda redonda y portátil de lana tejida que se coloca sobre una armazón de madera, **152**

Z

ziggurats/zigurates templos en forma de pirámide construidos por los sumerios, **90**

Zionism/sionismo Movimiento que trata de establecer un país o comunidad judía en Palestina, **115**

zonal/zonal Clima del este de África que se extiende en franjas de este a oeste, **222**

S *indicates Skills Handbook*　　g *indicates graphic*　　m *indicates map*　　p *indicates photograph*

wadis, 127
Wake Island, *m423,* 453. *See also* Pacific Islands
water cycle 27
water vapor, 27
water: characteristics of, 23; geographic distribution of, 25; groundwater, 26, *p25;* hydroelectric power, 40; oceans, 25; surface water, 25; water cycle, 27, *g27;* water vapor, 27
weather, 32; global warming, 31; greenhouse effect, 31, *g31;* weather maps, *m34*
weathering, 20
Wellington, New Zealand, *m431,* 443
West Africa, 220–37, *m221;* challenges of independence, 226; coastal region, 232–35; culture, 228; Gold Coast, 196; history, 224–26; landforms and climate, 222–23; Niger River, 223; resources, 169, 223; Sahel region, 222, *p222, p228,* 229–31, *g230, p230;* slave trade, 225, *p225;* statistics, *g230, g231, g237. See also* specific countries
West Bank, *m107, m116;* climate, 108–09; as Israeli occupied territory, 116–17; physical features, 108; resources, 109. *See also* Israel
Western Ghats, *m303,* 304
Western Hemisphere, S3, *gS3*

Western New Guinea *See* Irian; Jaya
Western Plateau, 432
Western Rift Valley, *m255,* 256
Western Sahara, *m201,* 207, *m207*
White Nile, 203, *m239,* 240–41
wind: as energy resource, 41; land breezes, 340; monsoons, 355, 305; sea breezes, 340; turbines, *p40;* typhoons, 355
Windhoek, Namibia, *m271,* 282
Witwatersrand, *m271,* 280
Wolong Nature Reserve, *p354*
work ethic, 386
world population growth, *gS10;* issues, 58–59
World Wildlife Fund, 338
writing: development of, 87; cuneiform, *p82,* 90; hieroglyphics, 179, *g179,* 205, *p205;* Sanskrit, 307; skills, S16–S17, *gS16*
Wuhan, China, *m353,* 365

Xi River, *m353,* 355

Yahweh, 95
Yalu River, 376
Yangon, Myanmar, *m397, p402,* 405
Yangtze River. *See* Chang River

Yaoundé, Cameroon, *m255,* 265
Yellow Sea, 355
Yemen, *m125,* 130, 133, *p133;* climate, 126–27; physical features, 126; resources, 127; statistics, 79, *g132*
Yoruba, *p185,* 232, 235
yurt, 152, 155, *p155*

Zaire, 262–63. *See also* Congo, Democratic Republic of the
Zambezi River, *m187, m255,* 256, *p256*
Zambia, *m255,* 266–67; climate, plants, animals, 256–57; culture, 259–261, 259; economy, 267; history, 196, 258–59; people, *p259,* 266–67, *p266;* physical features, 256, *p256;* resources, 257; statistics, 175, *g267;* student profile, 254, *p254*
Zanzibar, 243, 246, 247. *See also* Tanzania
ziggurats, 90, *p90*
Zimbabwe, 188, *m271,* 283; ancient history, 274–75; European colonization in, 276–77; Great, *m187,* 188, *p188;* physical features and climate, *p256,* 272–73; resources, 273; statistics, 175, *g283*
Zionism, 115
zonal, 222
Zulu, Zululand, 193, *p193*

ACKNOWLEDGMENTS

For permission to reproduce copyrighted material, grateful acknowledgment is made to the following sources:

Doubleday, a division of Random House, Inc.; electronic format by permission of Harold Ober Associates Incorporated: From "Marriage Is a Private Affair" from *Girls at War and Other Stories* by Chinua Achebe. Copyright © 1972, 1973 by Chinua Achebe.

FocalPoint f/8: From "October 5—Galtai" from "Daily Chronicles" and from "Buddhist Prayer Ceremony" from "Road Stories" by Gary Matoso and Lisa Dickey from *The Russian Chronicles* from *FocalPoint f/8*, accessed October 14, 1999, at http://www.f8.com/FP/Russia.

HarperCollins Publishers, Inc.; electronic format by permission of Wallace Literary Agency: From *My Days* by R. K. Narayan. Copyright © 1973, 1974 by R. K. Narayan.

International Rescue Committee: From "IRC Staff Members Talk About 'The Bigggest Humanitarian Crisis on the Planet'" by Werner Vansant from *International Rescue Committee* web site, accessed October 19, 2003, at http://www.theirc.org/index.cfm?section = where& wwwID = 1708. Copyright © 2003 by International Rescue Committee.

Professor Hugh Kawharu: From "Treaty of Waitangi, 1840," translated by Prof. Sir Hugh Kawharu from *Government of New Zealand* web site, accessed October 30, 2003, at http://www.govt.nz/en/ aboutnz/?id = a32f7d70e71e9632aad1016cb343f900.

James Li, M.D.: From "Africa" by James Li, M.D from *eMedicine*, accessed October 11, 1999, at http://www.emedicine.com/emerg/topic726.htm. Copyright © 1999 by James Li.

Ms. Magazine: From "Foresters Without Diplomas" by Wangari Maathai from *Ms.*, vol. 1, no. 5, March/April 1991. Copyright © 1991 by *Ms.* Magazine.

Penguin Books Ltd.: From *The Epic of Gilgamesh*, translated by N. K. Sandars (Penguin Classics 1960, Third Edition, 1972). Copyright © 1960, 1964, 1972 by N. K. Sandars.

Taylor & Francis, Inc.: "Kurdish Present and Near Future Demographic Trends" (table) from *The Kurds: A Concise Handbook* by Mehrad R. Izady. Copyright © 1992 by Taylor & Francis. All rights reserved.

Writer's House, Inc. c/o The Permissions Company: From *For Love Alone* by Christina Stead. Copyright © 1944 by Harcourt, Inc.; copyright renewed © 1972 by Christina Stead.

Sources Cited:

"B. Ospanova, a citizen of Almaty, 50 years old, December 1998" from *President of the Republic of Kazakhstan* web site, accessed December 2, 2003, at http://www.president.kz/articles/Sover_Kaz.asp?lng = en&art = kazakh_10. Published by the Analysis and Strategic Research Center of the Administration of the President of the Republic of Kazakhstan, 1998.

From "Weekender: Woman of Courage (Tales of the Century: A Filipino writer recalls an interview with Aung San Suu Kyi)" from *Businessworld*, Manila, March 5, 1999, pg.1.

From "President Khatami's Interview with the NY Times" from *The New York Times*, November 9, 2001.

From "Courage, the Spirit of Daring" from *Bushido: The Warrior's Code* by Inazo Nitobe. Published by Ohara Publications, Inc., Burbank, CA, 1979.

From "Ancient Ghana and the Customs of Its Inhabitants" by Al Bakri from *Africa in the Days of Exploration*, edited by Roland Oliver and Caroline Oliver. Published by Prentice-Hall, Inc., Englewood Cliffs, NJ, 1965.

ART CREDITS

Abbreviated as follows: (t) top, (b) bottom, (l) left, (r) right, (c) center.

Unit flags of United States created by One Mile Up, Inc. Unit flags of Canadian provinces created by EyeWire, Inc. Other flags, country silhouettes, feature maps and atlas maps created by MapQuest.com., Inc. All other illustrations, unless otherwise noted, contributed by Holt, Rinehart and Winston.

Table of Contents: Page VII, Nick Rotondo; XVI, Dave Henderson.

Atlas: Page A2, MapQuest.com, Inc.; A4, MapQuest.com, Inc.; A6, MapQuest.com, Inc.; A8, MapQuest.com, Inc.; A10, MapQuest.com, Inc.; A11, MapQuest.com, Inc.; A12, MapQuest.com, Inc.; A13, MapQuest.com, Inc.; A14, MapQuest.com, Inc.; A15, MapQuest.com, Inc.; A16, MapQuest.com, Inc.; A17, MapQuest.com, Inc.; A18, MapQuest.com, Inc.; A19, MapQuest.com, Inc.; A20, MapQuest.com, Inc.; A21, MapQuest.com, Inc.; A22, MapQuest.com, Inc.

Geography and Map Skills Handbook: Page S2, MapQuest.com, Inc.; S3, MapQuest.com, Inc.; S4 (cl, bl), MapQuest.com, Inc.; S5, MapQuest.com, Inc.; S6, MapQuest.com, Inc.; S7, MapQuest.com, Inc.; S8, MapQuest.com, Inc.; S9, MapQuest.com, Inc.; S10 (t, br), Leslie Kell; S11 (t), Leslie Kell; S11 (b), Ortelius Design; S12 (b), Leslie Kell; S13, Uhl Studios, Inc.; S14, MapQuest.com, Inc.; S16, Robert Hynes.

Chapter 1: Page 5 (cl), MapQuest.com, Inc.; 6 (bl), MapQuest.com, Inc.; 8 (l, bc), MapQuest.com, Inc.; 9 (tr), MapQuest.com, Inc.; 10 (tc), MapQuest.com, Inc.; 11 (bc), MapQuest.com, Inc.; 14 (b), MapQuest.com, Inc.; 16 (b), MapQuest.com, Inc.

Chapter 2: Page 19, MapQuest.com, Inc.; 27, Uhl Studios, Inc.; 28 HRW Art; 31, Uhl Studios, Inc.; 33, Uhl Studios, Inc.; 35 (tl), Uhl Studios, Inc.; 37, MapQuest.com, Inc.; 41, MapQuest.com, Inc.; 42 (t), MapQuest.com, Inc.; 42 (b), MapQuest.com, Inc.; 44, MapQuest.com, Inc.; 45, Leslie Kell.

Chapter 3: Page 48 (t), MapQuest.com, Inc.; 48 (b), MapQuest.com, Inc.; 49 (tr), MapQuest.com, Inc.; 50 (bl), MapQuest.com, Inc.; 53 (t), MapQuest.com, Inc.; 54, MapQuest.com, Inc.; 55 (t), MapQuest.com, Inc.; 58, MapQuest.com, Inc.; 64, MapQuest.com, Inc.: 67, MapQuest.com, Inc.

Unit 2: Page 72 (bl, t), Ortelius Design; 73, MapQuest.com, Inc.; 74, MapQuest.com, Inc.; 75, MapQuest.com, Inc.; 76, MapQuest.com, Inc.; 77, MapQuest.com, Inc.; 78–81, MapQuest.com, Inc.

Chapter 4: Page 85, MapQuest.com, Inc.; 87 (b), MapQuest.com, Inc.; 89 (b), MapQuest.com, Inc.; 95, MapQuest.com, Inc.; 97, MapQuest.com, Inc.; 101, MapQuest.com, Inc.; 104, MapQuest.com, Inc.; 105, MapQuest.com, Inc.

Chapter 5: Page 107 (b), MapQuest.com, Inc.; 108, (bl) MapQuest.com, Inc.; 109 (t), MapQuest.com, Inc.; 110, (b) MapQuest.com, Inc.; 113 (t), MapQuest.com, Inc.; 114 (bl), MapQuest.com, Inc.; 116, MapQuest.com, Inc.; 117, MapQuest.com, Inc.; 118 (bc), MapQuest.com, Inc.; 122 (b), MapQuest.com, Inc.

Chapter 6: Page 125, MapQuest.com, Inc.; 126, MapQuest.com, Inc.; 128, MapQuest.com, Inc.; 129, MapQuest.com, Inc.; 130, MapQuest.com, Inc.; 133, MapQuest.com, Inc.; 134 MapQuest.com, Inc.; 139 Uhl Studios, Inc.; 140 MapQuest.com, Inc.; 142 MapQuest.com, Inc.; 143, Leslie Kell.

Chapter 7: Page 145, MapQuest.com, Inc.; 147, MapQuest.com, Inc.; 148, MapQuest.com, Inc.; 149, MapQuest.com, Inc.; 152, MapQuest.com, Inc.; 155, Leslie Kell; 156, MapQuest.com, Inc.; 159, MapQuest.com, Inc.

Unit 3: Page 164 (bl, t), Ortelius Design; 165, MapQuest.com, Inc.; 166, MapQuest.com, Inc.; 167, MapQuest.com, Inc.; 168, MapQuest.com, Inc.; 169, MapQuest.com, Inc.; 170–175, MapQuest.com, Inc.

Chapter 8: Page 177 (bl), MapQuest.com, Inc.; 179, Stephen Brayfield; 181, Nick Rotondo; 183, MapQuest.com,Inc.; 187 (tl), MapQuest.com, Inc.; 191, MapQuest.com, Inc.; 198, MapQuest.com, Inc.; 199, MapQuest.com, Inc..

Chapter 9: Page 201, MapQuest.com, Inc.; 202, MapQuest.com, Inc.; 203, MapQuest.com, Inc.; 207, MapQuest.com, Inc.; 208, MapQuest.com, Inc.; 206, Ralph Voltz; 209, MapQuest.com, Inc.; 210, MapQuest.com, Inc.; 211 (r, l), Joe LeMonnier; 212, MapQuest.com, Inc.; 213 (tr), MapQuest.com, Inc.; 216 (tr), MapQuest.com, Inc.; 218, MapQuest.com, Inc.; 219, Leslie Kell.

Chapter 10: Page 221 (b), MapQuest.com, Inc.; 222 (bl), MapQuest.com, Inc.; 224 (bl), MapQuest.com, Inc.; 225 (br), MapQuest.com, Inc.; 226 (bl), MapQuest.com, Inc.; 228 (tl), MapQuest.com, Inc.; 229 (br), MapQuest.com, Inc.; 230 (tl), MapQuest.com, Inc.; 231 (tr), Leslie Kell; 232 (bl), MapQuest.com, Inc.; 233 (t), MapQuest.com, Inc.; 234, MapQuest.com, Inc.; 236, MapQuest.com, Inc.; 237, Leslie Kell.

Chapter 11: Page 239 (b), MapQuest.com, Inc.; 240 (br), MapQuest.com, Inc.; 241 (tr), MapQuest.com, Inc.; 245 (br), MapQuest.com, Inc.; 246 (bl), MapQuest.com, Inc.; 250 (br), MapQuest.com, Inc.; 251 (tr), MapQuest.com, Inc.; 252, MapQuest.com, Inc.

Chapter 12: Page 255 (b), MapQuest.com, Inc.; 256 (bl), MapQuest.com, Inc.; 259 (br), MapQuest.com, Inc.; 261 (tr), MapQuest.com, Inc.; 264 (tr), MapQuest.com, Inc.; 265 (br), MapQuest.com, Inc.; 268, MapQuest.com, Inc.; 269, MapQuest.com, Inc.

Chapter 13: Page 271, MapQuest.com, Inc.; 272 (tl), MapQuest.com, Inc.; 273 (tr), MapQuest.com, Inc.; 276 (tl), MapQuest.com, Inc.; 282 (cl), MapQuest.com, Inc.; 285 (tr), MapQuest.com, Inc.; 286, MapQuest.com, Inc.; 287, Leslie Kell.

Unit 4: Page 294 (bl, t), Ortelius Design; 295, MapQuest.com, Inc.; 296, MapQuest.com, Inc.; 297, MapQuest.com, Inc.; 298, MapQuest.com, Inc.; 299, MapQuest.com, Inc.; 300–301, MapQuest.com, Inc.

Chapter 14: Page 303, MapQuest.com, Inc.; 304 (bl), MapQuest.com, Inc.; 306 (bl), MapQuest.com, Inc.; 309 (tr), MapQuest.com, Inc.; 312 (bl), MapQuest.com, Inc.; 314 (bl), MapQuest.com, Inc.; 315 (br), MapQuest.com, Inc.; 318, MapQuest.com, Inc.; 319, MapQuest.com, Inc.

Chapter 15: Page 321 (b), MapQuest.com, Inc.; 324 (bl), MapQuest.com, Inc.; 325 (br), MapQuest.com, Inc.; 326 (tl), MapQuest.com, Inc.; 328 (t), MapQuest.com, Inc.; 329, Joe LeMonnier; 330 (bl), MapQuest.com, Inc.; 332 (bl), MapQuest.com, Inc.; 333 (br), MapQuest.com, Inc.; 334 (tl), MapQuest.com, Inc.; 335 (tr), MapQuest.com, Inc.; 336, MapQuest.com, Inc.; 339, MapQuest.com, Inc.; 340, Stephen Durke/ Washington Artists; 341 (t), Ortelius Design.

Chapter 16: Page 353 (b), MapQuest.com, Inc.; 354 (tl), MapQuest.com, Inc.; 355 (br), MapQuest.com, Inc.; 358 (tl), MapQuest.com, Inc.; 359 (b), Leslie Kell; 361 (br, tr), MapQuest.com, Inc.; 363 (tr), MapQuest.com, Inc.; 364 (bl), Rosa + Wesley; 365 (br), MapQuest.com, Inc.; 366 (bl), MapQuest.com, Inc.; 367 (tr), MapQuest.com, Inc.; 369 (tl), MapQuest.com, Inc.; 370 (bl), MapQuest.com, Inc.; 372, MapQuest.com, Inc.; 373, Leslie Kell;

Unit 5: Page 344 (bl, t), Ortelius Design; 345, MapQuest.com, Inc.; 346, MapQuest.com, Inc.; 347, MapQuest.com, Inc.; 348, MapQuest.com, Inc.; 349, MapQuest.com, Inc.; 350–351, MapQuest.com, Inc.

Chapter 17: Page 375 (b), MapQuest.com, Inc.; 376 (bl), MapQuest.com, Inc.; 377 (br), MapQuest.com, Inc.; 379 (br), MapQuest.com, Inc.; 384 (tl, bl), MapQuest.com, Inc.; 387 (br), MapQuest.com, Inc.; 388 (tl), MapQuest.com, Inc.; 391 (br), MapQuest.com, Inc.; 392, (bl), MapQuest.com, Inc.

Chapter 18: Page 397, MapQuest.com, Inc.; 398 (bl), MapQuest.com, Inc.; 400, Dave Henderson; 403 (tr), MapQuest.com, Inc.; 404 (bl), MapQuest.com, Inc.; 405 (tr), MapQuest.com, Inc.; 407 (br), MapQuest.com, Inc.; 409 (br), MapQuest.com, Inc.; 410 (tl), MapQuest.com, Inc.; 411 (tr), MapQuest.com, Inc.; 412, MapQuest.com, Inc.; 413, Leslie Kell; 415, Leslie Kell; 417 (tr), MapQuest.com, Inc.

Unit 6: Page 422 (bl, t), Ortelius Design; 423, MapQuest.com, Inc.; 424, MapQuest.com, Inc.; 425, MapQuest.com, Inc.; 426, MapQuest.com, Inc.; 427, MapQuest.com, Inc.;428–429, MapQuest.com, Inc.

Chapter 19: Page 431 (b), MapQuest.com, Inc.; 432 (bl), MapQuest.com, Inc.; 436 (tl), MapQuest.com, Inc.; 437, Leslie Kell; 439, Nenad Jakesevic; 440 (bl), MapQuest.com, Inc.; 442 (bl), MapQuest.com, Inc.; 443 (tr), MapQuest.com, Inc.; 444, MapQuest.com, Inc.; 445, MapQuest.com, Inc.;

Chapter 20: Page 447 (b), Uhl Studios, Inc.; 448 (tr), MapQuest.com, Inc.; 449 (bl), MapQuest.com, Inc.; 455 (br), MapQuest.com, Inc.; 456 (tl), MapQuest.com, Inc.; 460, MapQuest.com, Inc.; 462, Uhl Studios, Inc.; 463, MapQuest.com, Inc.

PHOTO CREDITS

Cover and Title Page: (child image) Steve Vidler/ Nawrocki Stock Photo; (bkgd) Image Copyright © 2003 PhotoDisc, Inc./HRW

Table of Contents: iv (bl), © SuperStock; ix (b), © Marc Riboud/Magnum; x (bl), © Alex Wasinski/ FPG International LLC; xi (tl), © FPG International LLC; xi (b), © Daniel J. Cox/Liaison Agency; xii (tr), © Richard Bickel/CORBIS; xii (bl), © C. Rennie/TRIP Photo Library; xiii (cl), © CORBIS; xiv (br), © Digital Stock Corp./HRW; xiv (cl), © Frans Lanting/Minden Pictures; xxiii CORBIS Images/HRW; xxiv (tl), David Young-Wolf/PNI; xxiv (b), Klaus Lahnstein/ Getty Images; S2–S15, (border), © Delorme Mapping; S20 (b), © Nik Wheeler/CORBIS; S21 (cl), Jeffrey Aaronson/ Network Aspen; S21 (c), Index Stock Imagery, Inc.; S21 (tr), Amit Bhargava/Newsmakers/ Getty Images; S22 (l), Norman Owen Tomalin/Bruce Coleman, Inc.; S22 (cl), © Fritz Polking/Peter Arnold, Inc.; S22 (tl), Larry Kolvoord Photography; S22 (tr), Runk/ Schoenberger/Grant Heilman Photography; S22 (tr), Wolfgang Kaehler Photography; S27 (b), Rosenback/ ZEFA/Index Stock Imagery, Inc.;

Unit 1: 1 (b), Photo © Transdia/Panoramic Images, Chicago 1998; 1 (cl), © Joe Viesti/The Viesti Collection; 1 (tr), Francois Gohier/Photo Researchers, Inc.; 1 (t), © Norbert Wu/ www.norbertwu.com; 1 (br), Steven David Miller/Animals Animals/Earth Scenes; **Chapter 1:** 2 (cl), © Stone/Philip & Karen Smith; 2 (bl), Sam Dudgeon/HRW Photo; 2 (tr), CORBIS; 2 (c), © Joseph Sohm; ChromoSohm Inc./CORBIS; 3 (bl), © Stone/Ken McVey; 3 (tr), British Library, London, Great Britain/Art Resource, NY; 4, Luca Turi/AP/Wide World Photos; 5 (cl), The Stock Market/Jose Fuste Raga; 5 (cr), NASA; 6 (cl), Robert Caputo/Aurora; 6 (tr), © Stone/Robert Frerck; 7-8 © Bob Daemmrich; 8 (b), K.D. Frankel/Bilderberg/ Aurora; 9 (t,br), © Wolfgang Kaehler; 10, © Nik Wheeler/CORBIS; 11 (cr), © Ilene Perlman/Stock, Boston; 11 (tr), © Archivo Iconografico S.A./CORBIS; 13 (cr), © Chris Rainier/CORBIS; **Chapter 2:** 18 (tl), Image Copyright © 2002 PhotoDisc, Inc./HRW; 18 (tr), © Stone/A. Witte/C. Mahaney; 36 (b), © Stone/Brian Stablyk; 20, © Galen Rowell/CORBIS; 21 (t), Wendell Metzen/Bruce Coleman, Inc; 20 (b), 1996 CORBIS; Original image courtesy of NASA/CORBIS; 22, Nenad Jakesevic/HRW Art & Stone/Denis Waugh; 24, The Granger Collection, New York; 25, Carr Clifton/ Minden Pictures; 26, Grant Heilman/Grant Heilman Photography; 27, © Stone/Martin Puddy; 28, © Gary Braasch/CORBIS; 28, Wolfgang Kaehler Photography; 30, Steven Burr Williams/Liaison International; 31, HRW Art; 32, © Darrell Gulin/CORBIS; 34, Rosentiel School of Marine and Atmospheric Science, University of Miami; 35, David Madison/Bruce Coleman, Inc.; 38, © Michael Busselle/CORBIS; 39 (t), © Kevin Schafer; 39 (b), L. Linkhart/Visuals Unlimited; 40 (t), © Stone/Mike Abrahams; 40 (b), © Telegraph Colour Library/FPG International LLC; 41 (t), B. Brander/ Photo Researchers, Inc.; 41 (b), David R. Frazier Photolibrary; 42 (t), CORBIS/AFP Photo/Vanderlei Almeida; 42 (b), Ernest Manewal/FPG International LLC; 43, David Hiser/Photographers/Aspen;

Chapter 3: 46(t), © Gerald Brimacombe/International Stock Photography; 46 (cr), © Bob Firth/International Stock Photography; 46 (b), © Ahu Tongariki/Bruce Coleman, Inc.; 46 (c), © Wally McNamee/ CORBIS; 47 (b), © Bob Daemmrich/Stock, Boston; 48, © Bohdam Hrynewch/Stock, Boston/PNI; 49 (b), © Stone/Ron Sherman; 48 (t), © Stone/ Rich La Salle; 50 (b), Bruno Barbey/Magnum Photos; 50 (t), S. Sherbell/SABA Press Photos, Inc.; 51, © Werner Forman/ CORBIS; 52, © Eric and David Hosking/CORBIS; 53 (b), © Rich Iwasaki/AllStock/PNI; 55 (t), © Digital Vision; 55 (tl), © Michelle Gabel/The Image Works, Woodstock, NY; 55 (tr), © Richard Hamilton Smith/CORBIS; 55 (bl), Henry Friedman; 55 (br), © Stephen Frisch/Stock, Boston/PNI; 57, Carolyn Schaefer/SCHAE/Bruce Coleman, Inc.; 057, Martin Rogers/CORBIS; 60, © Pramod Mistry/The Image Works, Woodstock, NY; 61 (t), © Ed Kashi; 60, Richard T. Nowitz/CORBIS; 61, Ulrike Welsch; 61, Dave G. Houser/CORBIS; 62, Reuters/CORBIS; 63, Peter Turnley/Black Star; 65, Martin Guhl; 66 (t), Sam Dudgeon/HRW Photo; 66 (b), Dr. Bode; 68 (b), © Stone/Mike Abrahams; 68 (t), © Stone/Vince Streano; 69, © Ernest Manewal/FPG International LLC;

Unit 2: 70 (t), © Beryl Goldberg; 70 (b), Kevin Rushby; 71 (t), Annie Griffiths Belt/National Geographic Society Image Collection; 71 (b), Hill, M. Osf/Animals Animals/Earth Scenes; 79, Richard T. Nowitz/CORBIS; 80, © 1990 Abbas/Magnum Photos; 81, Gerard Degeorge/CORBIS; **Chapter 4:** 82, Gianni Dagli Orti/Corbis; 86 (l), Archivo Iconografico, S.A./ CORBIS; 86 (r), Bridgeman Art Library; 88, Randy Olson/Aurora; 90, Dean Conger/CORBIS; 91, Archivo Iconografico, S.A./CORBIS; 91, Gianni Dagli Orti/ Corbis; 92, Archives Charmet/Bridgeman Art Library; 93, Michael Holford; 94, Sonia Halliday Photographs; 94, Sonia Halliday Photographs; 95, Ali Meyer /CORBIS; 96, Giraudon/Bridgeman Art Library; 98, Peter Turnley/CORBIS; 99, Nabeel Turner/Stone/ Getty; 100, AKG London; 102, Werner Forman Archive/Art Resource, NY; 103 Madar-i-Shah Madrasa, Isfahan, Iran/Bridgman Art Library;

Chapter 5: 106, © Zafer KIZILKAYA; 108, © Robert Frerck/Odyssey/ Chicago; 111 (t), © AFP (Staton R. Winter)/CORBIS; 112 (t), Colossus of Gilgamesh Gripping a Lion, relief from the Palace of Sargon II at Khorsabad, Iraq, Assyrian Period, c. 725 BC (gypsum)/Ruenion des Musees Nationaux/Bridgeman Art Library, London/New York; 113, © Robert Frerck/ Odyssey/Chicago; 114 (l), Bill Curtsinger/NGS Image Collection; 115, t Peter Turnley/CORBIS; 116, © Alexandria Avakian/Contact Press Images; 117, © Richard T. Nowitz/CORBIS; 118 (b), © Ed Kashi; 119 (t), © Ed Kashi ; 119 (b), William Maynard Owen/NGS Image Collection; 120, bl Wolfgang Kaehler/CORBIS; 120 (t), © Tomas Muscionico/ Contact Press Images; 121, (t), Bettmann/CORBIS;

Chapter 6: 124, Steve Ewert Photography; 126, © Marc Riboud/Magnum; 127, © Stephen Frink/ CORBIS; 388 (b), © Abbas/Magnum; 129, © Adam Woolfitt/CORBIS; 130, NASA Johnson Space Center; 131, University Library Istanbul/The Art Archive; 132, (cl), Kate Brooks/Corbis; 132, © TRIP Photo Library/H Rogers; 133, © AbbieEnock; Travel Ink/ CORBIS; 135 (t), © Burnett H. Moody/Bruce Coleman, Inc.; 136 (b), © Stephen Wallace/Black Star; 137, Michael Macor/San Francisco Chronicle/Corbis; 137, © Alexandra Avakian/ Contact Press Images; 138, © Nik Wheeler/CORBIS; 140, ODD ANDERSEN/AFP/Getty Images; 140, © Alexandra Avakian/ Contact Press Images; **Chapter 7:** 144, Brian Vikander/ Vikander Photography; 146 (b), © Hans Reinhard/ Bruce Coleman Inc.; 146 (t), © Tass/Sovfoto/Eastfoto; 147, © Yann Arthus-Bertrand/CORBIS; 148 (b), © K.M. Westermann/CORBIS; 149, © Wolfgang Kaehler/CORBIS; 150, © Nevada Wier/CORBIS; 151 (b), © Wolfgang Kaehler/CORBIS; 152, © Dean Conger/CORBIS; 154, Alain Le Garsml/Panos Pictures; 155, Chris Stowers/ Panos Pictures; 158, © 1990 Abbas/Magnum Photos; 159 (c), Marc Garanger/ CORBIS; 161, Sovfoto/ Eastfoto; **Unit 3:** 162 (bl), STONE/Theo Allofs/Getty Images; 162 (t), Robert Frerck/Odyssey/Chicago; 162-163 (b) Herb Zulpier/Masterfile; 163 (cr), Charles Henneghien/Bruce Coleman, Inc.; 163 (br), S. Michael Bisceglie/Animals Animals/Earth Scenes; 175, Steve Ewert Photography; **Chapter 8:** 176, Boltin Picture Library; 176, (r), Roger Wood/CORBIS; 182, Gianni Dagli Orti/CORBIS; 184, Gallo Images/CORBIS; 189, Lauros/ Giraudon/Bridgeman Art Library; 192,Lauros/Giraudon/ Bridgeman Art Library; 194, Hulton-Deutsch Collection/CORBIS; 195, MARK KAUFFMAN/Getty images; 196, (bl), A. Ramey/ Woodfin Camp & Associates; 197 Marc & Evelyn Bernheim/Woodfin Camp & Associates;

Chapter 9: 200, Steve Ewert Photography; 202, Guiseppe Bizzarri/Panos Pictures; 203 (tl), © Staffan Widstrand/CORBIS; 203 (tr), Photo Researchers, Inc.; 204, © Roger Tidman/CORBIS; 205 (cr), Kenneth Garrett/NGS Image Collection; 207 (t), © M. Timothy O'Keefe/Bruce Coleman, Inc.; 207 (b), © Carmen Redondo/CORBIS; 207 (c), © Sharon Smith/Bruce Coleman, Inc.; 208 (t), Frank and Helen Schreider/ Photo Researchers, Inc.; 208 (bl), Jean-Léo Dugast/ Panos Pictures; 209, Kazuyoshi Nomachi/ Photo Researchers, Inc.; 210-211, (tr), Yann Arthus-Bertrand/ CORBIS; 211 (cl), Leonard de Selva/ CORBIS; 211 (bl), © SuperStock; 211 (t), Bettman/ CORBIS; 212 (t), Egyptian National Museum, Cairo, Egypt/SuperStock; 212 (b), © Christine Osborne/CORBIS; 213, © Yann Arthus-Bertrand/CORBIS; 214, (tl), Wally McNamee/ CORBIS; 214, © Jeffrey L. Rotman/CORBIS; 215, Jean-Léo Dugast/Panos Pictures; 215, (tl), K.M. Westermann/ CORBIS; 216, J. PH. Charbonnier/ Photo Researchers, Inc.; 217, James L. Stanfield/NGS Image Collection;

Chapter 10: 220, Steve Ewert Photography; 222, © Wolfgang Kaehler; 223, © Gail Shumway/FPG International LLC; 224 (b), 225, © Wolfgang Kaehler; 226, © Stone/Will Curtis; 227, M & M Bernheim/ Woodfin Camp & Associates; 228, © Peter Guttman/ LIFE Magazine; 229, © Wolfgang Kaehler; 230, © John Elk/Bruce Coleman, Inc.; 233 (b), © Alex Wasinski/ FPG International LLC; 233 (t), © Stone/James Nelson; 234, Daniel Lainé/CORBIS; 234, © SuperStock; 235, PELLETIER MICHELINE/CORBIS SYGMA;

Chapter 11: 238, Neil Cooper/Panos Pictures; 240, © Gerald Cubitt; 241, M. Denis-Huot/Liaison Agency; 242 (bl), Giraudon/Art Resource, NY; 244, Victor Englebert; 245 (br), Dave G. Houser; 246, Daniel J. Cox/Liaison Agency; 247 (tr), © Wolfgang Kaehler; 248, Khartoum, Sudan, in the 1860's, engraved by Alfred Louis Sargent (b.1828) (engraving)/Private Collection/ Bridgeman Art Library, London/New York; 249 (b), Victor Englebert; 489 (t), Dave G. Houser; 250, Betty Press/Woodfin Camp & Associates; 251, Maya Kardum/Panos Pictures; **Chapter 12:** 254, Steve Ewert Photography; 256, © Gerald Cubitt; 257, Michael Nichols/NGS Image Collection; 258 (bl), Christie's Images; 259, © Stone/Ian Murphy; 260, M. & E. Bernheim/Woodfin Camp & Associates; 261 (tl), M. Edwards/Still Pictures/Peter Arnold, Inc.; 261 (cr), © David Reed/CORBIS; 262 (bl), Jose Azel/Aurora; 263, © SuperStock; 264, Robert Caputo/Aurora; 265 (br), M & E Bernheim/Woodfin Camp & Associates; 266, Jason Lauré/Lauré Communications;

Chapter 13: 270, Trygve Bolstad/Panos Pictures; 272, © Stone/John Lamb; 273, © Gerald Cubitt; 274 (cl), © Gerald Cubitt; 275 (br), Peggy Kelsey; 275 (tr), Jason Lauré/Lauré Communications; 276 (tr), The Rabler off Table Mountain, Cape Town, © 1865/Jersey Museums Service, UK/Bridgeman Art Library, London/New York; 276 (bl), © Stone/Hulton Getty; 277, © Gerald Cubitt; 278, (cl), RUET STEPHANE/CORBIS SYGMA; 278 (cl), Archive Photos/Express Newspapers; 278 (all), Jason Lauré/Lauré Communications; 280, (cr), Bettmann/CORBIS; 281, © Stone/Steve Vidler; 282 (bl), © Gerald Cubitt; 283, © Gerald Cubitt; 284, The Granger Collection, New York; 285, © Gerald Cubitt; 288, © Fritz Polking/Peter Arnold, Inc.; 289 (b), Peter Arnold, Inc.; 289 (t), © William Campbell/Peter Arnold, Inc.; 290 Dianne Blell/ Peter Arnold, Inc.; **Unit 4:** 292 (t), © Stone/Hugh Sitton; 292 (b), © Stone; 292 (c), © Stone/Art Wolfe;

ACKNOWLEDGEMENTS

293 (c), © Stone; 293 (b), Robert Winslow/ Animals Animals/Earth Scenes; 300, © Adam Woolfit/ CORBIS; 301 (t), Index Stock Imagery, Inc.; 301 (b), Steve Ewert Photography; **Chapter 14:** 302, Steve Ewert Photography; 304, Ric Ergenbright; 306, © R Graham/ TRIP Photo Library; 307 (c), © H. Rogers/TRIP Photo Library; 307 (cr), The Memoirs of Babur/Nat'l Museum of India, New Delhi, India/Bridgeman Art Library, London/ New York; 308, © Cheryl Sheridan/ Odyssey/Chicago; 308, Craig Lovell/ Eagle Visions; 310 (bl), © Stone/Hulton Getty ; 310 (tl), Atkinson, George Franklin (1822-59)/British Library, London/ Bridgeman Art Library, London/New York; 311, © Stone/Hulton Getty; 312 (bl), Ric Ergenbright; 313, (b) AFP/CORBIS; 314 (tr), © Robert Frerck/ Odyssey/Chicago; 314 (b), © Mary Altier; 315 (b) Stringer/Reuters Newmedia Inc/Corbis; 315, © Robert Frerck/Odyssey/Chicago; 316 (tl), Martin Adler/Panos Pictures; 316 (b), Ric Ergenbright; 317, © Robert Frerck/ Odyssey/Chicago; **Chapter 15:** 320, Steve Ewert Photography; 322, © Galen Rowell/CORBIS; 324 (c), © Nik Wheeler/ CORBIS; 325, © Ed Kashi; 326, © Mike Goldwater/Network/ SABA; 328-329, AP Photo/ Pavel Rahman; 329, (tr), MAURY CHRISTIAN/CORBIS SYGMA; 330 (l), William Thompson; 331, CORBIS/ Bettmann; 332 (t), © Stone/Paula Bronstein; 332 (b), © Evelyn Scott/Bruce Coleman, Inc.; 333, © Robert Frerck/Odyssey/Chicago; 334 (b), © Robert Frerck/ Odyssey/Chicago; 334 (t), © Masha Nordbye/Bruce Coleman, Inc.; 335 (t), E. Valentin/Liaison Agency; 337, Paul Dlugokencky; 341, © Galen Rowell/CORBIS; **Unit 5:** 342 (bl), Vision Photo/Pacific Stock; 342 (br), © Stone/Margaret Gowan; 342-343 (c), © Ken Ross/ FPG International LLC; 343 (cr), © Dean Conger/ CORBIS; 343 (br), © John Giustina/FPG International LLC; **Chapter 16:** 352, Steve Ewert Photography; 354, © Stone/Colin Prior; 355, © Brian Vikander; 356, Courtesy of Freer Gallery of Art, Smithsonian Institution, Washington, D.C.; 357 © Stone/D. E. Cox; 358, (b), Bettmann/CORBIS; 358 (t), © James

Montgomery/ Bruce Coleman, Inc.; 358 (inset), Dennis Cox/China Stock; 359, Catalan Atlas, detail showing the family of Marco Polo (1254-1324) travelling by camel caravan/British Library, London, UK/ Bridgeman Art Library, London/New York; 360, (t), Bettmann/CORBIS; 360-361 (b), © James Montgomery/Bruce Coleman, Inc.; 361 (t), Jeffrey Aaronson/Network Aspen; 362, © Keren Su/FPG International LLC; 363, © 1997 Michele Burgess; 365, © Keren Su/FPG International LLC; 366, © Stone/ Yann Layma; 367, Jeffrey Aaronson/Network Aspen; 368, Mongolian Eight flags soldiers from Ching's military forces, engraved by R.Rancati (colour engraving)/Private Collection/Bridgeman Art Library, London/New York; 369 (t), © Stone/Michel Setboun; 369 (inset), © Wolfgang Kaehler; 370 (b), Orion Press/Pacific Stock; 370 (t), © Stone/Hulton Getty; 371, © Stone/Hugh Sitton; **Chapter 17:** 374, Steve Ewert Photography; 376, © Uniphoto Pictor ; 377, © SuperStock; 378, © Toyohiro Yamada/FPG International LLC; 379, © Michael S. Yamashita/COR-BIS; 381, © Bettmann/CORBIS; 382 (bl), © SuperStock; 384 (t), Toyohiro Yamada/FPG International LLC; 384 (bl), © David Wade/FPG International LLC; 385, Orion Press/Pacific Stock; 386, 387 (r), © Kim Newton/ Woodfin Camp & Associates, Inc.; 387 (l), City Art Gallery, Leeds/Bridgeman Art Library, London/ SuperStock; 388, © SuperStock; 391 (b), Nathan Benn/Woodfin Camp & Associates, Inc.; 391 (tr), © SuperStock; 393, Jeffrey Aaronson/ Network Aspen; **Chapter 18:** 396, Steve Ewert Photography; 3971, 398, © Gerald Cubitt; 399, Fred Hoogervorst/Panos Pictures; 400 (b), Brian Vikander; 401 (t), Bullit Marquez/AP/Wide World Photos; 401 (b), Charlyn Zlotnik/Woodfin Camp & Associates, Inc.; 402, © Richard Bickel/CORBIS; 403, Chris Sattlberger/ Panos Pictures; 404 (b), © John Elk III/Bruce Coleman, Inc.; 404 (t), Brian Vikander; 405, © Stefano Amantini/ Bruce Coleman, Inc.; 406, (tl), Christopher Loviny/ CORBIS; 406 (b), R. Ian Lloyd/The Stock Market;

408, Vision Photo/Pacific Stock; 412, © John Elk III/ Bruce Coleman, Inc.; 410 (b), Veronica Garbutt/Panos Pictures; 410 (t), © Wolfgang Kaehler; 411, © Chris Salvo/FPG International LLC; 413 (t), Michele Burgess/ The Stock Market; 416, © Frans Lanting/Minden Pictures; 417, © Picture Press/CORBIS; **Unit 6:** 420 (cl), © Stone/Glen Allison; 420 (t), © Frans Lanting/Minden Pictures; 420-421 (b), © Bill Bachman; 421 (cr), © Stone/Greg Probst; 421 (br), © Picture Finders Ltd./Leo de Wys; 429 Steve Ewert Photography; **Chapter 19:** 430, Penny Tweedie/HRW Photo; 432 (b), Digital Stock Corp./HRW; 433 (t), Digital Stock Corp./HRW; 434, W. Robert Moore/NGS Image Collection; 435, Aboriginal Bark painting showing the path taken by the soul on its journey to the other world/Private Collection/Bridgeman Art Library, London/New York; 436, Digital Stock Corp./HRW; 438 (c), Wayne Lawler/Photo Researchers, Inc.; 438 (b), © Four by Five/ SuperStock; 440 (b), © Clyde H. Smith/Peter Arnold, Inc.; 440 (t), Pendant in the form of the god Hei-Tiki from the Maori, New Zealand, late 18th century (nephrite)./ Bonhams, London/Bridgeman Art Library, London/New York; 441 (t), © Colin Monteath/Auscape; 441 (b), SEF/Art Resource, NY; 442 (t), Michael Steele/Allsport; 442 (b), John Eastcott/NGS Image Collection; 443, © Lance Nelson/The Stock Market; **Chapter 20:** 446, © Zafer KIZILKAYA; 448, © Stone/Paul Chelsey; 449 (b), © Bojan Brecelj/CORBIS; 449 (inset), © Arne Hodalic/ CORBIS; 450, 451 (t), © Frans Lanting/ Minden Pictures; 452 (l), Liaison Agency; 453 © David Austen/Stock, Boston/PNI; 454, (b), Robert Harding Picture Library Ltd /Alamy; 454 (t),Peter Essick/ Aurora; 455, © Jack Fields/CORBIS; 456, © Craig Lovell/CORBIS; 457 (cr), Bettmann/CORBIS; 458, © Norbert Wu/ www.norbertwu.com; 459, © Stone/ Art Wolfe; 463, © Allan Morgan/Peter Arnold, Inc.; 464, Douglas Faulkner/CORBIS/HRW; 465, Art Wolfe/ Getty Images.